Account Title	Normal Balance	Financial Report Found On	Category	Permanent or Temporary
Medicare Tax Payable	Credit	Balance Sheet	Liability	Permanent
Merchandise Inventory	Debit	Balance Sheet; Income Statement	Current Asset; Cost of Goods Sold	Permanent
Mortgage Payable	Credit	Balance Sheet	Long-Term Liability	Permanent
Notes Payable	Credit	Balance Sheet	Current Liability	Permanent
Notes Receivable	Debit	Balance Sheet	Current Asset	Permanent
Organization Costs	Debit	Balance Sheet	Intangible Asset	Permanent
Patents	Debit	Balance Sheet	Intangible Asset	Permanent
Paid-In Capital from Treasury Stock	Credit	Balance Sheet	Stockholders' Equity	Permanent
Paid-In Capital in Excess of (. . .)	Credit	Balance Sheet	Stockholder's Equity	Permanent
Payroll Tax Expense	Debit	Income Statement	Operating Expense	Temporary
Petty Cash	Debit	Balance Sheet	Current Asset	Permanent
Premium on Bonds Payable	Credit	Balance Sheet	Long-Term Liability	Permanent
Prepaid Insurance	Debit	Balance Sheet	Current Asset	Permanent
Prepaid Rent	Debit	Balance Sheet	Current Asset	Permanent
Preferred Stock	Credit	Balance Sheet	Stockholders' Equity	Permanent
Purchases	Debit	Income Statement	Cost of Goods Sold	Temporary
Purchases Discount	Credit	Income Statement	Contra Cost of Goods Sold	Temporary
Purchases Returns and Allowances	Credit	Income Statement	Contra Cost of Goods Sold	Temporary
Retained Earnings	Credit	Statement of Retained Earnings; Balance Sheet	Stockholders' Equity	Permanent
Salaries Expense	Debit	Income Statement	Operating Expense	Temporary
Salaries Payable	Credit	Balance Sheet	Current Liability	Permanent
Sales	Credit	Income Statement	Revenue	Temporary
Sales Discount	Debit	Income Statement	Contra Revenue	Temporary
Sales Returns and Allowances	Debit	Income Statement	Contra Revenue	Temporary
Sales Tax Payable	Credit	Balance Sheet	Current Liability	Permanent
Social Security Tax Payable	Credit	Balance Sheet	Liability	Permanent
Stock Dividend Distributable	Credit	Balance Sheet	Stockholders' Equity	Permanent
Stock Subscriptions Receivable	Debit	Balance Sheet	Current Asset	Permanent
Supplies	Debit	Balance Sheet	Current Asset	Permanent
Treasury Stock	Debit	Balance Sheet	Contra Stockholder's Equity	Permanent
Unearned Revenue	Credit	Balance Sheet	Current Liability	Permanent
Vouchers Payable	Credit	Balance Sheet	Current Liability	Permanent
Withdrawals	Debit	Statement of Owner's Equity; Balance Sheet	Owners' Equity	Temporary

KEY TO USE OF COLOR IN TEXT

	Yellow	journals, special journals, combination journals
	Green	general ledgers, trial balance, worksheets, payroll registers
	Blue	subsidiary ledgers, forms, documents
	Orange	financial reports
	Buff	tables
	Magenta	key numbers, emphasis, steps

SEVENTH EDITION

COLLEGE ACCOUNTING

A PRACTICAL APPROACH

CHAPTERS 1 – 26

SEVENTH EDITION

COLLEGE ACCOUNTING

A PRACTICAL APPROACH

CHAPTERS 1–26

JEFFREY SLATER

NORTH SHORE COMMUNITY COLLEGE
BEVERLY, MASSACHUSETTS

PRENTICE HALL

UPPER SADDLE RIVER, NEW JERSEY 07458

Library of Congress Cataloging-in-Publication Data
Slater, Jeffrey
   College accounting : a practical approach, Chapters 1–26/
Jeffrey Slater. —7th ed.
       p.   cm.
       Includes index.
       ISBN 0-13-788464-8 (chs. 1–26)
       1. Accounting.   I. Title.
HF5635.S6315   1998
657'.044—dc21   98-26455
                                                     CIP

Editorial/Production Credits

Editor in Chief: *P.J. Boardman*
Executive Editor: *Annie Todd*
Associate Editor: *Diane deCastro*
Director of Development: *Steve Deitmer*
Development Editor: *Mike Buchman*
Marketing Manager: *Beth Toland*
Sales Directors: Kris King, Iain MacDonald, Dana Simms
Director of Production: *Joanne Jay*
Managing Editor: *Bruce Kaplan*
Senior Production Manager: *Anne Graydon*
Copy Editor: *Sylvia Moore*
Proofreader: *Ann Koonce*
Design Manager: *Pat Smythe*
Interior Design: *Jill Yutkowitz, Lisa Delgado*
Art Design: *Ed Smith*
Cover Design: *Jill Yutkowitz*
Cover Art: *Dave Cutler*
Photo Permissions Supervisor: *Kay Dellosa*
Photo Permissions Editor: *Charles Morris*
Chapter-Opening Photos: *Jann Underwood*
Senior Manufacturing Supervisor: *Paul Smolenski*
Manufacturing Manager: *Vincent Scelta*
Compositor: *Progressive Information Technologies*

Prentice-Hall International (UK) Limited, *London*
Prentice-Hall of Australia Pty. Limited, *Sydney*
Prentice-Hall Canada Inc., *Toronto*
Prentice-Hall Hispanoamericana, S.A., *Mexico*
Prentice-Hall of India Private Limited, *New Delhi*
Prentice-Hall of Japan, Inc., *Tokyo*
Pearson Education Asia Pte. Ltd., *Singapore*
Editora Prentice-Hall do Brasil, Ltda., *Rio de Janeiro*

Printed in the United States of America
10 9 8 7 6 5 4

To   SCUPPER
        MOLLY
            MAGGIE
                AMBER

With love, JEFF

BRIEF CONTENTS

CONTENTS

8 THE EMPLOYER'S TAX RESPONSIBILITIES: PRINCIPLES AND PROCEDURES 267

9 SPECIAL JOURNALS: SALES AND CASH RECEIPTS 312

10 SPECIAL JOURNALS: PURCHASES AND CASH PAYMENTS   353

11 THE COMBINED JOURNAL   401

CONTENTS

DUNKIN' DONUTS BOXES

COMPUTER WORKSHOPS

PREFACE

Today's accounting students are learning the skills that will help them succeed in business. The seventh edition of *College Accounting: A Practical Approach* by Jeffrey Slater helps students integrate these skills by infusing the tried-and-true Slater system with real-world applications. Each chapter begins with a "Big Picture" introduction that puts the subject in a practical context. A "Continuing Problem" at the end of each chapter lets students apply their skills to a practical case. Throughout the book, students read about real accounting applications in thirteen Dunkin' Donuts boxes that feature both local franchise operations and corporate support functions. And students are taught computer accounting skills using *Simply Accounting*™ and *Peachtree® Accounting* software.

THE REAL WORLD

Whether students will keep the books for their own small business or function within a corporation, developing an understanding of how accounting procedures are applied in a business setting is crucial to their success. That is why the seventh edition of *College Accounting: A Practical Approach* now brings the real world to the classroom through the following **NEW features:**

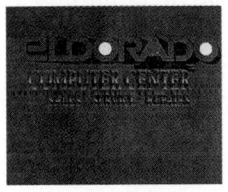

To provide a conceptual overview of topics that will be discussed in the chapters, each chapter now opens with a short vignette called "The Big Picture." The scenarios come from the experiences of Tony Freedman, who started his own business (Eldorado Computer Center) in California upon graduation from a local community college. Tony keeps his own books and shares with students how he uses accounting procedures to run a successful and growing business.

Based on interviews with members of the accounting department at Dunkin' Donuts corporate headquarters, thirteen boxes have been specially crafted to illustrate how accounting procedures are used at both franchise stores and corporate headquarters. By reading about how useful the worksheet is to a shop owner throughout the year (Chapter 4), or how new IBM point-of-sale terminals help store owners generate more accurate Cash Summaries (Chapter 6), students will see how the skills they learn in class are applied by this well-known company.

The Computer Workshops following Chapters 3, 4, 5, 8, 10, and 13 have been updated for Version 5.0 of Simply Accounting. Also, a new Workshop has been added following Chapter 16 to show students how to set up a perpetual inventory system, which is used by most businesses to track and manage inventory. This commercial software package is used by small- to medium-sized businesses to keep their books and the Computer Workshops teach students to set up the manual systems they learn in the book in a computerized format. Many businesses use computers in some way to manage their accounting records, so students that possess computer skills are a very valuable asset!

A new supplement, *Peachtree® for College Accounting,* is available for student purchase with the seventh edition of *College Accounting: A Practical Approach.* Peachtree is the most widely-used commercial software package on the market and this supplement is designed to teach students how to convert the manual procedures they learn in Chapters 1–16 of the text into a computerized environment using Peachtree Accounting for Windows.

THE SLATER SYSTEM

Jeffrey Slater developed his renowned teaching system through 28+ years of classroom experience. Broad goals are presented at the start of each chapter. Students are then presented with material in small, manageable units followed by immediate self-checks and feedback. Each chapter is limited to a small number of units, so students review and apply concepts before they move on. In addition, cumulative reviews in each chapter help students solidify their learning.

Textbook Options

You can use the Slater System in several configurations of *College Accounting: A Practical Approach:*

- ◆ Chapters 1–10 *(0-13-095489-6)* OR
  Chapters 1–10 with Simply Accounting disks for Computer Workshops *(0-13-082554-9)*
- ◆ Chapters 1–15 *(0-13-095488-8)* OR
  Chapters 1–15 with Simply Accounting disks for Computer Workshops *(0-13-082555-7)*
- ◆ Chapters 1–26 *(0-13-788464-8)* OR
  Chapters 1–26 with Simply Accounting disks for Computer Workshops *(0-13-082557-3)*
- ◆ Chapters 1–15 paperback text with Study Guide and Working Papers *(0-13-095487-X)* OR
  Chapters 1–15 paperback text with Study Guide and Working Papers and Simply Accounting disks for Computer Workshops *(0-13-082556-5)*

SEVENTH EDITION HIGHLIGHTS AND CHANGES

The Slater System   The seventh edition retains the proven pedagogy that has made *College Accounting* a classic.

The Big Picture   New introductions open each chapter providing a conceptual preview and relating topics to an actual business, Eldorado Computer Center.

Continuing Problem A new Continuing Problem runs through Chapters 1 – 16, asking students to apply skills to the business scenario set in the Big Picture.

Dunkin' Donuts Boxes The real-world accounting issues facing franchise owners and corporate staff are presented in boxed features based on research of the nationally known company. Discussion questions tie the boxes to chapter concepts.

Quiz Tips "Quiz Tips" provide additional guidance to help students complete the self-review activities at the end of each learning unit.

Check Figures "Check Figures" provide quick feedback for students to monitor progress in all A and B problems.

Expanded Coverage of Perpetual Inventory An Appendix to Chapter 12 now introduces perpetual inventory, the most prevalent method of tracking inventory in business today. Chapter 16 focuses on this method in depth.

Simply Accounting™ Computer Workshops These popular workshop activities are updated for Version 5.0, and a new perpetual inventory workshop now follows Chapter 16.

Peachtree Accounting® A new *Peachtree for College Accounting* supplement is tied directly to the text and allows students to learn how to apply accounting principles using Peachtree software.

Practical Accounting Tutor The expanded, highly visual, interactive study guide allows students to review Chapters 1 – 10 at their own pace and includes a grading tool.

Self-Quiz Videotapes New videotapes produced by the author recreate the Self-Review Quizzes at the end of each learning unit.

Real-World Applications End-of-chapter materials, including "You Make the Call" sections, offer short cases that require critical thinking and cover ethical issues while stressing oral and written communications.

Extensive End-of-Chapter Framework Each chapter offers extensive learning aides, including:

- Discussion Questions
- Mini Exercises
- Exercises
- Problem sets A and B
- Real World Applications
- Accounting Recall: a cumulative review that offers a two-part quiz including vocabulary and theory. Forms and worked-out solutions are in the *Study Guide and Working Papers.*
- Continuing Problem: a cumulative problem that runs through Chapters 1 – 16, asking students to work through the entire business cycle for Eldorado Computer Center.

SUPPLEMENTS
For the Student

- Study Guide and Working Papers, Chs. 1 – 10 *(0-13-096153-1)*
- Study Guide and Working Papers, Chs. 1 – 15 *(0-13-096154-X)*
- Study Guide and Working Papers, Chs. 16 – 26 *(0-13-096155-8)*
- One-on-One Videos *(0-13-080876-8)*

- ◆ Practical Accounting Tutor CD-ROM *(0-13-080879-2)*
- ◆ A-1 Photography Practice Set — Manual *(0-13-080310-3)*
- ◆ A-1 Photography Practice Set — Computerized *(0-13-080319-7)*
- ◆ Who-Dun-It Bookstore Practice Set — Manual *(0-13-082027-X)*
- ◆ Runners Corporation Practice Set — Manual *(0-13-080316-2)*
- ◆ Runners Corporation Practice Set — Computerized *(0-13-080315-4)*
- ◆ Peachtree for College Accounting Practice Sets — Computerized *(0-13-982216-X)*

For the Instructor

- ◆ Instructor's Resource and Solutions Manual, Chs. 1 – 15 *(0-13-080866-0)*
- ◆ Instructor's Resource and Solutions Manual, Chs. 16 – 26 *(0-13-080867-9)*
- ◆ Solutions and Teaching Transparencies, Chapters 1 – 15 *(0-13-080873-3)*
- ◆ Solutions and Teaching Transparencies, Chapters 16 – 26 *(0-13-080874-1)*
- ◆ Solutions Manual for Who-Dun-It Bookstore Practice Set *(0-13-080872-5)*
- ◆ Solutions Manual for A-1 Photography/Runners Corporation Practice Sets *(0-13-080314-6)*
- ◆ Solutions Manual for Peachtree for College Accounting Practice Set *(0-13-099657-2)*
- ◆ Test Item File with Achievement Tests, Chs. 1 – 15 *(0-13-080868-7)*
- ◆ Test Item File with Achievement Tests, Chs. 16 – 26 *(0-13-080869-5)*
- ◆ Windows PH Custom Test *(0-13-080871-7)*
- ◆ Achievement Tests 1 – 15A *(0-13-080858-X)*
- ◆ Achievement Tests 1 – 15B *(0-13-080897-0)*
- ◆ Tips on Teaching College Accounting Video *(0-13-080875-X)*
- ◆ PowerPoint Transparencies *(0-13-080878-4)*

ACKNOWLEDGMENTS

Writers and Checkers

Tim Carse (SunGard EBS)— His work on Chapters 7 and 8

Paul A. Concilio (McLennan Community College) — Appendix to Chapter 12

Sylvia Hearing (Clackamas Community College) — Simply Accounting Computer Workshops

Mary McGarry — Dunkin' Donuts boxes

Kathleen Murphrey (San Antonio College) — Solution checking the text, Study Guide and Working Papers, and Instructor's Resource and Solutions Manual

Jann Underwood (Eldorado College) — The Big Picture and the Continuing Problem

Al Walczak (Linn Benton Community College) — Revising Chapter 16

Reviewers

Bill Reynolds, St. Charles County Community College

Charles N. Calvin, Computer Learning Center

Dick D. Wasson, Southwestern College

Tom Kimberling, Ventura College

James Guyor, St. Clair County Community College

Noel McKeon, Florida Community College

Pete Rizzo, Heald Business College

Larry Ziegler, Highland College

Glen Rado, St. Phillips College

Sue Lynch, Florence-Darlington Technical College
Jeannelou Hodgens, Florence-Darlington Technical College
Charles J. Blumer, St. Charles County Community College
Marvin Dittman, Elgin Community College
Joan E. Cook, Milwaukee Area Technical College
Ray Lewis, San Antonio College
Delores G. Huerta, Del Mar College
Sophia B. Klopp, Palm Beach Community College
Albert J. Walczak, Linn-Benton Community College

Supplements Authors

Paul A. Concilio, McLennan Community College
Shari L. DeMarco, Bryant & Stratton Business College
Patricia Holmes, Des Moines Area Community College
Diane Mach, McLennan Community College
Larena McGinnity, Chadron State College
Errol Osteraa, Heald Business College
Lou Procopio, North Shore Community College
Barbara Roscher, McLennan Community College

Prentice Hall Staff

In addition to the people mentioned above, I would like to thank the dedicated Prentice Hall staff members who worked on this project: Diane DeCastro, Associate Editor, who did a tremendous amount of work in pulling together *both* the text and the supplements package; Annie Todd, Executive Editor, who worked on the last edition and served as a valuable resource on this edition; Elaine Oyzon-Mast, their Editorial Assistant; Beth Toland, Marketing Manager; Mike Buchman, Development Editor, and Steve Deitmer, Director of Development; Anne Graydon, Senior Production Editor, and Bruce Kaplan, Managing Editor; Paul Smolenski, Senior Manufacturing Supervisor; Pat Smythe, Design Manager, and Jill Yutkowitz, Designer; and last but not least, Richard Bretan, Supplements Production Manager.

—Jeff Slater

SEVENTH EDITION

COLLEGE ACCOUNTING

A PRACTICAL APPROACH

CHAPTERS 1 – 26

ACCOUNTING CONCEPTS AND PROCEDURES

An Introduction

THE BIG PICTURE

People start businesses for many reasons: to be their own boss; to be a success; to build their own financial empire; to bring a great idea to the market. But all businesses share one goal — to increase in value.

Tony Freedman, a graduate of Eldorado College, decided that he wanted to use his acquired skills as a computer technician and build his own business, Eldorado Computer Center. His technical skills would provide the services his customers needed, and his knowledge of accounting would show how his business was doing. He would provide added value to his customers and to his business at the same time. As he thought about his business, he asked these questions:

◆ What type of business organization shall I form?

◆ How much money will I need to start, and where will it come from?

◆ What will I charge my customers?

◆ What will my projected revenue and expenses be?

Tony had learned that accounting is the language of business because it helps translate events into numbers that show how a company is doing. He used this language to answer his questions and to write a business plan to open a sole proprietorship on July 1.

To the Student:

A business must have a way to track its financial activities. Accounting is the process of gathering, processing, reporting, and communicating this information. "The Big Picture" introduces each chapter by connecting accounting to the real world of business. At the end of each chapter, you will find the "Continuing Problem," which asks you to apply what you've learned in the chapter to a real business situation.

Accounting is the language of business; it provides information to managers, owners, investors, governmental agencies, and others inside and outside the organization. Accounting provides answers and insights to questions like these:

◆ Is Subway's cash balance sufficient?

◆ Should McDonald's expand its product line?

◆ Can American Airlines pay its debt obligations?

◆ What percentage of IBM's marketing budget is for television advertisement? How does this compare with the competition? What is the overall financial condition of IBM?

Smaller businesses also need answers to their financial questions:

◆ Did business increase enough over the last year to warrant hiring a new assistant?

◆ Should we spend more money to design, produce, and send out new brochures in an effort to create more business?

Accounting is as important to individuals as it is to businesses; it answers questions like

◆ Should I take out a loan for a new car or wait until I can afford to pay cash for it?

◆ Would my money work better in a savings bank or in a credit union savings plan?

Accounting is the process that analyzes, records, classifies, summarizes, reports, and interprets financial information to decision makers — whether individuals, small businesses, large corporations, or governmental agencies — in a timely fashion. It is important that students understand the "whys" of the accounting process. Just knowing the mechanics is not enough.

There are three main categories of business organization: (1) sole proprietorships, (2) partnerships, and (3) corporations. Let's define each of them and look at their advantages and disadvantages. This information also appears in Table 1-1.

Sole Proprietorship

A **sole proprietorship** is a business that has one owner. That person is both the owner and the manager of the business. An advantage of a sole proprietorship is that the owner makes all of the decisions for the business. A disadvantage is that if the business cannot pay its obligations, the business owner must pay them. This means that the owner could lose some of his personal assets (e.g., his house or his savings).

Sole proprietorships are easy to form. They end if the business closes or when the owner dies.

Partnership

A **partnership** is a form of business ownership that has at least two owners (partners). Each partner acts as an owner of the company. This is an advantage because the partners can share the decision making and the risks of the busi-

TABLE 1-1   TYPES OF BUSINESS ORGANIZATIONS

	Sole Proprietorship	Partnership	Corporation
Ownership	Business owned by one person.	Business owned by more than one person.	Business owned by stockholders.
Formation	Easy to form.	Easy to form.	More difficult to form.
Liability	Owner could lose personal assets to meet obligations of business.	Partners could lose personal assets to meet obligations of partnership.	Limited personal risk. Stockholders' loss is limited to their investment in the company.
Closing	Ends with death of owner or closing of business.	Ends with death of partner or exit of a partner.	Can continue indefinitely.

ness. A disadvantage is that, as in a sole proprietorship, the partners' personal assets could be lost if the partnership cannot meet its obligations.

Partnerships are easy to form. They end when a partner dies or leaves the partnership.

Corporation

A **corporation** is a business owned by stockholders. The corporation may have only a few stockholders or it may have many stockholders. The stockholders are not personally liable for the corporation's debts, and they usually do not have input into the business decisions.

Corporations are more difficult to form than sole proprietorships or partnerships. Corporations can exist indefinitely.

CLASSIFYING BUSINESS ORGANIZATIONS

Whether we are looking at a sole proprietorship, a partnership, or a corporation, the business can be classified by what the business does to earn money. Companies are categorized as either service, merchandise, or manufacturing businesses.

A local cab company is a good example of a **service company** because it provides a service. The first part of this book focuses on service businesses.

Stores like Sears and J.C. Penney sell products. They are called merchandise companies. **Merchandise companies** can either make their own products or sell products that are made by another supplier. Companies like Mattel and General Motors that make their own products are called **manufacturers.** (See Table 1-2.)

Disney is an example of a corporation.

TABLE 1-2   EXAMPLES OF SERVICE, MERCHANDISE, AND MANUFACTURING BUSINESSES

Service Businesses	Merchandise Businesses	Manufacturing Businesses
Pete's Taxi Service	Sears	Mattel
Jane's Painting Co.	J.C. Penney	General Motors
Dr. Wheeler, M.D.	L.L. Bean	Toro
Accountemps	Home Depot	Levi's
CellularOne Paging Services	Staples	Intel

DEFINITION OF ACCOUNTING

Accounting (also called the **accounting process**) is a system that measures the activities of a business in financial terms. It provides various reports and financial statements that show how the various transactions the business undertook (e.g., buying and selling goods) affected the business. It does this by performing the following functions:

- ◆ **Analyzing:** Looking at what happened and how the business was affected.
- ◆ **Recording:** Putting the information into the accounting system.
- ◆ **Classifying:** Grouping all of the same activities (e.g., all purchases) together.
- ◆ **Summarizing:** Explaining the results.
- ◆ **Reporting:** Issuing the reports that tell the results of the previous functions.
- ◆ **Interpreting:** Examining the reports to determine how the various pieces of information they contain relate to each other.

The system communicates the reports and financial statements to people who are interested in the information, such as the business's decision makers, investors, creditors, governmental agencies (e.g., the Internal Revenue Service), and so on.

As you can see, a lot of people use these reports. A set of procedures and guidelines were developed to make sure that everyone prepares and interprets them the same way. These guidelines are known as **generally accepted accounting principles (GAAP).**

Now let's look at the difference between bookkeeping and accounting. Keep in mind that we will use the terms "accounting" and "the accounting process" interchangeably.

DIFFERENCE BETWEEN BOOKKEEPING AND ACCOUNTING

Confusion often arises concerning the difference between bookkeeping and accounting. **Bookkeeping** is the recording (recordkeeping) function of the accounting process; a bookkeeper enters accounting information in the company's books. An accountant takes that information and prepares the financial reports that are used to analyze the company's financial position. Accounting involves many complex activities. Often, it includes the preparation of tax and financial reports, budgeting, and analyses of financial information.

Today, computers are used for routine bookkeeping operations that used to take weeks or months to complete. The text takes this into consideration by explaining how the advantages of the computer can be applied to a manual accounting system by using hands-on knowledge of how accounting works. Basic accounting knowledge is needed even though computers can do routine tasks.

LEARNING UNIT 1-1
The Accounting Equation

ASSETS, LIABILITIES, AND EQUITIES

Let's begin our study of accounting concepts and procedures by looking at a small business; Cathy Hall's law practice. Cathy decided to open her practice at the end of August. She consulted her accountant before she made her decision. The accountant told her some important things before she made this decision. First, he told her the new business would be considered a separate business entity whose finances had to be kept separate and distinct from Cathy's personal finances. The accountant went on to say that all transactions can be analyzed using the basic accounting equation: Assets = Liabilities + Owner's Equity.

Cathy had never heard of the basic accounting equation. She listened carefully as the accountant explained the terms used in the equation and how the equation works:

Assets

Cash, land, supplies, office equipment, buildings, and other properties of value *owned* by a firm are called **assets.**

Equities

The rights of financial claim to the assets are called **equities.** Equities belong to those who supply the assets. If you are the only person to supply assets to the firm, you have the sole rights, for financial claims, to them. For example, if you supply the law firm with $4,000 in cash and $3,000 in office equipment, your equity in the firm is $7,000.

Relationship Between Assets and Equities

The relationship between assets and equities is

Assets   **=**   **Equities**

(Total value of items *owned* by business)   (Total claims against the assets)

The total dollar value of the assets of your law firm will be equal to the total dollar value of the financial claims to those assets, that is, equal to the total dollar value of the equities.

The total dollar value is broken down on the left-hand side of the equation to show the specific items of value owned by the business and on the right-hand side to show the types of claims against the assets owned.

Liabilities

A firm may have to borrow money to buy more assets; when this occurs it means the firm is **buying assets *on account*** (buy now, pay later). Suppose the law firm purchases a desk for $400 on account from Joe's Stationery, and the store is willing to wait 10 days for payment. The law firm has created a **liability:** an obligation to pay that comes due in the future. Joe's Stationery is called the **creditor.** This liability — the amount owed to Joe's Stationery — gives the store the right, or the financial claim, to $400 of the law firm's assets. When Joe's Stationery is paid, the store's rights to the assets of the law firm will end, since the obligation has been paid off.

Basic Accounting Equation

To best understand the various claims to a business's assets, accountants divide equities into two parts. The claims of creditors — outside persons or businesses — are labeled **liabilities.** The claim of the business's owner are labeled **owner's equity.** Let's see how the accounting equation looks now.

Elements of the basic accounting equation.

Assets =   **Equities**

1. Liabilities: rights of creditors
2. Owner's equity: rights of owner

Assets = Liabilities + Owner's Equity

The total value of all the assets of a firm equals the combined total value of the financial claims of the creditors (liabilities) and the claims of the owners (owner's equity). This is known as the **basic accounting equation.** The basic accounting equation provides a basis for understanding the conventional accounting system of a business. The equation records business transactions in a logical and orderly way that shows their impact on the company's assets, liabilities, and owner's equity.

Importance of Creditors

Another way of presenting the basic accounting equation is:

Assets − Liabilities = Owner's Equity

This form of the equation stresses the importance of creditors. The owner's rights to the business's assets are determined after the rights of the creditors are subtracted. In other words, creditors have first claim to assets. If a firm has no liabilities — and therefore no creditors — the owner has the total rights to assets. Another term for the owner's current investment, or equity, in the business's assets is **capital.**

As Cathy Hall's law firm engages in business transactions (paying bills, serving customers, and so on), changes will take place in the assets, liabilities, and owner's equity (capital). Let's analyze some of these transactions.

Transaction (A)   Aug. 28: Cathy invests $7,000 in cash and $800 of office equipment into the business.

On August 28, Cathy withdraws $7,000 from her personal bank account and deposits the money in the law firm's newly opened bank account. She also invests $800 of office equipment in the business. She plans to be open for business on September 1. With the help of her accountant, Cathy begins to prepare the accounting records for the business. We put this information into the basic accounting equation as follows:

Note: Capital is part of owner's equity; it is not an asset.

In our analyses, assume that any number without a sign in front of it is a +.

ASSETS		= LIABILITIES +	OWNER'S EQUITY
Cash	**+ Office Equipment =**		**Cathy Hall, Capital**
$7,000 +	$800	=	$7,800
	$7,800 = $7,800		

Note that the total value of the assets, cash, and office equipment — $7,800 — is equal to the combined total value of liabilities (none, so far) and owner's equity ($7,800). Remember, Hall has supplied all the cash and office equipment, so she has the sole financial claim to the assets. Note how the heading "Cathy Hall, Capital" is written under the owner's equity heading. The $7,800 is Cathy's investment, or equity, in the firm's assets.

Transaction (B)   Aug. 29: Law practice buys office equipment for cash, $900.

From the initial investment of $7,000 cash, the law firm buys $900 worth of office equipment (such as a desk), which lasts a long time, while **supplies** (such as pens) tend to be used up relatively quickly.

	ASSETS	= LIABILITIES +	OWNER'S EQUITY
	Cash + Office Equipment =		Cathy Hall, Capital
BEGINNING BALANCE	$7,000 + $800	=	$7,800
TRANSACTION	−900 +900		
ENDING BALANCE	$6,100 + $1,700	=	$7,800

$$\$7,800 = \$7,800$$

Shift in Assets

As a result of the last transaction, the law office has less cash but has increased its amount of office equipment. This is called a **shift in assets** — the makeup of the assets has changed, but the total of the assets remains the same.

Suppose you go food shopping at the supermarket with $100 and spend $60. Now you have two assets, food and money. The composition of the assets has been *shifted* — you have more food and less money than you did — but the *total* of the assets has not increased or decreased. The total value of the food, $60, plus the cash, $40, is still $100. When you borrow money from the bank, on the other hand, you have an increase in cash (an asset) and an increase in liabilities; overall there is an increase in assets, not just a shift.

An accounting equation can remain in balance even if only one side is updated. The key point to remember is that the left-hand-side total of assets must always equal the right-hand-side total of liabilities and owner's equity.

Transaction (C)   Aug. 30: Buys additional office equipment on account, $400.

The law firm purchases an additional $400 worth of chairs and desks from Wilmington Company. Instead of demanding cash right away, Wilmington agrees to deliver the equipment and to allow up to 60 days for the law practice to pay the invoice (bill).

This liability, or obligation to pay in the future, has some interesting effects on the basic accounting equation. Wilmington Company has accepted as payment a partial claim against the assets of the law practice. This claim exists until the law firm pays off the bill. This unwritten promise to pay the creditor is a liability called **accounts payable.**

	ASSETS	= LIABILITIES	+ OWNER'S EQUITY
	Cash + Office Equipment =	Accounts Payable +	Cathy Hall, Capital
BEGINNING BALANCE	$6,100 + $1,700	=	$7,800
TRANSACTION	+400	+$400	
ENDING BALANCE	$6,100 + $2,100	= $400	$7,800

$$\$8,200 = \$8,200$$

When this information is analyzed, we can see that the law practice has increased what it owes (accounts payable) as well as what it owns (office equipment) by $400. The law practice gains $400 in an asset but has an obligation to pay Wilmington Company at a future date.

The owner's equity remains unchanged. This transaction results in an increase of total assets from $7,800 to $8,200.

Finally, note that after each transaction the basic accounting equation remains in balance.

LEARNING UNIT 1-1 REVIEW

AT THIS POINT you should be able to

◆ List the functions of accounting. (pp. 2, 4)
◆ Define and explain the differences between sole proprietorships, partnerships, and corporations. (p. 3)
◆ Compare and contrast bookkeeping and accounting. (p. 4)
◆ Explain the role of the computer as an accounting tool. (p. 4)
◆ State the purpose of the accounting equation. (p. 5)
◆ Explain the difference between liabilities and owner's equity. (p. 6)
◆ Define capital. (p. 6)
◆ Explain the difference between a shift in assets and an increase in assets. (p. 7)

To test your understanding of this material, complete Self-Review Quiz 1-1. The blank forms you need are in the *Study Guide and Working Papers* for Chapter 1. The solution to the quiz immediately follows here in the text. If you have difficulty doing the problems, review Learning Unit 1-1 and the solution to the quiz. Videotapes are available to review these quizzes. Check with your instructor on availability.

Keep in mind that learning accounting is like learning to type — the more you practice, the better you become. You will not be an expert in one day. Be patient. It will all come together.

SELF-REVIEW QUIZ 1-1

(The blank forms you need are on page 1 of the *Study Guide and Working Papers*.)

Record the following transactions in the basic accounting equation:

1. Pete O'Brien invests $14,000 to begin a real estate office.
2. The real estate office buys $600 of computer equipment for cash.
3. The real estate company buys $500 of additional computer equipment on account.

Quiz Tip: Note that transaction 2 below is a shift in assets, while transaction 3 is an increase in assets. Keep asking yourself: What did the business get and who supplied it to the business? Remember, capital is not cash. Cash is an asset, while capital is part of owner's equity.

Solution to Self-Review Quiz 1-1

	ASSETS		=	**LIABILITIES**	+	**OWNER'S EQUITY**
	Cash	**+ Computer Equipment**	**= Accounts Payable**		**+ Pete O'Brien, Capital**	
1.	+$14,000					+$14,000
BALANCE	14,000		=			14,000
2.	−600	+$600				
BALANCE	13,400 +	600	=			14,000
3.		+500		+$500		
ENDING BALANCE	$13,400 +	$1,100	=	$ 500	+	$14,000

$$\$14,500 = \$14,500$$

LEARNING UNIT 1-2
The Balance Sheet

The balance sheet shows the company's financial position as of a particular date. (In our example, that date is at the end of August.)

In the first learning unit, the transactions for Cathy Hall's law office were recorded in the accounting equation. The transactions we recorded occurred before the law firm opened for business. A report called a **balance sheet** or **statement of financial position** can show the history of a company before it opened. The balance sheet is a formal report that presents the information from the ending balances of both sides of the accounting equation. Think of the balance sheet as a snapshot of the business's financial position as of a particular date.

Let's look at the balance sheet of Cathy Hall's law practice for August 31, 19XX, shown in Figure 1-1. The figures in the balance sheet come from the ending balances of the accounting equation for the law practice as shown in Learning Unit 1-1.

Note that in Figure 1-1 the assets owned by the law practice appear on the left-hand side and that liabilities and owner's equity appear on the right-hand side. Both sides equal $8,200. This *balance* between left and right gives the balance sheet its name. In later chapters we will be looking at other ways to set up a balance sheet.

POINTS TO REMEMBER IN PREPARING A BALANCE SHEET
The Heading

The heading of the balance sheet provides the following information:

Do you remember the three elements that make up a balance sheet? Assets, liabilities, and owner's equity.

◆ The company name: Cathy Hall, Attorney At Law.
◆ The name of the report: Balance Sheet.
◆ The date for which the report is prepared: August 31, 19XX.

Use of the Dollar Sign

Note that the dollar sign is not repeated each time a figure appears. As shown in the balance sheet for Cathy Hall's law practice, it usually is placed to the left of each column's top figure and to the left of the column's total.

FIGURE 1-1
The Balance Sheet

Remember: The balance sheet is a formal report.

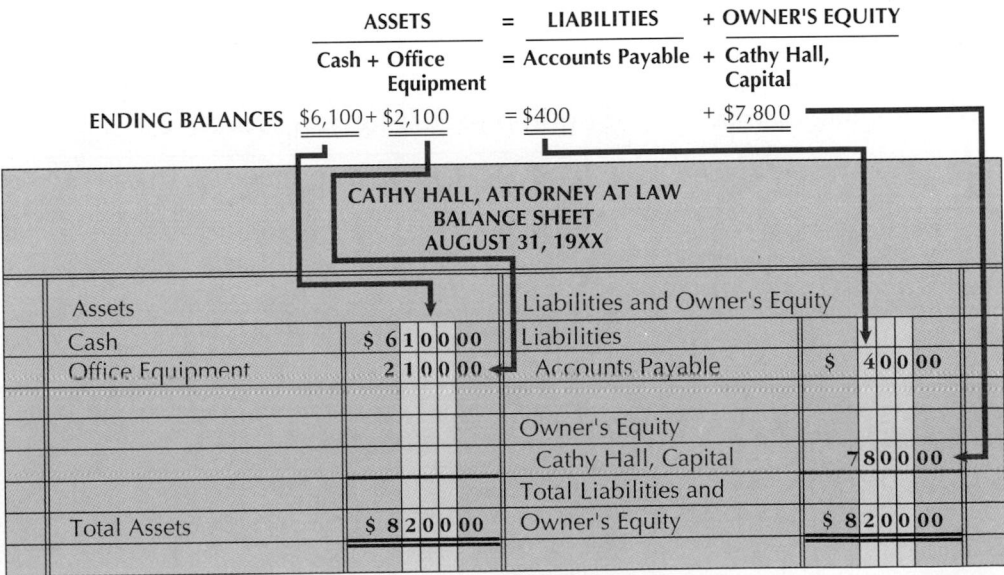

	ASSETS	=	LIABILITIES	+ OWNER'S EQUITY
	Cash + Office Equipment	= Accounts Payable	+ Cathy Hall, Capital
ENDING BALANCES	$6,100 + $2,100	= $400	+ $7,800

CATHY HALL, ATTORNEY AT LAW
BALANCE SHEET
AUGUST 31, 19XX

Assets		Liabilities and Owner's Equity	
Cash	$ 6 1 0 0 00	Liabilities	
Office Equipment	2 1 0 0 00	Accounts Payable	$ 4 0 0 00
		Owner's Equity	
		Cathy Hall, Capital	7 8 0 0 00
		Total Liabilities and	
Total Assets	$ 8 2 0 0 00	Owner's Equity	$ 8 2 0 0 00

CATHY HALL, ATTORNEY AT LAW BALANCE SHEET AUGUST 31, 19XX								
Assets								
Cash			$	6	1	0	0	00
Office Equipment				2	1	0	0	00
Total Assets			$	8	2	0	0	00

A single line means the numbers above it have been added or subtracted.

A double line indicates a total.

Distinguishing the Total

When adding numbers down a column, use a single line before the total and a double line beneath it. A single line means that the numbers above it have been added or subtracted. A double line indicates a total. It is important to align the numbers in the column; many errors occur because these figures are not lined up. These rules are the same for all accounting reports.

The balance sheet gives Cathy the information she needs to see the law firm's financial position before it opens for business. This information does not tell her, however, whether or not the firm will make a profit.

LEARNING UNIT 1-2 REVIEW

AT THIS POINT you should be able to

- ◆ Define and state the purpose of a balance sheet. (p. 9)
- ◆ Identify and define the elements making up a balance sheet. (p. 9)
- ◆ Show the relationship between the accounting equation and the balance sheet. (p. 9)
- ◆ Prepare a balance sheet in proper form from information provided. (p. 9)

SELF-REVIEW QUIZ 1-2

(The blank forms you need are on page 2 of the *Study Guide and Working Papers*.)

The date is November 30, 19XX. Use the following information to prepare in proper form a balance sheet for Janning Company:

Accounts Payable	$30,000
Cash	8,000
A. Janning, Capital	9,000
Office Equipment	31,000

Quiz Tip: The heading of a balance sheet answers the questions *who, what,* and *when.* Nov. 30, 19XX is the particular date.

Solution to Self-Review Quiz 1-2

JANNING COMPANY BALANCE SHEET NOVEMBER 30, 19XX																
Assets						Liabilities and Owner's Equity										
Cash	$	8	0	0	0	00	Liabilities									
Office Equipment		31	0	0	0	00	Accounts Payable		$	30	0	0	0	00		
							Owner's Equity									
							A. Janning, Capital			9	0	0	0	00		
							Total Liabilities and									
Total Assets	$	39	0	0	0	00	Owner's Equity		$	39	0	0	0	00		

Capital does not mean cash. The capital amount is the owner's current investment of assets in the business.

LEARNING UNIT 1-3
The Accounting Equation Expanded: Revenue, Expenses, and Withdrawals

As soon as Cathy Hall's office opened, she began performing legal services for her clients and earning revenue for the business. At the same time, as a part of doing business, she incurred various expenses, such as rent.

When Cathy asked her accountant how these transactions fit into the accounting equation, he began by defining some terms.

Revenue   A service company earns **revenue** when it provides services to its clients. Cathy's law firm earned revenue when she provided legal services to her clients for legal fees. When revenue is earned, owner's equity is increased. In effect, revenue is a subdivision of owner's equity.

Assets are increased. The increase is in the form of cash if the client pays right away. If the client promises to pay in the future, the increase is called **accounts receivable.** When revenue is earned, the transaction is recorded as an increase in revenue and an increase in assets (either as cash and/or as accounts receivable, depending on whether it was paid right away or will be paid in the future).

Expenses   A business's **expenses** are the cost the company incurs in carrying on operations in its effort to create revenue. Expenses are also a subdivision of owner's equity; when expenses are incurred, they *decrease* owner's equity. Expenses can be paid for in cash or they can be charged.

Net Income/Net Loss   When revenue totals more than expenses, **net income** is the result; when expenses total more than revenue, **net loss** is the result.

Withdrawals   At some point Cathy Hall may need to withdraw cash or other assets from the business to pay living or other personal expenses that do not relate to the business. We will record these transactions in an account called **withdrawals.** Sometimes this account is called the *owner's drawing account.* Withdrawals is a subdivision of owner's equity that records personal expenses not related to the business. Withdrawals decrease owner's equity (see Fig. 1-2).

It is important to remember the difference between expenses and withdrawals. Expenses relate to business operations; withdrawals are the result of personal needs outside the normal operations of the business.

Now let's analyze the September transactions for Cathy Hall's law firm using an **expanded accounting equation** that includes withdrawals, revenues, and expenses.

Sidebar notes:

When revenue is earned, it is recorded as an increase in Cathy's owner's equity and an increase in assets.

Accounts *receivable* is an asset. The law firm expects to be able to *receive* amounts owed from customers at a later date.

Remember: Accounts receivable results from earning revenue even when cash is not yet received.

Record an expense when it is incurred, whether it is paid then or is to be paid later.

FIGURE 1-2
Owner's Equity

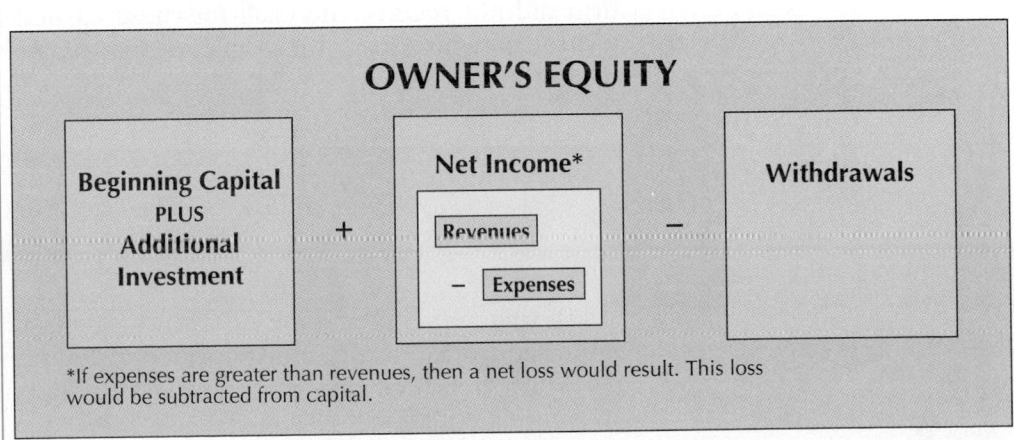

OWNER'S EQUITY

Beginning Capital PLUS Additional Investment

+

Net Income*
Revenues
− Expenses

−

Withdrawals

*If expenses are greater than revenues, then a net loss would result. This loss would be subtracted from capital.

EXPANDED ACCOUNTING EQUATION

Transaction (D)   Sept. 1–30: Provided legal services for cash, $3,000.

Transactions A, B, and C were discussed earlier, when the law office was being formed in August. See Learning Unit 1-1.

	ASSETS			= LIABILITIES +		OWNER'S EQUITY			
	Cash +	Accts. Rec.	+ Office Equip. =	Accts. Pay.	+ C. Hall, Capital	− C. Hall, Withdr.	+ Revenue	− Expenses
BALANCE FORWARD	$6,100		+ $ 2,100 =	$ 400	+ $7,800			
TRANSACTION	+3,000						+$3,000	
ENDING BALANCE	$9,100		+ $ 2,100 =	$ 400	+ $7,800		+ $3,000	
			$11,200 =	$11,200				

In the law firm's first month of operation a total of $3,000 in cash was received for legal services performed. In the accounting equation the asset Cash is increased by $3,000. Revenue is also increased by $3,000, resulting in an increase in owner's equity.

A revenue column was added to the basic accounting equation. Amounts are recorded in the revenue column when they are earned. They are also recorded in the assets column, either under Cash and/or under Accounts Receivable. Do not think of revenue as an asset. It is part of owner's equity. It is the revenue that creates an inward flow of cash and accounts receivable.

Transaction (E)   Sept. 1–30: Provided legal services on account, $4,000.

	ASSETS			= LIABILITIES +		OWNER'S EQUITY			
	Cash +	Accts. Rec.	+ Office Equip. =	Accts. Pay.	+ C. Hall, Capital	− C. Hall, Withdr.	+ Revenue	− Expenses
BAL. FOR.	$9,100		+ $ 2,100 =	$ 400	+ $7,800		+ $3,000	
TRANS.		+$4,000					+4,000	
END. BAL.	$9,100 +	$4,000	+ $ 2,100 =	$ 400	+ $7,800		+ $7,000	
			$15,200 =	$15,200				

Cathy's law practice performed legal work on account for $4,000. The firm did not receive the cash for these earned legal fees; it accepted an unwritten promise from these clients that payment would be received in the future.

Transaction (F)   Sept. 1–30: Received $700 cash as partial payment from previous services performed on account.

During September some of Cathy's clients who had received services and promised to pay in the future decided to reduce what they owed the practice by $700 when their bills came due. This is shown as follows on the expanded accounting equation.

	ASSETS			= LIABILITIES +		OWNER'S EQUITY			
	Cash +	Accts. Rec.	+ Office Equip. =	Accts. Pay.	+ C. Hall, Capital	− C. Hall, Withdr.	+ Revenue	− Expenses	
BALANCE FORWARD	$9,100 +	$4,000	+ $ 2,100 =	$ 400	+ $7,800		+ $7,000		
TRANSACTION	+700	−700							
ENDING BALANCE	$9,800 +	$3,300	+ $ 2,100 =	$ 400	+ $7,800		+ $7,000		
			$15,200 =	$15,200					

The law firm increased the asset Cash by $700 and reduced another asset, Accounts Receivable, by $700. The *total* of assets does not change. The right-hand side of the expanded accounting equation has not been touched because the total on the left-hand side of the equation has not changed. The revenue was recorded when it was earned, and the *same revenue cannot be recorded twice*. This transaction analyzes the situation *after* the revenue has been previously earned and recorded. Transaction (F) shows a shift in assets—more cash and less accounts receivable.

Transaction (G) Sept. 1–30: Paid salaries expense, $600.

	ASSETS			= LIABILITIES +		OWNER'S EQUITY			
	Cash +	Accts. Rec.	+ Office Equip. =	Accts. Pay.	+ C. Hall, Capital	− C. Hall, Withdr.	+ Revenue	− Expenses	
BAL. FOR.	$9,800 +	$3,300	+ $ 2,100 =	$ 400	+ $7,800		+ $7,000		
TRANS.	−600								+$600
END. BAL.	$9,200 +	$3,300	+ $ 2,100 =	$ 400	+ $7,800		+ $7,000 −	$600	
			$14,600 =	$14,600					

As expenses increase, they decrease owner's equity. This incurred expense of $600 reduces the cash by $600. Although the expense was paid, the total of our expenses to date has *increased* by $600. Keep in mind that owner's equity decreases as expenses increase, so the accounting equation remains in balance.

Transaction (H) Sept. 1–30: Paid rent expense, $700.

	ASSETS			= LIABILITIES +		OWNER'S EQUITY			
	Cash +	Accts. Rec.	+ Office Equip. =	Accts. Pay.	+ C. Hall, Capital	− C. Hall, Withdr.	+ Revenue	− Expenses	
BAL. FOR.	$9,200 +	$3,300	+ $ 2,100 =	$ 400	+ $7,800		+ $7,000 −	$ 600	
TRANS.	−700								+700
END. BAL.	$8,500 +	$3,300	+ $ 2,100 =	$ 400	+ $7,800		+ $7,000 −	$1,300	
			$13,900 −	$13,900					

During September the practice incurred rent expenses of $700. This rent was not paid in advance; it was paid when it came due. The payment of rent reduces the asset Cash by $700 as well as increases the expenses of the firm, resulting in a decrease in owner's equity. The firm's expenses are now $1,300.

Transaction (I)   Sept. 1–30: Incurred advertising expenses of $300, to be paid next month.

	ASSETS			= LIABILITIES +		OWNER'S EQUITY			
	Cash +	Accts. Rec.	+ Office Equip. =	Accts. Pay.	+ C. Hall, Capital	− C. Hall, Withdr.	+ Revenue	− Expenses
BALANCE FORWARD	$8,500 +	$3,300	+ $ 2,100 =	$ 400	+ $7,800		+ $7,000	− $1,300
TRANSACTION				+300				+300
ENDING BALANCE	$8,500 +	$3,300	+ $ 2,100 =	$ 700	+ $7,800		+ $7,000	− $1,600
			$13,900 =	$13,900				

Cathy ran an ad in the local newspaper and incurred an expense of $300. This increase in expenses caused a corresponding decrease in owner's equity. Since Cathy has not paid the newspaper for the advertising yet, she owes $300. Thus her liabilities (Accounts Payable) increase by $300. Eventually, when the bill comes in and is paid, both Cash and Accounts Payable will be decreased.

Transaction (J)   Sept. 1–30: Cathy withdrew $200 for personal use.

	ASSETS			= LIABILITIES +		OWNER'S EQUITY			
	Cash +	Accts. Rec.	+ Office Equip. =	Accts. Pay.	+ C. Hall, Capital	− C. Hall, Withdr.	+ Revenue	− Expenses
BAL. FOR.	$8,500 +	$3,300	+ $ 2,100 =	$ 700	+ $7,800		+ $7,000	− $1,600
TRANS.	−200					+$200		
END. BAL.	$8,300 +	$3,300	+ $ 2,100 =	$ 700	+ $7,800 −	$200	+ $7,000	− $1,600
			$13,700 =	$13,700				

By taking $200 for personal use, Cathy has *increased* her withdrawals from the business by $200 and decreased the asset Cash by $200. Note that as withdrawals increase, the owner's equity will *decrease*. Keep in mind that a withdrawal is *not* a business expense. It is a subdivision of owner's equity that records money or other assets an owner withdraws from the business for *personal* use.

Subdivision of Owner's Equity

Take a moment to review the subdivisions of owner's equity:

- As capital increases, owner's equity increases (see Transaction A).
- As withdrawals increase, owner's equity decreases (see Transaction J).
- As revenue increases, owner's equity increases (see Transaction D).
- As expenses increase, owner's equity decreases (see Transaction G).

Cathy Hall's Expanded Accounting Equation

The following is a summary of the expanded accounting equation for Cathy Hall's law firm.

Cathy Hall
Attorney at Law
Expanded Accounting Equation: A Summary

	ASSETS			= LIABILITIES +		OWNER'S EQUITY		
	Cash +	Accts. Rec.	+ Office Equip. =	Accts. Pay.	+ C. Hall, Capital	− C. Hall, Withdr.	+ Revenue	− Expenses
A.	$7,000		+$800 =		+$7,800			
BALANCE	7,000		+ 800 =		7,800			
B.	−900		+900					
BALANCE	6,100		+ 1,700 =		7,800			
C.			+400	+$400				
BALANCE	6,100		+ 2,100 =	400	+ 7,800			
D.	+3,000						+$3,000	
BALANCE	9,100		+ 2,100 =	400	+ 7,800		+ 3,000	
E.		+$4,000					+ 4,000	
BALANCE	9,100 +	4,000 +	2,100 =	400	+ 7,800		+ 7,000	
F.	+700	−700						
BALANCE	9,800 +	3,300 +	2,100 =	400	+ 7,800		+ 7,000	
G.	−600							+$600
BALANCE	9,200 +	3,300 +	2,100 =	400	+ 7,800		+ 7,000 −	600
H.	−700							+700
BALANCE	8,500 +	3,300 +	2,100 =	400	+ 7,800		+ 7,000 −	1,300
I.				+300				+300
BALANCE	8,500 +	3,300 +	2,100 =	700	+ 7,800		+ 7,000 −	1,600
J.	−200					+$200		
END BALANCE	$8,300 +	$3,300 +	$2,100 =	$700	+ $7,800	− $200	+ $7,000 −	$1,600

LEARNING UNIT 1-3 REVIEW

AT THIS POINT you should be able to

◆ Define and explain the difference between revenue and expenses. (p. 11)
◆ Define and explain the difference between net income and net loss. (p. 11)
◆ Explain the subdivision of owner's equity. (p. 14)
◆ Explain the effects of withdrawals, revenue, and expenses on owner's equity. (p. 14)
◆ Record transactions in an expanded accounting equation and balance the basic accounting equation as a means of checking the accuracy of your calculations. (p. 15)

SELF-REVIEW QUIZ 1-3

(The blank forms you need are on page 3 of the *Study Guide and Working Papers.*)
    Record the following transactions into the expanded accounting equation for the Bing Company. Note that all titles have a beginning balance.

1. Received cash revenue, $3,000.
2. Billed customers for services rendered, $6,000.
3. Received a bill for telephone expenses (to be paid next month), $125.
4. Bob Bing withdrew cash for personal use, $500.
5. Received $1,000 from customers in partial payment for services performed in transaction 2.

Solution to Self-Review Quiz 1-3

	ASSETS			=	LIABILITIES +		OWNER'S EQUITY			
	Cash +	Accts. Rec. +	Cleaning = Equip.		Accts. Pay.	+ B. Bing, Capital	− B. Bing, Withdr.	+ Revenue	− Expenses	
BEG. BALANCE	$10,000 +	$ 2,500 +	$6,500 =		$1,000	+ $11,800 −	$ 800 +	$ 9,000 −	$2,000	
1.	+3,000							+3,000		
BALANCE	13,000 +	2,500 +	6,500 =		1,000	+ 11,800 −	800 +	12,000 −	2,000	
2.		+6,000						+6,000		
BALANCE	13,000 +	8,500 +	6,500 =		1,000	+ 11,800 −	800 +	18,000 −	2,000	
3.					+125				+125	
BALANCE	13,000 +	8,500 +	6,500 =		1,125	+ 11,800 −	800 +	18,000 −	2,125	
4.	−500						+500			
BALANCE	12,500 +	8,500 +	6,500 =		1,125	+ 11,800 −	1,300 +	18,000 −	2,125	
5.	+1,000	−1,000								
END BALANCE	$13,500 +	$ 7,500 +	$6,500 =		$1,125	+ $11,800 −	$ 1,300 +	$18,000 −	$2,125	
			$27,500 =		$27,500					

LEARNING UNIT 1-4
Preparing Financial Reports

Cathy Hall would like to be able to find out whether her firm is making a profit, so she asks her accountant whether he can measure the firm's financial performance on a monthly basis. Her accountant replies that there are a number of financial reports that he can prepare, such as the income statement, which shows how well the law firm has performed over a specific period of time. The accountant can use the information in the income statement to prepare other reports.

THE INCOME STATEMENT

An **income statement** is an accounting report that shows business results in terms of revenue and expenses. If revenues are greater than expenses, the report shows net income. If expenses are greater than revenues, the report shows net loss. An income statement can cover one, three, six, or twelve months. It cannot cover more than one year. The report shows the result of all revenues and expenses throughout the entire period and not just as of a specific date. The income statement for Cathy Hall's law firm is shown in Figure 1-3.

CATHY HALL, ATTORNEY AT LAW
INCOME STATEMENT
FOR MONTH ENDED SEPTEMBER 30, 19XX

Revenue:		
Legal Fees		$ 7 000 00
Operating Expenses:		
Salaries Expense	$ 600 00	
Rent Expense	700 00	
Advertising Expense	300 00	
Total Operating Expenses		1 600 00
Net Income		$ 5 400 00

FIGURE 1-3
The Income Statement

The inside column of numbers ($600, $700, $300) is used to subtotal all expenses ($1,600) before subtracting from revenue.

Points to Remember in Preparing an Income Statement

Heading   The heading of an income statement tells the same three things as all other accounting reports: the company's name, the name of the report, and the period of time the report covers.

The Sct Up   As you can see on the income statement, the inside column of numbers ($600, $700, and $300) is used to subtotal all expenses ($1,600) before subtracting them from revenue ($7,000 − $1,600 = $5,400).

Operating expenses may be listed in alphabetical order, in order of largest amounts to smallest, or in a set order established by the accountant.

THE STATEMENT OF OWNER'S EQUITY

As we said, the income statement is a business report that shows business results in terms of revenue and expenses. But how does net income or net loss affect owner's equity? To find that out we have to look at a second type of report, the **statement of owner's equity.**

The statement of owner's equity shows for a certain period of time what changes occurred in Cathy Hall, Capital. The statement of owner's equity is shown in Figure 1-4.

The capital of Cathy Hall can be

If this statement of owner's equity is omitted, the information will be included in the owner's equity section of the balance sheet.

Increased by: Owner Investment	
Net Income (Revenue − Expenses)	
Decreased by: Owner Withdrawals	
Net Loss (Expenses Greater than Revenue)	

FIGURE 1-4 Statement of Owner's Equity

CATHY HALL, ATTORNEY AT LAW
STATEMENT OF OWNER'S EQUITY
FOR MONTH ENDED SEPTEMBER 30, 19XX

Cathy Hall, Capital, September 1, 19XX		$ 7 800 00
Net Income for September	$ 5 400 00	
Less Withdrawals for September	200 00	
Increase in Capital		5 200 00
Cathy Hall, Capital, September 30, 19XX		$ 13 000 00

Comes from Income Statement

Remember, a withdrawal is *not* a business expense and thus is not involved in the calculation of net income or net loss on the income statement. It appears on the statement of owner's equity. The statement of owner's equity summarizes the effects of all the subdivisions of owner's equity (revenue, expenses, withdrawals) on beginning capital. The ending capital figure ($13,000) will be the beginning figure in the next statement of owner's equity.

Suppose that Cathy's law firm had operated at a loss in the month of September. Suppose instead of net income there was a net loss, and an additional investment of $700 was made on September 15. This is how the statement would look if this had happened.

CATHY HALL, ATTORNEY AT LAW STATEMENT OF OWNER'S EQUITY FOR MONTH ENDED SEPTEMBER 30, 19XX		
Cathy Hall, Capital, September 1, 19XX		$ 7 8 0 0 00
Additional Investment, September 15, 19XX		7 0 0 00
Total Investment for September		$ 8 5 0 0 00
Less: Net Loss for September	$ 4 0 0 00	
Withdrawals for September	2 0 0 00	
Decrease in Capital		6 0 0 00
Cathy Hall, Capital, September 30, 19XX		$ 7 9 0 0 00

THE BALANCE SHEET

Now let's look at how to prepare a balance sheet from the expanded accounting equation (see Fig. 1-5). As you can see, the asset accounts (cash, accounts receivable, and office equipment) appear on the left of the balance sheet. Accounts payable and Cathy Hall, Capital appear on the right. Notice that the $13,000 of capital can be calculated within the accounting equation, or read from the statement of owner's equity.

FIGURE 1-5 The Accounting Equation and the Balance Sheet

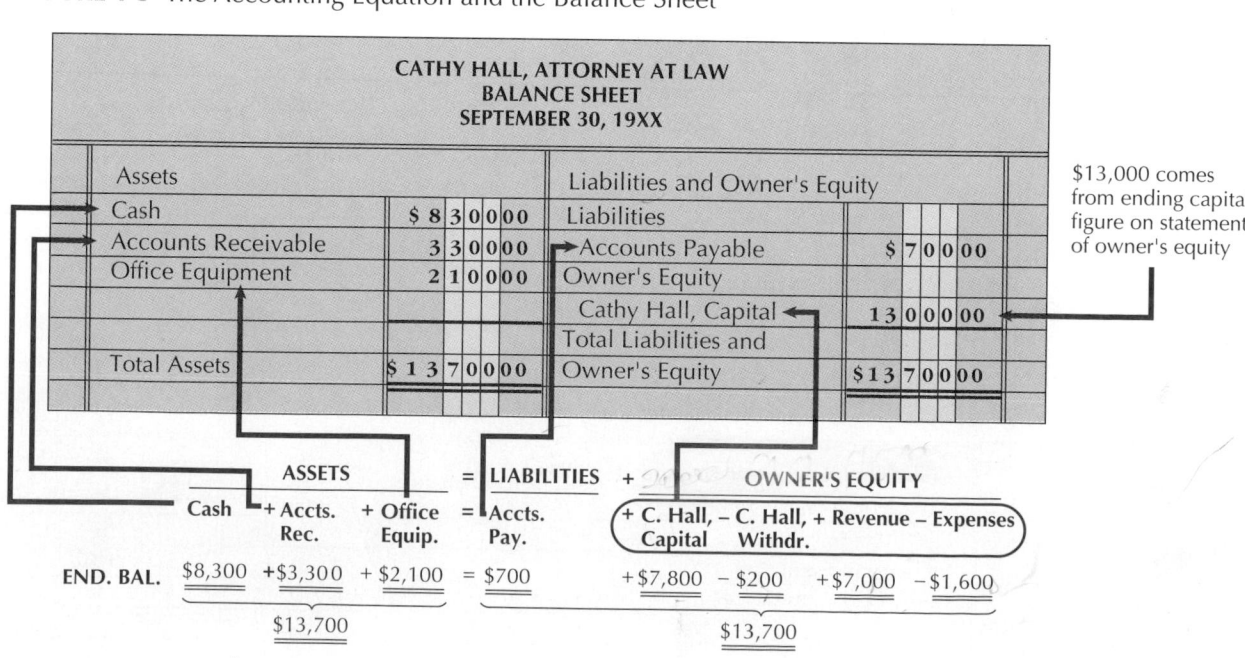

TABLE 1-3   WHAT GOES ON EACH FINANCIAL REPORT

	Income Statement	Statement of Owner's Equity	Balance Sheet
Assets			X
Liabilities			X
Capital† (beg)		X	
Capital (end)		X	X
Withdrawals		X	
Revenues	X		
Expenses	X		

† Note Additional Investments go on the Statement of Owner's Equity.

MAIN ELEMENTS OF THE INCOME STATEMENT, THE STATEMENT OF OWNER'S EQUITY, AND THE BALANCE SHEET

In this chapter we have discussed three financial reports: the income statement, the statement of owner's equity, and the balance sheet. There is a fourth report, called the statement of cash flows, that will not be covered at this time. Let us review what elements of the expanded accounting equation go into each report, and the usual order in which the reports are prepared. Figure 1-5 presents a diagram of the accounting equation and the balance sheet. Table 1-3 summarizes the following points:

◆ The income statement is prepared first; it includes revenues and expenses and shows net income or net loss. This net income or net loss is used to update the next report, the statement of owner's equity.

◆ The statement of owner's equity is prepared second; it includes beginning capital and any additional investments, the net income or net loss shown on the financial statement, withdrawals, and the total, which is the **ending capital.** The balance in Capital comes from the statement of owner's equity.

◆ The balance sheet is prepared last; it includes the final balances of each of the elements listed in the accounting equation under Assets and Liabilities. The balance in Capital comes from the statement of owner's equity.

LEARNING UNIT 1-4 REVIEW

AT THIS POINT you should be able to

◆ Define and state the purpose of the income statement, the statement of owner's equity, and the balance sheet. (p. 16)
◆ Discuss why the income statement should be prepared first. (p. 17)
◆ Compare and contrast these three financial reports. (p. 19)
◆ Calculate a new figure for capital on the statement of owner's equity and the balance sheet. (p. 17)
◆ Show what happens on a statement of owner's equity if there is a net loss. (p. 18)

SELF-REVIEW QUIZ 1-4

(The blank forms you need are on pages 4 and 5 of the *Study Guide and Working Papers.*)

From the following balances for Rusty Realty prepare:

1. Income statement for month ended November 30, 19XX.

R emember the TV ad in which Fred the Baker stumbles out of bed in the dark and drives to work—stopping only to wake up a rooster on the way! Fred is dedicated to making donuts (and the coffee and the bagels) fresh for the early morning customers at his Dunkin' Donuts store. Fred Baker, one of Dunkin' Donuts' newest shop owners, smiled as he thought of this commercial while he drove to work early one morning. Fred's name had been the source of lots of jokes—thousands of them—about his choice of companies, since it was also the name of the character in Dunkin' Donuts' long-running ad campaign. Like everyone else, Fred Baker was fond of Fred the Baker.

So what has this to do with accounting? Plenty, as it turns out. As one of Dunkin' Donuts' shop owners, Fred Baker wears two hats—his baker's cap and an accountant's green eyeshade. He makes the donuts, and he manages the accounts for his store. To learn how to do his job, Fred attended Dunkin' Donuts University. We'll share the financial lessons he learned there with you. The baking lessons—NO.

When you look at Fred's store, you are really seeing two businesses. Fred is the owner of his store, and he is a sole proprietor. He operates under an agreement with Dunkin' Donuts Inc. of Randolph, Massachusetts. Dunkin' Donuts Inc. supplies the business know-how and support (like training, national advertising, and recipes). Fred supplies capital (his investment) and his baking, management, and effort. Dunkin' Donuts Inc. and Fred operate interdependent businesses, and both rely on accounting information for their success.

Dunkin' Donuts Inc., in business since 1950, has grown dramatically over the years, to the point that it now has stores in 43 states and 20 countries. To manage this enormous service business requires very careful control of each of its 4,139 stores. At Dunkin' Donuts headquarters, Dwayne Goulding, Business Consultant for Fred's zone, monitors Fred's reports closely. It's his job to see that Fred makes money at making donuts, which in

TIME TO MAKE THE DONUTS

DUNKIN' DONUTS.

turn results in Dunkin' Donuts Inc. making money too.

Why does headquarters require accounting reports? Accounting reports give the information both Fred and the company need to make business decisions in a number of vital areas. For example:

1. Before Fred could buy his Dunkin' Donuts store, the company needed to know how much cash Fred had and his assets and liabilities. Fred prepared a personal Balance Sheet to give them this information.
2. Fred needs to know if his store is making a profit. He prepares an Income Statement to tell him that.
3. Dwayne needs to know if Fred's store is profitable and well run, compared to other shops in the zone. He compares the Income Statements of all shops to learn this. He also looks at competing businesses.
4. Fred must have the right amount of supplies on hand. If he has too few, he can't make the donuts. If he has too many, some may spoil. The Balance Sheet tells him what supplies are on hand. It also alerts Dwayne to potential problems Fred may have.
5. How often do Dunkin' Donuts stores report accounting information? Fred prepares a monthly Income Statement and Balance Sheet. He also prepares a daily Sales Report, which he summarizes every Saturday and sends to national headquarters. In addition, Fred does a weekly Payroll Report, which Dwayne reviews.

DISCUSSION QUESTIONS

1. What makes Fred a sole proprietor?
2. Why are Fred and Dunkin' Donuts interdependent businesses?
3. Why did Fred have to share his personal Balance Sheet with Dunkin' Donuts? Do you think most interdependent businesses do this?
4. What does Dunkin Donuts learn from Fred's Income Statement and Balance Sheet?

2. Statement of owner's equity for the month ended November 30, 19XX.
3. Balance sheet as of November 30, 19XX.

Cash	$4,000	R. Rusty, Capital	
Accounts Receivable	1,370	November 1, 19XX	$5,000
Store Furniture	1,490	R. Rusty, Withdrawals	100
Accounts Payable	900	Commissions Earned	1,500
		Rent Expense	200
		Advertising Expense	150
		Salaries Expense	90

Solution to Self-Review Quiz 1-4

Quiz Tip: Note that the inside column is only used for subtotaling.

RUSTY REALTY
INCOME STATEMENT
FOR MONTH ENDED NOVEMBER 30, 19XX

Revenue:			
Commissions Earned			$ 1 50 000
Operating Expenses:			
Rent Expense	$ 20 000		
Advertising Expense	15 000		
Salaries Expense	9 000		
Total Operating Expenses		44 000	
Net Income		$ 1 06 000	

Subtotal
Columns

The net income from the income statement is used to help build the statement of owner's equity.

RUSTY REALTY
STATEMENT OF OWNER'S EQUITY
FOR MONTH ENDED NOVEMBER 30, 19XX

R. Rusty, Capital, November 1, 19XX			$ 5 00 000
Net Income for November	$ 1 06 000		
Less Withdrawals for November	10 000		
Increase in Capital		96 000	
R. Rusty, Capital, November 30, 19XX		$ 5 96 000	

The new figure for capital from the statement of owner's equity is used as the capital figure on the balance sheet.

RUSTY REALTY
BALANCE SHEET
NOVEMBER 30, 19XX

Assets		Liabilities and Owner's Equity	
Cash	$ 4 00 000	Liabilities	
Accounts Receivable	1 37 000	Accounts Payable	$ 90 000
Store Furniture	1 49 000		
		Owner's Equity	
		R. Rusty, Capital	5 96 000
		Total Liabilities and	
Total Assets	$ 6 86 000	Owner's Equity	$ 6 86 000

CHAPTER REVIEW

COMPREHENSIVE DEMONSTRATION PROBLEM WITH SOLUTIONS TIPS

(The blank forms you need are on pages 6 and 7 of the *Study Guide and Working Papers.*)

Michael Brown opened his law office on June 1, 19XX. During the first month of operations Michael conducted the following transactions:

1. Invested $5,000 in cash into the law practice.
2. Paid $600 for office equipment.
3. Purchased additional office equipment on account, $1,000.
4. Performed legal services for clients receiving cash, $2,000.
5. Paid salaries, $800.
6. Performed legal services for clients on account, $1,000.
7. Paid rent, $1,200.
8. Withdrew $500 from his law practice for personal use.
9. Received $500 from customers in partial payment for legal services performed, transaction 6.

Assignment:

a. Record these transactions in the expanded accounting equation.
b. Prepare the financial statements at June 30 for Michael Brown, Attorney at Law.

Solution to Comprehensive Demonstration Problem

A.	Cash	+ Accts. Rec.	+ Office Equip.	= Accounts Payable	+ M. Brown, Capital	− M. Brown, Withdr.	+ Legal Fees	− Expenses
1.	+$5,000				+$5,000			
BAL.	5,000		=		5,000			
2.	−600		+$600					
BAL.	4,400	+	600 =		5,000			
3.			+1,000	+$1,000				
BAL.	4,400	+	1,600 =	1,000 +	5,000			
4.	+2,000						+$2,000	
BAL.	6,400	+	1,600 =	1,000 +	5,000		+ 2,000	
5.	−800							+$800
BAL.	5,600	+	1,600 =	1,000 +	5,000		+ 2,000 −	800
6.		+$1,000					+1,000	
BAL.	5,600 +	1,000 +	1,600 =	1,000 +	5,000		+ 3,000 −	800
7.	−1,200							+1,200
BAL.	4,400 +	1,000 +	1,600 =	1,000 +	5,000		+ 3,000 −	2,000
8.	−500					+$500		
BAL.	3,900 +	1,000 +	1,600 =	1,000 +	5,000 −	500	+ 3,000 −	2,000
9.	+500	−500						
END. BAL.	$4,400 +	$ 500 +	$1,600 =	$1,000 +	$5,000 −	$500	+ $3,000 −	$2,000
			$6,500 =	$6,500				

22

CH. 1 / ACCOUNTING CONCEPTS AND PROCEDURES: AN INTRODUCTION

Solution Tips to Expanded Accounting Equation

A.

◆ **Transaction 1:** The business increased its cash by $5,000. Owner's Equity (capital) increased when Michael supplied the cash to the business.

◆ **Transaction 2:** There was a shift in assets when the equipment was purchased. The business lowered its cash by $600, and a new column — Equipment — was increased for the $600 of equipment that was bought. The amount of capital is not touched because the owner did not supply any new funds.

◆ **Transaction 3:** When creditors supply $1,000 of additional equipment, the business Accounts Payable shows the debt. The business had increased what it *owes* the creditors.

◆ **Transaction 4:** Legal Fees, a subdivision of owner's equity, is increased when the law firm provides a service even if no money is received. The service provides an inward flow of $2,000 cash, an asset. Remember, legal fees are *not* an asset. As legal fees increase, owner's equity increases.

◆ **Transaction 5:** The salary paid by Michael shows an $800 increase in expenses, and a corresponding decrease in owner's equity.

◆ **Transaction 6:** Michael did the work and earned the $1,000. That $1,000 is recorded as revenue. This time the legal fees create an inward flow of assets called Accounts Receivable for $1,000. Remember legal fees are *not* an asset. They are a subdivision of owner's equity.

◆ **Transaction 7:** The $1,200 rent expense reduces owner's equity as well as cash.

◆ **Transaction 8:** Withdrawals are for personal use. Here, business decreases cash of $500 while Michael increases $500. Withdrawals decrease the owner's equity.

◆ **Transaction 9:** This transaction does not reflect new revenue in the form of legal feels. It is only a shift in assets: more cash and less Accounts Receivable.

B-1.

Michael Brown, Attorney at Law
Income Statement
For Month Ended June 30, 19XX

Revenue:		
Legal Fees		$3,000
Operating expenses:		
Salaries expense	$ 800	
Rent expense	1,200	
Total operating expenses		2,000
Net income		$1,000

B-2.

Michael Brown, Attorney at Law
Statement of Owner's Equity
For Month Ended June 30, 19XX

Michael Brown, Capital, June 1, 19XX		$5,000
Net income for June	$1,000	
Less withdrawals for June	500	
Increase in Capital		500
Michael Brown, Capital, June 30, 19XX		$5,500

B-3.

Michael Brown, Attorney at Law
Balance Sheet
June 30, 19XX

Assets		*Liabilities and Owner's Equity*	
Cash	$4,400	Liabilities	
Accounts Receivable	500	Accounts Payable	$1,000
Office equipment	1,600	Owner's Equity	
		M. Brown, Capital	5,500
Total Assets	$6,500	Total Liabilities and Owner's Equity	$6,500

Solution Tips to Financial Reports

B-1. Income statement lists only Revenues and Expenses for a period of time. Inside column for subtotaling. Withdrawals are not listed here.

B-2. The statement of Owner's Equity takes the net income figure of $1,000 and adds it to Beginning Capital less any withdrawals. This new capital figure of $5,500 will go on the balance sheet. This report shows changes in Capital for a period of time.

B-3. The $4,400, $500, $1,600, and $1,000 came from the totals of the expanded accounting equation. The Capital figure of $5,500 came from the statement of Owner's Equity. This balance sheet reports Assets, Liabilities, and a new figure for Capital at a specific date.

SUMMARY OF KEY POINTS

Learning Unit 1-1

1. The functions of accounting involve analyzing, recording, classifying, summarizing, reporting, and interpreting financial information.

2. A sole proprietorship is a business owned by one person. A partnership is a business owned by two or more persons. A corporation is a business owned by stockholders.

3. Bookkeeping is the recording part of accounting.

4. The computer is a tool to use in the accounting process.

5. Assets = Liabilities + Owner's Equity is the basic accounting equation that aids in analyzing business transactions.

6. Liabilities represents amounts owed to creditors while capital represents what is invested by the owner.

7. Capital does not mean cash. Capital is the owner's current investment. The owner could have invested equipment that was purchased before the new business was started.

8. In a shift of assets, the composition of assets changes, but the total of assets does not change. For example, if a bill is paid by a customer, the firm increases cash (an asset) but decreases accounts receivable (an asset), so there is no overall increase in assets; total assets remain the same. When you borrow money from a bank, you have an increase in cash (an asset) and an increase in liabilities: overall there is an increase in assets, not just a shift.

Learning Unit 1-2

1. The balance sheet is a report written as of a particular date. It lists the assets, liabilities, and owner's equity of a business. The heading of the balance sheet answers the questions *who, what,* and *when* (as of a specific date).

2. The balance sheet is a formal report of a financial position.

1. Revenue generates an inward flow of assets. Expenses generate an outward flow of assets or a potential outward flow. Revenue and expenses are subdivisions of owner's equity. Revenue is not an asset.

2. When revenue totals more than expenses, net income is the result; when expenses total more than revenue, net loss is the result.

3. Owner's equity can be subdivided into four elements: capital, withdrawals, revenue, and expenses.

4. Withdrawals decrease owner's equity; revenue increases owner's equity; expenses decrease owner's equity. A withdrawal is not a business expense; it is for personal use.

1. The income statement is a report written for a specific period of time that lists earned revenue and expenses incurred to produce the earned revenue. The net income or net loss will be used in the statement of owner's equity.

2. The statement of owner's equity reveals the causes of a change in capital. This report lists any investments, net income (or net loss), and withdrawals. The ending figure for capital will be used on the balance sheet.

3. The balance sheet uses the ending balances of assets and liabilities from the accounting equation and the capital from the statement of owner's equity.

4. The income statement should be prepared first because the information on it as to net income or net loss is used to prepare the statement of owner's equity, which in turn provides information about capital for the balance sheet. In this way one builds upon the next, and it begins with the income statement.

KEY TERMS

Accounting   A system that measures the business's activities in financial terms, provides written reports and financial statements about those activities, and communicates these reports to decision makers and others.

Accounts payable   Amounts owed to creditors that result from the purchase of goods or services on account: a liability.

Accounts receivable   An asset that indicates amounts owed by customers.

Assets   Properties (resources) of value owned by a business (cash, supplies, equipment, land).

Balance sheet   A report, as of a particular date, that shows the amount of assets owned by a business as well as the amount of claims (liabilities and owner's equity) against these assets.

Basic accounting equation   Assets = Liabilities + Owner's Equity.

Bookkeeping   The recording function of the accounting process.

Business entity   In *accounting* it is assumed that a business is separate and distinct from the personal assets of the owner. Each unit or entity requires separate accounting functions.

Capital   The owner's investment of equity in the company.

Corporation   A type of business organization that is owned by stockholders. Stockholders usually are not personally liable for the corporation's debts.

Creditor   Someone who has a claim to assets.

Ending capital   Beginning Capital + Additional Investments + Net Income − Withdrawals = Ending Capital. Or: Beginning Capital + Additional Investments − Net Loss − Withdrawals = Ending Capital.

Equities   The interest or financial claim of creditors (liabilities) and owners (owner's equity) who supply the assets to a firm.

Expanded accounting equation   Assets = Liabilities + Capital − Withdrawals + Revenue − Expenses.

Expense   A cost incurred in running a business by consuming goods or services in producing revenue; a subdivision of owner's equity. When expenses increase, there is a decrease in owner's equity.

Generally accepted accounting principles (GAAP)   The procedures and guidelines that must be followed during the accounting process.

Income statement   An accounting report that details the performance of a firm (revenue minus expenses) for a specific period of time.

Liabilities   Obligations that come due in the future. Liabilities result in increasing the financial rights or claims of creditors to assets.

Manufacturing company Business that makes a product and sells it to its customers.

Merchandising company Business that buys a product from a manufacturing company to sell to its customers.

Net income When revenue totals more than expenses, the result is net income.

Net loss When expenses total more than revenue, the result is net loss.

Owner's equity Rights or financial claims to the assets of a business (in the accounting equation, assets minus liabilities).

Partnership A form of business organization that has at least two owners. The partners usually are personally liable for the partnership's debts.

Revenue An amount earned by performing services for customers or selling goods to customers; can be in the form of cash and/or accounts receivable; a subdivision of owner's equity — as revenue increases, owner's equity increases.

Service company Business that provides a service.

Shift in assets A shift that occurs when the composition of the assets has changed, but the total of the assets remains the same.

Sole proprietorship A type of business ownership that has one owner. The owner is personally liable for paying the business's debts.

Statement of financial position Another name for a balance sheet.

Statement of owner's equity A financial report that reveals the change in capital. The ending figure for capital is then placed on the balance sheet.

Supplies One type of asset acquired by a firm; has a much shorter life than equipment.

Withdrawals A subdivision of owner's equity that records money or other assets an owner withdraws from a business for personal use.

BLUEPRINT OF FINANCIAL REPORTS

❶ Income Statement
Measuring performance

Revenue:		XXX
Operating	XX	
Expenses	XX	XXX
Net Income		XXX

❷ Statement of Owner's Equity
Calculating new figure for capital

Beginning Capital		XXX
Additional Investments		XXX
Total Investments		XXX
Net Income	XXX	
Less Withdrawals	XXX	
Increase in Capital		XXX
Ending Capital		XXX

❸ Balance Sheet
Where do we now stand

Assets		Liabilities and Owner's Equity	
	XXX	Liabilities	XXX
	XXX	Owner's Equity	
	XXX	Ending Capital	XXX
Total Assets	XXX	Total Liab. + OE	XXX

QUESTIONS, MINI EXERCISES, EXERCISES, AND PROBLEMS

Discussion Questions

1. What are the functions of accounting?
2. Define, compare, and contrast sole proprietorships, partnerships, and corporations.
3. How are businesses classified?
4. What is the relationship of bookkeeping to accounting?
5. List the three elements of the basic accounting equation.
6. Define capital.
7. The total of the left-hand side of the accounting equation must equal the total of the right-hand side. True or false? Please explain.
8. A balance sheet tells a company where it is going and how well it will perform. True or false? Please explain.
9. Revenue is an asset. True or false? Please explain.
10. What categories is owner's equity subdivided into?
11. A withdrawal is a business expense. True or false? Please explain.
12. As expenses increase they cause owner's equity to increase. Defend or reject.
13. What does an income statement show?
14. The statement of owner's equity only calculates ending withdrawals. True or false? Please explain.

Mini Exercises

(The blank forms you need are on page 9 of the *Study Guide and Working Papers*.)

Classifying Accounts

1. Classify each of the following items, as an Asset (A), Liability (L), or Part of Owner's Equity (OE).
   a. Land _____
   b. Accounts Payable _____
   c. P. Jean, Capital _____
   d. Supplies _____
   e. Cash _____
   f. Computer Equipment _____

The Accounting Equation

2. Complete
   a. A _____ _____ _____ results when the total of the assets remain the same but the makeup of the assets has changed.
   b. Assets − _____ = Owner's Equity.
   c. Capital does not mean _____.

Shift versus Increase in Assets

3. Identify which transaction results in a shift in assets (S) and which transaction causes an increase in assets (I).
   a. Ace Jewelry bought computer equipment for cash.
   b. Jake's Appliance bought office equipment on account.

The Balance Sheet

4. From the following, calculate what would be the total of assets on the Balance Sheet.

H. Anna, Capital	$8,000
Word Processing Equipment	600
Accounts Payable	2,000
Cash	9,400

The Accounting Equation Expanded

5. From the following, which are subdivisions of Owner's Equity?
   a. Land   _____
   b. B. Flynn, Capital   _____
   c. Accounts Receivable   _____
   d. B. Flynn, Withdrawals   _____
   e. Accounts Payable   _____
   f. Rent Expense   _____
   g. Office Equipment   _____
   h. Hair Salon Fees Earned   _____

Identifying Assets

6. Identify which of the following are *not* assets.
   a. Supplies   _____
   b. Accounts Payable   _____
   c. Legal Fees Earned   _____
   d. Accounts Receivable   _____

The Accounting Equation Expanded

7. Which of the following statements are false?
   a. _____ Revenue is an asset.
   b. _____ Revenue is a subdivision of Owner's Equity.
   c. _____ Revenue provides an inward flow of cash and/or Accounts Receivable.
   d. _____ Withdrawals are part of Total Assets.

Preparing Financial Reports

8. Indicate whether the following items would appear on the Income Statement (IS), Statement of Owner's Equity (OE), or Balance Sheet (BS).
   a. _____ B. Clo, Withdrawals
   b. _____ Supplies
   c. _____ Accounts Payable
   d. _____ Computer Equipment
   e. _____ Commission Fees Earned
   f. _____ Salaries Expense
   g. _____ B. Clo, Capital (Beg.)
   h. _____ Accounts Receivable

Preparing Financial Reports

9. Indicate next to each statement whether it refers to the Income Statement (IS), Statement of Owner's Equity (OE), or Balance Sheet (BS).

    a. _____ Calculate new figure for Capital

    b. _____ Prepared as of a particular date

    c. _____ Statement that is prepared first

    d. _____ Report Listing Revenues and Expenses

Exercises

(The forms you need are on pages 10–12 of the *Study Guide and Working Papers.*)

1-1. Complete the following table:

The accounting equation.

ASSETS = LIABILITIES + OWNER'S EQUITY

	ASSETS	=	LIABILITIES	+	OWNER'S EQUITY
a.	$7,000	=	?	+	$2,000
b.	?	=	$6,000	+	$8,000
c.	$10,000	=	$4,000	+	?

Recording transactions into the accounting equation.

1-2. Record the following transactions in the basic accounting equation. Treat each one separately.

ASSETS = LIABILITIES + OWNER'S EQUITY

    a. Jim invests $60,000 in company

    b. Bought equipment for cash, $600

    c. Bought equipment on account, $900

Preparing a balance sheet.

1-3. From the following, prepare a balance sheet for Avon's Cleaners at the end of November 19XX: Cash, $30,000; Cleaning Equipment, $8,000; Accounts Payable, $9,000; A. Avon, Capital?

Recording transactions into the expanded accounting equation.

1-4. Record the following transactions into the expanded accounting equation. The running balance may be omitted for simplicity.

ASSETS			= LIABILITIES +			OWNER'S EQUITY		
Cash +	Accounts Receivable	+ Computer Equipment	= Accounts Payable	+ B. Wong, Capital	− B. Wong, Withdrawals	+ Revenues	− Expenses	

    a. Bill Wong invested $60,000 in a computer company.

    b. Bought computer equipment on account, $7,000.

    c. Bill Wong paid personal telephone bill from company checkbook, $200.

    d. Received cash for services rendered, $14,000.

    e. Billed customers for services rendered for month, $30,000.

    f. Paid current rent expense, $4,000.

    g. Paid supplies expense, $1,500.

Preparing the income statement, statement of owner's equity, and balance sheet.

1-5. From the following account balances, prepare in proper form (a) an income statement for June, (b) a statement of owner's equity, and (c) a balance sheet for French Realty.

Cash	$3,310
Accounts Receivable	1,490
Office Equipment	6,700
Accounts Payable	2,000
S. French, Capital, June 1	8,000
S. French, Withdrawals	40
Professional Fees	2,900

Salaries Expense	500
Utilities Expense	360
Rent Expense	500

Group A Problems

(The forms you need are on pages 13 – 19 of the *Study Guide and Working Papers.*)

The accounting equation.

1A-1. Maggie Kay decided to open Kay's Realty. Maggie completed the following transactions:

Check Figure:

Total Assets $16,600

   a. Invested $16,000 cash from her personal bank account into the business.

   b. Bought equipment for cash, $4,000.

   c. Bought additional equipment on account, $1,000.

   d. Paid $400 cash to partially reduce what was owed from transaction C.

Based on the above information, record these transactions into the basic accounting equation.

Preparing a balance sheet.

1A-2. Joyce Hill is the accountant for Green's Advertising Service. From the following information, her task is to construct a balance sheet as of September 30, 19XX, in proper form. Could you help her?

Check Figure:

Total Assets $59,000

Building	$35,000
Accounts Payable	30,000
R. Green, Capital	29,000
Cash	10,000
Equipment	14,000

Recording transactions in the expanded accounting equation.

1A-3. At the end of November, Rick Fox decided to open his own typing service. Analyze the following transactions he completed by recording their effects on the expanded accounting equation.

   a. Invested $10,000 in his typing service.

   b. Bought new office equipment on account, $4,000.

   c. Received cash for typing services rendered, $500.

   d. Performed typing services on account, $2,100.

Check Figure:

Total Assets $15,640

   e. Paid secretary's salary, $350.

   f. Paid office supplies expense for the month, $210.

   g. Rent expenses for office due but unpaid, $900.

   h. Rick Fox withdrew cash for personal use, $400.

Preparing an income statement, statement of owner's equity, and balance sheet.

1A-4. Jane West, owner of West's Stenciling Service, has requested that you prepare from the following balances (a) an income statement for June 19XX, (b) a statement of owner's equity for June, and (c) a balance sheet as of June 30, 19XX.

Cash	$2,300
Accounts Receivable	400
Equipment	685
Accounts Payable	310
J. West, Capital, June 1, 19XX	1,200

Check Figure:

Total Assets $3,385

J. West, Withdrawals	300
Stenciling Fees	3,000
Advertising Expense	110
Repair Expense	25
Travel Expense	250
Supplies Expense	190
Rent Expense	250

Comprehensive problem.	**1A-5.** John, a retired army officer, opened Tobey's Catering Service. As his accountant, analyze the transactions listed below and present in proper form.

1. The analysis of the transactions by utilizing the expanded accounting equation.

Check Figure:

Total Assets, Nov. 30 $24,060

2. A balance sheet showing the position of the firm before opening on November 1, 19XX.
3. An income statement for the month of November.
4. A statement of owner's equity for November.
5. A balance sheet as of November 30, 19XX.

19XX

Oct.   25 John Tobey invested $20,000 in the catering business from his personal savings account.
       27 Bought equipment for cash from Munroe Co., $700
       28 Bought additional equipment on account from Ryan Co., $1,000.
       29 Paid $600 to Ryan Co. as partial payment of the October 28 transaction.

(You should now prepare your balance sheet as of October 31, 19XX)

Nov.   1 Catered a graduation and immediately collected cash, $2,400.
        5 Paid salaries of employees, $690.
        8 Prepared desserts for customers on account, $300.
       10 Received $100 cash as partial payment of November 8 transaction.
       15 Paid telephone bill, $60.
       17 Paid his home electric bill from the company's checkbook, $90.
       20 Catered a wedding and received cash, $1,800.
       25 Bought additional equipment on account, $400.
       28 Rent expense due but unpaid, $600.
       30 Paid supplies expense, $400.

Group B Problems

(The forms you need are on pages 13–19 of the *Study Guide and Working Papers*.)

The accounting equation.

1B-1. Maggie Kay began a new business called Kay's Realty. The following transactions resulted:

   a. Maggie invested $17,000 cash from her personal bank account into the realty company.

Check Figure:

Total Assets $18,000

   b. Bought equipment on account, $1,800.
   c. Paid $800 cash to partially reduce what was owed from transaction B.
   d. Purchased additional equipment for cash, $3,000.

Record these transactions into the basic accounting equation.

Preparing a balance sheet.

1B-2. Joyce Hill has asked you to prepare a balance sheet as of September 30, 19XX, for Green's Advertising Service. Could you assist Joyce?

R. Green, Capital	$19,000
Accounts Payable	70,000
Equipment	41,000
Building	16,000
Cash	32,000

Check Figure:

Total Assets $89,000

Recording transactions in the expanded accounting equation.

1B-3. Rick Fox decided to open his own typing service company at the end of November. Analyze the following transactions by recording their effects on the expanded accounting equation.

a. Rick Fox invested $9,000 in the typing service.

b. Purchased new office equipment on account, $3,000.

c. Received cash for typing services rendered, $1,290.

Check Figure:

Total Assets $14,820

d. Paid secretary's salary, $310.

e. Billed customers for typing services rendered, $2,690.

f. Paid rent expense for the month, $500.

g. Rick withdrew cash for personal use, $350.

h. Advertising expense due but unpaid, $100.

Preparing an income statement, statement of owner's equity, and balance sheet.

1B-4. Jane West, owner of West's Stenciling Service, has requested that you prepare from the following balances (a) an income statement for June 19XX, (b) a statement of owner's equity for June, and (c) a balance sheet as of June 30, 19XX.

Cash	$2,043
Accounts Receivable	1,140
Equipment	540
Accounts Payable	45
J. West, Capital, June 1, 19XX	3,720
J. West, Withdrawals	360
Stenciling Fees	1,098
Advertising Expense	135
Repair Expense	45
Travel Expense	90
Supplies Expense	270
Rent Expense	240

Check Figure:

Total Assets $3,723

Comprehensive Problem.

1B-5. John Tobey, a retired army officer, opened Tobey's Catering Service. As his accountant, analyze the transactions and present the following information in proper form:

1. The analysis of the transactions by utilizing the expanded accounting equation.

2. A balance sheet showing the financial position of the firm before opening on November 1, 19XX.

Check Figure:

Total Assets, Nov. 30 $25,005

3. An income statement for the month of November.

4. A statement of owner's equity for November.

5. A balance sheet as of November 30, 19XX.

19XX

Oct.   25 John Tobey invested $17,500 in the catering business.

27 Bought equipment on account from Munroe Co., $900.

28 Bought equipment for cash from Ryan Co., $1,500.

29 Paid $300 to Munroe Co. as partial payment of the October 27 transaction.

Nov.   1 Catered a business luncheon and immediately collected cash, $2,000.

5 Paid salaries of employees, $350.

8 Provided catering services to Northwest Community College on account, $4,500.

10 Received from Northwest Community College $1,000 cash as partial payment of November 8 transaction.

15 Paid telephone bill, $95.

17 Tobey paid his home mortgage from the company's checkbook, $650.

20 Provided catering services and received cash, $1,800.

25 Bought additional equipment on account, $300.

28 Rent expense due but unpaid, $750.

30 Paid supplies expense, $600.

REAL WORLD APPLICATIONS

1R-1.

You have just been hired to prepare, if possible, an income statement for the year ended December 31, 19XX, for Logan's Window Washing Company. The problem is that Bill Logan kept only the following records (on the back of a piece of cardboard).

Money in:
Window cleaning	$11,376
My investment	1,200
Loan from brother-in-law	4,000

Money out:
Salaries	$5,080
Withdrawals	6,200
Supplies expense	1,400

What I owe or they owe me

A. People that work for me but I still owe salaries to $1,800
B. Owe bank interest of $300
C. Work done but clients still owe me $2,900
D. Advertising bill due but not paid $95

Assume that Logan's Window Washing Company records all revenues when earned and all expenses when incurred.

You feel that it is part of your job to tell Bill how to organize his records better. What would you tell him?

1R-2.

While Jon Lune was on a business trip, he asked Abby Slowe, the bookkeeper for Lune Co., to try to complete a balance sheet for the year ended December 31, 19XX. Abby, who had been on the job only two months, submitted the following.

LUNE CO.
FOR THE YEAR ENDED DECEMBER 31, 19XX

Building	$44,600 00	Accounts Payable	$12,760 400
Land	72,935 00	Accounts Receivable	10,433 700
Notes Payable	75,328 00	Auto	14,268 00
Cash	10,016 00	Desks	6,825 00
J. Lune, Capital	?	Total Equity	$25,003 400

1. Could you help Abby fix as well as complete the balance sheet?
2. What written recommendations would you make about the bookkeeper? Should she be retained?
3. Suppose that (a) Jon Lune invested an additional $20,000 in cash as well as additional desks with a value of $8,000 and (b) Lune Co. bought an auto for $6,000 that was originally marked $8,000, paying $2,000 down and issuing a note for the balance. Could you prepare an updated balance sheet? Assume that these two transactions occurred on January 4.

YOU make the call

Critical Thinking/Ethical Case

(The forms you need are on page 8 of the *Study Guide and Working Papers*.)

1R-3.

Paul Kloss, Accountant for Lowe & Co., traveled to New York on company business. His total expenses came to $350. Paul felt that since the trip extended over the weekend he would "pad" his expense account with an additional $100 of expenses. After all, weekends represent his own time, not the company's. What would you do? Write your specific recommendations to Paul.

ACCOUNTING RECALL

A CUMULATIVE APPROACH

THIS EXAM REVIEWS CHAPTER 1

Your *Study Guide and Working Papers* has a form on page 23 to complete this exam, as well as solutions on page 26. The page references next to each question identify what page to turn back to if you answer the question incorrectly.

PART 1   Vocabulary Review

Match the terms to the appropriate definition or phrase.
Page Ref.

(6)	1. Capital	A. Prepared as of a particular date
(11)	2. Accounts receivable	B. A liability
(2)	3. Sole proprietorship	C. For personal use
(11)	4. Expense	D. Provides an inward flow of assets
(9)	5. Balance sheet	E. Company owned and managed by one person
(11)	6. Revenue	F. Amount owed by customers
(11)	7. Withdrawals	G. Owner's investment
(16)	8. Income statement	H. A cost of running a business
(7)	9. Accounts payable	I. Broken into four subdivisions
(5)	10. Owner's equity	J. Prepared for specific period of time

PART II   True or False (Accounting Theory)

(11) 11. Revenue is an asset.

(14) 12. The four subdivisions of owner's equity are capital, withdrawals, revenue, and expenses.

(14) 13. As expenses increase, owner's equity increases.

(18) 14. Accounts receivable goes on the income statement.

(17) 15. The statement of owner's equity calculates a new figure for capital.

CONTINUING PROBLEM

The following problem will continue from one chapter to the next carrying the balances forward of each month. Each chapter will focus on the learning experience of the chapter and add additional information as the business grows. Forms are on page 24 of the *Study Guide and Working Papers*.

Assignment

1. Set up an expanded accounting equation spreadsheet using the following accounts.

Assets	Liabilities	Owner's Equity
Cash	Accounts Payable	Freedman, Capital
Supplies		Freedman, Withdrawal
Computer Shop Equipment		Service Revenue
Office Equipment		Expenses (notate type)

2. Analyze and record each transaction in the expanded accounting equation.
3. Prepare the financial statements ending July 31 for Eldorado Computer Center.

On July 1, 19XX, Tony Freedman decided to begin his own computer service business. He named the business the Eldorado Computer Center. During the first month Tony conducted the following business transactions:

a) Invested $4,500 of his savings into the business
b) Paid $1,200 (check #8095) for the computer from Multi Systems, Inc.
c) Paid $600 (check # 8096) for office equipment from Office Furniture, Inc.
d) Set up a new account with Office Depot and purchased $250 in office supplies on credit
e) Paid July rent, $400 (check # 8087)
f) Repaired a system for a customer; collected $250
g) Collected $200 for system upgrade labor charge from a customer
h) Electric bill due but unpaid, $85
i) Collected $1,200 for services performed on Taylor Golf computers
j) Tony withdrew $100 (check # 8098) to take his wife Carol out in celebration of opening the new business

2

DEBITS AND CREDITS

Analyzing and Recording

Business Transactions

THE BIG PICTURE

As the owner of Eldorado Computer Center, Tony Freedman spends most of his time interacting with customers and performing services for them. Only some of Freedman's activities, however, are business transactions. In a business transaction an exchange takes place. Cash is paid for services. Credit is given to customers. Rent is paid for the use of space. Each transaction must be recorded in the accounts of Freedman's business.

In this chapter you will see how every transaction must affect at least two accounts. As you learned in Chapter 1, every account is categorized under a heading from the accounting equation: assets, liabilities, or owner's equity. When you analyze a transaction, you decide not only which accounts change in value, but also whether they increase or decrease. Remember the accounting equation must always be kept in balance, and the key to recording every transaction is the interpretation of what happened.

To analyze transactions accurately and to keep the accounting equation in balance, you will use T accounts and a system of debits and credits. The T account lets us write the value of a transaction as a credit or debit in a standard format. A T account can be easily totaled at any time. The rules for debits and credits assure us that if debits equal credits in every transaction, then the accounting equation will always balance. Whether you use a manual or a computerized accounting system, you must analyze transactions correctly to get correct results.

At the end of each monthly accounting period, Freedman conducts a trial balance, a test of the equality of debits and credits in all his accounts. He can then use the account balances to generate financial statements that he can compare from month to month.

In Chapter 1, we used the expanded accounting equation to document the financial transactions performed by Cathy Hall's law firm. Remember how long it was: the cash column had a long list of pluses and minuses, and there was no quick system of recording and summarizing the increases and decreases of cash or other items. Can you imagine the problem Compaq Computer or Dunkin' Donuts would have if they used the expanded accounting equation to track the thousands of business transactions they do each day?

LEARNING UNIT 2-1
The T Account

Let's look at the problem a little more closely. Each business transaction is recorded in the accounting equation under a specific **account.** There are different accounts for each of the subdivisions of the accounting equation — there are asset accounts, liabilities accounts, expense accounts, revenue accounts, and so on. What is needed is a way to record the increases and decreases in specific account *categories* and yet keep them together in one place. The answer is the **standard account** form (see Fig. 2-1). A standard account is a formal account that includes columns for date, explanation, posting reference, debit, and credit. Each account has a separate form and all transactions affecting that account are recorded on the form. All the business's account forms (which often are referred to as *ledger accounts*) are then placed in a **ledger.** Each page of the ledger contains one account. The ledger may be in the form of a bound or a loose-leaf book. If computers are used, the ledger may be part of a computer printout. For simplicity's sake, we will use the **T account** form. This form got its name because it looks like the letter T. Generally, T accounts are used for demonstration purposes.

FIGURE 2-1
The Standard Account Form is the source of the T account's Shape

Account Title								Account No.
Date	Item	PR	Debit	Date	Item	PR	Credit	

Each T account contains three basic parts:

$$\underset{\text{2} \qquad \text{Left side} \mid \text{Right side} \qquad \text{3}}{\overline{\underset{1}{\text{Title of Account}}}}$$

All T accounts have this structure. In accounting, the left side of any T account is called the **debit** side.

Left side
Dr. (debit)

Just as the word *left* has many meanings, the word *debit* for now in accounting means a position, the left side of an account. Don't think of it as good (+) or bad (−).

Amounts entered on the left side of any account are said to be *debited* to an account. The abbreviation for debit (Dr.) is from the Latin *debere*.

The right side of any T account is called the **credit** side.

Right side
Cr. (credit)

Amounts entered on the right side of an account are said to be *credited* to an account. The abbreviation for credit (Cr.) is from the Latin *credere*.

At this point, do not associate the definition of debit and credit with the words *increase* or *decrease*. Think of debit or credit as only indicating a *position* (left or right side) of a T account.

Debit defined:

1. The *left* side of any T account.
2. A number entered on the left side of any account is said to be *debited* to an account.

Credit defined:

1. The *right* side of any T account.
2. A number entered on the right side of any account is said to be *credited* to an account.

Dollar signs are not used in standard accounts or T accounts. However, dollar signs are used in formal financial reports.

BALANCING AN ACCOUNT

No matter which individual account is being balanced, the procedure used to balance it will be the same.

	Dr.	Cr.	
Entries {	**3,000**		**300**
	500		**400**
Footings →	3,500		700
Balance	2,800		

In the "real" world, the T account would also include the date of the transaction. The date would appear to the left of the entry:

	Dr.		Cr.
4/2	**3,000**	4/3	**300**
4/20	**500**	4/25	**400**
	3,500		700
Bal.	2,800		

Note that on the debit (left) side the numbers add up to $3,500. On the credit (right) side the numbers add up to $700. The $3,500 and the $700 written in small type are called **footings**. Footings help in calculating the new (or ending) balance. The **ending balance** ($2,800) is placed on the debit or left side, since the balance of the debit side is greater than that of the credit side.

Remember, the ending balance does not tell us anything about increase or decrease. It only tells us that we have an ending balance of $2,800 on the debit side.

Footings aid in balancing an account. The ending balance is the difference between the footings.

If the balance was greater on the credit side, that is the side the ending balance would be on.

LEARNING UNIT 2-1 REVIEW

AT THIS POINT you should be able to

- ◆ Define ledger. (p. 37)
- ◆ State the purpose of a T account. (p. 38)
- ◆ Identify the three parts of a T account. (p. 38)
- ◆ Define debit. (p. 38)
- ◆ Define credit. (p. 38)
- ◆ Explain footings and calculate the balance of an account. (p. 38)

SELF-REVIEW QUIZ 2-1

(The blank forms you need are on page 27 of the *Study Guide and Working Papers.*)

Respond True or False to the following:

1.

Dr.	Cr.
1,000	100
50	50

The balance of the account is $900 Cr.

2. A credit always means increase.

3. A debit is the left side of any account.

4. A ledger can be prepared manually or by computer.

5. Footings replace the need for debits and credits.

Quiz Tip:

Dr. + Dr. ⟶ Add to get Dr. balance

Cr. + Cr. ⟶ Add to get Cr. balance

Dr. − Cr. ⟶ Subtract to get balance for the larger side.

Solutions to Self-Review Quiz 2-1

1. False   2. False   3. True   4. True   5. False

LEARNING UNIT 2-2

Recording Business Transactions: Debits and Credits

Can you get a queen in checkers? In a baseball game does a runner rounding first base skip second base and run over the pitcher's mound to get to third? No — most of us don't do such things because we follow the rules of the game. Usually we learn the rules first and reflect on the reasons for them afterward. The same is true in accounting.

Instead of first trying to understand all the rules of debit and credit and how they were developed in accounting, it will be easier to learn the rules by "playing the game."

T ACCOUNT ENTRIES FOR ACCOUNTING IN THE ACCOUNTING EQUATION

Have patience. Learning the rules of debit and credit is like learning to play any game — the more you play, the easier it becomes. Table 2-1 shows the rules for the side on which you enter an increase or a decrease for each of the separate accounts in the accounting equation. For example, an increase is entered on the debit side in the asset account, but on the credit side for a liability account.

It might be easier to visualize these rules of debit and credit if we look at them in the T account form, using + to show increase and − to show decrease.

ASSETS = LIABILITIES + OWNER'S EQUITY

ASSETS			LIABILITIES		+	Capital		−	Withdrawals		−	Revenue		−	Expenses	
Dr.	Cr.		Dr.	Cr.		Dr.	Cr.		Dr.	Cr.		Dr.	Cr.		Dr.	Cr.
+	−		−	+		−	+		+	−		−	+		+	−

Rules for Assets Work in the Opposite Direction to Those for Liabilities

When you look at the equation you can see that the rules for assets work in the opposite direction to those for liabilities. That is, for assets the increases appear on the debit side and the decreases are shown on the credit side; the opposite is true for liabilities. As for the owner's equity, the rules for withdrawals and expenses, which *decrease* owner's equity, work in the opposite direction to the rules for capital and revenue, which *increase* owner's equity.

Assets		+	Withdrawals		+	Expenses		=	Liabilities		+	Capital		+	Revenue	
Dr.	Cr.		Dr.	Cr.		Dr.	Cr.		Dr.	Cr.		Dr.	Cr.		Dr.	Cr.
+	−		+	−		+	−		−	+		−	+		−	+

This setup may help you visualize how the rules for withdrawals and expenses are just the opposite of those for capital and revenue.

A **normal balance of an account** is the side that increases by the rules of debit and credit. For example, the balance of cash is a debit balance, because an asset is increased by a debit. We will discuss normal balances further in Chapter 3.

Balancing the Equation   It is important to remember that any amount(s) entered on the debit side of a T account or accounts also must be on the credit side of another T account or accounts. This ensures that the total amount added to the debit side will equal the total amount added to the credit side, thereby keeping the accounting equation in balance.

Chart of Accounts   Our job is to analyze Cathy Hall's business transactions — the transactions we looked at in Chapter 1 — using a system of accounts guided by the rules of debits and credits that will summarize increases and decreases of individual accounts in the ledger. The goal is to prepare an income statement, statement of owner's equity, and balance sheet for Cathy Hall. Sound familiar? If this system works, the rules of debits and credits and the use of accounts will give us the same answers as in Chapter 1, but with greater ease.

Normal Balance

Dr.	Cr.
Assets	Liabilities
Expenses	Capital
Withdrawals	Revenue

Be sure to follow the rules of debits and credits when recording accounts. They were designed to keep the accounting equation in balance.

TABLE 2-1   RULES OF DEBIT AND CREDIT

Account Category	Increase (Normal Balance)	Decrease
Assets	Debit	Credit
Liabilities	Credit	Debit
Owner's Equity		
Capital	Credit	Debit
Withdrawals	Debit	Credit
Revenue	Credit	Debit
Expenses	Debit	Credit

TABLE 2-2 CHART OF ACCOUNTS FOR CATHY HALL, ATTORNEY AT LAW

Balance Sheet Accounts	
Assets	**Liabilities**
111 Cash	211 Accounts Payable
112 Accounts Receivable	**Owner's Equity**
121 Office Equipment	311 Cathy Hall, Capital
	312 Cathy Hall, Withdrawals

Income Statement Accounts	
Revenue	**Expenses**
411 Legal Fees	511 Salaries Expense
	512 Rent Expense
	513 Advertising Expense

The chart of accounts aids in locating and identifying accounts quickly.

Large companies may have up to four digits assigned to each title.

Cathy's accountant developed what is called a **chart of accounts.** The chart of accounts is a numbered list of all of the business's accounts. It allows accounts to be located quickly. In Cathy's business, for example, 100s are assets, 200s are liabilities, and so on. As you see in Table 2-2, each separate asset and liability has its own number. Note the chart may be expanded as the business grows.

THE TRANSACTION ANALYSIS: FIVE STEPS

We will analyze the transactions in Cathy Hall's law firm using a teaching device called a *transaction analysis chart* to record these five steps. (Keep in mind that the transaction analysis chart is not a part of any formal accounting system.) There are five steps to analyzing each business transaction:

Steps to analyze and record transactions. Steps 1 and 2 will come from the chart of accounts.

Remember the rules of debit and credit only tell us on which side to place information. Whether the debit or credit represents increases or decreases depends on the account category—assets, liabilities, capital, and so on. Think of a business transaction as an exchange—you get something and you give or part with something.

Step 1: Determine which accounts are affected. Example: cash, accounts payable, rent expense. A transaction always affects at least two accounts.

Step 2: Determine which categories the accounts belong to — assets, liabilities, capital, withdrawals, revenue, or expenses. Example: cash is an asset.

Step 3: Determine whether the accounts increase or decrease. Example: If you receive cash, that account is increasing.

Step 4: What do the rules of debits and credits say (Table 2-1)?

Step 5: What does the T account look like? Place amounts into accounts either on the left or right side depending on the rules in Table 2-1.

This is how the five-step analysis looks in chart form:

1	2	3	4	5
Accounts Affected	Category	↓ or ↑ (decrease) (increase)	Rules of Dr. and Cr.	Appearance of T Accounts

Let us emphasize a major point: *Do not try to debit or credit an account until you have gone through the first three steps of the transaction analysis.*

APPLYING THE TRANSACTION ANALYSIS TO CATHY HALL'S LAW PRACTICE

Transaction (A)   August 28: Cathy Hall invests $7,000 cash and $800 of office equipment in the business

1 Accounts Affected	2 Category	3 ↓ ↑	4 Rules of Dr. and Cr.	5 Appearance of T Accounts
Cash	Asset	↑	Dr.	**Cash 111** (A) 7,000 |
Office Equipment	Asset	↑	Dr.	**Office Equipment 121** (A) 800 |
Cathy Hall, Capital	Capital	↑	Cr.	**Cathy Hall, Capital 311** |7,800 (A)

Note in column 3 of the chart: It doesn't matter if both arrows go up, as long as the sum of the debits equals the sum of the credits in the T accounts in column 5.

Note again that every transaction affects at least two T accounts, and that the total amount added to the debit side(s) must equal the total amount added to the credit side(s) of the T accounts of each transaction.

Analysis of Transaction A

Step 1:   Which accounts are affected? The law firm receives its cash and office equipment, so three accounts are involved: Cash, Office Equipment, and Cathy Hall, Capital. These account titles come from the chart of accounts.

Step 2:   Which categories do these accounts belong to? Cash and Office Equipment are assets. Cathy Hall, Capital, is capital.

Step 3:   Are the accounts increasing or decreasing? The Cash and Office Equipment, both assets, are increasing in the business. The rights or claims of Cathy Hall, Capital, are also increasing, since she invested money and office equipment in the business.

Step 4:   What do the rules say? According to the rules of debit and credit, an increase in assets (Cash and Office Equipment) is a debit. An increase in Capital is a credit. Note that the total dollar amount of debits will equal the total dollar amount of credits when the T accounts are updated in column 5.

Step 5:   What does the T account look like? The amount for Cash and Office Equipment is entered on the debit side. The amount for Cathy Hall, Capital, goes on the credit side.

A transaction that involves more than one credit or more than one debit is called a **compound entry.** This first transaction of Cathy Hall's law firm is a compound entry; it involves a debit of $7,000 to Cash and a debit of $800 to Office Equipment (as well as a credit of $7,800 to Cathy Hall, Capital).

There is a name for this double-entry analysis of transactions, where two or more accounts are affected and the total of debits and credits is equal. It is called **double-entry bookkeeping.** This double-entry system helps in checking the recording of business transactions.

Double-entry bookkeeping system: The total of all debits is equal to the total of all credits.

As we continue, the explanations will be brief, but do not forget to apply the five steps in analyzing and recording each business transaction.

Transaction (B)   Aug. 29: Law practice bought office equipment for cash, $900.

1 Accounts Affected	2 Category	3 ↓ ↑	4 Rules of Dr. and Cr.	5 T Account Update
Office Equipment	Asset	↑	Dr.	Office Equipment 121 (A) 800 (B) 900
Cash	Asset	↓	Cr.	Cash 111 (A) 7,000 | 900 (B)

Analysis of Transaction B

Step 1: The law firm paid cash for the office equipment it received. The accounts involved in the transaction are Cash and Office Equipment.

Step 2: The accounts belong to these categories: Office Equipment is an asset; Cash is an asset.

Step 3: The asset Office Equipment is increasing. The asset Cash is decreasing — it is being reduced in order to buy the office equipment.

Step 4: An increase in the asset Office Equipment is a debit; a decrease in the asset Cash is a credit.

Step 5: When the amounts are placed in the T accounts, the amount for Office Equipment goes on the debit side and the amount for Cash on the credit side.

Transaction (C)   Aug. 30: Bought more office equipment on account, $400.

1 Accounts Affected	2 Category	3 ↓ ↑	4 Rules of Dr. and Cr.	5 T Account Update
Office Equipment	Asset	↑	Dr.	Office Equipment 121 (A) 800 (B) 900 (C) 400
Accounts Payable	Liability	↑	Cr.	Accounts Payable 211 |400 (C)

Analysis of Transaction C

Step 1: The law firm receives office equipment by promising to pay in the future. An obligation or liability, Accounts Payable, is created.

Step 2: Office Equipment is an asset. Accounts Payable is a liability.

Step 3: The asset Office Equipment is increasing; the liability Accounts Payable is increasing because the law firm is increasing what it owes.

Step 4: An increase in the asset Office Equipment is a debit. An increase in the liability Accounts Payable is a credit.

Step 5: Enter the amount for Office Equipment on the debit side of the T account. The amount for the Accounts Payable goes on the credit side.

1 Accounts Affected	2 Category	3 ↓ ↑	4 Rules of Dr. and Cr.	5 T Account Update
Cash	Asset	↑	Dr.	**Cash 111** (A) 7,000 | 900 (B) (D) 3,000 |
Legal Fees	Revenue	↑	Cr.	**Legal Fees 411** | 3,000 (D)

Analysis of Transaction D

Step 1: The firm has earned revenue from legal services and receives $3,000 in cash.

Step 2: Cash is an asset. Legal Fees are revenue.

Step 3: Cash, an asset, is increasing. Legal Fees, or revenue, are also increasing.

Step 4: An increase in Cash, an asset, is debited. An increase in Legal Fees, or revenue, is credited.

Step 5: Enter the amount for Cash on the debit side of the T account. Enter the amount for Legal Fees on the credit side.

Transaction (E)   Sept. 1–30: Provided legal services on account, $4,000.

1 Accounts Affected	2 Category	3 ↓ ↑	4 Rules of Dr. and Cr.	5 T Account Update
Accounts Receivable	Asset	↑	Dr.	**Accounts Receivable 112** (E) 4,000 |
Legal Fees	Revenue	↑	Cr.	**Legal Fees 411** | 3,000 (D) | 4,000 (E)

Analysis of Transaction E

Step 1: The law practice has earned revenue but has not yet received payment (cash). The amounts owed by these clients are called Accounts Receivable. Revenue is earned at the time the legal services are provided, whether payment is received then or will be received sometime in the future.

Step 2: Accounts Receivable is an asset. Legal Fees are revenue.

Step 3: Accounts Receivable is increasing because the law practice has increased the amount owed to it for legal fees that have been earned but not paid. Legal Fees, or revenue, are increasing.

Step 4: An increase in the asset Accounts Receivable is a debit. An increase in Revenue is a credit.

Step 5: Enter the amount for Accounts Receivable on the debit side of the T account. The amount for Legal Fees goes on the credit side.

Transaction (F) Sept. 1–30: Received $700 cash from clients for services rendered previously on account.

1 Accounts Affected	2 Category	3 ↓	↑	4 Rules of Dr. and Cr.	5 T Account Update
Cash	Asset		↑	Dr.	**Cash 111** (A) 7,000 | 900 (B) (D) 3,000 | (F) 700 |
Accounts Receivable	Asset	↓		Cr.	**Accounts Receivable 112** (E) 4,000 | 700 (F)

Analysis of Transaction F

Step 1: The law firm collects $700 in cash from previous revenue earned. Since the revenue is recorded at the time it is earned, and not when the payment is made, in this transaction we are concerned only with the payment, which affects the Cash and Accounts Receivable accounts.

Step 2: Cash is an asset. Accounts Receivable is an asset.

Step 3: Since clients are paying what is owed, Cash (asset) is increasing and the amount owed (Accounts Receivable) is decreasing (the total amount owed by clients to Hall is going down). This transaction results in a shift in assets, more Cash for less Accounts Receivable.

Step 4: An increase in Cash, an asset, is a debit. A decrease in Accounts Receivable, an asset, is a credit.

Step 5: Enter the amount for Cash on the debit side of the T account. The amount for Accounts Receivable goes on the credit side.

Transaction (G) Sept. 1–30: Paid salaries expense, $600.

1 Accounts Affected	2 Category	3 ↓	↑	4 Rules of Dr. and Cr.	5 T Account Update
Salaries Expense	Expense		↑	Dr.	**Salaries Expense 511** (G) 600 |
Cash	Asset	↓		Cr.	**Cash 111** (A) 7,000 | 900 (B) (D) 3,000 | 600 (G) (F) 700 |

Analysis of Transaction G

Step 1: The law firm pays $600 worth of salaries expense by cash.

Step 2: Salaries Expense is an expense. Cash is an asset.

Step 3: The Salaries Expense of the law firm is increasing, which results in a decrease in Cash.

Step 4: An increase in Salaries Expense, an expense, is a debit. A decrease in Cash, an asset, is a credit.

Step 5: Enter the amount for Salaries Expense on the debit side of the T account. The amount for Cash goes on the credit side.

Transaction (H)   Sept. 1–30: Paid rent expense, $700.

1 Accounts Affected	2 Category	3 ↓ ↑	4 Rules of Dr. and Cr.	5 T Account Update
Rent Expense	Expense	↑	Dr.	**Rent Expense 512** (H) 700 |
Cash	Asset	↓	Cr.	**Cash 111** (A) 7,000 | 900 (B) (D) 3,000 | 600 (G) (F) 700 | 700 (H)

Analysis of Transaction H

Step 1: The law firm's rent expenses are paid in cash.

Step 2: Rent is an expense. Cash is an asset.

Step 3: The Rent Expense increases the expenses, and the payment for the Rent Expense decreases the cash.

Step 4: An increase in Rent Expense, an expense, is a debit. A decrease in Cash, an asset, is a credit.

Step 5: Enter the amount for Rent Expense on the debit side of the T account. Place the amount for Cash on the credit side.

Transaction (I)   Sept. 1–30: Received a bill for Advertising Expense (to be paid next month), $300.

1 Accounts Affected	2 Category	3 ↓ ↑	4 Rules of Dr. and Cr.	5 T Account Update
Advertising Expense	Expense	↑	Dr.	**Advertising Expense 513** (I) 300 |
Accounts Payable	Liability	↑	Cr.	**Accounts Payable 211** | 400 (C) | 300 (I)

Analysis of Transaction I

Step 1: The advertising bill has come in and payment is due but has not yet been made. Therefore the accounts involved here are Advertising Expense and Accounts Payable; the expense has created a liability.

Step 2: Advertising Expense is an expense. Accounts Payable is a liability.

Step 3: Both the expense and the liability are increasing.

Step 4: An increase in an expense is a debit. An increase in a liability is a credit.

Step 5: Enter the amount for Advertising Expense on the debit side of the T Account. Enter amount for Accounts Payable on the credit side.

Transaction (J) Sept. 1–30: Hall withdrew cash for personal use, $200.

1 Accounts Affected	2 Category	3 ↓ ↑	4 Rules of Dr. and Cr.	5 T Account Update
Cathy Hall, Withdrawals	Withdrawals	↑	Dr.	Cathy Hall, Withdrawals, 312 (J) 200
Cash	Asset	↓	Cr.	Cash 111 (A) 7,000 | 900 (B) (D) 3,000 | 600 (G) (F) 700 | 700 (H) | 200 (J)

Analysis of Transaction J

Step 1: Cathy Hall withdraws cash from business for *personal* use. This withdrawal is not a business expense.

Step 2: This transaction affects Withdrawal and Cash accounts.

Step 3: Cathy has increased what she has withdrawn from the business for personal use. The business cash has been decreased.

Step 4: An increase in withdrawals is a debit. A decrease in cash is a credit. (*Remember:* Withdrawals go on the statement of owner's equity; expenses go on the income statement.)

Step 5: Enter the amount for Cathy Hall, Withdrawals on the debit side of the T account. The amount for Cash goes on the credit side.

Withdrawals are always increased by debits.

SUMMARY OF TRANSACTIONS FOR CATHY HALL

ASSETS	=	LIABILITIES	+	OWNER'S EQUITY				
				Capital	− Withdrawals	+ Revenue	− Expenses	

ASSETS

Cash 111
(A) 7,000 | 900 (B)
(D) 3,000 | 600 (G)
(F) 700 | 700 (H)
 | 200 (J)

Accounts Receivable 112
(E) 4,000 | 700 (F)

Office Equipment 121
(A) 800 |
(B) 900 |
(C) 400 |

= LIABILITIES +

Accounts Payable 211
 | 400 (C)
 | 300 (I)

Capital

Cathy Hall, Capital 311
 | 7,800 (A)

− Withdrawals +

Cathy Hall, Withdrawals 312
(J) 200 |

+ Revenue −

Legal Fees 411
 | 3,000 (D)
 | 4,000 (E)

Expenses

Salaries Expense 511
(G) 600 |

Rent Expense 512
(H) 700 |

Advertising Expense 513
(I) 300 |

LEARNING UNIT 2-2 REVIEW

AT THIS POINT you should be able to

◆ State the rules of debit and credit. (p. 40)
◆ List the five steps of a transaction analysis. (p. 41)
◆ Show how to fill out a transaction analysis chart. (p. 41)
◆ Explain double-entry bookkeeping. (p. 42)

SELF-REVIEW QUIZ 2-2

(The blank forms you need are on pages 27 and 28 of the *Study Guide and Working Papers.*)

O'Malley Company uses the following accounts from its chart of accounts: Cash (111), Accounts Receivable (112), Equipment (121), Accounts Payable (211), Bill O'Malley, Capital (311), Bill O'Malley, Withdrawals (312), Professional Fees (411), Utilities Expense (511), and Salaries Expense (512).

Record the following transactions into transaction analysis charts.

a. Bill O'Malley invested in the business $900 cash and equipment worth $600 from his personal assets.

b. Billed clients for services rendered, $9,000.

c. Utilities bill due but unpaid, $125.

d. Bill O'Malley withdrew cash for personal use, $120.

e. Paid salaries expense, $250.

Solution to Self-Review Quiz 2-2

A.

1 Accounts Affected	2 Category	3 ↓　↑	4 Rules of Dr. and Cr.	5 T Account Update
Cash	Asset	↑	Dr.	Cash 111 (A)　900
Equipment	Asset	↑	Dr.	Equipment 121 (A)　600
Bill O'Malley, Capital	Capital	↑	Cr.	Bill O'Malley, Capital 311 |1,500　(A)

B.

1 Accounts Affected	2 Category	3 ↓　↑	4 Rules of Dr. and Cr.	5 T Account Update
Accounts Receivable	Asset	↑	Dr.	Accounts Receivable 112 (B)　9,000
Professional Fees	Revenue	↑	Cr.	Professional Fees 411 |9,000　(B)

Quiz Tip:

Column 1: Row titles must come from the chart of accounts. The order doesn't matter as long as the total of all debits equals the total of all credits.

When a business bills a client, it creates an asset—a claim for payment called an "account receivable."

C.

1 Accounts Affected	2 Category	3 ↓ ↑	4 Rules of Dr. and Cr.	5 T Account Update
Utilities Expense	Expense	↑	Dr.	Utilities Expense 511 (C) 125|
Accounts Payable	Liability	↑	Cr.	Accounts Payable 211 |125 (C)

Record an expense when it happens whether it is paid for or not.

D.

1 Accounts Affected	2 Category	3 ↓ ↑	4 Rules of Dr. and Cr.	5 T Account Update
Bill O'Malley, Withdrawals	Withdrawals	↑	Dr.	Bill O'Malley, Withdrawals 312 (D) 120|
Cash	Asset	↓	Cr.	Cash 111 (A) 900|120 (D)

Think of withdrawals as always increasing.

E.

1 Accounts Affected	2 Category	3 ↓ ↑	4 Rules of Dr. and Cr.	5 T Account Update
Salaries Expense	Expense	↑	Dr.	Salaries Expense 512 (E) 250|
Cash	Asset	↓	Cr.	Cash 111 (A) 900|120 (D) |250 (E)

Think of expenses as always increasing.

LEARNING UNIT 2-3
The Trial Balance and Preparation of Financial Reports

Let us look at all the transactions we have discussed, arranged by T accounts and recorded using the rules of debit and credit. (See the equation at the top of page 50.)

This grouping of accounts is much easier to use than the expanded accounting equation because all of the transactions that affect a particular account are in one place.

As we saw in Learning Unit 2-2, when all the transactions are recorded in the accounts, the total of all the debits should be equal to the total of all the credits. (If they are not, the accountant must go back and find the error by checking the numbers and adding every column again.)

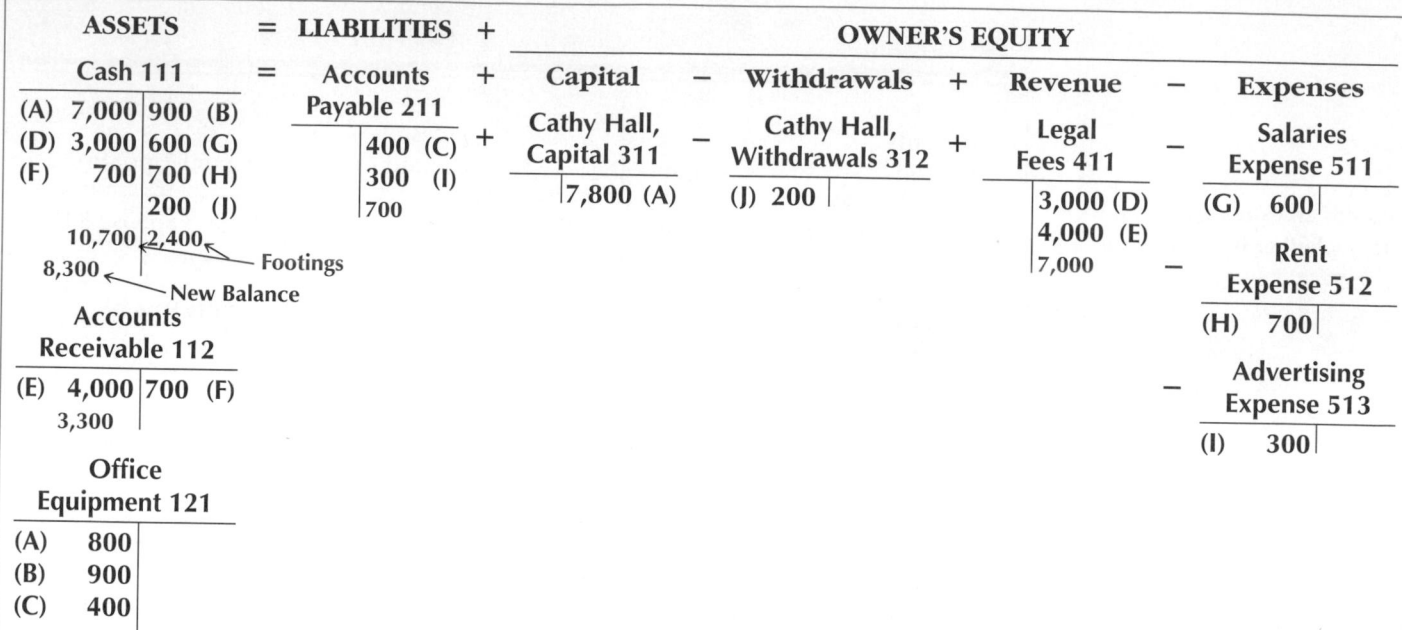

ASSETS	=	LIABILITIES	+	OWNER'S EQUITY				

Cash 111

Debit	Credit
(A) 7,000	900 (B)
(D) 3,000	600 (G)
(F) 700	700 (H)
	200 (J)
10,700	2,400 ← Footings
8,300 ← New Balance	

Accounts Receivable 112

Debit	Credit
(E) 4,000	700 (F)
3,300	

Office Equipment 121

Debit	Credit
(A) 800	
(B) 900	
(C) 400	
2,100	

Accounts Payable 211

Debit	Credit
	400 (C)
	300 (I)
	700

Capital — Cathy Hall, Capital 311

Debit	Credit
	7,800 (A)

Withdrawals — Cathy Hall, Withdrawals 312

Debit	Credit
(J) 200	

Revenue — Legal Fees 411

Debit	Credit
	3,000 (D)
	4,000 (E)
	7,000

Expenses

Salaries Expense 511

Debit	Credit
(G) 600	

Rent Expense 512

Debit	Credit
(H) 700	

Advertising Expense 513

Debit	Credit
(I) 300	

THE TRIAL BALANCE

Footings are used to obtain the balance of each side of the T account. They are not needed if there is only one entry in the account.

Footings are used to obtain the balance of each side of every T account that has more than one entry. The footings are used to find the ending balance. The ending balances are used to prepare a **trial balance.** The trial balance is not a financial report, although it is used to prepare financial reports. The trial balance lists all of the accounts with their balances in the same order as they appear in the chart of accounts. It proves the accuracy of the ledger. For example, look at the Cash account above. The footing for the debit side is $10,700 and the footing for the credit side is $2,400. Since the debit side is larger, we subtract $2,400 from

---

unkin' Donuts shop owners have many accounts to deal with: food costs, payroll, rent, utilities, supplies, advertising, promotion, and—biggest of all—cash. It's critical for them to keep debits and credits straight. If not, both they and Dunkin' Donuts Inc. could lose a lot of money—fast.

Many of Dunkin' Donuts smaller shop owners keep their own accounts, while most of the larger shops use accountants. In some areas of the United States, some accountants actually specialize in handling Dunkin' Donuts accounts for individual shop owners. But many shop owners, especially those with just one shop, handle the books themselves, both to save money and to keep a finger on the pulse of their business.

The Balance Sheet for each shop must be submitted to the zone's Business Consultant on the last Saturday of each month at noon. Fred had once been late in sending the Balance Sheet because he mistakenly debited both cash and supplies when he paid for an order of paper cups. Fred had been angry at himself for having made such a basic error. Dwayne had been understanding, but

TIME TO PUT THE DEBITS ON THE LEFT . . .

had encouraged him to review the rules for recording debits and credits.

"It's only going to get harder, Fred," Dwayne had said. "Once you computerize your accounts, debits and credits are not as visible as they are with your paper system. You will only enter the payables, and the computer does the other side of the Balance Sheet. So a thorough knowledge of debits and credits is critical to understanding the [computerized] system. And the way you're growing the business, it won't be long before you'll want to switch to the computer."

DISCUSSION QUESTIONS

1. Why is the cash account so important in Fred's business?
2. Why do you think that most of the larger shops use accountants to do their books instead of doing them themselves?
3. Is the difference between debits and credits important to shop owners who don't do their own books?

Since this is not a formal report, there is no need to use dollar signs; however, the single and double lines under subtotals and final totals are still used for clarity.

	Dr.	Cr.
Cash	8 3 0 0 00	
Accounts Receivable	3 3 0 0 00	
Office Equipment	2 1 0 0 00	
Accounts Payable		7 0 0 00
Cathy Hall, Capital		7 8 0 0 00
Cathy Hall, Withdrawals	2 0 0 00	
Legal Fees		7 0 0 0 00
Salaries Expense	6 0 0 00	
Rent Expense	7 0 0 00	
Advertising Expense	3 0 0 00	
Totals	15 5 0 0 00	15 5 0 0 00

FIGURE 2-2
Trial Balance for
Cathy Hall's Law Firm

As mentioned earlier, the ending balance of cash, $8,300, is a *normal balance* because it is on the side that increases the asset account.

Only the ending balance of each account is listed.

$10,700 to arrive at an *ending balance* of $8,300. Now look at the Rent Expense account. There is no need for a footing because there is only one entry. The amount itself is the ending balance. When the ending balance has been found for every account, we should be able to show that the total of all debits equals the total of all credits.

In the ideal situation, businesses would take a trial balance every day. The larger number of transactions most businesses conduct each day makes this impractical. Instead, trial balances are prepared periodically.

Keep in mind that the figure for capital might not be the beginning figure if any additional investment has taken place during the period. You can tell this by looking at the capital account in the ledger.

A more detailed discussion of the trial balance will be provided in the next chapter. For now, notice the heading, how the accounts are listed, the debits in the left column, the credits in the right, and the fact that the total of debits is equal to the total of credits.

A trial balance of Cathy Hall's accounts is shown in Figure 2-2.

PREPARING FINANCIAL REPORTS

The trial balance is used to prepare the financial reports. The diagram in Figure 2-3 on page 52 shows how financial reports can be prepared from a trial balance. Remember, financial reports do not have debit or credit columns. The left column is used only to subtotal numbers.

LEARNING UNIT 2-3 REVIEW

Loveness

AT THIS POINT you should be able to

- Explain the role of footings. (p. 50)
- Prepare a trial balance from a set of accounts. (p. 50)
- Prepare financial reports from a trial balance. (p. 52)

SELF-REVIEW QUIZ 2-3

(The blank forms you need are on page 29 of the *Study Guide and Working Papers*.)

As the bookkeeper of Pam's Hair Salon, you are to prepare from the following accounts on June 30, 19XX (1) a trial balance as of June 30; (2)

CATHY HALL, ATTORNEY AT LAW
INCOME STATEMENT
FOR MONTH ENDED SEPTEMBER 30, 19XX

Revenue:			
Legal Fees			$7 0 0 0 00
Operating Expenses:			
Salaries Expense	$6 0 0 00		
Rent Expense	7 0 0 00		
Advertising Expense	3 0 0 00		
Total Operating Expenses		1 6 0 0 00	
Net Income		$5 4 0 0 00	

CATHY HALL, ATTORNEY AT LAW
TRIAL BALANCE
SEPTEMBER 30, 19XX

	Dr.	Cr.
Cash	8 3 0 0 00	
Accounts Receivable	3 3 0 0 00	
Office Equipment	2 1 0 0 00	
Accounts Payable		7 0 0 00
Cathy Hall, Capital		7 8 0 0 00
C. Hall, Withdrawals	2 0 0 00	
Legal Fees		7 0 0 0 00
Salaries Expense	6 0 0 00	
Rent Expense	7 0 0 00	
Advertising Expense	3 0 0 00	
Totals	15 5 0 0 00	15 5 0 0 00

CATHY HALL, ATTORNEY AT LAW
STATEMENT OF OWNER'S EQUITY
FOR MONTH ENDED SEPTEMBER 30, 19XX

Cathy Hall, Capital			
September 1, 19XX			$7 8 0 0 00
Net Income for September	$5 4 0 0 00		
Less Withdrawals			
for September		2 0 0 00	
Increase in Capital		5 2 0 0 00	
Cathy Hall, Capital			
September 30, 19XX			$13 0 0 0 00

CATHY HALL, ATTORNEY AT LAW
BALANCE SHEET
SEPTEMBER 30, 19XX

Assets		Liabilities and Owner's Equity	
Cash	$8 3 0 0 00	Liabilities	
Accts. Receivable	3 3 0 0 00	Accounts Payable	$7 0 0 00
Office Equipm.	2 1 0 0 00	Owner's Equity	
		C. Hall, Capital	13 0 0 0 00
		Total Liab. and	
Total Assets	$13 7 0 0 00	Owner's Eq.	$13 7 0 0 00

FIGURE 2-3 Steps in Preparing Financial Reports from a Trial Balance.

an income statement for the month ended June 30; (3) a statement of owner's equity for the month ended June 30; and (4) a balance sheet as of June 30, 19XX.

Cash 111		Accounts Payable 211		Salon Fees 411	
4,500	300	300	700		3,500
2,000	100				1,000
1,000	1,200				
300	1,300				
	2,600				

Accounts Receivable 131		Pam Jay, Capital 311		Rent Expense 511	
1,000	300		4,000*	1,200	

* No additional investments.

Salon Equipment 131	Pam Jay, Withdrawals 321	Salon Supplies Expense 521
700		100		1,300	

		Salaries Expense 531
		2,600	

Solution to Self-Review Quiz 2-3

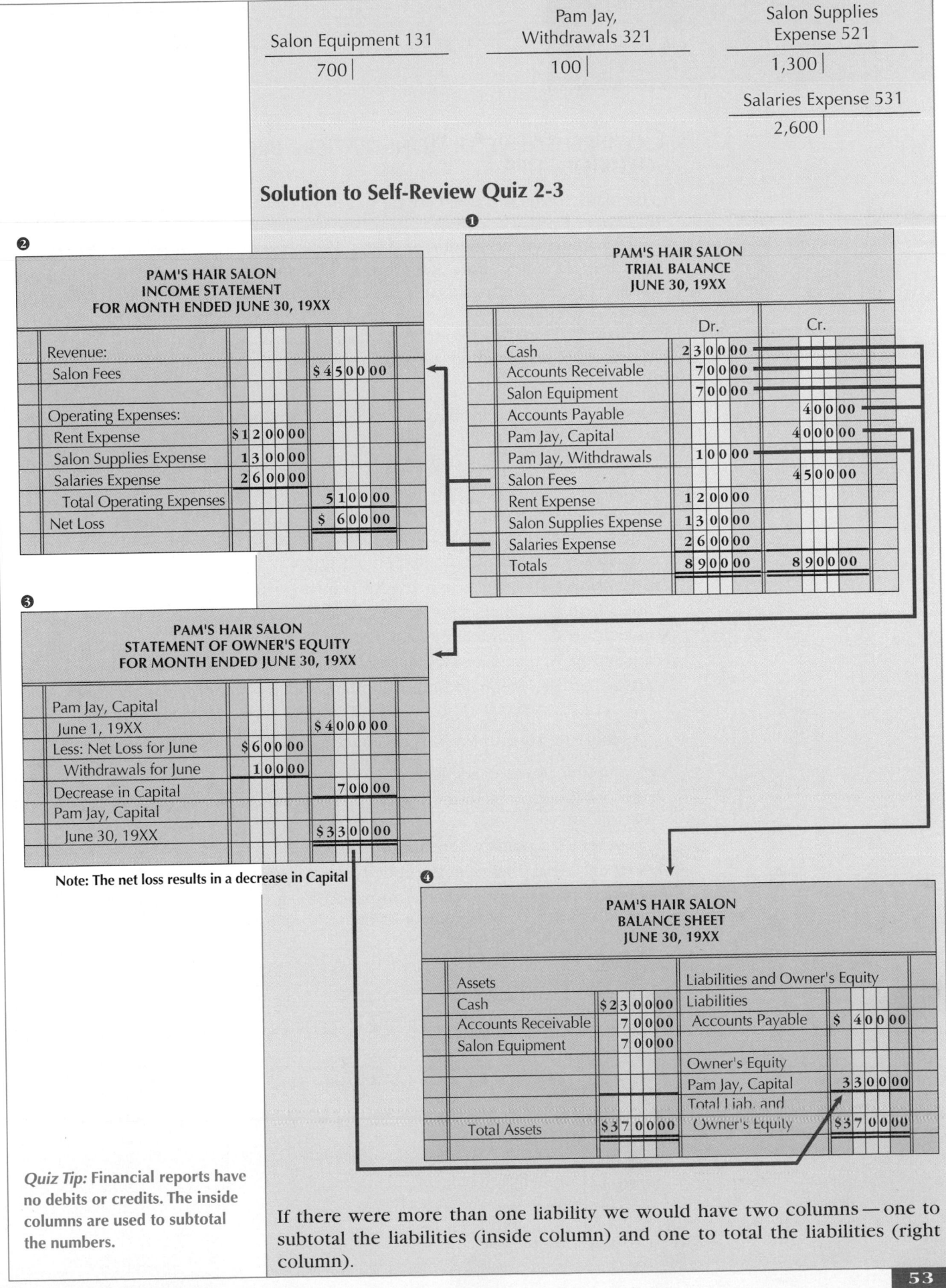

❶

PAM'S HAIR SALON
TRIAL BALANCE
JUNE 30, 19XX

	Dr.	Cr.
Cash	2 3 0 0 00	
Accounts Receivable	7 0 0 00	
Salon Equipment	7 0 0 00	
Accounts Payable		4 0 0 00
Pam Jay, Capital		4 0 0 0 00
Pam Jay, Withdrawals	1 0 0 00	
Salon Fees		4 5 0 0 00
Rent Expense	1 2 0 0 00	
Salon Supplies Expense	1 3 0 0 00	
Salaries Expense	2 6 0 0 00	
Totals	8 9 0 0 00	8 9 0 0 00

❷

PAM'S HAIR SALON
INCOME STATEMENT
FOR MONTH ENDED JUNE 30, 19XX

Revenue:		
Salon Fees		$ 4 5 0 0 00
Operating Expenses:		
Rent Expense	$ 1 2 0 0 00	
Salon Supplies Expense	1 3 0 0 00	
Salaries Expense	2 6 0 0 00	
Total Operating Expenses		5 1 0 0 00
Net Loss		$ 6 0 0 00

❸

PAM'S HAIR SALON
STATEMENT OF OWNER'S EQUITY
FOR MONTH ENDED JUNE 30, 19XX

Pam Jay, Capital		
June 1, 19XX		$ 4 0 0 0 00
Less: Net Loss for June	$ 6 0 0 00	
Withdrawals for June	1 0 0 00	
Decrease in Capital		7 0 0 00
Pam Jay, Capital		
June 30, 19XX		$ 3 3 0 0 00

Note: The net loss results in a decrease in Capital

❹

PAM'S HAIR SALON
BALANCE SHEET
JUNE 30, 19XX

Assets		Liabilities and Owner's Equity	
Cash	$ 2 3 0 0 00	Liabilities	
Accounts Receivable	7 0 0 00	Accounts Payable	$ 4 0 0 00
Salon Equipment	7 0 0 00		
		Owner's Equity	
		Pam Jay, Capital	3 3 0 0 00
		Total Liab. and	
Total Assets	$ 3 7 0 0 00	Owner's Equity	$ 3 7 0 0 00

Quiz Tip: Financial reports have no debits or credits. The inside columns are used to subtotal the numbers.

If there were more than one liability we would have two columns — one to subtotal the liabilities (inside column) and one to total the liabilities (right column).

COMPREHENSIVE DEMONSTRATION PROBLEM WITH SOLUTION TIPS

(The blank forms you need are on pages 32–34 of the *Study Guide and Working Papers.*)

The chart of accounts of Mel's Delivery Service includes the following: Cash, 111; Accounts Receivable, 112; Office Equipment, 121; Delivery Trucks, 122; Accounts Payable, 211; Mel Free, Capital, 311; Mel Free, Withdrawals, 312; Delivery Fees Earned, 411; Advertising Expense, 511; Gas Expense, 512; Salaries Expense, 513; and Telephone Expense, 514. The following transactions resulted for Mel's Delivery Service during the month of July:

Transaction A:	Mel invested $10,000 in the business from his personal savings account.
Transaction B:	Bought delivery trucks on account, $17,000.
Transaction C:	Advertising bill received but unpaid, $700.
Transaction D:	Bought office equipment for cash, $1,200.
Transaction E:	Received cash for delivery services rendered, $15,000.
Transaction F:	Paid salaries expense, $3,000.
Transaction G:	Paid gas expense for company trucks, $1,250.
Transaction H:	Billed customers for delivery services rendered, $4,000.
Transaction I:	Paid telephone bill, $300.
Transaction J:	Received $3,000 as partial payment of transaction H.
Transaction K:	Mel paid home telephone bill from company checkbook, $150.

As Mel's newly employed accountant, you must do the following:

1. Set up T accounts in a ledger.
2. Record transactions in the T accounts. (Place the letter of the transaction next to the entry.)
3. Foot the T accounts where appropriate.
4. Prepare a trial balance at the end of July.
5. Prepare from the trial balance, in proper form, (a) an income statement for the month of July, (b) a statement of owner's equity, and (c) a balance sheet as of July 31, 19XX.

Solution to Demonstration Problem

1, 2, 3.   **GENERAL LEDGER**

Cash 111				Acc. Payable 211			Advertising Expense 511	
(A)	10,000	1,200	(D)		17,000	(B)	(C)	700
(E)	15,000	3,000	(F)		700	(C)		
(J)	3,000	1,250	(G)		17,700			
	28,000	300	(I)					
	22,100	150	(K)					
		5,900						

Acc. Receivable 112		Mel Free, Capital 311		Gas Expense 512	
(H) 4,000	3,000 (J)		10,000 (A)	(G) 1,250	
1,000					

Office Equipment 121		Mel Free, Withdrawals 312		Salaries Expense 513	
(D) 1,200		(K) 150		(F) 3,000	

Delivery Trucks 122		Delivery Fees Earned 411		Telephone Expense 514	
(B) 17,000			15,000 (E)	(I) 300	
			4,000 (H)		
			19,000		

Solution Tips to Recording Transactions

A.	Cash	A	↑	Dr.	F.	Salaries Expense	Exp.	↑	Dr.
	Mel Free, Capital	Cap.	↑	Cr.		Cash	A	↓	Cr.
B.	Delivery Trucks	A	↑	Dr.	G.	Gas Expense	Exp.	↑	Dr.
	Acc. Payable	L	↑	Cr.		Cash	A	↓	Cr.
C.	Advertising Expense	Exp.	↑	Dr.	H.	Acc. Receivable	A	↑	Dr.
	Acc. Payable	L	↑	Cr.		Del. Fees Earned	Rev.	↑	Cr.
D.	Office Equipment	A	↑	Dr.	I.	Tel. Expense	Exp.	↑	Dr.
	Cash	A	↓	Cr.		Cash	A	↓	Cr.
E.	Cash	A	↑	Dr.	J.	Cash	A	↑	Dr.
	Del. Fees Earned	Rev.	↑	Cr.		Acc. Receivable	A	↓	Cr.
					K.	Mel Free, Withd.	Withd.	↑	Dr.
						Cash	A	↓	Cr.

4.
Mel's Delivery Service
Trial Balance
July 31, 19XX

	Dr.	Cr.
Cash	22,100	
Accounts Receivable	1,000	
Office Equipment	1,200	
Delivery Trucks	17,000	
Accounts Payable		17,700

Mel Free, Capital		10,000
Mel Free, Withdrawals	150	
Delivery Fees Earned		19,000
Advertising Expense	700	
Gas Expense	1,250	
Salaries Expense	3,000	
Telephone Expense	300	
TOTALS	46,700	46,700

Solution Tips to Footings and Preparation of a Trial Balance

3. Footings: Cash   Add left side $28,000

Add right side $5,900

Take difference $22,100 and stay on side

that is larger

Accounts Payable   Add $17,000 + $700 and stay on same side.

Total is $17,700

4. Trial balance is a list of the ledger's ending balances. The list is in the same order as the chart of accounts. Each title has only one number listed either as a debit or credit balance.

5a.

Mel's Delivery Service
Income Statement
for Month Ended July 31, 19XX

Revenue:		
Delivery Fees Earned		$19,000
Operating Expenses:		
Advertising Expense	$700	
Gas Expense	1,250	
Salaries Expense	3,000	
Telephone Expense	300	
Total Operating Expenses		5,250
Net Income		$13,750

b.

Mel's Delivery Service
Statement of Owner's Equity
for Month Ended July 31, 19XX

Mel Free, Capital July 1, 19XX		$10,000
Net Income for July	$13,750	
Less Withdrawals for July	150	
Increase in Capital		13,600
Mel Free, Capital, July 31, 19XX		$23,600

c.

Mel's Delivery Service
Balance Sheet
July 31, 19XX

Assets		Liabilities and Owner's Equity	
Cash	$ 22,100	Liabilities	
Accounts Receivable	1,000	Accounts Payable	$17,700
Office Equipment	1,200		
Delivery Trucks	17,000	Owner's Equity	
		Mel Free, Capital	23,600
		Total Liabilities and	
Total Assets	**$41,300**	**Owner's Equity**	**$41,300**

Solution Tips to Prepare Financial Reports from a Trial Balance

		Trial Balance	
		Dr.	Cr.
Balance Sheet	Assets	X	
	Liabilities		X
Statement of Equity	Capital		X
	Withdrawals	X	
Income Statement	Revenues		X
	Expenses	X	
		XX	XX

Net income on the income statement of $13,750 goes on the statement of owner's equity.

Ending capital of $23,600 on the statement of owner's equity goes on the balance sheet as the new figure for capital.

Note: There are no debits or credits on Financial Reports. The inside column is used for subtotaling.

SUMMARY OF KEY POINTS

Learning Unit 2-1

1. A T account is a simplified version of a standard account.
2. A ledger is a group of accounts.
3. A debit is the left-hand position (side) of an account and a credit is the right-hand position (side) of an account.
4. A footing is the total of one side of an account: the ending balance is the difference between the footings.

Learning Unit 2-2

1. A chart of accounts lists the account titles and their numbers for a company.
2. The transaction analysis chart is a teaching device, not to be confused with standard accounting procedures.
3. A compound entry is a transaction involving more than one debit or credit.

Learning Unit 2-3

1. In double-entry bookkeeping, the recording of each business transaction affects two or more accounts, and the total of debits equals the total of credits.
2. A trial balance is a list of the ending balances of all accounts, listed in the same order as on the chart of accounts.

3. Any additional investments during the period result in capital on the trial balance not being the beginning figure for capital.
4. There are *no* debit or credit columns on the three financial reports.

KEY TERMS

Account   An accounting device used in bookkeeping to record increases and decreases of business transactions relating to individual assets, liabilities, capital, withdrawals, revenue, expenses, and so on.

Chart of accounts   A numbering system of accounts that lists the account titles and account numbers to be used by a company.

Compound entry   A transaction involving more than one debit or credit.

Credit   The right-hand side of any account. A number entered on the right side of any account is said to be credited to an account.

Debit   The left-hand side of any account. A number entered on the left side of any account is said to be debited to an account.

Double-entry bookkeeping   An accounting system in which the recording of each transaction affects two or more accounts, and the total of the debits is equal to the total of the credits.

Ending balance   The difference between footings in a T account.

Footings   The totals of each side of a T account.

Ledger   A group of accounts that records data from business transactions.

Normal balance of an account   The side of an account that increases by the rules of debit and credit.

Standard account   A formal account that includes columns for date, explanation, posting reference, debit, and credit.

T account   A skeleton version of a standard account, used for demonstration purposes.

Trial balance   A list of the ending balances of all the accounts in a ledger. The total of the debits should equal the total of the credits.

BLUEPRINT FOR PREPARING FINANCIAL REPORTS FROM A TRIAL BALANCE

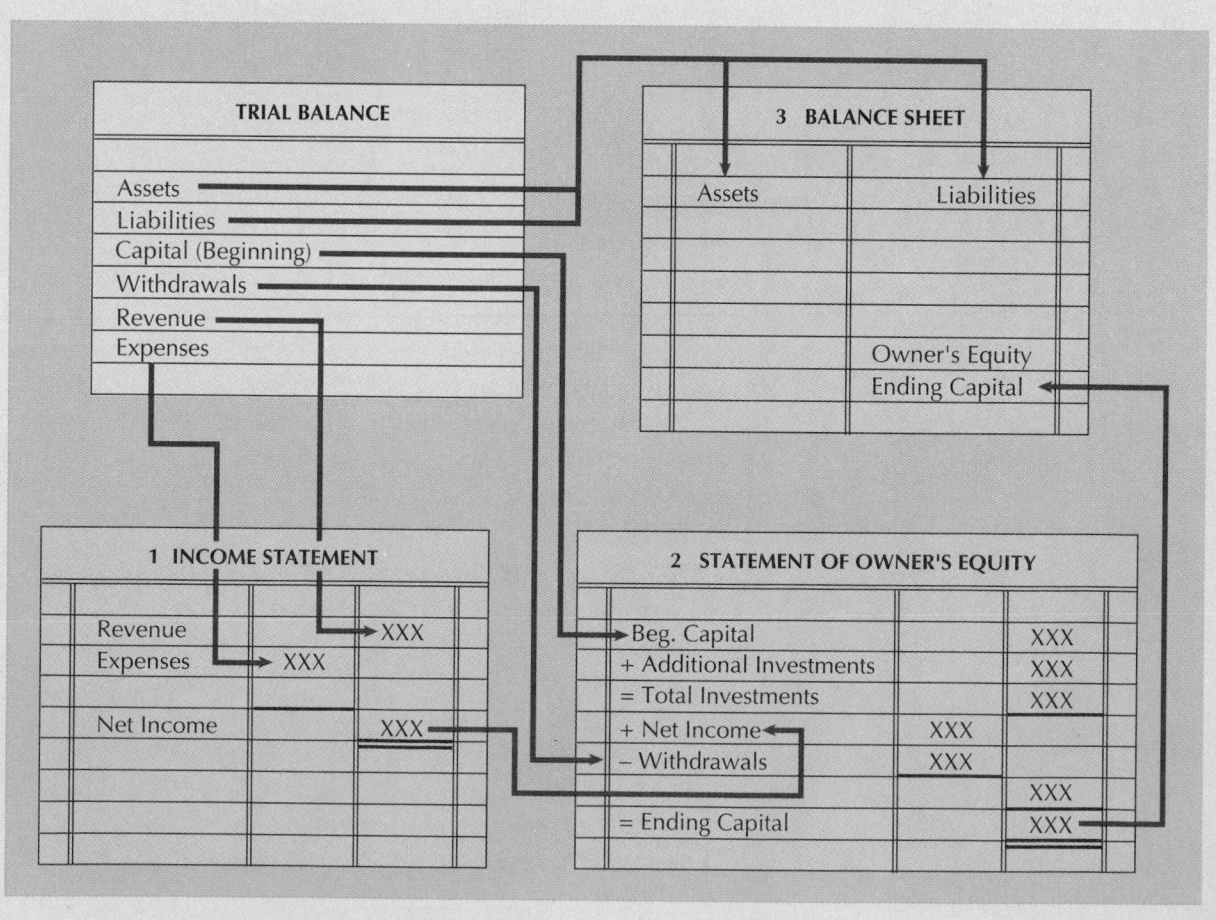

QUESTIONS, MINI EXERCISES, EXERCISES, AND PROBLEMS

Discussion Questions

1. Define a ledger.
2. Why is the left-hand side of an account called a debit?
3. Footings are used in balancing all accounts. True or false? Please explain.
4. What is the end product of the accounting process?
5. What do we mean when we say that a transaction analysis chart is a teaching device?
6. What are the five steps of the transaction analysis chart?
7. Explain the concept of double-entry bookkeeping.
8. A trial balance is a formal report. True or false? Please explain.
9. Why are there no debit or credit columns on financial reports?
10. Compare the financial statements prepared from the expanded accounting equation with those prepared from a trial balance.

Mini Exercises

(The blank forms you need are on page 36 in the *Study Guide and Working Papers*.)

The T Account

1. From the following, foot and balance each account.

Cash 110					R. Rich, Capital 311	
4/8	2,000	4/4	2,000		3/7	5,000
4/12	6,000				3/9	3,000
					4/12	6,000

Transaction Analysis

2. Complete the following:

Account	Category	↑	↓	Normal Balance
A. Cash				
B. Prepaid Rent				
C. Accounts Payable				
D. B. Block, Capital				
E. B. Block Withdrawals				
F. Legal Fees				
G. Salary Expense				

Transaction Analysis

3. Record the following transaction into the transaction analysis chart: Provided legal services for $4,000, receiving $3,000 cash with the remainder to be paid next month.

Accounts Affected	Category	↓	↑	Rules of Dr. and Cr.	T Accounts

Trial Balance

4. Rearrange the following titles in the order they would appear on a Trial Balance:

Selling Expense

Accounts Receivable

Accounts Payable

D. Cope, Capital

Computer Equipment

Legal Fees

D. Cope, Withdrawals

Rent Expense

Advertising Expense

Cash

Trial Balance/Financial Reports

5. From the following Trial Balance identify which report each title will appear on:

◆ Income Statement (IS)

◆ Statement of Owner's Equity (OE)

◆ Balance Sheet (BS)

Logan Co.
Trial Balance
Sept. 30, 19XX

		Dr.	Cr.
A._____	Cash	390	
B._____	Supplies	100	
C._____	Office Equipment	200	
D._____	Accounts Payable		100
E._____	D. Heath, Capital		450
F._____	D. Heath, Withdrawals	160	
G._____	Fees Earned		290
H._____	Hair Salon Fees		300
I._____	Salaries Expense	130	
J._____	Rent Expense	120	
K._____	Advertising Expense	40	
	TOTALS	1,140	1,140

Exercises

(The blank forms you need are on page 37 in the *Study Guide and Working Papers*.)

2-1. From the following, prepare a chart of accounts, using the same numbering system used in this chapter.

Word Processing Equipment   Professional Fees
Rent Expense   A. Sting, Capital
Accounts Payable   Cash
Accounts Receivable   Salaries Expense
Repair Expense   A. Sting, Withdrawals

2-2. Record the following transaction into the transaction analysis chart: Heather Reese bought a new piece of office equipment for $11,000, paying $2,000 down and charging the rest.

2-3. Complete the table: For each account listed on the left, fill in what category it belongs to, whether increases and decreases in the account are marked on the debit or credit sides, and which financial report the account appears on. A sample is provided.

Accounts Affected	Category	↑	↓	Appears on which Financial Report
Supplies	Asset	Dr.	Cr.	Balance Sheet
Legal Fees Earned				
D. Long, Withdrawals				
Accounts Payable				
Salaries Expense				
Auto				

2-4. Given the following accounts, complete the table by inserting appropriate numbers next to the individual transaction to indicate which account is debited and which account is credited.

1. Cash   **6.** B. Baker, Withdrawals
2. Accounts Receivable   **7.** Plumbing Fees Earned
3. Equipment   **8.** Salaries Expense
4. Accounts Payable   **9.** Advertising Expense
5. B. Baker, Capital   **10.** Supplies Expenses

	Transaction	Rules Dr.	Cr.
Example:	A. Paid salaries expense.	8	1
	B. Bob paid personal utilities bill from company checkbook.		
	C. Advertising bill received but unpaid.		
	D. Received cash from plumbing fees.		
	E. Paid supplies expense.		
	F. Bob invested additional equipment into the business.		
	G. Billed customers for plumbing services rendered.		
	H. Received one-half the balance from transaction G.		
	I. Bought equipment on account.		

2-5. From the following trial balance of Hall's Cleaners, prepare the following:

- ◆ Income Statement
- ◆ Statement of Owner's Equity
- ◆ Balance Sheet

HALL'S CLEANERS
TRIAL BALANCE
JULY 31, 19XX

	Dr.	Cr.
Cash	5 5 0 00	
Equipment	6 9 2 00	
Accounts Payable		4 5 5 00
J. Hall, Capital		8 0 0 00
J. Hall, Withdrawals	1 9 8 00	
Cleaning Fees		4 5 8 00
Salaries Expense	1 6 0 00	
Utilities Expense	1 1 3 00	
Totals	1 7 1 3 00	1 7 1 3 00

Group A Problems

(The forms you need are on pages 40–47 of the *Study Guide and Working Papers*.)

2A-1. The following transactions occurred in the opening and operation of Ted's Bookkeeping Service.

- **a.** Ted Williams opened the bookkeeping service by investing $6,000 from his personal savings account.
- **b.** Purchased store equipment on account, $3,000.
- **c.** Rent expense due but unpaid, $600.
- **d.** Received cash for bookkeeping services rendered, $800.
- **e.** Billed a client on account, $500.
- **f.** Ted Williams withdrew cash for personal use, $200.

Complete the transaction analysis chart in the *Study Guide and Working Papers*. The chart of accounts includes Cash; Accounts Receivable; Store Equipment; Accounts Payable; Ted Williams, Capital; Ted Williams, Withdrawals; Bookkeeping Fees Earned; and Rent Expense.

2A-2. Lee White opened a travel agency, and the following transactions resulted:

- **a.** Lee White invested $20,000 in the travel agency.
- **b.** Bought office equipment on account, $4,000.
- **c.** Agency received cash for travel arrangements that it completed for a client, $3,000.
- **d.** Lee White paid a personal bill from the company checkbook, $50.
- **e.** Paid advertising expense for the month, $700.
- **f.** Rent expense for the month due but unpaid, $900.
- **g.** Paid $800 as partial payment of what was owed from transaction **b.**

Check Figure:

After G:

	Cash		
(A)	20,000	50	(D)
(C)	3,000	700	(E)
		800	(G)

As Lee White's accountant, analyze and record the transactions in T account form. Set up the T accounts and label each entry with the letter of the transaction.

Chart of Accounts

Assets
Cash 111
Office Equipment 121
Liabilities
Accounts Payable 211
Owner's Equity
L. White, Capital 311
L. White, Withdrawals 312

Revenue
Travel Fees Earned 411
Expenses
Advertising Expense 511
Rent Expense 512

Preparing a trial balance from the T accounts.

2A-3. From the following T accounts of Mike's Window Washing Service, (a) record and foot the balances in the *Study Guide and Working Papers* where appropriate, and (b) prepare a trial balance in proper form for May 31, 19XX.

Check Figure:
Trial Balance Total $12,700

Cash 111

5,000	(A)	100	(D)
3,500	(G)	200	(E)
		400	(F)
		200	(H)
		900	(I)

Accounts Payable 211

| 100 | (D) | 1,300 | (C) |

Fees Earned 411

| | | 6,500 | (B) |

Accounts Receivable 112

| 6,500 | (B) | 3,500 | (G) |

Mike Frank, Capital 311

| | | 5,000 | (A) |

Rent Expense 511

| 400 | (F) | |

Office Equipment 121

| 1,300 | (C) | |
| 200 | (H) | |

Mike Frank, Withdrawals 312

| 900 | (I) | |

Utilities Expense 512

| 200 | (E) | |

2A-4. From the trial balance of Gracie Lantz, Attorney at Law, prepare (a) an

Check Figure:
Total Assets $6,400

GRACIE LANTZ, ATTORNEY AT LAW
TRIAL BALANCE
MAY 31, 19XX

	Dr.	Cr.
Cash	5 0 0 0 00	
Accounts Receivable	6 5 0 00	
Office Equipment	7 5 0 00	
Accounts Payable		4 3 0 0 00
Salaries Payable		6 7 5 00
G. Lantz, Capital		1 2 7 5 00
G. Lantz, Withdrawals	3 0 0 00	
Revenue from Legal Fees		1 3 5 0 00
Utilities Expense	3 0 0 00	
Rent Expense	4 5 0 00	
Salaries Expense	1 5 0 00	
Totals	7 6 0 0 00	7 6 0 0 00

income statement for the month of May, (b) a statement of owner's equity for the month ended May 31, and (c) a balance sheet as of May 31, 19XX.

2A-5. The chart of accounts for Angel's Delivery Service is as follows:

Chart of Accounts

Assets
Cash   111
Accounts Receivable   112
Office Equipment   121
Delivery Trucks   1,22

Liabilities
Accounts Payable   211

Owner's Equity
Alice Angel, Capital   311
Alice Angel, Withdrawals   312

Revenue
Delivery Fees Earned   411

Expenses
Advertising Expense   511
Gas Expense   512
Salaries Expense   513
Telephone Expense   514

Angel's Delivery Service completed the following transactions during the month of March:

Transaction A: Alice Angel invested $16,000 in the delivery service from her personal savings account.

Transaction B: Bought delivery trucks on account, $18,000.

Transaction C: Bought office equipment for cash, $600.

Transaction D: Paid advertising expense, $250.

Transaction E: Collected cash for delivery services rendered, $2,600.

Transaction F: Paid drivers' salaries, $900.

Transaction G: Paid gas expense for trucks, $1,200.

Transaction H: Performed delivery services for a customer on account, $800.

Transaction I: Telephone expense due but unpaid, $700.

Transaction J: Received $300 as partial payment of transaction H.

Transaction K: Alice Angel withdrew cash for personal use, $300.

As Alice's newly employed accountant, you must:

1. Set up T accounts in a ledger.
2. Record transactions in the T accounts. (Place the letter of the transaction next to the entry.)
3. Foot the T accounts where appropriate.
4. Prepare a trial balance at the end of March.
5. Prepare from the trial balance, in proper form, (a) an income statement for the month of March, (b) a statement of owner's equity, and (c) a balance sheet as of March 31, 19XX.

Group B Problems

(The forms you need are on pages 40–48 of the *Study Guide and Working Papers*.)

2B-1. Ted Williams decided to open a bookkeeping service. Record the following transactions into the transaction analysis charts:

Transaction A:	Ted invested $1,500 in the bookkeeping service from his personal savings account.
Transaction B:	Purchased store equipment on account, $900.
Transaction C:	Rent expense due but unpaid, $250.
Transaction D:	Performed bookkeeping services for cash, $1,200.
Transaction E:	Billed clients for bookkeeping services rendered, $700.
Transaction F:	Ted paid his home heating bill from the company checkbook, $275.

Check Figure:

After F:

Cash

| 1,500 | 275 |
| 1,200 | |

Recording transactions into ledger accounts.

The chart of accounts for the shop includes Cash; Accounts Receivable; Store Equipment; Accounts Payable; Ted Williams, Capital; Ted Williams, Withdrawals; Bookkeeping Fees Earned; and Rent Expense.

2B-2. Lee White established a new travel agency. Record the following transactions for Lee in T account form. Label each entry with the letter of the transaction.

Transaction A:	Lee White invested $18,000 in the travel agency from her personal bank account.
Transaction B:	Bought office equipment on account, $6,000.
Transaction C:	Travel agency rendered service to Jensen Corp. and received cash, $1,200.
Transaction D:	Lee White withdrew cash for personal use, $200.
Transaction E:	Paid advertising expense, $600.
Transaction F:	Rent expense due but unpaid, $500.
Transaction G:	Paid $400 in partial payment of transaction B.

Check Figure:

After G:

Cash

(A) 18,000	200	(D)
(C) 1,200	600	(E)
	400	(G)

The chart of accounts includes Cash, 111; Office Equipment, 121; Accounts Payable, 211; L. White, Capital, 311; L. White, Withdrawals, 312; Travel Fees Earned, 411; Advertising Expense, 511; and Rent Expense, 512.

2B-3. From the following T accounts of Mike's Window Washing Service, (a) record and foot the balances in the *Study Guide* where appropriate and (b) prepare a trial balance for May 31, 19XX.

Preparing a trial balance from the T accounts.

Cash 111

10,000 (A)	4,000	(C)
4,000 (F)	310	(D)
2,000 (G)	50	(E)
	600	(H)

Accounts Receivable 112

| 2,000 (G) | |

Office Equipment 121

| 2,000 | (B) |
| 4,000 | (C) |

Check Figure:

Trial Balance Total $20,000

Accounts Payable 211

| | 2,000 | (B) |

Mike Frank, Capital 311

| | 10,000 | (A) |

Mike Frank, Withdrawals 312

| 600 | (H) |

Fees Earned 411

| | 4,000 | (F) |
| | 4,000 | (G) |

Rent Expense 511

| 310 | (D) |

Utilities Expense 512

| 50 | (E) |

Preparing financial reports from the trial balance.

2B-4. From the trial balance of Gracie Lantz, Attorney at Law, prepare (a) an income from the statement for the month of May, (b) a statement of owner's equity for the month ended May 31, and (c) a balance sheet as of May 31, 19XX.

GRACIE LANTZ, ATTORNEY AT LAW		
TRIAL BALANCE		
MAY 31, 19XX		

	Debit	Credit
Cash	6 0 0 0 00	
Accounts Receivable	2 4 0 0 00	
Office Equipment	2 4 0 0 00	
Accounts Payable		2 0 0 00
Salaries Payable		6 0 0 00
G. Lantz, Capital		4 0 0 0 00
G. Lantz, Withdrawals	2 0 0 0 00	
Revenue from Legal Fees		8 8 0 0 00
Utilities Expense	1 0 0 00	
Rent Expense	3 0 0 00	
Salaries Expense	4 0 0 00	
Totals	13 6 0 0 00	13 6 0 0 00

Check Figure:

Total Assets $10,800

Comprehensive Problem

Check Figure:

Trial Balance Total $84,300

2B-5. The chart of accounts of Angel's Delivery Service includes the following: Cash, 111; Accounts Receivable, 112; Office Equipment, 121; Delivery Trucks, 122; Accounts Payable, 211; Alice Angel, Capital, 311; Alice Angel, Withdrawals, 312; Delivery Fees Earned, 411; Advertising Expense, 511; Gas Expense, 512; Salaries Expense, 513; and Telephone Expense, 514. The following transactions resulted for Angel's Delivery Service during the month of March:

Transaction A: Alice invested $40,000 in the business from her personal savings account.

Transaction B: Bought delivery trucks on account, $25,000.

Transaction C: Advertising bill received but unpaid, $800.

Transaction D: Bought office equipment for cash, $2,500.

Transaction E: Received cash for delivery services rendered, $13,000.

Transaction F: Paid salaries expense, $1,850.

Transaction G: Paid gas expense for company trucks, $750.

Transaction H: Billed customers for delivery services rendered, $5,500.

Transaction I: Paid telephone bill, $400.

Transaction J: Received $1,600 as partial payment of transaction H.

Transaction K: Alice paid home telephone bill from company checkbook, $88.

As Alice's newly employed accountant, you must

1. Set up T accounts in a ledger.
2. Record transactions in the T accounts. (Place the letter of the transaction next to the entry.)
3. Foot the T accounts where appropriate.
4. Prepare a trial balance at the end of March.
5. Prepare from the trial balance, in proper form, (a) an income statement for the month of March, (b) a statement of owner's equity, and (c) a balance sheet as of March 31, 19XX.

REAL WORLD APPLICATIONS

2R-1.

Andy Leaf is a careless bookkeeper. He is having a terrible time getting his trial balance to balance. Andy has asked for your assistance in preparing a correct trial balance. The following is the incorrect trial balance.

RANCH COMPANY
TRIAL BALANCE
JUNE 30, 19XX

	Dr.	Cr.
Cash	510 00	
Accounts Receivable		635 00
Office Equipment	360 00	
Accounts Payable	110 00	
Wages Payable	10 00	
H. Clo, Capital	635 00	
H. Clo, Withdrawals	1440 00	
Professional Fees		2240 00
Rent Expense		240 00
Advertising Expense	25 00	
Totals	3090 00	3115 00

Facts you have discovered:

◆ Debits to the Cash account were $2,640; credits to the Cash account were $2,150.

◆ Amy Hall paid $15 but was not updated in Accounts Receivable.

◆ A purchase of office equipment for $5 on account was never recorded in the ledger.

◆ Revenue was understated in the ledger by $180.

Show how these errors affected the ending balances for the accounts involved, and explain how the trial balance will indeed balance once they are corrected.

Tell Ranch Company how it can avoid this problem in the future. Write your recommendations.

2R-2.

Alice Groove, owner of Lonton Company, asked her bookkeeper how each of the following situations will affect the totals of the trial balance and individual ledger accounts.

◆ An $850 payment for a desk was recorded as a debit to Office Equipment, $85, and a credit to Cash, $85.

◆ A payment of $300 to a creditor was recorded as a debit to Accounts Payable, $300, and a credit to Cash, $100.

◆ The collection on an Accounts Receivable for $400 was recorded as a debit to Cash, $400, and a credit to J. Ray, Capital, $400.

◆ The payment of a liability for $400 was recorded as a debit to Accounts Payable, $40, and a credit to Supplies, $40.

◆ A purchase of equipment of $800 was recorded as a debit to Supplies, $800, and a credit to Cash, $800.

◆ A payment of $95 to a creditor was recorded as a debit to Accounts Payable, $95, and a credit to Cash, $59.

What did the bookkeeper tell her? Which accounts were overstated and understated? Which were correct? Explain in writing how mistakes can be avoided in the future.

YOU make the call

Critical Thinking/Ethical Case

2R-3.

Audrey Flet, the bookkeeper of ALN Co., was scheduled to leave on a three-week vacation at 5 o'clock on Friday. She couldn't get the company's trial balance to balance. At 4:30, she decided to put in fictitious figures to make it balance. Audrey told herself she would fix it when she got back from her vacation. Was Audrey right or wrong to do this? Why?

ACCOUNTING RECALL

A CUMULATIVE APPROACH

THIS EXAM REVIEWS CHAPTERS 1 AND 2

Your *Study Guide and Working Papers* (pages 51 and 55) have forms to complete this exam, as well as worked-out solutions. The page references next to each question identify what page to turn back to if you answer the question incorrectly.

PART 1   Vocabulary Review

Match the terms to the appropriate definition or phrase.
Page Ref.

(50)	1. Trial balance	A. Total remains the same
(38)	2. Debit	B. Entering numbers on right side
(40)	3. Normal balance	C. Subdivisions of owner's equity
(11)	4. Revenue	D. Group of accounts
(38)	5. Crediting	E. Numbering system
(9)	6. Balance sheet	F. Left side of an account
(7)	7. Shift in assets	G. Prepared as of a particular date
(40)	8. Chart of accounts	H. Not an asset
(37)	9. Ledger	I. Side of account that increases it
(11)	10. Capital, withdrawals, revenue, expenses	J. List of the ledger

PART II   True or False (Accounting Theory)

(38)   11. A debit always means increase.

(51)   12. There are no debit or credit columns on financial reports.

(50)   13. The trial balance lists only the ending figure for capital that goes on the balance sheet.

(40)   14. An increase in a withdrawal is a credit.

(50)   15. The trial balance is not a formal report.

CONTINUING PROBLEM

The Eldorado Computer Center created its chart of accounts as follows:

Chart of Accounts
As of June 1, 19XX

Assets
1000 Cash
1020 Accounts Receivable
1030 Supplies
1080 Computer Shop Equipment
1090 Office Equipment

Liabilities
2000 Accounts Payable

Owners Equity
3000 Freedman, Capital
3010 Freedman, Withdrawals

Revenue
4000 Service Revenue

Expenses
5010 Advertising Expense
5020 Rent Expense
5030 Utilities Expense
5040 Phone Expense
5050 Supplies Expense
5060 Insurance Expense
5070 Postage Expense

You will use this chart of accounts to complete the Continuing Problem. The following problem continues from Chapter 1. The balances as of July 31 have been brought forward in your *Working Papers* on page 52.

Assignment:

1. Set up T accounts in a ledger.
2. Record the transactions (k) through (q) in the appropriate T accounts.
3. Foot the T accounts where appropriate.
4. Prepare a trial balance at the end of August.
5. Prepare from the trial balance an income statement, statement of owner's equity, and a balance sheet for the two months ending with August 31, 19XX.

k) Received the phone bill for the month of July, $155
l) Paid $150 (check #8099) for insurance for the month
m) Paid $200 (check #8100) of the amount due from transaction (d) in Chapter 1
n) Paid advertising expense for the month, $1,400 (check #8101)
o) Billed a client (Jeannine Sparks) for services rendered, $850
p) Collected $900 for services rendered
q) Paid the electric bill in full for the month of July [check #8102 — transaction (h), Chapter 1].
r) Paid cash (check #8103) for $50 in stamps
s) Purchased $200 worth of supplies from Computer Connection on credit

BEGINNING THE ACCOUNTING CYCLE

Journalizing, Posting, and the Trial Balance

THE BIG PICTURE

At Eldorado Computer Center, Tony Freedman uses the standard accounting practice of keeping a journal. Later, he copies (or "posts") transactions to a ledger. Each account is separate in the ledger, so it can be totaled. Like a personal diary, an accounting journal lets you capture information as it happens. You first analyze each transaction to determine which ledger accounts will be affected. Then you record your analysis — along with descriptive notes — in the journal.

Eldorado's journal lets Freedman look up transactions easily. He can also check his analysis at any time. If an error is discovered when he prepares the trial balance, he can trace his steps back to the original transaction and make corrections.

The Eldorado Computer Center deals with many different source documents, such as checks, calculator tapes, receipts, invoices, purchase orders, and deposit slips. When customers enter Tony's store, they complete a repair order authorizing the center to do the work. Once the work is completed, Tony issues a bill or "invoice." The customer may pay in cash, or Tony may extend credit. Either way, Tony records the invoice as a business transaction.

Of course people make mistakes in accounting records. Nonetheless, these records are kept in ink, not pencil. Corrections are shown clearly and initialed. This record shows a complete and trustworthy record of events.

Learning Objectives	◆ Journalizing—analyzing and recording business transactions into a journal. (p. 71) ◆ Posting—transferring information from a journal to a ledger. (p. 80) ◆ Preparing a trial balance. (p. 86)

The normal accounting procedures that are performed over a period of time are called the **accounting cycle.** The accounting cycle takes place in a period of time called an **accounting period.** An accounting period is the period of time covered by the income statement. Although it can be any time period up to one year (e.g., one month or three months), most businesses use a one-year accounting period. The year can be either a **calendar year** (January 1 through December 31) or a **fiscal year.**

A fiscal year is an accounting period that runs for any twelve consecutive months, so it can be the same as a calendar year. A business can choose any fiscal year that is convenient. For example, some retailers may decide to end their fiscal year when inventories and business activity are at a low point, such as after the Christmas season. This is called a **natural business year.** Using a natural business year allows the business to count its year-end inventory when it is easiest to do so.

This chapter covers Steps 1 to 4 of the accounting cycle. (See diagram on page p. 72.)

Businesses would not be able to operate successfully if they only prepared financial reports at the end of their calendar or fiscal year. That is why most businesses prepare **interim reports** on a monthly, quarterly, or semiannual basis.

In this chapter, as well as in Chapters 4 and 5, we will follow Brenda Clark's new business, Clark's Word Processing Services. We will follow the normal accounting procedures that the business performs over a period of time. Clark has chosen to use a fiscal period of January 1 to December 31, which also is the calendar year.

The diagram (page 72) that follows lists the steps in the business accounting cycle for a manual and a computerized system. This diagram should be used as a reference figure. By the end of Chapter 5, every step in the manual accounting system will have been explained and illustrated.

LEARNING UNIT 3-1

Analyzing and Recording Business Transactions into a Journal: Steps 1 and 2 of the Accounting Cycle

THE GENERAL JOURNAL

A business uses a journal to record transactions in chronological order. A ledger accumulates information from a journal. The journal and the ledger are in two different books.

Chapter 2 taught us how to analyze and record business transactions into T accounts, or ledger accounts. However, recording a debit in an account on one page of the ledger and recording the corresponding credit on a different page of the ledger can make it difficult to find errors. It would be much easier if all of the business's transactions were located in the same place. That is the function of the **journal** or **general journal.** Transactions are entered in the journal in chronological order (January 1, 8, 15, etc.), and then this recorded information is used to update the ledger accounts. In computerized accounting, a journal may be recorded on disk or tape.

We will use a general journal, the simplest form of a journal, to record the transactions of Clark's Word Processing Services. A transaction [debit(s) + credit(s)] that has been analyzed and recorded in a journal is called a **journal entry.** The process of recording the journal entry into the journal is called **journalizing.**

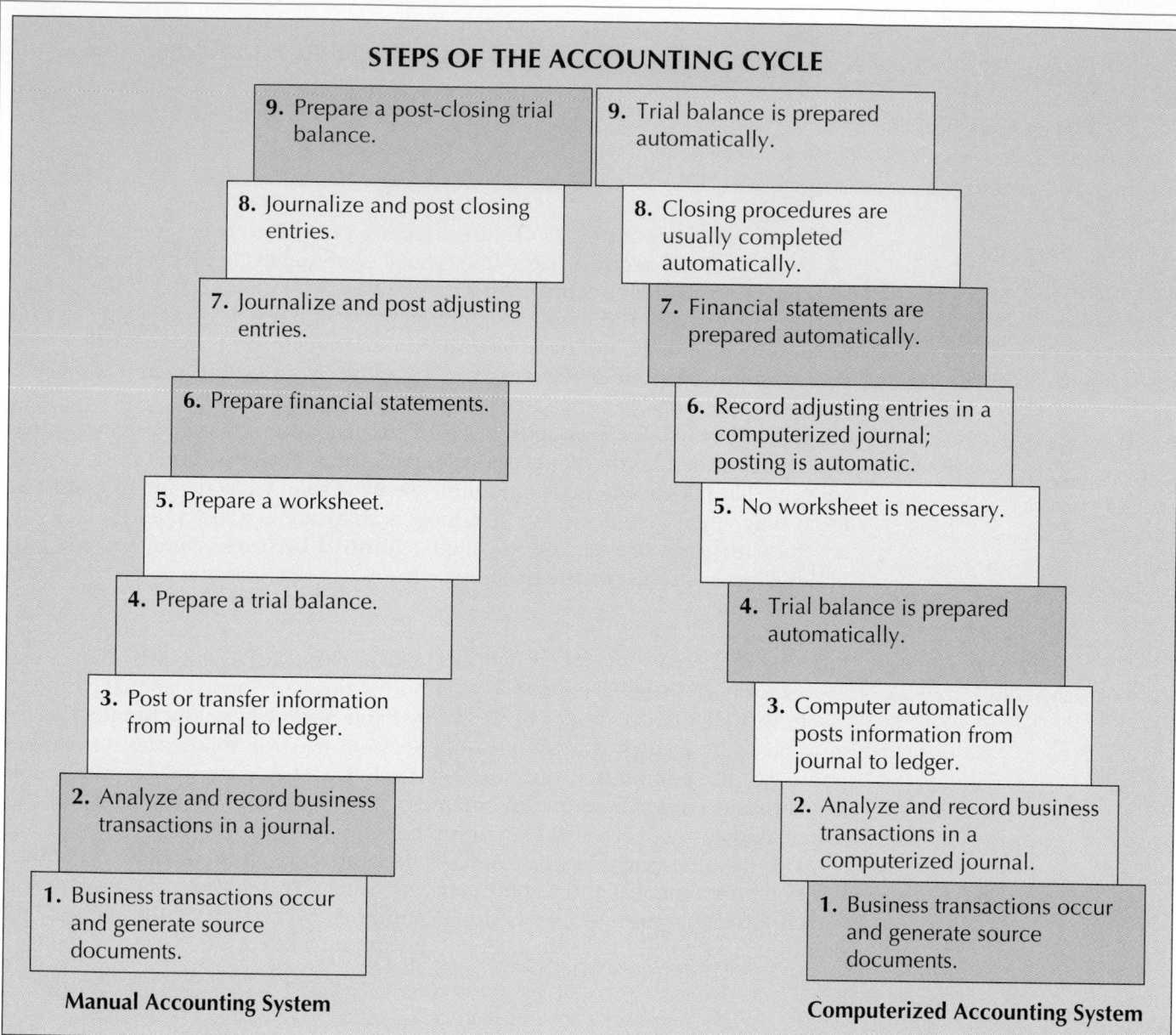

STEPS OF THE ACCOUNTING CYCLE

9. Prepare a post-closing trial balance.

9. Trial balance is prepared automatically.

8. Journalize and post closing entries.

8. Closing procedures are usually completed automatically.

7. Journalize and post adjusting entries.

7. Financial statements are prepared automatically.

6. Prepare financial statements.

6. Record adjusting entries in a computerized journal; posting is automatic.

5. Prepare a worksheet.

5. No worksheet is necessary.

4. Prepare a trial balance.

4. Trial balance is prepared automatically.

3. Post or transfer information from journal to ledger.

3. Computer automatically posts information from journal to ledger.

2. Analyze and record business transactions in a journal.

2. Analyze and record business transactions in a computerized journal.

1. Business transactions occur and generate source documents.

1. Business transactions occur and generate source documents.

Manual Accounting System

Computerized Accounting System

Journal—book of original entry.

The journal is called the **book of original entry,** since it contains the first formal information about the business transactions. The ledger is known as the **book of final entry,** because the information the journal contains will be transferred to the ledger. Like the ledger, the journal may be a bound or loose-leaf book. Each of the journal pages looks like the one in Figure 3-1. The pages of the journal are numbered consecutively from page 1. Keep in mind that the journal and the ledger are separate books.

Relationship Between the Journal and the Chart of Accounts

The accountant must refer to the business's chart of accounts for the account name that is to be used in the journal. Every company has its own "unique" chart of accounts.

The chart of accounts for Clark's Word Processing Services appears on page 73. By the end of Chapter 5, we will have discussed each of these accounts.

Note that we will continue to use transaction analysis charts as a teaching aid in the journalizing process.

FIGURE 3-1
The General Journal

	CLARK'S WORD PROCESSING SERVICES GENERAL JOURNAL			
				Page 1
Date	Account Titles and Description	PR	Dr.	Cr.

Clark's Word Processing Services
Chart of Accounts

Assets (100–199)
111   Cash
112   Accounts Receivable
114   Office Supplies
115   Prepaid Rent
121   World Processing Equipment
122   Accumulated Depreciation,
         Word Processing Equipment

Liabilities (200–299)
211   Accounts Payable
212   Salaries Payable

Owner's Equity (300–399)
311   Brenda Clark, Capital
312   Brenda Clark, Withdrawals
313   Income Summary

Revenue (400–499)
411   Word Processing Fees

Expenses (500–599)
511   Office Salaries Expense
512   Advertising Expense
513   Telephone Expense
514   Office Supplies Expense
515   Rent Expense
516   Depreciation Expense,
         Word Processing Equipment

Journalizing the Transactions of Clark's Word Processing Services

Certain formalities must be followed in making journal entries:

◆ The debit portion of the transaction always is recorded first.

◆ The credit portion of a transaction is indented one-half inch and placed below the debit portion.

◆ The explanation of the journal entry follows immediately after the credit and one inch from the date column.

◆ A one-line space follows each transaction and explanation. This makes the journal easier to read, and there is less chance of mixing transactions.

◆ Finally, as always, the total amount of debits must equal the total amount of credits. The same format is used for each of the entries in the journal.

May 1, 19XX: Brenda Clark began the business by investing $10,000 in cash.

1 Accounts Affected	2 Category	3 ↓ ↑	4 Rules of Dr. and Cr.
Cash	Asset	↑	Dr.
Brenda Clark, Capital	Capital	↑	Cr.

CLARK'S WORD PROCESSING SERVICES
GENERAL JOURNAL

Page 1

Date			Account Titles and Description	PR	Dr.	Cr.
19XX May	1		Cash		10000 00	
			Brenda Clark, Capital			10000 00
			Initial investment of cash by owner			

For now the PR (posting reference) column is blank; we will discuss it later.

Let's now look at the structure of this journal entry. The entry contains the following information:

1. Year of the journal entry   19XX
2. Month of the journal entry   May
3. Day of journal entry   1
4. Name(s) of accounts debited   Cash
5. Name(s) of accounts credited   Brenda Clark, Capital
6. Explanation of transaction   Investment of cash
7. Amount of debit(s) $10,000
8. Amount of credit(s) $10,000

May 1: Purchased word processing equipment from Ben Co. for $6,000, paying $1,000 and promising to pay the balance within 30 days.

1 Accounts Affected	2 Category	3 ↓ ↑	4 Rules of Dr. and Cr.
Word Processing Equipment	Asset	↑	Dr.
Cash	Asset	↓	Cr.
Accounts Payable	Liability	↑	Cr.

This transaction affects three accounts. When a journal entry has more than two accounts, it is called a **compound journal entry.**

		1	Word Processing Equipment		6000 00	
			Cash			1000 00
			Accounts Payable			5000 00
			Purchase of equipment from Ben Co.			

In this entry, only the day is entered in the date column. That is because the year and month were entered at the top of the page from the first transaction. There is no need to repeat this information until a new page is needed or a change of months occurs.

Note that in this compound entry we have one debit and two credits—but the total amount of debits equals the total amount of credits.

A journal entry that requires three or more accounts is called a compound journal entry.

1 Accounts Affected	2 Category	3 ↓ ↑	4 Rules of Dr. and Cr.
Prepaid Rent	Asset	↑	Dr.
Cash	Asset	↓	Cr.

Rent paid in advance is an asset.

In this transaction Clark gains an asset called prepaid rent and gives up an asset, cash. The prepaid rent does not become an expense until it expires.

1	Prepaid Rent	1 2 0 0 00	
	Cash		1 2 0 0 00
	Rent paid in advance—3 mos.		

1 Accounts Affected	2 Category	3 ↓ ↑	4 Rules of Dr. and Cr.
Office Supplies	Asset	↑	Dr.
Accounts Payable	Liability	↑	Cr.

Supplies become an *expense* when used up.

Remember, supplies are an asset when they are purchased. Once they are used up or consumed in the operation of business, they become an expense.

3	Office Supplies	6 0 0 00	
	Accounts Payable		6 0 0 00
	Purchase of supplies on account		
	from Norris		

1 Accounts Affected	2 Category	3 ↓ ↑	4 Rules of Dr. and Cr.
Cash	Asset	↑	Dr.
Word Processing Fees	Revenue	↑	Cr.

	7	Cash		3 0 0 0 00		
		Word Processing Fees			3 0 0 0 00	
		Cash received for services rendered				

May 15: Paid office salaries, $650.

1 Accounts Affected	2 Category	3 ↓ ↑	4 Rules of Dr. and Cr.
Office Salaries Expense	Expense	↑	Dr.
Cash	Asset	↓	Cr.

	15	Office Salaries Expense		6 5 0 00		
		Cash			6 5 0 00	
		Payment of office salaries				

Remember, expenses are recorded when they are incurred, no matter when they are paid.

May 18: Advertising bill from Al's News Co. comes in but is not paid, $250.

1 Accounts Affected	2 Category	3 ↓ ↑	4 Rules of Dr. and Cr.
Advertising Expense	Expense	↑	Dr.
Accounts Payable	Liability	↑	Cr.

	18	Advertising Expense		2 5 0 00		
		Accounts Payable			2 5 0 00	
		Bill in but not paid from Al's News				

Keep in mind that as withdrawals *increase,* owner's equity *decreases.*

May 20: Brenda Clark wrote a check on the bank account of the business to pay her home mortgage payment of $625.

1 Accounts Affected	2 Category	3 ↓ ↑	4 Rules of Dr. and Cr.
Brenda Clark, Withdrawals	Withdrawals	↑	Dr.
Cash	Asset	↓	Cr.

	20	Brenda Clark, Withdrawals		6 2 5 00	
		Cash			6 2 5 00
		Personal withdrawal of cash			

Reminder: Revenue is recorded when it is earned, no matter when the cash is actually received.

May 22: Billed Morris Company for a sophisticated word processing job, $5,000.

1 Accounts Affected	2 Category	3 ↓ ↑	4 Rules of Dr. and Cr.
Accounts Receivable	Asset	↑	Dr.
Word Processing Fees	Revenue	↑	Cr.

	22	Accounts Receivable		5 0 0 0 00	
		Word Processing Fees			5 0 0 0 00
		Billed Morris Co. for fees earned			

May 27: Paid office salaries, $650.

1 Accounts Affected	2 Category	3 ↓ ↑	4 Rules of Dr. and Cr.
Office Salaries Expense	Expense	↑	Dr.
Cash	Asset	↓	Cr.

Note: Since we are on page 2 of the journal, the year and month are repeated.

CLARK'S WORD PROCESSING SERVICES
GENERAL JOURNAL

Page 2

Date		Account Titles and Description	PR	Dr.	Cr.
19XX May	27	Office Salaries Expense		6 5 0 00	
		Cash			6 5 0 00
		Payment of office salaries			

May 28: Paid half the amount owed for word processing equipment purchased May 1 from Ben Co., $2,500.

1 Accounts Affected	2 Category	3 ↓ ↑	4 Rules of Dr. and Cr.
Accounts Payable	Liability	↓	Dr.
Cash	Asset	↓	Cr.

	28	Accounts Payable		2 5 0 0 00	
		Cash			2 5 0 0 00
		Paid half the amount owed Ben Co.			

May 29: Received and paid telephone bill, $220.

1 Accounts Affected	2 Category	3 ↓ ↑	4 Rules of Dr. and Cr.
Telephone Expense	Expense	↑	Dr.
Cash	Asset	↓	Cr.

	29	Telephone Expense		2 2 0 00	
		Cash			2 2 0 00
		Paid telephone bill			

This concludes the journal transactions of Clark's Word Processing Services. (See page 82 for a summary of all the transactions.)

LEARNING UNIT 3-1 REVIEW

AT THIS POINT you should be able to

- ◆ Define an accounting cycle. (p. 71)
- ◆ Define and explain the relationship of the accounting period to the income statement. (p. 71)
- ◆ Compare and contrast a calendar year to a fiscal year. (p. 71)
- ◆ Explain the term natural business year. (p. 71)
- ◆ Explain the function of interim reports. (p. 71)
- ◆ Define and state the purpose of a journal. (p. 71)
- ◆ Compare and contrast a book of original entry to a book of final entry. (p. 72)
- ◆ Differentiate between a chart of accounts and a journal. (p. 73)
- ◆ Explain a compound entry. (p. 74)
- ◆ Journalize a business transaction. (p. 75)

SELF-REVIEW QUIZ 3-1

(The blank forms you need are on pages 56–57 of the *Study Guide and Working Papers.*)

The following are the transactions of Lowe's Repair Service. Journalize the transactions in proper form. The chart of accounts includes Cash; Accounts Receivable; Prepaid Rent; Repair Supplies; Repair Equipment; Accounts Payable; A. Lowe, Capital; A. Lowe, Withdrawals; Repair Fees Earned; Salaries Expense; Advertising Expense; and Supplies Expense.

19XX
June   1 A. Lowe invested $6,000 cash and $4,000 of repair equipment in the business.
       1 Paid two months' rent in advance, $1,200.
       4 Bought repair supplies from Melvin Co. on account, $600. (These supplies have not yet been consumed or used up.)
      15 Performed repair work, received $600 in cash, and had to bill Doe Co. for remaining balance of $300.
      18 A. Lowe paid his home telephone bill, $50, with a check from the company.
      20 Advertising bill for $400 from Jones Co. received but payment not due yet. (Advertising has already appeared in the newspaper.)
      24 Paid salaries, $1,400.

Solution to Self-Review Quiz 3-1

LOWE'S REPAIR SERVICE
GENERAL JOURNAL

Page 1

Date			Account Titles and Description	PR	Dr.	Cr.
19XX June	1		Cash		6 0 0 0 00	
			Repair Equipment		4 0 0 0 00	
			A. Lowe, Capital			10 0 0 0 00
			Owner investment			
	1		Prepaid Rent		1 2 0 0 00	
			Cash			1 2 0 0 00
			Rent paid in advance—2mos.			
	4		Repair Supplies		6 0 0 00	
			Accounts Payable			6 0 0 00
			Purchase on account from Melvin Co.			
	15		Cash		6 0 0 00	
			Accounts Receivable		3 0 0 00	
			Repair Fees Earned			9 0 0 00
			Performed repairs for Doe Co.			
	18		A. Lowe, Withdrawals		5 0 00	
			Cash			5 0 00
			Personal withdrawal			
	20		Advertising Expense		4 0 0 00	
			Accounts Payable			4 0 0 00
			Advertising bill from Jones Co.			
	24		Salaries Expense		1 4 0 0 00	
			Cash			1 4 0 0 00
			Paid salaries			

Quiz Tip: All titles for the debits and credits come from the chart of accounts, debits against the date column and credits indented. The PR column is left blank in the journalizing process.

LEARNING UNIT 3-2
Posting to the Ledger: Step 3 of the Accounting Cycle

The general journal serves a particular purpose; it puts every transaction the business does in one place. There are things it cannot do, though. For example, if you were asked to find the balance of the cash account from the general journal, you would have to go through the entire journal and look for only the cash entries. Then you would have to add up the debits and credits for the cash account and determine the difference between the two.

What we really need to do to find balances of accounts is to transfer the information from the journal to the ledger. This is called **posting.** In the ledger we will accumulate an ending balance for each account so that we can prepare financial statements.

In Chapter 2, we used the T account form to make our ledger entries. T accounts are very simple, but they are not used in the real business world. They are only used for demonstration purposes. In practice, accountants often use a **four-column account form** that includes a column for the business's running balance. Figure 3-2 shows a standard four-column account. We will use that format in the text from now on.

Footings are not needed in four-column accounts.

POSTING

Now let's look at how to post the transactions of Clark's Word Processing Service from its journal. The diagram in Figure 3-3 shows how to post the cash line from the journal to the ledger. The steps in the posting process are numbered and illustrated in the figure.

Step 1: In the Cash account in the ledger, record the date (May 1, 19XX) and the amount of the entry ($10,000).

Step 2: Record the page number of the journal "GJ1" in the posting reference (PR) column of the Cash account.

Step 3: Calculate the new balance of the account. You keep a running balance in each account as you would in your checkbook. To do this you take the present balance in the account on the previous line and add or subtract the transaction as necessary to arrive at your new balance.

Step 4: Record the account number of Cash (111) in the posting reference (PR) column of the journal. This is called **cross referencing.**

The same sequence of steps occurs for each line in the journal. In a manual system like Clark's, the debits and credits in the journal may be posted in the order they were recorded, or all the debits may be posted first and then all the credits. If Clark used a computer system, the program menu would post at the press of a button.

FIGURE 3-2
Four-Column Account

Accounts Payable								Account No. 211	
Date	Explanation	Post. Ref.	Debit	Credit		Balance			
						Debit		Credit	
19XX May 1		GJ1		5 0 0 0 00				5 0 0 0 00	
3		GJ1		6 0 0 00				5 6 0 0 00	
18		GJ1		2 5 0 00				5 8 5 0 00	
28		GJ2	2 5 0 0 00						3 3 5 0 00	

FIGURE 3-3
How to Post from Journal to
Ledger

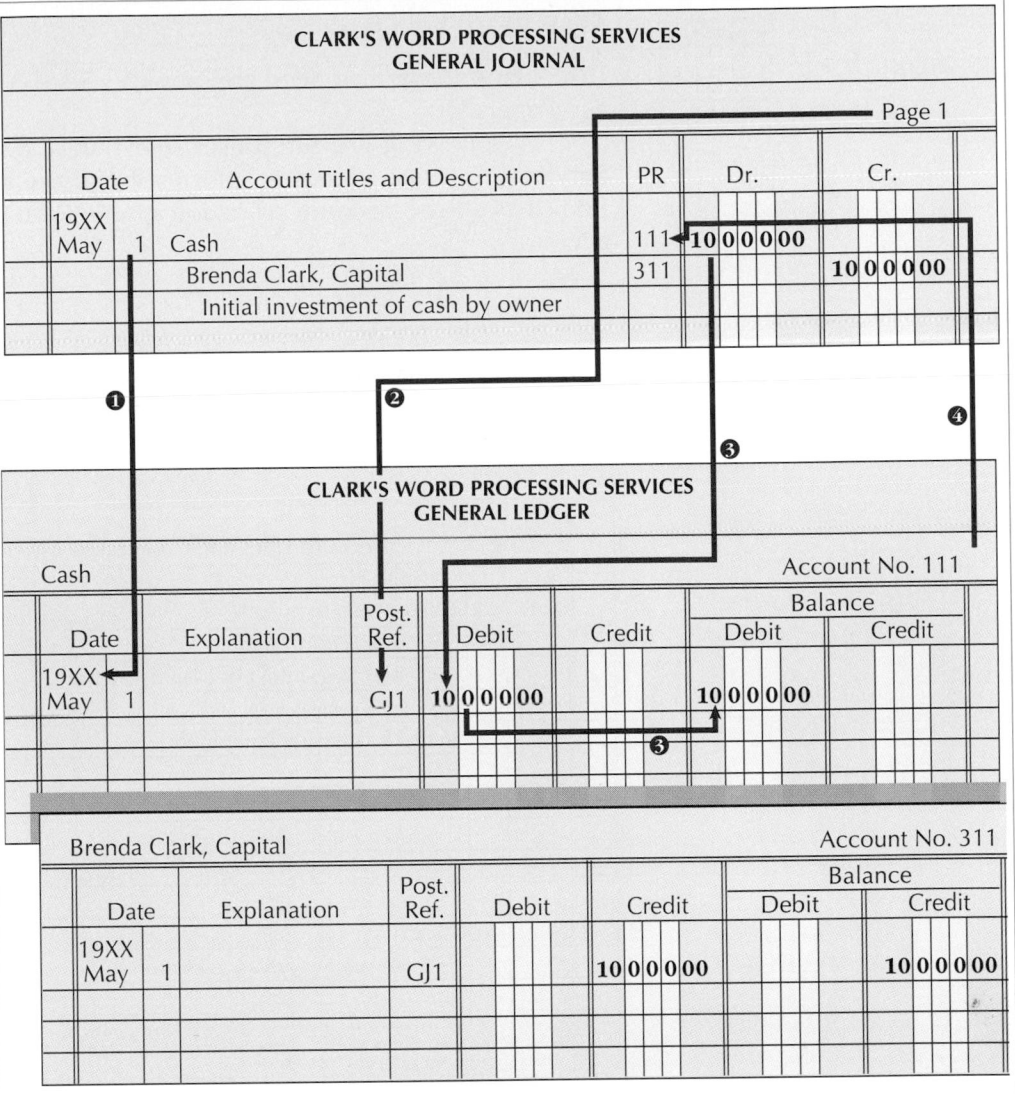

CLARK'S WORD PROCESSING SERVICES
GENERAL JOURNAL

Page 1

Date	Account Titles and Description	PR	Dr.	Cr.
19XX May 1	Cash	111	10 00 00 00	
	Brenda Clark, Capital	311		10 00 00 00
	Initial investment of cash by owner			

❶ ❷ ❸ ❹

CLARK'S WORD PROCESSING SERVICES
GENERAL LEDGER

Cash   Account No. 111

Date	Explanation	Post. Ref.	Debit	Credit	Balance Debit	Balance Credit
19XX May 1		GJ1	10 00 00 00		10 00 00 00	

❸

Brenda Clark, Capital   Account No. 311

Date	Explanation	Post. Ref.	Debit	Credit	Balance Debit	Balance Credit
19XX May 1		GJ1		10 00 00 00		10 00 00 00

Using Posting References

The posting references are very helpful. In the journal, the PR column tells us which transactions have or have not been posted and also to which accounts they were posted. In the ledger, the posting reference leads us back to the original transaction in its entirety, so that we can see why the debit or credit was recorded and what other accounts were affected. (It leads us back to the original transaction by identifying the journal and the page in the journal from which the information came.)

LEARNING UNIT 3-2 REVIEW

AT THIS POINT you should be able to

◆ State the purpose of posting. (p. 80)
◆ Discuss the advantages of the four-column account. (p. 80)
◆ Identify the elements to be posted. (p. 81)
◆ From journalized transactions, post to the general ledger. (p. 81)

SELF-REVIEW QUIZ 3-2

(The blank forms you need are on pages 58–63 of the *Study Guide and Working Papers.*)

The following are the journalized transactions of Clark's Word Processing Services. Your task is to post information to the ledger. The ledger in your workbook has all the account titles and numbers that were used from the chart of accounts.

CLARK'S WORD PROCESSING SERVICES
GENERAL JOURNAL

Page 1

Date			Account Titles and Description	PR	Dr.	Cr.
19XX May	1		Cash		10 0 0 0 00	
			Brenda Clark, Capital			10 0 0 0 00
			Initial investment of cash by owner			
	1		Word Processing Equipment		6 0 0 0 00	
			Cash			1 0 0 0 00
			Accounts Payable			5 0 0 0 00
			Purchase of equip. from Ben Co.			
	1		Prepaid Rent		1 2 0 0 00	
			Cash			1 2 0 0 00
			Rent paid in advance (3 months)			
	3		Office Supplies		6 0 0 00	
			Accounts Payable			6 0 0 00
			Purchase of supplies on acct. from Norris			
	7		Cash		3 0 0 0 00	
			Word Processing Fees			3 0 0 0 00
			Cash received for services rendered			
	15		Office Salaries Expense		6 5 0 00	
			Cash			6 5 0 00
			Payment of office salaries			
	18		Advertising Expense		2 5 0 00	
			Accounts Payable			2 5 0 00
			Bill received but not paid from Al's News			
	20		Brenda Clark, Withdrawals		6 2 5 00	
			Cash			6 2 5 00
			Personal withdrawal of cash			
	22		Accounts Receivable		5 0 0 0 00	
			Word Processing Fees			5 0 0 0 00
			Billed Morris Co. for fees earned			

CLARK'S WORD PROCESSING SERVICES
GENERAL JOURNAL

Page 2

Date		Account Titles and Description	PR	Dr.	Cr.
19XX May	27	Office Salaries Expense		65000	
		Cash			65000
		Payment of office salaries			
	28	Accounts Payable		250000	
		Cash			250000
		Paid half the amount owed Ben Co.			
	29	Telephone Expense		22000	
		Cash			22000
		Paid telephone bill			

Solution to Self-Review Quiz 3-2

CLARK'S WORD PROCESSING SERVICES
GENERAL JOURNAL

Page 1

Date		Account Titles and Description	PR	Dr.	Cr.
19XX May	1	Cash	111	1000000	
		Brenda Clark, Capital	311		1000000
		Initial investment of cash by owner			
	1	Word Processing Equipment	121	600000	
		Cash	111		100000
		Accounts Payable	211		500000
		Purchase of equip. from Ben Co.			
	1	Prepaid Rent	115	120000	
		Cash	111		120000
		Rent paid in advance (3 months)			
	3	Office Supplies	114	60000	
		Accounts Payable	211		60000
		Purchase of supplies on acct. from Norris			
	7	Cash	111	300000	
		Word Processing Fees	411		300000
		Cash received from services rendered			
	15	Office Salaries Expense	511	65000	
		Cash	111		65000
		Payment of office salaries			

(page 1, Clark's General Journal, cont. at top of p. 84)

CH. 3 / BEGINNING THE ACCOUNTING CYCLE: JOURNALIZING, POSTING, AND THE TRIAL BALANCE

83

	18	Advertising Expense	512	2 5 0 00	
		Accounts Payable	211		2 5 0 00
		Bill received but not paid from Al's News			
	20	Brenda Clark, Withdrawals	312	6 2 5 00	
		Cash	111		6 2 5 00
		Personal withdrawal of cash			
	22	Accounts Receivable	112	5 0 0 0 00	
		Word Processing Fees	411		5 0 0 0 00
		Billed Morris Co. for fees earned			

CLARK'S WORD PROCESSING SERVICES
GENERAL JOURNAL

Page 2

Date		Account Titles and Description	PR	Dr.	Cr.
19XX May	27	Office Salaries Expense	511	6 5 0 00	
		Cash	111		6 5 0 00
		Payment of office salaries			
	28	Accounts Payable	211	2 5 0 0 00	
		Cash	111		2 5 0 0 00
		Paid half the amount owed Ben Co.			
	29	Telephone Expense	513	2 2 0 00	
		Cash	111		2 2 0 00
		Paid telephone bill			

CLARK'S WORD PROCESSING SERVICES
PARTIAL GENERAL LEDGER

Cash   Account No. 111

Date		Explanation	Post. Ref.	Debit	Credit	Balance Debit	Balance Credit
19XX May	1		GJ1	10 0 0 0 00		10 0 0 0 00	
	1		GJ1		1 0 0 0 00	9 0 0 0 00	
	1		GJ1		1 2 0 0 00	7 8 0 0 00	
	7		GJ1	3 0 0 0 00		10 8 0 0 00	
	15		GJ1		6 5 0 00	10 1 5 0 00	
	20		GJ1		6 2 5 00	9 5 2 5 00	
	27		GJ2		6 5 0 00	8 8 7 5 00	
	28		GJ2		2 5 0 0 00	6 3 7 5 00	
	29		GJ2		2 2 0 00	6 1 5 5 00	

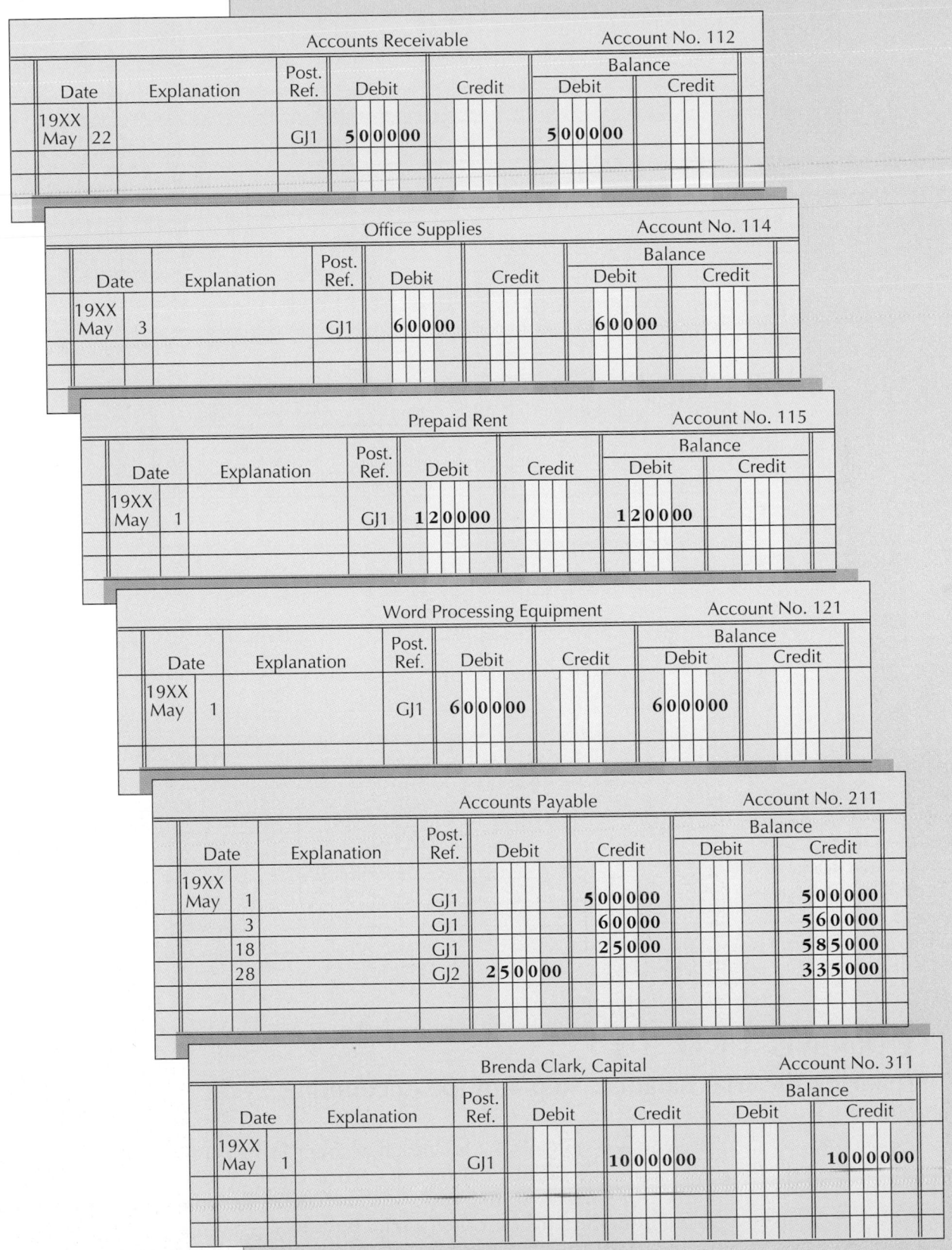

Accounts Receivable   Account No. 112

Date		Explanation	Post. Ref.	Debit	Credit	Balance Debit	Balance Credit
19XX May	22		GJ1	5 000 00		5 000 00	

Office Supplies   Account No. 114

Date		Explanation	Post. Ref.	Debit	Credit	Balance Debit	Balance Credit
19XX May	3		GJ1	60 000		60 000	

Prepaid Rent   Account No. 115

Date		Explanation	Post. Ref.	Debit	Credit	Balance Debit	Balance Credit
19XX May	1		GJ1	1 200 00		1 200 00	

Word Processing Equipment   Account No. 121

Date		Explanation	Post. Ref.	Debit	Credit	Balance Debit	Balance Credit
19XX May	1		GJ1	6 000 00		6 000 00	

Accounts Payable   Account No. 211

Date		Explanation	Post. Ref.	Debit	Credit	Balance Debit	Balance Credit
19XX May	1		GJ1		5 000 00		5 000 00
	3		GJ1		60 000		5 600 00
	18		GJ1		250 00		5 850 00
	28		GJ2	2 500 00			3 350 00

Brenda Clark, Capital   Account No. 311

Date		Explanation	Post. Ref.	Debit	Credit	Balance Debit	Balance Credit
19XX May	1		GJ1		10 000 00		10 000 00

Brenda Clark, Withdrawals					Account No. 312	
Date	Explanation	Post. Ref.	Debit	Credit	Balance	
					Debit	Credit
19XX May 20		GJ1	625 00		625 00	

Word Processing Fees					Account No. 411	
Date	Explanation	Post. Ref.	Debit	Credit	Balance	
					Debit	Credit
19XX May 7		GJ1		3000 00		3000 00
22		GJ1		5000 00		8000 00

Office Salaries Expense					Account No. 511	
Date	Explanation	Post. Ref.	Debit	Credit	Balance	
					Debit	Credit
19XX May 15		GJ1	650 00		650 00	
27		GJ2	650 00		1300 00	

Advertising Expense					Account No. 512	
Date	Explanation	Post. Ref.	Debit	Credit	Balance	
					Debit	Credit
19XX May 18		GJ1	250 00		250 00	

Telephone Expense					Account No. 513	
Date	Explanation	Post. Ref.	Debit	Credit	Balance	
					Debit	Credit
19XX May 29		GJ2	220 00		220 00	

Quiz Tip: The Post Reference column in the ledger tells which page of the journal the information came from. The Post Reference column in the journal (the last to be filled in) tells what account number in the ledger the information was posted to.

LEARNING UNIT 3-3
Preparing the Trial Balance: Step 4 of the Accounting Cycle

Did you note in Quiz 3-2 how each account had a running balance figure? Did you know the normal balance of each account in Clark's ledger? As we discussed in Chapter 2, the list of the individual accounts with their balances taken from the ledger is called a **trial balance.**

The trial balance shown in Figure 3-4 was developed from the ledger accounts of Clark's Word Processing Services that were posted and balanced in Quiz 3-2. If the information is journalized or posted incorrectly, the trial balance will not be correct.

CLARK'S WORD PROCESSING SERVICE TRIAL BALANCE MAY 31, 19XX		
	Debit	Credit
Cash	6 1 5 5 00	
Accounts Receivable	5 0 0 0 00	
Office Supplies	6 0 0 00	
Prepaid Rent	1 2 0 0 00	
Word Processing Equipment	6 0 0 0 00	
Accounts Payable		3 3 5 0 00
Brenda Clark, Capital		10 0 0 0 00
Brenda Clark, Withdrawals	6 2 5 00	
Word Processing Fees		8 0 0 0 00
Office Salaries Expense	1 3 0 0 00	
Advertising Expense	2 5 0 00	
Telephone Expense	2 2 0 00	
Totals	21 3 5 0 00	21 3 5 0 00

The trial balance lists the accounts in the same order as in the ledger. The $6,155 figure of cash came from the ledger, p. 84.

FIGURE 3-4 Trial Balance

There are some things the trial balance will not show:

♦ The capital figure on the trial balance may not be the beginning capital figure. For instance, if Brenda Clark had made additional investments during the period, the additional investment would have been journalized and posted to the capital account. The only way to tell if the capital balance on the trial balance is the original balance is to check the ledger capital account to see whether any additional investments were made. This will be important when we make financial reports.

♦ There is no guarantee that transactions have been properly recorded. For example, the following errors would remain undetected: (1) a transaction that may have been omitted in the journalizing process; (2) a transaction incorrectly analyzed and recorded in the journal; (3) a journal entry journalized or posted twice.

> The totals of a trial balance can balance and yet be incorrect.

WHAT TO DO IF A TRIAL BALANCE DOESN'T BALANCE

The trial balance of Clark's Word Processing Services shows that the total of debits is equal to the total of credits. But what happens if the trial balance is in balance, but the correct amount is not recorded in each ledger account? Accuracy in the journalizing and posting process will help ensure that no errors are made.

Even if there is an error, the first rule is "don't panic." Everyone makes mistakes, and there are accepted ways of correcting them. Once an entry had been made in ink, correcting an error in it must always show that the entry has been changed and who changed it. Sometimes the change has to be explained.

SOME COMMON MISTAKES

> Correcting the trial balance: What to do if your trial balance doesn't balance.
>
> Did you clear your adding machine?

If the trial balance does not balance, the cause could be something relatively simple. Here are some common errors and how they can be fixed:

♦ If the difference (the amount you are off) is 10, 100, 1,000, etc., there probably is a mathematical error in addition.

♦ If the difference is equal to an individual account balance in the ledger, the amount could have been omitted. It is also possible the figure was not posted from the general journal.

- ◆ Divide the difference by 2; then check to see if a debit should have been a credit and vice versa in the ledger or trial balance. Example: $150 difference ÷ 2 = $75. This means you may have placed $75 as a debit to an account instead of a credit or vice versa.

- ◆ If the difference is evenly divisible by 9, a **slide** or transposition may have occurred. A slide is an error resulting from adding or deleting zeros in writing numbers. For example, $4,175.00 may have been copied as $41.75. A **transposition** is the accidental rearrangement of digits of a number. For example, $4,175 might have been accidentally written as $4,157.

- ◆ Compare the balances in the trial balance with the ledger accounts to check for copying errors.

- ◆ Recompute balances in each ledger account.

- ◆ Trace all postings from journal to ledger.

If you cannot find the error after you have done all of this, take a coffee break. Then start all over again.

MAKING A CORRECTION BEFORE POSTING

Before posting, error correction is straightforward. Simply draw a line through the incorrect entry, write the correct information above the line, and write your initials near the change.

Correcting an Error in an Account Title   The following illustration shows an error and its correction in an account title:

	1	Word Processing Equipment		6 0 0 0 00			
		Cash			1 0 0 0 00		
		~~Accounts Payable~~ ᵃᵐᵖ Accounts Payable			5 0 0 0 00		
		Purchase of equipment from Ben Co.					

Correcting a Numerical Error   Numbers are handled the same way as account titles, as the next change from 520 to 250 shows:

	18	Advertising Expense		2 5 0 00			
		Accounts Payable			ᵃᵐᵖ 2 5 0 00 ~~5 2 0 00~~		
		Bill from Al's News					

Correcting an Entry Error   If a number has been entered in the wrong column, a straight line is drawn through it, and the number is then written in the correct column:

	1	Word Processing Equipment		6 0 0 0 00			
		Cash			1 0 0 0 00		
		Accounts Payable	ᵃᵐᵖ 5 0 0 0 00	~~5 0 0 0 00~~	5 0 0 0 00		
		Purchase of equip. from Ben Co.					

MAKING A CORRECTION AFTER POSTING

It is also possible to correct an amount that is correctly entered in the journal but posted incorrectly to the ledger of the proper account. The first step is to draw a line through the error and write the correct figure above it. The next step is changing the running balance to reflect the corrected posting. Here, too, a line is drawn through the balance and the corrected balance is written above it. Both changes must be initialed.

			Word Processing Fees			Account No. 411	
		Post.			Balance		
Date	Explanation	Ref.	Debit	Credit	Debit	Credit	
19XX May 7		GJ1		2500 00		2500 00	
22		GJ1		~~4100 00~~ *amp*		~~2600 00~~ *amp*	

CORRECTING AN ENTRY POSTED TO THE WRONG ACCOUNT

Drawing a line through an error and writing the correction above it is possible when a mistake has occurred within the proper account, but when an error involves a posting to the wrong account the journal must include a correction accompanied by an explanation. In addition, the correct information must be posted to the appropriate ledgers.

Suppose, for example, that as a result of tracing postings from journal entries to ledgers you find that a $180 telephone bill was incorrectly debited as an advertising expense. The following illustration shows how this is done.

Step 1: The journal entry is corrected and the correction is explained:

		GENERAL JOURNAL			Page 3	
Date	Account Titles and Description	PR	Dr.	Cr.		
19XX May 29	Telephone Expense	513	180 00			
	Advertising Expense	512		180 00		
	To correct error in which					
	Advertising Exp. was debited					
	for charges to Telephone Exp.					

Step 2: The Advertising Expense ledger account is corrected:

			Advertising Expense			Account No. 512	
		Post.			Balance		
Date	Explanation	Ref.	Debit	Credit	Debit	Credit	
19XX May 18		GJ1	175 00		175 00		
23		GJ1	180 00		355 00		
29	Correcting entry	GJ3		180 00	175 00		

Step 3: The Telephone Expense ledger is corrected:

			Telephone Expense			Account No. 513	
		Post.			Balance		
Date	Explanation	Ref.	Debit	Credit	Debit	Credit	
19XX May 29		GJ3	180 00		180 00		

AT THIS POINT you should be able to

◆ Prepare a trial balance with a ledger, using four-column accounts. (p. 87)
◆ Analyze and correct a trial balance that doesn't balance. (p. 87)
◆ Correct journal and posting errors. (p. 88)

SELF-REVIEW QUIZ 3-3

(The blank forms you need are on page 64 of the *Study Guide and Working Papers*.)

1.

MEMO

To: Al Vincent

From: Professor Jones

Re: Trial Balance

You have submitted to me an incorrect trial balance. Could you please re-work and turn in to me before next Friday?

Note: Individual amounts look OK.

A. RICE
TRIAL BALANCE
OCTOBER 31, 19XX

	Dr.	Cr.
Cash		8 0 6 0 00
Operating Expenses		1 7 0 0 00
A. Rice, Withdrawals		4 0 0 00
Service Revenue		5 4 0 0 00
Equipment	5 0 0 0 00	
Accounts Receivable	3 5 4 0 00	
Accounts Payable	2 0 0 0 00	
Supplies	3 0 0 00	
A. Rice, Capital		11 6 0 0 00

2. A $7,000 debit to office equipment was mistakenly journalized and posted on June 9, 19XX to office supplies. Prepare the appropriate journal entry to correct this error.

Solution to Self-Review Quiz 3-3

1.

A. RICE
TRIAL BALANCE
OCTOBER 31, 19XX

	Dr.	Cr.
Cash	8 0 6 0 00	
Accounts Receivable	3 5 4 0 00	
Supplies	3 0 0 00	
Equipment	5 0 0 0 00	
Accounts Payable		2 0 0 0 00
A. Rice, Capital		11 6 0 0 00
A. Rice, Withdrawals	4 0 0 00	
Service Revenue		5 4 0 0 00
Operating Expenses	1 7 0 0 00	
Totals	19 0 0 0 00	19 0 0 0 00

2.

GENERAL JOURNAL					Page 4	
Date		Account Titles and Description	PR	Dr.	Cr.
19XX June	9	Office Equipment		7 0 0 0 0 0	
		Office Supplies			7 0 0 0 0 0
		To correct error in which office supplies			
		had been debited for purchase of			
		office equipment			

COMPREHENSIVE DEMONSTRATION PROBLEM WITH SOLUTION TIPS

(The blank forms you need are on pages 65–69 in the *Study Guide and Working Papers.*)

In March, Abby's Employment Agency had the following transactions:

19XX

Mar. 1 Abby Todd invested $5,000 in the new employment agency.
4 Bought equipment for cash, $200.
5 Earned employment fee commission, $200, but payment from Blue Co. will not be received until June.
6 Paid wages expense, $300.
7 Abby Todd paid her home utility bill from the company checkbook, $75.
9 Placed Rick Wool at VCR Corporation, receiving $1,200 cash.
15 Paid cash for supplies, $200.
28 Telephone bill received but not paid, $180.
29 Advertising bill received but not paid, $400.

The chart of accounts includes: Cash, 111; Accounts Receivable, 112; Supplies, 131; Equipment, 141; Accounts Payable, 211; A. Todd, Capital, 311; A. Todd, Withdrawals, 321; Employment Fees Earned, 411; Wage Expense, 511; Telephone Expense, 521; Advertising Expense, 531.

Your task is to:

a. Set up a ledger based on the chart of accounts.
b. Journalize (all p. 1) and post transactions.
c. Prepare a trial balance for March 31.

		ABBY'S EMPLOYMENT AGENCY				Page 1
Date		Account Titles and Description	PR	Dr.	Cr.	

Date			Account Titles and Description	PR	Dr.	Cr.
19XX Mar.	1		Cash	111	5 0 0 0 00	
			A. Todd, Capital	311		5 0 0 0 00
			Owner investment			
	4		Equipment	141	2 0 0 00	
			Cash	111		2 0 0 00
			Bought equipment for cash			
	5		Accounts Receivable	112	2 0 0 00	
			Employment Fees Earned	411		2 0 0 00
			Fees on account from Blue Co.			
	6		Wage Expense	511	3 0 0 00	
			Cash	111		3 0 0 00
			Paid wages			
	7		A. Todd, Withdrawals	321	7 5 00	
			Cash	111		7 5 00
			Personal withdrawals			
	9		Cash	111	1 2 0 0 00	
			Employment Fees Earned	411		1 2 0 0 00
			Cash fees			
	15		Supplies	131	2 0 0 00	
			Cash	111		2 0 0 00
			Bought supplies for cash			
	28		Telephone Expense	521	1 8 0 00	
			Accounts Payable	211		1 8 0 00
			Telephone bill owed			
	29		Advertising Expense	531	4 0 0 00	
			Accounts Payable	211		4 0 0 00
			Advertising bill received			

Cash   111

Date		PR	Dr.	Cr.	Balance Dr.	Balance Cr.
19XX March	1	GJ1	5,000		5,000	
	4	GJ1		200	4,800	
	6	GJ1		300	4,500	
	7	GJ1		75	4,425	
	9	GJ1	1,200		5,625	
	15	GJ1		200	5,425	

Accounts Receivable   112

Date		PR	Dr.	Cr.	Balance Dr.	Balance Cr.
19XX March	5	GJ1	200		200	

Supplies   131

Date		PR	Dr.	Cr.	Balance Dr.	Balance Cr.
19XX March	15	GJ1	200		200	

Equipment   141

Date		PR	Dr.	Cr.	Balance Dr.	Balance Cr.
19XX March	4	GJ1	200		200	

Accounts Payable   211

Date		PR	Dr.	Cr.	Balance Dr.	Balance Cr.
19XX March	28	GJ1		180		180
	29	GJ1		400		580

A. Todd, Capital   311

Date		PR	Dr.	Cr.	Balance Dr.	Balance Cr.
19XX March	1	GJ1		5,000		5,000

A. Todd, Withdrawals   321

Date		PR	Dr.	Cr.	Balance Dr.	Balance Cr.
19XX March	7	GJ1	75		75	

Employment Fees Earned   411

Date		PR	Dr.	Cr.	Balance Dr.	Balance Cr.
19XX March	5	GJ1		200		200
	9	GJ1		1,200		1,400

Wage Expense   511

Date		PR	Dr.	Cr.	Balance Dr.	Balance Cr.
19XX March	6	GJ1	300		300	

Telephone Expense   521

Date		PR	Dr.	Cr.	Balance Dr.	Balance Cr.
19XX March	28	GJ1	180		180	

Advertising Expense   531

Date		PR	Dr.	Cr.	Balance Dr.	Balance Cr.
19XX March	29	GJ1	400		400	

Solution Tips to Journalizing

1. When journalizing, the PR column is not filled in.
2. Write the name of the debit against the date column. Indent credits and list them below debits. Be sure total debits for each transaction equal total credits.
3. Skip a line between each transaction.

THE ANALYSIS OF THE JOURNAL ENTRIES

Date	Account	Type		Dr/Cr	Amount
March 1	Cash	A	↑	Dr.	$5,000
	A. Todd, Capital	Capital	↑	Cr.	$5,000
4	Equipment	A	↑	Dr.	$ 200
	Cash	A	↓	Cr.	$ 200
5	Acc. Receivable	A	↑	Dr.	$ 200
	Empl. Fees Earned	Rev.	↑	Cr.	$ 200
6	Wage Expense	Exp.	↑	Dr.	$ 300
	Cash	A	↓	Cr.	$ 300
7	A. Todd, Withdrawals	Withd.	↑	Dr.	$ 75
	Cash	A	↓	Cr.	$ 75
9	Cash	A	↑	Dr.	$1,200
	Empl. Fees Earned	Rev.	↑	Cr.	$1,200
15	Supplies	A	↑	Dr.	$ 200
	Cash	A	↓	Cr.	$ 200
28	Telephone Expense	Exp.	↑	Dr.	$ 180
	Accounts Payable	L	↑	Cr.	$ 180
28	Advertising Expense	Exp.	↑	Dr.	$ 400
	Accounts Payable	L	↑	Cr.	$ 400

Solution Tips to Posting

The PR column in the ledger cash account tells you from which page a journal information came (see page 1). After the ledger cash account is posted, Account Number 111 is put in the PR column of the journal. (This is called cross-referencing.)

Note how we keep a running balance in the cash account. A $5,000 dr. balance and a $200 credit entry result in a new debit balance of $4,800.

ABBY'S EMPLOYMENT AGENCY
TRIAL BALANCE
MARCH 31, 19XX

	Dr.	Cr.
Cash	5,425	
Accounts Receivable	200	
Supplies	200	
Equipment	200	
Accounts Payable		580
A. Todd, Capital		5,000
A. Todd, Withdrawals	75	
Employment Fees Earned		1,400
Wage Expense	300	
Telephone Expense	180	
Advertising Expense	400	
Totals	**6,980**	**6,980**

Solution Tip to Trial Balance

The trial balance lists the ending balance of each title in the order in which they appear in the ledger. The total of $6,980 on the left equals $6,980 on the right.

SUMMARY OF KEY POINTS

Learning Unit 3-1

1. The accounting cycle is a sequence of accounting procedures that are usually performed during an accounting period.
2. An accounting period is the time period for which the income statement is prepared. The time period can be any period up to one year.
3. A calendar year is from January 1 to December 31. The fiscal year is any twelve-month period. A fiscal year could be a calendar year but does not have to be.
4. Interim reports are statements that are usually prepared for a portion of the business's calendar or fiscal year (e.g., a month or a quarter).
5. A general journal is a book that records transactions in chronological order. Here debits and credits are shown together on one page. It is the book of original entry.
6. The ledger is a collection of accounts where information is accumulated from the postings of the journal. The ledger is the book of final entry.
7. Journalizing is the process of recording journal entries.
8. The chart of accounts provides the specific titles of accounts to be entered in the journal.

9. When journalizing, the post reference (PR) column is left blank.
10. A compound journal entry occurs when more than two accounts are affected in the journalizing process of a business transaction.

Learning Unit 3-2

1. Posting is the process of transferring information from the journal to the ledger.
2. The journal and ledger contain the same information but in a different form.
3. The four-column account aids in keeping a running balance of an account.
4. The normal balance of an account will be located on the side that increases it according to the rules of debits and credits. For example, the normal balances of liabilities occur on the credit side.
5. The mechanical process of posting requires care in transferring to the appropriate account the dates, post references, and amounts.

Learning Unit 3-3

1. A trial balance can balance but be incorrect. For example, an entire journal entry may not have been posted.
2. If a trial balance doesn't balance, check for errors in addition, omission of postings, slides, transpositions, copying errors, and so on.
3. Specific procedures should be followed in making corrections in journals and ledgers.

KEY TERMS

Accounting cycle For each accounting period, the process that begins with the recording of business transactions or procedures into a journal and ends with the completion of a post-closing trial balance.

Accounting period The period of time for which an income statement is prepared.

Book of final entry Book that receives information about business transactions from a book of original entry (a journal). Example: a ledger.

Book of original entry Book that records the first formal information about business transactions. Example: a journal.

Calendar year January 1 to December 31.

Compound journal entry A journal entry that affects more than two accounts.

Cross-referencing Adding to the PR column of the journal the account number of the ledger account that was updated from the journal.

Fiscal year The twelve-month period a business chooses for its accounting year.

Four-column account A running balance account that records debits and credits and has a column for an ending balance (debit or credit). Replaces the standard two-column account we used earlier.

General journal The simplest form of a journal, which records information from transactions in chronological order as they occur. This journal links the debit and credit parts of transactions together.

Interim reports Financial reports that are prepared for a month, quarter, or some other portion of the fiscal year.

Journal A listing of business transactions in chronological order. The journal links on one page the debit and credit parts of transactions.

Journal entry The transaction (debits and credits) that is recorded into a journal once it is analyzed.

Journalizing The process of recording a transaction entry into the journal.

Natural business year A business's fiscal year that ends at the same time as a slow seasonal period begins.

Posting The transferring, copying, or recording of information from a journal to a ledger.

Slide The error that results in adding or deleting zeros in the writing of a number. Example: 79,200 → 7,920.

Transposition The accidental rearrangement of digits of a number. Example: 152 → 125.

Trial balance An informal listing of the ledger accounts and their balances in the ledger that aids in proving the equality of debits and credits.

BLUEPRINT OF FIRST FOUR STEPS OF ACCOUNTING CYCLE

Step 1: Business transactions occur and generate source documents.

Business Transactions (in monetary terms)

INVOICE
ACE SUPPLY

Moore Company
125 First Ave.
Lynn, MA 01970

Supplies *Paid Cash* $5.00

MOORE COMPANY
GENERAL JOURNAL

p.2

Date			PR	Dr.	Cr.
19XX Jan.	10	Supplies	114	5	
		Cash	111		5
		Bought supplies			

Step 2: Analyze and record business transactions in a journal.

Step 3: Post information from journal to ledger.

Book of original entry—records in chronological order

POST

Book of final entry accumulates information from journal

Step 4: Prepare a trial balance.

LEDGER

MOORE COMPANY
TRIAL BALANCE
JANUARY 31, 19XX

	Dr.	Cr.
Assets	X	
Liabilities		X
Capital		X
Withdrawals	X	
Revenues		X
Expenses	X	
Totals	XXX	XXX

List of balances from each of the ledger accounts

Cash 111

Date		Expl.	PR	Dr.	Cr.	Balance Dr.	Cr.
19XX Jan.	1	Bal.	✔			200	
	10		GJ2		5	195	

Supplies 114

Date		Expl.	PR	Dr.	Cr.	Balance Dr.	Cr.
19XX Jan.	10		GJ2	5		5	

QUESTIONS, MINI EXERCISES, EXERCISES, AND PROBLEMS

Discussion Questions

1. Explain the concept of the accounting cycle.
2. An accounting period is based on the balance sheet. Agree or disagree.
3. Compare and contrast a calendar year versus a fiscal year.
4. What are interim reports?
5. Why is the ledger called the book of final entry?
6. How do transactions get "linked" in a general journal?
7. What is the relationship of the chart of accounts to the general journal?
8. What is a compound journal entry?
9. Posting means updating the journal. Agree or disagree. Please comment.
10. The side that decreases an account is the normal balance. True or false?

11. The PR column of a general journal is the last item to be filled in during the posting process. Agree or disagree.

12. Discuss the concept of cross-referencing.

13. What is the difference between a transposition and a slide?

Mini Exercises

(The blank forms you need are on page 71 of the *Study Guide and Working Papers.*)

General Journal

1. Complete the following from the general journal of Ranger Co.

			RANGER COMPANY			
			GENERAL JOURNAL			Page 1
Date		Account Titles and Descriptions	PR	Dr.	Cr.	
19XX Aug	18	Cash		7 0 0 0 00		
		Equipment		2 0 0 00		
		B. Ranger, Capital			7 2 0 0 00	
		Initial Investment by Owner				

    a. Year of Journal Entry   _____

    b. Month of Journal Entry   _____

    c. Day of Journal Entry   _____

    d. Name(s) of Accounts Debited   _____

    e. Name(s) of Accounts Credited   _____

    f. Explanation of Transaction   _____

    g. Amount of Debit(s)   _____

    h. Amount of Credit(s)   _____

    i. Page of Journal   _____

General Journal

2. Provide the explanation for each of these general journal entries.

			GENERAL JOURNAL			
						Page 4
Date		Account Titles and Descriptions	PR	Debit	Credit	
19XX July	9	Cash		7 0 0 0 00		
		Office Equipment		5 0 0 0 00		
		A. Rye, Capital			12 0 0 0 00	
		(A)				
	15	Cash		3 0 00		
		Accounts Receivable		6 0 00		
		Hair Fees Earned			9 0 00	
		(B)				
	20	Advertising Expense		4 0 00		
		Accounts Payable			4 0 00	
		(C)				

Posting and Balancing

3. Balance this four-column account. What function does the PR column serve? When will the Account 111 be used in the journalizing and posting process?

Cash					Acct. 111	
					Balance	
Date	Explanation	PR	Dr.	Cr.	Dr.	Cr.
19XX June 4		GJ 1	15			
5		GJ 1	6			
9		GJ 2		4		
10		GJ 3	1			

The Trial Balance

4. The following Trial Balance was prepared *incorrectly.*

   a. Rearrange the accounts in proper order.

   b. Calculate the total of the Trial Balance. (Small numbers are used intentionally so you can do the calculations in your head.) Assume each account has a normal balance.

LARKIN CO.
TRIAL BALANCE
OCTOBER 31, 19XX

	Dr.	Cr.
B. Larkin, Capital	14	
Equipment	9	
Rent Expense		4
Advertising Expense		3
Accounts Payable		8
Taxi Fees	16	
Cash	17	
B. Larkin, Withdrawals	—	5
Totals	**56**	**19**

Correcting Entry

5. On May 1, 1998 a telephone expense for $180 was debited to Repair Expense. On June 12, 1999 this error was found. Prepare the corrected Journal Entry. When would a correcting entry *not* be needed?

Exercises

(The forms you need are on pages 72–77 of the *Study Guide and Working Papers.*)

Preparing journal entries.

3-1. Prepare journal entries for the following transactions that occurred during October:

19XX
Nov.　1　Ann Carter invested $20,000 cash and $2,000 of equipment into her new business.
　　　3　Purchased building for $60,000 on account.
　　12　Purchased a truck from Lange Co. for $18,000 cash.
　　18　Bought supplies from Green Co. on account, $700.

3-2. Record the following into the general journal of Fay's Repair Shop.

19XX
Jan.　1　Fay Hope invested $15,000 cash in the repair shop.
　　　5　Paid $7,000 for shop equipment.
　　　8　Bought from Lowell Co. shop equipment for $6,000 on account.
　　14　Received $900 for repair fees earned.
　　18　Billed Sullivan Co. $900 for services rendered.
　　20　Fay withdrew $300 for personal use.

3-3. Post the following transactions to the ledger of King Company. The partial ledger of King Company is Cash, 111; Equipment, 121; Accounts Payable, 211; and A. King, Capital, 311. Please use four-column accounts in the posting process.

							Page 4
Date 19XX			PR	Dr.		Cr.	
April	6	Cash		15 00 0 00			
		A. King, Capital				15 00 0 00	
		Cash investment					
	14	Equipment		9 00 0 00			
		Cash				4 00 0 00	
		Accounts Payable				5 00 0 00	
		Purchase of equipment					

3-4. From the following transactions for Lowe Company for the month of July, (a) prepare journal entries (assume that it is p. 1 of the journal), (b) post to the ledger (use four-column account), and (c) prepare a trial balance.

19XX
July　1　Joan Lowe invested $6,000 in the business.
　　　4　Bought from Lax Co. equipment on account, $800.
　　15　Billed Friend Co. for services rendered, $4,000.
　　18　Received $5,000 cash for services rendered.
　　24　Paid salaries expense, $1,800.
　　28　Joan withdrew $400 for personal use.

Partial chart of accounts includes: Cash, 111; Accounts Receivable, 112; Equipment, 121; Accounts Payable, 211; J. Lowe, Capital, 311; J. Lowe, Withdrawals, 312; Fees Earned, 411; Salaries Expense, 511.

3-5. You have been hired to correct the following trial balance that has been recorded improperly from the ledger to the trial balance.

Preparing journal entries.

Posting

Journalizing, posting, and preparing a trial balance.

SUNG CO. TRIAL BALANCE MARCH 31, 19XX		
	Dr.	Cr.
Accounts Payable	2 0 0 0 00	
A. Sung, Capital		6 5 0 0 00
A. Sung, Withdrawals		3 0 0 00
Services Earned		4 7 0 0 00
Concessions Earned	2 5 0 0 00	
Rent Expense	4 0 0 00	
Salaries Expense	2 5 0 0 00	
Miscellaneous Expense		1 3 0 0 00
Cash	10 0 0 0 00	
Accounts Receivable		1 2 0 0 00
Totals	17 4 0 0 00	14 0 0 0 00

3-6. On February 6, 19XX, Mike Sullivan made the following journal entry to record the purchase on account of office equipment priced at $1,400. This transaction had not yet been posted when the error was discovered. Make the appropriate correction.

GENERAL JOURNAL					
Date		Account Titles and Description	PR	Dr.	Cr.
19XX Feb.	6	Office Equipment		9 0 0 00	
		Accounts Payable			9 0 0 00
		Purchase of office equip. on account			

Group A Problems

(The forms you need are on pages 78–89 of the *Working Papers and Study Guide*.)

3A-1. Sue Vance operates Vance's Dog Grooming Center. As the bookkeeper, you have been requested to journalize the following transactions:

19XX

July
1 Paid rent for two months in advance, $3,000.
3 Purchased grooming equipment on account from Leek's Supply House, $2,500.
10 Purchased grooming supplies from Angel's Wholesale for $600 cash.
12 Received $1,400 cash from grooming fees earned.
20 Sue withdrew $400 for her personal use.
21 Advertising bill received from *Daily Sun* but unpaid, $120.
25 Paid cleaning expense, $90.
28 Paid salaries expense, $500.
29 Performed grooming work for $1,700, however, payment will not be received from Rick's Kennel until May.

30 Paid Leek's Supply House half the amount owed from July 3 transaction.

Your task is to journalize the above transactions. The chart of accounts for Vance's Dog Grooming Center is as follows:

Chart of Accounts

Assets		Owner's Equity	
111	Cash	311	Sue Vance, Capital
112	Accounts Receivable	312	Sue Vance, Withdrawals
114	Prepaid Rent	**Revenue**	
116	Grooming Supplies	411	Grooming Fees Earned
121	Grooming Equipment	**Expenses**	
Liabilities		511	Advertising Expense
211	Accounts Payable	512	Salaries Expense
		514	Cleaning Expense

Comprehensive Problem: Journalizing, posting, and preparing a trial balance.

3A-2. On June 1, 19XX, Molly Taylor opened Taylor's Dance Studio. The following transactions occurred in June:

19XX
June 1 Molly Taylor invested $8,000 in the dance studio.
      1 Paid three months' rent in advance, $1,000.
      3 Purchased $700 of equipment from Astor Co. on account.
      5 Received $900 cash for fitness-training workshop for dancers.
      8 Purchased $300 of supplies for cash.
      9 Billed Lester Co. $2,100 for group dance lesson for its employees.
     10 Paid salaries of assistants, $400.
     15 Molly Taylor withdrew $150 from the business for her personal use.
     28 Paid electrical expense, $125.
     29 Paid telephone bill for June, $190.

Your task is to

a. Set up the ledger based on the charts of accounts below.
b. Journalize (journal is p. 1) and post the June transactions.
c. Prepare a trial balance as of June 30, 19XX.

The chart of accounts for Taylor's Dance Studio is as follows:

Check Figure:
Trial Balance Total $11,700

Chart of Accounts

Assets		Owner's Equity	
111	Cash	311	Molly Taylor, Capital
112	Accounts Receivable	312	Molly Taylor, Withdrawals
114	Prepaid Rent	**Revenue**	
121	Supplies	411	Fees Earned
131	Equipment	**Expenses**	
Liabilities		511	Electrical Expense
211	Accounts Payable	512	Salaries Expense
		531	Telephone Expense

3A-3. The following transactions occurred in June 19XX for A. French's Placement Agency:

19XX
June 1 A. French invested $9,000 cash in the placement agency.
1 Bought equipment on account from Hook Co., $2,000.
3 Earned placement fees of $1,600, but payment will not be received until July.
5 A. French withdrew $100 for his personal use.
7 Paid wages expense, $300.
9 Placed a client on a local TV show, receiving $600 cash.
15 Bought supplies on account from Lyon Co., $500.
28 Paid telephone bill for June, $160.
29 Advertising bill from Shale Co. received but not paid, $900.

Check Figure:
Trial Balance Total $14,600

The chart of accounts for A. French Placement Agency is as follows:

Chart of Accounts

Assets
111 Cash
112 Accounts Receivable
131 Supplies
141 Equipment

Liabilities
211 Accounts Payable

Owner's Equity
311 A. French, Capital
312 A. French, Withdrawals

Revenue
411 Placement Fees Earned

Expenses
511 Wage Expense
512 Telephone Expense
531 Advertising Expense

Your task is to

a. Set up the ledger based on the chart of accounts.
b. Journalize (p. 1) and post the June transactions.
c. Prepare a trial balance as of June 30, 19XX.

Group B Problems

Journalizing

(The forms you need are on pages 78–89 of the *Study Guide and Working Papers.*)

3B-1. In April Sue Vance opened a new dog grooming center. Please assist her by journalizing the following business transactions:

Check Figure:
April 21
Dr. Advertising expense $75
Cr. Accounts payable $75

19XX
April 1 Sue Vance invested $4,000 of grooming equipment as well as $6,000 cash in the new business.
3 Purchased grooming supplies on account from Rex Co., $500.
10 Purchased office equipment on account from Ross Stationery, $400.
12 Sue paid her home telephone bill from the company checkbook, $60.
20 Received $600 cash for grooming services performed.
21 Advertising bill received but not paid, $75.
25 Cleaning bill received but not paid, $90.
28 Performed grooming work for Jay Kennels, $700; however, payment will not be received until May.

29 Paid salaries expense, $400.

30 Paid Ross Stationery half the amount owed from April 10 transaction.

The chart of accounts for Vance's Dog Grooming Center includes: Cash, 111; Accounts Receivable, 112; Prepaid Rent, 114; Grooming Supplies, 116; Office Equipment, 120; Grooming Equipment, 121; Accounts Payable, 211; Sue Vance, Capital, 311; Sue Vance, Withdrawals, 312; Grooming Fees Earned, 411; Advertising Expense, 511; Salaries Expense, 512; and Cleaning Expense, 514.

Comprehensive Problem: Journalizing, posting, and preparing a trial balance.

3B-2. In June the following transactions occurred for Taylor's Dance Studio.

19XX

June 1 Molly Taylor invested $6,000 in the dance studio.

1 Paid four months rent in advance, $1,200.

3 Purchased supplies on account from A.J.K., $700.

5 Purchased equipment on account from Reese Company, $900.

8 Received $1,300 cash for dance-training program provided to Northwest Junior College.

9 Billed Long Co. for dance lessons provided, $600.

10 Molly withdrew $400 from the dance studio to buy a new chain saw for her home.

15 Paid salaries expense, $400.

28 Paid telephone bill, $118.

29 Electric bill received but unpaid, $120.

Check Figure:
Total Trial Balance $9,620

Your task is to

a. Set up a ledger.

b. Journalize (all p. 1) and post the June transactions.

c. Prepare a trial balance as of June 30, 19XX.

Chart of accounts includes: Cash, 111; Accounts Receivable, 112; Prepaid Rent, 114; Supplies, 121; Equipment, 131; Accounts Payable, 211; M. Taylor, Capital, 311; M. Taylor, Withdrawals, 321; Fees Earned, 411; Electrical Expense, 511; Salaries Expense, 521; Telephone Expense, 531.

Comprehensive Problem: Journalizing, posting, and preparing a trial balance.

3B-3. In June, A. French's Placement Agency had the following transactions:

19XX

June 1 A. French invested $6,000 in the new placement agency.

2 Bought equipment for cash, $350.

3 Earned placement fee commission, $2,100, but payment from Avon Co. will not be received until July.

5 Paid wages expense, $400.

7 A. French paid his home utility bill from the company checkbook, $69.

9 Placed Jay Diamond on a national TV show, receiving $900 cash.

15 Paid cash for supplies, $350.

28 Telephone bill received but not paid, $185.

29 Advertising bill received but not paid, $200.

Check Figure:
Total Trial Balance $9,385

The chart of accounts includes: Cash, 111; Accounts Receivable, 112; Supplies, 131; Equipment, 141; Accounts Payable, 211; A. French, Capital, 311; A. French, Withdrawals, 321; Placement Fees Earned, 411; Wage Expense, 511; Telephone Expense, 521; Advertising Expense, 531.

Your task is to

a. Set up a ledger based on the chart of accounts.

b. Journalize (all p. 1) and post transactions.

c. Prepare a trial balance for June 30, 19XX.

REAL WORLD APPLICATIONS

3R-1.

Paul Regan, bookkeeper of Hampton Co., has been up half the night trying to get his trial balance to balance. Here are his results:

HAMPTON CO. TRIAL BALANCE JUNE 30, 19XX	Dr.	Cr.
Office Sales		5 7 2 0 00
Cash in Bank	3 2 6 0 00	
Accounts Receivable	5 6 6 0 00	
Office Equipment	8 4 0 0 00	
Accounts Payable		4 1 6 0 00
D. Hole, Capital		11 5 6 0 00
D. Hole, Withdrawals		7 0 0 00
Wage Expense	2 6 0 0 00	
Rent Expense	9 4 0 00	
Utilities Expense	2 6 00	
Office Supplies	1 2 0 00	
Prepaid Rent	1 8 0 00	

Ken Small, the accountant, compared Paul's amounts in the trial balance with those in the ledger, recomputed each account balance, and compared postings. Ken found the following errors:

1. A $200 debit to D. Hole, Withdrawals, was posted as a credit.
2. D. Hole, Withdrawals, was listed on the trial balance as a credit.
3. A Note Payable account with a credit balance of $2,400 was not listed on the trial balance.
4. The pencil footings for Accounts Payable were debits of $5,320 and credits of $8,800.
5. A debit of $180 to Prepaid Rent was not posted.
6. Office Supplies bought for $60 was posted as a credit to Supplies.
7. A debit of $120 to Accounts Receivable was not posted.
8. A cash payment of $420 was credited to Cash for $240.
9. The pencil footing of the credits to Cash was overstated by $400.
10. The Utilities Expense of $260 was listed in the trial balance as $26.

Assist Paul Regan by preparing a correct trial balance. What advice could you give Ken about Paul? Can you explain the situation to Paul? Put your answers in writing.

3R-2.

Lauren Oliver, an accountant lab tutor, is having a debate with some of her assistants. They are trying to find out how each of the following five unrelated situations would affect the trial balance:

1. A $5 debit to cash in the ledger was not posted.
2. A $10 debit to Computer Supplies was debited to Computer Equipment.
3. An $8 debit to Wage Expense was debited twice to the account.
4. A $4 debit to Computer Supplies was debited to Computer Sales.
5. A $35 credit to Accounts Payable was posted as a $53 credit.

Could you indicate to Lauren the effect that each situation will have on the trial balance? If a situation will have no effect, indicate that fact. Put in writing how each of these situations could be avoided in the future.

YOU make the call

Critical Thinking/Ethical Case

3R-3.
Jay Simons, the accountant of See Co., would like to buy a new software package for his general ledger. He couldn't do it because all funds were frozen for the rest of the fiscal period. Jay called his friend at Joor Industries and asked whether he could copy their software. Why should or shouldn't Jay have done that?

ACCOUNTING RECALL
A CUMULATIVE APPROACH

THIS EXAM REVIEWS CHAPTERS 1 THROUGH 3

Your *Study Guide and Working Papers* have forms (pages 93 and 105) to complete this exam, as well as worked-out solutions. The page references next to each question identify what page to turn back to if you answer the question incorrectly.

PART 1   Vocabulary Review

Match the terms to the appropriate definition or phrase.
Page Ref.

(40)	1. Chart of Accounts	A.	Process of recording transactions in a journal
(72)	2. Ledger	B.	Rearrangement of digits
(88)	3. Slide	C.	Book of original entry
(71)	4. Calendar year	D.	Running balance
(88)	5. Transposition	E.	Transferring information
(80)	6. Four-column account	F.	January 1 to December 31
(71)	7. Journalizing	G.	Adding or deleting numbers
(74)	8. Compound entry	H.	Numbering system
(80)	9. Posting	I.	More than two accounts
(71)	10. Journal	J.	Book of final entry

PART II   True or False (Accounting Theory)

(72)	11. The ledger is located in same book as a journal.
(81)	12. The PR column of a general journal is completed after the posting to the ledger is complete.
(88)	13. Correcting errors in journalizing can only be done before posting.
(71)	14. A calendar year could be a fiscal year.
(87)	15. A trial balance could balance but be incorrect.

CONTINUING PROBLEM

Tony's computer center is picking up in business, so he has decided to expand his bookkeeping system to a general journal/ledger system. The balances from August have been forwarded to the ledger accounts. The forms are in the *Study Guide and Working Papers,* pages 94–104.

Assignment:

1. Use the chart of accounts provided in Chapter 2 to record the following transactions.

Eldorado Computer Center
385 N. Escondido Blvd.
Escondido CA 92025

8104

September 1, -- 19xx

Pay
To the
Order of— *Capital Management* ------------------------------ $ 1200.00
One thousand and two hundred 00/100

First Union Bank
322 Glen Ave.
Escondido, CA 92025
memo *Prepaid Rent—Aug. Sept. Oct.* -------- *Tony Freedman* --------
0611 062 78 72

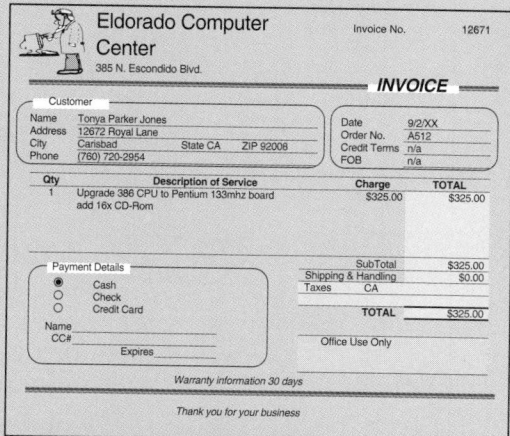

Eldorado Computer Center
385 N. Escondido Blvd.

Invoice No. 12671

INVOICE

Customer		
Name	Tonya Parker Jones	
Address	12672 Royal Lane	
City	Carlsbad State CA ZIP 92008	
Phone	(760) 720-2954	

Date	9/2/XX
Order No.	A512
Credit Terms	n/a
FOB	n/a

Qty	Description of Service	Charge	TOTAL
1	Upgrade 386 CPU to Pentium 133mhz board add 16x CD-Rom	$325.00	$325.00

Payment Details
○ Cash
○ Check
○ Credit Card
Name
CC#
Expires

SubTotal	$325.00
Shipping & Handling	$0.00
Taxes CA	
TOTAL	$325.00

Office Use Only

Warranty information 30 days

Thank you for your business

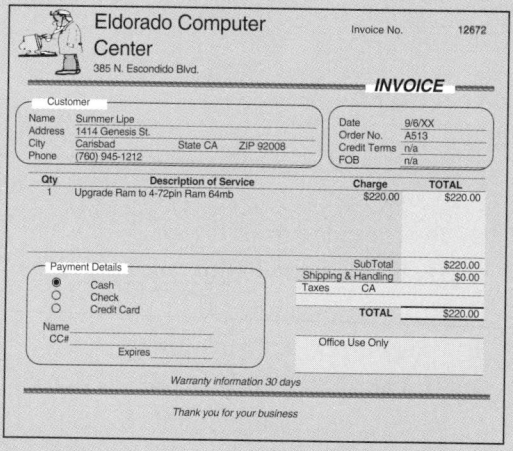

Eldorado Computer Center
385 N. Escondido Blvd.

Invoice No. 12672

INVOICE

Customer		
Name	Summer Lipe	
Address	1414 Genesis St.	
City	Carlsbad State CA ZIP 92008	
Phone	(760) 945-1212	

Date	9/6/XX
Order No.	A513
Credit Terms	n/a
FOB	n/a

Qty	Description of Service	Charge	TOTAL
1	Upgrade Ram to 4-72pin Ram 64mb	$220.00	$220.00

Payment Details
○ Cash
○ Check
○ Credit Card
Name
CC#
Expires

SubTotal	$220.00
Shipping & Handling	$0.00
Taxes CA	
TOTAL	$220.00

Office Use Only

Warranty information 30 days

Thank you for your business

Eldorado Computer Center
385 N. Escondido Blvd.
Escondido CA 92025

8105

September 8, -- 19xx

Pay
To the
Order of— *Pacific Bell* ------------------------------ $ 155.00
One hundred and fifty five 00/100

First Union Bank
322 Glen Ave.
Escondido, CA 92025
memo *August phone bill transaction (k) Chpt. 2* -------- *Tony Freedman* --------
0611 062 78 72

Refer back to Chapter 2 transaction (k).

Jeannine Sparks
1919 Sierra St.
Escondido CA 92025

251

September 12, -- 19xx

Pay
To the
Order of— *Eldorado Computer Center* ------------------------ $ 850.00
Eight Hundred and Fifty dollars 00/100

Bank First
322 Cardiff Ave.
Escondido, CA 92025

memo *Computer Fixed. Transaction (o) Chpt. 2* ------- *Jeannine Sparks* --------
0611 062 78 72

Eldorado Computer Center
385 N. Escondido Blvd.
Escondido CA 92025

8106

September 15, -- 19xx

Pay
To the
Order of— *Computer Connection* ------------------------ $ 200.00
Two hundred dollars and 00/100

First Union Bank
322 Glen Ave.
Escondido, CA 92025
memo *Account due from transaction (s) Chpt. 2* -------- *Tony Freedman* --------
0611 062 78 72

Refer back to Chapter 2 transaction (s).

Purchased computer shop equipment.

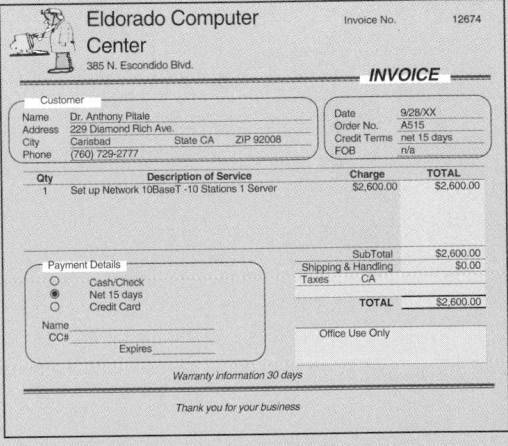

Refer back to Chapter 2 transaction (o).

2. Post all transactions to the general ledger accounts (the Prepaid Rent Account #1025 has been added to the chart of accounts).

3. Prepare a trial balance for Sept. 30, 19XX.

4. Prepare the financial statements for the three months ended September 30, 19XX.

COMPUTERIZED ACCOUNTING APPLICATION FOR CHAPTER 3

Journalizing, Posting, General Ledger, Trial Balance, and Chart of Accounts

Before starting on this assignment, read and complete the tasks discussed in Parts A, B, and F of the Computerized Accounting appendix at the back of this book.

How to Open the Company Data Files

1. Click on the Start button. Point to Programs; point to Simply Accounting; then click on Simply Accounting in the final menu presented.

2. The Simply Accounting copyright screen will appear briefly; then the Simply Accounting Open File dialog box will appear. Insert your Student Data Files disk into disk drive A. Enter the following path into the **File name** text box: A:\student\atlas.asc.

3. Click on the **Open** button. The program will respond with a request for the **Using Date for this Session.** The **Using** date is the date associated with the current work session. Once the **Using** date is advanced, it cannot be turned back to an earlier date.

4. Enter 12/31/97 into the **Using Date for this Session** text box; then click on the **OK** button. Click on the **OK** button in response to the message "The date entered is more than one week past your previous **Using** date of 12/1/97." When you start Simply Accounting, the file name for the company's data files (in this case Atlas) will appear in the title bar at the top of the Company Window. Your screen will look like this:

Note that the icons for Purchases, Payments, Sales, Receipts, Payroll, Transfers, and Adjustments Journals are shown with the no-entry symbol. The General Journal has no symbol. The Atlas Company will only be using the General Journal to record transactions.

How to Add Your Name to the Company Name

5. It is important for you to be able to identify the specific reports that you print for each assignment as your own, particularly if you are using a computer that shares a printer with other computers. Simply Accounting prints the name of the company you are working with at the top of each report. To personalize your reports so that you can identify both the company and your printed reports, the company name needs to be modified to include your name:

a. Click on the **Setup** menu; then click on Company Information. The Company Information dialog box will appear.

b. In the Company Information dialog box use the mouse to position the insertion point immediately before "Your Name" in the **Name** text box; drag through the "Your Name" text to highlight the text; then type your name. Your screen will look similar to the one shown below:

c. Click on the **OK** button to return to the Company Window.

How to Record a General Journal Entry

6. The owner of The Atlas Company has invested $10,000 in the business. Double-click on the General icon to open the General Journal dialog box. Enter the word "Memo" into the **Source** text box; press the TAB key; enter 12/1/97 into the **Date** text box; press the TAB key; enter "Initial investment of cash by owner" into the **Comment** text box; then press the TAB key.

The **Source** text box can be used for any reference number or notation you wish to associate with a general journal entry and the source document that authorizes the entry. The **Date** text box is used to record the date the transaction occurred. The **Comment** text box can be used for comments related to the journal entry in much the same way that an explanation is used when journal entries are recorded in a manual accounting system. Note that a flashing insertion point is positioned in the **Account** text box.

7. With the flashing insertion point positioned in the **Account** text box, press the ENTER key. The Select Account dialog box will appear. Double-click on 1110 Cash. The program will enter the account number and name into the **Account** text box, and the flashing insertion point will move to the **Debits** text box.

8. Enter 10000 into the **Debits** text box; then press the TAB key. Dollar amounts can be entered in several ways. For example, to enter $50.00, type 50, 50., or 50.00. To enter an amount containing a decimal point, type the decimal point as part of the amount. For example, enter five dollars and twenty-five cents as 5.25. Do not enter commas. The flashing insertion point will move to **Account** text box ready for the selection of the account to be credited for this entry.

9. With the flashing insertion point positioned in the **Account** text box, press the ENTER key to bring up the Select Account dialog box. Click on the down arrow button on the scroll bar to the right of the **Select account** listing to advance the display until 3110 Owner's, Capital appears. Double-click on 3110 Owner's, Capital. The program will offer the same amount as the **Debits** portion of the entry as a default amount in the **Credits** text box. The **Credits** amount remains highlighted.

10. Press the TAB key to accept the default **Credits** amount. This completes the data you need to enter into the General Journal dialog box to record the journal entry for the initial investment of cash by the owner. Your screen should look like this:

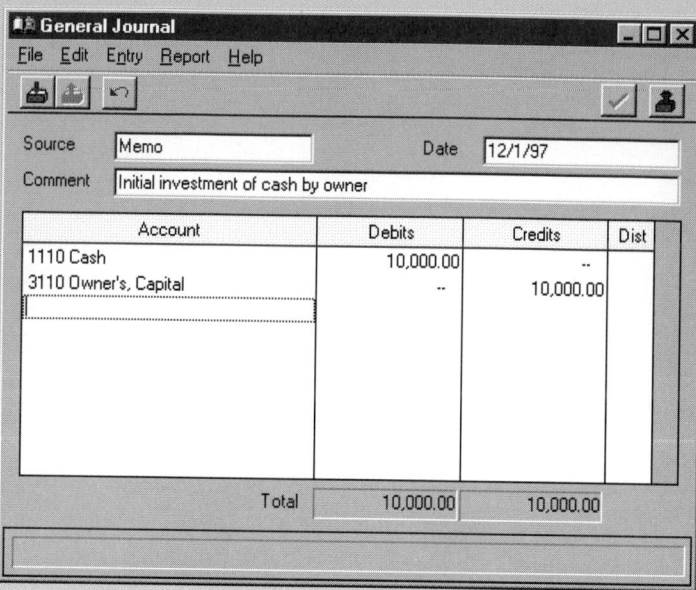

How to Review a Journal Entry

11. Before posting this transaction, you need to verify that the transaction data are correct by reviewing the journal entry. To review the entry, click on the General Journal Report menu; then click on Display General Journal Entry. The journal entry representing the data you have recorded in the General Journal dialog box is displayed. Review the journal entry for accuracy, noting any errors.

How to Edit an Entry Prior to Posting

12. Close the General Journal Entry window by clicking on the close button. If you have made an error, use the following editing techniques to correct the error.

Editing a General Journal Entry

◆ Move to the text box that contains the error by either pressing the TAB key to move forward through each text box or the SHIFT and TAB keys together to move to a previous text box. This will highlight the selected text box information so that you can change it. Alternatively, you can use the mouse to point to a text box and drag through the incorrect information to highlight it.

◆ Type the correct information; then press the TAB key to enter it.

◆ Note that when editing a dollar amount entered into the **Debits** or **Credits** text box, the program does not automatically change the corresponding **Debits** or **Credits** amount to agree with the new amount you have entered.

◆ If you have associated a transaction with an incorrect account, double-click on the incorrect account; then select the correct account from the Select Account dialog box. This will replace the incorrect account with the correct account.

◆ Note that the **Post** icon will be dimmed (unavailable) until the journal entry is in balance.

◆ To discard an entry and start over, click on the close button. Click on the **Yes** button in response to the question "Are you sure you want to discard this journal entry?"

◆ Review the journal entry for accuracy after any editing corrections.

◆ **It is IMPORTANT TO NOTE that the only way to edit a journal entry after it is posted is to reverse the entry and enter the correct journal entry.** To correct journal entries posted in error, see "Reversing an Entry Made in the General Journal Dialog Box" in Part C of the Computerized Accounting appendix.

How to Post an Entry

13. After verifying that the journal entry is correct, click on the **Post** icon to post this transaction. A blank General Journal dialog box is displayed, ready for additional General Journal transactions to be recorded.

Record Additional Transactions

14. Record the following additional journal entries (enter "Memo" into the **Source** text box for each transaction, then enter the **Date** listed for each transaction):

```
1997
Dec.    1  Paid rent for two months in advance, $400.
        3  Purchased office supplies on account, $100.
        9  Billed a customer for fees earned, $1,500.
       13  Paid telephone bill, $180.
       20  Owner withdrew $500 from the business.
       27  Received $450 for fees earned.
       31  Paid salaries expense, $700.
```

15. After you have posted the additional journal entries, click on the close button to close the General Journal dialog box. This will restore the Company Window screen, and the General Journal icon will remain highlighted.

How to Display and Print a General Journal

16. In the Company Window with the General Journal icon highlighted, click on the Reports menu; then click on Display General Journal. The General Journal Options dialog box will appear asking you to define the information you want displayed. Leave the **Current Year** and **By Posting Date** options buttons selected; leave the **All Ledger Entries** check box checked; enter 12/1/97 into the **Start** text box; leave the **Finish** text box date set at 12/31/97; then click on the **OK** button. The following General Journal Display will appear on your screen:

```
┌─────────────────────────────────────────────────────────────────────┐
│ ▣  General Journal Display                               _ □ ×       │
│ File  Help                                                           │
│ 12/1/97 to 12/31/97                                  Debits   Credits│
│ 12/1/97   J1   Memo, Initial investment of cash by owner          ▲  │
│                1110  Cash                        10,000.00    ·       │
│                3110    Owner's, Capital               ·    10,000.00  │
│                                                                      │
│ 12/1/97   J2   Memo, Rent paid in advance (2 months)                 │
│                1140  Prepaid Rent                   400.00    ·       │
│                1110    Cash                           ·       400.00  │
│                                                                      │
│ 12/3/97   J3   Memo, Purchased office supplies on account            │
│                1150  Office Supplies               100.00    ·       │
│                2110    Accounts Payable               ·       100.00  │
│                                                                      │
│ 12/9/97   J4   Memo, Billed customer for fees earned                 │
│                1120  Accounts Receivable         1,500.00    ·       │
│                4110    Fees Earned                    ·     1,500.00  │
│                                                                      │
│ 12/13/97  J5   Memo, Paid telephone bill                             │
│                5150  Telephone Expense             180.00    ·       │
│                1110    Cash                           ·       180.00  │
│                                                                      │
│ 12/20/97  J6   Memo, Personal withdrawal of cash                     │
│                3120  Owner's, Withdrawals          500.00    ·    ▼  │
│                1110    Cash                           ·       500.00  │
│ ◄                                                              ►      │
└─────────────────────────────────────────────────────────────────────┘
```

17. The scroll bars can be used to advance the display to view other portions of the report. Note: You may display the entire General Journal Display window by clicking the maximize icon.

18. Click on the General Journal Display File menu; then click on Print to print the General Journal. If you experience any difficulties with your printer (for example, the type size is too small), refer to Part F of the Computerized Accounting appendix for information on how to adjust the print and display settings.

What to Do if You Posted an Incorrect Entry

19. Review your printed General Journal. If you have made an error in a posted journal entry, see "Reversing an Entry Made in the General Journal Dialog Box" in Part C of the Computerized Accounting appendix at the back of this book for information on how to correct the error.

How to Display and Print a General Ledger Report

20. Click on the close button to close the General Journal Display window; click on the Company Window Reports menu; point to Financials; then click on General Ledger. The General Ledger Report Options dialog box will appear. Leave the Current Year option button selected. Enter 12/1/97 into the **Start** text box; leave the **Finish** text box date set at 12/31/97; click on the **Select All** button, then click on the **OK** button. Your screen will look like this:

General Ledger Report

File   Help

12/1/97 to 12/31/97

				Debits	Credits	E
1110 Cash						
12/1/97	Initial investment of cash by o...	Memo	J1	10,000.00	-	10
12/1/97	Rent paid in advance (2 months)	Memo	J2	-	400.00	9
12/13/97	Paid telephone bill	Memo	J5	-	180.00	9
12/20/97	Personal withdrawal of cash	Memo	J6	-	500.00	8
12/27/97	Cash received for fees earned	Memo	J7	450.00	-	9
12/31/97	Payment of salaries	Memo	J8	-	700.00	8
				10,450.00	1,780.00	
1120 Accounts Receivable						
12/9/97	Billed customer for fees earned	Memo	J4	1,500.00	-	1
				1,500.00	0.00	

21. The scroll bars can be used to advance the display to view other portions of the report.

22. In the General Ledger Report click on the File menu; then click on Print to print the General Ledger report.

How to Display and Print a Trial Balance

23. Click on the close button to close the General Ledger Report window; click on the Company Window Reports menu; point to Financials; then click on Trial Balance. The Trial Balance Options dialog box will appear. Leave the Select a Report text box set at Current Year. Leave the **As at** date set at 12/31/97; then click on the **OK** button. Your screen will look like this:

Trial Balance

File   Help

As At 12/31/97

		Debits	Credits
1110	Cash	8,670.00	-
1120	Accounts Receivable	1,500.00	-
1140	Prepaid Rent	400.00	-
1150	Office Supplies	100.00	-
1210	Office Equipment	0.00	-
1221	Accum. Dep.-Office Equipment	0.00	-
1230	Automobile	0.00	-
1241	Accum. Dep.-Automobile	0.00	-
1250	Store Equipment	0.00	-
1261	Accum. Dep.-Store Equipment	0.00	-
2110	Accounts Payable	-	100.00
3110	Owner's, Capital	-	10,000.00
3120	Owner's, Withdrawals	500.00	-
4110	Fees Earned	-	1,950.00
5110	Rent Expense	0.00	-

Double-click to display General Ledger Report for current account.

24. The scroll bar can be used to advance the display to view other portions of the report.

25. Click on the Trial Balance File menu; then click on Print to print the Trial Balance.

How to Display and Print a Chart of Accounts

26. Click on the close button to close the Trial Balance window; click on the Accounts icon under the General module column in the Company Window; click on the Company Window Reports menu; then click on Display Chart of Accounts. The Chart of Accounts window will appear. Move the mouse pointer opposite the Cash account. The mouse pointer will appear as a magnifying glass and the **Status Bar** will indicate that you can "Double-click to display General Ledger Report for current account." Your screen will look like this:

Chart of Accounts

File   Help

12/31/97

ASSETS

1000	**ASSETS**	H
1110	Cash	R
1120	Accounts Receivable	R
1140	Prepaid Rent	R
1150	Office Supplies	R
1210	Office Equipment	L
1221	Accum. Dep.-Office Equipment	L
1222	Net: Office Equipment	S
1230	Automobile	L
1241	Accum. Dep.-Automobile	L
1242	Net: Automobile	S
1250	Store Equipment	L
1261	Accum. Dep.-Store Equipment	L
1262	Net: Store Equipment	S

Double-click to display General Ledger Report for current account.

27. Double-click with your mouse. Your screen will look like this:

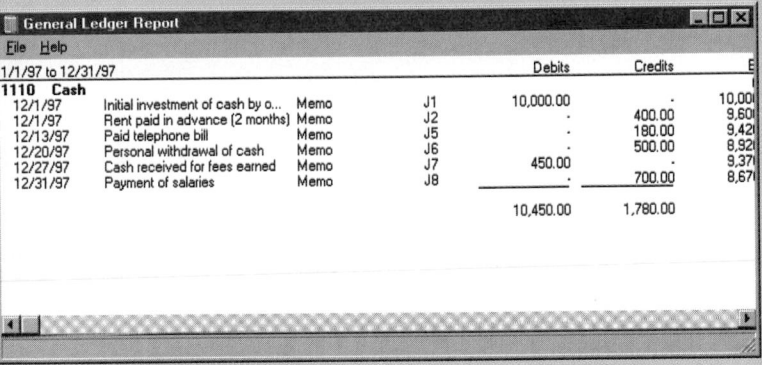

Simply Accounting's Drill-down Feature

28. Going deeper into the detail that supports a report in this manner is called "drill-down." You can drill-down to detailed supporting information on any Simply Accounting report where the mouse pointer changes to a magnifying glass. The **Status Bar** will tell you what information will appear when you double-click on an item in a report.

29. Click on the close button to close the General Ledger Report window: click on the Chart of Accounts File menu; then click on Print to print the Chart of Accounts.

30. Click on the close button to close the Chart of Accounts window and return to the Company Window.

How to Exit from the Program

31. Click on the Company Window File menu; then click on Exit to end the current work session and return to your Windows desktop. Your work will automatically be saved to your Student Data Files disk.

32. You can exit from Simply Accounting at any time during a current work session. Click on the Company Window File menu; then click on Exit. To resume working on an assignment, open the company data files; then leave the **Using Date for this Session** set at the default date offered.

How to Save your Work During a Current Work Session

33. To save your work during a lengthy current work session, click on the Company Window File menu. Click on Save; then continue with your current work session. It is a good practice to save your work about every 10 minutes when you are involved in a lengthy work session.

34. A Quick Reference Guide is in the Computerized Accounting appendix at the back of this textbook. You will find this guide useful for locating the page number on which frequently used Simply Accounting procedures are explained in detail.

Complete the Report Transmittal

35. Complete The Atlas Company Report Transmittal located in Appendix A in your *Study Guide and Working Papers.*

4

THE ACCOUNTING CYCLE CONTINUED

Preparing Worksheets and Financial Reports

THE BIG PICTURE

Revenue is increasing at Eldorado Computer Center. Tony Freedman can see the receipts from day to day. He has increased store hours, and now he's busier than ever making sure his customers are satisfied — so busy, in fact, that he was surprised when the fiscal year ended. "How well is the business doing?" Freedman wondered.

To answer that question he will have to prepare financial reports. But to prepare those reports he'll first have to gather information from his records and then make adjustments to be sure that he follows *GAAP*, "generally accepted accounting practices." Using the accrual method of accounting, GAAP's "revenue recognition principle" requires that revenue be recorded in the period in which it is earned. The GAAP "matching principle" requires that expenses be matched against the revenue generated. For instance, rental and utility expenses are recorded as they are used, not necessarily when they are paid.

Following these principles sometimes requires *adjustments,* actions that bring accounts up to date. They are internal transactions that do not involve an outside party. Adjusting entries usually are made at the end of the accounting period, but some businesses make them more frequently. Accounts commonly adjusted include: prepaid accounts, supplies, and long-term assets (which depreciate, or lose value, over time), interest, salaries, and taxes.

In this chapter you will learn to use a 10-column worksheet to help organize and check data in a trial balance. You'll make adjustments, adjust the trial balance, and complete the income-statement section and balance-sheet section of the worksheet. Using your worksheet, you will then prepare financial statements. These financial reports give a better picture of "how well the business is doing" than day-to-day receipts.

<table>
<tr><td rowspan="2">**Learning Objectives**</td><td>◆ **Adjustments: prepaid rent, office supplies, depreciation on equipment, and accrued salaries. (p. 117)**
◆ **Preparation of adjusted trial balance on the worksheet. (p. 126)**
◆ **The income statement and balance sheet sections of the worksheet. (pp. 127–129)**
◆ **Preparing financial reports from the worksheet. (p. 132)**</td></tr>
</table>

In the accompanying diagram, steps 1–4 show the parts of the manual accounting cycle that were completed for Clarke's Word Processing Services in the last chapter. This chapter continues the cycle with steps 5–6: the preparation of a worksheet and the three financial reports.

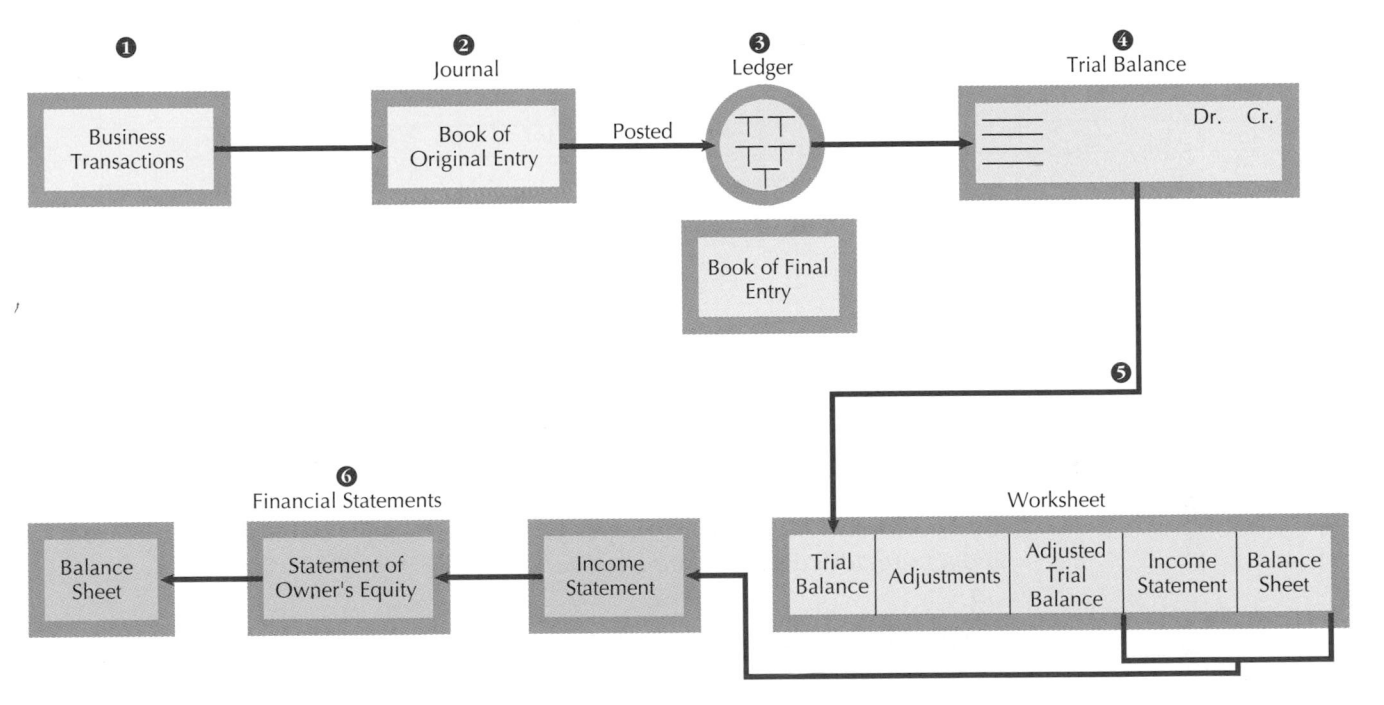

LEARNING UNIT 4-1
Step 5 of the Accounting Cycle: Preparing a Worksheet

The worksheet is not a formal report, so no dollar signs appear on it. Because it is a form, there are no commas, either.

As is true for all accounting reports, the heading includes the name of the company, the name of the report, the date, and the length of the accounting period.

An accountant uses a **worksheet** to organize and check data before preparing financial reports necessary to complete the accounting cycle. The most important function of the worksheet is to allow the accountant to find and correct errors before financial statements are prepared. In a way, a worksheet acts as the accountant's scratch pad. No one sees the worksheet once the formal reports are prepared. A sample worksheet is shown in Figure 4-1 on page 118.

The accounts listed on the far left of the worksheet are taken from the ledger. The rest of the worksheet has five sections: the trial balance, adjustments, adjusted trial balance, income statement, and balance sheet. Each of these sections is divided into debit and credit columns.

CLARK'S WORD PROCESSING SERVICES
WORKSHEET
FOR MONTH ENDING MAY 31, 19XX

Account Titles	Trial Balance Dr.	Trial Balance Cr.	Adjustments Dr.	Adjustments Cr.	Adjusted Trial Balance Dr.	Adjusted Trial Balance Cr.	Income Statement Dr.	Income Statement Cr.
Cash	6 1 5 5 00							
Accounts Receivable	5 0 0 0 00							
Office Supplies	6 0 0 00							
Prepaid Rent	1 2 0 0 00							
Word Processing Equipment	6 0 0 0 00							
Accounts Payable		3 3 5 0 00						
Brenda Clark, Capital		10 0 0 0 00						
Brenda Clark, Withdrawals	6 2 5 00							
Word Processing Fees		8 0 0 0 00						
Office Salaries Expense	1 3 0 0 00							
Advertising Expense	2 5 0 00							
Telephone Expense	2 2 0 00							
	21 3 5 0 00	21 3 5 0 00						

FIGURE 4-1 Sample Worksheet

THE TRIAL BALANCE SECTION

We discussed how to prepare a trial balance in Chapter 2. Some companies prepare a separate trial balance; others, such as Clark's Word Processing Services, prepare the trial balance directly on the worksheet. A trial balance is taken on every account listed in the ledger that has a balance. Additional titles from the ledger are added as they are needed. (We will show this later.)

THE ADJUSTMENTS SECTION

Chapters 1–3 discussed transactions that occurred with outside suppliers and companies. In a real business, though, inside transactions also occur during the accounting cycle. These transactions must be recorded, too. At the end of the worksheet process, the accountant will have all of the business's accounts up-to-date and ready to be used to prepare the formal financial reports. By analyzing each of Clark's accounts on the worksheet, the accountant will be able to identify specific accounts that must be **adjusted,** to bring them up to date. The accountant for Clark's Word Processing Services needs to adjust the following accounts:

Adjusting is like fine-tuning your TV set.

◆ Office Supplies
◆ Prepaid Rent
◆ Word Processing Equipment
◆ Office Salaries Expense

Let's look at how to analyze and adjust each of these accounts.

Adjusting the Office Supplies Account

On May 31, the accountant found out that the company had only $100 worth of office supplies on hand. When the company had originally purchased the

$600 of office supplies, they were considered an asset. But as the supplies were used up, they became an expense.

◆ Office supplies available, $600.
◆ Office supplies left or on hand as of May 31, $100.
◆ Office supplies used up in the operation of the business for the month of May, $500.

As a result, the asset Office Supplies is too high on the trial balance (it should be $100, not $600). At the same time, if we don't show the additional expense of supplies used, the company's *net income* will be too high.

If Clark's accountant does not adjust the trial balance to reflect the change, the company's net income would be too high on the income statement and both sides (assets and owner's equity) of the balance sheet would be too high.

Now let's look at the adjustment for office supplies in terms of the transaction analysis chart.

Will go on income statement

Accounts Affected	Category	↓ ↑	Rules
Office Supplies Expense	Expense	↑	Dr.
Office Supplies	Asset	↓	Cr.

Will go on balance sheet

The office supplies expense account comes from the Chart of Accounts on page 73. Since it is not listed in the account titles, it must be listed below the trial balance. Let's see how we enter this adjustment on the worksheet:

The adjustment for supplies deals with the amount of supplies *used up.*

Adjustments affect both the income statement and balance sheet.

Office Supplies Exp. 514

| 500 | |

This is supplies used up.

Office Supplies 114

| 600 | 500 |
| 100 | |

This is supplies on hand.

For our discussion, the letter "A" is used to code the Office Supplies Expense because it is the first account to be adjusted.

Note: All accounts listed *below* the trial balance will be *increasing.*

CLARK'S WORD PROCESSING SERVICES
WORKSHEET
FOR MONTH ENDED MAY 31, 19XX

Account Titles	Trial Balance Dr.	Trial Balance Cr.	Adjustments Dr.	Adjustments Cr.
Cash	6 1 5 5 00			
Accounts Receivable	5 0 0 0 00			
Office Supplies	6 0 0 00			(A) 5 0 0 00
Prepaid Rent	1 2 0 0 00			
Word Processing Equipment	6 0 0 0 00			
Accounts Payable		3 3 5 0 00		
Brenda Clark, Capital		10 0 0 0 00		
Brenda Clark, Withdrawals	6 2 5 00			
Word Processing Fees		8 0 0 0 00		
Office Salaries Expense	1 3 0 0 00			
Advertising Expense	2 5 0 00			
Telephone Expense	2 2 0 00			
	21 3 5 0 00	21 3 5 0 00		
Office Supplies Expense			(A) 5 0 0 00	

A decrease in Office Supplies, $500.

An increase in Office Supplies Expense, $500.

The Office Supplies Expense account indicates the amount of supplies used up. It is listed below other trial balance accounts, since it was not on the original trial balance.

A debit will increase the account Office Supplies Expense; a credit will reduce the account Office Supplies.

Adjusting Prepaid Rent: On p. 119 the trial balance showed a figure for Prepaid Rent of $1,200. The amount of rent *expired* is the adjustment figure used to update Prepaid Rent and Rent Expense.

Rent Expense 515

| 400 | |

Prepaid Rent 115

| 1,200 | 400 Adj. |
| 800 | |

Take this one slowly.

Original cost of $6,000 for word processing equipment remains *unchanged* after adjustments.

Place $500 in the debit column of the adjustments section on the same line as Office Supplies Expense. Place $500 in the credit column of the adjustments section on the same line as Office Supplies. The numbers in the adjustment column show what is used, *not* what is on hand.

Adjusting the Prepaid Rent Account

Back on May 1, Clark's Word Processing Services paid three months' rent in advance. The accountant realized that the rent expense would be $400 per month ($1,200 ÷ 3 months = $400).

Remember, when rent is paid in advance, it is considered an asset called *prepaid rent.* When the asset, prepaid rent, begins to expire or be used up it becomes an expense. Now it is May 31, and one month's prepaid rent has become an expense.

How is this handled? Should the account be $1,200, or is there really only $800 of prepaid rent left as of May 31? What do we need to do to bring prepaid rent to the "true" balance? The answer is that we must increase Rent Expense by $400 and decrease Prepaid Rent by $400.

Without this adjustment, the expenses for Clark's Word Processing Services for May will be too low, and the asset Prepaid Rent will be too high. If unadjusted amounts were used in the formal reports, the net income shown on the income statement would be too high, and both sides (assets and owner's equity) would be too high on the balance sheet. In terms of our transaction analysis chart, the adjustment would look like this:

Will go on income statement

Accounts Affected	Category	↓ ↑	Rules
Rent Expense	Expense	↑	Dr.
Prepaid Rent	Asset	↓	Cr.

Will go on balance sheet

Like the Office Supplies Expense account, the Rent Expense account comes from the chart of accounts on p. 73.

The worksheet on page 121 shows how to enter an adjustment to Prepaid Rent.

Adjusting the Word Processing Equipment Account for Depreciation

The life of the asset affects how it is adjusted. The two accounts we discussed above, Office Supplies and Prepaid Rent, involved things that are used up relatively quickly. Equipment—like word processing equipment—is expected to last much longer. Also, it is expected to help produce revenue over a longer period. That is why accountants treat it differently. The balance sheet reports the **historical cost,** or original cost, of the equipment. The original cost also is reflected in the ledger. The adjustment shows how the cost of the equipment is allocated (spread) over its expected useful life. This spreading is called **depreciation.** To depreciate the equipment, we have to figure out how much its cost goes down each month. Then we have to keep a running total of how that depreciation mounts up over time. The Internal Revenue Service (IRS) issues guidelines, tables, and formulas that must be used to estimate the amount of depreciation. Different methods can be used to calculate depreciation (see the Appendix at the end of the text). We will use the simplest method—straight-line depreciation—to calculate the depreciation of Clark Word Processing Services'

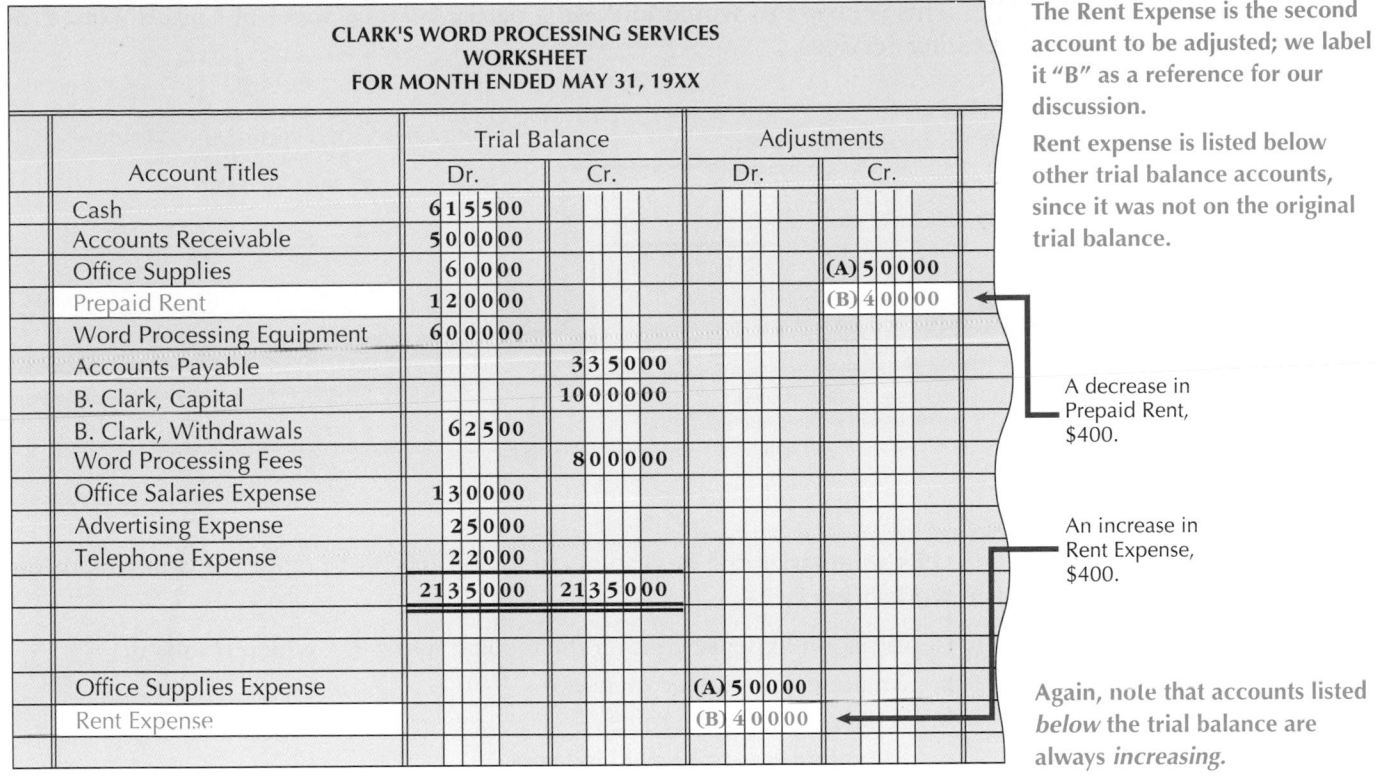

The Rent Expense is the second account to be adjusted; we label it "B" as a reference for our discussion.

Rent expense is listed below other trial balance accounts, since it was not on the original trial balance.

A decrease in Prepaid Rent, $400.

An increase in Rent Expense, $400.

Again, note that accounts listed *below* the trial balance are always *increasing*.

CLARK'S WORD PROCESSING SERVICES
WORKSHEET
FOR MONTH ENDED MAY 31, 19XX

Account Titles	Trial Balance Dr.	Trial Balance Cr.	Adjustments Dr.	Adjustments Cr.
Cash	6 1 5 5 00			
Accounts Receivable	5 0 0 0 00			
Office Supplies	6 0 0 00			(A) 5 0 0 00
Prepaid Rent	1 2 0 0 00			(B) 4 0 0 00
Word Processing Equipment	6 0 0 0 00			
Accounts Payable		3 3 5 0 00		
B. Clark, Capital		10 0 0 0 00		
B. Clark, Withdrawals	6 2 5 00			
Word Processing Fees		8 0 0 0 00		
Office Salaries Expense	1 3 0 0 00			
Advertising Expense	2 5 0 00			
Telephone Expense	2 2 0 00			
	21 3 5 0 00	21 3 5 0 00		
Office Supplies Expense			(A) 5 0 0 00	
Rent Expense			(B) 4 0 0 00	

equipment. Under the straight-line method, equal amounts are taken over successive periods of time.

The calculation of depreciation for the year for Clark's Word Processing Services is as follows:

$$\frac{\text{cost of equipment} - \text{residual value}}{\text{estimated years of usefulness}}$$

According to the IRS, word processing equipment has an expected life of five years. At the end of that time, the property's value is called its "residual value." Think of **residual value** as the estimated value of the equipment at end of the fifth year. For Clark, the equipment has an estimated residual value of $1,200.

Assume equipment has a 5-year life.

Clark will record $960 of depreciation each year.

Depreciation is an expense reported on the income statement.

$$\frac{\$6,000 - \$1,200}{5 \text{ years}} = \frac{\$4,800}{5} = \$960 \text{ depreciation per year}$$

Our trial balance is for one month, so we must determine the adjustment for that month:

$$\frac{\$960}{12 \text{ months}} = \$80 \text{ depreciation per month}$$

This $80 is known as *Depreciation Expense* and will be shown on the income statement.

Next, we have to create a new account that can keep a running total of the depreciation amount apart from the original cost of the equipment. That account is called **Accumulated Depreciation.**

The Accumulated Depreciation account shows the relationship between the original cost of the equipment and the amount of depreciation that has been taken or accumulated over a period of time. This is a *contra-asset* account; it has the opposite balance of an asset such as equipment. Accumulated Depreciation will summarize, accumulate, or build up the amount of depreciation that is taken on the word processing equipment over its estimated useful life.

Accumulated Depreciation

Dr.	Cr.

is a contra asset account found on the balance sheet.

This is how this would look on a partial balance sheet of Clark's Word Processing Services.

❶ Historical cost of $6,000 of equipment is not changed.

❷ Amount of accumulated depreciation is $80.

❸ This shows the unused amount of the equipment that may be depreciated in future periods of time. This figure, the cost of the asset less its accumulated depreciation, is often termed *book value* or carrying value.

CLARK'S WORD PROCESSING SERVICES
BALANCE SHEET
MAY 31, 19XX

Assets

- - - - - - -		XXXX
Word Processing Equip.	$6,000	
Less accumulated depreciation	80	5,920

Let's summarize the key points before going on to mark the adjustment on the worksheet:

1. Depreciation Expense goes on the income statement, which results in
   a. An increase in total expenses.
   b. A decrease in net income.
   c. Therefore, less to be paid in taxes.
2. Accumulated depreciation is a contra-asset account found on the balance sheet next to its related equipment account.
3. The original cost of equipment is not reduced; it stays the same until the equipment is sold or removed.
4. Each month the amount in the Accumulated Depreciation account grows larger, while the cost of the equipment remains the same.

Now, let's analyze the adjustment on the transaction analysis chart:

Will go on income statement

Accounts Affected	Category	↓ ↑	Rules
Depreciation Expense, Word Processing Equipment	**Expense**	↑	**Dr.**
Accumulated Depreciation, Word Processing Equipment	**Contra Asset**	↑	**Cr.**

Will go on balance sheet

Remember, the original cost of the equipment never changes: (1) the equipment account is not included among the affected accounts because the original cost of equipment remains the same; and (2) the original cost does not change. Even though the Accumulated Depreciation increases (as a credit), the equipment's book value decreases.

The worksheet on page 123 shows how we enter the adjustment for depreciation of word processing equipment.

Because this is a new business, neither account had a previous balance. Therefore, neither is listed in the account titles of the trial balance. We need to list both accounts below Rent Expense in the account titles section. On the worksheet, put $80 in the debit column of the adjustments section on the same line as Depreciation Expense, W. P. Equipment, and put $80 in the credit column

CLARK'S WORD PROCESSING SERVICES
WORKSHEET
FOR MONTH ENDED MAY 31, 19XX

Account Titles	Trial Balance Dr.	Trial Balance Cr.	Adjustments Dr.	Adjustments Cr.
Cash	6155 00			
Accounts Receivable	5000 00			
Office Supplies	600 00			(A) 500 00
Prepaid Rent	1200 00			(B) 400 00
Word Processing Equipment	6000 00			
Accounts Payable		3350 00		
B. Clark, Capital		10000 00		
B. Clark, Withdrawals	625 00			
Word Processing Fees		8000 00		
Office Salaries Expense	1300 00			
Advertising Expense	250 00			
Telephone Expense	220 00			
	21350 00	21350 00		
Office Supplies Expense			(A) 500 00	
Rent Expense			(B) 400 00	
Depreciation Exp., W.P. Equip.			(C) 80 00	
Accum. Deprec., W.P. Equip.				(C) 80 00

An increase in Depreciation Expense, W.P. Equipment.

An increase in Accumulated Depreciation, W.P. Equipment.

The third account to be adjusted is assigned the letter "C."

Accumulated Depreciation	
Dr.	Cr.
	History of amount of depreciation taken to date

Adjusting Salaries

of the adjustments section on the same line as Accumulated Depreciation, W. P. Equipment.

Next month, on June 30, $80 would be entered under Depreciation Expense, and Accumulated Depreciation would show a balance of $160. Remember, in May, Clark's was a new company, so no previous depreciation was taken.

Now let's look at the last adjustment for Clark's Word Processing Services.

Adjusting the Salaries Accrued Account

Clark's Word Processing Services paid $1,300 in Office Salaries Expense (see the trial balance of any previous worksheet in this chapter). The last salary checks for the month were paid on May 27. How can we update this account to show the salary expense as of May 31?

John Murray worked for Clark on May 28, 29, 30, and 31, but his next paycheck is not due until June 3. John earned $350 for these four days. Is the $350 an expense to Clark in May, when it was earned, or in June when it is due and is paid?

May						
S	M	T	W	T	F	S
						1
2	3	4	5	6	7	8
9	10	11	12	13	14	15
16	17	18	19	20	21	22
23	24	25	26	27	28	29
30	31					

Think back to Chapter 1, when we first discussed revenue and expenses. We noted then that revenue is recorded when it is earned, and expenses are recorded when they are incurred, not when they are actually paid off. This principle will be discussed further in a later chapter; for now it is enough to remember that we record revenue and expenses when they occur, because we want to match earned revenue with the expenses that resulted in earning those revenues. In this case, by working those four days, John Murray created some revenue for Clark in May. Therefore, the office salaries expense must be shown in May — the month the revenue was earned.

The results are:

Office Salaries Expense is increased by $350. This unpaid and unrecorded expense for salaries for which payment is not yet due is called **accrued salaries.** In effect, we now show the true expense for salaries ($1,650 instead of $1,300):

Office Salaries Expense	
1,300	
350	

The second result is that salaries payable is increased by $350. Clark's has created a liability called Salaries Payable, meaning that the firm owes money for salaries. When the firm pays John Murray, it will reduce its liability, Salaries Payable, as well as decrease its cash.

In terms of the transaction analysis chart, the following would be done:

Office Salaries Exp. 511	
1,300	
350	

Salaries Payable 212	
	350

Accounts Affected	Category	↓ ↑	Rules
Office Salaries Expense,	Expense	↑	Dr.
Salaries Payable	Liability	↑	Cr.

How the adjustment for accrued salaries is entered is shown at the top of page 125.

The account Office Salaries Expense is already listed in the account titles, so $350 is placed in the debit column of the adjustments section on the same line as Office Salaries Expense. However, because the Salaries Payable is not listed in the account titles, it is added below the trial balance under Accumulated Depreciation, W. P. Equipment. Also, $350 is placed in the credit column of the adjustments section on the same line as Salaries Payable.

Now that we have finished all the adjustments that we intended to make, we total the adjustments section, as shown in Figure 4-2.

THE ADJUSTED TRIAL BALANCE SECTION

The adjusted trial balance is the next section on the worksheet. To fill it out, we must summarize the information in the trial balance and adjustments sections, as shown in Figure 4-3 on page 126.

Note that when the numbers are brought across from the trial balance to the adjusted trial balance, two debits will be added together and two credits will be added together. If the numbers include a debit and a credit, take the difference between the two and place it on the side that is larger.

Now that we have completed the adjustments and adjusted trial balance sections of the worksheet, it is time to move on to the income statement and the balance sheet sections. Before we do that though, look at the chart shown

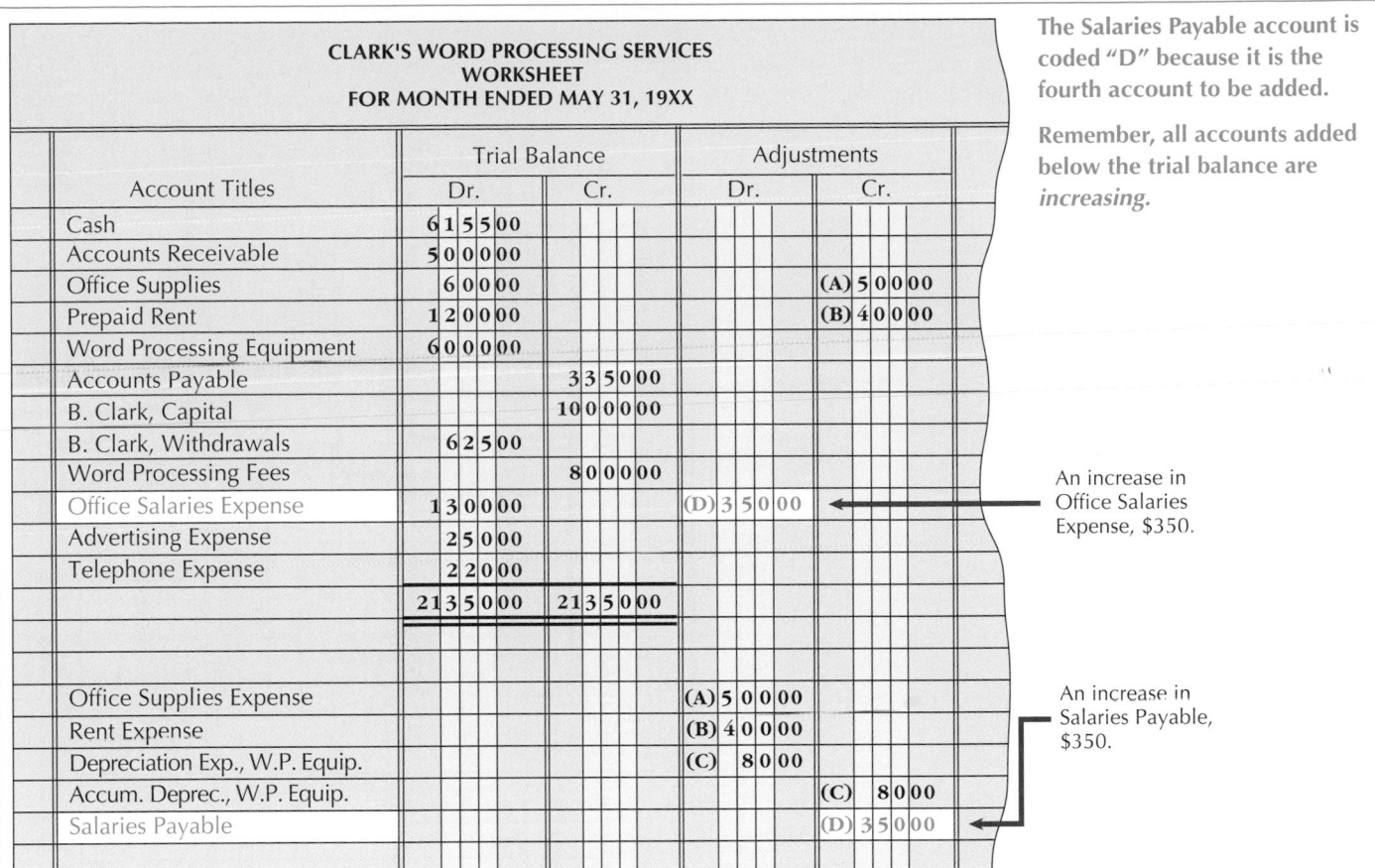

CLARK'S WORD PROCESSING SERVICES
WORKSHEET
FOR MONTH ENDED MAY 31, 19XX

Account Titles	Trial Balance Dr.	Cr.	Adjustments Dr.	Cr.
Cash	6155 00			
Accounts Receivable	5000 00			
Office Supplies	600 00			(A) 500 00
Prepaid Rent	1200 00			(B) 400 00
Word Processing Equipment	6000 00			
Accounts Payable		3350 00		
B. Clark, Capital		10000 00		
B. Clark, Withdrawals	625 00			
Word Processing Fees		8000 00		
Office Salaries Expense	1300 00		(D) 350 00	
Advertising Expense	250 00			
Telephone Expense	220 00			
	21350 00	21350 00		
Office Supplies Expense			(A) 500 00	
Rent Expense			(B) 400 00	
Depreciation Exp., W.P. Equip.			(C) 80 00	
Accum. Deprec., W.P. Equip.				(C) 80 00
Salaries Payable				(D) 350 00

The Salaries Payable account is coded "D" because it is the fourth account to be added.

Remember, all accounts added below the trial balance are *increasing.*

An increase in Office Salaries Expense, $350.

An increase in Salaries Payable, $350.

FIGURE 4-2
The Adjustments Section of
the Worksheet

CLARK'S WORD PROCESSING SERVICES
WORKSHEET
FOR MONTH ENDED MAY 31, 19XX

Account Titles	Trial Balance Dr.	Cr.	Adjustments Dr.	Cr.
Cash	6155 00			
Accounts Receivable	5000 00			
Office Supplies	600 00			(A) 500 00
Prepaid Rent	1200 00			(B) 400 00
Word Processing Equipment	6000 00			
Accounts Payable		3350 00		
B. Clark, Capital		10000 00		
B. Clark, Withdrawals	625 00			
Word Processing Fees		8000 00		
Office Salaries Expense	1300 00		(D) 350 00	
Advertising Expense	250 00			
Telephone Expense	220 00			
	21350 00	21350 00		
Office Supplies Expense			(A) 500 00	
Rent Expense			(B) 400 00	
Depreciation Exp., W.P. Equip.			(C) 80 00	
Accum. Deprec., W.P. Equip.				(C) 80 00
Salaries Payable				(D) 350 00
			1330 00	1330 00

FIGURE 4-3 The Adjusted Trial Balance Section of the Worksheet

CLARK'S WORD PROCESSING SERVICES
WORKSHEET
FOR MONTH ENDED MAY 31, 19XX

Account Titles	Trial Balance Dr.	Trial Balance Cr.	Adjustments Dr.	Adjustments Cr.	Adjusted Trial Balance Dr.	Adjusted Trial Balance Cr.
Cash	615500				615500	
Accounts Receivable	500000				500000	
Office Supplies	60000			(A) 50000	10000	
Prepaid Rent	120000			(B) 40000	80000	
Word Processing Equipment	600000				600000	
Accounts Payable		335000				335000
Brenda Clark, Capital		1000000				1000000
Brenda Clark, Withdrawals	62500				62500	
Word Processing Fees		800000				800000
Office Salaries Expense	130000		(D) 35000		165000	
Advertising Expense	25000				25000	
Telephone Expense	22000				22000	
	2135000	2135000				
Office Supplies Expense			(A) 50000		50000	
Rent Expense			(B) 40000		40000	
Depreciation Exp., W.P. Equip.			(C) 8000		8000	
Accum. Deprec., W.P. Equip.				(C) 8000		8000
Salaries Payable				(D) 35000		35000
			133000	133000	2178000	2178000

Annotations:

- If no adjustment is made, just carry over amount from trial balance on same side.
- Supplies were $600 but we used up $500, leaving us with a $100 balance in supplies. *Note:* If there are a debit and a credit, take the *difference* between the two and place it on the side that is larger.
- *Note:* Equipment is *not* adjusted here.
- Two debits are added together. If two credits, they also would have been added together.
- Carry these amounts over to adjusted trial balance in the same positions.
- *Note:* The total of the left (debit) must equal the total of the right (credit) ($21,780).

TABLE 4-1   NORMAL BALANCES AND ACCOUNT CATEGORIES

Account Titles	Category	Normal Balance on Adjusted Trial Balance	Income Statement Dr.	Income Statement Cr.	Balance Sheet Dr.	Balance Sheet Cr.
Cash	Asset	Dr.			X	
Accounts Receivable	Asset	Dr.			X	
Office Supplies	Asset	Dr.			X	
Prepaid Rent	Asset	Dr.			X	
Word Proc. Equip.	Asset	Dr.			X	
Accounts Payable	Liability	Cr.				X
Brenda Clark, Capital	Capital	Cr.				X
Brenda Clark, Withdrawals	Withdrawal	Dr.			X	
Word Proc. Fees	Revenue	Cr.		X		
Office Salaries Exp.	Expense	Dr.	X			
Advertising Expense	Expense	Dr.	X			
Telephone Expense	Expense	Dr.	X			
Office Supplies Exp.	Expense	Dr.	X			
Rent Expense	Expense	Dr.	X			
Dep. Exp., W. P. Equip.	Expense	Dr.	X			
Acc. Dep., W. P. Equip.	Contra Asset	Cr.				X
Salaries Payable	Liability	Cr.				X

in Table 4-1. This table should be used as a reference to help you in filling out the next two sections of the worksheet.

Keep in mind that the numbers from the adjusted trial balance are carried over to one of the last four columns of the worksheet before the bottom section is completed.

THE INCOME STATEMENT SECTION

As shown in Figure 4-4 on page 128, the income statement section lists only revenue and expenses from the adjusted trial balance. Note that accumulated depreciation and salaries payable do not go on the income statement. Accumulated depreciation is a contra-asset found on the balance sheet. Salaries payable is a liability found on the balance sheet.

The revenue ($8,000) and all the individual expenses are listed in the income statement section. The revenue is placed in the credit column of the income statement section because it has a credit balance. The expenses have debit balances, so they are placed in the debit column of the income statement section. The following steps must be taken after the debits and credits are placed in the correct columns:

In the worksheet, net income is placed in the debit column of the income statement. Net loss goes on the credit column.

Step 1: Total the debits and credits.

Step 2: Calculate the balance between the debit and credit columns and place the difference on the smaller side.

Step 3: Total the columns.

The difference between $3,100 Dr. and $8,000 Cr. indicates a net income of $4,900. Do not think of the Net Income as a Dr. or Cr. The $4,900 is placed in the debit column to balance both columns to $8,000. Actually, the credit side is larger by $4,900.

The worksheet in Figure 4-4 shows that the label Net Income is added in the account title column on the same line as $4,900. When there is a net income, it will be placed in the debit column of the income statement section of the worksheet. If there is a net loss, it is placed in the credit column. The $8,000 total indicates that the two columns are in balance.

Account Titles	Adjusted Trial Balance Dr.	Adjusted Trial Balance Cr.	Income Statement Dr.	Income Statement Cr.
Cash	6 1 5 5 00			
Accounts Receivable	5 0 0 0 00			
Office Supplies	1 0 0 00			
Prepaid Rent	8 0 0 00			
Word Processing Equipment	6 0 0 0 00			
Accounts Payable		3 3 5 0 00		
B. Clark, Capital		10 0 0 0 00		
B. Clark, Withdrawals	6 2 5 00			
Word Processing Fees		8 0 0 0 00		8 0 0 0 00
Office Salaries Expense	1 6 5 0 00		1 6 5 0 00	
Advertising Expense	2 5 0 00		2 5 0 00	
Telephone Expense	2 2 0 00		2 2 0 00	
Office Supplies Expense	5 0 0 00		5 0 0 00	
Rent Expense	4 0 0 00		4 0 0 00	
Depreciation Exp., W.P. Equip.	8 0 00		8 0 00	
Accum. Deprec., W.P. Equip.		8 0 00		
Salaries Payable		3 5 0 00		
	21 7 8 0 00	21 7 8 0 00	3 1 0 0 00	8 0 0 0 00
Net Income			4 9 0 0 00	
			8 0 0 0 00	8 0 0 0 00

FIGURE 4-4 The Income Statement Section of the Worksheet

THE BALANCE SHEET SECTION

To fill out the balance sheet section of the worksheet, the following are carried over from the adjusted trial balance section: assets, contra-assets, liabilities, capital, and withdrawals. Because the beginning figure for capital* is used on the worksheet, the net income is brought over to the credit column of the balance sheet so both columns balance.

Let's now look at the completed worksheet in Figure 4-5 to see how the balance sheet section is completed. Note how the net income of $4,900 is brought over to the credit column of the worksheet. The figure for capital is also on the credit column, while the figure for withdrawals is on the debit column. By placing the net income in the credit column both sides total $18,680. If a net loss were to occur it would be placed in the debit column of the balance sheet column.

Now that we have completed the worksheet, we can go on to the three financial reports. But first let's summarize our progress.

Remember: The ending figure for capital is not on the worksheet.

To see whether additional investments occurred for the period you must check the capital account in the ledger.

The amounts come from the adjusted trial balance, except the $4,900, which was carried over from the income statement section.

---
* We assume no additional investments during the period.

FIGURE 4-5 The Completed Worksheet

CLARK'S WORD PROCESSING SERVICES
WORKSHEET
FOR MONTH ENDED MAY 31, 19XX

Account Titles	Trial Balance Dr.	Trial Balance Cr.	Adjustments Dr.	Adjustments Cr.	Adjusted Trial Balance Dr.	Adjusted Trial Balance Cr.	Income Statement Dr.	Income Statement Cr.	Balance Sheet Dr.	Balance Sheet Cr.
Cash	6155 00				6155 00				6155 00	
Accounts Receivable	5000 00				5000 00				5000 00	
Office Supplies	600 00			(A) 500 00	100 00				100 00	
Prepaid Rent	1200 00			(B) 400 00	800 00				800 00	
Word Processing Equipment	6000 00				6000 00				6000 00	
Accounts Payable		3350 00				3350 00				3350 00
B. Clark, Capital		10000 00				10000 00				10000 00
B. Clark, Withdrawals	625 00				625 00				625 00	
Word Processing Fees		8000 00				8000 00		8000 00		
Office Salaries Expense	1300 00		(D) 350 00		1650 00		1650 00			
Advertising Expense	250 00				250 00		250 00			
Telephone Expense	220 00				220 00		220 00			
	21350 00	21350 00								
Office Supplies Expense			(A) 500 00		500 00		500 00			
Rent Expense			(B) 400 00		400 00		400 00			
Depreciation Exp., W.P. Equip.			(C) 80 00		80 00		80 00			
Accum. Deprec., W.P. Equip.				(C) 80 00		80 00				80 00
Salaries Payable				(D) 350 00		350 00				350 00
			1330 00	1330 00	21780 00	21780 00	3100 00	8000 00	18680 00	13780 00
Net Income							4900 00			4900 00
							8000 00	8000 00	18680 00	18680 00

LEARNING UNIT 4-1 REVIEW

AT THIS POINT you should be able to

◆ Define and explain the purpose of a worksheet. (p. 117)
◆ Explain the need as well as the process for adjustments. (p. 118)
◆ Explain the concept of depreciation. (p. 120)
◆ Explain the difference between depreciation expense and accumulated depreciation. (p. 121)
◆ Prepare a worksheet from a trial balance and adjustment data. (p. 129)

SELF-REVIEW QUIZ 4-1

From the accompanying trial balance and adjustment data, complete a worksheet for P. Logan Co. for the month ended Dec. 31, 19XX. (You can use the blank fold-out worksheet located at the end of the *Study Guide and Working Papers.*)

Note: The numbers used on this quiz may seem impossibly small, but we have done that on purpose, so that at this point you don't have to worry about arithmetic, just about preparing the worksheet correctly.

P. LOGAN
TRIAL BALANCE
DECEMBER 31, 19XX

	Dr.	Cr.
Cash	15 00	
Accounts Receivable	3 00	
Prepaid Insurance	3 00	
Store Supplies	5 00	
Store Equipment	6 00	
Accumulated Depreciation, Store Equipment		4 00
Accounts Payable		2 00
P. Logan, Capital		14 00
P. Logan, Withdrawals	3 00	
Revenue from Clients		25 00
Rent Expense	2 00	
Salaries Expense	8 00	
	45 00	45 00

Adjustment Data:

a. Depreciation Expense, Store Equipment, $1.
b. Insurance Expired, $2
c. Supplies on hand, $1.
d. Salaries owed but not paid to employees, $3.

Solution to Self-Review Quiz 4-1

Don't adjust this line! Store Equipment always contains the historical cost.

Quiz Tip: The adjustment for supplies of $4 represents the amount *used up.* The *on hand* amount of $1 ends up on the adjusted trial balance.

P. LOGAN COMPANY
WORKSHEET
FOR MONTH ENDED DECEMBER 31, 19XX

Account Titles	Trial Balance Dr.	Trial Balance Cr.	Adjustments Dr.	Adjustments Cr.	Adjusted Trial Balance Dr.	Adjusted Trial Balance Cr.	Income Statement Dr.	Income Statement Cr.	Balance Sheet Dr.	Balance Sheet Cr.
Cash	1500				1500				1500	
Accounts Receivable	300				300				300	
Prepaid Insurance	300			(B) 200	100				100	
Store Supplies	500			(C) 400	100				100	
Store Equipment	600				600				600	
Accum. Depr., Store Equipment		400		(A) 100		500				500
Accounts Payable		200				200				200
P. Logan, Capital		1400				1400				1400
P. Logan, Withdrawals	300				300				300	
Revenue from Clients		2500				2500		2500		
Rent Expense	200				200		200			
Salaries Expense	800		(D) 300		1100		1100			
	4500	4500								
Depr. Exp., Store Equipment			(A) 100		100		100			
Insurance Expense			(B) 200		200		200			
Supplies Expense			(C) 400		400		400			
Salaries Payable				(D) 300		300				300
			1000	1000	4900	4900	2000	2500	2900	2400
Net Income							500			500
							2500	2500	2900	2900

Note that Accumulated Depreciation is listed in trial balance, since this is not a new company. Store Equipment has already been depreciated $4.00 from an earlier period.

CH. 4 / THE ACCOUNTING CYCLE CONTINUED: PREPARING WORKSHEETS AND FINANCIAL REPORTS

LEARNING UNIT 4-2
Step 6 of the Accounting Cycle: Preparing the Financial Statements from the Worksheet

The formal financial reports can be prepared from the worksheet completed in Learning Unit 4-1. Before beginning, we must check that the entries on the worksheet are correct and in balance. To do this, we have to be sure that (1) all entries are recorded in the appropriate column, (2) the correct amounts are entered in the proper places, (3) the addition is correct across the columns (i.e., from the trial balance to the adjusted trial balance to the financial reports), and (4) the columns are added correctly.

PREPARING THE INCOME STATEMENT

The first report to be prepared for Clark's Word Processing Services is the income statement. When preparing the income statement, it is important to remember that:

1. Every figure on the formal report is on the worksheet. Figure 4-6 shows where each of these figures goes on the income statement.
2. There are no debit or credit columns on the formal report.
3. The inside column on financial reports is used for subtotaling.
4. Withdrawals do not go on the income statement; they go on the statement of owner's equity.

Take a moment to look at the income statement in Figure 4-6. Note which items go where from the income statement section of the worksheet onto the formal report.

PREPARING THE STATEMENT OF OWNER'S EQUITY

Figure 4-7 is the statement of owner's equity for Clark's. The figure shows where the information comes from on the worksheet. It is important to remember that if there were additional investments, the figure on the worksheet for capital would not be the beginning figure for capital. Checking the ledger account for capital will tell you whether the amount is correct. Note how net income and withdrawals aid in calculating the new figure for capital.

PREPARING THE BALANCE SHEET

In preparing the balance sheet (p. 134), remember that the balance sheet section totals on the worksheet ($18,680) do *not* match the totals on the formal balance sheet ($17,975). This is because information is grouped differently on the formal report. First, in the formal report Accumulated Depreciation ($80) is subtracted from Word Processing Equipment, reducing the balance. Second, Withdrawals ($625) are subtracted from Owner's Equity, reducing the balance further. These two reductions (−$80 − $625 = −$705) represent the difference between the worksheet and the formal version of the balance sheet ($17,975 − $18,680 = −$705). Figure 4-8 on page 134 shows how to prepare the balance sheet from the worksheet.

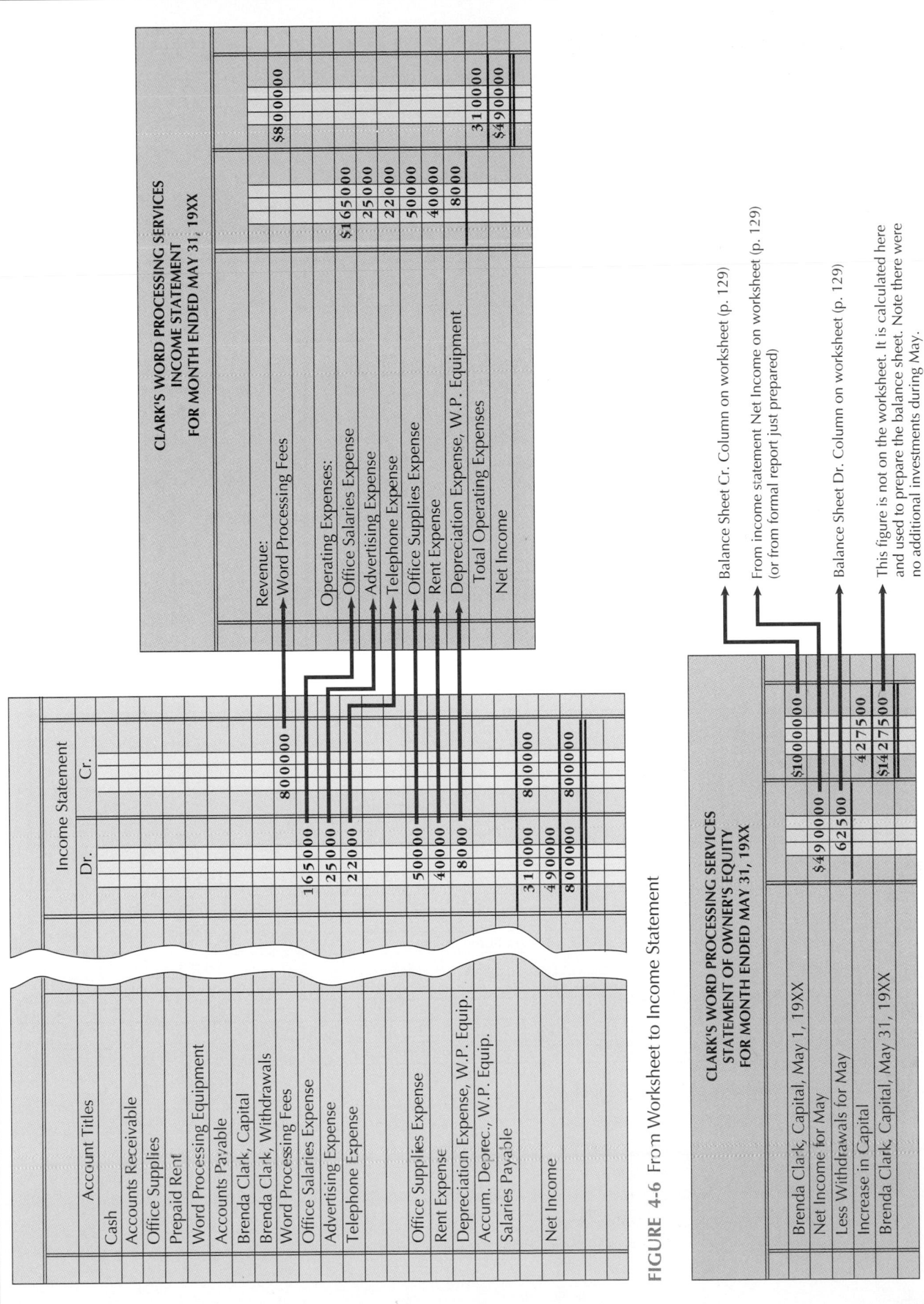

FIGURE 4-6 From Worksheet to Income Statement

CLARK'S WORD PROCESSING SERVICES
INCOME STATEMENT
FOR MONTH ENDED MAY 31, 19XX

Revenue:		
Word Processing Fees		$8 000 00
Operating Expenses:		
Office Salaries Expense	$1 650 00	
Advertising Expense	250 00	
Telephone Expense	220 00	
Office Supplies Expense	500 00	
Rent Expense	400 00	
Depreciation Expense, W.P. Equipment	80 00	
Total Operating Expenses		3 100 00
Net Income		$4 900 00

Income Statement

Account Titles	Dr.	Cr.
Cash		
Accounts Receivable		
Office Supplies		
Prepaid Rent		
Word Processing Equipment		
Accounts Payable		
Brenda Clark, Capital		
Brenda Clark, Withdrawals		
Word Processing Fees		8 000 00
Office Salaries Expense	1 650 00	
Advertising Expense	250 00	
Telephone Expense	220 00	
Office Supplies Expense	500 00	
Rent Expense	400 00	
Depreciation Expense, W.P. Equip.	80 00	
Accum. Deprec., W.P. Equip.		
Salaries Payable		
	3 100 00	8 000 00
Net Income	4 900 00	
	8 000 00	8 000 00

CLARK'S WORD PROCESSING SERVICES
STATEMENT OF OWNER'S EQUITY
FOR MONTH ENDED MAY 31, 19XX

Brenda Clark, Capital, May 1, 19XX		$10 000 00
Net Income for May	$4 900 00	
Less Withdrawals for May	625 00	
Increase in Capital		4 275 00
Brenda Clark, Capital, May 31, 19XX		$14 275 00

→ Balance Sheet Cr. Column on worksheet (p. 129)

→ From income statement Net Income on worksheet (p. 129) (or from formal report just prepared)

→ Balance Sheet Dr. Column on worksheet (p. 129)

→ This figure is not on the worksheet. It is calculated here and used to prepare the balance sheet. Note there were no additional investments during May.

FIGURE 4-7 Completing a Statement of Owner's Equity

FIGURE 4-8 From Worksheet to Balance Sheet

Fred has dreams. Big ones. He wants to grow his business to the point where he can start another Dunkin' Donuts shop. To do that, Fred realizes that he will have to manage his current shop more efficiently. His donuts and muffins are widely praised, and his bagel line is so successful that he has hired more help. But along with this success has come more paperwork. Fred now spends hours on his accounts. What to do?

Dunkin' Donuts' Business Consultant, Dwayne Goulding, knows that Fred needs to reduce the time he spends handling his accounts. Dwayne has suggested that Fred hire an accountant, or that he switch to a computerized accounting system, as many owners have done recently. Fred has been hesitant to do either, because he wants to control the finances himself. And save money. And he fears computers. What to do?

Seeing Fred's dilemma, Dwayne encourages him to contact his zone's Advisory Council. This Advisory Council, like hundreds across the country, offers fellow Dunkin' Donuts shop owners from the same zone a chance to get together to share ways to improve their operations and discuss common problems. They work with Dwayne and the rest of the Dunkin' Donuts managerial team to keep their interdependent businesses running smoothly and profitably.

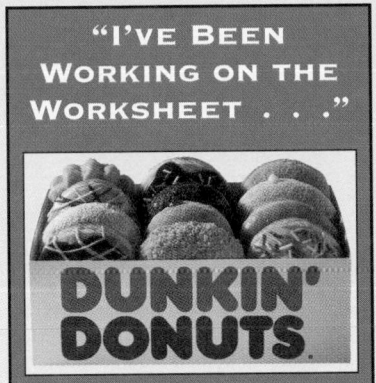

"I'VE BEEN WORKING ON THE WORKSHEET . . ."

When Fred approaches the Council, they are very supportive. "I've been there, Fred, so I know how you feel," said Joe Franklin, from two towns away. "First, you're on the right track when you prepare a worksheet. It's too easy to mess up if you try to skip this step. Next, you might want to try keeping a clean copy of last month's worksheet. Even though you don't have to submit it to Dwayne, you frequently have to go back and refer to it when questions come up on your Income Statement or Balance Sheet. When your worksheet is all crossed out and doodled on, like this one is, you can't find info fast. Also, you may need your worksheets at tax time. I sure found that out the hard way!"

DISCUSSION QUESTIONS

1. What is an Advisory Council? Why do you think that Dwayne recommended that Fred seek their advice?
2. Why do you think that some small business owners fear computerization and equate it with a loss of financial control?
3. Why is a clear worksheet helpful even after that month's statements have been prepared?

LEARNING UNIT 4-2 REVIEW

AT THIS POINT you should be able to

◆ Prepare the three financial reports from a worksheet. (p. 132)
◆ Explain why totals of the formal balance sheet don't match totals of balance sheet columns on the worksheet. (p. 132)

SELF-REVIEW QUIZ 4-2

(The forms you need are located on pages 107 and 108 of the *Study Guide and Working Papers*.)

From the worksheet on page 131 for P. Logan, please prepare (1) an income statement for December; (2) a statement of owner's equity; and (3) a balance sheet for December 31, 19XX. No additional investments took place during the period.

Solution to Self-Review Quiz 4-2

P. LOGAN
INCOME STATEMENT
FOR THE MONTH ENDED DECEMBER 31, 19XX

Revenue:		
Revenue from clients		$25 00
Operating Expenses:		
Rent Expense	$2 00	
Salaries Expense	11 00	
Depreciation Expense, Store Equipment	1 00	
Insurance Expense	2 00	
Supplies Expense	4 00	
Total Operating Expenses		20 00
Net Income		$5 00

Quiz Tips:

The income statement is made up of revenue and expenses. Use the inside column for subtotaling.

The $5 on the income statement is used to update the statement of owner's equity.

P. LOGAN
STATEMENT OF OWNER'S EQUITY
FOR THE MONTH ENDED DECEMBER 31, 19XX

P. Logan, Capital, December 1, 19XX		$14 00
Net Income for December	$5 00	
Less Withdrawals for December	3 00	
Increase in Capital		2 00
P. Logan, Capital, December 31, 19XX		$16 00

P. LOGAN
BALANCE SHEET
DECEMBER 31, 19XX

Assets			Liabilities and Owner's Equity		
Cash		$15 00	Liabilities		
Accounts Receivable		3 00	Accounts Payable	$2 00	
Prepaid Insurance		1 00	Salaries Payable	3 00	
Store Supplies		1 00	Total Liabilities		$5 00
Store Equipment	$6 00		Owner's Equity		
Less Acc. Dep., St. Eq.	5 00	1 00	P. Logan, Capital		16 00
			Total Liabilities and		
Total Assets		$21 00	Owner's Equity		$21 00

The ending capital figure on the statement of owner's equity ($16) is used as the capital figure on the balance sheet.

COMPREHENSIVE DEMONSTRATION PROBLEM WITH SOLUTION TIPS

(The blank forms you need are on pages 109 and 110 of the *Study Guide and Working Papers.*)

From the following trial balance and additional data complete (1) a worksheet and (2) the three financial reports (numbers are intentionally small so you may concentrate on the theory).

FROST COMPANY
TRIAL BALANCE
DECEMBER 31, 19XX

	Dr.	Cr.
Cash	14	
Accounts Receivable	4	
Prepaid Insurance	5	
Plumbing Supplies	3	
Plumbing Equipment	7	
Accumulated Depreciation, Plumbing Equipment		5
Accounts Payable		1
J. Frost, Capital		12
J. Frost, Withdrawals	3	
Plumbing Fees		27
Rent Expense	4	
Salaries Expense	5	
Totals	45	45

Adjustment Data:

a. Insurance Expired $3
b. Plumbing Supplies on Hand $1
c. Depreciation Expense, Plumbing Equipment $1
d. Salaries owed but not paid to employees $2

Solution Tips to Building a Worksheet

1. Adjustments (Used up)

a.

Insurance Expense	Expense	↑	Dr.	$3
Prepaid Insurance	Asset	↓	Cr.	$3

Expired means used up

b.

Plumbing Supplies Expense	Expense	↑	Dr.	$2
Plumbing Supplies	Asset	↓	Cr.	$2

$3 − 1 = $2 *used up*
on hand

(cont. on p. 139)

Solution to Worksheet

FROST COMPANY
WORKSHEET
FOR MONTH ENDED DECEMBER 31, 19XX

Account Titles	Trial Balance Dr.	Trial Balance Cr.	Adjustments Dr.	Adjustments Cr.	Adjusted Trial Balance Dr.	Adjusted Trial Balance Cr.	Income Statement Dr.	Income Statement Cr.	Balance Sheet Dr.	Balance Sheet Cr.
Cash	1400				1400				1400	
Accounts Receivable	400				400				400	
Prepaid Insurance	500			(A) 300	200				200	
Plumbing Supplies	300			(B) 200	100				100	
Plumbing Equipment	700				700				700	
Accum. Depr., Plumb. Equip.		500		(C) 100		600				600
Accounts Payable		100				100				100
J. Frost, Capital		1200				1200				1200
J. Frost, Withdrawals	300				300				300	
Plumbing Fees		2700				2700		2700		
Rent Expense	400				400		400			
Salaries Expense	500		(D) 200		700		700			
	4500	4500								
Insurance Expense			(A) 300		300		300			
Plumbing Supplies Expense			(B) 200		200		200			
Depr. Exp. Plumb. Equip.			(C) 100		100		100			
Salaries Payable				(D) 200		200				200
			800	800	4800	4800	1700	2700	3100	2100
Net Income							1000			1000
							2700	2700	3100	3100

c.

Depreciation Expense, Plumbing Equipment	Expense	↑	Dr.	$1
Accumulated Depreciation, Plumbing Equipment	Contra Asset	↑	Cr.	$1

The original cost of equipment of $7 is not "touched."

d.

Salaries Expense,	Expense	↑	Dr.	$2
Salaries Payable	Liability	↑	Cr.	$2

2. Last four columns of worksheet prepared from adjusted trial balance.

3. Capital of $12 is the old figure. Net income of $10 (revenue − expenses) is brought over to same side as capital on the balance sheet Cr. column to balance columns.

FROST COMPANY
INCOME STATEMENT
FOR MONTH ENDED DECEMBER 31, 19XX

Revenue:		
Plumbing Fees		$27
Operating Expenses:		
Rent Expense	$4	
Salaries Expense	7	
Insurance Expense	3	
Plumbing Supplies Expense	2	
Depreciation Expense, Plumbing Equipment	1	
Total Operating Expenses		17
Net Income		$10

FROST COMPANY
STATEMENT OF OWNER'S EQUITY
FOR MONTH ENDED DECEMBER 31, 19XX

J. Frost Capital, Dec. 1, 19XX		$12
Net Income for December	$10	
Less Withdrawals for December	3	
Increase in Capital		7
J. Frost, Capital Dec. 31, 19XX		$19

FROST COMPANY
BALANCE SHEET
DECEMBER 31, 19XX

Assets			Liabilities and Owner's Equity		
Cash		$14	Liabilities		
Accounts Receivable		4	Accounts Payable	$1	
Prepaid Insurance		2	Salaries Payable	2	
Plumbing Supplies		1	Total Liabilities		$ 3
Plumbing Equipment	$7				
Less Accumulated Dep.	6	1	Owner's Equity		
			J. Frost, Capital		19
			Total Liabilities and		
Total Assets		$22	Owner's Equity		$22

Solution Tips for Preparing Financial Reports from a Worksheet

Inside columns of the three financial reports are used for subtotal. There are no debits or credits on the formal reports.

REPORT

◆ **Income Statement**	From Income Statement columns of worksheet for revenue and expenses.
◆ **Statement of Owner's Equity**	From Balance Sheet Cr. column for old figure for Capital. Net Income from Income Statement. From Balance Sheet Dr. Column for Withdrawal figure.
◆ **Balance Sheet**	From Balance Sheet Dr. column for Assets. From Balance Sheet Cr. Column for liabilities and Accumulated Depreciation. New Figure for Capital from Statement of Owner's Equity.

Note how plumbing equipment $7 and Accumulated Depreciation $6 are rearranged on the formal balance sheet. The total assets of $22 is not on the worksheet. Remember there are no debits or credits on formal reports.

SUMMARY OF KEY POINTS

Learning Unit 4-1

1. The worksheet is not a formal report.
2. Adjustments update certain accounts so that they will be up to their latest balance before financial reports are prepared. Adjustments are the result of internal transactions.
3. Adjustments will affect both the income statement and the balance sheet.
4. Accounts listed *below* the account titles on the trial balance of the worksheet are *increasing*.
5. The original cost of a piece of equipment is not adjusted, historical cost is not lost.
6. Depreciation is the process of spreading the original cost of the asset over its expected useful life.
7. Accumulated depreciation is a contra-asset on the balance sheet that summarizes, accumulates, or builds up the amount of depreciation that an asset has accumulated.
8. Book value is the original cost less accumulated depreciation.
9. Accrued salaries are unpaid and unrecorded expenses that are accumulating but for which payment is not yet due.
10. Revenue and Expenses go on income statement sections of the worksheet. Assets, contra-assets, liabilities, capital, and withdrawals go on balance sheet sections of the worksheet.

Learning Unit 4-2

1. The formal reports prepared from a worksheet do not have debit or credit columns.
2. Revenue and expenses go on the income statement. Beginning capital plus net income less withdrawals (or: beginning capital minus net loss, less withdrawals) go on the statement of owner's equity. Be sure to check capital account in ledger to see if any additional investments took place. Assets, contra-assets, liabilities, and the new figure for capital go on the balance sheet.

KEY TERMS

Accrued salaries Salaries that are earned by employees but unpaid and unrecorded during the period (and thus need to be recorded by an adjustment) and will not come due for payment until the next accounting period.

Accumulated depreciation A contra-asset account that summarizes or accumulates the amount of depreciation that has been taken on an asset.

Adjusting The process of calculating the latest up-to-date balance of each account at the end of an accounting period.

Book value Cost of equipment less accumulated depreciation.

Depreciation The allocation (spreading) of the cost of an asset (such as an auto or equipment) over its expected useful life.

Historical cost The actual cost of an asset at time of purchase.

Residual value Estimated value of an asset after all the allowable depreciation has been taken.

Worksheet A columnar device used by accountants to aid them in completing the accounting cycle. It is not a formal report. Often called a spreadsheet.

BLUEPRINT OF STEPS 5 AND 6 OF THE ACCOUNTING CYCLE

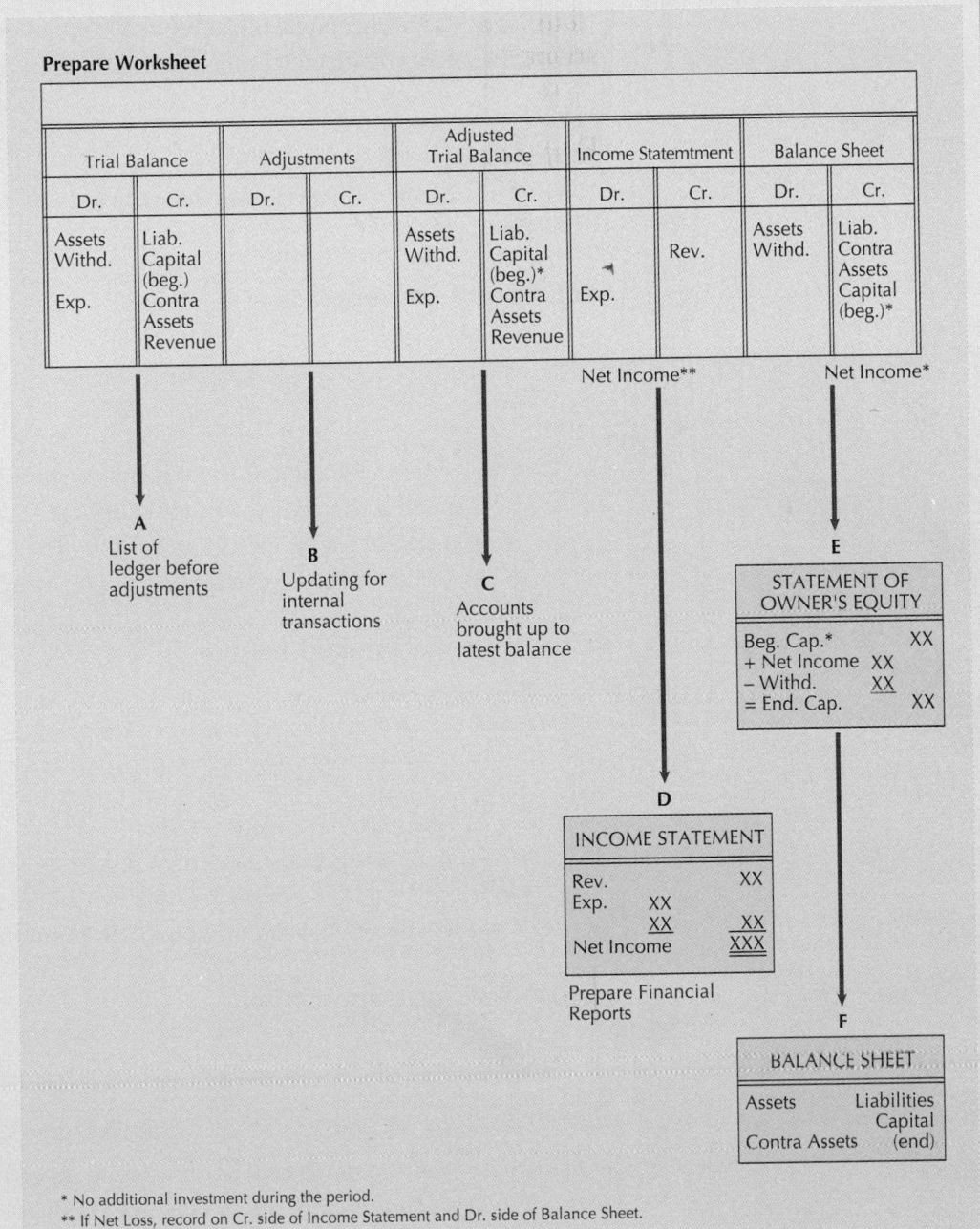

Prepare Worksheet

	Trial Balance		Adjustments		Adjusted Trial Balance		Income Statemtment		Balance Sheet	
	Dr.	Cr.	Dr.	Cr.	Dr.	Cr.	Dr.	Cr.	Dr.	Cr.
	Assets Withd. Exp.	Liab. Capital (beg.) Contra Assets Revenue			Assets Withd. Exp.	Liab. Capital (beg.)* Contra Assets Revenue	Exp.	Rev.	Assets Withd.	Liab. Contra Assets Capital (beg.)*

Net Income**   Net Income*

A
List of ledger before adjustments

B
Updating for internal transactions

C
Accounts brought up to latest balance

E
STATEMENT OF OWNER'S EQUITY

Beg. Cap.*	XX
+ Net Income	XX
– Withd.	XX
= End. Cap.	XX

D
INCOME STATEMENT

Rev.		XX
Exp.	XX	
	XX	XX
Net Income		XXX

Prepare Financial Reports

F
BALANCE SHEET

Assets	Liabilities
	Capital
Contra Assets	(end)

* No additional investment during the period.
** If Net Loss, record on Cr. side of Income Statement and Dr. side of Balance Sheet.

CH. 4 / THE ACCOUNTING CYCLE CONTINUED: PREPARING WORKSHEETS AND FINANCIAL REPORTS

QUESTIONS, MINI EXERCISES, EXERCISES, AND PROBLEMS

Discussion Questions

1. Worksheets are required in every company's accounting cycle. Please agree or disagree and explain why.
2. What is the purpose of adjusting accounts?
3. What is the relationship of internal transactions to the adjusting process?
4. Explain how an adjustment can affect both the income statement and balance sheet. Please give an example.
5. Why do we need the accumulated depreciation account?
6. Depreciation expense goes on the balance sheet. True or false. Why?
7. Each month the cost of accumulated depreciation grows while the cost of equipment goes up. Agree or disagree. Defend your position.
8. Define accrued salaries.
9. Why don't the formal financial reports contain debit or credit columns?
10. Explain how the financial reports are prepared from the worksheet.

Mini Exercises

(The blank forms you need are on pages 112–113 of the *Study Guide and Working Papers*.)

Adjustment for Supplies

1. *Before Adjustment*

Supplies	Supplies Expense
400	

Given: At year end an inventory of supplies showed $50.
   a. How much is the adjustment for supplies?
   b. Draw a transaction analysis box for this adjustment.
   c. What will the balance of supplies be on the Adjusted Trial Balance?

Adjustment for Prepaid Rent

2. *Before Adjustment*

Prepaid Rent	Rent Expense
700	

Given: At year end rent expired is $300.
   a. How much is the adjustment for Prepaid Rent?
   b. Draw a transaction analysis box for this adjustment.
   c. What will be the balance of Prepaid Rent on the Adjusted Trial Balance?

Adjustment for Depreciation

3. *Before Adjustment*

Equip.	Acc. Dep., Equip.	Dep. Exp., Equip.
6,000	1,000	

Given: At year end depreciation on Equipment is $1,000.
   a. Which of the three T Accounts above is not affected?
   b. Which Title is a contra-asset?

c. Draw a transaction analysis box for this adjustment.

d. What will be the balance of these three accounts on the Adjusted Trial Balance?

Adjustment for Accrued Salaries

4. *Before Adjustment*

Salaries Expense	Salaries Payable
900	

Given: Accrued Salaries, $200.

a. Draw a transaction analysis box for this adjustment.

b. What will be the balance of these two accounts on the Adjusted Trial Balance?

Worksheet

5. From the following Adjusted Trial Balance titles of a worksheet identify in which column each account will be listed on the last four columns of the worksheet.

(ID) Income Statement Dr. Column

(IC) Income Statement Cr. Column

(BD) Balance Sheet Dr. Column

(BC) Balance Sheet Cr. Column

	ATB	IS	BS
A. Supplies	~~~ ~~~	___	___
B. Acc. Receivable	~~~ ~~~	___	___
C. Cash	~~~ ~~~	___	___
D. Prepaid Rent	~~~ ~~~	___	___
E. Equipment	~~~ ~~~	___	___
F. Acc. Depreciation	~~~ ~~~	___	___
G. B., Capital	~~~ ~~~	___	___
H. B., Withdrawals	~~~ ~~~	___	___
I. Taxi Fees	~~~ ~~~	___	___
J. Advertising Expense	~~~ ~~~	___	___
K. Off. Supplies Expense	~~~ ~~~	___	___
L. Rent Expense	~~~ ~~~	___	___
M. Depreciation Expense	~~~ ~~~	___	___
N. Salaries Payable	~~~ ~~~	___	___

6. From the following Balance Sheet (which was made from the worksheet and other financial reports) explain why the lettered numbers were not found on the worksheet. *Hint:* There are no debits or credits on the formal financial reports.

H. WELLS
BALANCE SHEET
DECEMBER 31, 19XX

Assets			Liabilities and Owner's Equity			
Cash		$ 6	Liabilities			
Acc. Receivable		2	Accounts Payable	$2		
Supplies		2	Salaries, Payable	1		
Equipment	$10		Total Liabilities		$ 3	(B)
Less Acc. Dep.	4	6	Owner's Equity			
			H. Wells, Capital		13	(C)
			Total Liability and			
(A) Total Assets		$16	Owner's Equity		$16	(D)

(The blank forms you need are on pages 114–116 of the *Study Guide and Working Papers.*)

4-1. Complete the following table.

Account	Category	Normal Balance	Which Financial Report(s) Found
Salary Expense			
Prepaid Insurance			
Equipment			
Accumulated Depreciation			
A. Jax, Capital			
A. Jax, Withdrawals			
Salaries Payable			
Depreciation Expense			

Categorizing accounts.

Reviewing adjustments and the transaction analysis charts.

4-2. Use transaction analysis charts to analyze the following adjustments:
  a. Depreciation on equipment, $500.
  b. Rent expired, $200.

4-3. From the following adjustment data, calculate the adjustment amount and record appropriate debits or credits:

Recording adjusting entries.

  a. Supplies purchased, $600.
      Supplies on hand, $200.
  b. Store equipment, $10,000.
      Accumulated depreciation before adjustment, $900.
      Depreciation expense, $100.

Preparing a worksheet.

4-4. From the following trial balance and adjustment data, complete a worksheet for J. Trent as of December 31, 19XX:

  a. Depreciation expense, equipment $2.00
  b. Insurance expired   1.00
  c. Store supplies on hand   4.00
  d. Wages owed, but not paid for (they are an expense in the old year)   5.00

J. TRENT TRIAL BALANCE DECEMBER 31, 19XX	Dr.	Cr.
Cash	9 00	
Accounts Receivable	2 00	
Prepaid Insurance	7 00	
Store Supplies	6 00	
Store Equipment	7 00	
Accumulated Depreciation, Equipment		2 00
Accounts Payable		4 00
J. Trent, Capital		1 7 00
J. Trent, Withdrawals	6 00	
Revenue from Clients		2 4 00
Rent Expense	4 00	
Wage Expense	6 00	
	4 7 00	4 7 00

Preparing financial reports from a worksheet.

4-5. From the completed worksheet in Exercise 4-4, prepare

    a. An income statement for December.

    b. A statement of owner's equity for December.

    c. A balance sheet as of December 31, 19XX.

Group A Problems

(The blank forms you need are on pp. 117–120 of the *Study Guide and Working Papers.*)

4A-1.

Completing a partial worksheet up to the adjusted trial balance.

Check Figure:
Total Adjusted Trial Balance
$26,550

SILVER'S FITNESS CENTER TRIAL BALANCE DECEMBER 31, 19XX	Debit	Credit
Cash in Bank	4 1 0 0 00	
Accounts Receivable	5 0 0 0 00	
Gym Supplies	5 4 0 0 00	
Gym Equipment	7 2 0 0 00	
Accumulated Depreciation, Gym Equipment		3 7 5 0 00
J. Silver, Capital		10 7 0 0 00
J. Silver, Withdrawals	3 0 0 0 00	
Gym Fees		11 3 0 0 00
Rent Expense	9 0 0 00	
Advertising Expense	1 5 0 00	
	25 7 5 0 00	25 7 5 0 00

Given the following adjustment data on December 31:

    a. Gym supplies on hand, $1,500.

    b. Depreciation taken on gym equipment, $800.

Complete a partial worksheet up to the adjusted trial balance.

4A-2. On the next page is the trial balance for Fred's Plumbing Service for December 31, 19XX.

Adjustment data to update the trial balance:

    a. Rent expired, $500.

    b. Plumbing supplies on hand (remaining), $100.

    c. Depreciation expense, plumbing equipment, $200.

    d. Wages earned by workers but not paid or due until January, $350.

Your task is to prepare a worksheet for Fred's Plumbing Service for the month of December.

FRED'S PLUMBING SERVICE
TRIAL BALANCE
DECEMBER 31, 19XX

	Dr.	Cr.
Cash in Bank	3 6 0 6 00	
Accounts Receivable	7 0 0 00	
Prepaid Rent	8 0 0 00	
Plumbing Supplies	7 4 2 00	
Plumbing Equipment	1 4 0 0 00	
Accumulated Depreciation, Plumbing Equipment		1 0 6 0 00
Accounts Payable		4 4 2 00
Fred Jack, Capital		3 2 5 0 00
Plumbing Revenue		4 3 5 6 00
Heat Expense	4 0 0 00	
Advertising Expense	2 0 0 00	
Wage Expense	1 2 6 0 00	
	9 1 0 8 00	9 1 0 8 00

4A-3. The following is the trial balance for Kevin's Moving Co.

KEVIN'S MOVING CO.
TRIAL BALANCE
OCTOBER 31, 19XX

	Dr.	Cr.
Cash	5 0 0 0 00	
Prepaid Insurance	2 5 0 0 00	
Moving Supplies	1 2 0 0 00	
Moving Truck	11 0 0 0 00	
Accumulated Depreciation, Moving Truck		9 0 0 0 00
Accounts Payable		2 7 6 8 00
K. Hoff, Capital		5 4 4 2 00
K. Hoff, Withdrawals	1 4 0 0 00	
Revenue from Moving		9 0 0 0 00
Wage Expense	3 7 1 2 00	
Rent Expense	1 0 8 0 00	
Advertising Expense	3 1 8 00	
	26 2 1 0 00	26 2 1 0 00

Adjustment data to update trial balance:

a. Insurance expired, $700.

b. Moving supplies on hand, $900.

c. Depreciation on moving truck, $500.

d. Wages earned but unpaid, $250.

Your task is to

1. Complete a worksheet for Kevin's Moving Co. for the month of October.

2. Prepare an income statement for October, a statement of owner's equity for October, and a balance sheet as of October 31, 19XX.

4A-4.

Adjustment data to update trial balance:

a. Insurance expired, $700.

b. Repair supplies on hand, $3,000.

c. Depreciation on repair equipment, $200.

d. Wages earned but unpaid, $400.

Your task is to

1. Complete a worksheet for Dick's Repair Service for the month of November.

2. Prepare an income statement for November, a statement of owner's equity for November, and a balance sheet as of November 30, 19XX.

Comprehensive Problem

Check Figure:
Net Income $1,830

DICK'S REPAIR SERVICE TRIAL BALANCE NOVEMBER 30, 19XX	Dr.	Cr.
Cash	3 2 0 0 00	
Prepaid Insurance	4 0 0 00	
Repair Supplies	4 6 0 0 00	
Repair Equipment	3 0 0 0 00	
Accumulated Depreciation, Repair Equipment		7 0 0 00
Accounts Payable		5 5 7 0 00
D. Horn, Capital		3 8 0 0 00
Revenue from Repairs		7 0 0 0 00
Wages Expense	1 8 0 0 00	
Rent Expense	3 6 0 00	
Advertising Expense	1 1 0 00	
	17 0 7 0 00	17 0 7 0 00

Group B Problems

(The blank forms you need are on pages 117–120 of the *Study Guide and Working Papers*.)

4B-1.

Completing a partial worksheet up to adjusted trial balance.

Check Figure:
Total of Adjusted Trial Balance
$18,600

SILVER'S FITNESS CENTER TRIAL BALANCE DECEMBER 31, 19XX	Dr.	Cr.
Cash	2 0 0 0 00	
Accounts Receivable	2 0 0 0 00	
Gym Supplies	4 2 0 0 00	
Gym Equipment	8 0 0 0 00	
Accumulated Depreciation, Gym Equipment		5 7 0 0 00
J. Silver, Capital		11 0 0 0 00
J. Silver, Withdrawals	1 0 0 0 00	
Gym Fees		1 4 0 0 00
Rent Expense	8 0 0 00	
Advertising Expense	1 0 0 00	
	18 1 0 0 00	18 1 0 0 00

Please complete a partial worksheet up to the adjusted trial balance using the following adjustment data:

a. Gym supplies on hand, $2,600.

b. Depreciation taken on gym equipment, $500.

4B-2.

4B-2. Given the following trial balance and adjustment data of Fred's Plumbing Service, your task is to prepare a worksheet for the month of December.

Completing a worksheet.

Check Figure:

Net Income $673

FRED'S PLUMBING SERVICE
TRIAL BALANCE
DECEMBER 31, 19XX

	Dr.	Cr.
Cash in Bank	3 9 6 00	
Accounts Receivable	2 8 4 00	
Prepaid Rent	4 0 0 00	
Plumbing Supplies	3 1 0 00	
Plumbing Equipment	1 0 0 0 00	
Accumulated Depreciation, Plumbing Equipment		2 0 0 00
Accounts Payable		3 4 6 00
Fred Jack, Capital		4 5 6 00
Plumbing Revenue		4 6 8 0 00
Heat Expense	6 3 2 00	
Advertising Expense	1 2 0 0 00	
Wage Expense	1 4 6 0 00	
Total	5 6 8 2 00	5 6 8 2 00

Adjustment data:

  a. Plumbing supplies on hand, $60.
  b. Rent expired, $150.
  c. Depreciation on plumbing equipment, $200.
  d. Wages earned but unpaid, $115.

4B-3. Using the following trial balance and adjustment data of Kevin's Moving Co., prepare

  1. A worksheet for the month of October.
  2. An income statement for October, a statement of owner's equity for October, and a balance sheet as of October 31, 19XX.

Comprehensive Problem

Check Figure:

Net Loss $1,628

KEVIN'S MOVING CO.
TRIAL BALANCE
OCTOBER 31, 19XX

	Dr.	Cr.
Cash	3 9 2 0 00	
Prepaid Insurance	3 2 8 8 00	
Moving Supplies	1 4 0 0 00	
Moving Truck	10 6 5 8 00	
Accumulated Depreciation, Moving Truck		3 6 6 0 00
Accounts Payable		1 3 1 2 00
K. Hoff, Capital		17 4 8 2 00
K. Hoff, Withdrawals	4 2 4 0 00	
Revenue from Moving		8 1 6 2 00
Wages Expense	5 7 1 2 00	
Rent Expense	1 0 8 0 00	
Advertising Expense	3 1 8 00	
	30 6 1 6 00	30 6 1 6 00

Adjustment Data:

  a. Insurance expired $600
  b. Moving supplies on hand $310

c. Depreciation on moving truck $580
d. Wages earned but unpaid $410

4B-4. As the bookkeeper of Dick's Repair Service, use the information that follows to prepare

1. A worksheet for the month of November.
2. An income statement for November, a statement of owner's equity for November, and a balance sheet as of November 30, 19XX.

Comprehensive Problem

Check Figure:
Net Income $1,012

DICK'S REPAIR SERVICE TRIAL BALANCE NOVEMBER 30, 19XX		
	Dr.	Cr.
Cash	3 2 0 4 00	
Prepaid Insurance	4 0 0 0 00	
Repair Supplies	7 7 0 00	
Repair Equipment	3 1 0 6 00	
Accumulated Depreciation, Repair Equipment		6 5 0 00
Accounts Payable		1 9 0 4 00
D. Horn, Capital		6 2 5 8 00
Revenue from Repairs		5 6 3 4 00
Wages Expense	1 6 0 0 00	
Rent Expense	1 5 6 0 00	
Advertising Expense	2 0 6 00	
	14 4 4 6 00	14 4 4 6 00

Adjustment Data:
a. Insurance expired $300
b. Repair supplies on hand $170
c. Depreciation on repair equipment $250
d. Wages earned but unpaid $106

REAL WORLD APPLICATIONS

4R-1.

MEMO

To: Hal Hogan, Bookkeeper

From: Pete Tennant, V. P.

Re: Adjustments for year ended December 31, 19XX

Hal, here is the information you requested. Please supply me with the adjustments needed ASAP. Also, please put in writing why we need to do these adjustments.

Thanks.

Attached to memo:

a. Insurance data:

Policy No.	Date of Policy Purchase	Policy Length	Cost
100	November 1 of previous year	4 years	$480
200	May 1 of current year	2 years	600
300	September 1 of current year	1 year	240

b. Rent data: Prepaid rent had a $500 balance at beginning of year. An additional $400 of rent was paid in advance in June. At year end, $200 of rent had expired.

c. Revenue data: Accrued storage fees of $500 were earned but uncollected and unrecorded at year end.

4R-2.

> *Hint: Unearned Rent is a liability on the balance sheet.*

On Friday, Harry Swag's boss asks him to prepare a special report, due on Monday at 8:00 A.M. Harry gathers the following material in his briefcase:

	Dec. 31	
	19X1	**19X2**
Prepaid Advertising	$300	$600
Interest Payable	150	350
Unearned Rent	500	300

Cash paid for:	Advertising	$1,900
	Interest	1,500
Cash received for:	Rent	2,300

As his best friend, could you help Harry show the amounts that are to be reported on the 19XX income statement for (a) Advertising Expense, (b) Interest Expense, and (c) Rent Fees Earned. Please explain in writing why unearned rent is considered a liability.

YOU make the call

Critical Thinking/Ethical Case

4R-3.

Janet Fox, President of Angel Co., went to a tax seminar. One of the speakers at the seminar advised the audience to put off showing expenses until next year because doing so would allow them to take advantage of a new tax law. When Janet returned to the office, she called in her accountant, Frieda O'Riley. She told Frieda to forget about making any adjustments for salaries in the old year so more expenses could be shown in the new year. Frieda told her that putting off these expenses would not follow generally accepted accounting procedures. Janet said she should do it anyway. You make the call. Write your specific recommendations to Frieda.

ACCOUNTING RECALL
A CUMULATIVE APPROACH

THIS EXAM REVIEWS CHAPTERS 1 THROUGH 4

Pages 125 and 129 of the *Study Guide and Working Papers* have the forms to complete this exam, as well as worked-out solutions. The page references next to each question identify what page to turn back to if you answer the question incorrectly.

PART 1   Vocabulary Review

Match the terms to the appropriate definition or phrase.

Page Ref.

(120)	1. Prepaid rent E	A. Estimated value of an asset after all depreciation taken
(123)	2. Accrued salaries B	
(122)	3. Depreciation expense	B. Earned but unpaid
(121)	4. Accumulated depreciation	C. Actual cost at time of purchase

(40)	5. Normal balance	D. Columnar device
(121)	6. Residual value	E. Rent paid in advance
(5)	7. An Asset	F. Cost — accumulated depreciation
(117)	8. Worksheet	G. Supplies
(122)	9. Book value	H. Shown on the income statement
(122)	10. Historical cost	I. Side that increases it
		J. Contra asset

PART II   True or False (Accounting Theory)

(118)   11. Adjustments are the result of external transactions.

(119)   12. Adjustments affect only the balance sheet.

(122)   13. Accumulated depreciation and equipment will both go on the balance sheet.

(121)   14. The normal balance of accumulated depreciation is a debit.

(132)   15. All financial reports could be prepared from a worksheet.

CONTINUING PROBLEM

At the end of September, Tony took a complete inventory of his supplies and found the following:

5 dozen ¼" screws at a cost of $8.00 a dozen

2 dozen ½" screws at a cost of $5.00 a dozen

2 cartons of computer inventory paper at a cost of $14 a carton

3 feet of coaxial cable at a cost of $4.00 per foot

After speaking to his accountant, he found that a reasonable depreciation amount for each of his long-term assets is as follows:

Computer purchased July 5, 19XX	Depreciation $33 a month
Office Equipment purchased July 17, 19XX	Depreciation $10 a month
Computer Workstations purchased Sept. 17, 19XX	Depreciation $20 a month

Tony uses the straight-line method of depreciation and declares no salvage value for any of the assets. If any long-term asset is purchased in the first fifteen days of the month, he will charge depreciation for the full month. If an asset is purchased on the sixteenth of the month, or later, he will not charge depreciation in the month it was purchased.

August and September's rent has now expired.

Assignment:

Use your trial balance from the completed problem in Chapter 3 and the above adjusting information to complete the worksheet for the three months ended September 30, 19XX. From the worksheets prepare the financial statements. (See pp. 126–127 in your *Study Guide and Working Papers.*)

COMPUTERIZED ACCOUNTING APPLICATION FOR CHAPTER 4

PART A: Compound Journal Entries, Adjusting Entries, and Financial Reports

PART B: Backup Procedures

Before starting on this assignment, read and complete the tasks discussed in Parts A, B, and F of the Computerized Accounting appendix at the back of this book and complete the Computerized Accounting Application assignment at the end of Chapter 3.

PART A: Compound Journal Entries, Adjusting Entries, and Financial Reports

Open the Company Data Files

1. Click on the Start button. Point to Programs; point to Simply Accounting; then click on Simply Accounting in the final menu presented. The Simply Accounting Open File dialog box will appear.

2. Insert your Student Data Files disk into disk drive A. Enter the following path into the **File name** text box: A:\student\zell.asc

3. Click on the **Open** button; enter 12/31/97 into the **Using Date for this Session** text box; then click on the **OK** button. Click on the **OK** button in response to the message "The date entered is more than one week past your previous Using date of 12/1/97." The Company Window for Zell will appear.

Add Your Name to the Company Name

4. Click on the Company Window Setup menu; then click on Company Information. The Company Information dialog box will appear. Insert your name in place of the text "Your Name" in the **Name** text box. Click on the **OK** button to return to the Company Window.

How to Record a Compound Journal Entry

5. In the Computerized Accounting Application assignment in Chapter 3 you learned how to record journal entries in the General Journal dialog box. Compound journal entries can also be recorded in the General Journal dialog box. The owner of The Zell Company has made an investment in the business consisting of $5,000 in cash and an automobile valued at $12,000. Open the General Journal dialog box. Enter the word Memo into the **Source** text box; press the TAB key; enter 12/1/97 into the **Date** text box; press the TAB key; enter "Initial investment by owner" into the **Comment** text box; then press the TAB key. The flashing insertion point will be positioned in the **Account** text box.

6. With the flashing insertion point positioned in the **Account** text box, press the ENTER key. The Select Account dialog box will appear. Double-click on 1110 Cash; enter 5000 into the **Debits** text box; then press the TAB key.

7. Press the ENTER key to bring up the Select Account dialog box. Double-click on 1230 Automobile. The program will offer 5000.00 as a default amount in the **Credits** text box. The **Credits** amount remains highlighted. You do not want to accept the default. To override the default, enter − 12000 (Be sure to enter the minus sign!); then press the TAB key. The 12000.00 amount will move to the **Debits** text box.

8. Press the ENTER key to bring up the Select Account dialog box; then double-click on 3110 Owner's Capital. The program will offer the total of the **Debits** portion of the compound journal entry (17000.00) as a default amount in the **Credits** text box. The **Credits** amount remains highlighted. Press the TAB key

to accept the default **Credits** amount. This completes the data you need to enter into the General Journal dialog box to record the compound journal entry for the initial investment by the owner. Your screen should look like this:

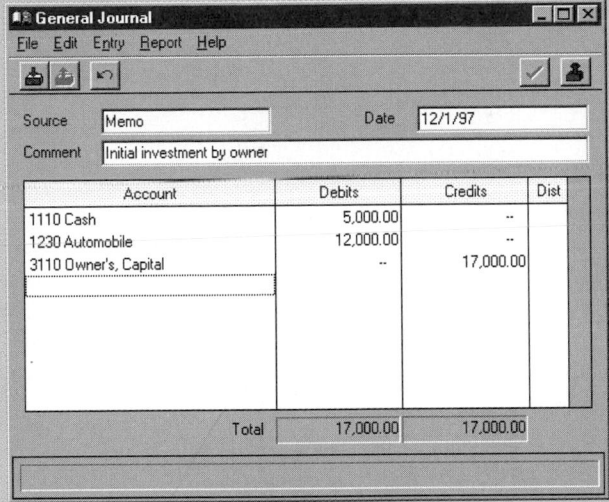

Review the Compound Journal Entry

9. Click on the General Journal Report menu; then click on Display General Journal Entry. Review the compound journal entry for accuracy, noting any errors.

10. Close the General Journal Entry window; then make any editing corrections required.

Post the Entry

11. After verifying that the compound journal entry is correct, click on the **Post** icon to post this transaction.

Record Additional Transactions

12. Record the following additional journal entries (enter "Memo" into the **Source** text box for each transaction; then enter the Date listed for each transaction):

1997
Dec.   1   Paid rent for two months in advance, $500.
       3   Purchased office supplies ($200) and office equipment ($1,100) both
           on account.
       9   Billed a customer for fees earned, $2,000.
       13 Paid telephone bill, $150.
       20 Owner withdrew $475 from the business for personal use.
       27 Received $600 for fees earned.
       30 Paid salaries expense, $800.

Display and Print a General Journal and Trial Balance

13. After you have posted the additional journal entries, close the General Journal; then print the following reports:

   a. General Journal (By posting date, All ledger entries, Start: 12/1/97, Finish: 12/31/97).

   b. Trial Balance As at 12/31/97.

14. Review your printed reports. If you have made an error in a posted journal entry, see "Reversing an Entry Made in the General Journal Dialog Box" in Part C of the Computerized Accounting appendix for information on how to correct the error.

How to Record Adjusting Journal Entries

15. Open the General Journal; then record adjusting journal entries based on the following adjustment data (*Source:* Memo; *Date:* 12/31/97; *Comment:* Adjusting entry):

   a. One month's rent has expired.

   b. An inventory shows $25 of office supplies remaining.

   c. Depreciation on office equipment, $50.

   d. Depreciation on automobile, $150.

Display and Print a General Journal, General Ledger, and Trial Balance

16. After you have posted the adjusting journal entries, close the General Journal; then print the following reports:

  a. General Journal (By posting date, All ledger entries, Start: 12/31/97, Finish: 12/31/97).

  b. General Ledger Report (Start: 12/1/97, Finish: 12/31/97, Select All).

  c. Trial Balance As at 12/31/97.

17. Review your printed reports. If you have made an error in a posted journal entry, see "Reversing an Entry Made in the General Journal Dialog Box" in Part C of the Computerized Accounting appendix for information on how to correct the error.

How to Display and Print an Income Statement

18. Click on the Company Window Reports menu; point to Financials; then click on Income Statement. The Income Statement Options dialog box will appear asking you to define the information you want displayed. Leave the Select a Report text box set at Current Year. Leave the **Start** text box date set at 1/1/97; leave the **Finish** text box date set at 12/31/97; then click on the **OK** button. Your screen will look like this:

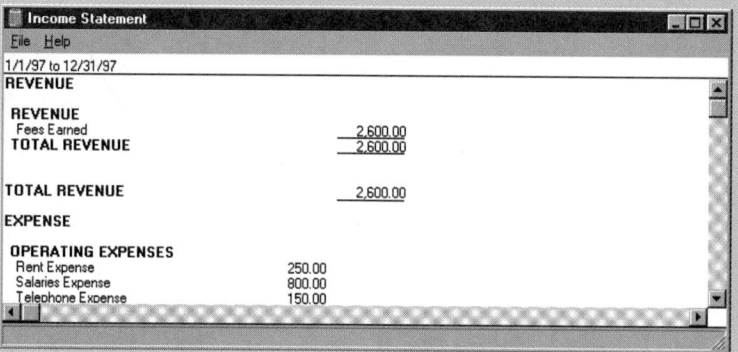

19. The scroll bar can be used to advance the display to view other portions of the report.

20. Click on the Income Statement File menu; then click on Print to print the Income Statement.

How to Display and Print a Balance Sheet

21. Close the Income Statement window; click on the Company Window Reports menu; point to Financials; then click on Balance Sheet. The Balance Sheet Options dialog box will appear asking you to define the information you want displayed. Leave the Select a Report text box set at Current Year. Leave the **As at** date set as 12/31/97; then click on the **OK** button. Your screen will look like this:

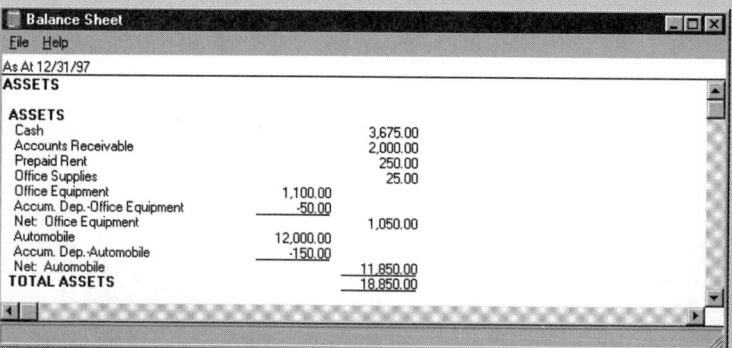

22. Use the scroll bar to advance the display to the Owner's Equity section of the Balance Sheet. Note that the program has included the Statement of Owner's Equity information directly in the Owner's Equity section of the Balance Sheet.

23. Click on the Balance Sheet File menu; click on Print to print the Balance Sheet; then close the Balance Sheet window to return to the Company Window.

Exit from the Program

24. Click on the Company Window File menu; then click on Exit to end the current work session and return to your Windows desktop.

PART B: Backup Procedures

Companies that use computerized accounting systems make frequent backup copies of their accounting data for two major reasons:

1. To ensure that they have a copy of the accounting data in case the current data becomes damaged.
2. To permit the printing of historical reports after the **Using** date has been advanced to a new month.

The methods used to make backup copies of company data files vary greatly. Large companies may backup daily using sophisticated high-speed tape backup devices while small companies may backup weekly on floppy disks using the backup program supplied with their operating system or applications software.

Normally all backup copies of a company's data files are stored on a secondary storage medium separate from the original data files in case the original secondary storage medium becomes damaged. However, for the purposes of this introduction to computerized accounting systems, you will be using the working copy of your Student Data Files disk to store backup copies of a company's data files. You will be using a backup method known as the Save As method.

How to Make a Backup Copy of a Company's Data Files

1. Click on the Start button. Point to Programs; point to Simply Accounting; then click on Simply Accounting in the final menu presented. The Simply Accounting Open File dialog box will appear.
2. Insert your Student Data Files disk into disk drive A. Enter the following path into the **File name** text box: A:\student\zell.asc
3. Click on the **Open** button; leave the **Using date for this session** set at 12/31/97; then click on the **OK** button. The Company Window for Zell will appear on your screen.
4. Click on the Company Window File menu; then click on Save As. The Save As dialog box will appear. Enter the following new file name into the **File name** text box: A:\student\zelldec.asc
5. Click on the **Save** button. Note that the company name in the Company Window has changed from Zell to Zelldec. Click on the Company Window File menu again; then click on Save As. Enter the following new file name into the **File name** text box: A:\student\zell.asc
6. Click on the **Save** button. Click on the **Yes** button to confirm that you want to replace the existing file. Note that the company name in the Company Window has changed back from Zelldec to Zell.
7. You now have two sets of company data files for The Zell Company on your Student Data Files disk. The current data is stored under the file name zell.asc. The backup data for December is stored under the file name zelldec.asc.

Exit from the Program

8. Click on the Company Window File menu; then click on Exit to end the current work session and return to your Windows desktop.
9. For information on when you might want to use the backup copy of a company's data files, see Part E of the Computerized Accounting appendix in the back of this book.

Complete the Report Transmittal

10. Complete The Zell Company Report Transmittal located in Appendix A in your *Study Guide and Working Papers.*

THE ACCOUNTING CYCLE COMPLETED

Adjusting, Closing, and Post-Closing Trial Balance

THE BIG PICTURE

As Tony Freedman began to prepare for his busiest season, he thought it might be a good time to end the fiscal year for Eldorado Computer Center and record the adjusting entries before closing the books.

Under GAAP, every business is required to complete an accounting cycle within 12 months of doing business. Freedman has chosen to end his cycle using a fiscal year date of September 30. He chose this date because it was a good time to complete inventory and take time to analyze his books. As Christmas gets closer he knows there will be a lot of potential new business because it's the "giving" season.

Adjusting entries must be recorded and posted to the permanent books to reflect the changes. This will bring each ledger account up to date with the balances reflected on the financial statements.

The final step ends with closing the books. This process closes the temporary accounts (revenue, expenses, and withdrawals) into the permanent account (capital). Remember that owner's equity is made up with several temporary accounts that reflect how the business is doing. Profits (when revenue exceeds expenses) from the business increase the worth of a business. On the other hand, a net loss will decrease the worth of a business. Similarly, when an owner personally withdraws assets from the business, that too will decrease the value of the business. Closing the books is simply a process of moving the temporary account balances to the permanent account.

<table>
<tr>
<td>

Learning Objectives

</td>
<td>

◆ **Journalizing and posting adjusting entries. (p. 157)**
◆ **Journalizing and posting closing entries. (p. 160)**
◆ **Preparing a post-closing trial balance. (p. 171)**

</td>
</tr>
</table>

Remember, for ease of presentation we are using a month as the accounting cycle for Clark. In the "real" world, the cycle can be any time period that does not exceed one year.

In Chapters 3 and 4 we completed these steps of the manual accounting cycle for Clark's Word Processing Services:

Step 1: Business transactions occurred and generated source documents.

Step 2: Business transactions were analyzed and recorded into a journal.

Step 3: Information was posted or transferred from journal to ledger.

Step 4: A trial balance was prepared.

Step 5: A worksheet was completed.

Step 6: Financial statements were prepared.

This chapter covers the following steps. This will complete Clark's accounting cycle for the month of May:

Step 7: Journalizing and posting adjusting entries.

Step 8: Journalizing and posting closing entries.

Step 9: Preparing a post-closing trial balance.

LEARNING UNIT 5-1

Journalizing and Posting Adjusting Entries: Step 7 of the Accounting Cycle

RECORDING JOURNAL ENTRIES FROM THE WORKSHEET

At this point, many ledger accounts are *not up to date*.

Purpose of adjusting entries.

The information in the worksheet is up to date. The financial reports prepared from that information can give the business's management and other interested parties a good idea of where the business stands as of a particular date. The problem is that the worksheet is an informal report. The information concerning the adjustments has not been placed into the journal, or posted to the ledger accounts. This means that the books are not up to date and ready for the next accounting cycle to begin. For example, the ledger shows $1,200 of prepaid rent (p. 85), but the balance sheet we prepared in Chapter 4 shows an $800 balance. Essentially, the worksheet is a tool for preparing financial reports. Now we must use the adjustment columns of the worksheet as a basis for bringing the ledger up to date. We do this by **adjusting journal entries** (see Figs. 5-1, 5-2). Again, the updating must be done before the next accounting period starts. For Clark's Word Processing Services, the next period begins on June 1.

Figure 5-2 shows the adjusting journal entries for Clark taken from the adjustments section of the worksheet. Once the adjusting journal entries are posted to the ledger, the accounts making up the financial statements that were prepared from the worksheet will equal the updated ledger. (Keep in mind that this is the same journal we have been using.) Let's look at some simplified T accounts to show how Clark's ledger looked before and after the adjustments were posted (see Adjustments A – D on pp. 118 – 124).

FIGURE 5-1
Journalizing and Posting Adjustments from the Adjustments Section of the Worksheet

Account Titles	Trial Balance Dr.	Trial Balance Cr.	Adjustments Dr.	Adjustments Cr.
Cash	6 1 5 5 00			
Accounts Receivable	5 0 0 0 00			
Office Supplies	6 0 0 00			(A) 5 0 0 00
Prepaid Rent	1 2 0 0 00			(B) 4 0 0 00
Word Processing Equipment	6 0 0 0 00			
Accounts Payable		3 3 5 0 00		
Brenda Clark, Capital		10 0 0 0 00		
Brenda Clark, Withdrawals	6 2 5 00			
Word Processing Fees		8 0 0 0 00		
Office Salaries Expense	1 3 0 0 00		(D) 3 5 0 00	
Advertising Expense	2 5 0 00			
Telephone Expense	2 2 0 00			
	21 3 5 0 00	21 3 5 0 00		
Office Supplies Expense			(A) 5 0 0 00	
Rent Expense			(B) 4 0 0 00	
Depreciation Exp., W.P. Equip.			(C) 8 0 00	
Accum. Deprec., W.P. Equip.				(C) 8 0 00
Salaries Payable				(D) 3 5 0 00
			1 3 3 0 00	1 3 3 0 00

Adjustment (A)

Before Posting:

Office Supplies 114
600 |

Office Supplies Expense 514
|

After Posting:

Office Supplies 114
600 | 500

Office Supplies Expense 514
500 |

FIGURE 5-2
Adjustments A–D in the adjustments section of the worksheet must be recorded in the journal and posted to the ledger.

**CLARK'S WORD PROCESSING SERVICES
GENERAL JOURNAL**

Page 2

Date		Account Titles and Description	PR	Dr.	Cr.
		Adjusting Entries			
May	31	Office Supplies Expense	514	5 0 0 00	
		Office Supplies	114		5 0 0 00
	31	Rent Expense	515	4 0 0 00	
		Prepaid Rent	115		4 0 0 00
	31	Depreciation Expense, W.P. Equip.	516	8 0 00	
		Accumulated Depreciation, W.P. Equip.	122		8 0 00
	31	Office Salaries Expense	511	3 5 0 00	
		Salaries Payable	212		3 5 0 00

Adjustment (B)

Before Posting:

Prepaid Rent 115	Rent Expense 515
1,200	

After Posting:

Prepaid Rent 115	Rent Expense 515
1,200 | 400	400 |

Adjustment (C)

Before Posting:

Word Processing Equipment 121	Depreciation Expense, W. P. Equipment 516	Accumulated Depreciation, W. P. Equipment 122
6,000 |		

After Posting:

Word Processing Equipment 121	Depreciation Expense, W. P. Equipment 516	Accumulated Depreciation, W. P. Equipment 122
6,000 |	80 |	| 80

The first adjustment in (C) shows the same balances for Depreciation Expense and Accumulated Depreciation. However, in subsequent adjustments the Accumulated Depreciation balance will keep getting larger, but the debit to Depreciation Expense and the credit to Accumulated Depreciation will be the same. We will see why in a moment.

Adjustment (D)

Before Posting:

Office Salaries Expense 511	Salaries Payable 212
650 |	
650 |	

After Posting:

Office Salaries Expense 511	Salaries Payable 212
650 |	| 350
650 |	
350 |	

LEARNING UNIT 5-1 REVIEW

SELF-REVIEW QUIZ 5-1

(The blank forms you need are on pages 129–130 of the *Study Guide and Working Papers.*)

Turn to the worksheet of P. Logan (p. 131) and (1) journalize and post the adjusting entries and (2) compare the adjusted ledger accounts before and after the adjustments are posted. T accounts are provided in your study guide with beginning balances.

Solution to Self-Review Quiz 5-1

								Page 2	
Date		Account Titles and Description	PR	Dr.			Cr.		
		Adjusting Entries							
Dec.	31	Depreciation Expense, Store Equip.	511		1	00			
		Accumulated Depreciation, Store Equip.	122					1	00
	31	Insurance Expense	516		2	00			
		Prepaid Insurance	116					2	00
	31	Supplies Expense	514		4	00			
		Store Supplies	114					4	00
	31	Salaries Expense	512		3	00			
		Salaries Payable	212					3	00

Quiz Tip: These journalized entries come from the Adjustments column of the worksheet.

PARTIAL LEDGER

Before Posting

Depreciation Expense, Store Equipment 511	Accumulated Depreciation, Store Equipment 122
	4

Prepaid Insurance 116	Insurance Expense 516
3	

Store Supplies 114	Supplies Expense 514
5	

Salaries Expense 512	Salaries Payable 212
8	

After Posting

Depreciation Expense, Store Equipment 511	Accumulated Depreciation Store Equipment 122
1	4 / 1

Prepaid Insurance 116	Insurance Expense 516
3 / 2	2

Store Supplies 114	Supplies Expense 514
5 / 4	4

Salaries Expense 512	Salaries Payable 212
8 / 3	3

LEARNING UNIT 5-2
Journalizing and Posting Closing Entries: Step 8 of the Accounting Cycle

To make recording of the next period's transactions easier, a mechanical step, called *closing,* is taken by Clark's accountant. Closing is intended to end — or close off — the revenue, expense, and withdrawal accounts at the end of the accounting period. The information needed to complete closing entries will be found in the income statement and balance sheet sections of the worksheet.

To make it easier to understand this process, we will first look at the difference between temporary (nominal) accounts and permanent (real) accounts. Here is the expanded accounting equation we used in an earlier chapter:

Assets = Liabilities + Capital − Withdrawals + Revenues − Expenses

Permanent accounts are found on the balance sheet.

Three of the items in that equation—assets, liabilities, and capital—are known as **real** or **permanent accounts** because their balances are carried over from one accounting period to another. The other three items—withdrawals, revenue, and expenses—are called **nominal** or **temporary accounts,** because their balances are not carried over from one accounting period to another. Instead, their "balances" are set at zero at the beginning of each accounting period. This allows us to accumulate new data about revenue, expenses, and withdrawals, in the new accounting period. The process of closing summarizes the effects of the temporary accounts on capital for that period using **closing journal entries.** When the closing process is complete, the accounting equation will be reduced to:

Assets = Liabilities + Ending Capital

After all closing entries are journalized and posted to the ledger; all temporary accounts have a zero balance in the ledger. Closing is a step-by-step process.

If you look back to page 134 in Chapter 4, you will see that we already calculated the new capital on the balance sheet to be $14,275 for Clark's Word Processing Services. But before the mechanical closing procedures are journalized and posted, the capital account of Clark in the ledger is only $10,000 (Chapter 3, p. 85). Let's look now at how to journalize and post closing entries.

How to journalize closing entries

There are four steps to be performed in journalizing closing entries:

An Income Summary is a temporary account located in the chart of accounts under owner's equity. It does not have a normal balance of a debit or a credit.

Step 1: Clear the revenue balance and transfer it to Income Summary. **Income Summary** is a temporary account in the ledger needed for closing. At the end of the closing process there will be no balance in Income Summary.

Revenue ⟶ Income Summary

Step 2: Clear the individual expense balances and transfer them to Income Summary.

Expenses ⟶ Income Summary

Sometimes, closing the accounts is referred to as "clearing the accounts."

Step 3: Clear the balance in Income Summary and transfer it to Capital.

Income Summary ⟶ Capital

Step 4: Clear the balance in Withdrawals and transfer it to Capital.

Withdrawals ⟶ Capital

Figure 5-3 on page 162 is a visual representation of these four steps. Keep in mind that this information must first be journalized and then posted to the appropriate ledger accounts. The worksheet presented in Figure 5-4 on page 162, contains all the figures we will need for the closing process.

Step 1: Clear Revenue Balance and Transfer to Income Summary

Here is what is in the ledger before closing entries are journalized and posted:

Word Processing Fees 411	Income Summary 313
8,000	

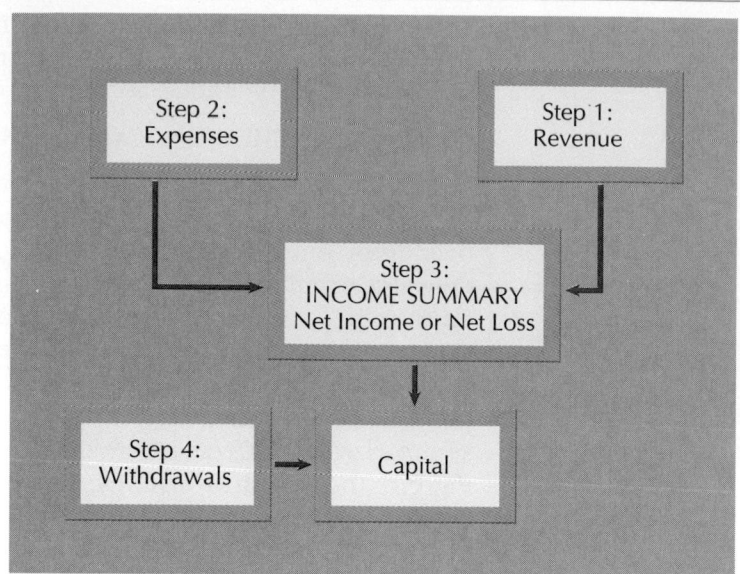

FIGURE 5-3 Four Steps in Journalizing Closing Entries. All numbers can be found on the worksheet in Figure 5-4.

The income statement section on the worksheet below shows that the Word Processing Fees have a credit balance of $8,000. To close or clear this to zero, a debit of $8,000 is needed. But if we add an amount to the debit side, we must also add a credit—so we add $8,000 on the credit side of the Income Summary.

FIGURE 5-4 Closing Figures on the Worksheet

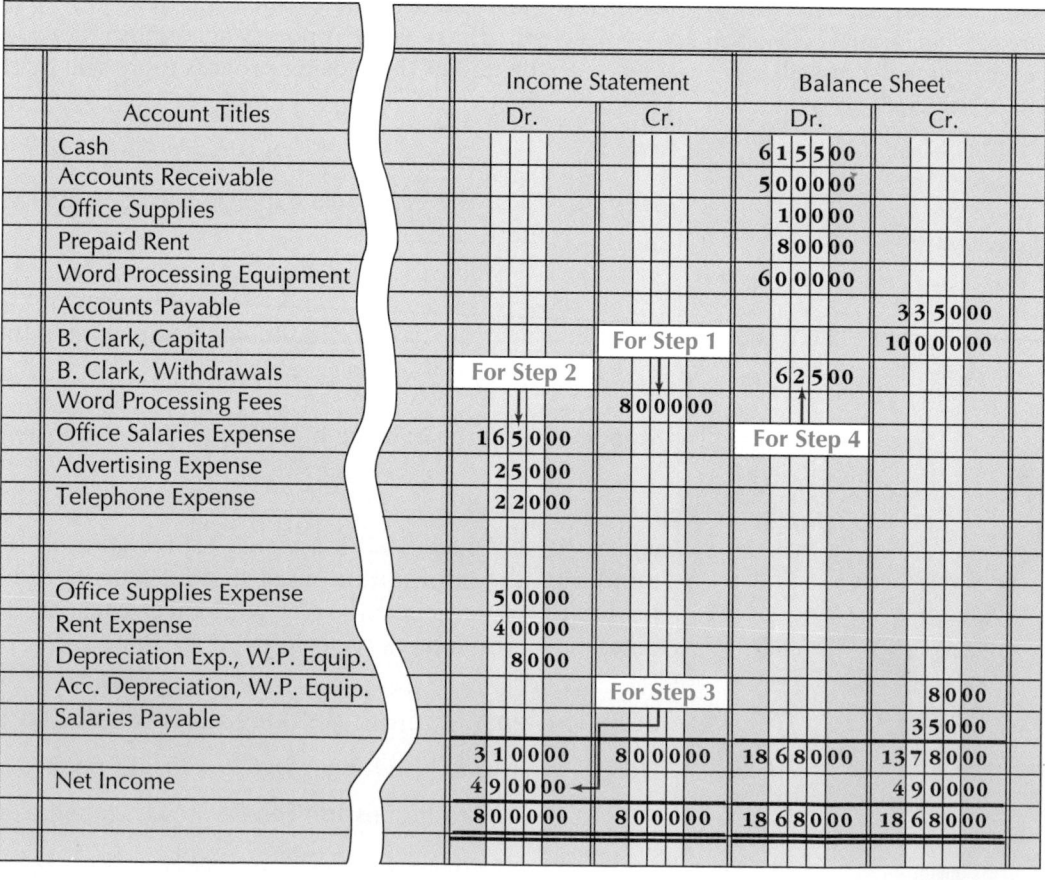

Account Titles	Income Statement Dr.	Income Statement Cr.	Balance Sheet Dr.	Balance Sheet Cr.
Cash			6 1 5 5 00	
Accounts Receivable			5 0 0 0 00	
Office Supplies			1 0 0 00	
Prepaid Rent			8 0 0 00	
Word Processing Equipment			6 0 0 0 00	
Accounts Payable				3 3 5 0 00
B. Clark, Capital		For Step 1		10 0 0 0 00
B. Clark, Withdrawals	For Step 2		6 2 5 00	
Word Processing Fees		8 0 0 0 00		
Office Salaries Expense	1 6 5 0 00	For Step 4		
Advertising Expense	2 5 0 00			
Telephone Expense	2 2 0 00			
Office Supplies Expense	5 0 0 00			
Rent Expense	4 0 0 00			
Depreciation Exp., W.P. Equip.	8 0 00			
Acc. Depreciation, W.P. Equip.		For Step 3		8 0 00
Salaries Payable				3 5 0 00
	3 1 0 0 00	8 0 0 0 00	18 6 8 0 00	13 7 8 0 00
Net Income	4 9 0 0 00			4 9 0 0 00
	8 0 0 0 00	8 0 0 0 00	18 6 8 0 00	18 6 8 0 00

The following is the journalized closing entry for Step 1:

May	31	Word Processing Fees	411	8 0 0 0 00			
		Income Summary	313			8 0 0 0 00	

This is what Word Processing Fees and Income Summary should look like in the ledger after the first step of closing entries is journalized and posted:

Word Processing Fees 411		Income Summary 313	
8,000	8,000		8,000
Closing	Revenue		Revenue

Note that the revenue balance is cleared to zero and transferred to Income Summary, a temporary account also located in the ledger.

Step 2: Clear Individual Expense Balances and Transfer the Total to Income Summary

Here is what is in the ledger for each expense before Step 2 of closing entries is journalized and posted. Each expense is listed on the worksheet in the debit column of the income statement section on page 162.

Office Salaries Expense 511		Advertising Expense 512	
650		250	
650			
350			

Telephone Expense 513		Office Supplies Expense 514	
220		500	

Rent Expense 515		Depreciation Expense, W. P. Equipment 516	
400		80	

The income statement section of the worksheet lists all the expenses as debits. If we want to reduce each expense to zero, each one must be credited. The following is the journalized closing entry for Step 2:

Remember, the worksheet is a tool. The accountant realizes that the information about the total of the expenses will be transferred to the Income Summary.

The $3,100 is the total of the expenses on the worksheet.

	31	Income Summary	313	3 1 0 0 00			
		Office Salaries Expense	511			1 6 5 0 00	
		Advertising Expense	512			2 5 0 00	
		Telephone Expense	513			2 2 0 00	
		Office Supplies Expense	514			5 0 0 00	
		Rent Expense	515			4 0 0 00	
		Depreciation Expense, W.P.Equip.	516			8 0 00	

The following is what individual expenses and Income Summary should look like in the ledger after Step 2 of closing entries is journalized and posted:

Office Salaries Expense 511		Advertising Expense 512	
650	Closing 1,650	250	Closing 250
650			
350			

Telephone Expense 513		Office Supplies Expense 514	
220	Closing 220	500	Closing 500

Rent Expense 515		Depreciation Expense, W. P. Equipment 516	
400	Closing 400	80	Closing 80

Income Summary 313

Expenses	Revenue
Step 2 3,100	8,000 Step 1

Step 3: Clear Balance in Income Summary (Net Income) and Transfer It to Capital

This is how the Income Summary and B. Clark, Capital, accounts look before Step 3:

Income Summary 313		B. Clark, Capital 311	
3,100	8,000		10,000
	4,900		

Note that the balance of Income Summary (Revenue minus Expenses or $8,000 − $3,100) is $4,900. That is the amount we must clear from the Income Summary account and transfer to the B. Clark, Capital, account.

In order to transfer the balance of $4,900 from Income Summary (check the bottom debit column of the income statement section on the worksheet in Fig. 5-4) to Capital, it will be necessary to debit Income Summary for $4,900 (the difference between the revenue and expenses) and credit or increase Capital of B. Clark for $4,900.

This is the journalized closing entry for Step 3:

	31	Income Summary	313	4 9 0 0 00	
		B. Clark, Capital	311		4 9 0 0 00

This is what the Income Summary and B. Clark, Capital, accounts will look like in the ledger after Step 3 of closing entries is journalized and posted:

Income Summary 313

	Income Summary 313		B. Clark, Capital 311	
Total of Expenses →	3,100	8,000 ← Revenue		10,000
Debit to close account →	4,900	4,900 ← Net Income		4,900 ← Net Income

The opposite would take place if the business had a net loss.

At the end of these three steps, the Income Summary has a zero balance. If we had a net loss the end result would be to decrease capital. Entry would be debit capital and credit income summary for the loss.

Step 4: Clear the Withdrawals Balance and Transfer it to Capital

Next, we must close the withdrawals account. The B. Clark, Withdrawals, and B. Clark, Capital, accounts now look like this:

```
    B. Clark, Withdrawals 312          B. Clark, Capital 311
         625          |                        |  10,000
                      |                        |   4,900
```

To bring the Withdrawals account to a zero balance, and summarize its effect on Capital, we must credit Withdrawals and debit Capital.

Remember, withdrawals are a nonbusiness expense and thus not transferred to Income Summary. The closing entry is journalized as follows:

	31	B. Clark, Capital	311	625 00	
		B. Clark, Withdrawals	312		625 00

At this point the B. Clark, Withdrawals, and B. Clark, Capital, accounts would look like this in the ledger.

```
    B. Clark, Withdrawals 312              B. Clark, Capital 311
       625 | Closing   625          ──→  625 | 10,000  ←
                                      Withdrawals    Beg. Balance
                                              |  4,900  ←
                                              |   Net Income
```

Now let's look at a summary of the closing entries.

<table>
<tr><th colspan="6">SUMMARY OF
CLOSING ENTRIES</th></tr>
<tr><td>Date</td><td>Account Titles and Description</td><td>PR</td><td>Dr.</td><td>Cr.</td><td></td></tr>
<tr><td></td><td>Closing Entries</td><td></td><td></td><td></td><td></td></tr>
<tr><td>19XX</td><td></td><td></td><td></td><td></td><td></td></tr>
<tr><td>May 31</td><td>Word Processing Fees</td><td>411</td><td>8000 00</td><td></td><td></td></tr>
<tr><td></td><td>Income Summary</td><td>313</td><td></td><td>8000 00</td><td></td></tr>
<tr><td></td><td></td><td></td><td></td><td></td><td></td></tr>
<tr><td>31</td><td>Income Summary</td><td>313</td><td>3100 00</td><td></td><td></td></tr>
<tr><td></td><td>Office Salaries Expense</td><td>511</td><td></td><td>1650 00</td><td></td></tr>
<tr><td></td><td>Advertising Expense</td><td>512</td><td></td><td>250 00</td><td></td></tr>
<tr><td></td><td>Telephone Expense</td><td>513</td><td></td><td>220 00</td><td></td></tr>
<tr><td></td><td>Office Supplies Expense</td><td>514</td><td></td><td>500 00</td><td></td></tr>
<tr><td></td><td>Rent Expense</td><td>515</td><td></td><td>400 00</td><td></td></tr>
<tr><td></td><td>Depreciation Expense, W.P. Equip.</td><td>516</td><td></td><td>80 00</td><td></td></tr>
<tr><td></td><td></td><td></td><td></td><td></td><td></td></tr>
<tr><td>31</td><td>Income Summary</td><td>313</td><td>4900 00</td><td></td><td></td></tr>
<tr><td></td><td>B. Clark, Capital</td><td>311</td><td></td><td>4900 00</td><td></td></tr>
<tr><td></td><td></td><td></td><td></td><td></td><td></td></tr>
<tr><td>31</td><td>B. Clark, Capital</td><td>311</td><td>625 00</td><td></td><td></td></tr>
<tr><td></td><td>B. Clark, Withdrawals</td><td>312</td><td></td><td>625 00</td><td></td></tr>
</table>

Note that the $10,000 is a beginning balance since no additional investments were made during the period.

The following is the complete ledger for Clark's Word Processing Services (see Fig. 5-5). Note how the word "adjusting" or "closing" is written in the explanation column of individual ledgers, as for example in the one for Office Supplies. If the goals of closing have been achieved, only permanent accounts will have balances carried to the next accounting period. All temporary accounts should have zero balances.

FIGURE 5-5
Complete Ledger

CLARK'S WORD PROCESSING SERVICES
GENERAL LEDGER

Cash   Account No. 111

Date		Explanation	Post. Ref.	Debit	Credit	Balance Debit	Balance Credit
19XX May	1		GJ1	10 000 00		10 000 00	
	1		GJ1		1 000 00	9 000 00	
	1		GJ1		1 200 00	7 800 00	
	7		GJ1	3 000 00		10 800 00	
	15		GJ1		650 00	10 150 00	
	20		GJ1		625 00	9 525 00	
	27		GJ2		650 00	8 875 00	
	28		GJ2		2 500 00	6 375 00	
	29		GJ2		220 00	6 155 00	

Accounts Receivable   Account No. 112

Date		Explanation	Post. Ref.	Debit	Credit	Balance Debit	Balance Credit
19XX May	22		GJ1	5 000 00		5 000 00	

Office Supplies   Account No. 114

Date		Explanation	Post. Ref.	Debit	Credit	Balance Debit	Balance Credit
19XX May	3		GJ1	600 00		600 00	
	31	Adjusting	GJ2		500 00	100 00	

(Fig. 5.5 cont.)

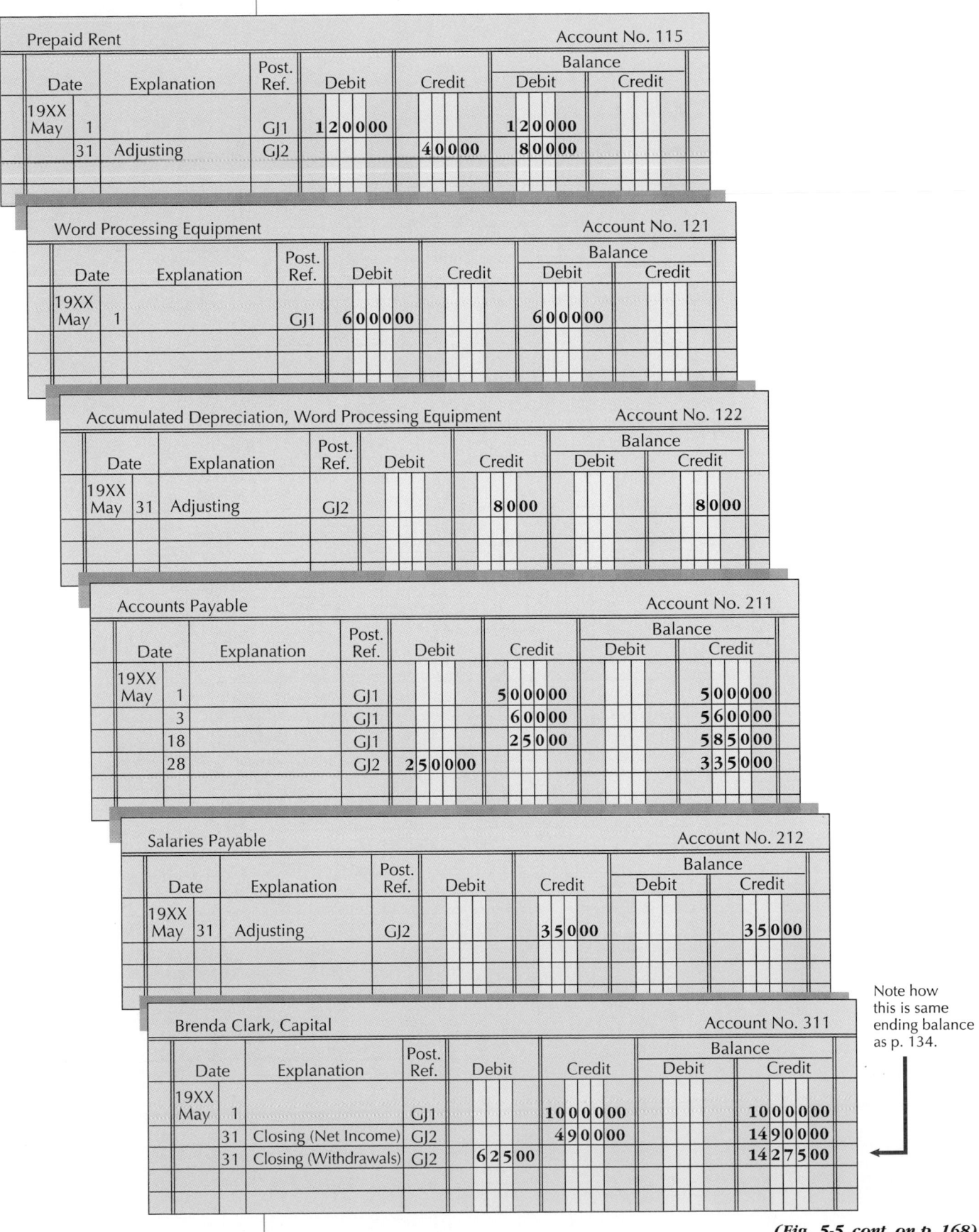

Prepaid Rent — Account No. 115

Date		Explanation	Post. Ref.	Debit	Credit	Balance Debit	Balance Credit
19XX May	1		GJ1	1 20 00		1 20 00	
	31	Adjusting	GJ2		40 00	80 00	

Word Processing Equipment — Account No. 121

Date		Explanation	Post. Ref.	Debit	Credit	Balance Debit	Balance Credit
19XX May	1		GJ1	6 00 00		6 00 00	

Accumulated Depreciation, Word Processing Equipment — Account No. 122

Date		Explanation	Post. Ref.	Debit	Credit	Balance Debit	Balance Credit
19XX May	31	Adjusting	GJ2		80 00		80 00

Accounts Payable — Account No. 211

Date		Explanation	Post. Ref.	Debit	Credit	Balance Debit	Balance Credit
19XX May	1		GJ1		5 00 00		5 00 00
	3		GJ1		60 00		5 60 00
	18		GJ1		25 00		5 85 00
	28		GJ2	2 50 00			3 35 00

Salaries Payable — Account No. 212

Date		Explanation	Post. Ref.	Debit	Credit	Balance Debit	Balance Credit
19XX May	31	Adjusting	GJ2		35 00		35 00

Brenda Clark, Capital — Account No. 311

Date		Explanation	Post. Ref.	Debit	Credit	Balance Debit	Balance Credit
19XX May	1		GJ1		10 00 00		10 00 00
	31	Closing (Net Income)	GJ2		4 90 00		14 90 00
	31	Closing (Withdrawals)	GJ2	62 50			14 27 50

Note how this is same ending balance as p. 134.

(Fig. 5-5 cont. on p. 168)

(Fig. 5.5 cont.)

Brenda Clark, Withdrawals — Account No. 312

Date		Explanation	Post. Ref.	Debit	Credit	Balance Debit	Balance Credit
19XX May	20		GJ1	6 2 5 00		6 2 5 00	
	31	Closing	GJ2		6 2 5 00	—	—

Income Summary — Account No. 313

Date		Explanation	Post. Ref.	Debit	Credit	Balance Debit	Balance Credit
19XX May	31	Closing (Revenue)	GJ2		8 0 0 0 00		8 0 0 0 00
	31	Closing (Expenses)	GJ2	3 1 0 0 00			4 9 0 0 00
	31	Closing (Net Income)	GJ2	4 9 0 0 00		—	

Word Processing Fees — Account No. 411

Date		Explanation	Post. Ref.	Debit	Credit	Balance Debit	Balance Credit
19XX May	7		GJ1		3 0 0 0 00		3 0 0 0 00
	22		GJ1		5 0 0 0 00		8 0 0 0 00
	31	Closing	GJ2	8 0 0 0 00		—	—

Office Salaries Expense — Account No. 511

Date		Explanation	Post. Ref.	Debit	Credit	Balance Debit	Balance Credit
19XX May	15		GJ1	6 5 0 00		6 5 0 00	
	27		GJ2	6 5 0 00		1 3 0 0 00	
	31	Adjusting	GJ2	3 5 0 00		1 6 5 0 00	
	31	Closing	GJ2		1 6 5 0 00	—	—

Advertising Expense — Account No. 512

Date		Explanation	Post. Ref.	Debit	Credit	Balance Debit	Balance Credit
19XX May	18		GJ1	2 5 0 00		2 5 0 00	
	31	Closing	GJ2		2 5 0 00	—	—

(Fig. 5.5 cont.)

Telephone Expense — Account No. 513

Date		Explanation	Post. Ref.	Debit	Credit	Balance Debit	Balance Credit
19XX May	29		GJ2	2 2 0 00		2 2 0 00	
	31	Closing	GJ2		2 2 0 00		

Office Supplies Expense — Account No. 514

Date		Explanation	Post. Ref.	Debit	Credit	Balance Debit	Balance Credit
19XX May	31	Adjusting	GJ2	5 0 0 00		5 0 0 00	
	31	Closing	GJ2		5 0 0 00	—	

Rent Expense — Account No. 515

Date		Explanation	Post. Ref.	Debit	Credit	Balance Debit	Balance Credit
19XX May	31	Adjusting	GJ2	4 0 0 00		4 0 0 00	
	31	Closing	GJ2		4 0 0 00	—	—

Depreciation Expense, Word Processing Equipment — Account No. 516

Date		Explanation	Post. Ref.	Debit	Credit	Balance Debit	Balance Credit
19XX May	31	Adjusting	GJ2	8 0 00		8 0 00	
	31	Closing	GJ2		8 0 00	—	—

LEARNING UNIT 5-2 REVIEW

AT THIS POINT you should be able to

- Define closing. (p.160)
- Differentiate between temporary (nominal) and permanent (real) accounts. (p. 161)
- List the four mechanical steps of closing. (p. 161)
- Explain the role of the Income Summary account. (p. 161)
- Explain the role of the worksheet in the closing process. (p. 161)

SELF-REVIEW QUIZ 5-2

(The blank forms you need are on pages 131–132 of the *Study Guide and Working Papers.*)

Go to the worksheet for P. Logan on p. 131. Then (1) journalize and post the closing entries and (2) calculate the new balance for P. Logan, Capital.

Solution to Self-Review Quiz 5-2

		Closing Entries				
Dec.	31	Revenue from Clients	410	25 00		
		Income Summary	312		25 00	
	31	Income Summary	312	20 00		
		Rent Expense	518		2 00	
		Salaries Expense	512		11 00	
		Depreciation Expense, Store Equip.	510		1 00	
		Insurance Expense	516		2 00	
		Supplies Expense	514		4 00	
	31	Income Summary	312	5 00		
		P. Logan, Capital	310		5 00	
	31	P. Logan, Capital	310	3 00		
		P. Logan, Withdrawals	311		3 00	

PARTIAL LEDGER

P. Logan, Capital 310	Revenue from Clients 410	Supplies Expense 514
3 | 14	25 | 25	4 | 4
5		
16		

P. Logan, Withdrawals 311	Dep. Exp., Store Equip. 510	Insurance Expense 516
3 | 3	1 | 1	2 | 2

Income Summary 312	Salaries Expense 512	Rent Expense 518
20 | 25	11 | 11	2 | 2
5 | 5		

Quiz Tip: No calculations are needed in the closing process. ALL numbers come from the worksheet. Income summary is a temporary account in the ledger.

P. Logan, Capital		$14
Net Income	$5	
Less Withdrawals	3	
Increase in Capital		2
P. Logan, Capital (ending)		$16

CLOSING TIME

The doorbell rang at 1 A.M. "The cavalry has arrived!" said the giant in the doorway. "You're a real friend in need, Lou," said Fred gratefully, as he opened the door. "I've been over and over this, and I can't get it to balance. And my monthly closing is due to Dwayne at noon tomorrow! I hate to bother you so late, but . . ." Fred had called Lou Jacobs, his roommate at Dunkin' Donuts University. Lou had ridden hard to the rescue—one and a half hours on the Expressway.

"You look as if you haven't slept in days, Fred," interrupted Lou. "This is what friends are for. Let me at those accounts! You put a pot of coffee on. I'll start with payroll, because you hired someone this month."

Dunkin' Donuts company policy calls for a closing every month, on the last Saturday, before noon. This way comparisons between shops are most valid. Dunkin' Donuts University stresses to all shop owners that the monthly closing grows more difficult as the year progresses. Errors get harder to find, and accuracy becomes ever more critical. There is, unfortunately, no set way to find errors, and even no set place to start. Lou chose payroll because it is one of the largest expenses and because of the new hire.

At 2:45 A.M. Lou woke Fred, who was dozing. "I think I've got it, Fred! It looks like you messed up on ad-justing the Salaries Expense account. I looked at the Payroll Register and compared the total to the Salaries Payable account. It didn't match! Remember, you hired Maria Sanchez on the 26th, so you have to increase *both* the Salaries Expense *and* the Salaries Payable lines, because she has accrued wages. Salaries Expense is a debit and Salaries Payable is a credit. You skipped the payable. Now, If you make this adjusting entry in the General Journal, the worksheet will balance."

Fred's sigh of relief turned into a big yawn, and they both laughed. "Thank heavens *you* stayed awake in Accounting class!," said Fred, with another huge yawn.

DISCUSSION QUESTIONS

1. How would the adjustment be made if Maria Sanchez received $6.50 per hour and worked 25 hours? Where would you place her accrued wages?
2. Fred bought six new uniforms for Maria Sanchez for $72 each, but forgot to post it to the Uniforms account. How much will the closing balance be off? In what way will it be off?
3. Why does Dunkin' Donuts require a monthly closing from each shop, no matter how much—or little—business each does?

LEARNING UNIT 5-3
The Post-Closing Trial Balance: Step 9 of the Accounting Cycle and the Cycle Reviewed

PREPARING A POST-CLOSING TRIAL BALANCE

The post-closing trial balance helps prove the accuracy of the adjusting and closing process. It contains the true ending figure for capital.

The last step in the accounting cycle is the preparation of a **post-closing trial balance,** which lists only permanent accounts in the ledger and their balances after adjusting and closing entries have been posted. This post-closing trial balance aids in checking whether the ledger is in balance. This checking is important to do because so many new postings go to the ledger from the adjusting and closing process.

The procedure for taking a post-closing trial balance is the same as for a trial balance, except that, since closing entries have closed all temporary accounts, the post closing trial balance will contain only permanent accounts (balance sheet). Keep in mind, however, that adjustments have occurred.

THE ACCOUNTING CYCLE REVIEWED

Table 5-1 on the next page lists the steps we completed in the manual accounting cycle for Clark's Word Processing Services for the month of May:

TABLE 5-1   STEPS OF THE MANUAL ACCOUNTING CYCLE

Steps	Explanation
1. Business transactions occur and generate source documents.	Cash register tape, sales tickets, bills, checks, payroll cards.
2. Analyze and record business transactions into a journal.	Called journalizing.
3. Post or transfer information from journal to ledger.	Copying the debits and credits of the journal entries into the ledger acounts.
4. Prepare a trial balance.	Summarizing each individual ledger account and listing those accounts to test for mathematical accuracy in recording transactions.
5. Prepare a worksheet.	A multicolumn form that summarizes accounting information to complete the accounting cycle.
6. Prepare financial statements.	Income statement, statement of owner's equity, and balance sheet.
7. Journalize and post adjusting entries.	Use figures in the adjustment columns of worksheet.
8. Journalize and post closing entries.	Use figures in the income statement and balance sheet sections of worksheet.
9. Prepare a post-closing trial balance.	Prove the mathematical accuracy of the adjusting and closing process of the accounting cycle.

Insight: Most companies journalize and post adjusting and closing entries only at the end of their fiscal year. A company that prepares interim reports may complete only the first six steps of the cycle. Worksheets allow the preparation of interim reports without the formal adjusting and closing of the books. If this happens, footnotes on the interim report will indicate the extent to which adjusting and closing were completed.

Insight: To prepare a financial report for April, the data needed can be obtained by subtracting the worksheet accumulated totals from the end of March from the worksheet prepared at the end of April. In this chapter, we chose a month that would show the completion of an entire cycle for Clark's Word Processing Services.

LEARNING UNIT 5-3 REVIEW

AT THIS POINT you should be able to

- ◆ Prepare a post-closing trial balance. (p. 171)
- ◆ Explain the relationship of interim reports to the accounting cycle. (p. 172)

SELF-REVIEW QUIZ 5-3

(The blank forms you need are on page 132 of the *Study Guide and Working Papers.*)

From the ledger on page 166, prepare a post-closing trial balance.

Solution to Self-Review Quiz 5-3

Quiz Tip: The post-closing trial balance contains only permanent accounts because all temporary accounts have been closed. All temporary accounts are summarized in the capital account.

	Dr.	Cr.
CLARK'S WORD PROCESSING SERVICES		
POST-CLOSING TRIAL BALANCE		
MAY 31, 19XX		
Cash	6 1 5 5 00	
Accounts Receivable	5 0 0 0 00	
Office Supplies	1 0 0 00	
Prepaid Rent	8 0 0 00	
Word Processing Equipment	6 0 0 0 00	
Accumulated Depreciation, Word Processing Equip.		8 0 00
Accounts Payable		3 3 5 0 00
Salaries Payable		3 5 0 00
Brenda Clark, Capital		14 2 7 5 00
Totals	18 0 5 5 00	18 0 5 5 00

COMPREHENSIVE DEMONSTRATION PROBLEM WITH SOLUTION TIPS

(The blank forms you need are on pages 133–141 of the *Study Guide and Working Papers.*)

From the following transactions for Rolo Co. complete the entire accounting cycle. The Chart of Accounts includes:

Assets	**Owner's Equity**
111 Cash	311 Rolo Kern, Capital
112 Accounts Receivable	312 Rolo Kern, Withdrawals
114 Prepaid Rent	313 Income Summary
115 Office Supplies	**Revenue**
121 Office Equipment	411 Fees Earned
122 Accumulated Depreciation, Office Equipment	**Expenses**
Liabilities	511 Salaries Expense
211 Accounts Payable	512 Advertising Expense
212 Salaries Payable	513 Rent Expense
	514 Office Supplies Expense
	515 Depreciation Expense, Office Equipment

We will use unusually small numbers to simplify calculation and emphasize the theory.

19XX

Jan.
1 Rolo Kern invested $1,200 cash and $100 of office equipment to open Rolo Co.
1 Paid rent for three months in advance, $300
4 Purchased office equipment on account, $50
6 Bought office supplies for cash, $40
8 Collected $400 for services rendered
12 Rolo paid his home electric bill from the company checkbook, $20
14 Provided $100 worth of services to clients who will not pay till next month
16 Paid salaries, $60
18 Advertising bill received for $70 but will not be paid until next month

Adjustment Data on January 31

a. Supplies on hand	$6
b. Rent Expired	$100
c. Depreciation, Office Equipment	$20
d. Salaries Accrued	$50

General Journal					Page 1
Date		Account Titles and Description	PR	Dr.	Cr.
19XX Jan	1	Cash	111	1 2 0 0 00	
		Office Equipment	121	1 0 0 00	
		R. Kern, Capital	311		1 3 0 0 00
		Initial Investment			
	1	Prepaid Rent	114	3 0 0 00	
		Cash	111		3 0 0 00
		Rent Paid in Advance—3 mos.			
	4	Office Equipment	121	5 0 00	
		Accounts Payable	211		5 0 00
		Purchased Equipment on Account			
	6	Office Supplies	115	4 0 00	
		Cash	111		4 0 00
		Supplies purchased for cash			
	8	Cash	111	4 0 0 00	
		Fees Earned	411		4 0 0 00
		Services rendered			
	12	R. Kern, Withdrawals	312	2 0 00	
		Cash	111		2 0 00
		Personal payment of a bill			
	14	Accounts Receivable	112	1 0 0 00	
		Fees Earned	411		1 0 0 00
		Services rendered on account			
	16	Salaries Expense	511	6 0 00	
		Cash	111		6 0 00
		Paid salaries			
	18	Advertising Expense	512	7 0 00	
		Accounts Payable	211		7 0 00
		Advertising bill, but not paid			

Solution Tips to Journalizing and Posting Transactions

Jan 1	Cash	Asset	↑	Dr.	$1,200
	Office Equipment	Asset	↑	Dr.	$ 100
	R. Kern, Capital	Capital	↑	Cr.	$1,300

2	Prepaid Rent	Asset	↑	Dr.	$ 300
	Cash	Asset	↓	Cr.	$ 300

4	Office Equipment Accounts Payable	Asset Liability	↑ ↑	Dr. Cr.	$ 50 $ 50
6	Office Supplies Cash	Asset Asset	↑ ↓	Dr. Cr.	$ 40 $ 40
8	Cash Fees Earned	Asset Revenue	↑ ↑	Dr. Cr.	$ 400 $ 400
12	R. Kern, Withdrawals Cash	Withdrawals Asset	↑ ↓	Dr. Cr.	$ 20 $ 20
14	Accounts Receivable Fees Earned	Asset Revenue	↑ ↑	Dr. Cr.	$ 100 $ 100
16	Salaries Expense Cash	Expense Asset	↑ ↓	Dr. Cr.	$ 70 $ 70
18	Advertising Expense Accounts Payable	Expense Liability	↑ ↑	Dr. Cr.	$ 70 $ 70

Note: All account titles come from the chart of accounts. When journalizing, the PR column of the general journal is blank. It is in the posting process that we update the ledger. The PR column in the ledger accounts tells us from what journal page the information came. After the title in ledger is posted to, we fill in the PR column of the journal telling us to what account number the information was transferred.

COMPLETING THE WORKSHEET
See worksheet on page 177.

Solution Tips to the Trial Balance and Completion of the Worksheet

After the posting process is complete from the journal to the ledger, we take the ending balance in each account and prepare a Trial Balance on the worksheet. If a title has no balance, it is not listed on the trial balance. New titles on the worksheet will be added below as needed.

ROLO CO
WORKSHEET
FOR MONTH ENDED JANUARY 31, 19XX

Account Titles	Trial Balance Dr.	Trial Balance Cr.	Adjustments Dr.	Adjustments Cr.	Adjusted Trial Balance Dr.	Adjusted Trial Balance Cr.	Income Statement Dr.	Income Statement Cr.	Balance Sheet Dr.	Balance Sheet Cr.
Cash	1 1 8 0 00				1 1 8 0 00				1 1 8 0 00	
Accounts Receivable	1 0 0 00				1 0 0 00				1 0 0 00	
Prepaid Rent	3 0 0 00			(B) 1 0 0 00	2 0 0 00				2 0 0 00	
Office Supplies	4 0 00			(A) 3 4 00	6 00				6 00	
Office Equipment	1 5 0 00				1 5 0 00				1 5 0 00	
Accounts Payable		1 2 0 00				1 2 0 00				1 2 0 00
R. Kern, Capital		1 3 0 0 00				1 3 0 0 00				1 3 0 0 00
R. Kern, Withdrawals	2 0 00				2 0 00				2 0 00	
Fees Earned		5 0 0 00				5 0 0 00		5 0 0 00		
Salaries Expense	6 0 00		(D) 5 0 00		1 1 0 00		1 1 0 00			
Advertising Expense	7 0 00				7 0 00		7 0 00			
	1 9 2 0 00	1 9 2 0 00								
Office Supplies Expense			(A) 3 4 00		3 4 00		3 4 00			
Rent Expense			(B) 1 0 0 00		1 0 0 00		1 0 0 00			
Depr. Exp., Office Equip.			(C) 2 0 00		2 0 00		2 0 00			
Acc. Dep., Office Equip.				(C) 2 0 00		2 0 00				2 0 00
Salaries Payable				(D) 5 0 00		5 0 00				5 0 00
			2 0 4 00	2 0 4 00	1 9 9 0 00	1 9 9 0 00	3 3 4 00	5 0 0 00	1 6 5 6 00	1 4 9 0 00
Net Income							1 6 6 00			1 6 6 00
							5 0 0 00	5 0 0 00	1 6 5 6 00	1 6 5 6 00

ADJUSTMENTS

Office Supplies Expense	Expense	↑	Dr.	$ 34	($40 − $6)
Office Supplies	Asset	↓	Cr.	$ 34	

On hand of $6 is *not* the Adjustment. Need to calculate amount used up.

Rent Expense	Expense	↑	Dr.	$100
Prepaid Rent	Asset	↓	Cr.	$100

Expired.

Depr. Exp., Office Equip.	Expense	↑	Dr.	$ 20
Accum. Dep., Office Equip.	Contra-Asset	↑	Cr.	$ 20

Do not touch original cost of equipment.

Salaries Expense	Expense	↑	Dr.	$ 50
Salaries Payable	Liability	↑	Cr.	$ 50

Owed but not paid.

Note: This information is on the worksheet but has *not* been updated in the ledger. (This will happen when we journalize and post adjustments at end of cycle.)

Note that the last four columns of the worksheet come from numbers on the Adjusted Trial Balance.

We move the Net Income of $166 to the Balance Sheet credit column since the capital figure is the old one on the worksheet.

PREPARING THE FORMAL FINANCIAL REPORTS

ROLO CO.
INCOME STATEMENT
FOR MONTH ENDED JANUARY 31, 19XX

Revenue:			
Fees Earned			$ 5 0 0 00
Operating Expenses			
Salaries Expense	$ 1 1 0 00		
Advertising Expense	7 0 00		
Office Supplies Expense	3 4 00		
Rent Expense	1 0 0 00		
Depreciation Expense, Office Equipment	2 0 00		
Total Operating Expenses		3 3 4 00	
Net Income		$ 1 6 6 00	

ROLO CO.
STATEMENT OF OWNER'S EQUITY
FOR MONTH ENDED JANUARY 31, 19XX

R. Kern, Capital, January 1, 19XX			$1 3 0 0 00
Net Income for January	$ 1 6 6 00		
Less Withdrawals for January	2 0 00		
Increase in Capital		1 4 6 00	
R. Kern, Capital, January 31, 19XX			$1 4 4 6 00

ROLO CO.
BALANCE SHEET
JANUARY 31, 19XX

Assets		Liabilities & Owner's Equity		
Cash	$1 1 8 0 00	Liabilities		
Accounts Receivable	1 0 0 00	Accounts Payable	$1 2 0 00	
Prepaid Rent	2 0 0 00	Salaries Payable	5 0 00	
Office Supplies	6 00	Total Liabilities		$1 7 0 00
Office Equipment $1 5 0 00		Owner's Equity		
Less Accum. Depr. 2 0 00	1 3 0 00	R. Kern, Capital		1 4 4 6 00
		Total Liabilities &		
Total Assets	$1 6 1 6 00	Owner's Equity		$1 6 1 6 00

Solution Tips to Preparing the Financial Reports

The reports are prepared from the worksheet. (Many of the ledger accounts are not up to date.) The Income Statement lists revenue and expenses. The net income figure of $166 is used to update the Statement of Owner's Equity. The Statement of Owner's Equity calculates a new figure for Capital, $1,446 (Beginning Capital + Net Income − Withdrawals). This new figure is then listed on the Balance Sheet (Assets, Liabilities, and a new figure for Capital).

JOURNALIZING AND POSTING ADJUSTING AND CLOSING ENTRIES

See journal at top of page 180.

Solution Tips to Journalizing and Posting Adjusting and Closing Entries

ADJUSTMENTS

The adjustments from the worksheet are journalized (same journal) and posted to the ledger. Now ledger accounts will be brought up to date. Remember, we have already prepared the financial reports from the worksheet. Our goal now is to get the ledger up to date.

CLOSING

Note Income Summary is a temporary account located in the ledger.

Goals:

1. Wipe out all temporary accounts in the ledger to zero balances.
2. Get a new figure for capital in the ledger.

	Date		Account Titles and Description	PR	Dr.	Cr.
			ADJUSTING ENTRIES			
	Jan.	31	Office Supplies Expense	514	3 4 00	
			Office Supplies	115		3 4 00
		31	Rent Expense	513	1 0 0 00	
			Prepaid Rent	114		1 0 0 00
		31	Depr. Expense, Office Equipment	515	2 0 00	
			Accum. Depr., Office Equip.	122		2 0 00
		31	Salaries Expense	511	5 0 00	
			Salaries Payable	212		5 0 00
			CLOSING ENTRIES			
Step 1 →		31	Fees Earned	411	5 0 0 00	
			Income Summary	313		5 0 0 00
Step 2 →		31	Income Summary	313	3 3 4 00	
			Salaries Expense	511		1 1 0 00
			Advertising Expense	512		7 0 00
			Office Supplies Expense	514		3 4 00
			Rent Expense	513		1 0 0 00
			Depr. Expense, Office Equip.	515		2 0 00
Step 3 →		31	Income Summary	313	1 6 6 00	
			R. Kern, Capital	311		1 6 6 00
Step 4 →		31	R. Kern, Capital	311	2 0 00	
			R. Kern, Withdrawals	312		2 0 00

Closing { Step 1, Step 2, Step 3, Step 4 }

STEPS IN THE CLOSING PROCESS

Where do I get my information for closing?

Step 1:   Close revenue to Income Summary.

Step 2:   Close individual expenses to Income Summary.

Step 3:   Close balance of Income Summary to capital. (This really is the net income figure on the worksheet.)

Step 4:   Close balance of withdrawals to capital.

All the journal closing entries (no new calculations needed since all figures are on the worksheet) are posted. The result in the ledger is that all temporary accounts have a zero balance.

Cash   111

Date	PR	Dr.	Cr.	Balance Dr.	Balance Cr.
1/1	GJ1	1,200		1,200	
1/1	GJ1		300	900	
1/6	GJ1		40	860	
1/8	GJ1	400		1,260	
1/12	GJ1		20	1,240	
1/16	GJ1		60	1,180	

Accounts Receivable   112

Date	PR	Dr.	Cr.	Balance Dr.	Balance Cr.
1/14	GJ1	100		100	

Prepaid Rent   114

Date	PR	Dr.	Cr.	Balance Dr.	Balance Cr.
1/1	GJ1	300		300	
1/31 Adj.	GJ2		100	200	

Office Supplies   115

Date	PR	Dr.	Cr.	Balance Dr.	Balance Cr.
1/6	GJ1	40		40	
1/31 Adj	GJ2		34	6	

Office Equipment   121

Date	PR	Dr.	Cr.	Balance Dr.	Balance Cr.
1/1	GJ1	100		100	
1/4	GJ1	50		150	

Accumulated Depreciation, Equipment   122

Date	PR	Dr.	Cr.	Balance Dr.	Balance Cr.
1/31 Adj.	GJ2		20		20

Accounts Payable   211

Date	PR	Dr.	Cr.	Balance Dr.	Balance Cr.
1/4	GJ1		50		50
1/18	GJ1		70		120

Salaries Payable   212

Date	PR	Dr.	Cr.	Balance Dr.	Balance Cr.
1/31 Adj.	GJ2		50		50

Rolo Kern, Capital   311

Date	PR	Dr.	Cr.	Balance Dr.	Balance Cr.
1/1	GJ1		1,300		1,300
1/31 Clos.	GJ2		166		1,466
1/31 Clos.	GJ2	20			1,446

Rolo Kern, Withdrawals   312

Date	PR	Dr.	Cr.	Balance Dr.	Balance Cr.
1/12	GJ1	20		20	
1/31 Clos.	GJ2		20	—	

Income Summary   313

Date	PR	Dr.	Cr.	Balance Dr.	Balance Cr.
1/31 Clos.	GJ2		500		500
1/31 Clos.	GJ2	334			166
1/31 Clos.	GJ2	166		—	

Fees Earned   411

Date	PR	Dr.	Cr.	Balance Dr.	Balance Cr.
1/8	GJ1		400		400
1/14	GJ1		100		500
1/31 Clos.	GJ2	500			——

Rent Expense   513

Date	PR	Dr.	Cr.	Balance Dr.	Balance Cr.
1/31 Adj.	GJ2	100		100	
1/31 Clos.	GJ2		100	——	

Salaries Expense   511

Date	PR	Dr.	Cr.	Balance Dr.	Balance Cr.
1/16	GJ1	60		60	
1/31 Adj.	GJ2	50		110	
1/31 Clos.	GJ2		110	——	

Office Supplies Expense   514

Date	PR	Dr.	Cr.	Balance Dr.	Balance Cr.
1/31 Adj.	GJ2	34		34	
1/31 Clos.	GJ2		34	——	

Advertising Expense   512

Date	PR	Dr.	Cr.	Balance Dr.	Balance Cr.
1/18	GJ1	70		70	
1/31 Clos.	GJ2		70	——	

Depreciation Expenses Office Equipment   515

Date	PR	Dr.	Cr.	Balance Dr.	Balance Cr.
1/31 Adj.	GJ2	20		20	
1/31 Clos.	GJ2		20	——	

These are all permanent accounts.

ROLO CO.
POST-CLOSING TRIAL BALANCE
JANUARY 31, 19XX

	Dr.	Cr.
Cash	1 1 8 0 00	
Accounts Receivable	1 0 0 00	
Prepaid Rent	2 0 0 00	
Office Supplies	6 00	
Office Equipment	1 5 0 00	
Accum. Dep., Office Equipment		2 0 00
Accounts Payable		1 2 0 00
Salaries Payable		5 0 00
R. Kern, Capital		1 4 4 6 00
TOTAL	1 6 3 6 00	1 6 3 6 00

Solution Tips for the Post-Closing Trial Balance

The Post-Closing Trial Balance is a list of the ledger *after* adjusting and closing entries have been completed. Note the figure for capital $1,446 is the new figure.

Beginning Capital	$1,300
+ Net Income	166
− Withdrawals	20
= Ending Capital	$1,446

Next accounting period we will enter new amounts in the Revenues, Expenses, and Withdrawal accounts. For now, the post-closing trial balance is only made up of permanent accounts.

SUMMARY OF KEY POINTS

Learning Unit 5-1

1. After formal financial reports have been prepared, the ledger has still not been brought up to date.
2. Information for journalizing adjusting entries comes from the adjustments section of the worksheet.

Learning Unit 5-2

1. Closing is a mechanical process that aids the accountant in recording transactions for the next period.
2. Assets, liabilities, and capital are permanent (real) accounts; their balances are carried over from one accounting period to another. Withdrawals, revenue, and expenses are temporary (nominal) accounts; their balances are *not* carried over from one accounting period to another.
3. Income Summary is a temporary account in the general ledger and does not have a normal balance. It will summarize revenue and expenses and transfer the balance to capital. Withdrawals do not go into Income Summary, because they are *not* business expenses.
4. All information for closing can be obtained from the worksheet or ledger.
5. When closing is complete, all temporary accounts in the ledger will have a zero balance, and all this information will be updated in the capital account.
6. Closing entries are usually done only at year end. Interim reports can be prepared from worksheets that are prepared monthly, quarterly, etc.

Learning Unit 5-3

1. The post-closing trial balance is prepared from the ledger accounts after the adjusting and closing entries have been posted.
2. The accounts on the post-closing trial balance are all permanent titles.

KEY TERMS

Adjusting journal entries Journal entries that are needed in order to update specific ledger accounts to reflect correct balances at the end of an accounting period.

Closing journal entries Journal entries that are prepared to (a) reduce or clear all temporary accounts to a zero balance, or (b) update capital to a new balance.

Income Summary A temporary account in the ledger that summarizes revenue and expenses and transfers its balance (net income or net loss) to capital. Does not have a normal balance.

Permanent accounts (real) Accounts whose balances are carried over to the next accounting period. Examples: assets, liabilities, capital.

Post-closing trial balance The final step in the accounting cycle that lists only permanent accounts in the ledger and their balances after adjusting and closing entries have been posted.

Temporary accounts (nominal) Accounts whose balances at end of an accounting period are not carried over to the next accounting period. These accounts — revenue, expenses, withdrawals — help summarize a new or ending figure for capital to begin the next accounting period. Keep in mind that Income Summary is also a temporary account.

BLUEPRINT OF CLOSING PROCESS FROM THE WORKSHEET

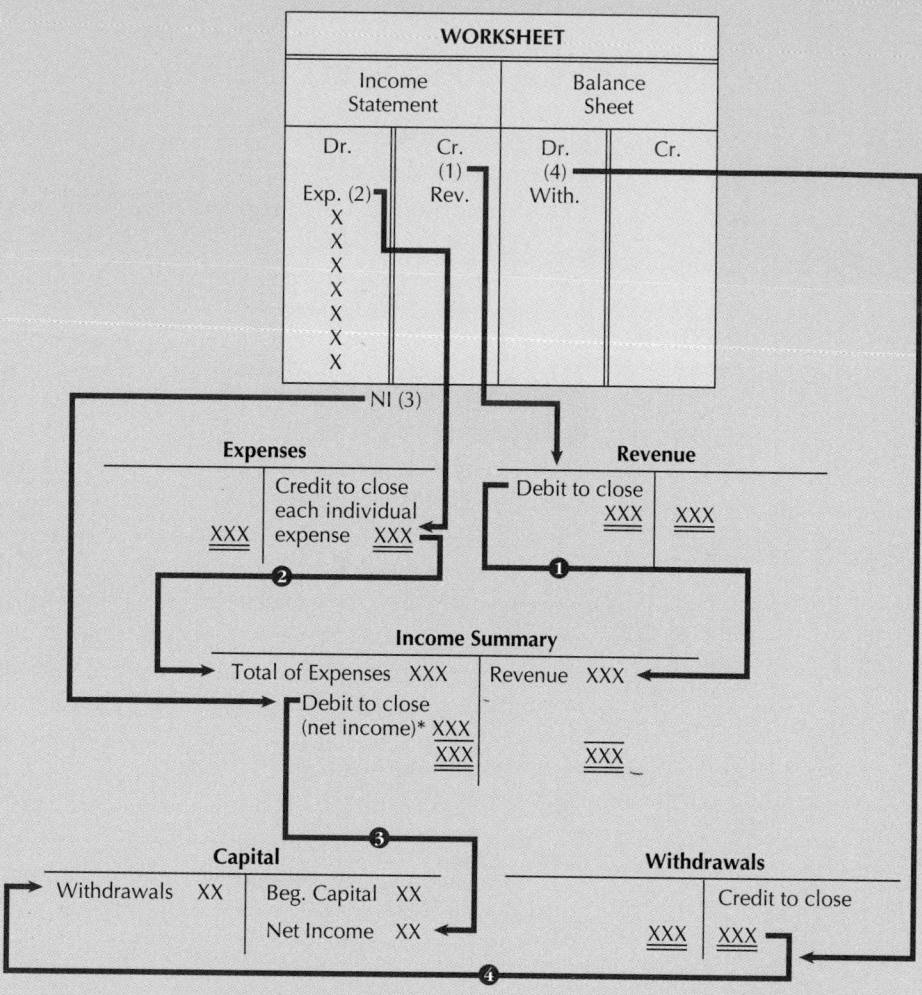

* If a net loss, it would be a Credit to close.

THE CLOSING STEPS

1. Close revenue balance to Income Summary.

2. Close each *individual* expense and transfer *total* of all expenses to Income Summary.

3. Transfer balance in Income Summary (Net Income or Net Loss) to Capital.

4. Close Withdrawals to Capital.

QUESTIONS, MINI EXERCISES, EXERCISES, AND PROBLEMS

Discussion Questions

1. When a worksheet is completed, what balances are found in the general ledger?

2. Why must adjusting entries be journalized even though the formal reports have already been prepared?

3. "Closing slows down the recording of next year's transactions." Defend or reject this statement with supporting evidence.
4. What is the difference between temporary and permanent accounts?
5. What are the two major goals of the closing process?
6. List the four steps of closing.
7. What is the purpose of Income Summary and where is it located?
8. How can a worksheet aid the closing process?
9. What accounts are usually listed on a post-closing trial balance?
10. Closing entries are always prepared once a month. Agree or disagree. Why?

Mini Exercises

(The blank forms you need are on pages 143–144 of the *Study Guide and Working Papers.*)

Journalizing and Posting Adjusting Entries

1. Post the following Adjusting Entries (be sure to cross-reference back to Journal) that came from the Adjustment columns of the worksheet.

Ledger Accounts Before Adjusting Entries Posted

Prepaid Insurance 115	Insurance Expense 510
10	

Store Supplies 116	Dep. Exp., Store Equip. 512
15	

Acc. Dep., Store Equip. 119	Supplies Expense 514
12	

Salaries Payable 210	Salaries Expense 516
	7

General Journal						Page 3
Date	Account Titles and Description	PR	Dr.		Cr.	
Dec. 31	Insurance Expense		6 00			
	Prepaid Insurance				6 00	
31	Supplies Expense		3 00			
	Store Supplies				3 00	
31	Depr. Exp., Store Equipment		7 00			
	Accum. Depr., Store Equipment				7 00	
31	Salaries Expense		4 00			
	Salaries Payable				4 00	

Steps of Closing and Journalizing Closing Entries

2.

```
                    Worksheet

            IS                      BS

    Dr.     Cr.             Dr.      Cr.
    (2)     Rev. (1)        Withd.   (4)
    E
    X
    P
    E
    N
    S
    E
    S
    ___    ___
           NI (3)
```

Goals of Closing:

1. Temporary accounts in the ledger should have a zero balance.
2. New figure for capital in closing.

Note: All closing can be done from the worksheet. Income Summary is a temporary account in the ledger.

From the above worksheet explain the four steps of closing. Keep in mind that each *individual* expense normally would be listed in the closing process.

Journalizing Closing Entries

3. From the following accounts, journalize the closing entries (assume December 31).

Mel Blanc, Capital 310		Gas Expense 510	
	30	5	

Mel Blanc, Withdr. 312		Advertising Exp. 512	
6		4	

Income Summary 314		Dep. Exp., Taxi 516	
		6	

Taxi Fees 410	
	18

Posting to Income Summary

4. Draw a T Account of Income Summary and post to it all entries from Question 3 that affect it. Is Income Summary a temporary or permanent account?

Posting to Capital

5. Draw a T Account for Mel Blanc, Capital, and post to it all entries from Question 3 that affect it. What is the final balance of the capital account?

Exercises

(The blank forms you need are on pages 145–147 of the *Study Guide and Working Papers*.)

5-1. From the adjustments section of a worksheet presented here, prepare adjusting journal entries for end of December.

Journalize adjusting entries

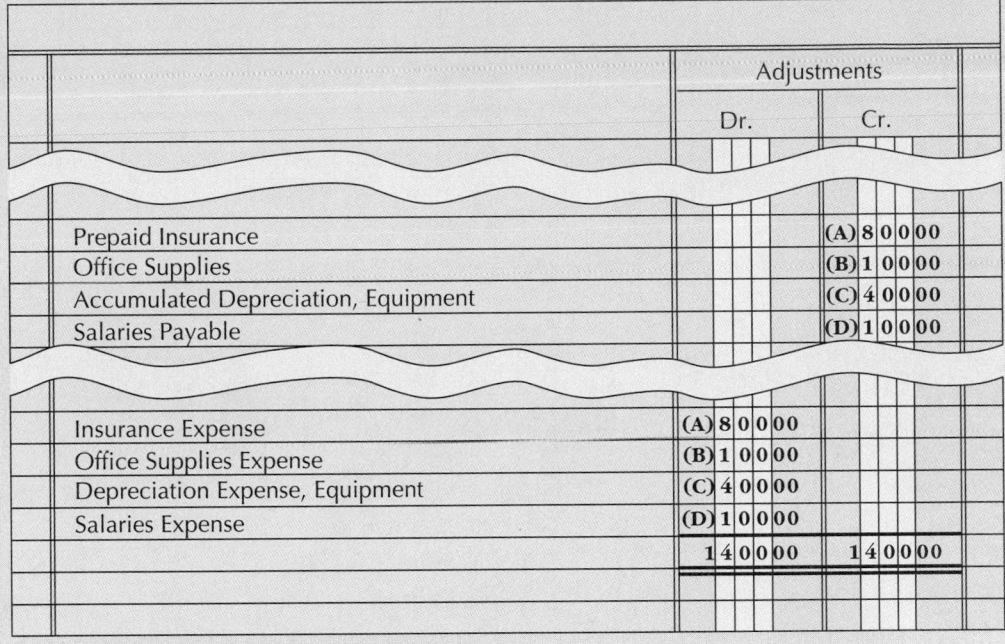

	Adjustments	
	Dr.	Cr.
Prepaid Insurance		(A) 8 0 0 00
Office Supplies		(B) 1 0 0 00
Accumulated Depreciation, Equipment		(C) 4 0 0 00
Salaries Payable		(D) 1 0 0 00
Insurance Expense	(A) 8 0 0 00	
Office Supplies Expense	(B) 1 0 0 00	
Depreciation Expense, Equipment	(C) 4 0 0 00	
Salaries Expense	(D) 1 0 0 00	
	1 4 0 0 00	1 4 0 0 00

5-2. Complete the following table by placing an X in the correct column.

Temporary vs. permanent accounts.

	Temporary	Permanent	Will be Closed
Ex. Accounts Receivable		X	
1. Income Summary			
2. A. Rose, Capital			
3. Salary Expense			
4. A. Rose, Withdrawals			
5. Fees Earned			
6. Accounts Payable			
7. Cash			

Closing entries.

5-3. From the following T accounts, journalize the four closing entries on December 31, 19XX.

J. King, Capital	Rent Expense
14,000	5,000

J. King, Withdrawals	Wage Expense
4,000	7,000

Income Summary	Insurance Expense
	1,200

Fees Earned	Dep. Expense, Office Equipment
33,000	900

Reconstructing closing entries.

5-4. From the following posted T accounts, reconstruct the closing journal entries for December 31, 19XX.

M. Foster, Capital

Withdrawals 100	2,000 (Dec. 1)
	700 Net Income

M. Foster, Withdrawals

100	Closing 100

Income Summary

Expenses 600	Revenue 1,300
700	Net Income 700

Salon Fees

Closing 1,300	1,300

Insurance Expense

50	Closing 50

Wage Expense

100	Closing 100

Rent Expense

200	Closing 200

Depreciation Expense, Equipment

250	Closing 250

Post-closing trial balance.

5-5. From the following accounts (not in order), prepare a post-closing trial balance for Wey Co. on December 31, 19XX. **Note:** These balances are **before** closing.

Accounts Receivable	$18,875
Legal Supplies	14,250
Office Equipment	59,700
Repair Expense	2,850
Salaries Expense	1,275
P. Wey, Capital	63,450
P. Wey, Withdrawals	1,500
Legal Fees Earned	12,000
Accounts Payable	45,000
Cash	22,000

Group A Problems

(The blank forms you need are on pages 148–165 of the *Study Guide and Working Papers*.)

5A-1. Given the following data for Marc's Consulting Service:

Review in preparing a worksheet and journalizing adjusting and closing entries.

Check Figure:
Net Income $4,600

MARC'S CONSULTING SERVICE TRIAL BALANCE JUNE 30, 19XX	Dr.	Cr.
Cash	18 0 0 0 00	
Accounts Receivable	6 0 0 0 00	
Prepaid Insurance	4 0 0 00	
Supplies	1 5 0 0 00	
Equipment	3 0 0 0 00	
Accumulated Depreciation, Equipment		9 0 0 00
Accounts Payable		10 0 0 0 00
M. Key, Capital		12 3 0 0 00
M. Key, Withdrawals	3 0 0 00	
Consulting Fees Earned		9 0 0 0 00
Salaries Expense	1 4 0 0 00	
Telephone Expense	1 0 0 0 00	
Advertising Expense	6 0 0 00	
	32 2 0 0 00	32 2 0 0 00

CH. 5 / THE ACCOUNTING CYCLE COMPLETED: ADJUSTING, CLOSING, AND POST-CLOSING TRIAL BALANCE

Adjustment Data:

a. Insurance expired $300.
b. Supplies on hand $700.
c. Depreciation on equipment $100.
d. Salaries earned by employees but not to be paid till July $200.

Your task is to

1. Prepare a worksheet.
2. Journalize adjusting and closing entries.

Journalizing and posting adjusting and closing entries. Preparing a post-closing trial balance.

Check Figure:
Post-closing Trial Balance $3,504

5A-2. Enter beginning balance in each account in your working papers from the trial balance columns of the worksheet. From the worksheet on page 190, (1) journalize and post adjusting and closing entries after entering beginning balance in each account in the ledger, and (2) prepare from the ledger a post-closing trial balance for the month of March.

Comprehensive review of the entire accounting cycle, Chapters 1–5.

5A-3. As the bookkeeper of Pete's Plowing, you have been asked to complete the entire accounting cycle for Pete from the following information:

19XX
Jan.

1 Pete invested $7,000 cash and $6,000 worth of snow equipment into the plowing company.
1 Paid rent for three months in advance for garage space, $2,000.
4 Purchased office equipment on account from Ling Corp., $7,200.
6 Purchased snow supplies for $700 cash.
8 Collected $15,000 from plowing local shopping centers.
12 Pete Mack withdrew $1,000 from the business for his own personal use.
20 Plowed North East Co. parking lots, payment not to be received until March, $5,000.
26 Paid salaries to employees, $1,800.
28 Paid Ling Corp. one-half amount owed for office equipment.
29 Advertising bill received from Bush Co. but will not be paid until March, $900.
30 Paid telephone bill, $210.

Check Figure:
Net Income $15,780

Adjustment Data:

a. Snow supplies on hand $400.
b. Rent expired $600.
c. Depreciation on office equipment $120.
   ($7,200 ÷ 5 yr. = $1,440/12 = $120)
d. Depreciation on snow equipment $100.
   ($6,000 ÷ 5 = $1,200/12 mo. = $100)
e. Accrued salaries $190.

POTTER CLEANING SERVICE
WORKSHEET
FOR MONTH ENDED MARCH 31, 19XX

Account Titles	Trial Balance Dr.	Trial Balance Cr.	Adjustments Dr.	Adjustments Cr.	Adjusted Trial Balance Dr.	Adjusted Trial Balance Cr.	Income Statement Dr.	Income Statement Cr.	Balance Sheet Dr.	Balance Sheet Cr.
Cash	40000				40000				40000	
Prepaid Insurance	52000			(A) 18000	34000				34000	
Cleaning Supplies	14400			(B) 10000	4400				4400	
Auto	272000				272000				272000	
Accum. Depr. Auto		86000		(C) 15000		101000				101000
Accounts Payable		22400				22400				22400
B. Potter, Capital		54000				54000				54000
B. Potter, Withdrawals	46000				46000				46000	
Cleaning Fees		468000				468000		468000		
Salaries Expense	144000		(D) 16000		160000		160000			
Telephone Expense	26400				26400		26400			
Advertising Expense	19600				19600		19600			
Gas Expense	16000				16000		16000			
	630400	630400								
Insurance Expense			(A) 18000		18000		18000			
Cleaning Supplies Expense			(B) 10000		10000		10000			
Depr. Expense Auto			(C) 15000		15000		15000			
Salaries Payable				(D) 16000		16000				16000
			59000	59000	661400	661400	265000	468000	396400	193400
Net Income							203000			203000
							468000	468000	396400	396400

Chart of Accounts

Assets
111 Cash
112 Accounts Receivable
114 Prepaid Rent
115 Snow Supplies
121 Office Equipment
122 Accumulated Depreciation,
      Office Equipment
123 Snow Equipment
124 Accumulated Depreciation,
      Snow Equipment

Liabilities
211 Accounts Payable
212 Salaries Payable

Owner's Equity
311 Pete Mack, Capital
312 Pete Mack, Withdrawals
313 Income Summary

Revenue
411 Plowing Fees

Expenses
511 Salaries Expense
512 Advertising Expense
513 Telephone Expense
514 Rent Expense
515 Snow Supplies Expense
516 Depreciation Expense,
      Office Equipment
517 Depreciation Expense,
      Snow Equipment

Group B Problems

(The blank forms you need are on pages 148–165 of the *Study Guide and Working Papers.*)

5B-1.

Review in preparing a worksheet and journalizing and closing entries.

MEMO

To: Ron Ear

From: Sue French

Re: Accounting Needs

Please prepare ASAP from the following information (attached) (1) a worksheet along with (2) journalized adjusting and closing entries.

Check Figure:

Net Income $3,530

MARC'S CONSULTING SERVICE
TRIAL BALANCE
JUNE 30, 19XX

	Dr.	Cr.
Cash	10 1 5 0 00	
Accounts Receivable	5 0 0 0 00	
Prepaid Insurance	7 0 0 00	
Supplies	3 0 0 00	
Equipment	12 9 5 0 00	
Accumulated Depreciation, Equipment		4 0 0 0 00
Accounts Payable		5 7 5 0 00
M. Key, Capital		15 1 5 0 00
M. Key, Withdrawals	4 0 0 00	
Consulting Fees Earned		5 2 0 0 00
Salaries Expense	4 5 0 00	
Telephone Expense	7 0 00	
Advertising Expense	8 0 00	
	30 1 0 0 00	30 1 0 0 00

Adjustment Data:

a. Insurance expired $100.
b. Supplies on hand $20.
c. Depreciation on equipment $200.
d. Salaries earned by employees but not due to be paid till July $490.

Journalizing and posting adjusting and closing entries. Preparing a post-closing trial balance.

Check Figure:

Post-closing Trial Balance $3,294

Comprehensive review of entire accounting cycle. Review of Chapters 1–5.

5B-2. Enter beginning balance in each account in your working papers from the trial balance columns of the worksheet. From the worksheet on page 193, (1) journalize and post adjusting and closing entries after entering beginning balances in each account in the ledger, and (2) prepare from the ledger a post-closing trial balance at end of March.

5B-3. From the following transactions as well as additional data, please complete the entire accounting cycle for Pete's Plowing (use the chart of accounts on page 191).

19XX

Check Figure:

Net Income $9,610

Jan.   1 To open the business, Pete invested $8,000 cash and $9,600 worth of snow equipment.
       1 Paid rent for five months in advance, $3,000.
       4 Purchased office equipment on account from Russell Co., $6,000.
       6 Bought snow supplies, $350.
       8 Collected $7,000 for plowing during winter storm emergency.
       12 Pete paid his home telephone bill from the company checkbook, $70.
       20 Billed Eastern Freight Co. for plowing fees earned but not to be received until March, $6,500.
       24 Advertising bill received from Jones Co. but will not be paid until next month, $350.
       26 Paid salaries to employees, $1,800.
       28 Paid Russell Co. one-half of amount owed for office equipment.
       29 Paid telephone bill of company, $165.

Adjustment Data:

a. Snow supplies on hand $200.
b. Rent expired $600.
c. Depreciation on office equipment $125.
   ($6,000/4 yr = $1,500 \div 12 = $125)
d. Depreciation on snow equipment $400.
   ($9,600 \div 2 = $4,800 \div 12 = $400)
e. Salaries accrued $300.

REAL WORLD APPLICATIONS

5R-1. Ann Humphrey needs a loan from the Charles Bank to help finance her business. She has submitted to the Charles Bank the following unadjusted trial balance. As the loan officer, you will be meeting with Ann tomorrow. Could you make some specific written suggestions to Ann regarding her loan report?

Cash in Bank	770	
Accounts Receivable	1,480	
Office Supplies	3,310	
Equipment	7,606	
Accounts Payable		684
A. Humphrey, Capital		8,000
Service Fees		17,350
Salaries	11,240	

POTTER CLEANING SERVICE
WORKSHEET
FOR MONTH ENDED MARCH 31, 19XX

Account Titles	Trial Balance Dr.	Trial Balance Cr.	Adjustments Dr.	Adjustments Cr.	Adjusted Trial Balance Dr.	Adjusted Trial Balance Cr.	Income Statement Dr.	Income Statement Cr.	Balance Sheet Dr.	Balance Sheet Cr.
Cash	172400				172400				172400	
Prepaid Insurance	35000			(A) 20000	15000				15000	
Cleaning Supplies	80000			(B) 60000	20000				20000	
Auto	122000				122000				122000	
Accumulated Depreciation, Auto		66000		(C) 15000		81000				81000
Accounts Payable		67400				67400				67400
B. Potter, Capital		248000				248000				248000
B. Potter, Withdrawals	60000				60000				60000	
Cleaning Fees		370000				370000		370000		
Salaries Expense	200000		(D) 17500		217500		217500			
Telephone Expense	28400				28400		28400			
Advertising Expense	27600				27600		27600			
Gas Expense	26000				26000		26000			
	751400	751400								
Insurance Expense			(A) 20000		20000		20000			
Cleaning Supplies Expense			(B) 60000		60000		60000			
Depreciation Expense, Auto			(C) 15000		15000		15000			
Salaries Payable				(D) 17500		17500				17500
			112500	112500	783900	783900	394500	370000	389400	413900
Net Loss								24500	24500	
							394500	394500	413900	413900

Utilities Expense	842	
Rent Expense	360	
Insurance Expense	280	
Advertising Expense	146	
Totals	26,034	26,034

5R-2. Janet Smother is the new bookkeeper who replaced Dick Burns, owing to his sudden illness. Janet finds on her desk a note requesting that she close the books and supply the ending capital figure. Janet is upset, since she can only find the following:

a. Revenue and expense accounts all were zero balance.

b. Income Summary

14,360 | 19,300

c. Owner withdrew $8,000.

d. Owner beginning capital was $34,400.

Could you help Janet accomplish her assignment? What written suggestions should Janet make to her supervisor so that this situation will not happen again?

YOU make the call

Critical Thinking/Ethical Case

5R-3. Todd Silver is the purchasing agent for Moore Co. One of his suppliers, Gem Co., offers Todd a free vacation to France if he buys at least 75 percent of Moore's supplies from Gem Co. Todd, who is angry because Moore Co. has not given him a raise in over a year, is considering the offer. Write your recommendation to Todd.

ACCOUNTING RECALL
A CUMULATIVE APPROACH

THIS EXAM REVIEWS CHAPTERS 1 THROUGH 5

Page 170 and 179 of the *Study Guide and Working Papers* has forms to complete this exam, as well as worked-out solutions. The page references next to each question identify what page to turn back to if you answer the question incorrectly.

PART 1 Vocabulary Review

Match the terms to the appropriate definition or phrase.

Page Ref.

(160)	1. Closing entries	A. Updates specific ledger accounts
(122)	2. Book value	B. A temporary account usually with debit balance
(161)	3. Income summary	
(121)	4. Contra-asset	C. A permanent account
(119)	5. Supplies	D. Lists only permanent account
(71)	6. Journal	E. Clears all temporary accounts

(172)	7. Post-closing trial balance	F. Book of original entry
(157)	8. Adjusting journal entries	G. A temporary account in the ledger
(81)	9. Ledger	H. Cost — accumulated depreciation
(11)	10. Withdrawals	I. Book of final entry
		J. Accumulated depreciation

PART II   True or False (Accounting Theory)

(161)   11. Income summary has a normal balance of a debit.

(161)   12. After closing, all temporary accounts will be cleared to zero balance.

(161)   13. Closing entries cannot be made from a worksheet.

(128)   14. The worksheet shows the beginning figure for capital.

(157)   15. Financial reports are prepared after journalizing and posting adjusting and closing entries.

CONTINUING PROBLEM

Tony has decided to end the Eldorado Computer Center's first year as of September 30, 19XX. Below is an updated chart of accounts.

Assets
1000   Cash
1020   Accounts Receivable
1025   Prepaid Rent
1030   Supplies
1080   Computer Shop Equip.
1081   Accum. Depr. CS Equip.
1090   Office Equipment
1091   Accum. Depr. Office Equip.

Liabilities
2000   Accounts Payable

Owner's Equity
3000   T. Freedman, Capital
3010   T. Freedman, W/D
3020   Income Summary

Revenue
4000   Service Revenue

Expenses
5010   Advertising Expense
5030   Utilities Expense
5050   Supplies Expense
5070   Postage Expense
5090   Depr. Exp. Office Equip.
5020   Rent Expense
5040   Phone Expense
5060   Insurance Expense
5080   Depr. Exp. C.S. Equip.

Assignment:

(See pp. 171–178 in your *Study Guide and Working Papers*.)

1. Journalize the adjusting entries from Chapter 4.
2. Post the adjusting entries to the ledger.
3. Journalize the closing entries.
4. Post the closing entries to the ledger.
5. Prepare a post-closing trial balance.

Valdez Realty

Reviewing the Accounting Cycle Twice

This comprehensive review problem requires you to complete the accounting cycle for Valdez Realty twice. This will allow you to review Chapters 1–5 while reinforcing the relationships between all parts of the accounting cycle. By completing two cycles, you will see how the ending June balances in the ledger are used to accumulate data in July. (The blank forms you need are on pages 180–200 of the *Study Guide and Working Papers.*)

The following chart shows the steps of the accounting cycle and the pages in the text where each step is covered. You can use it to review the accounting cycle before you start and as a reference while you are working.

Steps in the Accounting Cycle	Pages in Text Where Covered
1. Business transactions occur and generate source documents.	**1.** p. 72
↓	
2. Analyze and record business transactions into a journal.	**2.** p. 73
↓	
3. Post or transfer information from journal to ledger.	**3.** p. 81
↓	
4. Prepare a trial balance.	**4.** p. 87
↓	
5. Prepare a worksheet.	**5.** p. 117
↓	
6. Prepare financial statements.	**6.** p. 132
↓	
7. Journalize and post adjusting entries.	**7.** p. 157
↓	
8. Journalize and post closing entries.	**8.** p. 160
↓	
9. Prepare a post-closing trial balance.	**9.** p. 171

First, let's look at the chart of accounts for Valdez Realty (top of page 197).

On June 1 Juan Valdez opened a real estate office called Valdez Realty. The following transactions were completed for the month of June:

19XX
June   1   Juan Valdez invested $7,000 cash in the real estate agency along with $3,000 of office equipment.
         1   Rented office space and paid three months rent in advance, $2,100.

Valdez Realty
Chart of Accounts

Assets

111   Cash
112   Accounts Receivable
114   Prepaid Rent
115   Office Supplies
121   Office Equipment
122   Accumulated Depreciation,
       Office Equipment
123   Automobile
124   Accumulated Depreciation,
       Automobile

Liabilities

211   Accounts Payable
212   Salaries Payable

Owner's Equity

311   Juan Valdez, Capital
312   Juan Valdez, Withdrawals
313   Income Summary

Revenue

411   Commissions Earned

Expenses

511   Rent Expense
512   Salaries Expense
513   Gas Expense
514   Repairs Expense
515   Telephone Expense
516   Advertising Expense
517   Office Supplies Expense
518   Depreciation Expense,
       Office Equipment
519   Depreciation Expense,
       Automobile
524   Miscellaneous Expense

  1   Bought an automobile on account, $12,000.
  4   Purchased office supplies for cash, $300.
  5   Purchased additional office supplies on account, $150.
  6   Sold a house and collected a $6,000 commission.
  8   Paid gas bill, $22.
15   Paid the salary of the office secretary, $350.
17   Sold a building lot and earned a commission, $6,500. Payment is to
      be received on July 8.
20   Juan Valdez withdrew $1,000 from the business to pay personal
      expenses.
21   Sold a house and collected a $3,500 commission.
22   Paid gas bill, $25.
24   Paid $600 to repair automobile.
30   Paid the salary of the office secretary, $350.
30   Paid the June telephone bill, $510.
30   Received advertising bill for June, $1,200. The bill is to be paid on
      July 2.

Required Work for June:

1. Journalize transactions and post to ledger accounts.

2. Prepare a trial balance in the first two columns of the worksheet and complete the worksheet using the following adjustment data:

  a. One month's rent had expired.

  b. An inventory shows $50 of office supplies remaining.

  c. Depreciation on office equipment, $100.

  d. Depreciation on automobile, $200.

3. Prepare a June income statement, statement of owner's equity, and balance sheet.

4. From the worksheet, journalize and post adjusting and closing entries (p. 3 of journal).

5. Prepare a post-closing trial balance.

During July, Valdez Realty completed these transactions:

19XX

July
1 Purchased additional office supplies on account, $700.
2 Paid advertising bill for June.
3 Sold a house and collected a commission, $6,600.
6 Paid for gas expense, $29.
8 Collected commission from sale of building lot on June 17.
12 Paid $300 to send employees to realtor's workshop.
15 Paid the salary of the office secretary, $350.
17 Sold a house and earned a commission of $2,400. Commission to be received on August 10.
18 Sold a building lot and collected a commission of $7,000.
22 Sent a check for $40 to help sponsor a local road race to aid the poor. (This is not to be considered an advertising expense, but it is a business expense.)
24 Paid for repairs to automobile, $590.
28 Juan Valdez withdrew $1,800 from the business to pay personal expenses.
30 Paid the salary of the office secretary, $350.
30 Paid the July telephone bill, $590.
30 Advertising bill for July, $1,400. The bill is to be paid on August 2.

Required Work for July:

1. Journalize transactions in a general journal (p. 4) and post to ledger accounts.

2. Prepare a trial balance in the first two columns of the worksheet and complete the worksheet using the following adjustment data:

   a. One month's rent had expired.

   b. An inventory shows $90 of office supplies remaining.

   c. Depreciation on office equipment, $100.

   d. Depreciation on automobile, $200.

3. Prepare a July income statement, statement of owner's equity, and balance sheet.

4. From the worksheet, journalize and post adjusting and closing entries (p. 6 of journal).

5. Prepare a post-closing trial balance.

COMPUTERIZED ACCOUNTING APPLICATION FOR VALDEZ REALTY MINI PRACTICE SET (CHAPTER 5)

Closing Process and Post-Closing Trial Balance

Before starting on this assignment, read and complete the tasks discussed in Parts A, B, and F of the Computerized Accounting appendix at the back of this book and complete the Computerized Accounting Application assignments at the end of Chapters 3 and 4.

This comprehensive review problem requires you to complete the accounting cycle for Valdez Realty twice. This will allow you to review Chapters 1–5 while reinforcing the relationships between all parts of the accounting cycle. By completing two cycles, you will see how the ending June balances in the ledger are used to accumulate data in July.

PART A: The June Accounting Cycle

On June 1, Juan Valdez opened a real estate office called Valdez Realty.

Open the Company Data Files

1. Click on the Start button. Point to Programs; point to Simply Accounting; then click on Simply Accounting in the final menu presented. The Simply Accounting Open File dialog box will appear.

2. Insert your Student Data Files disk into disk drive A. Enter the following path into the **File name** text box: A:\student\valdez.asc

3. Click on the **Open** button, enter 6/30/97 into the **Using Date for this Session** text box; then click on the **OK** button. Click on the **OK** button in response to the message "The date entered is more than one week past your previous **Using** date of 6/1/97." The Company Window for Valdez will appear.

Add Your Name to the Company Name

4. Click on the Company Window Setup menu; then click on Company Information. The Company Information dialog box will appear. Insert your name in place of the text "Your Name" in the **Name** text box. Click on the **OK** button to return to the Company Window.

Record June Transactions

5. Open the General Journal dialog box; then record the following journal entries (enter "Memo" into the **Source** text box for each transaction; then enter the **Date** listed for each transaction):

1997
June
  1 Juan Valdez invested $7,000 cash in the real estate agency along with $3,000 in office equipment.
  1 Rented office space and paid three months rent in advance, $2,100.
  1 Bought an automobile on account, $12,000.
  4 Purchased office supplies for cash, $300.
  5 Purchased additional office supplies on account, $150.
  6 Sold a house and collected a $6,000 commission.
  8 Paid gas bill, $22.
  15 Paid the salary of the office secretary, $350.
  17 Sold a building lot and earned a commission, $6,500. Expected receipt 7/8/97.
  20 Juan Valdez withdrew $1,000 from the business to pay personal expenses.
  21 Sold a house and collected a $3,500 commission.
  22 Paid gas bill, $25.
  24 Paid $600 to repair automobile.

30 Paid the salary of the office secretary, $350.

30 Paid the June telephone bill, $510.

30 Received advertising bill for June, $1,200. The bill is to be paid on 7/2/97.

Print Reports

6. After you have posted the journal entries, close the General Journal; then print the following reports:

   a. General Journal (By posting date, All ledger entries, Start: 6/1/97, Finish: 6/30/97).

   b. Trial Balance As at 6/30/97.

   Review your printed reports. If you have made an error in a posted journal entry, see "Reversing an Entry Made in the General Journal Dialog Box" in Part C of the Computerized Accounting appendix for information on how to correct the error.

Record June Adjusting Entries

7. Open the General Journal; then record adjusting journal entries based on the following adjustment data (Source: Memo; Date: 6/30/97; Comment: Adjusting entry):

   a. One month's rent has expired.

   b. An inventory shows $50 of office supplies remaining.

   c. Depreciation on office equipment, $100.

   d. Depreciation on automobile, $200.

Print Reports

8. After you have posted the adjusting journal entries, close the General Journal; then print the following reports:

   a. General Journal (By posting date, All ledger entries, Start: 6/1/97, Finish: 6/30/97).

   b. Trial Balance As at 6/30/97.

   c. General Ledger Report (Start: 6/1/97, Finish: 6/30/97, Select All).

   d. Income Statement (Start: 6/1/97, Finish: 6/30/97).

   e. Balance Sheet As at 6/30/97.

   Review your printed reports. If you have made an error in a posted journal entry, see "Reversing an Entry Made in the General Journal Dialog Box" in Part C of the Computerized Accounting appendix for information on how to correct the error.

How to Close the Accounting Records

9. Simply Accounting has the capability of performing the first three steps of the closing process automatically.

   Done automatically by the program.

   Step 1: Clear Revenue Balance and Transfer to Income Summary.

   Step 2: Clear Individual Expense Balances and Transfer the Total to Income Summary.

   Step 3: Clear Balance in Income Summary and Transfer it to Capital.

   It does not have the capability of performing the fourth step of the closing process automatically, so you will need to record this closing journal entry.

   You need to record this closing entry.

   Step 4: Clear the Withdrawals Balance and Transfer it to Capital.

Record Entry to Close Withdrawals Account

10. Open the General Journal; then record the closing journal entry for Juan Valdez's Withdrawals account.

11. After you have posted the closing entry for Juan Valdez's Withdrawals account, close the General Journal to return to the Company Window.

Make a Backup Copy of June Accounting Records.

12. Click on the Company Window File menu; click on Save As; then enter the following new file name into the **File name** text box: A:\student\valdjune.asc

13. Click on the **Save** button. Note that the company name in the Company Window has changed from Valdez to Valdjune. Click on the Company Window File menu again; then click on Save As. Enter the following new file name into the **File name** text box:A:\student\valdez.asc

14. Click on the **Save** button. Click on the **Yes** button to confirm that you want to replace the existing file. Note that the company name in the Company Window has changed back from Valdjune to Valdez.

15. You now have two sets of company data files for Valdez Realty on your Student Data Files disk. The current data is stored under the file name valdez.asc. The backup data for June is stored under the file name valdjune.asc.

Important Information About the Closing Process.

16. The next instruction will ask you to advance the **Using** date to a new month. It is this procedure that instructs the program to complete the first three steps in the closing process. It is important that you make a backup copy of a company's data files prior to advancing the **Using** date to a new month. When you advance the **Using** date to a new month the program will permanently remove all journal entries from all Journals and all individual postings of journal entries to the general ledger accounts. You will not be able to display or print a General Journal or General Ledger report based on dates in the prior month, nor will you be able to record journal entries for dates in the prior month. If for some reason you need to print a General Journal or General Ledger, or record a transaction that occurred in the prior month, you can do so by using the backup copy of the company's data files that you created prior to advancing the **Using** date. See Part E of the Computerized Accounting appendix at the end of this book for information on how and when to use a backup copy of a company's data files.

How to Advance the Using Date

17. Click on the Company Window Maintenance menu; then click on Advance Using Date. Click on the **No** button in response to the question "Would you like to backup now?" Enter 7/1/97 into the **New Using Date** text box; then click on the **OK** button. Click on the **OK** button in response to the message "You have entered both a new calendar quarter and a new fiscal year. If you proceed, the program will zero all employees' quarter-to-date payroll information, move the current year's data into last year, close all Revenue and Expense account balances into the Retained Earnings integration account, and set the new fiscal year's dates. Print all employee reports and make a backup before proceeding."

18. The warning message stated that the revenue and expense accounts would be closed to an account titled Retained Earnings. This is the account that corporations use to accumulate earnings. Valdez Realty is a sole proprietorship, and the program will correctly close the revenue and expense accounts to Income Summary and close Income Summary to the Juan Valdez, Capital account even though the message used a different account name. The backup you created using the Save As method will serve as the backup suggested in the warning message.

Print a Post-closing Trial Balance

19. Print a post-closing Trial Balance As at 7/1/97.

Exit from the Program

20. Click on the Company Window File menu; then click on Exit to end the current work session and return to your Windows desktop.

Complete the Report Transmittal

21. Complete the Valdez Realty Report Transmittal for June located in Appendix A of your *Study Guide and Working Papers*.

PART B: The July Accounting Cycle

Open the Company Data Files

1. Click on the Start button. Point to Programs: point to Simply Accounting; then click on Simply Accounting in the final menu presented. The Simply Accounting Open File dialog box will appear.

2. Insert your Student Data Files disk into disk drive A. Enter the following path into the **File name** text box:A:\student\valdez.asc

3. Click on the **Open** button; enter 7/31/97 into the **Using Date for this Session** text box; then click on the **OK** button. Click on the **OK** button in

response to the message "The date entered is more than one week past your previous **Using** date of 7/1/97." The Company Window for Valdez Realty will appear.

Modify the Fiscal End Date

4. Click on the Company Window Setup menu; then click on Company Information. The Company Information dialog box will appear. Enter 7/31/97 as the new **Fiscal End** date; then click on the **OK** button.

Record July Transactions

5. Open the General Journal dialog box; then record the following journal entries (enter "Memo" into the **Source** text box for each transaction; then enter the **Date** listed for each transaction):

1997
July
   1 Purchased additional office supplies on account, $700.
   2 Paid advertising bill for June.
   3 Sold a house and collected a commission, $6,600.
   6 Paid for gas expense, $29.
   8 Collected commission from sale of building lot on 6/17/97.
  12 Paid $300 to send employees to realtor's workshop.
  15 Paid the salary of the office secretary, $350.
  17 Sold a house and earned a commission of $2,400. Expected receipt 8/10/97.
  18 Sold a building lot and collected a commission of $7,000.
  22 Sent a check for $40 to help sponsor a local road race to aid the poor. (This is not to be considered an advertising expense, but it is a business expense.)
  24 Paid for repairs to automobile, $590.
  28 Juan Valdez withdrew $1,800 from the business to pay personal expenses.
  30 Paid the salary of the office secretary, $350.
  30 Paid the July telephone bill, $590.
  30 Advertising bill for July, $1,400. The bill is to be paid on 8/2/97.

Print Reports

6. After you have posted the journal entries, close the General Journal; then print the following reports:

   a. General Journal (By posting date, All ledger entries, Start: 7/1/97, Finish: 7/31/97).

   b. Trial Balance As at 7/31/97.

   Review your reports. If you have made an error in a posted journal entry, see "Reversing an Entry Made in the General Journal Dialog Box" in Part C of the Computerized Accounting appendix for information on how to correct the error.

Record July Adjusting Entries

7. Open the General Journal; then record adjusting journal entries based on the following adjustment data (Source: Memo; Date: 7/31/97; Comment: Adjusting entry):

   a. One month's rent has expired.

   b. An inventory shows $90 of office supplies remaining.

   c. Depreciation on office equipment, $100.

   d. Depreciation on automobile, $200.

Print Reports

8. After you have posted the adjusting journal entries, close the General Journal; then print the following reports:

   a. General Journal (By posting date, All ledger entries, Start: 7/1/97, Finish: 7/31/97).

   b. Trial Balance As at 7/31/97.

   c. General Ledger Report (Start: 7/1/97, Finish: 7/31/97, Select All).

   d. Income Statement (Start: 7/1/97, Finish: 7/31/97).

   e. Balance Sheet As at 7/31/97.

Review your reports. If you have made an error in a posted journal entry, see "Reversing an Entry Made in the General Journal Dialog Box" in Part C of the Computerized Accounting appendix for information on how to correct the error.

Record Entry to Close Withdrawals Account

9. Record the closing journal entry for Juan Valdez's Withdrawals account.

10. After you have posted the closing entry for Juan Valdez's Withdrawals account, close the General Journal to return to the Company Window.

Make a Backup Copy of July Accounting Records

11. Click on the Company Window File menu; click on Save As; then enter the following new file name into the **File name** text box: A:\student\valdjuly.asc

12. Click on the **Save** button. Note that the company name in the Company Window has changed from Valdez to Valdjuly. Click on the Company Window File menu again; then click on Save As. Enter the following new file name into the **File name** text box: A:\student\valdez.asc

13. Click on the **Save** button. Click on the **Yes** button in response to the question "Replace existing file?" Note that the company name in the Company Window has changed back from Valdjuly to Valdez.

14. You now have three sets of company data files for Valdez Realty on your Student Data Files disk. The current data is stored under the file name valdez.asc. The backup data for June is stored under the file name valdjune.asc and the backup data for July is stored under the file name valdjuly.asc.

Advance the Using Date

15. Click on the Company Window Maintenance menu; then click on Advance Using Date. Click on the **No** button in response to the question "Would you like to backup now?" Enter 8/1/97 into the **New Using Date** text box; then click on the **OK** button. Click on the **OK** button in response to the warning message. The backup you created using the Save As method will serve as the backup suggested in the warning message.

Print a Post-closing Trial Balance

16. Print a post-closing Trial Balance As at 8/1/97.

Exit from the Program

17. Click on the Company Window File menu; then click on Exit to end the current work session and return to your Windows desktop.

Complete the Report Transmittal

18. Complete the Valdez Realty Report Transmittal for July located in Appendix A of your *Study Guide and Working Papers*.

BANKING PROCEDURES AND CONTROL OF CASH

THE BIG PICTURE

As Tony Freedman planned for the upcoming months, he thought about the problems he'd had managing cash. In particular, he often ran short of change and frequently lost track of small cash purchases. Eldorado Computer Center was currently using one checking account for paying bills and making deposits. Maybe new banking technology was the solution, Tony thought; so he prepared some questions to ask of a customer service representative at his bank:

◆ Should I have an ATM card for my business versus a small cash account kept on site?

◆ Is there an advantage to having an on-line machine for ATM or credit card transactions for my customers?

◆ Is there a benefit to banking on line?

The bank's customer service representative responded:

Using an ATM card certainly has advantages when you want to make deposits or withdraw cash outside of banking hours, and it beats standing in long teller lines during banking hours. However, an ATM card will not solve your problem of making change for customers at your place of business or small cash expenditures on an as-needed basis.

There is an advantage to having an on-line debit machine for your business. For a small monthly expense, your customers can make payments from their checking accounts without writing a check. The bank will clear the transaction only if the funds are available, which eliminates your possible expense of accepting non-sufficient checks. Some of our customers choose to handle their banking transactions via the computer. They like not having to leave their home or their office for most banking transactions — although there are still some security measures to be concerned with.

Even though technology offered some new options that Tony might make use of in the future, he decided that basic accounting was the answer to his current cash control woes. First he would reconcile his cash ledger accounts for the past four months with his bank statements. He also decided that it would be necessary to establish a petty cash fund.

Learning Objectives	◆ Depositing, writing, and endorsing checks for a checking account. (p. 205) ◆ Reconciling a bank statement. (p. 211) ◆ Establishing and replenishing a petty cash fund; setting up an auxiliary petty cash record. (p. 216) ◆ Establishing and replenishing a change fund. (p.220) ◆ Handling transactions involving cash short and over. (p. 220)

The internal control policies of a company will depend on things such as number of employees, company size, sources of cash, etc.

I n the first five chapters of this book, we analyzed the accounting cycle for businesses that perform personal services (for example, word processing or legal services). In this chapter, we turn our attention to Debbie's Wholesale Stationery Company, a merchandising company that earns revenue by selling goods (or merchandise) to customers. When Debbie found that her business was increasing, she became concerned that she was not monitoring the business's cash closely enough. To try and remedy the situation, Debbie and her accountant decided to develop a system of **internal controls.**

After studying the situation carefully, Debbie began a series of procedures that were to be followed by all company employees. These are the new company policies that Debbie's Wholesale Stationery Company put into place:

1. Responsibilities and duties of employees will be divided. For example, the person receiving the cash, whether at the register or by opening the mail, will not record this information into the accounting records. The accountant, for his part, will not be handling the cash receipts.

2. All cash receipts of Debbie's Wholesale will be deposited into the bank the same day they arrive.

3. All cash payments will be made by check (except petty cash, which will be discussed later in this chapter).

4. Employees will be rotated. This allows workers to become acquainted with the work of others as well as to prepare for a possible changeover of jobs.

5. Debbie Lawrence will sign all checks after receiving authorization to pay from the departments concerned.

6. At time of payment, all supporting invoices or documents will be stamped paid. That will show when the invoice or document is paid as well as the number of the check used.

7. All checks will be prenumbered. This will control the use of checks and make it difficult to use a check fraudulently without its being revealed at some point.

Now let's look at how Debbie's Wholesale implemented these policies.

LEARNING UNIT 6-1
Bank Procedures, Checking Accounts, and Bank Reconciliations

Before Debbie's Wholesale opened on April 1, 19XX, Debbie had a meeting at Security National Bank to discuss the steps in opening up and using a checking account for the company.

OPENING A CHECKING ACCOUNT

Purpose of a signature card.

The bank manager gave Debbie a signature card to fill out. The signature card included space for signature(s), business and home addresses, references, type of account, etc. Because Debbie would be signing all of the checks for her company, she was the only employee who had to sign the card. The bank keeps the signature card in its files. When checks are presented for payment, the bank checks it to validate Debbie's signature. This helps avoid possible forgeries.

Once the account was opened, Debbie received a set of checks and **deposit tickets** that were preprinted with the business's name, address, and account number (see Fig. 6-1). Debbie's Wholesale was to use the deposit tickets when it received cash or checks from any source and deposited them into the checking account.

In a deposit ticket, check amounts are listed separately along with the code number of city and bank on which they are drawn. The code can be found in the upper right corner of a check (see Fig. 6-3 on p. 208). The top part of the fraction (53-393) is known as the *American Banker's Association Transit Number:* 53 identifies the large city or state the bank is located in; 393 identifies the bank.

The lower part of the fraction (113) is split in two; 1 represents the First Federal Reserve District; 13 is a routing number used by the Federal Reserve Bank. This is the way the code number appears on a check.

Deposit tickets usually come in duplicate. The bank keeps one copy, and the company keeps the other so it can verify that the items making up the deposit have actually been deposited correctly. The bank manager told Debbie

FIGURE 6-1 A Deposit Ticket

CH. 6 / BANKING PROCEDURES AND CONTROL OF CASH

that she could give the deposits to a bank teller or she could use an automated teller machine **(ATM).** The ATM could also be used for withdrawing cash, transferring funds, or paying bills.

Often, Debbie makes her deposits after business hours, when the bank is closed. When this happens, she puts the deposit into a locked bag (provided by the bank) and places the bag in the night depository. The bank will credit Debbie's account in the morning, when the deposit is processed. All payments of money are by written check (except petty cash), and all money (checks) received is deposited in the bank account.

Many checking accounts earn interest. However, for our purposes, we will assume that the checking account for Debbie's Wholesale does not pay interest. Also assume that the checking account has a monthly service charge, and that there is no individual charge for each check written.

CHECK ENDORSEMENT

Checks have to be *endorsed* (signed) by the person to whom the check is made out before they can be deposited or cashed. **Endorsement** is the signing or stamping of one's name on the back left-hand side of the check.

This signature means that the drawer has transferred the right to deposit or cash the check to someone else (the bank). The bank can then collect the money from the person or company that issued the check.

Three different types of endorsement can be used (see Fig. 6-2). The first is a **blank endorsement.** A blank endorsement does not specify that a particular person or firm must endorse it. It can be further endorsed by someone else. The bank will pay the last person who signs the check. This type of endorsement is not very safe. If the check is lost, the person who finds it can sign it and get the money.

FIGURE 6-2
Types of Check Endorsement

Types of Check Endorsement

Debbie Lawrence

204109

A signature on the back left side of a check of the person or firm the check is payable to. This can be *further* endorsed by someone else– the bank will give the money to the last person who signs the check. This is not a very safe type of endorsement. If the check is lost, anyone who picks it up can sign it and get the money.

Blank Endorsement

Pay to the order of
Security National Bank.

Debbie's Wholesale Stationery Co.
204109

This is a safer type of endorsement, since the person or company signing (or stamping) the back of the check indicates the name of the company or person to whom the check is to be paid. Only the person or company named in the endorsement can transfer the check to someone else.

Full Endorsement

Payable to the order of
Security National Bank
for deposit only.

Debbie's Wholesale Stationery Co.
204109

This is the safest endorsement for businesses. Debbie's Wholesale stamps the back of the check so that it must be deposited in the firm's account. This limits any further use to the check (it can only be deposited in the specified account).

Restrictive Endorsement

FIGURE 6-3 A Company Check

Check stub is used to record journal entries.

No. 2		
April 7		$ 4,000 XX/100
TO Joe Francis Co.		19 XX
For: Equipment		

BAL. FOR'D	7,100	00
DEPOSITS	784	00
TOTAL	7,884	00
THIS PAYMENT	4,000	00
THIS PAYMENT		
BAL. FOR'D	3,884	00

Drawee is the bank at which the drawer has an account.

To whom check is payable or payee.

The word "and" should be used only to signify the decimal position (i.e., to distinguish between dollars and cents).

Debbie's Wholesale Stationery Company
1528 Belle Ave.
New York, NY 10022

No. 2
53-393
113

PAY TO THE ORDER OF   Joe Francis Co. $ 4,000 XX/100

4/7   19 XX

Four Thousand and   XX/100   DOLLARS

Debbie Lawrence

MEMO

⑈:0130393⑈: 204109   2   0000 4000 00

Date check written.

Check number.

Code number to identify bank.

Amount of check.

Signature (same as on the signature card) of drawer, or one who orders the bank to pay a sum of money.

When it processes the check, the bank imprints the amount it paid here. Note this should match what is written for amount of check.

A line is drawn after XX/100 to fill up space and ensure that the amount cannot be changed.

Check number (preprinted).

Debbie's Wholesale account number (preprinted).

Preprinted bank identification

1st 2 digits - 01- Designates Federal Reserve District (1–12).

3rd digit - 1- Identifies Federal Reserve Bank.

4th digit - 3- Identifies the state.
0393   - Identifies the bank.
Last digit - 2- Used for computer checking.

SECURITY NATIONAL BANK
LYNN, MASSACHUSETTS 01903

The second type of endorsement is a **full endorsement.** The person or company signing (or stamping) the back of the check indicates the name of the company or the person to whom the check is to be paid. Only the person or company named in the endorsement can transfer the check to someone else.

Restrictive endorsements are the third type of endorsement. This is the safest endorsement for businesses. Debbie's Wholesale stamps the back of the check, so that it must be deposited in the firm's account. This limits any further use of the check.

THE CHECKBOOK

When Debbie opened her business's checking account, she received checks. These checks could be used to buy things for the business or to pay bills or salaries.

Drawer—one who writes the check.
Drawee—one who pays money to payee.
Payee—one to whom check is payable.

A **check** is a written order signed by a **drawer** (the person who writes the check) instructing a **drawee** (the person who pays the check) to pay a specific sum of money to the **payee** (the person to whom the check is payable). Figure 6-3 (p. 208) shows a check issued by Debbie's Wholesale Stationery Company. Debbie Lawrence is the drawer; Security National Bank is the drawee; and Joe Francis Company is the payee.

Look at the check in Figure 6-3. Notice that certain things, such as the company's name and address and the check number, are preprinted. Other things you should notice are (1) the line drawn after $\frac{xx}{100}$ is to fill up the empty space and ensure that the amount cannot be changed and (2) the word "and" should be used only to differentiate between dollars and cents.

Figure 6-3 includes a check stub. The check stub is used to record transactions, and it is kept for future reference. The information found on the stub includes the beginning balance ($7,100), the amount of any deposits ($784), the total amount in the account ($7,884), the amount of the check being written ($4,000), and the ending balance ($3,884). The check stub should be filled out before the check is written.

If the written amount on the check doesn't match the amount expressed in figures, Security National Bank may either pay the amount written in words, return the check unpaid, or contact the drawer to see what was meant.

Many companies use checkwriting machines to type out the information on the check.

Many companies use checkwriting machines to type out the information on the check. This prevents anyone from making fraudulent changes on handwritten checks.

During the same time period, in-company records must be kept for all transactions affecting Debbie's Wholesale Stationery Company's checkbook balance. Figure 6-4 (p. 210) shows these records. Note that the bank deposits ($14,324) minus the checks written ($6,994) give an ending checkbook balance of $7,330.

MONTHLY RECORDKEEPING: THE BANK'S STATEMENT OF ACCOUNT AND IN-COMPANY RECORDS

This is just one format for a bank statement. Different banks use different formats.

Each month, Security National Bank will send Debbie's Wholesale Stationery Company a Statement of Account. This statement reflects all of the activity in the account during that period. It begins with the beginning balance of the account at the start of the month, along with the checks the bank has paid and any deposits received (see Fig. 6-5, p. 210). Any other charges or additions to the bank balance are indicated by codes found on the statement. All checks that have been paid by the bank are sent back to Debbie's Wholesale. These are called **cancelled checks** because they have been processed by the bank and are no longer negotiable. The ending balance in Figure 6-5 is $6,919.

BANK DEPOSITS MADE FOR APRIL

Date of Deposit	Amount	Received From
April 1	$8,000	Debbie Lawrence, Capital
4	784	Check — Hal's Clothing
16	1,880	Cash sales/Check — Bevans Company
22	1,960	Check — Roe Company
27	500	Sale of equipment
30	1,200	Cash sales

Total deposits for month: $14,324

CHECKS WRITTEN FOR MONTH OF APRIL

Date	Check No.	Payment To	Amount	Description
April 2	1	Peter Blum	$ 900	Insurance paid in advance
7	2	Joe Francis Co.	4,000	Paid equipment
9	3	Rick Flo Co.	800	Cash purchases
12	4	Thorpe Co.	594	Paid purchases
28	5	Payroll	700	Salaries

Total amount of checks written: $6,994

Cash/checks deposited	$14,324
Checks paid	− 6,994
Balance in company checkbook	$ 7,330

FIGURE 6-4
Transactions Affecting
Checkbook Balance

FIGURE 6-5 A Bank Statement

SECURITY NATIONAL BANK

Debbie's Wholesale Stationery Company
1528 Belle Ave.
New York, New York 10022

ACCOUNT NUMBER 20 410 9

CLOSING PERIOD 4/30/XX

AMOUNT ENCLOSED $ _____

RETURN THIS PORTION WITH YOUR PAYMENT IF YOU ARE NOT USING OUR AUTOMATIC PAYMENT PLAN   Address Correction on Reverse Side ☐

CHECKING ACCOUNT

ON	YOUR BALANCE WAS	NO.	WE SUBTRACTED CHECKS TOTALING	LESS SERVICE CHARGE	NO.	WE ADDED DEPOSITS OF	MAKING YOUR PRESENT BALANCE
	0	3	5,700.00	5.00	5	12,624.00	6,919.00

DATE	CHECKS • WITHDRAWALS • PAYMENTS	DEPOSITS • INTEREST • ADVANCES	BALANCE
4/1		8,000.00	8,000.00
4/2	900		7,100.00
4/4		784.00	7,884.00
4/7	4,000		3,884.00
4/9	800		3,084.00
4/16		1,880.00	4,964.00
4/22		1,960.00	6,924.00
4/25	5.00 SC		6,919.00

THE BANK RECONCILIATION PROCESS

The problem is that the ending bank balance of $6,919 does not agree with the amount in Debbie's checkbook, $7,330, or the balance in the cash amount in the ledger, $7,330. Such differences are caused partly by the time a bank takes to process a company's transactions. A company records a transaction when it occurs. A bank cannot record a deposit until it receives the funds, and it cannot pay a check until the check is presented by the payee. In addition, the bank statement will report fees and transactions that the company did not know about.

Debbie's accountant has to find out why there is a $411 difference between the balances and how the records can be brought into balance. The process of reconciling the bank balance on the bank statement versus the company's checkbook balance is called a **bank reconciliation.** Bank reconciliations involve several steps, including calculating the deposits in transit and the outstanding checks. The bank reconciliation usually is done on the back of the **bank statement** (see Fig. 6-6). However, it can also be done by computer software.

Deposits in Transit

In comparing the list of deposits received by the bank with the checkbook, the accountant notices that the two deposits made on April 27 and 30 for $500 and $1,200 were not on the bank's statement. The accountant realizes that in order to prepare this statement, the bank only included information about Debbie's Wholesale Stationery up to April 25. These two deposits made by Debbie were not shown on the monthly bank statement, since they arrived at the bank after the statement was printed. Thus, timing becomes a consideration in the reconciliation process. The deposits not yet added onto the bank balance are called **deposits in transit.** These two deposits need to be added to the bank balance

---

Deposits in transit: These unrecorded deposits could result if a deposit were placed in a night depository on the last day of the month.

FIGURE 6-6
Bank Reconciliation Using Back of Bank Statement

Keep in mind that both the bank and the depositor can make mistakes that will not be discovered until the reconciliation process.

CHECKS OUTSTANDING				
NUMBER	AMOUNT		1. Enter balance shown on this statement	6,919 : 00
4	594 : 00			
5	700 : 00		2. If you have made deposits since the date of this statement add them to the above balance.	
				1,700 : 00
			3. SUBTOTAL	8,619 : 00
			4. Deduct total of checks outstanding	1,294 : 00
			5. ADJUSTED BALANCE This should agree with your checkbook.	
TOTAL OF CHECKS OUTSTANDING	1,294 : 00			7,325 : 00

TO VERIFY YOUR CHECKING BALANCE
1. Sort checks by number or by date issued and compare with your check stubs and prior outstanding list. Make certain all checks paid have been recorded in your checkbook. If any of your checks were not included with this statement, list the numbers and amounts under "CHECKS OUTSTANDING".
2. Deduct the Service Charge as shown on the statement from your checkbook balance.
3. Review copies of charge advices included with this statement and check for proper entry in your checkbook.

IF THE ADJUSTED BALANCE DOES NOT AGREE WITH YOUR CHECKBOOK BALANCE, THE FOLLOWING SUGGESTIONS ARE OFFERED FOR YOUR ASSISTANCE.

- Recheck additions and subtractions in your checkbook and figures to the left.
- Make certain checkbook balances have been carried forward properly.
- Verify deposits recorded on statement against deposits entered in checkbook.
- Compare amount on each checkbook stub.

shown on the bank statement. Debbie's checkbook is not affected, since the two deposits have already been added to its balance. The bank has no way of knowing that the deposits are coming until they are received.

Outstanding Checks

Checks #4 and #5 are outstanding.

The first thing the accountant does when the bank statement is received is put the checks in numerical order (1, 2, 3, etc.). In doing so, the accountant notices that two payments were not made by the bank and two checks, no. 4 and no. 5, were not returned by the bank.

Checks outstanding are checks drawn by the depositor but not yet presented to the bank for payment by the payee.

Debbie's books showed that these two checks had been deducted from the checkbook balance. However, these **outstanding checks** were not yet presented to the bank for payment or deducted from the bank balance. When these checks do reach the bank, the bank will reduce the amount of the balance.

Service Charges

Debbie's accountant also notices a bank service charge of $5. This means Debbie's checkbook balance should be lowered by $5.

Nonsufficient Funds

An **NSF (nonsufficient funds)** check is a check that has been returned because the drawer did not have enough money in its account to pay the check. Accountants are continually on the lookout for NSF (nonsufficient funds) checks. If there is an NSF funds check, it means that there is less money in the checking account than was thought. Debbie's Wholesale will have to (1) lower the checkbook balance and (2) try to collect the amount from the customer. The bank would notify Debbie's Wholesale of an NSF (or other deductions) check by a **debit memorandum.** Think of a debit memorandum as a deduction from the depositor's balance.

Debit memorandum:
Deducted from balance

Credit memorandum:
Addition to balance

If the bank acts as a collecting agent for Debbie's Wholesale, say in collecting notes, it will charge Debbie a small fee, and the net amount collected will be added to Debbie's bank balance. The bank will send to Debbie a **credit memorandum** verifying the increase in the depositor's balance.

A journal entry is also needed to bring the ledger accounts of cash and service charge expense up to date. Any adjustment to the checkbook balance results in a journal entry. The following entry was made to accomplish this:

Adjustments to the checkbook balance must be journalized and posted. This keeps the depositor's ledger accounts (especially cash) up to date.

This charge could be recorded as a miscellaneous expense.

April	30	Service Charge Expense			5 00			
		Cash					5 00	
		Bank service charge for April						

Example of a More Comprehensive Bank Reconciliation

The bank reconciliation of Debbie's Stationery was not as complicated as it is for many other companies. Let's take a moment to look at the bank reconciliation for Monroe Company, which is based on the following:

Checkbook balance: $3,978.

Balance reported by bank: $5,230.

Recorded in journal check no. 108 for $54 *more* than amount of check when store equipment was purchased.

Bank collected a note ($2,000) for Monroe, charging a collection fee of $10.

DM: Remember, a debit memorandum is sent by the bank indicating a reduction in depositor's balance. Examples: NSF, check printing.

CM: A credit memorandum is sent by a bank indicating an increase in depositor's balance. Example: collecting a note.

A bounced check for $252 (NSF) has to be covered by Monroe. The bank has lowered Monroe's balance by $252 (see Fig. 6-7 on p. 214).

Bank service charge of $10.

Deposits in transit, $1,084.

Checks not yet processed by the bank:

Check	Amount
191	$204
198	250
201	100

MONROE COMPANY
BANK RECONCILIATION AS OF JUNE 30, 19XX

Checkbook Balance			Balance per Bank	
Checkbook Balance		$3,978	Bank Statement Balance	$5,230
Add:			Add:	
Error in recording			Deposits in Transit	1,084
Check no. 108	$54			$6,314
Proceeds of a note*				
less collection				
charge by bank	1,990	2,044	Deduct:	
		$6,022	Check no. 191..$204	
			198.. 250	
Deduct:			201.. 100	554
NSF Check	$252			
Bank Service				
Charge	10	262		
Reconciled Balance		$5,760	Reconciled Balance	$5,760

Note that every time an adjustment is made in the reconciliation process to the checkbook balance, a journal entry is needed. Monroe Company has to make the following journal entries:

Date		Account Title and Description	PR	Dr.	Cr.
19XX June	30	Cash		1990 00	
		Collection Expense		10 00	
		Notes Receivable*			2000 00
		Note collected			
	30	Cash		54 00	
		Store Equipment			54 00
		Error recording check no. 108			
	30	Accounts Receivable		252 00	
		Cash			252 00
		Alvin Sooth NSF check			
	30	Miscellaneous Expense		10 00	
		Cash			10 00
		Bank service charge			

* We will discuss Notes Receivable in a later chapter—for now, think of it as a kind of written Accounts Receivable.

FIGURE 6-7
Sample Debit Memorandum

Debit:	Monroe Co. 170 Roe Rd. Dallas, TX 75208	Valley Bank
2/4–10–60811		Date: 6/30/XX
NSF Check – Alvin Sooth		$252.00
	Approved JS	

FIGURE 6-7
Sample Debit Memorandum

Banking services on the Internet was cleared by U.S. regulators in 1995. Today banking by computer continues to expand.

TRENDS IN BANKING

Electronic Funds Transfer

Many financial institutions have developed or are developing ways to transfer funds electronically, without the use of paper checks. Such systems are called **electronic funds transfers (EFT).** Most EFTs are established to save money and avoid theft.

Automatic payroll deposits are an example of an EFT. This is how it works: The company asks its employees if they would like their paychecks deposited automatically into their checking accounts. Employees who agree to do this are asked to sign an authorization form. The bank, on receiving computer-coded payroll data, adds each worker's payroll amount to his or her checking account. Employees who do not sign the authorization continue to get paper checks that they must cash themselves.

Another good example is the automatic teller machine (ATM). In some states, ATMs now issue postage stamps, railroad tickets, and grocery coupons. **Debit cards** are still another example of an EFT. If a customer buys a service or a product with a debit card, the amount of the purchase is deducted directly from the customer's bank account.

Check Truncation (Safekeeping)

Some banks do not return cancelled checks to the depositor but use a procedure called **check truncation** or **safekeeping.** What this means is that the bank holds a cancelled check for a specific period of time (usually 90 days) and then keeps a microfilm copy handy and the original check is destroyed. In Texas, for example, some credit unions and savings and loan institutions do not send back checks. Instead, the check date, number, and amount are listed on the bank statement. If the customer needs a copy of a check, the bank will provide the check or a photocopy for a small fee. (Photocopies are accepted as evidence in Internal Revenue Service tax returns and audits.)

Truncation cuts down on the amount of "paper" that is returned to customers and thus provides substantial cost savings. It is estimated that over 60 million checks are written each day in the United States.

LEARNING UNIT 6-1 REVIEW

AT THIS POINT you should be able to

◆ Define and explain the need for deposit tickets. (p. 206)
◆ Explain where the American Bankers' Association transit number is located on the check and what its purpose is. (p. 206)

- List as well as compare and contrast the three common types of check endorsement. (p. 207)
- Explain the structure of a check. (p. 208)
- Define and state the purpose of a bank statement. (p. 210)
- Explain deposits in transit, checks outstanding, service charge, and NSF. (p. 217)
- Explain the difference between a debit memorandum and a credit memorandum. (p. 212)
- Explain how to do a bank reconciliation. (p. 213)
- Explain electronic funds transfer and check truncation. (p. 214)

SELF-REVIEW QUIZ 6-1

(The blank forms you need are on page 201 of the *Study Guide and Working Papers.*)

Indicate, by placing an X under it, the heading that describes the appropriate action for each of the following situations:

Situation	Add to Bank Balance	Deduct from Bank Balance	Add to Checkbook Balance	Deduct from Checkbook Balance
1. Bank service charge				X
2. Deposits in transit		X		
3. NSF check				X
4. A $50 check was written and recorded by the company as $60				
5. Proceeds of a note collected by the bank				
6. Check outstanding				

Solution to Self-Review Quiz 6-1

Situation	Add to Bank Balance	Deduct from Bank Balance	Add to Checkbook Balance	Deduct from Checkbook Balance
1				X
2	X			
3				X
4			X	
5			X	
6		X		

Quiz Tip: Deposits in transit are added to the bank balance while checks outstanding are subtracted from the bank balance.

LEARNING UNIT 6-2
The Establishment of Petty Cash and Change Funds

Petty Cash is an asset on the balance sheet.

Debbie realized how time-consuming and expensive it would be to write checks for small amounts to pay for postage, small supplies, etc., so she set up a **petty cash fund.** Similarly, she established a *change fund* to make cash transactions more convenient. This unit will explain how to manage petty cash and change funds.

SETTING UP THE PETTY CASH FUND

The *petty cash fund* is an account dedicated to paying small day-to-day expenses. These petty cash expenses are recorded in an auxiliary record and later summarized, journalized, and posted. Debbie estimated that the company would need a fund of $60 to cover small expenditures during the month of May. This petty cash was not expected to last longer than one month. She gave one of her employees responsibility for overseeing the fund. This person is called the *custodian.*

The check for $60 is drawn to the order of the custodian, cashed, and the proceeds turned over to John Sullivan, the custodian.

Debbie named her office manager, John Sullivan, as custodian. In other companies the cashier or secretary may be in charge of petty cash. Check no. 6 was drawn to the order of the custodian and cashed to establish the fund. John keeps the petty cash fund in a small tin box in the office safe.

Shown here is the transaction analysis chart for the establishment of a $60 petty cash fund, which would be journalized on May 1, 19XX as follows:

Petty Cash is an asset, which is established by writing a new check. The Petty Cash account is debited only once unless a greater or lesser amount of petty cash is needed on a regular basis.

Accounts Affected	Category	↑	↓	Rules
Petty Cash	Asset	↑		Dr.
Cash (checks)	Asset		↓	Cr.

	Date		Account Title and Description	PR	Dr.	Cr.
	19XX May	1	Petty Cash		60 00	
			Cash			60 00
			Establishment			

GENERAL JOURNAL — Page 1

Note the new asset called *Petty Cash,* which was created by writing check no. 6, reduced the asset Cash. In reality, the total assets stay the same; what has occurred is a shift from the asset Cash (check no. 6) to a new asset account called Petty Cash.

The Petty Cash account is not debited or credited again if the size of the fund is not changed. If the $60 fund is used up quickly, the fund should be increased. If the fund is too large, the Petty Cash account should be reduced. We will take a closer look at this when we discuss replenishment of petty cash.

MAKING PAYMENTS FROM THE PETTY CASH FUND

John Sullivan has the responsibility for filling out a **petty cash voucher** for each cash payment made from the petty cash fund. The petty cash vouchers are numbered in sequence.

FIGURE 6-8
Petty Cash Voucher

Petty Cash Voucher No. 1

Date: May 2, 19XX   Amount: $3.00
Paid To: Al's Cleaning
For: Cleaning

                                    Approved By: *John Sullivan*

                              Payment Received By: *Debbie Lawrence*

Debit Account No.: 619

Note that when the voucher (shown in Fig. 6-8) is completed, it will include:

◆ The voucher number (which will be in sequence)
◆ The date
◆ The person or organization to whom the payment was made
◆ The amount of payment
◆ The reason for payment: cleaning
◆ The signature of the person who approved the payment
◆ The signature of the person who received the payment from petty cash
◆ The account to which the expense will be charged.

The completed vouchers are placed in the petty cash box. No matter how many vouchers John Sullivan fills out, *the total of (1) the vouchers in the box and (2) the cash on hand should equal the original amount of petty cash with which the fund was established ($60).*

Assume that at the end of May the following items are documented by petty cash vouchers in the petty cash box as having been paid by John Sullivan:

19XX
May   2 Cleaning package, $3.00
         5 Postage stamps, $9.00
         8 First-aid supplies, $15.00
         9 Delivery expense, $6.00
        14 Delivery expense, $15.00
        27 Postage stamps, $6.00

John records this information in the **auxiliary petty cash record** shown in Figure 6-9 (p. 218). It is not a required record but an aid to John—an auxiliary record that is not essential but is quite helpful as part of the petty cash system. You may want to think of the auxiliary petty cash record as an optional worksheet. Let's look at how to replenish the petty cash fund.

HOW TO REPLENISH THE PETTY CASH FUND

No postings are done from the auxiliary book because it is not a journal. At some point the summarized information found in the auxiliary petty cash record is used as a basis for a journal entry in the general journal and eventually posted to appropriate ledger accounts to reflect up-to-date balances.

This $54 of expenses (see Figure 6-9) is recorded in the general journal (Fig. 6-10 on p. 219) and a new check, no. 17, for $54 is cashed and returned to John Sullivan. In replenishment, old expenses are updated in journal and ledger to show where money has gone. Auxiliary before replenishment. The petty cash box now once again reflects $60 cash. The old vouchers that were used are stamped to indicate that they have been processed and the fund replenished.

A new check is written in the replenishment process, which is payable to the custodian, cashed by Sullivan, and the cash placed in the petty cash box.

Date	Voucher No.	Description	Receipts	Payments	Postage Expense	Delivery Expense	Sundry Account	Sundry Amount
							Category of Payments	
19XX May 1		Establishment	60 00					
2	1	Cleaning		3 00			Cleaning	3 00
5	2	Postage		9 00	9 00			
8	3	First Aid		15 00			Misc.	15 00
9	4	Delivery		6 00		6 00		
14	5	Delivery		15 00		15 00		
27	6	Postage		6 00	6 00			
		Total	60 00	54 00	15 00	21 00		18 00

FIGURE 6-9 Auxiliary Petty Cash Record

Note that in the replenishment process the debits are a summary of the totals (except sundry, since individual items are different) of expenses or other items from the auxiliary petty cash record. Posting of these specific expenses will assure that the expenses will not be understated on the income statement. The credit to cash allows us to draw a check for $54 to put money back in the petty cash box. The $60 in the box now agrees with the petty cash account balance. The end result is that our petty cash box is filled, and we have justified which accounts the petty cash money was spent for. Think of replenishment as a single, summarizing entry.

Remember, if at some point the petty cash fund is to be greater than $60, a check can be written that will increase Petty Cash and decrease Cash. If the Petty Cash account balance is to be reduced, we can credit or reduce Petty Cash. But for our present purpose Petty Cash will remain at $60.

The auxiliary petty cash record after replenishment would look as follows (keep in mind no postings are made from the auxiliary):

AUXILIARY PETTY CASH RECORD

Date	Voucher No.	Description	Receipts	Payments	Postage Expense	Delivery Expense	Sundry Account	Sundry Amount
							Category of Payments	
19XX May 1		Establishment	60 00					
2	1	Cleaning		3 00			Cleaning	3 00
5	2	Postage		9 00	9 00			
8	3	First Aid		15 00			Misc.	15 00
9	4	Delivery		6 00		6 00		
14	5	Delivery		15 00		15 00		
27	6	Postage		6 00	6 00			
		Total	60 00	54 00	15 00	21 00		18 00
		Ending Balance		6 00				
			60 00	60 00				
		Ending Balance	6 00					
31		Replenishment	54 00					
31		Balance (New)	60 00					

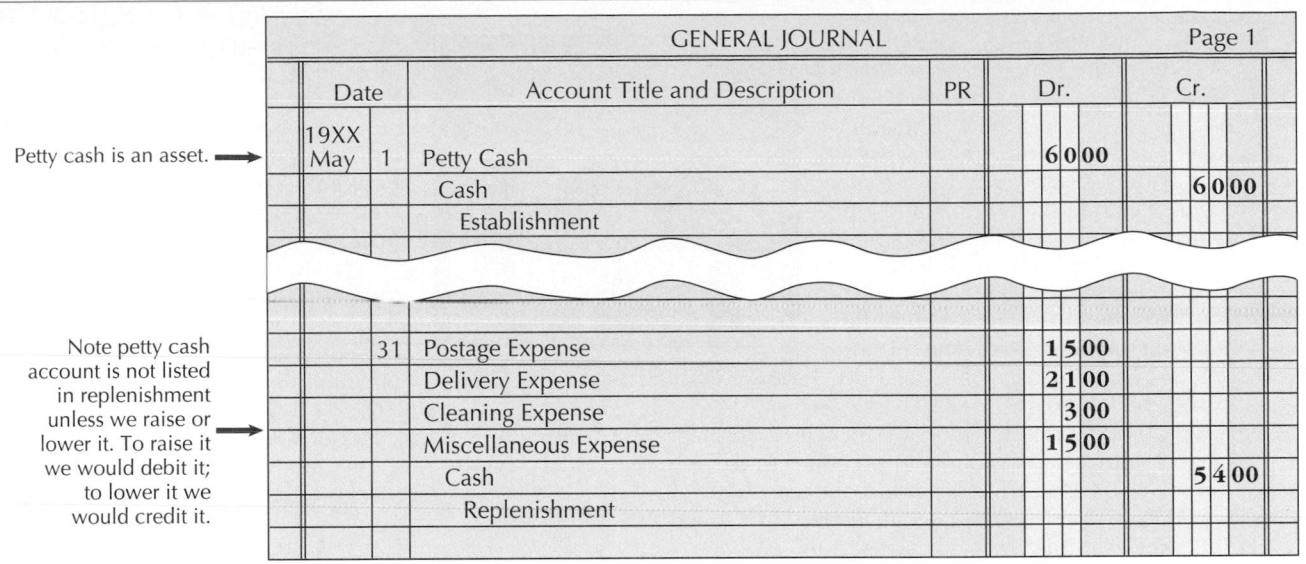

General Journal table:

	Date		Account Title and Description	PR	Dr.	Cr.
			GENERAL JOURNAL			**Page 1**
Petty cash is an asset. →	19XX May	1	Petty Cash		6 0 00	
			Cash			6 0 00
			Establishment			
Note petty cash account is not listed in replenishment unless we raise or lower it. To raise it we would debit it; to lower it we would credit it. →		31	Postage Expense		1 5 00	
			Delivery Expense		2 1 00	
			Cleaning Expense		3 00	
			Miscellaneous Expense		1 5 00	
			Cash			5 4 00
			Replenishment			

FIGURE 6-10 Establishment and Replenishment of Petty Cash Fund

Figure 6-11, below, may help you put the sequence together.

Before concluding this unit, let's look at how Debbie will handle setting up a change fund and problems with cash shortages and overages.

SETTING UP A CHANGE FUND AND INSIGHT INTO CASH SHORT AND OVER

If a company like Debbie's Stationery expects to have many cash transactions occurring, it may be a good idea to establish a **change fund.** This is a fund that is placed in the cash register drawer and used to make change for customers who pay cash. Debbie decides to put $120 in the change fund, made up of various denominations of bills and coins. Let's look at a transaction analysis chart and the journal entry (on p. 220) for this sort of procedure.

FIGURE 6-11 Which transactions involve petty cash and how to record them.

	Date		Description	New Check Written	Petty Cash Voucher Prepared	Recorded in Auxiliary Petty Cash Record	
	19XX Jan.	1	Establishment of petty cash for $60	X		X	} Dr. petty cash Cr. cash
Has nothing to do with petty cash (amounts too great). →		2	Paid salaries, $2,000	X			
		10	Paid $10 from petty cash for Band-Aids		X	X	} No journal entries
In this step the old expenses are listed in general journal and a new check is written to → replenish. All old vouchers removed from petty cash box.		19	Paid $8 from petty cash for postage		X	X	
		24	Paid light bill, $200	X			
		29	Replenishment of petty cash to $60	X		X	} Dr. individual expenses Cr. cash

unkin' Donuts is urging its shop owners to get rid of their cash registers and switch to a new IBM point-of-sale terminal. With these new machines, clerks just use a touch screen to punch in the number and type of items bought. This is faster than using the old cash registers and easier to learn. Training staff to handle cash is a critical component of a cash business like Dunkin' Donuts. Every sale must be recorded—and recorded correctly. Cash control is built into the new IBM system, which also provides the owners with information that will help them spot problems and track trends.

Fred was pleased when he heard about the new system at the company's annual convention in Orlando, Florida. Register training was a recurring problem for him and for most store owners. Now the terminals in the store would be easier to learn. They are linked, so he would be able to see consolidated data quickly. But the chore of closing out the cash drawer at the end of a shift remained. And it was still a critical control point.

"I gotta remember that," said Fred, thinking back to the convention, "when I explain how to close out her cash register drawer to Sally again. Even though she messes up my Cash Summary almost every day, getting

TIME TO CHECK THAT CASH

mad sure hasn't helped. Maybe if I go through it with her step-by-step." Fred had spent hours figuring out a discrepancy between the cash in the drawer and the register tape. Sally had forgotten to void a mistaken entry for $99.99. Fred had first suspected that Sally had made a huge error in counting change.

Nodding happily to himself, Fred treated himself to one of his glazed donuts. Doing the daily Cash Summary normally gave Fred a sense of accomplishment (when Sally wasn't working). And the monthly chore of reconciling the shop's bank account had been no problem. The cash on the monthly financials that he submitted to Dwayne were right on the money.

DISCUSSION QUESTIONS

1. How would Fred catch a discrepancy in the cash account?
2. How would Fred record a loss?
3. Why is cash register training so important to a service business like Fred's?
4. Why does Dunkin' Donuts invest time, money, and effort in investigating new cash handling systems like the IBM point-of-sale terminals?

Accounts Affected	Category	↑	↓	Dr./Cr.
Change Fund	Asset	↑		Dr.
Cash	Asset		↓	Cr.

April	1	Change Fund		1 2 0 00		
		Cash			1 2 0 00	
		Establish change fund				

At the close of the business day Debbie will place the amount of the change fund back in the safe in the office. She will set up the change fund (the same $120) in the appropriate denominations for the next business day. She will deposit in the bank the *remainder* of the cash taken in for the day.

Now, in the next section, we'll look at how to record errors that are made in making change, called **cash short and over.**

Cash Short and Over

Beg. change fund
+ Cash register total
= Cash should have on hand
− Counted cash
= Shortage or overage of cash

In a local pizza shop the total sales for the day did not match the amount of cash on hand. Errors often happen in making change. To record and summarize the differences in cash, an account called *cash short and over* is used. This account will record both overages (too much money) and shortages (not enough money). Lets first look at the account (in T account form).

Cash Short and Over

Dr.	Cr.
shortage	overage

All shortages will be recorded as debits and all overages will be recorded as credits. This account is temporary. If the ending balance of the account is a debit (a shortage) it is considered a miscellaneous expense that would be reported on the income statement. If the balance of the account is a credit (an overage) it is considered as other income reported on the income statement. Let's look at how the cash short and over account could be used to record shortages or overages in sales as well as in the petty cash process.

Example 1: Shortages and Overages in Sales:

Dec. 5 pizza shop rang up sales of $560 for the day but only had $530 in cash.

Accounts Affected	Category	↑ ↓	Dr./Cr.
Cash	Asset	↑	Debit $530
Cash Short and Over	Misc. Exp.	↑	Debit $30
Sales	Revenue	↑	Credit $560

The journal entry would look as follows:

Dec	5	Cash		5 3 0 00	
		Cash Short and Over		3 0 00	
		Sales			5 6 0 00
		Cash shortage			

Note the shortage $30 is a debit and would be recorded on the income statement as a miscellaneous expense.

What would the entry look like if the pizza shop showed a $50 overage?

Accounts Affected	Category	↑ ↓	Dr./Cr.
Cash	Asset	↑	Debit $610
Cash Short and Over	Other Income	↑	Credit $50
Sales	Revenue	↑	Credit $560

The journal entry would be as follows:

Dec	5	Cash		6 1 0	
		Cash Short and Over			5 0 00
		Sales			5 6 0 00
		Cash shortage			

Note the cash short and over account would be reported as other income on the income statement. Now let's look at how to use this cash short and over account to record petty cash transactions.

Example 2: Cash Short and Over in Petty Cash

A local computer company had established petty cash for $200. Today, November 30, the petty cash box had $160 in vouchers as well as $32 in coin and currency. What would be the journal entry to replenish petty cash? Assume the vouchers were made up of $90 for postage and $70 for supplies expense.

If you add up the vouchers and cash in the box, cash is short by $8.

Accounts Affected	Category	↑	↓	Dr./Cr.
Postage Expense	Expense	↑		Debit $90
Supplies Expense	Expense	↑		Debit $70
Cash Short and Over	Misc. Expense	↑		Debit $8
Cash	Asset		↓	Credit $168

The journal entry is as follows:

Nov	8	Postage Expense			9 0 00			
		Supplies Expense			7 0 00			
		Cash Short and Over			8 00			
		Cash					1 6 8 00	

If there had been an overage, the cash short and over would be a credit as other income. Note in Self-Review Quiz 6-2 the Solution shows how a fund shortage would be recorded in the auxiliary record.

LEARNING UNIT 6-2 REVIEW

AT THIS POINT you should be able to

◆ State the purpose of a petty cash fund. (p. 216)
◆ Prepare a journal entry to establish a petty cash fund. (p. 216)
◆ Prepare a petty cash voucher. (p. 217)
◆ Explain the relationship of the auxiliary petty cash record to the petty cash process. (p. 217)
◆ Prepare a journal entry to replenish Petty Cash to its original amount. (p. 218)
◆ Explain why individual expenses are debited in the replenishment process. (p. 218)
◆ Explain how a change fund is established. (p. 220)
◆ Explain how Cash Short and Over could be a miscellaneous expense. (p. 221)

SELF-REVIEW QUIZ 6-2

(The blank forms you need are on pages 201–202 of the *Study Guide and Working Papers.*)

As the custodian of the petty cash fund it is your task to prepare entries to establish the fund on October 1, as well as to replenish the fund on October 31. Please keep an auxiliary petty cash record.

19XX
Oct. 1 Establish petty cash fund for $90, check no. 8.
      5 Voucher 11, delivery expense, $21.
      9 Voucher 12, delivery expense, $15.
     10 Voucher 13, office repair expense, $24.
     17 Voucher 14, general expense, $12.
     30 Replenishment of petty cash fund, $78, check no. 108. (Check would be payable to the custodian.)

Solution to Self-Review Quiz 6-2

GENERAL JOURNAL
Page 6

Date		Account Title and Description	PR	Dr.	Cr.
19XX Oct.	1	Petty Cash		90 00	
		Cash			90 00
		Establishment, Check 8			

Date		Account Title and Description	PR	Dr.	Cr.
	31	Delivery Expense		36 00	
		General Expense		12 00	
		Office Repair Expense		24 00	
		Cash Short and Over		6 00	
		Cash			78 00
		Replenishment, Check 108			

AUXILIARY PETTY CASH RECORD

Date	Voucher No.	Description	Receipts	Payments	Delivery Expense	General Expense	Sundry Account	Sundry Amount
19XX Oct. 1		Establishment	90 00					
5	11	Delivery		21 00	21 00			
9	12	Delivery		15 00	15 00			
10	13	Repairs		24 00			Office Repair	24 00
17	14	General		12 00		12 00		
25		Fund Shortage		6 00			Cash Short and Over	6 00
		Totals	90 00	78 00	36 00	12 00		30 00
		Ending Balance		12 00				
				90 00				
30		Ending Balance	12 00					
31		Replenishment	78 00					
Nov. 1		New Balance	90 00					

Quiz Tip:

How to calculate shortage:

$21 + $15 + $24 + $12 = $72 of vouchers

Replenished with $78 check. Thus there was a $6 shortage.

Note how cash short and over was entered in the auxiliary petty cash record.

SUMMARY OF KEY POINTS

Learning Unit 6-1

1. Restrictive endorsement limits any further negotiation of a check.

2. Check stubs are filled out before a check is written.

3. The payee is the person the check is payable to. The drawer is the one who orders the bank to pay a sum of money. The drawee is the bank that the drawer has an account with.

4. The process of reconciling the bank balance with the company's balance is called the bank reconciliation. The timing of deposits, when the bank statement was issued, etc., often results in differences between the bank balance and the checkbook balance.

5. Deposits in transit are added to the bank balance.

6. Checks outstanding are subtracted from the bank balance.

7. NSF means that a check has insufficient funds to be credited (deposited) to a checking account; therefore, the amount is not included in the bank balance and thus the checking account balance is lowered.

8. When a bank debits your account they are deducting an amount from your balance. A credit to the account is an increase to your balance.

9. All adjustments to the checkbook balance require journal entries.

Learning Unit 6-2

1. Petty Cash is an asset found on the balance sheet.

2. The auxiliary petty cash record is an auxiliary book; thus no postings are done from this book. Think of it as an optional worksheet.

3. When a petty cash fund is established, the amount is entered as a debit to Petty Cash and a credit to Cash.

4. At time of replenishment of the petty cash fund, all expenses are debited (by category) and a credit to Cash (a new check) results. This replenishment, when journalized and posted, updates the ledger from the journal.

5. The only time the Petty Cash account is used is to establish the fund to begin with or bring the fund to a higher or lower level. If the petty cash level is deemed sufficient, all replenishments will debit specific expenses and credit cash (new check written). The asset Petty Cash account balance will remain unchanged.

6. A change fund is an asset that is used to make change for customers.

7. Cash Short and Over is an account that is either a miscellaneous expense or miscellaneous income, depending on whether the ending balance is shortage or overage.

KEY TERMS

ATM Automatic teller machine.

Auxiliary petty cash record A supplementary record for summarizing petty cash information.

Bank reconciliation This is the process of reconciling the checkbook balance with the bank balance given on the bank statement.

Bank statement A report sent by a bank to a customer indicating the previous balance, individual checks processed, individual deposits received, service charges, and ending bank balance.

Cancelled check A check that has been processed by a bank and is no longer negotiable.

Cash Short and Over The account that records cash shortages and overages. If ending balance is a debit, it is recorded on the income statement as a miscellaneous expense; if it is a credit, it is recorded as miscellaneous income.

Change fund Fund made up of various denominations that are used to make change for customers.

Check A form used to indicate a specific amount of money that is to be paid by the bank to a named person or company.

Check truncation (safekeeping) Procedure whereby checks are not returned to drawer with the bank statement but are instead kept at the bank for a certain amount of time before being first transferred to microfilm and then destroyed.

Credit memorandum Increase in depositor's balance.

Debit card A card similar to a credit card, except that the amount of a purchase is deducted directly from the customer's bank account.

Debit memorandum Decrease in depositor's balance.

Deposits in transit Deposits that were made by customers of a bank but did not reach, or were not processed by, the bank before the preparation of the bank statement.

Deposit ticket A form provided by a bank for use in depositing money or checks into a checking account.

Drawee Bank that drawer has an account with.

Drawer Person who writes a check.

Endorsement *Blank* — could be further endorsed. *Full* — restricts further endorsement to only the person or company named. *Restrictive* — restricts any further endorsement.

EFT (electronic funds transfer) An electronic system that transfers funds without use of paper checks.

Internal control A system of procedures and methods to control a firm's assets as well as monitor its operations.

NSF (nonsufficient funds) Notation indicating that a check has been written on an account that lacks sufficient funds to back it up.

Outstanding checks Checks written by a company or person that were not received or not processed by the bank before the preparation of the bank statement.

Payee The person or company the check is payable to.

Petty cash fund Fund (source) that allows payment of small amounts without the writing of checks.

Petty cash voucher A petty cash form to be completed when money is taken out of petty cash.

BLUEPRINT OF A BANK RECONCILIATION

Checkbook Balance			Balance Per Bank		
Ending Balance per Books		$XXX	Ending Bank Statement Balance (last figure on bank statement)		$XXX
Add:			Add:		
Recording of errors that understate balance	$XXX		Deposits in transit (amount not yet credited by bank)	$XXX	
Proceeds of notes collected by bank or other items credited (added) by bank but not yet updated in checkbook	XXX		Bank errors	XXX	
					XXX
		XXX			

(Cont. on page 226)

Deduct:			Deduct:		
Recording of errors that over-state balance	XXX		List of outstand-ing checks (amount not yet debited by bank)	XXX	
Service charges	XXX		Bank errors	XXX	
Printing charges	XXX				XXX
NSF, check, etc., or other items debited (charged) by bank but not yet updated in checkbook	XXX				
		XXX			
Reconciled Balance (Adjusted Balance)		$XXX	Reconciled Balance (Adjusted Balance)		$XXX

QUESTIONS, MINI EXERCISES, EXERCISES, AND PROBLEMS

Discussion Questions

1. What is the purpose of internal control?
2. What is the advantage of having preprinted deposit tickets?
3. Explain the difference between a blank endorsement and a restrictive endorsement.
4. Explain the difference between payee, drawer, and drawee.
5. Why should check stubs be filled out first, before the check itself is written?
6. A bank statement is sent twice a month. True or false? Please explain.
7. Explain the end product of a bank reconciliation.
8. Why are checks outstanding subtracted from the bank balance?
9. An NSF results in a bank issuing the depositor a credit memorandum. Agree or disagree. Please support your response.
10. Why do adjustments to the checkbook balance in the reconciliation process need to be journalized?
11. What is EFT?
12. What is meant by check truncation or safekeeping?
13. Petty cash is a liability. Accept or reject. Explain.
14. Explain the relationship of the auxiliary petty cash record to the recording of the cash payment.
15. At time of replenishment, why are the totals of individual expenses debited?
16. Explain the purpose of a change fund.
17. Explain how Cash Short and Over can be a miscellaneous expense.

Mini Exercises

(The blank forms you need are on page 204 in the *Study Guide and Working Papers*.)

Bank Reconciliation

1. Indicate what effect each situation will have on the bank reconciliation process:
   1. Add to bank balance
   2. Deduct from bank balance
   3. Add to checkbook balance
   4. Deduct from checkbook balance

   _____ a. $5 bank service charge
   _____ b. $100 deposit in transit
   _____ c. $30 NSF check
   _____ d. A $15 check was written and recorded as $25
   _____ e. Bank collected a $1,000 note less $50 collection fee
   _____ f. Check no. 111 was outstanding for $55

Journal Entries in Reconciliation Process

2. Which of the transactions in Mini Exercise 1 would require a journal entry?

Bank Reconciliation

3. From the following, construct a bank reconciliation for Woody Co. as of May 31, 19XX.

Checkbook balance	$10 CR
Bank statement balance	15
Deposits in transit	5
Outstanding checks	15
Bank service charge	5

Petty Cash

4. Indicate what effect each situation will have:
   1. New check written
   2. Recorded in general journal
   3. Petty cash voucher prepared
   4. Recorded in auxiliary petty cash record

   _____ a. Established petty cash   _____ d. Paid $3.00 for stamps
   _____ b. Paid $1,000 bill   from petty cash
   _____ c. Paid $2 for band-aids   _____ e. Paid electric bill, $250
           from petty cash   _____ f. Replenished petty cash

Replenishment of Petty Cash

5. Petty cash was originally established for $20. During the month $5 was paid out for band-aids and $6 for stamps. During replenishment custodian discovered balance in petty cash was $8. Record using a general journal entry the replenishment of petty cash back to $20.

Increasing Petty Cash

6. In Mini Exercise 5, if the custodian decided to raise the level of petty cash to $30, what would be the journal entry to replenish (use a general journal entry)?

(The blank forms you need are on pages 205–206 of the *Study Guide and Working Papers.*)

Bank reconciliation.

6-1. From the following information, construct a bank reconciliation for Norry Co. as of July 31, 19XX. Then prepare journal entries if needed.

Checkbook balance	$420	Outstanding checks	95
Bank statement balance	300	Bank service charge	15
Deposits (in transit)	200	(debit memo)	

Establishing and replenishing petty cash.

6-2. In general journal form, prepare journal entries to establish a petty cash fund on July 1 and replenish it on July 31.

19XX

July   1 A $40 petty cash fund is established.

       31 At end of month $12 cash plus the following paid vouchers exist: donations expense, $10; postage expense, $7; office supplies expense, $7; miscellaneous expense, $4.

Cash shortage in replenishment.

6-3. If in Exercise 6-2 cash on hand is $11, prepare the entry to replenish the petty cash on July 31.

Cash overage in replenishment.

6-4. If in Exercise 6-2 cash on hand is $13, prepare the entry to replenish the petty cash on July 31.

Calculate cash shortage with Change Fund.

6-5. At the end of the day the clerk for Pete's Variety Shop noticed an error in the amount of cash he should have. Total cash sales from the sales tape were $1,100 while the total cash in the register was $1,056. Pete keeps a $30 change fund in his shop. Prepare an appropriate general journal entry to record the cash sale as well as reveal the cash shortage.

Group A Problems

(The blank forms you need are on pages 207–214 of the *Study Guide and Working Papers.*)

Preparing a bank reconciliation including collection of a note.

Check Figure:
Reconciled Balance $6,460

6A-1. Rose Company received a bank statement from Macy Bank indicating a bank balance of $6,950. Based on Rose's check stubs, the ending checkbook balance was $5,825. Your task is to prepare a bank reconciliation for Rose Company as of July 31, 19XX, from the following information (journalize entries as needed):

  a. Checks outstanding: no. 124, $600; no. 126, $850

  b. Deposits in transit, $960

  c. Bank service charge, $18

  d. Macy Bank collected a note for Rose, $660, less a $7 collection fee.

Preparing a bank reconciliation with NSF using back side of a bank statement.

Check Figure:
Reconciled Balance $6,270

6A-2. From the bank statement on page 229, please (1) complete the bank reconciliation for Rick's Deli found on the reverse of the bank statement, and (2) journalize the appropriate entries as needed.

  a. A deposit of $3,000 is in transit.

  b. Rick's Deli has an ending checkbook balance of $6,600.

  c. Checks outstanding: no. 111, $600; no. 119, $1,200; no. 121, $330

  d. Jim Rice's check for $300 bounced due to lack of sufficient funds.

Establishment and replenishment of petty cash.

Check Figure:
Cash Replenishment $36

6A-3. The following transactions occurred in April for Merry Co.:

19XX

April   1 Issued check no. 14 for $80 to establish a petty cash fund.

      5 Paid $5 from petty cash for postage, voucher no. 1.

      8 Paid $10 from petty cash for office supplies, voucher no. 2.

JAMES NATIONAL BANK
RIO MEAN BRAND
BUGNA, TEXAS

RICK'S DELI
8811 2ND ST.
BUGNA, TEXAS

Old Balance	Checks in Order of Payment		Deposits	Date	New Balance
6,000				2/2	6,000
	90.00	210.00		2/3	5,700
	150.00		300.00	2/10	5,850
	600.00		600.00	2/15	5,850
	300.00	NSF	300.00	2/20	5,850
	1,200.00		1,200.00	2/24	5,850
	600.00	30.00 SC	180.00	2/28	5,400

15 Issued check no. 15 to Reliable Corp. for $200 from past purchases on account.

17 Paid $8 from petty cash for office supplies, voucher no. 3.

20 Issued check no. 16 to Roger Corp., $600 from past purchases on account.

24 Paid $4 from petty cash for postage, voucher no. 4.

26 Paid $9 from petty cash for local church donation, voucher no. 5 (this is a miscellaneous payment).

28 Issued check no. 17 to Roy Kloon to pay for office equipment, $700.

30 Replenish petty cash, check no. 18.

Your task is to

1. Record the appropriate entries in the general journal as well as the auxiliary petty cash record as needed.

2. Be sure to replenish the petty cash fund on April 30 (check no. 18).

Establishing and replenishing petty cash including a cash shortage.

6A-4. From the following, record the transactions into Logan's auxiliary petty cash record and general journal (p. 2) as needed:

19XX

Oct.   1 A check was drawn (no. 444) payable to Roberta Floss, petty cashier, to establish a $100 petty cash fund.

5 Paid $14 for postage stamps, voucher no. 1.

9 Paid $12 for delivery charges on goods for resale, voucher no. 2.

12 Paid $8 for donation to a church (Miscellaneous Expense), voucher no. 3.

Check Figure:
Cash Replenishment $66

14 Paid $9 for postage stamps, voucher no. 4.

17 Paid $8 for delivery charges on goods for resale, voucher no. 5.

27 Purchased computer supplies from petty cash for $8, voucher no. 6.

28 Paid $4 for postage, voucher no. 7.

29 Drew check no. 618 to replenish petty cash and a $3 shortage.

Group B Problems

(The blank forms you need are on pages 207-214 of the *Study Guide and Working Papers.*)

Preparing a bank reconciliation including collection of a note.

6B-1. As the bookkeeper of Rose Company you received the bank statement from Macy Bank indicating a balance of $9,185. The ending checkbook balance was $8,215. Prepare the bank reconciliation for Rose Company as of July 31, 19XX, and prepare journal entries as needed based on the following:

a. Deposits in transit, $3,600
b. Bank service charges, $29
c. Checks outstanding: no. 111, $590; no. 115, $1,255
d. Macy Bank collected a note for Rose, $2,760, less a $6 collection fee.

Check Figure:

Reconciled Balance $10,940

Preparing a bank reconciliation
with NSF using back side of a
bank statement.

Check Figure:

Reconciled Balance $756

6B-2. Based on the following, please (1) complete the bank reconciliation for Rick's Deli found on the reverse of the bank statement below, and (2) journalize the appropriate entries as needed.

a. Checks outstanding: no. 110, $80; no. 116, $160; no. 118, $52.
b. A deposit of $416 is in transit.
c. The checkbook balance of Rick's Deli shows an ending balance of $798.
d. Jim Rice's check for $40 bounced due to lack of sufficient funds.

Establishment and replenishment
of petty cash.

JAMES NATIONAL BANK
RIO MEAN BRAND
BUGNA, TEXAS

RICK'S DELI
8811 2ND ST.
BUGNA, TEXAS

Old Balance	Checks in Order of Payment		Deposits	Date	New Balance
718				4/2	718.00
	12.00	36.00		4/3	670.00
	20.00		40.00	4/10	690.00
	80.00		80.00	4/15	690.00
	40.00	NSF	40.00	4/20	690.00
	160.00		160.00	4/24	690.00
	80.00	2.00 SC	24.00	4/28	632.00

6B-3. From the following transactions, (1) record the entries as needed in the general journal of Merry Co. as well as the auxiliary petty cash record, and (2) replenish the petty cash fund on April 30 (check no. 8).

19XX
April   1 Issued check no. 4 for $60 to establish a petty cash fund.
        5 Paid $9 from petty cash for postage, voucher no. 1.
        8 Paid $12 from petty cash for office supplies, voucher no. 2.
       15 Issued check no. 5 to Reliable Corp. for $400 from past purchases on account.

Check Figure:

Cash Replenishment $46

       17 Paid $7 from petty cash for office supplies, voucher no. 3.
       20 Issued check no. 6 to Roger Corp, $300 from past purchases on account.
       24 Paid $6 from petty cash for postage, voucher no. 4.
       26 Paid $12 from petty cash for local church donation, voucher no. 5 (this is a miscellaneous payment).
       28 Issued check no. 7 to Roy Kloon to pay office equipment, $800.
       30 Replenish petty cash.

Establishing and replenishing
petty cash including a cash
shortage.

6B-4. From the following, record the transactions into Logan's auxiliary petty cash record and general journal (p. 2) as needed:

19XX
Oct.   1 Roberta Floss, the petty cashier, cashed a check, no. 444, to establish a $90 petty cash fund.
       5 Paid $16 for postage stamps, voucher no. 1.

9 Paid $14 for delivery charges on goods for resale, voucher no. 2.

12 Paid $6 for donation to a church (Miscellaneous Expense), voucher no. 3.

14 Paid $10 for postage stamps, voucher no. 4.

17 Paid $7 for delivery charges on goods for resale, voucher no. 5.

27 Purchased computer supplies from petty cash for $9, voucher no. 6.

28 Paid $3 for postage, voucher no. 7.

29 Drew check no. 618 to replenish petty cash and a $4 shortage.

Check Figure:

Cash Replenishment $69

REAL WORLD APPLICATIONS

6R-1.

Karen Johnson, the bookkeeper of Hoop Co., has appointed Jim Pool as the petty cash custodian. The following transactions occurred in November:

19XX

Nov. 25 Check no. 441 was written and cashed to establish a $50 petty cash fund.

27 Paid $8.50 delivery charge for goods purchased for resale.

29 Purchased office supplies for $12 from petty cash.

30 Purchased postage stamps for $15 from petty cash.

On December 3 Jim received the following internal memo:

MEMO

To: Jim Pool

From: Karen Johnson

Re: Petty Cash

Jim, I'll need $5 for postage stamps. By the way, I noticed that our petty cash account seems to be too low. Let's increase its size to $100.

Could you help Jim replenish petty cash on December 3 by providing him with a general journal entry? Support your answer and indicate in writing whether Karen was correct.

6R-2.

Ginger Company has the policy of depositing all receipts and making all payments by check. On receiving the bank statement, Bill Free, a new bookkeeper, is quite upset that the balance in cash in the ledger is $4,209.50 while the ending bank balance is $4,440.50. Bill is convinced the bank has made an error. Based on the following facts, is Bill's concern warranted? What other written suggestions could you offer Bill in the bank reconciliation process?

a. The Nov. 30 cash receipts, $611, had been placed in the bank's night depository after banking hours and consequently did not appear on the bank statement as a deposit.

b. Two debit memorandums and a credit memorandum were included with the returned check. None of the memorandums had been recorded at the time of the reconciliation. The first debit memorandum had a $130 NSF check written by Abby Ellen. The second was a $6.50 debit memorandum for service charges. The credit memorandum was for $494 and represented the proceeds less a $6 collection fee from a $500 non-interest-bearing note collected for Ginger Company by the bank.

c. It was also found that checks no. 942 for $71.50 and no. 947 for $206.50, both written and recorded on Nov. 28, were not among the cancelled checks returned.

d. Bill found that check no. 899 was correctly drawn for $1,094, in payment for a new cash register. However, this check had been recorded as though it were for $1,148.

e. The October bank reconciliation showed two checks outstanding on September 30, no. 621 for $152.50 and no. 630 for $179.30. Check no. 630 was returned with the November bank statement, but check no. 621 was not.

YOU make the call

Critical Thinking/Ethical Case

6R-3.

Jerry Ary, the bookkeeper of Logan Co., received a bank statement from Ajax Bank. Jerry noticed a $200 mistake made by the bank in the company's favor. Jerry called his supervisor, who said that as long as it benefits the company, he should not tell the bank about the error. You make the call. Write your specific recommendations to Jerry.

ACCOUNTING RECALL
A CUMULATIVE APPROACH

THIS EXAM REVIEWS CHAPTERS 1 THROUGH 6

Your *Study Guide and Working Papers* (pp. 218 and 230) have forms to complete this exam, as well as worked-out solutions. The page references next to each question identify what page to turn back to if you answer the question incorrectly.

PART 1   Vocabulary Review

Match the terms to the appropriate definition or phrase.

Page Ref.

(161)	1. Permanent account	A. A supplementary record
(207)	2. Blank endorsement	B. Revenues, Expenses, Withdrawals
(209)	3. Payee	C. A process of reconciling
(161)	4. Temporary accounts	D. Assets, Contra-assets, Liabilities, Capital
(212)	5. Outstanding checks	E. Person or company to whom the check is payable
(211)	6. Bank reconciliation	
(217)	7. Auxiliary petty cash record	F. Lacks sufficient funds
		G. Contra-asset on the Balance Sheet
(122)	8. Accumulated depreciation	H. Add to bank balance
(211)	9. Deposits in transit	I. Checks written but not processed by bank
(212)	10. NSF	J. Could be further endorsed

PART II   True or False (Accounting Theory)

(216)   11. Petty cash is a liability.

(217)   12. The auxiliary petty cash record is a journal.

(161)   13. The closing process reduces all temporary accounts to a zero balance.

(212)   14. NSF results in lowering the bank balance in the reconciliation process.

(219)   15. In replenishment, the old expenses are shown and a new check is written.

CONTINUING PROBLEM

The books have been closed for the first year of business for Eldorado Computer Center. The company ended up with a marginal profit for the first three months in operation. Tony expects faster growth as he enters into a busy season.

Following is a list of transactions for the month of October. Petty Cash Account #1010 and Miscellaneous Expense Account #5100 have been added to the chart of accounts.

Assignment:

(See pp. 219 – 220 in your *Study Guide and Working Papers*.)

1. Record the transactions in general journal or petty cash format.
2. Post the transactions to the general ledger accounts.
3. Prepare a trial balance.

Oct.
1 Paid rent for November, December, and January, $1,200 (check #8107)
2 Established a petty cash fund for $100
4 Collected $3,600 from a cash customer for building five systems
5 Collected $2,600, the amount due from A. Pitale's invoice #12674, customer on account
6 Purchased $25 worth of stamps, using petty cash voucher #101
7 Withdrew $2,000 (check #8108) for personal use.
8 Purchased $22 worth of supplies, using petty cash voucher #102
12 Paid the newspaper carrier $10, using petty cash voucher #103
16 Paid the amount due on the September phone bill, $65 (check #8109)
17 Paid the amount due on the September electric bill, $95 (check #8110)
22 Performed computer services for Taylor Golf; billed the client $4,200 (invoice #12675)
23 Paid $20 for computer paper, using petty cash voucher #104
30 Took $15 out of petty cash for lunch, voucher #105
31 Replenished the petty cash. Coin and currency in drawer $8.00

Since Tony was so busy trying to close his books, he forgot to reconcile his last three months of bank statements. What follows on pages 234 and 235 is a list of all deposits and checks written for the past three months (Each entry is identified by chapter, transaction date, or transaction letter.) and bank statements for July through September. The statement for October won't arrive until the first week of November.

Chapter	Transaction	Payor/Payee	Amount
		DEPOSITS	
1	(a)	Tony Freedman	$4,500
1	(f)	Cash customer	250
1	(i)	Taylor Golf	1200
1	(g)	Cash customer	200
2	(p)	Cash customer	900
3	Sept. 2	Tonya Parker Jones	325
3	Sept. 6	Summer Lipe	220
3	Sept. 12	Jeannine Sparks	850
3	Sept. 26	Mike Hammer	140

Chapter	Transaction	Check #	Payor/Payee	Amount
			CHECKS	
1	(b)	8095	Multi Systems	$1200
1	(c)	8096	Office Furniture, Inc.	600
1	(e)	8097	Capital Management	400
1	(j)	8098	Tony Freedman	100
2	(l)	8099	Insurance Protection, Inc.	150
2	(m)	8100	Office Depot	200
2	(n)	8101	Computer Edge Magazine	1400
2	(q)	8102	San Diego Electric	85
2	(r)	8103	U.S. Postmaster	50
3	Sept. 1	8104	Capital Management	1200
3	Sept. 8	8105	Pacific Bell USA	155
3	Sept. 15	8106	Computer Connection	200
3	Sept. 16	8107	Multi Systems, Inc.	1200

BANK STATEMENT
First Union Bank 322 Glen Ave. Escondido, CA 92025

Eldorado Computer Center   Statement Date: July 22 , 19XX

Checks Paid:

Date paid	Number	Amount	Date received	Amount
7-4	8095	1200.00	7-1	4500.00
7-7	8096	600.00	7-10	250.00
7-15	8097	400.00	7-20	1200.00
Total 3 checks paid for $2,200.00			7-21	200.00
			Total Deposits	**$6,150.00**

Deposits and Credits: (column header)

Ending Balance on July 22 — $3,950.00

Received Statement July 29, 19XX.

BANK STATEMENT
First Union Bank 322 Glen Ave. Escondido, CA 92025

Eldorado Computer Center   Statement Date: August 21 , 19XX

Checks Paid:

Date paid	Number	Amount	Date received	Amount
8-2	8098	100.00	8-12	900.00
8-3	8099	150.00		
8-10	8100	200.00		
8-15	8101	1400.00		
8-20	8102	85.00	**Total Deposits**	**$900.00**
Total 5 checks paid for $1935.00				

Deposits and Credits: (column header)

Beginning balance on July 22 — $3,950.00   **Ending balance on August 21 — $2,915.00**

Received statement August 27, 19XX.

BANK STATEMENT
First Union Bank 322 Glen Ave. Escondido, CA 92025

Eldorado Computer Center   *Statement Date: September 20 , 19XX*

Checks Paid:

Date paid	Number	Amount
9-2	8103	50.00
9-6	8104	1200.00
9-12	8105	155.00

Deposits and Credits:

Date received	Amount
9-4	325.00
9-7	220.00
9-14	850.00

Total 3 checks paid for $1405.00   *Total Deposits* $1,395.00

Beginning balance on August 21   *Ending balance on September 20*
$2,915.00 $2,905.00

Received statement September 29, 19XX.

Assignment:

1. Compare the Computer Center's deposits and checks with the bank statements, and complete a bank reconciliation as of September 30.

PAYROLL CONCEPTS AND PROCEDURES

Employee Taxes

THE BIG PICTURE

The Eldorado Computer Center ended its first year so successfully that owner Tony Freedman decided to hire two employees. He would pay them based on an hourly wage, using time cards to track the hours they worked. Freedman knew that this would involve significant expense and effort. In many companies the cost of payroll is more than half of total expenses. Beyond the cost of wages, however, a business becomes responsible for complying with rules that govern payroll deductions.

In addition to paying wages on time, the business must deduct taxes and other amounts. It must account for this money very strictly and pass it on to the proper agency according to government rules and regulations. These regulations are constantly changing, and the person handling payroll must be aware of all changes in order to stay in compliance with the law.

Some companies choose an outside service to prepare the payroll and issue the checks. Much of the work is done with computer accounting payroll software. Since Freedman will have only two employees (in addition to himself), he has decided to take the task on himself to save the expense of hiring an outside service.

In this chapter you will learn how to calculate hourly wages and overtime. You will also learn the basic rules and procedures for making payroll deductions, withholding taxes, and paying taxes withheld.

Learning Objectives	◆ Calculating overtime pay, FICA deductions for Social Security and Medicare, and federal income tax withholding. (p. 237) ◆ Preparing a payroll register. (p. 244) ◆ Journalizing and posting the payroll entry from the payroll register. (p. 251) ◆ Maintaining an individual employee earnings record. (p. 254)

Payroll can be a significant factor in running a business. Besides the money issue, business expenses (including payroll) must comply with a growing number of federal and state payroll regulations. That is why it is important to completely understand the step-by-step process involved in manual payroll systems. An accurate payroll system has (1) continual checks and balances and (2) strong internal control.

In this chapter we will take a close look at the employees of Fred's Market and see how their payroll is calculated; how it is affected by federal, state, and local taxes and deductions; and how the accountant for Fred's Market handles a weekly payroll. (In Chapter 8 we will continue to look at Fred's Market, but from the employer's point of view rather than that of the employees.)

LEARNING UNIT 7-1
Introduction to Payroll

A number of laws and regulations at the federal and state level govern payroll. We will look at several of them here.

FAIR LABOR STANDARDS ACT AND OVERTIME PAY

The Fair Labor Standards Act also deals with such issues as employing minors under the age of 18, recordkeeping, and the concept of equal pay for equal work, regardless of sex.

The **Fair Labor Standards Act** (also known as **Federal Wage and Hour Law**) applies to all employers involved directly or indirectly in **interstate commerce**. "Interstate commerce" is defined as one business communicating or doing business with another business in some other state. Since simple activities such as mailing or making long-distance phone calls are considered activities that pass the interstate commerce test, nearly all employers must comply with the law.

Two of the most important requirements of the Fair Labor Standards Act are that workers (1) must receive a minimum hourly rate of pay and (2) be paid at a higher rate of pay for any hours beyond 40 worked during a week. Once a worker reaches 40 hours, he or she must be paid at least time and a half (or 1.5 times the worker's regular rate of pay). Some employers, such as retailers, may pay double time (or 2 times the worker's regular rate of pay) to employees who work on a national holiday. This is commonly known as *overtime pay* (or premium pay).

Depending on the industry, either 40 or 44 hours represents the total hours worked before considering overtime.

Not all employers are subject to the 40-hour standard: restaurants, hotels, and the like are not required to pay overtime until a worker has worked more than 44 hours in one week. Also, workers who are considered to be executives, professionals, or administrative personnel of a company are exempt from the 40-hour requirement.

Two methods are commonly used to calculate overtime for a worker. Both are contained in the regulations to the Fair Labor Standards Act. Let's say that a person whose standard rate of pay is $6 an hour worked four hours of overtime. He works in an industry where overtime is considered beyond 40 hours. His pay would be calculated as follows:

METHOD 1

$$\text{Total hours} \times \text{Regular rate} = 44 \times \$6 = \$264$$
$$+ \ \underline{\text{Overtime hours} \times \tfrac{1}{2} \text{ rate}} \ = \ 4 \times \$3 = \ \underline{\quad 12}$$
$$\text{Total pay} \qquad\qquad = \qquad\qquad \$276$$

METHOD 2

$$\text{Regular hours} \times \text{Regular rate} = 40 \times \$6 = \$240$$
$$+ \ \underline{\text{Overtime hours} \times 1\tfrac{1}{2} \text{ rate}} \ = \ 4 \times \$9 = \ \underline{\quad 36}$$
$$\text{Total pay} \qquad\qquad = \qquad\qquad \$276$$

Using Method 1, the employer is clearly able to see that pure overtime wages cost $12 over the regular cost of labor. Because it is the more common method, we will use Method 2, which calculates the overtime rates at time and a half.

WITHHOLDING FOR FEDERAL INCOME TAXES (FIT)

Many rules and regulations govern the federal income taxes that a person must pay. Here, however, we will discuss only those that relate to withholding.

Every U.S. citizen must pay income tax each year. The tax is due on April 15 of the year after the tax year. (For example, taxes for 1997 are due on April 15, 1998; taxes for 1998 are due on April 15, 1999, etc.) Instead of each individual or company paying the tax due on April 15, employers are required to withhold taxes for each employee, deposit them in a special account, and then send them to the government at regular intervals. The funds sent to the government are called **payroll tax deposits.** We will discuss the specifics of payroll tax deposits in Chapter 8.

To facilitate this, the employer must have each employee fill out a **Form W-4** (an **Employee's Withholding Allowance Certificate**), which is kept on file by the employer (see Fig. 7-1). Using the Form W-4 along with the special withholding tables provided by the Internal Revenue Service (or IRS), an employer can determine the amount of **federal income tax withholding** (or

FIGURE 7-1 Form W-4, Employee's Withholding Allowance Certificate

Form **W-4** Department of the Treasury Internal Revenue Service	**Employee's Withholding Allowance Certificate** ▶ **For Privacy Act and Paperwork Reduction Act Notice, see reverse.**	OMB No. 1545-0010 **199X**

1 Type or print your first name and middle initial	Last name	**2** Your social security number
SUSAN	O'MALLY	021 ┆ 36 ┆ 9494

Home address (number and street or rural route) 80 GARFIELD STREET	**3** ☐ Single ☐ Married ☒ Married, but withhold at higher Single rate. **Note:** If married, but legally separated, or spouse is a nonresident alien, check the Single box.
City or town, state, and ZIP code MARBLEHEAD, MA 01945	**4** If your last name differs from that on your social security card, check here and call 1-800-772-1213 for more information ▸ · · · · ▶ ☐

5	Total number of allowances you are claiming (from line G above or from the worksheets on page 2 if they apply) .	**5**	3
6	Additional amount, if any, you want withheld from each paycheck	**6**	$
7	I claim exemption from withholding for 1994 and I certify that I meet **BOTH** of the following conditions for exemption:		

- Last year I had a right to a refund of **ALL** Federal income tax withheld because I had **NO** tax liability; **AND**
- This year I expect a refund of **ALL** Federal income tax withheld because I expect to have **NO** tax liability.

If you meet both conditions, enter "EXEMPT" here . . . . ▶ | **7** |

Under penalties of perjury, I certify that I am entitled to the number of withholding allowances claimed on this certificate or entitled to claim exempt status.

Employee's signature ▶ *Susan O'Malley*	**Date** ▶ January 2 , 19 9X

8 Employer's name and address (Employer: Complete 8 and 10 only if sending to the IRS)	**9** Office code (optional)	**10** Employer identification number

Cat. No. 10220Q

FIT) required. The FIT takes the employee's gross earnings, marital state, and number of exemptions claimed into consideration. An **exemption** (or **allowance**) represents the specific income that will be considered *non*taxable for FIT purposes.

Usually a worker is entitled to an allowance for himself or herself, one for his or her spouse (unless the spouse is working and claiming an allowance), and one for each dependent (e.g., a child) for whom the worker is providing more than one-half the support in a given year.

To properly calculate federal income tax withholding, the employee uses the **wage bracket table** in an IRS publication known as Circular E or *Employer's Tax Guide* (Publication 15). The wage bracket tables in this publication show the amount of federal income tax to be withheld for individuals who are paid weekly, biweekly, semimonthly, or monthly. These periods of time used to determine how much an employee earns are called **pay** (or **payroll**) **periods.** There are separate tables for married persons and for single persons (see Figs. 7-2 and 7-3, respectively, on pages 240–241).

Let's assume that an employee who has filled out a Form W-4 stating that he is married and has three withholding allowances earns $1,175 each week. Using the first table in Figure 7-2 (called MARRIED Persons — WEEKLY Payroll Period) we go down the left-hand column until we arrive at $1,170 in the column labeled "At least." Notice that the column to the immediate right of the first column says "But less than" $1,180. The $1,175 amount falls between these two amounts. Since the employee claims three allowances, we slide over to the right. Where the three allowances intersect with the "At least" $1,170, we see a federal withholding tax of $166. If the employee had earned $1,169, his or her tax would have been $164.

WITHHOLDING FOR FEDERAL INSURANCE CONTRIBUTIONS ACT (FICA)

The **Federal Insurance Contributions Act** (better known as **FICA**) helps fund the payments related to (1) monthly retirement benefits for those over 62 years of age, (2) medical benefits after age 65, (3) benefits for workers who have become disabled, and (4) benefits for families of deceased workers who were covered by the federal Social Security Act. Under this act, passed into law in 1935, employees, self-employed persons, and employers must all pay a FICA tax. The employer must match the amounts contributed by each employee. The employer's share of these taxes will be further discussed in Chapter 8.

FICA taxes are broken down into two parts: Social Security and Medicare. Employers must calculate and report each of these taxes separately to the government and to each employee. Employees are notified on their paycheck stubs and on their Form W-2, which they will receive after the end of the tax year.

Each year rates and maximum dollar amounts are set for Social Security. For example, in 1937, the first year FICA tax was collected, the rate was 1 percent on the first $3,000 of an employee's earnings during the year. This meant that the most an employee could contribute to Social Security that year was $30.

It is important to realize that the rate and the maximum dollar amount of earnings subject to FICA taxes, called a wage base limit, continually change. For this text, we use $65,400 as the wage base limit for Social Security (Old Age, Survivors, and Disability Insurance). There is no wage base limit for Medicare (Hospital Insurance). This means that the employee and employer pay 1.45 percent on all of the employee's earnings for the year. As of this writing, the rate of tax for Social Security is 6.2 percent (both the employee and employer would pay this). For Medicare, the rate is 1.45 percent.[1]

---

[1] 1997 Social Security rate is 6.2 percent on a base of $65,400. The 1998 rate is 6.2 percent on a base of $68,400.

MARRIED Persons—WEEKLY Payroll Period

If the wages are—		And the number of withholding allowances claimed is—										
At least	But less than	0	1	2	3	4	5	6	7	8	9	10
		The amount of income tax to be withheld is—										
$740	$750	$93	$86	$79	$72	$65	$58	$51	$44	$37	$30	$23
750	760	95	88	81	74	67	60	53	45	38	31	24
760	770	96	89	82	75	68	61	54	47	40	33	26
770	780	98	91	84	77	70	63	56	48	41	34	27
780	790	99	92	85	78	71	64	57	50	43	36	29
790	800	101	94	87	80	73	66	59	51	44	37	30
800	810	102	95	88	81	74	67	60	53	46	39	32
810	820	105	97	90	83	76	69	62	54	47	40	33
820	830	108	98	91	84	77	70	63	56	49	42	35
830	840	111	100	93	86	79	72	65	57	50	43	36
840	850	114	101	94	87	80	73	66	59	52	45	38
850	860	116	103	96	89	82	75	68	60	53	46	39
860	870	119	106	97	90	83	76	69	62	55	48	41
870	880	122	109	99	92	85	78	71	63	56	49	42
880	890	125	112	100	93	86	79	72	65	58	51	44
890	900	128	114	102	95	88	81	74	66	59	52	45
900	910	130	117	104	96	89	82	75	68	61	54	47
910	920	133	120	107	98	91	84	77	69	62	55	48
920	930	136	123	110	99	92	85	78	71	64	57	50
930	940	139	126	112	101	94	87	80	72	65	58	51
940	950	142	128	115	102	95	88	81	74	67	60	53
950	960	144	131	118	105	97	90	83	75	68	61	54
960	970	147	134	121	108	98	91	84	77	70	63	56
970	980	150	137	124	110	100	93	86	78	71	64	57
980	990	153	140	126	113	101	94	87	80	73	66	59
990	1,000	156	142	129	116	103	96	89	81	74	67	60
1,000	1,010	158	145	132	119	106	97	90	83	76	69	62
1,010	1,020	161	148	135	122	108	99	92	84	77	70	63
1,020	1,030	164	151	138	124	111	100	93	86	79	72	65
1,030	1,040	167	154	140	127	114	102	95	87	80	73	66
1,040	1,050	170	156	143	130	117	104	96	89	82	75	68
1,050	1,060	172	159	146	133	120	106	98	90	83	76	69
1,060	1,070	175	162	149	136	122	109	99	92	85	78	71
1,070	1,080	178	165	152	138	125	112	101	93	86	79	72
1,080	1,090	181	168	154	141	128	115	102	95	88	81	74
1,090	1,100	184	170	157	144	131	118	104	96	89	82	75
1,100	1,110	186	173	160	147	134	120	107	98	91	84	77
1,110	1,120	189	176	163	150	136	123	110	99	92	85	78
1,120	1,130	192	179	166	152	139	126	113	101	94	87	80
1,130	1,140	195	182	168	155	142	129	116	102	95	88	81
1,140	1,150	198	184	171	158	145	132	118	105	97	90	83
1,150	1,160	200	187	174	161	148	134	121	108	98	91	84
1,160	1,170	203	190	177	164	150	137	124	111	100	93	86
→ 1,170	1,180	206	193	180	166	153	140	127	114	101	94	87
1,180	1,190	209	196	182	169	156	143	130	116	103	96	89
1,190	1,200	212	198	185	172	159	146	132	119	106	97	90
1,200	1,210	214	201	188	175	162	148	135	122	109	99	92
1,210	1,220	217	204	191	178	164	151	138	125	112	100	93
1,220	1,230	220	207	194	180	167	154	141	128	114	102	95
1,230	1,240	223	210	196	183	170	157	144	130	117	104	96
1,240	1,250	226	212	199	186	173	160	146	133	120	107	98
1,250	1,260	228	215	202	189	176	162	149	136	123	110	99
1,260	1,270	231	218	205	192	178	165	152	139	126	112	101
1,270	1,280	234	221	208	194	181	168	155	142	128	115	102
1,280	1,290	237	224	210	197	184	171	158	144	131	118	105
1,290	1,300	240	226	213	200	187	174	160	147	134	121	108
1,300	1,310	242	229	216	203	190	176	163	150	137	124	110
1,310	1,320	245	232	219	206	192	179	166	153	140	126	113
1,320	1,330	248	235	222	208	195	182	169	156	142	129	116
1,330	1,340	251	238	224	211	198	185	172	158	145	132	119
1,340	1,350	254	240	227	214	201	188	174	161	148	135	122
1,350	1,360	256	243	230	217	204	190	177	164	151	138	124
1,360	1,370	259	246	233	220	206	193	180	167	154	140	127
1,370	1,380	262	249	236	222	209	196	183	170	156	143	130
1,380	1,390	265	252	238	225	212	199	186	172	159	146	133

$1,390 and over   Use Table 1(b) for a **MARRIED person** on page 29. Also see the instructions on page 27.

FIGURE 7-2 Wage Bracket Tables—Married Persons. The federal income tax (FIT) withholding for a married person earning $1,175 per week with 3 exemptions is $166.

CH. 7 / PAYROLL CONCEPTS AND PROCEDURES: EMPLOYEE TAXES

SINGLE Persons—WEEKLY Payroll Period

If the wages are—		And the number of withholding allowances claimed is—										
At least	But less than	0	1	2	3	4	5	6	7	8	9	10
		The amount of income tax to be withheld is—										
$600	$610	$102	$89	$75	$62	$55	$48	$41	$34	$27	$20	$13
610	620	105	91	78	65	57	49	42	35	28	21	14
620	630	107	94	81	68	58	51	44	37	30	23	16
630	640	110	97	84	71	60	52	45	38	31	24	17
640	650	113	100	87	73	61	54	47	40	33	26	19
650	660	116	103	89	76	63	55	48	41	34	27	20
660	670	119	105	92	79	66	57	50	43	36	29	22
670	680	121	108	95	82	69	58	51	44	37	30	23
680	690	124	111	98	85	71	60	53	46	39	32	25
690	700	127	114	101	87	74	61	54	47	40	33	26
700	710	130	117	103	90	77	64	56	49	42	35	28
710	720	133	119	106	93	80	67	57	50	43	36	29
720	730	135	122	109	96	83	69	59	52	45	38	31
730	740	138	125	112	99	85	72	60	53	46	39	32
740	750	141	128	115	101	88	75	62	55	48	41	34
750	760	144	131	117	104	91	78	65	56	49	42	35
760	770	147	133	120	107	94	81	67	58	51	44	37
770	780	149	136	123	110	97	83	70	59	52	45	38
780	790	152	139	126	113	99	86	73	61	54	47	40
790	800	155	142	129	115	102	89	76	63	55	48	41
800	810	158	145	131	118	105	92	79	65	57	50	43
810	820	161	147	134	121	108	95	81	68	58	51	44
820	830	163	150	137	124	111	97	84	71	60	53	46
830	840	166	153	140	127	113	100	87	74	61	54	47
840	850	169	156	143	129	116	103	90	77	63	56	49
850	860	172	159	145	132	119	106	93	79	66	57	50
860	870	175	161	148	135	122	109	95	82	69	59	52
870	880	177	164	151	138	125	111	98	85	72	60	53
880	890	180	167	154	141	127	114	101	88	75	62	55
890	900	183	170	157	143	130	117	104	91	77	64	56
900	910	186	173	159	146	133	120	107	93	80	67	58
910	920	189	175	162	149	136	123	109	96	83	70	59
920	930	191	178	165	152	139	125	112	99	86	73	61
930	940	194	181	168	155	141	128	115	102	89	75	62
940	950	197	184	171	157	144	131	118	105	91	78	65
950	960	200	187	173	160	147	134	121	107	94	81	68
960	970	203	189	176	163	150	137	123	110	97	84	71
970	980	206	192	179	166	153	139	126	113	100	87	73
980	990	209	195	182	169	155	142	129	116	103	89	76
990	1,000	212	198	185	171	158	145	132	119	105	92	79
1,000	1,010	215	201	187	174	161	148	135	121	108	95	82
1,010	1,020	218	203	190	177	164	151	137	124	111	98	85
1,020	1,030	221	206	193	180	167	153	140	127	114	101	87
1,030	1,040	224	210	196	183	169	156	143	130	117	103	90
1,040	1,050	227	213	199	185	172	159	146	133	119	106	93
1,050	1,060	230	216	201	188	175	162	149	135	122	109	96
1,060	1,070	233	219	204	191	178	165	151	138	125	112	99
1,070	1,080	237	222	207	194	181	167	154	141	128	115	101
1,080	1,090	240	225	210	197	183	170	157	144	131	117	104
1,090	1,100	243	228	214	199	186	173	160	147	133	120	107
1,100	1,110	246	231	217	202	189	176	163	149	136	123	110
1,110	1,120	249	234	220	205	192	179	165	152	139	126	113
1,120	1,130	252	237	223	208	195	181	168	155	142	129	115
1,130	1,140	255	241	226	211	197	184	171	158	145	131	118
1,140	1,150	258	244	229	214	200	187	174	161	147	134	121
1,150	1,160	261	247	232	218	203	190	177	163	150	137	124
1,160	1,170	264	250	235	221	206	193	179	166	153	140	127
1,170	1,180	268	253	238	224	209	195	182	169	156	143	129
1,180	1,190	271	256	241	227	212	198	185	172	159	145	132
1,190	1,200	274	259	245	230	215	201	188	175	161	148	135
1,200	1,210	277	262	248	233	218	204	191	177	164	151	138
1,210	1,220	280	265	251	236	222	207	193	180	167	154	141
1,220	1,230	283	268	254	239	225	210	196	183	170	157	143
1,230	1,240	286	272	257	242	228	213	199	186	173	159	146
1,240	1,250	289	275	260	245	231	216	202	189	175	162	149

$1,250 and over   Use Table 1(a) for a **SINGLE person** on page 29. Also see the instructions on page 27.

FIGURE 7-3 Wage Bracket Tables—Single Persons

Thus, the most an employee could contribute for Social Security tax from January 1 through December 31 (known as a **calendar year**) would be $4,054.80, calculated as follows:

$$\textit{Base} \qquad \textit{Rate}$$
$$\$65,400 \times .062 = \$4,054.80$$

Let's look at how two different employees would be taxed. Employee A earns $75,000 for the year while Employee B earns $125,000. Both employees have earned over $65,400, the Social Security wage base limit, so both will pay the maximum Social Security tax. However, they will pay different amounts for Medicare tax.

Employee A	Earnings	Wage Base Limit	Rate	
Social Security	$75,000	$65,400	× .062 =	$4,054.80
Medicare	$75,000	None	× .0145 =	1,087.50
			=	$5,142.30

Employee B	Earnings	Wage Base Limit	Rate	
Social Security	$125,000	$65,400	× .062 =	$4,054.80
Medicare	$125,000	None	× .0145 =	1,812.50
			=	$5,867.30

Please note that every employee pays Social Security tax up to the wage base limit, which is subject to change each year. Every employee pays Medicare tax on every dollar earned — there is no wage base limit for Medicare.

STATE AND CITY INCOME TAXES (SIT)

Employees in 41 states also have to pay a state income tax. The rates and rules vary too much for us to discuss them here, but all states that tax income publish charts and tables like those of the federal government. This allows employers to calculate the proper amount of **state income tax withholding.**

Many counties and/or cities also tax income. Such county and/or city income taxes are in addition to federal and state taxes.

WORKERS' COMPENSATION INSURANCE

Workers' Compensation Insurance protects employees against losses due to injury or death incurred while on the job. Each employer (in cooperation with an insurance agent) must estimate the cost of the insurance. The premium must be paid in advance. In Chapter 8 we will look at how the premium is calculated as well as specific tax responsibilities of the employer. Keep in mind that this tax is on the employer, not on the employee.

LEARNING UNIT 7-1 REVIEW

AT THIS POINT you should be able to

◆ Explain the purpose of the Federal Wage and Hour Law. (p. 237)
◆ Calculate overtime pay. (p. 238)
◆ Complete a W-4 form. (p. 238)
◆ Explain the term "claiming an allowance." (p. 239)

- ◆ Define and state the purpose of FICA. (p. 239)
- ◆ Calculate the FICA deductions for Social Security and Medicare. (p. 242)
- ◆ Utilize a wage bracket table to arrive at deductions from federal income tax. (p. 239)
- ◆ Explain the purpose of Workers' Compensation Insurance. (p. 242)

SELF-REVIEW QUIZ 7-1

(The forms you need are on page 231 of the *Study Guide and Working Papers*.)

John Small earns $1,300 each week as a software engineer. To date this year, before the current payroll, he earned a total of $65,000. Please calculate the amount of FICA tax for Social Security and Medicare, federal income tax, and state income tax deducted in the current pay period.

- ◆ FICA: Social Security is 6.2 percent on $65,400; Medicare is 1.45 percent with no wage base limit.
- ◆ John is married, claiming two allowances (please use Figure 7-2).
- ◆ The state income tax rate is 8 percent.
- ◆ No other deductions are taken out by John's employer.

Solution to Self-Review Quiz 7-1

This is how John's tax would be calculated:

FICA: Social Security:	$ 400 × .062 =	$ 24.80
Medicare	$1,300 × .0145 =	$ 18.85
Federal income tax		$216.00 by IRS table
State income tax	$1,300 × .08 =	$104.00

The wage base limit for Social Security is $65,400. John has earned—and been taxed on—$65,000. Therefore, in the current pay period, he only has to pay Social Security tax on $400 of his pay; the remaining $900 is not taxed for that purpose. However, John's total check of $1,300 is taxed for Medicare since there is no wage base limit for this tax.

LEARNING UNIT 7-2
The Payroll Process

Fred Stone, owner of Fred's Market, has five employees working for him. They are:

Bob Jones	$16 per hour
Abby King	$14 per hour
Susan O'Mally	$1,375 salary per week
Pat Regan	$900 salary per week
Jim Zott	$1,380 salary per week

Fred does not receive a salary since he is the owner of the sole proprietorship, but he does plan to eventually withdraw portions of the profit.

RECORDING PAYROLL DATA IN THE PAYROLL REGISTER

Fred's Market pays its employees on a weekly basis. The **payroll register** shown in Figure 7-4 on pages 244–245 contains the payroll information for the week of November 25. The payroll register is a multicolumn form used specifically for the purpose of recording the earnings of the employees of a business for a given pay period. Let's look closely at each column to see how the numbers were determined.

FIGURE 7-4 Payroll Register for Fred's Market

FRED'S MARKET
PAYROLL REGISTER
NOVEMBER 25, 19XX

Employee Name	Allowances and Marital Status	Cumulative Earnings	Salary per Week	No. of Hrs.	Wages per Hour	Earnings Regular	Earnings Overtime	Earnings Gross	Cumulative Earnings	Taxable Earnings Federal Unemployment	Taxable Earnings Soc. Sec.	Taxable Earnings Medicare
Jones, Bob	S-0	6800 00	—	39	16 00	624 00		624 00	7424 00	2000 00	624 00	624 00
King, Abby	S-1	6600 00	—	44	14 00	560 00	84 00	644 00	7244 00	400 00	644 00	644 00
O'Mally, Susan	M-3	64625 00	1375 00			1375 00		1375 00	66 000 00	—	775 00 ①	1375 00
Regan, Pat	M-1	42300 00	900 00			900 00		900 00	43200 00	—	900 00	900 00
Zott, Jim	M-2	64860 00	1380 00			1380 00		1380 00	66240 00	—	540 00	1380 00
TOTALS		185185 00	3655 00			4839 00	84 00	4923 00	190 108 00	6000 00	3483 00	4923 00
Discussions in this chapter are keyed to these letters	(A)	(B)	(C)			(D)	(E)	(F)	(G)	(H)	(I)	(J)

① $65,400
 −64,625
 $ 775

FIGURE 7-4 (cont.)

FRED'S MARKET
PAYROLL REGISTER
NOVEMBER 25, 19XX

FICA Soc. Sec.	FICA Medicare	Federal Income Tax	State Income Tax	Medical Insurance	Net Pay	Check No.	Office Salaries Expense	Market Wages Expense
			Deductions				Distribution of Expense Accounts	
3869	905	10700	3120	2200	41606	840		62400
3993	934	10000	3220	2200	44053	841		64400
4805	1994	22200	6875	4400	97226	842	137500	
5580	1305	11700	4500	4400	62515	843	90000	
3348	2001	23800	6900	4400	97551	844	138000	
21595	7139	78400	24615	17600	342951		365500	126800
(K)	(L)	(M)	(N)	(O)	(P)	(Q)	(R)	(S)

② over Soc. Sec. column; ③ over Medicare column

Discussions in this chapter are keyed to these letters

② $624 x .062
③ $624 x .0145

Note: Figure 7-4 should be used as a reference guide for both Chapters 7 and 8.

(A) Allowance and Marital Status

As previously mentioned, employees must complete Form W-4 (see Fig. 7-1 on p. 238). The form indicates the employee's marital status so that the correct amount of federal income tax withholding can be calculated. Remember, individual workers completing the form are entitled to claim one allowance for themselves and one for each dependent.

Fred's bookkeeper uses information from Form W-4 to determine how much money for federal income tax (column M). When more allowances are claimed, less tax is deducted from the employee's earnings when the check is issued. The opposite is also true: the fewer the allowances, the larger the deduction.

> **Example:** Bob Jones is single and claims zero allowances. A high amount of federal income taxes are taken out with each paycheck. If Bob overpays FIT, he may receive a refund at year end after he files his individual income tax return.

(B) Cumulative Earnings

This column represents each employee's cumulative earnings for the calendar year *before* the new payroll period. As we will show later, the cumulative figure can be obtained from the employee's individual earnings record.

Salary per Week, Number of Hours, and Wages per Hour

> **Example:** Abby King has earnings $6,600 before this payroll in the calendar year.

(C) Salary per Week, Number of Hours, and Wages per Hour

The weekly salary or hours worked with rate of pay per hour provides the basis for computing the gross earnings of the employees.

> **Example:** Bob Jones is paid $16 per hour and worked 39 hours for this pay period.

(D) Earnings

To calculate the regular earnings for an employee paid by the hour, multiply the number of hours (40 or less) times the rate per hour. Salaried employee amounts are listed with no calculations.

> **Example:** Bob Jones has earned $624 for this pay period.
>
> | Hours worked | | Rate per hour | | Regular pay |
> |:---:|:---:|:---:|:---:|:---:|
> | 39 | $\times$ | $16 | $=$ | $624 |

(E) Overtime

After 40 hours, hourly employees earn overtime pay (time and a half). *Note:* salaried employees do not receive overtime.

Example: Abby King has worked 4 hours of overtime at a rate of $21 per hour.

$$\underset{\$14}{\text{Hourly rate}} \times \underset{1.5}{\text{Time and a half}} = \underset{\$21}{\text{Overtime rate}}$$

$$\underset{\$21}{\text{Overtime rate}} \times \underset{4}{\text{Overtime hours}} = \underset{\$84}{\text{Overtime earnings}}$$

(F) Gross Earnings

Gross earnings is the total amount that has been earned (including overtime) before any deductions. We will use these numbers to fill columns (R) and (S).

Example: Abby King's gross earnings are $644.

$$\underset{\$560}{\text{Regular pay}} + \underset{\$84}{\text{Overtime}} = \underset{\$644}{\text{Gross pay}}$$

(G) Cumulative Earnings

This column provides an up-to-date picture of how much each employee has earned *after* this pay period for the calendar year. This column tells whether an employee has reached the Social Security tax wage base limit.

Example: Pat Regan has now earned a total of $43,200 for this calendar year.

$$\underset{\$42,300}{\substack{\text{Cumulative earnings} \\ \text{before pay period}}} + \underset{\$900}{\substack{\text{Gross earnings for} \\ \text{the pay period}}} = \underset{\$43,200}{\substack{\text{Cumulative earnings} \\ \text{to date}}}$$

(H) Taxable Earnings: Unemployment Insurance

In the next chapter we will see that certain taxes for state and federal unemployment insurance are paid only by the employer. Federal unemployment taxes, which are based on **taxable earnings,** are paid on the first $7,000 of earnings of each employee. The first $7,000 that each employee earns during the year is the wage base limit for federal unemployment insurance purposes. *This column doesn't show the tax amount: it shows the earnings that are subject to being taxed.*

Example: Before this payroll, Bob Jones has cumulative earnings of $6,800. In this pay period, he earns $624. Since the employer pays these unemployment taxes on the first $7,000 of earnings, only $200 will be taxed (we will provide tax rates in next chapter) of the $624.

Total taxable earnings for unemployment taxes per employee	$7,000
Cumulative earnings before pay period for Jones	6,800
Taxable earnings	$ 200

Now look at the lines on the payroll register for Susan O'Mally, Pat Regan, and Jim Zott. No federal unemployment insurance tax needs to be paid for any of these employees because each of them had earned $7,000 before this pay period.

(I) Taxable Earnings FICA: Social Security

All employees are taxed for Social Security until they have earned $65,400 for the calendar year. This column shows the amount of earnings that will be taxed for Social Security. It *does not* show the actual tax.

Example: Susan O'Mally has earned $64,625 before this pay period. Since she has earned more than the maximum of $65,400 after this payroll, only $775 will be taxed for Social Security:

$$\begin{array}{r} \$65,400 \\ -\ 64,625 \\ \hline \$\quad 775 \end{array}$$

(J) Taxable Earnings FICA: Medicare

All employee earnings are subject to the FICA Medicare tax.

(K) FICA Deduction—Social Security

The rate for Social Security is 6.2 percent on $65,400. In column (I) we see the taxable earnings for Social Security. By multiplying the 6.2 percent times the taxable earnings for each employee, we arrive at the Social Security tax.

Example: For this pay period for Jim Zott only $540 of the $1,380 is taxable for Social Security (column I)

$$\begin{array}{r} \$65,400 \\ -\ 64,860 \\ \hline \$\quad 540 \times .062 = \$33.48 \end{array}$$

(L) FICA Deduction—Medicare

The rate for Medicare is 1.45 percent on all employee earnings.

Example: Jim Zott's whole earnings of $1,380 is multiplied times 1.45 percent to arrive at a Medicare tax of $20.01.

$$\$1,380 \times .0145 = \$20.01$$

(M) Federal Income Tax

Federal income tax does not have a cutoff point. Employees are taxed on the total amount of their earnings for the year. The amount of tax withheld depends upon the person's (1) income, (2) marital status, and (3) number of exemptions claimed. Withholding tables are provided in *Circular E* of the *Employer's Tax Guide* published by the IRS.

> **Example:** Susan O'Mally is married, earning $1,375 per week, and claims three allowances. Using Figure 7-2 (p. 240), we get a tax of $222.

At the end of the year, the employee must prepare a federal tax return (Form 1040) and file it with the IRS. If too much tax has been withheld, the employee can request a refund; if too little has been taken out, the employee must pay the amount due when his or her tax return is filed. Various tax deductions and tax credits affect the amount of tax due.

(N) State Income Tax

Assume a 5 percent state income tax rate. Like federal income tax, there is no cutoff point. All of the employee's earnings are taxed.

> **Example:** Pat Regan's state income tax is $45.
>
> | Gross pay | | Tax rate | | State income tax |
> |---|---|---|---|---|
> | $900 | × | .05 | = | $45 |

(O) Medical Insurance

Fred's Market deducts $22 from hourly workers and $44 from salaried workers to pay for **medical insurance.**

(P) Net Pay

Net pay, or *take home pay,* is gross pay less deductions. Gross pay is what we wished we had; net pay is what we are stuck with.

> **Example:** Abby King, who is single, has worked a 44-hour week this pay period. Therefore, her gross earnings for the week are $644. Abby has one allowance. She will take home $429.53 as her net pay. This is what Abby's check showed.
>
> | Gross Pay | | | $644.00 |
> |---|---|---:|---:|
> | *Less:* | FICA — Social Security | $ 39.93 | |
> | | FICA — Medicare | 9.34 | |
> | | Federal Income Tax | 100.00 | |
> | | State Income Tax | 32.20 | |
> | | Medical Insurance | 22.00 | 203.47 |
> | Net Pay | | | $440.53 |

(Q) Check Number

When the payroll is paid, the check number is recorded in the payroll register.

(R & S) Distribution of Expense Accounts

These two columns identify the specific accounts to which the total gross earnings of $4,923 [column (F)] will be charged. For Fred's Market some employee earnings are allocated to office salaries and some to market wages. (We will show how this is done in the next unit when data from the payroll register is used to journalize and post the payroll entry.)

LEARNING UNIT 7-2 REVIEW

AT THIS POINT you should be able to

- ◆ Explain and prepare a payroll register. (p. 244)
- ◆ Explain the purpose of the taxable earnings columns and how they relate to the cumulative earnings columns. (p. 247)

SELF-REVIEW QUIZ 7-2

(The forms you need are on pages 231–232 of the *Study Guide and Working Papers.*)

Ryan Leter is an hourly employee who is paid weekly. He is paid overtime at a rate of 1.5 times his hourly pay for any hours he works over 40 each week. Ryan Leter has cumulative earnings of $64,600 before this pay period. This week he earns $1,200. Calculate his net pay, assuming the following facts:

1. FICA: Social Security, 6.2 percent on $65,400; Medicare, 1.45 percent with no wage base limit.
2. He is married claiming two allowances (use the table in Figure 7-2).
3. State income tax rate is 7 percent.
4. No other deductions are taken out by his employer.

Solutions to Self-Review Quiz 7-2

1. FICA: Social Security — $800 × .062 = $49.60;
   Medicare — $1,200 × .0145 = $17.40.
2. Federal income tax is $188 by table.
3. State income tax is $84.
   Thus, his net pay = $861 ($1,200 − $49.60 − $17.40 − $188 − $84).

Quiz Tip: Only the first $800 of Leter's wages is subject to social security tax ($65,400 − $64,600).

LEARNING UNIT 7-3
Recording and Paying the Payroll

Since the payroll register is a multicolumn form used only to record payroll data, we must take the data from the payroll register and prepare a journal entry in the general journal to record the payroll and then post to the specific accounts in the general ledger. Refer to the payroll register shown in Figure 7-4, pp. 244–245.

For Fred's Market, the payroll for the week ending on November 25, 19XX is recorded in the general journal as follows:

General Journal																	
Nov	25	Office Salaries Expense			3	6	5	5	00								
		Market Wages Expense			1	2	6	8	00								
		FICA — Social Security Payable										2	1	5	95		
		FICA — Medicare Payable											7	1	39		
		Federal Income Tax Payable										7	8	4	00		
		State Income Tax Payable										2	4	6	15		
		Medical Insurance Payable										1	7	6	00		
		Wages and Salaries Payable										3	4	2	9	51	
		Records payroll from payroll															
		register for week ended Nov. 25															

Note that the debits to **Office Salaries Expense** and **Market Wages Expense** come from the totals of the distribution of expense accounts on the payroll register (p. 245). The credits to **FICA—Social Security Payable** and **FICA—Medicare Payable,** the FIT Payable, SIT Payable, and Medical Insurance Payable are from the totals of these deductions on the payroll register. Keep in mind that these deductions are liabilities. The credit to **Wages and Salaries Payable** (a liability account) is from the total of the net pay column on the payroll register. The ledger of Fred's Market will look as follows *after* the posting process has been completed:

Wages and Salaries Payable 202	FICA — Social Security Payable 203	FICA — Medicare Payable 204
3,429.51	215.95	71.39
Liability on the balance sheet	Liability on the balance sheet	Liability on the balance sheet

Federal Income Tax Payable 205	State Income Tax Payable 206	Medical Insurance Payable 207
784.00	246.15	176.00
Liability on the balance sheet	Liability on the balance sheet	Liability on the balance sheet

Office Salaries Expense 601	Market Wages Expense 602
3,655.00	1,268.00
Expense on the income statement	Expense on the income statement

Figure 7-5 on page 252 summarizes this process.

PAYROLL CHECKING ACCOUNTS: PAYING THE PAYROLL

Fred's Market pays payroll by check from a special payroll checking account. The account is called Payroll Checking Cash. Most medium- to large-size firms have a separate checking account *for payroll checks* and a regular checking account for all other checks. Employers use a payroll checking account for paychecks for two reasons: 1) it gives them better internal control over the amounts deposited for a pay period, and 2) it allows for easier reconciliation of the account at the end of each month.

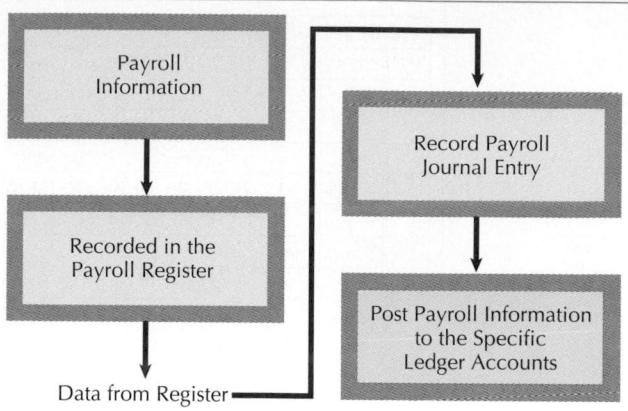

FIGURE 7-5 The Payroll Recording and Posting Process (see p. 253.)

A deposit for the total net amount of the payroll is placed in this separate checking account. When all the checks are written, the payroll checking account balance should be zero. The following journal entries would result in paying the payroll.

Payroll Checking Cash ← Separate account for payroll
   Cash   set up.

Wages and Salaries Payable ← Payroll paid and balance in
   Payroll Checking Cash   Payroll Checking is zero.

The checks from Fred's Market provide space to list amounts earned along with deductions, as shown in Figure 7-6 for Susan O'Mally. Keep in mind that if

FIGURE 7-6
Check from Fred's Market.

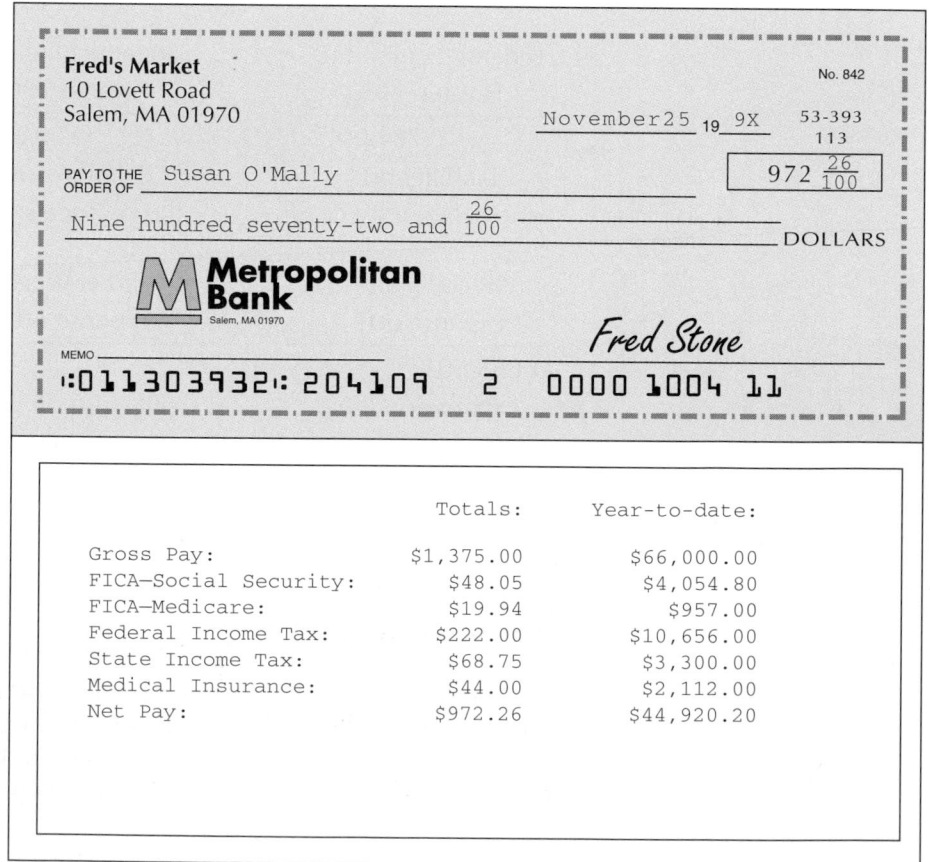

	Totals:	Year-to-date:
Gross Pay:	$1,375.00	$66,000.00
FICA—Social Security:	$48.05	$4,054.80
FICA—Medicare:	$19.94	$957.00
Federal Income Tax:	$222.00	$10,656.00
State Income Tax:	$68.75	$3,300.00
Medical Insurance:	$44.00	$2,112.00
Net Pay:	$972.26	$44,920.20

the account Payroll Checking Cash is not used, payroll can be paid by debiting Wages and Salaries Payable and crediting Cash.

THE INDIVIDUAL EMPLOYEE EARNINGS RECORD

Before concluding this chapter, it is important to look at how Fred keeps an individual record of each person's earnings and deductions, as required to meet federal employment laws and state regulations.

Fred maintains a summary of each employee's earnings, deductions, net pay for each payroll period, and cumulative earnings during the year. Figure 7-7 on page 254 is a partial **individual employee earnings record** for Susan O'Mally. This record will help Fred gather information to pay taxes and report quarterly and yearly payroll amounts. Individual employee earnings records generally break the calendar year into quarters, showing quarterly totals and year-to-date totals for earnings and taxes withheld. Keep in mind that each quarter is 13 weeks.

Note in the record for Susan that in the fourth quarter in week 48, she pays no more tax for Social Security since she is over the maximum $65,400. However, she will continue to pay Medicare on all of her earnings.

Figure 7-8 reviews the payroll function for Fred.

FIGURE 7-8 Payroll Function for Fred's Market

LEARNING UNIT 7-3 REVIEW

AT THIS POINT you should be able to

♦ Explain how to enter payroll information into the general journal from the payroll register. (p. 250)
♦ Journalize entries to pay a payroll. (p. 251)
♦ Update an individual employee earnings record. (p. 254)

SELF-REVIEW QUIZ 7-3

(The forms you need are on page 232 of the *Study Guide and Working Papers.*) Indicate which of the following statements are false:

(Cont. on p. 255)

FIGURE 7-7 Employee Individual Earnings Record

3375.24

INDIVIDUAL EMPLOYEE EARNINGS RECORD
FOR SUSAN O'MALLEY
FOURTH QUARTER, 19XX

Week #	Hours Worked Regular	Overtime	Total Earnings	Deductions Soc. Sec.	Medicare	Fed. Inc. Tax	State Inc. Tax	Med. Ins.	Net Pay	Check No.	Cumulative Pay
40			1375 00	85 25	19 94	222 00	68 75	44 00	935 06	710	53625 00
41			1375 00	85 25	19 94	222 00	68 75	44 00	935 06	750	55000 00
42			1375 00	85 25	19 94	222 00	68 75	44 00	935 06	780	56375 00
43			1375 00	85 25	19 94	222 00	68 75	44 00	935 06	812	57750 00
44			1375 00	85 25	19 94	222 00	68 75	44 00	935 06	830	59125 00
45			1375 00	85 25	19 94	222 00	68 75	44 00	935 06	842	60500 00
46			1375 00	85 25	19 94	222 00	68 75	44 00	935 06	871	61875 00
47			1375 00	85 25	19 94	222 00	68 75	44 00	935 06	893	63250 00
48			1375 00	48 05	19 94	222 00	68 75	44 00	972 26	915	64625 00
											66000 00
Total 4th Quarter			17875 00	730 05	259 22	2886 00	893 75	572 00	12533 98		
Total for Year			71500 00	4054 80	1036 88	11544 00	3575 00	2288 00	49001 32		

All Dunkin' Donuts shops keep a master file of employee information, containing every employee's name, address, phone number, Social Security number, rate of pay, hours worked per week, and W-4 form. Different shop owners offer different rates of pay, depending on local conditions. They offer different benefits as well. They employ mostly part-time workers, usually with a core of full-timers. Fred, for example, pays clerks with less than one year's experience the minimum wage. He offers health and dental insurance. Some of the bigger shop owners also offer profit sharing to employees with a minimum of five years of service. The frequency of pay varies by state, and sometimes by city or county. So, of course, do tax rates.

All this information must be recorded and reported to the various state, local, and federal authorities—and to Dunkin' Donuts headquarters, through the zone's Business Consultant.

Scheduling workers and keeping payroll records are Fred's least-favorite jobs. He was pleased to hear Dwayne announce at an Advisory Council meeting that

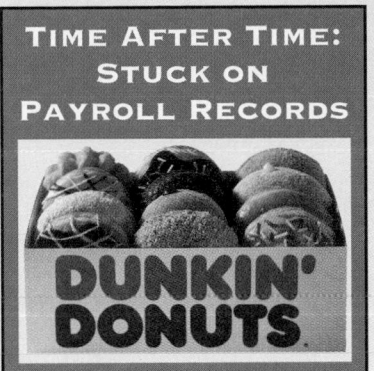

TIME AFTER TIME: STUCK ON PAYROLL RECORDS

the company's new IBM terminals will offer an electronic scheduling package.

"Wow! That will really help, Dwayne!" said Fred joyously. "No more different colors of ink just to keep track of who will work when! Now we can plan around the exam schedules of the part-timers without a hassle! Scheduling will be my favorite module in the new system!"

"Sure," said Molly Harris, another shop owner. "Now you can concentrate on payroll records. What fun!"

Fred groaned.

DISCUSSION QUESTIONS

1. What payroll records does Fred need to keep for his donut shop?
2. What other information might Fred want in order to schedule working hours for each employee?
3. How does the payroll register help Fred prepare the payroll? Consult the process outlined on page 253.

---

1. The use of a payroll register to record a company's payroll is optional.
2. FICA — Social Security Payable is a liability on the income statement.
3. Wages and Salaries Expense has a normal credit balance.
4. Individual employee earnings records are used by employees to keep track of their wages.
5. Every calendar quarter has 13 weeks.

Quiz Tip: There are four quarters in a year.

Solution to Self-Review Quiz 7-3

Statements 1, 2, 3, and 4 are false.

SUMMARY OF KEY POINTS

Learning Unit 7-1

1. The Fair Labor Standards Act states that a worker (1) will receive a minimum hourly rate of pay and (2) will work a maximum of 40 hours during the week at the regular rate of pay with time and a half after 40 hours.
2. In order for the rules of the Fair Labor Standards Act to apply to an employer, the employer must be involved in interstate commerce.
3. The employee and employer equally contribute to Social Security tax an amount that is based on a given yearly rate and wage base for a calendar year. Only Social Security tax has a wage base limit of $65,400 as of this writing. Medicare has no wage base limit, so an employee and employer will pay this tax on all of the employee's earnings during the calendar year.
4. Tax tables for federal income tax withholding can be found in IRS *Circular E, Employer's Tax Guide* (also known as Publication 15).

Learning Unit 7-2

1. Gross pay less deductions equals net pay.
2. The taxable earnings columns do not show the tax. They show amount of earnings to be taxed for unemployment taxes, Social Security, and Medicare. Note that FICA is made up of two taxes, Social Security and Medicare.

Learning Unit 7-3

1. A payroll register provides the data for journalizing the payroll entry in the general journal.
2. Deductions for payroll represent liabilities for the employer until paid.
3. The account distribution columns of the payroll register indicate which accounts will be debited to record the total payroll wages and salaries expense when a journal entry is prepared.
4. The accounts *FICA – Social Security Payable* and *FICA – Medicare Payable* accumulate the tax liabilities of both the employer and the employee for Medicare and Social Security.
5. Paying a payroll results in debiting *Wages and Salaries Payable* and crediting *Cash* (or Payroll Checking Cash).
6. The individual employee earnings records are updated soon after the payroll register is prepared.

KEY TERMS

Allowance (also called exemption) A certain dollar amount of a person's income that will be considered non-taxable for income tax withholding purposes.

Calendar year A one-year period beginning on January 1 and ending on December 31. Employers must use a calendar year for payroll purposes, even if the employer uses a fiscal year for financial statements and for any other reasons.

Fair Labor Standards Act (Federal Wage and Hour Law) A law the majority of employers must follow that contains rules stating the minimum hourly rate of pay and the maximum number of hours a worker will work before being paid time and a half for overtime hours worked. This law also has other rules and regulations that employers must follow for payroll purposes.

Federal income tax withholding Amount of federal income tax withheld by the employer from the employee's gross pay; the amount withheld is determined by the employee's gross pay, the pay period, the number of allowances claimed by the employee on the W-4 form, and by the marital status indicated on the W-4 form.

FICA (Federal Insurance Contributions Act) Part of the Social Security Act of 1935, this law requires that a tax be levied on both the employer and employee up to a certain maximum rate and wage base for Social Security tax purposes. Furthermore, there is a tax for Medicare purposes with no employer or employee wage base maximum.

FICA—Medicare Payable A liability account that accumulates tax for Medicare.

FICA—Social Security Payable A liability account that accumulates tax for Social Security.

Gross earnings Amount of pay received before any deductions.

Individual employee earnings record An accounting document that summarizes the total amount of wages paid and the deductions for the calendar year. It aids in preparing governmental reports. A new record is prepared for each employee each year.

Interstate commerce Test that is applied to determine whether an employer must follow the rules of the Fair Labor Standards Act. If an employer communicates or does business with another business in some other state it is usually considered to be involved in interstate commerce.

Market Wages Expense An account that records from the payroll register gross wages earned by employees of a market (grocery) outlet.

Medical insurance A deduction from employee's paycheck for health insurance.

Net pay Gross pay less deductions. Net pay (or *take home pay*) is what the worker actually takes home.

Office Salaries Expense An account that records from the payroll gross salaries earned by employees of an office.

Pay (or payroll) period A length of time used by an employer to calculate the amount of an employee's earnings. Pay periods can be weekly, biweekly (once every two weeks), semimonthly (twice each month), or monthly.

Payroll register A multicolumn form that can be used to record payroll data. The data in the payroll register is then used to prepare the general journal entry to record the paying of employees for a pay period.

Payroll tax deposits Amounts an employer pays to the government for payroll taxes. We will discuss these deposits in more detail in Chapter 8.

State income tax withholding Amount of state income tax withheld by the employer from the employee's gross pay.

Taxable earnings Shows amount of earnings subject to a tax. This *does not* show the tax itself.

W-4 (Employee's Withholding Allowance Certificate) A form filled out by employees used by employers to supply needed information about the number of allowances claimed, marital status, etc. The form is used for payroll purposes to determine federal income tax withholding from an employee's paycheck.

Wage bracket tables Various charts in IRS Circular E providing information about deductions for federal income tax based on earnings and data supplied on the W-4 form.

Wages and Salaries Payable A liability account that shows net pay for payroll before employees are paid. Account zeros out after employees are paid.

Workers' Compensation Insurance Insurance required by employers to protect their employees against losses due to injury or death incurred while on the job.

QUESTIONS, MINI EXERCISES, EXERCISES, AND PROBLEMS

Discussion Questions

1. What is the purpose of the Fair Labor Standards Act (also called Federal Wage and Hour Law)?
2. Explain how to calculate overtime.
3. Define and state the purpose of completing a W-4 form (called the *Employee's Withholding Allowance Certificate*).
4. The more allowances an employee claims on a W-4 form the more take home pay the employee gets with each paycheck. Please comment.
5. Why should a business prepare a payroll register before employees are paid? Please explain.

(Cont. on p. 259)

BLUEPRINT FOR RECORDING, POSTING, AND PAYING THE PAYROLL

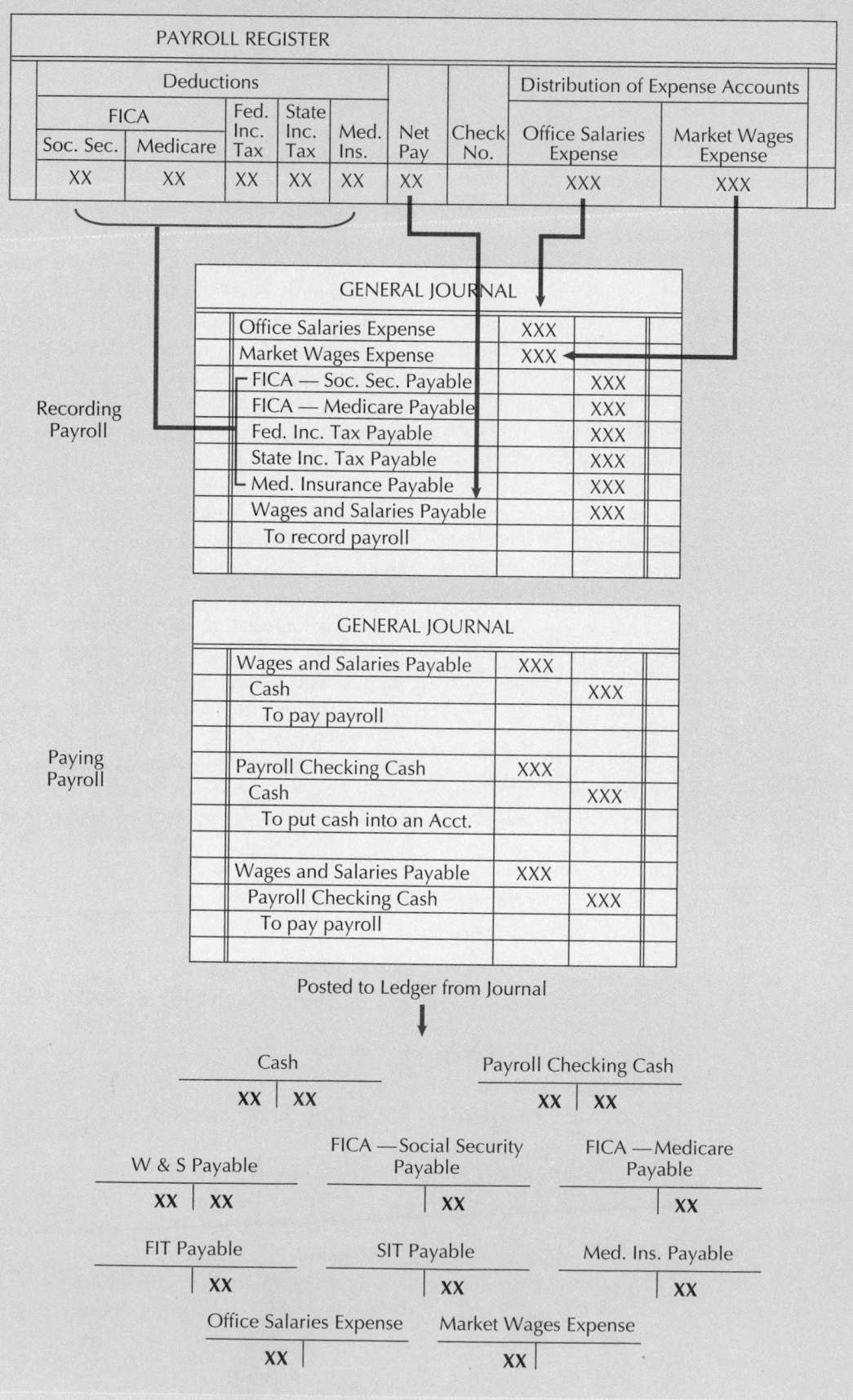

6. True or false: the taxable earnings column of a payroll register records the amount of tax due.

7. Define and state the purpose of FICA taxes.

8. Explain how to calculate Social Security and Medicare.

9. Do you agree or disagree with the following statement: the employer doesn't have to contribute to Social Security.

10. Explain how federal and state income tax withholding are determined.

11. What is a calendar year?

12. True or false: an employer must always use a calendar year for payroll purposes.

13. What purpose does the individual employee earnings record serve?

14. Why does payroll information center on 13-week quarters?

15. Please draw a diagram showing how the following items relate to each other: (A) a weekly payroll; (B) a payroll register; (C) individual employees' earnings; (D) general journal entries for payroll; (E) a payroll checking account.

16. If you earned $130,000 this year, you would pay more Social Security and Medicare tax than your partner who earned $75,000. Do you agree or disagree? Please provide calculations to support your answer.

Mini Exercises

(The forms you need are on page 234 of the *Study Guide and Working Papers.*)

Calculating Gross Earnings

1. Calculate the total wages earned (assume an overtime rate of time and a half over 40 hours).

Employee	Hourly Rate	No. of Hours Worked
A. Dawn Slow	$10	37
B. Jill Jones	12	50

FICA

2. Pete Martin, single claiming 1, has cumulative earnings before this weekly pay period of $80,000. Assuming he is paid $1,200 this week, what will his deduction be for FIT and FICA (Medicare and Social Security)? Use tables and rates in text.

Net Pay

3. Calculate Pete's Net Pay from 2 above. State income tax is 5 percent and death insurance is $40.

Payroll Register

4. From the following identify:

1. Total of gross pay — comes from distribution of expense accounts
2. A deduction
3. Net Pay

_____ A. Office Salaries Expense and Wages Expense

_____ B. FICA — SS Payable

_____ C. FICA — Medicare Payable

_____ D. Federal Income Tax Payable

_____ E. Medical Insurance Payable

_____ F. Wages and Salaries Payable

Payroll Account

5. From the following indicate if the title is:

1. An Asset	**4.** Appears in the Income Statement
2. A Liability	**5.** Appears on the Balance Sheet
3. An Expense	

_____ **a.** FICA — Social Security Payable

_____ **b.** Office Salaries Expense

_____ **c.** Federal Income Tax Payable

_____ **d.** FICA — Medicare Payable

_____ **e.** Wages and Salaries Payable

Exercises

(The forms you will need are on pages 235 – 236 of the *Study Guide and Working Papers.*)

7-1. Calculate the total wages earned for each employee (assume an overtime rate of time and a half over 40 hours):

Employee	Hourly Rate	No. of Hours Worked
Bob Role	$ 8	35
Jill West	12	44
Dale Aster	11	46

7-2. Compute the Net Pay for each employee using the federal income tax withholding tables in Figure 7-2 (Assume the following for FICA: Social Security tax is 6.2 percent on a wage base limit of $65,400; Medicare is 1.45 percent on all earnings; the payroll is paid weekly; there is no state income tax).

Employee	Status	Claiming	Cumulative Pay	This Week's Pay
Alvin Cell	Married	1	$50,000	$1,190
Angel Lowe	Single	0	$64,300	$1,200

7-3. Complete the table:

	Category	↑	Normal Balance	Account Appears on Which Financial Report?
Medical Insurance Payable				
Wages and Salaries Payable				
Office Salaries Expense				
Market Wages Expense				
FICA—Social Security Payable				
Federal Income Tax Payable				
State Income Tax Payable				

7-4. The following weekly payroll journal entry was prepared by Luster Company from its payroll register. Which columns of the payroll register has the data come from? How does the *taxable earnings* column of the payroll register relate to this entry?

Payroll register and the journal entry.

Oct.	7	Shop Salaries Expense	4 0 0 0 00			
		Factory Wages Expense	2 0 0 0 00			
		FICA–Social Security Payable			3 7 2 00	
		FICA–Medicare Payable			8 7 00	
		Federal Income Tax Payable			1 2 0 0 00	
		State Income Tax Payable			1 2 5 6 00	
		Union Dues Payable			1 1 0 00	
		Wages and Salaries Payable			2 9 7 5 00	

7-5. The following amounts have been taken from the weekly payroll register for the Debra Company on October 9, 19XX. Using the same account title headings that we have used in this chapter, please prepare the general journal entry to record the payroll for Debra Company for October 9.

Recording payroll by journal entry.

Factory Wages Expense	$3,579.00
Office Salaries Expense	1,597.00
Deduction for FICA — Social Security	296.15
Deduction for FICA — Medicare	75.05
Deduction for federal income tax	1,112.84
Deduction for state income tax	258.80
Deduction for union dues	350.00

Group A Problems

(The forms you need are on pages 237–241 of the *Study Guide and Working Papers*.)

7A-1. From the following information, please complete the chart for gross earnings for the week. (Assume an overtime rate of time and one half over 40 hours.)

Calculating gross earnings with overtime.

Check Figure:

d. $660   Gross Earnings

	Hourly Rate	No. of Hours Worked	Gross Earnings
a. Joe Jackson	$ 6	40	
b. Edna Kane	8	47	
c. Dick Wall	10	42	430
d. Pat Green	12	50	660

7A-2. March Company has five salaried employees. Your task is to record the following information into a payroll register.

Completing a payroll register.

Employee	Allowance and Marital Status	Cumulative Earnings Before this Payroll	Weekly Salary	Department
Kool, Alice	M-1	$42,000	$1,200	Sales
Lose, Bob	S-1	30,000	680	Office
Moore, Linda	M-2	59,200	1,240	Office
Relt, Rusty	M-3	64,000	1,270	Sales
Veel, Larry	S-0	29,000	610	Sales

Assume the following:

1. **FICA:** Social Security, 6.2 percent on $65,400; Medicare, 1.45 percent on all earnings.
2. Each employee contributes $25 per week for union dues.
3. State income tax is 6 percent of gross pay.
4. FIT is calculated from tables in Figures 7-2 and 7-3.

Check Figure:

Net Pay $3,382.49

Completing a payroll register and journalizing the payroll entry.

7A-3. The bookkeeper of Gore Co. gathered the following data from individual employees' earnings records and daily time cards. Your task is to (1) complete a payroll register on December 12 and (2) journalize the appropriate entry to record the payroll.

Employee	Allowance and Marital Status	Cumulative Earnings Before this Payroll	M	T	W	T	F	Hourly Rate of Pay	Department
Boy, Pete	M-1	$64,100	5	11	9	8	8	$18	Sales
Heat, Donna	S-0	15,000	8	10	9	9	4	16	Office
Pyle, Ray	M-3	66,000	8	10	10	10	10	16	Sales
Vent, Joan	S-1	19,000	8	8	8	8	8	20	Office

Assume the following:

1. **FICA:** Social Security, 6.2 percent on $65,400; Medicare, 1.45 percent on all earnings.
2. Federal income tax is calculated from tables in Figures 7-2 and 7-3.
3. Each employee contributes $25 per week for health insurance.
4. Overtime is paid at a rate of time and a half over 40 hours.

Check Figure:

Net Pay $2,309.64

Payroll register completed; journalizing and posting.

7A-4. Gary Nelson, Accountant, has gathered the following data from the time cards and individual employee earnings records. Your task is to

1. On December 5, 19XX, prepare a payroll register for this weekly payroll.
2. Journalize (p. 4) in the general journal and post to the general ledger accounts.

Employee	Allowance and Marital Status	Cumulative Earnings Before this Payroll	Weekly Salary	Check No.	Department
Aulson, Andy	M-3	$30,000	$ 950	30	Factory
Flynn, Jacki	M-1	50,000	$1,000	31	Office
Moore, Jeff	M-2	60,000	1,200	32	Factory
Sullivan, Alison	M-1	65,000	1,300	33	Office

Check Figure:

Net Pay $3,235.87

Assume the following:

1. **FICA:** Social Security, 6.2 percent on $65,400; Medicare, 1.45 percent on all earnings.
2. Federal income tax is calculated from tables in Figure 7-2.
3. State income tax is 5 percent of gross pay.
4. Union dues are $10 per week.

Group B Problems

(The forms you need are on pages 237–241 in the *Study Guide and Working Papers*.)

Calculating gross earnings with overtime.

7B-1. From the following information, please complete the chart for gross earnings for the week. (Assume an overtime rate of time and one half over 40 hours.)

		Hourly Rate	No. of Hours Worked	Gross Earnings
a.	Joe Jackson	$ 5	40	
b.	Edna Kane	9	47	
c.	Dick Wall	12	36	
d.	Pat Green	14	55	

Check Figure:
d. Gross Pay $875

Completing a payroll register.

7B-2. March Company has five salaried employees. Your task is to record the following information into a payroll register.

Employee	Allowance and Marital Status	Cumulative Earnings Before this Payroll	Weekly Salary	Department
Kool, Alice	M-1	$45,150	$1,290	Sales
Lose, Bob	S-1	22,575	645	Office
Moore, Linda	M-2	59,300	1,240	Office
Relt, Rusty	M-3	64,500	1,300	Sales
Veel, Larry	S-0	21,875	625	Sales

Check Figure:
Net Pay $3,468.65

Assume the following:

1. FICA: Social Security, 6.2 percent on $65,400; Medicare, 1.45 percent on all earnings.
2. Each employee contributes $25 per week for union dues.
3. State income tax is 6 percent of gross pay.
4. FIT is calculated from tables in Figures 7-2 and 7-3.

Completing a payroll entry and journalizing the payroll entry.

7B-3. The bookkeeper of Gore Co. gathered the following data from individual employees' earnings records and daily time cards. Your task is to (1) complete a payroll register on December 12 and (2) journalize the appropriate entry to record the payroll.

Employee	Allowance and Marital Status	Cumulative Earnings Before this Payroll	M	T	W	T	F	Hourly Rate of Pay	Department
Boy, Pete	S-1	$64,900	12	11	7	7	7	$16	Sales
Heat, Donna	S-0	19,000	8	9	9	9	5	16	Office
Pyle, Ray	M-3	67,550	10	10	10	10	5	20	Sales
Vent, Joan	S-1	13,500	6	8	8	8	8	19	Office

Check Figure:
Net Pay $2,323.36

Assume the following:

1. FICA: Social Security, 6.2 percent on $65,400; Medicare, 1.45 percent on all earnings.
2. Federal income tax is calculated from tables in Figures 7-2 and 7-3.
3. Each employee contributes $25 per week for health insurance.
4. Overtime is paid at a rate of time and a half over 40 hours.

Payroll entry completed; journalizing and posting.

7B-4. Gary Nelson, Accountant, has gathered the following data from the time cards and individual employee earnings records. Your task is to

1. On December 5, 19XX, prepare a payroll register for this weekly payroll.
2. Journalize (p. 4) in the general journal and post to the general ledger accounts.

Employee	Allowance and Marital Status	Cumulative Earnings Before this Payroll	Weekly Salary	Check No.	Department
Aulson, Andy	M-3	$30,000	$ 800	30	Factory
Flynn, Jacki	M-1	50,000	$1,100	31	Office
Moore, Jeff	M-2	60,000	1,050	32	Factory
Sullivan, Alison	M-1	65,000	1,200	33	Office

Assume the following:

1. FICA: Social Security, 6.2 percent on $65,400; Medicare 1.45 percent on all earnings.
2. Federal income tax is calculated from tables in Figure 7-2.
3. State income tax is 6 percent of gross pay.
4. Union dues are $15 per week.

REAL WORLD APPLICATIONS

7R-1.

Small Company, a sole proprietorship, has two employees, Jim Roy and Janice Alter. The owner of Small Co. is Bert Ryan. During the current pay period, Jim worked 48 hours and Janice 56. The reason for these extra hours is that both Jim and Janice worked their regular 40-hour workweek, plus Jim worked 8 extra hours on Sunday while Janice worked 8 extra hours on Saturday and Sunday. Their contract with Small Co. is that they are each paid an hourly rate of $8 per hour with all hours over 40 to be time and a half and double time on Sunday. Bert, the owner, feels he is also entitled to a salary, since he works as many hours. He plans to pay himself $425.

As the accountant for Small Co., (1) calculate the gross pay for Jim and Janice and (2) write a letter to Bert Ryan with your recommendations regarding his salary.

7R-2.

Marcy Moore works for Moose Company during the day and GTA Company at night. Both her employers have deducted FICA taxes for Social Security and Medicare. At year end Marcy has earned $58,000 at her job at Moose Company and $8,000 at GTA.

At a party she tells Bill Barnes, an accountant, who tells her she has paid too much Social Security tax and that she is entitled to a refund or credit on her tax return she files for the year. Bill suggests she call the Internal Revenue Service's toll-free number and ask for taxpayer assistance. Assume Social Security of 6.2 percent on $65,400 and Medicare of 1.45 percent on all of Marcy's earnings during the year.

As Marcy's friend, (1) check to see if indeed she has overpaid any FICA tax, and (2) write a brief note to her and show her your calculations to support your answer.

YOU make the call

Critical Thinking/Ethical Case

7R-3.

Russ Todd works for a delicatessen. As the bookkeeper Russ has been asked by the owner to keep two separate books for meals tax. The owner has asked Todd to hire someone on the weekends to punch in false tapes that can be submitted to the state. These tapes would show low sales and thus less liability for meals tax payments. You make the call. Write down your specific recommendations to Russ.

ACCOUNTING RECALL
A CUMULATIVE APPROACH

THIS EXAM REVIEWS CHAPTERS 1 THROUGH 7

Your *Study Guide and Working Papers* (pages 244–255) have forms to complete this exam, as well as worked-out solutions. The page references next to each question identify what page to turn back to if you answer the question incorrectly.

PART 1 Vocabulary Review

Match the terms to the appropriate definition or phrase.

Page Ref.

(247)	1. Taxable earnings columns	A. Gross pay less deductions
(217)	2. Petty cash	B. In payroll register records, gross payroll
(212)	3. NSF	
(239)	4. Exemption	C. Liability accounts for social security and medicare
(161)	5. Closing	
(251)	6. Office salaries expense	D. An asset
(240)	7. Wage bracket tables	E. Does not show tax
(249)	8. Net pay	F. Found in Circular E
(254)	9. Employee individual earnings record	G. Result of a bounced check
		H. Not taxable
(251)	10. FICA — Social Security payable, and FICA — Medicare payable	I. Helps get updated figure for Capital in ledger
		J. Broken down into quarters

PART II True or False (Accounting Theory)

(216)	11.	Petty cash is a liability.
(243)	12.	A payroll register is always the same for each company.
(247)	13.	The taxable earnings column of a payroll register shows earnings that are subject to being taxed.
(254)	14.	Wages and Salaries Payable records gross pay.
(122)	15.	Accumulated depreciation is a contra-asset on the balance sheet.

CONTINUING PROBLEM

I n preparing for next year, Freedman has hired two employees to work hourly, assisting with some troubleshooting and repair work.

Assignment:

(See pp. 245 – 254 in your *Study Guide and Working Papers*.)

1. Record the following transactions in general journal format, and post to the general ledger.
2. Prepare a payroll register.
3. Prepare a trial balance as of November 30, 19XX.

Assume the following transactions:

   a) The following accounts have been added to the chart of accounts: Wage Expense #5110; FICA-Social Security Payable #2020; FICA-Medicare Payable #2030; FIT Payable #2040; State Income Tax Payable #2050; and Wages Payable #2010.

   b) FICA-Social Security is taxed at 6.2 percent up to $65,400 in earnings; and Medicare at 1.45 percent on all earnings.

   c) State income tax is 2 percent of gross pay.

   d) Both employees have no federal income tax taken out of their pay.

   e) Each employee earns $10 an hour and is paid 1½ times their salary for hours worked in excess of 40 weekly.

Nov	1	Billed Vita Needle Company $6,800; invoice #12675 for services rendered
	3	Billed Accu Pac, Inc. $3,900; invoice #12676 for services rendered
	5	Purchased new shop benches $1,400 on account from System Design Furniture
	7	Paid the two employee wages: Lance Kumm, 38 hours, and Anthony Hall, 42 hours
	9	Received the phone bill, $150.
	12	Collected $500 of the amount due from Taylor Golf
	14	Paid the two employee wages: Lance Kumm, 25 hours, and Anthony Hall, 36 hours.
	18	Collected $800 of the amount due from Taylor Golf.
	20	Purchased a fax machine for the office from Multi Systems on credit, $450.
	21	Paid the two employee wages: Lance Kumm, 26 hours, and Anthony Hall, 35 hours

8

THE EMPLOYER'S TAX RESPONSIBILITIES

Principles and Procedures

THE BIG PICTURE

The goals for Eldorado Computer Center this year are to increase earnings, expand into additional locations, and increase revenue by 30 percent. Freedman realizes that company growth will eventually mean hiring more people. Therefore, although his revenue will increase, his operating expenses will also increase because of the additional payroll expenses he will incur.

After studying Chapter 8, you will understand these extra expenses. They include employer payroll taxes and worker's compensation insurance, which the law requires the employer to pay. Although Freedman is not offering benefits to his part-time employees at this time, he realizes that this too could become an additional operating expense.

Quarterly and annual federal tax returns must be submitted as well, similar to the personal income tax return that you are required to submit once a year. And most states require the employer to pay state unemployment insurance (SUTA) for each employee.

♦ Calculating and journalizing employer payroll tax expenses. (p. 268)
♦ Completing the Employer's Quarterly Federal Tax Return and Deposit Coupon (Forms 941 and 8109) and paying tax obligations for FICA tax (Social Security and Medicare) and federal income tax. (p. 273)
♦ Preparing Forms W-2, W-3, 940-EZ, and estimates of workers' compensation insurance premiums. (p. 282)

In Chapter 7 we looked at how Fred's Market computed and recorded payroll data about its *employees*. This chapter focuses on specific tax responsibilities of the *employer*.

LEARNING UNIT 8-1
The Employer's Payroll Tax Expense

When opening a business, every employer must get a federal **employer identification number** (also known as an **EIN**) for purposes of reporting earnings, taxes, etc. When Fred opened Fred's Market, he filled out **Form SS-4** to obtain his EIN. The SS-4 form asks for the following information:

1. Name of applicant.
2. Trade name of business.
3. Address or place of business.
4. County in which business is located.
5. Name of the principle officer or owner of the business.
6. Type of business (sole proprietor, partnership, etc.).
7. The reason for applying for an EIN.
8. The date the business began.
9. The closing month of the accounting year.
10. First date that the business will pay its employees.
11. The potential number of employees in the coming year.
12. Main activity or nature of the business.

Fred's payroll tax obligations are recorded in the general journal when the payroll is recorded. Fred's Market is responsible for (1) Social Security and Medicare tax (or FICA), (2) federal unemployment tax (FUTA), and (3) state unemployment tax (SUTA). The total of these taxes are recorded in the **Payroll Tax Expense** account in the general ledger.

Let's look at how Fred calculates the amount of each tax.

CALCULATING THE EMPLOYER'S PAYROLL TAXES
FICA (Federal Insurance Contributions Act)

It is the responsibility of Fred's Market to match whatever its employees pay into FICA on a dollar-for-dollar basis each pay period. The accounts in the ledger, *FICA-Social Security Payable* and *FICA-Medicare Payable*, record the tax for *both* the employee and the employer. To determine the amount of FICA Fred's Market owes, we must use the FICA taxable earnings columns for Social Security and Medicare from the payroll register discussed in Chapter 7 and reproduced here for your convenience as Figure 8-1.

FRED'S MARKET
PAYROLL REGISTER
NOVEMBER 25, 19XX

Employee Name	Allowances and Marital Status	Cumulative Earnings	Salary per Week	No. of Hrs.	Wages per Hour	Earnings Regular	Earnings Overtime	Earnings Gross	Cumulative Earnings	Taxable Earnings Federal Unemployment	Taxable Earnings Soc. Sec.	Taxable Earnings Medicare
Jones, Bob	S-0	680000	—	39	1600	62400		62400	742400	20000	62400	62400
King, Abby	S-1	660000	—	44	1400	56000	8400	64400	724400	40000	64400	64400
O'Mally, Susan	M-3	6462500	137500			137500		137500	6600000	—	77500 ①	137500
Regan, Pat	M-1	4230000	90000			90000		90000	4320000	—	90000	90000
Zott, Jim	M-2	6486000	138000			138000		138000	6624000	—	54000	138000
TOTALS		18518500	365500			483900	8400	492300	19010800	60000	3483300	492300
Discussions in this chapter are keyed to these letters	(A)	(B)	(C)		(D)	(E)	(F)	(G)	(H)	(I)	(J)

① $65,400
  −64,625
   $ 775

FIGURE 8-1 Partial Payroll for Fred's Market

The payroll register shows that $3,483 [column (I)] of wages is subject to Social Security tax, while in column (J) we see $4,923 of wages is subject to tax for Medicare.

$$\text{Social Security} \quad \$3,483 \times .062 \ = \$215.95$$
$$\text{Medicare} \quad \$4,923 \times .0145 = \$\ 71.38$$

The employer must match the FICA contribution of the employee for Social Security *and* Medicare taxes.

FICA-Social Security Payable 203	FICA-Medicare Payable 204
215.95 (employee)	71.38 (employee)
215.95 (employer)	71.38 (employee)

FUTA (Federal Unemployment Tax Act)

Unemployment insurance is a joint effort on the part of the federal government, all 50 states, and U.S. territories. Each state is required to run its own unemployment program for its unemployed workers. The state programs are approved and monitored by the federal government.

To raise money for these unemployment programs, the federal government levies taxes on employers under a law called the **Federal Unemployment Tax Act (FUTA).** This law (1) induces states to create their own unemployment programs, and (2) allows the federal government to monitor state programs. As mentioned in Chapter 7, the FUTA tax currently is 6.2 percent of wages paid during the year and the wage base limit is $7,000.

Generally, the federal government allows employers a credit against FUTA tax as long as the employer has paid all monies due to the state unemployment fund on time. This credit, called the **normal FUTA tax credit,** cannot exceed 5.4 percent. So, an employer who is entitled to the normal FUTA credit will pay a net amount of eight-tenths of one percent, as shown below:

$$
\begin{array}{ll}
6.2\% & \text{FUTA tax} \\
-5.4\% & \text{normal FUTA tax credit} \\
.8\% & \text{net FUTA tax for federal purposes}
\end{array}
$$

In effect the federal law says to employees, "Comply with your state's unemployment tax laws and your total tax will not exceed a maximum of 6.2 percent: 0.8 percent to the federal government, and a state rate that will vary up to a maximum of 5.4 percent. Remember that employers alone are responsible for paying FUTA tax; it is never deducted from employees' wages.

In Learning Unit 8-3, we will look at how to complete the federal report and the deposit requirements for FUTA tax. For now, let's calculate the amount of accumulated federal unemployment tax for Fred's Market based on the unemployment column under taxable earnings in the payroll register. Remember the $600 in column H represents the amount of earnings taxable for federal unemployment.

To calculate the FUTA tax, we multiply the FUTA taxable earnings times the net FUTA tax rate.

Taxable FUTA Earnings		FUTA Rate		FUTA Tax	FUTA Tax Payable 209
$600	$\times$	.008	$=$	$4.80	4.80

FUTA tax is paid after the end of a calendar year if the total tax owed is less than $100 for the year. If the amount owed is more than $100, the tax is paid on a quarterly basis, no later than the end of the month following the end of the quarter.

SUTA (State Unemployment Tax Acts)

To support state unemployment programs, all states charge employers a certain percent in taxes under the **State Unemployment Tax Act (SUTA).** Generally, employers pay more in SUTA tax than FUTA tax.

Each state has its own state unemployment wage base limit. Currently, these limits range from a low of $7,000 to a high of $25,000. The limits vary according to the needs of each state unemployment fund and are subject to change. For the current rate in your state, check with the state department of labor and employment.

The states vary the percentage rates charged to employers. The differences are based on the total amount of contributions the employer makes into the state fund and the dollar amount of unemployment claim money paid out of the fund to former employees of the employer. For example, employers who do not lay off employees during slack seasons (such as after the Christmas season or at the end of a ski resort season) owe a smaller percentage for state unemployment tax purposes. The variance, which is called an **experience** or **merit rating,** motivates employers to stabilize their workforce.

Fred's current state unemployment tax rate is 5.4 percent of the first $7,000 paid to each of Fred's employees during the calendar year. From the taxable earnings column (H) of the payroll register in Figure 8-1, we multiply $600 by the SUTA rate of 5.4 percent.

$$\underset{\$600}{\text{Taxable Earnings}} \times \underset{.054}{\text{SUTA Rate}} = \underset{\$32.40}{\text{SUTA Tax}} \qquad \dfrac{\text{SUTA Tax Payable 208}}{\quad | 32.40}$$

SUTA taxes are paid after the end of each **calendar quarter.** Employers are required to complete a state unemployment tax report and pay any SUTA tax due at this time.

JOURNALIZING PAYROLL TAX EXPENSE

Before showing the general journal entry to record Fred's Market payroll tax expense, let's review the categories and rules that affect the specific payroll ledger accounts used to record this expense.

Accounts Affected	Category	↑ ↓	Rules
Payroll Tax Expense	Expense	↑	Dr.
FICA—Social Security Payable	Liability	↑	Cr.
FICA—Medicare Payable	Liability	↑	Cr.
State Unemployment Tax Payable (SUTA)	Liability	↑	Cr.
Federal Unemployment Tax Payable (FUTA)	Liability	↑	Cr.

The total of employer's portion of FICA for Social Security and Medicare tax, FUTA, and SUTA equals the total of Fred's payroll tax expense.

The Journal Entry

The following is the general journal entry recording Fred's payroll tax expense for the weekly payroll ending November 25. (We will look carefully at the general ledger entries in Learning Unit 8-2.)

GENERAL JOURNAL

Page 10

Nov	25	Payroll Tax Expense	610	3 2 4 53		
		FICA — Social Security Payable	203		2 1 5 95	$3,483 × .062 = $215.95
		FICA — Medicare Payable	204		7 1 38	$4,923 × .0145 = $71.38
		SUTA Tax Payable	208		3 2 40	$600 × .054 = $32.40
		FUTA Tax Payable	209		4 80	$600 × .008 = $4.80
		Records employer's payroll tax				

In Learning Unit 8-2 we'll look at how to complete the form that goes with the payment of FICA tax (Social Security and Medicare) of the employee *and* the employer along with the amounts of federal income tax deducted from employees' paychecks. It is important to keep in mind that FUTA and SUTA taxes also have separate report forms to be completed, which we will look at in Learning Unit 8-3.

LEARNING UNIT 8-1 REVIEW

AT THIS POINT you should be able to

◆ Explain the purpose of the Form SS-4. (p. 268)
◆ Explain the use of the taxable earnings column in calculating the employer's payroll tax expense. (p. 270)
◆ Calculate the employer's payroll taxes. (p. 268)
◆ Explain the difference between FUTA and SUTA taxes. (p. 270)
◆ Explain when FUTA and SUTA taxes are paid. (p. 270)
◆ Journalize the employer's payroll tax expense. (p. 272)

SELF-REVIEW QUIZ 8-1

(The forms you need are on page 256 of the *Study Guide and Working Papers.*)

Given the following, prepare the general journal entry to record the payroll tax expense for Bill Co. for the weekly payroll of July 8. Assume the following: (a) SUTA is paid at a rate of 5.6 percent on the first $7,000 of earnings; (b) FUTA is paid at the net rate of .8 percent on the first $7,000 of earnings; (c) FICA rate for Social Security is 6.2 percent on $65,400, and Medicare is 1.45 percent on all earnings.

Employee	Cumulative Pay Before This Week's Payroll	Gross Pay For Week
Bill Jones	$6,000	$800
Julie Warner	6,600	400
Al Brooks	7,900	700

Solution to Self-Review Quiz 8-1

July	8	Payroll Tax Expense		2 2 2 15				
		FICA — Social Security Payable				1 1 7 80	
		FICA — Medicare Payable				2 7 55	
		SUTA Tax Payable				6 7 20	
		FUTA Tax Payable				9 60	
		Record employer's payroll tax					

FICA:
SS: $1,900 × .062 = $117.80
Med: 1,900 × .0145 =   27.55
SUTA: 1,200 × .056 =   67.20
FUTA: 1,200 × .008 =   9.60
                        $222.15

Quiz Tip: Al Brooks earned more than $7,000; thus his employer takes no SUTA or FUTA taxes on the $700 of Al's gross pay.

LEARNING UNIT 8-2

Form 941: Completing the Employer's Quarterly Federal Tax Return and Paying Tax Obligations for FICA Tax and Federal Income Tax

In this unit, we will look at Fred's Market's last calendar quarter (October, November, and December). Our goals are (1) determining the timing for paying FICA (for both the employees and the employer) and federal income tax (or FIT) and (2) completing **Form 941,** the **Employer's Quarterly Federal Tax Return.**

Before getting into specific deposit rules and form completions, let's look at Figure 8-2, which is a worksheet that Fred's accountant prepared to monitor Fred's Market deposit requirements for the taxes reported on Form 941—Social Security, Medicare, and federal income taxes. These so-called **Form 941 taxes,** will be discussed later in this Learning Unit. (The worksheet in Figure 8-2 has nothing to do with unemployment taxes, which follow different rules.)

Do note on the worksheet that the quarter is 13 weeks. Since Form 941 requires FICA information to be separated by Social Security and Medicare, you can see how helpful the worksheet can be. Note in week 47 that some wages are not taxable for Social Security since the $65,400 wage base limit was met. However, *all* wages for Medicare are taxable since there is no wage base limit for this tax. This worksheet can be built from the information in each individual's employee's earnings record and the weekly payroll registers.

Now let's look at the deposit rules Fred's Market must follow regarding Form 941 taxes (which are FICA and FIT).

DEPOSITING FORM 941 TAXES

The amount of tax due must be deposited in what is called an authorized depository in Fred's area or a Federal Reserve Bank. Authorized depositories are banks that have been authorized by the Federal Reserve system to accept payroll tax deposits from their own checking account customers. Federal Reserve banks can accept payroll tax deposits from any business, no matter where the business maintains its checking account.

| Payroll Period | Week # | Earnings | FIT | Taxable FICA Wages for | | FICA | | Total Tax | Cumulative Tax |
				Soc. Sec.	Medicare	Soc. Sec. EE + ER	Medicare EE + ER		
Oct.	40	4819 00	756 00	4819 00	4819 00	597 56	139 75	1493 31	1493 31
	41	5013 25	810 00	5013 25	5013 25	621 64	145 38	1577 02	3070 33
	42	4819 00	756 00	4819 00	4819 00	597 56	139 75	1493 31	4563 64
	43	4892 75	768 00	4892 75	4892 75	606 70	141 89	1516 59	6080 23
		19544 00	3090 00	19544 00	19544 00	2423 46	566 77	6080 23	
Nov.	44	4819 00	756 00	4819 00	4819 00	597 56	139 75	1493 31	7573 54
	45	5007 15	809 00	5007 15	5007 15	620 89	145 21	1575 10	9148 64
	46	5152 50	832 00	5152 50	5152 50	638 91	149 42	1620 33	10768 97
	47	4923 00	784 00	3483 00	4923 00	431 89*	142 77*	1358 66	12127 63
		19901 65	3181 00	18461 65	19901 65	2289 25*	577 15*	6047 40	
Dec.	48	5090 50	822 00	1464 50	5090 50	181 60	147 62	1151 22	13278 85
	49	5121 75	827 00	1495 75	5121 75	185 47	148 53	1161 00	14439 85
	50	5629 00	909 00	2003 00	5629 00	248 37	163 24	1320 61	15760 46
	51	5700 75	921 00	2074 00	5700 75	257 18	165 32	1343 50	17103 96
	52	4819 00	756 00	1193 00	4819 00	147 93	139 75	1043 68	18147 64
		26361 00	4235 00	8230 25	26361 00	1020 55	764 46	6020 01	
Totals for the Quarter		65806 65	10506 00	46235 90	65806 65	5733 26*	1908 38*	18147 64	

*Off one or two cents due to rounding

FIGURE 8-2 Fred's Accountant has Prepared this Worksheet to Track the Form 941 Payroll Taxes for Fred's Market During the Last Quarter

Types of Payroll Tax Depositors

For payroll tax deposit purposes, employers are classified as either **monthly** or **semiweekly depositors.** A monthly depositor is an employer who only has to deposit Form 941 taxes on the fifteenth day of every month. Semi-weekly depositors must deposit their Form 941 taxes once or twice each week.

The employer's classification depends on the dollar amount of the Form 941 taxes it has paid in the past. The IRS has developed a rule known as the **look-back period** rule, to determine how to classify an employer for payroll tax deposits. Under this rule, the IRS will *look back* to a time period that begins on July 1 and ends the following June 30 of the past year. (For example, to determine the employer's status for 1997, the IRS will look at the period between July 1, 1995 and June 30, 1996.) If, during this look-back time period, the employer has paid under $50,000 of Form 941 taxes, the IRS considers the employer to be a *monthly depositor.* If the employer has paid $50,000 or more during this period, it is considered to be a *semiweekly depositor.* Figure 8-3 shows how the look-back period works for payroll purposes.

Fred's Market is a semiweekly depositor because it made in excess of $50,000 in FICA and FIT deposits during the look-back period. If Fred's Market had made less than $50,000 in payroll tax deposits during the look-back period, it would have been classified as a monthly depositor.

New employers are automatically classified as monthly depositors until they have been in business long enough to have a look-back period for evaluation purposes. The employer's status is reevaluated every year.

Rules for Monthly Depositors   The rules for monthly depositors are fairly simple. They are:

1. The employee and employer Social Security and Medicare taxes and the employees' FIT accumulated during any month must be deposited by the fifteenth of the next month.
2. If the fifteenth of the month is a Saturday, Sunday, or bank holiday, the employer must make the payroll tax deposit on the next banking day.

Rules for Semiweekly Depositors   Semiweekly depositors like Fred's Market may have to make up to two payroll tax deposits every week, depending on when employees are paid. For this purpose, each seven-day week begins on Wednesday and ends on the following Tuesday. The seven-day week is broken into two payday time periods: Wednesday through Friday, and Saturday through Tuesday. In addition, the following rules apply:

1. If the company's payday occurs on Wednesday, Thursday, or Friday, the payroll tax deposit is due on the following Wednesday. If the company's payday occurs

> The IRS examines the amount of Form 941 taxes paid during the period beginning on July 1 and ending on June 30 to determine whether the employer is a monthly depositor or a semi-weekly depositor. This is called the look-back period rule.

FIGURE 8-3 The level of payroll taxes paid during the look-back period determines how often employer deposits payroll taxes.

	Monday	Tuesday	Wednesday	Thursday	Friday	Saturday	Sunday
The payday occurs this week ⟶			■ If the payday occurs on one of these days, the deposit will be due Wednesday of the next week.			★ If the payday occurs on Saturday or Sunday, or...	
	★...Monday or Tuesday, then payroll tax deposit will be due and payable on Friday of this week.		■ Deposit day for Wednesday–Friday payday		★ Deposit day for Saturday–Tuesday payday		

FIGURE 8-4 The payday determines when the tax deposit is due.

on Saturday, Sunday, Monday, or Tuesday, the payroll tax deposit is due on the following Friday. Thus, if an employer pays its employees on a Thursday and a Monday, it must make two payroll tax deposits—one on Wednesday for the Thursday payday, and one on Friday for the Monday payday.

2. If a bank holiday occurs after the end of the payday time-period but before the day the payroll tax deposit is due, the employer gets one extra day in which to make the deposit. So, a deposit due on a Wednesday will be due on Thursday, and a Friday deposit will be due on the following Monday.

As a general rule, the depositor always has three banking days in which to make the payroll tax deposit. The diagram in Figure 8-4 shows how these rules are applied.

Here is how the rules apply to Fred's Market. First, look back at Figure 8-2 (p. 274) to locate the dates of each weekly payday. Next, look at Figure 8-5, which shows a calendar for the last quarter of the year.

Note that each payday falls on a Friday. Because Fred's Market is a semi-weekly payroll tax depositor, its Form 941 payroll tax deposits are due on the following Wednesday. Fred's first payday in October falls on October 7. Its first payroll tax deposit will be due on October 12. Another deposit will be due on every Wednesday from that date until the end of the year. However, if we look at week 51 in Figure 8-2 (p. 274), the payday for this week is December 23, which is two days before Christmas. Christmas is a bank holiday, but in looking at the December calendar in Figure 8-5, we see that it falls on a Sunday. Under the law, Monday, December 26 then becomes the legal holiday. Fred must then apply the rule regarding a holiday that falls between a payday and the tax deposit day, and will make the Form 941 tax deposit on Thursday, December 29.

FIGURE 8-5 Last calendar quarter for Fred's Market shows paydays falling on Fridays.

○ = Paydays
△ = Tax Deposit Days

FIGURE 8-6 Form 8109.

Completion of Form 8109 to Accompany Deposits

Fred's accountant informed Fred that the check that is written for the amount of the Form 941 payroll tax deposit each week must be accompanied by IRS **Form 8109,** Federal Tax Deposit Coupon.

Fred received a book of coupons when he got the EIN for Fred's Market. Figure 8-6 on page 277 shows Form 8109 completed for the week 47 Form 941 payroll tax deposit. Note that the dollar amount found at the top of the form ($1,358.66) is the same as the amount found in the "Total Tax" column for week 47 in Figure 8-2.

In looking at Figure 8-6 you will see that in the upper-right-hand corner the "Type of Tax" and "Tax Period" must be indicated by darkening the appropriate oval using a No. 2 pencil. Fred's bookkeeper has darkened the "941" and "4th Quarter" ovals for the week 47 payday.

Journalizing and Posting Payroll Tax Deposits

Payment of the payroll tax deposit for week 47 is made in the general journal as follows:

Accounts Affected	Category	↑	↓	Rules
FICA—Social Security Payable	Liability		↓	Dr.
FICA—Medicare Payable	Liability		↓	Dr.
Federal Income Tax Payable	Liability		↓	Dr.
Cash	Asset		↓	Cr.

			FRED'S MARKET GENERAL JOURNAL			
Nov	30	FICA — Social Security Payable	203	431 89	
		FICA — Medicare Payable	204	142 77	
		Federal Income Tax Payable	205	784 00	
		Cash	111		1358 66
		To record the Form 941 tax deposit for week			
		#47 payroll on November 25, 19XX			

Now let's look at the partial general ledger of Fred's Market to get a better understanding of how specific payroll accounts in the ledger are updated regarding FICA (Social Security and Medicare) and FIT. Note in the *FICA-Social Security* and *Medicare Payable* accounts (shown on p. 279) how the posting came from the general journal for the employees' and employer's share of FICA tax.* The general journal is also used when the payroll tax deposit is made, recording a debit to the *FICA-Social Security* and *Medicare Payable* accounts as well as the *Federal Income Tax Payable* account.

Under the Form 941 payroll tax deposit rules, the general journal entries to record the payroll are made weekly each Friday, while the entries to record the payment of the payroll taxes are made each Wednesday after the Friday payday. Check Figure 8-2 (p. 274) to see how the Form 941 tax liability has been recorded and then paid in the partial general ledger accounts shown on page 279.

Note: each credit would actually be 2 credits — one from the employee and one from the employer.

FICA–Social Security Payable				203
Date	PR	Dr.	Cr.	Cr. Bal.
19XX				
Nov. 4	GJ28		597 56	597 56
9	GJ28	597 56		0
11	GJ28		620 89	620 89
16	GJ28	620 89		0
18	GJ29		638 91	638 91
23	GJ29	638 91		0
25	GJ29		431 89	431 89
30	GJ29	431 89		0

FICA–Medicare Payable				204
Date	PR	Dr.	Cr.	Cr. Bal.
19XX				
Nov. 4	GJ28		139 75	139 75
9	GJ28	139 75		0
11	GJ28		145 21	145 21
16	GJ28	145 21		0
18	GJ29		149 42	149 42
23	GJ29	149 42		0
25	GJ29		142 77	142 77
30	GJ29	142 77		0

FORM 941: EMPLOYER'S QUARTERLY FEDERAL TAX RETURN

Fred's accountant used the worksheet in Figure 8-2 in preparing Form 941 for the last quarter for Fred's Market (see Fig. 8-7 on the next page). The top section of the form identifies the taxpayer (Fred's Market), its address, the date the quarter ended, and Fred's Market's EIN. The postal code for the state where Fred's Market is located is filled in on the left-hand side of the form.

This is how Fred's accountant filled out Form 941 using the dollar amounts from Figure 8-2:*

Line 1a: This line is only filled in for the first quarter of the year. It is left blank for the last quarter.

2: Total gross pay: $65,806.65 ($19,544.00 + $19,901.65 + $26,361.00)

3: Total income tax: $10,506.00 ($3,090.00 + $3,181.00 + $4,235.00)

4: No adjustment — this line is only used in special situations.

5: The same amount as is found on line 3: $10,506.00.

6a: The wages subject to Social Security tax are multiplied by 12.4 percent (6.2 percent for the employee and 6.2 percent for the employer). Total taxable wages are $46,235.90 ($19,544.00 + $18,461.65 + $8,230.25). Note that this line is different from Line 2 because of the $65,400 Social Security wage base limit. The tax is $5,733.25.

6b: No employees of Fred's Market receive any tip income, so this line is left blank.

7: Taxable wages for Medicare are $65,806.65 ($19,544.00 + $19,901.65 + $26,361.00). Note that this line *will* be the same as Line 2 because all earnings are subject to Medicare tax. The tax is $1,908.39 (1.45% for the employee and 1.45% for the employer).

8: Total of Social Security and Medicare is $7,641.64 ($5,733.25 + $1,908.39).

9: Due to rounding of the dollar amounts, additional cents might be added to Line 9 as an adjustment. The amount must be written on Line 9. The goal here is to have Line 13 equal Line 17(d), found at the bottom of the form. For this problem no adjustment is needed.

10: This line is the sum of Line 8 as adjusted by Line 9.

11: This line is the sum of Lines 5 and 10 added together.

12: If Fred's Market advanced any Earned Income to its employees, it would deduct the amount on this line.

13: This line is the net of Line 11 as adjusted by any amount found on Line 12.

14: Total of the deposits made by Fred for the last quarter is $18,147.64, under the semiweekly deposit rule. Note that the last Form 941 tax deposit

Fraction of cents: If there is a difference between the total tax on Line 8 and the total deducted from your employees' wages or tips because of fractions of cents added or dropped in collecting the tax, report the difference on Line 9. Use the center column on Line 9 with a + or − sign to show the amount of the adjustment.

---

* Note that the rounding results in a one cent difference for *both* Social Security and Medicare.

Department of the Treasury
Internal Revenue Service

4141

Employer's Quarterly Federal Tax Return

► See separate instructions for information on completing this return.

Please type or print.

OMB No. 1545-0029

Enter state code for state in which deposits made . ► M A (see page 2 of instructions).

Name (as distinguished from trade name)
Fred Stone

Trade name, if any
Fred's Market

Address (number and street)
10 Lovett Road

Date quarter ended
December 31,

Employer identification number
58-12134791

City, state, and ZIP code
Salem, MA 01970

T	
FF	
FD	
FP	
I	
T	

If address is different from prior return, check here ► ☐

IRS Use

1 1 1 1 1 1 1 1 1 1   2   3 3 3 3 3 3   4 4 4

5 5 5   6   7   8 8 8 8 8   9 9 9   10 10 10 10 10 10 10 10 10 10

If you do not have to file returns in the future, check here ► ☐ and enter date final wages paid ►

If you are a seasonal employer, see **Seasonal employers** on page 2 and check here (see instructions) ► ☐

1	Number of employees (except household) employed in the pay period that includes March 12th ►		
2	Total wages and tips subject to withholding, plus other compensation	**2**	65,806 | 65
3	Total income tax withheld from wages, tips, and sick pay	**3**	10,506 | 00
4	Adjustment of withheld income tax for preceding quarters of calendar year	**4**	
5	Adjusted total of income tax withheld (line 3 as adjusted by line 4—see instructions)	**5**	10,506 | 00
6a	Taxable social security wages . . . . $ 46,235.90 × 12.4% (.124) =	**6a**	5,733 | 25
b	Taxable social security tips . . . . $ × 12.4% (.124) =	**6b**	
7	Taxable Medicare wages and tips . . . . . $ 65,806.65 × 2.9% (.029) =	**7**	1,908 | 39*
8	Total social security and Medicare taxes (add lines 6a, 6b, and 7). Check here if wages are not subject to social security and/or Medicare tax . . . . ► ☐	**8**	7,641 | 64
9	Adjustment of social security and Medicare taxes (see instructions for required explanation) Sick Pay $ _____ ± Fractions of Cents $ _____ ± Other $ _____ =	**9**	
10	Adjusted total of social security and Medicare taxes (line 8 as adjusted by line 9—see instructions)	**10**	7,641 | 64
11	**Total taxes** (add lines 5 and 10)	**11**	18,147 | 64
12	Advance earned income credit (EIC) payments made to employees, if any	**12**	
13	Net taxes (subtract line 12 from line 11). **This should equal line 17, column (d) below** (or line D of Schedule B (Form 941))	**13**	18,147 | 64
14	Total deposits for quarter, including overpayment applied from a prior quarter	**14**	18,147 | 64
15	**Balance due** (subtract line 14 from line 13). Pay to Internal Revenue Service	**15**	-0-

16 Overpayment, if line 14 is more than line 13, enter excess here ► $ _____
and check if to be: ☐ Applied to next return **OR** ☐ Refunded.

- **All filers:** If line 13 is less than $500, you need not complete line 17 or Schedule B.
- **Semiweekly depositors:** Complete Schedule B and check here . . . . ► ☒
- **Monthly depositors:** Complete line 17, columns (a) through (d) and check here . . . . ► ☐

17 Monthly Summary of Federal Tax Liability.

(a) First month liability	(b) Second month liability	(c) Third month liability	(d) Total liability for quarter
6,080.23	6,047.40	6,020.01	18,147.64

Sign Here

Under penalties of perjury, I declare that I have examined this return, including accompanying schedules and statements, and to the best of my knowledge and belief, it is true, correct, and complete.

Signature ► *Fred Stone*   Print Your Name and Title ►Fred Stone, Owner   Date ► 1/31/9X

FIGURE 8-7 Employer's Quarterly Federal Tax Return

---

* Note that due to rounding in Figure 8-2 (page 274), we are off by one cent. Thus we are using $1908.39 instead of $1908.38. If any adjustment were needed, it would be entered on line 9. Here no adjustment is needed.

is made after the year ends, but is allowed to be taken as a last quarter deposit because it applies to the December 30 payday.

15: There is no balance due to Fred's.

16: There is no overpayment for Fred's. Note that directly below Line 16 are two boxes that only are checked under certain circumstances. The accountant will check off the box for semiweekly depositors and prepare Form 941 Schedule B, which is an itemized listing of the semiweekly deposits made for the last quarter. This schedule is not shown here.

17: This line is broken into four sections. The first three sections labeled (a), (b), and (c) are the monthly Form 941 liability. These amounts are found in the column "Total Tax" at the end of October, November, and December in Figure 8-2. Note that the sum of (a), (b), and (c) will equal (d). Recall that the amount found on Line 13 must equal the amount found in box 17(d).

LEARNING UNIT 8-2 REVIEW

AT THIS POINT you should be able to

- Explain which taxes are reported on Form 941. (p. 273)
- Understand how employers are classified as payroll tax depositors. (p. 275)
- Explain the summary of Form 941 payroll tax deposit rules for monthly depositors. (p. 275)
- Explain the summary of Form 941 payroll tax deposit rules for semiweekly depositors. (p. 275)
- Prepare and explain the purpose of Form 8109. (p. 278)
- Record the general journal entry to pay FICA (Social Security and Medicare) and federal income taxes when a payroll tax deposit is made. (p. 278)
- Review how the general journal entries are posted into the general ledger to record the paying of employees and the paying of payroll taxes. (p. 279)
- Complete an Employer's Quarterly Federal Tax Return from a worksheet. (p. 280)

SELF-REVIEW QUIZ 8-2

(The blank forms you need are on page 257 of the *Study Guide and Working Papers*.)

Carol Ann's Import Chalet is a business that employs five full-time employees and four part-time employees. The accountant for Carol Ann's has determined that the business is a monthly depositor. The accountant prepared a worksheet showing the following payroll tax liabilities for the month of October:

Date	Social Security (EE + ER)	Medicare (EE + ER)	FIT
10/7	$ 486.56	$169.05	$ 829.00
10/14	632.15	165.01	901.00
10/21	579.43	131.05	734.00
10/28	389.99	142.24	765.00
Totals	$2,088.13	$607.35	$3,229.00

1. What is the dollar amount of the Form 941 tax deposit and when must it be made under the monthly deposit rule. Use Fig. 8-5 (p. 276) for the date.

2. Assume that Carol Ann's is classified as a semiweekly depositor. Please calculate the amount of each Form 941 tax deposit and when it would be made by completing the table on the next page (Use Fig. 8-5 for the dates):

Payday Date	Date of Deposit	Amount of Deposit
10/7	?	?
10/14	?	?
10/21	?	?
10/28	?	?

Solutions to Self-Review Quiz 8-2

1. As a monthly depositor, Carol Ann's deposit date would be Tuesday, November 15. The total amount of the deposit would be $5,924.48 ($2,088.13 + $607.35 + $3,229.00).

2. As a semiweekly depositor, Carol Ann's deposit schedule would be completed as follows:

Payday Date	Date of Deposit	Amount of Deposit
10/7	10/12	$1,484.61
10/14	10/19	1,698.16
10/21	10/26	1,444.48
10/28	11/2*	1,297.23*

* Note that this deposit will be made in November given the calendar dates found in Figure 8-5.

Quiz Tip: The tax for 941 is:

FICA – SS: employee and employer

FICA – MED: employee and employer

FIT: employee, only

LEARNING UNIT 8-3
W-2, W-3, Form 940-EZ, and Workers' Compensation

W-2: WAGE AND TAX STATEMENT

Form W-2, Wage and Tax Statement is a multipart form that is prepared by the employer each year. Fred's Market is required to give (or mail) copies of Form W-2 to each person who was employed in the past year. These forms must be distributed by January 31 of the following year. Employees use the figures on Form W-2 to compute the amount of income tax they must pay. One copy of the form must be attached to his or her federal income tax return; other copies must be attached to state and local tax returns.

Anyone who stopped working for Fred before the end of that year may be given a Form W-2 at any time after the employment ends. If the former employee asks for it, the employer must supply completed copies within 30 days of the request or the final wage payment, whichever is later.

Additional copies of Form W-2 are sent to the Social Security Administration and state and local governments. The employer retains a copy of the W-2 form for each employee for its records.

Figure 8-8 shows the W-2 that Susan O'Mally received from Fred's Market. The information was obtained from her individual employee earnings record. Note that Social Security wages and taxes are shown separately from the amounts reported for Medicare wages and taxes. That is because there is a wage base limit for the Social Security tax, but not for the Medicare tax.

W-3: Transmittal of Income and Tax Statements

Form W-3, Transmittal of Income and Tax Statements, is prepared and sent by the employer to the Social Security Administration along with copies of

Form W-2 (Figure 8-8)

a Control number **22222**	Void ☐	For Official Use Only ▶ OMB No. 1545-0008

b Employer's identification number 58-12134791	**1** Wages, tips, other compensation 71,500.00	**2** Federal income tax withheld 11,544.00
c Employer's name, address, and ZIP code	**3** Social security wages 65,400.00	**4** Social security tax withheld 4,054.80
Fred's Market 10 Lovett Road Salem, MA 01920	**5** Medicare wages and tips 71,500.00	**6** Medicare tax withheld 1,036.88
	7 Social security tips	**8** Allocated tips
d Employee's social security number 021-36-9494	**9** Advance EIC payment	**10** Dependent care benefits
e Employee's name (first, middle initial, last) Susan O'Mally 80 Garfield Street Marblehead, MA 01945	**11** Nonqualified plans	**12** Benefits included in box 1
	13 See Instrs. for box 13	**14** Other

15 Statutory employee ☐ · Deceased ☐ · Pension plan ☐ · Legal rep. ☐ · 942 emp. ☐ · Subtotal ☐ · Deferred compensation ☐

f Employee's address and ZIP code

16 State	Employer's state I.D. No.	**17** State wages, tips, etc.	**18** State income tax	**19** Locality name	**20** Local wages, tips, etc.	**21** Local income tax
MA	6 21-8966-4	71,500	3,575.00			

Cat. No. 10134D   Department of the Treasury—Internal Revenue Service

Form **W-2** Wage and Tax Statement **199X**

Copy A For Social Security Administration

For Paperwork Reduction Act Notice, see separate instructions.

FIGURE 8-8 Completed Form W-2

each employees' Form W-2. The W-3 form reports the total amounts of wages, tips, and compensation paid to employees; the total federal income tax withheld; the total Social Security and Medicare taxes withheld; and some other information.

Employers are required to send Form W-3 and Forms W-2 to the Social Security Administration for FICA tax purposes. The Social Security Administration, under a special agreement with the IRS, makes all information found on individual W-2 forms electronically available to the IRS so that it can check to verify the accuracy of the employer's 941 Forms and individual employees' federal income tax returns.

The information used to complete the W-3 form in Figure 8-9 came from a summary of the individual employee earnings records that Fred's accountant prepared after the end of the year (see Fig. 8-10 on page 284).

Form 940-EZ: Employer's Annual Federal Unemployment Tax Return

There are two types of federal unemployment tax returns. **Form 940-EZ, Employer's Annual Federal Unemployment Tax Return** is used by a business that only employs workers in one state. Businesses that employ workers in several states (multistate employers) must file a **Form 940.** Form 940 asks for additional information that is not required on Form 940-EZ.

Fred's Market must file Form 940-EZ. After the first year it files this form, the IRS will send Fred a preaddressed Form 940-EZ, near the close of each calendar year. Form 940-EZ must be filed no later than January 31 unless all required

DO NOT STAPLE

a Control number	33333	For Official Use Only ▶ OMB No. 1545-0008		

| b Kind of Payer ▶ | 941 ☒ Military ☐ 943 ☐ | 1 Wages, tips, other compensation 252,668.00 | 2 Federal income tax withheld 40,664.00 |
| | CT-1 ☐ 942 ☐ Medicare govt. emp. ☐ | 3 Social security wages 240,208.00 | 4 Social security tax withheld 14,892.90 |

c Total number of statements 5	d Establishment number	5 Medicare wages and tips 252,668.00	6 Medicare tax withheld 3,663.82

e Employer's identification number 58-12134791	7 Social security tips	8 Allocated tips

f Employer's name Fred's Market 10 Lovett Road Salem, MA 01970	9 Advance EIC payments	10 Dependent care benefits
	11 Nonqualified plans	12 Deferred compensation
	13 Adjusted total social security wages and tips	
	14 Adjusted total Medicare wages and tips	

| g Employer's address and ZIP code | | |
| h Other EIN used this year | 15 Income tax withheld by third-party payer | |

| i Employer's state I.D. No. 6 21-8966-4 | | |

Under penalties of perjury, I declare that I have examined this return and accompanying documents, and, to the best of my knowledge and belief, they are true, correct, and complete.

Signature ▶ *Fred Stone* Title ▶ Owner Date ▶1/31/XX

Telephone number (617) 555-1212

Form **W-3** Transmittal of Wage and Tax Statements **199X**

Department of the Treasury
Internal Revenue Service

FIGURE 8-9 Completed Form W-3

FUTA deposits have been made during the year, in which case the return can be filed by February 10. The completed form is shown in Figure 8-11.

FUTA As we saw earlier, the FUTA tax rate is .8 percent (or eight tenths of one percent) on the first $7,000 of each employee's gross pay. If Fred's accumulated FUTA tax liability is $100 or more during the calendar year, Fred must make a FUTA tax deposit with a Federal Reserve bank or a bank authorized to

FIGURE 8-10 Employee Earnings Record Summary

Employee	Total Earnings	FICA Taxable Earnings Soc. Sec.	FICA Taxable Earnings Medicare	FICA Tax Soc. Sec.	FICA Tax Medicare	FIT
Jones, Bob	$29,120.00	$29,120.00	$29,120.00	$1,805.44	$422.24	$5,252.00
King, Abby	33,488.00	33,488.00	33,488.00	2,076.26	485.58	5,772.00
O'Mally, Susan	71,500.00	65,400.00	71,500.00	4,054.80	1,036.88	11,544.00
Regan, Pat	46,800.00	46,800.00	46,800.00	2,901.60	678.60	7,176.00
Zott, Jim	71,760.00	65,400.00	71,760.00	4,054.80	1,040.52	10,920.00
	$252,668.00	$240,208.00	$252,668.00	$14,892.90	$3,663.82	$40,664.00

Form **940-EZ**

Department of the Treasury
Internal Revenue Service

Employer's Annual Federal Unemployment (FUTA) Tax Return

OMB No. 1545-1110

199X

T	
FF	
FD	
FP	
I	
T	

Name (as distinguished from trade name)   Calendar year
Fred Stone   199X

Trade name, if any
Fred's Market

Address and ZIP code
10 Lovett Road, Salem, MA 01970

Employer identification number
58 : 1213479 1

If incorrect, make any necessary changes. ▲

*Follow the chart under **Who May Use Form 940-EZ** on page 2. If you cannot use Form 940-EZ, you must use Form 940 instead.*

A   Enter the amount of contributions paid to your state unemployment fund. (See instructions for line A on page 4.) ▶ $ ....1,890.00..

B   (1) Enter the name of the state where you have to pay contributions ....▶ ..MASSACHUSETTS..
    (2) Enter your state reporting number as shown on state unemployment tax return. ▶ 281-615

If you will not have to file returns in the future, check here (see **Who Must File**, on page 2) **complete, and sign the return** . . . . . ▶ ☐

If this is an Amended Return check here . . . . ▶ ☐

Part I   Taxable Wages and FUTA Tax

1	Total payments (including payments shown on lines 2 and 3) during the calendar year for services of employees		**1**	252,668 00
2	Exempt payments. (Explain all exempt payments, attaching additional sheets if necessary.) ▶	Amount paid		
		2		
3	Payments for services of more than $7,000. Enter only amounts over the first $7,000 paid to each employee. Do not include any exempt payments from line 2. Do not use your state wage limitation. The $7,000 amount is the Federal wage base. Your state wage base may be different	**3** 217,668 00		
4	Total exempt payments (add lines 2 and 3)		**4**	217,668 00
5	**Total taxable wages** (subtract line 4 from line 1)	▶	**5**	35,000 00
6	**FUTA tax.** Multiply the wages on line 5 by .008 and enter here. (If the result is over $100, also complete Part II.)		**6**	280 00
7	Total FUTA tax deposited for the year, including any overpayment applied from a prior year (from your records)		**7**	280 00
8	**Amount you owe** (subtract line 7 from line 6). This should be $100 or less. Pay to "Internal Revenue Service".	▶	**8**	-0-
9	**Overpayment** (subtract line 6 from line 7). Check if it is to be: ☐ Applied to next return, or ☐ Refunded ▶		**9**	-0-

Part II   Record of Quarterly Federal Unemployment Tax Liability (Do not include state liability.) Complete only if line 6 is over $100.

Quarter	First (Jan. 1 – Mar. 31)	Second (Apr. 1 – June 30)	Third (July 1 – Sept. 30)	Fourth (Oct. 1 – Dec. 31)	Total for year
Liability for quarter	280.00	-0-	-0-	-0-	280.00

Under penalties of perjury, I declare that I have examined this return, including accompanying schedules and statements, and, to the best of my knowledge and belief, it is true, correct, and complete, and that no part of any payment made to a state unemployment fund claimed as a credit was, or is to be, deducted from the payments to employees.

Signature ▶ *Fred Stone*   Title (Owner, etc.) ▶ Owner   Date ▶ 2/10/XX

Cat. No. 10983G   Form **940-EZ** (1993)

FIGURE 8-11 Completed Form 940-EZ

take payroll tax deposits. The FUTA tax deposit rule is quite simple: if the amount of FUTA tax owed is $100 or more during any calendar quarter, the employer must deposit the amount due no later than one month after the quarter ends.

At the end of the first quarter Fred owes $280 for FUTA taxes. Fred's accountant has prepared a schedule showing how the tax was computed by taking each employee's weekly earnings times the amount earned each payday. (See Table 8-1 below for the calculations.) If an employee earned over the $7,000 FUTA wage base limit, only the first $7,000 will be taxable for FUTA purposes. Note that all of Fred's employees earned over the $7,000 FUTA limit during the first quarter of the year. Remember, because all of the employees of Fred's Market earned over $7,000 during the first quarter of the year, no further FUTA tax is due for the rest of the year. Please see Part II of the Form 940-EZ in Figure 8-11.

Since Fred owes $280 in FUTA taxes, he will make the FUTA tax deposit on April 30 to comply with the FUTA deposit rule. The general journal entry is prepared as shown below.

			FRED'S MARKET GENERAL JOURNAL				
*	April	30	FUTA Payable	212	2 8 0 00		
			SUTA Payable	213	1 8 9 0 00		
			Cash	111		2 1 7 0 00	
			To record the FUTA and SUTA tax				
			deposits for the first quarter of the year.				

* Note this could be two separate entries.

SUTA Fred must also pay state unemployment tax to Massachusetts. The SUTA tax is also due one month after the quarter ends, on April 30. Fred will pay out $1,890 in tax, based on a SUTA percentage rate of 5.4 percent on the first $7,000 that each of his employees have earned ($35,000 × .054 = $1,890).

The amount of SUTA Fred pays is shown on Lines A and B of Form 940-EZ.

WORKERS' COMPENSATION INSURANCE

Fred's Market is required to have **workers' compensation insurance** to insure its employees against losses due to accidental injury or death incurred while on the job. Fred is required to estimate the cost of this insurance and pay the premium in advance.

The premium for workers' compensation insurance is based on the total estimated gross payroll and the rate is calculated per $100 of weekly payroll. At year end, the actual payroll is compared to the estimated payroll, and Fred either will receive credit for overpayment or be responsible for paying additional premiums.

TABLE 8-1 COMPUTATION OF FUTA TAX FOR A YEAR

Employee	Amount Earned During Quarter						Amount Taxable for FUTA
Jones, Bob	13 Weeks	×	$624	per Week	=	$8,112	$7,000
King, Abby	13 Weeks	×	$560			$7,280	$7,000
O'Mally, Susan	13 Weeks	×	$1,375			$17,875	$7,000
Regan, Pat	13 Weeks	×	$900			$11,700	$7,000
Zott, Jim	13 Weeks	×	$1,380			$17,940	$7,000
							$35,000 × .008 = $280

These are the facts on which Fred's insurance cost was calculated:

1. Estimated payroll for Fred: $230,000.
2. Two grades of workers: Office and stockroom.
3. Rate per $100 of payroll: Office, 14 cents; stockroom, $1.90.
4. Estimated payroll: Office, $150,000; stockroom, $80,000.

This is how the estimated premium was calculated:

Office:	$150,000/$100 = 1,500 × $ .14 =	$ 210
Stockroom:	$80,000/$100 = 800 × $1.90 =	1,520
	Total Estimated Premium:	$1,730

Accounts Affected	Category	↑ ↓	Dr./Cr.
Prepaid Insurance, Worker's Compensation	Asset	↑	Dr.
Cash	Asset	↓	Cr.

Fred would have to pay $1,730 in advance. At the end of the year, his records show that his office payroll was $155,000 and his stockroom payroll was $87,542.

Give those amounts, Fred's actual premium should be $1,880.30 calculated as follows:

Office:	$155,000/$100 = 1,550 × $ .14 =	$ 217.00
Stockroom:	$87,542/$100 = 875.42 × $1.90 =	1,663.30
	Total Estimated Premium:	$1,880.30

Since the actual premium is $150.30 higher than the estimate, Fred must pay this amount in January together with the estimated premium for the next year.

The $150.30 adjustment takes place on December 31 by debiting *Workers' Compensation Insurance Expense* and crediting *Workers' Compensation Insurance Payable.*

Accounts Affected	Category	↑ ↓	Dr./Cr.
Workers' Compensation Insurance Expense	Expense	↑	Dr.
Workers' Compensation Insurance Payable	Liability	↑	Cr.

LEARNING UNIT 8-3 REVIEW

AT THIS POINT you should be able to

◆ Prepare a W-2 form. (p. 283)
◆ Explain the difference between a W-2 form and a W-3 form. (p. 283)
◆ Prepare a 940-EZ form. (p. 285)
◆ Explain the difference between a Form 940-EZ and a Form 940. (p. 283)
◆ Calculate estimated premium for workers' compensation. (p. 286)
◆ Prepare journal entries to record as well as adjust the premiums for workers' compensation insurance. (p. 287)

SELF-REVIEW QUIZ 8-3

(The forms you need are on page 257 of the *Study Guide and Working Papers.*)
Are the following questions true or false?

1. W-4's must be received by employees by January 31 of the following year.
2. Form W-3 is sent to the Social Security Administration yearly.

3. A Form 940 is prepared by a business that employs workers in only one state.

4. The Employer's Annual Federal Unemployment Tax Return records the employer's FICA and FIT tax liabilities.

5. A FUTA tax liability of $100 must be paid 10 days after the quarter ends.

6. Premiums for Workers' Compensation Insurance may be adjusted based on actual payroll figures.

Solutions to Self-Review Quiz 8-3

1. **False.** W-2 forms must be sent to each employee by January 31 of the next year. The W-4 form is filled out by a new employee and is used for calculating federal and state income taxes.

2. **True.**

3. **False.** The Form 940 will be prepared by a business that employs workers in more than one state. Form 940-EZ will be prepared by an employer with workers in only one state.

4. **False.** The Employer's Annual Federal Unemployment Tax Return records and reports the FUTA tax liability. The Form 941 records and reports the FICA and FIT tax liabilities.

5. **False.** A FUTA tax liability of $100 must be paid one month after the quarter ends.

6. **True.**

Quiz Tip: If you are getting refunds for FIT, you may want to change your withholding.

"As an employer, Fred, what are your tax responsibilities?" asked George Olsen, president of the local Kiwanis club. They were at one of the luncheons sponsored by the club every month. Fred had been asked to join a panel discussion on The Role of Small Business in Our Local Economy. Luckily, George had told the panelists the questions in advance, so Fred had his answers ready.

"Well, of course, I pay city, state, and U.S. government taxes myself. I also have to file city, state, and federal withholding taxes for each of my employees. I have to withhold state unemployment taxes, as well as FICA, which is another name for Social Security and Medicare taxes, for each of them. I pay workers' compensation, too," said Fred quickly.

"That's funny," said a voice from the audience. "My brother-in-law has a Dunkin' Donuts shop in the southern part of the state, and he doesn't pay any city taxes. What's going on here?"

"Naturally, the situation is slightly different for Dunkin' Donuts shop owners in different cities and towns in our state," said Fred confidently. "Not all cities have city income taxes. Different states have different regulations about worker's comp, as well."

"Oh, right," said the voice, sounding embarrassed.

"What happens at the corporate level at Dunkin' Donuts, Fred?" asked George Olsen, shifting the topic diplomatically.

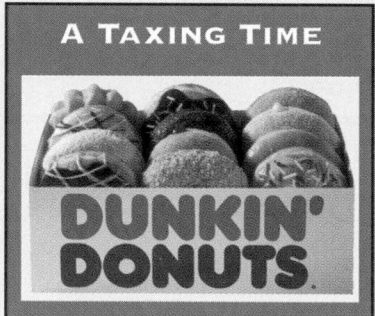

A TAXING TIME

"That's a really big operation, as you can imagine," said Fred. "We have corporate employees in some 20 states and countries, so a portion of the payroll function is not handled in-house. Instead it is outsourced to ADP, an international payroll processing service. They generate the checks and handle the tax reporting to the various cities, states, and countries. The corporate employees manage all the other aspects of the payroll process, from collecting information on hours worked to analysis of the labor dollars."

"Thanks, Fred," said George, "Now let's move on to Eva Jonet, who is going to tell us about advertising her new nail salon."

Fred nodded and breathed a sigh of relief as Eva took the microphone from him. He much preferred baking to public speaking!

DISCUSSION QUESTIONS

1. George had warned Fred not to use technical language in preparing his remarks, so Fred didn't mention Form 941 taxes. Define Form 941 taxes.

2. Fred is classified as a monthly depositor of Form 941 taxes. Why?

3. Assume that Fred owed $2,679.90 in Form 941 taxes for November. When would it be due? What would happen if that day were a Sunday?

SUMMARY OF KEY POINTS

Learning Unit 8-1

1. The Payroll Tax Expense for the employer is made up of FICA tax (Social Security and Medicare) and the state and federal unemployment insurance taxes.
2. The maximum amount of credit given for state unemployment taxes paid against the FUTA tax is 5.4 percent. This is known as the normal FUTA tax credit.
3. The Payroll Tax Expense is recorded at the time the payroll is recorded.

Learning Unit 8-2

1. Federal Form 941 is prepared and filed no later than one month after the calendar quarter ends. It reports the amount of Social Security, Medicare, and Federal Income taxes withheld from employees and the Social Security and Medicare taxes due from the employer during the quarter.
2. Social Security, Medicare, and federal income taxes are known as *Form 941 taxes.*
3. The total amount of Form 941 taxes paid by a business during a specific period of time determines how often the business will have to make its payroll tax deposits. This time period is called a *look-back period.*
4. Businesses will make their payroll tax deposits either monthly or semiweekly when paying Form 941 taxes.
5. Different deposit rules apply to monthly and semiweekly depositors.
6. Form 941 payroll tax deposits must be made using Form 8109 known as the Federal Tax Deposit Coupon.

Learning Unit 8-3

1. Information to prepare W-2 forms can be obtained from the individual employee earnings records.
2. The Form W-3 is used by the Social Security Administration in verifying that taxes have been withheld as reported on individual employee W-2 forms.
3. Form 940-EZ is prepared by January 31, after the end of the previous calendar year. This form can be filed by February 10 if all required deposits have been made by January 31.
4. If the amount of FUTA taxes is equal to or more than $100 during any calendar quarter, the deposit must be made no later than one month after the quarter ends. If the amount is less than $100, no deposit is required until the liability reaches the $100 point.
5. Workers' Compensation Insurance (the estimated premium) is paid at the beginning of the year by the employer to protect against potential losses to its employees due to accidental death or injury incurred while on the job.

KEY TERMS

Calendar Quarter A three-month time period. There are four calendar quarters in a calendar year (January 1 through December 31). The first quarter is January through March, the second is April through June, the third is July through September, and the fourth is October through December.

Employer identification number (EIN) This number assigned by the IRS is used by an employer when recording and paying payroll and income taxes.

Experience/merit rating A percentage rate that is assigned to a business by the state in calculating state unemployment taxes. The rate is based on the employment record and amount of contributions paid into the state unemployment fund. The lower the rating, the less tax that must be paid.

Federal Insurance Contributions Act (FICA) Part of the Social Security law that requires employees and employers to pay Social Security taxes and Medicare taxes.

Federal Unemployment Tax Act (FUTA) A tax paid by employers to the federal government. The 1997 rate is .8 percent after applying the normal FUTA tax credit (see below) on the first $7,000 of earnings of each employee.

Form 940, Employer's Annual Federal Unemployment Tax Return One version of the form used by employers at the end of the year to report the amount of unemployment tax due for the calendar year. This version of the form is used by an employer with workers in more than one state. If more than $100 is cumulatively owed in a quarter, it should be paid quarterly, one month after the end of the quarter. Normally payment is due January 31 after the calendar year, or February 10 if deposits have already been made by an employer.

Form 940-EZ, Employer's Annual Federal Unemployment Tax Return The other version of the form used by employers at the end of the year to report the amount of unemployment tax due for the calendar year. The "EZ" version of this form is used by an employer with workers in only one state.

Form 941, Employer's Quarterly Federal Tax Return A tax report that a business will complete after the end of each calendar quarter indicating the total FICA (Social Security and Medicare) owed plus the amount of federal income tax withheld from employees' pay for the quarter. If federal tax deposits have been made timely, the total amount deposited should equal the amount due on Form 941. If there is a difference, a payment may be due.

Form 941 taxes Another term used to describe Social Security, Medicare, and federal income taxes. This name comes from the form used to report these taxes.

Form 8109 A coupon that is completed and sent along with payments of tax deposits relating to either Forms 940-EZ or 941. This form can also be used to deposit other types of taxes a business may owe the federal government.

Form W-2, Wage and Tax Statement A form completed by the employer at the end of the calendar year to provide a summary of gross earnings and deductions to each employee. At least two copies go to the employee, one copy to the IRS, one copy to any state where employees' income taxes have been withheld, one copy to the Social Security Administration, and one copy into the records of the business.

Form W-3, Transmittal of Income and Tax Statements A form completed by the employer to verify the number of W-2's and amounts withheld as shown on them. This form is sent to a Social Security Administration data processing center along with copies of each employee's W-2 forms.

Look-back Period A period of time used to determine if a business will make its Form 941 tax deposits on a monthly or semiweekly basis. The IRS has defined this period as July 1 through June 30 of the year prior to the year in which Form 941 tax deposits will be made.

Monthly Depositor A business classified as a monthly depositor will make its payroll tax deposits only once each month for the amount of Form 941 due from the prior month.

Normal FUTA Tax Credit A credit given to employers who pay their state unemployment taxes on time. The credit is usually 5.4 percent, which is applied against a 6.2 percent rate. The result is a net FUTA tax of .8 percent.

Payroll Tax Expense The general ledger account that records the total of the employer's FICA (Social Security and Medicare), SUTA, and FUTA tax responsibilities.

Semiweekly depositor A business classified as a semiweekly depositor may make its payroll tax deposits up to twice in one week. Semiweekly depositors will make a minimum of one Form 941 payroll tax deposit each week.

SS-4 Form The form filled out by an employer in order to get an employer identification number. The form is sent to the IRS, who assigns the number to the business.

State Unemployment Tax Act (SUTA) A tax usually paid only by employers to the state for employee unemployment insurance.

Workers' Compensation Insurance Insurance paid for, in advance, by an employer to protect its employees against loss due to injury or death incurred during employment.

BLUEPRINT OF FORM 941 TAX DEPOSIT RULES

10 Questions and Answers About Depositing Social Security, Medicare, and Federal Income Taxes to the Government

Here is a summary of questions and answers that will help you to understand the payroll tax deposit rules for Form 941 taxes.

1. **What are Form 941 taxes?** This term is used to describe the amount of Social Security, Medicare, and federal income tax paid by employees, and the amount of Social Security and Medicare taxes that are matched and paid by an employer. The total of these taxes are known as Form 941 taxes because they are reported on Form 941 each quarter.

2. **When does an employer deposit Form 941 taxes?** How often an employer deposits Form 941 taxes depends on how the employer is classified for this purpose. The IRS classifies an employer as either a *monthly* or *semiweekly depositor* based on the amount of Form 941 taxes paid during a time-period known as a *look-back period.*

3. **When is a look-back period?** This time period is a fiscal year that begins on July 1 and ends on June 30 of the year before the calendar year when the deposits will be made. For example, for the 1998 calendar year, an employer's look-back period will begin on July 1, 1996 and end June 30, 1997.

4. **What is the dollar amount used to classify an employer for Form 941 tax deposits?** The key dollar amount used to determine if an employer is a *monthly* or *semiweekly* depositor is $50,000 in Form 941 taxes. Two rules apply here:

   a. If the total amount deposited in Form 941 taxes is less than $50,000 during the look-back period, the employer is considered a *monthly tax depositor.*

   b. If the total amount deposited in Form 941 taxes is $50,000 or more during the look-back period, the employer is considered a *semiweekly tax depositor.*

5. **How do employers deposit Form 941 taxes?** An employer will fill out a Form 8109 (Federal Tax Deposit Coupon) and give this form with a check to a bank authorized to receive payroll tax deposits or to a Federal Reserve Bank. Generally authorized banks will only take checks written from an account maintained at that same bank. So, an employer usually cannot make a Form 941 deposit at bank A using a check written from an account maintained at bank B. A Federal Reserve Bank will accept a check from any U.S. bank for payroll tax deposit purposes.

6. **When do monthly depositors make their deposits?** A monthly depositor will figure the total amount of Form 941 taxes owed in a calendar month and then pay this amount by the fifteenth of the next month. So, if an employer owes $3,125 in Form 941 taxes for the month of June, it will deposit this same amount no later than July 15 of the same year.

7. **When do semiweekly depositors make their deposits?** These rules are a little more complicated. A semiweekly depositor may have to make up to two Form 941 deposits each week. When a tax deposit is due depends on when the employees are paid. To keep the rules consistent, the IRS has taken a calendar week and divided it into two payday time-periods. It is easiest to think of a two-week period of time when discussing these time periods: *Wednesday, Thursday, and Friday* of week one; and, *Saturday and Sunday* of week one and *Monday and Tuesday* of week two.

   Two deposit rules apply to these two time-periods. We can call these rules the **Wednesday** and **Friday rules.**

   a. **Wednesday rule:** If employees are paid during the week one Wednesday–Friday period, the tax deposit will be due on Wednesday of week two.

b. Friday rule: If employees are paid anytime from Saturday or Sunday of week one, or Monday or Tuesday of week two, the tax deposit will be due on Friday of week two.

What these rules mean is that the payroll tax deposit will be due three banking days after the payday time-period ends. For the Wednesday rule, the deposit is due three banking days after Friday of week one, on the following Wednesday (in week two). For the Friday rule, the deposit is due three banking days after Tuesday of week two, on Friday of week two.

8. **What is a *banking day?*** This term refers to any day that a bank is open to the public for business. This means that Saturdays, Sundays, and legal holidays are not banking days.

9. **How do legal holidays affect payroll tax deposits?** If a legal holiday occurs after the last day of a payday time-period, the employer will get one extra day to make its Form 941 tax deposit as follows:

    a. For monthly depositors: If the fifteenth of the month is a Saturday, Sunday, or legal holiday, the deposit will be due and payable on the next banking day.

    b. For semiweekly depositors: A deposit due on Wednesday will be due on Thursday of the same week, and a Friday deposit will be due on Monday of the following week. Remember that the employer will always have three banking days after the last day of either payday time-period to make its payroll tax deposit.

10. **What happens if an employer is late with its Form 941 tax deposit?** If a Form 941 tax deposit is not made the day it should be deposited, the employer may be assessed a fine for lateness and even charged interest depending on how late the deposit is.

QUESTIONS, MINI EXERCISES, EXERCISES, AND PROBLEMS

Discussion Questions

1. What taxes make up *Payroll Tax Expense?*

2. Explain how an employer can receive a credit against the FUTA tax due.

3. Explain what an experience or merit rating is, and how it affects the amount paid by an employer for state unemployment insurance.

4. How is an employer classified as a monthly or semiweekly depositor for Form 941 tax purposes?

5. What is the purpose of Form 8109?

6. How often is Form 941 completed?

7. Please comment on the following statement: The amount found on Line 20(d) of Form 941 must always be the same amount found on Line 16 of the form.

8. Bill Smith leaves his job on July 9. He requests a copy of his W-2 form when he leaves. His boss tells him to wait until January of next year. Please discuss whether Bill's boss is correct in making this statement.

9. Why would one employer prepare a Form 940 while another would prepare a 940-EZ?

10. Employer "A" has a FUTA tax liability of $67.49 on March 31 of the current year. When does the employer have to make the deposit for this liability?

11. Employer "B" has a FUTA tax liability of $553.24 on January 31 of the current year. When does the employer have to make the deposit for this liability?

12. Why is the year-end adjusting entry needed for Workers' Compensation Insurance?

Mini Exercises

(The forms you need are on page 259 of the *Study Guide and Working Papers*.)

Account Classifications

1. Complete the following table:

Accounts Affected	Category	↑	Rules
a. Payroll Tax Expense			
b. FICA-SS Payable			
c. FICA-Medicare Payable			
d. State Unemployment Tax Payable			
e. Federal Unemployment Tax Payable			

Exempt Wages

2. Given: Pete Bole cumulative earnings before this pay period $6,800; gross pay for week $500. How much of *this* week's pay will be subject to taxes for: FICA-Medicare; FICA-Social Security; SUTA; FUTA. Assume base and rates in text.

Look-Back Periods

3. Label the following Look-Back Periods for 1998 by months

A	B	C	D
1996		1997	

Monthly versus Semiweekly Depositor

4. In November 1997, Pete also is trying to find out if he is a monthly or semi-weekly depositor for FICA (SS + Med.) and Federal Income Tax for 1998. Please advise based on the following taxes owed:

1996	Quarter 3	$28,000
	Quarter 4	12,000
1997	Quarter 1	3,000
	Quarter 2	10,000

Paying the Tax

5. Complete the following table:

Depositor	Four Quarter Look-Back Period Tax Liability	Payroll Paid	Tax Paid by
Monthly	$28,000	Nov.	A.
Semiweekly	$66,000	On Wed.	B.
		On Thur.	C.
		On Fri.	D.
		On Sat.	E.
		On Sun.	F.
		On Mon.	G.

(The forms you need are on pages 260–262 of the *Study Guide and Working Papers.*)

Journalizing the payroll tax

8-1. From the following information, prepare a general journal entry to record the payroll tax expense for Asty Company for the payroll of August 9:

Employee	Cumulative Earnings Before Weekly Payroll	Gross Pay For Week
J. Kline	$3,500	$900
A. Met	6,600	750
D. Ring	7,900	300

The FICA tax rate for Social Security is 6.2 percent on $65,400, and Medicare is 1.45 percent on all earnings. Federal unemployment tax is .8 percent (.008 when expressed as a decimal) on the first $7,000 earned by each employee. The experience or merit rating for Asty Co. is 5.6 percent on the first $7,000 of employee earnings for state unemployment purposes.

Change in merit rating

8-2. Using 8-1 above, the state changed Asty's experience/merit rating to 4.9 percent. What effect would this change have on the total payroll tax expense?

Change in payroll tax expense

8-3. Using exercise 8-1, if D. Ring earned $2,000 for the week instead of $300, what effect would this change have on the total payroll tax expense?

Journalizing payment of deposit

8-4. At the end of January 19XX, the total amount of Social Security, $610, and Medicare, $200, was withheld as tax deductions from the employees of Cornfield Acres Inc. Federal income tax of $3,000 was also deducted from their paychecks. Cornfield Acres has been classified as a monthly depositor of Form 941 taxes. Indicate when this payroll tax deposit is due and provide a general journal entry to record the payment.

Calculating total payroll tax expense

8-5. The total wage expense for Howie Co. was $150,000. Of this total, $30,000 was beyond the Social Security wage base limit and not subject to this tax. All earnings are subject to Medicare tax, and $60,000 was beyond the federal and state unemployment wage base limits and not subject to unemployment taxes. Please calculate the total payroll tax expense for Howie Co. given the following rates and wage base limits:

   a. FICA tax rate — Social Security, 6.2 percent; Medicare, 1.45 percent.

   b. State unemployment tax rate, 5.9 percent.

   c. Federal unemployment tax rate (after credit), .8 percent.

Determining when tax deposits are due

8-6. Carol's Grocery Store made the following Form 941 payroll tax deposits during the look-back period of July 1, 19X1 through June 30, 19X2:

Quarter Ended	Amount Paid in 941 Taxes
September 30, 19X1	$13,783.26
December 31, 19X1	14,893.22
March 31, 19X2	14,601.94
June 30, 19X2	15,021.01

Should Carol's Grocery Store make Form 941 tax deposits monthly or semiweekly for 19X3?

Determining when tax deposits are due

8-7. If Carol's Grocery Store downsized its operation during the second quarter of 19X2 and as a result paid only $6,121.93 in Form 941 taxes for the quarter that ended on June 30, 19X2, should Carol's Grocery make its Form 941 payroll tax deposits monthly or semiweekly for 19X3?

8-8. From the following accounts, record the payment of (a) July 3 payment for FICA (Social Security and Medicare) and federal income taxes; (b) July 30 payment of state unemployment tax; and (c) July 30 deposit of FUTA tax that may be required. Please prepare general journal entries from the following T accounts:

FICA-Social Security Payable 203	FICA-Medicare Payable 204
June 30 400 (EE)	June 30 100 (EE)
400 (ER)	100 (ER)

FIT Payable 205	FUTA Tax Payable 206
June 30 3,005	June 30 119

SUTA Tax Payable 207
June 30 411

8-9. At the end of the first quarter of 19XX, you have been asked to determine the FUTA tax liability for Oscar Company as well as to record any payment of tax liability. The following information has been supplied to you: FUTA tax rate is .8 percent on the first $7,000 each employee earns during the year.

Employee	Gross Pay Per Week
J. King	$400
A. Lane	500
B. Move	600
C. Slade	900

8-10. From the following data, estimate the annual premium and record it by preparing a general journal entry:

Type of Work	Estimated Payroll	Rate per $100
Office	$15,000	$ .17
Sales	42,000	1.90

Group A Problems

(The forms you need are on pages 263-269 of the *Study Guide and Working Papers.*)

8A-1. For the week of April 8 at Kane's Hardware, the partial payroll summary shown below is taken from the individual employee earnings records. Both Jill Reese and Jeff Vatack have earned more than $7,000 before this payroll.

Your task is to:

1. Complete the table.
2. Prepare a journal entry to record the payroll tax expense for Kane's. Use the federal income tax withholding tables in Figures 7-2 and 7-3 (Chapter 7 — pp. 240-242) to figure the amount of income tax withheld. Please show the calculations for FICA taxes.

Employee	Allowance and Marital Status	Gross	FICA Soc. Sec.	FICA Medicare	Federal Income Tax
Al Jones	S-1	$ 600	37.20	8.70	89.00
Janice King	S-0	850	52.70	12.33	172.00
Alice Long	S-2	750	46.50	10.88	117.00
Jill Reese	M-0	1,060	65.72	15.37	175.00
Jeff Vatack	M-2	1,365	84.63	19.79	233.00

Assume: FICA tax rate for Social Security is 6.2 percent up to $65,400 in earnings (no one has earned this much as of April 8); Medicare is 1.45 percent on all earnings. The state unemployment tax rate is 5.1 percent on the first $7,000 of earnings, and the federal unemployment tax rate is .8 percent of the first $7,000 of earnings. In cases where the amount of FICA tax calculates to one-half cent, round up to the next cent.

8A-2. The following is the monthly payroll of Hogan Co., owned by Dean Hogan. Employees are paid on the last day of each month.

Employer's tax responsibilities

JANUARY

Employee	Monthly Earnings	Year-to-Date Earnings	FICA Soc. Sec.	Medicare	Federal Income Tax
Sam Koy	$1,800	$1,800	$111.60	$ 26.10	$ 241
Joy Lane	3,150	3,150	195.30	45.68	361
Amy Hess	4,100	4,100	254.20	59.45	500
	$9,050	$9,050	$561.10	$131.23	$1,102

FEBRUARY

Employee	Monthly Earnings	Year-to-Date Earnings	FICA Soc. Sec.	Medicare	Federal Income Tax
Sam Koy	$1,975	$ 3,775	$122.45	$ 28.64	$ 265
Joy Lane	2,900	6,050	179.80	42.05	325
Amy Hess	3,775	7,875	234.05	54.74	426
	$8,650	$17,700	$536.30	$125.43	$1,016

MARCH

Check Figure:
Deposit of SUTA Tax $1,195.58

Employee	Monthly Earnings	Year-to-Date Earnings	FICA Soc. Sec.	Medicare	Federal Income Tax
Sam Koy	$ 3,200	$ 6,975	$198.40	$ 46.40	$ 608
Joy Lane	4,080	10,130	252.96	59.16	558
Amy Hess	4,250	12,125	263.50	61.63	545
	$11,530	$29,230	$714.86	$167.19	$1,711

Hogan Company is located at 2 Roundy Road, Marblehead, MA 01945. Employer identification number is 29-3458821. FICA tax rate for Social Security is 6.2 percent up to $65,400 in earnings during the year; Medicare is 1.45 percent on all earnings. The SUTA tax rate is 5.7 percent on the first $7,000. The FUTA tax rate is .8 percent on the first $7,000 of earnings. Hogan Company is classified as a monthly depositor for Form 941 taxes.

Your task is to:

1. Journalize entries to record the employer's payroll tax expense for each pay period in the general journal.
2. Journalize entries for the payment of each tax liability including SUTA tax in the general journal.

Journal entries and Form 941

Check Figure:
Total Liability for Quarter
$8,301.22

8A-3. Ed Ward, accountant of Hogan Company, has been requested to complete Form 941 for the first quarter of the current year. Using Problem 8A-2, Ed gathers the needed data. Ed has suddenly been called away to an urgent budget meeting and has requested you to assist him by preparing the Form 941 for the first quarter. Please note that the difference in the tax liability, a few cents, should be adjusted in the middle column of Line 9 — this difference is due to the rounding of FICA tax amounts.

Journal entries and Form 941

Check Figure:
Dec. 31 Payroll Tax Expense
$736.67

8A-4. The following is the monthly payroll for the last three months of the year for Henson's Sporting Goods Shop, 1 Roe Road, Lynn, MA 01945. The shop is a sole proprietorship owned and operated by Bill Henson. The employer ID number for Henson's Sporting Goods is 28-93118921.

The employees at Henson's are paid once each month on the last day of the month. Pete Avery is the only employee who has contributed the maximum into Social Security. None of the other employees will reach the Social Security wage base limit by the end of the year. Assume the rate for Social Security to be 6.2 percent with a wage base maximum of $65,400, and the rate for Medicare to be 1.45 percent on all earnings. Henson's is classified as a monthly depositor for Form 941 payroll tax deposit purposes.

OCTOBER

Check Figure:

Dec. 31 Payroll Tax Expense

$736.67

Employee	Monthly Earnings	Year-to-Date Earnings	FICA Soc. Sec.	Medicare	Federal Income Tax
Pete Avery	$ 2,950	$ 61,450	$182.90	$ 42.78	$ 530
Janet Lee	3,590	40,150	222.58	52.06	427
Sue Lyons	3,800	43,900	235.60	55.10	536
	$10,340	$145,500	$641.08	$149.94	$1,493

NOVEMBER

Employee	Monthly Earnings	Year-to-Date Earnings	FICA Soc. Sec.	Medicare	Federal Income Tax
Pete Avery	$ 3,180	$ 64,630	$197.16	$ 46.11	$ 597
Janet Lee	3,772	43,922	233.86	54.69	468
Sue Lyons	3,891	47,791	241.24	56.42	559
	$10,843	$156,343	$672.26	$157.22	$1,624

DECEMBER

Employee	Monthly Earnings	Year-to-Date Earnings	FICA Soc. Sec.	Medicare	Federal Income Tax
Pete Avery	$ 4,250	$ 68,880	$ 47.74	$ 61.63	$ 902
Janet Lee	3,800	47,722	235.60	55.10	479
Sue Lyons	4,400	52,191	272.80	63.80	704
	$12,450	$168,793	$556.14	$180.53	$2,085

Your task is to:

1. Journalize entries to record the employer's payroll tax expense for each pay period in the general journal.

2. Journalize entries for the payment of each tax for FICA tax (Social Security and Medicare) and federal income tax given that Henson's is a monthly Form 941 tax depositor.

3. Complete Form 941 for the fourth quarter of the current year.

Form 940-EZ

Check Figure:

Total Exempt Payments

$147,793

8A-5. Using the information from Problem 8A-4 above, please complete a Form 940-EZ for Henson's Sporting Goods for the current year. Additional information needed to complete the form is as follows:

a. FUTA tax deposit for first quarter, $168.00

b. SUTA rate, 5.7 percent; state reporting number, 025-319-2.

Please note that there were no FUTA tax deposits for the second, third, or fourth quarters of the year. Henson's has three employees for the year who all earned over $7,000.

Group B Problems

(The forms you need are on pages 263–269 of the *Study Guide and Working Papers.*)

Journal entry to record payroll tax expense

8B-1. For the week of April 8 at Kane's Hardware, the following partial payroll summary is taken from the individual employee earnings records. Both Jill Reese and Jeff Vatack have earned more than $7,000 before this payroll.

Your task is to:

1. Complete the table.
2. Prepare a journal entry to record the payroll tax expense for Kane's. Use the federal income tax withholding tables in Figures 7-2 and 7-3 (Chapter 7) to figure the amount of income tax withheld. Please show the calculations for FICA taxes.

Employee	Allowance and Marital Status	Gross	FICA Soc. Sec.	Medicare	Federal Income Tax
Al Jones	S-1	$ 620			
Janice King	S-2	890			
Alice Long	S-0	750			
Jill Reese	M-1	1,100			
Jeff Vatack	M-2	1,340			

Assume: FICA tax rate for Social Security is 6.2 percent up to $65,400 in earnings (no one has earned this much as of April 8); Medicare is 1.45 percent on all earnings. The state unemployment tax rate is 5.2 percent on the first $7,000 of earnings, and the federal unemployment tax rate is .8 percent of the first $7,000 of earnings. In cases where the FICA tax calculates to one-half cent, round up to the next cent.

Employers tax responsibilities

8B-2. The following is the monthly payroll of Hogan Co., owned by Dean Hogan. Employees are paid on the last day of each month.

JANUARY

Employee	Monthly Earnings	Year-to-Date Earnings	FICA Soc. Sec.	Medicare	Federal Income Tax
Sam Koy	$1,675	$1,675	$103.85	$ 24.29	$217
Joy Lane	3,000	3,000	186.00	43.50	343
Amy Hess	3,590	3,590	222.58	52.06	396
	$8,265	$8,265	$512.43	$119.85	$956

FEBRUARY

Employee	Monthly Earnings	Year-to-Date Earnings	FICA Soc. Sec.	Medicare	Federal Income Tax
Sam Koy	$1,975	$ 3,650	$122.45	$ 28.64	$ 265
Joy Lane	2,900	5,900	179.80	42.05	325
Amy Hess	3,775	7,365	234.05	54.74	426
	$8,650	$16,915	$536.30	$125.43	$1,016

MARCH

Employee	Monthly Earnings	Year-to-Date Earnings	FICA Soc. Sec.	Medicare	Federal Income Tax
Sam Koy	$ 3,220	$ 6,870	$199.64	$ 46.69	$ 608
Joy Lane	4,000	9,900	248.00	58.00	535
Amy Hess	4,300	11,665	266.60	62.35	556
	$11,520	$28,435	$714.24	$167.04	$1,699

Hogan Company is located at 2 Roundy Road, Marblehead, MA 01945. Employer identification number is 29-3458821. FICA tax rate for Social Security is 6.2 percent up to $65,400 in earnings during the year; Medicare is 1.45 percent on all earnings. The SUTA tax rate is 5.7 percent on the first $7,000. The FUTA tax rate is .8 percent on the first $7,000 of earnings. Hogan Company is classified as a monthly depositor for Form 941 taxes.

Your task is to:

1. Journalize entries to record the employer's payroll tax expense for each pay period in the general journal.
2. Journalize entries for the payment of each tax liability including SUTA tax in the general journal.

Journal entries and Form 941

Check Figure:

Liability for Quarter $8,021.58

8B-3. Ed Ward, accountant of Hogan Company, has been requested to complete Form 941 for the first quarter of the current year. Using Problem 8B-2, Ed gathers the needed data. Ed has suddenly been called away to an urgent budget meeting and has requested you to assist him by preparing the Form 941 for the first quarter. Please note that the difference in the tax liability, a few cents, should be adjusted in the middle column of Line 9 — this difference is due to the rounding of FICA tax amounts.

Journal entries and Form 941

8B-4. The following is the monthly payroll for the last three months of the year for Henson's Sporting Goods Shop, 1 Roe Road, Lynn, MA 01945. The shop is a sole proprietorship owned and operated by Bill Henson. The employer ID number for Henson's Sporting Goods is 28-93118921.

The employees at Henson's are paid once each month on the last day of the month. Pete Avery is the only employee who has contributed the maximum into Social Security. None of the other employees will reach the Social Security wage base limit by the end of the year. Assume the rate for Social Security to be 6.2 percent with a wage base maximum of $65,400, and the rate for Medicare to be 1.45 percent on all earnings. Henson's is classified as a monthly depositor for Form 941 payroll taxes.

OCTOBER

Employee	Monthly Earnings	Year-to-Date Earnings	FICA Soc. Sec.	Medicare	Federal Income Tax
Pete Avery	$ 2,950	$ 62,600	$182.90	$ 42.78	$ 530
Janet Lee	3,590	41,075	222.58	52.06	427
Sue Lyons	3,800	44,000	235.60	55.10	536
	$10,340	$147,675	$641.08	$149.94	$1,493

NOVEMBER

Check Figure:

Dec 31 Payroll Tax Expense
$654.51

Employee	Monthly Earnings	Year-to-Date Earnings	FICA Soc. Sec.	Medicare	Federal Income Tax
Pete Avery	$ 3,000	$ 65,600	$173.60	$ 43.50	$ 552
Janet Lee	3,650	44,725	226.30	52.93	439
Sue Lyons	3,710	47,710	230.02	53.80	503
	$10,360	$158,035	$629.92	$150.23	$1,494

DECEMBER

Employee	Monthly Earnings	Year-to-Date Earnings	FICA Soc. Sec.	Medicare	Federal Income Tax
Pete Avery	$ 4,250	$ 69,850	—	$ 61.63	$ 902
Janet Lee	3,850	48,575	$238.70	55.83	490
Sue Lyons	3,900	51,610	241.80	56.55	559
	$12,000	$170,035	$480.50	$174.01	$1,951

Your task is to:

1. Journalize entries to record the employer's payroll tax expense for each pay period in the general journal.
2. Journalize entries for the payment of each tax for FICA tax (Social Security and Medicare) and federal income tax.
3. Complete Form 941 for the fourth quarter of the current year.

8B-5. Using the information from Problem 8B-4 above, please complete a 940-EZ form for Henson's Sporting Goods for the current year. Additional information needed to complete the form is as follows:

  a. FUTA tax deposit for first quarter, $168.

  b. SUTA tax rate, 5.7 percent; state reporting number, 025-319-2.

    Please note that there were no FUTA tax deposits for the third or fourth quarters of the year. Henson's has three employees for the year who all earned over $7,000.

REAL WORLD APPLICATIONS

8R-1.

Sunshine School Supplies is a leading manufacturer of back-to-school kits and other items used by students in elementary and middle schools. Each summer Sunshine needs additional help to assemble, pack, and ship school items sold in stores around the country. Sunshine's company policy has been to hire 30 additional workers for 12 weeks during the summer. Each employee works 40 hours per week and earns $6 per hour. At the end of August these additional workers are laid off.

Sunshine's state unemployment rate has risen to 5.4 percent with no experience/merit rating allowed due to these layoffs in the last few years.

Miriam Holtz, who is the president of Sunshine, asks for your help to find a way to reduce Sunshine's 5.4 state unemployment rate. When Miriam called the state department of labor and employment, she was told that Sunshine's unemployment rate could drop to 4.1 percent if it stopped laying off workers.

Miriam has thought about using temporary employment agency workers during the summer months as a way to obtain the help the company needs and at the same time stop the seasonal layoffs.

Miriam asks you if this is a good idea. She gives you the following facts to use in analyzing this idea:

1. Five hundred workers who are permanent employees of Sunshine earn in excess of $7,000 each by September of each year.

2. A temporary employment agency told Miriam it would charge Sunshine $7.00 per hour for each worker it supplied during the summer.

3. The current federal unemployment tax rate is .8 percent up to the first $7,000 each employee earns during a year.

4. The current SUTA wage base limit is the first $7,000 each employee earns during a year.

5. Sunshine pays a FICA tax rate of 6.2 percent for Social Security and 1.45 percent for Medicare. The Social Security wage base limit is $65,400; there is no wage base limit for Medicare.

Please write a short memo to Miriam Holtz that shows your analysis of two options: (1) Continue to hire 30 additional workers for the summer and then lay them off; and, (2) have the temporary employment agency provide 30 additional workers for the summer.

In your memo be sure to show the financial effect of both options in terms of the tax calculations on employee earnings for SUTA, FUTA, and FICA. For option (1) be sure to include the SUTA and FUTA tax effects for *both* the permanent and temporary workers. At the end of your memo please provide Miriam with your conclusion so she can make a good decision for her company.

8R-2.

Cathy Johnson has just been hired as a bookkeeper for the Small Fry Dog Toy Company. She recently graduated from the local community college with an associates degree in business. She took several accounting courses at school but was unable to take the school's payroll accounting course.

Cathy is confused about payroll tax forms and their purpose. She wants to learn more about the forms the business must prepare and send in to the government.

You are the accountant for Small Fry. Your boss has asked you to help teach Cathy about the forms and why they are used. The boss feels it is best to give Cathy a brief written summary about the following forms:

1. Form 941
2. Form 940-EZ
3. Form 8109
4. Form W-2
5. Form W-3

Please write a brief report to Cathy to help her to understand the following points about these payroll tax forms:

a. The purpose of each form.
b. What is reported on each form.
c. When each form is sent to the government.
d. Where the amounts found on each form come from in the accounting system.

make the call

Critical Thinking/Ethical Case

8R-3.
Abby Ross works in the Payroll Department for Lange Co. as a junior accountant. Abby also is going to school for an advanced degree in accounting. After work each day she uses the company's photocopy machine to make extra copies of her assignments. Should she be photocopying personal material on a company machine? You make the call. Write down your specific recommendations to Abby.

ACCOUNTING RECALL
A CUMULATIVE APPROACH

THIS EXAM REVIEWS CHAPTERS 1 THROUGH 8

Your *Study Guide and Working Papers* have forms (pp. 274 and 279) to complete this exam, as well as worked-out solutions. The page references next to each question identify what page to turn back to if you answer the question incorrectly.

PART 1 Vocabulary Review

Match the terms to the appropriate definition or phrase.

Page Ref.

(212)	1. Checks outstanding	A.	Total of employer's tax responsibilities
(271)	2. SUTA		

(268)	3. SS-4	B. Used up
(271)	4. Payroll tax expense	C. Four quarters
(255)	5. Quarter	D. Merit rating
(282)	6. W-2	E. Federal employer identification
(280)	7. 941	number
(275)	8. Look-back periods	F. FICA (EE + ER) + FIT
(248)	9. Medicare — tax payable	G. 13 weeks
(281)	10. Adjustments	H. Not processed by bank
		I. A liability
		J. Provides summary of gross earnings

PART II True or False (Accounting Theory)

(271) 11. SUTA is not part of Payroll Tax Expense.

(212) 12. NSF means check did not have sufficient funds.

(278) 13. Quarterly return (941) records taxes for FIT and SUTA.

(270) 14. FUTA is always paid once a year.

(171) 15. The post-closing trial balance is the last step of the Accounting Cycle.

CONTINUING PROBLEM

As December comes to an end, Tony Freedman wants to take care of his payroll obligations. He will complete Form 941 for the first quarter of the current year and Form 940-EZ for federal unemployment taxes. Freedman will make the necessary deposits and payments associated with his payroll.

Assignment:

(See pp. 275 – 278 in your *Study Guide and Working Papers*.)

1. Record the payroll tax expense entry in general journal format for the quarter, using the information in the Chapter 7 problem.

2. Journalize entries for the payment of each tax liability including SUTA tax in the general journal. Freedman is classified as a quarterly depositor.

3. Prepare Form 941 for the first quarter. Eldorado Computer Center's employer identification number is 35-41325881.

4. Complete Form 940 for Eldorado Computer Center. FUTA tax ceiling is $7,000 and SUTA tax ceiling is $10,000 in cumulative wages for each employee. The Eldorado Computer Center's FUTA rate is .8 percent and SUTA rate is 2.7 percent. No deposits have been made.

Hint: Sometimes the amount of Social Security taxes paid by the employee for the quarter will not equal the employee's tax liability because of rounding. Any overage/difference should be reported on line 9 of Form 941.

Pete's Market

Completing Payroll Requirements for First Quarter and Preparing Form 941

This Mini Practice Set will aid in putting the pieces of payroll together. In this project, you are the bookkeeper and will have the responsibility of recording payroll in the payroll register, paying the payroll, recording the employer's tax responsibilities, and paying tax deposits, as well as completing the quarterly report. (The forms you need are on pages 278-283 of the *Study Guide and Working Papers.*)

Pete's Market, owned by Pete Reel, is located at 4 Sun Avenue, Swampscott, MA 01970. His employer identification number is 42-4583312. Please assume the following:

1. FICA: Social Security, 6.2 percent on $65,400; Medicare, 1.45 percent on all earnings.
2. SUTA: 4.9 percent (due to favorable merit rating) on $7,000.
3. FUTA: .8 percent on first $7,000.
4. Employees are paid monthly. The payroll is recorded the last day of each month and is paid on the first day of the next month.
5. FIT table provided with problem from IRS Circular E, *Employer's Tax Guide* (see p. 241).
6. State income tax is 8 percent.

The following are the employees of Pete's Market along with their monthly salary exemptions, etc.

SALARY PER MONTH

		January	February	March	
Fred Flynn	S-0	$2,500	$2,590	$2,475	(Sales Salaries)
Mary Jones	S-2	3,000	3,000	4,000	(Market Salaries)
Lilly Vron	S-1	3,000	3,000	4,260	(Sales Salaries)

Partial Ledger Accounts as of December 31, 19XX

FICA-Social Security Payable 210	FICA-Medicare Payable 212	FIT Payable 220
410.90 (EE)	100 (EE)	600
410.90 (ER)	100 (ER)	

SIT Payable 225	FUTA Payable 230	SUTA Payable 240
150	88	155

Using the general journal and payroll register provided, please complete the following:

19XX

Jan.   15   Record the entry for the deposit of Social Security, Medicare, and FIT from last month's payroll. (For simplicity we will not record the payment of state income tax.)

31 Pay state unemployment tax due from last quarter.

31 Pay federal unemployment tax owed.

31 Complete payroll register for January payroll, journalize payroll entry, and journalize entry for employer's payroll tax expense.

Feb.

1 Transfer cash for the January Net Pay from Cash to Payroll Checking Cash.

1 Pay payroll.

15 Pay taxes due for Social Security, Medicare, and FIT.

28 Complete payroll register for February payroll. Journalize payroll entry as well as journalize entry for employer's payroll tax expense.

Mar.

1 Transfer cash for the February Net Pay from Cash to Payroll Checking Cash.

1 Pay payroll.

15 Pay taxes due for Social Security, Medicare, and FIT.

31 Complete payroll register for March payroll. Journalize payroll entry as well as journalize entry for employer's payroll tax expense.

Apr.

1 Transfer cash for the March Net Pay from Cash to Payroll Checking Cash.

1 Pay payroll.

15 Pay taxes due for Social Security, Medicare, and FIT.

30 Pay federal unemployment tax due for quarter 1.

30 Pay state unemployment tax due for quarter 1.

30 Complete Form 941 for the first quarter.

If the wages are—		And the number of withholding allowances claimed is—										
At least	But less than	0	1	2	3	4	5	6	7	8	9	10
		The amount of income tax to be withheld is—										
$2,440	$2,480	$396	$338	$281	$245	$214	$184	$153	$122	$92	$61	$31
2,480	2,520	407	350	292	251	220	190	159	128	98	67	37
2,520	2,560	418	361	304	257	226	196	165	134	104	73	43
2,560	2,600	429	372	315	263	232	202	171	140	110	79	49
2,600	2,640	440	383	326	269	238	208	177	146	116	85	55
2,640	2,680	452	394	337	280	244	214	183	152	122	91	61
2,680	2,720	463	406	348	291	250	220	189	158	128	97	67
2,720	2,760	474	417	360	302	256	226	195	164	134	103	73
2,760	2,800	485	428	371	314	262	232	201	170	140	109	79
2,800	2,840	496	439	382	325	268	238	207	176	146	115	85
2,840	2,880	508	450	393	336	279	244	213	182	152	121	91
2,880	2,920	519	462	404	347	290	250	219	188	158	127	97
2,920	2,960	530	473	416	358	301	256	225	194	164	133	103
2,960	3,000	541	484	427	370	312	262	231	200	170	139	109
3,000	3,040	552	495	438	381	324	268	237	206	176	145	115
3,040	3,080	564	506	449	392	335	278	243	212	182	151	121
3,080	3,120	575	518	460	403	346	289	249	218	188	157	127
3,120	3,160	586	529	472	414	357	300	255	224	194	163	133
3,160	3,200	597	540	483	426	368	311	261	230	200	169	139
3,200	3,240	608	551	494	437	380	322	267	236	206	175	145
3,240	3,280	620	562	505	448	391	334	277	242	212	181	151
3,280	3,320	631	574	516	459	402	345	288	248	218	187	157
3,320	3,360	642	585	528	470	413	356	299	254	224	193	163
3,360	3,400	653	596	539	482	424	367	310	260	230	199	169
3,400	3,440	664	607	550	493	436	378	321	266	236	205	175
3,440	3,480	676	618	561	504	447	390	333	275	242	211	181
3,480	3,520	687	630	572	515	458	401	344	287	248	217	187
3,520	3,560	698	641	584	526	469	412	355	298	254	223	193
3,560	3,600	709	652	595	538	480	423	366	309	260	229	199
3,600	3,640	720	663	606	549	492	434	377	320	266	235	205
3,640	3,680	732	674	617	560	503	446	389	331	274	241	211
3,680	3,720	743	686	628	571	514	457	400	343	285	247	217
3,720	3,760	754	697	640	582	525	468	411	354	297	253	223
3,760	3,800	765	708	651	594	536	479	422	365	308	259	229
3,800	3,840	776	719	662	605	548	490	433	376	319	265	235
3,840	3,880	788	730	673	616	559	502	445	387	330	273	241
3,880	3,920	799	742	684	627	570	513	456	399	341	284	247
3,920	3,960	810	753	696	638	581	524	467	410	353	295	253
3,960	4,000	821	764	707	650	592	535	478	421	364	307	259
4,000	4,040	832	775	718	661	604	546	489	432	375	318	265
4,040	4,080	844	786	729	672	615	558	501	443	386	329	272
4,080	4,120	855	798	740	683	626	569	512	455	397	340	283
4,120	4,160	866	809	752	694	637	580	523	466	409	351	294
4,160	4,200	877	820	763	706	648	591	534	477	420	363	305
4,200	4,240	889	831	774	717	660	602	545	488	431	374	317
4,240	4,280	902	842	785	728	671	614	557	499	442	385	328
4,280	4,320	914	854	796	739	682	625	568	511	453	396	339
4,320	4,360	926	865	808	750	693	636	579	522	465	407	350
4,360	4,400	939	876	819	762	704	647	590	533	476	419	361
4,400	4,440	951	888	830	773	716	658	601	544	487	430	373
4,440	4,480	964	900	841	784	727	670	613	555	498	441	384
4,480	4,520	976	913	852	795	738	681	624	567	509	452	395
4,520	4,560	988	925	864	806	749	692	635	578	521	463	406
4,560	4,600	1,001	937	875	818	760	703	646	589	532	475	417
4,600	4,640	1,013	950	887	829	772	714	657	600	543	486	429
4,640	4,680	1,026	962	899	840	783	726	669	611	554	497	440
4,680	4,720	1,038	975	911	851	794	737	680	623	565	508	451
4,720	4,760	1,050	987	924	862	805	748	691	634	577	519	462
4,760	4,800	1,063	999	936	874	816	759	702	645	588	531	473
4,800	4,840	1,075	1,012	949	885	828	770	713	656	599	542	485
4,840	4,880	1,088	1,024	961	898	839	782	725	667	610	553	496
4,880	4,920	1,100	1,037	973	910	850	793	736	679	621	564	507
4,920	4,960	1,112	1,049	986	922	861	804	747	690	633	575	518
4,960	5,000	1,125	1,061	998	935	872	815	758	701	644	587	529
5,000	5,040	1,137	1,074	1,011	947	884	826	769	712	655	598	541

$5,040 and over — Use Table 4(a) for a **SINGLE person** on page 29. Also see the instructions on page 27.

MINI PRACTICE SET (CH 8): PETE'S MARKET

COMPUTERIZED ACCOUNTING APPLICATION FOR PETE'S MARKET MINI PRACTICE SET (CHAPTER 8)

Completing Payroll Requirements for First Quarter and Preparing Form 941

Before starting on this assignment, read and complete the tasks discussed in Parts A, B, and F of the Computerized Accounting appendix at the end of this book and complete the Computerized Accounting Application assignments for Chapter 3, Chapter 4, and the Valdez Realty Mini Practice Set (Chapter 5).

Pete's Market, owned by Pete Reel, is located at 4 Sun Avenue, Swampscott, Massachusetts, 01970. His employer identification number is 42-4583312. The educational version of Simply Accounting packaged with this text uses the state and federal tax laws in effect on April 15, 1997. Federal Income Tax (FIT), State Income Tax (SIT), Social Security, Medicare, FUTA, and SUTA are all calculated automatically by the program based on the following assumptions and built-in tax rates:

1. FICA: Social Security, 6.2 percent on $65,400; Medicare, 1.45 percent on all earnings.

2. SUTA: 4.9 percent on the first $10,800 in earnings.

3. FUTA: .8 percent on the first $7,000 in earnings.

4. Employees are paid monthly. The payroll is recorded and paid on the last day of each month. The cash amount for the first quarter's net pay has been transferred from the Cash account to the Payroll Checking Cash account.

5. FIT is calculated automatically by the program based on the marital status and number of exemptions claimed by each employee.

6. SIT for Massachusetts is calculated automatically by the program based on the marital status and number of exemptions claimed by each employee.

The Payroll Journal in Simply Accounting is designed to work with the General Ledger module in an integrated fashion. When transactions are recorded in the Payroll Journal, the program automatically updates the employee records, records the journal entry, and posts all accounts affected in the general ledger.

The following are the employees of Pete's Market and their monthly wages for the first payroll quarter:

	January	February	March
Fred Flynn	$2,500	$2,590	$2,475
Mary Jones	3,000	3,000	4,000
Lilly Vron	3,000	3,000	4,260

The trial balance for Pete's Market as at 1/1/97 appears below:

		Debits	Credits
1010	Cash	65,183.37	—
1020	Payroll Checking Cash	19,780.67	—
2310	FIT Payable	—	1,415.94
2320	SIT Payable	—	535.50
2330	Social Security Tax Payable	—	1,116.00
2335	Medicare Tax Payable	—	261.00
2340	FUTA Payable	—	48.00

2350	SUTA Payable	—	1,587.60
3560	Pete Reel, Capital	—	80,000.00
		84,964.04	84,964.04

Open the Company Data Files

1. Click on the Start button. Point to Programs; point to Simply Accounting; then click on Simply Accounting in the final menu presented. The Simply Accounting Open File dialog box will appear.

2. Insert your Student Data Files disk into disk drive A. Enter the following path into the **File name** text box: A:\student\pete.asc

3. Click on the **Open** button; enter 1/31/97 into the **Using Date for this Session** text box; then click on the **OK** button. Click on the **OK** button in response to the message "The date entered is more than one week past your previous **Using date** of 1/1/97." The Company Window for Pete will appear.

Add Your Name to the Company Name

4. Click on the Company Window Setup menu; then click on Company Information. The Company Information dialog box will appear. Insert your name in place of the text "Your Name" in the **Name** text box. Click on the **OK** button to return to the Company Window.

Record Payment of December Payroll Liabilities and Taxes

5. Open the General Journal dialog box; then record the following general journal entries (Enter "Memo" into the **Source** text box for each transaction; then enter the **Date** listed for each transaction.):

1997
Jan. 15 Record the compound journal entry for the deposit of Social Security, Medicare, and FIT from last month's payroll. (For simplicity we will not record the payment of state income tax.)
31 Record the payment of SUTA from last quarter.
31 Record the payment of FUTA tax owed.

How to Record Payroll Journal Entries

6. Close the General Journal; then double-click on the Payroll Journal icon. The Payroll Journal dialog box will appear.

7. Click on the arrow button to the right of the **To the Order of** text box. Click on Fred Flynn's name; then press the TAB key.

8. Click on the **Wages** text box; enter 2500; then press the TAB key. This completes the data you need to enter into the Payroll Journal dialog box to record the payroll journal entry for Fred Flynn's January payroll check. Your screen should look like this:

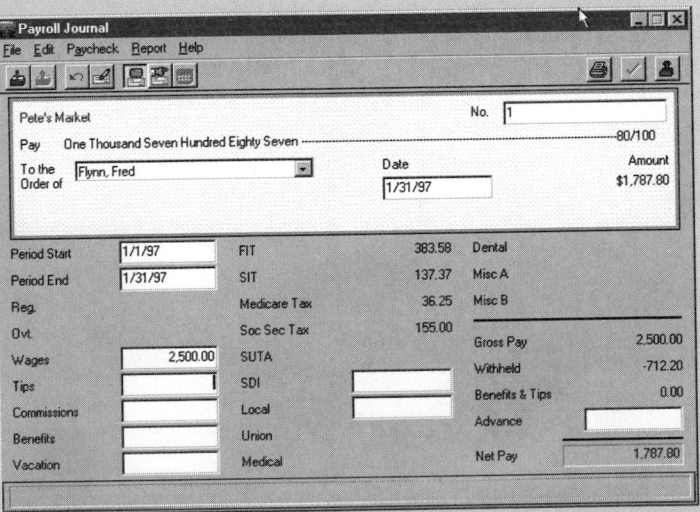

How to Review a Payroll Journal Entry

9. Before posting this transaction, you need to verify that the transaction data are correct by reviewing the payroll journal entry. To review the entry, click on the Payroll Journal Report menu; then click on Display Payroll Journal Entry. The journal entry representing the data you have recorded in the Payroll Journal dialog box is displayed.

Note that the program has combined the journal entry to record and pay the payroll with the journal entry to record the employer's payroll tax expense into a single compound journal entry. Also note that the program uses four individual payroll tax expense accounts (Social Security Tax Expense, Medicare Tax Expense, FUTA Expense, and SUTA Expense) in place of a single Payroll Tax Expense account. Review the payroll entry for accuracy noting any errors.

How to Edit a Payroll Journal Entry Prior to Posting

10. Close the Payroll Journal Entry window. If you have made an error, use the following editing techniques to correct the error:

Editing a Payroll Journal Entry

◆ Move to the text box that contains the error by either pressing the TAB key to move forward through each text box or the SHIFT and TAB keys together to move to a previous text box. This will highlight the selected text box information so that you can change it. Alternatively, you can use the mouse to point to a text box and drag through the incorrect information to highlight it.

◆ Type the correct information; then press the TAB key to enter it.

◆ If you have associated the transaction with an incorrect employee, re-select the correct employee from the employee list display after clicking on the arrow button to the right of the **To the Order of** text box.

◆ To discard an entry and start over, click on the close button. Click on the **Yes** button in response to the question "Are you sure you want to discard this journal entry?"

◆ Review the journal entry for accuracy after any editing corrections.

◆ **It is IMPORTANT TO NOTE that the only way to edit a payroll journal entry after it is posted is to reverse the entry and enter the correct journal entry.** To correct payroll journal entries posted in error, see Part C of the Computerized Accounting appendix in the back of this book.

How to Post a Payroll Entry

11. After verifying that the payroll journal entry is correct, click on the **Post** icon to post this transaction. A blank Payroll Journal dialog box is displayed, ready for additional Payroll Journal transactions to be recorded.

Record Remaining January Payroll

12. Record the January payroll journal entries for Mary Jones and Lilly Vron.

13. After you have posted the additional payroll journal entries, close the Payroll Journal dialog box. This will restore the Company Window screen, and the Payroll Journal icon will remain highlighted.

How to Display and Print an Employee Detail Report

14. Click on the Company Window Reports menu; point to payroll and then click on Employee. The Employee Report Options dialog box will appear. Click on the **Select All** button; click on the **Detail** option button; leave the **Start** date set at 1/1/97; leave the **Finish** date set at 1/31/97; leave the FIT, SIT, Medicare, and Soc. Sec. check boxes checked; then click on the **OK** button. Your screen will look like this:

```
┌─────────────────────────────────────────────────────────────┐
│ 🖳 Employee Detail                                  _ □ ✕    │
│ File  Help                                                    │
│ 1/1/97 to 1/31/97                                             │
│ Flynn, Fred                                                ▲  │
│ Date      PP    Gross      FIT      SIT  Medicare Tax  Soc Sec Tax │
│ 1/31/97   12   2,500.00   383.58   137.37    36.25      155.00    │
│                                                              │
│                2,500.00   383.58   137.37    36.25      155.00    │
│                                                              │
│                                                              │
│ Jones, Mary                                                  │
│ Date      PP    Gross      FIT      SIT  Medicare Tax  Soc Sec Tax │
│ 1/31/97   12   3,000.00   399.92   164.85    43.50      186.00    │
│                                                              │
│                3,000.00   399.92   164.85    43.50      186.00    │
│                                                              │
│                                                              │
│ Vron, Lilly                                                  │
│ Date      PP    Gross      FIT      SIT  Medicare Tax  Soc Sec Tax │
└─────────────────────────────────────────────────────────────┘
```

Print Reports

15. Click on the Employee Detail File menu; then click on Print to print the report. Close the Employee Detail window and return to the Company Window. Print the following reports:

a. General Journal (By posting date; All ledger entries; Start: 1/1/97, Finish: 1/31/97).

b. Trial Balance As at 1/31/97.

The program can display and print separate Journal Reports that list transactions recorded in a specific Journal (General, Purchases, Payments, Sales, Receipts, Payroll, Transfers, or Adjustments) and the program can display and print a single General Journal report that lists transactions recorded in all Journals. To display or print a General Journal report that includes all transactions recorded in all Journals, check the **All Ledger Entries** check box in the General Journal options dialog box. To save time and reduce the amount of printing involved in the Computer Workshop assignments, always check the **All Ledger Entries** check box.

Review your printed reports. If you have made an error in a posted journal entry, see Part C of the Computerized Accounting appendix (Reversing an Entry Made in the General Journal or Payroll Journal Dialog Box) for information on how to correct the error.

Make a January Backup Copy

16. Click on the Company Window File menu; click on Save As; then enter the following new file name into the **File name** text box: A:\student\petejan.asc

17. Click on the **Save** button. Note that the company name in the Company Window has changed from Pete to Petejan. Click on the Company Window File menu again; then click on Save As. Enter the following new file names into the **File name** text box: A:\student\pete.asc

18. Click on the **Save** button. Click on the **Yes** button in response to the question "Replace existing file?" Note that the company name in the Company Window has changed back from Petejan to Pete.

19. You now have two sets of company data files for Pete's Market on your Student Data Files disk. The current data is stored under the file name pete.asc. The January backup data is stored under the file name petejan.asc

Advance Dates

20. Click on the Company Window Maintenance menu; then click on Advance Using Date. Click on the **No** button in response to the question "You have never backed up your data. Would you like to backup now?" Enter 2/1/97 into the **New Using Date** text box; then click on the **OK** button. Click on the **OK** button in response to the warning message. The backup you created using the Save As method will serve as the backup suggested in both warning messages.

21. Click on the Company Window Setup menu; then click on Company Information. The Company Information dialog box will appear. Enter 2/28/97 as the new **Fiscal end** date; then click on the **OK** button.

22. Click on the Company Window Maintenance menu; then click on Advance Using Date. Click on the **No** button in response to the question "You have never backed up your data. Would you like to backup now?" Enter 2/28/97 into the **New Using Date** text box; then click on the **OK** button. Click on the **OK** button in response to the warning message.

Record Payment of January Payroll Liabilities and Taxes

23. Record the following general journal entry:

1997
Feb.   15   Record the compound journal entry for the deposit of Social Security, Medicare, and FIT from last month's payroll.

Record February Payroll

24. Record the February payroll journal entries for Fred Flynn, Mary Jones, and Lilly Vron.

Print Reports

25. Print the following reports:

a. Employee Detail (Select All; Start: 2/1/97; Finish: 2/28/97).

b. General Journal (By posting date; All ledger entries; Start: 2/1/97; Finish: 2/28/97).

c. Trial Balance As at 2/28/97.

Make a February Backup Copy	**26.** Click on the Company Window File menu; click on Save As; then enter the following new file name into the **File name** text box: A:\student\petefeb.asc
	27. Click on the **Save** button. Note that the company name in the Company Window has changed from Pete to Petefeb. Click on the Company Window File menu again; then click on Save As. Enter the following new file name into the **File name** text box: A:\student\pete.asc
	28. Click on the **Save** button. Click on the **Yes** button in response to the question "Replace existing file?" Note that the company name in the Company Window has changed back from Petefeb to Pete.
	29. You now have three sets of company data files for Pete's Market on your Student Data Files disk. The current data is stored under the file name pete.asc. The January backup data is stored under the file name petejan.asc and the February backup data is stored under the file name petefeb.asc.
Advance Dates	**30.** Click on the Company Window Maintenance menu; then click on Advance Using Date. Click on the **No** button in response to the question "You have never backed up your data. Would you like to backup now?" Enter 3/1/97 into the **New Using Date** text box; then click on the **OK** button. Click on the **OK** button in response to the warning message. The backup you created using the Save As method will serve as the backup suggested in both warning messages.
	31. Click on the Company Window Setup menu; then click on Company Information. The Company Information dialog box will appear. Enter 3/31/97 as the new **Fiscal end** date; then click on the **OK** button.
	32. Click on the Company Window Maintenance menu; then click on Advance Using Date. Click on the **No** button in response to the question "You have never backed up your data. Would you like to backup now?" Enter 3/31/97 into the **New Using Date** text box; then click on the **OK** button. Click on the **OK** button in response to the warning message.
Record Payment of February Payroll Liabilities and Taxes	**33.** Record the following general journal entry:

1997
Mar.   15   Record the compound journal entry for the deposit of Social Security, Medicare, and FIT from last month's payroll.

Record March Payroll	**34.** Record the March payroll journal entries for Fred Flynn, Mary Jones, and Lilly Vron.
Print Reports	**35.** Print the following reports:
	a. Employee Detail (Select All; Start: 3/1/97; Finish: 3/31/97).
	b. General Journal (By posting date; All ledger entries; Start: 3/1/97; Finish: 3/31/97).
	c. Trial Balance As at 3/31/97.
How to Display and Print 941 Summary Reports	**36.** Click on the Company Window Reports menu; point to Payroll; then click on 941 Summary. The 941 Summary Options dialog box will appear. Leave the **FIT** option button checked; click on the **Select All** button; then click on the **OK** button. The 941 FIT Summary display will appear. Click on the 941 FIT Summary File menu; then click on Print to print the report.
	37. Close the 941 FIT Summary window; click on the Company Window Reports menu; point to Payroll; then click on 941 Summary. The 941 Summary Options dialog box will appear. Click on the **SS/Med Tax** option button; click on the **Select All** button; then click on the **OK** button. The 941 Social Security/Medicare Summary display will appear. Click on the 941 Social Security/Medicare Summary File menu; click on Print to print the report; then close the 941 Social Security/Medicare Summary window.
Make a March Backup Copy	**38.** Click on the Company Window File menu; click on Save As; then enter the following new file name into the **File Name** text box: A:\student\petemar.asc
	39. Click on the **Save** button. Note that the company name in the Company Window has changed from Pete to Petemar. Click on the Company Window File

menu again; then click on Save As. Enter the following new file name into the **File Name** text box: A:\student\pete.asc

40. Click on the **Save** button. Click on the **Yes** button in response to the question "Replace existing file?" Note that the company name in the Company Window has changed back from Petemar to Pete.

41. You now have four sets of company data files for Pete's Market on your Student Data Files disk. The current data is stored under the file name pete.asc. The January backup data is stored under the file name petejan.asc, the February backup data is stored under the file name petefeb.asc, and the March backup data is stored under the file name petemar.asc.

Advance Dates

42. Click on the Company Window Maintenance menu; then click on Advance Using Date. Click on the **No** button in response to the question "You have never backed up your data. Would you like to backup now?" Enter 4/1/97 into the **New Using Date** text box; then click on the **OK** button. Click on the **OK** button in response to the warning message. The backup you created using the Save As method will serve as the backup suggested in both warning messages.

43. Click on the Company Window Maintenance menu again; then click on Advance Using Date. Click on the **No** button in response to the question "You have never backed up your data. Would you like to backup now?" Enter 4/30/97 into the **New Using Date** text box; then click on the **OK** button. Click on the **OK** button in response to the warning message.

Record Payment of March Payroll Liabilities and Taxes

44. Record the following general journal entries:

1997
Apr.   15 Record the compound journal entry for the deposit of Social Security, Medicare, and FIT from last month's payroll.
        30 Record the payment of SUTA from last quarter.
        30 Record the payment of FUTA tax owed.

Print Reports

45. Print the following reports:
   a. General Journal (By posting date; All ledger entries; Start: 4/1/97, Finish: 4/30/97).
   b. Trial Balance As at 4/30/97.

Exit from the Program

46. Click on the Company Window File menu; then click on Exit to end the current work session and return to your Windows desktop.

Complete the Report Transmittal and Form 941

47. Complete the Pete's Market Report Transmittal and Form 941 located in Appendix A of your *Study Guide and Working Papers*.

SPECIAL JOURNALS

Sales and Cash Receipts

THE BIG PICTURE

In reviewing the records last month for the Eldorado Computer Center, Tony Freedman discovered that his retail business has increased his revenue and profits. He also discovered that it is important to keep accurate detailed records of sales transactions. He decided to experiment with some specialized journals to track his sales activity and receipt of cash payments.

The cash receipts journal will assist Freedman in trimming down the number of entries he has to post daily for the business. Since controlling cash is one of the most important things a business must do in order to avoid financial difficulty, cash transactions must be posted accurately. The retail side of his business has increased the cash inflow, and also, by its very nature, the increased potential of loss or theft. Protecting this cash requires implementing some internal control procedures to avoid loss or theft.

The other specialized journal Tony has decided to experiment with is the sales journal. This journal will allow him to keep track of his sales to customers on credit. Freedman has extended more credit to his customers, and he wants to keep a closer look at his sales on account. He wants to know how he is collecting from those sales.

In this chapter you will learn the importance of protecting your cash and collecting your accounts receivable from the credit customers. The schedule of accounts receivable prepared at the end of the month will give you a detail of what dollar amount is owed by each customer. The ease of posting from specialized journals will help reduce the potential for errors when you have a lot of repetitive transactions.

	Learning Objectives
	◆ Journalizing sales on account in a sales journal. (p. 313) ◆ Posting from a sales journal to the general ledger. (p. 317) ◆ Recording to the accounts receivable subsidiary ledger from a sales journal. (p. 319) ◆ Preparing, journalizing, recording, and posting a credit memorandum. (p. 322) ◆ Journalizing and posting transactions using a cash receipts journal, as well as recording to the accounts receivable subsidiary ledger. (p. 327)

In Chapters 9 and 10 we will take a look at how merchandise companies operate. Chapter 9 focuses on sellers of goods; Chapter 10 discusses buyers. Let's first look at Chou's Toy Shop to get an overview of merchandise terms and journal entries. After that, we will take an in-depth look at how Art's Wholesale Clothing Company keeps its books.

LEARNING UNIT 9-1
Chou's Toy Shop: Seller's View of a Merchandise Company

Chou's Toy Shop is a **retailer.** It buys toys, games, bikes, etc., from manufacturers and **wholesalers** and resells these goods (or **merchandise**) to its customers. The shelving, display cases, and so on are called "fixtures" or "equipment." These items are not for resale.

GROSS SALES

Gross sales: Revenue earned from sale of merchandise to customers.

Each cash or charge sale made at Chou's Toy Shop is rung up at the register. Suppose the shop had $3,000 in sales on July 18. Of that amount, $1,800 were cash sales and $1,200 were charges. This is how the account that recorded those sales would look:

Sales (Gross)

Dr.	Cr.
	3,000 ◄—— Revenue account with a credit balance

This account is a revenue account with a credit balance and will be found on the income statement. Here is the journal entry for the day. **Note:** We will talk about sales tax later.

Accounts Affected	Category	↑	↓	Rules	T-Account Update
Cash	Asset	↑		Dr.	Cash 1,800 |
Accounts Receivable	Asset	↑		Dr.	Accounts Receivable 1,200 |
Sales	Revenue	↑		Cr.	Sales | 3,000

July	18	Cash		1 8 0 0 00		
		Accounts Receivable		1 2 0 0 00		
		Sales				3 0 0 0 00
		Sales for July 18				

SALES RETURNS AND ALLOWANCES

It would be great for Chou if all the customers were completely satisfied, but that rarely is the case. On July 19, Michelle Reese brought back a doll she bought on account for $50. She told Chou that the doll was defective and she wanted either a price reduction or a new doll. They agreed on a $10 price reduction. Michelle now owes Chou $40. The account called **Sales Returns and Allowances (SRA)** would record this information.

Sales Returns and Allowances

Contra-revenue account with a debit balance ⟶
Dr. | Cr.
10 |

This account is a contra-revenue account with a debit balance. It will be recorded on the income statement. This is how the journal entry would look:

Accounts Affected	Category	↑	↓	Rules	T Account Update
Sales Returns and Allowances	Contra-revenue	↑		Dr.	Sales Ret. & Allow. Dr. | Cr. 10 |
Accounts Receivable, Michelle Reese	Asset		↓	Cr.	Accounts Receivable Dr. | Cr. 1,200 | 10

Look at how the sales returns and allowances increase.

July	19	Sales Returns and Allowances			1 0 00		
		Accounts Receivable, Michelle Reese					1 0 00
		Issued credit memorandum					

SALES DISCOUNT

Chou gives a 2 percent **sales discount** to customers who pay their bills early. He wants his customers to know about this policy, so he posted the following sign at the cash register:

Sales Discount Policy

2/10, n/30	2% discount is allowed off price of bill if paid within the first 10 days or full amount is due within 30 days
n/10, EOM	No discount, full amount of bill is due within 10 days after the end of the month.

Note the **discount period** is the time when a discount is granted. The discount period is less time than the **credit period,** which is the length of time allowed to pay back the amount owed on the bill.

If Michelle pays her $40 bill early she will get an $.80 discount. This is the account that records this information:

$$\text{Sales Discount}$$

	Dr.	Cr.

Contra-revenue �te account with a debit balance.   Dr. .80 | Cr.

This is how Michelle's discount is calculated:

$$.02 \times \$40 = \$.80$$

Michelle pays her bill on July 24. She is entitled to the discount because she paid her bill within 10 days. Let's look at how Chou would record this on his books.

Gross sales
− Sales discount
− SRA
= Net sales

Accounts Affected	Category	↑	↓	Rules	T Account Update
Cash	Asset	↑		Dr.	**Cash** Dr. 39.20 | Cr.
Sales Discount	Contra-revenue	↑		Dr.	**Sales Discount** Dr. .80 | Cr.
Accounts Receivable	Asset		↓	Cr.	**Accounts Receivable** Dr. 1,200 | Cr. 40

July	24	Cash			3 9 20			
		Sales Discount			80			
		Accounts Receivable, Michelle Reese				4 0 00		

Although Michelle pays $39.20, her Accounts Receivable is credited for the full amount, $40.

In the examples so far we have not shown any transactions with sales tax. Note the actual or **net sales** for Chou would be **gross sales** less sales returns and allowances less any sales discounts. Let's look at how Chou would record his monthly sales if sales tax were charged.

SALES TAX PAYABLE

None of the examples shown above show state sales tax. Still, like it or not, Chou must collect that tax from his customers and send it to the state. Sales tax represents a liability to Chou.

Assume the state Chou's is located in charges a 5 percent sales tax. Remember, Chou's sales on July 18 were $3,000. Chou must figure out the sales tax on the purchases. For this purpose, let's assume that there were only two sales on that date: the cash sale ($1,800) and the charge sale ($1,200).

The sales tax on the cash purchase is calculated as follows:

$$1,800 \times .05 = \$90 \text{ tax}$$
$$1,800 + \$90 \text{ tax} = \$1,890 \text{ cash}$$

Here is how the sales tax on the charge sale is computed:

$$1,200 \times .05 = \$60 \text{ tax} + \$1,200 \text{ charge} = \$1,260 \text{ Accounts Receivable}$$

This is how it would be recorded:

Accounts Affected	Category	↑	↓	Rules	T Account Update
Cash	Asset	↑		Dr.	Cash Dr. | Cr. 1,890 |
Accounts Receivable	Asset	↑		Dr.	Accounts Receivable Dr. | Cr. 1,260 |
Sales Tax Payable	Liability	↑		Cr.	Sales Tax Payable Dr. | Cr. | 90 | 60
Sales	Revenue	↑		Cr.	Sales Dr. | Cr. | 3,000

July	18	Cash			1 8 9 0 00			
		Accounts Receivable			1 2 6 0 00			
		Sales Tax Payable					1 5 0 00	
		Sales					3 0 0 0 00	
		July 18 Sales						

In a later unit in this chapter, we will show you how to record a credit memorandum with sales tax.

LEARNING UNIT 9-1 REVIEW

AT THIS POINT you should be able to

◆ Explain the purpose of a contra-revenue account. (p. 314)
◆ Explain how to calculate net sales. (p. 315)
◆ Define, journalize, and explain gross sales, sales returns and allowances, and sales discounts. (p. 314)
◆ Journalize an entry for sales tax payable. (p. 316)

SELF-REVIEW QUIZ 9-1

(The forms you need can be found on page 285 of the *Study Guide and Working Papers.*)

LEARNING UNIT 9-2
The Sales Journal and Accounts Receivable Subsidiary Ledger

SPECIAL JOURNALS

Now let's examine how Art's Wholesale Clothing Company keeps its books. Art's business conducts many transactions. The following partial general journal shows the journal entries Art's must make for these sales on account transactions.

ART'S WHOLESALE CLOTHING COMPANY GENERAL JOURNAL					
April	3	Accounts Receivable, Hal's		80000	
		Sales			80000
		Sales on Account			
	6	Accounts Receivable, Bevans		160000	
		Sales			160000
		Sales on Account			
	18	Accounts Receivable, Roe		200000	
		Sales			200000
		Sales on Account			

This method is not very efficient. However, if Art's Wholesale Clothing Company kept a **special journal** for each type of transaction he conducts, the number of postings and recordings required for each transaction would be reduced. After carefully looking at the situation with his accountant, Art decided to use the following special journals:

For a discussion of recording of credit cards in special journals see appendix.

Special Journal Type	What It Records	
Sales journal	Sale of merchandise on account	Covered in this chapter
Cash receipts journal	Receiving cash from any source	
Purchases journal	Buying merchandise or other items on account	Covered in next chapter
Cash payments journal (cash disbursement journal)	Paying of cash for any purpose	

SUBSIDIARY LEDGERS

In the same way Art's Wholesale Clothing Company needs more than just a general journal, the business needs more than just a general ledger. For example, so far in this text, the only title we have used for recording amounts owed to the seller has been Accounts Receivable. Art could have replaced the Accounts Receivable title in the general ledger with the following list of customers who owe him money:

◆ Accounts Receivable, Bevans Company
◆ Accounts Receivable, Hal's Clothing
◆ Accounts Receivable, Mel's Department Store
◆ Accounts Receivable, Roe Company

As you can see, this would not be manageable if Art had 1,000 credit customers. To solve this problem, Art sets up a separate **accounts receivable subsidiary ledger.** Such a special ledger, often simply called a **subsidiary ledger,** contains a single type of account, such as credit customers. An account is opened for each customer and the accounts are arranged alphabetically.

The diagram in Figure 9-1 shows how the accounts receivable subsidiary ledger fits in with the general ledger. To clarify the difference in updating the general ledger versus the subsidiary ledger we will *post* to the general ledger and *record* to the subsidiary ledger. The word "post" refers to information that is moved from the journal to the general ledger; the word "record" refers to information that is transferred from the journal into the individual customer's account in the subsidiary ledger.

The accounts receivable subsidiary ledger, or any other subsidiary ledger, can be in the form of a card file, a binder notebook, or computer tapes or disks. It will not have page numbers. The accounts receivable subsidiary ledger is organized alphabetically based on customers' names and addresses; new customers can be added and inactive customers deleted.

The general ledger is *not* in the same book as the accounts receivable subsidiary ledger.

Proving: At the end of the month, the sum of the accounts receivable subsidiary ledger will equal the ending balance in accounts receivable, the controlling account in the general ledger.

FIGURE 9-1 Partial General Ledger of Art's Wholesale Clothing Company and Accounts Receivable Subsidiary Ledger

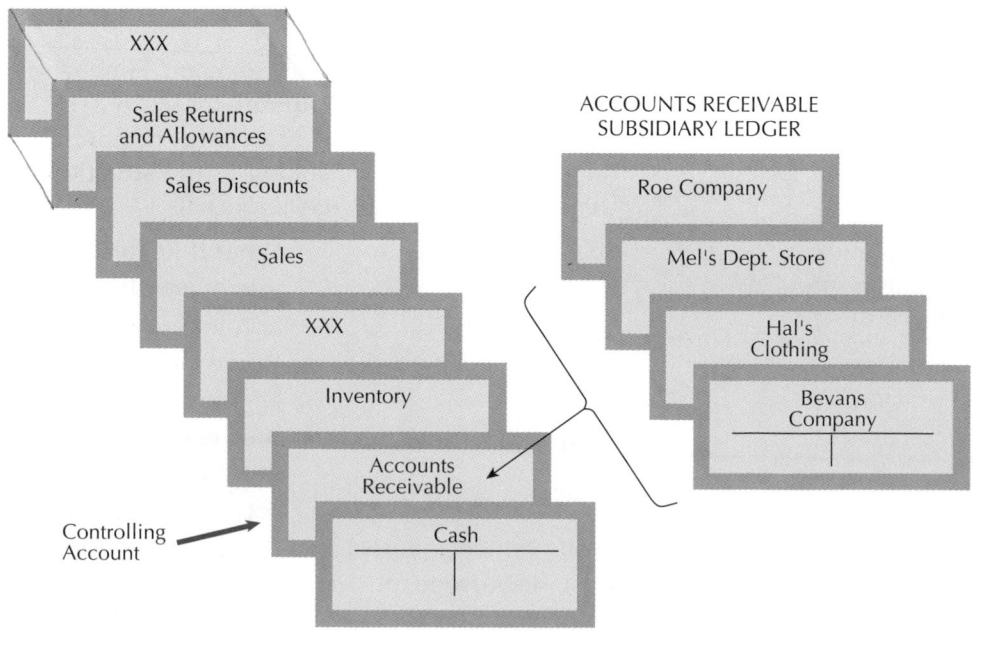

PARTIAL GENERAL LEDGER

ACCOUNTS RECEIVABLE SUBSIDIARY LEDGER

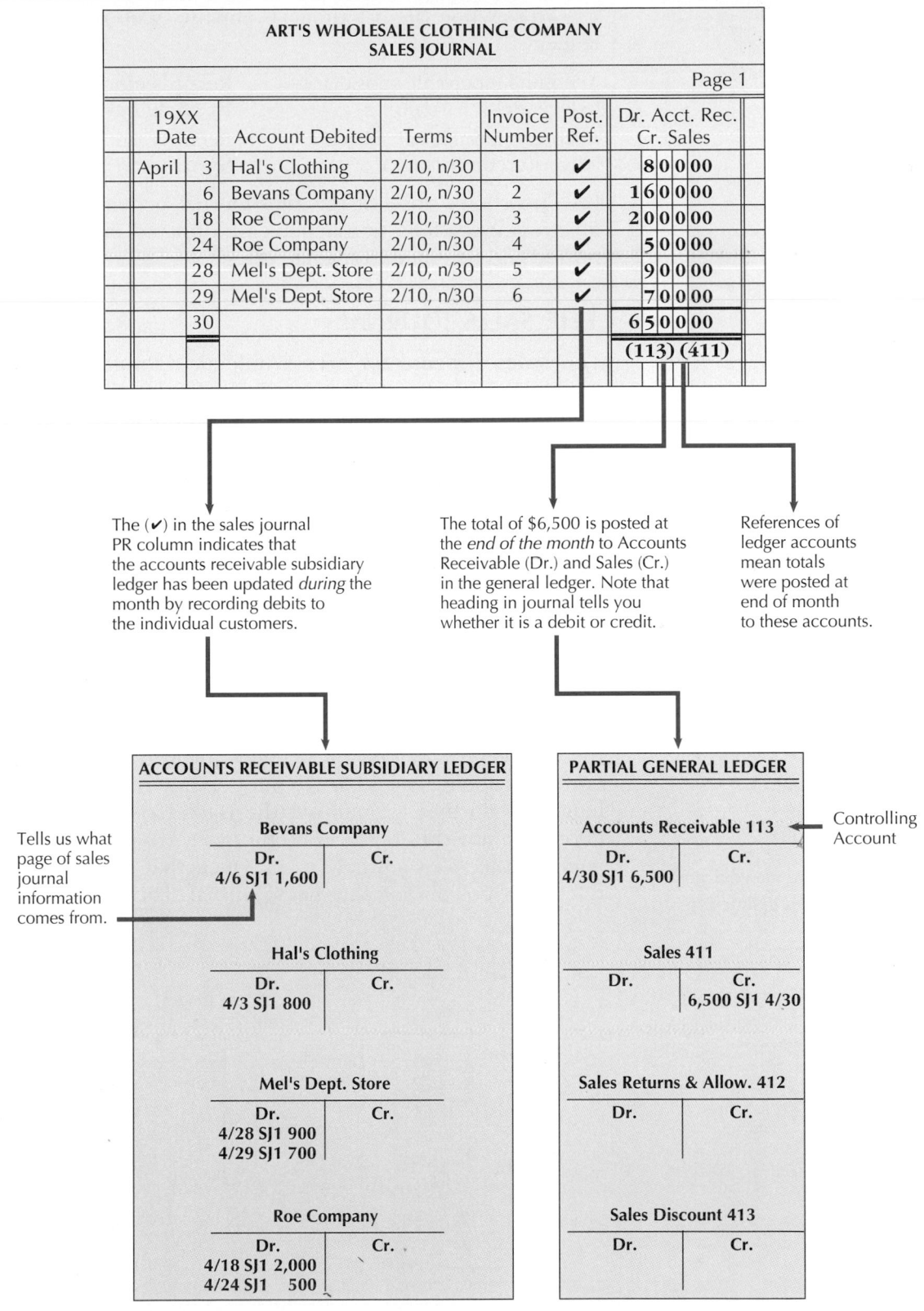

FIGURE 9-2 Sales Journal Recording and Postings

When using an accounts receivable subsidiary ledger, the title Accounts Receivable in the general ledger is called the **controlling account,** since it summarizes or controls the accounts receivable subsidiary ledger. At the end of the month the total of the individual accounts in the accounts receivable ledger will equal the ending balance in Accounts Receivable in the general ledger.

Art's Wholesale Clothing Company will use the following subsidiary ledgers:

Accounts receivable subsidiary ledger (debit balance)	Records money owed by credit customers	Covered in this chapter
Accounts payable subsidiary ledger (credit balance)	Records money owed by Art to creditors	Covered in next chapter

Let's now look closer at the sales journal, general ledger, and subsidiary ledger for Art's to see how transactions are updated in the special journal as well as posted and recorded to specific titles.

THE SALES JOURNAL

The **sales journal** for Art's Wholesale Clothing Company records all sales made on account to customers. Figure 9-2 on page 319 shows the sales journal at the end of the first month in operation, along with the recordings to the accounts receivable ledger and posting to the general ledger. Keep in mind that the reason the balances in the accounts receivable subsidiary ledger are *debit* balances is that the customers listed *owe* Art's Wholesale money. For some other companies, a sales journal might have multiple revenue account columns.

Look at the first transaction listed in the sales journal. It shows that on April 3 Art's Wholesale Clothing Company sold merchandise on account to Hal's Clothing for $800. The bill or **sales invoice** for this sale is shown in Figure 9-3.

Recording from the Sales Journal to the Accounts Receivable Subsidiary Ledger

As shown on the first line of the sales journal in Figure 9-2, the information on the invoice is recorded in the sales journal. However, the *PR column is left blank.* As soon as possible we now update the accounts receivable subsidiary ledger. To do this, we pull out the Hal's Clothing file card and update it: the debit side must show the $800 he owes Art along with the date (April 3) and page of the sales journal (p. 1). Once that is done, place a ✓ in the post-reference column of the sales journal. The accounts receivable subsidiary

---

Recording to the accounts receivable subsidiary ledger occurs daily.

Hal's Clothing	
Dr.	Cr.
4/3 SJ1	
800	

✓ means accounts receivable ledger has been updated.

FIGURE 9-3
Sales Invoice

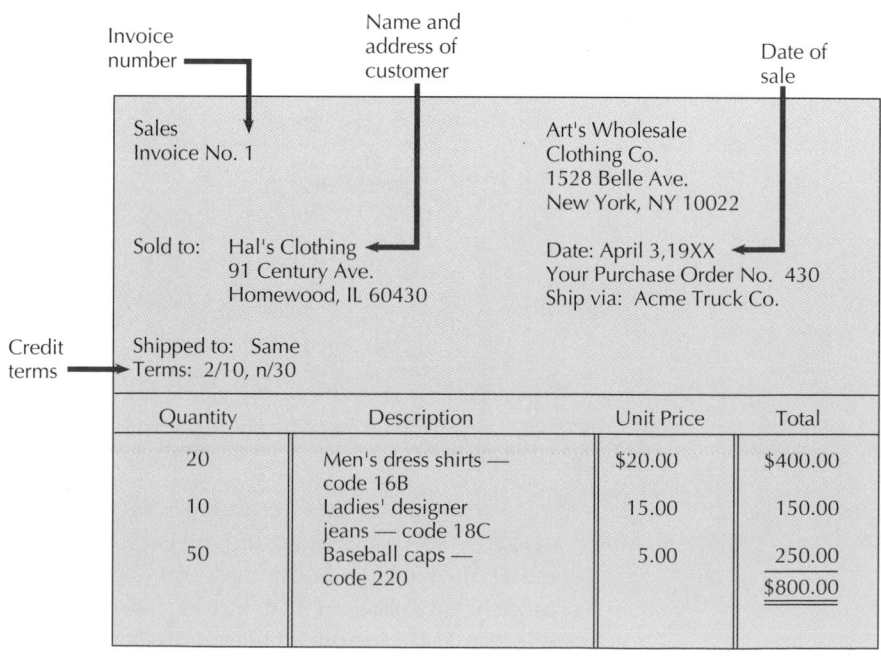

---

ledger shows us Hal's outstanding balance at any moment in time. We do not have to go through all the invoices. Note how the sales journal only needs one line instead of the three lines that would have been required in a general journal.

Posting at End of Month from the Sales Journal to the General Ledger

The sales journal is totaled ($6,500) at the end of the month. Looking back at page 319, you can see that the heading of Art's sales journal is a debit to accounts receivable and a credit to sales. Therefore, at the end of the month the $6,500 total is posted to Accounts Receivable (debit) *and* to Sales (credit) in the general ledger. In the general ledger we record the date (4/30), the initials of the journal (SJ), the page of the sales journal (1), and appropriate debit or credit ($6,500). Once the account in the general ledger is updated, we place below the totals in the sales journal the account numbers to which the information was posted (in this case accounts 113 and 411).

Sales Tax

Art's Wholesale Clothing Company does not have to deal with sales tax because it sells goods wholesale. However, if Art's was a retail company, it would have to pay sales tax.

Let's look at how Munroe Menswear Company, a retailer, handles sales tax on a purchase made by Jones Company. Figure 9-4 shows Munroe's sales journal.

Also, a new account, **Sales Tax Payable,** must be created. That account is a liability account in the general ledger with a credit balance. The customer owes Munroe the sale amount plus the tax.

Keep in mind that if sales discounts are available, they are not calculated on the sales tax. The discount is on the selling price less any returns before the tax. For example, if Jones receives a 2 percent discount, he pays the following:

$5,000 × .02 = $100 savings →

$5,250	Total owed (tax is $250)
−100	Savings (discount)
$5,150	Amount paid

Margin notes (left column):

Recording to the general ledger occurs at end of month.

Acc. Rec. 113

Dr.	Cr.
4/30 SJ1	
6,500	

Sales 411

Dr.	Cr.
	6,500 SJ1
	4/30

Sales Tax Payable

	XXX

A liability in general ledger.

FIGURE 9-4
Munroe Sales Journal

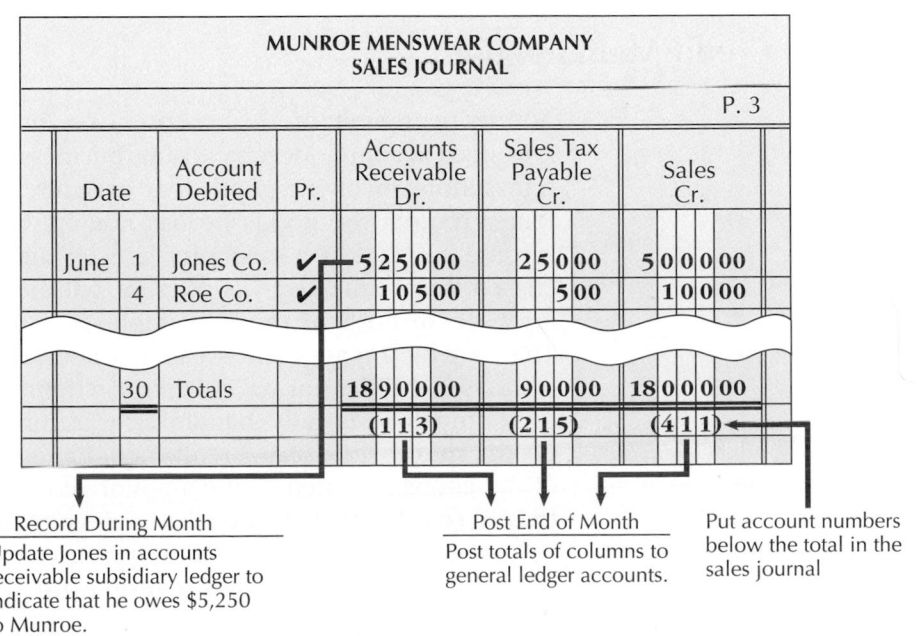

CH. 9 / SPECIAL JOURNALS: SALES AND CASH RECEIPTS

LEARNING UNIT 9-2 REVIEW

AT THIS POINT you should be able to

◆ Define and state the purposes of special journals. (p. 317)
◆ Define and state the purposes of the accounts receivable subsidiary ledger. (p. 318)
◆ Define and state the purpose of the controlling account, Accounts Receivable. (p. 318)
◆ Journalize, record, or post sales on account to a sales journal and its related accounts receivable and general ledgers. (p. 319)

SELF-REVIEW QUIZ 9-2

(The forms you need are on page 285 of the *Study Guide and Working Papers*.) Which of the following statements are false?

1. Special journals completely replace the general journal.
2. Special journals aid the division of labor.
3. The subsidiary ledger makes the general ledger less manageable.
4. The subsidiary ledger is separate from the general ledger.
5. The controlling account is located in the accounts receivable subsidiary ledger.
6. The total(s) of a sales journal are posted to the general ledger at the end of the month.
7. The accounts receivable subsidiary ledger is arranged in alphabetical order.
8. Transactions recorded into a sales journal are recorded only weekly to the accounts receivable subsidiary ledger.

Quiz Tip: The normal balance of the accounts receivable subsidiary ledger is a debit.

Solution to Self-Review Quiz 9-2

Numbers 1, 3, 5, and 8 are false.

LEARNING UNIT 9-3
The Credit Memorandum

A credit memorandum *reduces* accounts receivable.

Remember, no sales tax was involved because Art's is a wholesale company.

At the beginning of this chapter we introduced the Sales Returns and Allowances account. Merchandising businesses often use this account to handle transactions involving goods that have already been sold. For example, if a customer returns the goods he has bought, his account will be credited for the amount he paid; if a customer gets an allowance because the goods he purchased were damaged, his account will be credited for the amount of the allowance. In both of these examples, the company's sales revenue decreases. That is why the account is called a contra-revenue account: the sales revenue decreases and the normal balance is a debit.

Companies usually handle sales returns and allowances by means of a **credit memorandum.** Credit memoranda inform customers that the amount of the goods returned or the amount allowed for damaged goods has been subtracted (credited) from the customer's ongoing account with the company.

A sample credit memorandum from Art's Wholesale Clothing Company appears in Figure 9-5. It shows that on April 12 credit memo No. 1 was issued to Bevans Company for defective merchandise that had been returned. (Figure 9-2

End result is that Bevan owes Art's Wholesale less money.

Art's Wholesale
Clothing Co.
1528 Belle Ave.
New York, NY 10022

Credit
Memorandum No. _1_
Date: _April 12_
Credit to Bevans Company
110 Aster Rd.
Cincinnati, Ohio 45227
We credit your account as follows:
Merchandise returned 60 model 8 B men's dress gloves—$600

FIGURE 9-5
Credit Memorandum

Sales Returns and Allowances	
Dr.	Cr.
+	−

A contra-revenue account

Note that the Sales Returns and Allowances account is increasing, which in turn reduces sales revenue and reduces amount owed by customer (accounts receivable).

Remember, sales discounts are *not* taken on returns.

shows that Art's Wholesale Clothing Company sold Bevans Company $1,600 of merchandise on April 6.)

Let's assume that Art's Clothing has high-quality goods and does not expect many sales returns and allowances. Based on this assumption, no special journal for sales returns and allowances will be needed. Instead, any returns and allowances will be recorded in the general journal, and all postings and recordings will be done when journalized. Let's look at a transaction analysis chart before we journalize, record, and post this transaction.

Accounts Affected	Category	↑	↓	Rules
Sales Returns and Allowances	**Contra-revenue account**	↑		**Dr.**
Accounts Receivable, Bevans Co.	**Asset**		↓	**Cr.**

JOURNALIZING, RECORDING, AND POSTING THE CREDIT MEMORANDUM

The credit memorandum results in two postings to the general ledger and one recording to the accounts receivable subsidiary ledger (see Fig. 9-6 on page 324).

Note in the PR column next to Accounts Receivable, Bevans Co., that there is a diagonal line with the account number 113 above and a ✓ below. This is to show that the amount of $600 has been credited to Accounts Receivable in the controlling account in the general ledger *and* credited to the account of Bevans Company in the accounts receivable subsidiary ledger.

If the accountant for Art's Wholesale Clothing Company decided to develop a special journal for sales allowances and returns, the entry for a credit memorandum such as the one we've been discussing would look like this:

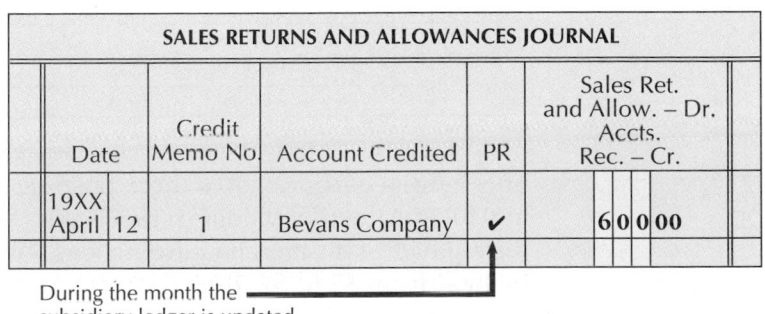

							Sales Ret. and Allow. – Dr. Accts. Rec. – Cr.				
Date		Credit Memo No.	Account Credited	PR							
19XX April	12	1	Bevans Company	✓			6	0	0	00	

During the month the subsidiary ledger is updated

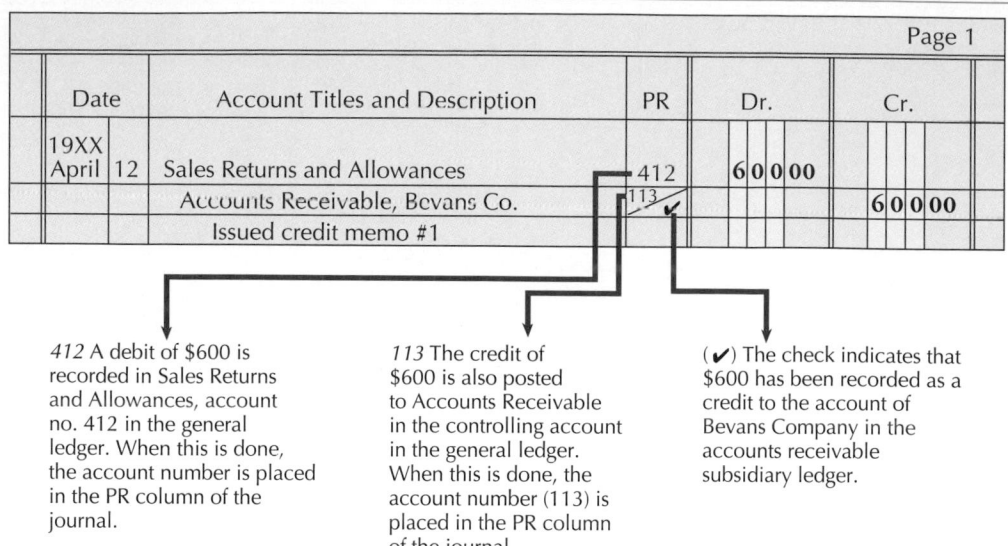

Date	Account Titles and Description	PR	Dr.	Cr.
19XX April 12	Sales Returns and Allowances	412	6 0 0 00	
	Accounts Receivable, Bevans Co.	113 ✔		6 0 0 00
	Issued credit memo #1			

412 A debit of $600 is recorded in Sales Returns and Allowances, account no. 412 in the general ledger. When this is done, the account number is placed in the PR column of the journal.

113 The credit of $600 is also posted to Accounts Receivable in the controlling account in the general ledger. When this is done, the account number (113) is placed in the PR column of the journal.

(✔) The check indicates that $600 has been recorded as a credit to the account of Bevans Company in the accounts receivable subsidiary ledger.

FIGURE 9-6
Postings and Recordings for the Credit Memorandum into the Subsidiary and General Ledger.

THE CREDIT MEMORANDUM WITH SALES TAX

Figure 9-4 (p. 321) shows the sales journal for Munroe Menswear Company. Remember, since Munroe is a retail company, its customers must pay sales tax. Let's assume that on June 8 Roe returns $50 worth of the $100 of merchandise he bought earlier in the month. Let's analyze and journalize the credit memo that Munroe issued. Keep in mind that the customer is no longer responsible for paying for either the returned merchandise or the tax on it.

Accounts Affected	Category	↑ ↓	Rules	T Account Update	
Sales Returns and Allowances	**Contra-revenue**	↑	**Dr.**	**Sales Ret. & Allow.** Dr. Cr. 50	
Sales Tax Payable ($5 tax on $100) ($2.50 tax on $50)	**Liability**	↓	**Dr.**	**Sales Tax Payable** Dr. Cr. 2.50	
Accounts Receivable, Roe	**Asset**	↓	**Cr.**	**Acc. Rec.** Dr. Cr. 52.50	**Roe Co.** Dr. Cr. 105 52.50

June	8	Sales Returns and Allowances		5 0 00		
		Sales Tax Payable		2 50		
		Accounts Receivable, Roe Co.			5 2 50	
		Received credit memo				

This journal entry requires three postings to the general ledger and one recording to Roe in the accounts receivable subsidiary ledger. Note since Roe returned half of his merchandise he was able to reduce what he pays for sales tax by half (from $5 to $2.50).

AT THIS POINT you should be able to

◆ Explain Sales Tax Payable in relation to Sales Discount. (p. 324)
◆ Explain, journalize, post, and record a credit memorandum with or without sales tax. (p. 324)

SELF-REVIEW QUIZ 9-3

(The forms you need are on pages 285–287 of the *Study Guide and Working Papers.*)

Journalize the following transactions into the sales journal or general journal for Moss Co. Record to the accounts receivable subsidiary ledger and post to general ledger accounts as appropriate. Use the same journal headings that we used for Art's Wholesale Clothing Company. (All sales carry credit terms of 2/10, n/30.) There is no tax.

19XX
May   1   Sold merchandise on account to Jane Company, invoice no. 1, $600.
      5   Sold merchandise on account to Ralph Company, invoice no. 2, $2,500.
    20   Issued credit memo no. 1 to Jane Company for $200 due to defective merchandise returned.

Solution to Self-Review Quiz 9-3

Quiz Tip: Total of accounts receivable subsidiary ledger $400 +$2,500 does indeed equal the balance in the controlling account, accounts receivable $2,900 at end of month, in the general ledger.

MOSS COMPANY
SALES JOURNAL

Page 1

Date		Account Debited	Terms	Invoice No.	Post Ref.	Dr. Acct. Rec. Cr. Sales
19XX May	1	Jane Company	2/10, n/30	1	✔	6 0 0 00
	5	Ralph Company	2/10, n/30	2	✔	2 5 0 0 00
	31					3 1 0 0 00
						(112) (411)

MOSS COMPANY
GENERAL JOURNAL

Page 1

Date		Account Titles and Description	PR	Dr.	Cr.
19XX May	20	Sales Ret. and Allowances	412	2 0 0 00	
		Acct. Rec., Jane Company	112 ✔		2 0 0 00
		Issued credit memo #1			

PARTIAL GENERAL LEDGER

Note the unusual credit balance of $200 due to the return. Why? Because total of sales journal is not posted till end of month.

Accounts Receivable — Account No. 112

Date		Explanation	Post. Ref.	Debit	Credit	Balance Debit	Balance Credit
19XX May	20		GJ1		2 0 0 00		2 0 0 00
	31		SJ1	3 1 0 0 00		2 9 0 0 00	

Sales — Account No. 411

Date		Explanation	Post. Ref.	Debit	Credit	Balance Debit	Balance Credit
19XX May	31		SJ1		3 1 0 0 00		3 1 0 0 00

Sales Returns and Allowances — Account No. 412

Date		Explanation	Post. Ref.	Debit	Credit	Balance Debit	Balance Credit
19XX May	20		GJ1	2 0 0 00		2 0 0 00	

ACCOUNTS RECEIVABLE SUBSIDIARY LEDGER

Customers owe Moss money and thus have a debit balance.

NAME Jane Company
ADDRESS 118 Morris Rd., Boston, MA 01935

Date		Explanation	Post. Ref.	Debit	Credit	Dr. Balance
19XX May	1		SJ1	6 0 0 00		6 0 0 00
	20		GJ1		2 0 0 00	4 0 0 00

NAME Ralph Company
ADDRESS 31 Norris Rd., Boston, MA 01935

Date		Explanation	Post. Ref.	Debit	Credit	Dr. Balance
19XX May	5		SJ1	2 5 0 0 00		2 5 0 0 00

Cash Receipts Journal and Schedule of Accounts Receivable

A **cash receipts journal** is another special journal often used in a merchandising operation. The cash receipts journal records the receipt of cash (or checks) from any source. The number of columns in the cash receipts journal depends on how frequently certain types of transactions occur. Figure 9-7 shows the headings in the cash receipts journal for Art's Wholesale, describes the purpose of each column, and tells when to update the accounts receivable ledger as well as general ledger.

The following transactions occurred and affected the cash receipts journal for Art's Clothing in April:

19XX

April   1 Art Newner invested $8,000 in the business.

          4 Received check from Hal's Clothing for payment of invoice no. 1 less discount.

       15 Cash sales for first half of April, $900.

FIGURE 9-7 Cash Receipts Journal

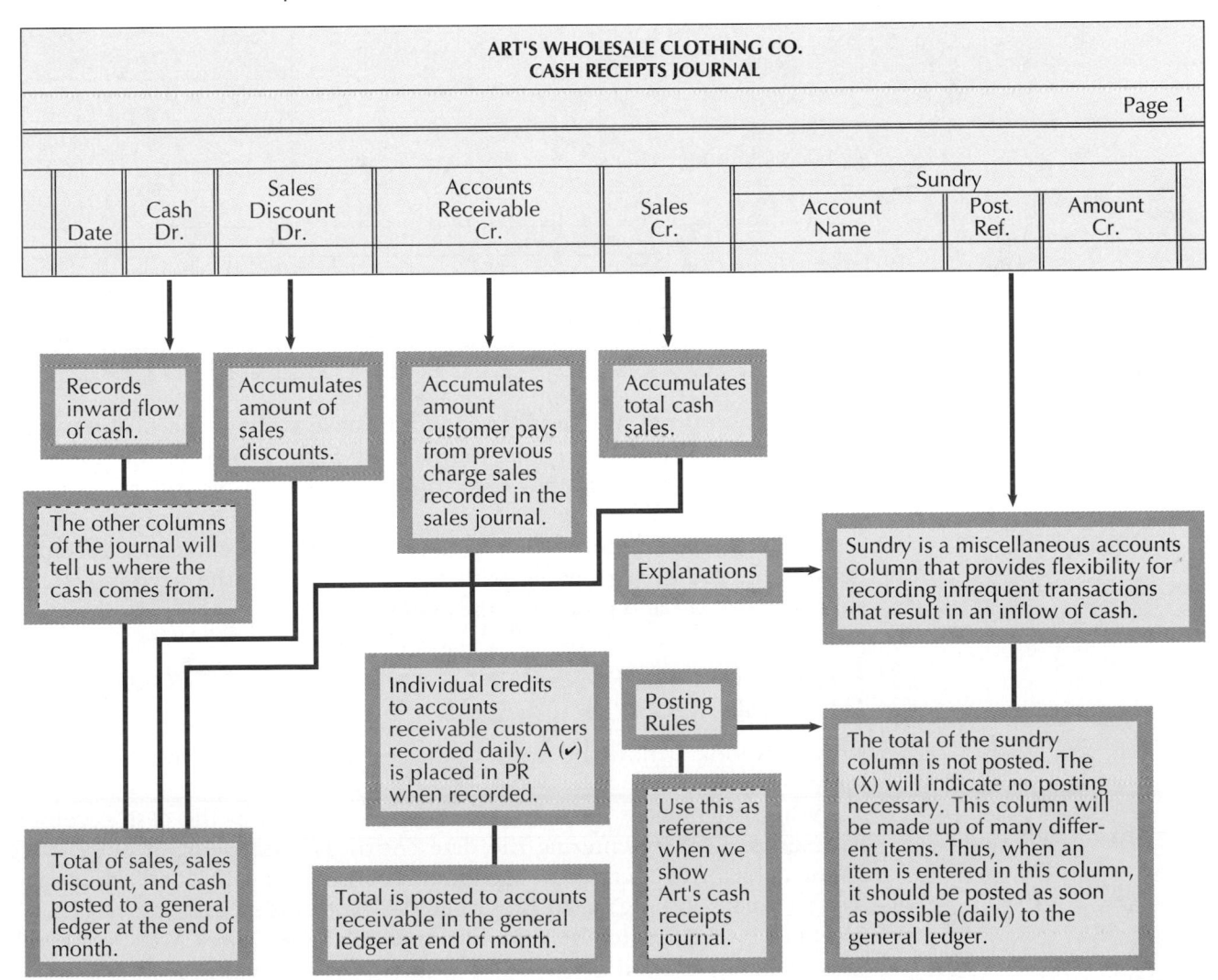

16 Received check from Bevans Company in settlement of invoice no. 2 less returns and discount.
22 Received check from Roe Company for payment of invoice no. 3 less discount.
27 Sold store equipment, $500.
30 Cash sales for second half of April, $1,200.

Benefits of a Cash Receipts Journal

Before we look at how these transactions will look in the cash receipts journal, let's see how the April 4 transaction would look if it were put into a general journal. This will illustrate the benefits of using a cash receipts journal.

19XX
April   4   Received check from Hal's Clothing for payment of invoice no. 1 less discount. (Keep in mind the sales journal showed the invoice at $800 on April 3.)

Hal's Clothing is located in the Accounts Receivable Subsidiary Ledger.

Accounts Affected	Category	↓ ↑	Rules	T Account Update	
Cash	Asset	↑	Dr.	**Cash** Dr. | Cr. / 784 |	
Sales Discount	Contra-revenue	↑	Dr.	**Sales Discount** Dr. | Cr. / 16 |	
Accounts Receivable, Hal's Clothing	Asset	↓	Cr.	**Acc. Rec.** Dr. | Cr. / 800 | 800	**Hal's Clothing** Dr. | Cr. / 800 | 800

April	4	Cash			7 8 4 00		
		Sales Discount			1 6 00		
		Accounts Receivable, Hal's Clothing				8 0 0 00	

If a general journal was used there would have to be three postings and one recording. Using a cash receipts journal (see Fig. 9-7, p. 327), the totals of cash sales discount and accounts receivable are not posted till the end of the month.

The diagram in Figure 9-8 on pages 329–330 shows the cash receipts journal for the end of April along with the recordings in the accounts receivable subsidiary ledger and posting to the general ledger.

JOURNALIZING, RECORDING, AND POSTING FROM THE CASH RECEIPTS JOURNAL

Now let's look at how the April 4 transaction is recorded in the cash receipts journal.

Remember, subsidiary ledgers can be in the form of a card file, a binder notebook, or computer tapes or disks.

When payment is received, Art's Wholesale updates the cash receipts journal (see p. 329) by entering the date (April 4), cash debit of $784, sales discount debit of $16, credit to accounts receivable of $800, and which account name (Hal's Clothing) is to be credited. The terms of sale indicate that Hal's Clothing is entitled to the discount and no longer owes Art's Wholesale the $800 balance. As soon as this line is entered into the cash receipts journal, Art's

FIGURE 9-8
Cash Receipts Journal
and Posting

(cont. on p. 330)

FIGURE 9-8 (cont.)

PARTIAL GENERAL LEDGER

Store Equipment   Account No. 121

Date	Explanation	Post. Ref.	Debit	Credit	Balance Debit	Balance Credit
19XX April 1	Balance	✔			400000	
27		CRJ1		50000	350000	

Art Newner, Capital   Account No. 311

Date	Explanation	Post. Ref.	Debit	Credit	Balance Debit	Balance Credit
19XX April 1		CRJ1		800000		800000

Sales   Account No. 411

Date	Explanation	Post. Ref.	Debit	Credit	Balance Debit	Balance Credit
19XX April 30		SJ1		650000		650000
30		CRJ1		210000		860000

Sales Discount   Account No. 413

Date	Explanation	Post. Ref.	Debit	Credit	Balance Debit	Balance Credit
19XX April 30		CRJ1	7600		7600	

ACCOUNTS RECEIVABLE SUBSIDIARY LEDGER

NAME Mel's Dept. Store
ADDRESS 181 Foss Rd., Swampscott, MA 01907

Date	Explanation	Post. Ref.	Debit	Credit	Dr. Balance
19XX April 28		SJ1	90000		90000
29		SJ1	70000		160000

NAME Roe Company
ADDRESS 18 Rantool St., Beverly, MA 01915

Date	Explanation	Post. Ref.	Debit	Credit	Dr. Balance
19XX April 18		SJ1	200000		200000
22		CRJ1		200000	-0-
24		SJ1	50000		50000

Wholesale will update the card file of Hal's Clothing. Note in the accounts receivable subsidiary ledger of Hal's Clothing how the date (April 4), post reference (CRJ1), and credit amount ($800) are recorded. The balance in the accounts receivable ledger is zero. The last step of this transaction is to go back to the cash receipts journal and put a ✓ in the post reference column.

In looking back at this cash receipts journal, note that:

Sundry: Miscellaneous accounts column(s) in a special journal, which record transactions that seldom occur.

◆ All totals of cash receipts journal *except* **sundry** were posted to the general ledger at the end of the month.

◆ Art Newner, Capital, and Store Equipment were posted to the general ledger when entered in the sundry column. For now in the general ledger it was assumed that the equipment account had a beginning balance of $4,000.

The last step is to put a ✓ back in the PR of the cash receipts journal to show the accounts receivable ledger is up to date.

◆ The cash sales were not posted when entered (thus the X to show no posting is needed). The sales and cash totals are posted at the *end* of the month.

◆ A (✓) means information was recorded daily to the accounts receivable subsidiary ledger.

◆ The Account Name column was used to describe each transaction.

Crossfooting special journals makes it easier to look for journalizing or posting errors.

We can prove the accuracy of recording transactions of the cash receipts journal by totaling the columns with debit balances and credit balances. This process, called **crossfooting,** is done before the totals are posted.

If a bookkeeper was using more than one page for the cash receipts journal, the balances on the bottom of one page would be brought forward to the next page. Let's crossfoot the cash receipts journal of Art's Wholesale (Fig. 9-8, p. 329).

Proving the cash receipts journal.

$$\begin{array}{cc} \textbf{Debit Columns} & \textbf{Credit Columns} \\ \text{Cash} + \text{Sales Discount} = \text{Accounts Receivable} + \text{Sales} + \text{Sundry} \\ \$14{,}324 + \$76 \qquad\quad = \$3{,}800 \qquad\quad + \$2{,}100 + \$8{,}500 \\ \$14{,}400 = \$14{,}400 \end{array}$$

Recording Sales Tax

The total of sales tax payable would be posted to Sales Tax Payable in the general ledger at the end of the month.

Consider the following situation. It involves Ryan Stationery, a retail stationer that must charge 5 percent sales tax to its customers. Hope Co. bought on July 1 $600 of equipment for cash from Ryan.

Here is how the transaction would be recorded in the general journal:

Accounts Affected	Category	↑	↓	Rules	T Account Update
Cash	Asset	↑		Dr.	Cash 630 |
Sales Tax Payable	Liability	↑		Cr.	Sales Tax Payable |30
Sales	Revenue	↑		Cr.	Sales |600

July	1	Cash		630 00		
		Sales Tax Payable			30 00	
		Sales			600 00	
		Cash Sale				

This is how the transaction would be recorded in a cash receipts journal.

	Date		Cash Dr.		Sales Discount Dr.		Accounts Receivable Cr.		Sales Tax Payable Cr.		Sales Cr.		Sundry		
													Acct.	Post Ref.	Amt.
	July	1	6 3 0 00						3 0 00		6 0 0 00			X	

CASH RECEIPTS JOURNAL

The total of the sales tax as a result of cash sales would be posted to Sales Tax Payable in the general ledger at the end of the month. It represents a liability of the merchant to forward the tax to the government. Remember, no cash discounts are taken on the sales tax.

Now let's prove the accounts receivable subsidiary ledger to the controlling account — accounts receivable — at the end of April for Art's Wholesale Clothing Company.

SCHEDULE OF ACCOUNTS RECEIVABLE

The **schedule of accounts receivable** is an alphabetical list of the companies that have an outstanding balance in the accounts receivable subsidiary ledger. This total should be equal to the balance of the accounts receivable controlling account in the general ledger at the end of the month.

Let's examine the schedule of accounts receivable for Art's Wholesale Clothing Company:

Schedule is listed in alphabetical order.

ART'S WHOLESALE CLOTHING COMPANY SCHEDULE OF ACCOUNTS RECEIVABLE APRIL 30, 19XX	
Mel's Dept. Store	$1 6 0 0 00
Roe Company	5 0 0 00
Total Accounts Receivable	$ 2 1 0 0 00

The balance of the controlling account, Accounts Receivable ($2,100), in the general ledger (p. 329) does indeed equal the sum of the individual customer balances in the accounts receivable ledger ($2,100) as shown in the schedule of accounts receivable. The schedule of accounts receivable can help forecast potential cash inflows as well as possible credit and collection decisions.

LEARNING UNIT 9-4 REVIEW

AT THIS POINT you should be able to

◆ Journalize, record, and post transactions using a cash receipts journal with or without sales tax. (p. 328)
◆ Prepare a schedule of accounts receivable. (p. 332)

SELF-REVIEW QUIZ 9-4

(The forms you need are on pages 288–290 of the *Study Guide and Working Papers*.)

Journalize, crossfoot, record, and post when appropriate the following transactions into the cash receipts journal of Moore Co. Use the same headings as for Art's Wholesale Clothing.

ACCOUNTS RECEIVABLE SUBSIDIARY LEDGER

NAME	BALANCE	INVOICE NO.
Irene Welch	$500	1
Janis Fross	200	2

PARTIAL GENERAL LEDGER

	Acct. No.	Balance
Cash	110	$600
Accounts Receivable	120	700
Store Equipment	130	600
Sales	410	700
Sales Discount	420	

19XX

May 1 Received check from Irene Welch for invoice no. 1 less 2 percent discount.

8 Cash sales collected, $200.

15 Received check from Janis Fross for invoice no. 2 less 2 percent discount.

19 Sold store equipment at cost, $300.

Solution to Self-Review Quiz 9-4

MOORE COMPANY
CASH RECEIPTS JOURNAL

Page 2

Date	Cash Dr.	Sales Discount Dr.	Accounts Receivable Cr.	Sales Cr.	Sundry Account Name	Post. Ref.	Amount Cr.
19XX May 1	490 00	10 00	500 00		Irene Welch	✔	
8	200 00			200 00	Cash Sales	✗	
15	196 00	4 00	200 00		Janis Fross	✔	
19	300 00				Store Equipment	130	300 00
31	1186 00	14 00	700 00	200 00			300 00
	(110)	(420)	(120)	(410)			(X)

Crossfooting: $1,200 = $1,200

PARTIAL GENERAL LEDGER

Cash   Account No. 110

Date	Explanation	Post. Ref.	Debit	Credit	Balance Debit	Balance Credit
19XX May 1	Balance	✔			600 00	
31		CRJ2	1186 00		1786 00	

Accounts Receivable   Account No. 120

Date	Explanation	Post. Ref.	Debit	Credit	Balance Debit	Balance Credit
19XX May 1	Balance	✔			700 00	
31		CRJ2		700 00	——	——

Quiz Tip: Sum of all debits equals sum of all credits

Quiz Tip: The total of the sundry column $300 is not posted. Only individual amounts are posted to the general ledger during the month.

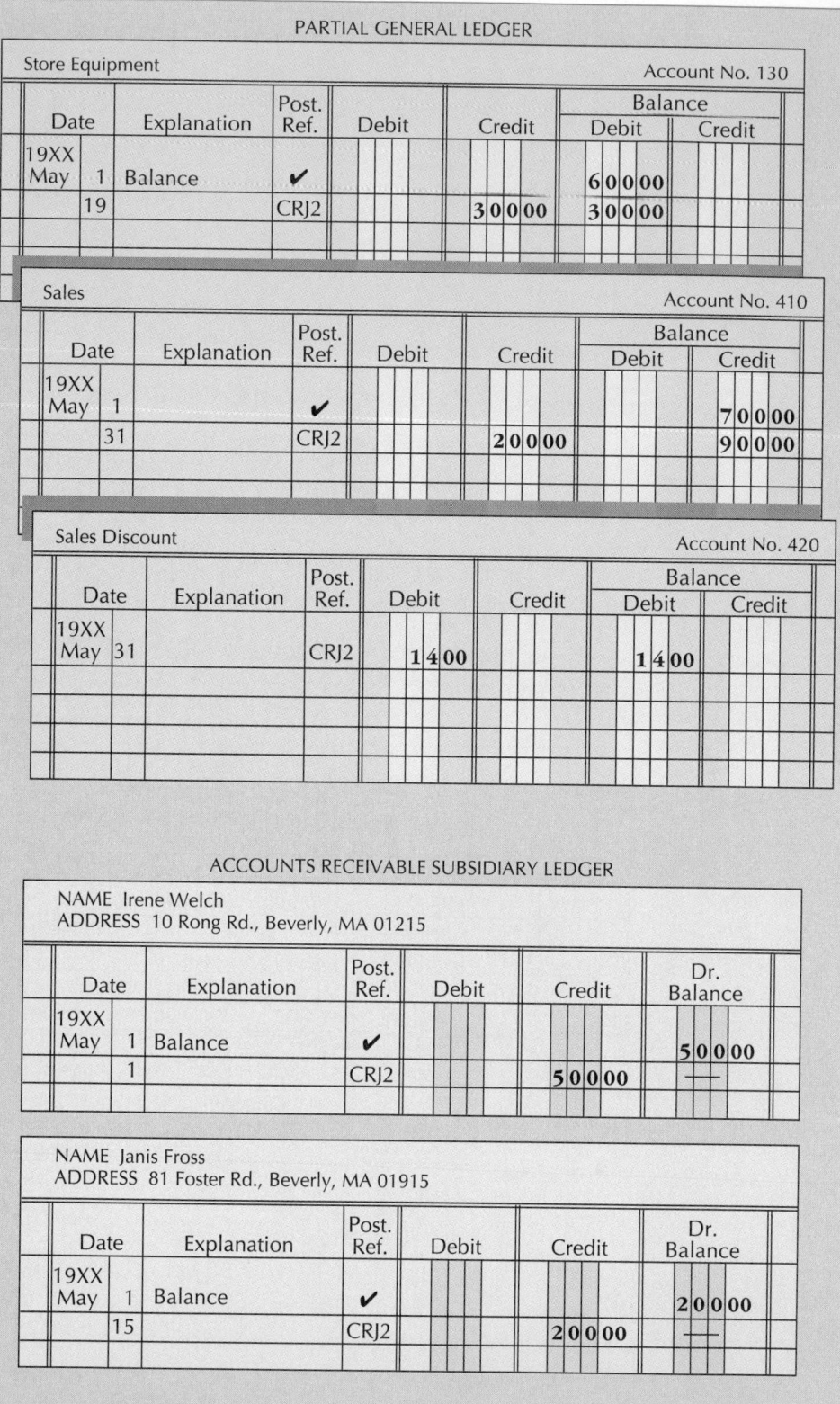

PARTIAL GENERAL LEDGER

Store Equipment — Account No. 130

Date		Explanation	Post. Ref.	Debit	Credit	Balance Debit	Balance Credit
19XX May	1	Balance	✔			6 0 0 00	
	19		CRJ2		3 0 0 00	3 0 0 00	

Sales — Account No. 410

Date		Explanation	Post. Ref.	Debit	Credit	Balance Debit	Balance Credit
19XX May	1		✔				7 0 0 00
	31		CRJ2		2 0 0 00		9 0 0 00

Sales Discount — Account No. 420

Date		Explanation	Post. Ref.	Debit	Credit	Balance Debit	Balance Credit
19XX May	31		CRJ2	1 4 00		1 4 00	

ACCOUNTS RECEIVABLE SUBSIDIARY LEDGER

NAME Irene Welch
ADDRESS 10 Rong Rd., Beverly, MA 01215

Date		Explanation	Post. Ref.	Debit	Credit	Dr. Balance
19XX May	1	Balance	✔			5 0 0 00
	1		CRJ2		5 0 0 00	—

NAME Janis Fross
ADDRESS 81 Foster Rd., Beverly, MA 01915

Date		Explanation	Post. Ref.	Debit	Credit	Dr. Balance
19XX May	1	Balance	✔			2 0 0 00
	15		CRJ2		2 0 0 00	—

COMPREHENSIVE DEMONSTRATION PROBLEM WITH SOLUTION TIPS

(The forms you need are on pages 291–294 of the *Study Guide and Working Papers.*)

a. Journalize, record, and post as needed, the following transactions to the sales, cash receipts, and general journal. All terms are 2/10, n/30.

b. Prepare a schedule of Accounts Receivable.

Solution Tips to Journalizing

19XX

CRJ	July	1	Walter Lantze invested $2,000 into the business.
SJ		1	Sold merchandise on account to Panda Co., invoice no. 1 — $300.
SJ		2	Sold merchandise on account to Buzzard Co., invoice no. 2 — $600.
CRJ		3	Cash sale — $400.
GJ		9	Issued Credit Memorandum no. 1 to Panda Co. for defective merchandise — $100.
CRJ		10	Received check from Panda Co. for invoice no. 1 less returns and discount.
CRJ		16	Cash sale — $500.
SJ		19	Sold merchandise on account to Panda Co. — $550, invoice no. 3.

Record immediately to subsidiary ledger.

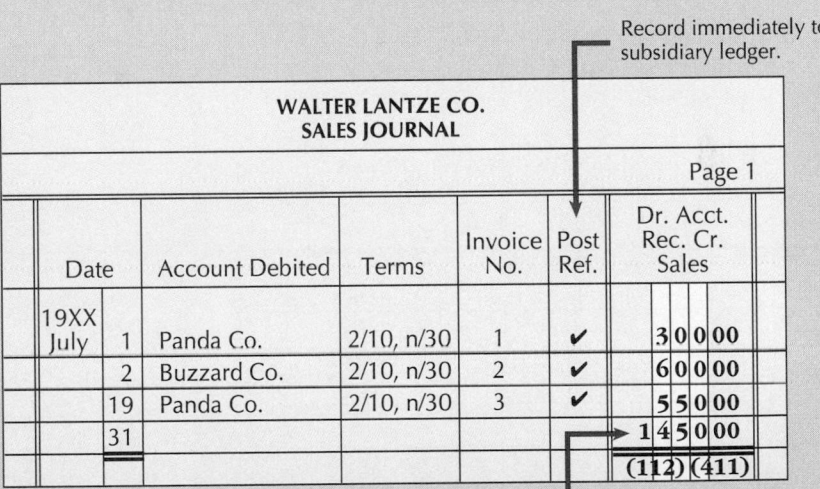

WALTER LANTZE CO.
SALES JOURNAL

Page 1

Date		Account Debited	Terms	Invoice No.	Post Ref.	Dr. Acct. Rec. Cr. Sales
19XX July	1	Panda Co.	2/10, n/30	1	✔	3 0 0 00
	2	Buzzard Co.	2/10, n/30	2	✔	6 0 0 00
	19	Panda Co.	2/10, n/30	3	✔	5 5 0 00
	31					1 4 5 0 00
						(112) (411)

Total posted at end of month to General Ledger Accounts.

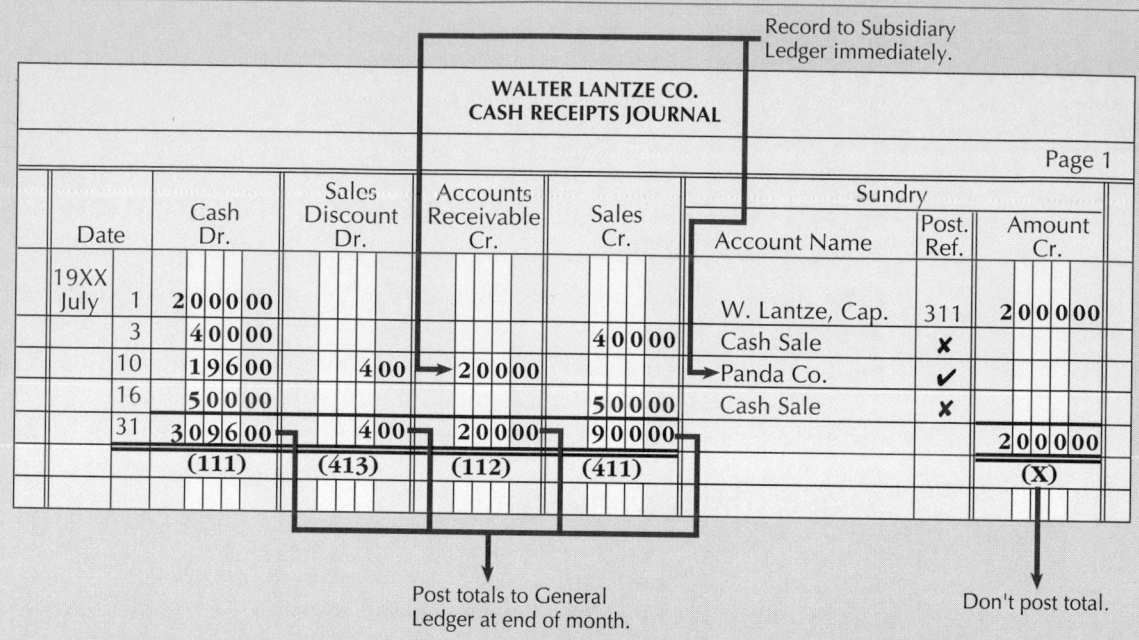

Record to Subsidiary Ledger immediately.

WALTER LANTZE CO.
CASH RECEIPTS JOURNAL

Page 1

Date	Cash Dr.	Sales Discount Dr.	Accounts Receivable Cr.	Sales Cr.	Sundry Account Name	Post. Ref.	Amount Cr.
19XX July 1	2 000 00				W. Lantze, Cap.	311	2 000 00
3	400 00			400 00	Cash Sale	✗	
10	196 00	4 00	200 00		Panda Co.	✓	
16	500 00			500 00	Cash Sale	✗	
31	3 096 00	4 00	200 00	900 00			2 000 00
	(111)	(413)	(112)	(411)			(X)

Post totals to General Ledger at end of month.

Don't post total.

GENERAL JOURNAL

Page 1

Date	Account Title and Description	PR	Dr.	Cr.
19XX July 9	Sales Returns and Allowances	412	100 00	
	Accounts Receivable, Panda Co.	112 ✓		100 00
	Issued credit memo #1			

Post immediately to General Ledger.

Record immediately to Subsidiary Ledger.

Accounts Receivable Subsidiary Ledger is usually a debit balance.

Accounts Receivable Subsidiary Ledger

Buzzard Co.

Date	PR	Debit	Credit	Dr. Balance
19XX July 2	SJ1	600 00		600 00

Panda Co.

Date	PR	Debit	Credit	Dr. Balance
19XX July 1	SJ1	300 00		300 00
9	GJ1		100 00	200 00
10	CRJ1		200 00	—
19	SJ1	550 00		550 00

General Ledger

Cash 111

July 31	CRJ1	3,096

Controlling Account

Accounts Receivable 112

July 31	SJ1	1,450	100	GJ1	July 9
			200	CRJ1	July 31
			Balance 1,150		

Walter Lantze, Capital 311

	2,000	July 1	CRJ1

Sales 411

	1,450	July 31	SJ1
	900	July 31	CRJ1
	Balance 2,350		

Sales Returns and Allowances 412

July 9	GJ1	100

Sales Discount 413

July 31	CRJ1	4

The controlling account at end of the month equals the sum of the Accounts Receivable Subsidiary Ledger.

LANTZE CO. SCHEDULE OF ACCOUNTS RECEIVABLE JULY 31, 19XX		
Buzzard Co.	$	6 0 0 00
Panda Co.		5 5 0 00
Total Accounts Receivable	$1	1 5 0 00

SUMMARY OF KEY POINTS

Learning Unit 9-1

1. Sales Returns and Allowances and Sales Discount are contra-revenue accounts.
2. Net Sales = Gross Sales − Sales Returns and Allowances − Sales Discounts.
3. Discounts are not taken on sales tax, freight, or goods returned. The discount period is shorter than the credit period.

Learning Unit 9-2

1. A general journal is still used with special journals.
2. A sales journal records sales on account.
3. The accounts receivable subsidiary ledger, organized in alphabetical order, is not in the same book as Accounts Receivable, the controlling account in the general ledger.
4. At the end of the month the total of all customers' ending balances in the accounts receivable subsidiary ledger should be equal to the ending balance in Accounts Receivable, the controlling account in the general ledger.

Learning Unit 9-3

1. The ✓ in the post-reference column of the sales journal means a customer's account in the accounts receivable ledger (or the accounts receivable subsidiary ledger) (on the debit side) has been updated (or recorded) during the month.
2. At the end of the month the total(s) of the sales journal is posted to general ledger accounts.
3. Sales Tax Payable is a liability found in the general ledger.
4. When a credit memorandum is issued, the result is that Sales Returns and Allowances is increasing, and Accounts Receivable is decreasing. When we record this into a general journal we assume that all parts of the transaction will be posted to the general ledger and recorded in the subsidiary ledger when the entry is journalized.

Learning Unit 9-4

1. The cash receipts journal records receipt of cash from any source.
2. The sundry column records the credit part of a transaction that does not occur frequently. Never post the *total* of sundry. Post items in sundry column to the general ledger when entered.
3. A ✓ in the post reference column of the cash receipts journal means that the accounts receivable ledger (or the accounts receivable subsidiary ledger) has been updated (recorded) with a credit.

4. An X in the cash receipts journal post-reference column means no posting was necessary, since the totals of these columns will be posted at the end of the month.

5. Crossfooting means proving that the total of debits and the total of credits are equal in the special journal, thus verifying the accuracy of recording.

6. A schedule of accounts receivable is a listing of the ending balances of customers in the accounts receivable subsidiary ledger. This total should be the same balance as found in the controlling account, Accounts Receivable, in the general ledger.

KEY TERMS

Accounts receivable subsidiary ledger A book or file that contains in alphabetical order the individual records of amounts owed by various credit customers.

Cash receipts journal A special journal that records all transactions involving the receipt of cash from any source.

Controlling account—Accounts Receivable The Accounts Receivable account in the general ledger, after postings are complete, shows a firm the total amount of money owed to it. This figure is broken down in the accounts receivable ledger, where it indicates specifically who owes the money.

Credit memorandum *Sales Returns* A piece of paper sent by the seller to a customer who has returned merchandise previously purchased on credit. The credit memorandum indicates to the customer that the seller is reducing the amount owed by the customer.

Credit period Length of time allowed for payment of goods sold on account.

Crossfooting The process of proving that the total debit columns of a special journal are equal to the total credit columns of a special journal.

Discount period A period shorter than the credit period when a discount is available to encourage early payment of bills.

Gross sales The revenue earned from sale of merchandise to customers.

Merchandise Goods brought into a store for resale to customers.

Net sales Gross sales less sales returns and allowances less sales discounts.

Retailers Merchants who buy goods from wholesalers for resale to customers.

Sales discount account A contra-revenue account that records cash discounts granted to customers for payments made within a specific period of time.

Sales invoice A bill sent to customer(s) reflecting a sale on credit.

Sales journal A special journal used to record only sales made on account.

Sales Returns and Allowances (SRA) account A contra-revenue account that records price adjustments and allowances granted on merchandise that is defective and has been returned.

Sales Tax Payable account An account in the general ledger that accumulates the amount of sales tax owed. It has a credit balance.

Schedule of accounts receivable A list of the customers, in alphabetical order, that have an outstanding balance in the accounts receivable ledger (or the accounts receivable subsidiary ledger). This total should be equal to the balance of the Accounts Receivable controlling account in the general ledger at the end of the month.

Special journal A journal used to record similar groups of transactions. Example: The sales journal records all sales on account.

Subsidiary ledger A ledger that contains accounts of a single type. Example: The accounts receivable subsidiary ledger records all credit customers.

Sundry (Miscellaneous) accounts column(s) in a special journal, which records part of transactions that do not occur too often.

Wholesalers Merchants who buy goods from suppliers and manufacturers for sale to retailers.

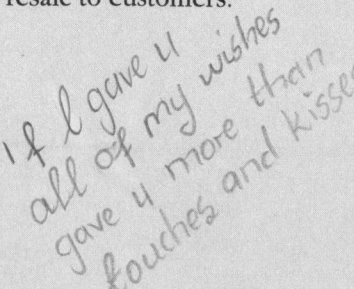
If I gave u all of my wishes gave u more than touches and kisses

QUESTIONS, MINI EXERCISES, EXERCISES, AND PROBLEMS

Discussion Questions

1. Explain the purpose of a contra-revenue account. ???
2. What is the normal balance of sales discount? DR
3. Give two examples of contra-revenue accounts. S D

4. What is the difference between a discount period and a credit period?

5. Explain the terms A. 2/10, n/30; B. n/10, EOM.

6. If special journals are used, what purpose will a general journal serve?

7. Compare and contrast the controlling account Accounts Receivable to the accounts receivable subsidiary ledger.

8. Why is the accounts receivable subsidiary ledger organized in alphabetical order?

9. When is a sales journal used?

10. What is an invoice? What purpose does it serve?

11. Why is sales tax a liability to the business?

12. Sales discounts are taken on sales tax. Agree or disagree and tell why.

13. When a seller issues a credit memorandum (assume no sales tax), what accounts will be affected?

14. Explain the function of a cash receipts journal.

15. When is the sundry column of the cash receipts journal posted?

16. Explain the purpose of a schedule of accounts receivable.

Mini Exercises

(The forms you need are on pages 296–297 of the *Study Guide and Working Papers*.)

Overview

1. Complete the table below for Sales, Sales Returns and Allowances, and Sales Discounts.

Accounts Affected	Category	↓ ↑	Temporary or Permanent

Calculating Net Sales

2. Given the following, calculate net sales:

Gross sales	$20
Sales Returns and Allowances	2
Sales Discounts	1

Sales Journal and General Journal

3. Match the following to the three journal entries (more than one number can be used)

> 1. Journalized into Sales Journal.
> 2. Record immediately to Subsidiary Ledger.
> 3. Post totals from Sales Journal at end of month to General Ledger.
> 4. Journalized in General Journal.
> 5. Record and post immediately to Subsidiary and General Ledger.

a. ____ Sold merchandise on account to Ree Co., invoice no. 1 — $50.

b. ____ Sold merchandise on account to Flynn Co., invoice no. 2 — $100.

c. ____ Issued credit memorandum no. 1 to Flynn Co. for defective merchandisc — $25.

(cont. on p. 341)

BLUEPRINT OF SALES AND CASH RECEIPTS JOURNALS

SUMMARY OF HOW TO POST AND RECORD
Single-Column Sales Journal

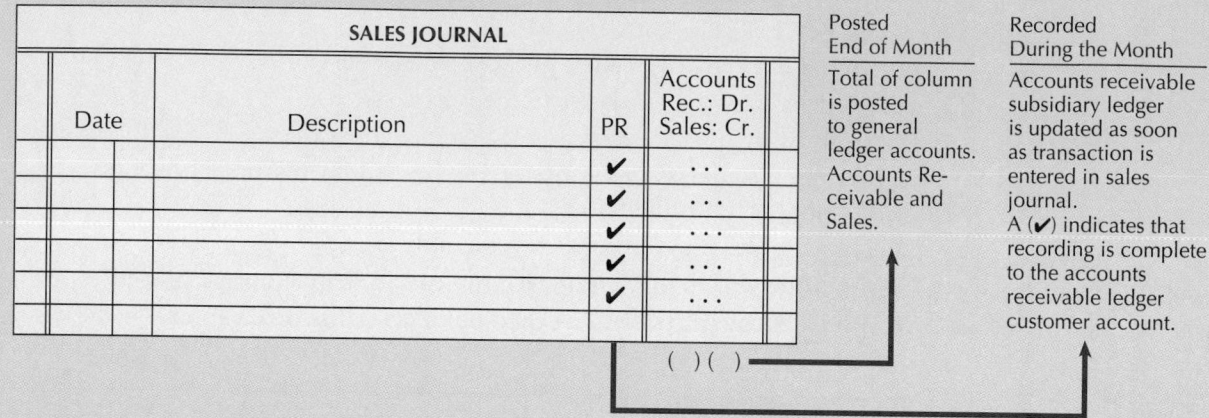

SALES JOURNAL

Date	Description	PR	Accounts Rec.: Dr. Sales: Cr.
		✔	...
		✔	...
		✔	...
		✔	...
		✔	...

( )( )

Posted End of Month

Total of column is posted to general ledger accounts. Accounts Receivable and Sales.

Recorded During the Month

Accounts receivable subsidiary ledger is updated as soon as transaction is entered in sales journal.
A (✔) indicates that recording is complete to the accounts receivable ledger customer account.

Multicolumn Sales Journal

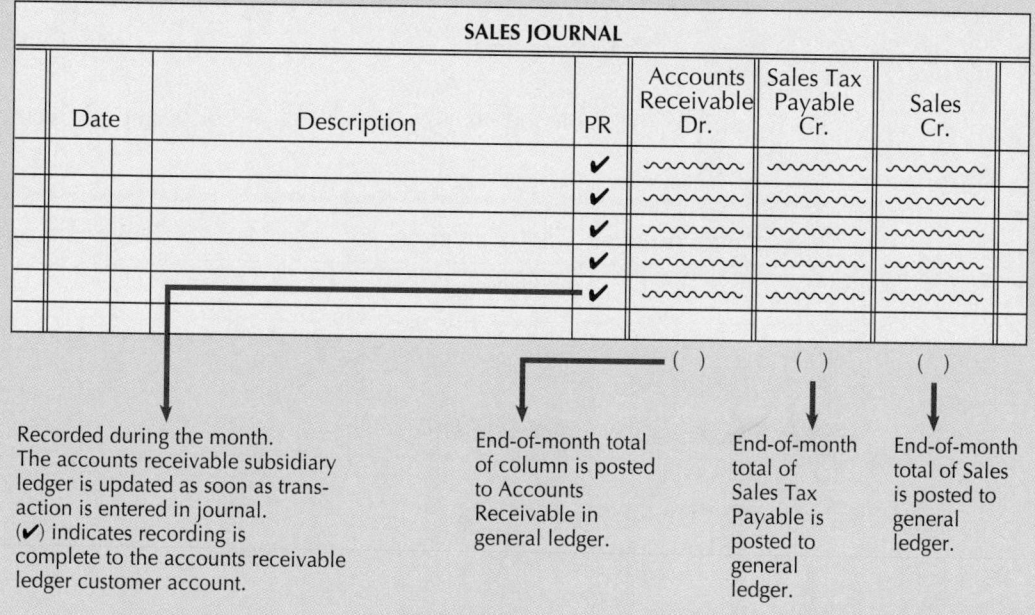

SALES JOURNAL

Date	Description	PR	Accounts Receivable Dr.	Sales Tax Payable Cr.	Sales Cr.	
		✔	~~~~	~~~~	~~~~	
		✔	~~~~	~~~~	~~~~	
		✔	~~~~	~~~~	~~~~	
		✔	~~~~	~~~~	~~~~	
		✔	~~~~	~~~~	~~~~	

( ) ( ) ( )

Recorded during the month. The accounts receivable subsidiary ledger is updated as soon as transaction is entered in journal. (✔) indicates recording is complete to the accounts receivable ledger customer account.

End-of-month total of column is posted to Accounts Receivable in general ledger.

End-of-month total of Sales Tax Payable is posted to general ledger.

End-of-month total of Sales is posted to general ledger.

Issuing a Credit Memo without Sales Tax Recorded in a General Journal

GENERAL JOURNAL

Date	Account Title and Description	PR	Dr.	Cr.
	Sales Returns and Allowances	~~	~~~~	
	Accounts Receivable, XXX	✔		~~~~
	Issued credit memo			

POSTED AND RECORDED WHEN TRANSACTION ENTERED
Two postings and one recording:

1. Post to SRA in general ledger
2. Post to Accounts Receivable in general ledger
3. Record to XXX in accounts receivable subsidiary ledger

(continued)

Issuing a Credit Memo with Sales Tax Recorded in a General Journal

GENERAL JOURNAL					POSTED AND RECORDED WHEN TRANSACTION ENTERED

Date	Account Title and Description	PR	Dr.	Cr.
	Sales Returns and Allowances	∿∿	∿∿∿∿	
	Sales Tax Payable	∿∿	∿∿∿∿	
	Accounts Receivable, XXX	∿✔		∿∿∿
	Issued credit memo			

POSTED AND RECORDED WHEN TRANSACTION ENTERED
Three postings and one recording:

1. Post to SRA in general ledger
2. Post to Sales Tax Payable in general ledger
3. Post to Accounts Receivable in general ledger
4. Record to XXX in accounts receivable subsidiary ledger

The Cash Receipts Journal

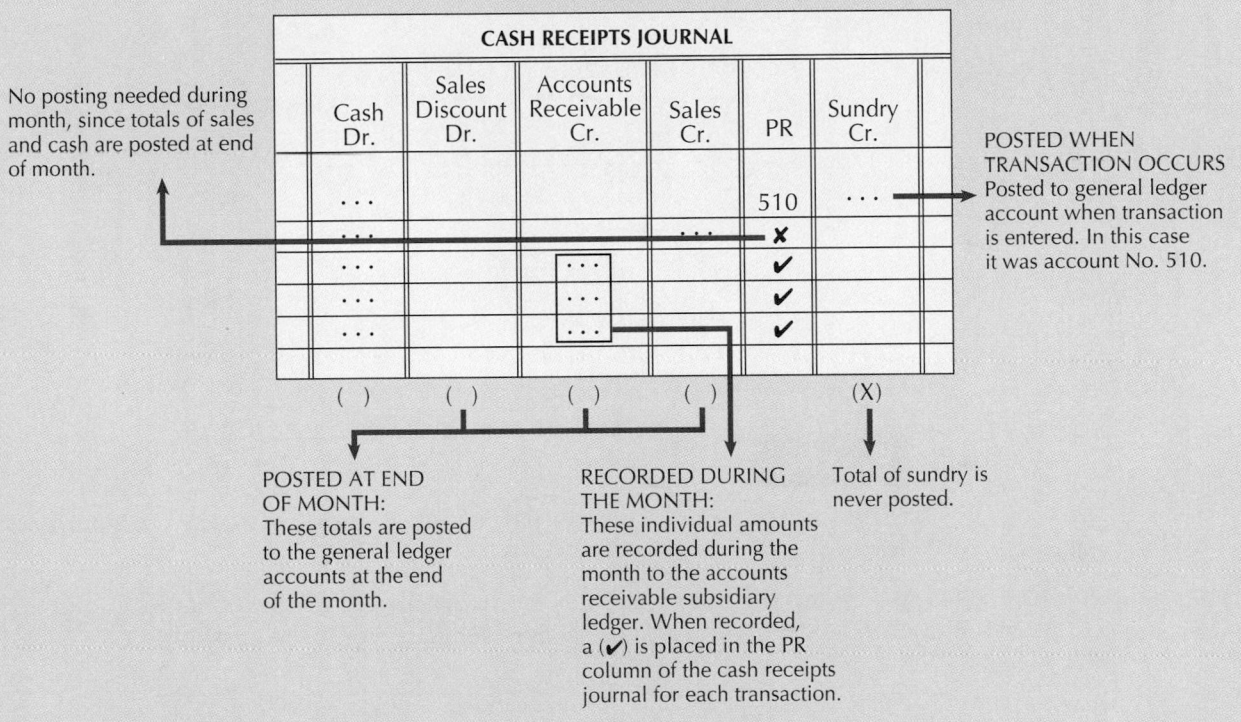

No posting needed during month, since totals of sales and cash are posted at end of month.

CASH RECEIPTS JOURNAL					
Cash Dr.	Sales Discount Dr.	Accounts Receivable Cr.	Sales Cr.	PR	Sundry Cr.
. . .				510	. . .
. . .			. . .	✗	
. . .		. . .		✔	
. . .		. . .		✔	
. . .		. . .		✔	
( )	( )	( )	( )		(X)

POSTED WHEN TRANSACTION OCCURS
Posted to general ledger account when transaction is entered. In this case it was account No. 510.

POSTED AT END OF MONTH:
These totals are posted to the general ledger accounts at the end of the month.

RECORDED DURING THE MONTH:
These individual amounts are recorded during the month to the accounts receivable subsidiary ledger. When recorded, a (✔) is placed in the PR column of the cash receipts journal for each transaction.

Total of sundry is never posted.

Note: If a Sales Tax Payable column were added, total of column would be posted at end of month.

Credit Memorandum

4. Draw a transactional analysis box for the following credit memorandum: Issued credit memorandum to Bob Corp. for defective merchandise — $50.

Sales and Cash Receipts Journal

5. Match the following to the four journal entries (a number can be used more than once).

1. Journalized into Sales Journal.
2. Journalized into Cash Receipts Journal.
3. Record immediately to Subsidiary Ledger.
4. Totals of Special Journals will be posted at end of month (except Sundry column).
5. Post to General Ledger immediately.
6. Journalize into General Journal.

a. ____ Sold merchandise on account to Ally Co., invoice no. 10 — $40.
b. ____ Received check from Moore Co. — $100 less 2 percent discount.
c. ____ Cash Sales — $100.
d. ____ Issued credit memorandum no. 2 to Ally Co. for defective merchandise — $20.

6. From the following, prepare a schedule of Accounts Receivable for Blue Co., for May 31, 19XX.

Accounts Receivable Subsidiary Ledger

Bon Co.

5/6 SJ1	100		

Peke Co.

5/20 SJ1	30	5/27 CRJ1	10

Green Co.

5/9 SJ1	10		

General Ledger

Accounts Receivable

5/31 SJ1	140	5/31 CRJ1	10

Exercises

(The forms you need are on pages 298–300 of the *Study Guide and Working Papers*.)

Recording to accounts receivable ledger and posting to general ledger.

9-1. From the following sales journal, record to the accounts receivable subsidiary ledger and post to the general ledger accounts as appropriate.

SALES JOURNAL					
					P. 1
Date		Account Debited	Invoice No.	PR	Dr. Accts. Receivable Cr. Sales
19XX April	18	Kevin Stone Co.	1		4 0 0 00
	19	Bill Valley Co.	2		6 0 0 00

ACCOUNTS RECEIVABLE SUBSIDIARY LEDGER

Kevin Stone Co.

Bill Valley Co.

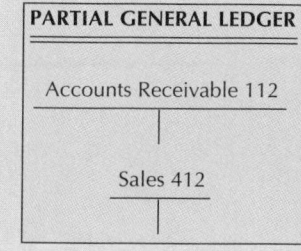

PARTIAL GENERAL LEDGER

Accounts Receivable 112

Sales 412

9-2. Journalize, record, and post when appropriate the following transactions into the sales journal (same heading as Exercise 9-1) and general journal (p. 1) (all sales carry terms of 2/10, n/30):

Journalizing, recording, and posting that includes credit memorandum.

19XX
May   16 Sold merchandise on account to Ronald Co., invoice no. 1, $1,000.
       18 Sold merchandise on account to Bass Co., invoice no. 2, $1,700.
       20 Issued credit memorandum no. 1 to Bass Co. for defective merchandise, $700.

Use the following account numbers: Accounts Receivable, 112; Sales, 411; Sales Returns and Allowances, 412.

Journalizing transaction into cash receipts journal.

9-3. From Exercise 9-2, journalize in the cash receipts journal the receipt of check from Ronald Co. for payment of invoice no. 1 on May 24. Use the same headings as for Art's Wholesale Clothing (on p. 329).

Journalizing, recording, and posting sales and cash receipts journal; schedule of accounts receivable.

9-4. From the following transactions for Edna Co., when appropriate, journalize, record, post, and prepare a schedule of accounts receivable. Use the same journal headings (all p. 1) and chart of accounts (use Edna Cares, Capital) that Art's Wholesale Clothing used in the text. You will have to set up your own accounts receivable subsidiary ledger and partial general ledger as needed. All sales terms are 2/10, n/30.

19XX
June   1 Edna Cares invested $3,000 in the business.
        1 Sold merchandise on account to Boston Co., invoice no. 1, $700.
        2 Sold merchandise on account to Gary Co., invoice no. 2, $900.
        3 Cash sale, $200.
        8 Issued credit memorandum no. 1 to Boston for defective merchandise, $200.
       10 Received check from Boston for invoice no. 1 less returns and discount.
       15 Cash sale, $400.
       18 Sold merchandise on account to Boston Co., invoice no. 3, $600.

9-5. From the following facts calculate what Ann Frost must pay Blue Co. for the purchase of a dining room set. Sale terms are 2/10, n/30.

Sales tax and cash discount calculation.

    a. Sales ticket price before tax, $4,000 — dated April 5.
    b. Sales tax, 7 percent.
    c. Returned one defective chair for credit of $400 on April 8.
    d. Paid bill on April 13.

Group A Problems

(The forms you need are on pages 301–320 of the *Study Guide and Working Papers*.)

9A-1. Jill Blue has opened Max Co., a wholesale grocery and pizza company. The following transactions occurred in June:

Multicolumn journal: Journalizing and posting to general ledger, recording to accounts receivable subsidiary ledger, and preparing a schedule of accounts receivable.

19XX
June   ╳ 1 Sold grocery merchandise to Joe Kase Co. on account, $400, invoice no. 1.
         4 Sold pizza merchandise to Sue Moore Co. on account, $600, invoice no. 2.
         8 Sold grocery merchandise to Long Co. on account, $700, invoice no. 3.
        10 Issued credit memorandum no. 1 to Joe Kase for $150 of grocery merchandise returned due to spoilage.
        15 Sold pizza merchandise to Sue Moore Co. on account, $160, invoice no. 4.

Check Figure:
Schedule of Accounts Receivable
$3,210

19 Sold grocery merchandise to Long Co. on account, $300, invoice no. 5.

25 Sold pizza merchandise to Joe Kase Co. on account, $1,200, invoice no. 6.

Required:

1. Journalize the transactions in the appropriate journals.

2. Record to the accounts receivable subsidiary ledger and post to general ledger as appropriate.

3. Prepare a schedule of accounts receivable.

9A-2. The following transactions of Ted's Auto Supply occurred in November (your working papers have balances as of Nov. 1 for certain general ledger and accounts receivable ledger accounts):

19XX

Nov. 1 Sold auto parts merchandise to R. Volan on account, $1,000, invoice no. 60, plus 5 percent sales tax.

5 Sold auto parts merchandise to J. Seth on account, $800, invoice no. 61, plus 5 percent sales tax.

8 Sold auto parts merchandise to Lance Corner on account, $9,000, invoice no. 62, plus 5 percent sales tax.

10 Issued credit memorandum no. 12 to R. Volan for $500 for defective auto parts merchandise returned from Nov. 1 transaction. (Be careful to record the reduction in sales tax payable as well.)

12 Sold auto parts merchandise to J. Seth on account, $600, invoice no. 63, plus 5 percent sales tax.

Required:

1. Journalize the transactions in the appropriate journals.

2. Record to the accounts receivable subsidiary ledger and post to general ledger as appropriate.

3. Prepare a schedule of accounts receivable.

9A-3. Mark Peaker owns Peaker's Sneaker Shop. (In your working papers balances as of May 1 are provided for the accounts receivable and general ledger accounts.) The following transactions occurred in May:

19XX

May 1 Mark Peaker invested an additional $12,000 in the sneaker store.

3 Sold $700 of merchandise on account to B. Dale, sales ticket no. 60, terms 1/10, n/30.

4 Sold $500 of merchandise on account to Ron Lester, sales ticket no. 61, terms 1/10, n/30.

9 Sold $200 of merchandise on account to Jim Zon, sales ticket no. 62, terms 1/10, n/30.

10 Received cash from B. Dale in payment of May 3 transaction, sales ticket no. 60, less discount.

20 Sold $3,000 of merchandise on account to Pam Pry, sales ticket no. 63, terms 1/10, n/30.

22 Received cash payment from Ron Lester in payment of May 4 transaction, sales ticket no. 61.

23 Collected cash sales, $3,000.

24 Issued credit memorandum no. 1 to Pam Pry for $2,000 of merchandise returned from May 20 sales on account.

26 Received cash from Pam Pry in payment of May 20, sales ticket no. 63. (Don't forget about the credit memo and discount.)

28 Collected cash sales, $7,000.

30 Sold sneaker rack equipment for $300 cash. (Beware.)

30 Sold merchandise priced at $4,000, on account to Ron Lester, sales ticket no. 64, terms 1/10, n/30. Sales.

31 Issued credit memorandum no. 2 to Ron Lester for $700 of merchandise returned from May 30 transaction, sales ticket no. 64. GJ

Required:

1. Journalize the transactions.
2. Record to the accounts receivable subsidiary ledger and post to general ledger as needed.
3. Prepare a schedule of accounts receivable.

9A-4. Bill Murray opened Bill's Cosmetic Market on April 1. There is a 6 percent sales tax on all cosmetic sales. Bill offers no sales discounts. The following transactions occurred in April:

19XX

April

1 Bill Murray invested $8,000 in the Cosmetic Market from his personal savings account.

5 From the cash register tapes, lipstick cash sales were $5,000 plus sales tax. X

5 From the cash register tapes, eye shadow cash sales were $2,000 plus sales tax. ✓

8 Sold lipstick on account to Alice Koy Co., $300, sales ticket no. 1, plus sales tax.

9 Sold eye shadow on account to Marika Sanchez Co., $1,000, sales ticket no. 2, plus sales tax.

15 Issued credit memorandum no. 1 to Alice Koy Co. for $150 for lipstick returned. (Be sure to reduce sales tax payable for Bill.)

19 Marika Sanchez Co. paid half the amount owed from sales ticket no. 2, dated April 9.

21 Sold lipstick on account to Jeff Tong Co., $300, sales ticket no. 3, plus sales tax.

24 Sold eye shadow on account to Rusty Neal Co., $800, sales ticket no. 4, plus sales tax.

25 Issued credit memorandum no. 2 to Jeff Tong Co. for $200 for lipstick returned from sales ticket no. 3, dated April 21.

29 Cash sales taken from the cash register tape showed:
1. Lipstick — $1,000 + $60 sales tax collected.
2. Eye shadow — $3,000 + $180 sales tax collected.

29 Sold lipstick on account to Marika Sanchez Co., $400, sales ticket no. 5, plus sales tax.

30 Received payment from Marika Sanchez Co. of sales ticket no. 5, dated April 29.

Required:

1. Journalize the above in the sales journal, cash receipts journal, or general journal.
2. Record to the accounts receivable subsidiary ledger and post to general ledger when appropriate.
3. Prepare a schedule of accounts receivable for the end of April.

Comprehensive problem: Using sales tax in recording transactions into sales, cash receipts, and general journals. Recording to accounts receivable subsidiary ledger and posting to general ledger. Crossfooting and preparing a schedule of accounts receivable.

Check Figure:

Schedule of Accounts Receivable
$1,643

Group B Problems

(The forms you need are on pages 301 – 320 of the *Study Guide and Working Papers.*)

9B-1. The following transactions occurred for Max Co. for the month of June:

	19XX	
Multicolumn journal: Journalizing and posting to general ledger, recording to accounts receivable subsidiary ledger, and preparing a schedule of accounts receivable.	June	1 Sold grocery merchandise to Joe Kase Co. on account, $800, invoice no. 1.
		4 Sold pizza merchandise to Sue Moore Co. on account, $550, invoice no. 2.
		8 Sold grocery merchandise to Long Co. on account, $900, invoice no. 3.
Check Figure:		10 Issued credit memorandum no. 1 to Joe Kase for $160 of grocery merchandise returned due to spoilage.
Schedule of Accounts Receivable $3,040		15 Sold pizza merchandise to Sue Moore Co. on account, $700, invoice no. 4.
		19 Sold grocery merchandise to Long Co. on account, $250, invoice no. 5.

Required:

1. Journalize the transactions in the appropriate journals.
2. Record to the accounts receivable subsidiary ledger and post to general ledger as appropriate.
3. Prepare a schedule of accounts receivable.

9B-2. In November the following transactions occurred for Ted's Auto Supply (your working papers have balances as of Nov. 1 for certain general ledger and accounts receivable ledger accounts):

19XX

	Nov.	
Multicolumn sales journal: Use of sales tax; journalizing and posting to general ledger and recording to accounts receivable subsidiary ledger; and preparing a schedule of accounts receivable.		1 Sold merchandise to R. Volan on account, $4,000, invoice no. 70, plus 5 percent sales tax.
		5 Sold merchandise to J. Seth on account, $1,600, invoice no. 71, plus 5 percent sales tax.
		8 Sold merchandise to Lance Corner on account, $15,000, invoice no. 72, plus 5 percent sales tax.
Check Figure:		10 Issued credit memorandum no. 14 to R. Volan for $2,000 for defective merchandise returned from Nov. 1 transaction. (Be careful to record the reduction in sales tax payable as well.)
Schedule of Accounts Receivable $22,600		12 Sold merchandise to J. Seth on account, $1,400, invoice no. 73, plus 5 percent sales tax.

Required:

1. Journalize the transactions in the appropriate journals.
2. Record to the accounts receivable subsidiary ledger and post to general ledger as appropriate.
3. Prepare a schedule of accounts receivable.

9B-3. (In your working papers all the beginning balances needed are provided for the accounts receivable subsidiary and general ledger.) The following transactions occurred for Peaker's Sneaker Shop:

19XX

	May	
Check Figure:		1 Mark Peaker invested an additional $14,000 in the sneaker store.
Schedule of Accounts Receivable $8,000		3 Sold $2,000 of merchandise on account to B. Dale, sales ticket no. 60, terms 1/10, n/30.
		4 Sold $900 of merchandise on account to Ron Lester, sales ticket no. 61, terms 1/10, n/30.
		9 Sold $600 of merchandise on account to Jim Zon, sales ticket no. 62, terms 1/10, n/30.
Comprehensive Problem: Recording transactions into sales, cash receipts, and general journals. Recording to accounts receivable subsidiary ledger and posting to general ledger. Preparing a schedule of accounts receivable.		10 Received cash from B. Dale in payment of May 3 transaction, sales ticket no. 60, less discount.
		20 Sold $4,000 of merchandise on account to Pam Pry, sales ticket no. 63, terms 1/10, n/30.
		22 Received cash payment from Ron Lester in payment of May 4 transaction, sales ticket no. 61.
		23 Collected cash sales, $6,000.

24 Issued credit memorandum no. 1 to Pam Pry for $500 of merchandise returned from May 20 sales on account.

26 Received cash from Pam Pry in payment of May 20 sales ticket no. 63. (Don't forget about the credit memo and discount.)

28 Collected cash sales, $12,000.

30 Sold sneaker rack equipment for $200 cash. (Beware.)

30 Sold $6,000 of merchandise on account to Ron Lester, sales ticket no. 64, terms 1/10, n/30.

31 Issued credit memorandum no. 2 to Ron Lester for $800 of merchandise returned from May 30 transaction, sales ticket no. 64.

Required:

1. Journalize the transactions in the appropriate journals.
2. Record and post as appropriate.
3. Prepare a schedule of accounts receivable.

9B-4. Bill's Cosmetic Market began operating in April. There is a 6 percent sales tax on all cosmetic sales. Bill offers no discounts. The following transactions occurred in April:

19XX
April

1 Bill Murray invested $10,000 in the Cosmetic Market from his personal account.

5 From the cash register tapes, lipstick cash sales were $5,000 plus sales tax.

5 From the cash register tapes, eye shadow cash sales were $3,000 plus sales tax.

8 Sold lipstick on account to Alice Koy Co., $400, sales ticket no. 1, plus sales tax.

9 Sold eye shadow on account to Marika Sanchez Co., $900, sales ticket no. 2, plus sales tax.

15 Issued credit memorandum no. 1 to Alice Koy Co. for lipstick returned, $200. (Be sure to reduce sales tax payable for Bill.)

19 Marika Sanchez Co. paid half the amount owed from sales ticket no. 2, dated April 9.

21 Sold lipstick on account to Jeff Tong Co., $600 sales ticket no. 3, plus sales tax.

24 Sold eye shadow on account to Rusty Neal Co., $1,000, sales ticket no. 4, plus sales tax.

25 Issued credit memorandum no. 2 to Jeff Tong Co. for $300, for lipstick returned from sales ticket no. 3, dated April 21.

29 Cash sales taken from the cash register tape showed:
 1. Lipstick — $4,000 + $240 sales tax collected.
 2. Eye shadow — $2,000 + $120 sales tax collected.

29 Sold lipstick on account to Marika Sanchez Co., $700, sales ticket no. 5 plus sales tax.

30 Received payment from Marika Sanchez Co. of sales ticket no. 5, dated April 29.

Comprehensive Problem: Using sales tax in recording transactions into sales, cash receipts, and general journals. Recording to accounts receivable subsidiary ledger and posting to general ledger, and preparing a schedule of accounts receivable.

Check Figure:

Schedule of Accounts Receivable $2,067

Required:

1. Journalize, record, and post as appropriate.
2. Prepare a schedule of accounts receivable for the end of April.

REAL WORLD APPLICATIONS

9R-1.
Ronald Howard has been hired by Green Company to help reconstruct the sales journal, general journal, and cash receipts journal, which were recently

destroyed in a fire. The owner of Green has supplied him with the following data. Please ignore dates, invoice numbers, etc., and enter the entries into the reconstructed sales journal, general journal, and cash receipts journal. What written recommendation should Ron make so reconstruction will not be needed in the future?

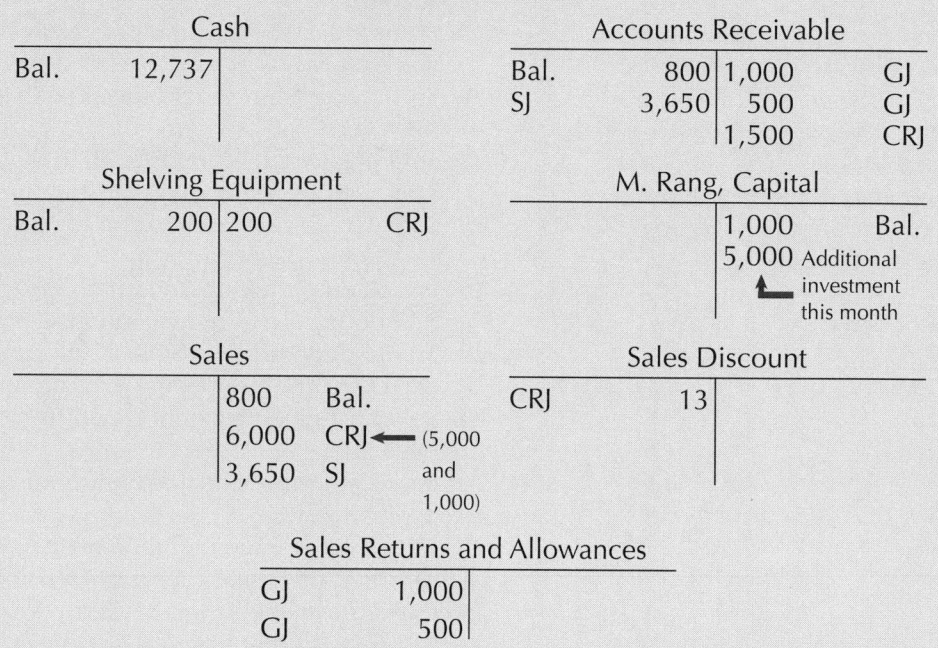

Accounts Receivable Subsidiary Ledger

P. Bond			
Bal.	100	150	CRJ
SJ	150	Entitled to 2% discount	

M. Raff			
Bal.	200		
SJ	100		

J. Smooth			
Bal.	300	1,000	GJ
SJ	2,000	1,000	CRJ
SJ	1,000	500	GJ
		Entitled to 1% discount	

R. Venner			
Bal.	200	400	CRJ
SJ	400		

Partial General Ledger

Cash		
Bal.	12,737	

Accounts Receivable			
Bal.	800	1,000	GJ
SJ	3,650	500	GJ
		1,500	CRJ

Shelving Equipment			
Bal.	200	200	CRJ

M. Rang, Capital		
	1,000	Bal.
	5,000	Additional investment this month

Sales		
	800	Bal.
	6,000	CRJ ← (5,000 and 1,000)
	3,650	SJ

Sales Discount		
CRJ	13	

Sales Returns and Allowances		
GJ	1,000	
GJ	500	

9R-2.

The bookkeeper of Floore Company records credit sales in a sales journal and returns in a general journal. The bookkeeper did the following:

1. Recorded an $18 credit sale as $180 in the sales journal.
2. Correctly recorded a $40 sale in the sales journal but posted it to B. Blue's account as $400 in the accounts receivable ledger.
3. Made an additional error in determining the balance of J. B. Window Co. in the accounts receivable ledger.
4. Posted a sales return that was recorded in the general journal to the Sales Returns and Allowance account and the Accounts Receivable account but forgot to record it to the B. Katz Co.
5. Added the total of the sales column incorrectly.

6. Posted a sales return to the Accounts Receivable account but not to the Sales Returns and Allowances account. Accounts Receivable ledger was recorded correctly.

Could you inform the bookkeeper in writing as to when each error will be discovered?

YOU make the call

Critical Thinking/Ethical Case

9R-3.
Amy Jak is the National Sales Manager of Rowe Co. In order to get sales up to the projection for the old year, Amy asked the accountant to put the first two weeks of sales in January back into December. Amy told the accountant that this secret would only be between them. Should Amy move the new sales into the old sales year? You make the call. Write down your specific recommendations to Amy.

ACCOUNTING RECALL
A CUMULATIVE APPROACH

THIS EXAM REVIEWS CHAPTERS 1 THROUGH 9

Your *Study Guide and Working Papers* has forms (pp. 325 and 331) to complete this exam, as well as worked-out solutions. The page references next to each question identify what page to turn back to if you answer the question incorrectly.

PART 1 Vocabulary Review

Match the terms to the appropriate definition or phrase.

Page Ref.

(318)	1. Accounts receivable subsidiary ledger	A. The results of a cash discount
(327)	2. Sundry	B. Records sales on account
(251)	3. Medicare payable	C. A contra-revenue account
(161)	4. Closing	D. Clears temporary accounts
(211)	5. Deposit in transit	E. In alphabetical order
(323)	6. Sales returns and allowances	F. Miscellaneous
(319)	7. Controlling account	G. Records receipt of cash
(320)	8. Sales journal	H. A liability
(329)	9. Cash receipts journal	I. Deposits not received by the bank
(314)	10. Sales discount	J. Accounts receivable

(216)   11. Petty cash is a liability.

(319)   12. The controlling account balance at end of month will equal the sum of the subsidiary ledger.

(323)   13. Issuing a credit memo results in sales returns and allowances decreasing.

(248)   14. There is no tax base for Medicare.

(319)   15. A (✓) means the controlling account has been updated.

CONTINUING PROBLEM

Freedman will use two specialized journals for recording business transactions in the month of January. To assist you in recording the transactions, at the end of this problem is the Schedule of Accounts Receivable as of December 31 and an updated chart of accounts with the current balance listed for each account.

Assignment:

(See p. 326 in your *Study Guide and Working Papers.*)

1. Journalize the transactions in the appropriate journals (cash receipts, sales journal, or general journal).
2. Record in the accounts receivable subsidiary ledger and post to the general ledger as appropriate. A partial general ledger is included in the *Working Papers.*
3. Prepare a schedule of accounts receivable as of January 31, 19X1.

The January transactions are as follows.

Jan   1   Sold $700 worth of merchandise to Taylor Golf on credit, sales invoice #5000; terms are 2/10/n30
      10   Sold $3,000 worth of merchandise on account to Anthony Pitale, sales invoice #5001; terms are 2/10/n30
      11   Received $3,000 from Accu Pac, Inc. toward payment of their balance; no discount allowed
      12   Collected $2,000 cash sales.
      19   Sold $4,000 worth of merchandise on account to Vita Needle, sales invoice #5002, terms are 4/10/n30.
      20   Collected balance in full from invoice #5001, Anthony Pitale.
      29   Issued credit memorandum to Taylor Golf for $400 worth of merchandise returned, invoice #5000.
      29   Collect full payment from Vita Needle, invoice #5002.

Schedule of Accounts Receivable
Eldorado Computer Center
December 31, 19XX

Taylor Golf	$ 2,900.00
Vita Needle	6,800.00
Accu Pac	$ 3,900.00
Total Amount Due	**$13,600.00**

Account #	Account Name	Debit Balance	Credit Balance
1000	Cash	$ 3,336.65	
1010	Petty Cash	100	
1020	Accounts Receivable	13,600	
1025	Prepaid Rent	1,600	
1030	Supplies	132	
1040	Merchandise Inventory	0	
1080	Computer Shop Equipment	3,800	
1081	Accumulated Depr. CS Equip.		$ 99
1090	Office Equipment	1,050	
1091	Accumulated Depr. Office Equip.		20
2000	Accounts Payable		2,050
2010	Wages Payable		0
2020	FICA-SS Payable		0
2030	FICA-Medicare Payable		0
2040	FIT Payable		0
2050	SIT Payable		0
2060	FUTA Payable		0
2070	SUTA Payable		0
3000	Freedman Capital		7,406
3010	Freedman Withdrawals	2,015	
3020	Income Summary		0
4000	Service Revenue		18,500
4010	Sales		0
4020	Sales Returns and Allowances	0	
4030	Sales Discounts	0	
5010	Advertising Expense	0	
5020	Rent Expense	0	
5030	Utilities Expense	0	
5040	Phone Expense	150	
5050	Supplies Expense	0	
5060	Insurance Expense	0	
5070	Postage Expense	25	
5080	Depreciation Exp. C.S. Equipment	0	
5090	Depreciation Exp. Office Equipment	0	
5100	Miscellaneous Expense	10	
5110	Wage Expense	2,030	
5120	Payroll Tax Expense	226.35	
5130	Interest Expense	0	
5140	Bad Debt Expense	0	
6000	Purchases	0	
6010	Purchases Returns and Allowances		0
6020	Purchases Discounts		0
6030	Freight In	0	

SPECIAL JOURNALS

Purchases and Cash Payments

THE BIG PICTURE

Tony Freedman was delighted to see the difference he made in using the specialized sales and cash receipts journal last month. He has decided to continue his efforts in using two more specialized journals: a purchases journal to track the merchandise Eldorado Computer Center is selling, and a cash payments journal.

You have learned how specialized journals can benefit the company in easing the posting of transactions. In this chapter you will learn how to use a purchases and cash payment journal.

A purchases journal is used to record purchases of merchandise on account, and the cash payments journal is used to record all cash payments. Each creditor you purchase merchandise from will have an individual ledger account showing the volume of business you are giving that creditor on account. The schedule of accounts payable, like the schedule of accounts receivable, will show a detailed list of each creditor and the amount owed.

Freedman has two primary objectives for using all of the specialized journals. One is to increase efficiency, and the other is to improve accuracy and detail.

Chapter 9 focused on the sellers in merchandise companies. This chapter will look at the buyers. Many of the concepts and rules related to special journals will carry over to this chapter.

LEARNING UNIT 10-1
Chou's Toy Shop: Buyer's View of a Merchandise Company

PURCHASES

Chou brings merchandise into his toy store for resale to customers. The account that records the cost of this merchandise is called **Purchases.** Suppose that Chou buys $4,000 worth of Barbie dolls on account from Mattel Manufacturing on July 6. The Purchases account records all merchandise bought for resale. Here's how this would be recorded if special journals were not used.

Purchases is a cost.
The rules work just like they were an expense.

Purchases	
Dr.	Cr.
4,000	

This account has a debit balance and is classified as a cost. Purchases represent costs that are directly related to bringing merchandise into the store for resale to customers. The July 6 entry would be analyzed and journalized as follows:

If Chou's purchased a new display case for the store, it would not show up in the Purchase account. The case is considered equipment that is not for resale to customers.

Accounts Affected	Category	↑ ↓	Rules	T Account Update	
Purchases	Cost	↑	Dr.	**Purchases** Dr. | Cr. 4,000 |	
Accounts Payable, Mattel	Liability	↑	Cr.	Acc. Payable Dr. | Cr. | 4,000	Mattel | 4,000

	July	6	Purchases	4 0 0 0 00		
			Accounts Payable, Mattel		4 0 0 0 00	
			Purchases on account			

Keep in mind we would have to record to Mattel in the accounts payable subsidiary ledger. We will talk about the subsidiary ledger in Learning Unit 10-2.

PURCHASES RETURNS AND ALLOWANCES

Chou noticed that some of the dolls he received were defective, and he notified the manufacturer of the defects. On July 9, Mattel issued a debit memorandum indicating that Chou would get a $500 reduction from the original selling price. Chou then agreed to keep the dolls. The account that records a decrease to a buyer's cost is a contra-cost account called **Purchases Returns and Allowances.** The account lowers the cost of purchases.

Purchases Returns and Allowances

Dr.	Cr.
	500

◄— Normal balance is a credit.

Let's analyze this reduction to cost and prepare a general journal entry.

Accounts Affected	Category	↑ ↓	Rules	T Account Update	
Accounts Payable, Mattel	Liability	↓	Dr.	Acc. Payable Dr. | Cr. 500 | 4,000	Mattel 500 | 4,000
Purchases Returns and Allowances	Contra-cost	↑	Cr.	Purchases Ret. & Allow. Dr. | Cr. | 500	

July	9	Accounts Payable, Mattel		5 0 0 00	
		Purchases Returns and Allowances			5 0 0 00
		Received debit memorandum			

When posted to general ledger accounts as well as recording to Mattel in the accounts payable subsidiary ledger, Chou owes $500 less.

PURCHASES DISCOUNT

Now let's look at the analysis and journal entry when Chou pays Mattel. Mattel offers a 2 percent cash discount if the invoice is paid within 10 days. To take advantage of this cash discount, Chou sent a check to Mattel on July 15. The discount is taken after the allowance.

$4,000
− 500 allowance
$3,500 × .02 = $70 purchases discount

The account that records this discount is called **Purchases Discount.** It, too, is a contra-cost account because it lowers the cost of purchases.

Purchases Discount

Dr.	Cr.
	70

◄— Normal balance is a credit.

Let's analyze and prepare a general journal entry:

Remember, for Mattel this is a sales discount, while for Chou this is a purchases discount.

Remember, purchases were a debit; purchases discounts are credits.

Accounts Affected	Category	↑ ↓	Rules	T Account Update
Accounts Payable, Mattel	Liability	↓	Dr.	**Acc. Payable** **Mattel** Dr. | Cr. 500 | 4,000 500 | 4,000 3,500 3,500 |
Purchases Discount	Contra-cost	↑	Cr.	**Purchases Discounts** Dr. | Cr. | 70
Cash	Asset	↓	Cr.	**Cash** Dr. | Cr. | 3,430

July	15	Accounts Payable, Mattel		3 5 0 0 00		
		Purchases Discount			7 0 00	
		Cash			3 4 3 0 00	
		Paid Mattel balance owed				

After the journal entry is posted and recorded to Mattel, the result will show that Chou saved $70 and totally reduced what he owed to Mattel. The actual — or net — cost of his purchase is $3,430, calculated as follows:

Purchases	$4,000
− Purchases Returns and Allowances	500
− Purchases Discounts	70
= Net Purchases	$3,430

Freight charges are not taken into consideration in calculating net purchases. Still, they are very important. If the seller is responsible for paying the shipping cost until the goods reach their destination, the freight charges are **F.O.B. destination.** For example, if a seller located in Boston sold goods F.O.B. destination to a buyer in New York, the seller would have to pay the cost of shipping the goods to the buyer.

If the buyer is responsible for paying the shipping costs, the freight charges are **F.O.B. shipping point.** In this situation, the seller sometimes will prepay the freight charges as a matter of convenience and will add it to the invoice of the purchaser.

Example:

Bill amount ($800 + $80 prepaid freight)	$880
Less 5% cash discount (.05 × $800)	40
Amount to be paid by buyer	$840

Purchases discounts are not taken on freight. The discount is based on the purchase price.

If the seller ships goods F.O.B. shipping point, legal ownership (title) passes to the buyer *when the goods are shipped.* If goods are shipped by the seller F.O.B. destination, title will change *when goods have reached their destination.*

F.O.B. stands for "free on board" the carrier.

F.O.B. Destination: Seller pays freight to point of destination.

F.O.B. Shipping Point: Buyer pays freight from seller's shipping point.

When does title change to goods shipped?

LEARNING UNIT 10-1 REVIEW

AT THIS POINT you should be able to

◆ Explain and calculate purchases, purchases returns and allowances, and purchases discounts. (p. 354)
◆ Calculate net purchases. (p. 356)
◆ Explain why purchase discounts are not taken on freight. (p. 356)
◆ Compare and contrast F.O.B. destination with F.O.B. shipping point. (p. 356)

SELF-REVIEW QUIZ 10-1

(The forms you need can be found on page 332 of the *Study Guide and Working Papers*.)

Which of the following statements are false?

1. Net purchases = Purchases − Purchases Returns and Allowances − Purchases Discount.
2. Purchases is a contra-cost.
3. F.O.B. destination means the seller covers shipping cost and retains title till goods reach their destination.
4. Purchases discounts are not taken on freight.
5. Purchases Discount is a contra-cost account.

Solution to Self-Review Quiz 10-1

Number 2 is false.

Quiz Tip:

Buyer			*Seller*		
Purchase	Dr.	Cost	Sale	Cr	Revenue
PRA	Cr.	Contra-cost	SRA	Dr.	Contra-revenue
PD	Cr.	Contra-cost	SD	Dr.	Contra-revenue

LEARNING UNIT 10-2

Steps Taken in Purchasing Merchandise and Recording Purchases

Merchandising companies must take specific steps when they purchase goods for resale. Let's look at the steps Art's Wholesale Clothing Company took when it ordered goods from Abby Blake Company on April 3.

Step 1: Prepare a Purchase Requisition at Art's Wholesale Clothing Company

Authorized personnel initiate purchase requisition.

The inventory clerk notes a low inventory level of ladies' jackets for resale, so he sends a **purchase requisition** to the purchasing department. A duplicate copy is sent to the accounting department. A third copy remains with the department that initiated the request, to be used as a check on the purchasing department.

PURCHASE ORDER NO. 1
ART'S WHOLESALE CLOTHING COMPANY
1528 BELLE AVE.
NEW YORK, NY 10022

Purchased From:	Abby Blake Company 12 Foster Road Englewood Cliffs, NJ 07632	Date: April 1, 19XX Shipped VIA: Freight Truck Terms: 2/10, n/60 FOB: Englewood Cliffs	

Quantity	Description	Unit Price	Total
100	Ladies' Jackets Code 14-0	$50	$5,000

Art's Wholesale
By: Bill Joy

Purchase order number must appear on all invoices.

FIGURE 10-1
Purchase Order

Four copies of purchase order: (1) (original) to supplier, (2) to accounting department, (3) remains with department that initiated purchase requisition, (4) to file of purchasing department.

Step 2: Purchasing Department of Art's Wholesale Clothing Company Prepares a Purchase Order

After checking various price lists and suppliers' catalogs, the purchasing department fills out a form called a **purchase order.** This form gives Abby Blake Company the authority to ship the ladies' jackets ordered by Art's Wholesale Clothing Company (see Fig. 10-1).

Step 3: Sales Invoice Prepared by Abby Blake Company

Abby Blake Company receives the purchase order and prepares a sales invoice. The sales invoice for the seller is the **purchase invoice** for the buyer. A sales invoice is shown in Figure 10-2.

The invoice shows that the goods will be shipped F.O.B. Englewood Cliffs. This means that Art's Wholesale Clothing Company is responsible for paying the shipping costs.

The sales invoice also shows a freight charge. This means that Abby Blake prepaid the shipping costs as a matter of convenience. Art's will repay the freight charges when it pays the invoice.

Step 4: Receiving the Goods

When goods are received, Art's Wholesale inspects the shipment and completes a **receiving report.** The receiving report verifies that the exact merchandise that was ordered was received in good condition.

FIGURE 10-2
Sales Invoice

SALES INVOICE NO. 228
ABBY BLAKE COMPANY
12 FOSTER ROAD
ENGLEWOOD, CLIFFS, NJ 07632

Sold To:	Art's Wholesale Clothing Co. 1528 Belle Ave. New York, NY 10022	Date: April 3, 19XX Shipped VIA: Freight Truck Terms: 2/10, n/60 Your Order No: 1 FOB: Englewood Cliffs	

Quantity	Description	Unit Price	Total
100	Ladies' Jackets Code 14-0 Freight	$50	$5,000 50 $5,050

```
                    INVOICE APPROVAL FORM
                    Art's Wholesale Clothing Co.

    Purchase Order #          _____
    Requisition check         _____
    Purchase Order check      _____
    Receiving Report check    _____
    Invoice check             _____
    Approved for Payment      _____
```

FIGURE 10-3
Invoice Approval Form

Step 5: Verifying the Numbers

Before the invoice is approved for recording and payment, the accounting department must check the purchase order, invoice, and receiving report to make sure that all are in agreement and that no steps have been omitted. The form used for checking and approval is an **invoice approval form** (see Fig. 10-3).

Keep in mind that Art's Wholesale Clothing Company does not record this purchase until the *invoice is approved for recording and payment.* However, Abby Blake Company records this transaction in its records when the sales invoice is prepared.

THE PURCHASES JOURNAL AND ACCOUNTS PAYABLE SUBSIDIARY LEDGER

Let's look at how Art's Wholesale Clothing Company journalizes, posts, and records to the accounts payable subsidiary ledger. We will also look at the **purchases journal,** a multicolumn special journal Art's uses to record the buying of merchandise or other items on account, and the **accounts payable subsidiary ledger,** an alphabetical list of the amounts owed to creditors from purchases on account.

For example, on April 3 Art's Wholesale Clothing Company records in its purchases journal the following:

◆ Date: April 3, 19XX
◆ Account Credited: Abby Blake Company
◆ Date of Invoice: April 3
◆ Invoice Number: 228
◆ Terms: 2/10, n/60
◆ Accounts payable: $5,050; Purchases: $5,000; Freight-In, $50

See Figure 10-4 for complete purchases journal.

Note that the normal balance in the accounts payable subsidiary ledger is a credit.

As soon as the information is journalized in the purchases journal (see Fig. 10-4 on p. 360), you should:

1. Record to Abby Blake Co. in the accounts payable subsidiary ledger to indicate that the amount owed is now $5,050. When this is complete, place a (✓) in the PR column of the purchases journal.
2. Post to Freight-In, account no. 514, in the general ledger right away. When this is complete, record the 514 in the PR column under sundry in the purchases journal.

The posting and recording rules are similar to those in the previous chapter, but here we are looking at the buyer rather than at the seller.

Page 1

Date	Account Credited	Date of Invoice	Inv. No.	Terms	PR	Accounts Payable Credit	Purchases Debit	Sundry–Dr.		
								Account	PR	Amount
19XX April 3	Abby Blake Company	April 3	228	2/10, n/60	✔	5 0 5 0 00	5 0 0 0 00	Freight-In	514	5 0 00
4	Joe Francis Company	April 5	388		✔	4 0 0 0 00		Equip.	121	4 0 0 0 00
6	Thorpe Company	April 6	415	1/10, n/30	✔	8 0 0 00	8 0 0 00			
7	John Sullivan Company	April 6	516	n/10, EOM	✔	9 8 0 00	9 8 0 00			
12	Abby Blake Company	April 13	242	1/10, n/30	✔	6 0 0 00	6 0 0 00			
25	John Sullivan Company	April 26	612		✔	5 0 0 00		Supplies	115	5 0 0 00
30						11 9 3 0 00	7 3 8 0 00			4 5 5 0 00
						(211)	(511)			(X)

The (✔) in the purchases journal indicates the accounts payable subsidiary ledger has been recorded *during* the month.

Total of Accounts Payable and Purchases posted to general ledger accounts at *end of month*.

Total of sundry *not* posted.

Posted when transaction is entered: Posted to general ledger account when transaction is entered.

ACCOUNTS PAYABLE SUBSIDIARY LEDGER

Abby Blake Co.

Dr.	Cr.
	5,050 PJ1 4/3
	600 PJ1 4/12

Joe Francis Co.

Dr.	Cr.
	4,000 PJ1 4/4

Tells us what page of journal information came from.

John Sullivan Co.

Dr.	Cr.
	980 PJ1 4/17
	500 PJ1 4/25

Thorpe Co.

Dr.	Cr.
	800 PJ1 4/6

PARTIAL GENERAL LEDGER

Supplies 115

4/25 PJ1 500

Purchases 511

4/30 PJ1 7,380

Equipment 121

4/4 PJ1 4,000

Freight-In 514

4/3 PJ1 50

Accounts Payable 211

Controlling Account

11,930 PJ1 4/30

FIGURE 10-4 Purchases Journal

THE DEBIT MEMORANDUM

In Chapter 9, Art's Wholesale Clothing Company had to handle returned goods as a seller. It did this by issuing credit memoranda to customers who returned or received an allowance on the price. In this chapter, Art's must handle returns as a buyer. It does this by using debit memoranda. A **debit memorandum** is a

FIGURE 10-5
Debit Memorandum

A debit memo shows that Art's does not owe as much money as was indicated in the company's purchases journal.

DEBIT MEMORANDUM			No. 1
Art's Wholesale Clothing Company 1528 Belle Ave. New York, NY 10022			
TO: Thorpe Company 3 Access Road Beverly, MA 01915			April 9, 19XX
WE DEBIT your account as follows:			
Quantity		Unit Cost	Total
20 Men's Hats Code 827 – defective brims		$10	$200

piece of paper issued by a customer to a seller. It indicates that a return or allowance has occurred.

Suppose that on April 6 Art's Wholesale had purchased men's hats for $800 from Thorpe Company (p. 360). On April 9, 20 hats valued at $200 were found to have defective brims. Art's issued a debit memorandum to Thorpe Company, as shown in Figure 10-5. At some point in the future, Thorpe will issue Art's a credit memorandum. Let's look at how Art's Wholesale Clothing Company handles such a transaction in its accounting records.

Journalizing and Posting the Debit Memo

First, let's look at a transactional analysis chart.

Result of debit memo: "debits" or reduces Accounts Payable. On seller's books, accounts affected would include Sales Returns and Allowances and Accounts Receivable.

Accounts Affected	Category	↑	↓	Rules
Accounts Payable	Liability		↓	Dr.
Purchases Returns and Allowances	Contra-cost	↑		Cr.

Next, let's examine the journal entry for the debit memorandum:

Purchases Returns and Allowances

Dr.	Cr.
–	+

A contra-cost-of-goods-sold account.

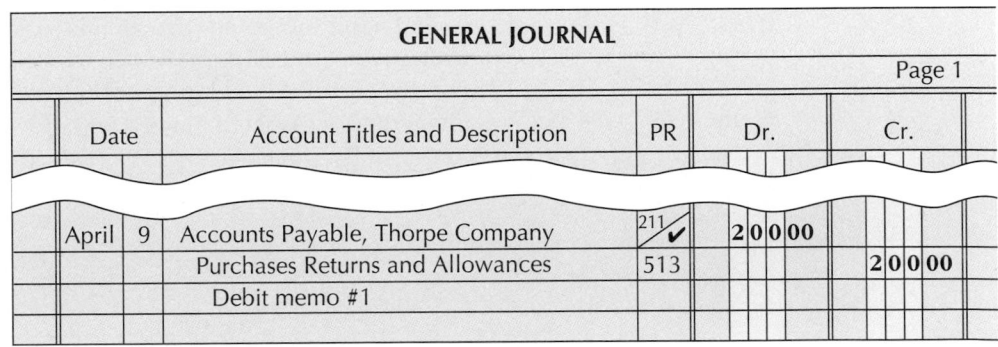

GENERAL JOURNAL					
					Page 1
Date	Account Titles and Description	PR	Dr.	Cr.	
April 9	Accounts Payable, Thorpe Company	211/✓	2 0 0 00		
	Purchases Returns and Allowances	513		2 0 0 00	
	Debit memo #1				

The two postings and one recording are:

1. 211—Post to Accounts Payable as a debit in the general ledger account no. 211. When this is done, place in the PR column the account number, 211, above the diagonal on the same line as Accounts Payable in the journal.
2. ✓—Record to Thorpe Co. in the accounts payable subsidiary ledger to show that Art's doesn't owe Thorpe as much money. When this is done, place a (✓) in

the journal in the PR column below the diagonal line on the same line as Accounts Payable in the journal.

3. 513 — Post to Purchases Returns and Allowances as a credit in the general ledger (account no. 513). When this is done, place the account number, 513, in the posting reference column of the journal on the same line as Purchases Returns and Allowances. (If equipment was returned that was not merchandise for resale, we would credit Equipment and not Purchases Returns and Allowances.)

LEARNING UNIT 10-2 REVIEW

AT THIS POINT you should be able to

◆ Explain the relationship between a purchase requisition, a purchase order, and a purchase invoice. (p. 358)
◆ Explain why a typical invoice approval form may be used. (p. 359)
◆ Journalize transactions into a purchases journal. (p. 360)
◆ Explain how to record the accounts payable subsidiary ledger and post to the general ledger from a purchases journal. (p. 360)
◆ Explain a debit memorandum and be able to journalize an entry resulting from its issuance. (p. 361)

SELF-REVIEW QUIZ 10-2

(The forms you need are on pages 333–335 of the *Study Guide and Working Papers*.)

Journalize the following transactions into the purchases journal or general journal for Munroe Co. Record to accounts payable subsidiary ledger and post to general ledger accounts as appropriate. Use the same journal headings we used for Art's Wholesale Clothing Company.

19XX

May   5   Bought merchandise on account from Flynn Co., invoice no. 512, dated May 6, terms 1/10, n/30, $900.

7   Bought merchandise from John Butler Company, invoice no. 403, dated May 7, terms n/10 EOM, $1,000.

13   Issued debit memo no. 1 to Flynn Co. for merchandise returned, $300, from invoice no. 512.

17   Purchased $400 of equipment on account from John Butler Company, invoice no. 413, dated May 18.

Solution to Self-Review Quiz 10-2

Date	Account Credited	Date of Invoice	Inv. No.	Terms	PR	Accounts Payable Credit	Purchases Debit	Sundry–Dr. Account	PR	Amount
19XX May 5	Flynn Co.	May 6	512	1/10, n/30	✔	9 0 0 00	9 0 0 00			
7	John Butler	May 7	403	n/10, EOM	✔	1 0 0 0 00	1 0 0 0 00			
17	John Butler	May 18	413		✔	4 0 0 00		Equip.	121	4 0 0 00
31						2 3 0 0 00	1 9 0 0 00			4 0 0 00
						(212)	(512)			(X)

MUNROE CO.
GENERAL JOURNAL

Date	Account Titles and Description	PR	Dr.	Cr.
19XX May 13	Accounts Payable, Flynn Co.	212 ✔	3 0 0 00	
	Purchases Returns and Allowances	513		3 0 0 00

ACCOUNTS PAYABLE SUBSIDIARY LEDGER

JOHN BUTLER COMPANY
18 REED RD.
HOMEWOOD, ILLINOIS 60430

Date	Explanation	Post. Ref.	Debit	Credit	Cr. Balance
19XX May 7		PJ2		1 0 0 0 00	1 0 0 0 00
17		PJ2		4 0 0 00	1 4 0 0 00

FLYNN COMPANY
15 FOSS AVE.
ENGLEWOOD CLIFFS, NEW JERSEY 07632

Date	Explanation	Post. Ref.	Debit	Credit	Cr. Balance
19XX May 5		PJ2		9 0 0 00	9 0 0 00
13		GJ1	3 0 0 00		6 0 0 00

FIGURE 10-6 Cash Payments Journal Recording and Posting

CASH PAYMENTS JOURNAL

Page 1

Cash

Purchases Discount

Accounts Payable

Sundry

Trade Discounts

Trade discounts are reductions from the purchase price. Usually, they are given to customers who buy items to resell or to use to produce other salable goods.

$$\text{Amount of Trade Discount} = \text{List Price} - \text{Net Price}$$

Different trade discounts are available to different classes of customers. Often, trade discounts are listed in catalogs that contain the list price and the amount of trade discount available. Such catalogs usually are updated by discount sheets.

Trade discounts are not reflected on the books.

Trade discounts have *no relationship* to whether a customer is paying a bill early. Trade discounts and list prices are not shown in the accounts of either the purchaser or the seller. Cash discounts are not taken on the amount of trade discount.

For example, look at the following:

◆ List price, $800
◆ 30% Trade discount
◆ 5% Cash discount
◆ Thus: Invoice cost of $560 ($800 − $240) less the cash discount of $28 ($560 × .05) results in a final cost of $532 if the cash discount is taken.

The purchaser as well as the seller would record the invoice amount at $560.

LEARNING UNIT 10-3 REVIEW

AT THIS POINT you should be able to

◆ Journalize, post, and record transactions utilizing a cash payments journal. (p. 365)
◆ Prepare a schedule of accounts payable. (p. 367)
◆ Compare and contrast a cash discount to a trade discount. (p. 367)

SELF-REVIEW QUIZ 10-3

(The forms you need are on pages 335–337 of the *Study Guide and Working Papers.*)

Given the following information, journalize, crossfoot, and when appropriate record and post the transactions of Melissa Company. Use the same headings as used for Art's Clothing. All purchases discounts are 2/12, n/30. The cash payments journal is page 2.

ACCOUNTS PAYABLE SUBSIDIARY LEDGER

Name	Balance	Invoice No.
Bob Finkelstein	$300	488
Al Jeep	200	410

PARTIAL GENERAL LEDGER

Account No.	Balance
Cash 110	$700
Accounts Payable 210	500
Purchases Discount 511	——
Advertising Expense 610	——

19XX

June 1 Issued check no. 15 to Al Jeep in payment of its May 25 invoice no. 410 less purchases discount.

8 Issued check no. 16 to Moss Advertising Co. to pay advertising bill due, $75, no discount.

9 Issued check no. 17 to Bob Finkelstein in payment of its May 28 invoice no. 488 less purchases discount.

Solution to Self-Review Quiz 10-3

MELISSA COMPANY
CASH PAYMENTS JOURNAL

Page 2

Date		Ck. No.	Account Debited	Post. Ref.	Sundry Accounts Dr.	Accounts Payable Dr.	Purchases Discount Cr.	Cash Cr.
19XX June	1	15	Al Jeep	✔		2 0 0 00	4 00	1 9 6 00
	8	16	Advertising Expense	610	7 5 00			7 5 00
	9	17	Bob Finkelstein	✔		3 0 0 00	6 00	2 9 4 00
	30				7 5 00	5 0 0 00	1 0 00	5 6 5 00
					(X)	(210)	(511)	(110)

$75 + $500 = $10 + $565
$575 = $575

ACCOUNTS PAYABLE SUBSIDIARY LEDGER

NAME Bob Finkelstein
ADDRESS 112 Flying Highway, Trenton, New Jersey 08611

Date		Explanation	Post. Ref.	Debit	Credit	Cr. Balance
19XX June	1	Balance	✔			3 0 0 00
	9		CPJ2	3 0 0 00		−0−

NAME Al Jeep
ADDRESS 118 Wang Rd., Saugus, Mass. 01432

Date		Explanation	Post. Ref.	Debit	Credit	Cr. Balance
19XX June	1	Balance	✔			2 0 0 00
	1		CPJ2	2 0 0 00		−0−

Accounts Payable 210				Purchases 510	
3/18 GJ1	500	1,800 3/31 PJ1		3/31 PJ1 1,500	
3/31 CPJ1	1,000				
		300 Balance			

J. Ling, Capital 310		Purchase Ret. + Allow. 520	
	2,000 3/1 CRJ1		500 3/18 GJ1

Purchase Discount 530	
	30 3/31 CPJ1

Salaries Expense 610	
3/20 CPJ1 300	

Summary of Solution Tips

Chapter 9 — Seller	Chapter 10 — Buyer
Sales Journal	Purchases Journal
Cash Receipts Journal	Cash Payments Journal
Accounts Receivable Subsidiary Ledger	Accounts Payable Subsidiary Ledger
Sales (Cr.)	Purchases (Dr.)
Sales Returns + Allowances (Dr.)	Purchase Returns + Allowances (Cr.)
Sales Discounts (Dr.)	Purchase Discounts (Cr.)
Accounts Receivable (Dr.)	Accounts Payable (Cr.)
Issue a Credit Memo	Receive a Credit Memo
or	or
Receive a Debit Memo	Issue a Debit Memo
Schedule of Accounts Receivable	Schedule of Accounts Payable

When Do I Do What?

A Step-by-Step Walk-Through of This Comprehensive Demonstration Problem

Transaction	What to Do Step by Step
19XX	
March 1	*Money Received:* Record in Cash Receipts Journal. Post immediately to J. Ling, Capital, since it is in Sundry.
1	*Sale on Account:* Record in Sales Journal. Record immediately to Balder Co., in Accounts Receivable Subsidiary Ledger. Place a (✓) in PR column of Sales Journal when subsidiary is updated.
2	*Buy Merchandise on Account:* Record in Purchases Journal. Record to Case Co. immediately in the Accounts Payable Subsidiary Ledger.
4	*Money In:* Record in Cash Receipts Journal. No posting needed (Put an X in PR column.)
6	*Money Out:* Record in Cash Payments Journal. Save $15, which is a Purchase Discount. Record immediately to Case Co. in Accounts Payable Subsidiary Ledger (the full amount of $500).

Transaction	What to Do Step by Step
8	**Sales on Account:** Record in Sales Journal. Update immediately to Lewis in Accounts Receivable Subsidiary Ledger.
10	**Money In:** Record in Cash Receipts Journal. Since Balder pays within 10 days, they get a $10 discount. Record immediately to Balder in the Accounts Receivable Subsidiary Ledger, the full amount.
12	**Returns:** Record in General Journal. Seller issues credit memo resulting in higher sales returns and customers owing less. All postings and recordings are done immediately.
14	**Money In:** Record in Cash Receipts Journal:

$$\$1{,}000 - \$200 \text{ returns} = \$800$$
$$\underline{\times .02}$$
$$\$\ 16 \text{ discount}$$

	Record immediately the $800 to Lewis in the Accounts Receivable Subsidiary Ledger.
16	*Buy Now, Pay Later:* Record in Purchases Journal. Record immediately to Noone Co. in the Accounts Payable Subsidiary Ledger.
17	*Buy Now, Pay Later:* Record in Purchases Journal in Sundry. This is not merchandise for resale. Record and Post immediately.
18	*Returns:* Record in General Journal. Buyer issues a debit memo reducing their Accounts Payable due to Purchases Return and Allowances. Post and Record immediately.
20	*Salaries:* Record in Cash Payments Journal, Sundry column. Post immediately to Salaries Expense.
24	*Money Out:* Record in Cash Payments Journal. Save 3 percent — $15, a Purchase Discount. Record immediately to Accounts Payable Subsidiary Ledger that you reduce Noone by $500.

End of Month: Post totals (except Sundry) of Special Journal to the General Ledger.

Note: In this problem at end of month (1) Accounts Receivable in the General Ledger, the controlling account, has a zero balance, as does each title in the Accounts Receivable Subsidiary Ledger. (2) The Balance in Accounts Payable (the controlling account) is $300. In the Accounts Payable Subsidiary Ledger, we owe Case $300. The sum of the Subsidiary does equal the balance in the controlling account at the end of the month.

SUMMARY OF KEY POINTS

Learning Unit 10-1

1. Purchases are merchandise for resale. It is a cost.

2. Purchases Returns and Allowances and Purchases Discount are contra-cost.

3. *F.O.B. shipping point* means that the purchaser of the goods is responsible for covering the shipping costs. If the terms were *F.O.B. destination,* the seller would be responsible for covering the shipping costs until the goods reached their destination.

4. Purchases discounts are not taken on freight.

Learning Unit 10-2

1. The steps for buying merchandise from a company may include:
   a. The requesting department prepares a purchase requisition.
   b. The purchasing department prepares a purchase order.
   c. Seller receives the order and prepares a sales invoice (a purchase invoice for the buyer).
   d. Buyer receives the goods and prepares a receiving report.
   e. Accounting department verifies and approves the invoice for payment.
2. The purchases journal records the buying of merchandise or other items on account.
3. The accounts payable subsidiary ledger, organized in alphabetical order, is not in the same book as Accounts Payable, the controlling account in the general ledger.
4. At the end of the month the total of all creditors' ending balances in the accounts payable subsidiary ledger should equal the ending balance in Accounts Payable, the controlling account in the general ledger.
5. A debit memorandum (issued by the buyer) indicates that the amount owed from a previous purchase is being reduced because some goods were defective or not up to a specific standard and thus were returned or an allowance requested. On receiving the debit memorandum, the seller will issue a credit memorandum.

Learning Unit 10-3

1. All payments of cash (check) are recorded in the cash payments journal.
2. At the end of the month, the schedule of accounts payable, a list of ending amounts owed individual creditors, should equal the ending balance in Accounts Payable, the controlling account in the general ledger.
3. Trade discounts are deductions off the list price that have nothing to do with early payments (cash discounts). Invoice amounts are recorded *after* the trade discount is deducted. Cash discounts are not taken on trade discounts.

KEY TERMS

Accounts payable subsidiary ledger A book or file that contains in alphabetical order the name of the creditor and amount owed from purchases on account.

Cash payments journal (Cash disbursements journal) A special journal that records all transactions involving the payment of cash.

Controlling account The account in the general ledger that summarizes or controls a subsidiary ledger. Example: The Accounts Payable account in the general ledger is the controlling account for the accounts payable subsidiary ledger. After postings are complete, it shows the total amount owed from purchases made on account.

Debit memorandum A memo issued by a purchaser to a seller, indicating that some Purchases Returns and Allowances have occurred and therefore the purchaser now owes less money on account.

F.O.B. Free on Board, which means without shipping charge either to the buyer or seller up to or from a specified location. In the view of one or the other, the shipment is *free* on board the carrier.

F.O.B. destination *Seller* pays or is responsible for the cost of freight to purchaser's location or destination.

F.O.B. shipping point *Purchaser* pays or is responsible for the shipping costs from seller's shipping point to purchaser's location.

Invoice approval form The accounting department uses this form in checking the invoice and finally approving it for recording and payment.

Purchases Merchandise for resale. It is a cost.

Purchases Discount A contra-cost account in the general ledger that records discounts offered by suppliers of merchandise for prompt payment of purchases by buyers.

Purchase invoice The seller's sales invoice, which is sent to the purchaser.

Purchases journal A multicolumn special journal that records the buying of merchandise or other items on account.

Purchase order A form used in business to place an order for the buying of goods from a seller.

Purchase requisition A form used within a business by the requesting department asking the purchasing department of the business to buy specific goods.

Purchases Returns and Allowances A contra-cost account in the ledger that records the amount of defective or unacceptable merchandise returned to suppliers and/or price reductions given for defective items.

Receiving report A business form used to notify the appropriate people of the ordered goods received along with the quantities and specific condition of the goods.

QUESTIONS, MINI EXERCISES, EXERCISES, AND PROBLEMS

Discussion Questions

1. Explain how net purchases is calculated.
2. What is the normal balance of Purchases Discount?
3. What is a contra-cost?
4. Explain the difference between F.O.B. shipping point and F.O.B. destination.
5. F.O.B. destination means that title to the goods will switch to the buyer when goods are shipped. Agree or disagree. Why?
6. What is the normal balance of each creditor in the accounts payable subsidiary ledger?
7. Why doesn't the balance of the controlling account, Accounts Payable, equal the sum of the accounts payable subsidiary ledger during the month?
8. What is the relationship between a purchase requisition and a purchase order?
9. What purpose could a typical invoice approval form serve?
10. Explain the difference between merchandise and equipment.
11. Why would the purchaser issue a debit memorandum?
12. Explain the relationship between a purchases journal and a cash payments journal.
13. Explain why a trade discount is not a cash discount.

Mini Exercises

(The forms you need are on page 342 of the *Study Guide and Working Papers.*)

Overview

1. Complete the following table:

To the Seller		To the Buyer
Sales	↔	a. _____
Sales Returns and Allowances	↔	b. _____
Sales Discount	↔	c. _____
Sales Journal	↔	d. _____
Cash Receipts Journal	↔	e. _____
Credit Memorandum	↔	f. _____
Schedule of Accounts Receivable	↔	g. _____
Accounts Receivable Subsidiary Ledger	↔	h. _____

BLUEPRINT OF PURCHASES AND CASH PAYMENTS JOURNALS

Purchase of Merchandise or Other Items on Account

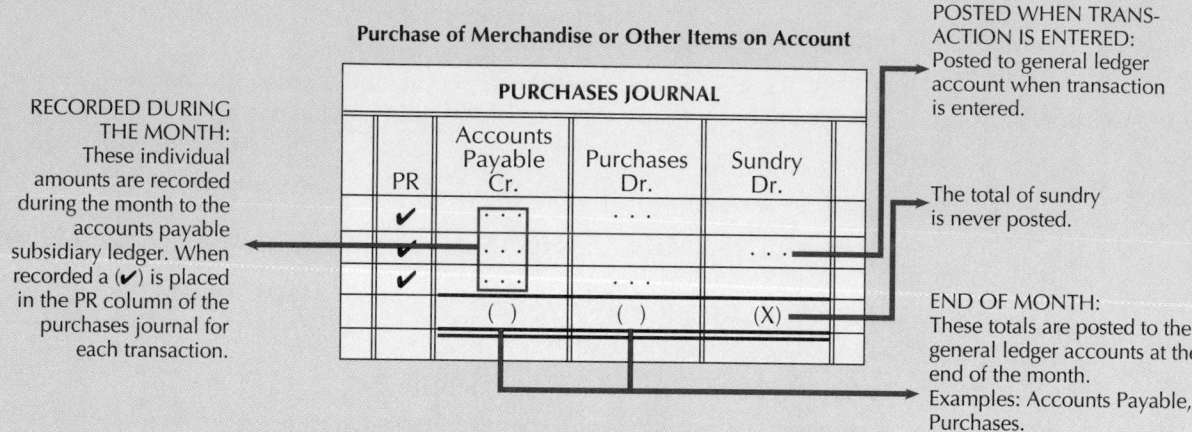

RECORDED DURING THE MONTH: These individual amounts are recorded during the month to the accounts payable subsidiary ledger. When recorded a (✔) is placed in the PR column of the purchases journal for each transaction.

POSTED WHEN TRANSACTION IS ENTERED: Posted to general ledger account when transaction is entered.

The total of sundry is never posted.

END OF MONTH: These totals are posted to the general ledger accounts at the end of the month. Examples: Accounts Payable, Purchases.

Issuing a Debit Memo (or Receiving a Credit Memo)

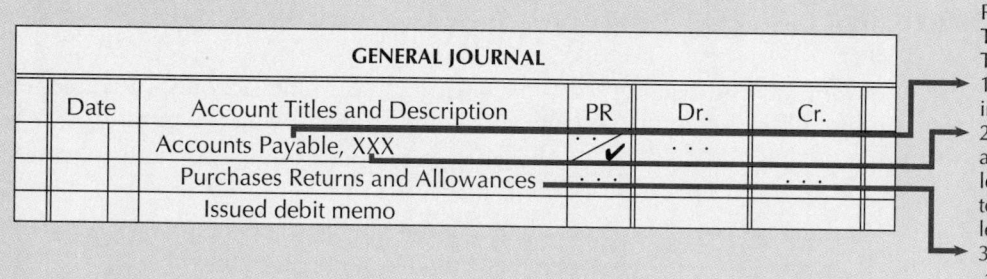

POSTED AND RECORDED WHEN TRANSACTION IS ENTERED
Two postings and one recording:
1. Posted to Accounts Payable in the general ledger.
2. Recorded to XXX in the accounts payable subsidiary ledger. A (✔) indicates recording to the accounts payable subsidiary ledger is complete.
3. Posted to Purchases Returns and Allowances in general ledger.

Outward Flow of Cash

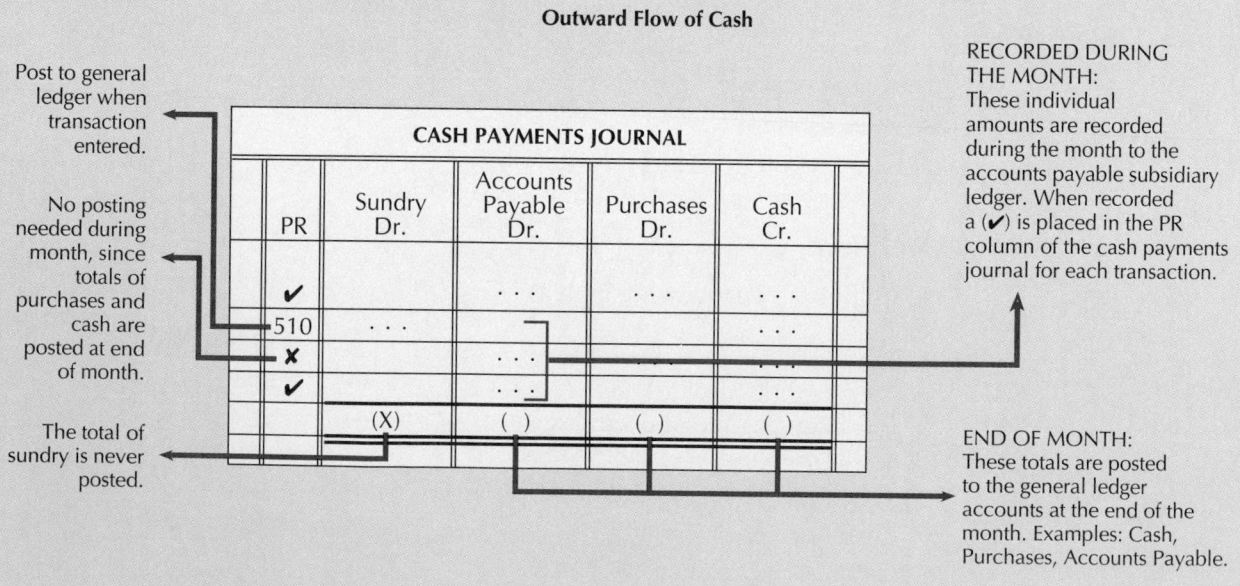

Post to general ledger when transaction entered.

No posting needed during month, since totals of purchases and cash are posted at end of month.

The total of sundry is never posted.

RECORDED DURING THE MONTH: These individual amounts are recorded during the month to the accounts payable subsidiary ledger. When recorded a (✔) is placed in the PR column of the cash payments journal for each transaction.

END OF MONTH: These totals are posted to the general ledger accounts at the end of the month. Examples: Cash, Purchases, Accounts Payable.

2. Complete the following table:

	Category	↑	↓	Temporary or Permanent
Purchases				
Purchases Returns and Allowances				
Purchases Discount				

Calculating Net Purchases

3. Calculate Net Purchases from the following: Purchases, $6; Purchases Returns and Allowances, $2; Purchases Discounts, $1.

Purchases Journal, General Journal, Recording and Posting

4. Match the following to the three journal entries (more than one number can be used).

1. Journalized into Purchases Journal.
2. Record immediately to Subsidiary Ledger.
3. Post totals from Purchases Journal (except Sundry total) at end of month to General Ledger.
4. Journalized in General Journal.
5. Record and post immediately to Subsidiary and General Ledger.

a. Bought merchandise on account from Also Co., invoice no. 12, $20.

b. Bought Equipment on account from Jone Co., invoice no. 13, $40.

c. Issued debit memo no. 1 to Also Co. for merchandise returned, $4, from invoice no. 12.

Recording Transactions in Special Journals

5. Indicate in which journal each transaction will be journalized:

1. SJ   **4.** CPJ

2. PJ   **5.** GJ

3. CRJ

_____ **a.** Issued credit memo no. 2, $13.

_____ **b.** Cash sales, $20.

_____ **c.** Received check from Blue Co., $50 less 3 percent discount.

_____ **d.** Bought merchandise on account from Mel Co., $35, 1/10, n/30, invoice no. 20.

_____ **e.** Cash Purchase, $15.

_____ **f.** Issued debit memo to Mel Co., $15 for merchandise returned from invoice no. 20.

6. From the following prepare a schedule of Accounts Payable for AVE Co. for May 31, 19XX:

Accounts Payable Subsidiary Ledger		General Ledger			

Rowe Co.		Accounts Payable			
	5/7 PJ1 60	5/31 CPJ 10	5/31 PJ1 110

Bloss Co.			
5/25 CPJ1 10	5/20 PJ1 · 50		

Exercises

(The forms you need are on pages 343–345 of the *Study Guide and Working Papers.*)

10-1. From the accompanying purchases journal, please record to the accounts payable subsidiary ledger and post to general ledger accounts as appropriate.

PURCHASES JOURNAL										

Page 1

Date		Account Credited	Date of Invoice	Terms	Post Ref.	Accounts Payable Credit	Purchases Debit	Sundry-Dr.		
								Account	PR	Amount
19XX June	3	Barr Co.	May 3	1/10, n/30		6 0 0 00	6 0 0 00			
	4	Jess Co.	May 4	n/10, EOM		9 0 0 00	9 0 0 00			
	8	Rey Co.	May 8			4 0 0 00		Equipment		4 0 0 00

Recording to the accounts payable subsidiary ledger and posting to the general ledger from a purchases journal.

Partial Accounts Payable Subsidiary Ledger

Barr Co.

Jess Co.

Rey Co.

Partial General Ledger

Equipment 120

Accounts Payable 210

Purchases 510

Journalizing, recording, and posting a debit memorandum.

10-2. On July 10, 19XX, Aster Co. issued debit memorandum no. 1 for $400 to Reel Co. for merchandise returned from invoice no. 312. Your task is to journalize, record, and post this transaction as appropriate. Use the same account numbers as found in the text for Art's Wholesale Clothing Company. The general journal is page 1.

Journalizing, recording, and posting a cash payments journal.

10-3. Journalize, record, and post when appropriate the following transactions into the cash payments journal (p. 2) for Morgan's Clothing. Use the same headings as found in the text (p. 365). All purchases discounts are 2/10, n/30.

ACCOUNTS PAYABLE SUBSIDIARY LEDGER

Name	Balance	Invoice No.
A. James	$1,000	522
B. Foss	400	488
J. Ranch	900	562
B. Swanson	100	821

PARTIAL GENERAL LEDGER

Account	Balance
Cash 110	$3,000
Accounts Payable 210	2,400
Purchases Discount 511	
Advertising Expense 610	

19XX
April 1 Issued check no. 20 to A. James Company in payment of its March 28 invoice no. 522.

8 Issued check no. 21 to Flott Advertising in payment of its advertising bill, $100, no discount.

15 Issued check no. 22 to B. Foss in payment of its March 25 invoice no. 488.

Schedule of accounts payable.

10-4. From Exercise 10-3, prepare a schedule of accounts payable and verify that the total of the schedule equals the amount in the controlling account.

F.O.B. destination.

10-5. Record the following transaction in a transaction analysis chart for the buyer: Bought merchandise for $9,000 on account. Shipping terms were F.O.B. destination. The cost of shipping was $500.

Trade and cash discounts.

10-6. Angie Rase bought merchandise with a list price of $4,000. Angie was entitled to a 30 percent trade discount, as well as a 3 percent cash discount. What was Angie's actual cost of buying this merchandise after the cash discount?

Group A Problems

(The forms you need are on pages 346–367 of the *Study Guide and Working Papers*.)

Journalizing, recording, and posting a purchases journal.

10A-1. Judy Clark recently opened a sporting goods shop. As the bookkeeper of her shop, please journalize, record, and post when appropriate the following transactions (account numbers are: Store Supplies, 115; Store Equipment, 121; Accounts Payable, 210; Purchases, 510):

Check Figure:

Total of Purchases Column $2,300

19XX
June 4 Bought merchandise on account from Aster Co., invoice no. 442, dated June 5, terms 2/10, n/30, $900.

5 Bought store equipment from Norton Co., invoice no. 502, dated June 6, $4,000.

8 Bought merchandise on account from Rolo Co., invoice no. 401, dated June 9; terms 2/10, n/30, $1,400.

14 Bought store supplies on account from Aster Co., invoice no. 419, dated June 14, $900.

10A-2. Mabel's Natural Food Store uses a purchases journal (p. 10) and a general journal (p. 2) to record the following transactions (continued from April):

Journalizing, recording, and posting a purchases journal as well as recording debit memorandum and preparing a schedule of accounts payable.

19XX
May 8 Purchased merchandise on account from Aton Co., invoice no. 400, dated May 9, terms 2/10, n/60, $600.

10 Purchased merchandise on account from Broward Co., invoice no. 420, dated May 11, terms 2/10, n/60, $1,200.

12 Purchased store supplies on account from Midden Co., invoice no. 510, dated May 13, $500.

14 Issued debit memo no. 8 to Aton Co. for merchandise returned, $400, from invoice no. 400.

Check Figure:

Total Schedule of Accounts
Payable $5,810

17 Purchased office equipment on account from Relar Co., invoice no. 810, dated May 18, $560.

24 Purchased additional store supplies on account from Midden Co., invoice no. 516, dated May 25, terms 2/10, n/30, $650.

The food store has decided to keep a separate column for the purchases of supplies in the purchases journal. Your task is to

1. Journalize the transactions.
2. Post and record as appropriate.
3. Prepare a schedule of accounts payable.

ACCOUNTS PAYABLE SUBSIDIARY LEDGER

Name	Balance
Aton Co.	$ 400
Broward Co.	600
Midden Co.	1,200
Relar Co.	500

PARTIAL GENERAL LEDGER

Account	Number	Balance
Store Supplies	110	$ —
Office Equipment	120	—
Accounts Payable	210	2,700
Purchases	510	16,000
Purchases Returns and Allowances	512	—

Journalizing, recording, and posting a cash payments journal. Preparing a schedule of accounts payable.

Check Figure:

Total of Schedule of Accounts
Payable $1,900

10A-3. Wendy Jones operates a wholesale computer center. All transactions requiring the payment of cash are recorded in the cash payments journal (p. 5). The account balances as of May 1, 19XX, are as follows:

ACCOUNTS PAYABLE SUBSIDIARY LEDGER

Name	Balance
Alvin Co.	$1,200
Henry Co.	600
Soy Co.	800
Xon Co.	1,400

PARTIAL GENERAL LEDGER

Account	Number	Balance
Cash	110	$17,000
Delivery Truck	150	—
Accounts Payable	210	4,000
Computer Purchases	510	—
Computer Purchases Discount	511	—
Rent Expense	610	—
Utilities Expense	620	—

Your task is to

1. Journalize the following transactions.

2. Record to the accounts payable subsidiary ledger and post to general ledger as appropriate.

3. Prepare a schedule of accounts payable.

19XX

May 1 Paid half the amount owed Henry Co. from previous purchases of appliances on account, less a 2 percent purchases discount, check no. 21.

3 Bought a delivery truck for $8,000 cash, check no. 22, payable to Bill Ring Co.

6 Bought computer merchandise from Lectro Co., check no. 23, $2,900.

18 Bought additional computer merchandise from Pulse Co., check no. 24, $800.

24 Paid Xon Co. the amount owed less a 2 percent purchases discount, check no. 25.

28 Paid rent expense to King's Realty Trust, check no. 26, $2,000.

29 Paid utilities expense to Stone Utility Co., check no. 27, $300.

30 Paid half the amount owed Soy Co., no discount, check no. 28.

10A-4. Abby Ellen opened Abby's Toy House. As her newly hired accountant, your task is to

1. Journalize the transactions for the month of March.

2. Record to subsidiary ledgers and post to general ledger as appropriate.

3. Total and rule the journals.

4. Prepare a schedule of accounts receivable and a schedule of accounts payable.

The following is the partial chart of accounts for Abby's Toy House:

Comprehensive Problem: All special journals and the general journal. Schedule of accounts payable and accounts receivable.

Abby's Toy House Chart of Accounts

Assets
110 Cash
112 Accounts Receivable
114 Prepaid Rent
121 Delivery Truck

Liabilities
210 Accounts Payable

Owner's Equity
310 A. Ellen, Capital

Revenue
410 Toy Sales
412 Sales Returns and Allowances
414 Sales Discounts

Cost of Goods
510 Toy Purchases
512 Purchases Returns and Allowances
514 Purchases Discount

Expenses
610 Salaries Expense
612 Cleaning Expense

Check Figures:

Total of Schedule of Accounts Receivable $7,600

Total of Schedule of Accounts Payable $9,000

19XX

March 1 Abby Ellen invested $8,000 in the toy store.

1 Paid three months' rent in advance, check no. 1, $3,000.

1 Purchased merchandise from Earl Miller Company on account, $4,000, invoice no. 410, dated March 2, terms 2/10, n/30.

3 Sold merchandise to Bill Burton on account, $1,000, invoice no. 1, terms 2/10, n/30.

6 Sold merchandise to Jim Rex on account, $700, invoice no. 2, terms 2/10, n/30.

8 Purchased merchandise from Earl Miller Co. on account, $1,200, invoice no. 415, dated March 9, terms 2/10, n/30.

9 Sold merchandise to Bill Burton on account, $600, invoice no. 3, terms 2/10, n/30.

9 Paid cleaning service $300, check no. 2.

10 Jim Rex returned merchandise that cost $300 to Abby's Toy House. Abby issued credit memorandum no. 1 to Jim Rex for $300.

10 Purchased merchandise from Minnie Katz on account, $4,000, invoice no. 311, dated March 11, terms 1/15, n/60.

12 Paid Earl Miller Co. invoice no. 410, dated March 2, check no. 3.

13 Sold $1,300 of toy merchandise for cash.

13 Paid salaries, $600, check no. 4.

14 Returned merchandise to Minnie Katz in the amount of $1,000. Abby's Toy House issued debit memorandum no. 1 to Minnie Katz.

15 Sold merchandise for $4,000 cash.

16 Received payment from Jim Rex, invoice no. 2 (less returned merchandise) less discount.

16 Bill Burton paid invoice no. 1.

16 Sold toy merchandise to Amy Rose on account, $4,000, invoice no. 4, terms 2/10, n/30.

20 Purchased delivery truck on account from Sam Katz Garage, $3,000, invoice no. 111, dated March 21 (no discount).

22 Sold to Bill Burton merchandise on account, $900, invoice no. 5, terms 2/10, n/30.

23 Paid Minnie Katz balance owed, check no. 5.

24 Sold toy merchandise on account to Amy Rose, $1,100, invoice no. 6, terms 2/10, n/30.

25 Purchased toy merchandise, $600, check no. 6.

26 Purchased toy merchandise from Woody Smith on account, $4,800, invoice no. 211, dated March 27, terms 2/10, n/30.

28 Bill Burton paid invoice no. 5, dated March 22.

28 Amy Rose paid invoice no. 6, dated March 24.

28 Abby invested an additional $5,000 in the business.

28 Purchased merchandise from Earl Miller Co., $1,400, invoice no. 436, dated March 29, terms 2/10, n/30.

30 Paid Earl Miller Co. invoice no. 436, check no. 7.

30 Sold merchandise to Bonnie Flow Company on account, $3,000, invoice no. 7, terms 2/10, n/30.

Group B Problems

(The forms you need are on pages 346–367 of the *Study Guide and Working Papers.*)

Journalizing, recording, and posting a purchases journal.

Check Figure:
Total of Purchases Column
$2,200

10B-1. From the following transactions of Judy Clark's sporting goods shop, journalize in the purchases journal and record and post as appropriate:

19XX
June 4 Bought merchandise on account from Rolo Co., invoice no. 400, dated June 5, terms 2/10, n/30, $1,800.

5 Bought store equipment from Norton Co., invoice no. 518, dated June 6, $6,000.

8 Bought merchandise on account from Aster Co., invoice no. 411, dated June 5, terms 2/10, n/30, $400.

14 Bought store supplies on account from Aster Co., invoice no. 415, dated June 13, $1,200.

Journalizing, recording, and posting a purchases journal as well as recording the issuing of a debit memorandum and preparing a schedule of accounts payable.

Check Figure:
Total of Schedule of Accounts
Payable $6,000

10B-2. As the accountant of Mabel's Natural Food Store (1) journalize the following transactions into the purchases (p. 10) or general journal (p. 2), (2) record and post as appropriate, and (3) prepare a schedule of accounts payable. Beginning balances are in your *Working Papers.*

19XX
May

8   Purchased merchandise on account from Broward Co., invoice no. 420, dated May 9, terms 2/10, n/60, $500.

10   Purchased merchandise on account from Aton Co., invoice no. 400, dated May 11, terms 2/10, n/60, $900.

12   Purchased store supplies on account from Midden Co., invoice no. 510, dated May 13, $700.

14   Issued debit memo no. 7 to Aton Co. for merchandise returned, $400, from invoice no. 400.

17   Purchased office equipment on account from Relar Co., invoice no. 810, dated May 18, $750.

24   Purchased additional store supplies on account from Midden Co., invoice no. 516, dated May 25, $850.

Journalizing, recording, and posting a cash payments journal. Preparing a schedule of accounts payable.

Check Figure:
Total of Schedule of Accounts
Payable $1,900

10B-3. Wendy Jones has hired you as her bookkeeper to record the following transactions in the cash payments journal. She would like you to record and post as appropriate and supply her with a schedule of accounts payable. (Beginning balances are in your workbook or Problem 10A-3, p. 355 in the text.)

19XX
May

1   Bought a delivery truck for $8,000 cash, check no. 21, payable to Randy Rosse Co.

3   Paid half the amount owed Henry Co. from previous purchases of computer merchandise on account, less a 5 percent purchases discount, check no. 22.

6   Bought computer merchandise from Jane Co. for $900 cash, check no. 23.

18   Bought additional computer merchandise from Jane Co., check no. 24, $1,000.

24   Paid Xon Co. the amount owed less a 5 percent purchases discount, check no. 25.

28   Paid rent expense to Regan Realty Trust, check no. 26, $3,000.

29   Paid half the amount owed Soy Co., no discount, check no. 27.

30   Paid utilities expense to French Utility, check no. 28, $425.

10B-4. As the new accountant for Abby's Toy House, your task is to

1. Journalize the transactions for the month of March.

2. Record to subsidiary ledgers and post to the general ledger as appropriate.

3. Total and rule the journals.

4. Prepare a schedule of accounts receivable and a schedule of accounts payable.

Check Figures:
Total of Schedule of Accounts
Receivable $9,900

Total of Schedule of Accounts
Payable $9,200

(Use the same chart of accounts as in Problem 10A-4, p. 383. Your workbook has all the forms you need to complete this problem.)

19XX
March

1   Abby invested $4,000 in the new toy store.

1   Paid two months' rent in advance, check no. 1, $1,000.

1   Purchased merchandise from Earl Miller Company, invoice no. 410, dated March 2, terms 2/10, n/30, $6,000.

3   Sold merchandise to Bill Burton on account, $1,600, invoice no. 1, terms 2/10, n/30.

6 Sold merchandise to Jim Rex on account, $800, invoice no. 2, terms 2/10, n/30.

8 Purchased merchandise from Earl Miller Company, $800, invoice no. 415, dated March 9, terms 2/10, n/30.

9 Sold merchandise to Bill Burton on account, $700, invoice no. 3, terms 2/10, n/30.

9 Paid cleaning service, $400, check no. 2.

10 Jim Rex returned merchandise that cost $200 to Abby. Abby issued credit memorandum no. 1 to Jim Rex for $200.

10 Purchased merchandise from Minnie Katz, $7,000, invoice no. 311, dated March 11, terms 1/15, n/60.

12 Paid Earl Miller Co. invoice no. 410, dated March 2, check no. 3.

13 Sold $1,500 of toy merchandise for cash.

13 Paid salaries, $700, check no. 4.

14 Returned merchandise to Minnie Katz in the amount of $500. Abby issued debit memorandum no. 1 to Minnie Katz.

15 Sold merchandise for cash, $4,800.

16 Received payment from Jim Rex for invoice no. 2 (less returned merchandise) less discount.

16 Bill Burton paid invoice no. 1.

16 Sold toy merchandise to Amy Rose on account, $6,000, invoice no. 4, terms 2/10, n/30.

20 Purchased delivery truck on account from Sam Katz Garage, $2,500, invoice no. 111, dated March 21 (no discount).

22 Sold to Bill Burton merchandise on account, $2,000, invoice no. 5, terms 2/10, n/30.

23 Paid Minnie Katz balance owed, check no. 5.

24 Sold toy merchandise on account to Amy Rose, $2,000, invoice no. 6, terms 2/10, n/30.

25 Purchased toy merchandise, $800, check no. 6.

26 Purchased toy merchandise from Woody Smith on account, $5,900, invoice no. 211, dated March 27, terms 2/10, n/30.

28 Bill Burton paid invoice no. 5, dated March 22.

28 Amy Rose paid invoice no. 6, dated March 24.

28 Abby invested an additional $3,000 in the business.

28 Purchased merchandise from Earl Miller Co., $4,200, invoice no. 436, dated March 29, terms 2/10, n/30.

30 Paid Earl Miller Co. invoice no. 436, check no. 7.

30 Sold merchandise to Bonnie Flow Company on account, $3,200, invoice no. 7, terms 2/10, n/30.

REAL WORLD APPLICATIONS

10R-1.

Hint: $R = \dfrac{I}{PT}$

Angie Co. bought merchandise for $1,000 with credit terms of 2/10, n/30. Owing to the bookkeeper's incompetence, the 2 percent cash discount was missed. The bookkeeper told Pete Angie, the owner, not to get excited. After all, it was a $20 discount that was missed—not hundreds of dollars. Could you please act as Mr. Angie's assistant and show the bookkeeper that his $20 represents a sizeable equivalent interest cost? In your calculation assume a 360-day year. Make some written recommendations so that this will not happen again.

SALES JOURNAL

Account	PR			
Blue Co.		4 8 0 0 0 0		
Jon Co.		5 6 0 0 0 0		
Roff Co.		6 4 0 0 0 0		
Totals		16 8 0 0 0 0		

PURCHASES JOURNAL

Account	PR			
Ralph Co.		4 0 0 0 0 0		
Sos Co.		6 0 0 0 0 0		
Jingle Co.		8 0 0 0 0 0		
Totals		18 0 0 0 0 0		

GENERAL JOURNAL

Sales Returns and Allowances		1 6 0 0 0 0		
Accounts Receivable, Jon Co.			1 6 0 0 0 0	
Customer returned merchandise				
Accounts Payable, Jingle Co.		8 0 0 0 0		
Purchases, Returns, and Allowances			8 0 0 0 0	
Returned defective merchandise				

CASH RECEIPTS JOURNAL*

Cash Dr.	Sales Discount Dr.	Accounts Receivable Cr.	Sales Cr.	Sundry-Dr.		
				Account Name	PR	Amount Cr.
4 7 0 4 00	9 6 00	4 8 0 0 00		Blue Co.		
1 9 6 0 00	4 0 00	2 0 0 0 00		Jon Co.		
5 0 0 0 00			5 0 0 0 00	Sales		
20 0 0 0 00				Notes Payable		20 0 0 0 00
3 1 3 6 00	6 4 00	3 2 0 0 00		Roff Co.		
4 6 0 0 00			4 6 0 0 00	Sales		
39 4 0 0 00	2 0 0 00	10 0 0 0 00	9 6 0 0 00	Totals		20 0 0 0 00

* Note: This company's set of columns differs from that shown in the chapter.

CASH PAYMENTS JOURNAL

Account	PR	Sundry	Accounts Payable	Purchases Discount	Cash	
Sos Co.			3 0 0 0 00	6 0 00	2 9 4 0 00	
Salaries Expense		2 6 0 0 00			2 6 0 0 00	
Jingle Co.			4 0 0 0 00	8 0 00	3 9 2 0 00	
Salaries Expense		2 6 0 0 00			2 6 0 0 00	
Totals		5 2 0 0 00	7 0 0 0 00	1 4 0 00	12 0 6 0 00	

10R-2.

Jeff Ryan completed an Accounting I course and was recently hired as the book-keeper of Spring Co. The special journals have not been posted, nor are *Dr.* and *Cr.* used on the column headings. Please assist Jeff by marking the Dr. and Cr. headings as well as setting up and posting to the general ledger and recording to the subsidiary ledger. (Only post or record the amounts, since no chart of accounts is provided.) Make some written recommendations on how a new computer system may lessen the need for posting.

YOU make the call

Critical Thinking/Ethical Case

10R-3.

Spring Co. bought merchandise from All Co. with terms 2/10, n/30. Joanne Ring, the bookkeeper, forgot to pay the bill within the first 10 days. She went to Mel Ryan, Head Accountant, who told her to backdate the check so it looked like the bill was paid within the discount period. Joanne told Mel that she thought they could get away with it. Should Joanne and Mel backdate the check to take advantage of the discount? You make the call. Write down your specific recommendations to Joanne.

ACCOUNTING RECALL
A CUMULATIVE APPROACH

THIS EXAM REVIEWS CHAPTERS 1 THROUGH 10

Your *Study Guide and Working Papers* has forms (pp. 372 and 379) to complete this exam, as well as worked-out solutions. The page references next to each question identify what page to turn back to if you answer the question incorrectly.

PART 1   Vocabulary Review

Match the terms to the appropriate definition or phrase.

Page Ref.

(212)	1. Checks outstanding	A. A contra-cost account
(356)	2. F.O.B. destination	B. Issued by a buyer to the seller
(360)	3. Purchases journal	C. Special journal that records buying on account
(319)	4. Sales journal	
(355)	5. Purchases discount	D. Sales on account
(314)	6. Credit memorandum	E. Seller pays cost of freight
(280)	7. 941	F. Form completed quarterly for FIT, Social Security, and Medicare
(360)	8. Debit memorandum	

(365)	9. Cash payments journal	G. Merchandise for resale
(354)	10. Purchases	H. Payment of cash
		I. Issued by seller
		J. Checks not yet processed by the bank

PART II True or False (Accounting Theory)

(314) 11. Issuing a credit memo results in seller increasing its purchases returns and allowances.

(355) 12. Purchases discounts have a normal balance of a debit.

(248) 13. Medicare and Social Security have different rates.

(365) 14. Each creditor in the accounts payable subsidiary ledger usually has a debit balance.

(216) 15. Petty cash is an asset that will only be debited with establishment or when raising to a higher amount.

CONTINUING PROBLEM

Freedman was very happy to see the progress made by using the specialized journals. For the month of February he will add two additional journals (purchases journal and the cash payments journal). To assist you in recording the transactions, the following is an updated schedule of accounts payable as of January 31:

Schedule of Accounts Payable

Office Depot	$50
System Design Furniture	$1,400
Pac Bell	$150
Multi Systems	$450
Total Accounts Payable	$2,050

Assignment:

(See pp. 373 – 378 in your *Study Guide and Working Papers.*)

4. Journalize the transactions in the appropriate journals (cash payments, purchase journal, or general journal).

5. Record in the accounts payable subsidiary ledger and post to the general ledger as appropriate. A partial general ledger is included in the *Working Papers.*

6. Prepare a schedule of accounts payable as of February 28, 19XX.

The transactions for the month of February are:

Feb.   1 Prepaid the rent for the months of February, March, and April, $1,200; check #2585

4 Bought merchandise on account from Multi Systems (purchase order #4010), $450; terms are 3/10, n/30

8 Bought office supplies on account from Office Depot (purchase order #4011), $250; terms are n/30

9 Purchased merchandise on account from Computer Connection (purchase order #4012), $500; terms are 1/30, n/60

15 Paid (purchase order #4010) in full to Multi Systems; check #2586

21 Issued debit memorandum #10 to Computer Connection for merchandise returned from (purchase order #4012), $100

27 Paid for office supplies, $50; check #2587

COMPUTERIZED ACCOUNTING APPLICATION FOR CHAPTER 10

PART A: Recording Transactions in the Sales, Receipts, Purchases, and Payments Journals

PART B: Computerized Accounting Instructions for Abby's Toy House (Problem 10A-4)

Before starting on this assignment, read and complete the tasks discussed in Parts A, B, and F of the Computerized Accounting appendix at the back of this book and complete the Computerized Accounting Application assignments for Chapter 3, Chapter 4, the Valdez Realty Mini Practice Set (Chapter 5), and the Pete's Market Mini Practice Set (Chapter 8).

PART A: Recording Transactions in the Sales, Receipts, Purchases, and Payments Journals

What to Record in a Computerized Sales or Receipts Journal

The Sales and Receipts Journals in Simply Accounting are designed to work with the Receivables and General Ledgers modules in an integrated fashion. When transactions are recorded in the Sales and Receipts journals, the program automatically posts the customer's account in the accounts receivable subsidiary ledger, records the journal entry, and posts all accounts affected in the general ledger. However, the type of transactions recorded in the Sales and Receipts journals in Simply Accounting differ from the types of transactions recorded in these journals in a manual accounting system. An explanation of the differences appears in the following chart:

Name of Computerized Journal	Types of Transactions Recorded in Computerized Journal
Sales Journal	Sales of merchandise on account
	Sales returns and allowances (credit memos)
Receipts Journal	Cash receipts from credit customers
General Journal	Cash receipts from all sources other than credit customers

Computerized Schedule of Accounts Receivable

A Customer Aged Detail report (the computerized version of a schedule of accounts receivable) for The Mars Company appears below (terms of 2/10, n/30 are offered to all credit customers of The Mars Company):

The Mars Company: Customer Aged Detail As at 3/1/97

			Total	Current	31 to 60	61 to 90	91+
John Dunbar							
909	2/25/97	Invoice	500.00	500.00	—	—	—
Kevin Tucker							
911	2/26/97	Invoice	550.00	550.00	—	—	—
			1,050.00	1,050.00	—	—	—

What to Record in a Computerized Purchases or Payments Journal

The Purchases and Payments Journals in Simply Accounting are also designed to work with the Payables and General Ledgers modules in an integrated fashion.

When transactions are recorded in the Purchases and Payments journals, the program automatically posts the vendor's account in the accounts payable subsidiary ledger, records the journal entry, and posts all accounts affected in the general ledger. However, the type of transactions recorded in the Purchases and Payments journals in Simply Accounting differ from the types of transactions recorded in these journals in a manual accounting system. An explanation of the differences appears in the following chart:

Name of Computerized Journal	Types of Transactions Recorded in Computerized Journal
Purchases Journal	Purchases of merchandise and other items on account
	Purchase returns and allowances (debit memos)
Payments Journal	Cash payments to credit vendors
General Journal	Cash payments for all purposes other than payments to credit vendors

Computerized Schedule of Accounts Payable

A Vendor Aged Detail report (the computerized version of a schedule of accounts payable) for The Mars Company appears below:

The Mars Company: Vendor Aged Detail As at 3/1/97

			Total	Current	31 to 60	61 to 90	91+
Laurie Snyder							
567	2/27/97	Invoice	435.00	435.00	—	—	—
Pat Young							
789	2/25/97	Invoice	112.00	112.00	—	—	—
			547.00	547.00	—	—	—

Open the Company Data Files

1. Click on the Start button. Point to Programs; point to Simply Accounting; then click on Simply Accounting in the final menu presented. The Simply Accounting Open File dialog box will appear.

2. Insert your Student Data Files disk into disk drive A. Enter the following path into the **File name** text box: A:\student\mars.asc

3. Click on the **Open** button; enter 3/31/97 into the **Using Date for this Session** text box; then click on the **OK** button. Click on the **OK** button in response to the message "The date entered is more than one week past your previous **Using** date of 3/1/97." The Company Window for Mars will appear.

Add Your Name to the Company Name

4. Click on the Company Window Setup menu; then click on Company Information. The Company Information dialog box will appear. Insert your name in place of the text "Your Name" in the **Name** text box. Click on the **OK** button to return to the Company Window.

How to Record a Sale on Account

5. On March 1, 1997 sold merchandise to Kevin Tucker on account, $800, invoice no. 913, terms 2/10, n/30. Double-click on the Sales icon to open the Sales Journal dialog box. Note that the program automatically offers **Invoice** 913 as the invoice number for this transaction through the program's automatic invoice numbering feature. Click on the arrow button to the right of the **Sold to** text box to display a list of customers; then click on Kevin Tucker. Note that the company's standard payment terms of 2/10, n/30 are presented. Highlight the **Date** text box; enter 3/1/97; then press the TAB key until the insertion point is positioned in the **Amount** text box. Enter 800; then press the TAB key. The flashing insertion point will move to the **Acct** text box. Press the ENTER key to display the Select Account dialog box; then select 4110 Sales. Your screen should look like this:

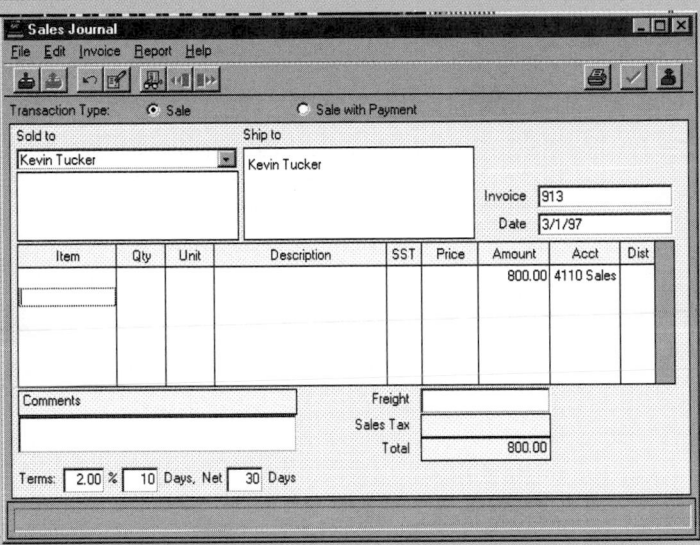

How to Review a Sales Journal Entry

6. Before posting this transaction, you need to verify that the transaction data are correct by reviewing the journal entry. To review the entry, click on the Sales Journal Report menu; then click on Display Sales Journal Entry. The journal entry representing the data you have recorded in the Sales Journal dialog box is displayed. Review the journal entry for accuracy noting any errors. Note that the program has automatically debited the accounts receivable account through its integration feature.

How to Edit a Sales or Purchases Journal Entry Prior to Posting

7. Close the Sales Journal Entry window. If you have made an error, use the following editing techniques to correct the error:

Editing a Sales or Purchases Journal Entry

◆ Move to the text box that contains the error by either pressing the TAB key to move forward through each text box or the SHIFT and TAB keys together to move to a previous text box. This will highlight the selected text box information so that you can change it. Alternatively, you can use the mouse to point to a text box and drag through the incorrect information to highlight it.

◆ Type the correct information; then press the TAB key to enter it.

◆ If you have associated the transaction with an the incorrect customer or vendor, reselect the correct customer or vendor from the customer or vendor list display after clicking on the arrow button to the right of the **Sold to** text box (customers) or **Purchased From** text box (vendors).

◆ If you have associated a transaction with an incorrect account, double-click on the incorrect account; then select the correct account from the Select Account dialog box. This will replace the incorrect account with the correct account.

◆ To discard an entry and start over, click on the close button. Click on the **Yes** button in response to the question "Are you sure you want to discard this journal entry?"

◆ Review the journal entry for accuracy after any editing corrections.

◆ **It is IMPORTANT TO NOTE that the only way to edit a journal entry after it is posted is to reverse the entry and enter the correct journal entry.** To correct journal entries posted in error, see Part C of the Computerized Accounting appendix at the back of this book.

How to Post a Sales Journal Entry

8. After verifying that the journal entry is correct, click on the **Post** icon to post this transaction. A blank Sales Journal dialog box is displayed, ready for additional Sales Journal transactions to be recorded.

How to Record a Credit Memo

9. On March 5, 1997 issued credit memorandum no. 14 to Kevin Tucker for returned merchandise that cost $50. Click on the arrow button to the right of the **Sold to** text box; then click on Kevin Tucker. Highlight the **Invoice** text box; enter Cm 14; then press the TAB key. Enter 3/5/97 into the **Date** text box; then press the TAB key until the insertion point is positioned in the **Amount** text box. Enter − 50 (don't forget the minus sign!); then press the TAB key. The flashing insertion point will move to the **Acct** text box. Press the ENTER key to display the Select Account dialog box; then select 4120 Sales Returns and Allowances. Your screen should look like this:

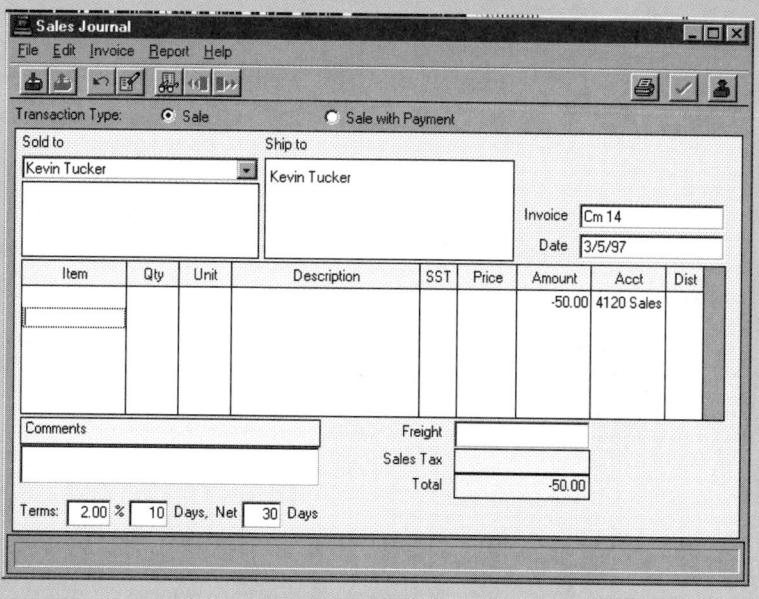

Review the Entry

10. Click on the Sales Journal Report menu; then click on Display Sales Journal Entry. Review the journal entry for accuracy noting any errors. Note that the program has automatically credited the accounts receivable account through its integration feature.

11. Close the Sales Journal Entry window; then make any editing corrections required.

Post the entry

12. After verifying that the journal entry is correct, click on the **Post** icon to post this transaction; then close the Sales Journal dialog box.

How to Record a Cash Receipt from a Credit Customer

13. On March 7, 1997 received check no. 1634 from Kevin Tucker in the amount of $735 in payment of invoice no. 913 ($800), dated March 1, less credit memorandum no. 14 ($50), less 2 percent discount ($16 − 1 = $15 net sales discount).

    Open the Receipts Journal dialog box by double-clicking on the Receipts Journal icon. Click on the arrow button to the right of the **From** text box; click on Kevin Tucker; then press the TAB key. Enter 1634 into the **No.** text box; then press the TAB key. Enter 3/7/97 into the **Date** text box; then press the TAB key. Click in the **Disc. Taken** field for invoice no. 913; click in the **Payment Amt.** field for invoice no. 913; click in the **Disc. Taken** field for Cm 14; click in the **Payment Amt.** field for Cm 14; then press the TAB key. Your screen should look like the one at the top of page 395.

How to Review a Receipts Journal Entry

14. Before posting this transaction, you need to verify that the transaction data are correct by reviewing the journal entry. To review the entry, click on the Receipts Journal Report menu; then click on Display Receipts Journal Entry. The journal entry representing the data you have recorded in the Receipts Journal dialog box is displayed. Review the journal entry for accuracy noting any errors. Note that the program has automatically debited the cash and sales

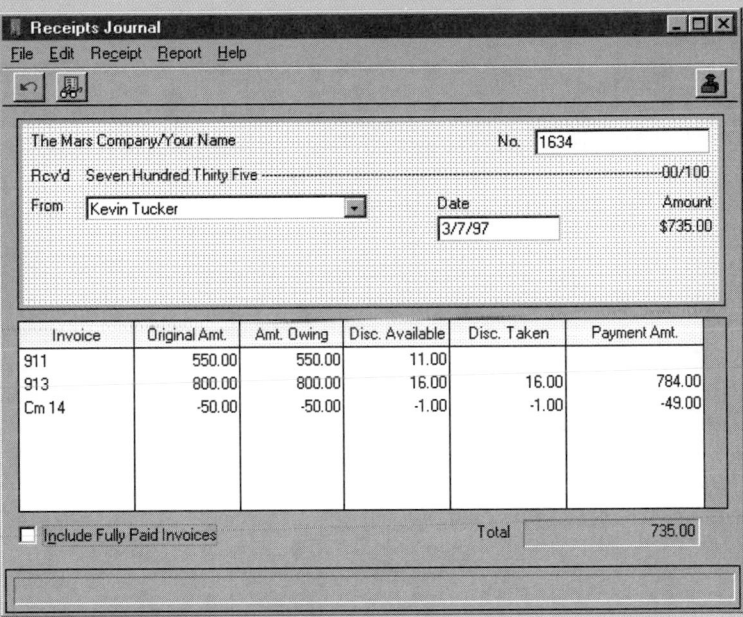

discounts accounts and credited the accounts receivable account through its integration feature.

How to Edit a Receipts or Payments Journal Entry Prior to Posting

15. Close the Receipts Journal Entry window. If you have made an error, use the following editing techniques to correct the error:

Editing a Receipts or Payments Journal Entry

◆ Move to the text box that contains the error by either pressing the TAB key to move forward through each text box or the SHIFT and TAB keys together to move to a previous text box. This will highlight the selected text box information so that you can change it. Alternatively, you can use the mouse to point to a text box and drag through the incorrect information to highlight it.

◆ Type the correct information; then press the TAB key to enter it.

◆ If you have associated the transaction with an incorrect customer or vendor, re-select the correct customer or vendor from the customer or vendor list display after clicking on the arrow button to the right of the **From** text box (customers) or **To the Order of** text box (vendors). You will be asked to confirm that you want to discard the current transaction. Click on the **Yes** button to discard the incorrect entry and display the outstanding invoices for the correct customer or vendor.

◆ To discard an entry and start over, click on the close button. Click on the **Yes** button in response to the question "Are you sure you want to discard this journal entry?"

◆ Review the journal entry for accuracy after any editing corrections.

◆ **It is IMPORTANT TO NOTE that the only way to edit a journal entry after it is posted is to reverse the entry and enter the correct journal entry.** To correct journal entries posted in error, see Part C of the Computerized Accounting appendix at the back of this book.

How to Post a Receipts Journal Entry

16. After verifying that the journal entry is correct, click on the **Post** icon to post this transaction. A blank Receipts Journal dialog box is displayed, ready for additional Receipts Journal transactions to be recorded. Close the Receipts Journal dialog box.

How to Record a Purchase on Account

17. On March 15, 1997 purchased merchandise from Pat Young on account, $275, invoice no. 796, terms 3/15, n/30. Double-click on the Purchases icon to open the Purchases Journal dialog box. Click on the arrow button to the right of the **Purchased from** text box; then click on Pat Young. Note that Pay Young's stan-

dard payment terms of 3/15, n/30 are presented. Click on the **Invoice** text box; enter 796; then press the TAB key. Enter 3/15/97 into the **Date** text box; then press the TAB key until the insertion point is positioned in the **Amount** text box. Enter 275; then press the TAB key. The flashing insertion point will move to the **Acct** text box. Press the ENTER key to display the Select Account dialog box; then select 5100 Purchases. Your screen should look like this:

How to Review a Purchases Journal Entry

18. Before posting this transaction, you need to verify that the transaction data are correct by reviewing the journal entry. To review the entry, click on the Purchases Journal Report menu; then click on Display Purchases Journal Entry. The journal entry representing the data you have recorded in the Purchases Journal dialog box is displayed. Review the journal entry for accuracy noting any errors. Note that the program has automatically credited the accounts payable account through its integration feature.

19. Close the Purchases Journal Entry window; then make any editing corrections required.

How to Post a Purchases Journal Entry

20. After verifying that the journal entry is correct, click on the **Post** icon to post this transaction. A blank Purchases Journal dialog box is displayed, ready for additional Purchases Journal transactions to be recorded.

How to Record a Debit Memo

21. On March 17, 1997 returned merchandise to Pat Young in the amount of $75. Issued debit memorandum no. 27. Click on the arrow button to the right of the **Purchased From** text box; then click on Pat Young. Click on the **Invoice** text box; enter Dm 27; then press the TAB key. Enter 3/17/97 into the **Date** text box; then press the TAB key until the insertion point is positioned in the **Amount** text box. Enter − 75 (don't forget the minus sign!); then press the TAB key. The flashing insertion point will move to the **Acct** text box. Press the ENTER key to display the Select Account dialog box; then select 5120 Purchase Returns and Allowances. Your screen should look like the one at the top of page 397.

Review the Entry

22. Click on the Purchases Journal Report menu; then click on Display Purchases Journal Entry. Review the journal entry for accuracy noting any errors. Note that the program has automatically debited the accounts payable account through its integration feature.

23. Close the Purchases Journal Entry window; then make any editing corrections required.

Post the Entry

24. After verifying that the journal entry is correct, click on the **Post** icon to post this transaction; then close the Purchases Journal dialog box.

How to Record a Cash Payment to a Credit Vendor

25. On March 25, 1997 issued check no. 437 to Pat Young in the amount of $194 in payment of invoice no. 796 ($275), dated March 15, less debit memorandum

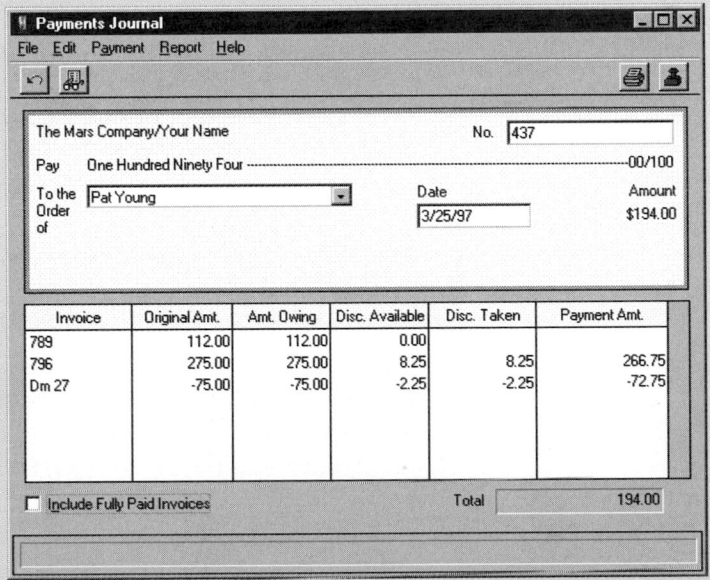

no. 27 ($75), less 3 percent discount ($8.25 − 2.25 = $6 net purchases discount).

Open the Payments Journal dialog box by double-clicking on the Payments icon. Click on the arrow button to the right of the **To the Order of** text box; click on Pat Young; then press the TAB key. Enter 437 into the **No.** text box; then press the TAB key. (The program has offered a default check **No.** of 435 which is the next check number in the program's automatic check numbering sequence. However, since certain cash payments are recorded in the General Journal and the checks used are not recorded in the Payments Journal the check **No.** needs to be advanced to the next check number in The Mars Company's checkbook.) Enter 3/25/97 into the **Date** text box; then press the TAB key. Click in the **Disc. Taken** field for invoice no. 796; click in the **Payment Amt.** field for invoice no. 796; click in the **Disc. Taken** field for Dm 27; click in the **Payment Amt.** field for Dm 27; then press the TAB key. Your screen should look like this:

How to Review a Payments Journal Entry

26. Before posting this transaction, you need to verify that the transaction data are correct by reviewing the journal entry. To review the entry, click on the Payments Journal Report menu; then click on Display Payments Journal Entry. The journal entry representing the data you have recorded in the Payments Journal dialog box is displayed. Review the journal entry for accuracy noting any

errors. Note that the program has automatically debited the accounts payable account and credited the cash and purchases discount accounts through its integration feature.

27. Close the Payments Journal Entry window; then make any editing corrections required.

How to Post a Payments Journal Entry

28. After verifying that the journal entry is correct, click on the **Post** icon to post this transaction. A blank Payments Journal dialog box is displayed, ready for additional Payments Journal transactions to be recorded. Close the Payments Journal dialog box.

How to Display and Print a Customer Aged Detail Report

29. Click on the Company Window Reports menu; point to Receivables; then click on Customer Aged. The Customer Aged Report Options dialog box will appear asking you to define the information you want displayed. Click on the **Detail** option button, click on the **Select All** button; leave the As at date set at 3/31/97; then click on the **OK** button. Click on the Customer Aged Detail File menu; then click on Print to print the report.

How to Display and Print a Vendor Aged Detail Report

30. Close the Customer Aged Detail window; click on the Company Window Reports menu; point to Payables; then click on Vendor Aged. The Vendor Aged Report Options dialog box will appear asking you to define the information you want displayed. Click on the **Detail** option button, click on the **Select All** button; leave the As at date set at 3/31/97; then click on the **OK** button. Click on the Vendor Aged Detail File menu; then click on Print to print the report.

Print Reports

31. Close the Vendor Aged Detail window, then print the following reports:
   a. General Journal (By posting date, All ledger entries, Start: 3/1/97, Finish: 3/31/97).
   b. General Ledger Report (Start: 3/1/97, Finish: 3/31/97, Select All).

   Note that by checking the **All Ledger Entries** check box in the General Journal Options dialog box, all transactions recorded in the Sales, Receipts, Purchases, and Payments Journals are reflected in the General Journal report.

   Review your printed reports. If you have made an error in a posted journal entry, see Part C (Reversing an Entry Made in the Sales Journal, Receipts Journal, Purchases Journal, or Payments Journal Dialog Box) of the Computerized Accounting appendix for information on how to correct the error.

Exit from the Program

32. Click on the Company Window File menu; then click on Exit to end the current work session and return to your Windows desktop.

Complete the Report Transmittal

33. Complete The Mars Company Report Transmittal located in Appendix A of your *Study Guide and Working Papers*.

PART B: Computerized Accounting Instructions for Abby's Toy House (Problem 10A-4)

Open the Company Data Files

1. Click on the Start button. Point to Programs; point to Simply Accounting; then click on Simply Accounting in the final menu presented. The Simply Accounting Open File dialog box will appear.

2. Insert your Student Data Files disk into disk drive A. Enter the following path into the **File name** text box: A:\student\abby.asc

3. Click on the **Open** button; enter 3/31/97 into the **Using Date for this Session** text box; then click on the **OK** button. Click on the **OK** button in response to the message "The date entered is more than one week past your previous **Using** date of 3/1/97." The Company Window for Abby will appear.

Add your Name to the Company Name

4. Click on the Company Window Setup menu; then click on Company Information. The Company Information dialog box will appear. Insert your name in place of the text "Your Name" in the **Name** text box. Click on the **OK** button to return to the Company Window.

5. Record the following transactions using the General, Sales, Receipts, Purchases, and Payments journals:

1997

March — 1 Abby Ellen invested $8,000 in the toy store. ✓

1 Paid three months' rent in advance, check no. 1, $3,000. ✓

2 Purchased merchandise from Earl Miller Company on account, $4,000, invoice no. 410, terms 2/10, n/30. ✓

3 Sold merchandise to Bill Burton on account, $1,000, invoice no. 1, terms 2/10, n/30. ✓

6 Sold merchandise to Jim Rex on account, $700, invoice no. 2, terms 2/10, n/30. ✓

9 Purchased merchandise from Earl Miller Co. on account, $1,200, invoice no. 415, terms 2/10, n/30. ✓

9 Sold merchandise to Bill Burton on account, $600, invoice no. 3, terms 2/10, n/30.

9 Paid cleaning service $300, check no. 2.

10 Jim Rex returned merchandise that cost $300 to Abby's Toy House. Abby issued credit memorandum no. 1 to Jim Rex for $300.

11 Purchased merchandise from Minnie Katz on account, $4,000, invoice no. 311, terms 1/15, n/60.

12 Issued check no. 3 to Earl Miller Co. in the amount of $3,920 in payment of invoice no. 410 ($4,000), dated March 2, less 2 percent discount ($80). (*Note:* Use the DELETE key to remove amounts in the **Disc. Taken** and **Payment Amt.** fields that do not apply to this payment.)

13 Sold $1,300 of toy merchandise for cash. (*Reminder:* Cash sales are recorded in the General Journal.) ✓

13 Paid salaries, $600, check no. 4.

14 Returned merchandise to Minnie Katz in the amount of $1,000. Abby's Toy House issued debit memorandum no. 1 to Minnie Katz.

15 Sold merchandise for $4,000 cash. (*Reminder:* Cash sales are recorded in the General Journal.)

16 Received check no. 9823 from Jim Rex in the amount of $392 in payment of invoice no. 2 ($700), dated March 6, less credit memorandum no. 1 ($300), less 2 percent discount ($14 − 6 = $8 net sales discount).

16 Received check no. 4589 from Bill Burton in the amount of $1,000 in payment of invoice no. 1, dated March 2. (*Note:* Use the DELETE key to remove amounts in the **Disc. Taken** and **Payment Amt.** fields that do not apply to this payment.)

16 Sold toy merchandise to Amy Rose on account, $4,000, invoice no. 4, terms 2/10, n/30.

21 Purchased delivery truck on account from Sam Katz Garage, $3,000, invoice no. 111, (no discount). (*Reminder:* Purchases of merchandise and other items on account are recorded in the Purchases Journal.)

22 Sold to Bill Burton merchandise on account, $900, invoice no. 5, terms 2/10, n/30.

23 Issued check no. 5 to Minnie Katz in the amount of $2,970 in payment of invoice no. 311 ($4,000), dated March 11, less debit memorandum no. 1 ($1,000), less 1 percent discount ($40 − 10 = $30 net purchases discount).

24 Sold toy merchandise on account to Amy Rose, $1,100, invoice no. 6, terms 2/10, n/30.

25 Purchased toy merchandise, $600, check no. 6. (*Reminder:* Cash purchases are recorded in the General Journal.)

27 Purchased toy merchandise from Woody Smith on account, $4,800, invoice no. 211, terms 2/10, n/30.

28 Received check no. 4598 from Bill Burton in the amount of $882 in

payment of invoice no. 5 ($900), dated March 22, less 2 percent discount ($18).

28 Received check no. 3217 from Amy Rose in the amount of $1,078 in payment of invoice no. 6, dated March 24, less 2 percent discount ($22).

28 Abby invested an additional $5,000 in the business.

29 Purchased merchandise from Earl Miller Co., $1,400, invoice no. 436, terms 2/10, n/30.

30 Issued check no. 7 to the Earl Miller Co. in the amount of $1,372 in payment of invoice no. 436 ($1,400), dated March 29, less 2 percent discount ($28).

30 Sold merchandise to Bonnie Flow Company on account, $3,000 invoice no. 7, terms 2/10, n/30.

Print Reports

6. Print the following reports:

   a. Customer Aged report As at 3/31/97 (Detail, Select All).

   b. Vendor Aged report As at 3/31/97 (Detail, Select All).

   c. General Journal (By posting date, All ledger entries, Start: 3/1/97, Finish: 3/31/97).

   d. General Ledger Report (Start: 3/1/97, Finish: 3/31/97, Select All).

Review your printed reports. If you have made an error in a posted journal entry, see Part C of the Computerized Accounting appendix at the back of this book for information on how to correct the error.

Exit from the Program

7. Click on the Company Window File menu; then click on Exit to end the current work session and return to your Windows desktop.

Complete the Report Transmittal

8. Complete The Abby's Toy House Report Transmittal located in Appendix A of your *Study Guide and Working Papers*.

11

THE COMBINED JOURNAL

THE BIG PICTURE

The Eldorado Computer Center continues to grow in sales and profit. Tony Freedman met one of his objectives by keeping accurate detailed records in the specialized journals. However, he found the use of so many specialized journals increased his accounting time significantly. It was just not efficient. This month he decided to try a different specialized journal that he hopes will help him accomplish both objectives.

The combined journal replaces the use of all special journals and the general journal. It is similar to an accounting worksheet and can be used in a spreadsheet format on computer. Since Freedman is the only one who handles the day-to-day accounting for the business, he can tailor this journal to his exact business needs.

In this chapter you will learn to use a combined journal. You will also learn the difference between keeping the books using cash basis of accounting, modified cash, or accrual basis of accounting. Many businesses will use the cash basis if they operate as a service company offering no credit and handling no inventory. Freedman keeps his books under the accrual system, since he has inventory for resale, offers credit terms to his customers, and makes purchases for the computer center on credit himself. No system is better than the other. The best choice simply depends on the nature of the business.

Accrual accounting:

◆ earning revenue

◆ incurred expenses

Cash accounting:

◆ cash received

◆ cash paid

Many service companies will use the cash method if they have no inventories.

In the first ten chapters of this text, we used general journals and special journals to record business transactions. Often, students want to know how to set up journals for their own small business. They feel that the general journals are too simple and special journals are too detailed.

The solution is a combined journal. A combined journal is a special journal that replaces the general journal and other special journals. It has the same basic features as other special journals. Combined journals are an option for small businesses that do not have many transactions. Lawyers, doctors, dentists, and other professionals may use a combined journal, which may be modified in many ways to suit their individual needs. If the volume of transactions increases, more specialized journals may be required. For example, if a company adds bookkeepers to its accounting department, management must be prepared to provide a system of dividing the work to be done. This division of labor may play an important part in determining the types of special journals that are needed.

Before we can discuss combined journals, however, we must first learn the difference between cash basis accounting and accrual basis accounting.

The *accrual basis of accounting* is based on the matching principle, which says that revenue is recorded when it is earned (not when the money actually comes in), and expenses are recorded when they are incurred (not when they are paid). Companies often choose the accrual basis because they want to show earned revenue along with the expenses that were incurred to earn that revenue. All of the businesses we have discussed so far used accrual basis accounting.

In the *cash basis of accounting*, revenue is recorded when cash is received, and expenses are recorded when they are paid. Service companies use the cash basis because it is simpler and more convenient. Companies with inventory do not use this method. Also, if this accounting method is used, the revenue and expenses may not show up in the same accounting period.

Let's look at the difference between accrual and cash basis with the following example: John Mills earned real estate commissions of $100,000, of which he received $60,000 in cash. He incurred $25,000 in expenses. Of that amount, $10,000 was paid in cash.

COMPARISON OF CASH BASIS WITH ACCRUAL BASIS
FOR MONTH OF JULY 19XX

Cash Basis		Accrual Basis	
Revenue (received)	$60,000	Revenue (earned)	$100,000
Expenses (paid)	10,000	Expenses (incurred)	25,000
Net income	$50,000	Net income	$ 75,000

Note how net income differs according to which system is used.

LEARNING UNIT 11-1
Combined Journal: A Modified Cash System for a Professional or Business Service Company

This learning unit focuses on Dr. Gary Wheeler, a dentist who uses a modified cash system in his professional service company. He wanted to use a strictly cash-basis system, but his accountant told him that doing so would distort his financial reports and violate IRS guidelines. The accountant said that the best system for a dentist is the **modified cash-basis** or **hybrid method,** which is a combination of the cash and accrual methods. Many professional services (e.g., attorneys, doctors, dentists, architects, etc.) and business services (e.g., real estate, insurance, dry cleaning, etc.) use this method.

Using the modified cash basis, Dr. Wheeler will record professional fees and his expenses when cash is received. Long-lived assets (equipment, building, etc.) are depreciated (i.e., the amount paid for these items are not treated as expense of just that period). For example, Dr. Wheeler must depreciate (or allocate) the cost of his dental equipment over a period of years. These items are treated the same way under cash and accrual accounting. Insurance premiums and purchases of a large amount of supplies are treated the same under cash and accrual accounting. This means that the amount consumed or used up is shown as an expense in the current year and that the amount on hand is carried over into the next accounting period.

These exceptions require adjusting entries.

Chart of Accounts

The chart of accounts for Dr. Wheeler is shown in Figure 11-1. Note that, unlike a chart of accounts on the accrual basis, there are no categories for Accounts Receivable, Accounts Payable, or Salaries Payable. This chart of accounts does have titles for handling the exceptions (for example, Accumulated Depreciation, Prepaid Insurance, etc.). There is no supplies account under assets, since Dr. Wheeler is *not* buying a large amount of supplies, and thus all will be shown as Dental Supplies Expense without distorting the financial reports.

The transactions that occurred for the month of November are listed below:

Transactions for Dr. Wheeler

19XX
Nov.
1 Paid $200 office rent for November, check no. 61.
1 Received checks for $3,000 from patients for dental work.
4 Paid telephone bill, $80, check no. 62.
4 Issued check no. 63 to Bill Blan Insurance Agency for premium on insurance for three years, $600.
7 Purchased dental supplies from Roe Suppliers, $150, check no. 64.
8 Received checks from patients, $1,600.
8 Calculated current cash balance.
11 Issued check no. 65 to Moe Gas for automobile expenses charged during October, $80.
11 Dr. Wheeler withdrew $500 for personal use, check no. 66.
14 Issued check no. 67 to V. P. Suppliers Company for dental supplies charged during October, $250.
15 Paid office salaries for the period Nov. 1 to Nov. 15, $2,000, check no. 68.
15 Cash receipts from patients totaled $2,800 for the week.

Dr. Wheeler
Chart of Accounts

Assets
111   Cash
113   Petty Cash Fund
131   Prepaid Insurance
141   Office Furniture
142   Accum. Dep., Office Furniture
151   Dental Equipment
152   Accum. Dep., Dental Equipment
161   Auto
162   Accum. Dep., Auto

Liabilities
211   FICA—Social Security Payable
212   FICA—Medicare Payable
213   Federal Income Tax Payable
214   Notes Payable

Owner's Equity
311   G. Wheeler, Capital
312   G. Wheeler, Withdrawals
313   Income Summary

Revenue
411   Professional Fees

Expenses
511   Automobile Expense
512   Rent Expense
513   Salaries Expense
514   Telephone Expense
515   Dep. Exp., Office Furniture
516   Dep. Exp., Dental Equipment
517   Dep. Exp., Auto
518   Miscellaneous Expense
519   Insurance Expense
520   Dental Supplies Expense
521   Payroll Tax Expense

FIGURE 11-1 Chart of Accounts

15   Calculated current cash balance.
19   Collected $800 from insurance companies for patients' accounts.
21   Purchased dental supplies from J. Labs, $200, check no. 69.
22   Cash receipts for the week totaled $2,900.
22   Calculated current cash balance.
27   Issued check no. 70 for charitable contributions, $300.
27   Purchased dental supplies from J. Labs, $100, check no. 71.
28   Received checks from patients' insurance companies totaling $3,300.
29   Paid office salaries for the period November 15 to November 30, $1,500, check no. 72.
30   Calculated current cash balance and crossfooted journal.

Monthly Transactions

These transactions are recorded in the **combined journal**—the special journal that replaces the general journal. The combined journal has the same basic features as other special journals that we introduced in Chapters 9 and 10. Each business designs the headings of the combined journal to fit its individual needs. Accounts that are used most often are the ones that should have a special column. This saves time in journalizing and posting.

RECORDING TRANSACTIONS IN THE COMBINED JOURNAL

The combined journal for Dr. Wheeler is shown in Figure 11-2 (p. 405). Note that the bank balance can be calculated at any time. For example, in the

FIGURE 11-2 The Combined Journal

DR. WHEELER
COMBINED JOURNAL

Month: November

Cash Deposits Dr.	Checks Cr.	Check No.	Date 19XX Nov.		Explanation	PR	Sundry Dr.	Sundry Cr.	Prof. Fees Cr.	Dental Supplies Expense Dr.
					Cash Balance *end of month* 9,500					
	2000 00	61		1	Rent Expense	512	2000 00			
3000 00				1	Professional Fees *end of month*	X			3000 00	
	800 00	62		4	Telephone Expense	514	800 00			
	600 00	63		4	Prepaid Insurance	131	600 00			
	150 00	64		7	Roe Suppliers	X				150 00
1600 00				8	Professional Fees 13,070	X			1600 00	
	800 00	65		11	Auto. Exp.	511	800 00			
	500 00	66		11	G. Wheeler, Withdrawals	312	500 00			
	250 00	67		14	V.P. Suppliers	X				250 00
	2000 00	68		15	Salaries Expense	513	2000 00			
2800 00				15	Professional Fees 13,040	X			2800 00	
800 00				19	Professional Fees	X			800 00	
	200 00	69		21	J. Labs	X				200 00
2900 00				22	Professional Fees 16,540	X			2900 00	
	300 00	70		27	Miscellaneous Expense	518	300 00			
	100 00	71		27	J. Labs	X				100 00
3300 00				28	Professional Fees	X			3300 00	
	1500 00	72		29	Salaries Expense 17,940	513	1500 00			
14400 00	5960 00						5260 00		14400 00	700 00
(111)	(111)						(X)		(411)	(520)

$20,360 = $20,360

Post at ē end of month.

don't post

Post at ē end of month.

explanation column, note the beginning balance of $9,500. On Nov. 8 the current balance was calculated as follows:

Beg. Balance	$ 9,500
+ Deposits	4,600
− Checks written	1,030
Ending Balance	$13,070 ← recorded in explanation column

This combined journal is proved this way:

	Dr.	Cr.
Cash	$14,400	$ 5,960
Sundry	5,260	
Professional Fees		14,400
Dental Sup. Exp.	700	
	$20,360	$20,360

Proving the journal. This is the same method that is used for proving special journals. The sum of all the debit columns should equal the sum of all the credit columns.

Memorandum records can be used in a modified cash system.

POSTING THE COMBINED JOURNAL

Since this is a modified cash system, there are no subsidiary ledgers for accounts receivable or accounts payable. Companies using a modified cash basis usually keep information about any receivables or payables in an informal memorandum record until cash is received or paid. During the month, items entered into the sundry column can be updated in the general ledger. At end of month the totals of Cash, Professional Fees, and Dental Supplies Expense would be posted to the general ledger. The account numbers are shown at the bottom of the columns of the combined journal to show that the totals were posted. The (X) means that no posting is necessary. The total of the sundry column is not posted.

RECORDING PAYROLL DEDUCTIONS AND EMPLOYER'S TAX EXPENSE

Back in Chapters 7 and 8 we studied payroll. The payroll register recorded gross pay, deductions, and net pay. A general journal entry is prepared from the payroll register to record the payroll. We also discussed using a general journal to record the employer's payroll tax expense before it is paid (for FICA – Social Security Payable, FICA – Medicare Payable, FUTA, and SUTA). The recordkeeping involved in paying an employee is similar in a combined journal using the cash-basis method, but the employer's payroll tax expense is recorded differently.

This is because the owner's share of Social Security, Medicare, FUTA, and SUTA are recorded when they are paid under the cash basis method. In accrual accounting they are recorded when they are incurred.

Let's look at a partially completed combined journal on page 407 and explain each entry. For simplicity we are ignoring the deposit requirements for quarterly reports that we covered in the payroll chapters.

(A) Bill Smith's gross salary of $500 is recorded as a salary expense, and the deductions for FICA – Social Security, FICA – Medicare, and FIT are listed as liabilities until the employer makes the deposit. Note that the check is written for $371.75 (net pay). The same procedure is followed for Joe Ring.

(B) On June 3 the deposit for the quarterly Form 941 is assumed made. This means the employer pays the FICA (SS and Med.) for the employee as well as the employer's matching share, along with the FIT taken out of the employees' paychecks.

COMBINED JOURNAL

	Voe Bank Deposits Dr.	Checks Cr.	Check No.	Date	Accounts or Explanations	PR	Sundry Dr.	Sundry Cr.	Professional Fees Cr.	Salary Expense Dr.	FICA SS. Cr.	FICA Med. Cr.	Fed. Inc. Tax Payable Cr.
(A)		371 75	33	May 5	Bill Smith	x				500 00	31 00	7 25	90 00
		227 05	34	5	Joe Ring	x				300 00	18 60	4 35	50 00
(B)		262 40	50	June 3	Employee FIT Payable	211	140 00						
					FICA Soc. Sec. Payable	211	49 60						
					FICA-Medicare Payable	212	11 60						
					Payroll Tax Expense	612	61 20						

The payroll tax expense is now being recorded for the employer's FICA share of Social Security and Medicare since it is now being paid.

The payroll tax expense is now being recorded for the employer's FICA share of Social Security and Medicare since it is now being paid. Note that the check amount is for $262.40, which includes the total of the following three taxes:

Federal Income Tax Payable	140.00
FICA — Social Security Payable	49.60
FICA — Medicare Payable	11.60
This is employer's FICA share for Social Security and Medicare → Payroll Tax Expense	61.20

The end result is to reduce the three liabilities owed as well as record the employer's share of FICA for Social Security and Medicare as payroll tax expense. When FUTA or SUTA tax is *paid,* the employer's payroll tax expense will be recorded for these taxes.

In summary:

WHEN FICA TAX AND FEDERAL INCOME TAX PAID

Employee Fed. Inc. Tax Payable	
FICA—Social Security Payable	
FICA—Medicare Payable	
Payroll Tax Expense	
Cash	

WHEN FUTA TAX OR SUTA TAX PAID

Payroll Tax Expense	
Cash	

Some systems will record the FICA portion of the employer when the payroll is paid, instead of when the FICA tax deposit is made. Then when the deposit is made they will record the entry as follows:

Fed. Inc. Tax Payable	
FICA—Social Security Payable	
FICA—Medicare Payable	
Cash	

LEARNING UNIT 11-1 REVIEW

AT THIS POINT you should be able to

◆ Explain the modified cash basis of accounting. (p. 403)
◆ Journalize transactions into a combined journal. (p. 405)
◆ Calculate the current bank balance of a combined journal. (p. 406)
◆ Prove a combined journal. (p. 406)
◆ Explain how to record payroll as well as payroll tax expense into a combined journal. (p. 406)

SELF-REVIEW QUIZ 11-1

(The forms you need are on page 380 of the *Study Guide and Working Papers.*)
Answer true or false to the following:

1. A modified cash system will only have one exception, long-lived assets, in the adjustment process.

LEARNING UNIT 11-2
Combined Journal for Art's Wholesale Clothing Company

In Chapters 9 and 10, we developed the sales journal, cash receipts journal, purchases journal, cash payments journal, and general journal for Art's Wholesale Clothing Company. However, many small businesses that are concerned with saving journalizing, recording, and posting labor only have one bookkeeper. Such businesses are likely to want the advantages provided by special journals but would like to reduce the number of journals needed. This unit will develop a combined journal, a book of original entry, that dispenses with the special journals, yet gains their advantages in journalizing, recording, and posting for a company that uses an accrual accounting approach.

Note: In order to focus on the combined journal here, we will save specific details of payroll for Chapter 13.

Our goal in this unit is to place all the special journals for Art's Wholesale Clothing Company into the following combined journal:

COMBINED JOURNAL																
												Month: April				Page 1
Date	Explanation	Check No.	PR	Sundry Dr.	Cr.	Cash Dr.	Cr.	Acct. Rec. Dr.	Cr.	Acct. Pay. Dr.	Cr.	Sales Cr.	Sales Dis. Dr.	Pur. Dr.	Pur. Dis. Cr.	

Note that since Art uses accrual *accounting, we now have columns for Accounts Receivable and Accounts Payable.*

The first thing Art and his accountant must do is go over the chart of accounts. Their goal would be to set up columns in the combined journal for accounts in which transactions would occur frequently. In the case of Art's Wholesale Clothing Company, the following special columns would be needed:

◆ *Cash Dr.:* Used to record increases in cash.

◆ *Cash Cr.:* Used to record decreases in cash.

◆ *Accounts Receivable Dr.:* Used to record amounts owed from sales on account.

◆ *Accounts Receivable Cr.:* Used to record amounts paid by customers from past sales on account.

◆ *Accounts Payable Dr.:* Used to record amounts paid to creditors.

◆ *Accounts Payable Cr.:* Used to record amounts owed to creditors.

◆ *Sales Cr.:* Used to record all sales made for cash or on account.

◆ *Sales Discount Dr.:* Used to record the amounts of discounts taken by customers.

◆ *Purchases Dr.:* Used to record all purchases of merchandise for resale.

ART'S WHOLESALE CLOTHING COMPANY
COMBINED JOURNAL

Date	Explanation	Ck. No.	PR	Sundry Dr.	Sundry Cr.	Cash Dr.	Cash Cr.	Accounts Receivable Dr.	Accounts Receivable Cr.
19XX Apr. 1	Art Newner, Cap.		311		800000	800000			
2	Prepaid Ins.	1	116	90000			90000		
3	Hal's Clothing		✔					80000	
3	Freight-In, Abby Blake		512 ✔	5000					
4	Equip., Joe Francis		121 ✔	400000					
4	Hal's Clothing		✔			78400			80000
6	Thorpe Co.		✔						
6	Bevans Co.		✔					160000	
7	J. Francis Co.	2	✔				400000		
7	J. Sullivan Co.		✔						
9	Purchases	3	✘				80000		
9	Pur. R&A, Thorpe Co.		514 ✔		20000				
12	Thorpe Co.	4	✔				59400		
12	Sales R&A, Bevans Co.		412 ✔	60000					60000
12	Abby Blake Co.		✔						
15	Cash Sales		✘			90000			
16	Bevans Co.		✔			98000			100000
18	Roe Co.		✔					200000	
22	Roe Co.		✔			196000			200000
24	Roe Co.		✔					50000	
25	Sup., J. Sullivan		115 ✔	50000					
27	Store Equip.		121		50000	50000			
28	Salaries Expense	5	611	70000			70000		
28	Mel's Dept. St.		✔					90000	
29	Mel's Dept. St.		✔					70000	
30	Cash Sales		✘			120000			
	Totals			675000	870000	1432400	699400	650000	440000
				(X)	(X)	(111)	(111)	(113)	(113)

FIGURE 11-3 Combined Journal Completed

Proving the accuracy of the combined journal.

Account Title	Dr.	Cr.
Sundry	$ 675000	$ 870000
Cash	1432400	699400
Accounts Receivable	650000	440000
Accounts Payable	480000	1193000
Sales		860000
Sales Discount	7600	
Purchases	818000	
Purchases Discount		600
Totals	$4063000	$4063000

	Accounts Payable		Sales Cr.	Sales Discount Dr.	Purchases Dr.	Purchases Discount Cr.
	Dr.	Cr.				
			800 00			
		5050 00			5000 00	
		4000 00				
				16 00		
		800 00			800 00	
			1600 00			
	4000 00					
		980 00			980 00	
					800 00	
	200 00					
	600 00					6 00
		600 00			600 00	
			900 00			
				20 00		
			2000 00			
				40 00		
			500 00			
		500 00				
			900 00			
			700 00			
			1200 00			
	4800 00	11930 00	8600 00	76 00	8180 00	6 00
	(211)	(211)	(411)	(413)	(511)	(513)

Month: April

FIGURE 11-3 (cont.)

◆ *Purchases Discount Cr.:* Used to record the amounts of discounts Art receives by paying for purchases before the discount period expires.
◆ *Sundry Dr., Cr.:* Used to record transactions that do not occur very frequently. If a transaction occurs and no special columns are set up to record part or all of it, it can be recorded in the sundry columns.

Figure 11-3 (pp. 410–411) shows the completed combined journal for the month of April for Art's Wholesale Clothing Company. The combined journal can be proved as shown on the same page.

RECORDING AND POSTING THE COMBINED JOURNAL

The recording and posting rules we learned for Art's special journals will hold true for the combined journal. Here are some key points:

◆ (✓): Record to accounts receivable or accounts payable subsidiary ledgers daily.
◆ *Sundry:* Update the general ledger account on a daily basis. Use the ledger account number as a posting reference.

FIGURE 11-4 Combined Journal with Sales Tax Payable Column

COMBINED JOURNAL

Page 3

Date		Explanation	Ck. No.	PR	Sundry Dr.	Sundry Cr.	Cash Dr.	Cash Cr.	Acct. Rec. Dr.	Acct. Rec. Cr.	Acct. Pay.	Sales Cr.	Sales Tax Pay. Cr.
19XX May	1	Bill Jones		✓					105 00			100 00	5 00
	8	Alice Smith		✓					420 00			400 00	20 00
	31	Totals							945 00			900 00	45 00
									(12)			(41)	(23)

Recorded immediately to accounts receivable ledger.

Totals posted at end of the month to the general ledger.

CJ1 (Combined Journal, p. 1) will be placed in PR of ledger account, where information from journal is updated in ledger.

Adjusting and closing entries would be recorded in the sundry columns of a combined journal.

If a company has many sales returns and allowances a special column could be developed.

◆ An (X) in the PR column indicates no posting, since the total is posted at the end of the month. An (X) below the total means that the total of the column is not posted.

The total of each column except sundry will be posted to the general ledger at the end of the month. Note that the account number from the ledger is placed at the bottom of the column in the combined journal, indicating that the total was posted to that account.

Note the following when a combined journal is used:

1. Charge *and* cash sales are recorded in the sales column.
2. Purchases returns, sales returns, etc., are recorded in sundry, since no general journal is used with a combined journal.
3. Adjusting and closing entries will be recorded in the sundry columns.

Whether Art uses a combined journal or a set of special journals, the schedule of accounts receivable and accounts payable will be the same, as will the trial balance.

SPECIAL SITUATIONS

A sample of how a combined journal might look if it included Sales Tax Payable is shown in Figure 11-4. Note that the totals of accounts receivable, sales, and sales tax payable must be posted to the general ledger at the end of the month. Keep in mind that sales tax payable is a liability located on the general ledger.

LEARNING UNIT 11-2 REVIEW

AT THIS POINT you should be able to

◆ Journalize transactions into the combined journal for a merchandise company. (pp. 410–411)
◆ Explain how to record and post the combined journal. (p. 411)
◆ Compare special journals (cash payments, receipts, etc.) and the combined journal. (p. 411)
◆ Explain how sales tax could be recorded in a combined journal. (p. 413)

SELF-REVIEW QUIZ 11-2

(The forms you need are on page 380 of the *Study Guide and Working Papers.*)
Based on the combined journal presented in this unit, classify each statement as true or false.

1. Combined journals are less efficient than other types of special journals.
2. The total of the cash column is posted daily.
3. The total of the sundry column is not posted.
4. The total of the sales column is not posted.
5. All combined journals have the same headings.
6. Combined journals cannot be proved.
7. Subsidiary ledgers are posted from the cash column.
8. The combined journal is used for large companies.
9. A dentist could use a combined journal.
10. A lawyer will always use a combined journal.

Solution to Self-Review Quiz

1. False   2. False   3. True   4. False   5. False
6. False   7. False   8. False   9. True   10. False

SUMMARY OF KEY POINTS

Learning Unit 11-1

1. A company with inventory will not use the cash method.
2. The modified cash system is used because federal and state requirements make a strictly cash-basis system difficult to implement without distorting financial reports.
3. The modified cash system requires adjustments for depreciation, insurance premiums, and large amounts of supplies purchased. Adjustments are recorded in the sundry columns of the combined journal.
4. No accounts for Accounts Payable or Accounts Receivable are used in the chart of accounts for a modified cash system. Companies use memorandums to keep track of receivables or payables until money is received or paid.
5. The bank balance (cash balance) can be determined at any time when a combined journal is used.
6. A combined journal can be proved by crossfooting the totals to verify that total debits equal total credits.
7. The payroll tax expense for the employer using a cash-basis system is recorded when the tax is paid. There are in the cash-basis system no liability accounts for FUTA or SUTA; you record them when paid as part of Payroll Tax Expense.

Learning Unit 11-2

1. A combined journal for Art's Wholesale Clothing Company replaces the individual special journals (SJ, CRJ, PJ, CPJ, GJ).
2. Many small companies use a combined journal.
3. A combined journal on an accrual basis uses columns for accounts receivable and accounts payable. Subsidiary ledgers will be recorded during the month. The total of the sundry columns is not posted.
4. Adjusting and closing entries will be recorded in the sundry columns.

KEY TERMS

Combined journal A special journal that combines the features of the sales, cash payments, cash receipts, purchases, and general journals.

Modified cash-basis method (hybrid) The accounting method that records revenue when cash is received, and expenses when they are paid. Adjustments to long-lived assets, as well as insurance premiums and amounts of supplies on hand, are required by state and federal laws so that financial reports will not be distorted.

QUESTIONS, MINI EXERCISES, EXERCISES, AND PROBLEMS

Discussion Questions

1. All companies with inventory must use the cash basis of accounting. Agree or disagree.

BLUEPRINT OF A TYPICAL CHART OF ACCOUNTS FOR AN ATTORNEY USING A MODIFIED CASH BASIS (INCLUDING PAYROLL)

ASSETS

No Accounts Receivable account

Village National Bank	111
Petty Cash	112
Office Supplies	113
Prepaid Insurance	114
Office Equip.	115
Accum. Dep. Office Equip.	116
Automobiles	117
Accum. Dep., Auto	118

LIABILITIES

No Accounts Payable account

FICA — Social Security Payable	211	
FICA — Medicare Payable	212	For payroll, note no titles for FUTA or SUTA
Federal Income Tax Payable	213	
Notes Payable	214	

OWNER'S EQUITY

Jack Smith, Capital	311
Jack Smith, Withdrawals	312
Income Summary	313

REVENUE

Only recorded when cash received →

Professional Fees	411

EXPENSES

Dep. Exp., Office Equip.	511	
Dep. Exp., Auto	512	For adjustments so financial reports will not be distorted
Insurance Expense	513	
Office Supplies Expense	514	
Dues	515	
Postage	516	
Payroll Tax Expense	517	← Records the tax expense for employer when the Social Security, Medicare, FUTA, or SUTA is *paid*
Rent Expense	518	
Salary Expense	519	
Telephone Expense	520	
Miscellaneous Expense	521	

2. Why does the strictly cash basis tend to distort financial reports?

3. List three adjustments that may result in a modified cash system.

4. Explain how a company can change its method of accounting.

5. A modified cash system has an accounts receivable as well as accounts payable ledger. Agree or disagree. Please support your answer.

6. Explain how a cash balance can be calculated during the month when using a combined journal.

7. How is a combined journal proved?

8. Explain why there are no accounts for SUTA or FUTA in the chart of accounts in the cash basis.

9. What purpose would an informal memorandum serve when dealing with accounts payable and accounts receivable in a modified cash system?

10. Explain when the Payroll Tax Expense account will be updated in a modified cash system.

11. Explain how a combined journal for an accrual-based company will aid in reducing the number of special journals needed.

12. If a company is expanding, a combined journal could be efficient. Please respond.

Mini Exercises

(The forms you need are on page 382 of the *Study Guide and Working Papers*.)

Accounts Needing Adjustment

1. Which of the following titles may require adjusting entries using modified cash basis?

	Yes	No
Cash	_____	_____
Accounts Receivable	_____	_____
Equipment	_____	_____
Supplies	_____	_____
Accounts Payable	_____	_____
Salaries Payable	_____	_____
Accumulated Depreciation	_____	_____
Prepaid Insurance	_____	_____

Employees Deposit of Taxes

2. Using the modified cash basis the following balances have been found in the ledger: FIT, $250; FICA – SS Payable, $50; FICA – Medicare Payable, $70. Prepare a journal entry to record the employees deposit of these taxes along with the employees payroll tax expense.

SUTA Payment

3. Mel Blanc uses a modified cash basis system. He pays a SUTA tax of $150. Please record the general journal entry.

Combined Journal Headings

4. Match the following partial list of column headings of Pete Moore's combined journal to the statements below. Use only one number for each letter.
   1. Cash   Cr.
   2. Accounts Payable   Cr.
   3. Sales Discounts   Dr.
   4. Sundry   Dr./Cr.
   5. Sales   Cr.

   _____ a. Reflects amounts owed to creditors.
   _____ b. Records the amounts of discounts taken by customers.

      c. Records transactions that do not occur very often.

      d. Records sales made for cash or on account.

      e. Records decreases in cash.

Recording to Subsidiary Ledgers

5. Indicate which of the following transactions would result in a recording to a subsidiary ledger. The company uses a combined journal with an accrual accounting approach.

    a. Pete Daving invests $20,000 into the business.

    b. Sold $300 of merchandise to French Co. on account.

    c. Cash sales $200.

    d. Received half the amount owed by French from sales on account in **b.**

Exercises

(The forms you need are on page 383 of the *Study Guide and Working Papers.*)

Identifying adjustment titles for a modified cash system.

11-1. In a modified cash system, which of the following titles may need adjustments?

Cash	A. Swan, Capital
Supplies	A. Swan, Withdrawals
Prepaid Insurance	Commission Sales
Equipment	Salary Expense
Notes Payable	

Posting a combined journal using the accrual approach.

11-2. Avon Company uses a combined journal with the following headings:

Sundry	Dr.	Cr.
Accounts Receivable	Dr.	Cr.
Accounts Payable	Dr.	Cr.
Commission Sales	Cr.	
Salary Expense	Dr.	
Cash	Dr.	Cr.

    a. How can the balance of cash be determined at any point in the month?

    b. Which column total will not be posted?

    c. Do you think Avon Company has subsidiary ledgers? Please explain.

    d. Which columns will be used to record the payment of advertising expense?

Preparing a chart of accounts for a modified cash system.

11-3. Listed below are the accounts used by Dr. Jonson, who keeps his records on a strictly cash basis. As his accountant, which titles do you think could be added to use a modified cash system? Assume that a large amount of supplies is bought. Cash; Notes Payable; L. Jonson, Capital; L. Jonson, Withdrawals; Professional Fees; Auto Expense; Rent Expense; Office Furniture Expense; Insurance Expense; Medical Supplies Expense.

Explaining postings of a combined journal for a modified cash basis.

11-4. Using the headings of the combined journal for Dr. Wheeler (p. 405), indicate when postings would occur in a modified cash basis.

19XX

May   3 Al Henson invested $4,000 in the dental business.

         8 Paid three months' insurance premiums, $1,200.

15 Received checks from patients, $900.
19 Paid office salaries, $500.

Explaining recordings and postings of a combined journal using an accrual approach.

11-5. Using the headings of the combined journal for Art's Wholesale Clothing Company (p. 410), indicate when recordings and postings would occur in an accrual approach.

19XX
May
  2 Joe Davis invested $12,000 in the business.
  5 Bought $600 of merchandise for cash.
  8 Cash sale, $600.
 19 Received $400 less a 3 percent discount from Alvie Corp. from past sale on account.

Group A Problems

(The forms you need are on pages 384–386 of the *Study Guide and Working Papers.*)

11A-1. Dr. Lovejoy, M.D., uses the following chart of accounts:

Journalizing transactions of a modified cash system in a combined journal.

Check Figure:
Crossfooting Total $18,040

Chart of Accounts

Assets
111 Borne Bank
113 Petty Cash
114 Prepaid Insurance
115 Medical Supplies
121 Medical Equipment
122 Accumulated Depreciation, Medical Equipment
123 Office Furniture
124 Accumulated Depreciation, Office Furniture
125 Auto
126 Accumulated Depreciation, Auto

Liabilities
211 Notes Payable

Owner's Equity
311 Pete Lovejoy, Capital
312 Pete Lovejoy, Withdrawals
313 Income Summary

Revenue
411 Professional Fees

Expenses
511 Rent Expense
512 Donation Expense
513 Salaries Expense
514 Medical Supplies Expense
515 Depreciation Expense, Medical Equipment
516 Depreciation Expense, Office Furniture
517 Depreciation Expense, Automobile
518 Insurance Expense
519 Telephone Expense
610 Cleaning Expense
611 Miscellaneous Expense

The headings of the combined journal are as follows:

			Sundry		Medical Supplies	Pete Lovejoy, Withdrawals	Cleaning Expense	Prof. Fees		Borne Bank		P. 1
Date	Explanation	PR	Dr.	Cr.	Dr.	Dr.	Dr.	Cr.	Ck. No.	Dr.	Cr.	

From the transactions listed below:

1. Journalize them in the combined journal for a modified cash basis.
2. Prove the combined journal. *make sure that the*

19XX
May
1   Dr. Lovejoy deposited $6,000 in the practice.
3   Paid rent for the month to Foster Realty, $800, check no. 1.
8   Bought medical equipment from Ace Supply Co., $1,500, check no. 2.
12 Bought medical supplies from Lone Co., $700, check no. 3.
15 Received cash from patients, $2,800.
18 Bought additional medical supplies from Lone Co., $1,200, check no. 4.
19 Dr. Lovejoy withdrew $600 for personal use, check no. 5.
21 Paid Al's Janitorial Service, $300, check no. 6.
24 Received cash from patients, $1,900.
25 Paid for postage stamps, $40 (miscellaneous expense), check no. 7.
27 Paid salaries for month, $1,400, check no. 8.
28 Paid Al's Janitorial Service, $400, check no. 9.
29 Dr. Lovejoy withdrew $400 for personal use, check no. 10.

11A-2. The following is the chart of accounts of Dr. Fox, M.D.:

Journalizing transactions of a modified cash system into a combined journal with headings for payroll deductions as well as recording payroll tax expense.

Check Figure:
Crossfooting $31,534

Assets
111 Valley Blue Bank
112 Prepaid Insurance
113 Medical Supplies
121 Office Equipment
122 Accumulated Depreciation, Office Equipment

Liabilities
211 FICA—Social Security Payable
212 FICA—Medicare Payable
213 Federal Income Tax Payable

Owner's Equity
311 Al Fox, Capital
312 Al Fox, Withdrawals
313 Income Summary

Revenue
411 Professional Fees

Expenses
511 Rent Expense
512 Medical Supplies Expense
513 Salaries Expense
514 Payroll Tax Expense
515 Telephone Expense
516 Depreciation Expense, Office Equipment
517 Insurance Expense
518 Cleaning Expense
519 Miscellaneous Expense

The headings of Dr. Fox's combined journal are as follows:

Date	Explanation	PR	Valley Blue Bank Dr.	Valley Blue Bank Cr.	Ck. No.	Prof. Fees Cr.	Sal. Exp. Dr.	FICA SS. Cr.	FICA Med. Cr.	Fed. Inc. Tax Payable Cr.	Med. Supp. Dr.	Sundry Dr.	Sundry Cr.

From the transactions listed on page 420:

1. Journalize them in the combined journal (beginning balances are provided in the *Study Guide and Working Papers.*)
2. Prove the combined journal.

19XX
May 1 Received $3,000 from patients.
3 Issued check no. 480 to Lane Drug for medical supplies, $600.
5 Issued check no. 481 to A. Realty to pay three months' insurance premiums, $1,200.
9 Received checks from patients, $2,000.
12 Issued the following payroll checks to his staff:

	Check No.	Gross Pay	Social Security	Medicare	FIT	Net Pay
Abby Slat	482	$ 700	$ 43	$10	$140	$ 507
Jane Reeves	483	600	38	8	120	434
Bob Swan	484	500	31	7	100	362
		$1,800	$112	$25	$360	$1,303

18 Issued check no. 485 to Lane Drug for medical supplies, $400.
25 Dr. Fox withdrew $700 for personal use, check no. 486.
28 Dr. Fox paid Social Security, Medicare, and federal income tax from payroll of May 12, check no. 487. (Don't forget Dr. Fox's share of FICA.)

11A-3. Dick Clark, a recent graduate of a medical school, has decided to open his own office. Based on the advice of his accountant, he will use a combined journal. The following is the chart of accounts for Dr. Clark's office:

Journalizing and proving combined journal, recording transactions using an accrual basis of accounting.

Check Figure:
Total of Sundry Dr. Column $2,060

Assets
111 Cash
112 Accounts Receivable
113 Prepaid Insurance
121 Office Equipment
Liabilities
211 Accounts Payable
Owner's Equity
311 D. Clark, Capital
312 Income Summary

Revenue
411 Medical Fees
Expenses
511 Telephone Expense
512 Cleaning Expense
513 Utilities Expense

The headings of Dr. Clark's combined journal are:

				COMBINED JOURNAL								
										Month		Page 1
Date	Explanation	Ck. No.	PR	Sundry Dr.	Sundry Cr.	Cash Dr.	Cash Cr.	Acct. Rec. Dr.	Acct. Rec. Cr.	Acct. Pay. Dr.	Acct. Pay. Cr.	Office Equip. Dr.	Medical Fees Cr.

Your task is to

1. Record the following transactions in the combined journal. Complete the PR column as if you were recording and posting.
2. Prove the combined journal.

19XX
July 1 Dick Clark invested $7,000 cash and $4,000 of office equipment in the practice.

1 Paid insurance on the office for one year in advance, $1,700, check no. 1.

9 Purchased office equipment on account from Smith Stationery Co., $400.

12 Purchased office equipment on account from Vole Stationery Co., $700.

18 Completed physical examinations on each schoolchild at Salem Elementary School, $3,000 on account.

18 Received $900 cash for medical fees earned.

19 Performed a complete examination for Alvin Ray's son, $75 on account.

20 Paid Smith Stationery one-half the amount owed from July 9 transaction, check no. 2.

26 Paid telephone bill, $90, check no. 3.

27 Paid utilities, $170, check no. 4.

28 Paid Toby Cleaning Co. for cleaning service performed, $100, check no. 5.

29 Paid one-half the amount owed Vole Stationery Company from July 12 transaction, check no. 6.

11A-4. Buzzy Sullivan opened a dry-cleaning store that also sold accessories. The following is the chart of accounts for Buzzy's Cleaning Company.

Journalizing, recording, and *posting* combined journal for a company using the accrual basis of accounting.

Check Figure:
Total of Sundry Dr. Column $2,400

Assets		Revenue	
111	Cash	411	Cleaning Sales
112	Accounts Receivable	412	Cleaning Sales Discount
113	Prepaid Insurance	**Cost of Goods Sold**	
121	Cleaning Equipment	511	Purchases
Liabilities		512	Purchases Returns and Allowances
211	Accounts Payable	513	Purchases Discounts
212	Note Payable	**Expenses**	
Owner's Equity		611	Utilities Expense
311	B. Sullivan, Capital	612	Advertising Expense
312	Income Summary		

Here are the transactions for the month of January:

19XX
Jan.
1 Buzzy Sullivan invested $8,000 cash in the business.

8 Paid a five-year insurance policy in advance, $1,500, check no. 1.

10 Purchased merchandise on account from Role Company, $900.

12 Cleaned shirts for cash, $650.

15 Cleaned suits on account for Pete Daley, $200.

17 Purchased cleaning equipment on account from Ral Co., $900.

20 Borrowed $6,000 from Frank National Bank.

21 Cleaned shirts for Pete Daley for $50 on account.

24 Received payment from Pete Daley for $200 less a 2 percent discount from January 15 transaction.

25 Purchased merchandise on account from Bomb Co., $250.

26 Cleaned pants on account for Alice Small, $15.

27 Paid Role Company $900 less a 2 percent discount for merchandise that was purchased on January 10, check no. 2.

28 Returned $100 of cleaning equipment to Ral Company for faulty workmanship.

29 Paid Bomb Company $250 less a 10 percent discount on purchases made on account on January 25, check no. 3.

30 Cash sales, $800.

30 Received payment from Alice Small, $15, less a 20 percent sales discount.

Your task is to

1. Set up accounts in the general ledger (some accounts may not be used in January).

2. Set up accounts in the accounts payable and accounts receivable subsidiary ledger as needed.

3. Journalize the above transactions.

4. Record to the accounts payable and accounts receivable subsidiary ledger as appropriate.

5. Post to the general ledger as appropriate.

6. Prove the sum of the subsidiary ledgers equal the controlling accounts.

7. Prove the combined journal.

The headings of the combined journal of Buzzy's Cleaning Company will be as follows:

				COMBINED JOURNAL											
							Month								
										Cleaning Sales Disc.	Cleaning Sales				
Date	Explanation	Ck. No.	PR	Sundry		Cash		Acct. Rec.		Acct. Pay.		Dr.	Cr.	Purch. Dr.	Purch. Dis. Cr.
				Dr.	Cr.	Dr.	Cr.	Dr.	Cr.	Dr.	Cr.				

Group B Problems

(The forms you need are on pages 384–396 of the *Study Guide and Working Papers*.)

Journalizing transactions of a modified cash system into a combined journal.

Check Figure:
Crossfooting Total $25,280

11B-1. Using the chart of accounts of Dr. Lovejoy from Problem 11A-1 (p. 418), record the following transactions in the combined journal and then prove the journal:

19XX

May
1 Dr. Lovejoy deposited $9,000 in the practice.
3 Paid rent for the month to Jane Jones Realty, $700, check no. 1.
8 Bought medical supplies from Able Co., $750, check no. 2.
12 Bought medical equipment from Jane's Supply, $4,000, check no. 3.
15 Received cash from patients, $3,000.
18 Bought additional medical supplies from Able Co., $910, check no. 4.
19 Dr. Lovejoy withdrew $790 for personal use, check no. 5.
21 Paid Ron's Janitorial Service, $500, check no. 6.
24 Received cash from patients, $3,400.
25 Paid for postage stamps, $30 (miscellaneous expense), check no. 7.
27 Paid salaries for month, $1,600, check no. 8.
28 Paid Ron's Janitorial Service, $300, check no. 9.
29 Dr. Lovejoy withdrew $300 for personal use, check no. 10.

11B-2. Using the chart of accounts for Dr. Fox from Problem 11A-2 (p. 419), record the following transactions in the combined journal and then prove the journal. (Beginning balances are in the *Study Guide and Working Papers*.)

Journalizing transactions of a modified cash system into a combined journal with headings for payroll deductions, and recording payroll tax expenses.

Check Figure:
Crossfooting Total $34,212

19XX
May

1 Received $4,000 from patients.
3 Issued check no. 400 to Lane Drug for medical supplies, $700.
5 Issued check no. 401 to J. Realty to pay three months' insurance premiums, $900.
9 Received checks from patients, $3,000.
12 Issued the following payroll checks:

	Check No.	Gross Pay	Social Security	Medicare	FIT	Net Pay
Amy Wand	402	$ 900	$ 56	$13	$180	$ 651
Jessie Fire	403	800	49	12	160	579
Willard Scott	404	600	37	9	120	434
		$2,300	$142	$34	$460	$1,664

18 Issued check no. 405 to Lane Drug for medical supplies, $900.
25 Dr. Fox withdrew $400 for personal use, check no. 406.
28 Dr. Fox paid Social Security, Medicare, and FIT from payroll of May 12, check no. 407. (Don't forget Dr. Fox's share of Social Security and Medicare.)

Journalizing, recording, and posting combined journal used to record transactions utilizing accrual basis of accounting.

Check Figure:
Total of Sundry Dr. Column
$1,430

11B-3. Using the chart of accounts of Dick Clark from Problem 11A-3 (p. 420), journalize the following transactions and prove the combined journal. Fill in the PR column as if you were actually recording and posting to the ledger.

19XX
July

1 Dick Clark invested $6,000 cash and $4,000 of office equipment in the practice.
1 Paid insurance on the office for one year in advance, $1,200, check no. 1.
9 Purchased office equipment on account from Smith Stationery Co., $1,400.
12 Completed physical examinations on each schoolchild at Salem Elementary School, $2,000 on account.
18 Received $700 cash for medical fees earned.
19 Performed a complete examination for Alvin Ray's son, $200 on account.
20 Paid Smith Stationery one-half the amount owed from July 9 transaction, check no. 2.
26 Paid telephone bill, $95, check no. 3.
27 Paid utilities, $60, check no. 4.
28 Paid Toby Cleaning Co. for cleaning service performed, $75, check no. 5.

11B-4. Buzzy Sullivan opened a dry-cleaning store that also sold accessories. The chart of accounts for Buzzy's Cleaning Company is given in Problem 11A-4 (p. 421). Here are the transactions for the month of January:

Check Figure:
Total of Sundry Dr. Column
$1,800

19XX
Jan.

1 Buzzy Sullivan invested $6,000 cash in the business.
8 Paid for a five-year company insurance policy in advance, $1,200, check no. 1.
10 Purchased merchandise on account from Role Company, $700.
12 Cleaned shirts for cash, $950.
15 Cleaned suits on account for Pete Daley, $500.
17 Purchased cleaning equipment on account from Ral Co., $600.
20 Borrowed $4,000 from Frank National Bank.

21 Cleaned shirts on account for P. Daley, $50.
24 Received payment from P. Daley for $500 less a 2 percent discount from January 15 transaction.
25 Purchased merchandise on account from Bomb Company, $90.
26 Cleaned pants on account for Alice Small, $20.
27 Paid Role Company $700 less a 2 percent discount for merchandise that was purchased on January 10, check no. 2.
28 Returned $200 of cleaning equipment to Ral Company for faulty workmanship.
29 Paid Bomb Company $90 less a 10 percent discount on purchases made on account on January 25, check no. 3.
30 Cash sales, $700.

Your task is to journalize, record, post, and prove the combined journal for Buzzy.

REAL WORLD APPLICATIONS

11R-1.

Jeff Smith has been running his business on a strictly cash basis. At a party over the weekend he met an accountant who told him that his business should use a modified cash system. Jeff has brought you his chart of accounts so that you may revise it as well as lay out a combined journal. Using the following chart of accounts, please design a combined journal for Jeff. Allow columns for payroll deductions. Tell Jeff in writing some of the benefits of a modified cash system.

Dr. Smith—Chart of Accounts

Assets		Revenue	
111	Cash	411	Professional Fees
113	Petty Cash	**Expenses**	
Liabilities		511	Insurance Expense
211	Notes Payable	512	Furniture Expense
Owner's Equity		514	Medical Equipment Expense
311	J. Smith, Capital	515	Medical Supplies Expense
312	J. Smith, Withdrawals	516	Salary Expense
313	Income Summary	517	Telephone Expense
		518	Miscellaneous Expense

11R-2.

Margie Heaves is about to open a dry-cleaning shop. She has hired you to design a combined journal for her shop. It will definitely be a small business with a limited number of transactions that are not too complicated. After analyzing Margie's company, you develop the following chart of accounts:

1. Cash
2. Accounts Receivable
3. Equipment
4. Accounts Payable
5. Cleaning Sales
6. Wage Expense
7. Supplies Expense
8. Miscellaneous Expense

Margie has asked you to provide her, as soon as possible, a written justification for your design of the parts of the combined journal. Be prepared to support the combined journal you present to her. Please label all headings of the journal in terms of Debits and Credits. What titles are missing from the chart of accounts?

YOU make the call

Critical Thinking/Ethical Case

11R-3.

Angel Shower, the bookkeeper of Aster Co., also collects the payments of invoices by customers. Angel noticed that Rume Co. paid the April 10 invoice twice. Angel, who is in need of extra cash, does not plan to inform Rume Co. of the double payment. Do you agree with Angel's decision? You make the call. Write down your specific recommendations to Angel.

ACCOUNTING RECALL
A CUMULATIVE APPROACH

THIS EXAM REVIEWS CHAPTERS 1 THROUGH 11

Your *Study Guide and Working Papers* (pp. 401 and 414) has forms to complete this exam, as well as worked-out solutions. The page references next to each question identify what page to turn back to if you answer the question incorrectly.

PART 1 Vocabulary Review

Match the terms to the appropriate definition or phrase.

Page Ref.

(403)	1. Hybrid	A. A special journal
(411)	2. Sundry	B. Determines monthly versus semiweekly deposits
(406)	3. (X)	C. Records revenue when cash is received
(402)	4. Accrual accounting	
(412)	5. (✓)	D. Accounts payable
(275)	6. Look-back periods	E. Verification
(406)	7. Payroll tax expense	F. No posting
(319)	8. Controlling account	G. Record to subsidiary
(406)	9. Crossfoot	H. Records revenue when earned
(405)	10. Combined journal	I. Miscellaneous
		J. Social Security, Medicare (er) + SUTA, FUTA

PART II True or False (Accounting Theory)

(318)	11. We post to subsidiary ledgers and record to general ledgers.
(402)	12. Small businesses could use combined journals.

(413) 13. Adjusting entries would be recorded in the sundry columns of a special journal.

(321) 14. Sales tax payable has a normal balance of a debit.

(318) 15. The total of accounts receivable is posted to the subsidiary ledger.

CONTINUING PROBLEM

Using the combined journal to replace all previously used journals, record the following transactions for the month of March.

Assignment:

(See pp. 402–413 in your *Study Guide and Working Papers.*)
Post all transactions to the required ledger accounts and prepare a trial balance as of March 31.

March   2   Billed Vita Needle for services performed; invoice #12686, $1,300

  5   Paid a balance owed on the phone bill received in November, $150

  6   Received the electric bill for the month, $290, due in 30 days

  10   Collected balance in full from Taylor Golf, sales invoice #5000

  11   Paid for advertising with Pacific Bell, $800

  20   Paid the insurance premium for the month, $100

  28   Bought postage on account for direct mail piece from Mail Boxes, Etc., $150

12

PREPARING A WORKSHEET FOR A MERCHANDISE COMPANY

With Special Appendix on Perpetual Inventory

THE BIG PICTURE

Six months into Eldorado Computer Center's second year of operation Tony Freedman decides to update his books. He wants to prepare an accurate financial statement to give to the bank. He will make all necessary adjustments to his accounts as he did before. The first step in completing these adjustments is preparing a worksheet that includes merchandise transactions.

The Eldorado Computer Center has purchased and sold merchandise inventory for computers. To make sure he's had accessories available in stock to increase customer satisfaction, Tony has kept an inventory of many parts and accessories. However, all have not been sold in the first six months of this year.

The worksheet you will prepare for the Eldorado Computer Center will include new accounts to track the actual inventory Freedman purchased. Some of that inventory became an expense in this time period, and some is still to be sold. Although Freedman tracks purchases of inventory on a monthly basis, accurate value for all inventory cannot be determined until a physical count is completed. This physical count also allows Freedman to see if there has been a problem with theft or breakage of parts.

Freedman updates his inventory as he does the rest of his accounts, at the end of an accounting period. Since his inventory is not that large in quantity or in dollars, he feels a six-month update is something he can accomplish without hiring additional people to handle the workload of the business or shutting down operations for a few days.

<table>
<tr><td>

Learning Objectives

</td><td>

◆ Figuring adjustments for merchandise inventory, unearned rent, supplies used, insurance expired, depreciation expense, and salaries accrued. (p. 428)

◆ Preparing a worksheet for a merchandise company. (p. 431)

</td></tr>
</table>

In Chapters 9 and 10 we discussed the special journals and subsidiary ledgers of a merchandise company, and in Chapters 7 and 8 we looked at payroll recordkeeping practices and procedures. Now we will shift our attention to recording adjustments and completing a worksheet for a merchandise company.

LEARNING UNIT 12-1

Adjustments for Merchandise Inventory and Unearned Rent

Gross Sales
− Sales Ret. + Allow.
− Sales discount
= Net Sales

Net Sales
− Cost of goods sold
= Gross profit
− Operating expenses
= Net Income

Cost of goods sold:
  Beginning inventory
+ Net purchases
+ Freight-in
− Ending inventory
= Cost of goods sold

The Merchandise Inventory account shows the goods that a merchandise company has available to sell to customers. There are several ways of keeping track of the **cost of goods sold** (the total cost of the goods sold to customers) and quantity of inventory that a company has on hand. In this chapter we will discuss the **periodic inventory system,** in which the balance in inventory is updated only at the end of the accounting period. This system is used by companies like Art's Wholesale Clothing Company, which sell a variety of merchandise with low unit prices. In the appendix at the end of this chapter another system called the **Perpetual Inventory System** is discussed. In this system, businesses with large inventories can have current information about inventory on hand and the actual cost of goods sold.

Assume that Art's Wholesale Clothing Company started the year with $19,000 worth of merchandise. This is called **beginning merchandise inventory** or simply **beginning inventory.** The balance of beginning inventory never changes. Instead, all purchases of merchandise are recorded in the Purchases account. During the accounting period $52,000 worth of such purchases were made and recorded in the Purchases account.

At the end of the period, the company takes a physical count of the merchandise in stock; this amount is called **ending merchandise inventory** or simply **ending inventory.** It is calculated on an inventory sheet as shown in Figure 12-1.

This $4,000, which is the ending inventory for this period, will be the beginning inventory for the next period.

When the income statement is prepared, the cost of goods sold section requires two distinct numbers for inventory. The beginning inventory adds to the cost of goods sold, and the ending inventory is subtracted from the cost of goods sold (see margin aids at left). Remember that the two figures for beginning and ending inventory were calculated months apart. Thus combining these amounts to come up with one inventory figure would not be accurate.

Note that in the calculation (in the margin) of cost of goods sold that a new title called **Freight-In** is shown. This is a cost of goods sold account that records the shipping cost to the buyer. Note that net sales less cost of goods sold equals **gross profit.** Subtracting operating expenses from gross profits equals net income.

ART'S WHOLESALE CLOTHING COMPANY ENDING INVENTORY SHEET AS OF DECEMBER 31, 19X2			
Amount	Explanation	Unit Cost	Total
20	Ladies' Jackets code 14-0	$50	$1,000
10	Men's Hats code 327	10	100
90	Men's Shirts code 423	10	900
100	Ladies' Blouses code 481	20	2,000
			$4,000

Counted by ———— Checked and priced by ————

FIGURE 12-1
Ending Inventory Sheet

First adjustment transfers amount in beginning inventory from Merchandise Inventory to Income Summary.

Note that Income Summary has no normal balance of debit or credit.

ADJUSTMENT FOR MERCHANDISE INVENTORY

Adjusting the Merchandise Inventory account is a two-step process because we must record the beginning inventory and ending inventory amounts separately. The first step deals with beginning merchandise inventory.

Given: Beginning Inventory, $19,000

Our first adjustment removes beginning inventory from the asset account (Merchandise Inventory) and transfers it to Income Summary. We do this by crediting Merchandise Inventory for $19,000 and debiting Income Summary for the same amount. This is shown below in T account form and on a transaction analysis chart:

```
     Merchandise Inventory 114          Income Summary 313
     Bal.  19,000 | Adj.  19,000      Adj.  19,000 |
                        |_____(A)____↑
```

Accounts Affected	Category	↑	↓	Rules
Income Summary	—	—		Dr.
Merchandise Inventory	Asset		↓	Cr.

(The adjusting entries would be recorded first on the worksheet and then in the general journal.)

The second step is entering the amount of ending inventory ($4,000) in the Merchandise Inventory account. This is done to record the amount of goods on hand at the end of the period as an asset, and to subtract this amount from the cost of goods sold (since we have not sold this inventory yet). To do this we debit Merchandise Inventory for $4,000 and credit Income Summary for the same amount. This is shown below in T account form and on a transaction analysis chart:

```
     Merchandise Inventory 114          Income Summary 313
     Bal.  19,000 | Adj.  19,000      Adj.  19,000 | Adj.  4,000
     Adj.   4,000 |
          ↑_____(B)_____↑
```

Second adjustment updates inventory account with a figure for ending inventory.

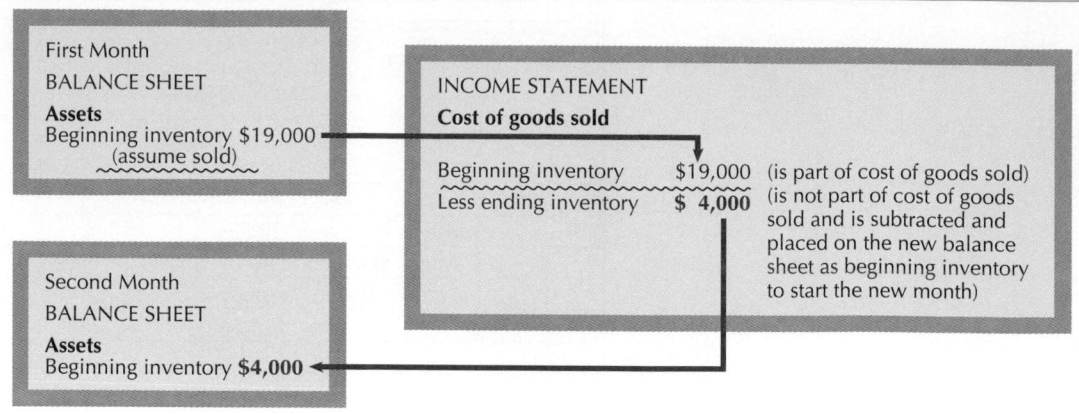

FIGURE 12-2 Recording Inventory on a Partial Balance Sheet and Income Statement

Accounts Affected	Category	↑ ↓	Rules
Merchandise Inventory	Asset	↑	Dr.
Income Summary	—	—	Cr.

Beginning inventory $19,000
+ Net cost of purchases   50,910
= Cost of goods
  available for sale $69,910
− Ending inventory   4,000
= Cost of goods sold $65,910

Note: If freight-in was involved, it would have been added to net cost of purchases.

Let's look at how this process or method of recording merchandise inventory is reflected in the balance sheet and income statement (see Figure 12-2). Note that the $19,000 of beginning inventory is assumed sold and is shown on the income statement as part of the cost of goods sold. The ending inventory of $4,000 is assumed not to be sold and is subtracted from the cost of goods sold on the income statement. The ending inventory becomes next month's beginning inventory on the balance sheet. When the income statement is prepared, we will need a figure for beginning inventory as well as a figure for ending inventory.

ADJUSTMENT FOR UNEARNED RENT

A second new account we have not seen before is a liability called Unearned Rent or Rent Received in Advance. This account records the amount collected for rent before the service (renting the space) has been provided.

Suppose Art's Wholesale Clothing Company is subletting a portion of its space to Jesse Company for $200 per month. Jesse Company sends Art a check for $600 for three months' rent paid in advance. This unearned rent ($600) is a liability on the balance sheet because Art's Wholesale owes Jesse Company three months' worth of occupancy.

Received cash for renting space in future.

Cash	Asset	↑	Dr.
Unearned Rent	Liab.	↑	Cr.

The *adjustment* when rental income is earned:

Unearned Rent	Liab.	↓	Dr.
Rental Income	Rev.	↑	Cr.

When Art's Wholesale fulfills a portion of the rental agreement — when Jesse Company has been in the space for a period of time — this liability account will be reduced and the Rental Income account will be increased. Rental Income is another type of revenue for Art's Wholesale.

Remember, under accrual accounting revenue is recognized when it is earned, whether payment is received then or not. Here, Art's Wholesale collected cash in advance for a service that it has not performed as yet. A liability called Unearned Rent is the result. Art's Wholesale may have the cash, but the Rental Income is not recorded until it is earned. There are other types of unearned revenue besides unearned rent — examples would be subscriptions for magazines, legal fees collected before the work is performed, insurance, etc.

LEARNING UNIT 12-1 REVIEW

AT THIS POINT you should be able to

◆ Define the periodic method of inventory accounting. (p. 428)
◆ Explain why beginning and ending inventory are two separate figures in the cost of goods sold section on the income statement. (p. 428)
◆ Calculate net sales, cost of goods sold, gross profit, and net income. (p. 428)
◆ Show how to calculate a figure for ending inventory. (p. 429)
◆ Explain why unearned rent is a *liability* account. (p. 430)

SELF-REVIEW QUIZ 12-1

(The forms you need are on page 415 of the *Study Guide and Working Papers.*)

Given the following, prepare the two *adjusting* entries for Merchandise Inventory on 12/31/XX.

Merchandise Inventory, 1/1/XX	$ 6,000
Purchases	9,000
Merchandise Inventory, 12/31/XX	5,000
Cost of Goods Sold	10,000
Unearned Magazine Subscriptions	8,000

Solution to Self-Review Quiz 12-1

Quiz Tip: Note Unearned Magazine Subscriptions is a liability and not involved in the adjustment for Merchandise Inventory.

Dec.	31	Income Summary	6 0 0 0 00	
		Merchandise Inventory		6 0 0 0 00
	31	Merchandise Inventory	5 0 0 0 00	
		Income Summary		5 0 0 0 00

LEARNING UNIT 12-2
Completing the Worksheet

In this unit we will prepare a worksheet for Art's Wholesale Clothing Company. For convenience we reproduce the company's chart of accounts in Figure 12-3 on page 432.

Figure 12-4 (p. 433) shows the trial balance that was prepared on Dec. 1, 19XX, from the special journals of Art's Wholesale (note it is placed directly on the first two columns of the worksheet).

In looking at the trial balance, we see many new titles that have appeared since we completed a trial balance for a service company back in Chapter 5. Let's look specifically at these new titles in the summary in Table 12-1 (p. 434).

Note the following:

◆ **Mortgage Payable** is a liability account that records the increases and decreases in the amount of debt owed on a mortgage. We will discuss this more in the next chapter, when financial reports are prepared.

Chart of Accounts

Assets 100–199
111 Cash
112 Petty Cash
113 Accounts Receivable
114 Merchandise Inventory
115 Supplies
116 Prepaid Insurance
121 Store Equipment
122 Accum. Depreciation, Store Equipment

Liabilities 200–299
211 Accounts Payable
212 Salaries Payable
213 Federal Income Tax Payable
214 FICA–Social Security Payable
215 FICA–Medicare Payable
216 State Income Tax Payable
217 SUTA Tax Payable
218 FUTA Tax Payable
219 Unearned Rent*
220 Mortgage Payable

Owner's Equity 300–399
311 Art Newner, Capital
312 Art Newner, Withdrawals
313 Income Summary

Revenue 400–499
411 Sales
412 Sales Returns and Allowances
413 Sales Discount
414 Rental Income

Cost of Goods Sold 500–599
511 Purchases
512 Purchases Discount
513 Purchases Returns and Allowances
514 Freight-In

Expenses 600–699
611 Salaries Expense
612 Payroll Tax Expense
613 Depreciation Expense, Store Equipment
614 Supplies Expense
615 Insurance Expense
616 Postage Expense
617 Miscellaneous Expense
618 Interest Expense
619 Cleaning Expense
620 Delivery Expense

* Although this is the only term under Liabilities not using payable, it is a liability.

FIGURE 12-3 Art's Wholesale Clothing Company Chart of Accounts

- **Interest Expense** represents a nonoperating expense for Art's Wholesale and thus is categorized as Other Expense. The interest would be a regular expense if it were incurred for business purposes. We will also be looking at this in the next chapter.
- **Unearned Revenue** is a liability account that records receipt of payment for goods and services in advance of delivery. Unearned Rent is a particular example of this general type of account.

We have already discussed Adjustments A and B (p. 429), which make up the two-step process involved in adjusting Merchandise Inventory at the end of the accounting period. Now we will go on to show T accounts and transaction analysis charts for some more adjustments that need to be made at this point in a merchandise firm, just as they do in a service company.

Adjustment (C) Rental Income Earned by Art's Wholesale, $200

A month ago, Cash was increased by $600, as was a liability, Unearned Rent. Art's Wholesale received payment in advance but had not earned the rental income. Now, since $200 has been earned, the liability is reduced and Rental Income can be recorded for the $200. This is shown on the facing page below Figure 12-4.

			Trial Balance	
			Dr.	Cr.
		Cash	12 9 2 0 00	
		Petty Cash	1 0 0 00	
		Accounts Receivable	14 5 0 0 00	
		Merchandise Inventory	19 0 0 0 00	
		Supplies	8 0 0 00	
		Prepaid Insurance	9 0 0 00	
		Store Equipment	4 0 0 0 00	
		Acc. Dep., Store Equipment		4 0 0 00
		Accounts Payable		17 9 0 0 00
		Federal Income Tax Payable		8 0 0 00
		FICA-Soc. Sec. Payable		4 5 4 00
		FICA-Medicare Payable		1 0 6 00
		State Income Tax Payable		2 0 0 00
		SUTA Tax Payable		1 0 8 00
		FUTA Tax Payable		3 2 00
		Unearned Rent		6 0 0 00
		Mortgage Payable		2 3 2 0 00
		Art Newner, Capital		79 0 5 00
		Art Newner, Withdrawals	8 6 0 0 00	
		Income Summary		
		Sales		95 0 0 0 00
		Sales Returns and Allowances	9 5 0 00	
		Sales Discount	6 7 0 00	
		Purchases	52 0 0 0 00	
		Purchases Discount		8 6 0 00
		Purchases Returns and Allowances		6 8 0 00
		Freight-In	4 5 0 00	
		Salaries Expense	11 7 0 0 00	
		Payroll Tax Expense	4 2 0 00	
		Postage Expense	2 5 00	
		Miscellaneous Expense	3 0 00	
		Interest Expense	3 0 0 00	
			127 3 6 5 00	127 3 6 5 00

FIGURE 12-4
Trial Balance Section of the Worksheet

Unearned Rent	**Liability**	↓	**Dr.**	**$200**
Rental Income	**Revenue**	↑	**Cr.**	**$200**

Adjustment (D) Supplies on Hand, $300

$500 worth of supplies has been used up; thus there is a need to increase Supplies Expense and decrease the asset Supplies.

TABLE 12-1   SUMMARY OF NEW ACCOUNT TITLES

Title	Category	Report(s) Found on	Normal Balance	Temporary or Permanent
Petty Cash	Asset	Balance Sheet	Dr.	Permanent
Merchandise Inventory* (Beginning)	Asset	Balance Sheet from prior period	Dr.	Permanent
	Cost of Goods Sold	Income Statement of current period		
Federal Income Tax Payable	Liability	Balance Sheet	Cr.	Permanent
FICA—Social Security Payable	Liability	Balance Sheet	Cr.	Permanent
FICA—Medicare Payable	Liability	Balance Sheet	Cr.	Permanent
State Income Tax Payable	Liability	Balance Sheet	Cr.	Permanent
SUTA Tax Payable	Liability	Balance Sheet	Cr.	Permanent
FUTA Tax Payable	Liability	Balance Sheet	Cr.	Permanent
Unearned Rent**	Liability	Balance Sheet	Cr.	Permanent
Mortgage Payable	Liability	Balance Sheet	Cr.	Permanent
Sales	Revenue	Income Statement	Cr.	Temporary
Sales Returns and Allowances	Contra Revenue	Income Statement	Dr.	Temporary
Sales Discount	Contra Revenue	Income Statement	Dr.	Temporary
Purchases***	Cost of Goods Sold	Income Statement	Dr.	Temporary
Purchases Discount	Contra-Cost of Goods Sold	Income Statement	Cr.	Temporary
Purchases Returns and Allowances	Contra-Cost of Goods Sold	Income Statement	Cr.	Temporary
Freight-In	Cost of Goods Sold	Income Statement	Dr.	Temporary
Payroll Tax Expense	Expense	Income Statement	Dr.	Temporary
Postage Expense	Expense	Income Statement	Dr.	Temporary
Interest Expense	Other Expense	Income Statement	Dr.	Temporary

* The ending inventory of current period is a contra-cost of goods sold on the income statement and will be an asset on the balance sheet for next period.

** Referred to as Unearned Revenue.

*** Note the category for Purchases and Freight-In are Cost of Goods Sold while Purchases Discounts and Purchases Returns and Allowances are Contra-Cost of Goods Sold.

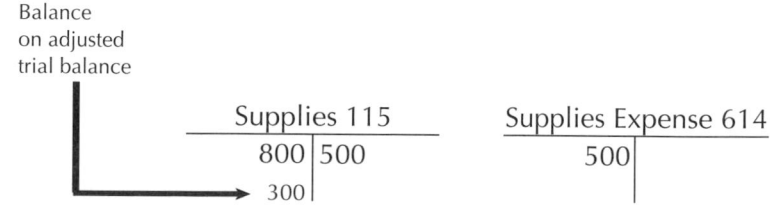

Supplies Expense	Expense	↑	Dr.	$500
Supplies	Asset	↓	Cr.	$500

Adjustment (E) Insurance Expired, $300

Since insurance has expired by $300, Insurance Expense is increased by $300 and the asset Prepaid Insurance is decreased by $300 (see p. 435).

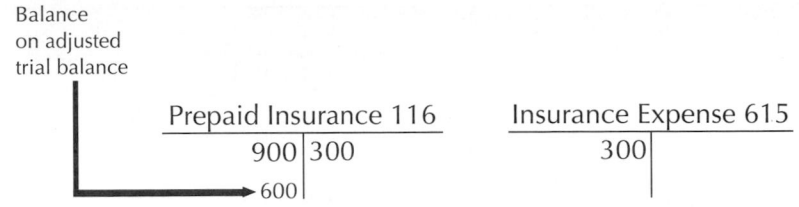

Balance on adjusted trial balance

Prepaid Insurance 116		Insurance Expense 615	
900	300	300	
→ 600			

Insurance Expense	Expense	↑	Dr.	$300
Prepaid Insurance	Asset	↓	Cr.	$300

Adjustment (F) Depreciation Expense, $50

When depreciation is taken, Depreciation Expense and Accumulated Depreciation are both increased by $50. Note that the cost of the store equipment remains the same.

Store Equipment 121	Accumulated Depreciation, Store Equipment 122	Depreciation Expense, Store Equipment 613
4,000	400	50
(remains	50	
unchanged)	450 ←	

Balance on adjusted trial balance

Dep. Exp., Store Equip.	Expense	↑	Dr.	$50
Acc. Dep., Store Equip.	Contra-Asset	↑	Cr.	$50

Adjustment (G) Salaries Accrued, $600

The $600 in Salaries Accrued causes an increase in Salaries Expense and Salaries Payable.

Salaries Payable 212	Salaries Expense 611
600	11,700
	600
	12,300

Balances on adjusted trial balance

Salaries Expense	Expense	↑	Dr.	$600
Salaries Payable	Liability	↑	Cr.	$600

Figure 12-5 shows the worksheet with the adjustments and adjusted trial balance column filled out. Note that the adjustment numbers in Income Summary from beginning and ending inventory are also carried over to the adjusted trial balance and are not combined.

The next step in completing the worksheet is to fill out the income

	Trial Balance Dr.	Trial Balance Cr.	Adjustments Dr.	Adjustments Cr.	Adjusted Trial Balance Dr.	Adjusted Trial Balance Cr.
Cash	12 9 2 0 00				12 9 2 0 00	
Petty Cash	1 0 0 00				1 0 0 00	
Accounts Receivable	14 5 0 0 00		(B)	(A)	14 5 0 0 00	
Merchandise Inventory	19 0 0 0 00		4 0 0 0 00	19 0 0 0 00	4 0 0 0 00	
Supplies	8 0 0 00			(D) 5 0 0 00	3 0 0 00	
Prepaid Insurance	9 0 0 00			(E) 3 0 0 00	6 0 0 00	
Store Equipment	4 0 0 0 00				4 0 0 0 00	
Acc. Dep., Store Equipment		4 0 0 00		(F) 5 0 00		4 5 0 00
Accounts Payable		17 9 0 0 00				17 9 0 0 00
Federal Income Tax Payable		8 0 0 00				8 0 0 00
FICA-Soc. Sec. Payable		4 5 4 00				4 5 4 00
FICA-Medicare Payable		1 0 6 00				1 0 6 00
State Income Tax Payable		2 0 0 00				2 0 0 00
SUTA Tax Payable		1 0 8 00				1 0 8 00
FUTA Tax Payable		3 2 00				3 2 00
Unearned Rent		6 0 0 00	(C) 2 0 0 00			4 0 0 00
Mortgage Payable		2 3 2 0 00				2 3 2 0 00
Art Newner, Capital		7 9 0 5 00				7 9 0 5 00
Art Newner, Withdrawals	8 6 0 0 00		(A)	(B)	8 6 0 0 00	
Income Summary			19 0 0 0 00	4 0 0 0 00	19 0 0 0 00	4 0 0 0 00
Sales		95 0 0 0 00				95 0 0 0 00
Sales Returns and Allowances	9 5 0 00				9 5 0 00	
Sales Discount	6 7 0 00				6 7 0 00	
Purchases	52 0 0 0 00				52 0 0 0 00	
Purchases Discount		8 6 0 00				8 6 0 00
Purchases Returns and Allowances		6 8 0 00				6 8 0 00
Freight-In	4 5 0 00				4 5 0 00	
Salaries Expense	11 7 0 0 00		(G) 6 0 0 00		12 3 0 0 00	
Payroll Tax Expense	4 2 0 00				4 2 0 00	
Postage Expense	2 5 00				2 5 00	
Miscellaneous Expense	3 0 00				3 0 00	
Interest Expense	3 0 0 00				3 0 0 00	
	127 3 6 5 00	127 3 6 5 00				
Rental Income				(C) 2 0 0 00		2 0 0 00
Supplies Expense			(D) 5 0 0 00		5 0 0 00	
Insurance Expense			(E) 3 0 0 00		3 0 0 00	
Depreciation Expense, Store Equip.			(F) 5 0 00		5 0 00	
Salaries Payable				(G) 6 0 0 00		6 0 0 00
			24 6 5 0 00	24 6 5 0 00	132 0 1 5 00	132 0 1 5 00

FIGURE 12-5 Worksheet with Three Columns Filled Out

Remember, we do *not* combine the $19,000 and $4,000 in Income Summary. When we prepare the cost of goods sold section for the formal financial report, we will need both a beginning and an ending figure for inventory.

statement columns from the adjusted trial balance, as shown in Figure 12-6.

The next step in completing the worksheet is to fill out the balance sheet columns (Fig. 12-7, p. 438). Note how ending inventory is carried over to the balance sheet from the adjusted trial balance column. Take time also to look at the placement of the payroll tax liabilities as well as Unearned Rent on the worksheet.

Figure 12-8 is the completed worksheet, on pages 440–441.

FIGURE 12-6 Income Statement Section of the Worksheet

$19,000 of beginning inventory is assumed sold during the period and thus is part of the cost of goods sold. By placing it in the debit column of Income Summary we increase the cost of goods sold.

$4,000 is the cost of ending inventory at the end of the period. It is assumed to be unsold and therefore is not part of the cost of goods sold. By placing it in the credit column of Income Summary we reduce the cost of goods sold.

$95,000 is the credit balance of Sales. The Sales Returns and Allowances, $950, and Sales Discount, $670, are placed on the debit side, which represents a reduction to total sales:
(Cr.) Sales
(Dr.) Less: Sales Returns and Allowances
(Dr.) Less: Sales Discount

The purchases account, $52,000, is on the debit side, reflecting an increase in costs due to purchasing additional merchandise. The Purchases Discount, $860, and Purchases Returns and Allowances, $680, are on the credit side, which reduces cost of purchases:
(Dr.) Purchases
(Cr.) Less: Purchases Returns and Allowances
(Cr.) Less: Purchases Discount

Freight-In adds to the cost of goods sold.

Rental Income, which falls under the category "other income" for Art's Wholesale, is increased by $200, because the first month's rental agreement has been fulfilled.

	Income Statement	
	Dr.	Cr.
Income Summary	19 000 00	4 000 00
Sales		95 000 00
Sales Returns and Allowances	950 00	
Sales Discount	670 00	
Purchases	52 000 00	
Purchases Discount		860 00
Purchases Returns and Allowances		680 00
Freight-In	450 00	
Salaries Expense	12 300 00	
Payroll Tax Expense	420 00	
Postage Expense	25 00	
Miscellaneous Expense	30 00	
Interest Expense	300 00	
Rental Income		200 00
Supplies Expense	500 00	
Insurance Expense	300 00	
Depreciation Expense, Store Equip.	50 00	
Salaries Payable		
	86 995 00	100 740 00
Net Income	13 745 00	
	100 740 00	100 740 00

FIGURE 12-7 Balance Sheet Section of the Worksheet

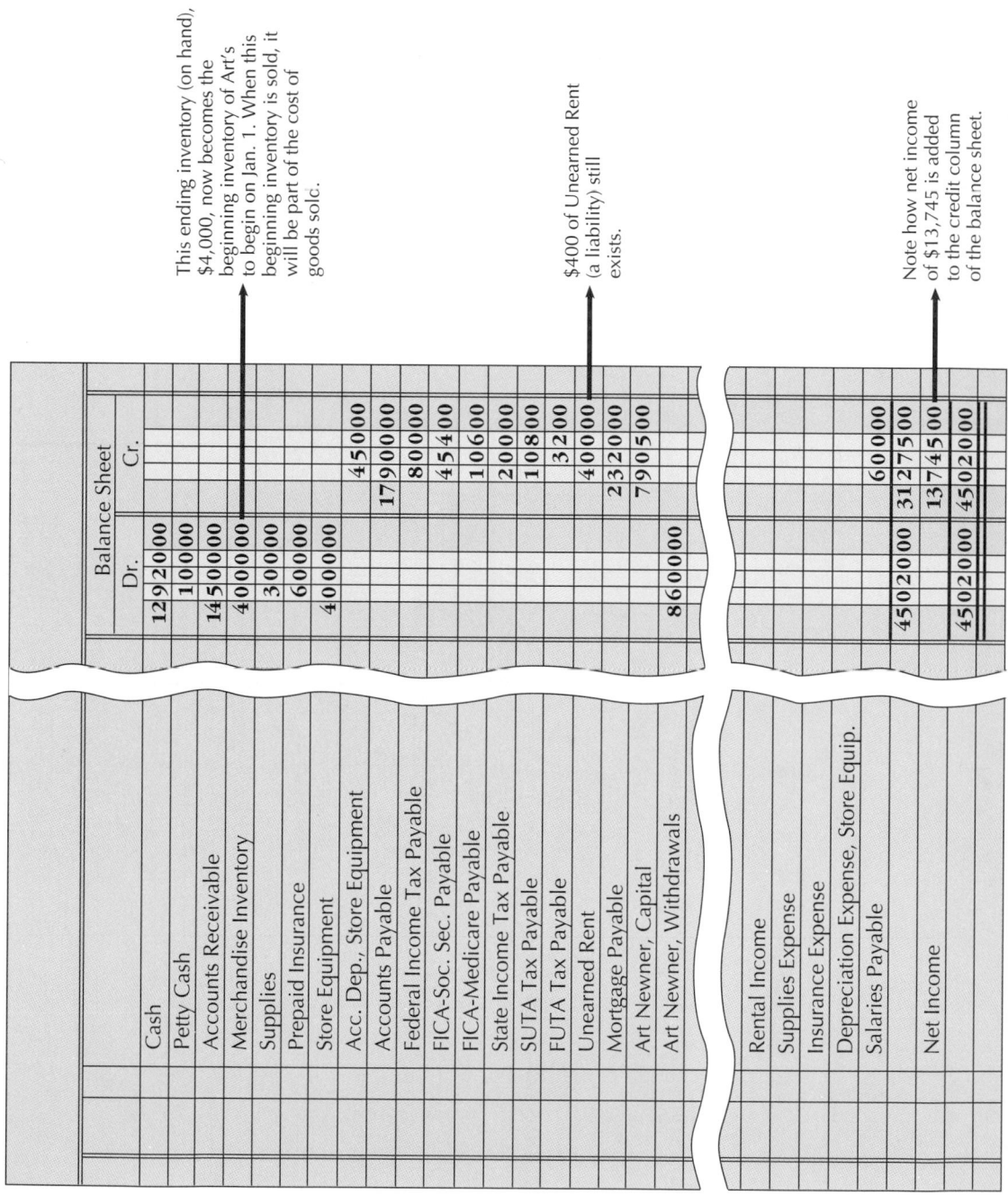

This ending inventory (on hand), $4,000, now becomes the beginning inventory of Art's to begin on Jan. 1. When this beginning inventory is sold, it will be part of the cost of goods sold.

$400 of Unearned Rent (a liability) still exists.

Note how net income of $13,745 is added to the credit column of the balance sheet.

	Balance Sheet	
	Dr.	Cr.
Cash	1292000	
Petty Cash	10000	
Accounts Receivable	1450000	
Merchandise Inventory	400000	
Supplies	30000	
Prepaid Insurance	60000	
Store Equipment	400000	
Acc. Dep., Store Equipment		45000
Accounts Payable		1790000
Federal Income Tax Payable		80000
FICA-Soc. Sec. Payable		45400
FICA-Medicare Payable		10600
State Income Tax Payable		20000
SUTA Tax Payable		10800
FUTA Tax Payable		3200
Unearned Rent		40000
Mortgage Payable		232000
Art Newner, Capital		790500
Art Newner, Withdrawals	860000	
Rental Income		
Supplies Expense		
Insurance Expense		
Depreciation Expense, Store Equip.		
Salaries Payable		60000
	4502000	3127500
Net Income		1374500
	4502000	4502000

LEARNING UNIT 12-1 REVIEW

AT THIS POINT you should be able to

◆ Complete adjustments for a merchandise company. (pp. 432, 435)
◆ Complete a worksheet. (pp. 440 – 441)

SELF-REVIEW QUIZ 12-2

(Use the foldout worksheet at the end of the *Study Guide and Working Papers.*)
    From the trial balance shown here, complete a worksheet for Ray Company. Additional data includes: (A and B) On December 31, 19XX, ending inventory was calculated as $200; (C) Storage Fees Earned, $516; (D) Rent expired, $100; (E) Depreciation Expense, Office Equipment, $60; (F) Salaries Accrued, $200.

Account Title	Trial Balance Dr.	Trial Balance Cr.
Cash	2 4 8 6 00	
Merchandise Inventory	8 2 4 00	
Prepaid Rent	1 1 5 2 00	
Prepaid Insurance	6 0 00	
Office Equipment	2 1 6 0 00	
Accumulated Depreciation, Office Equipment		5 6 0 00
Unearned Storage Fees		2 5 1 6 00
Accounts Payable		1 0 0 00
B. Ray, Capital		1 9 3 2 00
Income Summary		
Sales		11 0 4 0 00
Sales Returns and Allowances	5 4 6 00	
Sales Discount	2 1 6 00	
Purchases	5 2 5 6 00	
Purchases Returns and Allowances		1 6 8 00
Purchases Discount		1 0 2 00
Salaries Expense	2 0 1 6 00	
Insurance Expense	1 3 9 2 00	
Utilities Expense	9 6 00	
Plumbing Expense	2 1 4 00	
	16 4 1 8 00	16 4 1 8 00

Quiz Tip: The ending inventory of $200 becomes next month's beginning inventory.

Solution to Self-Review Quiz 12-2

Solution is shown on page 442.

WORKSHEET
FOR YEAR ENDED DECEMBER 31, 19XX

	Trial Balance Dr.	Trial Balance Cr.	Adjustments Dr.	Adjustments Cr.
Cash	12920 00			
Petty Cash	100 00			
Accounts Receivable	1450 00			
Merchandise Inventory	19000 00		(B)4000 00	(A)19000 00
Supplies	800 00			(D)500 00
Prepaid Insurance	900 00			(E)300 00
Store Equipment	4000 00			
Acc. Dep., Store Equipment		400 00		(F)50 00
Accounts Payable		17900 00		
Federal Income Tax Payable		800 00		
FICA-Soc. Sec. Payable		454 00		
FICA-Medicare Payable		106 00		
State Income Tax Payable		200 00		
SUTA Tax Payable		108 00		
FUTA Tax Payable		32 00		
Unearned Rent		600 00	(C)200 00	
Mortgage Payable		2320 00		
Art Newner, Capital		79050 00		
Art Newner, Withdrawals	8600 00			
Income Summary			(A)19000 00	(B)4000 00
Sales		95000 00		
Sales Returns and Allowances	950 00			
Sales Discount	670 00			
Purchases	52000 00			
Purchases Discount		860 00		
Purchases Returns and Allowances		680 00		
Freight-In	450 00			
Salaries Expense	11700 00		(G)600 00	
Payroll Tax Expense	420 00			
Postage Expense	25 00			
Miscellaneous Expense	30 00			
Interest Expense	300 00			
	127365 00	127365 00		
Rental Income				(C)200 00
Supplies Expense			(D)500 00	
Insurance Expense			(E)300 00	
Depreciation Expense, Store Equip.			(F)50 00	
Salaries Payable				(G)600 00
			24650 00	24650 00
Net Income				

FIGURE 12-8 Completed Worksheet

Adjusted Trial Bal.		Income Statement		Balance Sheet	
Dr.	Cr.	Dr.	Cr.	Dr.	Cr.
1292000				1292000	
10000				10000	
1450000				1450000	
400000				400000	
30000				30000	
60000				60000	
400000				400000	
	45000				45000
	1790000				1790000
	80000				80000
	45400				45400
	10600				10600
	20000				20000
	10800				10800
	3200				3200
	40000				40000
	232000				232000
	790500				790500
860000				860000	
1900000	400000	1900000	400000		
	9500000		9500000		
95000		95000			
67000		67000			
5200000		5200000			
	86000		86000		
	68000		68000		
45000		45000			
1230000		1230000			
42000		42000			
2500		2500			
3000		3000			
30000		30000			
	20000		20000		
50000		50000			
30000		30000			
5000		5000			
	60000				60000
13201500	13201500	8699500	10074000	4502000	3127500
		1374500			1374500
		10074000	10074000	4502000	4502000

FIGURE 12-8 (cont.)

RAY COMPANY
WORKSHEET
FOR YEAR ENDED DECEMBER 31, 19XX

Account	Trial Balance Dr.	Trial Balance Cr.	Adjustments Dr.	Adjustments Cr.	Adjusted Trial Balance Dr.	Adjusted Trial Balance Cr.	Income Statement Dr.	Income Statement Cr.	Balance Sheet Dr.	Balance Sheet Cr.
Cash	248600				248600				248600	
Merchandise Inventory	82400		(B) 20000	(A) 82400	20000				20000	
Prepaid Rent	115200			(D) 10000	105200				105200	
Prepaid Insurance	6000				6000				6000	
Office Equipment	216000				216000				216000	
Acc. Dep., Store Equipment		56000		(E) 6000		62000				62000
Unearned Storage Fees		251600	(C) 51600			200000				200000
Accounts Payable		10000				10000				10000
B. Ray, Capital		193200				193200				193200
Income Summary			(A) 82400	(B) 20000	82400	20000	82400	20000		
Sales		952000				952000		952000		
Sales Returns and Allowances	54600				54600		54600			
Sales Discount	21600				21600		21600			
Purchases	525600				525600		525600			
Purchases Returns and Allowances		168800				168800		168800		
Purchases Discount		10200				10200		10200		
Salaries Expense	201600		(F) 20000		221600		221600			
Insurance Expense	139200				139200		139200			
Utilities Expense	9600				9600		9600			
Plumbing Expense	21400				21400		21400			
	1641800	1641800								
Storage Fees Earned				(C) 51600		51600		51600		
Rent Expense			(D) 10000		10000		10000			
Depreciation Expense, Equipment			(E) 6000		6000		6000			
Salaries Payable				(F) 20000		20000				20000
			190000	190000	1687800	1687800	1092000	1202600	595800	485200
Net Income							110600			110600
							1202600	1202600	595800	595800

SUMMARY OF KEY POINTS

Learning Unit 12-1

1. The periodic inventory system updates the record of goods on hand only at the *end* of the accounting period. This system is used for companies with a variety of merchandise with low unit prices.

2. In the periodic inventory system, additional purchases of merchandise during the accounting period will be recorded in the Purchases account. The amount in beginning inventory will remain unchanged during the accounting period. At the end of the period a new figure for ending inventory will be calculated.

3. Beginning inventory at the end of the accounting period is part of the cost of goods sold, while ending inventory is a reduction to cost of goods sold.

4. The perpetual inventory system keeps a continuous record of inventory: it is used by companies with high amounts of inventory.

5. Net Sales less cost of goods sold equals gross profit. Gross profit less operating expenses equals Net Income.

6. Unearned Revenue is a liability account that accumulates revenue that has *not* been earned yet, although the cash has been received. It represents a liability to the seller until the service or product is performed or delivered.

Learning Unit 12-2

1. Two important adjustments in the accounting for a merchandise company deal with the Merchandise Inventory account and with the Unearned Revenue account (unearned rent).

2. When a company delivers goods or services for which it has been paid in advance, an adjustment is made to reduce the liability account Unearned Revenue and to increase an earned revenue account.

KEY TERMS

Beginning merchandise inventory (beginning inventory)   The cost of goods on hand in a company to *begin* an accounting period.

Cost of goods sold   Total cost of goods sold to customers.

Ending merchandise inventory (ending inventory)   The cost of goods that remain unsold at the *end* of the accounting period. It is an asset on the new balance sheet.

Freight-In   A cost of goods sold account that records shipping cost to buyer.

Gross profit   Net sales less cost of goods sold.

Interest Expense   The cost of borrowing money.

Mortgage Payable   A liability account showing amount owed on a mortgage.

Periodic inventory system   An inventory system that, at the *end* of each accounting period, calculates the cost of the unsold goods on hand by taking the cost of each unit times the number of units of each product on hand.

Perpetual inventory system   An inventory system that keeps *continual track* of each type of inventory by recording units on hand at beginning, units sold, and the current balance after each sale or purchase.

Unearned Revenue   A liability account that records receipt of payment for goods or services in advance of delivery.

BLUEPRINT OF A WORKSHEET FOR A MERCHANDISE COMPANY

Account Titles	Adjustments Dr.	Adjustments Cr.	Adjusted Trial Balance Dr.	Adjusted Trial Balance Cr.	Income Statement Dr.	Income Statement Cr.	Balance Sheet Dr.	Balance Sheet Cr.
Cash			X				X	
Petty Cash			X				X	
Accounts Receivable			X				X	
Merchandise Inventory	X-E	X-B	X-E				X-E	
Supplies			X				X	
Equipment			X				X	
Acc. Dep., Store Equipment				X				X
Accounts Payable				X				X
Federal Income Tax Payable				X				X
FICA-Social Security Payable				X				X
FICA-Medicare Payable				X				X
State Income Tax Payable				X				X
SUTA Tax Payable				X				X
FUTA Tax Payable				X				X
Unearned Sales				X				X
Mortgage Payable				X				X
A. Flynn, Capital				X				X
A. Flynn, Withdrawals			X				X	
Income Summary*	X-B	X-E	X-B	X-E	X-B	X-E		
Sales				X		X		
Sales Returns and Allow.			X		X			
Sales Discount			X		X			
Purchases			X		X			
Purchases Ret. and Allow.				X		X		
Purchases Discount				X		X		
Freight-In			X		X			
Salaries Expense			X		X			
Payroll Tax Expense			X		X			
Insurance Expense			X		X			
Depreciation Expense			X		X			
Salaries Payable				X				X
Rental Income				X		X		

* Note that the figures for beginning (X-B) and ending inventory (X-E) are never combined on the Income Summary line of the worksheet. When the formal income statement is prepared, two distinct figures for inventory will be used to explain and calculate cost of goods sold. Beginning inventory adds to cost of goods sold; ending inventory reduces cost of goods sold.

QUESTIONS, MINI EXERCISES, EXERCISES, AND PROBLEMS

Discussion Questions

1. When would a company consider using a periodic inventory system?
2. What is the function of the Purchases account?

3. A low-volume, high-unit-price inventory requires a company to use a periodic inventory system. Accept or reject, and support your answer.

4. Explain why Unearned Revenue is a liability account.

5. In a periodic system of inventory, the balance of beginning inventory will remain unchanged during the period. True or false?

6. What is the purpose of an inventory sheet?

7. Why do many Unearned Revenue accounts have to be adjusted?

8. Explain why figures for beginning and ending inventory are not combined on the Income Summary line of the worksheet.

Mini Exercises

(The forms you need are on page 417 of the *Study Guide and Working Papers.*)

Adjustment for Merchandise Inventory

1. Given the following, journalize the adjusting entries for merchandise inventory. Note ending inventory has a balance of $12,000.

Merchandise Inventory 114	Income Summary 313
20,000	

Adjustment for Unearned Fees

2.

   a. Given the following, journalize the adjusting entry. By Dec. 31, $300 of the unearned dog walking fees were earned.

Unearned Dog Walking Fees 225	Earned Dog Walking Fees 441
650 12/1/XX	4,000 12/1/XX

   b. What is the category of unearned dog walking fees?

Worksheet

3. Match the following:

   1. Located on the Income Statement debit column of the worksheet

   2. Located on the Income Statement credit column of the worksheet

   3. Located on the Balance Sheet debit column of the worksheet

   4. Located on the Balance Sheet credit column of the worksheet

   _____ **a.** Ending Merchandise Inventory

   _____ **b.** Unearned Rent

   _____ **c.** Sales Discount

   _____ **d.** Purchases

   _____ **e.** Rental Income

   _____ **f.** Petty Cash

Merchandise Inventory Adjustment on Worksheet

4. Adjustment column of a worksheet:

Merchandise Inventory   (A)   (B)

Income Summary   (B)   (A)

Explain what the letters A and B represent. Why are they never combined?

Income Summary on the Worksheet

5.

	Adj.		ATB		Income Statement	
	Dr.	Cr.	Dr.	Cr.	Dr.	Cr.
Income Summary	A	B	C	D	E	F

Given a figure of Beginning Inventory of $500 and a $700 figure for Ending Inventory, place these numbers on the Income Summary line of this partial worksheet.

Exercises

(The forms you need are on page 418 of the *Study Guide and Working Papers*.)

Categorizing account titles.

12-1. Indicate the normal balance and category of each of the following accounts.
   a. Purchases Returns and Allowances
   b. Merchandise Inventory (beginning of period)
   c. Freight-In
   d. Payroll Tax Expense
   e. Purchases Discount
   f. Sales Discount
   g. FICA — Social Security Payable
   h. Unearned Revenue

Calculating net sales, cost of goods sold, gross profit, and net income.

12-2. From the following, calculate (a) net sales, (b) cost of goods sold, (c) gross profit, and (d) net income: Sales, $22,000; Sales Discount, $500; Sales Returns and Allowances, $250; Beginning Inventory, $650; Net Purchases, $13,200; Ending Inventory, $510; Operating Expenses, $3,600.

Unearned revenue.

12-3. Allan Co. had the following balances on December 31, 19XX:

Cash		Unearned Janitorial Service	
2,100			600

Janitorial Service	
	7,200

The accountant for Allan has asked you to make an adjustment, since $400 of janitorial services has just been performed for customers who had paid two months. Construct a transaction analysis chart.

Calculating cost of goods sold.

12-4. Lesan Co. purchased merchandise costing $400,000. Calculate the cost of goods sold under the following different situations:
   a. Beginning inventory $40,000 and no ending inventory.
   b. Beginning inventory $50,000 and a $60,000 ending inventory.
   c. No beginning inventory and a $30,000 ending inventory.

Preparing a worksheet.

12-5. Prepare a worksheet from the following information:
   a/b. Merchandise Inventory — ending   13
   c. Store Supplies on hand   4
   d. Depreciation on Store Equipment   4
   e. Accrued Salaries   2

MOORE CO.
TRIAL BALANCE
DECEMBER 31, 19XX

	Dr.	Cr.
Cash	800	
Accounts Receivable	500	
Merchandise Inventory	1100	
Store Supplies	1000	
Store Equipment	2000	
Accumulated Depreciation, Store Equipment		600
Accounts Payable		500
J. Moore, Capital		3400
Income Summary	—	—
Sales		6400
Sales Returns and Allowances	900	
Purchases	2300	
Purchases Discount		300
Freight-In	300	
Salaries Expense	1000	
Advertising Expense	1300	
Totals	11200	11200

Group A Problems

Calculating net sales, cost of goods sold, gross profit and net income.

Check Figure:
Net Income $1,241

(The forms you need are on page 419 of the *Study Guide and Working Papers.* Also you can use the foldout worksheets at the end of the *Study Guide and Working Papers.*)

12A-1. Based on the accounts listed below, calculate:
  a. Net sales.
  b. Cost of goods sold.
  c. Gross profit.
  d. Net income.

Accounts Payable	$ 3,200
Operating Expenses	1,490
J. Jensen, Capital	18,200
Purchases	1,250
Freight-In	60
Ending Merchandise Inventory, Dec. 31, 19XX	44
Sales	4,210
Accounts Receivable	389
Cash	656
Purchases Discount	32
Sales Returns and Allowances	185
Beg. Merchandise Inventory, Jan. 1, 19XX	55
Purchases Returns and Allowances	47
Sales Discount	52

Comprehensive Problem.
Completing a worksheet for
a merchandise company.

12A-2. From the following trial balance, complete a worksheet for Jim's Hardware.

Check Figure:

Net Income $1,984

JIM'S HARDWARE TRIAL BALANCE DECEMBER 31, 19XX	Dr.	Cr.
Cash	786 00	
Accounts Receivable	1 152 00	
Merchandise Inventory	600 00	
Prepaid Insurance	684 00	
Store Equipment	2 160 00	
Accumulated Depreciation, Store Equipment		660 00
Accounts Payable		516 00
Jim Spool, Capital		1 632 00
Income Summary	—	—
Hardware Sales		1 104 0 00
Hardware Sales Returns and Allowances	546 00	
Hardware Sales Discount	216 00	
Purchases	5 256 00	
Purchases Discount		168 00
Purchases Returns and Allowances		102 00
Wages Expense	1 716 00	
Rent Expense	792 00	
Telephone Expense	114 00	
Miscellaneous Expense	96 00	
	14 118 00	14 118 00

Assume the following:

a/b. Ending inventory on Dec. 31 is calculated at $310.

  c. Insurance expired, $150.

  d. Depreciation on store equipment, $60.

  e. Accrued wages, $90.

Comprehensive Problem. Completing a worksheet.

Check Figure:

Net Income $5,300

12A-3. The owner of Waltz Company has asked you to prepare a worksheet from the following trial balance.

WALTZ COMPANY TRIAL BALANCE DECEMBER 31, 19XX	Dr.	Cr.
Cash	5 4 0 8 00	
Petty Cash	2 4 0 00	
Accounts Receivable	2 5 1 2 00	
Beginning Merchandise Inventory, Jan. 1	5 0 9 2 00	
Prepaid Rent	6 1 6 00	
Office Supplies	9 4 4 00	
Office Equipment	9 2 8 0 00	
Accumulated Depreciation, Office Equipment		7 6 0 0 00
Accounts Payable		5 9 6 4 00
K. Waltz, Capital		5 4 7 6 00
K. Waltz, Withdrawals	4 8 0 0 00	
Income Summary		
Sales		5 2 4 8 4 00
Sales Returns and Allowances	9 6 00	
Sales Discount	2 4 0 0 00	
Purchases	2 9 3 1 6 00	
Purchases Discount		1 6 00
Purchases Returns and Allowances		3 4 8 00
Office Salaries Expense	7 4 0 8 00	
Insurance Expense	2 4 0 0 00	
Advertising Expense	8 0 0 00	
Utilities Expense	5 7 6 00	
	7 1 8 8 8 00	7 1 8 8 8 00

Additional data:

a/b. Ending merchandise inventory on December 31, $1,805.

   c. Office supplies used up, $210.

   d. Rent expired, $195.

   e. Depreciation expense on office equipment, $550.

   f. Office salaries earned but not paid, $310.

Comprehensive Problem. Completing a worksheet with payroll and unearned revenue.

12A-4. From the following trial balance and additional data, complete the worksheet for Ron's Wholesale Clothing Company.

RON'S WHOLESALE CLOTHING COMPANY TRIAL BALANCE DECEMBER 31, 19XX		
	Dr.	Cr.
Cash	4 4 6 0 00	
Petty Cash	3 0 0 00	
Accounts Receivable	7 5 0 0 00	
Merchandise Inventory	9 0 0 0 00	
Supplies	1 0 0 0 00	
Prepaid Insurance	8 5 0 00	
Store Equipment	2 5 0 0 00	
Acc. Dep., Store Equipment		1 5 0 0 00
Accounts Payable		10 6 3 5 00
Federal Income Tax Payable		5 0 0 00
FICA-Social Security Payable		4 5 4 00
FICA-Medicare Payable		1 0 6 00
State Income Tax Payable		1 5 0 00
SUTA Tax Payable		1 0 8 00
FUTA Tax Payable		3 2 00
Unearned Storage Fees		3 2 5 00
Ron Win, Capital		12 5 0 0 00
Ron Win, Withdrawals	4 3 0 0 00	
Income Summary	—	—
Sales		45 0 0 0 00
Sales Returns and Allowances	1 4 7 5 00	
Sales Discount	1 3 3 5 00	
Purchases	26 0 0 0 00	
Purchases Discount		5 5 0 00
Purchases Returns and Allowances		4 0 0 00
Freight-In	2 2 5 00	
Salaries Expense	12 0 0 0 00	
Payroll Tax Expense	4 2 0 00	
Interest Expense	8 9 5 00	
	72 2 6 0 00	72 2 6 0 00

Additional data:

a/b. Ending merchandise inventory on December 31, $6,000.

c. Supplies on hand, $400.

d. Insurance expired, $600.

e. Depreciation on store equipment, $400.

f. Storage fees earned, $176.

(The forms you need are on page 419 of the *Study Guide and Working Papers.*)

Calculating net sales, cost of goods sold, gross profit, and net income.

12B-1. From the following accounts, calculate (a) net sales, (b) cost of goods sold, (c) gross profit, (d) net income.

Sales Discount	$ 452
Purchases Returns and Allowances	64
Beginning Merchandise Inventory, Jan 1, 19XX	79
Sales Returns and Allowances	191
Purchases Discounts	42
Cash	3,895
Accounts Receivable	441
Sales	3,950
Ending Merchandise Inventory, Dec. 31, 19XX	75
Freight-In	41
Purchases	1,152
R. Roland, Capital	1,950
Operating Expenses	895
Accounts Payable	129

Check Figure:

Net Income $1,321

Comprehensive Problem. Completing a worksheet for a merchandise company.

12B-2. As the accountant for Jim's Hardware, you have been asked to complete a worksheet from the following trial balance as well as additional data.

Check Figure:

Net Income $1,336

JIM'S HARDWARE
TRIAL BALANCE
DECEMBER 31, 19XX

	Dr.	Cr.
Cash	9 6 0 00	
Accounts Receivable	1 6 0 0 00	
Merchandise Inventory	7 3 6 00	
Prepaid Insurance	1 1 1 2 00	
Store Equipment	3 2 0 0 00	
Accumulated Depreciation, Store Equipment		1 6 8 0 00
Accounts Payable		1 4 0 8 00
J. Spool, Capital		2 5 7 6 00
Income Summary	—	—
Hardware Sales		1 4 8 0 0 00
Hardware Sales Returns and Allowances	7 2 8 00	
Hardware Sales Discount	6 8 8 00	
Purchases	7 0 8 8 00	
Purchases Discounts		2 4 0 00
Purchases Returns and Allowances		2 4 8 00
Wages Expense	2 3 0 4 00	
Rent Expense	1 8 4 0 00	
Telephone Expense	5 5 2 00	
Miscellaneous Expense	1 4 4 00	
	2 0 9 5 2 00	2 0 9 5 2 00

Additional data:

a/b. Cost of ending inventory on December 31, $480.

c. Insurance expired, $112.

d. Depreciation on store equipment, $90.

e. Accrued wages, $150.

12B-3. From the following, complete a worksheet for Waltz Company.

WALTZ COMPANY TRIAL BALANCE DECEMBER 31, 19XX		
	Dr.	Cr.
Cash	3 8 0 0 00	
Petty Cash	1 0 0 00	
Accounts Receivable	3 4 0 0 00	
Merchandise Inventory	5 2 0 4 00	
Prepaid Rent	1 2 0 0 00	
Office Supplies	1 3 6 0 00	
Office Equipment	9 6 8 0 00	
Accumulated Depreciation, Office Equipment		4 0 4 0 00
Accounts Payable		7 9 6 4 00
K. Waltz, Capital		5 4 7 6 00
K. Waltz, Withdrawals	5 0 0 0 00	
Income Summary	—	—
Sales		52 4 6 2 00
Sales Returns and Allowances	1 1 6 00	
Sales Discount	2 2 0 0 00	
Purchases	29 2 9 6 00	
Purchases Discounts		1 2 0 8 00
Purchases Returns and Allowances		1 3 5 0 00
Office Salaries Expense	7 4 0 8 00	
Insurance Expense	2 2 0 0 00	
Advertising Expense	8 0 0 00	
Utilities Expense	7 3 6 00	
	72 5 0 0 00	72 5 0 0 00

Additional data:

a/b. Ending merchandise inventory on December 31, $1,600.

  c. Office supplies on hand, $90.

  d. Rent expired, $110.

  e. Depreciation expense on office equipment, $250.

  f. Salaries accrued, $180.

12B-4. From the following trial balance and additional data, complete the worksheet for Ron's Wholesale Clothing Company.

Check Figure:

Net Loss $8,686

RON'S WHOLESALE CLOTHING COMPANY TRIAL BALANCE DECEMBER 31, 19XX		
	Dr.	Cr.
Cash	2 6 0 0 00	
Petty Cash	3 0 00	
Accounts Receivable	3 0 0 0 00	
Merchandise Inventory	3 6 0 0 00	
Supplies	2 7 0 00	
Prepaid Insurance	1 8 0 00	
Store Equipment	1 0 0 0 00	
Accumulated Depreciation, Store Equipment		4 9 6 00
Accounts Payable		4 5 9 0 00
FIT Payable		3 5 0 00
FICA-Soc Sec Payable		1 9 4 00
FICA-Medicare Payable		4 6 00
SIT Payable		1 0 0 00
SUTA Tax Payable		6 0 00
FUTA Tax Payable		1 4 00
Unearned Storage Fees		3 5 0 00
Ron Win, Capital		2 7 3 4 00
Ron Win, Withdrawals	1 8 0 0 00	
Income Summary	—	—
Sales		19 4 0 0 00
Sales Returns and Allowances	5 6 0 00	
Sales Discount	4 8 0 00	
Purchases	8 6 0 0 00	
Purchases Discount		2 4 0 00
Purchases Returns and Allowances		1 6 0 00
Freight-In	1 0 0 00	
Salaries Expense	6 0 0 0 00	
Payroll Tax Expense	1 9 4 00	
Interest Expense	3 2 0 00	
	28 7 3 4 00	28 7 3 4 00

Additional data:

a/b. Ending merchandise inventory on December 31, $9,000.

c. Supplies on hand, $50.

d. Insurance expired, $55.

e. Depreciation on store equipment, $100.

f. Storage fees earned, $115.

REAL WORLD APPLICATIONS

12R-1.

Kim Andrews prepared the following income statement on a cash basis for Ed Sloan, M.D.

ED SLOAN, M.D. INCOME STATEMENT FOR YEAR ENDED DECEMBER 31, 19X2		
Professional Fees Earned		50 0 0 0 00
Expenses		18 0 0 0 00
Net Income		32 0 0 0 00

Ed Sloan has requested written information from Kim as to what his professional fees earned would be under the accrual-basis system of accounting. Kim has asked you to provide Dr. Sloan with this information, based on the following facts that Kim ignored in the original preparation of the financial report:

	19X1	19X2
Accrued Professional Fees	$4,200	$5,300
Unearned Professional Fees	6,200	4,250

Make a written recommendation of the advantages of an accrual system to Dr. Sloan.

12R-2.

Abby Jay is having a difficult time understanding the relationship of sales, cost of goods sold, gross profit, and net income for a merchandise company. As the accounting lab tutor, you have been asked to sit down with Abby and explain how to calculate the missing amounts in each situation listed below. Keep in mind that each situation is a distinct and separate business problem.

	Sales	Beg. Inv.	Purchases	End Inv.	Cost of Goods Sold	Gross Profit	Expense	Net Income or Loss
Sit. 1	320,000	200,000	160,000	?	260,000	?	80,000	?
Sit. 2	380,000	140,000	?	180,000	200,000	?	100,000	80,000
Sit. 3	480,000	200,000	?	160,000	?	220,000	140,000	80,000
Sit. 4	?	160,000	280,000	140,000	?	160,000	140,000	?
Sit. 5	440,000	160,000	260,000	?	240,000	?	100,000	?
Sit. 6	280,000	120,000	?	140,000	160,000	?	?	40,000
Sit. 7	?	160,000	200,000	120,000	?	160,000	?	−20,000
Sit. 8	320,000	?	200,000	140,000	?	120,000	?	40,000

Explain in writing why gross profit does not always mean cash.

YOU make the call

Critical Thinking/Ethical Case

12R-3.

Jim Heary is the custodian of petty cash. Jim, who is short of personal cash, decided to pay his home electrical and phone bill from petty cash. He plans to pay it back next month. Do you feel Jim should do this? You make the call. Write down your specific recommendations to Jim.

ACCOUNTING RECALL
A CUMULATIVE APPROACH

THIS EXAM REVIEWS CHAPTERS 1 THROUGH 12

Your *Study Guide and Working Papers* (pp. 424–425) has forms to complete this exam, as well as worked-out solutions. The page references next to each question identify what pages to turn back to if you answer the question incorrectly.

PART 1   Vocabulary Review

Match the terms to the appropriate definition or phrase.

Page Ref.

(432)	1. Interest expense	A. A liability
(314)	2. Sales return and allowance	B. Cost of goods sold account
(428)	3. Ending merchandise inventory	C. Continual track
(121)	4. Accumulated depreciation	D. Contra-asset
(430)	5. Income summary	E. Nonoperating expense
(430)	6. Rental Income	F. New figure for capital
(430)	7. Unearned revenue	G. Subtracted from cost of goods sold
(356)	8. Purchases	
(161)	9. Closing	H. Other income
(428)	10. Perpetual inventory	I. Contra-revenue account
		J. Used in adjusting merchandise inventory

PART II   True or False (Accounting Theory)

(430)	11. Unearned rent is an asset.
(436)	12. Beginning and ending inventory are combined on the worksheet.
(428)	13. Ending inventory is added to cost of goods sold.
(275)	14. Look-back periods involve Federal Income Tax, Social Security, and Medicare.
(430)	15. The normal balance of income summary is a debit.

CONTINUING PROBLEM

The first six months of the year have concluded for Eldorado Computer Center, and Freedman wants to make the necessary adjustments to his accounts in order to prepare accurate financial statements.

Assignment:

(The worksheet is in the envelope at the end of the *Study Guide and Working Papers*.)

To prepare these adjustments, use the trial balance from Chapter 11 and the following inventory that Tony took at the end of March.

10 dozen ¼″ screws at a cost of $10 a dozen

5 dozen ½″ screws at a cost of $7 a dozen

2 feet of coaxial cable at a cost of $5 per foot

There was $300 worth of merchandise left in stock.

Depreciation of Computer Equipment:

Computer depreciates at $33 a month; purchased July 5

Computer workstations depreciate at $20 per month; purchased Sept. 17

Shop benches depreciate at $25 per month; purchased November 5

Depreciation of Office Equipment:

Office Equipment depreciates at $10 per month; purchased July 17.

Fax machine depreciates at $10 per month; purchased November 20.

Six months worth of rent at a rental state of $400 per month has expired.

Remember: If any long-term asset is purchased in the first fifteen days of the month, Freedman will charge depreciation for the full month. If an asset is purchased later than the 16th, he will not charge depreciation in the month it was purchased.

Complete the ten-column worksheet for the six months ended March 31, 19XX.

The method of accounting for merchandise inventory that we have been using thus far is characterized by the fact that the inventory account is adjusted only once, at the end of the accounting period. Since the inventory account is brought up to date only periodically, this system is named the **Periodic Method.** Let's now look at the **Perpetual Method,** an inventory system in which the inventory account is kept perpetually up to date, (or up to date at all times).

In the perpetual inventory system we have two key accounts into which we record information every time we buy or sell merchandise. These accounts are the Merchandise Inventory and Cost of Goods Sold accounts.

The Merchandise Inventory account is an asset account, the same account that was used in the previous discussion of the periodic inventory system. However, in the periodic system the balance of the Merchandise Inventory was correct *only* at the end of each accounting period. In the perpetual system, we will be recording entries to the Merchandise Inventory account each time our store purchases new merchandise and each time we sell merchandise to a customer.

The other key account is the Cost of Goods Sold account. As we sell merchandise to our customers, we will record entries that remove the cost of the merchandise from the Merchandise Inventory account and transfer that cost to the Cost of Goods Sold account. Thus the Merchandise Inventory account will show the correct cost for the inventory on hand, and the Cost of Goods Sold account will show the cumulative total cost of all merchandise that has been sold to our customers during the accounting period.

The Perpetual Method requires more accounting effort but has the important advantage that our key accounts, Merchandise Inventory and Cost of Goods Sold, will always provide *current* information to managers about their investment in inventory and the cost of the merchandise sold to customers.

EXAMPLE TRANSACTIONS

Let us imagine a typical college bookstore and look at some sample transactions as this bookstore buys books from publishers and then resells those books to students. We will assume that all transactions are in cash so that we can focus on recording transactions with the Perpetual Method of accounting for inventory.

19XX
March 2   Purchased ten copies of the textbook for the Math 2301 course at a cost of $29 per package for a total of $290.

	Mar.	2	Merchandise Inventory			2	9	0	00						
			Cash								2	9	0	00	
			To record the purchase												
			of inventory												

The asset account, Merchandise Inventory, has been increased by the cost of the new merchandise we have purchased. Now let's look at a sales transaction.

19XX
March 3 Sold a copy of the Math 2301 text for $38.

Mar.	3	Cash		3 8 00					
		Sales Revenue				3 8 00			
		To record revenue							
	3	Cost of Goods Sold		2 9 00					
		Merchandise Inventory				2 9 00			
		To record the cost of							
		goods sold							

In the perpetual inventory system we record both the retail value of the sale in a transaction that records the revenue and the cost of the sale in a transaction that transfers the cost of the item sold to the Cost of Goods Sold account.

When a business is using the perpetual method, it will be necessary to keep a detailed record of the quantity and cost of each item on hand. A subsidiary ledger with an inventory record form for each item in inventory will be created. This is very similar to the way that we keep a detailed record for each credit customer in an Accounts Receivable ledger. On the right below is the inventory record form for our Math 2301 textbook. Note how the form relates to the Merchandise Inventory account.

GENERAL LEDGER ACCOUNT
Merchandise Inventory

	Dr.	Cr.	
3/2	290		
		3/3	29
Bal. 261			

INVENTORY RECORD FORM
Math 2301 Text

date	purchased	sold	balance
3/2	10 @ $29		$290
3/3		1 @ $29	$261

The Merchandise Inventory ledger will consist of as many inventory record forms as a company has items for sale, and the total value of all items on hand will equal the balance of the Merchandise Inventory account.

Let's summarize the journal entries for the Perpetual Method.

Purchases: Each time we purchase inventory from a supplier we debit the Merchandise Inventory account to increase the balance.

Sales: Each time we sell an item we do *two* entries. One entry records the selling price exactly as is done with the Periodic Method. The additional entry transfers the cost of the item sold out of the Merchandise Inventory account and into the Cost of Goods Sold account.

The result of these entries is that our Merchandise Inventory, Cost of Goods Sold, and Sales (revenue) accounts are *perpetually* up to date.

13

COMPLETION OF THE ACCOUNTING CYCLE FOR A MERCHANDISE COMPANY

THE BIG PICTURE

The Eldorado Computer Center is in need of expansion. It currently has 4,000 square feet of space for repairs, sales, and office activity. Freedman is planning to increase his space and remodel some of the current space he has. To finance his plan he will take his completed financial reports to the bank and request a line of credit. The bank will review his detailed records to form an opinion on how the business has done and determine the amount of credit the business will be able to repay.

In the last chapter you began the steps to bring the books up to date by completing the adjusting entries for the first six months of the year. In this chapter you will record those adjusting entries and prepare the financial reports.

Eldorado Computer Center's income statement will show more detail than those prepared before, so the bank can see expenses according to the activity of the company. Some expenses can be classified as *selling expenses* because they relate directly to the sale of the merchandise. Other expenses, including rent and utilities, are *administrative expenses,* relating to office activity or general expenses of the business.

The balance sheet will also include more detail by breaking down the assets and liabilities into current and long-term categories. Freedman prepares a classified balance sheet for his business to help him as well as creditors and suppliers understand the business's ability to repay current and long-term debt obligations.

In this chapter you will also review how to close a business year by completing the necessary closing entries and the reversing entries to prepare for the new year. Since this is not the year-end time for Eldorado Computer Center, only the adjusting entries will be recorded and financial statements prepared.

Learning Objectives	◆ Preparing financial reports for a merchandise company. (p. 460) ◆ Recording adjusting and closing entries. (p. 467) ◆ Preparing a post-closing trial balance. (p. 472) ◆ Completing reversing entries. (p. 474)

In this chapter, we will discuss the steps involved in completing the accounting cycle for a merchandise company. The steps involved include preparing financial reports, journalizing and posting adjusting and closing entries, preparing a post-closing trial balance, and reversing entries.

LEARNING UNIT 13-1
Preparing Financial Reports

As we discussed in Chapter 5, when we were dealing with a service company rather than a merchandise company, the three financial reports can be prepared from the worksheet. Let's begin by looking at how Art's Wholesale Clothing Company prepares the income statement.

THE INCOME STATEMENT

Art is interested in knowing how well his shop performed for the year ended December 31, 19XX. What were its net sales? Were there many returns of goods from dissatisfied customers? What was the cost of the goods brought into the store versus the selling price received? How many goods were returned to suppliers? What is the cost of the goods that have not been sold? What was the cost of the Freight-In account? The income statement in Figure 13-1 is prepared from the income statement columns of the worksheet. Note that there are no debit or credit columns on the formal income statement — the inside columns on financial reports are used for subtotaling, not for debit and credit.

The income statement is broken down into several sections. Remembering the sections can help you set it up correctly on your own. Basically, this is what the income statement shows:

$$
\begin{aligned}
&\text{Net Sales} \\
&-\ \text{Cost of Goods Sold} \\
\hline
&=\ \text{Gross Profit} \\
&-\ \text{Operating Expenses} \\
\hline
&=\ \text{Net Income from Operations} \\
&+\ \text{Other Income} \\
&-\ \text{Other Expenses} \\
\hline
&=\ \text{Net Income}
\end{aligned}
$$

Let's take these sections one at a time and see where the figures come from on the worksheet.

Revenue Section

Net Sales: The first major category of the income statement shows net sales. The figure here — $93,380 — is not on the worksheet. Instead, the accountant

ART'S WHOLESALE CLOTHING COMPANY
INCOME STATEMENT
FOR YEAR ENDED DECEMBER 31, 19XX

Revenue:			
Gross Sales			$95 000 00
Less: Sales Ret. and Allow.		$ 95000	
Sales Discount		67000	162000
Net Sales			$9338000
Cost of Goods Sold:			
Merchandise Inventory, 1/1/X2		$1900000	
Purchases	$5200000		
Less: Purch. Discount	$ 86000		
Purch. Ret. and Allow.	68000	154000	
Net Purchases		$5046000	
Add: Freight-In		45000	
Net Cost of Purchases		5091000	
Cost of Goods Available for Sale		$6991000	
Less: Merch. Inv., 12/31/X2		400000	
Cost of Goods Sold			6591000
Gross Profit			$2747000
Operating Expenses:			
Salaries Expense		$1230000	
Payroll Tax Expense		42000	
Dep. Exp., Store Equip.		5000	
Supplies Expense		50000	
Insurance Expense		30000	
Postage Expense		2500	
Miscellaneous Expense		3000	
Total Operating Expenses			1362500
Net Income from Operations			$1384500
Other Income:			
Rental Income		$ 20000	
Other Expenses:			
Interest Expense		30000	10000
Net Income			$1374500

ART'S WHOLESALE CLOTHING COMPANY
PARTIAL WORKSHEET
FOR YEAR ENDED DECEMBER 31, 19XX

	Income Statement	
	Dr	Cr
Income Summary	1900000	400000
Sales		9500000
Sales Returns and Allowances	95000	
Sales Discount	67000	
Purchases	5200000	
Purchases Discount		86000
Purchases Returns and Allowances		68000
Freight-In	45000	
Salaries Expense	1230000	
Payroll Tax Expense	42000	
Postage Expense	2500	
Miscellaneous Expense	3000	
Interest Expense	30000	
Rental Income		20000
Supplies Expense	50000	
Insurance Expense	30000	
Depreciation Expense, Store Equip.	5000	
Salaries Payable		
	8699500	10074000
Net Income	1374500	
	10074000	10074000

FIGURE 13-1 Partial Worksheet and Income Statement

Sales
− Sales Ret. & Allow.
− Sales Discount
= Net Sales

Beg. Inventory
+ Net Cost of Purchases
− Ending Inventory
= Cost of Goods Sold

Remember, in the periodic inventory system goods brought in during the accounting period are added to the Purchases account, not to the Merchandise Inventory account.

Net Sales
− Cost of Goods Sold
= Gross Profit

must combine the amounts for gross sales, sales returns and allowances, and sales discount found on the worksheet to arrive at a figure for net sales. Thus, these individual amounts are not summarized in a single figure for net sales until the formal income statement is prepared.

Cost of Goods Sold Section

The figures for Merchandise Inventory are shown separately on the worksheet. The $19,000 represents the beginning inventory of the period, and the $4,000, calculated from an inventory sheet, is the ending inventory. Note on the financial report how the cost of goods sold section uses two separate figures for inventory.

Note that the following numbers are not found on the worksheet but are shown on the formal income statement (they are combined by the accountant in preparing the income statement):

◆ Net Purchases: $50,460 (Purchases − Purchases Discount − Purchases Returns and Allowances)

◆ Net Cost of Purchases: $50,910 (Net Purchases + Freight-In)

◆ Cost of Goods Available for Sale: $69,910 (Beginning Inventory + Net Cost of Purchases)

◆ Cost of Goods Sold: $65,910 (Cost of Goods Available for Sale − Ending Inventory)

Gross Profit

Gross profit ($27,470) is calculated by subtracting the cost of goods sold from net sales ($93,380 − $65,910). The amount is not found on the worksheet.

Operating Expenses Section

Like the other figures we have discussed, the business's operating expenses do not appear on the worksheet. To get this figure ($13,625), the accountant adds up all the expenses on the worksheet.

Many operating companies break expenses down into those directly related to the selling activity of the company (**selling expenses**) and those related to administrative or office activity (**administrative expenses** or **general expenses**). Here's a sample list broken down into these two categories:

Operating Expenses
◆ Selling Expenses:
    Sales Salaries Expense
    Delivery Expense
    Advertising Expense
    Depreciation Expense, Store Equipment
    Insurance Expense
      Total Selling Expenses
◆ Administrative Expenses:
    Rent Expense
    Office Salaries Expense
    Utilities Expense
    Supplies Expense
    Depreciation Expense, Office Equipment
      Total Administrative Expenses
        Total Operating Expenses

Other Income (or Other Revenue) Section

This section is used to record any revenue other than revenue from sales. For example, Art's Wholesale makes a profit from subletting a portion of a building. The $200 of rental income the company earns from this is recorded in the **Other Income** section.

Other Expenses Section

This section is used to record nonoperating expenses—that is, expenses that are not related to the main operating activities of the business. For example, Art's Wholesale owes $300 interest on money it has borrowed. That expense is shown in the **Other Expenses** section.

STATEMENT OF OWNER'S EQUITY

The information used to prepare the statement of owner's equity comes from the balance sheet columns of the worksheet. Keep in mind the capital account in the ledger should be checked to see whether any additional investments have occurred during the period. The diagram below shows how the worksheet aids in this. The ending figure of $13,050 for Art Newner, Capital, is carried over to the balance sheet, which is the final report we will look at in this chapter.

Statement of owner's equity is the same for a merchandise business as for a service firm.

Any additional investment by owner would be added to his or her beginning capital amount.

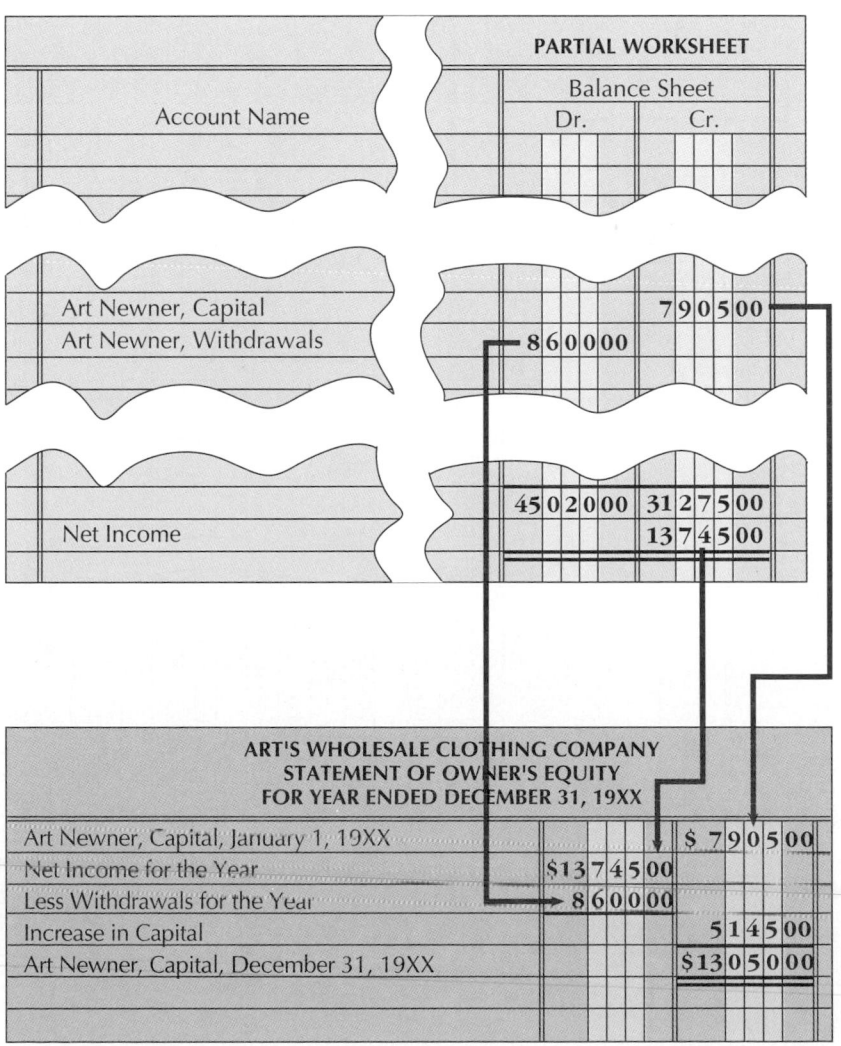

ART'S WHOLESALE CLOTHING COMPANY
CLASSIFIED BALANCE SHEET
FOR YEAR ENDED DECEMBER 31, 19XX

Assets

Current Assets:			
Cash	$12920 00		
Petty Cash	100 00		
Accounts Receivable	1450 00		
Merchandise Inventory	4000 00		
Supplies	300 00		
Prepaid Insurance	600 00		
Total Current Assets			$32420 00
Plant and Equipment:			
Store Equipment		$4000 00	
Less: Accum. Depreciation		450 00	3550 00
Total Assets			$35970 00

Liabilities

Current Liabilities:			
Mortgage Payable (current portion)	$ 320 00		
Accounts Payable	17900 00		
Federal Income Tax Payable	800 00		
FICA-Social Security Payable	454 00		
FICA-Medicare Payable	106 00		
State Income Tax Payable	200 00		
SUTA Tax Payable	108 00		
FUTA Tax Payable	32 00		
Salaries Payable	600 00		
Unearned Rent	400 00		
Total Current Liabilities			$20920 00
Long-Term Liabilities:			
Mortgage Payable			2000 00
Total Liabilities			$22920 00
Owner's Equity			
Art Newner, Capital, December 31, 19XX			13050 00
Total Liabilities and Owner's Equity			$35970 00

ART'S WHOLESALE CLOTHING COMPANY
WORKSHEET
FOR YEAR ENDED DECEMBER 31, 19XX

	Balance Sheet	
	Dr.	Cr.
Cash	12920 00	
Petty Cash	100 00	
Accounts Receivable	1450 00	
Merchandise Inventory	4000 00	
Supplies	300 00	
Prepaid Insurance	600 00	
Store Equipment	4000 00	
Acc. Dep., Store Equipment		450 00
Accounts Payable		17900 00
Federal Income Tax Payable		800 00
FICA-Social Security Payable		454 00
FICA-Medicare Payable		106 00
State Income Tax Payable		200 00
SUTA Tax Payable		108 00
FUTA Tax Payable		32 00
Unearned Rent		400 00
Mortgage Payable		2320 00
Art Newner, Capital		7905 00
Salaries Payable		600 00
	45020 00	31275 00
Net Income		13745 00
	45020 00	45020 00

FIGURE 13-2 Partial Worksheet and Classified Balance Sheet

THE BALANCE SHEET

Figure 13-2 on the facing page shows how a worksheet is used to aid in the preparation of a **classified balance sheet.** A classified balance sheet breaks down the assets and liabilities into more detail. Classified balance sheets provide management, owners, creditors, and suppliers with more information about the company's ability to pay current and long-term debts. They also provide a more complete financial picture of the firm.

These are the categories on the classified balance sheet:

◆ **Current assets** are defined as cash and assets that will be converted into cash or used up during the normal operating cycle of the company or one year, whichever is longer. (Think of the **operating cycle** as the time period it takes a company to buy and sell merchandise and then collect accounts receivable.)

Accountants list current assets in order of how easily they can be converted into cash (this is called liquidity). In some cases Accounts Receivable can be turned into cash more quickly than Merchandise Inventory — for example, it can be quite difficult to sell an outdated computer in a computer store, or to sell last year's model car this year.

◆ **Plant and Equipment** are long-lived assets that are used in the production or sale of goods or services. Art's Wholesale has only one plant asset, store equipment; other plant assets could include buildings and land. The assets are usually listed in order according to how long they will last; the shortest-lived assets are listed first. Land would always be the last asset listed (and land is never depreciated). Note that we still show the cost of the asset less its accumulated depreciation.

◆ **Current liabilities** are the debts or obligations of Art's Wholesale that must be paid within one year or one operating cycle. The order of listing accounts in this section is not always the same — many times companies will list their liabilities in the order they expect to pay them off. Note that the current portion of the mortgage, $320 (that portion due within one year), is listed before Accounts Payable.

Mortgage Payable:

	$2,320
−	320 current portion
	$2,000 long-term

◆ **Long-term liabilities** are debts or obligations that are not due and payable for a comparatively long period, usually for more than one year. For Art's Wholesale there is only one long-term liability — Mortgage Payable. The long-term portion of the mortgage is listed here; the current portion, due within one year, is listed under current liabilities.

LEARNING UNIT 13-1 REVIEW

AT THIS POINT you should be able to

◆ Prepare a detailed income statement from the worksheet. (p. 461)
◆ Explain the difference between selling and administrative expenses. (p. 462)
◆ Explain which columns of the worksheet are used in preparing a statement of owner's equity. (p. 463)
◆ Prepare a classified balance sheet from a worksheet. (p. 464)
◆ Explain as well as compare current assets with plant and equipment. (p. 465)
◆ Using Mortgage Payable as an example, explain the difference between current and long-term liabilities. (p. 465)

SELF-REVIEW QUIZ 13-1

(The forms you need are on pages 427–429 of the *Study Guide and Working Papers.*)

Using the worksheet on p. 442 from Self-Review Quiz 12-2, prepare in proper form (1) an income statement, (2) a statement of owner's equity, (3) a classified balance sheet for Ray Company.

Quiz Tip: Note Cost of Goods Sold has a separate figure for Beginning Inventory and Ending Inventory.

Solution to Self-Review Quiz 13-1

1.

RAY COMPANY INCOME STATEMENT FOR YEAR ENDED DECEMBER 31, 19XX					
Revenue:					
Sales					$11 04 0 00
Less: Sales Ret. and Allow.			$ 5 46 00		
Sales Discount			2 16 00		7 62 00
Net Sales					$10 27 8 00
Cost of Goods Sold:					
Merchandise Inventory, 1/1/XX			$ 8 24 00		
Purchases		$5 25 6 00			
Less: Pur. Ret. and Allow.	$ 1 68 00				
Purchases Discount	1 02 00	2 70 00			
Net Purchases			4 98 6 00		
Cost of Goods Available for Sale			$ 5 81 0 00		
Less: Merchandise Inv., 12/31/XX			2 00 00		
Cost of Goods Sold				5 61 0 00	
Gross Profit				$ 4 66 8 00	
Operating Expenses:					
Salaries Expense		$ 2 21 6 00			
Insurance Expense		1 39 2 00			
Utilities Expense		9 6 00			
Plumbing Expense		2 14 00			
Rent Expense		1 00 00			
Depreciation Exp., Equip.		6 0 00			
Total Operating Expenses				4 07 8 00	
Net Income from Operations				$ 5 9 0 00	
Other Income:					
Storage Fees				5 16 00	
Net Income				$ 1 10 6 00	

2.

RAY COMPANY STATEMENT OF OWNER'S EQUITY FOR YEAR ENDED DECEMBER 31, 19XX		
B. Ray, Capital, 1/1/XX		$1 9 3 2 00
Net Income for the Year		1 1 0 6 00
B. Ray, Capital, 12/31/XX		$3 0 3 8 00

3.

RAY COMPANY BALANCE SHEET DECEMBER 31, 19XX			
Assets			
Current Assets:			
Cash	$2 4 8 6 00		
Merchandise Inventory	2 0 0 00		
Prepaid Rent	1 0 5 2 00		
Prepaid Insurance	6 0 00		
Total Current Assets		$3 7 9 8 00	
Plant and Equipment:			
Office Equipment	$2 1 6 0 00		
Less: Accumulated Depreciation	6 2 0 00	1 5 4 0 00	
Total Assets		$5 3 3 8 00	
Liabilities			
Current Liabilities			
Accounts Payable	$ 1 0 0 00		
Salaries Payable	2 0 0 00		
Unearned Storage Fees	2 0 0 0 00		
Total Liabilities		$2 3 0 0 00	
Owner's Equity			
B. Ray, Capital, December 31, 19XX		3 0 3 8 00	
Total Liabilities and Owner's Equity		$5 3 3 8 00	

LEARNING UNIT 13-2

Journalizing and Posting Adjusting and Closing Entries; Preparing the Post-Closing Trial Balance

JOURNALIZING AND POSTING ADJUSTING ENTRIES

From the worksheet of Art's Wholesale, repeated here in Figure 13-3 (pp. 468–469) for your convenience, the adjusting entries can be journalized from the adjustments column and posted to the ledger. Keep in mind

ART'S WHOLESALE CLOTHING CO.
WORKSHEET
FOR YEAR ENDED DECEMBER 31, 19XX

	Trial Balance Dr.	Trial Balance Cr.	Adjustments Dr.	Adjustments Cr.
Cash	12 920 00			
Petty Cash	100 00			
Accounts Receivable	14 500 00			
Merchandise Inventory	19 000 00		(B) 4 000 00	(A) 19 000 00
Supplies	800 00			(D) 500 00
Prepaid Insurance	900 00			(E) 300 00
Store Equipment	400 00			
Acc. Dep., Store Equipment		400 00		(F) 50 00
Accounts Payable		17 900 00		
Federal Income Tax Payable		800 00		
FICA-Soc. Sec. Payable		454 00		
FICA-Medicare Payable		106 00		
State Income Tax Payable		200 00		
SUTA Tax Payable		108 00		
FUTA Tax Payable		32 00		
Unearned Rent		600 00	(C) 200 00	
Mortgage Payable		2 320 00		
Art Newner, Capital		7 905 00		
Art Newner, Withdrawals	8 600 00			
Income Summary			(A) 19 000 00	(B) 4 000 00
Sales		95 000 00		
Sales Returns and Allowances	950 00			
Sales Discount	670 00			
Purchases	52 000 00			
Purchases Discount		860 00		
Purchases Returns and Allowances		680 00		
Freight-In	450 00			
Salaries Expense	11 700 00		(G) 600 00	
Payroll Tax Expense	420 00			
Postage Expense	25 00			
Miscellaneous Expense	30 00			
Interest Expense	300 00			
	127 365 00	127 365 00		
Rental Income				(C) 200 00
Supplies Expense			(D) 500 00	
Insurance Expense			(E) 300 00	
Depreciation Expense, Store Equip.			(F) 50 00	
Salaries Payable				(G) 600 00
			24 650 00	24 650 00
Net Income				

FIGURE 13-3 Completed Worksheet

Adjusted Trial Bal. Dr.	Adjusted Trial Bal. Cr.	Income Statement Dr.	Income Statement Cr.	Balance Sheet Dr.	Balance Sheet Cr.
12920 00				12920 00	
100 00				100 00	
14500 00				14500 00	
4000 00				4000 00	
300 00				300 00	
600 00				600 00	
4000 00				4000 00	
	450 00				450 00
	17900 00				17900 00
	800 00				800 00
	454 00				454 00
	106 00				106 00
	200 00				200 00
	108 00				108 00
	32 00				32 00
	400 00				400 00
	2320 00				2320 00
	7905 00				7905 00
8600 00				8600 00	
19000 00	4000 00	19000 00	4000 00		
	95000 00		95000 00		
950 00		950 00			
670 00		670 00			
52000 00		52000 00			
	860 00		860 00		
	680 00		680 00		
450 00		450 00			
12300 00		12300 00			
420 00		420 00			
25 00		25 00			
30 00		30 00			
300 00		300 00			
	200 00		200 00		
500 00		500 00			
300 00		300 00			
50 00		50 00			
	600 00				600 00
132015 00	132015 00	86995 00	100740 00	45020 00	31275 00
		13745 00			13745 00
		100740 00	100740 00	45020 00	45020 00

FIGURE 13-3 (cont.)

that the adjustments have been placed only on the worksheet, not in the journal nor in the ledger. At this point the journal does not reflect adjustments, and the ledger still contains only unadjusted amounts.

ART'S WHOLESALE CLOTHING CO.
GENERAL JOURNAL

Page 2

Date		Account Titles and Description	PR	Dr.	Cr.
		Adjusting Entries			
	31	Income Summary	313	19 0 0 0 00	
		Merchandise Inventory	114		19 0 0 0 00
		Transferred beginning inventory			
		to Income Summary			
	31	Merchandise Inventory	114	4 0 0 0 00	
		Income Summary	313		4 0 0 0 00
		Records cost of ending inventory			
	31	Unearned Rent	219	2 0 0 00	
		Rental Income	414		2 0 0 00
		Rental Income earned			
	31	Supplies Expense	614	5 0 0 00	
		Supplies	115		5 0 0 00
		Supplies consumed			
	31	Insurance Expense	615	3 0 0 00	
		Prepaid Insurance	116		3 0 0 00
		Insurance expired			
	31	Dep. Exp., Store Equipment	613	5 0 00	
		Acc. Dep., Store Equipment	122		5 0 00
		Depreciation on equipment			
	31	Salaries Expense	611	6 0 0 00	
		Salaries Payable	212		6 0 0 00
		Accrued salaries			

PARTIAL LEDGER

Merchandise Inventory 114		Accum. Dep., Store Equipment 122		Income Summary 313		Dep. Expense, Store Equip. 613	
1,900	19,000		400	19,000	4,000	50	
4,000			50				

Supplies 115		Salary Payable 212		Supplies Expense 614		Salary Exp. 611	
800	500		600	500		12,000	
						600	

Prepaid Insurance 116		Unearned Rent 219		Insurance Expense 615		Rental Income 414	
900	300	200	600	300			200

The journalized and posted adjusting entries are shown above. Note that the liability Unearned Rent is reduced by $200 and Rental Income has increased by $200.

JOURNALIZING AND POSTING CLOSING ENTRIES

Back in Chapter 5, we discussed the closing process for a service company. The goals of closing are the same for a merchandise company. These goals are (1) to clear all temporary accounts in the ledger to zero and (2) to update capital in the ledger to its latest balance. The company must use the worksheet and the steps here and on page 472 to complete the closing process.

Step 1: Close all balances on the income statement credit column of the worksheet except Income Summary by debits.
Then credit the total to the Income Summary account.

Step 2: Close all balances on the income statement debit column of the worksheet except Income Summary by credits.
Then debit the total to the Income Summary account.

FIGURE 13-4 General Journal Closing Entries

	Date	Account Titles and Description	PR	Dr.	Cr.
		ART'S WHOLESALE CLOTHING CO. GENERAL JOURNAL			Page 2
		Closing Entries			
Step 1	31	Sales	411	95 00 0 00	
		Rental Income	414	2 0 0 00	
		Purchases Discount	512	8 6 0 00	
		Purchases Ret. and Allow.	513	6 8 0 00	
		Income Summary	313		96 74 0 00
		Transfers credit account balances			
		on income statement column of			
		worksheet to Income Summary			
Step 2	31	Income Summary	313	67 99 5 00	
		Sales Returns and Allowances	412		9 5 0 00
		Sales Discount	413		6 7 0 00
		Purchases	511		52 00 0 00
		Freight-In	514		4 5 0 00
		Salaries Expense	611		12 3 0 0 00
		Payroll Tax Expense	612		4 2 0 00
		Postage Expense	616		2 5 00
		Miscellaneous Expense	617		3 0 00
		Interest Expense	618		3 0 0 00
		Supplies Expense	614		5 0 0 00
		Insurance Expense	615		3 0 0 00
		Depreciation Expense, Store Equip.	613		5 0 00
		Transfers all expenses, and			
		deductions to Sales are			
		closed to Income Summary			
Step 3	31	Income Summary	313	13 74 5 00	
		A. Newner, Capital	311		13 74 5 00
		Transfer of net income to			
		Capital from Income Summary			
Step 4	31	A. Newner, Capital	311	8 6 0 0 00	
		A. Newner, Withdrawals	312		8 6 0 0 00
		Closes withdrawals to			
		Capital Account			

Step 3: Transfer the balance of the Income Summary account to the Capital account.

Step 4: Transfer the balance of the owner's Withdrawal account to the Capital account.

Let's look now at the journalized closing entries in Figure 13-4 (p. 471).

When these entries are posted, all the temporary accounts will have zero balances in the ledger, and the Capital account will be updated with a new balance.

Let's take a moment to look at the Income Summary account in T account form:

Income Summary 313

Adj.	19,000	4,000	Adj.
Clos.	67,995	96,740	Clos.
	86,995	100,740	
Net Income ➡ Clos.	13,745		

Note that Income Summary before the closing process contains the adjustments for Merchandise Inventory. The end result is that the net income of $13,745 is closed to the Capital account.

THE POST-CLOSING TRIAL BALANCE

The following post-closing trial balance is prepared from the general ledger. Note first that all temporary accounts have been closed and thus are not shown on this post-closing trial balance. Note also that the ending inventory figure of the last accounting period, $4,000, becomes the beginning inventory figure on Jan. 1, 19X3.

ART'S WHOLESALE CLOTHING COMPANY
POST-CLOSING TRIAL BALANCE
DECEMBER 31, 19XX

	Dr.	Cr.
Cash	12 9 2 0 00	
Petty Cash	1 0 0 00	
Accounts Receivable	14 5 0 0 00	
Merchandise Inventory	4 0 0 0 00	
Supplies	3 0 0 00	
Prepaid Insurance	6 0 0 00	
Store Equipment	4 0 0 0 00	
Accum. Depreciation, Store Equipment		4 5 0 00
Accounts Payable		17 9 0 0 00
Federal Income Tax Payable		8 0 0 00
FICA–Social Security Payable		4 5 4 00
FICA–Medicare Payable		1 0 6 00
State Income Tax Payable		2 0 0 00
SUTA Tax Payable		1 0 8 00
FUTA Tax Payable		3 2 00
Salary Payable		6 0 0 00
Unearned Rent		4 0 0 00
Mortgage Payable		2 3 2 0 00
Art Newner, Capital		13 0 5 0 00
	36 4 2 0 00	36 4 2 0 00

LEARNING UNIT 13-2 REVIEW

AT THIS POINT you should be able to

- ◆ Journalize and post adjusting entries for a merchandise company. (p. 467)
- ◆ Explain the relationship of the worksheet to the adjusting and closing process. (pp. 470)
- ◆ Complete the closing process for a merchandise company. (pp. 471)
- ◆ Prepare a post-closing trial balance and explain why ending merchandise inventory is not a temporary account. (p. 472)

SELF-REVIEW QUIZ 13-2

(The forms you need are on page 430 of the *Study Guide and Working Papers.*)

Using the worksheet from Self-Review Quiz 12-2 (p. 442), journalize the closing entries.

Solution to Self-Review Quiz 13-2

	Date	Account Titles and Description	PR	Dr.	Cr.
		Closing			
	Dec. 31	Sales		11 04 0 00	
		Storage Fees Earned		5 1 6 00	
		Purchases Returns and Allowances		1 6 8 00	
		Purchases Discount		1 0 2 00	
		Income Summary			11 82 6 00
	31	Income Summary		10 09 6 00	
		Sales Returns and Allowances			5 4 6 00
		Sales Discount			2 1 6 00
		Purchases			5 25 6 00
		Salaries Expense			2 21 6 00
		Insurance Expense			1 39 2 00
		Utilities Expense			9 6 00
		Plumbing Expense			2 1 4 00
		Rent Expense			1 0 0 00
		Depreciation Exp., Equipment			6 0 00
	31	Income Summary		1 10 6 00	
		B. Ray, Capital			1 10 6 00

Page 2

Quiz Tip: Note in the first closing entry that the four account titles (now listed as debits) were found on the worksheet as credits in the Income Statement column.

LEARNING UNIT 13-3
Reversing Entries (Optional Section)

Reversing entries are an option; they are not mandatory.

The accounting cycle for Art's Wholesale Clothing Company is completed. Now let's look at **reversing entries** — an optional way of handling some adjusting entries. Reversing entries are general journal entries that are the opposite of adjusting entries. Reversing entries help reduce potential errors and simplify the recordkeeping process. If Art's accountant does reversing entries, then routine transactions can be done in the usual steps.

To help explain the concept of reversing entries, let's look at these two adjustments that could be reversed:

1. When there is an increase in an asset account (no previous balance).
   Example: Interest Receivable
            Interest Income
   (Interest earned but not collected; we will cover this in later chapters)
2. When there is an increase in a liability account (no previous balance).
   Example: Wages Expense
            Wages Payable

With the exception of businesses in their first year of operation, accounts such as Accumulated Depreciation or Inventory cannot be reduced because they have previous balances.

This is how Art's bookkeeper handles an entry without reversing for salaries at the end of the year (see Fig. 13-5). Note that the permanent account, Salaries Payable, carries over to the new accounting period a $600 balance. Remember: The $600 was an expense of the prior year.

On January 8 of the new year the payroll to be paid is $2,000. If the optional reversing entry is *not* used, the bookkeeper must make the following journal entry:

Salaries Payable	600 00	
Salaries Expense	1 400 00	
Cash		2 000 00

Salaries Exp.	Salaries Pay.	Cash
1,400		600 | 600		2,000

To do this the bookkeeper has to refer back to the adjustment on December 31 to determine how much of the salary of $2,000 is indeed a new salary expense and what portion was shown in the old year although not paid. It is easy to see

FIGURE 13-5 Reversing Entries Not Used

ADJUSTING JOURNAL ENTRY   T ACCOUNT UPDATE

❶ On December 31 after adjusting entry was journalized and posted for $600 of salaries incurred but not paid.

Salaries Expense	600 00	
Salaries Payable		600 00

Salaries Exp.	Salaries Pay.
11,700	600
600	

❷ On January 1 after closing entries have been journalized and posted, Salaries expense has a zero balance.

Income Summary	XXX	
Salaries Expense		12 300 00

Salaries Exp.	Salaries Pay.
11,700 | 12,300	600
600	

❶

On December 31
adjustment for salary
was recorded.

Salaries Exp.		Salaries Pay.	
11,700			600
600			

❷

Closing entry on
December 31.

Salaries Exp.		Salaries Pay.	
11,700	12,300		600
600			

❸

On January 1 (first day of
the following fiscal period)
reverse adjusting entry
was made for salary on
December 31. (This means
"flipping" adjustment.)

Jan.	1	Salaries Payable	600 00		
		Salaries Expense		600 00	

Salaries Exp.		Salaries Pay.	
	600	600	600

By doing this the liability is reduced to 0. We know it will be paid in this new period but the salaries expense has a credit balance of $600 until the payroll is paid. When the payroll of $2,000 is paid, the following results:

❹

Paid Payroll $2,000.

Jan.	1	Salaries Expense	2000 00		
		Cash		2000 00	

Salaries Exp.		Cash	
2,000	600		2,000

FIGURE 13-6 Reversing Entries Used

how potential errors can result if the bookkeeper pays the payroll but forgets about the adjustment in the previous year. In this way reversing entries can help avoid potential errors.

Figure 13-6 shows the four steps the bookkeeper would take if reversing entries were used: Note that steps (1) and (2) are the same whether the accountant uses reversing entries or not.

Note that the balance of Salaries Expense is indeed only $1,400, the *true* expense in the new year. Reversing results in switching the adjustment the first day of the new period. Also note that each of the accounts ends up with the same balance no matter which method is chosen. However, using reversing entry for salaries allows the accountant to make the normal entry when it is time to pay salaries.

LEARNING UNIT 13-3 REVIEW

AT THIS POINT you should be able to

◆ Explain the purpose of reversing entries. (p. 474)
◆ Complete a reversing entry. (p. 475)
◆ Explain when reversing entries can be used. (p. 475)

SELF REVIEW QUIZ 13-3

Explain which of the following situations could be reversed:

1.
Supplies Exp.		Supplies	
200		800	200

2.

Wages Exp.		Wages Payable	
3,200			200
200			

3.

Sales		Unearned Sales	
	4,000	50	200
	50		

Solution to Self-Review Quiz 13-3

(The forms you need are on page 431 of the *Study Guide and Working Papers*.)

1. Not reversed — asset Supplies is decreasing, not increasing.
2. Reversed — liability is increasing and no previous balance exists.
3. Not reversed — liability is decreasing and a previous balance exists.

SUMMARY OF KEY POINTS

Learning Unit 13-1

1. The formal income statement can be prepared from the income statement columns of the worksheet.
2. There are no debit or credit columns on the formal income statement.
3. The cost of goods sold section has a figure for beginning inventory and a separate figure for ending inventory.
4. Operating expenses could be broken down into selling and administrative expenses.
5. The ending figure for capital is not found on the worksheet. It comes from the statement of owner's equity.
6. A classified balance sheet breaks assets into current and plant and equipment. Liabilities are broken down into current and long-term.

Learning Unit 13-2

1. The information for journalizing, adjusting, and closing entries can be obtained from the worksheet.
2. In the closing process all temporary accounts will be zero and the capital account is brought up to its new balance.
3. Inventory is not a temporary account. The ending inventory, along with other permanent accounts, will be listed in the post-closing trial balance.

Learning Unit 13-3

1. Reversing entries are optional and could aid in reducing potential errors and simplify the recordkeeping process.
2. The reversing entry "flips" the adjustment on the first day of a new fiscal period. Thus the bookkeeper need *not* look back at what happened in the old year when recording the current year's transactions.
3. Reversing entries are only used if (a) assets are increasing and have no previous balance, (b) liabilities are increasing and have no previous balance.

KEY TERMS

Administrative expenses (general expenses) Expenses such as general office expenses that are incurred indirectly in the selling of goods.

Classified balance sheet A balance sheet that categorizes assets as current or plant and equipment and groups liabilities as current or long-term.

Current assets Assets that can be converted into cash or used within one year or the normal operating cycle of the business, whichever is longer.

Current liabilities Obligations that will come due within one year or within the operating cycle, whichever is longer.

Long-term liabilities Obligations that are not due or payable for a long time, usually for more than a year.

Operating cycle Average time it takes to buy and sell merchandise and then collect accounts receivable.

Other expenses These are nonoperating expenses that do not relate to the main operating activities of the business; they appear in a separate section on the income statement. One example given in the text is Interest Expense — interest owed on money borrowed by the company.

Other income This includes any revenue other than revenue from sales and appears in a separate section on the income statement. Examples would be Rental Income and Storage Fees.

Plant and equipment Long-lived assets such as buildings or land that are used in the production or sale of goods or services.

Reversing entries Optional bookkeeping technique in which certain adjusting entries are reversed or switched on the first day of the new accounting period so that transactions in the new period can be recorded without referring back to prior adjusting entries.

Selling expenses Expenses directly related to the sale of goods.

QUESTIONS, MINI EXERCISES, EXERCISES, AND PROBLEMS

Discussion Questions

1. Which columns of the worksheet aid in the preparation of the income statement?
2. Explain the components of cost of goods sold.
3. Explain how operating expenses can be broken down into different categories.
4. What is the difference between current assets and plant and equipment?
5. What is an operating cycle?
6. Why journalize adjusting entries *after* the formal reports have been prepared?
7. Explain the steps of closing for a merchandise company.
8. Temporary accounts could appear on a post-closing trial balance. Agree or disagree.
9. What is the purpose of using reversing entries? Are they mandatory? When should they be used?

Mini Exercises

(The forms you need are on page 443 of the *Study Guide and Working Papers*.)

Calculate Net Sales

1. From the following calculate net sales:

Purchases	$ 50
Gross Sales	100
Sales Returns and Allowances	5
Sales Discount	2
Operating Expenses	12

Calculate Cost of Goods Sold

2. Calculate Cost of Goods Sold:

Freight-In	$ 5
Beginning Inventory	20
Ending Inventory	15
Net Purchases	50

Calculate Gross Profit and Net Income

3. Using Mini Exercises 1 and 2, calculate:
   a. Gross Profit
   b. Net Income or Net Loss

(Questions, Mini Exercises, Exercises, and Problems cont. on p. 480)

BLUEPRINT OF FINANCIAL REPORTS

(1) INCOME STATEMENT

Revenue:				
Sales				$ XXX
Less: Sales Ret. and Allow.			$ XXX	
Sales Discount			XXX	XXX
Net Sales				$ XXXX
Cost of Goods Sold:				
Merchandise Inventory, 1/1/XX			$ XXX	
Purchases		$XXX		
Less: Purchases Discount	$XXX			
Purch. Ret. and Allow.	XXX	XXX		
Net Purchases		XXX		
Add: Freight-In		XXX		
Net Cost of Purchases			XXX	
Cost of Goods Avail. for Sale			$XXXX	
Less: Merch. Inv., 12/31/XX			XXX	
Cost of Goods Sold				XXXX
Gross Profit				$XXXX
Operating Expenses:				
~~			$XXX	
~~			XXX	
~~			XXX	
Total Operating Expenses				XXX
Net Income from Operations				$ XXX
Other Income:				
Rental Income			$ XXX	
Storage Fees Income			XXX	
Total Other Income			$ XXX	
Other Expenses:				
Interest Expenses			XXX	XXX
Net Income:				$ XXX

(2) STATEMENT OF OWNER'S EQUITY

Beginning Capital		$XXX
Additional Investments		XXX
Total Investment		$XXX
Net Income	$XXX	
Less: Withdrawals	XXX	
Increase in Capital		XXX
Ending Capital		$XXX

(Cont. on p. 480)

(3) BALANCE SHEET				
Assets				
Current Assets:				
Cash		$ XXXX		
Acccounts Receivable		XXXX		
Merchandise Inventory		XXXX		
Prepaid Insurance		XXX		
Total Current Assets			$ XXXX	
Plant and Equipment:				
Store Equipment	$XXXX			
Less Accumulated Depreciation	XXXX	$XXXX		
Office Equipment	$XXXX			
Less Accumulated Depreciation	XXX	XXX		
Total Plant and Equipment			XXXX	
Total Assets			$XXXX	
Liabilities				
Current Liabilities:				
Unearned Revenue		$XXX		
Mortgage Payable (current portion)		XXX		
Accounts Payable		XXX		
Salaries Payable		XX		
FICA–Soc. Sec. Payable		XX		
FICA–Medicare Payable		XX		
Income Taxes Payable		XX		
Total Current Liabilities			$XXX	
Long-Term Liabilities				
Mortgage Payable			$XXX	
Total Liabilities			$XXXX	
Owner's Equity				
Capital*			XXXX	
Total Liabilities and Owner's Equity			$XXXX	

* From statement of owner's equity

Classification of Accounts

4. Match the following categories to each account listed below:
    1. Current Asset
    2. Plant and Equipment
    3. Current Liabilities

4. Long-Term Liabilities

_____ **a.** Merchandise Inventory

_____ **b.** Unearned Rent

_____ **c.** Prepaid Insurance

_____ **d.** SUTA Payable

_____ **e.** Store Equipment

_____ **f.** Mortgage Payable (Not Current)

_____ **g.** FUTA Payable

_____ **h.** Accumulated Depreciation

_____ **i.** FICA – Social Security Payable

_____ **j.** Petty Cash

Reversing Entries

5. a. On January 1 prepare a reversing entry. On January 8, journalize the entry to record the paying of salary expense, $900.

b. What will be the balance in Salary Expense on January 8 (after posting)?

December 31:

Salaries Expense			Salaries Payable	
900	1,200	closing		300 Adj.
Adj. 300				

(The forms you need are on pages 444–445 of the *Study Guide and Working Papers.*)

Exercises

Preparing cost of goods sold section.

13-1. From the following accounts, prepare a cost of goods sold section in proper form: Freight-In, $300; Merchandise Inventory, 12/31/X1, $5,000; Purchases Discount, $900; Merchandise Inventory, 12/1/X1, $4,000; Purchases, $58,000; Purchases Returns and Allowances, $1,000.

Categorizing and classifying account titles.

13-2. Give the category, the classification, and the report(s) on which each of the following appears (for example: Cash — asset, current asset, balance sheet):

a. Salaries Payable

b. Accounts Payable

c. Mortgage Payable

d. Unearned Legal Fees

e. SIT Payable

f. Office Equipment

g. Land

Journalizing closing entries.

13-3. From the partial worksheet on page 482, journalize the closing entries of December 31 for A. Slow Co.

Preparing partially completed balance sheet.

13-4. From the worksheet in Exercise 13-3, prepare the assets section of a classified balance sheet.

Reversing entry.

13-5. On December 31, 19X1, $300 of salaries has been accrued. (Salaries before accrued amount totaled $26,000.) The next payroll to be paid will be on February 3, 19X2, for $6,000. Please do the following:

a. Journalize and post the adjusting entry (use T accounts).

b. Journalize and post the reversing entry on January 1.

c. Journalize and post the payment of the payroll. Cash has a balance of $15,000 before the payment of payroll on February 3.

A. SLOW CO. WORKSHEET FOR YEAR ENDED DECEMBER 31, 19XX				
	Income Statement		Balance Sheet	
Account Titles	Dr.	Cr.	Dr.	Cr.
Cash			19300	
Merch. Inventory			45000	
Prepaid Advertising			56100	
Prepaid Insurance			3000	
Office Equipment			108000	
Accum. Depr., Office Equip.				21000
Accounts Payable				25800
A. Slow, Capital				96600
Income Summary	36200	45000		
Sales		552000		
Sales Returns and Allowances	22300			
Sales Discount	10800			
Purchases	262800			
Purchases Returns and Allow.		3400		
Purchases Discount		5100		
Salaries Expense	108300			
Insurance Expense	69600			
Utilities Expense	4800			
Plumbing Expense	5700			
Advertising Expense	1500			
Depr. Expenses, Office Equip.	3000			
Salaries Payable				7500
	525000	605500	231400	150900
Net Income	80500			80500
	605500	605500	231400	231400

Group A Problems

(The forms you need are on pages 446–463 of the *Study Guide and Working Papers*.)

13A-1. Prepare a formal income statement from the partial worksheet for Babe's Pants Co. on the next page.

Check Figure:

Net Income from operations $761

13A-2. Prepare a statement of owner's equity and a classified balance sheet from the worksheet for James Company (p. 483). *Note:* Of the Mortgage Payable, $200 is due within one year.

Check Figure:

Total Assets $33,340

13A-3. a. Complete the worksheet for Jay's Supplies on page 484.

   b. Prepare an income statement, a statement of owner's equity, and a classified balance sheet. (*Note:* The amount of the mortgage due the first year is $800.)

   c. Journalize the adjusting and closing entries.

Check Figure:

Net Income $4,340

13A-4. Using the ledger balances and additional data shown on page 484, do the following for Callahan Lumber for the year ended December 31, 19XX:

   1. Prepare the worksheet.

   2. Prepare the income statement, statement of owner's equity, and balance sheet.

BABE'S PANTS CO.
PARTIAL WORKSHEET
FOR YEAR ENDED DECEMBER 31, 19XX

Account Titles	Income Statement Dr.	Income Statement Cr.
Income Summary	37000	26000
Sales		280000
Sales Returns and Allowances	11900	
Sales Discount	6400	
Purchases	87000	
Purchases Returns and Allow.		16700
Purchases Discount		12900
Freight-In	10200	
Salaries Expense	30000	
Insurance Expense	20000	
Advertising Expense	15500	
Rental Income		20000
Rent Expense	21500	
Depr. Exp., Store Equip.	20000	
Salaries Payable		
	259500	355600
Net Income	96100	
	355600	355600

JAMES COMPANY
MONTWORKSHEET
FOR YEAR ENDED DECEMBER 31, 19XX

Account Titles	Balance Sheet Dr.	Balance Sheet Cr.
Cash	2350000	
Petty Cash	9000	
Accounts Receivable	135000	
Merchandise Inv.	400000	
Supplies	32500	
Prepaid Insurance	50000	
Store Equipment	280000	
Acc. Dep., Store Eq.		70000
Automobile	170000	
Acc. Dep., Auto.		22500
Accounts Payable		280000
Taxes Payable		240000
Unearned Rent		185000
Mortgage Payable		45000
H. James, Capital		1240000
H. James, With.	10000	
Salaries Payable		60000
	3436500	3807500
Net Loss	371000	
	3807500	3807500

Preparing a statement of owner's equity and a classified balance sheet from a worksheet.

JAY'S SUPPLIES
WORKSHEET
FOR YEAR ENDED DECEMBER 31, 19XX

Account Titles	Trial Balance Dr.	Trial Balance Cr.	Adjustments Dr.	Adjustments Cr.
Cash	2 0 0 0 00			
Accounts Receivable	3 0 0 0 00			
Merch. Inv., 1/1/XX	11 0 0 0 00	(B)	10 4 0 0 00	11 0 0 0 00 (A)
Prepaid Insurance	1 8 8 0 00			5 0 0 00 (E)
Equipment	3 4 0 0 00			
Accum. Depr., Equipment		1 0 8 0 00		4 0 0 00 (D)
Accounts Payable		5 0 8 0 00		
Unearned Training Fees		2 1 2 0 00	(C) 3 2 0 00	
Mortgage Payable		1 2 0 0 00		
P. Jay, Capital		10 5 6 0 00		
P. Jay, Withdrawals	4 2 8 0 00			
Income Summary		(A)	11 0 0 0 00	10 4 0 0 00 (B)
Sales		95 8 0 0 00		
Sales Returns and Allowances	3 2 0 0 00			
Sales Discount	2 6 0 0 00			
Purchases	63 6 0 0 00			
Purchases Returns and Allow.		13 6 0 0 00		
Purchases Discount		3 2 0 0 00		
Freight-In	2 6 8 0 00			
Advertising Expense	11 4 0 0 00			
Rent Expense	10 0 0 0 00			
Salaries Expense	13 6 0 0 00			
	132 6 4 0 00	132 6 4 0 00		
Training Fees Earned				3 2 0 00 (C)
Depr. Exp., Equipment			(D) 4 0 0 00	
Insurance Expense			(E) 5 0 0 00	
			22 6 2 0 00	22 6 2 0 00

Comprehensive Problem. Worksheet preparation: preparing financial reports; journalizing and posting adjusting and closing entries; preparing a post-closing trial balance; journalizing reversing entry.
Check Figure:
Net Income $4,336

3. Journalize and post adjusting and closing entries. (Be sure to put beginning balances in the ledger first.)
4. Prepare a post-closing trial balance.
5. Journalize the reversing entry for wages.

Acct. No.

110	Cash	$ 1,340
111	Accounts Receivable	1,300
112	Merchandise Inventory	4,550
113	Lumber Supplies	269
114	Prepaid Insurance	218
121	Lumber Equipment	3,000
122	Accum. Depr., Lumber Equipment	490
220	Accounts Payable	1,160
221	Wages Payable	
330	J. Callahan, Capital	7,352
331	J. Callahan, Withdrawals	3,000
332	Income Summary	—

440	Sales	22,800
441	Sales Returns and Allowances	200
550	Purchases	14,800
551	Purchases Discount	285
552	Purchases Returns and Allowances	300
660	Wages Expense	2,480
661	Advertising Expense	400
662	Rent Expense	830
663	Depr. Expense, Lumber Equipment	
664	Lumber Supplies Expense	
665	Insurance Expense	

Additional Data:

a./b.	Merchandise inventory, December 31	$4,900
c.	Lumber supplies on hand, December 31	75
d.	Insurance expired	150
e.	Depreciation for the year	250
f.	Accrued wages on December 31	95

Group B Problems

(The forms you need are on pages 446–463 of the *Study Guide and Working Papers.*)

Preparing an income statement from a worksheet.

Check Figure:

Net Income from operations $845

13B-1. From the partial worksheet shown below, prepare a formal income statement.

BABE'S PANTS CO.
PARTIAL WORKSHEET
FOR YEAR ENDED DECEMBER 31, 19XX

Account Titles	Income Statement Dr.	Income Statement Cr.
Income Summary	3000 00	2950 00
Sales		4100 00
Sales R & A	145 00	
Sales Dis.	175 00	
Purchases	2000 00	
Purchases R & A		175 00
Purchases Dis.		85 00
Freight-In	50 00	
Salaries Expense	360 00	
Insurance Expense	275 00	
Advertising Expense	165 00	
Rental Income		230 00
Rent Expense	225 00	
Dep. Exp., Store Eq.	115 00	
Salaries Payable		
	3810 00	4885 00
Net Income	1075 00	
	4885 00	4885 00

551	Purchases Discount	440
552	Purchases Returns and Allowances	545
660	Wages Expense	2,390
661	Advertising Expense	400
662	Rent Expense	840
663	Depr. Exp., Lumber Equipment	
664	Lumber Supplies Expense	
665	Insurance Expense	

Additional Data:

a./b.	Merchandise inventory, December 31	$3,900
c.	Lumber supplies on hand, December 31	60
d.	Insurance expired	50
e.	Depreciation for the year	400
f.	Accrued wages on December 31	175

REAL WORLD APPLICATIONS

13R-1.

Chan Company recently had most of its records destroyed in a fire. The information for 19X1 was discovered by the bookkeeper.

Beg. Inv. $1,400
End. Inv. 3,000

CHAN CORP.					
GENERAL JOURNAL					
					Page 2
Date	Description	PR	Dr.		Cr.
Dec. 31	Income Summary	312	3 6 3 0 00		
	Sales Returns and Allowances	420			1 4 0 00
	Sales Discount	430			3 0 00
	Purchases	500			2 4 0 0 00
	Delivery Expense	600			9 0 00
	Salaries Expense	610			8 4 0 00
	Rent Expense	620			3 0 00
	Office Supplies Expense	630			5 0 00
	Advertising Expense	640			1 0 00
	Dep. Exp., Store Equipment	650			4 0 00
31	Sales	410	5 5 4 2 00		
	Purchases Discount	510	1 2 0 00		
	Purchases Returns and Allowances	520	1 0 0 00		
	Income Summary	312			5 7 6 2 00
31	Income Summary	312	3 7 3 2 00		
	J. Chan, Capital	310			3 7 3 2 00

Please assist the bookkeeper in reconstructing an income statement for 19X1.

13R-2.

Hope Lang, a junior accountant, has the December 31, 19XX trial balance of Gregot Company sitting on her desk. Attached is a memo from her supervisor requesting that a classified balance sheet be prepared. Hope gathers the following data:

1. A physical inventory at December 31 showed $80,000 on hand.
2. Office supplies on hand was $600.
3. Insurance unexpired was $750.
4. Depreciation (straight-line) is based on a 25-year life.

Using the following trial balance of Gregot Co., please assist Hope with this project. *Hint:* Ending figure for capital is $115,850.

GREGOT COMPANY TRIAL BALANCE DECEMBER 31, 19XX	Dr.	Cr.
Cash	11 0 0 0 00	
Accounts Receivable	38 0 0 0 00	
Inventory, Jan. 1	80 0 0 0 00	
Prepaid Insurance	2 0 0 0 00	
Office Supplies	1 0 0 0 00	
Land	17 5 0 0 00	
Building	50 0 0 0 00	
Accumulated Depreciation, Building		10 0 0 0 00
Notes Payable		40 0 0 0 00
Accounts Payable		30 0 0 0 00
G. Gregot, Capital		98 4 0 0 00
G. Gregot, Withdrawals	13 0 0 0 00	
Income Summary		
Retail Sales		329 0 0 0 00
Sales Returns and Allowances	21 0 0 0 00	
Sales Discount	8 0 0 0 00	
Purchases	215 5 0 0 00	
Purchases Returns and Allowances		11 6 0 0 00
Purchases Discount		4 0 0 0 00
Transportation-In	5 0 0 0 00	
Advertising Expense	2 5 0 0 00	
Wage Expense	55 0 0 0 00	
Utilities Expense	3 5 0 0 00	
	523 0 0 0 00	523 0 0 0 00

 make the call

Critical Thinking/Ethical Case

13R-3.

Janet Flynn, owner of Reel Company, plans to apply for a bank loan at Petro National Bank. Since the company has a lot of debt on its balance sheet, Janet does not plan to show the loan officer the balance sheet. She plans only to bring the income statement. Do you feel this is a sound financial move by Janet? You make the call. Write down your specific recommendations to Janet.

ACCOUNTING RECALL
A CUMULATIVE APPROACH

THIS EXAM REVIEWS CHAPTERS 1 THROUGH 13

Your *Study Guide and Working Papers* (pp. 467 and 471) has forms to complete this exam, as well as worked-out solutions. The page references next to each question identify what page to turn back to if you answer the question incorrectly.

PART 1   Vocabulary Review

Match the terms to the appropriate definition or phrase.

Page Ref.

(465)	1. Current asset	A. General expenses
(465)	2. Current liabilities	B. Contra-asset
(355)	3. Purchases discount	C. Converted into cash or used within
(275)	4. Semiweekly depositor	one year
(462)	5. Administrative expenses	D. Contra-cost of goods sold
(121)	6. Accumulated	E. Land
	depreciation	F. Mortgage payable
(315)	7. Net sales	G. Optional bookkeeeping technique
(465)	8. Plant and equipment	H. Look-back periods over $50,000
(465)	9. Long-term liability	I. Sales − SRA − SD
(474)	10. Reversing entries	J. Due within one year

PART II   True or False (Accounting Theory)

(465) 11. There are debit and credit columns on the formal reports.

(474) 12. Reversing entries are the same as adjusting entries.

(474) 13. All adjustments can be reversed.

(465) 14. Equipment is a current asset.

(462) 15. Administrative expenses are directly incurred to the selling of goods.

CONTINUING PROBLEM

U sing the worksheet in Chapter 12 for Eldorado Computer Center, journalize and post the adjusting entries and prepare the financial statements. (See p. 458 in your *Study Guide and Working Papers*.)

The Corner Dress Shop

Reviewing the Accounting Cycle for a Merchandise Company

(The forms you need are on pages 472–494 of the *Study Guide and Working Papers.* This practice set will help you review all the key concepts of a merchandise company along with the integration of payroll, including the preparation of Form 941.)

Since you are the bookkeeper of The Corner Dress Shop, we have gathered the following information for you. It will be your task to complete the accounting cycle for March.

Betty Loeb's Dress Shop is located at 1 Milgate Rd., Marblehead, MA 01945. Her identification number is 33-4158215.

THE CORNER DRESS SHOP POST-CLOSING TRIAL BALANCE FEBRUARY 28, 19XX	1	2
Cash	1 7 7 4 90	
Accounts Receivable	2 2 0 0 00	
Petty Cash	3 5 00	
Merchandise Inventory	5 6 0 0 00	
Prepaid Rent	1 8 0 0 00	
Delivery Truck	6 0 0 0 00	
Accumulated Depreciation, Truck		1 5 0 0 00
Accounts Payable		1 9 0 0 00
FIT Payable		1 1 5 0 00
FICA–Social Security Payable		1 1 1 6 00
FICA–Medicare Payable		2 6 1 00
SIT Payable		6 3 0 00
SUTA Payable		8 1 5 40
FUTA Payable		1 3 4 40
Unearned Rent		8 0 0 00
B. Loeb, Capital		9 1 0 3 10
	17 4 0 9 90	17 4 0 9 90

Balances in subsidiary ledgers as of March 1:

Accounts Receivable		Accounts Payable	
Bing Co.	$2,200	Blew Co.	$1,900
Blew Co.	—	Jones Co.	—
Ronald Co.	—	Moe's Garage	—
		Morris Co.	—

Payroll is paid monthly:

FICA rate	Social Security 6.2 percent on $65,400 Medicare 1.45% on all earnings
SUTA rate	4.8 percent on $7,000

FUTA rate	.8 percent on $7,000
SIT rate	7 percent
FIT	Use tables provided on pp. 496–497

The payroll register for January and February is provided. In March, salaries are as follows:

Mel Case	$1,660
Jane Holl	4,120
Jackie Moore	4,760

Your task is to

1. Set up a general ledger, accounts receivable subsidiary ledger and accounts payable subsidiary ledger, auxiliary petty cash record and payroll register. (Be sure to update ledger accounts based on given information in post-closing trial balance for Feb. 28 before beginning.)
2. Journalize the transactions and prepare the payroll register.
3. Update the accounts payable and accounts receivable subsidiary ledgers.
4. Post to the general ledger.
5. Prepare a trial balance on a worksheet and complete the worksheet.
6. Prepare an income statement, statement of owner's equity, and classified balance sheet.
7. Journalize the adjusting and closing entries.
8. Post the adjusting and closing entries to the ledger.
9. Prepare a post-closing trial balance.
10. Complete Form 941 and sign it as of the last day in April.

Chart of Accounts for The Corner Dress Shop

Assets
110   Cash
111   Accounts Receivable
112   Petty Cash
114   Merchandise Inventory
116   Prepaid Rent
120   Delivery Truck
121   Accumulated Depreciation, Truck

Liabilities
210   Accounts Payable
212   Salaries Payable
214   Federal Income Tax Payable
216   FICA–Soc. Sec. Payable
218   FICA–Medicare Payable
220   State Income Tax Payable
222   SUTA Tax Payable
224   FUTA Tax Payable
226   Unearned Rent

Owner's Equity
310   B. Loeb, Capital
320   B. Loeb, Withdrawals
330   Income Summary

Revenue
410   Sales
412   Sales Returns and Allowances
414   Sales Discount
416   Rental Income

Cost of Goods Sold
510   Purchases
512   Purchases Returns and Allowances
514   Purchase Discount

Expenses
610   Sales Salaries Expense
611   Office Salaries Expense
612   Payroll Tax Expense
614   Cleaning Expense
616   Depreciation Expense, Truck
618   Rent Expense
620   Postage Expense
622   Delivery Expense
624   Miscellaneous Expense

Employees	Allow. and Marital Status	Cum. Earnings	Salary	Earnings Reg.	Earnings O/T	Earnings Gross	Cum. Earnings
Mel Case	S – 2	—	1500 00	1500 00	—	1500 00	1500 00
Jane Holl	M – 1	—	3400 00	3400 00	—	3400 00	3400 00
Jackie Moore	M – 0	—	4100 00	4100 00		4100 00	4100 00
			9000 00	9000 00		9000 00	9000 00
Mel Case	S – 2	1500 00	1500 00	1500 00	—	1500 00	3000 00
Jane Holl	M – 1	3400 00	3400 00	3400 00	—	3400 00	6800 00
Jackie Moore	M – 0	4100 00	4100 00	4100 00		4100 00	8200 00
			9000 00	9000 00		9000 00	18000 00

PAYROLL REGISTER

Taxable Earnings Unemp.	Taxable Earnings FICA Soc. Sec.	Taxable Earnings FICA Medicare	Deductions FICA Soc. Sec.	Deductions FICA Medicare	Deductions FIT	Deductions SIT	Net Pay	Ck. No.	Distribution Office Salary Expense	Distribution Sales Salary Expense
1500 00	1500 00	1500 00	93 00	21 75	132 00	105 00	1148 25		1500 00	
3400 00	3400 00	3400 00	210 80	49 30	403 00	238 00	2498 90			3400 00
4100 00	4100 00	4100 00	254 20	59 45	615 00	287 00	2884 35			4100 00
9000 00	9000 00	9000 00	558 00	130 50	1150 00	630 00	6531 50		1500 00	7500 00
1500 00	1500 00	1500 00	93 00	21 75	132 00	105 00	1148 25		1500 00	
3400 00	3400 00	3400 00	210 80	49 30	403 00	238 00	2498 90			3400 00
2900 00	2900 00	2900 00	254 20	59 45	615 00	287 00	2884 35			4100 00
7800 00	7800 00	7800 00	558 00	130 50	1150 00	630 00	6531 50		1500 00	7500 00

19XX

March

1 Bing paid balance owed, no discount.

2 Purchased merchandise from Morris Company on account, $10,000, terms 2/10, n/30.

2 Paid $6 from the petty cash fund for cleaning package, voucher no. 18 (consider this a cleaning expense).

3 Sold merchandise to Ronald Company on account, $7,000, invoice no. 51, terms 2/10, n/30.

5 Paid $3 from the petty cash fund for postage, voucher no. 19.

6 Sold merchandise to Ronald Company on account, $5,000, invoice no. 52, terms 2/10, n/30.

8 Paid $10 from the petty cash fund for First Aid emergency, voucher no. 20.

9 Purchased merchandise from Morris Company on account, $5,000, terms 2/10, n/30.

9 Paid $5 for delivery expense from petty cash fund, voucher no. 21.

9 Sold more merchandise to Ronald Company on account, $3,000, invoice no. 53, terms 2/10, n/30.

9 Paid cleaning service, $300, check no. 110.

10 Ronald Company returned merchandise costing $1,000 from invoice no. 52; The Corner Dress Shop issued credit memo no. 10 to Ronald Company for $1,000.

11 Purchased merchandise from Jones Company on account, $10,000, terms 1/15, n/60.

12 Paid Morris Company invoice dated March 2, check no. 111.

13 Sold $7,000 of merchandise for cash.

14 Returned merchandise to Jones Company in amount of $2,000; The Corner Dress Shop issued debit memo no. 4 to Jones Company.

14 Paid $5 from the petty cash fund for delivery expense, voucher no. 22.

15 Paid taxes due for FICA (Social Security and Medicare) and FIT for February payroll, check no. 112.

15 Sold merchandise for $29,000 cash.

15 B. Loeb withdrew $100 for her own personal expenses, check no. 113.

15 Paid state income tax for February payroll, check no. 114.

16 Received payment from Ronald Company for invoice no. 52, less discount.

16 Ronald Company paid invoice no. 51, $7,000.

16 Sold merchandise to Bing Company on account, $3,200, invoice no. 54, terms 2/10, n/30.

21 Purchased delivery truck on account from Moe's Garage, $17,200.

22 Sold merchandise to Ronald Company on account, $4,000, invoice no. 55, terms 2/10, n/30.

23 Paid Jones Company the balance owed, check no. 115.

24 Sold merchandise to Bing Company, $2,000, invoice no. 56, terms 1/10, n/30.

25 Purchased merchandise for $1,000, check no. 116.

27 Purchased merchandise from Blew Company on account, $6,000, terms 2/10, n/30.

27 Paid $2 postage from the petty cash fund, voucher no. 23.

28 Ronald Company paid invoice no. 55 dated March 22, less discount.

28 Bing Company paid invoice no. 54 dated March 16.

29 Purchased merchandise from Morris Company on account, $9,000, terms 2/10, n/30.

30 Sold merchandise to Blew Company on account, $10,000, invoice no. 57, terms 2/10, n/30.

30 Issued check no. 117 to replenish to the same level the petty cash fund.

30 Recorded payroll in payroll register.

30 Journalized payroll entry (to be paid on 31st).

30 Journalized employer's payroll tax expense.

31 Paid payroll checks no. 118, no. 119, and no. 120.

Additional data:

a./b. Ending merchandise inventory, $3,700.

c. During March, rent expired, $600.

d. Truck depreciated, $150.

e. Rental income earned, $200 (one month's rent from subletting).

SINGLE Persons—MONTHLY Payroll Period

If the wages are—		And the number of withholding allowances claimed is—										
At least	But less than	0	1	2	3	4	5	6	7	8	9	10
		The amount of income tax to be withheld is—										
$0	$220	$0	$0	$0	$0	$0	$0	$0	$0	$0	$0	$0
220	230	2	0	0	0	0	0	0	0	0	0	0
230	240	3	0	0	0	0	0	0	0	0	0	0
240	250	5	0	0	0	0	0	0	0	0	0	0
250	260	6	0	0	0	0	0	0	0	0	0	0
260	270	8	0	0	0	0	0	0	0	0	0	0
270	280	9	0	0	0	0	0	0	0	0	0	0
280	290	11	0	0	0	0	0	0	0	0	0	0
290	300	12	0	0	0	0	0	0	0	0	0	0
300	320	14	0	0	0	0	0	0	0	0	0	0
320	340	17	0	0	0	0	0	0	0	0	0	0
340	360	20	0	0	0	0	0	0	0	0	0	0
360	380	23	0	0	0	0	0	0	0	0	0	0
380	400	26	0	0	0	0	0	0	0	0	0	0
400	420	29	0	0	0	0	0	0	0	0	0	0
420	440	32	2	0	0	0	0	0	0	0	0	0
440	460	35	5	0	0	0	0	0	0	0	0	0
460	480	38	8	0	0	0	0	0	0	0	0	0
480	500	41	11	0	0	0	0	0	0	0	0	0
500	520	44	14	0	0	0	0	0	0	0	0	0
520	540	47	17	0	0	0	0	0	0	0	0	0
540	560	50	20	0	0	0	0	0	0	0	0	0
560	580	53	23	0	0	0	0	0	0	0	0	0
580	600	56	26	0	0	0	0	0	0	0	0	0
600	640	61	30	0	0	0	0	0	0	0	0	0
640	680	67	36	6	0	0	0	0	0	0	0	0
680	720	73	42	12	0	0	0	0	0	0	0	0
720	760	79	48	18	0	0	0	0	0	0	0	0
760	800	85	54	24	0	0	0	0	0	0	0	0
800	840	91	60	30	0	0	0	0	0	0	0	0
840	880	97	66	36	5	0	0	0	0	0	0	0
880	920	103	72	42	11	0	0	0	0	0	0	0
920	960	109	78	48	17	0	0	0	0	0	0	0
960	1,000	115	84	54	23	0	0	0	0	0	0	0
1,000	1,040	121	90	60	29	0	0	0	0	0	0	0
1,040	1,080	127	96	66	35	4	0	0	0	0	0	0
1,080	1,120	133	102	72	41	10	0	0	0	0	0	0
1,120	1,160	139	108	78	47	16	0	0	0	0	0	0
1,160	1,200	145	114	84	53	22	0	0	0	0	0	0
1,200	1,240	151	120	90	59	28	0	0	0	0	0	0
1,240	1,280	157	126	96	65	34	4	0	0	0	0	0
1,280	1,320	163	132	102	71	40	10	0	0	0	0	0
1,320	1,360	169	138	108	77	46	16	0	0	0	0	0
1,360	1,400	175	144	114	83	52	22	0	0	0	0	0
1,400	1,440	181	150	120	89	58	28	0	0	0	0	0
1,440	1,480	187	156	126	95	64	34	3	0	0	0	0
1,480	1,520	193	162	132	101	70	40	9	0	0	0	0
1,520	1,560	199	168	138	107	76	46	15	0	0	0	0
1,560	1,600	205	174	144	113	82	52	21	0	0	0	0
1,600	1,640	211	180	150	119	88	58	27	0	0	0	0
1,640	1,680	217	186	156	125	94	64	33	2	0	0	0
1,680	1,720	223	192	162	131	100	70	39	8	0	0	0
1,720	1,760	229	198	168	137	106	76	45	14	0	0	0
1,760	1,800	235	204	174	143	112	82	51	20	0	0	0
1,800	1,840	241	210	180	149	118	88	57	26	0	0	0
1,840	1,880	247	216	186	155	124	94	63	32	2	0	0
1,880	1,920	253	222	192	161	130	100	69	38	8	0	0
1,920	1,960	259	228	198	167	136	106	75	44	14	0	0
1,960	2,000	265	234	204	173	142	112	81	50	20	0	0
2,000	2,040	272	240	210	179	148	118	87	56	26	0	0
2,040	2,080	284	246	216	185	154	124	93	62	32	1	0
2,080	2,120	295	252	222	191	160	130	99	68	38	7	0
2,120	2,160	306	258	228	197	166	136	105	74	44	13	0
2,160	2,200	317	264	234	203	172	142	111	80	50	19	0
2,200	2,240	328	271	240	209	178	148	117	86	56	25	0
2,240	2,280	340	282	246	215	184	154	123	92	62	31	1
2,280	2,320	351	294	252	221	190	160	129	98	68	37	7
2,320	2,360	362	305	258	227	196	166	135	104	74	43	13
2,360	2,400	373	316	264	233	202	172	141	110	80	49	19
2,400	2,440	384	327	270	239	208	178	147	116	86	55	25

MARRIED Persons—MONTHLY Payroll Period

If the wages are—		And the number of withholding allowances claimed is—										
At least	But less than	0	1	2	3	4	5	6	7	8	9	10
		The amount of income tax to be withheld is—										
$3,240	$3,280	$410	$379	$348	$318	$287	$257	$226	$195	$165	$134	$103
3,280	3,320	416	385	354	324	293	263	232	201	171	140	109
3,320	3,360	422	391	360	330	299	269	238	207	177	146	115
3,360	3,400	428	397	366	336	305	275	244	213	183	152	121
3,400	3,440	434	403	372	342	311	281	250	219	189	158	127
3,440	3,480	440	409	378	348	317	287	256	225	195	164	133
3,480	3,520	447	415	384	354	323	293	262	231	201	170	139
3,520	3,560	458	421	390	360	329	299	268	237	207	176	145
3,560	3,600	469	427	396	366	335	305	274	243	213	182	151
3,600	3,640	480	433	402	372	341	311	280	249	219	188	157
3,640	3,680	492	439	408	378	347	317	286	255	225	194	163
3,680	3,720	503	446	414	384	353	323	292	261	231	200	169
3,720	3,760	514	457	420	390	359	329	298	267	237	206	175
3,760	3,800	525	468	426	396	365	335	304	273	243	212	181
3,800	3,840	536	479	432	402	371	341	310	279	249	218	187
3,840	3,880	548	490	438	408	377	347	316	285	255	224	193
3,880	3,920	559	502	444	414	383	353	322	291	261	230	199
3,920	3,960	570	513	456	420	389	359	328	297	267	236	205
3,960	4,000	581	524	467	426	395	365	334	303	273	242	211
4,000	4,040	592	535	478	432	401	371	340	309	279	248	217
4,040	4,080	604	546	489	438	407	377	346	315	285	254	223
4,080	4,120	615	558	500	444	413	383	352	321	291	260	229
4,120	4,160	626	569	512	454	419	389	358	327	297	266	235
4,160	4,200	637	580	523	466	425	395	364	333	303	272	241
4,200	4,240	648	591	534	477	431	401	370	339	309	278	247
4,240	4,280	660	602	545	488	437	407	376	345	315	284	253
4,280	4,320	671	614	556	499	443	413	382	351	321	290	259
4,320	4,360	682	625	568	510	453	419	388	357	327	296	265
4,360	4,400	693	636	579	522	464	425	394	363	333	302	271
4,400	4,440	704	647	590	533	476	431	400	369	339	308	277
4,440	4,480	716	658	601	544	487	437	406	375	345	314	283
4,480	4,520	727	670	612	555	498	443	412	381	351	320	289
4,520	4,560	738	681	624	566	509	452	418	387	357	326	295
4,560	4,600	749	692	635	578	520	463	424	393	363	332	301
4,600	4,640	760	703	646	589	532	474	430	399	369	338	307
4,640	4,680	772	714	657	600	543	486	436	405	375	344	313
4,680	4,720	783	726	668	611	554	497	442	411	381	350	319
4,720	4,760	794	737	680	622	565	508	451	417	387	356	325
4,760	4,800	805	748	691	634	576	519	462	423	393	362	331
4,800	4,840	816	759	702	645	588	530	473	429	399	368	337
4,840	4,880	828	770	713	656	599	542	485	435	405	374	343
4,880	4,920	839	782	724	667	610	553	496	441	411	380	349
4,920	4,960	850	793	736	678	621	564	507	450	417	386	355
4,960	5,000	861	804	747	690	632	575	518	461	423	392	361
5,000	5,040	872	815	758	701	644	586	529	472	429	398	367
5,040	5,080	884	826	769	712	655	598	541	483	435	404	373
5,080	5,120	895	838	780	723	666	609	552	495	441	410	379
5,120	5,160	906	849	792	734	677	620	563	506	449	416	385
5,160	5,200	917	860	803	746	688	631	574	517	460	422	391
5,200	5,240	928	871	814	757	700	642	585	528	471	428	397
5,240	5,280	940	882	825	768	711	654	597	539	482	434	403
5,280	5,320	951	894	836	779	722	665	608	551	493	440	409
5,320	5,360	962	905	848	790	733	676	619	562	505	447	415
5,360	5,400	973	916	859	802	744	687	630	573	516	459	421
5,400	5,440	984	927	870	813	756	698	641	584	527	470	427
5,440	5,480	996	938	881	824	767	710	653	595	538	481	433
5,480	5,520	1,007	950	892	835	778	721	664	607	549	492	439
5,520	5,560	1,018	961	904	846	789	732	675	618	561	503	446
5,560	5,600	1,029	972	915	858	800	743	686	629	572	515	457
5,600	5,640	1,040	983	926	869	812	754	697	640	583	526	469
5,640	5,680	1,052	994	937	880	823	766	709	651	594	537	480
5,680	5,720	1,063	1,006	948	891	834	777	720	663	605	548	491
5,720	5,760	1,074	1,017	960	902	845	788	731	674	617	559	502
5,760	5,800	1,085	1,028	971	914	856	799	742	685	628	571	513
5,800	5,840	1,096	1,039	982	925	868	810	753	696	639	582	525

$5,840 and over

MINI PRACTICE SET (CH. 13): THE CORNER DRESS SHOP

COMPUTERIZED ACCOUNTING APPLICATION FOR THE CORNER DRESS SHOP MINI PRACTICE SET (CHAPTER 13)

Inventory Adjusting Entries

Before starting on this assignment, read and complete the tasks discussed in Parts A, B, and F of the Computerized Accounting appendix at the end of this book and complete the Computerized Accounting Application assignments for Chapter 3, Chapter 4, Valdez Realty Mini Practice Set (Chapter 5), Pete's Market Mini Practice Set (Chapter 8), and Chapter 10.

This practice set will help you review all the key concepts of a merchandise company along with the integration of payroll, including the preparation of Form 941.

Since you are the bookkeeper of The Corner Dress Shop, we have gathered the following information for you. It will be your task to complete the accounting cycle for March.

The Corner Dress Shop: Trial Balance As at 3/1/97

		Debits	Credits
1110	Cash	1,774.90	—
1115	Petty Cash	35.00	—
1120	Accounts Receivable	2,200.00	—
1130	Inventory	5,600.00	—
1140	Prepaid Rent	1,800.00	—
1250	Delivery Truck	6,000.00	—
1251	Accum. Dep — Delivery Truck	—	1,500.00
2110	Accounts Payable	—	1,900.00
2310	FIT Payable	—	1,188.21
2320	SIT Payable	—	494.53
2330	Social Security Tax Payable	—	1,116.00
2335	Medicare Tax Payable	—	261.00
2340	FUTA Payable	—	134.40
2350	SUTA Payable	—	864.00
2400	Unearned Rent	—	800.00
3110	Betty Loeb, Capital	—	9,151.76
		17,409.90	17,409.90

The Corner Dress Shop: Customer Aged Detail As at 3/1/97

			Total	Current	31 to 60	61 to 90	91+
Bing. Co.							
12	12/31/96	Invoice	2,200.00	—	—	2,200.00	—

The Corner Dress Shop: Vendor Aged Detail As at 3/1/97

			Total	Current	31 to 60	61 to 90	91+
Blew Co.							
510	12/31/96	Invoice	1,900.00	—	—	1,900.00	—

The Corner Dress Shop, owned by Betty Loeb, is located at 1 Milgate Road, Marblehead, Massachusetts, 01945. Her employer identification number is 33-4158215. The educational version of Simply Accounting packaged with this text uses the state and federal tax laws in effect on April 15, 1997. Federal Income Tax (FIT), State Income Tax (SIT), Social Security, Medicare, FUTA, and SUTA are all calculated automatically by the program based on the following assumptions and built-in tax rates:

1. FICA: Social Security, 6.2 percent on $65,400; Medicare, 1.45 percent on all earnings.
2. SUTA: 4.8 percent on the first $10,800 in earnings.   *Federal Unemployment*
3. FUTA: .8 percent on the first $7,000 in earnings.
4. Employees are paid monthly. The payroll is recorded and paid on the last day of each month.
5. FIT is calculated automatically by the program based on the marital status and number of exemptions claimed by each employee.
6. SIT for Massachusetts is calculated automatically by the program based on the marital status and number of exemptions claimed by each employee.

Open the Company Data Files

1. Click on the Start button. Point to Programs; point to Simply Accounting; then click on Simply Accounting in the final menu presented. The Simply Accounting Open File dialog box will appear.
2. Insert your Student Data Files disk into disk drive A. Enter the following path into the **File name** text box: A:\student\dress.asc
3. Click on the **Open** button; enter 3/31/97 into the **Using date for this session** text box; then click on the **OK** button. Click on the **OK** button in response to the message "The date entered is more than one week past your previous **Using** date of 3/1/97." The Company Window for Dress will appear.

Add Your Name to the Company Name

4. Click on the Company Window Setup menu; then click on Company Information. The Company Information dialog box will appear. Insert your name in place of the text "Your Name" in the **Name** text box. Click on the **OK** button to return to the Company Window.

Record March Transactions

5. Record the following transactions using the General, Purchases, Payments, Sales, Receipts, and Payroll Journals:

1997

March 1 *Receipts* Received check no. 7634 from the Bing. Co. in the amount of $2,200 in payment of invoice no. 12 ($2,200), dated December 31.

2 *Purchases* Purchased merchandise from the Morris Co. on account, $10,000, invoice no. 1210, terms 2/10, n/30.

3 *Sales* Sold merchandise to the Ronold Co. on account, $7,000, invoice no. 51, terms 2/10, n/30.

6 *Sales* Sold merchandise to the Ronold Co. on account, $5,000, invoice no. 52, terms 2/10, n/30.

9 *Purch* Purchased merchandise from the Morris Co. on account, $5,000, invoice no. 1286, terms 2/10, n/30.

9 *Sales* Sold merchandise to the Ronold Co. on account, $3,000, invoice no. 53, terms 2/10, n/30.

9 *GJ* Paid cleaning service $300, check no. 110.

10 *Sales—use a minus sign* Ronold Co. returned merchandise that cost $1,000 from invoice no. 52. The Corner Dress Shop issued credit memorandum no. 10 to the Ronold Co. for $1,000.

11 *Purch* Purchased merchandise from the Jones Co. on account, $10,000, invoice no. 4639, terms 1/15, n/60.

12 *Payments* Issued check no. 111 to the Morris Co. in the amount of $9,800 in payment of invoice no. 1210 ($10,000), dated March 2, less 2 percent discount ($200).

13 *GJ* Sold $7,000 of merchandise for cash.

14 Returned merchandise to the Jones Co. in the amount of $2,000. The Corner Dress Shop issued debit memorandum no. 4 to the Jones Co.

15 *GJ* Paid FIT, Social Security, and Medicare taxes due for February payroll, check no. 112.

15 Sold merchandise for $29,000 cash.

15 B. Loeb withdrew $100 for her own personal expenses, check no. 113.

15 Paid SIT tax for February payroll, check no. 114.

16 Received check no. 5432 from the Ronold Co. in the amount of $3,920 in payment of invoice no. 52 ($5,000), dated March 6, less credit memorandum no. 10 ($1,000), less 2 percent discount ($100 − 20 = $80 net sales discount).

16 Received check no. 5447 from the Ronold Co. in the amount of $7,000 in payment of invoice no. 51, dated March 3.

16 Sold merchandise to the Bing Co. on account, $3,200, invoice no. 54, terms 2/10, n/30.

21 Purchased delivery truck on account from Moe's Garage, invoice no. 7113, $17,200.

22 Sold merchandise to the Ronold Co. on account, $4,000, invoice no. 55, terms 2/10, n/30.

23 Issued check no. 115 to the Jones Co. in the amount of $7,920 in payment of invoice no. 4639 ($10,000), dated March 11, less debit memorandum no. 4 ($2,000), less 1 percent discount ($100 − 20 = $80 net purchases discount).

24 Sold merchandise to the Bing Co. on account, $2,000, invoice no. 56, terms 2/10, n/30.

25 Purchased merchandise for $1,000, check no. 116.

27 Purchased merchandise from the Blew Co. on account, $6,000, invoice no. 437, terms 2/10, n/30.

28 Received check no. 5562 from the Ronold Co. in the amount of $3,920 in payment of invoice no. 55 ($4,000), dated March 22, less 2 percent discount ($80).

28 Received check no. 8127 from the Bing Co. in the amount of $3,200 in payment of invoice no. 54, dated March 16.

29 Purchased merchandise from the Morris Co. on account, $9,000, invoice no. 1347, terms 2/10, n/30.

30 Sold merchandise to the Blew Co. on account, $10,000, invoice no. 57, terms 2/10, n/30.

30 The Auxiliary Petty Cash Record for March listed the following: Postage Expense, $5; Delivery Expense, $10; Cleaning Expense, $6; Miscellaneous Expense, $10. Issued check no. 117 to replenish the petty cash fund.

31 Issued payroll checks for March wages as follows:

Employee	March Wages	Check no.
Case, Mel	$1,660	118
Holl, Jane	4,120	119
Moore, Jackie	4,760	120

Print Reports

6. Print the following reports:

   a. General Journal (By posting date, All ledger entries, Start: 3/1/97, Finish: 3/31/97).

   b. Trial Balance As at 3/31/97.

   c. Customer Aged report As at 3/31/97 (Detail, Select All).

   d. Vendor Aged report As at 3/31/97 (Detail, Select All).

   e. Employee Detail Report 1 (Select All, Start: 3/1/97, Finish: 3/31/97).

   f. 941 Summary (FIT, Select All).

   f. 941 Summary (SS/Med Tax, Select All).

   Review your printed reports. If you have made an error in a posted journal entry, see Part C of the Computerized Accounting appendix at the end of this book for information on how to correct the error.

| Record March Adjusting Entries | **7.** Open the General Journal; then record adjusting journal entries based on the following adjustment data: |

Record March Adjusting Entries

How to Record Inventory Adjusting Entries

7. Open the General Journal; then record adjusting journal entries based on the following adjustment data:

a./b. Ending inventory, $3,700. The format of the adjusting entries for inventory in a computerized accounting system, and specifically for The Corner Dress Shop are as follows:

	Debit	Credit
5050 Beginning Inventory	$5,600	
1130 Inventory		$5,600
1130 Inventory	$3,700	
5150 Ending Inventory		$3,700

c. During March, rent expired, $600.

d. Truck depreciated, $150.

e. Rental income earned, $200 (one month's rent from subletting).

Print Reports

8. After you have posted the adjusting journal entries, close the General Journal; then print the following reports:

a. General Journal (By posting date, All ledger entries, Start: 3/1/97, Finish: 3/31/97).

b. Trial Balance As at 3/31/97.

c. General Ledger Report (Start: 3/1/97, Finish: 3/31/97, Select All).

d. Income Statement (Start: 3/1/97, Finish: 3/31/97).

e. Balance Sheet As at 3/31/97.

Review your printed reports. If you have made an error in a posted journal entry, see Part C of the Computerized Accounting appendix for information on how to correct the error.

Record Entry to Close Withdrawals Account

9. Open the General Journal; then record the closing journal entry for Betty Loeb's Withdrawals account.

10. After you have posted the closing entry for Betty Loeb's Withdrawals account, close the General Journal to return to the Company Window.

Make a Backup Copy of March Accounting Records

11. Click on the Company Window File menu; click on Save As; then enter the following new file name into the **Filename** text box: A:\student\dressmar.asc

12. Click on the **Save** button. Note that the company name in the Company Window has changed from Dress to Dressmar. Click on the Company Window File menu again; then click on Save As. Enter the following new file name into the **Filename** text box: A:\student\dress.asc

13. Click on the **Save** button. Click on the **Yes** button in response to the question "Replace existing file?" Note that the company name in the Company Window has changed back from Dressmar to Dress.

14. You now have two sets of company data files for The Corner Dress Shop on your Student Data Files disk. The current data is stored under the file name dress.asc. The backup data is stored under the file name dressmar.asc.

Advance the Using Date

15. Click on the Company Window Maintenance menu; then click on Advance Using Date. Click on the **No** button in response to the question "You have never backed up your data. Would you like to backup now?" Enter 4/1/97 into the **New Using Date** text box; then click on the **OK** button. Click on the **OK** button in response to the warning message. The backup you created using the Save As method will serve as the backup suggested in both warning messages.

Print a Post-Closing Trial Balance

16. Print a post-closing Trial Balance As at 4/1/97.

Exit from the Program

17. Click on the Company Window File menu; then click on Exit to end the current work session and return to your Windows desktop.

Complete the Report Transmittal and Form 941

18. Complete The Corner Dress Shop Report Transmittal and Form 941 located in Appendix A of your *Study Guide and Working Papers.*

14

ACCOUNTING FOR BAD DEBTS

THE BIG PICTURE

After completing the detailed financial reports for Eldorado Computer Center, Tony Freedman noticed that his accounts receivable was extremely large for the amount of sales his business had done. He decided to take several steps to measure whether he is collecting accounts as he should. First, he looked at his new credit policy to see if he was giving out credit to customers without judging their ability to pay. He decided that his customers were generally creditworthy and that he would need to take a look at his accounts in further detail.

Any business would like to collect on all its debts, but every business that extends credit has to realize that some customers do not, or cannot, pay all or part of their debt. When this happens, the business incurs an account that becomes uncollectible, known as *bad debt*.

In this chapter you will learn how to determine the potential bad debt a business may incur. There are different methods used for making this determination. Some companies prefer to write off bad debt after a certain number of days; others may choose to set an allowance of what they expect to become uncollectible during the year. The allowance for bad debt can be determined by the aging of the accounts receivable or as a percentage of sales on credit. These methods usually require some history of account trends or comparison to another, similar business.

Since Freedman has not been in business that long, he has decided to start by writing off accounts that have not been paid in 90 days. If he continues to see a pattern of growing bad debt, he plans to review his new credit policy and possibly to hire an accounts receivable manager.

Learning Objectives	◆ Describing how the Bad Debts Expense account and the Allowance for Doubtful Accounts account are used to record bad debts. (p. 503)
	◆ Using the income statement approach and the balance sheet approach to estimate the amount of Bad Debts Expense. (p. 505)
	◆ Preparing an Aging of Accounts Receivable. (p. 508)
	◆ Writing off an account using the Allowance for Doubtful Accounts account. (p. 510)
	◆ Using the direct write-off method. (p. 511)

Eventually, all companies that sell goods or services on account will come upon a customer that does not pay its bill. The question of so-called *bad debts* affects the company's credit policy. If a company extends credit too easily, it may end up with too many uncollectible accounts. On the other hand, if the credit policy is too strict, the company will end up losing customers to other firms with easier credit policies — and that, too, could mean lost profit.

This chapter looks at how bad debts are recorded in the accrual system of accounting. It also discusses issues like these: When accounts receivable turn into bad debts (or uncollectible accounts), how and what to charge them to, and how to write them off.

LEARNING UNIT 14-1
Accrual Accounting and Recording Bad Debts

As we discussed in an earlier chapter, the accrual system of accounting matches earned revenue with expenses that have been incurred in producing revenue during an accounting period. One expense that is incurred as a result of sales on credit or on account is a bad debts expense. The problem is that it may take as long as a year for the seller to realize that the debt is uncollectible. What happens in the meantime? How can the books be kept up-to-date?

One way to do this is to estimate at the end of the year what percentage of sales made during that year will turn out to be bad debts. There are several ways of arriving at the percentage. At the moment, let's say Abby Ellen Company estimates that 1.6 percent of their sales of $100,000 for the year 19X1 will not be collectible; that means that the company expects not to collect $1,600 of the $100,000 owed them from sales. (Other ways to estimate the amount will be discussed in Learning Unit 14-2.)

Two accounts that we haven't dealt with before, Bad Debts Expense and Allowance for Doubtful Accounts, are needed. **Bad Debts Expense** is an expense account whose normal balance is a debit; it is a temporary account that is closed to Income Summary at year's end. **Allowance for Doubtful Accounts** is a contra-asset account that accumulates the expected amount of bad debts as of a given date; its normal balance is a credit. It is a permanent account that is *not* closed to Income Summary at the end of the year.

In the case of Abby Ellen Company, which expects to be unable to collect $1,600 of the $100,000 owed them from sales, at the end of the year (19X1) an adjustment is made debiting Bad Debts Expense and crediting Allowance for Doubtful Accounts for $1,600. This transaction is shown on page 504, along with a transaction analysis chart:

Dec.	31	Bad Debt Expense	1 6 0 0 00	
		Allowance for Doubtful Accounts		1 6 0 0 00
		Record estimate of bad debts.		

1 Accounts Affected	2 Category	3 ↑ ↓	4 Rules
Bad Debts Expense	Expense	↑	Dr.
Allowance for Doubtful Accounts	Contra-Asset	↑	Cr.

Will go on income statement as an operating expense and eventually be closed to Income Summary.

Will go on balance sheet as a reduction to Accounts Receivable. The normal balance of the allowance account is a credit. It will not be closed at the end of the period.

Accounts Receivable
− Allowance for Doubtful Accounts
= Net Realizable Value

The allowance account is subtracted from Accounts Receivable. This leaves a **net realizable value** of $98,400. Net realizable value is the amount Abby Ellen Company expects to collect. When an account is written off, the net realizable value doesn't change, because both the Accounts Receivable and the Allowance for Doubtful Accounts are reduced (see Fig. 14-1).

Think of the Allowance for Doubtful Accounts as a reservoir that is filled before bad debts occur. The reservoir is drained when a customer's bill is declared uncollectible. Abby Ellen Company estimates that out of its $100,000 of credit sales, $1,600 will prove to be uncollectible, but it does not know which accounts those will be.

WRITING OFF AN ACCOUNT DEEMED UNCOLLECTIBLE

At some point a customer's bill must be written off as uncollectible. Let's look at how Abby Ellen Company would write off the account of Jones Moore on June 5, 19X2. (The $200 sale was made in 19X1.)

Remember, at end of 19X1, Abby made an adjusting entry increasing Bad Debts Expense (debit) and filling the Allowance for Doubtful Accounts (credit) with the estimate of accounts receivable that will not be collectible. The following journal entry is recorded to write off this account:

The bad debts expense was recorded in old year when credit sales were earned.

Fill Cr.

Allowance for Doubtful Accounts

Drain Dr.

FIGURE 14-1
Partial Balance Sheet

Writing off an account.
Note: Bad Debts Expense is not involved.

19X2 June	5	Allowance For Doubtful Accounts	2 0 0 00	
		Accounts Receivable, J. Moore		2 0 0 00
		Writing off J. Moore account.		

ABBY ELLEN COMPANY PARTIAL BALANCE SHEET DECEMBER 31, 19X1			
Assets			
Current Assets:			
Cash		$ 51 4 0 0 00	
Accounts Receivable	$100 0 0 0 00		
Less: Allowance for Doubtful Accounts	1 6 0 0 00	98 4 0 0 00	
Merchandise Inventory		200 0 0 0 00	
Total Current Assets		$349 8 0 0 00	

Note that we did *not* debit the account Bad Debts Expense, since the estimate for this account was made on December 31, 19X1 (and applies to that year, not to 19X2). When that estimate was made, we did not know which bills would turn out to be uncollectible. Once the debt is identified as uncollectible, we reduce both the Allowance account and the controlling account Accounts Receivable and update the accounts receivable subsidary ledger. The subsidiary ledger will be credited just as the controlling account is.

LEARNING UNIT 14-1 REVIEW

AT THIS POINT you should be able to

◆ Define and explain the purpose of Bad Debts Expense and Allowance for Doubtful Accounts. (p. 503)
◆ Explain why the subsidiary ledger account cannot be updated at the time the Bad Debts Expense is estimated. (p. 503)
◆ Prepare an adjusting entry for Bad Debts Expense. (p. 504)
◆ Prepare a partial balance sheet showing the relationship between the Allowance for Doubtful Accounts and Accounts Receivable. (p. 504)
◆ Explain net realizable value. (p. 504)
◆ Prepare a journal entry to write off a customer's debt in a year following the sale. (p. 504)

SELF-REVIEW QUIZ 14-1

(The forms you need are on page 495 of the *Study Guide and Working Papers.*) Respond true or false to the following:

1. The Bad Debts Expense account should be updated only when the customer's debt is declared to be uncollectible.
2. The Allowance for Doubtful Accounts is a contra-asset account on the balance sheet.
3. Bad Debts Expense is part of cost of goods sold.
4. Net realizable value equals Accounts Receivable less Allowance for Doubtful Accounts.
5. When a customer's debt is written off as uncollectible, the account Allowance for Doubtful Accounts is credited.

Quiz Tip: The Allowance account fills with a credit and Drains with a debit.

Solutions to Self-Review Quiz 14-1

1. F   2. T   3. F   4. T   5. F

LEARNING UNIT 14-2
The Allowance Method: Two Approaches to Estimating the Amount of Bad Debts Expense

As mentioned earlier, at the end of each year companies must estimate what percentage of their sales for that year will turn out to be uncollectible accounts

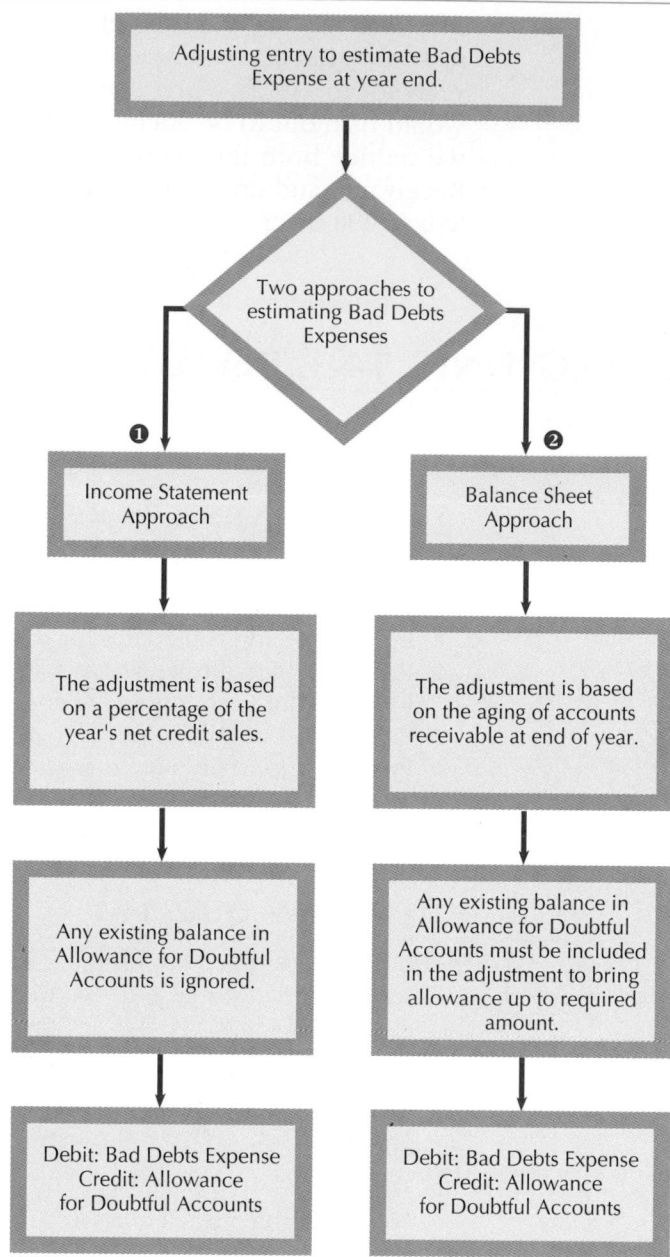

FIGURE 14-2
Two Approaches to Estimating
Amount of Bad Debts Expense

or bad debts. How is this estimate arrived at? In this unit we will look at two of the most common ways of arriving at this amount: the income statement approach and the balance sheet approach. The diagram in Figure 14-2 outlines these methods.

THE INCOME STATEMENT APPROACH

Bad Debts Expense can be based on a percentage of the dollar volume of net credit sales on the income statement.

Abby Ellen Company uses the **income statement approach** to calculate how much Bad Debts Expense will be associated with this year's sales. Based on the past several years, the company has averaged Bad Debts Expense of 1 percent of *net* credit sales. From the following facts, let's prepare an adjusting entry to record the Bad Debts Expense that is based on a percentage of net credit sales.

19X4	Dr.	Cr.
Sales (all credit)		$95,000
Sales Returns and Allowances	$10,000	
Sales Discount	5,000	
Accounts Receivable	7,000	
Allowance for Doubtful Accounts		100

Analysis:

	Analysis:
Sales	$95,000
− SRA	10,000
− SD	5,000
Net Credit Sales	$80,000

1 Accounts Affected	2 Category	3 ↑ ↓	4 Rules
Bad Debts Expense	Expense	↑	Dr.
Allowance for Doubtful Accounts	Contra-Asset	↑	Cr.

Dec.	31	Bad Debts Expense		80000	
		Allowance for Doubtful Accounts			80000
		Record estimate of bad debts.			
		(.01 × $80,000)			

When it is posted, the Allowance account looks like this:

Allowance for Doubtful Accounts

Dr.	
	100 → Balance *before* adjustment
	800 → Adjustment
	900 → New Balance

The income statement approach emphasizes the matching requirements of the income statement. The $100 in the Allowance account represents a carryover of potential bad debts from *prior* years. Thus the total of $900 represents total potential uncollectible accounts of several periods of sales. If, over the years, the estimate for Bad Debts Expense has been inaccurate, an adjusting entry can be made in the current year's Bad Debts Expense. If this happens, the company may reevaluate its percentage, and use 1½ percent instead of 1 percent.

Trudy Kakamba

THE BALANCE SHEET APPROACH

The **balance sheet approach** bases the new total Allowance for Doubtful Accounts on the current Accounts Receivable on the balance sheet. That means the adjustment is reduced by the old balance in Allowance for Doubtful Accounts. When the adjustment is credited, the new balance will reflect the state of Accounts Receivable. (See Fig. 14-2, page 506.) This approach focuses on the aging of Accounts Receivable.

Aging of Accounts Receivable

The longer a bill has been due and not paid, the more likely it is that it is not going to be paid. Therefore, one way of estimating the amount of bad debts for the year just past is to look at Accounts Receivable and analyze it according to how many days past due the accounts are. This is called **aging of Accounts**

Beginning balance in Allowance account represents potential bad debts from previous periods.

Aging classifies uncollected amounts of individual customers according to days past due.

TABLE 14-1 AGING OF ACCOUNTS RECEIVABLE

Name of Customer	Total Balance	Not Yet Due	Days Past Due			
			1–30	31–60	61–90	Over 90
Sarah Elliot	$ 100	$ 100				
Joshua Karras	30			$ 30		
Alan Ledbury	160	160				
John Sullivan	180				$160	$ 20
Sheri Missan	80	80				
Others	6,450	3,260	$2,000	840	40	310
Totals	$7,000	$3,600	$2,000	$870	$200	$330
Percent of total (rounded to nearest whole percent)	100%	51%	29%	12%	3%	5%
		$\left(\dfrac{\$3,600}{\$7,000}\right)$	$\left(\dfrac{\$2,000}{\$7,000}\right)$	$\left(\dfrac{\$870}{\$7,000}\right)$	$\left(\dfrac{\$200}{\$7,000}\right)$	$\left(\dfrac{\$330}{\$7,000}\right)$

Today, with the computer, an analysis of Accounts Receivable can be completed quickly.

Receivable.

Table 14-1 shows an analysis that the Abby Ellen Company did on December 31, 19X4. Note that 29 percent of the total receivables for Abby Ellen are past due from 1 to 30 days. (This analysis will also provide feedback to the credit department as to how well the current credit policy is working.) Now let's look at how the company will estimate what balance in the Allowance for Doubtful Accounts is required to meet probable bad debts.

The schedule shown in Table 14-2 is prepared to assist the company in calculating the needed balance. In this schedule Abby Ellen Company has applied a sliding scale of percents (3, 4, 10, 20, 50), based on previous experience, to the total amount of receivables due in each time period. For example, of the

TABLE 14-2 BALANCE REQUIRED TO MEET PROBABLE BAD DEBTS

	Amount	Estimated Percent Considered to be Bad Debts Expense	Amount Needed in Allowance for Doubtful Accounts to Cover Estimated Bad Debts Expense
Not Yet Due	$3,600	3	$108 ($3,600 × .03)
Days Past Due			
1–30	2,000	4	80
31–60	870	10	87
61–90	200	20	40
Over 90	330	50	165
Total Accounts Receivable ⟶	$7,000	Total Balance Required in ⟶ Allowance for Doubtful Accounts	$480
Less current balance			−100
Adjusting entry			$380

$3,600 not yet due, 3 percent or $108, will probably never be paid. Looking at this schedule reveals that Abby Ellen Company needs $480 to cover estimated bad debts. *Presently* the balance in the Allowance account is $100. Thus, to reach a balance of $480, we must adjust the balance of the account by the following adjusting journal entry:

The balance in the Allowance for Doubtful Accounts is *not* ignored.

19X4 Dec.	31	Bad Debts Expense	3 8 0 00	
		Allowance for Doubtful Accounts		3 8 0 00
		Estimate of bad debts		

Bad Debits Expense			Allowance for Doubtful Accounts	
Dr.	Cr.	Dr.		Cr.
380			100	Beg. Balance
			380	Adj.
			480	New balance in Allowance

Some companies that feel aging is too time-consuming may estimate bad debts based on a percentage of total Accounts Receivable.

The desired balance of $480 is now reached. If the Allowance had a *debit* balance of $100 before the adjustment, the amount of the adjusting entry would be $580 credit to the Allowance to arrive at the $480 balance. Once again, the adjustment *must* consider the existing balance in the Allowance account before the adjusting entry is prepared.

LEARNING UNIT 14-2 REVIEW

AT THIS POINT you should be able to

- ◆ Explain the two approaches to estimating Bad Debts Expense. (p. 506)
- ◆ Explain why the balance in the Allowance for Doubtful Accounts is ignored when an adjusting entry for bad debts is prepared in the income statement approach. (p. 507)
- ◆ Show how to prepare an aging of Accounts Receivable. (p. 508)
- ◆ Explain how the aging of Accounts Receivable is used to arrive at the balance required in the Allowance for Doubtful Accounts. (p. 509)

SELF-REVIEW QUIZ 14-2

(The forms you need are on page 495 of the *Study Guide and Working Papers*.)
From the following, prepare an adjusting journal entry for Bad Debts Expense for (1) the income statement approach and (2) the balance sheet approach.

Allowance for Doubtful Accounts		**Income Statement Approach**	
Dr.	Cr.	Net Sales	$160,000
	400	1% of Net Sales	

Balance Sheet Approach		Percent Considered Bad Debts
Not yet due:	$4,000	4
Days past due:		
1–30	3,000	5
31–60	400	10
Over 60	5,000	30

Solution to Self-Review Quiz 14-2

(1)	Dec.	31	Bad Debts Expense	1 6 0 0 00		
			Allowance for Doubtful Accounts		1 6 0 0 00	
			[.01 × $160,000]			
(2)		31	Bad Debts Expense	1 4 5 0 00		
			Allowance for Doubtful Accounts		1 4 5 0 00	
			$4,000 × .04 = $ 160			
			3,000 × .05 = 150			
			400 × .10 = 40			
			5,000 × .30 = 1,500			
			$1,850			

$1,850 is amount required

Quiz Tip: Note allowance adjusted: $1,850 − $400 = $1,450

LEARNING UNIT 14-3
Writing Off and Recovering Uncollectible Accounts

WRITING OFF AN ACCOUNT USING THE ALLOWANCE FOR DOUBTFUL ACCOUNTS

Let's assume that on March 18, 19X7, the Abby Ellen Company determines that the account of Jill Sullivan for $900 is uncollectible. (The sale to Jill Sullivan was back in 19X6.) This means that this Accounts Receivable amount should no longer be considered an asset and should be written off. The following journal entry reduces the Allowance for Doubtful Accounts and reduces the Accounts Receivable controlling account as well as the accounts receivable subsidiary ledger.

19X7					
Mar.	18	Allowance for Doubtful Accounts	9 0 0 00		
		Accounts Receivable, Jill Sullivan		9 0 0 00	
		Wrote off Sullivan account			

Key Points:

◆ This journal entry does *not* affect any expenses. Remember, Bad Debts Expense is not affected when an account is finally written off. The estimate for Bad

Debts Expense was recorded in the previous year before the bad debt actually occurred.

◆ If more than one customer is written off, a compound entry can be used, debiting Allowance for the total and crediting each individual account.

◆ The net realizable value of Accounts Receivable is unchanged. Let's prove this:

	Balances Before the Write-off		Balances After the Write-off
Accounts Receivable	$12,000	$900 write-off	$11,100
Less: Allowance for Doubtful Accounts	2,000	$900 drain	1,100
Estimated realizable value	$10,000	no change	$10,000
	(what to expect to collect)		

Recording Recovered Debts Using Allowance for Doubtful Accounts

But what would happen if Jill Sullivan paid all or part of the debt after Abby Ellen Company wrote it off? Consider this situation: Assume that Jill Sullivan is able to pay off half of her debt and send a check to Abby Ellen Company on February 1, 19X8. (Keep in mind the fact that her account was written off on March 18, 19X7, and the original sale was made in 19X6.) To record this, Abby Ellen Company reverses in part the entry that was made to write off the account in the amount expected to be recovered and records the amount received from Jill. The following are the journal entries to record the recovery of $450 out of the original amount of $900:

19X8 Feb.	1	Accounts Receivable, Jill Sullivan		450 00		
		Allowances for Doubtful Accounts			450 00	
		Restores collectible portion				
	1	Cash		450 00		
		Accounts Receivable, Jill Sullivan			450 00	
		Records payment received				

Reinstates the account → (first entry)

Records the amount received → (second entry)

The reason we record both a debit and a credit to Accounts Receivable is that it provides a clear picture of the transactions involving Jill Sullivan. If the company is considering giving credit again to Jill Sullivan, these previous records could be of assistance in determining how much if any credit could be extended. Note how the first entry reinstates the account and the second entry records the cash received.

THE DIRECT WRITE-OFF METHOD

The direct write-off method does not fulfill the matching principle but is acceptable for federal income tax reporting.

When a company cannot reasonably estimate its Bad Debts Expense, it may use the **direct write-off method.** Using this method, an account that is determined to be uncollectible would be directly written off to this year's Bad Debts Expense account without regard to when the original sale was made.

In this method, the Allowance for Doubtful Accounts is not used, since no adjustment is needed at the end of the year to estimate Bad Debts Expense. The Journal entry would be a debit to Bad Debts Expense and a credit to Accounts Receivable.

Recording Recovered Debts Using the Direct Method   Let's suppose that Jill Sullivan repays half of her outstanding debt after Abby Ellen Company has written it off. This is how the recovered debt would be accounted for using the direct write-off method.

Writing off Jill Sullivan on March 18, 19X7. Note that Allowance account is not used. See p. 510.

19X7 Mar.	18	Bad Debts Expense		9 0 0 00	
		Accounts Receivable, Jill Sullivan			9 0 0 00
		Wrote off account			

A new account title, **Bad Debts Recovered,** must be created. Think of this account as a revenue account found in the Other Income section of an income statement.

Recovery of half the amount owed by Jill Sullivan on Feb. 1, 19X8. Note that Bad Debts Recovered is used instead of Allowance for Doubtful Accounts.

19X8 Feb.	1	Acct. Rec., Jill Sullivan		4 5 0 00	
		Bad Debts Recovered			4 5 0 00
		Restores collectible portion			
	1	Cash		4 5 0 00	
		Acct. Rec., Jill Sullivan			4 5 0 00
		Records payment received			

On the balance sheet, Accounts Receivable is recorded at gross. No Allowance account or realizable amount is used.

Bad Debts Recov.	Other Revenue	↑	Cr.

In the direct write-off method, when the amount is written off, no Allowance for Doubtful Accounts is used. Instead, the debit is to Bad Debts Expense. If the debt is recovered later, the direct method credits Bad Debts Recovered (an account in the "Other Revenue" category). In effect, this increases the revenue and puts the Accounts Receivable back on the books. If recovery is made the same year (let's say on May 1) as the debt is written off, the entry made to write off the account is reversed:

19X7 May	1	Accounts Receivable, Jill Sullivan		4 5 0 00	
		Bad Debts Expense			4 5 0 00

LEARNING UNIT 14-3 REVIEW

AT THIS POINT you should be able to

♦ Write off an account using the Allowance for Doubtful Accounts method. (p. 510)

- ◆ Explain why net realizable value is unchanged after a write-off is complete. (p. 511)
- ◆ Prepare journal entries to recover entire or partial amounts that were once declared uncollectible. (p. 511)
- ◆ Explain the direct write-off method and prepare appropriate journal entries for write-off and recovery. (p. 512)

SELF-REVIEW QUIZ 14-3

(The forms you need are on page 496 of the *Study Guide and Working Papers.*) Respond true or false to the following:

1. When an account using the Allowance for Doubtful Accounts method is written off in a period following the sale, the result is a debit to Bad Debts Expense and a credit to Accounts Receivable.
2. The direct write-off method will sometimes use the Allowance for Doubtful Accounts.
3. When an account is written off (using the Allowance for Doubtful Accounts method), net realizable value is unchanged.
4. Bad Debts Recovered is an asset.
5. A debit balance in the Allowance for Doubtful Accounts indicates that the estimate for Bad Debts Expense was too low.

Solution to Self-Review Quiz 14-3

1. F   2. F   3. T   4. F   5. T

SUMMARY OF KEY POINTS

Learning Unit 14-1

1. If accrual accounting is used, Bad Debts Expense should be recognized in the year the sale was earned, even though the actual write-off may not yet have taken place.
2. Bad Debts Expense is an expense found on the income statement.
3. The Allowance for Doubtful Accounts is a contra-asset account found on the balance sheet that accumulates the amount of estimated uncollectibles before they are actually written off.
4. Net realizable value equals Accounts Receivable minus Allowance for Doubtful Accounts.
5. When an account is written off, the Allowance for Doubtful Accounts is debited and Accounts Receivable is credited (along with the subsidiary ledger account).

Learning Unit 14-2

1. The two approaches to estimating Bad Debts Expense are the income statement approach and the balance sheet approach.
2. The income statement approach estimates Bad Debts Expense based on a percent of net sales. (Some companies use credit sales, some use total sales.) The balance is ignored in the Allowance for Doubtful Accounts when the Bad Debts Expense is estimated from sales of the period.
3. The balance sheet approach estimates the balance required in the Allowance for Doubtful Accounts by aging the Accounts Receivable. The balance in the Allowance account will have to be adjusted based on the aging of the receivables.

Learning Unit 14-3

After the write-off, net realizable value is unchanged.

1. When an account is written off (using the Allowance account) in years following the sale, the result is to debit the Allowance for Doubtful Accounts and credit Accounts Receivable. Do not debit Bad Debts Expense, as it has already been recorded in the year the sale was earned.
2. When an uncollectible account has been written off and is now recovered, the entry reverses the original write-off by debiting Accounts Receivable and crediting the Allowance for Doubtful Accounts. Then the cash received is debited and the Accounts Receivable is credited.
3. The direct write-off method will recognize the Bad Debts Expense when the customer account is declared uncollectible. The direct method does *not* use the Allowance for Doubtful Accounts, since no estimate is made for bad debts. This method does not follow the matching principle in the accrual basis of accounting.
4. Bad Debts Recovered is classified as "other revenue" when a customer account is reinstated after being written off in the direct method.

KEY TERMS

Aging of Accounts Receivable The procedure of classifying accounts of individual customers by age group, where age is the number of days elapsed from due date.

Allowance for Doubtful Accounts A contra-asset account that is subtracted from the Accounts Receivable. This account accumulates the *expected* amount of uncollectibles as of a given date.

Bad Debts Expense The operating expense account that estimates the amount of credit sales that will probably not be collectible in a given accounting period when the Allowance method is used. For the direct write-off method, this account would be the actual amount written off.

Bad Debts Recovered When an Account Receivable has been written off and is recovered, this account, which is in the "Other Revenue" category, is credited in the direct write-off method if the recovery is in a year *following* the write-off.

Balance sheet approach A method used to calculate the amount *required* in the Allowance for Doubtful Accounts to cover expected uncollectibles. This method is based on the Accounts Receivable amount and the aging process. The adjustment to the Allowance for Doubtful Accounts will bring the new balance of that account to the new required level.

Direct write-off method The method of writing off uncollectibles when they occur and thus *not* using the Allowance for Doubtful Accounts. This method does not fulfill the matching principle of accrual accounting.

Income statement approach A method that estimates the amount of Bad Debts Expense that will result based on a percent of net credit sales for the period. The amount of the expected bad debt is added to the existing balance of Allowance for Doubtful Accounts.

Net realizable value The amount (Accounts Receivable − Allowance for Doubtful Accounts) that is expected to be collected.

QUESTIONS, MINI EXERCISES, EXERCISES, AND PROBLEMS

Discussion Questions

1. Explain the matching principle in relationship to recording Bad Debts Expense.
2. What is the purpose of the Allowance for Doubtful Accounts?
3. What is net realizable value?
4. When an Account Receivable is written off, Bad Debts Expense must be debited. True or false? Please discuss.
5. Explain why the Allowance for Doubtful Accounts is a contra-asset account.
6. Recording Bad Debts Expense is a closing entry. True or false? Defend your position.
7. The income statement approach used to estimate bad debts is based on Accounts Receivable on the balance sheet. Accept or reject. Why?
8. In which approach is the balance of the Allowance for Doubtful Accounts considered when the estimate of Bad Debts Expense is made? Please explain.
9. Why would a company age its Accounts Receivable?
10. Using the Allowance for Doubtful Accounts method, what journal entries would be made to write off an account as well as later record the recovery of the Accounts Receivable?
11. Why doesn't net realizable value change when an account is written off in the use of the Allowance account?

(Cont. on p. 517)

BLUEPRINT SUMMARY OF RECORDING BAD DEBTS EXPENSE, WRITE-OFFS, AND RECOVERY

Situation	ALLOWANCE FOR DOUBTFUL ACCOUNTS METHOD		DIRECT WRITE-OFF METHOD
	A. Income Statement Approach	B. Balance Sheet Approach	
Adjusting entry to record estimated uncollectible accounts	Bad Debts Expense XX Allowance for Doubtful Accounts XX Based on percent of net sales. Balance in Allowance account is ignored.	Bad Debts Expense XX Allowance for Doubtful Accounts XX Aging of Accounts Receivable determines amount needed in Allowance account. Balance in Allowance account is adjusted.	None
Accounts Receivable is determined to be uncollectible	Allowance for Doubtful Accounts XX Accounts Receivable, XX	Allowance for Doubtful Accounts XX Accounts Receivable, XX	Bad Debts Expense XX Accounts Receivable, XX
Bad Debts are recovered	Accounts Receivable, XX Allowance for Doubtful Accounts XX Cash XX Accounts Receivable, XX	Accounts Receivable, XX Allowance for Doubtful Accounts XX Cash XX Accounts Receivable, XX	Accounts Receivable, XX Bad Debts Recovered* XX Cash XX Accounts Receivable, XX
Balance sheet update	Shows net realizable value	Shows net realizable value	Does not show net realizable value

* Used if recovery is not in the same year as the sale.

12. What is the purpose of using a direct write-off method?

13. Explain the purpose of the Bad Debts Recovered account.

Mini Exercises

(The forms you need are on page 498 of the *Study Guide and Working Papers*.)

Categorizing Accounts

1. a. Complete the following transactional analysis chart:

	Category	↑ ↓	Rules
Bad Debts Expense			
Allowance for Doubtful Accounts			

    b. Which financial statement will each title be recorded on?

    c. Which account is temporary? Which account is permanent?

Allowance Method

2. Complete Table:

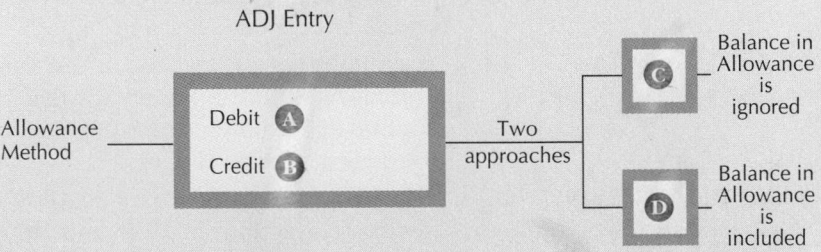

Journalize Adjusting Entries for Income Statement and Balance Sheet Approach

3. Given the balance in the Allowance for Doubtful Accounts of $100 credit. Prepare Adjusting entries for Bad Debts based on the following assumptions:

    a. Bad Debts to be 5 percent of Net Credit Sales or $400.

    b. Based on Aging of Accounts Receivable, Bad Debts should be $400.

Writing Off Uncollectible Accounts and Reinstatement— Allowance Method

4. Journalize entries for the following situations (assume allowance method):

    Situation 1: Wrote off Bill Allen as a Bad Debt 2 years after the sale for $50.

    Situation 2: Reinstated Bill Allen who sent in his past due amount.

Writing Off Uncollectible Account and Reinstatement—Direct Write-Off Method

5. Journalize entries for the following situation (assume direct write-off method).

Situation 1: Wrote off Bill Allen as a bad debt two years after the sale of $50.

Situation 2: Reinstated Bill Allen who sent in his past due amount two years after it had been written off.

Exercises

(The forms you need are on pages 499–500 of the *Study Guide and Working Papers.*)

Preparing a partial balance sheet with Allowance for Doubtful Accounts.

14-1. Jetson Co. has requested that you prepare a partial balance sheet on December 31, 19XX, from the following: Cash, $105,000; Petty Cash, $60; Accounts Receivable, $60,000; Bad Debts Expense, $40,000; Allowance for Doubtful Accounts, $12,000; Merchandise Inventory, $18,000.

Calculating Bad Debts Expense by income statement approach.

14-2. Given the following information:

Accounts Receivable	Sales	Sales Returns and Allowances
30,000	110,000	500

	Sales Discount	Allowance for Doubtful Accounts
	9,500	5,000

Journalize the adjusting entry on December 31, 19XX, for Bad Debts Expense, which is estimated to be 4 percent of net sales. The income statement approach is used.

Calculating Bad Debts Expense by balance sheet approach.

14-3. Assuming that in Exercise 2 the balance sheet approach is used, prepare a journalized adjusting entry for Bad Debts Expense. Based on an aging of Accounts Receivable, an $8,000 balance in the Allowance account will be needed to cover bad debts.

Journalizing adjustment for Bad Debts as well as reinstatement by Allowance method; comparison with direct write-off method.

14-4. The Austin Co., which uses an Allowance for Doubtful Accounts, had the following transactions in 19X5 and 19X6. (Use the income statement approach.)

19X5
Dec.   31   Recorded Bad Debts Expense of $12,000.

19X6
Apr.   3   Wrote off Angie Ring account of $4,000 as uncollectible.
June   4   Wrote off Mike Catuc account of $3,000 as uncollectible.

19X7
Aug.   5   Recovered $500 from Mike Catuc.

a. Journalize the transactions. (They use the income statement approach in estimating bad debts.)

b. Journalize how Austin Co. would record the Mike Catuc bad debt situation if the direct write-off method were used.

Journalizing adjustments for Bad Debts Expense (1) based on percent of sales, (2) based on aging of Accounts Receivable with balance of Allowance for Doubtful Accounts, a debit balance.

14-5. Rowe Company had credit sales of $200,000 during 19X7. The balance in the Allowance for Doubtful Accounts is a $1,000 debit balance. Journalize the Bad Debts Expense for December 31 using each of the following methods:

a. Bad Debts Expense is estimated at 1½ percent of credit sales.

b. The aging of Accounts Receivable indicates that $2,200 will be required in the Allowance account to cover Bad Debts Expense.

Group A Problems

(The forms you need are on pages 501–507 of the *Study Guide and Working Papers*.)

The income statement approach: journalizing Bad Debts Expense and writing accounts off.

14A-1. The Palter Co. has requested that you prepare journal entries from the following (this company uses the Allowance for Doubtful Accounts method based on the income statement approach).

Check Figure:

August 24:

Dr.: Allowance for Doubtful Accounts

Cr.: Accounts Receivable, Jill Neuman

19X7
Dec. 31 Recorded Bad Debts Expense of $11,000.

19X8
Jan. 7 Wrote off Gene Smore's account of $800 as uncollectible.
Mar. 5 Wrote off Paul Jane's account of $600 as uncollectible.
July 8 Recovered $300 from Paul Jane.
Aug. 19 Wrote off Bob Seager's account of $1,300 as uncollectible.
Aug. 24 Wrote off Jill Neuman's account of $750 as uncollectible.
Nov. 19 Recovered $400 from Bob Seager.

The balance sheet approach: aging analysis and journalizing of Bad Debts Expense.

Check Figure:

Net Realizable Value $146,650

14A-2. Given the information presented below:

a. Prepare on December 31, 19X8, the adjusting journal entry for Bad Debts Expense.

b. Prepare a partial balance sheet on December 31, 19X8, showing how net realizable value is calculated.

c. If the balance in the Allowance for Doubtful Accounts was a $300 debit balance, journalize the adjusting entry for Bad Debts Expense on December 31, 19X8.

		Amount	Estimated Percent Considered to Be Bad Debts Expense	Estimated Amount Needed in Allowance for Doubtful Accounts	
	Not yet due	$130,000	.01		
	0 – 60	9,000	.05		
	61 – 180	8,000	.20		
	Over six months	5,000	.40		
		$152,000			

ALVIE CO.
DECEMBER 31, 19X8

Balances: Cash, $30,000; Accounts Receivable, $152,000; Allowance for Doubtful Accounts, $300; Inventory, $12,000.

The direct write-off method.

Check Figure:

Dec. 7:

Dr.: Bad Debt Exp.

Cr.: Acct Rec, J. Miller

14A-3. T. J. Rack Company uses the direct write-off method for recording Bad Debts Expense. At the beginning of 19X8, Accounts Receivable has a $119,000 balance. Journalize the following transactions for T. J. Rack:

19X8
Mar. 13 Wrote off S. Rose's account for $1,800.
Apr. 14 Wrote off P. Soy's account for $750.

19X9

Nov.	8	P. Soy paid bad debt of $750 that was written off April 14, 19X8.
Dec.	7	Wrote off J. Miller's account as uncollectible, $285.
Dec.	12	Wrote off D. Lovejoy's account for $375 due from sales made on account in 19X7.

Journalizing and posting adjustments for Bad Debts Expense and write-offs and recovery based on balance sheet approach. Preparation of partial balance sheet.

14A-4. Simon Company completed the following transactions:

19X8

Jan.	9	Sold merchandise on account to Ray's Supply, $1,500.
Jan.	15	Wrote off the account of Pete Runnels as uncollectible because of his death, $600.
Mar.	17	Received $400 from Roland Co., whose account had been written off in 19X7. The account was reinstated and the collection recorded.
Apr.	9	Received 10 percent of the $4,000 owed by Lane Drug. The remainder was written off as uncollectible.
June	15	The account of Mel's Garage was reinstated for $1,200. The account was written off three years ago.
Oct.	18	Prepared a compound entry to write the following accounts off as uncollectible: Jane's Diner, $200; Keen Auto, $400; Ralph's Hardware, $600.
Nov.	12	Sold merchandise on account to J. B. Rug, $1,900.
Dec.	31	Based on an aging of Accounts Receivable, it was estimated that $7,000 will be uncollectible out of a total of $160,000 in Accounts Receivable.
Dec.	31	Closed Bad Debts Expense to Income Summary.

From the above as well as the following additional data:

	Acct. No.	Balance
Allowance for Doubtful Accounts	114	$4,100
Income Summary	312	—
Bad Debts Expense	612	—

Check Figure:
Total current assets $272,360

1. Journalize the transactions.

2. Post to Allowance for Doubtful Accounts, Income Summary, and Bad Debts Expense Accounts as needed. (Be sure to record beginning balance in the Allowance account in your *Study Guide and Working Papers.*)

3. Prepare a current assets section of the balance sheet. Ending balances needed: Cash, $13,000; Accounts Receivable, $160,000; Office Supplies, $2,110; Merchandise Inventory, $103,000; Prepaid Rent, $1,250.

Group B Problems

(The forms you need are on pages 501–507 of the *Study Guide and Working Papers.*)

The income statement approach: journalizing Bad Debts Expense and writing accounts off.

14B-1. The Palter Co. has requested that you prepare journal entries from the following (this company uses the Allowance for Doubtful Accounts method based on the income statement approach).

Check Figure:

Aug. 24:

Dr.: Allow for D.A.

Cr.: Acc Rec, Jim O'Reilly

19X7

Dec. 31 Recorded Bad Debts Expense of $14,800.

19X8

Jan.   7 Wrote off Woody Tree's Account of $1,200 as uncollectible.
Mar.   5 Wrote off Jim Lantz's account of $600 as uncollectible.
July   8 Recovered $600 from Jim Lantz.
Aug.   19 Wrote off Mabel Hest's account of $750 as uncollectible.
Aug.   24 Wrote off Jim O'Reilly's account of $950 as uncollectible.
Nov.   19 Recovered $500 from Mabel Hest.

The balance sheet approach: aging analysis and journalizing of Bad Debts Expense.

14B-2. Given the following information and the information below: Cash, Merchandise $42,000; Accounts Receivable, $173,000; Allowance for Doubtful Accounts, $400; Merchandise Inventory, $12,000:

a. Prepare on December 31, 19X8, the adjusting journal entry for Bad Debts Expense.

b. Prepare a partial balance sheet on December 31, 19X8, showing how net realizable value is calculated.

c. If the balance in the Allowance for Doubtful Accounts was a $400 debit balance, journalize the adjusting entry for Bad Debts Expense on December 31, 19X8.

Check Figure:

Net Realizable Value $166,000

ALVIE CO.
DECEMBER 31, 19X8

	Amount	Estimated Percent Considered to Be Bad Debts Expense	Estimated Amount Needed in Allowance for Doubtful Accounts
Not yet due	$150,000	.02	
0 – 60	10,000	.06	
61 – 180	9,000	.20	
Over six months	4,000	.40	
	$173,000		

The direct write-off method.

14B-3. T. J. Rack Company uses the direct write-off method for recording Bad Debts Expense. At the beginning of 19X8, Accounts Receivable has an $88,000 balance. Journalize the following transactions for T. J. Rack:

Check Figure:

Dec. 7:

Dr.: Bad Debt Expense

Cr.: Accounts Receivable, Joe Francis

19X8

Mar.   13 Wrote off Jill Diamond's account for $1,950.
Apr.   14 Wrote off Buffy Hall's account for $900.

19X9

Nov.   8 Buffy Hall paid debt of $900 that was written off April 14, 19X8.
Dec.   7 Wrote off Joe Francis's account as uncollectible, $880.
Dec.   12 Wrote off Joe Martin's account for $410 from sales made on account in 19X7.

Journalizing and posting adjustments for Bad Debts Expense and write-offs and recovery based on balance sheet approach. Partial balance sheet prepared.

14B-4. Simon Company completed the following transactions:

19X8

Jan.   9 Sold merchandise on account to Lowe's Supply, $1,900.
Jan.   15 Wrote off the account of Kevin Reese as uncollectible because of his death, $700.

Mar.	17	Received $300 from J. James whose account had been written off in 19X7. The account was reinstated and the collection recorded.
Apr.	9	Received 20 percent of the $5,000 owed by Long Drug. The remainder was written off as uncollectible.
June	15	The account of Morse's Garage was reinstated for $3,100. The account was written off three years ago.
Oct.	18	Prepared a compound entry to write the following accounts off as uncollectible: Sal's Diner, $800; Ring Auto, $1,300; Neel's Hardware, $800.
Nov.	12	Sold merchandise on account to Able Roy, $1,950.
Dec.	31	Based on an aging of Accounts Receivable, it was estimated that $8,000 will be uncollectible out of a total of $170,000 in Accounts Receivable.
Dec.	31	Closed Bad Debts Expense to Income Summary.

From the above as well as the following additional data:

	Acct. No.	Balance
Allowance for Doubtful Accounts	114	$3,300
Income Summary	312	—
Bad Debts Expense	612	—

1. Journalize the transactions.

2. Post to Allowance for Doubtful Accounts, Income Summary, and Bad Debts Expense Account as needed.

3. Prepare a current assets section of the balance sheet. Ending balances needed: Cash, $24,000; Accounts Receivable, $170,000; Office Supplies, $3,000; Merchandise Inventory, $94,000; Prepaid Rent, $1,200.

REAL WORLD APPLICATIONS

14R-1.

Joan Rivers, the newly hired bookkeeper of Lyon Company, has until 5:00 P.M. today to prepare an analysis on December 31 of Accounts Receivable by age as well as record the entry for Bad Debts Expense. Please assist Joan, who has found the following invoices and balances scattered on her desk (see top of p. 523). Terms of all sales are n/30. Explain in writing why the allowance method is used.

14R-2.

MEMO

To: Al Jones

From: Peter Flynn, Pres.

Re: Bad Debts

Sept. 30, 19XX

At a party last night a friend of mine told me that we should not be using the direct write-off method. He told me that it doesn't fulfill the matching principle of accounting. Check the Tax Reform Act of 1986 in your Research Department to support or reject this information. Please provide me with a written report.

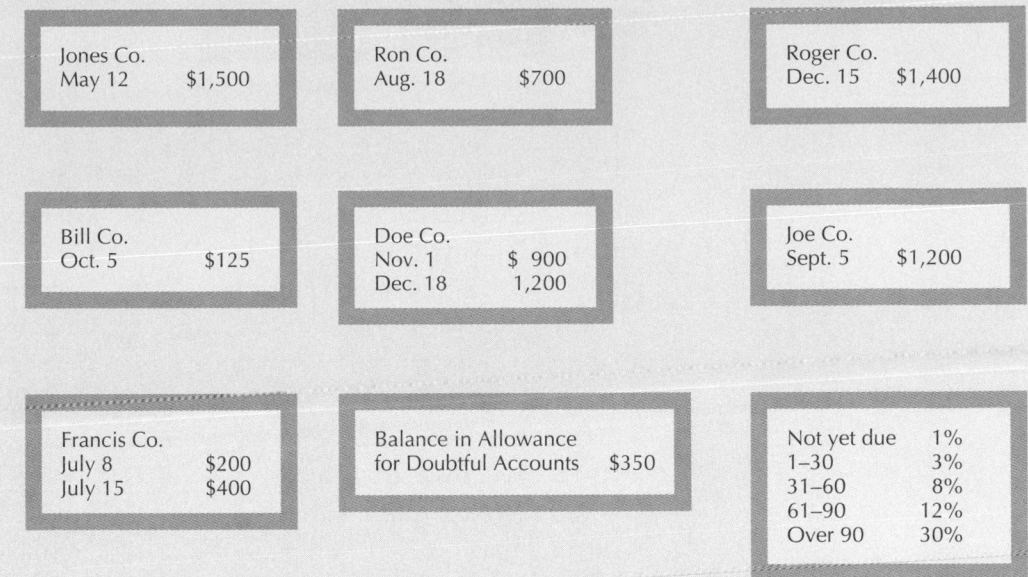

Jones Co.		Ron Co.		Roger Co.	
May 12	$1,500	Aug. 18	$700	Dec. 15	$1,400

Bill Co.		Doe Co.		Joe Co.	
Oct. 5	$125	Nov. 1	$ 900	Sept. 5	$1,200
		Dec. 18	1,200		

Francis Co.		Balance in Allowance for Doubtful Accounts $350	Not yet due	1%
July 8	$200		1–30	3%
July 15	$400		31–60	8%
			61–90	12%
			Over 90	30%

YOU make the call

Critical Thinking/Ethical Case

14R-3.
Pete Sazich, the accountant for Moore Company, feels that all bad debts will be eliminated if credit transactions are done by credit card. He also feels that the cost of the credit cards should be added on to the price of the goods. Pete feels that in the future, the allowance method will be totally eliminated. You make the call. Write a letter stating your opinion regarding this matter to Pete's boss.

ACCOUNTING RECALL
A CUMULATIVE APPROACH

THIS EXAM REVIEWS CHAPTERS 1 THROUGH 14

Your *Study Guide and Working Papers* (pp. 511 and 513) has forms to complete this exam, as well as worked-out solutions. The page references next to each question identify what page to turn back to if you answer the question incorrectly.

PART 1   Vocabulary Review

Match the terms to the appropriate definition or phrase.

Page Ref.

(508)	1. Aging of accounts receivable	A. In alphabetical order
(512)	2. Bad debts recovered	B. Balance in allowable account will have to be adjusted
(429)	3. Ending merchandise inventory	C. Operating expense
(503)	4. Allowance for doubtful accounts	D. Does not use allowance for doubtful accounts
(464)	5. Plant and Equipment	E. Classifying of accounts
(319)	6. Subsidiary ledgers	F. Land
(504)	7. Net realizable value	G. Contra-asset account
(511)	8. Direct write-off method	H. Other revenue
(507)	9. Balance sheet approach	I. Subtracted from cost of goods sold
(503)	10. Bad debt expense	J. Accounts receivable less allowance for doubtful accounts

PART II   True or False (Accounting Theory)

(506)   11. In the income statement approach any existing balance in the Allowance for Doubtful Accounts is ignored.

(506)   12. The income statement approach is based on aging of Accounts Receivable.

(511)   13. Allowance for Doubtful Accounts is used in the direct write-off method.

(503)   14. The Allowance for Doubtful Accounts is listed on the income statement.

(509)   15. A debit to the Allowance account will increase it.

CONTINUING PROBLEM

The Eldorado Computer Center currently has an $11,900 balance in accounts receivable. Here is a current schedule of accounts receivable:

Eldorado Computer Center
Schedule of Accounts Receivable
March 31, 19XX

Taylor Golf	$ 2,900
Vita Needle	8,100
Accu Pac	900
Total	$11,900

Assignment:

(See p. 512 in your *Study Guide and Working Papers*.)

Although Accu Pac's account is not 90 days past due, Freedman has determined that it is necessary to write off the entire balance because the business has foreclosed. Make the necessary journal entry using the direct write-off method.

15

Notes Receivable and Notes Payable

The Big Picture

Tony Freedman just received notice from the bank saying that Eldorado Computer Center may borrow money for the improvement and remodeling of its facility. Freedman realizes that although this is a necessary move for the business, there will be an additional expense incurred for borrowing money.

Most of us have borrowed money in some form. Before starting the business, Freedman borrowed money to buy his car and to go to school. When any person or business borrows money, there is a cost beyond the repayment of the money borrowed (principal). The borrower also pays interest. For a business, interest is usually accounted for either at the end of the accounting period or when the loan is repaid.

The money borrowed creates a note payable to the lender and has a time frame for the repayment of the principal and interest. Chapter 15 will show you how to determine interest calculations and maturity dates on notes. You will also learn what happens when a business doesn't pay back a loan and what accounting steps are necessary to dishonor a note.

Learning Objectives	◆ Determining interest calculations and maturity dates on notes. (p. 529) ◆ Journalizing entries to record renewal of a note, dishonoring of a note, eventual receipt of payment, and note given in exchange for equipment purchased. (p. 532) ◆ Discounting an interest-bearing note receivable and recording a discounted note that has been dishonored. (p. 537) ◆ Handling adjustments for interest expense and interest income. (p. 542)

Notes receivable—asset. Notes payable—liability.

So far the accounts receivable and accounts payable transactions we have been discussing have involved informal promises: Purchase orders and sales receipts are not formal written promises. In this chapter we will turn to transactions by buyers and sellers that require promissory notes (or notes), which are *formal written promises.* Notes receivable record amounts owed to a company by others. Notes payable record amounts the company itself owes.

Companies use notes instead of informal promises for many reasons, such as (1) recording sales of high-cost items like farm machinery or construction equipment that have long-term credit periods (usually over 60 days), (2) giving additional time to settle past due accounts, or (3) borrowing money from a bank for a fee. The fee that is charged for the use of one's money over a period of time is called **interest.** In addition, a note gives the seller or lender a stronger legal claim for collecting a past due account because the note acts as formal proof of the transaction.

LEARNING UNIT 15-1
Promissory Notes, Interest Calculations, and Determining Maturity Dates

Before looking at recording notes receivable and notes payable, let's discuss the structure of a note and how to determine interest calculations and *maturity dates* (when the note comes due).

A **promissory note** (often called simply a *note*) is a written promise by a borrower to pay a certain sum of money to the lender at a fixed future date. Figure 15-1 on page 528 is a promissory note that Able Company issued to Green Company. Take a moment to look at the structure of this note. The following explanation is keyed to the figure:

a. Able Company is borrowing $20,000; this amount is called the **principal.**

b. Money is being borrowed for 60 days.

c. The note is issued on October 2, 199X.

Think of the payee as the lender.

d. The Green Company is the **payee** to whom the note is payable.

e. The note carries a 12 percent annual interest rate. (Even though the note is for 60 days, interest is stated as a yearly rate.)

f. The date the note will come due, December 1, 199X, is called the **maturity date.**

The maker is often also called the payor or debtor.

g. Able Company is the **maker,** or the one promising to pay the note plus interest when it comes due.

FIGURE 15-1
A Promissory Note

```
$ 20,000        (A)          Bennington, Vermont  October 2nd   19 9X (C)

sixty days   (B)                        after date  we  promise to pay

to the order of  Green Company      (D)

Twenty - Thousand  and    00/100 ————————————————————— Dollars

Payable at  National Bank

Value received  12 %    (E)

No. 115    Due.  December 1, 199X  (F)

                                        Able Company  (G)

                                        Joe Mack

                                        Treasurer
```

Most interest on notes will be paid on maturity date. We will cover exceptions later in chapter.

The maker (Able Company) is the borrower. The borrower calls this obligation a **note payable.** The payee (Green Company) views this note as an asset called a **note receivable.** Able Company's interest expense is interest income for Green Company. Remember, interest expense is classified on the income statement as "other expenses," and interest income is "other income."

How to calculate interest

The formula for calculating the interest on a note is:

$$\text{Interest} = \text{Principal} \times \text{Rate} \times \text{Time}$$

| The face value or amount stated on note indicating amount borrowed | Percent per year | Years or fraction of year |

Let's look at some illustrative situations to show specific interest calculations:

Interest calculated for one year on a $6,000 12 percent note:

$$I = P \times R \times T$$

$12\% = .12 \text{ or } \frac{12}{100} \qquad I = \$6,000 \times .12 \times 1$

$$I = \$720$$

Interest calculated for five months on an $8,000 10 percent note: Time is expressed in twelfths of a year; thus 5 months is .

$$I = P \times R \times T$$
$$= \$8,000 \times .10 \times \frac{5}{12}$$
$$= \$333.33$$

Interest calculated for exact number of days based on a 360-day year, 60 days at 6 percent on a $4,000 note: When the note is given in days, the fraction for time is

$$\frac{\text{exact number of days}}{360}$$

Some federal agencies use 365 days, but common business practice is to use 360.

So we have

$$I = P \times R \times T$$
$$= \$4{,}000 \times .06 \times \frac{60}{360}$$
$$= \$40$$

Shortcut to figuring interest on notes—the 6 percent, 60-day method and its variations: The interest on any note that is 6 percent for 60 days is always equal to 1 percent of the principal of the note:

$$.06 \times \frac{60}{360} = .01$$

Thus when the rate times the number of days equals 360, it is equal to 1 percent, and the interest is calculated by moving the decimal two places to the left. For example:

$4{,}000 at 6 percent for 60 days = $40

$481.40 at 6 percent for 60 days = $4.81

$6{,}000 at 10 percent for 36 days = $60

Here are some other variations that equal 1 percent:

4 percent for 90 days = 1%

$4\frac{1}{2}$ percent for 80 days = 1%

8 percent for 45 days = 1%

10 percent for 36 days = 1%

12 percent for 30 days = 1%

Here's a variation on this shortcut. Take as an example a note for $4,000 at 9 percent for 60 days:

$4,000 at 6 percent for 60 days =	$40
$4,000 at 3 percent for 60 days =	$20
$4,000 at 9 percent for 60 days =	$60

Note that the 3 percent is half the 6 percent rate; thus interest is half of $40 or $20. Here's the proof: $4{,}000 \times .09 \times \frac{60}{360} = \$60$.

Next we'll look at how to determine the maturity date of a note when it is expressed in either exact days or months.

How to Determine Maturity Date

Maturity Date Determined by Exact Days

To determine the maturity date of a 90-day note dated June 21, the following could be set up (or you could count on a calendar):

Number of days remaining in June (30 − 21)	9
Days in July	31
Days in August	31
Number of days at end of August	71
Days in September to reach 90	19
Term of note	90

Thus the maturity date of the note is September 19.

Another way to calculate the maturity date is to use a table of days in a year (see Table 15-1 on p. 530).

The original note is dated June 21. Look at the top of the table for June and down the left column to day 21. The point of intersection reveals that June 21 is day 172 of the year. If we add 172 and 90 (length of note) we get 262. By searching in the table for 262, we see the date of maturity is September 19.

Note: Each rate multiplied times the number of days equals 360.

30 Days have September, April, June, and November, all the rest have 31, except February, which has 28 (29 during a leap year).

TABLE 15-1 DAYS IN A YEAR

Day of Month	Jan.	Feb.*	Mar.	Apr.	May	June	July	Aug.	Sept.	Oct.	Nov.	Dec.	Day of Month
1	1	32	60	91	121	152	182	213	244	274	305	335	1
2	2	33	61	92	122	153	183	214	245	275	306	336	2
3	3	34	62	93	123	154	184	215	246	276	307	337	3
4	4	35	63	94	124	155	185	216	247	277	308	338	4
5	5	36	64	95	125	156	186	217	248	278	309	339	5
6	6	37	65	96	126	157	187	218	249	279	310	340	6
7	7	38	66	97	127	158	188	219	250	280	311	341	7
8	8	39	67	98	128	159	189	220	251	281	312	342	8
9	9	40	68	99	129	160	190	221	252	282	313	343	9
10	10	41	69	100	130	161	191	222	253	283	314	344	10
11	11	42	70	101	131	162	192	223	254	284	315	345	11
12	12	43	71	102	132	163	193	224	255	285	316	346	12
13	13	44	72	103	133	164	194	225	256	286	317	347	13
14	14	45	73	104	134	165	195	226	257	287	318	348	14
15	15	46	74	105	135	166	196	227	258	288	319	349	15
16	16	47	75	106	136	167	197	228	259	289	320	350	16
17	17	48	76	107	137	168	198	229	260	290	321	351	17
18	18	49	77	108	138	169	199	230	261	291	322	352	18
19	19	50	78	109	139	170	200	231	(262)	292	323	353	19
20	20	51	79	110	140	171	201	232	263	293	324	354	20
21	21	52	80	111	141	(172)	202	233	264	294	325	355	21
22	22	53	81	112	142	173	203	234	265	295	326	356	22
23	23	54	82	113	143	174	204	235	266	296	327	357	23
24	24	55	83	114	144	175	205	236	267	297	328	358	24
25	25	56	84	115	145	176	206	237	268	298	329	359	25
26	26	57	85	116	146	177	207	238	269	299	330	360	26
27	27	58	86	117	147	178	208	239	270	300	331	361	27
28	28	59	87	118	148	179	209	240	271	301	332	362	28
29	29		88	119	149	180	210	241	272	302	333	363	29
30	30		89	120	150	181	211	242	273	303	334	364	30
31	31		90		151		212	243		304		365	31

* For leap years, February has 29 days, and the number of each day after February 28 is one greater than the number given in the table.

Maturity Date Determined by Number of Months

If the note were expressed in months rather than days, the table or calendar would not be needed. The maturity date could be found by counting the months from the date the note was issued, regardless of number of days in each month.

Here are some examples:

Date of Note	Length of Note	Maturity Date	
March 31	2 months	May 31	
April 30	3 months	July 31	(last day of
July 31	2 months	Sept. 30	month)

LEARNING UNIT 15-1 REVIEW

AT THIS POINT you should be able to

◆ Explain the advantages of using notes instead of informal promises. (p. 527)
◆ Define and explain the structure of a promissory note. (p. 528)
◆ Calculate interest on notes in days, monthly, or yearly. (p. 528)
◆ Calculate maturity date by days in the month, by special chart, or by months. (p. 529)

SELF-REVIEW QUIZ 15-1

(The forms you need are on page 514 of the *Study Guide and Working Papers.*)

1. Calculate the interest for the following:

   a. $10,000   12%   1 year
   b.   9,000   13%   7 months
   c.   7,000   10%   80 days

2. Find the maturity date of an 80-day note dated March 3 by (a) days in each month, (b) using a days-in-a-year chart.

3. Find the maturity date of a note dated March 31, due in 5 months.

Solution to Self-Review Quiz 15-1

1. **a.** $10,000 \times .12 \times 1 = \$1,200$.
   b. $\$ 9,000 \times .13 \times \frac{7}{12} = \$682.50$.
   c. $\$ 7,000 \times .10 \times \frac{80}{360} = \$155.56$.

2. **a.**

Number of days remaining in March $(31 - 3)$	28
Days in April	30
Number of days at end of April	58
Days in May to reach 80	22
Maturity date — May 22	80

   b. March 3   62 days
   $$\begin{array}{r} +80 \\ \hline 142 \end{array}\quad \text{May 22}$$

3. March 31, April, May, June, July, $\boxed{\text{August 31}}$.

"Coffee By The Pound! Why that's like money in the bank! I gotta get in on that," thought Fred happily. "I've got plenty of room for the big floor display. It costs twice as much as the countertop unit, but it's worth it. I might as well get the header panel too—it's less than $40, and it really finishes off the display. Then I'll buy the coffee grinder, and some rolls of the variety stickers . . . and . . . the bags of coffee too! The bigger my order, the lower my cost. But this is adding up fast—I'd better think about getting a loan."

Fred found himself in a position not uncommon for businesses of all sizes—the need to spend money to make more money. He checked the interest rates at his bank and calculated what it would cost him to repay a note with a principal of $3,000, an interest rate of 9 percent, and a time of 120 days.

$$\$3,000 \times .09 \times \frac{120}{360} = \$90.00$$

"$90 bucks," thought Fred. "That's steep. I wonder if I could do better at another bank?" Fred then checked

INTEREST: TIME IS MONEY

with Country Bank. They offered him $3,000, an interest rate of $8\frac{3}{4}$ percent, and a time of 90 days.

$$\$3,000 \times .0875 \times \frac{90}{360} = \$65.63$$

"$65 bucks is more like it," thought Fred. "But how can I pay it back in only 3 months? That really puts the pressure on. Is it worth the $25 difference to pay back the loan so fast? It's 30 days more or $25 more. An in either case I can deduct the interest from my taxes as a business expense. So it's really less than a $25 difference. Hmmm . . ."

DISCUSSION QUESTIONS

1. Which loan would you take if you were in Fred's place? Why?
2. Assume that Fred wanted the loan on October 1. What is the maturity date for the 60-day loan? The 90-day loan?
3. Always cautious, Fred expects slow coffee-by-the-pound sales for October and November, but brisk sales by December. How might this affect his decision to take a longer loan?

LEARNING UNIT 15-2
Recording Notes

We will use general journal entries to keep things simple instead of using special journals.

To understand how notes can be used to extend credit periods and to see how a note is paid off, let's look at some illustrative transactions involving Mace Company and Jane Company.

Sale of Merchandise on Account: On August 1, 19XX, Mace Company sold $6,000 of merchandise on account to Jane Company.

ON BOOKS OF SELLER — MACE COMPANY				
Aug.	1	Accounts Receivable, Jane Co.	6 0 0 0 00	
		Sales		6 0 0 0 00
		Sold merchandise on account		

ON BOOKS OF BUYER — JANE COMPANY				
Aug.	1	Purchases	6 0 0 0 00	
		Accounts Payable, Mace Co.		6 0 0 0 00
		Purchased merchandise on account		

On September 1, the end of the credit period, Jane Company gave a $6,000, 60-day, 13 percent note to Mace Company to gain additional time to settle the past due account. The following entries would be made on the books of the buyer and seller.

TIME EXTENSION WITH A NOTE

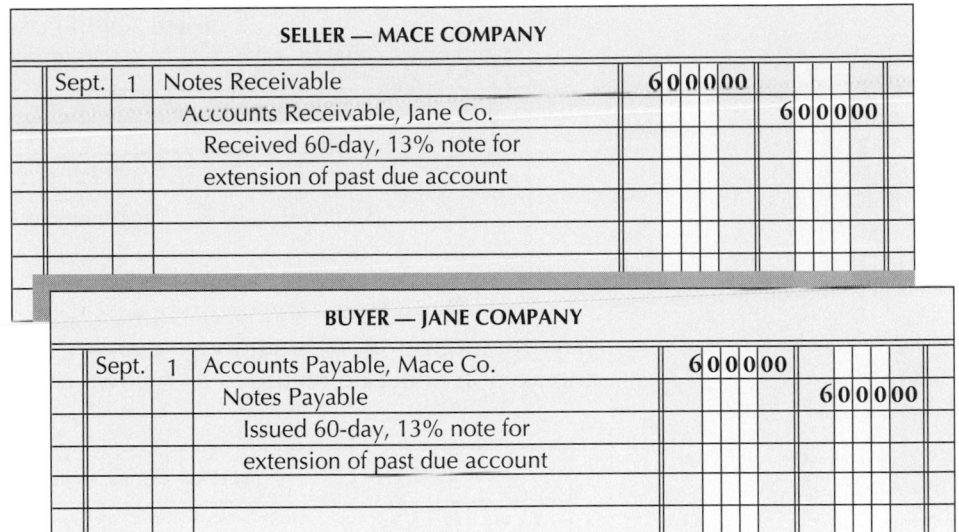

SELLER — MACE COMPANY

Sept.	1	Notes Receivable	6 0 0 0 00	
		Accounts Receivable, Jane Co.		6 0 0 0 00
		Received 60-day, 13% note for		
		extension of past due account		

BUYER — JANE COMPANY

Sept.	1	Accounts Payable, Mace Co.	6 0 0 0 00	
		Notes Payable		6 0 0 0 00
		Issued 60-day, 13% note for		
		extension of past due account		

Notes Receivable is a current asset on the balance sheet.

Notes Payable is a current liability on the balance sheet.

When this transaction is journalized, both Accounts Receivable and Accounts Payable are reduced. With *notes* a subsidiary ledger is usually *not* needed, since the file of the notes provides all the information.

Mace might accept this note as an extension because (1) if Jane Company doesn't pay, a formal written promise is in hand, and (2) interest is accumulating on the note.

Seller ➡️ The end result of this transaction is a shifting of assets of Mace Company from Accounts Receivable to Notes Receivable.

Buyer ➡️ For Jane Company the result is a shift in liabilities from Accounts Payable to Notes Payable.

NOTE DUE AND PAID AT MATURITY

Now let's look at the journal entries (top of p. 534) that will be made if Jane Company pays off the note on October 31.

It is important to emphasize that the interest is calculated on the maturity date of the note.

NOTE RENEWED AT MATURITY

If Jane Company is unable to pay the $6,130 at maturity, it is possible for the company to renew all or part of the note. Let's assume that the company can

SELLER — MACE COMPANY

Oct.	31	Cash	6 1 3 0 00		
		Notes Receivable		6 0 0 0 00	
		Interest Income		1 3 0 00	
		Collected Jane Company note.			

$$[\$6,000 \times .13 \times \tfrac{60}{360} = \$130 \text{ Interest Income}]$$

BUYER — JANE COMPANY

Oct.	31	Notes Payable	6 0 0 0 00		
		Interest Expense	1 3 0 00		
		Cash		6 1 3 0 00	
		Paid note to Mace Company.			

$$[\$6,000 \times .13 \times \tfrac{60}{360} = \$130 \text{ Interest Expense}]$$

pay the interest of $130 and give another note for 90 days at 13 percent. The transaction could be recorded as follows on the books of the buyer and seller:

SELLER — MACE COMPANY

Oct.	31	Cash	1 3 0 00		
		Notes Receivable (new)	6 0 0 0 00		
		Notes Receivable (old)		6 0 0 0 00	
		Interest Income		1 3 0 00	
		Interest of old note collected and			
		renewal of note for 90 days.			

BUYER — JANE COMPANY

Oct.	31	Notes Payable (old)	6 0 0 0 00		
		Interest Expense	1 3 0 00		
		Notes Payable (new)		6 0 0 0 00	
		Cash		1 3 0 00	
		Interest of old note paid and			
		renewal of note recorded.			

Note on the seller's books how the interest is received, the old note is canceled, and the new note is put on the books.

DISHONORED NOTE

Mace Company does not have to renew the note if Jane Company fails to pay it at maturity. In this situation, the note is said to be **dishonored.** Another way of saying this is to say that Jane Company has **defaulted** on its note.

On Jane's and Mace's books the amounts in Notes Receivable and Notes Payable will then be removed and transferred back to Accounts Receivable and Accounts Payable, because the note has reached the maturity date. At the same time, whether the note is paid or not, the interest expense is due and payable and should be recorded (for Mace Company this is Interest Income and for Jane Company it is Interest Expense).

Let's see what entries would look like if Jane Company first defaults and then finally pays the amount owed on December 1. To keep it simple, no additional charges will be calculated for the extra month Jane Company has taken to pay off the amount owed to Mace Company.

Only unmatured notes are in the Notes Receivable account.

SELLER — MACE COMPANY

(A) Oct.	31	Accounts Receivable, Jane Co.	6 1 3 0 00	
		Interest Income		1 3 0 00
		Notes Receivable		6 0 0 0 00
		Recorded note receivable dishonored.		

BUYER — JANE COMPANY

(A) Oct.	31	Notes Payable	6 0 0 0 00	
		Interest Expense	1 3 0 00	
		Accounts Payable, Mace Co.		6 1 3 0 00
		Recorded note payable dishonored.		

SELLER — MACE COMPANY

(B) Dec.	1	Cash	6 1 3 0 00	
		Accounts Receivable, Jane Co.		6 1 3 0 00
		Recorded payment of note		
		receivable dishonored.		

BUYER — JANE COMPANY

(B) Dec.	1	Accounts Payable, Mace Co.	6 1 3 0 00	
		Cash		6 1 3 0 00
		Payment of note payable dishonored.		

NOTE GIVEN IN EXCHANGE FOR EQUIPMENT PURCHASED

A note may be given in exchange for an asset that is purchased. For instance, suppose that Jane Company decided to buy from Ronald Company some display racks for $7,000. Because the price was high, Jane Company gave a note instead of buying the racks on account. The note issued by Jane Company was a 60-day, 9 percent interest-bearing note for $7,000. This transaction is recorded on the books of the buyer and seller as follows:

		SELLER — RONALD COMPANY					
May	9	Notes Receivable	7 0 0 0 00	
		Sales		7 0 0 0 00
		Sold display racks with a		
		60 day, 9% note.		

		BUYER — JANE COMPANY					
May	9	Store Equipment	7 0 0 0 00	
		Notes Payable		7 0 0 0 00
		Purchased display racks with a		
		60 day, 9% note.		

When the note is paid at maturity, the same transactions we discussed earlier would result.

LEARNING UNIT 15-2 REVIEW

AT THIS POINT you should be able to

◆ Journalize entries for buyer and seller to record the extension of a past due account by issuing a note. (p. 532)
◆ Explain why a subsidiary ledger may not be needed with Notes Payable and Notes Receivable. (p. 533)
◆ Journalize entries for the buyer and seller to record renewal of a note, dishonoring of a note, eventual receipt of payment, and a note given in exchange for equipment purchased. (pp. 532–536)

SELF-REVIEW QUIZ 15-2

(The forms you need are on page 515 of the *Study Guide and Working Papers.*) Journalize the following transactions for Action Company:

A. Action Company sold $8,000 of merchandise on account to Brian Company.

B. Action Company received a 60-day, $8,000, 12 percent note for a time extension of past due account of Brian Company.

C. Collected the Brian Company note on the maturity date.

D. Brian Company renewed the note for 90 days and paid interest on the old note. (Alternative to C.)

E. Assuming that Brian Company defaulted in (C), record the note receivable dishonored.

F. Brian Company paid note receivable dishonored.

Solution to Self-Review Quiz 15-2

(A)	Accounts Receivable, Brian Co.		8 0 0 0 00	
	Sales			8 0 0 0 00
	Sold merchandise on acct.			
(B)	Notes Receivable		8 0 0 0 00	
	Accounts Receivable, Brian Co.			8 0 0 0 00
	Started note at 12% for 60 days			
(C)	Cash		8 1 6 0 00	
	Interest Income			1 6 0 00
	Notes Receivable			8 0 0 0 00
	Collected Brian Co. note			
	[$8,000 × .12 × $\frac{60}{360}$ = $160]			
(D)	Cash		1 6 0 00	
	Notes Receivable		8 0 0 0 00	
	Notes Receivable			8 0 0 0 00
	Interest Income			1 6 0 00
	Collected interest and renewed note			
(E)	Accounts Receivable, Brian Company		8 1 6 0 00	
	Notes Receivable			8 0 0 0 00
	Interest Income			1 6 0 00
	Brian Co. defaulted on note			
(F)	Cash		8 1 6 0 00	
	Accounts Receivable, Brian Company			8 1 6 0 00
	Brian Co. paid dishonored note			

LEARNING UNIT 15-3
How to Discount Customers' Notes

Think of the bank discount as the cost *of cashing in a note before maturity.*

Many times a company that accepts notes from customers will not (or cannot) wait to receive its cash until the maturity date. Instead, it goes to a bank and exchanges the note for cash; this is called **discounting.** The company will endorse the note and receive the **maturity value** of the note (principal plus interest) less what the bank charges for holding the note from the date of discounting until the maturity date. The time period during which the bank holds the note (until maturity) is called the **discount period.**

The amount that the bank charges the company is called the **bank discount.** It is the difference between what the company receives from the bank and the maturity value of the note. The actual amount of money the company receives when a note is discounted is called the **proceeds** (maturity value less the bank discount).

Let's see how Marvin Company discounts an interest-bearing note receivable. The best way to understand the process is to take it step by step.

HOW TO DISCOUNT AN INTEREST-BEARING NOTE RECEIVABLE

What Marvin Company will receive from bank is called the *proceeds*.

Marvin Company received an $8,000, 90-day, 12 percent note from Jee Company dated Oct. 1. On October 31 Marvin Company needed cash to finance its inventory, so it discounted the note to Blue Bank, which charges a bank discount rate of 14 percent. An overview of the process is shown in Figure 15-2 at the bottom of this page.

Step 1: Find the *maturity* value of the note:

Find maturity value.

$$\text{(a) } \$8,000 \times .12 \times \frac{90}{360} = \$240 \text{ interest}$$

(b) Maturity value = principal + interest
= $8,000 + $240
= $8,240

Calculate discount period.

Step 2: Calculate the *discount* period (number of days from the date of discounting until the maturity date):

90 days	note
− 30 days	expired before discounting (Oct. 31 − Oct. 1)
= 60 days	that bank holds note until it comes due

Calculate bank discount.

Step 3: Calculate the bank discount (what the bank charges Marvin Company for holding the note until maturity: To do this we use the following formula:

$$\text{Bank discount} = \text{maturity value} \times \text{bank discount rate} \times \frac{\text{no. of days bank holds note until maturity}}{360 \text{ days}}$$

$$= \$8,240 \times .14 \times \frac{60}{360}$$

$$= \$192.27$$

Note that the bank discount is based on the maturity value, because we are borrowing the maturity value for the number of days in the discount period.

Calculate proceeds.

Step 4: Calculate the proceeds (what Marvin Company receives from the bank in the discounting process):

Proceeds = maturity value − bank discount
= $8,240 − $192.27
= $8,047.73

FIGURE 15-2 Discounting a Note Receivable, $8,000 @ 12 percent for 90 days

Issue Date October 1	Date of Discount October 31	Maturity Date
Oct. 31 – Oct. 1 = 30 days	90 days – 30 days = 60 days = Discount Period	
Marvin Company holds note	Bank holds note	
Face Value: $8,000		Maturity Value: $8,240

90 days

If Marvin Company could have waited until the maturity date, it would have received $8,240. By discounting the note the company lost interest of $192.27, or the cost charged by the bank to hold the note until maturity. Let's look at how Marvin Company would record this on its books (again for simplicity we use general journal entries rather than special journals).

Journalizing the discounted note receivable:

$8,047.73
− 8,000.00
───────────
$ 47.73

(Interest Income)

Oct.	31	Cash	8 0 4 7 73	
		Notes Receivable		8 0 0 0 00
		Interest Income		4 7 73
		Discounted Jee Company's		
		90-day, 12% note at 14%.		

There is Interest Income because the proceeds Marvin Company received were more than the face value of the note ($8,000). In actuality, if the proceeds had been *less* than the $8,000, Marvin Company would have incurred an interest expense. This could have happened, for example, if Marvin Company held the note for only a short period of time and Blue Bank had a bank discount rate much higher than the original note. Suppose the note was discounted after being held only 2 days, and the bank's discount rate was 18 percent. The bank discount, or amount the bank charges, would be calculated as follows:

$$\text{Bank discount} = \underset{\text{maturity value}}{\$8,240} \times .18 \times \underset{\text{discount period}}{\frac{88}{360}}$$

$$= \$362.56$$

Thus the proceeds to Marvin Company would be:

$$\text{Proceeds} = \$8,240 - \$362.56$$
$$= \$7,877.44$$

Note that here Marvin Company is receiving less than the $8,000 face value of the note. The general journal entry of Marvin Company would thus look as follows:

Oct.	31	Cash	7 8 7 7 44	
		Interest Expense	1 2 2 56	
		Notes Receivable		8 0 0 0 00
		To record discount of note		

PROCEDURE WHEN A DISCOUNTED NOTE IS DISHONORED

Note that if Marvin Company endorsed the note without recourse, it would not have any liability. Instead, the bank would have liability if Jee Company did not pay.

Who is liable for the note if Jee Company fails to pay the note at maturity? The answer is Marvin Company.

When Marvin Company endorsed the note to Blue Bank, it agreed to pay the note at maturity if Jee Company failed to. The potential liability is called a **contingent liability.** Until the note is paid, Marvin Company will state this contingent liability as a footnote on its balance sheet.

At some point before maturity, Jee Company is notified that Blue Bank is holding the note. Let's assume that the maturity date is reached and Jee

Company defaults. Blue Bank notifies Marvin Company and charges Marvin Company the full amount of the note, including interest and a $5 protest fee, which is the charge made by Blue Bank for notifying Marvin Company that the note was presented to the maker for payment and was not received. Thus the bank charges Marvin Company (and Marvin will in turn charge Jee Company) the following:

Note	$8,000
Interest	240
Protest Fee	5
	$8,245

The following entry is recorded on Marvin Company's book:

Dec.	30	Accounts Receivable, Jee Co.	8 2 4 5 00	
		Cash		8 2 4 5 00
		To record default		

You can be sure that Marvin Company will try to collect this $8,245 from Jee Company. Marvin Company may charge additional interest for this delay in paying the $8,245. For simplicity we have left this step out. If the $8,245 becomes uncollectible, the account could be written off as a bad debt using the Allowance for Doubtful Accounts method discussed in Chapter 14.

LEARNING UNIT 15-3 REVIEW

AT THIS POINT you should be able to

- Define and explain discounting, maturity value, discount period, bank discount, proceeds. (p. 537)
- Explain the four steps required in discounting an interest-bearing note receivable. (p. 531)
- Prepare a journal entry to record the proceeds of a note. (p. 539)
- Define contingent liability and compare it with an endorsement without recourse. (p. 539)
- Journalize the entry to record a discounted note that has been dishonored. (p. 540)

SELF-REVIEW QUIZ 15-3

(The forms you need are on pages 516–517 of the *Study Guide and Working Papers*.)

Al Gene Company received a $10,000, 60-day, 12 percent note from Broom Company dated July 5. On August 3 Al Gene Company discounted the note to Ryan Bank, which charged a bank discount rate of 15 percent.

a. Complete the four steps to discount the note.

b. Journalize the entry to record the proceeds.

c. Journalize the entry if a default occurs, assuming a $5 protest fee.

Solution to Self-Review Quiz 15-3

a. Step 1: Maturity value (principal + interest)

$$I = \$10,000 \times .12 \times \frac{60}{360}$$

$$= \$200.$$

$$MV = \$10,000 + \$200$$

$$= \$10,200$$

Step 2: Discount period:

July 31	
-5	
26	days Al Gene held note in July
3	days Al Gene held note in August
29	days Al Gene held note
60	days
-29	days
31	days bank holds note

Step 3: Bank discount:

$$\text{Bank discount} = \text{maturity value} \times \text{bank discount rate} \times \frac{\text{no. of days bank holds note until maturity}}{360}$$

$$= \$10,200 \times \quad .15 \quad \times \frac{31}{360}$$

$$\text{(step 1)} \quad \text{(given in facts)}$$

$$= \$131.75$$

Step 4: Proceeds:

$$\text{Proceeds} = \text{maturity value} - \text{bank discount}$$

$$= \$10,200 - \$131.75$$

$$= \$10,068.25$$

(b) Aug.	3	Cash	10 0 6 8 25		
		Notes Receivable		10 0 0 0 00	
		Interest Income		6 8 25	
		Discounted Broom Company			
		12% note at 15%.			
(c) Sept.	3	Accounts Receivable, Broom Company	10 2 0 5 00		
		Cash		10 2 0 5 00	
		To record default			

LEARNING UNIT 15-4
Discounting One's Own Note: Handling Adjustments for Interest Expense and Interest Income

DISCOUNTING ONE'S OWN NOTE

In the last unit we looked at how a note of a customer was discounted. Now our attention shifts to Jones Company, which is borrowing $10,000 by giving Alvin Bank its own 12 percent, 60-day note on December 16, 19XX. In this case Alvin Bank deducts the interest in advance. The following is the formula to calculate the bank discount (cost of borrowing) and the proceeds (what Jones Company gets):

$$\begin{array}{c}\text{Bank} \\ \text{discount}\end{array} = \left(\begin{array}{c}\text{maturity} \\ \text{value}\end{array}\right) \times \left(\begin{array}{c}\text{interest} \\ \text{rate}\end{array}\right) \times \dfrac{\begin{array}{c}\text{discount} \\ \text{period}\end{array}}{360}$$

$$= \$10,000 \quad \times \quad .12 \quad \times \quad \dfrac{60}{360}$$

$$= \$200$$

$$\text{Proceeds} = \text{maturity value} - \text{discount}$$

$$= \$10,000 - \$200$$

$$= \$9,800$$

Note that maturity value here is the same *as the original principal, since interest is deducted* in advance.

Thus, Jones Company receives $9,800 and at the time of maturity will pay back $10,000. The $200 of interest is recorded in a new account called **Discount on Notes Payable.** This is a contra-liability account that is subtracted from Notes Payable on the balance sheet, where it looks like this:

Discount on Notes Payable is a contra-liability.

Current Liabilities

Notes Payable	$10,000
Less: Discount on Notes Payable	200
	$9,800

Later in this unit, when we talk about adjustments, you will see that as the note matures, the discount will be reduced and then charged to Interest Expense. But for now let's record the journal entry for Jones Company as it discounts its own note with interest deducted in advance:

Dec.	16	Cash	9 8 0 0 00	
		Discount on Notes Payable	2 0 0 00	
		Notes Payable		10 0 0 0 00
		Discounted own note at 12%.		

Accounts Affected	Category	↑ ↓	Rules	
Cash	Asset	↑	Dr.	$9,800
Discount on Notes Payable	Contra-Liability	↑	Dr.	$200
Notes Payable	Liability	↑	Cr.	$10,000

Effective interest rate: The cost of borrowing the $10,000 is not 12 percent but really almost 12¼ percent.

When the note is paid, the accountant will debit Notes Payable for $10,000 and credit Cash for $10,000.

Note: Although the bank interest rate is stated at 12 percent, the truth is that Jones Company really has the use of only $9,800. To calculate the true interest rate, which is called the **effective interest rate,** the following formula applies:

$$\text{Effective interest rate} = \frac{(\text{Maturity value of note}) \times (\text{bank interest rate})}{\text{amount of cash proceeds received from note}}$$

$$= \frac{\$10,000 \times .12}{\$9,800}$$

$$= 12.24 \text{ percent}$$

Now let's look at how adjustments will be handled for some of the transactions presented in this chapter.

INTEREST: THE NEED FOR ADJUSTMENTS

Because interest-bearing notes are often taken out and then paid off in different accounting periods, it is necessary to adjust or bring up to date Interest Income and Interest Expense. The following diagram shows why we need to adjust, as well as who does the adjusting:

Accrued Interest Income	**Accrued Interest Expense**
Must adjust for income that has been earned during the period but has not been received or recorded because payment is not yet due.	Must adjust for interest that has been incurred during the period but has not been paid or recorded because payment is not yet due.

Notes Receivable
(payee)

(A) Note Payable
(maker)

(B) Company's own discounted note

The payee is the seller and the maker is the buyer.

Let's look at how to record adjustments for Interest Income and Interest Expense from the following: Bog Company receives a $24,000, 60-day, 10 percent note on December 16 from Jan Company.

Step 1: Calculate interest on the note:

$$\text{Interest} = \$24,000 \times .10 \times \frac{60}{360}$$

$$= \$400$$

Step 2: Calculate the number of days the note has already run before the end of the current period (see Fig. 15-3, top of p. 544):

Dec. 31	(end of period)
−Dec. 16	(starting date of note)
15	days

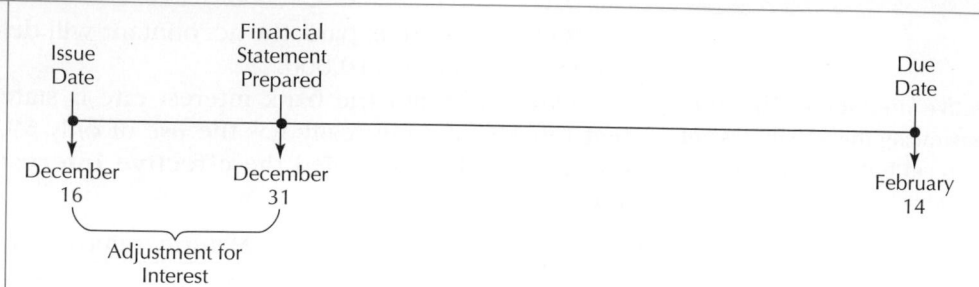

FIGURE 15-3
Adjusting for Interest Accrued

Step 3: Calculate interest incurred for this period:

$$\underset{\substack{\text{Length} \\ \text{of note}}}{} \longrightarrow \frac{15 \text{ days}}{60 \text{ days}} = \frac{1}{4} \times \$400$$

$$= \$100$$

Another way to calculate this would be:

$$\$24,000 \times .10 \times \frac{15}{360} = \$100$$

Step 4: Prepare the adjusting journal entries:

On Books of *Seller* (Holder of Note)

Dec.	31	Interest Receivable	1 0 0 00			
		Interest Income			1 0 0 00	
		Adj. for int.				

On Books of *Buyer* (Debtor)

Dec.	31	Interest Expense	1 0 0 00			
		Interest Payable			1 0 0 00	
		Adj. for int.				

Interest Receivable	
	100
Current Asset on balance sheet	

Interest Expense	
100	
Other Expense on income statement	

Interest Income	
	100
	Other Income on income statement

Interest Payable	
	100
	Current Liability on balance sheet

When the note is paid off on February 14, the first two entries on page 545 are made, assuming that no reversing entry is used.

(No Reversing Entry)

SELLER

Date		Account	Debit	Credit
Feb.	14	Cash	2440000	
		Interest Receivable		10000
		Notes Receivable		2400000
		Interest Income		30000
		Received payment of note		

BUYER

Date		Account	Debit	Credit
Feb.	14	Notes Payable	2400000	
		Interest Expense	30000	
		Interest Payable	10000	
		Cash		2440000
		Paid off note		

Note that by not using reversing entries the bookkeepers of the buyer and seller had to look up the amount of accrued interest that was recorded in the *old* year so that this year's interest expense or income would not be overstated.

If a reversing entry (which is optional) is used, the following entries are made:

(Reversing Entry Made)

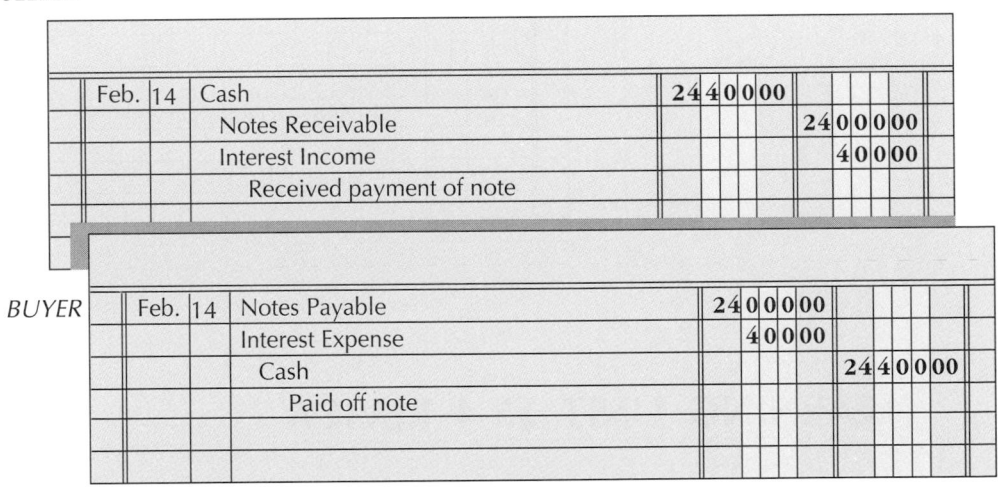

SELLER

Date		Account	Debit	Credit
Feb.	14	Cash	2440000	
		Notes Receivable		2400000
		Interest Income		40000
		Received payment of note		

BUYER

Date		Account	Debit	Credit
Feb.	14	Notes Payable	2400000	
		Interest Expense	40000	
		Cash		2440000
		Paid off note		

The last adjustment deals with a firm discounting its own note. Back on page 542, at the beginning of this unit, we saw Jones Company discounting its own note on December 16 for $10,000 for 60 days at 12 percent interest. Jones Company actually received $9,800 and recorded the $200 interest deducted in advance by the bank in a contra-liability account called *Discount on Notes Payable*.

Discount on Notes Payable		Interest Expense	
200			

At the end of December, 15 days out of the 60 days have passed. Thus one-fourth of the interest on this note should be recorded in the old year. To record this interest we reduce the amount in the Discount on Notes Payable by $50 ($\frac{1}{4} \times$ $200). The following journal entry is made:

Dec.	31	Interest Expense	50 00		
		Discount on Notes Payable		50 00	
		Recognition of expense incurred.			

Accounts Affected	Category	↑ ↓	Rules	
Interest Expense	Other Expense	↑	Dr.	$50
Discount on Notes Payable	Contra-Liability	↓	Dr.	$50

The current liability on the balance sheet will look as follows:

Current Liabilities

Notes Payable	$10,000
Less: Discount on Notes Payable	150
	$9,850

When the note is paid the following journal entry will result:

Feb.	14	Notes Payable	10000 00		
		Interest Expense	150 00		
		Discount on Notes Payable		150 00	
		Cash		10000 00	
		Note paid			

See p. 542 for comparison of this section before discount on note is reduced.

$$\frac{45 \text{ days}}{60 \text{ days}} \times \$200$$

LEARNING UNIT 15-4 REVIEW

AT THIS POINT you should be able to

- ◆ Explain the purpose of the Discount on Notes Payable account. (p. 542)
- ◆ Calculate the effective interest rate. (p. 543)
- ◆ Make adjustments for interest income and interest expense at end of period. (p. 544)
- ◆ Adjust the Discount on Notes Payable account. (p. 546)

SELF-REVIEW QUIZ 15-4

(The forms you need are on page 517 of the *Study Guide and Working Papers*.)
Answer true or false to the following:

1. No bank deducts interest in advance.

2. Discount on Notes Payable is a contra-liability account.

3. When Discount on Notes Payable is reduced, Interest Expense results.

4. Effective rate of interest is lower than the stated rate.

5. Reversing entries are never used to adjust interest at the end of a period of time.

Solution to Self-Review Quiz 15-4

1. F   **2.** T   **3.** T   **4.** F   **5.** F

SUMMARY OF KEY POINTS

Learning Unit 15-1

1. A promissory note is a written promise by a borrower to pay a certain sum of money to a lender at a fixed future date. The note may be interest-bearing or non-interest-bearing.
2. The payee is the party to whom the note is payable.
3. The maker is the one who will pay the promissory note.
4. Maturity date is the time when note comes due.
5. Interest = principal $\times$ rate $\times \dfrac{\text{number of days}}{360}$.

Learning Unit 15-2

1. Notes Payable is a current liability on the balance sheet.
2. Notes do not need subsidiary ledgers.
3. Interest Income for the payee is Interest Expense for the maker.
4. A note that is not paid at maturity is said to be dishonored.
5. Notes may be renewed as well as issued to buy assets.

Learning Unit 15-3

1. Maturity value = principal + interest.
2. Discount period = number of days from date of discounting until maturity date.
3. Bank discount = what the bank charges for holding a note until the maturity date, as shown in the formula:

$$\text{Bank discount} = \text{maturity value} \times \text{bank discount rate} \times \frac{\text{no. of days bank holds note till maturity}}{360 \text{ days}}$$

4. Proceeds = what one receives from bank in the discounting process (the maturity value minus the bank discount).
5. If a discounted note is dishonored, the original holder of the note may be liable for payment unless the note was endorsed without recourse. This is called contingent liability.

Learning Unit 15-4

1. In discounting one's own note, the interest is usually deducted in advance.
2. The interest that is deducted in advance is recorded in a contra-liability account called Discount on Notes Payable.
3. The effective interest rate is higher than the stated rate.

4. At the end of the period, adjustments are made for Interest Income and Interest Expense that have accrued or built up. These entries can be reversed on the first day starting the next period to simplify recording when interest is paid or received in the new period.

5. The interest in the Discount on Notes Payable account is adjusted by reducing the Discount on Notes Payable and recording it as Interest Expense.

Key Terms

Bank discount What the bank charges to hold a note until maturity (maturity value − proceeds).

Contingent liability Liability on the part of one who discounts a note to pay if the maker of the note defaults at maturity date.

Default Failure of maker to pay the maturity value of a note when due.

Discounting a note The process or act of transferring the note to a bank before the maturity date.

Discount on Notes Payable The amount of interest deducted in advance by the lender. This account reduces Notes Payable to actual cash value.

Discount period The amount of time the bank holds a note that was discounted until the maturity date.

Dishonored note A note that was not paid at maturity by the maker.

Effective interest rate The true rate of simple interest.

Interest The cost of using money for a period of time.

Maker One promising to pay a note.

Maturity date Due date of the promissory note.

Maturity value The value of the note that is due on the date of maturity (principal + interest).

Note payable A promissory note from the maker's point of view.

Note receivable A promissory note from the payee's point of view.

Payee One to whom note is payable.

Principal The face amount of the note.

Proceeds Maturity value less bank discount.

Promissory note A formal written promise by a borrower to pay a certain sum at a fixed future date.

Questions, Mini Exercises, Exercises, and Problems

Discussion Questions

1. List three reasons why a company may use Notes Payable instead of Accounts Payable.
2. Explain the parts of a promissory note.
3. What is the difference between finding a maturity date by (a) days or (b) months?
4. Notes Receivable is a current liability on the balance sheet. Accept or reject. Why?
5. Why is a subsidiary ledger not needed for notes?
6. Only matured notes are listed in the Notes Receivable account. Please discuss.
7. Explain what will happen if a maker defaults on a note. (Assume the note has not been discounted.)
8. List the four steps to arrive at proceeds in the process of discounting a note.
9. What is meant by contingent liability?

(Cont. on p. 553)

BLUEPRINT FOR NOTES PAYABLE AND NOTES RECEIVABLE

SELLER (Payee) | **BUYER (Maker)**

Sales of merchandise on account

SELLER (Payee)
Accounts Receivable, XXX
Sales
Sold on account

BUYER (Maker)
Purchases
Accounts Payable, XXX
Bought on account

Time extension with a note

SELLER (Payee)
Notes Receivable
Accounts Receivable, XXX
Transferred to note rec.

BUYER (Maker)
Accounts Payable, XXX
Notes Payable
Transferred to note pay.

Note due and paid

SELLER (Payee)
Cash
Interest Income
Notes Receivable
Received payment

BUYER (Maker)
Notes Payable
Interest Expense
Cash
Paid off note

Note renewed at maturity

SELLER (Payee)
Cash
Notes Receivable (new)
Notes Receivable (old)
Interest Income
Renewed note

BUYER (Maker)
Notes Payable
Interest Expense
Notes Payable (new)
Cash
Renewed note

Note given in exchange for equipment purchased

SELLER (Payee)
Notes Receivable
Sales
Sold on note rec.

BUYER (Maker)
Store Equipment
Notes Payable
Bought equip. for note

(Continued)

Blueprint for Notes Payable and Notes Receivable (cont.)

SITUATIONS AFFECTING SELLER ONLY

Discounting a note—
receiving more
than face value

Cash		
Interest Income		
Notes Receivable		
Loaned discounted note		

Discounting a note—
receiving less
than face value

Cash		
Interest Expense		
Notes Receivable		
Loaned discounted note		

SITUATION BORROWING FROM BANK

Discounted note
dishonored

Accounts Receivable, XXX		
Cash		
Discounted customer note		

Discounting one's
own note

Cash		
Discount on Notes Payable		
Notes Payable		
Borrowed with a discount		

(Continued)

BLUEPRINT FOR NOTES PAYABLE AND NOTES RECEIVABLE (cont.)

ADJUSTMENTS	SELLER	BUYER

Adjust interest	19X1 Dec. 31 Interest Receivable
	              Interest Income
	              Interest adj.
		19X1 Dec. 31 Interest Expense
		              Interest Payable
		              Interest adj.

Note paid
(no reversing entry
was made)
	19X2 Feb. 1 Cash
	            Interest Receivable
	            Interest Income
	            Notes Receivable
	            Received cash from note
		19X2 Feb. 1 Interest Expense
		            Interest Payable
		            Notes Payable
		            Cash
		            Paid cash for note

Note paid
(reversing entry
was made)
	Feb. 1 Cash
	         Interest Income
	         Notes Receivable
	         Received cash from note
		Feb. 1 Interest Expense
		         Notes Payable
		         Cash
		         Paid cash for note

Recognizing interest
from discount on
Notes Payable
	Dec. 31 Interest Expense
	         Discount on Notes Payable
	         Adjustment for interest	

10. When could interest be deducted in advance by a lender?
11. What is the normal balance of the Discount on Notes Payable account?
12. How is the effective interest rate calculated?
13. How could Discount on Notes Payable be adjusted?

Mini Exercises

(The forms you need are on pages 519–521 of the *Study Guide and Working Papers.*)

Determining Maturity Date

1. Find the maturity date of the following:
   a. 120-day note dated July 8.
   b. 90-day note dated October 8.

Calculate Maturity Value

2. Find the maturity value of the following:
   a. $6,000   6%   9 months
   b. $8,000   7%   70 days

Recording Notes for Buyer and Seller

3. For each of the following transactions for the Frank Co. (the seller), journalize what the entry would be for the buyer.

   a. Accounts Receivable, Bore Co.   7,000
          Sales   7,000
              Sold on account

   b. Notes Receivable   7,000
          Accounts Receivable, Bore Co.   7,000
              Transferred to note rec.

   c. Cash   7,140
          Notes Receivable   7,000
          Interest Income   140

Discounting a Note

4. Pete Jones discounted a $9,000, 8 percent, 90-day note at Friend Bank. He recorded the following entry:

   Cash   9,100
       Notes Receivable   9,000
       Interest Income   100

   How much interest did Pete Jones lose by discounting the note?

Four Steps in the Discounting Process

5. Blue Co. received a $1,000, 6 percent, 60-day note from Aluin Co. dated August 10. On August 30 Blue discounted the note at Reel Bank, which charged a discount rate of 8 percent. Calculate:

    a. maturity value

    b. discount period

    c. bank discount

    d. proceeds

Journal Entry for Discounting

6. Journalize the discounted note for Blue from Mini Exercise 5.

Defaulting

7. If Aluin defaults on the note what would be the journal entry for Blue Co. assuming a $5 protest fee?

Discounting One's Own Note

8. Aster Co. discounts their own note at a bank. This $5,000 note results in the bank deducting $300 interest in advance. Draw a transactional analysis box for this situation.

Adjusting the Discount

9. If in Mini Exercise 8 the discount of $100 needs to be adjusted at year end, what would be the journalized adjusting entry?

Exercises

(The forms you need are on pages 521–522 of the *Study Guide and Working Papers.*)

Calculating interest.

15-1. Calculate the interest for the following:

    a. $14,000   8%   1 year

    b. $20,000   10%   7 months

    c. $ 9,000   12%   80 days

Determining maturity date without tables.

15-2. Determine the maturity date for each of the following without the use of tables:

Note Issued	Length of Time
a. January 17, 19X4	30 days
b. July 14, 19X4	90 days
c. May 31, 19X4	4 months
d. June 25, 19X4	75 days

Determining maturity date by tables.

15-3. Using the table in the text (p. 530) prove your answers for Exercise 15-2.

Discounting a note and journalizing entry for proceeds.

15-4. On May 15, 19X4, Ralph Co. gave Blue Co. a 180-day, $9,000, 8 percent note. On July 21 Blue Co. discounted the note at 9 percent.

a. Journalize the entry for Blue to record the proceeds.

b. Record the entry for Blue if Ralph fails to pay at maturity.

Discount on Notes Payable.

15-5. Howard Slater negotiated a bank loan for $30,000 for 120 days at a bank rate of 10 percent. Assuming the interest is deducted in advance, prepare the entry for Howard to record the bank loan.

Group A Problems

(The forms you need are on pages 523–529 of the *Study Guide and Working Papers.*)

Journalizing Notes Receivable and Notes Payable along with note dishonored.

15A-1. Journalize the following entries for (1) the buyer and (2) the seller. Record all entries for the buyer first.

Check Figure:
Oct. 9 Interest income and interest expense $100

19X9

June	11	Morgan Company sold $5,000 of merchandise on account to Connors Company.
July	11	Morgan received a 90-day, $5,000, 8 percent note for a time extension of past due account of Connors Company.
Oct.	9	Collected the Connors Company note on the maturity date.
Oct.	9	Assuming Connors Company defaulted on its July 11 note, record the dishonored note.
Oct.	15	Connors Company paid the note receivable that was dishonored on October 9 (no additional interest is charged).

Identifying steps in discounting a note along with journal entry.

15A-2. On May 1, 19X4, Apples Company received a $30,000, 90-day, 9 percent note from Fletcher Company dated May 1. On June 20, 19X4, Apples discounted the note at Run Bank at a discount rate of 10 percent.

Check Figure:
Proceeds $30,334.17

1. Calculate the following:

a. Maturity value of the note.

b. Number of days the bank will hold the note till maturity date.

c. Bank discount.

d. Proceeds.

2. Journalize the entry to record the proceeds.

15A-3. Journalize the following transactions for Joye Company:

19X1

Discounting of one's own note.

June	18	Joye discounted its own $40,000, 90-day note at National Bank at 10 percent.
Sept.	16	Paid the amount due on the note of June 18. (Be sure to record interest expense from Discount on Notes Payable.)
Nov.	2	Joye discounted its own $20,000, 120-day note at National Bank at 1 percent.
Dec.	31	Record the adjusting entry for interest expense.

Check Figure:
Nov. 2 Discount on Notes Payable $733.33

Comprehensive Problem. Integration of Notes Receivable and Notes Payable with Allowance for Doubtful Accounts and discounting.

15A-4. Journalize the following transactions for Rochester Company:

19XX

Apr.	18	Received $15,000, 80-day, 11 percent note from Mark Castle in payment of account past due.
May	9	Wrote off the Hal Balmer account as uncollectible for $600. (Rochester uses the Allowance method to record bad debts.)
July	7	Mark Castle paid Rochester the note in full.
Nov.	11	Gave Reech Company a $9,000, 30-day, 12 percent note as a time extension of account now past due.

Check Figure:
Dec. 31 Interest expense $38.89

Nov.	15	Hal Balmer paid Rochester amount previously written off on May 9.
Dec.	3	Discounted its own $5,000, 90-day note at Tree Bank at 10 percent.
Dec.	5	Received a $10,000, 60-day, 12 percent note dated December 5 from Beverly Fields in payment of account past due.
Dec.	11	Paid principal and interest due on note issued to Reech Company from November 11 note.
Dec.	16	Received a $20,000, 60-day, 11 percent note from Larry Company in payment of account past due.
Dec.	28	Discounted the Beverly Fields note to Realty Bank at 13 percent.
Dec.	31	Recorded adjusting entries as appropriate.

Group B Problems

(The forms you need are on pages 523 – 529 of the *Study Guide and Working Papers.*)

Journalizing Notes Receivable and Notes Payable along with note dishonored.

Check Figure:

Nov. 8 Interest expense and interest income $135

15B-1. Journalize the following entries for (1) the buyer and (2) the seller.

19X9

July	10	Morgan Company sold $8,000 of merchandise on account to Connors Company.
Aug.	10	Morgan received a 90-day, $6,000, 9 percent note for a time extension of past due account of Connors Company.
Nov.	8	Collected the Connors Company note on the maturity date.
Nov.	8	Assuming Connors Company defaulted on November 8, record the dishonored note.
Nov.	16	Connors Company paid the note receivable that was dishonored on November 8 (no additional interest is charged).

Identifying steps in discounting a note along with journal entry.

Check Figure:

Proceeds $40,469.80

15B-2. On June 2, 19X4, Apples Company received a $40,000, 90-day, 11 percent note from Fletcher Company dated June 2. On July 16, 19X4, Apples discounted the note at Run Bank at a discount rate of 12 percent.

1. Calculate the following:
   a. Maturity value of the note.
   b. Number of days the bank will hold the note till maturity date.
   c. Bank discount.
   d. Proceeds.
2. Journalize the entry to record the proceeds.

Discounting of one's own note.

Check Figure:

Dec. 31 Interest expense $467.50

15B-3. As the bookkeeper of Joye Company, record in the general journal the following transactions:

19X2

May	9	Joye discounted its own $25,000, 90-day note at National Bank at 10 percent.
Aug.	7	Paid the amount due on the note of May 9. (Be sure to record interest expense from Discount on Note Payable.)
Oct.	7	Joye discounted its own $18,000, 120-day note at National Bank at 11 percent.
Dec.	31	Record the adjusting entry for interest expense.

15B-4. Record the following entries into the general journal of Rochester Company:

Comprehensive Problem.
Integration of Notes Receivable
and Notes Payable with
Allowance for Doubtful
Accounts and discounting.

Check Figure:

Dec. 31 Interest income $9.17

19XX

May   12 Received $13,000, 90-day, 9 percent note from Mark Castle in payment of account past due.

June   15 Wrote off the Hal Balmer account as uncollectible for $900 using the Allowance method.

Aug.   10 Mark Castle paid Rochester the note in full.

Nov.   2 Gave Reech Company a $20,000, 30-day, 8 percent note as a time extension of account now past due.

Nov.   18 Hal Balmer paid Rochester amount previously written off on June 15.

Dec.   2 Discounted its own $10,000, 90-day note at Tree Bank at 9 percent.

Dec.   2 Received a $6,000, 60-day, 11 percent note dated December 3 from Beverly Fields in payment of account past due.

Dec.   2 Paid principal and interest due on note issued to Reech Company from November 2 note.

Dec.   16 Received a $2,000, 60-day, 11 percent note from Larry Company in payment of account past due.

Dec.   28 Discounted the Beverly Fields note to Realty Bank at 12 percent.

Dec.   31 Recorded adjusting entries as appropriate.

REAL WORLD APPLICATIONS

15R-1.
Abby Scale, the bookkeeper of Roland Company, is having difficulty calculating the amount that is due Agent Company on March 19. Based on the following information, prepare a detailed calculation of the amount due Agent.

Roland issued Agent a $2,000, 60-day, 12 percent note dated December 19, 19X1. Roland was notified by Alvin Bank that the note had been discounted by Agent and the note would be payable to Alvin Bank. On February 18 the bookkeeper of Roland became ill and the note wasn't paid. Alvin Bank notified Agent and charged them an additional $9 protest fee. On March 19 Abby decided to pay Agent the amount owed. Agent indicated they were charging the maturity value of the note, the protest fee, and interest on *both* for 30 days beyond maturity at 14 percent. Do you think this is fair? Make your recommendation in writing.

15R-2.
Moe Ring has left the following notes on your desk. As the new bookkeeper of Ryan Company you realize that no adjusting entries were made in 19X1.

Notes Receivable	
11/25/X1	$20,000
12%	150 days

Notes Payable	
12/16/X1	$33,600
15%	30 days

a. Please prepare the appropriate adjusting entries.

b. Moe would like to know whether reversing entries are needed. Prepare a set of T accounts to show what would result on the books in the year 19X2 when the notes are paid (1) if there are no reversing entries, and (2) if reversing entries are made. Provide Moe with a written justification for the use of reversing entries.

Critical Thinking/Ethical Case

15R-3.

Kevin Hoffaman works as a teller in Victory Bank. Yesterday he looked up confidential information concerning several friends. Kevin told his girlfriend all about the confidential information. Do you think Kevin acted appropriately? You make the call. Write down your recommendations to Kevin.

ACCOUNTING RECALL

A CUMULATIVE APPROACH

THIS EXAM REVIEWS CHAPTERS 1 THROUGH 15

Your *Study Guide and Working Papers* (pp. 533 and 535) has forms to complete this exam, as well as worked-out solutions. The page references next to each question identify what page to turn back to if you answer the question incorrectly.

PART 1   Vocabulary Review

Match the terms to the appropriate definition or phrase.

Page Ref.

(541)	1. Proceeds	A. Face amount of note
(505)	2. Allowance for doubtful accounts	B. Principal and interest
		C. Cost of goods sold account
(528)	3. Notes payable	D. Bank charge
(527)	4. Maturity value	E. Contra-revenue account
(527)	5. Maker	F. A liability
(542)	6. Discount on notes payable	G. Maturity value less bank discount
(356)	7. Purchases	
(542)	8. Bank discount	H. Reduces notes payable to actual cash value
(314)	9. Sales returns and allowances	I. Contra-asset
(527)	10. Principal	J. One promising to pay a note

(542)   11. Discount on notes payable is a contra-asset account.

(542)   12. Maturity value less bank discount equals proceeds.

(539)   13. When a note is discounted and you receive more than face value it is interest expense.

(527)   14. The payee is the one who will pay the promissory note.

(271)   15. The three tax responsibilities of an employer include FICA (Social Security and Medicare), SUTA, and FUTA.

CONTINUING PROBLEM

S everal banks have offered loans to the Eldorado Computer Center for their expansion, however, Freedman wants to weigh each option to determine the best financial situation for the company. Currently the Eldorado Computer Center is trying to collect from its customers to strengthen the cash flow of the business.

Assignment:

(See p. 534 in your *Study Guide and Working Papers*.)

Using the information provided by each bank, determine the due date and interest amount for each.

Bank of America　　A 90-day note dated April 15 for $20,000 at a 6% interest rate

Bank One　　　　A 120-day note dated April 10 for $40,000 at a 5% interest rate

Capital One Bank　A 75-day note dated April 5 for $30,000 at a 4% interest rate

16

ACCOUNTING FOR MERCHANDISE INVENTORY

THE BIG PICTURE

With plans to handle all business entries on computer, the Eldorado Computer Center is in the process of evaluating several accounting software packages. Before implementing a new accounting method, Tony Freedman wants to take a closer look at how he evaluates his merchandise inventory.

For the first six months of the business, Freedman used an inventory method that created an adjustment at the end of the accounting period to bring his books up to date. Using that method did not give him an accurate picture of what he actually had in stock as items were sold. To remedy the situation he decided to track his inventory using the perpetual system, which updates the inventory account as items are sold. He realizes that this new method will not track stolen or damaged items that cannot be sold — so periodically he will need to do a physical count.

In this chapter you will also learn that there are different methods used to track the value of the inventory. Each method will give you a different dollar value for the cost of inventory sold and the amount of inventory still on hand. You must decide which method is best for your type of business. The Eldorado Computer Center has previously used the First-In, First-Out method to track its inventory. This method assumes that the merchandise first bought by the computer center is sold first. Freedman uses this method because it reflects his type of business: In the constantly changing computer business, merchandise becomes outdated quickly. Therefore it is necessary to sell the oldest merchandise first, before it cannot be sold at all.

Learning Objectives	◆ **Understanding and journalizing transactions using the perpetual inventory system, and explaining the difference between a perpetual and periodic inventory system.** (p. 562) ◆ **Maintaining a subsidiary ledger for inventory.** (p. 567) ◆ **Understanding periodic methods of determining the value of the ending inventory.** (p. 571) ◆ **Estimating ending inventory using the retail method and gross profit method, and how the ending inventory amount affects financial reports.** (p. 578)

Have you ever thought of the perfect present for someone at Christmas time only to find that everyone else in the world had the same idea, and the stores were out of stock? In recent years such gifts have included Lion King, Barney, Power Rangers, home computers, video games, and so on. Having the right quantities of inventory is crucial to a retail business. It's bad to run out of stock and miss out on sales revenue, especially at Christmas, but it's also harmful to have too much of an item. A store must consider the cost of carrying inventory, and it must also worry about product obsolescence or the possibility of a fad running its course before all the products are sold. A good example would be your local computer store. Models change so quickly that an inventory of old models could mean losing sales to competitors.

In Chapter 12 we discussed the periodic inventory system. A major weakness of the periodic system is that inventory is checked and counted only at the beginning and end of the accounting period, and managers do not know the actual amount of inventory on hand nor the actual cost of goods sold until the end of the accounting period. In businesses with large inventories, managers need to have *current* information about how much of their capital is tied up in inventory and they need to have *current* information about the profitability of their sales of merchandise. The *perpetual* system of accounting for merchandise inventory will provide this information on a transaction-by-transaction basis. Managers will know the balance of inventory and the profitability of sales as soon as each sale is completed. The perpetual system requires extra time and effort in order to gain these benefits but, fortunately, computers can handle much of the detail. In this chapter we will look at how the perpetual inventory system can be used in a merchandising business. We will also compare the perpetual system to the periodic system.

In the last part of the chapter we will discuss how to assign costs to inventory using the *periodic inventory system* — since many businesses with small inventories still use this system.

LEARNING UNIT 16-1
Perpetual Inventory System

In the **perpetual inventory system** we have two key accounts: Merchandise Inventory and Cost of Goods Sold.

The Merchandise Inventory account is an asset account which will reveal the current balance of inventory at all times (perpetually). This is the same account that was used in the previous discussion of the periodic inventory system, but in the periodic system the balance of the Merchandise Inventory was correct *only* at the end of each accounting period. In the perpetual system, entries will be recorded to the Merchandise Inventory account each time the store purchases new merchandise and each time the store sells merchandise to a customer.

The other key account is the Cost of Goods Sold account. As merchandise is sold to our customers, an entry will be recorded that will remove the cost of the merchandise from the Merchandise Inventory account and transfer that cost to the Cost of Goods Sold account. Thus the Merchandise Inventory account will show the correct cost for the inventory on hand, and the Cost of Goods Sold account will show the cumulative total cost of all merchandise that has been sold to customers during the accounting period.

With the perpetual inventory system the key accounts, Merchandise Inventory and Cost of Goods Sold, will always provide current information to managers about their investment in inventory and the cost of the merchandise sold to customers.

Accounts Affected	Category	↑ ↓	Rules
Merchandise Inventory	Asset	↑	Dr.
Cost of Goods Sold	Cost of Goods Sold	↑	Cr.

You have been hired to work for a software retail business called *Painless Bytes*. A best seller for *Painless Bytes* is an accounting software package called *A-I-B*, (<u>A</u>lways <u>I</u>n <u>B</u>alance). Let's record some transactions relating to buying and selling A-I-B software. Since most businesses buy their merchandise inventory on account, we will use Accounts Payable in the transactions.

19XX
June 2 Purchased 10 packages of A-I-B software at a cost $25 per package for a total of $250.

June	2	Merchandise Inventory		250 00	
		Accounts Payable			250 00
		To record the purchase of inventory			

Note that the asset account, Merchandise Inventory, has been increased by the cost of the new merchandise we have purchased. Now let's look at a sales transaction.

19XX
June 3 Sold three software packages for cash to a customer at $50 each for a total of $150.

June	3	Cash		150 00	
		Sales Revenue			150 00
		To record sale of 3 packages of A-I-B			
June	3	Cost of Goods Sold		75 00	
		Merchandise Inventory			75 00
		To record the cost of goods sold			

Note that in the perpetual inventory system we record both the retail value of the sale (3 units at $50) in the Sales Revenue account and the cost of the sale (3 units at $25) in the Cost of Goods Sold account with two related transactions. But what if the customer returns one of the packages? Assuming that the returned package is still in new condition, here is what we would record:

19XX
June   5   Allowed the customer to return one package for a cash refund, $50.

	June	5	Sales Returns and Allowances		50 00			
			Cash				50 00	
			To record the return of one					
			package A-I-B					

	June	5	Merchandise Inventory		25 00			
			Cost of Goods Sold				25 00	
			To record return of one package					
			A-I-B at cost					

In this transaction we must record the reduction in revenue of $50 and we must also record that we now have returned one package of software to our inventory by adding the $25 cost of that unit back to the Merchandise Inventory account.

Once in awhile a business may have to return some inventory that came in damaged or for some other reason. Painless Bytes would prepare a debit memo. Let's see how this transaction is handled in a perpetual inventory system.

19XX
June   6   Returned one damaged A-I-B software package from the June 2 purchase

	June	6	Accounts Payable		25 00			
			Merchandise Inventory				25 00	
			To record return of damaged A-I-B					
			package to vendor					

This transaction reduced what we owe our vendor by $25, the cost of the package, and we reduced the Asset account — Merchandise Inventory — because we returned the item to the vendor. Note: We do not use a Purchases Returns and Allowances account when we are recording in a perpetual inventory system. The Asset account Merchandise Inventory is directly reduced by the amount we returned to our vendor.

Now let's look at how these transactions relate to the accounts and to the financial statements. In the T accounts that follow you can see that the Merchandise Inventory account shows the correct balance for the seven software packages remaining in inventory and that the Cost of Goods Sold account

GENERAL LEDGER ACCOUNTS

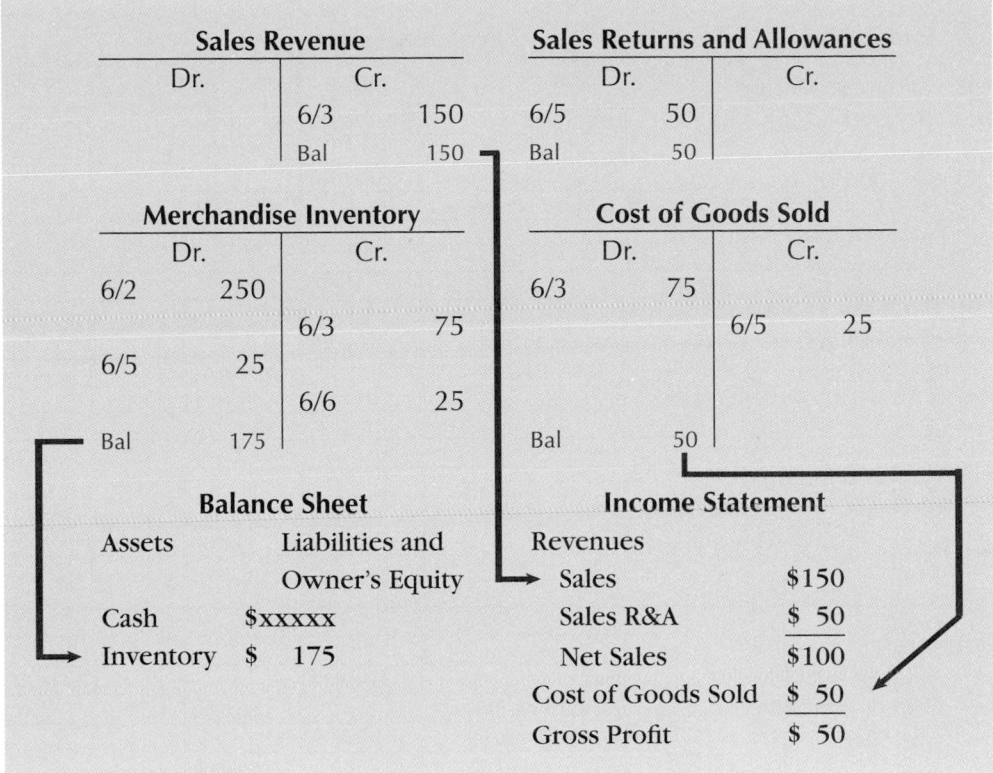

shows the correct amount for the cost of the two software packages actually sold. Asset accounts such as Merchandise Inventory are shown on the Balance Sheet and the Sales and Cost of Goods Sold accounts appear on the Income Statement. Remember that we calculate Gross Profit when we subtract Cost of Goods Sold from Sales. In fact, we know the gross profit on each sale just as soon as the sale is completed.

COMPARISON OF THE PERPETUAL AND PERIODIC INVENTORY SYSTEMS

In our discussion of the perpetual inventory system, the primary benefit from this system is that the value of merchandise inventory is known after every purchase and sale. The cost of goods sold is known after every sale. The merchandise inventory account becomes an active account. The Cost of Goods Sold is now an account in the general ledger rather than just a item on the Income Statement. The *periodic inventory system* does not give accurate or up-to-date information about merchandise inventory or cost of goods sold until after an ending inventory is taken.

The taking of a physical inventory at least once a year is not eliminated by a business that uses the perpetual inventory system. An inventory must be taken at least once a year to detect any inventory recording errors, shoplifting, or damages to the merchandise inventory.

The comparisons of recording of transactions in the two systems are revealed in the chart (top of p. 566).

The chart shows that in a perpetual inventory system, the Purchases, Purchases Returns and Allowances, and Freight accounts *do not* exist. Inventory and Cost of Goods Sold are updated immediately.

Transaction	Perpetual System	Periodic System
(A) Sold merchandise that cost $8,000 on account for $20,000	Acc. Receiv. 20 00 00 / Sales 20 00 00 / Cost of Goods Sold 80 00 00 / Merch. Inventory 80 00 00	Acc. Receiv. 20 00 00 / Sales 20 00 00
(B) Purchased $900 of merchandise on account	Merch. Inventory 9 00 00 / Acc. Payable 9 00 00	Purchases 9 00 00 / Acc. Payable 9 00 00
(C) Paid $50 freight charges.	Merch. Inventory 50 00 / Cash 50 00	Freight-In 50 00 / Cash 50 00
(D) Customer returned $200 of merchandise. Cost of merchandise was $100	Sales Ret. & Allow. 2 00 00 / Accounts Receiv. 2 00 00 / Merchandise Inv. 1 00 00 / Cost of Goods Sold 1 00 00	Sales Ret. & Allow. 2 00 00 / Accts. Receiv. 2 00 00
(E) Returned $400 of merchandise previously bought on account due to defects.	Acc. Payable 4 00 00 / Merch. Inv. 4 00 00	Acc. Payable 4 00 00 / Pur. Ret. and Allow 4 00 00

LEARNING UNIT 16-1 REVIEW

AT THIS POINT you should be able to

◆ Explain the perpetual inventory system. (p. 562)
◆ Journalize transactions for a perpetual inventory system. (p. 563)
◆ Explain the difference between the perpetual and periodic inventory systems. (p. 565)

SELF-REVIEW QUIZ 16-1

(The blank forms you need are on page 2 of the *Study Guide and Working Papers.*)

Journalize the following transactions for a firm that uses a perpetual inventory system:

a. Bought $200 of merchandise on account.
b. Sold $100 of merchandise on account that cost $50.

c. Allowed a customer to return for cash $30 worth of inventory. Our cost was $15.

d. We got permission from our vendor to return $30 worth of inventory.

Solutions to Self-Review Quiz 16-1

a.

Merchandise Inventory	2 0 0 00			
Accounts Payable			2 0 0 00	

b.

Accounts Receivable	1 0 0 00			
Sales			1 0 0 00	

Cost of Goods Sold	5 0 00			
Merchandise Inventory			5 0 00	

c.

Sales Returns and Allowances	3 0 00			
Cash			3 0 00	

Merchandise Inventory	1 5 00			
Cost of Goods Sold			1 5 00	

d.

Accounts Payable	3 0 00			
Merchandise Inventory			3 0 00	

LEARNING UNIT 16-2
Using a Subsidiary Ledger for Inventory

Suppose that the business Painless Bytes sells many different kinds of software packages. How can Painless Bytes keep track of the cost and balances of a variety of inventory items? How do stores such as Wal-Mart keep track of the thousands of items which they keep in inventory? The answer is found in the use of a subsidiary ledger for inventory and the use of computers to maintain the subsidiary ledger.

Do you recall from Chapters 9 and 10 that when we had a large number of account receivable or account payable accounts, we used subsidiary ledgers to maintain the details for each customer or vendor? This same accounting procedure can be used to keep track of inventory. Our Merchandise Inventory account becomes a control account keeping track of the total balance of inventory, while the details are kept in separate inventory records in a subsidiary ledger for inventory. Let's first show our existing inventory account with a subsidiary ledger and with the transactions from Learning Unit 16-1. On the left is our inventory account in T form and on the right is an inventory record form for our A-I-B product.

GENERAL LEDGER ACCOUNT

Merchandise Inventory

Dr.		Cr.	
6/2	250		
		6/3	75
6/5	25		
		6/6	25
Bal	175		

SUBSIDIARY LEDGER RECORDS

A-I-B Software

Date	Purchased	Sold	Balance
6/2	10 @ $25		$250
6/3		3 @ $25	$175
6/5		(1) @ $25	$200
6/6	(1) @ $25		$175

Notice that the inventory record form on the right contains the detail about the quantity and per unit cost for the transactions posted to the general ledger account on the left. Notice too, that the return of 6/5 is recorded in the inventory record as a negative sale and that the ending balances agree. The debit memo transaction of 6/6 is entered as a negative purchase and again the ending balances agree. Try using your calculator to see if you can also calculate the running balance shown in the inventory record.

In this next transaction, Painless Bytes adds *R&C,* (Rows and Columns), a spreadsheet software package, to the line of software that they sell.

June   6   Purchased 7 packages of R&C software on account at a cost $225 per package and a total of $1,575.

	June	6	Merchandise Inventory		1 5 7 5 00	
			Accounts Payable			1 5 7 5 00
			To record the purchase of inventory			

Note that the Merchandise Inventory account has again been increased by the cost of the new merchandise we have purchased. Since we now have two products in inventory, our inventory ledger will have a new inventory record form for the R&C product. Check out the way our inventory records relate to the Merchandise Inventory account.

GENERAL LEDGER ACCOUNT

Merchandise Inventory

Dr.		Cr.	
6/2	250		
		6/3	75
6/5	25		
6/6	1,575	6/6	25
Bal	1,750		

SUBSIDIARY LEDGER RECORDS

Product #1:   A-I-B Software

Date	Purchased	Sold	Balance
6/2	10 @ $25		$ 250
6/3		3 @ $25	$ 175
6/5		(1) @ $25	$ 200
6/6	(1) @ $25		$ 175

Product #2:   R&C Software

Date	Purchased	Sold	Balance
6/6	7 @ $225		$1,575

Does the total of the balances of the two inventory records agree with the Merchandise Inventory account?

Now let's try another sales transaction.

19XX
June   9   Sold two A-I-B packages at $50 each and three R&C packages at $295 each for a total of $985

June	9	Cash		985 00		
		Sales Revenue			985 00	
		Sold 2 A-I-B and 3 R&C				
June	3	Cost of Goods Sold		725 00		
		Merchandise Inventory			725 00	
		To record the cost of goods sold				

Again, we record both the total sales price of the transaction and the cost of the merchandise sold. Do you know how we arrived at the cost of goods sold figure of $725? A quick look at the inventory record forms will show us how we know the cost of goods sold.

GENERAL LEDGER ACCOUNT

Merchandise Inventory

Dr.		Cr.	
6/2	250		
		6/3	75
6/4	25		
6/6	1,575	6/6	25
		6/9	725
Bal	1,025		

SUBSIDIARY LEDGER RECORDS

Product #1:   A-I-B Software

Date	Purchased	Sold	Balance
6/2	10 @ $25		$ 250
6/3		3 @ $ 25	$ 175
6/4		(1) @ $195	$ 200
6/5	(1) @ $25		$ 175
6/9		2 @ $ 25	$ 125

Product #2:   R&C Software

Date	Purchased	Sold	Balance
6/6	7 @ $225		$1,575
6/9		3 @ $225	$ 900

We obtained the cost of goods sold total when we posted the quantities sold to each of the inventory records. Two units of A-I-B at $25 each plus three units of R&C at $225 each equals a total cost of $725. Notice that the ending balances of the two products will total to the same amount as the balance shown in the Merchandise Inventory account.

In summary, a business with a variety of products in inventory will use an inventory subsidiary ledger with an individual record for each different product. These records will keep the detail about the quantity and cost of inventory on hand and will allow us to calculate the cost of goods sold on each sale.

Computerized accounting systems can handle a perpetual inventory system with ease. You have no doubt seen such systems in operation when the clerk at your local store used a laser scanner or a bar code to enter your purchases into the cash register. The transaction put into the cash register will record the

FIGURE 16-1
An Inventory Record

Inventory Control									
Item VX113						Maximum 22			
Description Digital Clock						Reorder Level 12			
Location Storeroom 1						Reorder Quantity 10			
Received				Sold			Balance		
Date	Units	Cost per Unit	Total	Units	Cost per Unit	Total	Units	Cost per Unit	Total
19XX Jan. 1	Balance		FWD				14	50	$ 700
12				2	50	100	12	50	600
19	10	60	600				12	50	
							10	60	1,200
25				8	50	400	4	50	
							10	60	800

sale and update the cost of goods sold and inventory. Computerized systems keep track of inventory by many different methods. They could use average cost; first-in, first-out (FIFO); or last-in, first-out (LIFO) when figuring the value of the inventory. The example in Figure 16-1 uses the first-in, first-out (FIFO) method in determining the cost of the merchandise for each sale.

LEARNING UNIT 16-2 REVIEW

AT THIS POINT you should be able to

♦ Understand how a subsidiary ledger for inventory works with a controlling account for inventory. (pp. 567 – 568)
♦ Journalize and post transactions that affect the general ledger Merchandise Inventory account as well as the individual inventory records in the Merchandise Inventory Subsidiary Ledger. (pp. 568 – 569)

SELF-REVIEW QUIZ 16-2

(The forms you need are on page 3 of the *Study Guide and Working Papers*.)
Journalize and post the following transactions for a firm that uses a subsidiary ledger for Merchandise Inventory. Only post to the accounts that you have.

a. Bought 3 X-Products at $3 each on account.
b. Sold one of the X-Products we purchased above for cash, $6.
c. Bought 4 more X-Products at $3 and 5 Z-Products at $10 on account.
d. Sold for cash 2 more X-Products at $6 each and 3 Z-Products at $20 each.

Solutions to Self-Review Quiz 16-2

a.

Merchandise Inventory	114 ✔	9 00		
Accounts Payable			9 00	

b.

Cash		6 00		
Sales			6 00
Cost of Goods Sold		3 00		
Merchandise Inventory	114 ✓		3 00

c.

Merchandise Inventory	114 ✓	6 2 00		
Accounts Payable			6 2 00

d.

Cash		7 2 00		
Sales			7 2 00
Cost of Goods Sold		3 6 00		
Merchandise Inventory	114 ✓		3 6 00

GENERAL LEDGER ACCOUNT

Merchandise Inventory

	Dr.		Cr.
a.	9	b.	3
c.	62	d.	36
Bal.	32		

SUBSIDIARY LEDGER RECORDS

Product #1:   X Product

Date	Purchased	Sold	Balance
a.	3 @ $3		9
b.		1 @ $3	6
c.	4 @ $3		18
d.		2 @ $3	12

Product #2:   Z Product

Date	Purchased	Sold	Balance
c.	5 @ $10		50
d.		3 @ $10	20

LEARNING UNIT 16-3
Methods of Determining the Value of the Ending Inventory When Using the Periodic Inventory System

For a small business or any business using the **periodic inventory system,** the method used to assign costs to ending inventory will have a direct effect on the company's cost of goods sold and gross profit. Look at the table on the next page, and note how the ending inventory does in fact have an effect on the Gross Profit.

If all inventory brought into a store had the same cost, it would be simple to calculate the ending inventory, and we would not have to have this discussion. Unfortunately, things are not that easy; often the very same products are

	Situation A		Situation B		Situation C		Situation D	
Net Sales		$50,000		$50,000		$50,000		$50,000
Beginning Inventory	$ 4,000		$ 4,000		$ 4,000		$ 4,000	
Net Purchases	20,000		20,000		20,000		20,000	
Cost of Goods Available for Sale	24,000		24,000		24,000		24,000	
Ending Inventory	5,000		6,000		7,000		8,000	
Cost of Goods Sold		19,000		18,000		17,000		16,000
Gross Profit		$31,000		$32,000		$33,000		$34,000

purchased and brought into the store at different costs during the same accounting period. Over the years, four generally accepted methods have been developed to assign a cost to ending inventory. The reason these methods are needed is that often inventory is brought in at different times. The result is that the inventory is made up of many past purchases at *different* prices. Think of the inventory methods as a way of tracing costs. These methods are: (1) specific invoice; (2) first-in, first-out; (3) last-in, first-out; and (4) weighted average. Each is based on an assumed flow of costs, not on the actual physical movement of goods sold in a store.

We will now look at how the four inventory cost assumptions are applied within the periodic inventory system. The following situation occurred at Jones Hardware. Jones Hardware sells rakes. The job before us is to come up with the value of the ending inventory and cost of goods sold using the four methods we have listed. The following table provides us with all the information needed to accomplish our task.

Goods Available for Sale

		Units	Cost	Total
January 1	Beginning Inventory	10	@ $10 =	$100
March 15	Purchases	9	@ 12 =	108
August 18	Purchases	20	@ 13 =	260
November 15	Purchases	5	@ 15 =	75
		44		$543

Actual inventory on December 31 revealed that 12 rakes remained in stock.

SPECIFIC INVOICE METHOD

In the **specific invoice method,** the cost of ending inventory is assigned by identifying each item in that inventory by a specific purchase price and invoice number, and maybe even by serial number.

For our example of this method, let's assume that Jones Hardware knew that six of the rakes not sold were from the March 15 invoice and the other six were from the August 18 purchase. Thus $150 was assigned as the actual cost of ending inventory. If the total cost of goods available for sale is $543, and we subtract the actual cost of ending inventory ($150), this method provides a figure of $393 for cost of goods sold.

	Goods Available For Sale			Calculating Cost of Ending Inventory		
	Units	Cost	Total	Units	Cost	Total
January 1 Beg. Inventory	10	@ $10	= $100			
March 15 Purchased	9	@ 12	= 108	6	@ $12	$ 72
August 18 Purchased	20	@ 13	= 260	6	@ 13	78
November 15 Purchased	5	@ 15	= 75			
	44		$543	12		$150

Cost of Goods Available for Sale → $543
Less: Cost of Ending Inventory   150 ←
= Cost of Goods Sold $393

Let's look at the pros and cons of this method.

Pros	Cons
1. Simple to use if company has small amount of high-cost goods—for example, autos, jewels, boats, antiques, etc.	1. Difficult to use for goods with large unit volume and small unit prices—for example, nails at a hardware store, packages of toothpaste at a drug store.
2. Flow of goods and flow of cost are the same	2. Difficult to use for decision-making purposes—ordinarily an impractical approach since companies usually deal with high-cost unique items.
3. Costs are matched with the sales they helped to produce.	

FIRST-IN, FIRST-OUT METHOD (FIFO)

In the **FIFO method,** we assume that the oldest goods are sold first. Therefore, the items in the ending inventory will be valued at the costs shown on the most recent invoices.

	Goods Available For Sale			Calculating Cost of Ending Inventory		
	Units	Cost	Total	Units	Cost	Total
January 1 Beg. Inventory	10	@ $10	= $100			
March 15 Purchased	9	@ 12	= 108			
August 18 Purchased	20	@ 13	= 260	7	@ $13	= $ 91
November 15 Purchased	5	@ 15	= 75	5	@ 15	= 75
	44		$543	12		$166

Cost of Goods Available for Sale → $543
Less: Cost of Ending Inventory   166 ←
= Cost of Goods Sold $377

In our Jones Hardware example, the ending inventory of 12 rakes on hand is assigned a cost from the last two purchase invoices of rakes (purchases made on November 15 and part of the purchases made on August 18), totaling $166. If you are having difficulty with this, think of the inventory as being taken from the bottom layer first, then the next one up. If our ending inventory is valued at $166, then our cost of goods sold must be $377.

The following are the pros and cons of this method.

Pros	Cons
1. The cost flow tends to follow the physical flow (most businesses try to sell the old goods first—for example, perishables such as fruit or vegetables).	1. During periods of inflation this method will produce higher income on the income statement—thus more taxes to be paid. (We will discuss this later in the chapter.)
2. The figure for ending inventory is made up of current costs on the balance sheet (since inventory left over is assumed to be from goods last brought into the store).	2. Recent costs are not matched with recent sales, since we assume *old* goods are sold first.

LAST-IN, FIRST-OUT METHOD (LIFO)

Under the LIFO method, it is assumed that the goods *most recently acquired* are sold first. Therefore, the items in the ending inventory will be valued at the invoice costs shown from the top of the list down.

For the Jones Hardware this assumption means that the 12 rakes not sold were assigned costs from the 10 listed in beginning inventory and 2 from the March 15 invoice. The ending inventory totals $124 and the cost of goods sold would be $419.

LAST-IN, FIRST-OUT METHOD

	Goods Available For Sale			Calculating Cost of Ending Inventory		
	Units	Cost	Total	Units	Cost	Total
January 1 Beg. Inventory	10	@ $10 =	$100	10	@ $10 =	$100
March 15 Purchased	9	@ 12 =	108	2	@ 12 =	24
August 18 Purchased	20	@ 13 =	260			
November 15 Purchased	5	@ 15 =	75			
	44		$543	12		$124

Cost of Goods Available for Sale → $543
Less: Cost of Ending Inventory   124
= Cost of Goods Sold $419

These are the pros and cons of this method.

WEIGHTED AVERAGE METHOD

The **weighted-average method** calculates an average unit cost by dividing the *total cost* of goods available for sale by the *total units* of goods available for sale. In this example, the total cost of goods available for sale was $543 and the total units available for sale was 44. Taking the $543 and dividing that number by the 44 total units for the period would give a $12.34 weighted average per unit.

In this illustration, Jones Hardware assumes that the 12 units left on hand are *average* units and therefore assigns an *average* cost figure of $12.34 to each of the 12 rakes left in inventory. Thus we have a fair approximation of the cost of the ending inventory at $148.08 and of the amount of cost of goods sold, $394.92.

WEIGHTED-AVERAGE METHOD

	Goods Available For Sale		
	Units	Cost	Total
January 1 Beg. Inventory	10	@ $10 =	$100
March 15 Purchased	9	@ 12 =	108
August 18 Purchased	20	@ 13 =	260
November 15 Purchased	5	@ 15 =	75
	44		$543

$$\frac{\$543}{44} = \$12.34 \text{ weighted-average cost per unit}$$

12 rakes × $12.34 = $148.08

Cost of Goods Available for Sale	$543.00
Less: Cost of Ending Inventory	148.08
= Cost of Goods Sold	$394.92

The pros and cons of this method are as follows:

WEIGHTED-AVERAGE METHOD: A REFERENCE GUIDE

Pros	Cons
1. Weighted-average takes into account the number of units purchased at each amount, not a simple average cost. Good for products sold in large volume, such as grains and fuels.	1. Current prices have no more significance than prices of goods bought months earlier.
2. Accountant assigns an equal unit cost to each unit of inventory; thus, when the income statement is prepared, net income will not fluctuate as much as with other methods.	2. Compared with other methods, the most recent costs are *not* matched with current sales. This is important in financial reporting so as to provide an accurate picture of the company.
	3. Cost of ending inventory is not as up to date as it could be using another method.

Remember that all four methods are acceptable accounting procedures. Management needs to select the method best suited to their business and be consistent in their application of that method.

WHEN CAN AN INVENTORY METHOD BE CHANGED

In accounting there is a principle of **consistency,** which means that once a business selects a particular accounting method, it should follow it consistently from one year to the next without switching to another method. In the previous part of this chapter we saw four methods of inventory valuations causing four different results for a business in terms of cost of goods sold and, ultimately, net income. Therefore, if a company kept switching from LIFO to FIFO each year, significant changes would result in the profit it reported. The financial reports would become undependable. Keeping with the same method, readers of the financial reports can make meaningful comparisons of the cost of ending inventory, cost of goods sold, etc., from year to year.

The principle of consistency doesn't mean that a company can *never* change from one method of inventory valuation to another. If a change is decided upon, however, the company should fully disclose the change, the effects of the change on profit and inventory valuation, and the justification for change in a footnote on the financial report. This is called the **full disclosure principle** in accounting.

ITEMS THAT SHOULD BE INCLUDED IN THE COST OF INVENTORY

Goods in Transit

On the date inventory is taken, goods in transit should be added to inventory if the ownership of the inventory has been transferred to the buyer. For example, if the merchandise was purchased *F.O.B. shipping point,* the buyer becomes the owner of the merchandise when the merchandise is placed on the carrier at the shipping point. On the other hand, if the buyer purchases the merchandise *F.O.B. destination,* the seller has ownership of the merchandise until the merchandise reaches the destination and it should not be included in the cost of the buyer's inventory.

Merchandise on Consignment

Consignment means that a business (the **consignor**) is selling its merchandise through an agent (the **consignee**) who doesn't own the merchandise but has possession of it. Consigned merchandise belongs to the consignor and should not be included in the consignee's inventory cost.

Damaged or Obsolete Merchandise

If the merchandise is not saleable, it should *not* be added to the cost of the inventory. For merchandise that is saleable but at a lower cost, the value of that inventory should be estimated at a conservative figure and added to the cost of the inventory.

LEARNING UNIT 16-3 REVIEW

AT THIS POINT you should be able to

- ◆ Calculate cost of ending inventory and cost of goods sold by specific invoice: first-in, first-out; last-in, first-out; and weighted-average method. (pp. 571–575)
- ◆ Explain the pros and cons of each method used to calculate cost of ending inventory and cost of goods sold. (pp. 571–575)
- ◆ Explain the principles of consistency and full disclosure. (p. 576)
- ◆ Explain how merchandise in transit, merchandise on consignment, and damaged or obsolete merchandise are counted in calculating inventory. (pp. 576–577)

SELF-REVIEW QUIZ 16-3

(The forms you need are on page 4 of the *Study Guide and Working Papers.*)

1. From the information given below, calculate the cost of inventory as well as the cost of goods sold, using the (a) specific invoice, (b) weighted-average, (c) first-in, first-out, and (d) last-in, first-out methods.

	Goods Available For Sale			Additional Fact: Inventory Not Sold
	Units	Cost	Total	
January 1 Beg. Inventory	40	@ $ 8 =	$ 320	
April 1 Purchased	20	@ 9 =	180	40 from January 1
May 1 Purchased	20	@ 10 =	200	4 from May 1
October 1 Purchased	20	@ 12 =	240	4 from October 1
December 1 Purchased	20	@ 13 =	260	
	120		$1,200	

2. Respond true or false to the following:

   a. It is possible for a company to change from LIFO to FIFO if the company follows specific guidelines.

   b. Goods in transit (shipped F.O.B. shipping point) will not be included as part of the inventory for the purchaser.

c. Damaged goods are always added to the cost of inventory.

Solution to Self-Review Quiz 16-3

1. a. Total cost of goods available for sale $1,200

Less ending inventory based on specific invoices:

40 units from Jan. 1 purchased at $8	$320	
4 units from May 1 purchased at $10	40	
4 units from Oct. 1 purchased at $12	48	
48 units in ending inventory		408
Cost of goods sold		$ 792

b. $1,200 ÷ 120 units = $10 weighted-average cost per unit.

Total cost of goods available for sale	$1,200
Less ending inventory priced at weighted-average basis: 48 units at $10.00	480
Cost of goods sold	$ 720

c. Total cost of goods available for sale $1,200

Less ending inventory priced on FIFO:

20 units from Dec. 1 at $13	$260	
20 units from Oct. 1 at $12	240	
8 units from May 1 at $10	80	
48 units in ending inventory		580
Cost of goods sold		$ 620

d. Total cost of goods available for sale $1,200

Less ending inventory priced on LIFO:

40 units from Jan. 1 at $8	$320	
8 units from April 1 purchased at $9	72	
48 units in ending inventory		392
Cost of goods sold		$ 808

2. a. True   **b.** False   **c.** False

LEARNING UNIT 16-4
Estimating Ending Inventory

The actual taking of a physical inventory is time-consuming and expensive. Because of the time and expense involved, most businesses take a physical inventory only once a year. For the business using the periodic inventory system, the need to have an inventory cost figure more often may become necessary. This is especially true when a business makes interim financial reports. This business may find that estimating the inventory rather than taking a physical inventory is accurate enough. Another reason to estimate the ending inventory is in case of a fire when the inventory may be destroyed. The business would need an inventory cost figure when it submits a claim of loss to the insurance company.

Two common and recognized ways to estimate ending inventory are the **Retail Method** and the **Gross Profit Method.**

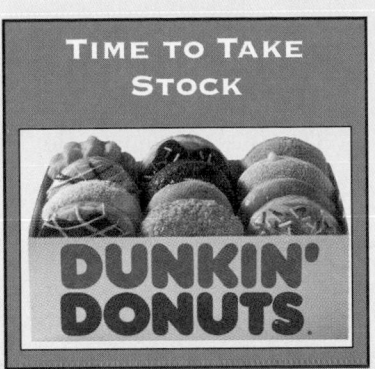

TIME TO TAKE STOCK

"Not again!" moaned Sally. "Didn't we just take an inventory of the stockroom last month? My sister works at Wal-Mart, and they only take inventory once a year!"

"Yes, we did. And now we're doing it again," said Fred patiently. "We have a very different business than Wal-Mart—we have to make sure that we get enough cream cheese and milk—but not too much, or it will spoil. And I don't want to run out of Coffee Coolatta™ mix again. That special rush shipping cost extra."

"I'm selling lots of Coolatta, 'specially the hazelnut," said Sally. "It's my favorite, too. We can't run out of it!" With that, she sped to the stockroom and started work on the inventory.

The popularity of the new Coffee Coolatta™ had taken Dunkin' Donuts by surprise. The test marketing in 1996 had been successful, but the roll-out had surpassed all expectations. Shop owners reported that their regular morning coffee and donut customers were returning in the afternoon for a Coolatta—and often another donut. Fears that the Coolatta would just replace hot coffee sales were unfounded. Instead, Coolatta sales accounted for 30 percent of all coffee sales in just six months. Hot coffee sales were unaffected.

The necessity of managing physical inventory is clear in a business that sells prepared food and drinks. In terms of physical flow, perishable inventory must be FIFO; the first inventory in is the first used, so that nothing is allowed to get stale or spoiled. If a Dunkin' Donuts shop uses the FIFO method for accounting, the cost follows the physical flow. While every Dunkin' Donuts shop owner uses the FIFO method for physical flow, not every shop owner chooses the FIFO method of accounting. Some prefer LIFO for financial accounting, because with this method, the cost of goods sold is matched to current selling prices. In a time of inflation, when prices rise quickly, LIFO saves taxes because it lowers net income.

Dunkin' Donuts currently uses a periodic inventory system. It is encouraging the use of new computerized cash registers because they will create a perpetual inventory system. But a physical count of inventory will still be needed—because spoilage and shrinkage are always possible.

DISCUSSION QUESTIONS

1. Learning Unit 16-4 discusses the retail inventory method. Why does Fred insist on a physical count?
2. The different benefits LIFO and FIFO offer Fred are discussed above. Why might Fred choose a weighted average method of accounting for inventory costs?
3. The price of coffee is subject to rapid changes, depending on growing conditions in Brazil, Colombia, Kenya, and other parts of the world. What effect might this changeability have on the method of financial accounting a Dunkin' Donuts shop owner chooses?

RETAIL METHOD

To use the Retail Method, a business must have the following information available:

1. Beginning inventory at cost and at retail (selling price).
2. Cost of net purchases at both cost and at retail.
3. The net sales at retail.

Let's look at the diagram on the next page to see how French Company estimates ending inventory at cost by the retail method.

French completed the following steps to arrive at ending inventory cost of $3,600.

Step 1: Calculate cost of merchandise available for sale at cost and retail.

Step 2: Calculate the cost ratio (cost of goods available for sale at cost divided by cost of goods available for sale at retail). It cost French Company .60 or 60 cents for each $1 of sales for the merchandise.

Step 3: Deduct net sales from retail value of merchandise available for sale to arrive at an estimated ending inventory at retail.

Step 4: Multiply cost ratio (.60 in this case) times ending inventory at retail to arrive at ending inventory at cost of $3600.

Keep in mind that at year-end French will take a physical inventory.

			Cost	Retail
	Goods Available for Sale:			
	Beginning Inventory		$ 4,100	$ 6,900
	Net Purchases		7,900	13,100
Step 1 →	Cost of Goods Available for Sale		$12,000	$20,000
Step 2 →	Cost Ratio (relationship between cost and retail)	$\dfrac{\$12,000}{\$20,000} = 60\%$		
Step 3 →	Net Sales at Retail			14,000
⌐→	Inventory at Retail			$ 6,000
Step 4 →	Ending Inventory at Cost, $6,000 × .60		$ 3,600	

GROSS PROFIT METHOD

Another method of estimating ending inventory without taking a physical count is the gross profit method. The method develops a relationship among sales, cost of goods sold, and gross profit in estimating the cost of ending inventory.

To use this method a company would have to keep track of the following:

1. Average gross profit rate.
2. Net sales, beginning inventory, net purchases.

The steps Moose Company takes to estimate its ending inventory are shown in the accompanying diagram. We assume a normal gross profit rate of 30 percent of net sales. If 30 cents on a dollar is profit, 70 cents on a dollar is cost.

	Goods Available for Sale:		
	Inventory, January 1, 19XX		$10,000
	Net Purchases		4,000
Step 1 →	Cost of Goods Available for Sale		$14,000
	Less: Estimated Cost of Goods Sold:		
	Net Sales at Retail	$6,000	
Step 2 →	Cost percentage (100% − 30%)	.70	
	Estimated Cost of Goods Sold		4,200
Step 3 →	Estimated Inventory, January 31, 19XX		$ 9,800

Step 1: Moose determines cost of goods available for sale (beginning inventory plus net purchases).

Step 2: Moose estimates cost of goods sold by multiplying cost percentage (70 percent) times net sales.

Step 3: Moose subtracts cost of goods sold from cost of goods available for sale to arrive at an estimated inventory of $9,800.

This method, besides helping prepare financial reports, can help determine the amount of inventory on hand due to a fire or can verify at year's end the accuracy of the physical inventory.

Freight, if any, would be added to cost of net purchases.

Before concluding this unit, let's look at how an error made in calculating ending inventory will affect financial reports.

How INCORRECT CALCULATION OF ENDING INVENTORY AFFECTS FINANCIAL REPORTS

As we have stated before, assigning costs to ending inventory can have an effect on cost of goods sold, gross profit, net income, and current assets, as well as owner's capital. Let's look at the diagram below to see — if a mistake is in fact made — what items on the income statement will be affected and what the mistake's impact will be over time.

	Correct		Incorrect	
	19X1	**19X2**	**19X1**	**19X2**
Sales	$200	$300	$200	$300
Cost of Goods Sold:	correct		incorrect	
Beginning Inventory	$ 30	$ 70	$ 30	$ 60
Purchases	95	85	95	85
Goods Available for Sale	125	155	125	145
Ending Inventory	−70 55	−100 55	−60 65	−100 45
Gross Profit	$145	$245	$135	$255

SUMMARY:

	Correct	Incorrect	Difference
Year X1, Gross Profit	$145	$135	−$10
Year X2, Gross Profit	245	255	+ 10
Total effect of mistake after two periods			0

Note when the incorrect figure of $60 is used for ending inventory in 19X1, it causes cost of goods sold to be $65 instead of $55 and profit to be $135 instead of $145. In other words, when ending inventory is understated ($60 instead of $70), cost of goods sold is overstated and profit is understated.

As we look next at 19X2, we see that the ending incorrect inventory of 19X1 is carried as the beginning inventory of 19X2. The understatement of beginning inventory in 19X2 of $60 (instead of $70) causes cost of goods sold to be understated and gross profit to be overstated.

Thus, at the end of 19X2, the error will be self-correcting.

To review, look at the diagram that follows and prove it to yourself by going back over the previous explanation.

Ending Inventory works in same direction as Profit. Beginning Inventory is inversely related.

If the Item Is	Overstated	Understated
Beginning Inventory	Profit is Understated	Profit is Overstated
Ending Inventory	Profit is Overstated	Profit is Understated

Keep in mind that since ending inventory is recorded as a current asset on the balance sheet, any mistake will cause the assets to be under- or overstated. The statement of owner's equity will also be affected, since we have seen that the net income will be over- and understated.

LEARNING UNIT 16-4 REVIEW

AT THIS POINT you should be able to

◆ Calculate ending inventory by the retail method. (p. 579)
◆ Calculate ending inventory by the gross profit method. (p. 580)
◆ Explain how understating or overstating ending inventory will affect financial reports. (p. 581)

SELF-REVIEW QUIZ 16-4

(The forms you need are on page 5 of the *Study Guide and Working Papers*.)

1. Alon Company needs to estimate its month-end inventory. From the following, estimate the cost of ending inventory on September 30 by the retail method.

	Cost	Retail
Beginning Inventory	$ 8,000	$10,000
Net Purchases	40,000	60,000
Net Sales		30,000

(Carry out the cost ratio to nearest hundredth percent.)

2. Respond true or false to the following:
   a. The retail inventory method is an estimate.
   b. The cost ratio in the gross profit method represents only sales, not costs.
   c. The first step in the gross profit method is to determine cost of goods available for sale.
   d. If ending inventory is overstated, net income will be overstated.
   e. If beginning inventory is overstated, net income will be overstated.

Solution to Self-Review Quiz 16-4

	Cost	Retail
1. Beginning Inventory	$ 8,000	$10,000
Net Purchases	40,000	60,000
Cost of Goods Available for Sale	$48,000	70,000
Cost Ratio, $48,000/$70,000 = 68.57%		
Net Sales at Retail		30,000
Inventory at Retail		$40,000
Ending Inventory at Cost, $40,000 × .6857	$27,428	

2. a. True   b. False   c. True   d. True   e. False.

SUMMARY OF KEY POINTS

Learning Unit 16-1

1. In the perpetual inventory method we have two key accounts that are kept up to date at all times. These accounts are Merchandise Inventory and Cost of Goods Sold.
2. Each purchase of merchandise is recorded by a debit to the Merchandise Inventory account.
3. Each sale requires two entries. One entry records the revenue or selling price of the merchandise and the other entry transfers the cost of the items sold from the Merchandise Inventory account to the Cost of Goods Sold account.
4. Sales returns also require two entries. One to record the reduction in revenue in a Sales Returns and Allowance account and the other entry to move the cost of the items returned back to the Merchandise Inventory account from the Cost of Goods Sold account.
5. When the business returns merchandise to the vendor because of damage or some other reason, the Merchandise Inventory account is credited because we no longer have the merchandise to sell.
6. The comparison of the perpetual inventory system and the periodic inventory system reveals the Purchases, Purchases Returns and Allowances, and Freight accounts do not exist in the perpetual inventory system. The accounts Merchandise Inventory and Cost of Goods Sold become active accounts in the perpetual inventory system.

Learning Unit 16-2

1. If there are many items in inventory, a subsidiary inventory ledger will be used to keep track of the details of quantities and cost for each item in inventory.
2. An inventory record form will be used for each item in the inventory. This form has columns for recording the quantities and cost of units purchased and units sold, and it provides a running balance of inventory on hand.
3. When selling an item, the inventory record form provides the cost information for the debit to Cost of Goods sold and the credit to Merchandise Inventory.
4. The total cost represented by all of the inventory record forms will equal the balance of the Merchandise Inventory account in the General Ledger.

Learning Unit 16-3

1. In assigning a cost to ending inventory, the flow of goods may *not* follow the actual flow of costs.
2. The specific invoice method identifies each item in inventory with a specific invoice in assigning a cost of ending inventory. It matches costs exactly with revenues.
3. FIFO assumes the old goods are sold first. Since ending inventory is valued at most recent costs, FIFO provides the most realistic figure for ending merchandise inventory.
4. LIFO assumes the newest goods are sold first. It provides the most realistic figure for cost of goods sold. LIFO may also reduce income taxes.

5. The weighted-average method provides an average unit cost of all inventory. Weighted-average inventory value generally falls somewhere between LIFO and FIFO.
6. Accounting principles require that we be consistent in the use of the inventory method that is adopted.
7. Goods in transit should be added to the value of the inventory. Merchandise on consignment and damaged or obsolete merchandise should not be included in the value of the inventory.

Learning Unit 16-4

1. Taking a physical inventory is costly and time-consuming.
2. If a business needs to take an inventory more often than once a year, the retail method or gross profit method is used to prepare interim financial reports or in submitting a claim for insurance purposes.
3. The ending inventory amount has an effect on the financial reports, and a mistake will cause the assets to be under- or overstated. Net income will also be under- or overstated by this mistake.

KEY TERMS

Consignee A company or person to whom merchandise is consigned but who doesn't have ownership.

Consignment Sales of goods through an agent who has possession but not ownership.

Consignor The one who consigns merchandise to the consignee.

Consistency The accounting principle that requires companies to follow the same accounting methods or procedures from period to period.

FIFO (First-in, First-out) method Valuing of inventory assuming that the company sells the first goods received in the store.

Full disclosure principle The accounting principle that requires companies to fully disclose on their financial reports changes in accounting procedures and methods along with effects of the change, as well as justification for change.

Gross Profit method A method used to determine the value of the ending inventory using a predetermined gross profit rate. This method can be used to determine value of ending inventory if a loss from fire occurs.

LIFO (Last-in, Last-out) method Valuing of inventory with the assumption the last goods received in the store are the first to be sold.

Periodic inventory system An inventory system that does not keep continuous inventory of merchandise on hand.

Perpetual inventory system The inventory system of a company that keeps a continuous (perpetual) record of inventory on hand and of the cost of goods sold.

Retail method A method used to determine the value of the ending inventory using a cost to retail ratio. Often used for interim financial reports.

Specific invoice method Valuing of inventory where each item is identified with a specific invoice.

Weighted-average method Valuing of inventory where each item is assigned the same unit cost. This unit cost is found by dividing cost of goods available for sale by the total number of units for sale.

QUESTIONS, MINI EXERCISES, EXERCISES, AND PROBLEMS

Discussion Questions

1. Why would a manager prefer the perpetual inventory system over the periodic system of inventory?
2. What are the two key accounts in the perpetual inventory system?
3. In the perpetual system, what account is debited to record the cost of merchandise purchased?
4. Why are there two entries required to record each sale in the perpetual inventory system?
5. Explain the relationship between the merchandise inventory account and the subsidiary inventory ledger.

BLUEPRINT: METHODS OF ESTIMATING INVENTORY

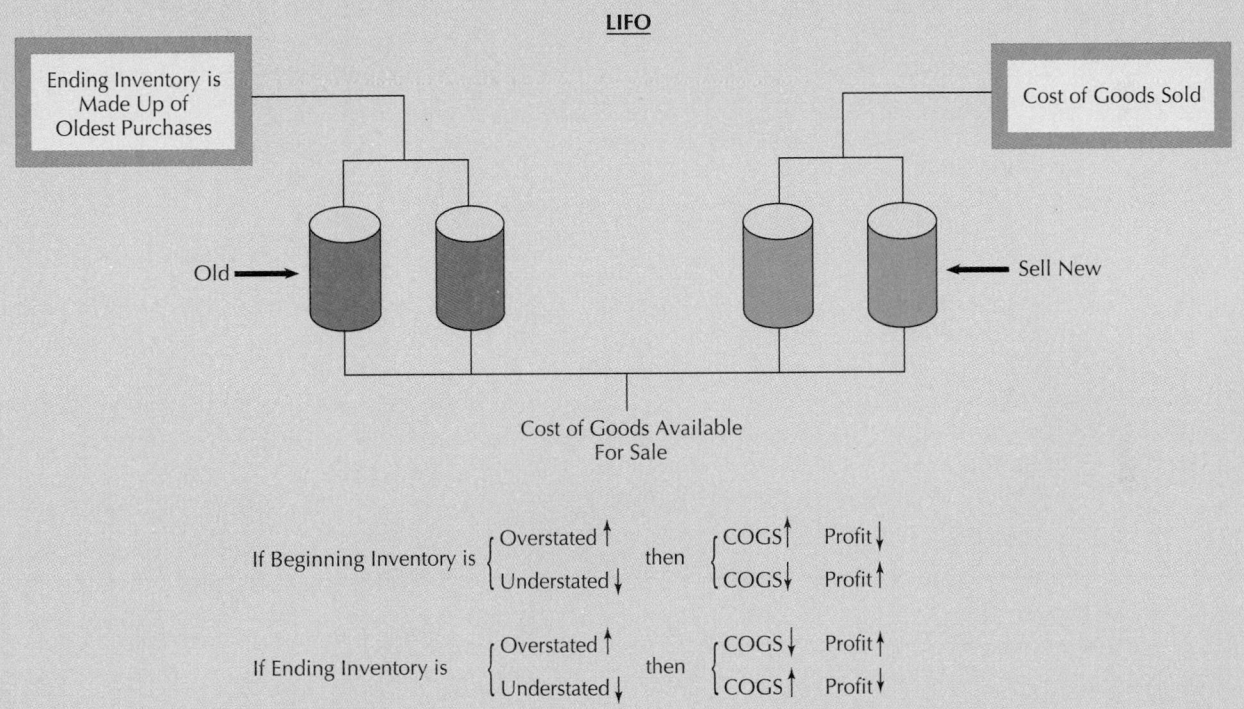

(Cont. on p. 586)

6. Must the flow of cost in inventory match the physical movement of merchandise? Please explain.

7. What are the four methods of inventory valuation? Explain each.

8. During inflation, which inventory method will provide the lowest income on the income statement?

9. Which inventory method provides the most current valuation of inventory on the balance sheet? Please explain.

10. Explain why goods in transit (F.O.B. shipping point) to buyer and goods issued on consignment are added to inventory valuations.

11. When Ending Inventory is understated, what effect will this have on cost of goods sold and net income?

SUMMARY OF PROS AND CONS OF INVENTORY, VALUATION METHODS

	Pros	Cons
Specific Invoice	1. Simple to use if company has small amount of high-cost goods—for example, autos, jewels, boats, antiques, etc. 2. Flow of goods and flow of cost are the same. 3. Costs are matched with the sales they helped to produce.	1. Difficult to use for goods with large unit volume and small unit prices—for example, nails at a hardware store, packages of toothpaste at a drug store. 2. Difficult to use for decision-making purposes—ordinarily an impractical approach.

	Pros	Cons
Weighted-Average Method	1. Weighted-average takes into account the number of units purchased at each amount, not a simple average cost. Good for products sold in large volume, such as grains and fuels. 2. Accountant assigns an equal unit cost to each unit of inventory; thus when the income statement is prepared, net income will not fluctuate as much as with other methods.	1. Current prices have no more significance than prices of goods bought months earlier. 2. Compared with other methods, the most recent costs are *not* matched with current sales. 3. Cost of ending inventory is not as up to date as it could be using another method.

	Pros	Cons
FIFO	1. The cost flow tends to follow the physical flow (most businesses try to sell the old goods first—for example, perishables such as fruit or vegetables). 2. The figure for ending inventory is made up of current costs on the balance sheet (since inventory left over is assumed to be from goods last brought into the store).	1. During inflation this method will produce higher income on the income statement—thus more taxes to be paid. 2. Recent costs are not matched with recent sales, since we assume *old* goods are sold first.

	Pros	Cons
LIFO	1. Cost of goods sold is stated at or near current costs, since costs of *latest* goods acquired are used. 2. Matches current costs with current selling prices. 3. During inflation this method produces the lowest net income, which is a tax advantage. (The lower cost of ending inventory means a higher cost of goods sold; with a higher cost of goods sold, gross profit and ultimately net income are smaller, and thus taxes are lower.)	1. Ending inventory is valued at very old prices. 2. Doesn't match physical flow of goods (but can still be used to calculate flow of costs).

12. Why would a company use the retail method to determine the value of the ending inventory? Why would they use the gross profit method?

Mini Exercises

(The blank forms you need are on pages 6–9 of the *Study Guide and Working Papers.*)

Transaction Analysis

1. Complete the following transaction analysis:

Accounts Affected	Category	↑	↓	Rules
Merchandise Inventory			↓	
Cost of Goods Sold		↑		

Journal Entries   Use the perpetual inventory system.

2. Journalize the following transaction in correct form:

19XX
Mar.   1   Sold merchandise on account, $500. The merchandise cost $300.

3. Journalize the following transaction in correct form:

19XX
Mar.   15   A customer returned merchandise for a cash refund of $250. The item cost the seller $125.

4. Journalize the following transaction in correct form:

19XX
Mar.   20   The business returned to the vendor a damaged inventory item that cost $150.

Estimating Inventory Value

5. From the following information calculate the cost of ending inventory and cost of goods sold using (1) FIFO, (2) LIFO, and (3) Weighted-Average.

		Units	Cost
January 1	Beginning Inventory	5	$1
March 6	Purchased	3	2
August 9	Purchased	2	3
December 10	Purchased	4	4

The ending inventory reveals six items unsold.

Retail Inventory Method

6. Complete the following using the retail inventory method. (Round cost ratio is nearest whole percent.)

	Cost	Retail
Goods available for Sale		
Beginning Inventory	$50	$100
Net Purchases	70	90
Cost of Goods Available for Sale	A	B

Cost Ratio	C	
Net Sales at Retail		140
Inventory at Retail		D
Ending Inventory	E	

Gross Profit Method

7. Complete the following using the gross profit method. Assume a normal gross profit rate of 40 percent of Net Sales.

Goods Available for Sale

Inventory Jan. 1, 19XX		$50
Net Purchases		10
Cost of Goods Available for Sale		A
Less: Estimated Cost of Goods Sold:		
Net Sales at Retail	$40	
Cost Percentage	B	
Estimated Cost of Goods Sold		C
Estimated Inventory Jan. 31, 19XX		D

Exercises

(The blank forms you need are on pages 10–13 of the *Study Guide and Working Papers.*)

Journalizing perpetual entries

16-1. The DMM Electric Company uses the perpetual inventory system. Record these transactions in a two-column journal.

19XX
Feb
  3 Purchased 10 model 77DX light fixtures on account from Dealer's Electric at total cost of $230, terms n/30.
  5 Sold 3 model U67 light fixtures for cash for $84 total. The cost of these three fixtures amounted to $54.
  6 Our customer returned 1 model U67 light fixture. We gave the customer a $28 cash refund.
 10 We issued a debit memo for $23 to Dealer's Electric for 1 model 77DX light fixture that came in damaged in the shipment of Feb. 3.

Perpetual inventory—subsidiary ledgers.

16-2. The RJM Company uses the perpetual inventory system with a subsidiary ledger for inventory. Enter the following information into the inventory record form for product U47. Be sure to keep the balance on hand up to date.

19XX
Nov
  5 Purchased 5 units at a cost of $10 each. (There were no units on hand prior to this purchase.)
  6 Sold 3 units for $16 each. (*Hint:* The inventory record form only contains information about the cost of a product, not the selling price!)
  7 Sold 1 unit for $15.50.
 10 Purchased 12 additional units at a cost of $10 each.

Journalizing perpetual entries.

16-3. Journalize and post the above transactions using a two-column journal.

FIFO—perpetual method.

16-4. CVR Sales uses the FIFO method with the perpetual inventory system. Enter the following information into the inventory record form for product 44BX. Be sure to keep the balance on hand up to date.

19XX

Oct   1   Balance on hand—3 units at a cost of $21 each.
      2   Purchased 5 units at a cost of $23 each.
      5   Sold 2 units for $31 each. (*Remember,* use cost and not selling price in the inventory record.)
      6   Sold 5 units for $31 each.
      8   Purchased 6 units at a cost of $24 each.

Periodic method.

16-5. The Loyola Company uses the periodic inventory system. Calculate the cost of ending inventory and cost of goods sold using the (a) FIFO, (b) LIFO, and (c) weighted-average methods. Loyola sells only one product called SM57.

		Units	Cost per Unit
Jan. 1	Beginning inventory	50	$ 9
Mar. 18	Purchased	12	10
Aug. 19	Purchased	40	12
Nov. 8	Purchased	48	13

Ending inventory is 52 units.

Shipping goods.

16-6. From the following facts, calculate the correct cost of inventory for Ray Company. The facts:

◆ Cost of inventory on shelf, $4,000, which includes $300 of goods received on consignment.

◆ Goods in transit en route to Ray Company shipped F.O.B. shipping point, $22,000.

◆ Goods in transit en route to Ray shipped F.O.B. destination, $300. Ray has $600 worth of goods on consignment in Alice's Dress Shop.

Retail inventory.

16-7. Miles Company's May 1 inventory had a cost of $58,000 and a retail value of $72,000. During May, net purchases cost $255,000 with a retail value of $405,000. Net sales at retail for Miles Company during May were $225,000. Calculate the ending inventory at cost using the retail inventory method. (Round the cost ratio to the nearest hundredth percent.)

Gross profit method.

16-8. Amy Company on January 1 had inventory costing $30,000 and during January had net purchases of $67,000. Over recent years Amy Company's gross profit has averaged 40 percent on sales. Given that the company has net sales of $106,000, calculate an estimated cost of ending inventory using the gross profit method.

Group A Problems

(The blank forms you need are on pages 14–23 of the *Study Guide and Working Papers.*)

Journalizing perpetual inventory.

16A-1. The Wren Company uses the perpetual inventory system. Record these transactions in a two-column journal. All credit sales are n/30.

Check Figure:

Mar. 13

Dr.   Cost of goods sold $290

Cr.   Merch. inventory $290

19XX

March   5   Purchased merchandise on account totaling $1,750. Terms n/30.
        6   Sold merchandise on account to Tommy Dorsey for $85. This merchandise cost $63.
        8   Returned $100 of defective merchandise purchased March 5.
        9   Sold $125 of merchandise for cash. This merchandise cost $98.
        9   Allowed a return for credit of $7 of merchandise sold on March 6. The cost of the returned merchandise was $5. (*Hint:* Don't forget to

return the cost of the merchandise to the Merchandise Inventory account.)

10 Purchased $800 of merchandise on account from BG Supply. Terms n/30.

12 Received payment from Tommy Dorsey for the March 6 sale less the return.

13 Sold $380 of merchandise for cash. The cost was $290.

Journalizing perpetual inventory.

16A-2. Mr. E. L. Best owns an electronics supply company called Best Electronics. His company uses the perpetual inventory system with a subsidiary inventory ledger to maintain control over an inventory of thousands of electronic parts. Here are the quantities and costs for three of the parts in his inventory:

Check Figure:
KT88   Ending balance $192.50

Part #	Quantity on hand	Cost per unit
KT88	3	$17.50
EL34	22	16.40
12AX7	5	8.70

Your job is to

1. Enter the above beginning balances in the inventory record forms; beginning inventory is $456.80.

2. Journalize and post the following transactions.

19XX

Oct   10   Purchased the following on account:

Part #	Quantity	Cost per unit
KT88	24	$17.50
12AX7	36	8.70

(Hint: Be sure to update each inventory record.)

11 Sold four number KT88 units for cash at a selling price of $27.50 each. (*Hint:* Remember to record both the revenue and the cost. The cost data will be found in the inventory record form for this part number. Don't forget to update the form.)

13 Sold the following for cash:

Part #	Quantity	Sales price per unit
KT88	12	$27.50
EL34	8	25.00
12AX7	14	12.90

15 A customer brought back one of KT88 bought two days ago because it did not work.

16 Best Electronics sent back to the vendor the faulty KT88 that the customer brought back.

Perpetual—LIFO
                FIFO

16A-3. Agree Company uses a perpetual inventory system. From the information given below, prepare an inventory record form (a) assuming that the FIFO method is in use and (B) assuming that the LIFO method is in use. Assume on January 1, 19XX, a beginning inventory of 800 units at a cost of $8 each.

Check Figure:
Ending balance $11,960

RECEIVED			SOLD	
Date	Quantity	Cost per Unit	Date	Quantity
Apr. 15	220	$7	Mar. 8	500
Nov. 12	800	9	Oct. 5	350
Dec. 31	700	10	Nov. 30	400

16A-4. Ashley Company, using the periodic inventory system, began the year with 250 units of product B in inventory with a unit cost of $35. The following additional purchases of the product were made:

Apr. 1	300 units @ $40 each
July 5	400 units @ 50 each
Aug. 15	500 units @ 60 each
Nov. 20	150 units @ 70 each

At end of year Ashley Company had 500 units of its product unsold. Your task is to calculate cost of ending inventory as well as cost of goods sold by (a) FIFO, (b) LIFO, (c) weighted-average. (Round weighted-average to nearest cent.)

16A-5. Marge Company uses the retail method to estimate cost of ending inventory for its monthly interim reports. From the following facts, estimate Marge's ending inventory at cost for the end of January. (Round the cost ratio to the nearest tenth percent.)

January 1 inventory at cost	$ 16,500
January 1 inventory at retail	32,000
Net purchases at cost	110,800
Net purchases at retail	195,000
Net sales at retail	191,000

16A-6. Over the past four years the gross profit rate for Hall Company was 30 percent. Last week a fire destroyed all of Hall's inventory. Luckily all the records for Hall were in a fireproof safe and indicated the following facts:

Inventory (January 1, 19XX)	$ 39,000
Sales	128,500
Sales Returns	3,200
Purchases	78,000
Purchases Returns and Allowances	3,000

Please estimate the cost of inventory that was destroyed in the fire.

Group B Problems

(The blank forms you need are on pages 14–23 of the *Study Guide and Working Papers.*)

16B-1. The Wren Company uses the perpetual inventory system. Record these transactions in a two-column journal. All credit sales are n/30.

19XX

March 15 Purchased merchandise on account totaling $1,450. Terms n/30.

16 Sold merchandise on account to Bobby Hackett for $92. This merchandise cost $71.

18 Returned $120 of defective merchandise purchased March 15.

19 Sold $230 of merchandise for cash. This merchandise cost $175.

19 Allowed a return for credit of $14 of merchandise sold on March 16. The cost of the returned merchandise was $11. (*Hint:* Don't forget to return the cost of the merchandise to the Merchandise Inventory account.)

20 Purchased $900 of merchandise on account from JT Supply. Terms n/30.

22 Received payment from Bobby Hackett for the March 16 sale less the return.

23 Sold $410 of merchandise for cash. The cost was $320.

16B-2. Mr. E. L. Best owns an electronics supply company called Best Electronics. His company uses the perpetual inventory system with a subsidiary inventory ledger to maintain control over an inventory of thousands of electronic parts. Here are the quantities and costs for three of the parts in his inventory:

Part #	Quantity on hand	Cost per unit
6L6	4	$12.50
EL84	18	9.40
12AU7	3	7.80

Your job is to:

1. Enter the above beginning balances in the inventory record forms; beginning inventory is $242.60.

2. Journalize and post the following transactions.

19XX

Oct 10 Purchased the following on account:

Part #	Quantity	Cost per unit
6L6	18	$12.50
12AU7	28	7.80

(*Hint:* Be sure to update each inventory record.)

11 Sold four number 12AU7 units for cash at a selling price of $18.50 each. (*Hint:* Remember to record both the revenue and the cost. The cost data will be found in the inventory record form for this part number. Don't forget to update the form.)

13 Sold the following for cash:

Part #	Quantity	Sales price per unit
6L6	10	$18.50
EL84	9	14.00
12AU7	12	11.80

15 A customer brought back one 6L6 that was bought two days ago because it did not work.

16 Best Electronics returned to the vendor the faulty part that was returned yesterday.

16B-3. Agree Company uses a perpetual inventory system. From the information given below, prepare an inventory record form (a) assuming that the FIFO method is in use and (b) assuming that the LIFO method is in use. Assume on January 1, 19XX, a beginning inventory of 500 units at a cost of $7 each.

RECEIVED			SOLD	
Date	Quantity	Cost per Unit	Date	Quantity
Apr. 15	200	$8	Mar. 8	400
Nov. 12	300	9	Oct. 5	300
Dec. 31	600	10	Nov 30	200

16B-4. On January 1, 19XX, Ashley Company, a company which uses the periodic inventory system, began with 150 units of product B in inventory with a unit cost of $20. The following additional purchases of the product were made:

Apr. 1	210 units @ $30 each
Jul. 5	500 units @ 40 each
Aug. 15	450 units @ 50 each
Nov. 20	200 units @ 60 each

At end of year Ashley Company had 400 units of its product unsold. Your task is to calculate cost of ending inventory as well as cost of goods sold by (a) FIFO, (b) LIFO, (c) weighted-average. (Round weighted-average to nearest cent.)

Retail inventory method.

Check Figure:

$28,450   Ending inventory

16B-5. Marge Company uses the retail method to estimate cost of ending inventory for its monthly interim reports. From the facts given below, estimate Marge's ending inventory at cost for the end of January. (Round the cost ratio to the nearest hundredth percent.)

January 1 inventory at cost	$ 17,000
January 1 inventory at retail	35,000
Net purchases at cost	119,000
Net purchases at retail	204,000
Net sales at retail	189,000

Gross profit method.

Check Figure:

$15,762.50   Estimated inventory

16B-6. Over the past four years the gross profit rate for Hall Company was 35 percent. Last week a fire destroyed all of Hall's inventory. Luckily all the records for Hall were in a fireproof safe and indicated the following facts:

Inventory (January 1, 19XX)	$ 5,400
Sales	127,000
Sales Returns	3,250
Purchases	94,900
Purchases Returns and Allowances	4,100

Using the gross profit method, estimate the cost of inventory that was destroyed in the fire.

REAL WORLD APPLICATIONS

16R-1.

The following inventory errors were discovered during an internal audit:

a. The beginning inventory was overstated by $200.

b. The ending inventory was understated by $300.

c. $900 of purchases were unrecorded.

d. A sales return of $1,500 was not recorded.

Indicate what effect these mistakes (treat each one separately) will have on (1) the cost of goods sold, (2) the gross profit, and (3) the owner's equity. Please provide a written explanation.

 make the call

Critical Thinking/Ethical Case

16R-2.

Lyon Co. has used a perpetual inventory system for six months. The President has issued a memo stating that the new computer system has failed to deliver acceptable standards in servicing his customers—too many goods out of stock. Fran, Lyon's accountant, blames the Computer Department and tells the President to fire the head of that department. The President wants to return immediately to a periodic inventory system. You make the call. Write down your recommendations to the President.

ACCOUNTING RECALL

A CUMULATIVE APPROACH

THIS EXAM REVIEWS CHAPTERS 1 THROUGH 16

Your *Study Guide and Working Papers* (pp. 27 – 29) has forms to complete this exam, as well as worked-out solutions. The page references next to each question identify what page to turn back to if you answer the question incorrectly.

PART 1   Vocabulary Review

Match the terms to the appropriate definition or phrase.

Page Ref.

(562)	1. Perpetual inventory system	A. Reduces cost of goods sold
(574)	2. LIFO	B. Improves control of cash
(271)	3. SUTA	C. Newest units sold first
(573)	4. FIFO	D. Social Security tax
(216)	5. Petty Cash	E. A "hot" check
(248)	6. FICA	F. Equals total of subsidiary ledger
(355)	7. Purchases discount	G. Inventory always up to date
(365)	8. Controlling account	H. Doesn't have ownership
(577)	9. Consignee	I. Oldest units sold first
(212)	10. NSF	J. Unemployment tax

PART II   True or False (Accounting Theory)

(572)   11. If ending inventory is understated then COGS is overstated.

(474)   12. LIFO assumes the old goods are sold first.

(314)   13. Sales Returns and Allowances is a contra-revenue account.

(315)   14. Net sales less cost of goods sold equals gross profit.

(562)   15. In the perpetual system the purchases account is not used.

CONTINUING PROBLEM

The Eldorado Computer Center had 300 pieces of merchandise inventory as of March 31, 19XX. The inventory was purchased with prices as follows:

Lot	Price each Piece	Number of Pieces	Total Cost
1st lot	$1.00	100	$100
2nd lot	$1.75	100	$175
3rd lot	$2.00	80	$160
4th lot	$2.50	100	$250
5th lot	$1.65	100	$165

Lot numbers represent oldest to newest.

Assignment:

(See p. 28 in your *Study Guide and Working Papers.*)

Using the FIFO, LIFO, and Weighted-Average methods, calculate the dollar value of the Eldorado Computer Center's ending inventory.

COMPUTERIZED ACCOUNTING APPLICATION FOR CHAPTER 16

Perpetual Inventory System

Before starting on this assignment, read and complete the tasks discussed in Parts A, B and F of the Computerized Accounting appendix at the end of this book and complete the Computerized Accounting Application assignments for Chapter 3, Chapter 4, Valdez Realty Mini Practice Set (Chapter 5), Pete's Market Mini Practice Set (Chapter 8), Chapter 10, and The Corner Dress Shop Mini Practice Set (Chapter 13).

One of the most powerful features of a computerized accounting system is its ability to maintain perpetual inventory records easily and accurately. In the prior Computer Workshops this feature was not demonstrated as you focused on the tasks associated with maintaining a periodic inventory system. Simply Accounting has the ability to maintain perpetual inventory records through its Inventory module. Simply Accounting uses the weighted-average method as its inventory cost flow assumption.

In this Computer Workshop you will be working with the data files for a company called The Paint Place. The Paint Place uses the General, Payables, Receivables, and Inventory modules of Simply Accounting to maintain its accounting and perpetual inventory records. The Paint Place extends terms of 2/10, n/30 to all of its credit customers. An Inventory Synopsis (a computerized schedule of the current status of the perpetual inventory records) for The Paint Place appears below:

Computerized Perpetual Inventory Schedule

The Paint Place
Inventory Synopsis 3/1/97

Number	Description	Unit	Price	Quantity	Cost	Value	Margin (%)
1	Latex Flat	Gallon	16.95	642	7.47	4,795.74	55.93
2	Latex Semi-gloss	Gallon	16.95	1,066	7.47	7,963.02	55.93
3	Latex High-gloss	Gallon	16.95	600	7.47	4,482.00	55.93
4	Oil High-gloss	Gallon	17.95	801	8.97	7,184.97	50.03
5	Oil Semi-gloss	Gallon	17.95	502	8.97	4,502.94	50.03
						28,928.67	

Open the Company Data Files

1. Click on the Start button. Point to Programs; point to Simply Accounting; then click on Simply Accounting in the final menu presented. The Simply Accounting-Open File dialog box will appear.

2. Insert your Student Data Files disk into disk drive A. Enter the following path into the **File name** text box: A:\student\paint.asc

3. Click on the **Open** button; enter 3/31/97 into the **Using Date for this Session** text box; then click on the **OK** button. Click on the **OK** button in response to the message "The date entered is more than one week past your previous **Using** date of 3/1/97." The Company Window for The Paint Place will appear. Note that the two journals associated with the Inventory module (Transfers and Adjustments) are available. The Transfers and Adjustments Journals are used to record nonroutine types of transactions that affect inventory quantities and values such as adjustments to the perpetual inventory records for items that have been damaged or become obsolete. Routine perpetual inventory transactions such as the sale or purchase of an inventory item are recorded in the Sales and Purchases Journal dialog boxes.

Add Your Name to the Company Name	**4.** Click on the Company Window Setup menu; then click on Company Information. The Company Information dialog box will appear. Insert your name in place of the text "Your Name" in the **Name** text box. Click on the **OK** button to return to the Company Window.
How to Record a Sale on Account	**5.** On March 1, 1997 sold 5 gallons of Oil High-gloss (Item #4) at $17.95 per gallon to Elaine Anderson on account, invoice no. 5468, $89.75, terms 2/10, n/30.

Double-click on the Sales icon to open the Sales Journal dialog box. Note that the program automatically offers **Invoice** 5468 as the invoice number for this transaction through the program's automatic invoice numbering feature. Click on the arrow button to the right of the **Sold to** text box to display a list of customers; then click on Elaine Anderson. Highlight the **Date** text box; enter 3/1/97; then press the TAB key. The insertion point will be positioned in the **Item** text box. Press the ENTER key to display the Select Inventory item dialog box; then highlight Item #4 Oil High-gloss, and click on the Select button. Note that the program automatically enters the **Unit, Description,** default sales **Price,** and sales **Acct** (4010 Sales) associated with this inventory item (Item #4). If the item is being sold at a price other than the default sales price shown, the **Price** offered by the program can be modified. For example, the item may be on sale, or a volume discount may be offered to the customer.

6. The flashing insertion point appears in the **Qty** text box. Enter 5; then press the TAB key. The program will automatically multiply the **Qty** times the **Price** and enter the result in the **Amount** text box. Your screen should look like this:

How to Review a Sales Journal Entry	**7.** Before posting this transaction, you need to verify that the transaction data are correct by reviewing the journal entry. To review the entry, click on the Sales Journal Report menu; then click on Display Sales Journal Entry. The journal entry representing the data you have recorded in the Sales Journal dialog box is displayed. Review the journal entry for accuracy, noting any errors. Note that the program has automatically created a compound journal entry recording the retail value of the sale and the cost of the sale through its perpetual inventory integration feature. Close the Sales Journal Entry window; then make any editing corrections required.
How to Post a Sales Journal Entry	**8.** After verifying that the journal entry is correct, click on the **Post** icon to post this transaction. A blank Sales Journal dialog box is displayed, ready for additional Sales Journal transactions to be recorded. Close the Sales Journal dialog box.
How to Record a Purchase on Account	**9.** On March 2, 1997 received invoice no. 6892 from Wholesale Paints in the amount of $1,504 for the purchase of 200 gallons of Latex High-gloss (Item #3) at $7.52 per gallon, terms 2/10, n/30.

Double-click on the Purchases icon to open the Purchases Journal dialog box. Click on the arrow button to the right of the **Purchased From** text box; then click on Wholesale Paints. Click on the **Invoice** text box; enter 6892; then press the TAB key. Enter 3/2/97 into the **Date** text box; then press the TAB key. The insertion point will be positioned in the **Item** text box. Press the ENTER key to display the Select Inventory item dialog box; then highlight Item #3 Latex High-gloss, and click on the Select button. Note that the program automatically enters the **Unit, Description, Price** (current weighted-average cost per unit), and **Acct** (1300 Merchandise Inventory) associated with this inventory item (Item #3). For some purchases the default **Price** offered by the program will need to be modified to agree with the per unit price stated on the vendor's invoice. For example, the price of the item being purchased may be increased or decreased, or a volume discount may be extended by the vendor.

10. The flashing insertion point appears in the **Rec'd** text box. Enter 200; then press the TAB key until the insertion point is positioned in the **Price** field. Change the **Price** to 7.52 (don't forget to change the **Price!**); then press the TAB key. The program will automatically multiply the number of items in the **Rec'd** text box times the **Price** and enter the result in the **Amount** text box. Your screen should look like this:

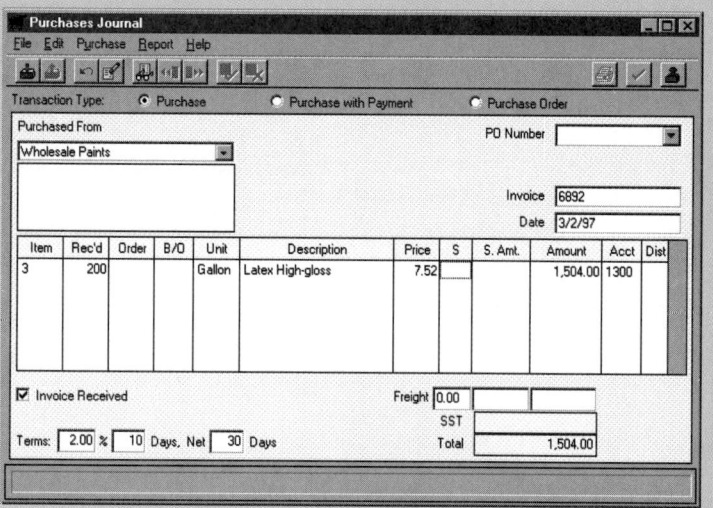

How to Review a Purchases Journal Entry

11. Before posting this transaction, you need to verify that the transaction data are correct by reviewing the journal entry. To review the entry, click on the Purchases Journal Report menu; then click on Display Purchases Journal Entry. The journal entry representing the data you have recorded in the Purchases Journal dialog box is displayed. Review the journal entry for accuracy noting any errors.

12. Close the Purchases Journal Entry window; then make any editing corrections required.

How to Post a Purchases Journal Entry

13. After verifying that the journal entry is correct, click on the **Post** icon to post this transaction. A blank Purchases Journal dialog box is displayed, ready for additional Purchases Journal transactions to be recorded. Close the Purchases Journal dialog box.

Record Transactions

14. Record the following additional transactions:

1997
March   3   Received invoice no. CC675 from Painter's Supply in the amount of $906 for the purchase of 100 gallons of Oil High-gloss (Item #4) at 9.06 per gallon (don't forget to change the **Price!**), terms 2/10, n/30.

4 Sold 5 gallons of Oil High-gloss paint (Item #4) at $17.95 per gallon to Jake Kerns on account, invoice no. 5469, $89.75, terms 2/10, n/30.

6 Received check no. 8723 from Wes Young in the amount of $3,225.13 in payment of invoice no. 5468 ($3,290.95), dated February 28, less 2 percent discount ($65.82).

7 Issued check no. 2345 to Vantage Tints in the amount of $1,082.84 in payment of invoice no. E5658 ($1,116.33), dated February 28, less 3 percent discount ($33.49).

14 Sold 10 gallons of Latex Semi-gloss (Item #2) at $16.95 per gallon to Elaine Anderson on account, $169.50, invoice no. 5470, terms 2/10, n/30.

16 Received invoice no. 6943 from Wholesale Paints in the amount of $1,134 for the purchase of 150 gallons of Latex Semi-gloss (Item #2) at 7.56 per gallon (don't forget to change the **Price!**), terms 2/10, n/30.

19 Received invoice no. CC691 from Painter's Supply in the amount of $1,618.75 for the purchase of 175 gallons of Oil Semi-gloss (Item #5) at 9.25 per gallon (don't forget to change the **Price!**), terms 2/10, n/30.

21 Sold 10 gallons of Latex Semi-gloss (Item #2) at $16.95 per gallon to Jake Kerns on account, $169.50, invoice no. 5471, terms 2/10, n/30.

24 Sold 25 gallons of Oil Semi-gloss paint (Item #5) at $17.95 per gallon to Elaine Anderson on account, $448.75, invoice no. 5472, terms 2/10, n/30.

25 Received invoice no. CC787 from Painter's Supply in the amount of $465 for the purchase of 50 gallons of Oil Semi-gloss (Item #5) at 9.30 per gallon (don't forget to change the **Price!**), terms 2/10, n/30.

31 Sold 25 gallons of Oil Semi-gloss (Item #5) at $17.95 per gallon to Jake Kerns on account, $448.75, invoice no. 5473, terms 2/10, n/30.

How to Display an Inventory Activity Detail Report

15. Click on the Company Window Reports menu; point to Inventory; then click on Inventory Activity. Click on the **Detail** option button, click on the **Select All** button; leave the **Select Assets** option button checked; change the **Start** date to 3/1/97; leave the **Finish** date set at 3/31/97; then check the check boxes for **Purchases, Sales, Transfers, Adjustments,** and **Balance forward.** Your screen will look like this:

16. Click on the **OK** button. Your screen will look like this:

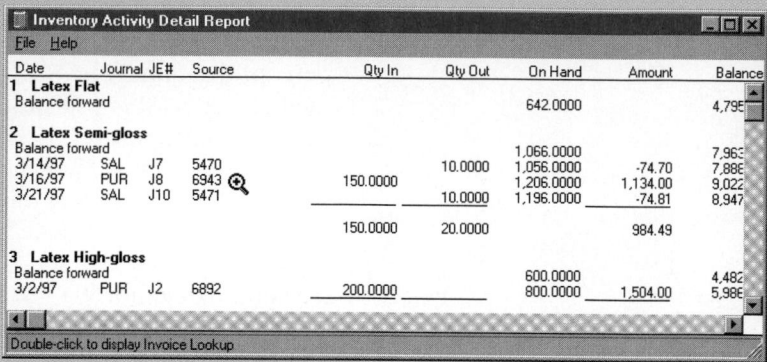

How to Access Invoice Lookup

17. Move the mouse pointer opposite the 3/16/97 purchase of Latex Semi-gloss. The mouse pointer will appear as a magnifying glass and the **Status Bar** will indicate that you can "Double-click to display Invoice Lookup." Double-click with your mouse. Your screen will look like this:

Important Information about Automatic Journal Entry Reversals

18. The program has drilled-down to show the details of this transaction in the Purchases Journal dialog box. In addition to viewing the details of the transaction from this dialog box, you can also use Simply Accounting's automatic reversing feature for incorrect journal entries from this dialog box. Instead of using the procedures described in Part C of the Computerized Accounting appendix for correcting a posted transaction, certain types of journal entries can be reversed automatically by drilling-down to the detail of the journal entry and deleting the entry. This feature is available for reversing purchase and sales invoices and is especially useful for companies that use a perpetual inventory system because the program automatically updates the inventory item records for the reversal. If you find an error in a purchases or sales journal entry you can reverse the entry by drilling-down to the invoice and removing each detail line on the invoice. The program will automatically create and post the reversing entry, inserting the letters ADJ in front of the original invoice number. The accounting records will be in the same position as if the original transaction had not been posted in the first place, but a complete record of the original entry and the reversing entry will appear in the journal you are working with and in the General Journal. You can then re-enter the journal entry correctly.

	19. Let's try it! We are going to assume that the purchase of 150 gallons of Latex Semi-gloss at $7.56 per gallon from Wholesale Paints on March 16 was recorded incorrectly. The price should be $7.65 per gallon. Click on the Purchase menu in the Purchases Journal-Invoice Lookup window; then click on Adjust Invoice. Click on the **Description** of the item; click on the Edit menu in the Purchases Journal-Adjust Invoice window; then click on Remove Line. Click on the **Yes** button in response to the question, "Are you sure you want to delete the item?"

20. Click on the **Post** icon; then click on the **Yes** button in response to the statement, "Are you sure you want to reverse this invoice? All original inventory quantities will be reversed, new quantities on the invoice will not be recorded; you must use the Adjustments journal to record the new quantities."

21. A blank Purchases Journal dialog box will appear. Enter and post the following transaction:

March   16   Received invoice no. 6943 from Wholesale Paints in the amount of $1,147.50 for the purchase of 150 gallons of Latex Semi-gloss (Item #2) at 7.65 per gallon (don't forget to change the **Price!**), terms 2/10, n/30.

22. Close the Purchases Journal dialog box. Click on the Company Window Reports menu; point to Inventory; then click on Inventory Activity. The Inventory Activity Detail Report will appear showing the reversed and correct entry. Note that the program did not adjust the sale on 3/21/97 to reflect the new weighted-average cost for the Latex Semi-gloss inventory item. To update the accounting records to reflect the correct weighted-average cost for this sale you need to reverse the sale and re-record the sale.

23. Move the mouse pointer opposite the 3/21/97 sale of Latex Semi-gloss. The mouse pointer will appear as a magnifying glass and the **Status Bar** will indicate that you can "Double-click to display Invoice Lookup." Double-click with your mouse. The program has drilled-down to show the details of this transaction in the Sales Journal dialog box.

24. Click on the Invoice menu in the Sales Journal-Invoice Lookup window; then click on Adjust Invoice. Click on the **Description** of the item; click on the Edit menu in the Sales Journal-Adjust Invoice window; then click on Remove Line. Click on the **Yes** button in response to the question, "Are you sure you want to delete the item?"

25. Click on the **Post** icon; then click on the **Yes** button in response to the statement, "Are you sure you want to reverse this invoice? All original inventory quantities will be reversed, new quantities on the invoice will not be recorded; you must use the Adjustments journal to record the new quantities."

26. A blank Sales Journal dialog box will appear. Enter and post the following transaction:

March   21   Sold 10 gallons of Latex Semi-gloss (Item #2) at $16.95 per gallon to Jake Kerns on account, $169.50, invoice no. 5471, terms 2/10, n/30.

27. Close the Sales Journal dialog box. Click on the Company Window Reports menu; point to Inventory; then click on Inventory Activity. The Inventory Activity Detail Report will appear showing the two entries that you have reversed and corrected. The sale on 3/21/97 to Jake Kerns will reflect the correct weighted-average cost amount based on the corrected purchase from Wholesale Paints. Click on the Inventory Activity Detail Report File menu; then click on Print to print the report. Close the Inventory Activity Detail Report window.

28. Click on the Company Window Reports menu; point to Inventory; then click on Inventory in the final menu presented. Click on the **Select All** button; leave the **Select Assets** and **Synopsis** option buttons checked; then click on the **OK** button. Your screen will look like the one at the top of page 602.

Learning Objectives	◆ Calculating the cost of an asset. (p. 604) ◆ Calculating depreciation using one of four methods: straight-line, declining-balance, units-of-production, and sum-of-the-years'-digits. (p. 606) ◆ Calculating depreciation for tax purposes using the Modified Accelerated Cost Recovery System. (p. 610) ◆ Explaining the difference between capital expenditures and revenue expenditures. (p. 613) ◆ Journalizing entries for discarding, selling, or exchanging plant assets. (p. 615) ◆ Explaining amortization and how it applies to intangible assets. (p. 621)

In Chapter 13 we classified assets as either current or plant and equipment. Current assets are those that are used up in a company's operations or converted into cash within one year or one accounting cycle, whichever is longer. Long-term assets, such as plant and equipment, provide benefits to a company for more than one year or one accounting cycle. Types of long-term assets include property (such as land), plant (such as buildings), and equipment (such as trucks and tools). There is another classification of assets called **intangible assets.** These are rights owned by a business that do not involve a *physical* object. Examples are patents or franchises. Intangible assets are also considered long-term assets.

In this chapter we will look at how to calculate a long-term asset's overall cost and its depreciation (depreciation being the allocation of the cost of the asset over its lifetime). We will also show how to record expenditures involved in improving or repairing an asset, and how to account for the disposal of these assets.

LEARNING UNIT 17-1
Cost of Property, Plant, and Equipment

The cost of property, plant, and equipment is not just the price one pays to buy it. One must also include the cost involved in getting it into position and in condition for use in the company. Thus the cost of a machine includes freight, assembly, and all other costs that are needed to get the machine up and ready to run.

For example, Smith ordered a machine with a list price of $20,000 with terms of 3/10, n/30. There was a freight charge of $1,500 to cover transportation to the railroad station. Smith had to pay $250 to transport the machine from the railroad station to corporate headquarters. Total costs of assembling and installation amounted to $700. In addition Smith purchased a special concrete foundation to keep the machine from tilting when operational for $900. The life of the machine is expected to be 15 years.

HOW SMITH CALCULATES COST OF MACHINE
List price	$20,000
Less: Cash discount (.03 × $20,000)	600
Net purchase price	19,400
Freight	1,500
Transportation from railroad station	250
Assembly and installation	700
Special foundation	900
Total cost of machine	$22,750

Note that cash discount is deducted in arriving at total cost of machine. If sales tax were involved, it too would be added to the cost of the asset.

Cost of machine will be matched with revenue.	Entries to record freight, assembly, installation, etc., would be made as a debit to the Machinery account and as a credit to Cash.

The $22,750 cost of the asset will be spread over the years the machine helps Smith produce revenue. This is an example of the matching principle. But notice that all these additional costs were reasonable and necessary to get the machine *ready for use*. If the buyer causes negligence, illegal acts, or gross inefficiencies to occur, these would be charged to an expense and not to the cost of the asset.

Let's look now at how to record the cost of land.

LAND AND LAND IMPROVEMENTS |
| **Land does not depreciate, since it has an unlimited life.** | When land (which has unlimited useful life) is purchased, there are usually many incidental costs that are considered part of the *cost* of the land. These would include surveying, commissions to attorneys and real estate brokers, title searches, grading, draining, and clearing the property. If there is a special one-time assessment made for paving a street or installing sewers, it should be charged to cost of land, since it adds "permanent value" to the land.

Now let's look at some items related to land that will not be added to cost of land. **Land Improvements** is an asset account that records improvements to land that have a *limited* useful life. Some examples could include driveways, fences, shrubbery, paving of parking lots, and sprinkler systems. These are improvements subject to depreciation, and thus we need an account that is kept separate from the Land account, which does *not* depreciate.

BUILDINGS

The cost of buying a building would include the purchase price and all the cost of repairs and other expenses to get the building *ready for use*. For construction of a new building, the cost would include all reasonable and necessary payments for labor, insurance, building permits, architect's fees, legal fees, and so on, to get the building ready for use.

If a building and land are purchased for one lump-sum payment, the cost must be separated (allocated) for each, since land will not depreciate, but buildings will. |

LEARNING UNIT 17-1 REVIEW

AT THIS POINT you should be able to

◆ Explain how to classify property, plant, and equipment. (p. 604)
◆ Calculate the cost of an asset. (p. 604)
◆ Explain the difference between land and land improvements. (p. 605)

SELF-REVIEW QUIZ 17-1

(The forms you need are on page 30 of the *Study Guide and Working Papers*.)
Answer true or false to the following:

1. Land does not depreciate.
2. Total cost of acquiring an asset cannot include cost of freight.
3. Land improvements are not subject to depreciation.
4. A cash discount is added to list price.
5. Sales tax is added to cost of asset.

Solution to Self-Review Quiz 17-1

1. T **2.** F **3.** F **4.** F **5.** T

LEARNING UNIT 17-2
Depreciation Methods

Now that students know which long-term assets are depreciable, let's look at different methods for computing depreciation. If you want to check any of the concepts of depreciation we discussed in Chapter 4, take a moment to refer back to page 122.

When a company calculates its periodic depreciation expense, different methods will produce significantly different results. Thus the method of depreciation chosen will affect the net income for current as well as future periods, as well as the **book value** (cost of asset less accumulated depreciation) of the asset on the balance sheet.

Let's assume that Melvin Company purchased a truck on January 1, 19XX, for $20,000, with a **residual value (salvage value)** of $2,000 and an estimated life of five years. The following are the four common depreciation methods that Melvin Company could use:

Think of residual value as trade-in value at end of estimated life.

1. Straight-line method.
2. Units-of-production method.
3. Sum-of-the-years'-digits method.
4. Double declining-balance method.

STRAIGHT-LINE METHOD

The **straight-line method** is simple to use, because it allocates the cost of the asset (less residual value) evenly over its estimated useful life. (At the time an asset is acquired, an estimate is made of its usefulness or **useful life** in terms of number of years it would last, amount of output expected, etc.) Let's look at how Melvin Company calculates its depreciation expense for each of the estimated five years of usefulness using the straight-line method. Take a moment to read the key points in the parentheses below the accompanying table.

The formula:

$$\frac{\text{cost} - \text{residual value}}{\text{service useful life in years}} = \frac{\$20,000 - \$2,000}{5} = \$3,600$$

End of Year	Cost of Delivery Truck	Yearly* Depreciation Expense	Accumulated Depreciation, End of Year	Book Value, End of Year (Cost − Accum. Dep.)
1	$20,000	$3,600	$ 3,600	$16,400
2	20,000	3,600	7,200	12,800
3	20,000	3,600	10,800	9,200
4	20,000	3,600	14,400	5,600
5	20,000	3,600	18,000	2,000
	↑	↑	↑	↑
	(Cost of machine doesn't change)	(Note that depreciation expense is the same each year)	(Accumulated depreciation increases by $3,600 each year)	(Book value each year is lowered by $3,600 until residual value of $2,000 is reached)

* The depreciation rate is 100 percent ÷ 5 years = 20 percent. The 20 percent is then multiplied times the cost minus the residual value.

UNITS-OF-PRODUCTION METHOD

Depreciation expense is directly related to use, not to passage of time.

With the **units-of-production method** it is assumed that *passage of time* does not determine the amount of depreciation taken. Depreciation expense is based on *use*, be it total estimated miles, tons hauled, or estimated units of production — for example, the number of shoes a machine could produce in its expected useful life. The accompanying table shows the calculations that Melvin Company makes for its truck using the units-of-production method (note that for this example the truck is assumed to have an estimated life of 90,000 miles).

The formula:

$$\frac{cost - residual\ value}{estimated\ units\ of\ production} = \frac{\$20,000 - \$2,000}{90,000\ miles} = \$.20\ per\ mile$$

$$(\$.20) \times (number\ of\ miles\ driven) = Depreciation\ expense\ for\ period$$

End of Year	Cost of Delivery Truck	Miles Driven In Year	Yearly Depreciation Expense	Accumulated Depreciation, End of Year	Book Value, End of Year (Cost − Accum. Dep.)
1	$20,000	30,000	$6,000	$ 6,000	$14,000
2	20,000	21,000	4,200	10,200	9,800
3	20,000	15,000	3,000	13,200	6,800
4	20,000	5,000	1,000	14,200	5,800
5	20,000	19,000	3,800	18,000	2,000
		↑ (After 5 years, truck has been driven 90,000 miles)	↑ (Depreciation expense is directly related to number of miles driven)		↑ (Residual value of $2,000 is reached)

SUM-OF-THE-YEARS'-DIGITS METHOD

The **sum-of-the-years'-digits method** places more depreciation expense in the early years rather than in the later years in order to better match revenue and expenses, since an asset's productivity may be reduced in later years. For this reason, it is called an **accelerated depreciation** method. To use it, you multiply cost minus residual times a certain fraction. This fraction is made up of the following:

1. *The denominator.* The denominator is based on how many years the asset is likely to last (say 5). You then add the sum of the digits of five years (1 + 2 + 3 + 4 + 5), which equals 15; 15 is the denominator. [There is also a formula to use for the denominator: $N(N + 1)/2$, where N stands for number of years of useful life (in our case, five years). In our case the formula would look like this: $5(5 + 1)/2 = 15$.]

2. *The numerator.* The years in reverse order are the numerator (in our case, 5, 4, 3, 2, 1).

Thus in year 1 the fraction would be $\frac{5}{15}$; in year 2, $\frac{4}{15}$; in year 3, $\frac{3}{15}$; in year 4, $\frac{2}{15}$; in year 1, $\frac{1}{15}$. And in each year you would multiply this fraction times cost minus residual to find the depreciation expense. This is shown in the table on page 608.

End of Year	$\begin{pmatrix} \text{Cost} \\ \text{Minus} \\ \text{Residual} \end{pmatrix} \times \begin{pmatrix} \text{Fraction} \\ \text{for Year} \end{pmatrix} =$	Yearly Depreciation Expense	Accumulated Depreciation, End of Year	Book Value, End of Year (Cost − Accum. Dep.)
1	$\$18,000 \times \dfrac{5}{15}$ (20,000 − 2,000)	= $6,000	$ 6,000	$14,000 ($20,000 − $6,000)
2	$18,000 \times \dfrac{4}{15}$	= 4,800	10,800	9,200
3	$18,000 \times \dfrac{3}{15}$	= 3,600	14,400	5,600
4	$18,000 \times \dfrac{2}{15}$	= 2,400	16,800	3,200
5	$18,000 \times \dfrac{1}{15}$	= 1,200	18,000	2,000
	↑ (Fraction for year is multiplied times cost minus residual)	↑ (Depreciation expense in first year is highest)	↑ (Each year depreciation accumulates by a smaller amount)	↑ (Book value goes down each year until residual is reached)

Take a moment to make sure you see how the figures for these calculations are arrived at before moving on to the next method.

DOUBLE DECLINING-BALANCE METHOD

The **double declining-balance method** is also an accelerated method, in which a larger depreciation expense is taken in earlier years and smaller amounts in later years. This method depreciates at twice the straight-line rate, which is why it is called the *double* declining-balance method.

A key point in this method is that *residual value* is *not* deducted from cost in the calculations, although the asset cannot be depreciated below its residual value. To calculate depreciation, take the following steps:

1. Calculate the straight-line rate and double it:

$$\frac{100\%}{\text{useful life}} \times 2$$

2. At the *end of each year* multiply the rate times the book value of the asset at the beginning of the year.

Let's look at how Melvin Company calculates the depreciation on its truck (top of p. 609) using this method.

Be sure to note the $592 in year 5 of depreciation expense. We could not take more than the $592, or we would have depreciated the asset below the residual value.

Now let's look at how Melvin Company could handle depreciation calculations for partial years (if it bought a truck on May 4).

DEPRECIATION FOR PARTIAL YEARS

When depreciating for partial years we assume that for any asset purchased before the 15th of the month, depreciation is calculated for a full month. After the 15th of the month, the depreciation is disregarded for the month.

Note rate of .40 is not changed (20% × 2)

End of Year	Cost	Accumulated Depreciation Beg. of Year	Book Value Beg. of Year (Cost − Acc. Dep.)	Dep. Exp. (B.V. Beg. of Year × Rate)	Accumulated Depreciation, End of Year	Book Value, End of Year (Cost − Acc. Dep.)
1	$20,000		$20,000	$8,000 ($20,000 × .40)	$ 8,000	$12,000 (20,000 − 8,000)
2	20,000	$ 8,000	12,000	4,800 (12,000 × .40)	12,800 (8,000 + 4,800)	7,200
3	20,000	12,800	7,200	2,880 (7,200 × .40)	15,680	4,320
4	20,000	15,680	4,320	1,728 (4,320 × .40)	17,408	2,592
5	20,000	17,408	2,592	592	18,000	2,000
	↑ (Original cost remains the same)			↑ (Depreciation is limited to $592, since the asset cannot depreciate below the residual value)		↑ (The book value now equals the residual value)

Straight-Line

Original calculation on p. 606.

For Melvin Company, if the truck was purchased on May 4, depreciation expense would be calculated as follows:

$$\frac{\$20,000 - \$2,000}{5 \text{ years}} \times \frac{8}{12} = \$2,400$$

We use 8 since the truck was bought on May 4. Do not count the first four months of the year in the calculation of depreciation. The following year the full yearly depreciation would be taken.

Units-of-Production

This method would not be affected, since depreciation is based on usage, not passage of time.

Sum-of-the-Years'-Digits

Original calculation on p. 607.

If the truck is bought on May 4, Melvin would receive benefits of eight months of $4,000 ($18,000 × $\frac{5}{15}$) × $\frac{8}{12}$. In the following year Melvin would assume benefits of the last four months of the first year and the first eight months of the second year. Let's look at the calculation for year 2:

$$\text{year 2} = (\$18,000 \times \tfrac{5}{15}) \times \tfrac{4}{12} + (18,000 \times \tfrac{4}{15}) \times \tfrac{8}{12}$$

↑ Depreciation completed from old year first

Double Declining-Balance

Original calculation on p. 608.

Since Melvin has the benefit of the truck for eight months, his depreciation on year 1 would be

$$(\$20,000 \times .40) \times \tfrac{8}{12}$$

In year 2 and in future years the annual rate of 40 percent is multiplied times the *current* book value. In this method there is no need to apportion the months as we did in sum-of-the-years'-digits, because we are using current book value.

DEPRECIATION FOR TAX PURPOSES—MACRS (MODIFIED ACCELERATED COST RECOVERY SYSTEM), INCLUDING THE TAX ACT OF 1989

The 1986 tax act generally overhauled the depreciation setup of property placed in service after December 31, 1986. This **Modified Accelerated Cost Recovery System** is known as MACRS.* Previous methods we have discussed have been for financial reporting. They have not been for tax purposes. This tax law requires a business to depreciate assets placed in service after December 31, 1986. To do this, two factors must be known:

1. Recovery classification

2. MACRS depreciation rates

Look for a moment at Figure 17-1.

According to the 1986 act, classes 3, 5, 7, and 10 use 200 percent declining-balance, switching to straight-line, while classes 15 and 20 use 150 percent declining-balance, switching to straight-line. Both residential and nonresidential real property must use straight-line. Note that the recovery period is $27\frac{1}{2}$ years for residential property and $31\frac{1}{2}$ years for nonresidential property.

Let's use Table 17-1 to calculate depreciation on the purchase of a nonluxury car for $5,000 on March 19, 1990.

---

* Has been renamed the General Depreciation System (GDS).

FIGURE 17-1
Summary of Classes for the Tax Reform Act of 1986

The following classes use a 200 percent declining-balance, switching to straight-line:

◆ 3-year: Race horses more than two years old or any horse other than a race horse that is more than 12 years old at time placed into service; special tools of certain industries.

◆ 5-year: Automobiles (not luxury); taxis; light general-purpose trucks, semiconductor manufacturing equipment; computer-based telephone central office switching equipment; qualified technological equipment; property used in connection with research and experimentation:

◆ 7-year: Railroad track; single-purpose agricultural (pigpens) or horticultural structure; fixtures, equipment, and furniture.

◆ 10-year: The 1986 law doesn't add any specific property under this class.

The following classes use a 150 percent declining-balance, switching to straight-line:

◆ 15-year: Municipal wastewater treatment plants; telephone distribution plants and comparable equipment used for two-way exchange of voice and data communications.

◆ 20-year: Municipal sewers.

The following classes use straight-line:

◆ 27.5-year: Only residential rental property.

◆ 31.5-year: Only nonresidential real property.

Note that auto is now a five-year class.

TABLE 17-1 ANNUAL RECOVERY (PERCENT OF ORIGINAL DEPRECIABLE BASIS)

Recovery Year	3-Year Class (200% D.B.)	5-Year Class (200% D.B.)	7-Year Class (200% D.B.)	10-Year Class (200% D.B.)	15-Year Class (150% D.B.)	20-Year Class (150% D.B.)
1	33.00	20.00	14.28	10.00	5.00	3.75
2	45.00	32.00	24.49	18.00	9.50	7.22
3	15.00*	19.20	17.49	14.40	8.55	6.68
4	7.00	11.52*	12.49	11.52	7.69	6.18
5		11.52	8.93*	9.22	6.93	5.71
6		5.76	8.93	7.37	6.23	5.28
7			8.93	6.55*	5.90*	4.89
8			4.46	6.55	5.90	4.52
9				6.55	5.90	4.46*
10				6.55	5.90	4.46
11				3.29	5.90	4.46
12					5.90	4.46
13					5.90	4.46
14					5.90	4.46
15					5.90	4.46
16					3.00	4.46
17						

* Identifies when switch is made to straight-line.

When we use this table, we do not have to decide which year we should switch from declining-balance to straight-line.

YEAR	DEPRECIATION
1	.20 × $5,000 = $1,000
2	.32 × $5,000 = 1,600
3	.1920 × $5,000 = 960
4	.1152 × $5,000 = 576
5	.1152 × $5,000 = 576
6	.0576 × $5,000 = 288

THE TAX ACT OF 1989

In 1989 the Omnibus Budget Reconciliation Act was passed. One section of the act dealt with depreciation of cellular phones and similar equipment under MACRS. Since cellular phones are subject to personal use, the tax act now treats them as listed property. This means that unless business use is greater than 50 percent, the straight-line method of depreciation is required.

LEARNING UNIT 17-2 REVIEW

AT THIS POINT you should be able to

◆ Explain and calculate the four methods of depreciation. (pp. 606–608)
◆ Calculate depreciation for partial years. (pp. 608–609)
◆ Explain and calculate depreciation for MACRS. (pp. 610–611)

SELF-REVIEW QUIZ 17-2

(The forms you need are on pages 30 and 31 of the *Study Guide and Working Papers.*)

From the following facts complete depreciation schedules for the **a.** straight-line; **b.** units-of-production; **c.** sum-of-the-years'-digits; and **d.** declining-balance methods.

Cost of equipment	$40,000
Residual value	7,000
Service life	5 years
Estimated units of output	20,000
Units produced in year 1:	8,000
2:	2,000
3:	5,000
4:	2,800
5:	2,200

Remember: Residual value is not subtracted in declining-balance, although the equipment cannot be depreciated below residual value.

Solution to Self-Review Quiz 17-2

a.

End of Year	Cost of Equipment	Yearly Depreciation Expense	Accumulated Depreciation, End of Year	Book Value, End of Year (Cost − Acc. Dep.)
1	$40,000	$6,600	$ 6,600	$33,400 ($40,000 − $6,600)
2	40,000	6,600	13,200	26,800
3	40,000	6,600	19,800	20,200
4	40,000	6,600	26,400	13,600
5	40,000	6,600	33,000	7,000 ◄— Book value now equals residual

value

b.

$$\frac{\$40,000 - \$7,000}{20,000 \text{ units}} = \$1.65$$

End of Year	Cost of Equipment	Units of Output in Year	Yearly Depreciation Expense	Accumulated Depreciation, End of Year	Book Value, End of Year
1	$40,000	8,000	$13,200 (8,000 × $1.65)	$13,200	$26,800
2	40,000	2,000	3,300	16,500	23,500
3	40,000	5,000	8,250	24,750	15,250
4	40,000	2,800	4,620	29,370	10,630
5	40,000	2,200	3,630	33,000	7,000

c.

End of Year	Cost Less Residual × Rate = Yearly Depreciation Expense	Accumulated Depreciation, End of Year	Book Value End of Year
1	$33,000 \times \dfrac{5}{15} = \$11,000$	$11,000	$29,000
			($40,000 − $11,000)
2	$33,000 \times \dfrac{4}{15} = 8,800$	19,800	20,200
3	$33,000 \times \dfrac{3}{15} = 6,600$	26,400	13,600
4	$33,000 \times \dfrac{2}{15} = 4,400$	30,800	9,200
5	$33,000 \times \dfrac{1}{15} = 2,200$	33,000	7,000

d.

End of Year	Cost	Accumulated Depreciation, Beg. of Year	Book Value Beg. of Year (Cost − Acc. Dep.)	Dep. Exp. (B.V. Beg. of Year × Rate)	Acc. Dep., End of Year	Book Value, End of Year (Cost − Acc. Dep.)
1	$40,000	—	$40,000	$16,000 ($40,000 × .40)	$16,000	$24,000 ($40,000 − $16,000)
2	40,000	$16,000	24,000	9,600 ($24,000 × .40)	25,600	14,400 ($40,000 − $25,600)
3	40,000	25,600	14,400	5,760	31,360	8,640
4	40,000	31,360	8,640	1,640	33,000	7,000

Only $1,640 could be taken so that book value would not go below residual value.

Rate is 40 percent

$$\dfrac{100\%}{5 \text{ yr}} = \dfrac{1.00}{5}$$

$$= .20 = 20\%$$

$$2 \times 20\% = 40\%$$

LEARNING UNIT 17-3
Capital and Revenue Expenditures and Disposal of Plant Assets

Now that we have seen depreciation calculations, let's look at capital and revenue expenditures and the disposal of plant assets.

CAPITAL EXPENDITURES

Capital expenditures include the original cost of an asset as well as payments that improve on or enlarge existing assets. Capital expenditures may be broken down into three categories: additions or enlargements; extraordinary repairs; and betterments. The differences among these three categories are based on whether or not the change will add to the value of the asset, extend the life of the asset, or only improve its efficiency. For example, adding a new wing to a school building will increase the value of the asset, so it is categorized as an **addition or enlargement.** Overhauling an aircraft engine definitely extends the life of the asset, so it is categorized as an **extraordinary repair.** Adding a CB radio to a fleet of delivery trucks improves the efficiency of the asset but does not extend its life, so it is categorized as a **betterment.** These three categories are shown in the chart in Figure 17-2.

It may be a little difficult at first to see the difference between betterments and extraordinary repairs. Betterments do not extend the life of the asset: the cost of a betterment is debited to the asset account. Extraordinary repairs do extend the life of the asset. The result of the extraordinary repair is to cancel some of the past depreciation.

The following is an example of how to analyze and record an extraordinary repair to a machine whose cost is $20,000, has no residual value, and has an estimated life of ten years.

Additions or enlargements and betterments are charged to the asset account.

Machine	Accumulated Depreciation, Machine
20,000	16,000 (after 8 years)

Note that after eight years the book value of the machine is $4,000 ($20,000 − $16,000). On March 30, a major overhaul of the machine is completed for $3,000. It is believed that this overhaul will extend the machine's life by three years. Thus the journal entry to record this extraordinary repair is as follows:

March	30	Accumulated Depreciation, Machine	3 0 0 0 00		
		Cash		3 0 0 0 00	
		To record extraordinary repair.			

Since the machine's life is extended by three years, there are now five years of depreciation to be taken. The new annual depreciation of $1,400 (instead of $1,000) is calculated on the next page.

FIGURE 17-2 Three Categories of Capital Expenditures

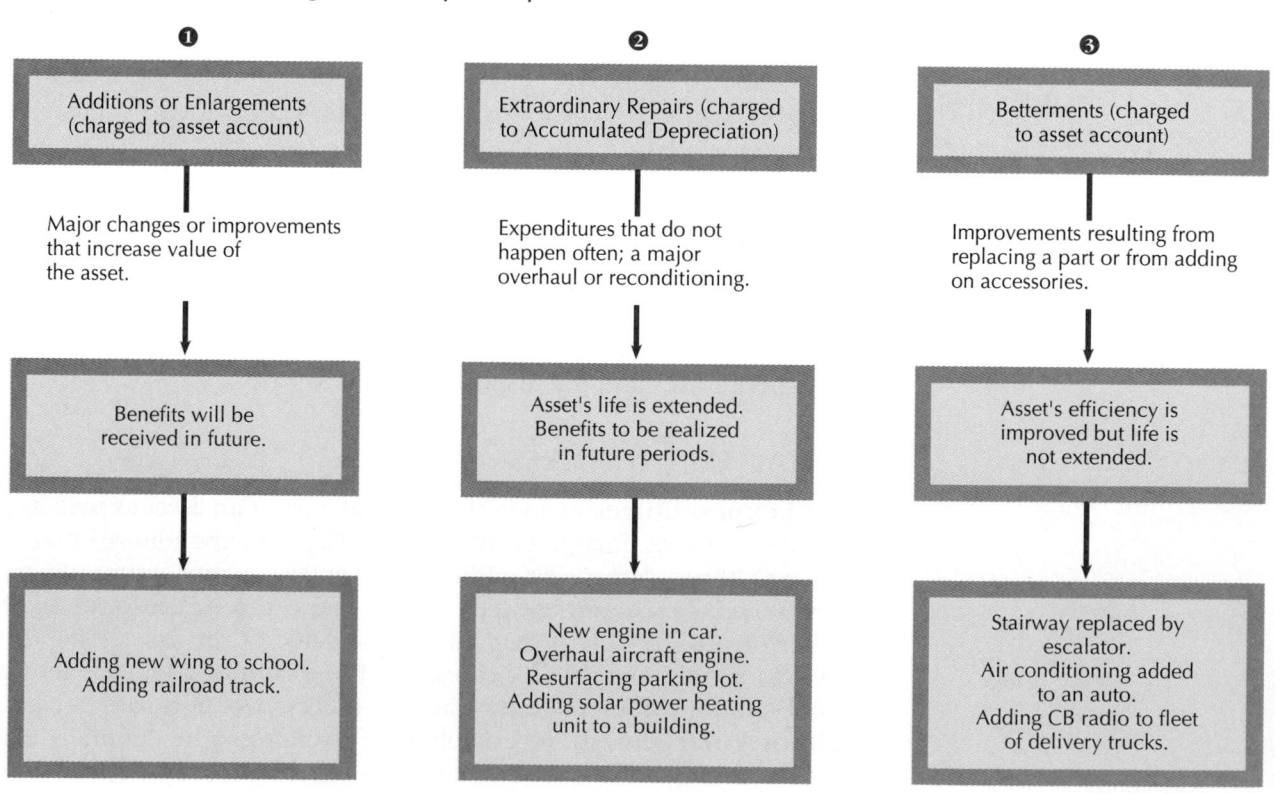

❶ Additions or Enlargements (charged to asset account)

Major changes or improvements that increase value of the asset.

Benefits will be received in future.

Adding new wing to school. Adding railroad track.

❷ Extraordinary Repairs (charged to Accumulated Depreciation)

Expenditures that do not happen often; a major overhaul or reconditioning.

Asset's life is extended. Benefits to be realized in future periods.

New engine in car. Overhaul aircraft engine. Resurfacing parking lot. Adding solar power heating unit to a building.

❸ Betterments (charged to asset account)

Improvements resulting from replacing a part or from adding on accessories.

Asset's efficiency is improved but life is not extended.

Stairway replaced by escalator. Air conditioning added to an auto. Adding CB radio to fleet of delivery trucks.

	Book value before extraordinary repair	$4,000
	Extraordinary repair	3,000
	New book value	$7,000 ÷ 5 years = $1,400 per year

If there were an estimated residual value, it would be subtracted from the new book value.

REVENUE EXPENDITURES

Another type of expenditure occurs after an asset has been acquired. *Revenue expenditures* are payments made for ordinary maintenance of an asset or unnecessary or unreasonable situations. These expenditures occur on a regular basis and are recorded as expenses. Examples would include changing oil and greasing a car, replacing window panes, changing tires on a truck, repainting a car, adding a sun roof, etc. When an expenditure is treated as a revenue expenditure, it is recorded on the income statement as an expense and thus reduces net income in the period in which it occurred. Now let's turn our attention to the disposal of certain plant assets.

DISPOSAL OF PLANT ASSETS

We will now move on to the basic accounting procedures followed when disposing of plant assets in the following ways:

a. Discarding plant assets.
b. Selling plant assets.
c. Exchanging for similar plant assets.

We will present a different example for each category (A, B, or C). It is important to remember that depreciation is recorded up until the date a plant asset is disposed of. Take time to compare journal entries to T accounts in each example.

A. Disposal by Discarding Plant Assets

A company discards a plant asset when it is no longer operational—for example, machinery or a truck that no longer works. This also means that no other company is willing to buy or exchange something for the asset.

Situation 1: No Gain or Loss. Boulder Company is disposing of a $7,000 truck with no residual value that has been fully depreciated (remember, it is possible to keep using a fully depreciated asset, but in this case the asset—the truck—is no longer in working order). Since the asset has been fully depreciated, there will be no need to bring any depreciation up to date before getting rid of it.

The following journal entry is made after disposing of the truck:

Accumulated Depreciation, Truck			7 0 0 0 00	
Truck				7 0 0 0 00

Here is how the ledger for these accounts would look after posting:

Truck		Accumulated Depreciation, Truck	
7,000	7,000	7,000	7,000

Therefore, the truck and the accumulated depreciation associated with it are off our books. Note that there was no gain or loss here.

Situation 2: Loss on Disposal. Moore Company disposed of a partially depreciated truck. The truck costing $6,000 was considered worthless (depreciation of $5,000 to date). Because we are receiving nothing for this asset that has a book value of $1,000, the difference between the cost of the truck and the accumulated depreciation is a loss. The Loss on Disposal account is categorized as Other Expense on the income statement. Let's look at the journal entry for this loss on disposal and see how the ledger would look after posting.

Loss on Disposal of Plant Asset	1 0 0 0 00	
Accumulated Depreciation, Truck	5 0 0 0 00	
Truck		6 0 0 0 00

Truck	Accumulated Depreciation, Truck	Loss on Disposal of Plant Asset
6,000 | 6,000	5,000 | 5,000	1,000 |

Situation 3: Loss from Fire. Missan Company received a check for $500 from an insurance company, settling a claim on a machine costing $1,500 that was damaged by fire before the end of its useful life. There was a balance in Accumulated Depreciation of $900. The following is the journal entry Missan Company records when it receives the $500 check:

Cash	5 0 0 00	
Loss from Fire	1 0 0 00	
Accumulated Depreciation, Machinery	9 0 0 00	
Machinery		1 5 0 0 00

There is a loss from the fire of $100; the book value of the machine was $600 ($1,500 − $900), and the amount received from the insurance company was $500.

Here is how the ledger would look after posting:

Machinery	Accumulated Depreciation, Machinery	Loss from Fire
1,500 | 1,500	900 | 900	100 |

Now our attention turns to situations when assets could be sold rather than discarded.

B. Disposal by Selling Plant Assets

Situation 4: Gain on Sale. Mason Company sold a truck costing $7,000 for $1,500 cash. The balance in Accumulated Depreciation is $6,000.

To see whether this sale results in a gain or loss, Mason Company must calculate whether the amount of cash received is greater or less than the book value of the truck. If the amount received is greater than the book value, there is a gain. A gain on the sale of a plant asset is categorized as Other Income on the income statement. Let's look at the calculation:

Cost of truck	$7,000	Amount received	$1,500
Less accumulated depreciation	6,000	Less book value	1,000
Book value	$1,000	Gain on sale	$ 500

Since there is a gain on the sale, the following journal entry is made:

Cash	1500 00	
Accumulated Depreciation, Truck	6000 00	
Truck		7000 00
Gain on Sale of Plant Asset		500 00

Here is what the ledger would look like after posting:

Truck			Accumulated Depreciation, Truck	
7,000	7,000		6,000	6,000

Gain on Sale of Plant Asset	
	500

Situation 5: Loss on Sale. Let's assume that in the previous situation Mason Company receives only $900 cash for the truck.

Now let's look at the calculation Mason Company does to see whether there is a loss or gain:

Cost of truck	$7,000
Less accumulated depreciation	− 6,000
Book value	1,000
Amount received	− 900
Loss on sale	$ 100

When price is less than book value, there is a loss. Since Mason's truck has a book value of $1,000 and the cash received is $900, the end result is a loss of $100 on the sale of the plant asset. This is categorized as Other Expense on the income statement. The following is the journal entry prepared by Mason to record this loss:

Cash	900 00	
Accumulated Depreciation, Truck	6000 00	
Loss on Sale of Plant Asset	100 00	
Truck		7000 00

Here is what the ledger would look like after posting:

Truck			Accumulated Depreciation, Truck			Loss on Sale of Plant Asset
7,000	7,000		6,000	6,000		100

The final category of disposal is exchanging a plant asset rather than discarding or selling.

C. Disposal by Exchanging for Similar Plant Assets

Situation 6: Loss on Exchange. VTR Company trades its old machine costing $19,000 for a new one for a cash price of $22,000 less a trade-in allowance of $2,000. Accumulated Depreciation of the old machine has a balance of $16,000. A **trade-in allowance** is given when you are buying a new car, for example, and trade in your old one for a sum of money that is applied to the price of the new car. A loss on exchange will result if the book value of the old machine is greater than what is received for the trade-in allowance. Let's look at how VTR calculates its loss on this machine exchange:

Step 1: Calculate book value of old machine:

Cost	$19,000
− Accumulated Depreciation	16,000
Book Value	$ 3,000

Step 2: Compare book value of old machine with trade-in:

$3,000	B.V. of old
2,000	Trade-in
$1,000	Loss

Since the book value of the old machine is $3,000 and VTR receives only a $2,000 trade-in, the result is a $1,000 loss. The following is the journal entry prepared by VTR:

Machinery	22000 00	
Loss on Exchange of Machinery	1000 00	
Acc. Dep., Machinery	16000 00	
Machinery		19000 00
Cash		20000 00

The entry puts on the books the cost of the new machine as well as recording the loss on the exchange and the removal of the old machine and the related accumulated depreciation. Note that cash is reduced by $20,000 (cash price less trade-in). Here is what the ledger would look like after posting:

Machinery (Old)		Accumulated Depreciation, Machinery	
19,000	19,000	16,000	16,000

Machinery (New)		Loss on Exchange of Machinery	
22,000		1,000	

Situation 7: Gain is Absorbed into Cost of New Machine. The Accounting Principles Board has ruled that when a gain exists on an exchange of a similar asset it should not be recorded as a gain, but the new asset should be equal to the book value of the old asset plus cash given in the exchange. In other words, no account called Gain is used, *but the actual gain is absorbed into the cost of the new machine.* The reason behind this decision was that an exchange of similar assets is not the result of an earnings process. In this situation we assume that VTR (situation 6) will receive a $5,000 trade-in allowance (instead of the $2,000) for trading in an old machine for a new machine for a cash price of $22,000. VTR will complete the following steps to calculate the new cost of the machine (assuming a gain). Remember that a

gain would be absorbed into the cost of the new machine for exchanges of similar assets.

1. Calculate book value of old machine.
2. Identify cash paid (cash price less trade-in).
3. Calculate the value of the new machine as it will show up on the books. (This is called the cash basis of the machine.) This is done by adding steps 1 and 2.

Let's now look at VTR's actual calculation of these steps:

Step 1: Calculate book value of old machine:

$$\begin{array}{r} \$19,000 \\ -\ \underline{16,000} \\ =\ \$\ 3,000 \end{array}$$

Step 2: Identify cash paid:

$$\$17,000\ (\$22,000 - \$5,000)$$

Step 3: New cash basis (step 1 + step 2):

$$\$20,000\ (\$3,000 + \$17,000)$$

Note that the cash basis is $20,000, not $22,000 as stated as original cost of new equipment. Note also that the new machine shows up on the books at the value of the things that were given up for it: an old machine with a book value of $3,000 and cash of $17,000.

Now let's look at how VTR records this exchange on its books:

Machinery	20000 00	
Accumulated Depreciation, Machinery	16000 00	
Machinery		19000 00
Cash		17000 00

Note that there is no account that records the gain. The gain is absorbed into the cost of the new asset. Remember that a gain results in *less* depreciation in the future, since the cost of the machine has a value of $20,000, not $22,000. The ledger when posted would look as follows:

Machinery (Old)		Accumulated Depreciation, Machinery	
19,000	19,000		16,000	16,000

Machinery (New)	
20,000	

Income tax rules agree with accountants regarding nonrecognition of gains and absorbing them into cost of new asset (situation 7). The Internal Revenue Service also believes losses should not be recognized and thus should be absorbed into cost of new assets.* Often two sets of records are kept. Situation 6 followed guidelines of the Accounting Principles Board. Situation 8 follows tax rules of the Internal Revenue Service. Compare the two.

Situation 8: Loss Is Absorbed in Cost of New Asset. Let's assume that VTR receives only a $2,000 trade-in allowance instead of $5,000 (situation 7) when the old machine is traded in for the new machine for a cash price of $22,000. VTR calculates the cost basis of the new machine (assuming it uses the **income tax method** of absorbing losses into the cost of the new machine) as follows:

---

* Accountants will do this only if loss is considered to be immaterial.

Cost of old machine		$19,000																
− Accumulated Depreciation		16,000																
= Book Value		3,000																
+ Cash paid		20,000																
($22,000 − $2,000)																		
= Cost basis of new machine		$23,000																

This loss of $1,000 (VTR having received $1,000 less than the book value) is *added on* to the cost of the new machine, resulting in a cost basis of $23,000. VTR records the exchange in the journal as follows:

Machinery			23 0 0 0 00							
Accumulated Depreciation, Machinery			16 0 0 0 00							
Machinery					19 0 0 0 00	
Cash					20 0 0 0 00	

Note that there is no Loss account. The loss has been absorbed into the cost of the equipment, the result being that more depreciation will be taken in future periods ($23,000 versus $22,000), since the cost of the new equipment is $1,000 higher.

Here is what the ledger would look like after posting:

Machinery (Old)		Accumulated Depreciation, Machinery	
19,000	19,000	16,000	16,000

Machinery (New)	
23,000	

LEARNING UNIT 17-3 REVIEW

AT THIS POINT you should be able to

- ◆ Compare and contrast capital and revenue expenditures. (pp. 613–614)
- ◆ Prepare journal entries to record discarding, selling, or exchanging plant assets. (pp. 615–618)
- ◆ Compare and contrast Internal Revenue procedures with those of the Financial Accounting Principles Board regarding gains and losses that result from exchanges of plant assets. (pp. 618–619)

SELF-REVIEW QUIZ 17-3

(The forms you need are on page 31 of the *Study Guide and Working Papers.*) Respond true or false to the following:

1. In selling a plant asset, a gain results if cash received is greater than the book value of the asset sold.

2. A loss on exchange of equipment can result if the book value of the old equipment is less than the trade-in allowance.

3. The Financial Accounting Principles Board does not recognize gains on exchange of similar assets.

4. Internal Revenue Service rules are consistent with the Financial Accounting Principles Board in recognizing losses when assets are exchanged.

LEARNING UNIT 17-4
Natural Resources and Intangible Assets

There's another type of long-term asset, natural resources, which we haven't discussed yet—it consists of natural assets such as oil, coal, or timber. The acquisition of oil wells or timber is recorded at cost, and as the oil or timber or coal is extracted from the earth, the allocation of that cost occurs through a process known as **depletion**. Depletion is similar to the units-of-production method of depreciation, which we discussed earlier in the chapter, and is listed as an operating expense on the income statement.

Let's take the example of a coal deposit. If a coal deposit has 200,000 tons available and was purchased for $200,000, the depletion per ton is $1. Thus if in 19X1 91,000 tons were removed from the deposit, the depletion charge that year would be recorded as follows:

Accumulated Depletion is a contra-asset on the balance sheet.

	19X1					
	Dec.	31	Depletion of Coal Deposit	91 00 0 00	
			Accumulated Depletion, Coal		91 00 0 00

Coal Deposit		Accumulated Depreciation, Coal	
200,000			91,000
(on balance sheet)		(on balance sheet)	

Depletion of Coal Deposit	
91,000	
(on income statement)	

INTANGIBLE ASSETS

Intangible assets are long-lived assets that have no physical existence but do represent valuable legal rights and monetary relationships that benefit a company. (In fact, Prepaid Insurance, Notes, and Accounts Receivable are intangible, but they are classified as *current* assets.) We are looking at intangible assets classified in the *long-term* asset section. Examples include patents, copyrights, franchises, and goodwill. Intangible assets are recorded at cost on the balance sheet and usually have no contra-accounts.

The process of allocating the cost of an intangible asset over all the periods it provides benefits is called amortization. The expense incurred in acquiring these assets is **amortized**—that means that it is written off over a fixed number of years. **Amortization expense** is an operating expense on the income statement.

Patents

A patent is good for 17 years but is amortized for a shorter period.

A **patent** is an exclusive right to the owner to sell or produce his or her discovery or invention. Let's assume that on Jan. 1, 19XX, a patent costing $100,000 is amortized over ten years. The following adjusting entry is made:

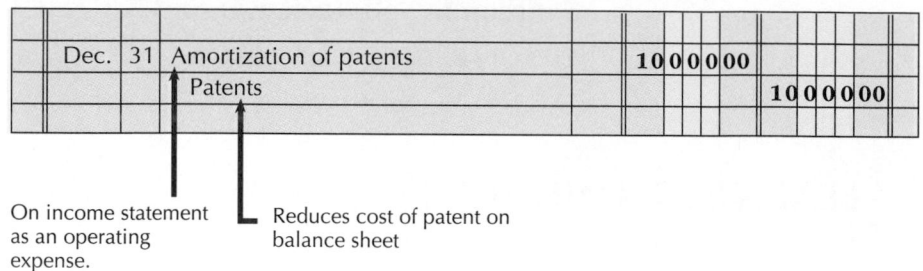

Dec.	31	Amortization of patents		10 0 0 0 00	
		Patents			10 0 0 0 00

On income statement as an operating expense.

Reduces cost of patent on balance sheet

Copyrights

Copyrights are exclusive rights to publish an artistic or literary work granted to owners by the federal government. In the United States a copyright is granted for the life of the creator and for 50 years thereafter. The cost of the copyright is recorded as a cost and amortized over its expected useful life in an account called Amortization Expense, Copyrights.

Franchises

A **franchise** is the result of someone purchasing an exclusive privilege or right to sell a manufacturer's product or a service in a specifically defined geographical location. Holiday Inns, for example, are franchises. The cost of obtaining a franchise is amortized over its life or 40 years, whichever is shorter.

Goodwill

Cost of assets purchased
− Value of assets identified
= Goodwill

When all or part of a business is purchased, the difference between the price paid and the value of the identifiable assets is called **goodwill.** This occurs when the expected rate of future earnings is greater than the rate of earnings for the industry standard. Some considerations that may cause goodwill could include brand names, business location, service, etc. It is not easy to pinpoint the exact amount of goodwill in each accounting period. Thus in the accounting profession it is agreed not to put a cost on goodwill until a company is bought or sold.

LEARNING UNIT 17-4 REVIEW

AT THIS POINT you should be able to

- ◆ Define depletion and accumulated depletion and indicate their normal balances and on which financial reports they are located. (p. 621)
- ◆ Explain amortization. (p. 621)
- ◆ Discuss how a patent is amortized. (p. 622)
- ◆ Explain the life of a copyright. (p. 622)
- ◆ Define and explain how goodwill is calculated. (p. 622)

SELF-REVIEW QUIZ 17-4

(The forms you need are on page 31 of the *Study Guide and Working Papers.*)
Respond true or false to the following:

CH. 17 / ACCOUNTING FOR PROPERTY, PLANT EQUIPMENT, AND INTANGIBLE ASSETS

1. Intangible assets are depleted, not amortized.
2. The life of a patent is 12 years.
3. A copyright lasts for 25 years.
4. The cost of a franchise must be amortized over 40 years.
5. Goodwill represents excess earning power for a company.

Solution to Self-Review Quiz 17-4

1. F   **2.** F   **3.** F   **4.** F   **5.** T

SUMMARY OF KEY POINTS

Learning Unit 17-1

1. Total cost of an asset includes all expenditures that are reasonable and necessary in acquiring it and getting it into position and in condition for use in the company.
2. Cash discounts are deducted from the cost of an asset.
3. Incidental costs related to the purchase of land and special costs that add a permanent value are added to the cost of land.
4. The Land Improvements account records improvements to land that have a limited useful life (such as driveways or fences). This account is subject to depreciation.
5. The cost of buying a building would include purchase price and all cost of repairs and other expenses to get the building ready for use. When constructing a new building, the cost would include all payments necessary to get the building ready for use.

Learning Unit 17-2

In this unit we look at four different depreciation methods.

1. Straight-line:
   a. Depreciation expense is the same each year.
   b. Book value each year is lowered till residual value is reached.
2. Units-of-production: Depreciation expense is directly related to output or usage of asset.
3. Sum-of-the-years'-digits:
   a. Fraction for the year is multiplied times cost less residual value.
   b. Depreciation in year 1 is highest.
4. Double declining-balance:
   a. Residual value is not deducted from cost.
   b. Depreciation expense is book value at beginning of year times rate.
   c. Asset cannot depreciate below book value.
5. Depreciation can be taken for partial years. If an asset is purchased in the first 15 days of the month, the whole month is considered in the depreciation calculation.
6. MACRS are for tax reporting, while the other four depreciation methods are used for financial reports.

Learning Unit 17-3

1. Capital expenditures include the original cost of an asset and three categories of additional payments:
   a. additions or enlargements — major changes or improvements that increase the value of an asset;
   b. extraordinary repairs, which extend the life of the asset;
   c. betterments — improvements that increase efficiency but do not extend the

life of an asset. Additions or enlargements and betterments are charged to the asset account: extraordinary repairs are charged to Accumulated Depreciation.

2. After an asset is acquired, the expenditures for ordinary maintenance and unnecessary or unreasonable situations that do not try to extend useful life are treated as expenses of the current period and are called revenue expenditures.

3. A plant asset can be disposed of by discarding, selling, or exchanging it.

4. The Loss on Disposal account appears as Other Expense on the income statement.

5. A gain on sale of an asset occurs if the cash received is greater than the book value of the asset. Such a gain appears as Other Income on the income statement.

6. When a plant asset is exchanged, loss occurs when the trade-in allowance is less than the book value of the asset.

7. In an exchange of similar assets, the Financial Accounting Principles Board has ruled that gains are to be absorbed into the cost of the new asset.

8. Income tax rules require that gains *and losses* on exchange of assets be absorbed into the cost of the new asset. This is inconsistent with the Financial Accounting Principles Board's ruling on losses.

Learning Unit 17-4

1. Natural resources, such as oil, coal, or timber, will deplete over a period of time as resources are extracted. Depletion expense is listed as an operating expense on the income statement.

2. Accumulated depletion is a contra-asset on the balance sheet.

3. Intangible assets, such as patents, copyrights, franchises, and goodwill, are also used up over a period of years. Amortization is the process of estimating and recording the charges as these intangible assets are used up.

4. Amortization expenses are operating expenses on the income statement.

5. A patent is good for 17 years; a copyright is granted for the life of the creator and 50 years thereafter.

6. The cost of obtaining a franchise is amortized over its life or 40 years, whichever is shorter.

7. Since it is not easy to put a price on goodwill in each accounting period, it is not until a company is bought or sold that a cost is placed on goodwill.

KEY TERMS

Accelerated depreciation More depreciation taken in early years of asset's life, decreasing amounts in later years.

Additions or enlargements Major changes or improvements that increase the value of an asset (such as adding a new wing to a school).

Amortize To charge a portion of an expenditure over a fixed number of years.

Amortization expense An operating expense on the income statement relating to intangible assets.

Betterments Improvements that increase the efficiency of an asset by adding accessories or replacing parts.

Book value Cost of asset less accumulated depreciation.

Capital expenditures Original cost of an asset as well as additions or enlargements, extraordinary repairs, and betterments.

Copyright The exclusive right that is granted by the federal government to sell and reproduce literary, musical, or artistic works for a period of time.

Depletion Amount of natural resources that has been exhausted by mining, pumping, etc., for a period of time.

Double declining-balance method An accelerated depreciation method that uses up to twice the straight-line rate times book value of asset to calculate depreciation expense. Residual value is not subtracted from cost of asset in determining depreciation.

Extraordinary repairs Infrequent expenditures that extend an asset's life (such as a new engine in a car).

Franchise A right granted by business or government to produce or sell goods in a specific geographic region. Examples would be a Burger King or Holiday Inn.

Goodwill When a business is purchased, the difference between the price paid and the value of the identifiable assets is goodwill. Goodwill may depend on brand names, business location, service, or other elements; it is a valuable asset that plays an important part in the expected rate of future earnings of a business.

Income tax method When plant assets are exchanged, tax law says the gain or loss must be absorbed into the cost of new asset.

Intangible assets Assets having no physical substance (such as patents or franchises).

Land Improvements An asset account that records improvements made to land; such improvements have a limited life and are subject to depreciation (an example would be a driveway or fences).

Modified Accelerated Cost Recovery System (MACRS) A system for businesses to calculate depreciation for tax purposes based on the Tax Laws of 1986 and 1989. Also known as the General Depreciation System (GDS).

Residual (salvage) value The amount of the asset's cost that will be recovered when the asset is sold, traded in, or scrapped.

Straight-line method Method that allocates an equal amount of depreciation over an asset's period of usefulness.

Sum-of-the-years'-digits method An accelerated method that allocates depreciation each period of an asset's life by multiplying a fraction for that period times cost less residual value.

Trade-in allowance A value received when one asset is traded in on the purchase of another asset. For example, when you buy a new car you may trade in your old car for an amount of money that is applied toward the purchase of the new car.

Useful life At the time an asset is acquired an estimate is made of its usefulness in terms of years, output, etc.

Units-of-production method A depreciation method that is based on usage and not on time. An example of units of production would be the numbers of shoes a machine could produce in its expected useful life.

BLUEPRINT OF KEY ACCOUNTS

REVIEW OF KEY ACCOUNTS

Account	Category*	↑	Normal Balance	Financial Report Found on
Equipment	Plant Asset	Dr.	Dr.	Balance Sheet
Buildings	Plant Asset	Dr.	Dr.	Balance Sheet
Land	Plant Asset	Dr.	Dr.	Balance Sheet
Loss on Disposal of Plant Asset	Other Expense	Dr.	Dr.	Income Statement
Loss from Fire	Other Expense	Dr.	Dr.	Income Statement
Gain on Sale of Plant Asset	Other Income	Cr.	Cr.	Income Statement
Loss on Exchange of Machinery	Other Expense	Dr.	Dr.	Income Statement
Depletion of Coal Deposit	Operating Expense	Dr.	Dr.	Income Statement
Accumulated Depletion	Contra-Asset	Cr.	Cr.	Balance Sheet
Coal Deposit	Natural Resource	Dr.	Dr.	Balance Sheet
Patents	Intangible Asset	Dr.	Dr.	Balance Sheet
Amortization Expense	Operating Expense	Dr.	Dr.	Income Statement
Copyrights, Franchises, or Goodwill	Intangible Assets	Dr.	Dr.	Balance Sheet

* We use Plant Assets to represent property, plant, and equipment.

QUESTIONS, MINI EXERCISES, EXERCISES, AND PROBLEMS

Discussion Questions

1. What types of payment are considered "reasonable and necessary" when determining cost of an asset?
2. What is the purpose of the Land Improvements account?
3. What is the difference between revenue and capital expenditures?
4. What are four methods of calculating depreciation? Briefly explain the key points of each.
5. What is the purpose of the Modified Accelerated Cost Recovery System?
6. A betterment is a revenue expenditure. True or false? Please explain.
7. Which method of depreciation does *not* deduct residual value in its calculation?
8. When a plant asset is sold, a loss results if the cash received is greater than book value. Defend or reject. Please explain.
9. A loss on an exchange of plant assets occurs when the book value of the old machine is more than the trade-in allowance. True or false?
10. Explain how the income tax method differs from the Accounting Principles Board ruling with regard to the recording exchanges of plant assets that result in a loss.
11. What is the purpose of the accumulated depletion account?
12. List and describe three intangible assets.

Mini Exercises

(The forms you need are on pages 33 and 34 of the *Study Guide and Working Papers.*)

Cost of Property, Plant, and Equipment

1. Calculate the total cost of the machine given:

List Price	$2,000
Cash Discount	5%
Freight	$ 50
Assembly	150
Special Foundation	50

Straight-Line

2. Mel Jones depreciates his truck by the straight-line method. Calculate the yearly depreciation expense given the following:

Cost	$6,000
Residual Value	$1,000
Service of useful life	10 years

Book Value

3. If a machine had a cost of $4,000 with an accumulated depreciation of $1,000, what would be its book value?

Units-of-Production

4. If Mel Jones (Mini Exercise 2) depreciated his truck by the units-of-production method, calculate the first year's depreciation based on the following: Cost $6,000; residual value $1,000. Estimated mileage is 100,000. The truck was driven 8,000 miles in year 1.

Sum-of-the-Year's-Digits

5. If Mel Jones (Mini Exercise 2) depreciated his truck by the sum-of-the-year's-digits method, calculate the first year's depreciation. Round the answer to the nearest dollar.

Double Declining-Balance

6. If Mel Jones (Mini Exercise 2) depreciated his truck by the double declining-balance method, calculate the depreciation expense for year 1.

Capital and Revenue Expenditures

7. Identify each situation as a Capital or Revenue Expenditure.

Situation	Capital Expenditure		Revenue Expenditure
	Addition	Betterment/ Extraordinary Repair	
A. New tires			
B. New air conditioning for a car			
C. New car engine			
D. New addition on school			

Loss and Gains

8. Complete the following:

	Account	Category	Financial Report Found on
A. Accumulated Depletion			
B. Loss on Disposal of Plant Assets			
C. Gain on Sale of Plant Assets			

Exchange with Loss

9. Pete Co. traded in an old machine costing $10,000 for a new machine for a cash price of $13,000 with a trade-in allowance of $3,000. Accumulated Depreciation on the old machine was $6,000.

a. What is book value of the old machine? What is the loss?

b. Provide a journal entry to record the exchange.

Exchange with Gain

10. Assume in Mini Exercise 9 the trade-in value was $5,000. Prepare a journal entry to record the exchange.

Income Tax Method

11. If in Mini Exercise 9 the income tax method was used, prepare the journal entry to record the exchange.

Exercises

(The forms you need are on pages 35–38 of the *Study Guide and Working Papers.*)

Calculating cost of equipment.

17-1. Mack Company incurred the following expenditures to buy a new machine:
- Invoice, $30,000 — less 10 percent cash discount
- Freight charges, $500
- Assembly charges, $1,400
- Special base to support machine, $505
- Machine dropped and repaired, $350

What is the actual cost of the machine?

Depreciation schedules.

17-2. From the following, prepare depreciation schedules for the first two years for (a) straight-line, (b) units-of-production, (c) double declining-balance at twice the straight-line rate, and (d) sum-of-the-years'-digits.
- Machine purchased on Jan. 1, $1,440
- Residual value, $240
- Estimated useful life, five years
- Total estimated output, 600 units
- Output year 1, 100 units
- Output year 2, 200 units

Depreciation schedules.

17-3. Larson Co., whose accounting period ends on December 31, purchased a machine for $6,800 on January 1 with an estimated residual value of $800 and estimated useful life of ten years. Prepare depreciation schedules for the current as well as the following year using (a) straight-line, (b) sum-of-the-years'-digits, and (c) double declining-balance at twice the straight-line rate.

Loss on exchange — and income tax methods.

17-4. A machine that cost $9,000 with $3,900 of accumulated depreciation was traded in for a similar machine having a $5,800 cash price. An $800 trade-in was offered by the seller.
- **a.** Calculate the book value of the old machine.
- **b.** Calculate the loss on the exchange.
- **c.** Prepare the journal entry for the exchange.
- **d.** Calculate the cost basis of the new equipment if the income tax method is used, and prepare a journal entry.

Patent.

17-5. On May 1, 19X1, Osgood Company bought a patent at a cost of $5,000. It is estimated the patent will give Osgood a competitive advantage for ten years. Record in general journal form amortization for 19X1 and 19X2. (Assume December 31 is the end of the accounting period for Osgood.)

MACRS and Tax Reform Act of 1986.

17-6. Pultzer Company bought a light general-purpose truck for $9,000 on March 8, 1991. Calculate the yearly depreciation using the MACRS method.

Group A Problems

(The forms you need are on pages 39–44 of the *Study Guide and Working Papers.*)

Property, plant, and equipment transactions.

17A-1. Record the following transactions into the general journal of Orange Company:

19XX

Feb. 5 Purchased land for $86,000. The $86,000 included attorney's fees of $5,000.

18 Orange Company decided to pave the parking lot for $5,400.

Mar. 24 Purchased a building for $90,000, putting down 30 percent and mortgaging the remainder.

29 Bought equipment for $32,000. Freight and assembly were an additional $4,000.

May 10 Added a new wing for $175,000 to building that was purchased on March 24.

June 15 Performed ordinary repair work on equipment purchased March 29, $750, to maintain its normal operations.

July 1 Bought a truck for $14,000.

Oct. 15 Added a hydraulic loader to truck, $2,200.

Nov. 30 Truck purchased in July was brought in for grease and oil, $33.

Dec. 30 Overhauled truck's motor for $900, extending its life by more than one year.

Dec. 31 Changed tires on truck, $325.

Check Figure:

Feb. 18

Dr Land Improvement $5,400

Cr Cash $5,400

Methods of computing depreciation.

Check Figure:

(c) Depr. expense 19X3 $8,000

17A-2. On January 1, 19X1, a machine was installed at Lavy Factory at a cost of $58,000. Its estimated residual value at the end of its estimated life of four years is $18,000. The machine is expected to produce 80,000 units with the following production schedule:

◆ 19X1: 12,000 units

◆ 19X2: 27,000 units

◆ 19X3: 15,000 units

◆ 19X4: 26,000 units

Complete depreciation schedules for (a) straight-line, (b) units-of-production, (c) sum-of-the-years'-digits, and (d) double declining-balance at twice the straight-line rate.

Check Figure:

(c) Depr. expense 19X1 $896

17A-3. On June 13, 19X1, Cook Company bought equipment for $4,080. Its estimated life is four years with a residual value of $240. Prepare depreciation schedules for 19X1, 19X2, and 19X3 for (a) straight-line, (b) double declining-balance at twice the straight-line rate, and (c) sum-of-the-years'-digits.

Disposing of plant assets.

17A-4. Journalize the following transactions for the Robe Company, and below each entry show all calculations:

19XX

Jan. 1 Sold a truck for $1,250 that cost $6,750 and had accumulated depreciation of $6,100.

Feb. 10 A machine costing $3,200 with accumulated depreciation of $2,450 was destroyed in a fire. The insurance company settled the claim for $300.

Check Figure:

May:

Loss on exchange $200 Dr.

May 1 Traded in a machine costing $19,400 with $16,500 of accumulated depreciation for a new machine costing $25,100 with a trade-in allowance of $2,700. Note that depreciation is up to date. The loss is to be recognized.

July 8 Traded in a machine costing $40,000 with $34,000 of accumulated depreciation (which is up to date) for a new machine for a cash price of $45,000 and a trade-in allowance of $8,000.

Aug. 9 Journalize the May 1 transaction using the income tax method.

Sept. 12 A truck costing $7,000 and fully depreciated was disposed of.

Group B Problems

(The forms you need are on pages 39–44 of the *Study Guide and Working Papers*.)

Property, plant, and equipment transactions.

17B-1. Journalize the following transactions for Orange Company.

19XX

Apr.   1   Purchased a machine for $89,500 along with an additional charge for freight and assembly of $1,500.

      8   Purchased land at a cost of $22,000. The $22,000 included attorney's fees of $2,500.

   15   Purchased a building for $90,000, putting down 10 percent and mortgaging the remainder.

   29   At a cost of $1,900, cleared and graded the land purchased on April 8 (the additional cost considered as part of cost of land).

May   1   Performed regular maintenance work on machinery, $160, to maintain its normal operations.

      8   Painted the building purchased on April 15, $2,900. This was necessary to have the building ready for proper use.

   30   Purchased a second airplane for company business, $65,000.

June 30   Installed a hydraulic loader on a truck at a cost of $2,900.

July   30   First airplane's engine was overhauled for $7,900.

Sept. 30   Building is completely renovated at a cost of $30,000, which will extend its life by ten years.

Methods of computing depreciation.

17B-2. On January 1, 19X1, Lavy Factory installed a new machine at a cost of $117,000. Its estimated residual value at the end of its estimated life of four years is $9,000. The machine is expected to produce 90,000 units with the following production schedule:

- ◆ 19X1: 11,000 units
- ◆ 19X2:   9,000 units
- ◆ 19X3: 11,000 units
- ◆ 19X4: 59,000 units

Complete depreciation schedules for (a) straight-line, (b) units-of-production, (c) sum-of-the-years'-digits, and (d) double declining-balance at twice the straight-line rate.

17B-3. On April 5, 19X1, Cook Company bought equipment for $6,200. Its estimated life is five years with a residual value of $200. Prepare depreciation schedules for 19X1, 19X2, and 19X3 for (a) straight-line, (b) double declining-balance at twice the straight-line rate, and (c) sum-of-the-years'-digits.

Disposing of plant assets.

17B-4. Journalize the following transactions for the Robe Company, and below each entry show all calculations:

19XX

Jan.   1   Sold a truck for $3,600 that cost $12,800 and had accumulated depreciation of $10,900.

Feb.   8   A machine costing $4,000 with accumulated depreciation of $3,390 was destroyed in a fire. The insurance company settled the claim for $150.

May   9   Traded in a machine costing $18,500 with $15,750 of accumulated depreciation (which is up to date) for a new machine costing $26,200 with a trade-in allowance of $2,600. The loss is to be recognized.

July 10   Traded in a machine costing $39,500 with $35,700 of accumulated depreciation (depreciation is up to date) for a new machine for a cash price of $44,000 and a trade-in allowance of $11,500.

Aug. 19   Journalize the May 9 transaction using the income tax method.

Sept. 12   A truck costing $11,000 and fully depreciated was disposed of.

REAL WORLD APPLICATIONS

17R-1.

On August 1, 19X1, Hope Co. purchased a customized light truck for $96,000 cash. On August 3 special shelving was added to the truck for $6,000. The truck has a useful life of six years with a trade-in value of $12,000 and is depreciated by the straight-line method. On January 1, 19X4, Hope Co. was trying to decide whether to overhaul the truck at a cost of $15,000 or buy a new truck for $100,000 and depreciate it by MACRS. Overhauling the truck would increase its useful life by two years, and residual value would remain at $12,000.

As the accountant of Hope Co. you have been called into a meeting with Mr. Reynolds, V. P., to further discuss this matter. Bring all your data with you, along with a written recommendation.

17R-2.

MEMO

To: Hal Owen

From: Pete Sanchez

Re: Decision on general-purpose truck

We need your assistance on which depreciation method would be best for us to use. I'm thinking that we should use MACRS instead of straight-line for both financial and tax purposes. We could save lots of dollars! Could you verify my decision (or not) and work up the numbers for me based on the following:

Cost:	$20,000
Life:	Five years
Residual:	$5,000

Work up a comparison of MACRS and straight-line depreciation along with a written recommendation to help Pete Sanchez make his decision.

 make the call

Critical Thinking/Ethical Case

17R-3.

Pete went to an auto dealer to buy a new Jeep. The salesperson told Pete that cars really appreciate in value. He cited antique cars as a perfect example. The dealer went on to tell Pete that buying a car represents some great tax savings. He told Pete that leasing is getting less and less popular. Should Pete buy a new car? You make the call. Write down your recommendations to Pete.

ACCOUNTING RECALL
A CUMULATIVE APPROACH

THIS EXAM REVIEWS CHAPTERS 1 THROUGH 17

Your *Study Guide and Working Papers* (pp. 49 and 50) has forms to complete this exam, as well as worked-out solutions. The page references next to each question identify what page to turn back to if you answer the question incorrectly.

PART 1 Vocabulary Review

Match the terms to the appropriate definition or phrase.

Page Ref.

(121)	1. Accumulated depreciation	A. Cost of asset less accumulated depreciation
(614)	2. Betterment	
(615)	3. Equipment	B. Other expense
(608)	4. Declining balance	C. Patent
(618)	5. Loss on exchange of machinery	D. Extraordinary repairs
		E. Residual value is not subtracted from cost of asset
(604)	6. Intangible asset	
(619)	7. Income tax method	F. Plant asset
(613)	8. Capital expenditures	G. Contra-asset
(606)	9. Straight-line method	H. Gain or loss absorbed when plant assets are exchanged
(606)	10. Book value	
		I. Increase the efficiency of an asset
		J. Equal amount of depreciation

PART II True or False (Accounting Theory)

(605) 11. Land improvements account is not subject to depreciation.

(608) 12. In double declining-balance an asset can be depreciated below book value.

(614) 13. Adding a wing on to a school is an example of a revenue expenditure.

(614) 14. Extraordinary repairs are charged to accumulated depreciation.

(618) 15. In an exchange of similar assets the Accounting Principles Board has ruled that gains are to be absorbed into the cost of the new asset.

18

PARTNERSHIPS

THE BIG PICTURE

Tony Freedman would like to expand the Eldorado Computer Center by selling to small and medium-sized businesses. To realize his goal, however, he'll need more investment dollars to make his operation grow, and he'll need a highly motivated manager to run the shop while he does the marketing. A partner might be the answer. The right partner would bring in additional capital, share the work, and add moral support.

After speaking with several associates about the possibility of bringing another owner into his business, Freedman decided that Charles West would be ideal. He began to consult with West about the type of partnership they would have, how the profits would be distributed, and the percentage of ownership each partner would have according to their capital investment.

In this chapter you will learn how to calculate a partner's share of net income based on the investment in the business. You will also learn about the advantages and disadvantages of forming a partnership — and how to liquidate this type of ownership, if it should become necessary.

Although the Eldorado Computer Center has become a partnership, it uses the same accounting principles as a sole proprietorship. The biggest differences are how the equity portion of the balance sheet may look and how the profits are distributed.

Learning Objectives	◆ Journalizing the entry for formation of a partnership. (p. 635) ◆ Calculating a partner's share of net income based on fractional ratio, beginning capital investment, and salary and interest allowances. (p. 638) ◆ Preparing a statement of partners' equity. (p. 641) ◆ Journalizing entries to record admitting a new partner, withdrawal of a partner, and bonuses to partners. (p. 642) ◆ Journalizing entries involved in the liquidation process and preparing a statement of liquidation. (p. 647)

Up to this point we have been using the sole proprietorship form of business organization in discussing the accounting process. We are now ready to look at another form of business organization, the **partnership.**

A partnership, as defined by the **Uniform Partnership Act,** is "an association of two or more persons to carry on as co-owners a business for profit." Examples of partnerships include service businesses and professional practitioners, such as physicians, dentists, attorneys, and accountants. Many small wholesale as well as retail companies are formed as partnerships. Your local convenience store may be a partnership.

The recording of business transactions involving assets, liabilities, revenue, and expenses is handled the same for both a sole proprietorship and a partnership. The major difference in recording business transactions for these two forms of organization lies in the capital account(s). A sole proprietorship has only one capital and withdrawals account, while in a partnership each owner has his or her own separate capital and withdrawals account. First we will look at the characteristics of a partnership and how it is formed.

LEARNING UNIT 18-1
Partnership Characteristics and Formation of Partnerships

It is quite easy to form a partnership. When two or more people agree orally or in writing to be partners, a contract results. Although the oral agreement is binding, it makes more sense to seek legal advice and have a formal written agreement prepared. Putting agreements in writing may minimize conflicts in the future. This written agreement, which formalizes the partners' relationship, is called the **articles of partnership.**

Some things that should be included in the written articles of partnership are:

The more partners a partnership has, (1) the easier it may be to finance the business with the owners' investments and (2) the more unique abilities may result from the different backgrounds of the owners.

1. Name and address of each partner, along with the date of agreement.

2. Rights and responsibilities of each partner.

3. Amount that each partner is investing.

4. Specific manner in which partners' profits or losses will be shared.

5. Provisions for one or more partners quitting the partnership.

6. How new partners will be admitted.

7. How assets will be distributed if the business is completely terminated.

8. How accounting records will be maintained.

CHARACTERISTICS OF PARTNERSHIPS

Limited Life

A partnership has a *limited life*. An advantage is that it does have more flexibility than some other forms of ownership to react to the marketplace since legal restrictions are minimal. However, when there is a change in the membership of a partnership—when someone new joins or when someone leaves—the partnership is dissolved. Dissolution can occur if a partner dies, becomes incapacitated, goes bankrupt, or withdraws. Admission of a new partner or expiration of the life of the partnership as stated in the articles of partnership could also result in the partnership being dissolved.

If a partnership is dissolved, a new partnership can be formed and the business can continue to operate without any interruptions.

Mutual Agency

Mutual agency means that the actions of one partner are binding on all of the other partners. For example, Jill Joy, who is a partner in a merchandise business, enters into a contract with Flynn Company to lease a building. This contract is binding on all of Jill's partners, since the transaction was within the scope of the business. If Jill, on the other hand, entered into a contract to provide *legal* work to another company, it would not be binding on the partners, since legal work is not in the normal scope of a merchandise company.

Mutual agency allows each partner to act for the partnership as a whole, since all of the partners are agents for the business. However, poor judgment on the part of one partner could, through mutual agency, result in heavy losses to all partners. An advantage of a partnership is that a credit rating is usually higher because one partner is responsible for the company's debt. So this characteristic of a partnership can be both an advantage and a disadvantage.

Unlimited Liability

Unlimited liability means that if a partnership is unable to pay its obligations, each **general partner** is individually liable to cover with his or her *personal* assets the obligations the partnership cannot meet. Think of a general partner as one who risks not only their investment in the partnership, but also their own personal assets. If the personal assets of some of the partners are exhausted, the other partners have the responsibility for covering the debts outstanding. There are, however, a few exceptions to this rule. First, a partner just entering an existing partnership is not held liable for past obligations before he or she joined the partnership. Second, in some states some members of a partnership have liability only up to the amount they have invested in the partnership. These people are called **limited partners.**

Co-Ownership of Property

Co-ownership of property means that all partners share all the assets of the partnership. For example, if Bill Boyd invests cash and Joyce Regan invests a building in their partnership, the assets become the property of the partnership. Joyce no longer has a specific claim to the building. Ownership is now shared by Bill and Joyce.

Taxation

The partnership itself does not pay taxes, but each partner pays taxes on his or her share of net income that has been allocated. (Note that the tax is on the net income and not on the amount that a partner has withdrawn from the partnership.) Remember, in a sole proprietorship, like a partnership, owners are not paid salaries. They take withdrawals from the company.

FORMATION OF A PARTNERSHIP

Let's look now at the journal entries that are needed when a partnership is formed. The important point is that when partners invest in a business, the assets should be recorded at their current fair value. This value is established by having the assets appraised. Partners have to agree on the amounts assigned to the noncash assets. These costs now represent the true acquisition cost to the partnership. Appraising of assets at their current fair value avoids inequities in the balances of the capital accounts of the partners.

Let's look at the following situation: On June 1, 19XX, Jane Reedy and Bill Burr enter into a partnership. Reedy invests from her old business $9,000 cash and store equipment worth $25,000 with accumulated depreciation of $5,000. The current appraised value of the equipment is $28,000. Also on the books is Accounts Receivable of $2,000 with an Allowance for Doubtful Accounts of $500. The partnership will take on the responsibility for a $6,000 note issued by Reedy. Burr invests $20,000 cash in the partnership. The following journal entries record this information:

These entries could be recorded in the cash receipts journal. Note that the $32,500 is the assets minus the liabilities.

19XX June	1	Cash	9 0 0 0 00	
		Accounts Receivable	2 0 0 0 00	
		Store Equipment	28 0 0 0 00	
		Allowances for Doubtful Accounts		5 0 0 00
		Notes Payable		6 0 0 0 00
		J. Reedy, Capital		32 5 0 0 00
	1	Cash	20 0 0 0 00	
		B. Burr, Capital		20 0 0 0 00

Note that the store equipment has no accumulated depreciation associated with it, since the appraised value is now the new book value. If the old book value was used, Reedy's capital would be understated. Reedy should not be penalized, since her investment has increased. Any additional investments made by the partners will result in a journal entry that debits Cash and credits the partners' capital account.

LEARNING UNIT 18-1 REVIEW

AT THIS POINT you should be able to

◆ Define a partnership and compare its equity section with that of a sole proprietorship. (p. 635)
◆ List the characteristics of a partnership. (p. 636)
◆ Journalize the formation of a partnership, recording assets of current fair value. (p. 637)

SELF-REVIEW QUIZ 18-1

(The forms you need are on page 51 of the *Study Guide and Working Papers*.)
Respond true or false to the following:

LEARNING UNIT 18-2
Division of Net Income and Net Loss among Partners

Partners work in order to gain a share of the net income of their partnership; they do not earn salaries as their employees do. As a matter of fact, they cannot legally hire themselves and pay themselves a salary. There are several ways to divide up net income and net loss among partners, based on partners' differing talent and abilities, time spent working for the partnership, and amount of investment in the partnership.

We need to introduce two terms to help describe how net income is divided among partners. One way is through a **salary allowance.** This is not the same thing as the Salary Expense involved in paying employees, and it is not in fact a salary at all; it is just a way to divide net income. It is usually used to account for unequal service contributions among partners—for example, if one partner worked full time for the business and the other put in only 20 hours a week. In such a case the partners might agree to pay $1,000 per week to the first partner and $500 per week to the other. This money would come out of the net income earned by the partnership.

Another way to divide net income among partners is through **interest allowance.** This is usually used when partners have put different amounts into the partnership as an initial investment. Let's say that one has invested $5,000 and the other has invested $10,000. At the end of the accounting period they would each get 10 percent interest on their investment—the first would get $500 ($5,000 × .10) and the second would get $1,000 ($10,000 × .10). This is done because it would be unfair to give half of net income to the first partner when he or she invested only one-third of the capital.

Now let's look at several different situations to see how a partnership might divide its net income or net loss. These situations will be based on the following facts:

Dot Alexander, John Sullivan, and Sheldon Brown invested $8,000, $6,000, and $4,000, respectively, in a partnership. The partnership in the first year had a net income of $24,300.

Situation 1

Partners could not agree on how to share net income of $24,300. The law states that if an agreement is not reached on how partners share earnings, they will be divided equally.

The Calculation: $24,300 ÷ 3 = $8,100 to each partner.

The journal entry at closing to allocate net income will look like this:

	19XX						
	Dec.	31	Income Summary	24 3 0 0 00		
			Dot Alexander, Capital			8 1 0 0 00
			John Sullivan, Capital			8 1 0 0 00
			Sheldon Brown, Capital			8 1 0 0 00

Note that the closing process now divides the net income into the *three* capital accounts. In a sole proprietorship, the net income was closed to the one capital account. If this situation involved net loss instead of net income, each capital account would be debited and the credit would be to Income Summary.

Situation 2

Partners share net income of $24,300 in the ratio of their beginning capital investments.

The Calculation:

Step 1: Find total capital invested:

Alexander	$ 8,000
Sullivan	6,000
Brown	4,000
	$18,000

Step 2: Set up a ratio (fraction) of each partner's investment to the total of capital invested ($18,000):

ALEXANDER	**SULLIVAN**	**BROWN**
$\dfrac{\$8,000}{\$18,000}$	$\dfrac{\$6,000}{\$18,000}$	$\dfrac{\$4,000}{\$18,000}$

Step 3: Multiply the ratio in step 2 by the amount of income to be distributed.

Alexander: $\dfrac{\$8,000}{\$18,000} \times \$24,300 = \$10,800$

Sullivan: $\dfrac{\$6,000}{\$18,000} \times \$24,300 = \$8,100$

Brown: $\dfrac{\$4,000}{\$18,000} \times \$24,300 = \$5,400$

The journal entry at closing to allocate net income will look like this:

	19XX						
	Dec.	31	Income Summary	24 3 0 0 00		
			Dot Alexander, Capital			10 8 0 0 00
			John Sullivan, Capital			8 1 0 0 00
			Sheldon Brown, Capital			5 4 0 0 00

This ratio in step 2 may be used if the net income of the company is related only to the amount the partners have invested. Alexander has invested the most ($8,000) and thus receives the largest portion of the earnings ($10,800).

Alternative to Ratio Based on Investment Only: Some partnerships share net income according to an agreed-upon ratio. If a ratio is 3:2:1, it means that 3/6 of net income goes to one partner, 2/6 to the next, and 1/6 to the last. Such a fractional ratio could be based on service as well as capital investment. Such ratios are called **profit and loss ratios.**

Situation 3

Partners' services and capital contributions are unequal, but net income does cover salary and interest allowance. The salary allowance is used to compensate for the partners' unequal service contributions, and the interest allowance is used to compensate for their unequal investments. One way to share net income in this situation is as follows:

a. Annual salary allowance of $6,000 to Alexander, $6,000 to Sullivan, and $9,000 to Brown.

b. Ten percent interest on each partner's capital investment.

c. Remaining net income or net loss shared equally.

		ALEXANDER		SULLIVAN		BROWN		TOTAL
a. Salary Allowance		$6,000	+	$6,000	+	$9,000	=	$21,000
b. Interest on Capital Investments								
.10 × $8,000		800						
.10 × $6,000			+	600				
.10 × $4,000					+	400		
Total Interest Allowance							=	1,800
Total Salary and Interest Allowance		$6,800	+	$6,600	+	$9,400	=	$22,800
c. Net Income	$24,300							
Less: Salary and Interest	22,800							
Income to be distributed equally	$ 1,500	500		500		500		
Share of Net Income to Partners		$7,300	+	$7,100	+	$9,900	=	$24,300

The journal entry at closing to allocate net income will look like this:

19XX					
Dec.	31	Income Summary	24 3 0 0 00		
		D. Alexander, Capital		7 3 0 0 00	
		J. Sullivan, Capital		7 1 0 0 00	
		S. Brown, Capital		9 9 0 0 00	

Note that in this case there was still net income remaining after salary and interest allowances. In the next situation we will see that net income doesn't always cover all the salary and interest allowance.

Situation 4

Partners' services and capital contributions are unequal, but net income does not cover salary and interest allowance.

Assume that (1) net income is $20,700, and (2) salary and interest allowance are the same as in Situation 3.

Whether net income covers the salaries and interest makes *no difference* in calculating the salary or interest allowance. As shown in the accompanying calculation, the total of salaries and allowances is $22,800. Net income is only $20,700; thus the partners must all share in a reduction of the profits allocated to them by $700 each. Remember that items (a) and (b) are calculated first *before* we consider the difference between net income and the amount that is needed to cover salary and interest allowance. There is no need to think of the $700 **deficit** as a loss; think of it as a reduction in the share of profits, since all of the interest and salary allowance was not covered.

	ALEXANDER		SULLIVAN		BROWN		TOTAL
a. Salary Allowance	$6,000	+	$6,000	+	$9,000	=	$21,000
b. Interest on Capital Investments:							
.10 × $8,000	800						
.10 × $6,000		+	600				
.10 × $4,000				+	400		
Total Interest Allowance						=	1,800
Total Salary and Interest Allowance	$6,800	+	$6,600	+	$9,400	=	$22,800
c. Net Income	$20,700						
Less: Salary and Interest	22,800						
Deficit to be shared equally	<$ 2,100>		<700>		<700>		<700>
Share of Net Income to Partners			$6,100	+	$5,900	+	$8,700	=	$20,700

	19XX					
	Dec.	31	Income Summary	20 70 0 00		
			D. Alexander, Capital			6 10 0 00
			J. Sullivan, Capital			5 90 0 00
			S. Brown, Capital			8 70 0 00

PARTNERSHIP FINANCIAL STATEMENT

Just as we had a statement of owner's equity for a sole proprietorship, we can prepare a statement of partners' equity. The accompanying statement was prepared from Situation 3.

On their personal tax returns, partners are taxed on their net income in the partnership, whether they withdraw it or not. For example, Alexander would pay taxes on $7,300, even though she withdrew only $4,000.

ALEXANDER, SULLIVAN, AND BROWN STATEMENT OF PARTNERS' EQUITY FOR YEAR ENDED DECEMBER 31, 19XX			
	Alexander	Sullivan	Brown
Capital Balances, January 1, 19XX	$ 8 00 0 00	$ 6 00 0 00	$ 4 00 0 00
Add: Net Income for 19XX	7 30 0 00	7 10 0 00	9 90 0 00
Totals	$15 30 0 00	$13 10 0 00	$13 90 0 00
Less: Withdrawals	4 00 0 00	5 00 0 00	8 00 0 00
Capital Balances, December 31, 19XX	$11 30 0 00	$ 8 10 0 00	$ 5 90 0 00

The ending balances for each partner would then be reported on the balance sheet. Think of the statement of partner's equity as a supporting document to arrive at a new figure for each capital account on the balance sheet.

AT THIS POINT you should be able to

◆ Explain why salary and interest allowances are not expenses when used to divide up earnings of a partnership. (p. 638)
◆ Calculate partners' earnings if shared (a) equally, (b) by ratio of beginning capital or fractional ratio, and (c) by salary and interest allowances. (p. 639)
◆ Prepare a statement of partner's equity. (p. 641)

SELF-REVIEW QUIZ 18-2

(The forms you need are on page 52 of the *Study Guide and Working Papers.*)
    From the following information, calculate the partners' share of net income. J. French and J. Small receive salary allowances of $60,000 and $48,000, respectively. The interest allowance is 12 percent of their beginning balances of $160,000 and $120,000, respectively. The remainder of the net income will be divided evenly. Net income for the year was $150,000.

Solution to Self-Review Quiz 18-2

	FRENCH		SMALL	=	TOTAL
Salary Allowance	$60,000	+	$48,000	=	$108,000
Interest on Capital Investments:					
.12 × $160,000	19,200				
.12 × $120,000		+	14,400		
Total Interest Allowance				=	33,600
Total Salary and Interest Allowance	$79,200	+	$62,400	=	$141,600
Net Income $150,000					
Less: Salary and Interest 141,600					
Income to be					
Distributed Equally $8,400 ⟶	4,200		4,200		
Share of Net Income to Partners	$83,400	+	$66,600	=	$150,000

LEARNING UNIT 18-3

Recording Admissions and Withdrawals of Partners

This unit looks at how the capital structure of a partnership may change due to (1) admission of a new partner or (2) withdrawal of a partner.

ADMISSION OF A NEW PARTNER

There are two ways to join a partnership:

1. **Purchase an equity interest** from one or more of the existing partners.
2. Make an investment into the business.

No matter what approach is taken, the admission of a new partner will technically dissolve the old partnership. Let's look at how Peter Mix bought into the partnership of Jones and Ryan.

Buying an Equity Interest from an Original Partner

The partners' balance sheet of Jones and Ryan looked as follows before Peter Mix purchased an interest in the company (there are no liabilities):

JONES AND RYAN				
Assets			**Partners' Equity**	
Cash	$ 5 0 0 0 00		Jones, Capital	$ 6 0 0 0 00
Other Assets	7 0 0 0 00		Ryan, Capital	6 0 0 0 00
Total Assets	$12 0 0 0 00		Total Equities	$12 0 0 0 00

On April 3 Ryan sold Peter Mix his equity in the company for $9,000. The following entry is recorded on the books of the partnership:

April	3	Ryan, Capital		6 0 0 0 00	
		Mix, Capital			6 0 0 0 00

The end result of this transaction is to transfer the $6,000 capital account of Ryan to Mix. Note that the difference in the selling price of $3,000 ($9,000 − $6,000) doesn't affect the books of the partnership, since the cash is paid directly to Ryan and not to the business. Think of it as a side transaction. All this transaction does is transfer the equity amounts. Any personal profit the former partner makes is of a personal nature and is not reflected in the accounts of the business.

Keep in mind also that Jones must agree to the equity exchange by Ryan if Mix is to become a partner. If Jones agrees, a new partnership contract is formed along with new profit or loss ratios. If Jones doesn't accept Mix as a partner, Mix still has the right to share in Ryan's profits and losses, but he will have no voice in the running of the company until he is admitted as a partner.

Ryan cannot force Jones to accept Mix as a partner.

Investing in an Existing Partnership

As an alternative to buying equity from an existing partner, one may simply invest assets in the partnership on one's own. For example, assume that on July 8 Roger Foss wants to invest cash in a business so that he will have a one-third interest in the partnership. Before Roger makes his investment, the partners' equity is as follows:

Having a one-third interest doesn't mean Roger has rights to one-third of the net income. The partners must agree on how to share profit and loss.

PARTNERS' EQUITY

B. Blee, Capital	$3,000
A. Jarvis, Capital	1,000

Roger wants one-third interest, and the $4,000 ($3,000 + $1,000) represents two-thirds interest; therefore Roger will have to contribute $2,000

$$\left(\frac{\$2,000}{\$6,000} \quad \begin{array}{l} \text{Roger's contribution} \\ \text{Total capital with Roger's contribution} \end{array} \right)$$

to gain the one-third interest. The entry to record the admission of Roger Foss would be as follows:

$$\frac{\$4,000}{2 \text{ parts}} = \$2,000 \text{ per part}$$

OR

$$\frac{\$4,000}{X} = \frac{2}{3}$$
$$2X = \$12,000$$
$$X = \$6,000$$

July	8	Cash		2 0 0 0 00	
		R. Foss, Capital			2 0 0 0 00

Recording a Bonus to the Old Partners When Admitting a New Partner

When the equity of a partnership in reality is worth more than the amounts recorded in its accounting records, the partners may require an incoming partner to pay an additional amount or **bonus.** This could result if a company had an outstanding earnings record with even higher expectations in the future compared with other companies in the industry. Let's see how this would work from the previous example of Roger Foss, assuming that the partners Blee and Jarvis on July 8 require a payment of $3,500 (instead of $2,000) to give Foss a one-third interest.

Blee and Jarvis, Capital	$4,000
Investment of Foss	3,500
Capital of New Partnership	$7,500
$\frac{1}{3}$ interest of Foss ($\frac{1}{3}$ × $7,500)	$2,500

Foss only needed to invest $2,000 to gain a one-third interest, but the old partners required $3,500.

$$\frac{\$7,500}{3 \text{ parts}} = \$2,500 \text{ per part}$$

Note that $1,000 ($3,500 − $2,500) difference represents the bonus the old partners will share. The old partners share all losses and gains equally. Thus the journal entry to admit Foss is as follows:

July	8	Cash	3 5 0 0 00		
		B. Blee, Capital		5 0 0 00	
		A. Jarvis, Capital		5 0 0 00	
		R. Foss, Capital		2 5 0 0 00	

Recording a Bonus to a New Partner

A firm often is anxious to bring into the company a new partner who has special skills, business contacts, or abilities. The old partners then must accept a reduction in their capital balances to make up the difference in what the new partner invests compared with his capital balance. Let's play back the previous example by looking at how "anxious" Blee and Jarvis are to obtain the managerial talents of Roger Foss. Now the old partners have required Foss on July 8 to invest only $1,400 to have a one-third interest in the business.

Blee and Jarvis, Capital	$4,000
Investment by Foss	1,400
Capital of New Partnership	$5,400
$\frac{1}{3}$ interest of Foss ($\frac{1}{3}$ × $5,400)	$1,800

$$\frac{\$5,400}{3 \text{ parts}} = \$1,800 \text{ per part}$$

Note that Foss invested only $1,400, while in reality he needed to invest $1,800. Thus the old partners are absorbing equally the bonus of $400 ($1,800 − $1,400) by reducing their capital balance. The journal entry to record the admitting of Foss to the partnership is as follows:

July	8	Cash	1 4 0 0 00		
		B. Blee, Capital	2 0 0 00		
		A. Jarvis, Capital	2 0 0 00		
		R. Foss, Capital		1 8 0 0 00	

RECORDING PERMANENT WITHDRAWAL OF A PARTNER

Any loss or gain in the revaluation is shared according to the partners' profit and loss ratio.

When a partnership contract is drawn up, it usually states the procedures to be followed when a partner withdraws. Often the procedures include an audit of the accounting records and the adjustment of the assets to their current fair market value. This is done so that the capital of the retiring partner does indeed reflect the current value of his or her equity. Let's look at (1) the balance sheet before revaluation of Ring, Rotter, and Freeze, (2) the entry made to record revaluation, (3) the new, revalued balance sheet, and (4) withdrawal of J. Freeze (assume no liabilities). Partners of Ring, Rotter, and Freeze have a profit and loss ratio of 1/2, 1/4, and 1/4, respectively.

1. The balance sheet before revaluation is as follows:

RING, ROTTER, AND FREEZE				
Assets			**Partners' Equity**	
Cash		$ 2 2 0 0 00	A. Ring, Capital	$ 4 4 0 0 00
Merchandise Inventory		3 2 0 0 00	B. Rotter, Capital	2 0 0 0 00
Store Equipment	$ 4 0 0 0 00		J. Freeze, Capital	2 0 0 0 00
Less Acc. Dep.	1 0 0 0 00	3 0 0 0 00		
Total Assets		$ 8 4 0 0 00	Total Equities	$ 8 4 0 0 00

2. When the accountant completes the audit, it is reported that inventory, owing to market conditions, is overvalued by $400. The journal entry to record the revaluation is as follows:

$$\text{Ring} = \tfrac{1}{2} \times \$400$$
$$= \$200$$
$$\text{Rotter} = \tfrac{1}{4} \times \$400$$
$$= \$100$$
$$\text{Freeze} = \tfrac{1}{4} \times \$400$$
$$= \$100$$

Nov.	30	A. Ring, Capital	2 0 0 00	
		B. Rotter, Capital	1 0 0 00	
		J. Freeze, Capital	1 0 0 00	
		Merchandise Inventory		4 0 0 00

3. Here is the new, revalued balance sheet:

RING, ROTTER, AND FREEZE				
Assets			**Partners' Equity**	
Cash		$ 2 2 0 0 00	A. Ring, Capital	$ 4 2 0 0 00
Merchandise Inventory		2 8 0 0 00	B. Rotter, Capital	1 9 0 0 00
Store Equipment	$ 4 0 0 0 00		J. Freeze, Capital	1 9 0 0 00
Less Acc. Dep.	1 0 0 0 00	3 0 0 0 00		
Total Assets		$ 8 0 0 0 00	Total Equities	$ 8 0 0 0 00

The withdrawal means a new partnership and a new profit and loss ratio for Ring and Rotter.

4. The entry to record the withdrawal of Freeze from the partnership is as follows:

Nov.	30	J. Freeze, Capital	1 9 0 0 00	
		Cash		1 9 0 0 00

RECORDING PERMANENT WITHDRAWAL WHEN A PARTNER TAKES ASSETS OF LESS VALUE THAN HIS BOOK EQUITY

In the last situation Freeze received the revalued amount of his capital by taking out $1,900 in cash. Often, when a partner retires, the assets may not be revalued. In this case the partners have to agree whether the assets are overvalued and whether the withdrawing partner should settle for less than the book value of his equity. For example, let's look at the following balance sheet for Joll, Smoot, and Jangles to see what will happen if Smoot settles for less than his book value on July 31 (assume a profit and loss ratio of 2:2:1):

JOLL, SMOOT, AND JANGLES				
Assets			Partners' Equity	
Cash	$25 0 0 0 00		R. Joll, Capital	$28 0 0 0 00
Merchandise Inventory	29 0 0 0 00		A. Smoot, Capital	18 0 0 0 00
			B. Jangles, Capital	8 0 0 0 00
Total Assets	$54 0 0 0 00		Total Equities	$54 0 0 0 00

Smoot is extremely anxious to withdraw from the partnership and is willing to accept a cash settlement of $12,000. Joll and Jangles will share the $6,000 ($18,000 − $12,000) of capital that Smoot does not take with him in the ratio of 2:1. The journal to record the withdrawal of Smoot is as follows:

July	31	A. Smoot, Capital	18 0 0 0 00		
		Cash		12 0 0 0 00	
		R. Joll, Capital		4 0 0 0 00	
		B. Jangles, Capital		2 0 0 0 00	

Now let's look at what could happen if Smoot withdrew assets valued at *more* than his book equity.

RECORDING PERMANENT WITHDRAWAL WHEN A PARTNER TAKES ASSETS OF GREATER VALUE THAN BOOK EQUITY

Using the above example, Smoot might withdraw assets valued at *more* than book equity if:

1. Partnership assets are undervalued, and
2. Joll and Jangles are anxious to have him retire.

Assume that the assets are undervalued by $12,000 and the owners want to leave them this way. Thus, Smoot's capital would be increased by $4,800 ($\frac{2}{5} \times \$12,000$), and the other owners' equity would be reduced to cover this $4,800 increase to Smoot's capital. The following entry would be recorded when Smoot leaves the partnership:

July	31	A. Smoot, Capital	18 0 0 0 00	
		R. Joll, Capital	3 2 0 0 00	
		B. Jangles, Capital	1 6 0 0 00	
		Cash		22 8 0 0 00

Note that Smoot receives in cash the $18,000 value of his capital plus the $4,800 to reflect the capital of $22,800 agreed upon by the other owners. Note also how the capital of Joll and Jangles was reduced according to their profit and loss ratio.

Remember, when a partner dies, the partnership ends, and his or her estate is entitled to receive the proper value of the capital account of the deceased after an audit and revaluation of the assets. Journal entries for the death of a partner are similar to those for other situations when a partner leaves. In order to have enough cash to pay the full value of the deceased partner's capital account, partnerships often carry life insurance policies on partners.

LEARNING UNIT 18-3 REVIEW

AT THIS POINT you should be able to

◆ Explain how a new partner can be admitted in a partnership. (p. 642)
◆ Journalize the entry to record the admitting of a partner. (p. 643)
◆ Explain why a one-third interest doesn't mean the net income is split three ways. (p. 643)
◆ Calculate as well as journalize a bonus to old partners when a new partner is admitted. (p. 644)
◆ Calculate as well as journalize a bonus to a new partner. (p. 644)
◆ Explain how assets might be revalued when a partner withdraws. (p. 645)
◆ Calculate as well as journalize entries to record withdrawal of a partner taking assets for less or more than book equity if assets are not revalued. (p. 646)

SELF-REVIEW QUIZ 18-3

(The forms you need are on page 53 of the *Study Guide and Working Papers*.) Answer true or false to the following:

1. When new partner, Cohen, buys an equity of existing partner, Lee-Ying, the cash account is always increased in the business.
2. The profit and loss ratio must be based on the capital balances of the partners.
3. A bonus to old partners is based on their profit and loss ratio.
4. A bonus to a new partner could result if the old partners are anxious to recruit the new partner.
5. Any loss or gain when assets are revalued is shared in the partners' profit and loss ratio.
6. Assets of a partnership cannot be revalued.
7. A partner, Jaworski, can never withdraw assets that are valued at less than his book equity.
8. A partner who withdraws assets of greater value than book equity causes the capital of the remaining partners to decrease when assets are not revalued.

Solution to Self-Review Quiz 18-3

1. F   **2.** F   **3.** T   **4.** T   **5.** T   **6.** F   **7.** F   **8.** T

LEARNING UNIT 18-4
The Liquidation of a Partnership

Up to this point we have looked at the admission and withdrawal of partners. Each time this happens, a new partnership is formed and any losses or gains are shared in an agreed-upon ratio. The operations of the business continue, of course, even when the new partnership is formed. In this unit we look at three situations in which a partnership is **liquidated.** This means that the business is completely ended by converting assets into cash and paying off obligations and equity. The following steps complete a liquidation:

1. Assets are sold for cash with any loss or gain recognized.
2. Any loss or gain is divided among the partners based on their profit or loss ratio.
3. Creditors are paid off.
4. Remaining cash is distributed to the partners based on their capital balances.

We will be looking at three different situations based on the following information:

Peters, French, and Smith are liquidating their business on May 31, 19XX. The partners have a profit and loss ratio of 3:2:1. The following is the updated balance sheet at the end of May. Note that at this point we've closed out the temporary accounts.

PETERS, FRENCH, AND SMITH BALANCE SHEET MAY 31, 19XX	
Assets	
Cash	$ 7 0 0 0 00
Other Assets	138 0 0 0 00
Total Assets	$145 0 0 0 00
Liabilities and Partners' Equity	
Liabilities	$ 25 0 0 0 00
Jane Peters, Capital	30 0 0 0 00
Joe French, Capital	70 0 0 0 00
Alan Smith, Capital	20 0 0 0 00
Total Liabilities and Partners' Equity	$145 0 0 0 00

Using this information, let's look at three different situations in which liquidation occurs.

Situation 1

Selling assets at a gain (assets sold for $144,000).

The Liquidation Process:

Step 1: Record sale of assets along with any loss or gain from realization* (gain = $144,000 − $138,000) on June 7:

June	7	Cash	144 0 0 0 00		
		Other Assets		138 0 0 0 00	
		Loss or Gain from Realization*		6 0 0 0 00	

---

* **Realization** means the conversion of noncash assets into cash as part of the liquidation process. It can result in either gain or loss. The account Loss or Gain from Realization is similar to the Cash Short and Over account that we discussed in Chapter 6. The account will be closed separately, since closing entries take place before liquidation. In using this account, think of loss as a debit and gain as a credit.

Step 3: Pay claims of creditors on June 15:

June	15	Liabilities	25 00 00	
		Cash		25 00 00

Step 4: Distribute remaining cash on June 30:

June	30	J. French, Capital	24 00 00	
		Cash		24 00 00

The accompanying statement of liquidation provides a comprehensive report of this liquidation process.

PETERS, FRENCH, AND SMITH
STATEMENT OF LIQUIDATION
FOR MONTH OF JUNE 19XX

				Capital		
	Cash	+ Other Assets	= Liabilities	+ Peters	+ French	+ Smith
Balances before realization	$7,000	+ $138,000	= $25,000	+ $30,000	+ $70,000	+ $20,000
Recording loss from sale of assets	+42,000	– $138,000 =		– 48,000	– 32,000	– 16,000
Balances updated	$49,000		$25,000	– $18,000	+ $38,000	+ $ 4,000
Deficit of Peters covered by partners in ratio 2:1				+ $18,000	– $12,000	– 6,000
Balances updated	$49,000		= $25,000		+ $26,000	– $2,000
Deficit of Smith covered by French					– $2,000	+ $2,000
Balances updated	$49,000		= $25,000		+ $24,000	
Paying of liabilities	–$25,000		–$25,000			
Balances updated	$24,000		=		$24,000	
Distribution of cash to French	–$24,000				– $24,000	

LEARNING UNIT 18-4 REVIEW

AT THIS POINT you should be able to

- Explain the steps of the liquidation process. (p. 648)
- Explain why the profit and loss ratio is not used to pay off the partners in the liquidation process. (p. 649)
- Prepare a liquidation statement. (p. 649)

SELF-REVIEW QUIZ 18-4

(The forms you need are on page 54 of the *Study Guide and Working Papers.*)
From the information given below, journalize the (A) sale of assets, (B) loss or gain from realization, (C) payment of liabilities, and (D) distribution of remaining cash to the partners.

1. Cash, $4,000; Other Assets, $13,000; Liabilities, $2,000; Jay, Capital, $3,000; Joger, Capital, $5,000; and Ynet, Capital, $7,000.

2. Partners share losses or gains in a $3:1:1$ ratio.
3. Assets sold for $16,000.

Solution to Self-Review Quiz 18-4

Jay: $\frac{3}{5} \times \$3,000$
Joger: $\frac{1}{5} \times \$3,000$
Ynet: $\frac{1}{5} \times \$3,000$

(A)	Cash		16 000 00	
	Other Assets			13 000 00
	Loss of Gain from Realization			3 000 00
(B)	Loss or Gain from Realization		3 000 00	
	Jay, Capital			1 800 00
	Joger, Capital			600 00
	Ynet, Capital			600 00
(C)	Liabilities		2 000 00	
	Cash			2 000 00
(D)	Jay, Capital		4 800 00	
	Joger, Capital		5 600 00	
	Ynet, Capital		7 600 00	
	Cash			18 000 00

SUMMARY OF KEY POINTS

Learning Unit 18-1

1. Forming a partnership is quite easy and can be agreed upon in writing or orally. Having a written articles of partnership clearly spells out the "specifics" of the partnership.
2. Although the life of a partnership is limited, dissolving a partnership does not mean that the business will cease operations.
3. Mutual agency means that in most cases all partners are bound by the acts of one partner who enters in to a contract as an agent of the company.
4. In the formation of a partnership, one records assets at their current fair value.

Learning Unit 18-2

1. Salary and interest allowances are not expenses but mechanisms used to divide net income or net loss among partners. Salary is based on personal service; interest is based on a percent of each partner's capital balance.
2. Whether net income covers the salary and interest allowances makes no difference in calculating them; they are allocated, and *then* one looks to see the effect on partners' equity.
3. The statement of partners' equity is a supporting document that calculates the ending capital balance found on the balance sheet for each partner.

Learning Unit 18-3

1. When a new partner buys an equity interest from an existing partner, any personal profit belongs to the existing partner and is not recorded in the partnership. All that results on the partnership's books is a change of equity.
2. One partner cannot force other partners to accept a new partner.
3. A one-quarter equity interest doesn't necessarily mean a one-quarter share of all earnings—this would depend on the profit and loss ratio agreed upon by the partners.
4. A bonus is given to old partners if a new partner contributes more than his or her equity interest. On the other hand, a bonus is given to a new partner if he or she invests less than equity interest. The bonus is shared based on the profit and loss ratio.
5. At the time a partner leaves, a partnership may be audited and assets adjusted to their current fair market value. Revaluations are shared between the partners based on the profit and loss ratio.
6. A partner may withdraw for less than or more than book equity. The difference is then shared by the other partners based on the profit and loss ratio. If assets are not revalued, partners must agree whether assets are overstated or not, and then the equity change of the partner who is leaving is shared in profit and loss ratio by the other partners.

1. Liquidation is the winding-up process involved in ending a business.
2. Liquidation steps include:
   a. Selling assets for cash.
   b. Dividing loss or gain for realization among partners.
   c. Paying creditors.
   d. Paying remaining cash to partners based on capital balances.

KEY TERMS

Articles of partnership The written contract that spells out the details of the agreement among the partners.

Bonus When a new partner is admitted, he or she may pay more or less than equity interest. If the new partner pays more, the old partners share a bonus in the profit and loss ratio. Of course the opposite could result, and the new partner could receive a bonus if he or she invests less than equity interest.

Co-ownership of property Each partner owns a share of the assets.

Deficit Amount by which net income falls short of salary and interest allowance.

General partner A partner who has unlimited liability.

Interest allowance A mechanism for dividing earnings of a partnership based on a percent of capital balances of the partners (not an expense).

Limited life Partnership is dissolved by admission, withdrawal, or death of a partner. Although the partnership is dissolved, the operations of the business continue.

Limited partner The partner's liability is limited to the amount of his or her investment in the partnership.

Liquidation Occurs when a business is terminated, the assets are sold, and liabilities and partners are paid off.

Mutual agency Act of a single partner is binding on all members of the partnership.

Partnership The association of two or more persons who act as co-owners of a business.

Profit and loss ratio An agreed-upon ratio used to divide earnings or losses of a partnership.

Purchase of an equity interest Transfer of ownership between an existing partner and a new partner.

Realization The conversion of noncash assets into cash in the liquidation process.

Salary allowance A mechanism for dividing earnings of a partnership based on personal services provided by the partners (not an expense).

Uniform Partnership Act Laws enacted in most states that govern how a partnership is formed, operated, and liquidated.

Unlimited liability Partners may be personally liable for debts of partnership.

BLUEPRINT—ADVANTAGES AND DISADVANTAGES OF A PARTNERSHIP

Advantages	Disadvantages
1. Ease of formation—legal status under Uniform Partnership Act.	1. Limited life expectancy—any changes in membership dissolve the partnership.
2. Ability to raise more capital than a sole proprietorship.	2. Mutual agency—action by one partner binds all other partners.
3. Pooled resource of talents.	3. Unlimited liability—each partner must cover partnership debts with his or her personal assets.
4. Flexibility to react to the marketplace, since legal restrictions are minimal.	4. Cannot admit a new partner without agreement of all other partners; a partner cannot withdraw without agreement of all other partners.
5. Credit rating usually higher because more than one partner is responsible for company's debts.	

QUESTIONS, MINI EXERCISES, EXERCISES, AND PROBLEMS

Discussion Questions

1. How is the equity of a partnership different from that of a sole proprietorship?
2. List five characteristics of a partnership.
3. What is the function of the Articles of Partnership?
4. Explain how a company could operate even when being dissolved.
5. Mutual agency could create unlimited liability. Agree or disagree. Defend your position.
6. Explain why salary and interest allowances are not expenses for a partnership.
7. Give an example of a fractional ratio.
8. The statement of partners' capital is a required report. Accept or reject. Defend your position.
9. What is meant by a "side transaction" when a new partner is admitted by an existing partner's selling the new partner his or her equity?
10. What is meant by a "bonus" when a partner is admitted?
11. When a partner withdraws, why would a partnership revalue its assets?
12. Why would a partner who is withdrawing take more or less than his book equity?
13. What are the four steps of the liquidation process?

Mini Exercises

(The forms you need are on pages 54–56 of the *Study Guide and Working Papers*.)

Forming a Partnership

1. Alice Hall and Jim Brown enter into a partnership. On July 1, 19XX Alice invests $5,000 cash in the partnership. Jim invests $2,000 cash and store equipment worth $6,000 with accumulated depreciation of $2,000. The equipment has a current appraised value of $7,000. Prepare a journal entry to record this information.

Division of Net Income

2. Jamie Slater, Scupper Ring, and Molly Flynn invested $2,000, $4,000, and $6,000. At the end of the first year the company's net income was $21,000. Assuming no agreement was reached on how to share net income, prepare a journal entry at closing to allocate net income.

Division of Net Income Based on Beginning Capital Balances

3. If partners in Mini Exercise 2 share net income based on their beginning capital investments, what would be the journal entry at closing to allocate net income?

Calculating Total Salary and Interest Allowance

4. If partners in Mini Exercise 2 have the following agreement, please calculate the total salary and interest allowance.
   a. *Salary Allowance:* Slater, $7,000; Ring, $6,000; and Flynn, $4,000.
   b. 10 percent interest on capital investments.

Share of Net Income to Partners; Deficit Sharing

5. Using your answer in Mini Exercise 4, how much more income is to be distributed to the partners (assume each shares equally) after the salary and interest allowance? If net income was $17,990, how much would partners share in the deficit?

Admission of a New Partner

6. On March 8, Alan Oll sold his equity in the partnership to B. Mills for $4,000. Alan's capital account had a $3,000 balance. Record the journal entry.

Investing into an Existing Partnership

7. Pete Raul wants to have a one-third interest in a law practice that has two partners with capital balances as follows:

R. Seel, Capital	$4,000
A. Pool, Capital	1,000

How much must Pete invest into the partnership?

Calculating Profit and Loss Ratio

8. From the following capital balances, calculate the profit and loss ratio for each account:

B. Bool, Capital	100
A. Jones, Capital	500
T. Pool, Capital	400

Liquidation

9. From the following journalize the (a) sale of assets and (b) loss or gain from liquidation realization. Given:

Cash	$ 3,000
Other Assets	$15,000
Liabilities	3,000
Moxie, Capital	4,000
Carol, Capital	6,000
Earl, Capital	5,000

Partners agreed to share losses or gains in a 4:1:2 ratio and sold assets for $19,200.

Exercises

(The forms you need are on pages 58 and 59 of the *Study Guide and Working Papers.*)

Journal entries to record investing into a partnership.

18-1. Earl Munroe and Carol Rogers form a partnership on May 1, 19XX. Munroe contributes $40,000. Rogers contributes $28,000 cash and land costing $18,000 with a current fair value of $29,000. A $30,000 note payable due Rogers is assumed by the new partnership. Please prepare the journal entries to record Munroe's and Rogers's investment in the partnership.

Interest allowance.

18-2. A. Lot and B. Stall have decided their partnership earnings will be shared as follows: (a) 10 percent interest allowance on capital balances at beginning of year, (b) remainder to be shared equally. Capital balances of A. Lot and B. Stall at the beginning of the year are $80,000 and $30,000, respectively. Net income is $16,000 for the year. Record the journal entry to update the capital balances of A. Lot and B. Stall on December 31.

Withdrawal of partner taking assets greater than book equity.

18-3. Julie Elliott, Tami DiVito, and Abby Ellen are partners who share losses and gains in a ratio of 2:2:1. Their capital balances are $5,000, $6,000, and $4,000, respectively. The partners are anxious to have Tami retire and have paid her $12,000. Give the journal entry to record the payment to Tami along with the absorption of the amount over book equity by Julie and Abby on July 31, 19XX.

Admission of new partner.

18-4. L. White, V. Slye, and E. Rothe are partners with capital balances of $90,000, $80,000, and $70,000, respectively. Rothe sells his interest in the company

18B-3. Lane, Right, and Von are partners of LRV Repairs Service. On July 31, 19XX, the balance sheet was as follows:

Cash	$50,000	Lane, Capital	$30,000
Other Assets	20,000	Right, Capital	15,000
Other Assets	10,000	Von, Capital	35,000
Total Assets	$80,000	Total Liab. + Equity	$80,000

The partners agree to share all losses and gains in a 2:1:2 ratio. Von is withdrawing from the partnership. From the following independent situations, journalize the withdrawal of Von.

Situation 1: Von sells his equity to Jones for $120,000. Partners agree to admission of Jones.

Situation 2: On withdrawal of Von, inventory is determined to be overvalued by $6,000. (Before withdrawal, assets are revalued to current fair market value.)

Situation 3: Von is paid $32,000 out of the assets of the partnership. Although the assets are overvalued, the partners do not want to decrease the recorded asset values.

Situation 4: Von is paid $44,000 out of the assets of the partnership. Since the assets are undervalued, partners do not want to increase the recorded asset values.

18B-4. Jones, Reston, and Sullivan are liquidating their partnership. All losses and gains are shared in a 4:2:1 ratio (not based on investment). Before liquidation their balance sheet looked as follows:

Cash	$ 800	Liabilities	$ 6,000
Other Assets	19,200	A. Jones, Capital	4,000
		C. Reston, Capital	8,000
		J. Sullivan, Capital	2,000
Total Assets	$20,000	Total Liab. + Equity	$20,000

Journalize the entries needed in the liquidation process under the following independent situations (assume a date of July 1, 19XX, for sale of assets and a date of July 15 to pay off liabilities and distribute cash that is left to partners):

Situation 1: Sold other assets for $26,200.

Situation 2: Sold other assets for $17,800.

Situation 3: Sold other assets for $10,800; Jones cannot cover his deficit. (For simplicity round any calculations to the nearest dollar.)

REAL WORLD APPLICATIONS

18R-1.

Al Ring and Marvin Smoy are partners who are extremely worried about the financial condition of their company. As of December 31, 19XX, their balance sheet revealed the following:

Assets		**Liabilities and Owner's Equity**	
Cash	$ 30,000	Liabilities	$ 60,000
Noncash assets	400,000	A. Ring, Capital	200,000
		M. Smoy, Capital	170,000
Total Assets	$430,000	Total Liab. + Equity	$430,000

There is a pending lawsuit that could result in a settlement of more than $400,000 against the company for negligence. Al wants out of the partnership before the case is settled. Marvin claims they are both in this together. As the accountant, could you explain in writing to Al how the situation looks? All losses and gains are shared in a 2 : 1 ratio.

18R-2.

On May 15 Peter Rig and Joan Fess formed a partnership in the catering business. Peter invested $30,000 in cash and $8,000 in equipment. Joan invested land worth $15,000, a building worth $24,000, and merchandise worth $8,000.

The partners decided that they would insure the building and its contents beginning June 1. On May 28 a fire broke out and destroyed half of the merchandise, the building, and the equipment. That night Rig and Fess decided to liquidate the business.

Rig told Fess that he would take his cash (which was in a fireproof safe) while Fess would take the land. Fess argued that in a partnership Rig couldn't do this. Could you settle this dispute? Make your recommendations in writing.

YOU make the call

Critical Thinking/Ethical Case

18R-3.

Jee Jones is in a partnership with Alvin Scott and Morry Flynn. Jee signed a long-term contract with a supplier without telling either partner. When Alvin heard about it he hit the roof. He told Jee the partnership could not afford this contract and he would have nothing to do with it. Do you think Alvin should be upset? You make the call. Write down your recommendations to Alvin.

ACCOUNTING RECALL

A CUMULATIVE APPROACH

THIS EXAM REVIEWS CHAPTERS 1 THROUGH 18

Your *Study Guide and Working Papers* (pp. 70 – 71) have forms to complete this exam, as well as worked-out solutions. The page references next to each question identify what page to turn back to if you answer the question incorrectly.

PART 1 Vocabulary Review

Match the terms to the appropriate definition or phrase.

Page Ref.

(638)	1. Salary allowance	A. Written contract
(505)	2. Allowance for doubtful accounts	B. Extends an asset's life
		C. Other income
(651)	3. Realization	D. A mechanism for dividing earnings
(614)	4. Extraordinary repairs	E. Sell old goods first
(617)	5. Gain on sale of plant asset	F. Operating expense
(636)	6. Mutual agency	G. Conversion of noncash assets
(573)	7. FIFO	H. Contra-asset

(621)	8.	Depletion of coal deposit	I.	Sell new goods first
(574)	9.	LIFO	J.	Act of a single partner is binding on all members of the partnership
(635)	10.	Articles of partnership		

PART II True or False (Accounting Theory)

(648)	11.	Dissolving a partnership means the business operation will cease.
(638)	12.	Salary and interest allowances are not expense.
(644)	13.	A bonus can never be based on the profit and loss ratio.
(636)	14.	An advantage of a partnership is mutual agency.
(636)	15.	A partnership has a limited life.

19

CORPORATIONS

Organization and Capital Stock

THE BIG PICTURE

When the Eldorado Computer Center ended its second year of business, Tony Freedman and Charles West were happy with their success. They had just opened an additional store and had also hired three more employees: Bobbi Castro, the bookkeeper for the south location, and Don Reyes and Kyle Underwood, the new computer technicians.

In the first meeting of the year, the partners considered incorporating the business. An incorporated business would stand as a separate legal entity, protecting the partners from the liabilities of the business. A disadvantage, however, is that a corporation pays taxes on its income, and its owners pay taxes on their income from the business, as well. Tony and Charles had to weigh the benefits against the costs.

This chapter talks about the advantages and disadvantages of a corporation. You will learn how to record entries for issuing stock, dividends, and capital gains. Day-to-day corporate accounting is exactly the same as for the other forms of ownership. The biggest difference is in the ownership itself — that is, each share of stock represents a unit of ownership, and the owners are called stockholders instead of partners.

Learning Objectives	◆ Defining a corporation; establishing a corporation; listing the advantages and disadvantages of a corporation. (p. 664) ◆ Journalizing entries for issuing par-value stock, no-par stock, and no-par with stated value stock. (p. 667) ◆ Calculating dividends on preferred and common stock. (p. 671) ◆ Recording capital stock transactions under a stock subscription plan. (p. 678)

So far we've learned about sole proprietorships and partnerships; now we're going to learn about corporations. A **corporation,** like Disney, is a separate legal entity. We will first look at how a corporation is formed, along with its main characteristics.

LEARNING UNIT 19-1
Forming a Corporation; Characteristics of the Corporate Structure

Four steps are involved in forming a corporation.

Step 1: The **incorporators,** those wishing to form the corporation, apply to a state for a charter. They do this by submitting an **articles of incorporation** drawn up by an attorney, together with a fee. The articles of incorporation consist of the following information:

1. Name of the corporation and incorporation date.
2. Purpose of business.
3. Organizational structure.
4. Expected life — usually "forever."
5. Primary location of business.
6. Types of stock to be offered. (Stock is what owners purchase to gain ownership rights in the company. We will look at this in detail in a few moments.)

Step 2: The Office of the Secretary of State reviews the application and, if deemed in order, a **charter** (often called a **certificate of incorporation**) is issued to the incorporators. Copies of the charter and the articles of incorporation are placed on file for public record.

Step 3: The stock is issued by the corporation to the owners (called **stockholders**).

Step 4: The stockholders meet to elect a board of **directors** and adopt the bylaws of the corporation. Often in a new corporation the stockholders become the directors. As the company grows, people are appointed to the board who are not stockholders. Records of meetings of the board of directors and stockholders are kept in a **minute book,** as directed by law. The board of directors appoints the officers to run the company; it is the board's job to oversee the overall management of the corporation, while the officers follow the policies set up by the board.

> When the charter is issued, the corporation's legal entity is established.

ADVANTAGES OF THE CORPORATE FORM OF ORGANIZATION

1. Limited Liability/Separate Legal Entity

Stockholders have **limited liability;** they are not personally liable for the obligations of the corporation, because a corporation is a separate and distinct legal entity. The corporation enters into contracts, buys or sells property, and sues or is sued in its own name. Thus the only amount the stockholders can lose is the amount of their investment in the business. Of course, stockholders can still be held liable for any fraudulent or negligent actions they perform in connection with the corporation.

2. Unlimited Life

A corporation's life is perpetual (goes on forever) except in the case of bankruptcy, mergers, or vote of the stockholders.

3. Ease of Transferring Ownership Interest

When an owner invests in a corporation, each share of ownership is represented by one or more formal documents called **stock certificates.** The stockholder can sell or transfer shares of some corporations through *brokerage firms* — companies that act as middlemen in the trading of stock. This trading occurs at various marketplaces called *stock exchanges.* On the back of the certificate is a form that the seller endorses. A key point is that when the shares of stock are sold by the stockholder, the sale has *no* effect on the company's assets and liabilities. What happens is really a *shift* in the ownership.

4. No Mutual Agency

In a corporation there is no mutual agency as there is in a partnership. For example, if John Jones is a stockholder of Passon Corporation and enters into a contract with the city of Lynn, this action by John cannot bind the corporation to complete the contract with the city of Lynn.

5. Ease of Raising Capital

With no mutual agency, with limited liability, and with the ease of transferring ownership interest, the investment in a corporation becomes attractive to many people. As a result, the corporation can raise large amounts of capital by assembling investment groups of stockholders.

DISADVANTAGES OF THE CORPORATE STRUCTURE

1. Difficulties in Forming a Corporation/Government Regulations

As we have seen, a corporation is more difficult to form than a sole proprietorship or a partnership. Incorporators must complete the articles of incorporation and pay an incorporation fee. The complexity of forming a corporation also usually means hiring a lawyer to deal with legal aspects. When granted a certificate of incorporation, corporations are required to fulfill many state and federal regulations and to file many governmental reports.

2. Corporate Taxation

Since the corporation is a separate legal entity, its income is taxed by the federal government. The corporation may also be taxed at the state and local levels. At the same time, any income that is distributed to the stockholders is taxable to the stockholders. Thus there is double taxation of a corporation's earnings. Later in the text we will show tax advantages that can be gained by forming a corporation. On page 666 are the corporate tax rates for 1998 and after:

"But WHY can't I buy stock in Dunkin' Donuts, Fred?" asked Marv. "Well, Marv, it's a long story," said Fred. "Pull up a chair, and I'll explain. "The 4,139 Dunkin' Donuts shops are individually owned businesses, "Fred continued, "working under a franchise agreement with Dunkin' Donuts Inc. The shops (called franchises) may be organized as sole proprietorships, partnerships, or corporations. Most shop owners (called franchisees) have chosen the corporate form, because corporations offer the advantage of limited liability. A wage is paid to the manager, and a franchise fee is paid to Dunkin' Donuts, Inc. Then the profits are distributed to the stockholders/owners as dividends on their common stock."

"But what does Dunkin' Donuts Inc. do?" asked Marv.

"Well," Fred continued, "the corporate structure for Dunkin' Donuts Inc. is complex. Dunkin' Donuts Inc. is owned by the British conglomerate, Allied Domecq PLC, which owns a number of different kinds of companies located throughout the world. As a British corporation, Allied Domecq operates under different accounting rules than American corporations. Allied Domecq's Retailing USA Division is composed of three different companies: Dunkin' Donuts, Baskin-Robbins (the ice cream shops), and Togos (sandwich shops).

"I'll sketch it out for you," said Fred, grabbing a paper napkin. (His sketch appears to the right.)

"So that's the story, Marv," said Fred. "You can't buy stock in Dunkin' Donuts Inc., but you could buy stock in Allied Domecq, on the London Stock Exchange. Or you could buy a franchise yourself."

DISCUSSION QUESTIONS

1. Why might Fred want to become a corporation?
2. How can Dunkin' Donuts Inc.'s profits be distributed to stockholders, if no one owns stock in Dunkin Donuts' Inc.?

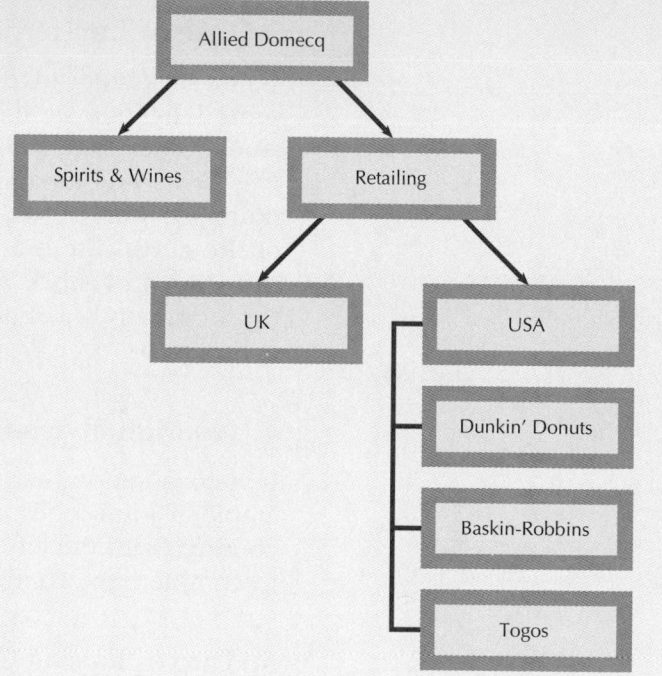

FEDERAL CORPORATE INCOME TAX RATE*

Taxable Income

Over	But Not Over	Tax Is	Of the Amount Over
$ 0	$ 50,000	15%	0
50,000	75,000	7,500 + 25%	50,000
75,000	100,000	13,750 + 34%	75,000
100,000	335,000	22,250 + 39%	100,000
335,000	10,000,000	113,900 + 34%	335,000
10,000,000	15,000,000	3,400,000 + 35%	10,000,000
15,000,000	18,333,333	5,150,000 + 38%	15,000,000
18,333,333	—	6,416,667 + 35%	18,333,333

* Check with IRS for latest rates.

CH. 19 / CORPORATIONS: ORGANIZATION AND CAPITAL STOCK

LEARNING UNIT 19-1 REVIEW

AT THIS POINT you should be able to

◆ Explain the steps in forming a corporation. (p. 664)
◆ List as well as explain the advantages and disadvantages of the corporate form of organization. (pp. 664–665)

SELF-REVIEW QUIZ 19-1

(The forms you need are on page 72 of the *Study Guide and Working Papers.*) Respond true or false to the following:

1. The articles of incorporation is quite easy to fill out.
2. A corporation is a separate legal entity.
3. The officers of a corporation always elect the board of directors.
4. Stocks can be transferred by stockholders without affecting the operations of a corporation.
5. Double taxation does exist in a corporate structure.

Solution to Self-Review Quiz 19-1

1. F   **2.** T   **3.** F   **4.** T   **5.** T

LEARNING UNIT 19-2
Stockholders' Equity: Retained Earnings and Capital Stock

The equity section of a corporation differs from that of a sole proprietorship or a partnership. In the sole proprietorship we have simply a capital account and a withdrawals account. In the partnership there is a separate capital and withdrawals account for each partner. With the corporation, the stockholders' equity section is broken down into two major parts:

1. **Paid-in Capital:** This is the amount that stockholders have invested in the business. It is equal to the values of the assets (usually cash) that have been contributed to the business.
2. **Retained Earnings:** These are accumulated profits that are retained or kept in the corporation. Retained earnings does not mean cash—cash is an *asset*, retained earnings is part of stockholders' *equity.*

CORPORATION

A = L + Stockholders' Equity

Paid-In Capital: *Retained Earnings:*

Capital Stock   Retained Earnings

Let's look more closely at the term "Capital Stock."

CAPITAL STOCK

In return for their investment in the corporation, stockholders are issued shares of **capital stock.** Think of ownership of a corporation as being represented by

In Chapter 20, we will look at the difference between issued and outstanding stock.

shares of stock. There are two classes of capital stock, common and preferred. The charter of the corporation indicates the maximum amount of shares of each class of capital stock that a company can legally issue, but the company does not have to issue all of it. **Authorized capital stock** is the amount listed in the charter; **issued capital stock** refers to the shares sold to the stockholders; **outstanding capital stock** means shares sold and in the stockholders' possession. Let's look at the two classes of capital stock, beginning with common stock.

Characteristics of common stock

The most prevalent type of capital stock is called **common stock.** When a corporation has only one kind of capital stock, it will be common stock. When the stock is issued, the owners receive certain rights from the corporation. These rights include:

1. The right to vote at stockholders' meetings.
2. The right to share in profits by receiving dividends.
3. The right to dispose of or sell their stock.
4. The right to maintain their proportionate ownership interest in the company. This is called **preemptive right.** For example, if Jill Evans owns 15 percent of the common stock of the corporation, she would have the chance to also purchase 15 percent of any *additional* common stock that is issued, before it is offered to the public at large.
5. The right, when a company is liquidated, to share in assets after creditors and others with prior claims are paid off.

Characteristics of preferred stock

Another type of capital stock some corporations may issue is called **preferred stock.** Basically it is stock that provides stockholders with prior claim to a corporation's profits and assets over holders of common stock. Corporations watch current market conditions and try to offer preferred stock that will be attractive to investors. Holders of preferred stock often give up some of the rights that go with common stock — such as voting rights, preemptive rights, or even some earnings potential — in return for their more stable earnings that come from preferred stock. In many ways preferred stock is a less risky investment than common stock.

Dividends on common and preferred stock

We show how to calculate dividends for preferred and common stock on pp. 675–676.

Dividends are paid to stockholders as their share of the corporation's profits. A dividend must be voted by the board of directors, and if it has been a bad year for profits, the board may refuse to vote a dividend. Keep in mind a company may decide against a dividend in a good year, feeling it may be wise to invest money in research and development, etc.

As we mentioned, preferred stock gives its stockholders a prior claim to a corporation's profits over holders of common stock. There are several ways this could happen:

1. If a preferred stock is **cumulative,** the holders have a right to a certain dividend every year. If in some years the board does not issue a dividend, then the amount payable will accumulate until the earnings justify the payout. At this

time the preferred stockholders will get dividends for all past years as well as the current year before the holders of common stock get any dividend.

For example, Moore Company has 3,000 shares of cumulative preferred stock that is entitled to a dividend of $3 per share. In 19X7, owing to financial problems, Moore Company decided to pay no dividend. Thus the company has **dividends in arrears** of $9,000. This means that no dividends can be paid to common stockholders until the preferred dividends are paid off in full—the amount in arrears plus the current year's dividend. Since financial conditions improved in 19X8, Moore paid the $9,000 of dividends in arrears (3,000 shares × $3) to holders of preferred stock plus the current year's dividend of $9,000.

2. If a preferred stock is **noncumulative,** holders have a right to the current year's dividend, but there are no holdovers from past years when dividends were not declared.

3. If a preferred stock is **nonparticipating,** each year the holders of preferred stock receive a certain percent as dividend and the remainder goes to common stock. Thus if a company declared a dividend of $50,000, the preferred stockholders would get their usual percent and the common stockholders would get all the rest, even if it was a greater percent dividend than preferred got.

4. If a preferred stock is **participating,** preferred stockholders get their yearly dividend and can get a percent of what's left over, splitting it in various ways with common stockholders.

STOCK VALUE (FOR CAPITAL STOCK)

When a corporation is created, it issues a certain number of shares of stock, which are then sold to stockholders. At the time that the corporation receives its charter, the board of directors may assign a **par value** to the stock—something like $25 or $50 a share. This value is entirely arbitrary—no one can say that the stock is really worth that much. It is a way of dividing up ownership of the corporation into a number of units and putting a value on each unit. Many companies have par values of 5 or 10 cents per share. The key point par value is a value assigned arbitrarily. It is stated on the stock certificate. Figure 19-1 on page 670 can be used as a summary as you read the rest of the chapter.

In most states the assigning of par value per share times the number of shares issued for a corporation represents the **legal capital**—an amount that a corporation must retain in the business for protection of creditors.

Since the concept of par value can be quite misleading, some corporations will issue **no-par stock**—stock with no par value. Thus the *entire* proceeds from selling this issue represents the legal capital (number of shares issued times amount investors paid for each share).

Most states permit (or some require) that the directors of a company set a **stated value** on the shares. This also is an arbitrary value but can be changed by the board of directors. Stated value, which has the same purpose as par value, may be less confusing to investors, since it is not printed on the stock certificates.

Whether a stock is issued at par value, no par value with no stated value, or no par value with stated value, the capital stock account can be updated with entries that indicate whether investors paid more or less than par value or stated value. We will look at specific examples of recording capital stock in the next unit.

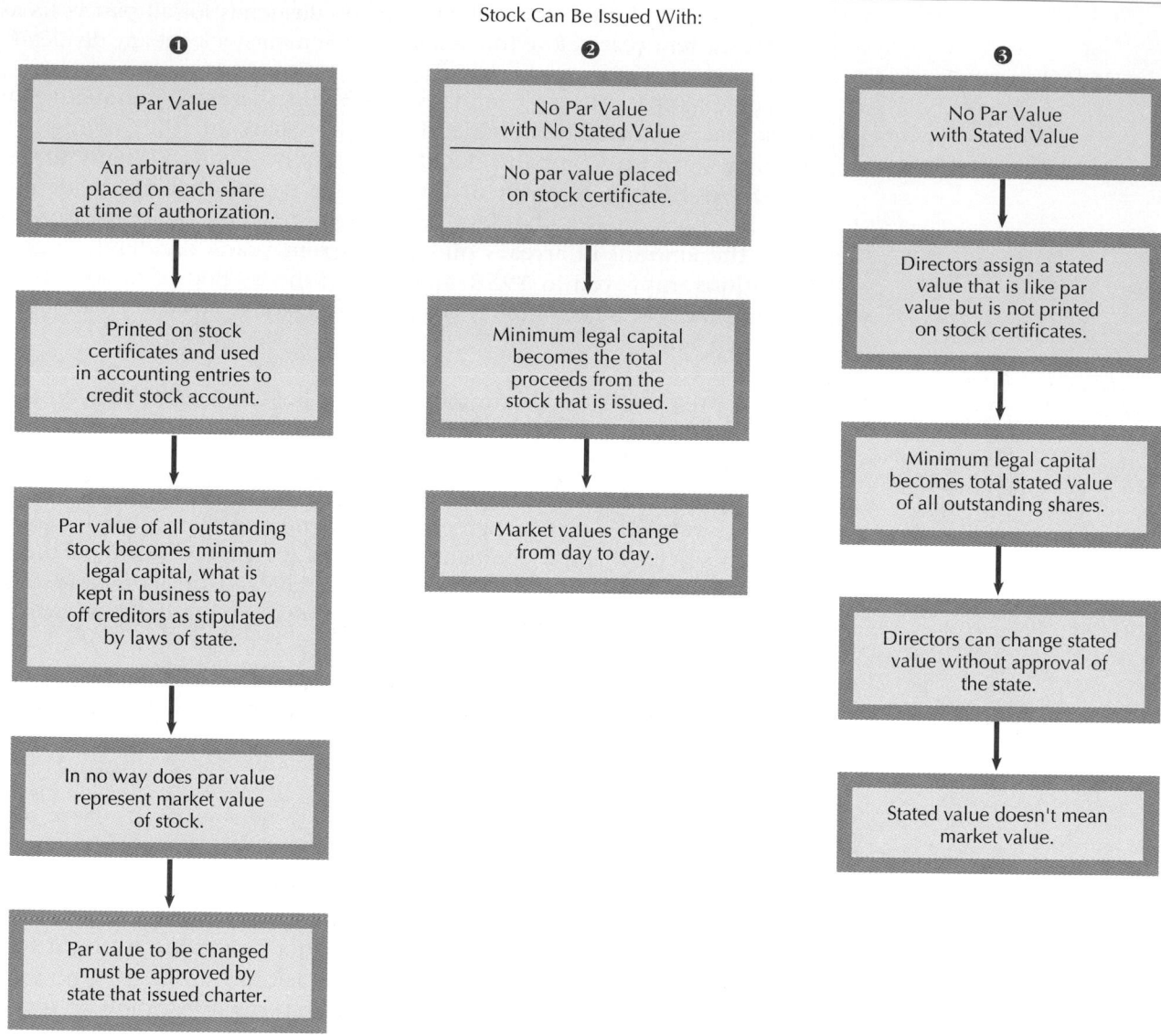

FIGURE 19-1 Par, No Par, and Stated Value

LEARNING UNIT 19-2 REVIEW

AT THIS POINT you should be able to

◆ Explain the difference between authorized and issued stock. (p. 668)
◆ List the characteristics of common and preferred stock. (pp. 668–669)
◆ Define and explain cumulative, noncumulative, participating, and nonparticipating preferred stock. (p. 669)
◆ Define and explain par value, legal capital, no-par stock, and stated value. (pp. 669–670)

SELF-REVIEW QUIZ 19-2

(The forms you need are on page 72 of the *Study Guide and Working Papers*.) Answer true or false to the following:

1. Retained Earnings is part of Paid-in Capital.
2. Preferred stock is the most prevalent type of capital stock.

The following text appears inside Figure 19-1:

Stock Can Be Issued With:

❶ Par Value — An arbitrary value placed on each share at time of authorization.

Printed on stock certificates and used in accounting entries to credit stock account.

Par value of all outstanding stock becomes minimum legal capital, what is kept in business to pay off creditors as stipulated by laws of state.

In no way does par value represent market value of stock.

Par value to be changed must be approved by state that issued charter.

❷ No Par Value with No Stated Value — No par value placed on stock certificate.

Minimum legal capital becomes the total proceeds from the stock that is issued.

Market values change from day to day.

❸ No Par Value with Stated Value

Directors assign a stated value that is like par value but is not printed on stock certificates.

Minimum legal capital becomes total stated value of all outstanding shares.

Directors can change stated value without approval of the state.

Stated value doesn't mean market value.

3. Preemptive right allows one to maintain one's proportionate ownership interest in a company.

4. Preferred stock that is cumulative is entitled to dividends in arrears.

5. Par value doesn't represent the market value of the stock.

6. Stock cannot be issued at par value.

Solution to Self-Review Quiz 19-2

1. F   **2.** F   **3.** T   **4.** T   **5.** T   **6.** F

LEARNING UNIT 19-3

Recording Capital Stock Transactions and Calculating Dividends

In this unit we will look at how to record the issuing of stock that has (1) par value, (2) no par value, and (3) no par value with stated value. We will also see how to record transactions in which stock is exchanged for noncash assets. We will then look at how to calculate dividends for preferred and common stock.

RECORDING THE SALE OF STOCK THAT HAS PAR VALUE

Situation 1: Selling Common Stock at Par

Roger Company sells 200 shares of a $10 par value common stock at $10 per share on February 3, 19XX.

Here is an analysis of the transaction.

Accounts Affected	Category	↑	↓	Rules	
Cash	Asset	↑		Dr. $2,000	$10 par
Common Stock	SE	↑		Cr. $2,000	× 200 shares = $2,000

Common Stock is recorded at number of shares times par value. This represents the legal capital. The journal entry would be as follows:

19XX Feb.	3	Cash		2 0 0 0 00	
		Common Stock			2 0 0 0 00

Situation 2: Selling Preferred Stock at Par

Roger Co. sells 300 shares of $50 par value preferred stock at $50 on March 18, 19XX.

Once again, here is an analysis of the transaction.

Accounts Affected	Category	↑	↓	Rules	
Cash	Asset	↑		Dr. $15,000	300 shares
Preferred Stock	SE	↑		Cr. $15,000	× $50 par = $15,000

Preferred Stock is recorded at number of shares times par value. The journal entry would be as shown on page 672.

19XX March	18	Cash			15	0	0	0	00								
		Preferred Stock									15	0	0	0	00	

Situation 3: Selling Common Stock at a Premium (More than Par Value)

Roger Co. sells 50 shares of $10 par value common stock at $15 on June 8, 19XX.

The Analysis: The common stock is recorded at par value. Since this stock is sold at a **premium** (more than par value), the excess of the par value will be recorded in a new account called **Paid-in Capital in Excess of Par Value— Common**. Note in the transactional analysis that follows that this account is part of stockholders' equity. On the balance sheet it will be listed below common stock in the paid-in capital section of stockholders' equity.

Accounts Affected	Category	↑	↓	Rules	
Cash	Asset	↑		Dr. $750	⟶ 50 shares × $15
Common Stock	SE	↑		Cr. $500	⟶ 50 shares × $10 par
Paid-in Capital in Excess of Par Value—Common	SE	↑		Cr. $250	⟶ 50 shares × $ 5 excess per share over par

The journal entry will be as follows:

19XX June	8	Cash			7	5	0	00									
		Common Stock									5	0	0	00		
		Paid-in Capital in															
		Excess of Par Value—Common									2	5	0	00		

Situation 4: Selling Common Stock at a Discount (Below Par)*

Roger Co. sells 100 shares of $10 par value common stock at $8 on July 3, 19XX.

The Analysis: When a stock is sold below par, a **discount** results. An account called *Discount on Common Stock* records the discount. It is a contra-stockholders' equity account that will reduce the common stock account it is related to. Some states do not allow stock to be sold at a discount.

Accounts Affected	Category	↑	↓	Rules	
Cash	Asset	↑		Dr. $800	⟶ 100 shares × $8
Discount on Common Stock	Contra SE	↑		Cr. $200	⟶ 100 shares × $2 ($10 par − $8)
Common Stock	SE	↑		Cr. $1,000	⟶ 100 shares × $10 par

* This situation does not occur very often.

The journal entry will be as follows:

	19XX July	3	Cash		8 0 0 0 00	
			Discount on Common Stock		2 0 0 0 00	
			Common Stock			1 0 0 0 00

Now let's look at how to record the sale of stock with no par value, with or without stated value.

RECORDING SALE OF STOCK WITH NO PAR VALUE AND STATED VALUE

Situation 5: Selling No-Par Common Stock with No Stated Value

Moss Co. sells 300 shares of no-par common stock for $20 per share on July 19, 19XX.

Our transaction analysis chart shows the following:

Accounts Affected	Category	↑	↓	Rules	
Cash	Asset	↑		Dr. $6,000	} 300 shares × $20
Common Stock	SE	↑		Cr. $6,000	

The journal entry will be as follows:

	19XX July	19	Cash		6 0 0 0 00	
			Common Stock			6 0 0 0 00

Situation 6: Selling No-Par Common Stock with a Stated Value

Reese Co. sells 200 shares of no-par common stock with a stated value of $40 for $50 pcr share on June 19, 19XX.

The Analysis: An excess over the stated value will be recorded in a stockholders' equity account called **Paid-in Capital in Excess of Stated Value— Common.**

Accounts Affected	Category	↑	↓	Rules	
Cash	Asset	↑		Dr. $10,000	→ 200 shares × $50
Common Stock	SE	↑		Cr. $8,000	→ 200 shares × $40
Paid-in Capital in Excess of Stated Value— Common	SE	↑		Cr. $2,000	→ 200 shares × $10 ($50 − $40)

The journal entry will be as follows, on page 674.

Note: Corporations cannot legally sell stock at less than the stated value.

	19XX July	19	Cash		1 0 0 0 0 0 0		
			Common Stock			8 0 0 0 0 0	
			Paid-in Capital in Excess of				
			Stated Value—Common			2 0 0 0 0 0	

RECORDING TRANSACTIONS IN WHICH STOCK IS EXCHANGED FOR NONCASH ASSETS

Situation 7: Exchanging Stock for Noncash Assets

On July 8, Moss Corporation exchanged 3,000 shares of $10 par-value common stock for machinery, buildings, and land. The assets had fair market value of $5,000, $10,000, and $20,000, respectively.

The Analysis: Assets are recorded at fair market value; common stock is recorded at par value. If fair market value is not available for assets, one can try to find the market (not par) value of the stock. In this chapter we assume fair market value of assets is available. The difference between fair market value and par is recorded in the account Paid-in Capital in Excess of Par. Par value is *never* used to measure the selling price of the assets.

Accounts Affected	Category	↑	↓	Rules	
Machinery	Asset	↑		Dr. $5,000	⎫
Buildings	Asset	↑		Dr. $10,000	⎬ Fair market value
Land	Asset	↑		Dr. $20,000	⎭
Common Stock	SE	↑		Cr. $30,000	→ 300 shares × $10 par
Paid-in Capital in Excess of Par—Common	SE	↑		Cr. $5,000	→ ($35,000 − $30,000)

The journal entry will be as follows:

	19XX July	8	Machinery		5 0 0 0 0 0		
			Buildings		1 0 0 0 0 0 0		
			Land		2 0 0 0 0 0 0		
			Common Stock			3 0 0 0 0 0 0	
			Paid-in Capital in				
			Excess of Par—Common			5 0 0 0 0 0	

Situation 8: Issuing Stock to Organizers of a Business for Services Performed

On June 8, Rose Corporation issued 2,000 shares of $10 par common stock to the organizers of the business for services performed.

The Analysis: **Organization Cost** in the formation of a corporation (legal fees, printing of stock certificates, etc.) is an intangible asset on the balance sheet. It is usually amortized over five years (can be up to 40 years) because that life is used for income tax returns.

Accounts Affected	Category	↑ ↓	Rules
Organization Cost	Asset	↑	Dr. $20,000
Common Stock	SE	↑	Cr. $20,000

The journal entry will be as follows:

19XX June	8	Organization Cost		20 00 0 00	
		Common Stock			20 00 0 00

HOW TO CALCULATE DIVIDENDS

Table 19-1 summarizes the process, which is divided into four steps. For our calculation we will use these basic facts:

◆ $150,000 dividend declared
◆ Preferred stock is 6 percent and fully participating

TABLE 19-1 FOUR-STEP PROCEDURE FOR CALCULATING DIVIDENDS

The Formula	The Calculation	Preferred Stock	Common Stock	Total Dividends
Step 1: Dividend for preferred Number of shares × par value per share × rate of dividend	1,000 shares × $200 × .06 = $12,000	$12,000		$12,000
Step 2: Dividend for common Number of shares × par value per share × rate of dividend	6,000 shares × $100 × .06 = $36,000		$36,000	36,000
Step 3: Find total par value Number of shares × par value per share (preferred) *plus* Number of shares × par value per share (common)	1,000 shares × $200 = $200,000 6,000 shares × $100 = 600,000 Total par = $800,000			
Step 4: Allocate remainder of dividend based on par value Preferred = $\dfrac{\text{Par value of preferred}}{\text{Total par value}}$ → $\dfrac{\$200,000}{\$800,000}$ × Remainder of dividend	$\dfrac{\$200,000}{\$800,000}$ × $102,000* = $25,500	25,500		25,500
Common = $\dfrac{\text{Par value of common}}{\text{Total par value}}$ × Remainder of dividend	$\dfrac{\$600,000}{\$800,000}$ × $102,000* = $76,500		76,500	76,500
		$37,500	$112,500	$150,000

* $150,000 − $48,000 = $102,000.

◆ Preferred stock: 1,000 shares, $200 par
◆ Common stock: 6,000 shares, $100 par

Step 1: To calculate preferred dividends you multiply the number of shares (1,000) times the par value ($200) per share times the rate of dividend (6 percent). This results in a $12,000 dividend to preferred.

Step 2: To calculate the common stock dividend you multiply the number of shares (6,000) times the par value per share ($100) times the same rate of dividend (6 percent). This results in a dividend of $36,000.

Step 3: At this point $48,000 of the $150,000 of dividends has been apportioned. Since the preferred is participating — which means it can share in additional dividends beyond the 6 percent dividend — the next step is to find the total par value and allocate the remainder of the dividend based on the total par.

Note in step 3 how the number of shares of preferred is multiplied by the $200 par and the number of common shares is multiplied by the $100 par. Thus total par is $800,000.

Step 4: Since preferred is one-fourth of the total par, preferred is allocated $25,500 ($\frac{1}{4}$ × $102,000) and common is allocated three-fourths of the $102,000 or $76,500.

We can see that both were paid the same percent on par by the following calculations:

PREFERRED:

$$\frac{\text{Total dividends}}{\text{Total par value of preferred}} = \frac{\$37,500}{\$200,000} = 18.75 \text{ percent}$$

COMMON:

$$\frac{\text{Total vidends}}{\text{Total par value of common}} = \frac{\$112,500}{\$600,000} = 18.75 \text{ percent}$$

The end result is that the dividends were equally divided in terms of percentage, because preferred was fully participating.

LEARNING UNIT 19-3 REVIEW

AT THIS POINT you should be able to

◆ Record transactions that issue stock with or without par value. (p. 671)
◆ Explain the account called Paid-in Capital in Excess of Par Value. (p. 672)
◆ Tell what the normal balance is for the account Discount on Common Stock. (p. 672)
◆ Explain when the account Paid-in Capital in Excess of Stated Value is used. (p. 672)
◆ Calculate capital in excess of par value when stock is exchanged for noncash assets. (p. 673)
◆ Explain when one uses the account called Organization Cost. (p. 675)
◆ Calculate dividends on common and preferred stock. (pp. 675 – 676)

SELF-REVIEW QUIZ 19-3

(The forms you need are on pages 73 and 74 of the *Study Guide and Working Papers*.)

1. Journalize the following transactions:

19XX
July 5 Boston Company sells 200 shares of $20 par-value common stock at $20.
Aug. 8 Jess Company sells 100 shares of $10 par-value common stock at $25.
Oct. 9 Mellisa Company sells 300 shares of no-par common stock with a stated value of $30 for $50 per share.
Nov. 12 Moss Company issued 1,000 shares of $25 par-value common stock to the organizers of the firm for services rendered costing $30,000.

2. From the following, calculate the dividends for common and preferred stock.

   ◆ Fourteen percent fully participating preferred stock
   ◆ Board declared a $210,000 dividend
   ◆ Preferred stock—3,000 shares, $100 par
   ◆ Common stock—7,000 shares, $100 par

Solution to Self-Review Quiz 19-3

1.

19XX					
July	5	Cash	4 0 0 0 00		
		Common Stock		4 0 0 0 00	
Aug.	8	Cash	2 5 0 0 00		
		Common Stock		1 0 0 0 00	
		Paid-in Capital in Excess			
		of Par Value—Common		1 5 0 0 00	
Oct.	9	Cash	15 0 0 0 00		
		Common Stock		9 0 0 0 00	
		Paid-in Capital in Excess			
		of Stated Value—Common		6 0 0 0 00	
Nov.	12	Organization Cost	30 0 0 0 00		
		Common Stock		25 0 0 0 00	
		Paid-in Capital in Excess			
		of Par Value—Common		5 0 0 0 00	

2.

	PREFERRED	COMMON
Dividends for preferred:		
(3,000 shares × $100 par) × .14 =	$42,000	
Dividends for common:		
(7,000 shares × $100 par) × .14 =		$ 98,000
Amount to be divided based on total par value:		
($210,000 − $140,000) = $70,000		

Total Par:
Preferred: 3,000 shares × $100 par = $ 300,000
Common: 7,000 shares × $100 par =   700,000
                        Total $1,000,000

Preferred: $\dfrac{\$300,000}{\$1,000,000}$ × $70,000 = $21,000   21,000

Common: $\dfrac{\$700,000}{\$1,000,000}$ × $70,000 = $49,000   49,000

                        Totals $63,000 $147,000

Proof:

$$\text{Preferred: } \frac{\$63,000}{\$300,000} = 21\%$$

$$\text{Common: } \frac{\$147,000}{\$700,000} = 21\%$$

LEARNING UNIT 19-4
Recording Capital Stock Transactions under a Stock Subscription Plan

In the last unit we assumed that stocks were immediately issued and full payment or cash or other assets were received. In this unit we examine stock transactions under **stock subscription** plans. Under such plans, buyers pledge to buy certain stocks but pay in installments or in a later lump sum. In most cases, companies will not issue the actual stock certificates to these buyers until payment is complete.

Let's look at how Krump Corporation receives subscriptions for 1,000 shares of $100 par-value common stock at $160 per share on April 1, 19XX. Two equal installments will be paid on August 1 and November 1 by the buyer.

April 1: Accepted Subscription for 1,000 Shares at $160 per Share

Since the stock certificates will not be issued until paid in full, Krump Corporation records the ownership at par value in a temporary stockholders' equity account called **Common Stock Subscribed.** This account is shown in the paid-in capital section below the issue of the common stock. The amount due is recorded in an account called **Subscriptions Receivable—Common Stock.** The difference between the par value and the issue price is accumulated in a permanent account called Paid-in Capital in Excess of Par Value — Common.

Here is an analysis of the transaction.

Represents amount due on stock subscription. It is a current asset on the balance sheet. ⟶

Stock reserved but not fully paid. (1,000 shares × $100 par) ⟶

Accounts Affected	Category	↑	↓	Rules
Subscriptions Receivable— Common Stock	Asset	↑		Dr. $160,000
Common Stock Subscribed	SE	↑		Cr. $100,000
Paid-in Capital in Excess of Par Value—Common	SE	↑		Cr. $60,000

1,000 shares × $160

1,000 shares × $60 par

The journal entry will be as follows:

	19XX					
	April	1	Subscriptions Receivable—			
			Common Stock	160 0 0 0 00		
			Common Stock Subscribed		100 0 0 0 00	
			Paid-in Capital in Excess of Par		60 0 0 0 00	

August 1: Received First Installment on Common Stock Subscription

Accounts Affected	Category	↑	↓	Rules
Cash	Asset	↑		Dr. $80,000
Subscriptions Receivable— Common Stock	Asset		↓	Cr. $80,000

The journal entry will be as follows:

19XX Aug.	1	Cash		80 00 0 00		
			Subscriptions Receivable—			
			Common Stock			80 00 0 00

November 1: Received Final Installment on Common Stock Subscription

Accounts Affected	Category	↑	↓	Rules
Cash	Asset	↑		Dr. $80,000
Subscriptions Receivable— Common Stock	Asset		↓	Cr. $80,000

The journal entry will be as follows:

19XX Nov.	1	Cash		80 00 0 00		
			Subscriptions Receivable—			
			Common Stock			80 00 0 00

November 1: Issued 1,000 Shares of Fully Paid Common Stock

Accounts Affected	Category	↑	↓	Rules
Common Stock Subscribed	SE		↓	Dr. $100,000
Common Stock	SE	↑		Cr. $100,000

The journal entry will be as follows:

Nov.	1	Common Stock Subscribed	100 00 0 00		
		Common Stock		100 00 0 00	

Remember, stock is recorded at par value. At this point the Common Stock Subscribed account in the ledger (when posted) is reduced to a zero balance, and the Common Stock account records the issued stock (which has been paid for).

STOCKHOLDERS' EQUITY

Before concluding this chapter, let's take a moment to set up a simplified stockholders' equity section of a balance sheet. The numbers in the following illustration are not related to the previous situations. The goal here is to show you the structure of paid-in capital and retained earnings. In the blueprint on page 685, the complete layout of stockholders' equity is illustrated by the **source-of-capital approach,** which lists classes of stockholders first. There is an alternative way, called the **legal capital approach,** we will illustrate in the next chapter; it lists all legal capital first. Both approaches are acceptable.

Stockholders' Equity	
Paid in Capital:	
Common Stock, $100 par value; authorized 10,000 shares, 7,000 issued and outstanding	$ 700 0 0 0 00
Common Stock Subscribed, 2,000 shares at par	200 0 0 0 00
Paid-in Capital in Excess of Par Value—Common	300 0 0 0 00
Total Paid-in Capital	$1200 0 0 0 00
Retained Earnings	400 0 0 0 00
Total Stockholders' Equity	$1600 0 0 0 00

LEARNING UNIT 19-4 REVIEW

AT THIS POINT you should be able to

◆ Journalize the entries in a stock subscription plan. (pp. 678–679)
◆ Explain the purpose of Common Stock Subscribed. (p. 679)
◆ Prepare a simplified stockholders' section. (p. 680)

SELF-REVIEW QUIZ 19-4

(The forms you need are on page 75 of the *Study Guide and Working Papers.*)

Journalize the entries to record the stock subscription plan for Moose Corp. On October 1 Moose Corp. received subscriptions for 500 shares of $50 par-value common stock at $80 per share. The buyer will pay two equal installments on December 31 and March 31.

Solution to Self-Review Quiz 19-4

				Debit	Credit
Oct.	1	Subscriptions Receivable—			
			Common Stock	4 0 0 0 0 00	
			Common Stock Subscribed		2 5 0 0 0 00
			Paid-in Capital in Excess of Par		
			Value—Common		1 5 0 0 0 00
Dec.	31	Cash		2 0 0 0 0 00	
			Subscriptions Receivable—		
			Common Stock		2 0 0 0 0 00
March	31	Cash		2 0 0 0 0 00	
			Subscriptions Receivable—		
			Common Stock		2 0 0 0 0 00
	31	Common Stock Subscribed		2 5 0 0 0 00	
			Common Stock		2 5 0 0 0 00

SUMMARY OF KEY POINTS

Learning Unit 19-1

1. The articles of incorporation is submitted to the state when one wants to form a corporation. It contains all the specifics of the proposed corporation. If approved, a charter (certificate of incorporation) is issued to incorporators.
2. Advantages of a corporation include limited liability, a separate legal entity, unlimited life, ease of transferring ownership interest, no mutual agency, and ease in raising capital. Disadvantages include difficulties in forming a corporation, government regulations, and double taxation.

Learning Unit 19-2

1. Stockholders' equity is broken down in Paid-in Capital and Retained Earnings.
2. Retained Earnings records the accumulated profits that are retained or kept in the corporation.
3. Authorized stock represents the total amount of stock that can be legally issued. Outstanding stock represents the amount of stock issued.
4. Common stockholders have the right to vote, share in profits, sell their ownership, and receive assets at liquidation if available; they also have preemptive rights (the right to maintain their proportionate ownership interest in the company).
5. Buyers of preferred stock, to gain stability of earnings, may give up voting rights, preemptive rights, etc. Preferred stock can be cumulative, noncumulative, participating, or nonparticipating or a combination of the above.
6. Par value is an arbitrary value. It doesn't mean market value. Stocks may have a par value, no par, or no par with a stated value.
7. Legal capital is the amount that a corporation must retain in the business for the protection of the creditors. It may be based on par value, no par value, or stated value.

Learning Unit 19-3

1. Common stock or preferred stock with par value is recorded by number of shares times par value. If stock is sold for more than par, the difference is recorded in a stockholders' equity account called Paid-in Capital in Excess of Par Value. If a stock is sold below par, the difference is recorded in a contra-stockholders' equity account called Discount on Common Stock.
2. If no-par stock with a stated value is sold at a price higher than stated value, the difference is recorded in a stockholders' equity account called Paid-in Capital in Excess of Stated Value.
3. Assets are recorded at fair market value when exchanged for stock. Any difference between par value of stock and fair market value is recorded in a stockholders' equity account called Capital in Excess of Par.
4. Organization Cost is an intangible asset on the balance sheet.
5. The calculation for a dividend to common or preferred with par value is: (number of shares × par) × rate. If preferred is fully participating, the allocation of the remainder is based on par value of each class of stock over the total par value. This fraction is multiplied times remainder of dividend.

1. The source-of-capital approach will present the paid-in capital component of stockholders' equity by classes of stockholders. There is no attempt to list legal capital first.

2. Subscriptions Receivable is an asset representing amounts due on stock that has been subscribed to. It is a current asset on the balance sheet.

3. Common Stock Subscribed is a stockholders' equity account that acts as a temporary account until a subscription is paid for. When paid, the Common Stock Subscribed account is reduced and the Common Stock account is increased.

KEY TERMS

Articles of incorporation Document submitted by incorporators when applying for a charter.

Authorized stock As stated in its charter, the number of shares of capital stock (common and preferred) that a corporation can sell.

Capital stock Classes of stock that represent the fractional elements of ownership of a corporation.

Certificate of incorporation Document granted by the state authorizing the creation of a corporation.

Charter Document issued to a corporation by the state that includes certificate of incorporation along with articles of incorporation.

Common stock Part of paid-in capital representing the basic ownership equity of the corporation. If corporation has only one class of stock, it will be common stock.

Common Stock Subscribed Temporary stockholders' equity account that records at par value stock that has been subscribed to but not fully paid for.

Corporation Business organization that is both a legal and accounting entity.

Cumulative preferred stock Stock that entitles its holders to any undeclared dividends that have accumulated before common stockholders receive their dividends.

Directors Officers elected by stockholders to represent the company and establish policies for the company.

Discount on stock The difference between the par value of the stock and an amount less than the par value that the stockholders have contributed. Discounts do not happen very often.

Dividend Cash, other assets, or shares of stock that a corporation issues to the stockholders.

Dividends in arrears Dividends owed to preferred stockholders that must be paid before common stockholders can receive their dividends.

Incorporators Persons responsible for getting the corporation formed.

Issued capital stock Stock that the corporation issues for assets or services contributed by the stockholders.

Legal capital Minimum amount of capital that a corporation must leave in the company (cannot be withdrawn by stockholders) for protection of the creditors.

Legal capital approach Method of preparing paid-in capital by listing the legal section first. (See blueprint at end of Chapter 20.)

Limited liability Freedom of stockholders from *personal* liability for the debts of the corporation.

Minute book Book that records meetings of board of directors and/or stockholders.

Noncumulative preferred Preferred stock that does not entitle its holders to a dividend for any year in which a dividend is not declared.

Nonparticipating preferred Preferred stock that entitles its holders only to a certain percent dividend, the remainder going to holders of common stock.

No-par stock Stock with no par value. A stated value could be placed on it.

Organization Cost An intangible asset that records the initial cost of forming the corporation, such as legal and incorporating fees.

Outstanding capital stock Stock that is held and owned by stockholders.

Paid-in Capital Section of stockholders' equity representing what stockholders have invested into the corporation.

Paid-in Capital in Excess of Par Value Difference between what stockholders invest and par value. This amount is not credited to the Stock account.

Paid-in Capital in Excess of Stated Value Difference between what stockholders invest and the stated value placed on stock by the board of directors. This amount is not credited to the Stock account.

Participating preferred Stock that entitles its holders not only to a fixed dividend but also to an opportunity to share in additional dividends with common stockholders.

Par value An arbitrary value that is placed on each share of stock. Par value represents legal capital and not market value.

Preemptive right The right of the stockholder to purchase additional shares of stock to maintain his or her proportionate interest when the corporation issues additional stock.

Preferred stock Class of capital stock that has preference to a corporation's profits and assets.

Preferred stock Class of capital stock that has preference to a corporation's profits and assets.

Premium A term that records the sale of stock at more than par value. In this book we use the account "Paid-in Capital in Excess of Par" to record the premium received.

Retained earnings Accumulated profits of a corporation that have been kept in the business and not paid out as dividends. Retained Earnings is part of stockholders' equity.

Source-of-capital approach Method of preparing paid-in capital by listing classes of stockholder sources of capital (see p. 685 for example).

Stated value Arbitrary value placed by the board of directors on each share of no-par stock to fulfill legal capital requirements.

Stock certificate Formal document issued to investors in a corporation that shows the number of shares purchased.

Stock subscription A contractual agreement to buy a certain number of shares of stock from a corporation at a specific price.

Stockholders Owners of the stock of the corporation.

Subscriptions Receivable Current asset on balance sheet that represents amount due on stock subscriptions.

QUESTIONS, MINI EXERCISES, EXERCISES, AND PROBLEMS

Discussion Questions

1. What is the difference between the Articles of Incorporation and a charter?
2. Who elects the board of directors?
3. List the advantages of the corporate form of organization.
4. Explain the difference between paid-in capital and retained earnings.
5. Why can't a company issue more stock than is authorized?
6. What does preemptive right mean?
7. Distinguish between legal capital, par value, no par value, and no par value with a stated value.
8. Preferred stock can never be cumulative *and* nonparticipating. True or false? Support your answer.
9. What is the normal balance and the category of the account Discount on Common Stock?
10. How does one calculate Paid-in Capital in Excess of Par Value or Stated Value?
11. Explain the account Paid-in Capital in Excess of Par Value as it relates to exchange of stock for noncash assets.
12. What is the purpose of the account Organization Costs?
13. In stock subscriptions why does one credit Common Stock Subscribed?

Mini Exercises

(The forms you need are on pages 77 and 78 of the *Study Guide and Working Papers*.)

Stockholder's Equity

1. Marci Corporation has capital stock of $5,000. Its retained earnings account has a $12,000 balance. Cash has a balance of $10,000. What is the total of stockholder's equity for Marci Corporation?

Cumulative Preferred

2. Moore Co. owed $10,000 each year for three years to holders of cumulative preferred stock. This year Moore pays out $100,000 in dividends to preferred and common. How much did each class of stock receive?

Journalizing Sales of Stock

3. Journalize the following:

VALLEY CO. PARTIAL BALANCE SHEET			
Assets			
Current Assets:			
Subscriptions Receivable, Common 8%			
Stock	XXX		
Intangible Assets:			
Organization Cost		XXX	
Total Assets			XXX
Liabilities			

Stockholders' Equity			
Paid-in Capital:			
Preferred 12% stock, $10 par value,			
authorized 20,000 shares, 8,000 shares			
issued	XXX		
Paid-in Capital in Excess of Par			
Value—preferred	XXX		
Total Paid-in Capital by preferred			
stockholders		XXX	
Common Stock, no par value, stated			
value $10 per share, authorized			
100,000 shares, 30,000 issued and			
outstanding	XXX		
Common Stock Subscribed, 1,000 shares			
at par	XXX		
Paid-in Capital in Excess of Stated			
Value—Common	XXX		
Total Paid-in Capital by common			
stockholders		XXX	
Total Paid-in Capital		XXX	
Retained Earnings		XXX	
Total Stockholders' Equity			XXX

Note that preferred stock is listed before common stock.

19XX

July	8	Pete Co. sells 300 shares of $10 par-value common stock at $10.
Oct.	15	Jon Co. sells 200 shares of $10 par-value common stock at $15.
Nov.	28	Angel Co. sells 200 shares of no-par common stock with a stated value $20 for $30 per share.
Dec.	30	Lowe Co. issues 500 shares of $10 par-value common stock to organizers of the firm for services rendered costing $7,500.

Cumulative and Participating Preferred

4. From the following calculate the dividends for common and preferred stock:

- ◆ 7 percent fully participating preferred stock.
- ◆ The board declared a $150,000 dividend.
- ◆ Preferred stock 2,000 shares, $100 par-value; common stock 8,000 shares, $100 par.

Stock Subscriptions

5. Journalize the entries to record the stock subscription plan for Blue Co. On October 1, Blue received subscriptions for 200 shares of $25 par-value common stock at $40 per share. The buyer will pay two equal installments on December 31 and March 31.

Exercises

(The forms you need are on pages 79 and 80 in the *Study Guide and Working Papers*.)

Journalizing transactions for sale of stock.

19-1. Val Corporation was authorized to issue 30,000 shares of common stock. Record the journal entry for each of the following independent situations, assuming that Val issues 6,000 shares at $11 on July 20, 19XX:

    a. Common stock has a $10 par value.

    b. Common stock has no par and no stated value.

    c. Common stock is no-par stock with a stated value of $8.

Exchange of stock for noncash assets.

19-2. On July 10, 19XX, Zeron Corporation issued 3,000 shares of common stock with a par value of $100 in exchange for equipment with a fair market value of $320,000. Journalize the appropriate entry.

Calculating dividends to preferred and common.

19-3. Vetco Corporation in its first three years of operation paid out the following dividends:

- ◆ Year 1: 0
- ◆ Year 2: $30,000
- ◆ Year 3: $90,000

Given that Vetco has 3,000 shares of $100 par 9 percent cumulative, non-participating preferred stock and 15,000 shares of $25 par value common stock, what would be the total dividends paid each year to holders of common and preferred?

Stock Subscription.

19-4. On January 1, 19XX, Lavrel Corporation issued on a subscription basis 1,000 shares of $50 par-value common stock at $90 per share. Two equal installments were to be made on July 1 and December 31. Prepare the appropriate journal entries on January 1, July 1, and December 31 to record this stock subscription for Lavrel Corporation.

Stockholders' equity.

19-5. Scupper Corporation began its business on January 1, 19XX. It sold at $30 per share 6,000 shares of no-par common stock with a stated value of $20 per share. The charter of Scupper indicated 40,000 shares were authorized. Retained earnings were $60,000 on December 31. Prepare the stockholders' equity section for Scupper on December 31, 19XX, using page 685 as a guide.

Group A Problems

(The forms you need are on pages 81–89 of the *Study Guide and Working Papers*.)

19A-1. The following is the Paid-in Capital section of stockholders' equity for the Larson Corporation on June 1, 19XX:

Recording capital stock transactions; preparing Paid-in Capital section of stockholders' equity.	Paid-in Capital:

Preferred Stock, $100 par, authorized 20,000 shares, 4,000 shares issued	$ 400,000
Paid-in Capital in Excess of Par Value — Preferred Stock	120,000
Common Stock, $25 par, authorized 50,000 shares, 20,000 shares issued	500,000
Paid-in Capital in Excess of Par Value — Common Stock	160,000
Total Paid-in Capital	$1,180,000

Check Figure:

Paid-in capital $2,732,000

The following transactions occurred in the months of June and July:

19XX

June   1 Issued 3,000 shares of preferred stock at $102 per share.

         2 Issued 7,000 shares of common stock at $40 per share.

      15 Issued 8,000 shares of common stock at $42 per share.

July   2 Issued 5,000 shares of preferred stock at $104 per share.

      18 Issued 2,000 shares of common stock in exchange for building and land with a fair market value of $60,000 and $50,000, respectively.

1. Journalize the above entries and update the stockholders' equity ledger. Accounts are provided in the workbook.

2. Prepare a new Paid-in Capital section of stockholders' equity as of July 31, 19XX.

19A-2. Katie Corporation has 20,000 shares outstanding of $10 par value 8 percent preferred stock and 40,000 shares outstanding of $10 par-value common stock. In its first five years of operation the company paid the following dividends: 19X1, 0; 19X2, $16,000; 19X3, $48,000; 19X4, 0; 19X5, $82,000. Calculate the dividends paid to preferred and common stockholders under the following three independent situations:

Calculating dividends for preferred and common stock.

Check Figure:

(b) Pref: $16,000   19X2
          32,000   19X3
          38,000   19X5

a. Preferred stock is noncumulative and nonparticipating.

b. Preferred stock is cumulative and nonparticipating.

c. Preferred stock is cumulative and fully participating.

19A-3. From the following partial mixed list, select the appropriate titles and prepare a stockholders' equity section (use the source-of-capital approach as shown on the blueprint, p. 685), for Xenon Corporation on July 31, 19XX.

Preparing a stockholders' equity section of a balance sheet.

Office Equipment	$100,000
Land	200,000
Paid-in Capital in Excess of Par Value — Preferred Stock	100,000
Building	80,000
Accounts Receivable	120,000
Notes Receivable	40,000
Organization Costs	10,000
Common Stock, $10 Par Value (60,000 shares issued and outstanding; 80,000 shares authorized)	600,000
Retained Earnings	200,000
Subscriptions Receivable — Common Stock	80,000
Patents	10,000
Preferred 14 percent Stock, $50 Par (6,000 shares issued; 7,000 shares authorized)	300,000
Common Stock Subscribed at Par	225,000
Paid-in Capital in Excess of Par Value — Common Stock	20,000

Check Figure:

Stockholders' equity $1,445,000

19-A4. Joilet Company has just been issued a charter by the state of New York. This charter gives Joilet the authority to issue 400,000 shares of $10 par-value common stock. From the following transactions:

1. Prepare journal entries to record the transactions of Joilet Co. for the month of August.
2. Prepare the Paid-in Capital section of Joilet's balance sheet at the end of the month.

19XX
Aug. 11 Issued 1,800 shares of stock for land and building with a fair market value of $13,000 and $17,500, respectively.
      16 Accepted subscriptions to 20,000 shares of stock for $250,000 to be paid in two equal installments.
      22 Collected first installment on 10,000 shares of the common stock subscribed on August 16.
      28 Sold 7,000 shares of stock for $88,000.
      30 Collected last installment on 10,000 shares of the common stock subscribed on August 16 and issued the shares.

Group B Problems

(The forms you need are on pages 81–89 of the *Study Guide and Working Papers*.)

19B-1. The following is the Paid-in Capital section of stockholders' equity for the Larson Corporation on June 1, 19XX:

Paid-in Capital:

Preferred Stock, $25, par, authorized 20,000 shares, 5,000 shares issued	$125,000
Paid-in Capital in Excess of Par Value — Preferred Stock	37,500
Common Stock, $10 par, authorized 100,000 shares, 20,000 shares issued	200,000
Paid-in Capital in Excess of Par Value — Common Stock	45,000
Total Paid-in Capital	$407,500

The following transactions occurred in the months of June and July:

19XX
June   1 Issued 2,000 shares of preferred stock at $28 per share.
       4 Issued 4,000 shares of common stock at $13 per share.
      15 Issued 5,000 shares of common stock at $16 per share.
July   2 Issued 1,000 shares of preferred stock at $29 per share.
      18 Issued 2,000 shares of common stock in exchange for building and land with a fair market value of $25,000 and $29,000, respectively.

1. Journalize and post the above entries and update the stockholders' equity ledger accounts provided in the workbook.
2. Prepare a new Paid-in Capital section of stockholders' equity as of July 31, 19XX.

19B-2. Katie Corporation has 10,000 shares outstanding of $20 par-value 10 percent preferred stock and 120,000 shares outstanding of $5 par-value common stock. In its first five years of operation, the company paid the following dividends: 19X1, 0; 19X2, $16,000; 19X3, $80,000; 19X4, $84,000; 19X5, $120,000. Calculate the dividends paid to preferred and common stockholders under the following three independent situations:

a. Preferred stock is noncumulative and nonparticipating.

b. Preferred stock is cumulative and nonparticipating.

c. Preferred stock is cumulative and fully participating.

19B-3. From the following partial mixed list, select the appropriate titles and prepare a stockholders' equity section using the source-of-capital approach for Xenon Corporation on July 31, 19XX.

Preparing a stockholders' equity section of a balance sheet.

Check Figure:
Total stockholders' equity
$150,200

Paid-in Capital in Excess of Par Value — Common Stock	$ 1,400
Common Stock Subscribed at Par	8,800
Paid-in Capital in Excess of Par Value — Preferred Stock	12,000
Land	15,000
Office Equipment	7,600
Preferred 14 percent Stock, $50 Par (400 shares issued; 8,000 shares authorized)	20,000
Patents	1,600
Subscriptions Receivable — Common Stock	12,000
Retained Earnings	28,000
Common Stock $10 Par Value (8,000 shares issued; and outstanding; 50,000 shares authorized)	80,000
Organization Costs	1,200
Notes Receivable	5,000
Accounts Receivable	18,000
Building	5,000

Stock subscriptions and exchange of stock for noncash assets.

Check Figure:
Total paid-in capital $151,000

19B-4. The state of New York has issued a charter to Joilet Company with the authorization to issue 10,000 shares of $100 par-value common stock. From the following transactions:

1. Journalize the transactions for Joilet for the month of September.

2. Prepare the Paid-in Capital section of Joilet Company's balance sheet at the end of the month.

19XX

Sept.　8　Issued 500 shares of stock for land and building with a fair market value of $29,000 and $24,000, respectively.

14　Accepted subscriptions to 300 shares of its stock for $39,000 to be paid in two equal installments.

22　Collected first installment on 150 shares of the common stock subscribed on September 14.

24　Sold 500 shares of stock for $59,000.

30　Collected last installment on 150 shares of the common stock subscribed on September 14 and issued the shares.

REAL WORLD APPLICATIONS

19R-1.

The partial balance sheet of Freedom Corporation had as of July 31, 19XX, the following balances:

Preferred Stock, $10 Par	$ 95,000
Paid-in Capital in Excess of Par — Preferred	65,000
Common Stock, $100 Par	180,000
Paid-in Capital in Excess of Par — Common	220,000
Common Stock Subscribed	10,000
Retained Earnings	520,000
Subscriptions Receivable	60,000
Bonds Payable	$300,000

The bookkeeper, Alice Fall, is quite concerned that the company has not kept enough legal capital in the business. She wants the board of directors to immediately change the par value, since the market value of the stock has increased. She believes it is only fair to protect the rights of the creditors.

Support or rebut Alice Fall's position in writing.

19R-2.

Bill Murray and Jim Smith, full-time high school teachers, had worked together in overnight camping for years. They both felt it was time to start their own overnight camp. Bill estimated he would be able to invest $30,000 while Jim could invest $2,000. Both agreed that they would need at least $200,000 to finance the purchase of land as well as the building of bunks and administrative offices.

Jim felt that forming a corporation was too involved and wanted to form a partnership. Bill, on the other hand, who trusted no one, felt the corporate structure was best.

Jim and Bill have come to you to recommend what form of organization is best for them and how they can or should raise the money. Please write them a recommendation.

YOU make the call

Critical Thinking/Ethical Case

19R-3.

Avan Co. just published its financial reports. The president of Avan told the accountants not to include in the annual report any information about a pending lawsuit. The president thought it would only worry the stockholders. Do you think the president is correct in not including any information about the pending lawsuit in the annual report? You make the call. Write down your recommendations to the president.

ACCOUNTING RECALL

A CUMULATIVE APPROACH

THIS EXAM REVIEWS CHAPTERS 1 THROUGH 19

Your *Study Guide and Working Papers* (pp. 94, 95) has forms to complete this exam, as well as worked-out solutions. The page references next to each question identify what page to turn back to if you answer the question incorrectly.

PART 1   Vocabulary Review

Match the terms to the appropriate definition or phrase.

Page Ref.

(672)	1. Premium	A. Intangible asset
(669)	2. Par value	B. Number of shares of stock a company can sell
(664)	3. Limited liability	
(668)	4. Outstanding stock	C. An asset
(574)	5. LIFO	D. Represents legal capital and not market value
(674)	6. Organization cost	
(121)	7. Accumulated depreciation	E. Contra-asset

(668)	8. Authorized stock	F.	Sale of stock at more than par
(678)	9. Subscriptions receivable	G.	Sell new inventory first
(667)	10. Retained earnings	H.	Stock held and owned by stockholders
		I.	Freedom from personal liability
		J.	Accumulated profits

PART II True or False (Accounting Theory)

(680) 11. The legal approach and source-of-capital approach are the same.

(678) 12. Common stock subscribed is a temporary stockholders' equity account.

(669) 13. Par value represents market value.

(672) 14. The usual balance of paid-in capital in excess of par is a debit.

(670) 15. No par-value stock can have a stated value.

CORPORATIONS

Stock Values, Dividends, Treasury Stock, and Retained Earnings

20

THE BIG PICTURE

After weighing the pros and cons, Tony Freedman and Charles West decided to incorporate the Eldorado Computer Center. Now the owners would become both stockholders and salaried employees.

Every corporation has to decide how much of its profits it will pay out to stockholders as dividends, and how much it will reinvest in its operations. These "retained earnings" can be an important source of capital to help the business grow. Of course, as more earnings are retained, fewer are available for dividends. Freedman and West have to decide what is best for the business — and for themselves, as stockholders.

In this chapter you will learn about the differences among common, preferred, and treasury stock. You will also learn how dividends are paid to the stockholders and why it is sometimes necessary to restrict part of the retained earnings to finance a special project.

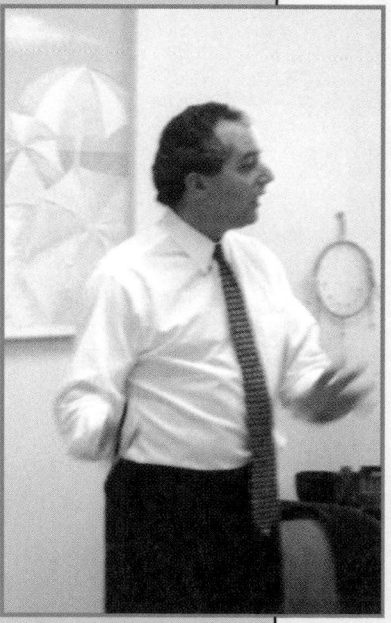

Learning Objectives	◆ Calculating the book value of preferred and common stock. (p. 693)
	◆ Journalizing entries to record issuance of a cash dividend and a stock dividend. (p. 696)
	◆ Journalizing the purchase and sale of treasury stock. (p. 701)
	◆ Preparing a statement of retained earnings. (p. 704)

In this chapter we continue the study of aspects of corporate equity that we began in the last chapter. We will discuss a number of topics, including stock values, how and why dividends are declared and paid, why a corporation buys back its own stock, and the restrictions on retained earnings.

In Chapter 19 we discussed two types of stock value — par value and stated value. In Learning Unit 20-1 we will turn our attention to other stock values.

LEARNING UNIT 20-1
Understanding Stock Values: Redemption, Market, and Book Value

REDEMPTION VALUE

When a corporation issues preferred stock, it often reserves the right to retire or redeem that stock for a specific price. At the time the stock is issued, this price per share, called **redemption value,** is determined, and people buy the stock knowing that the corporation can redeem it at this price.

MARKET VALUE

The price at which shares of capital stock are bought and sold in the open market is called the **market value.** Economic conditions, a company's earnings, and investors' expectations all play a factor in determining the market price.

BOOK VALUE PER SHARE

Book value per share is basically the total of stockholders' equity (assets minus liabilities) divided by the number of shares issued.

Why is book value used? For several reasons:

1. When a company seeks a loan, banks may specify a minimum book value for a loan to be approved.
2. If a merger is being negotiated, book value may be used as a factor in setting an exchange ratio of stock. For example, based on book value, 1 share of Octon Co. stock could fairly be issued for 3 shares of Xeron Co. stock, if book value of Octon stock is $30 and book value of Xeron stock is $10.
3. Book value may be used when contracts are made. For example, an individual may receive in the future an option to buy or sell stock based on future book value. (This is *not* market value, which is based on current prices.)

It is important to emphasize that book value doesn't represent what an owner might receive if the assets of a company were *liquidated.* At the time of liquidation the assets may be sold at prices quite different from the values on the books, which are based on cost and not current market prices.

CALCULATING BOOK VALUE WITH ONLY ONE CLASS OF STOCK

When a corporation has only common stock, book value is calculated using the following equation:

$$\text{book value per share} = \frac{\text{total stockholders' equity}}{\text{total shares outstanding}}$$

As an example, we will use the stockholders' equity shown below for Jones Corporation and calculate book value per share of common stock.

The book value is $45 per share ($450,000/10,000 shares). Thus for each share of stock owned $45 would be received *if* the corporation were liquidated without any losses from disposing of assets. By the time assets are disposed of the owner might get much less than book value.

JONES CORPORATION STOCKHOLDERS' EQUITY		
Paid-in Capital:		
Common Stock, $25 par value; 10,000 shares		
authorized, issued, and outstanding	$250 00 0 00	
Paid-in Capital in Excess of Par Value—Common	110 0 0 0 00	
Total Paid-in Capital	$360 0 0 0 00	
Retained Earnings	90 0 0 0 00	
Total Stockholders' Equity	$450 0 0 0 00	

CALCULATING BOOK VALUE WITH BOTH PREFERRED AND COMMON STOCK

When there are two classes of stock, before book value can be calculated the stockholders' equity must be allocated (divided up) for each class of stock. First, for preferred stock, a corporation assigns the redemption value (or par value if there is no redemption value) of the stock along with any dividends in arrears (any dividends that are owed to holders of preferred stock but have not yet been paid out). This total of redemption value plus dividends in arrears is divided by the number of preferred shares outstanding. The *remainder* of stockholders' equity is assigned to the common stockholders, and the book value of the common stock is calculated by that amount divided by the number of common stock shares outstanding. This can be shown in the following formulas:

$$\text{book value preferred} = \frac{\text{redemption value} + \text{dividends in arrears}}{\text{number of shares of preferred stock outstanding}}$$

$$\text{book value common} = \frac{\text{stockholders' equity} - \text{amount assigned to preferred}}{\text{number of shares of common stock outstanding}}$$

Let's illustrate this situation by looking at the stockholders' equity of Ryan Corporation (top of p. 695) and performing the necessary calculations.

Given: Redemption value of preferred is $103; there are $14,000 worth of dividends in arrears.

Thus,

$$\text{book value preferred} = \frac{\$206,000 + \$14,000}{2,000 \text{ shares}}$$

$$= \frac{\$220,000}{2,000 \text{ shares}} = \$110 \text{ per share}$$

STOCKHOLDERS' EQUITY			
Paid-in Capital:			
Preferred 7% Stock, $100 per value, authorized			
3,000 shares cumulative and nonparticipating,			
2,000 shares issued and outstanding	$200 0 0 0 00		
Paid-in Capital in Excess of Par Value—Preferred	10 0 0 0 00		
Total Paid-in Capital by Preferred Stockholders		$210 0 0 0 00	
Common Stock, $50 par value, authorized 12,000			
shares, 10,000 shares issued and outstanding	500 0 0 0 00		
Paid-in Capital in Excess of Par Value—Common	20 0 0 0 00		
Total Paid-in Capital by Common Stockholders		520 0 0 0 00	
Total Paid-in Capital		$730 0 0 0 00	
Retained Earnings		164 0 0 0 00	
Total Stockholders' Equity		$894 0 0 0 00	

Redemption value
$103 × 2,000 shares

Total Stockholders' Equity		$894 0 0 0 00	
Less: Equity Applicable to Preferred Stock:			
Redemption Value	$206 0 0 0 00		
Dividends in Arrears	14 0 0 0 00	(220 0 0 0 00)	
Equity Allocated to Common Stock			$674 0 0 0 00

and

$$\text{book value common} = \frac{\$894,000 - \$220,000}{10,000 \text{ shares}}$$

$$= \frac{\$674,000}{10,000 \text{ shares}} = \$67.40 \text{ per share}$$

Note: When preferred stock is redeemed, the paid-in capital in excess of par is *not* returned and thus is *not* included as part of the preferred equity in the book-value calculation.

LEARNING UNIT 20-1 REVIEW

AT THIS POINT you should be able to

◆ List and define other stock values besides par value. (p. 693)
◆ Explain the purpose of book value. (p. 693)
◆ Calculate the book value of preferred and common stock. (p. 694)

SELF-REVIEW QUIZ 20-1

(The forms you need are on page 97 of the *Study Guide and Working Papers*.)
From the following information calculate the book value for preferred and common stock:

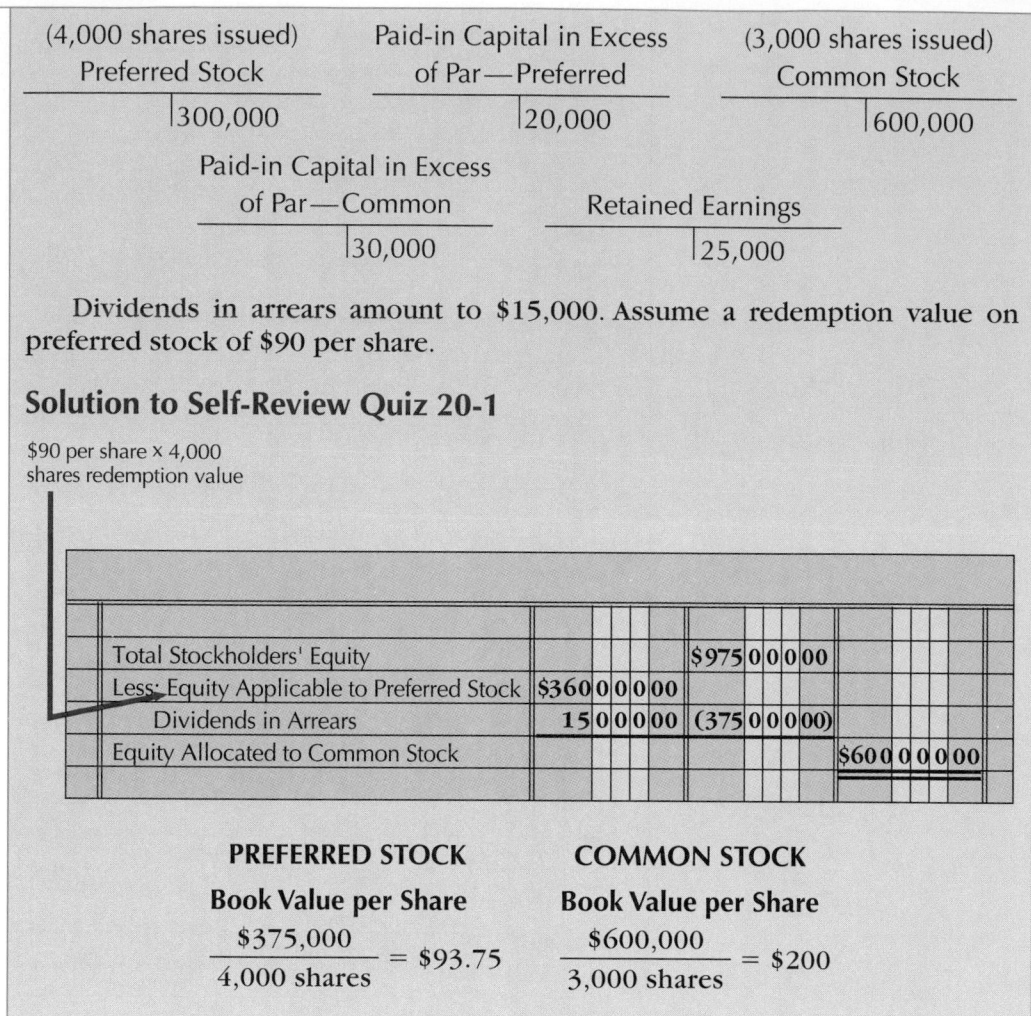

	(4,000 shares issued) Preferred Stock			Paid-in Capital in Excess of Par—Preferred			(3,000 shares issued) Common Stock	
		300,000			20,000			600,000

	Paid-in Capital in Excess of Par—Common			Retained Earnings	
		30,000			25,000

Dividends in arrears amount to $15,000. Assume a redemption value on preferred stock of $90 per share.

Solution to Self-Review Quiz 20-1

$90 per share × 4,000 shares redemption value

Total Stockholders' Equity		$975 0 0 0 00	
Less: Equity Applicable to Preferred Stock	$360 0 0 0 00		
Dividends in Arrears	15 0 0 0 00	(375 0 0 0 00)	
Equity Allocated to Common Stock			$600 0 0 0 00

PREFERRED STOCK
Book Value per Share
$$\frac{\$375,000}{4,000 \text{ shares}} = \$93.75$$

COMMON STOCK
Book Value per Share
$$\frac{\$600,000}{3,000 \text{ shares}} = \$200$$

LEARNING UNIT 20-2
Dividends

In this unit we will discuss the distribution of cash, stock, or other assets that the board of directors declares as dividends. **Dividends,** as we have seen, are the distribution of earnings of the corporation. It is important to realize that only the board of directors of a corporation has the authority to determine whether a dividend is to be paid, how much it will be, who receives it, and when and how it will be paid.

There are three important dates associated with the dividend process:

1. **Date of declaration.** This is the day the board of directors announces its decision to pay a dividend. This date creates a liability to the company called **Dividend Payable.**
2. **Date of record.** This is the date established by the board of directors that determines which stockholders will receive the dividend. These stockholders can be identified in the corporation's subsidiary stockholders' ledger at this date of record.
3. **Date of payment.** This is the date that the dividend is actually paid to stockholders of record.

CASH DIVIDENDS

The board of directors declares the dividend.

The distribution of earnings of a corporation in the form of cash to its stockholders is called a **cash dividend.** For example, on March 8, 19XX, the board

Date of record is usually two to four weeks after date of declaration.

There must be a sufficient balance in retained earnings *and* cash to pay the dividend.

of directors of Tell Corporation declares a $2 cash dividend per share on the 5,000 shares issued and outstanding. The dividend will be paid on April 16, 19XX, to stockholders of record on March 25, 19XX. Let's look at how to analyze as well as record this cash dividend.

Date of Declaration: March 8, 19XX: The following chart analyzes this transaction.

Declaration of dividends reduces Retained Earnings.
A legally declared dividend is a current liability on the balance sheet.

Accounts Affected	Category	↑	↓	Rules
Retained Earnings	SE		↓	Dr. $10,000
Dividends Payable	Liability	↑		Cr. $10,000

The journal entry will look like this:

March	8	Retained Earnings		1000000	
		Dividends Payable			1000000
		Dividends declared of $2 to stockholders			
		of record March 25, 19XX: payable on			
		April 16, 19XX, as declared by board			
		of directors.			

Note that no entry is made on date of record.

Date of Payment: April 16, 19XX: Here is an analysis of the dividend payment.

Accounts Affected	Category	↑	↓	Rules
Dividends Payable	Liability		↓	Dr. $10,000
Cash	Asset		↓	Cr. $10,000

The journal entry will look like this:

April	16	Dividends Payable		1000000	
		Cash			1000000
		Payment of dividend to stockholders of			
		record on March 25, 19XX			

The end result of these transactions is to reduce Cash and Retained Earnings. (*Remember, Retained Earnings doesn't mean Cash.* Cash is an asset, while Retained Earnings is part of stockholders' equity.) In effect, the company is distributing part of its accumulated income to stockholders.

THE STOCK DIVIDEND

A stock dividend doesn't reduce cash or the total of stockholders' equity.

A **stock dividend** occurs when a corporation issues its own stock instead of a distribution of assets to its stockholders. There are a number of reasons why a stock dividend is declared instead of a cash dividend:

1. To satisfy stockholders' expectations. The corporation doesn't have enough cash to pay a cash dividend and offers the stock dividend instead. The stockholders make no new investment to receive this type of dividend.

2. To increase permanent capital in the business (because more stock is issued).

3. To reduce the market value of the stock, because the price may be too high in the trading on the open market. When more stock is supplied with no demand for it, stock prices go down.

4. Income tax is avoided until the stock received is sold.

RECORDING A STOCK DIVIDEND

A stock dividend will *not* reduce total stockholders' equity the way a cash dividend does. The end result of a stock dividend is to transfer an amount based on market value from Retained Earnings to Paid-in Capital.* A stockholder after a stock dividend will own a larger number of shares, but the *total* ownership equity stays the same. Let's look at Jesse Corporation to illustrate recording a stock dividend.

On December 27, 19XX, Jesse Corporation declared a 10 percent stock dividend distributable January 27 to stockholders of record on January 13. Below is the stockholders' equity of Jesse Corporation before the dividend was declared. The current fair market value of the stock is $30 per share.

Stockholders' Equity		
Paid-in Capital:		
Common Stock, $20 par value,		
15,000 shares authorized, 10,000 shares issued		
and outstanding	$200 000 00	
Paid-in Capital in Excess of Par, Common	24 000 00	
Total Paid-in Capital by Common Stockholders	224 000 00	
Retained Earnings	62 000 00	
Total Stockholders' Equity		$286 000 00

Recording the Declaration of the Dividend: The following chart is an analysis of this transaction:

Accounts Affected	Category	↑	↓	Rules
Retained Earnings	SE		↓	Dr. $30,000
Common Stock Dividend Distributable	SE	↑		Cr. $20,000
Paid-in Capital in Excess of Par Value — Stock Dividend	SE	↑		Cr. $10,000

Retained Earnings is decreased by $30,000. To get that figure we multiply the market value of the stock ($30) times the number of shares issued in the dividend (1,000). The number of shares issued in the dividend is the number of shares issued and outstanding (10,000) times the percent of dividend declared (10 percent). The Common Stock Dividend Distributable is 1,000 shares times the par value of the common stock ($20).

---

* For larger stock dividends (over 25 percent of the outstanding stock) the amount is based on par. We will look at small stock dividends.

The journal entry will look like this:

19XX						
Dec.	27	Retained Earnings		30000 00		
		Common Stock Dividend Distributable			20000 00	
		Paid-in Capital in Excess of Par				
		Value—Stock Dividend			10000 00	
		Records declaration of a 10% stock				
		dividend to stockholders of record				
		as of Jan. 13; payable Jan. 27 as				
		declared by the board of directors.				

Note that the **Common Stock Dividend Distributable** account, which records the par value of the stock, is *not* a liability; it is not payable with assets. It is part of stockholders' equity. When the stock is issued, this account will be reduced and transferred into Common Stock.

Let's first see what the stockholders' equity would look like if it were prepared between the declaration and the payment date. Note in the layout to follow that the stocks are listed first, followed by all the additional paid-in capital. This type of layout is called the *legal approach;* earlier we showed the *source-of-capital* approach. Both ways are acceptable.

Stockholders' Equity			
Paid-in Capital:			
Common Stock, $20 par value,			
15,000 shares authorized, 10,000 shares issued			
and outstanding	$200000 00		
Common Stock Dividend Distributable,			
1,000 shares	20000 00		
Total Common Stock issued and			
to be issued		$220000 00	
Additional Paid-in Capital:			
Paid-in Capital in Excess of Par			
Value—Common	24000 00		
Paid-in Capital in Excess of Par			
Value—Stock Dividend	10000 00		
Total Additional Paid-in Capital		34000 00	
Total Paid-in Capital		$254000 00	
Retained Earnings		32000 00	
Total Stockholders' Equity		$286000 00	

Recording the Issuance of the Stock Dividend: First the analysis:

Accounts Affected	Category	↑	↓	Rules
Common Stock Dividend Distributable	SE		↓	Dr. $20,000
Common Stock	SE	↑		Cr. $20,000

Then the journal entry:

Jan.	27	Common Stock Dividend Distributable	2 0 0 0 0 0			
		Common Stock			2 0 0 0 0 0	
		Issuance of stock dividend declared				
		on Dec. 27 to stockholders of record				
		as of Jan. 13.				

The Stock Split

When a corporation issues additional stock to cause a large drop in the market price of the outstanding stock and receives no assets in return, this is called a **stock split.** The corporation reduces the par value or stated value of the authorized stock with an increase in the number of shares authorized, issued, and outstanding. However, the stock split doesn't change the Retained Earnings account as a stock dividend did. To repeat, the stock split will

1. Increase the number of shares outstanding.
2. Reduce the par or stated value in proportion.

For example, a two-for-one split on 10,000 shares of $20 par would result in 20,000 shares with a $10 par value. The total equity remains the same. Since the stock split doesn't change the balance of any ledger account, only a *memorandum notation** in the journal, as well as in the Stock account, would be needed to update the accounting record. The number of shares in this transaction has doubled, but the corporation total equity has not changed; thus the market price of $80 per share would drop to approximately $40. If Jay Owen owned 100 shares before the split, he would own 200 now, but his market value would be the same.

* An example of such a notation would be, "Called in the outstanding $20 par value 10,000 shares of common stock and issued 20,000 shares of $10 par-value common stock for old shares previously outstanding."

The American group of companies, Allied Domecq Retailing USA, pays dividends to Allied Domecq in England. In order to keep profits high for both shop owners and its parent, Allied Domecq Retailing USA has established a long-term goal for its three companies: Dunkin' Donuts, Baskin-Robbins, and Togos. They want to create a "multibrand environment." That means that they are encouraging shop owners to combine a Dunkin' Donuts shop with a Baskin-Robbins shop, or even to combine them with Togos—and put all three shops under one roof. In this way, Allied Domecq Retailing USA hopes to maximize traffic to the shops by combining what had been businesses with three different peak traffic periods:

♦ Dunkin' Donuts = morning
♦ Togos = lunchtime
♦ Baskin-Robbins = afternoons and evenings
♦ Under one roof, these businesses could probably stay open 12 to 24 hours. Since the real estate investment in each shop is so large, it makes sense to use the shop to full capacity around the clock,

ROCK AROUND THE CLOCK

or as close to it as practical, depending on the location and the traffic.

This combination plan also helps to even out the seasonal demand for ice cream, which peaks in the summer months. To a lesser extent, the demand for donuts and muffins peaks in the fall and winter. This means that sales—and cash flow—and profits—are also seasonal. Uneven cash flow can create a huge problem for a small business. Recognizing this, Allied Domecq Retailing USA aims to use the owner's investment dollars to best advantage—all day, all year. Or as Fred says; "This combo will keep us rockin' around the clock!"

DISCUSSION QUESTIONS

1. How might combining two or three retail food outlets into a single shop reduce expenses?
2. How might this combination increase sales?
3. Like all corporations, Allied Domecq's goal is to increase value to its stockholders. How could the plan to combine stores help achieve this goal?

CH. 20 / CORPORATIONS: STOCK VALUES, DIVIDENDS, TREASURY STOCK, AND RETAINED EARNINGS

	BEFORE	AFTER
	100 shares × $80 = $8,000	200 shares × $40 = $8,000

Jay will benefit from the stock split if

1. The stock price rises on the market.
2. Dividends per share are increased.

LEARNING UNIT 20-2 REVIEW

AT THIS POINT you should be able to

- List as well as explain the three important dates associated with the dividend process. (p. 696)
- Journalize the appropriate entries for a cash dividend. (p. 697)
- List possible reasons for a stock dividend. (p. 698)
- Journalize appropriate entries for a stock dividend. (p. 698)
- Compare and contrast a stock split to a stock dividend. (p. 699)

SELF-REVIEW QUIZ 20-2

(The forms you need are on page 98 of the *Study Guide and Working Papers*.)

Journalize the appropriate entries from the following facts: On September 24, 19XX, the Directors of Movy Co. declared a 5 percent stock dividend to be issued on November 8 to stockholders of record on October 10. There are 20,000 shares outstanding. The stock has a par value of $10 and a current market value of $15 per share.

Solution to Self-Review Quiz 20-2

($15 × 1,000 shares)
($10 par × 1,000 shares)

19XX					
Sept.	24	Retained Earnings	1 5 0 0 0 00		
		Common Stock Dividend Distributable		1 0 0 0 0 00	
		Paid-in Capital in Excess of Par			
		Value—Stock Dividend		5 0 0 0 00	
Nov.	8	Common Stock Dividend Distributable	1 0 0 0 0 00		
		Common Stock		1 0 0 0 0 00	

LEARNING UNIT 20-3
Treasury Stock

Previously issued preferred or common stock that has been reacquired by the corporation (or given as a gift to the corporation) is known as **treasury stock.** Why would a corporation reacquire previously issued stock? Some reasons might include:

1. A need to issue more stock for stock option plans or for use in acquiring other corporations.

2. A desire to reduce the number of shares of stock outstanding. This might be done to create a favorable market for the sale of the stock.

3. Anticipation of an opportunity at a later date to reissue stock at a higher price.

The following are some of the characteristics of treasury stock:

1. The purchase of treasury stock does not change the amount of issued stock.

2. The purchase of treasury stock does reduce outstanding stock. Remember, stock can be issued but not outstanding.

3. Treasury stock does not have rights to dividends or voting situations (since it is not outstanding).

4. Treasury stock is a contra-stockholders' equity account.

5. When treasury stock is bought, it is recorded at the purchase price. This purchase of treasury stock does not reduce the balance in the Retained Earnings account.

6. Many state laws will restrict the amount of retained earnings available for dividends if treasury stock exists, because the purchase of treasury stock reduces assets and stockholders' equity (like a cash dividend). This is commonly shown on a footnote on the balance sheet.

Let's look now at how to record the purchase of treasury stock.

PURCHASE OF TREASURY STOCK

On June 1, 19XX, Ashly Corporation has 5,000 shares of $10 par-value common stock and 2,000 shares of preferred stock outstanding. The corporation on June 1 purchases 1,000 shares of its own common stock at a price of $12 per share. The following is the analysis as well as journal entry to record the purchase:

Accounts Affected	Category	↑	↓	Rules
Treasury Stock—Common	Contra SE	↑		Dr. $12,000
Cash	Asset		↓	Cr. $12,000

(1,000 shares × 12) →

Record treasury stock at the purchase price of $12. Note that the par value of common is not affected. Think of an *increase* in treasury stock as a reduction to stockholders' equity.

	June	1	Treasury Stock—Common	1 2 0 0 0 00	
			Cash		1 2 0 0 0 00
			Purchase at $12 per share of		
			1,000 shares of previously		
			issued stock.		

SALE OF TREASURY STOCK

Treasury stock can be reissued at a price above or below the cost of reacquiring the stock. Let's look at how Ashly Company could sell on July 8 100 shares of the treasury stock at $15 per share that was reacquired on June 1 for $12 per share.

This chart analyzes the transaction:

Accounts Affected	Category	↑	↓	Rules
Cash	Asset	↑		Dr. $1,500
Treasury Stock—Common	Contra SE		↓	Cr. $1,200
Paid-in Capital from Treasury Stock	SE	↑		Cr. $300

(100 shares × $15) →
(100 shares × $12) →
(100 shares × $3) →

Think of a *decrease* in treasury stock resulting in an increase to stockholders' equity.

This is what the journal entry looks like:

July	8	Cash	1 5 0 0 00		
		Treasury Stock—Common		1 2 0 0 00	
		Paid-in Capital from Treasury Stock		3 0 0 00	
		Sold 100 shares of Treasury stock			
		purchased at $12.			

The Treasury Stock account is decreased by the number of shares reissued times the *cost* when the stock was reacquired by the company. The credit to **Paid-in Capital from Treasury Stock** represents the amount over what was paid for acquiring the treasury stock.

If a corporation sells treasury stock for less than cost, the result is a decrease in stockholders' equity that is recorded in Paid-in Capital from Treasury Stock until the balance of the account is 0. Any further decrease in this account will directly reduce Retained Earnings, since Paid-in Capital from Treasury Stock will not be a negative balance.

EXAMPLE OF STOCKHOLDERS' EQUITY WITH TREASURY STOCK

Now let's see what stockholders' equity will look like with the accounts Treasury Stock and Paid-in Capital from Treasury Stock.

The 900 shares of treasury stock don't reduce the number of shares *issued,* they reduce the number of shares *outstanding.*

Paid-in Capital:			
Preferred Stock, 14/%, $100 par value,			
authorized 6,000 shares, 2,000 shares			
issued and outstanding		$200 0 0 0 00	
Common Stock $10 par, authorized 9,000			
shares, 5,000 shares issued and 4,100			
outstanding, 900 shares in treasury		50 0 0 0 00*	
Additional Paid-in Capital:			
Paid-in Capital in Excess of Par			
Value—Preferred	10 0 0 0 00		
Paid-in Capital in Excess of Par			
Value—Common	30 0 0 0 00		
Paid-in Capital from Treasury Stock	3 0 0 00		
Total Additional Paid-in Capital		40 3 0 0 00	
Total Paid-in Capital		$290 3 0 0 00	
Retained Earnings		60 0 0 0 00	
		$350 3 0 0 00	
Deduct: Treasury Stock—Common			
(900 shares at cost)		10 8 0 0 00	
Total Stockholders' Equity		$339 5 0 0 00	

* $50,000 = shares issued (5,000) x par ($10)

LEARNING UNIT 20-3 REVIEW

AT THIS POINT you should be able to

◆ Define and explain the characteristics of treasury stock (p. 701)
◆ Journalize the purchase as well as sale of treasury stock. (pp. 702–703)
◆ Explain why treasury stock is a contra-stockholders' equity account. (pp. 702–703)

SELF-REVIEW QUIZ 20-3

(The forms you need are on page 98 of the *Study Guide and Working Papers*.)
Record the following transactions in general journal form (no explanation needed):

1. Also Company acquired 100 shares of its own $10 par common stock at $15 per share.
2. Fifty of the treasury shares are reissued at $18 per share.
3. Forty of the treasury shares are reissued at $6.

Solution to Self-Review Quiz 20-3

❶	Treasury Stock (100 × $15)	1 5 0 0 00	
	Cash		1 5 0 0 00
❷	Cash ($18 × 50)	9 0 0 00	
	Treasury Stock (50 × $15)		7 5 0 00
❸	Paid-in Capital from Treasury		
	Stock (50 × $3)		1 5 0 00
	Cash ($6 × 40)	2 4 0 00	
	Paid-in Capital from Treasury Stock	1 5 0 00	
	Retained Earnings	2 1 0 00	
	Treasury Stock (40 × $15)		6 0 0 00

Note that Retained Earnings is reduced by $210, because Paid-in Capital is down to a zero balance:

$$\begin{array}{ll} \$150 & (50 \times \$3) \\ \underline{-360} & (40 \times \$9) \\ \${<}210{>} & \end{array}$$

LEARNING UNIT 20-4

Appropriation of Retained Earnings and the Statement of Retained Earnings

In the first three units of this chapter we have seen that cash dividends as well as stock dividends reduce the amount of Retained Earnings. Now we look at how companies indicate to those reading their financial reports that some of the Retained Earnings are not available for declaration of dividends — they are **Appropriated (Restricted) Retained Earnings.**

This *appropriating* of retained earnings could be either voluntary or contractual. For example, the board of directors could voluntarily decide that a portion of earnings should be used for plant expansion instead of for dividends. If a company enters into a loan with a bank, the bank may require the company to keep a minimum balance in Retained Earnings to protect their rights until the loan is repaid. Companies in many states are required to keep a minimum in the Retained Earnings account at the level of legal capital. We saw in the last unit that treasury stock could result in Retained Earnings being restricted to the cost of the treasury stock.

In years past these special appropriations were recorded by transferring portions of the Retained Earnings account to accounts such as Retained Earnings Appropriated for Plant Expansion or Retained Earnings Appropriated for Contra Obligations. In reality, these appropriations didn't reduce total Retained Earnings; they just *shifted* a portion into an account that revealed its special purpose. For example, an entry to restrict $20,000 for plant expansion would be as follows:

Retained Earnings	20 00 0 00	
Appropriation for Plant Expansion		20 00 0 00

After the appropriation or restriction has passed (the loan has been paid off, or whatever), the balance is transferred back to the Retained Earnings account. No cash is involved in the appropriation.

Today, in order to make things clear to investors, most companies report restrictions by using a footnote to the Retained Earnings account. Restrictions about Retained Earnings do not have to be updated in the ledger; thus the use of a footnote is a common practice. (It is good practice to write a memo in the Retained Earnings account to identify each appropriation.) A footnote to announce such restrictions would look like this:

> The loan agreement with Jones Bank contains a restriction on the payment of cash dividends. Approximately $600,000 of retained earnings was free of such a restriction as of June 30, 19XX.

PREPARING THE STATEMENT OF RETAINED EARNINGS

In past chapters we have discussed the income statement, balance sheet, statement of owners' equity, and statement of partners' equity. We will now turn our attention to a **statement of retained earnings** that will reveal the changes of retained earnings over a period of time. Basically the changes in retained earnings result from:

1. Net income or loss.
2. Dividends declared.
3. Effects of prior period adjustments.

Often an error in a financial report of a company from a prior period may not be discovered until a later period. If the error is considered *material,* a

prior period adjustment should be made to the beginning balance of Retained Earnings. Let's look at a specific example.

Eight months after the close of its books Ralston Company discovered that depreciation was understated by $12,000. This meant in the old period that Depreciation Expense was understated by $12,000 and Net Income was overstated by $12,000. If Net Income was overstated, Retained Earnings also was overstated, since Net Income is closed into Retained Earnings. Thus the following entry is recorded in the *new* year to adjust the prior period error (we ignore tax effect here):

Retained Earnings	12 0 0 0 00	
Accumulated Depreciation, Equipment		12 0 0 0 00

The following is an example of what a statement of retained earnings would look like for the Ralston Company.

RALSTON COMPANY
STATEMENT OF RETAINED EARNINGS
YEAR ENDED DECEMBER 31, 19X2

Retained Earnings, Jan. 1, 19X2	$350 0 0 0 00
Less: Prior Period Adjustment:	
Correction of 19X1 error	12 0 0 0 00
Retained Earnings, Jan. 19X2, corrected	$338 0 0 0 00
Add: Net Income for 19X2	40 0 0 0 00
Total	$378 0 0 0 00
Deduct: Dividends declared in 19X2	28 0 0 0 00
Retained Earnings, Dec. 31, 19X2	$350 0 0 0 00

This ending figure of $350,000 will appear in the stockholders' equity section of the balance sheet.

ACCOUNTING CYCLE FOR A CORPORATION

Before we conclude our discussion of corporations, page 707 provides a simplified sample of a worksheet for a corporation. This will give you a better idea of what titles such as Subscriptions Receivable, Common Stock, Paid-in Capital, and Retained Earnings look like when all combined on one worksheet.

The cycle is then to prepare financial reports as well as journalize and post the adjusting and closing entries. We use Retained Earnings instead of Capital in the closing process. Also in the adjusting process we adjust the income tax owed. The Income Tax account is closed to Income Summary. The steps are quite similar to those we discussed for a merchandise company.

A key point is that the net income shown on the income statement could be substantially different from that reported for tax purposes. This is because certain deductions on the tax return will differ from the expenses on the corporation's books.

The statement of retained earnings is a formal report.

JANE CORPORATION
WORKSHEET
FOR YEAR ENDED DECEMBER 31, 19X3

Account Name	Trial Balance Dr.	Trial Balance Cr.	Adjustments Dr.	Adjustments Cr.	Adjusted Trial Balance Dr.	Adjusted Trial Balance Cr.	Income Statement Dr.	Income Statement Cr.	Balance Sheet Dr.	Balance Sheet Cr.
Cash	X				X				X	
Notes Receivable	X				X				X	
Accounts Receivable	X				X				X	
Subscriptions Rec., Com. Stock	X				X				X	
Merch. Inventory	X		O	X	O				O	
Prepaid Rent	X			X	X				X	
Office Equipment	X				X				X	
Acc. Dep., Office Equip.		X		X		X				X
Organization Costs	X				X				X	
Notes Payable		X				X				X
Accounts Payable		X				X				X
Dividends Payable, Com.		X				X				X
Common Stock		X				X				X
Common Stock Div. Dist.		X				X				X
Paid-in Capital in Excess of Par — Common Stock		X				X				X
Common Stock Subscribed		X				X				X
Paid-in Capital from Treasury Stock		X				X				X
Retained Earnings		X				O				X
Income Summary			X	O	X	O	X	O		
Sales (totals)		X				X		X		
Purchases	X				X		X			
Purch. Ret. And Allow.		X				X		X		
Expenses (totals)	X									
Expenses (Adj.)			X		X		X			
Income Tax	X		X		X		X			
Income Tax Payable				X		X				X

O = Ending inventory

AT THIS POINT you should be able to

♦ Explain what could lead to appropriations of Retained Earnings. (p. 705)
♦ Explain why footnotes are used on financial reports instead of appropriation accounts to report restrictions to Retained Earnings. (p. 705)
♦ Prepare a statement of retained earnings. (p. 705)

SELF-REVIEW QUIZ 20-4

(The forms you need are on page 99 of the *Study Guide and Working Papers.*)
From the following data prepare a statement of retained earnings for Janet Corporation for the year ended December 31, 19X3:

♦ Retained Earnings, Jan. 1, 19X3, $650,000
♦ Dividends, 19X3, $50,000
♦ Correction of error from 19X1, $50,000 for Net Income that was discovered to be understated
♦ Net Income, 19X3, $80,000

Solution to Self-Review Quiz 20-4

JANET CORPORATION STATEMENT OF RETAINED EARNINGS YEAR ENDED DECEMBER 31, 19X3		
Retained Earnings, Jan. 1, 19X3		$650 00 0 00
Add: Prior Period Adjustment,		
Correction of 19X1 error		50 00 0 00
Retained Earnings, Jan. 19X3, corrected		$700 00 0 00
Add: Net Income for 19X3		80 00 0 00
Total		$780 00 0 00
Deduct: Dividends declared in 19X3		50 00 0 00
Retained Earnings, Dec. 31, 19X3		$730 00 0 00

SUMMARY OF KEY POINTS

Learning Unit 20-1

1. Redemption value is the price per share a corporation pays to holders of preferred stock when the stock is retired or redeemed.
2. Market value represents the open-market price of stock bought and sold. Market value doesn't mean the same thing as book value.
3. Book value per share is the amount or value of net assets on a company's books for each share of stockholders' stock in the equity of the corporation. Book value is calculated for preferred and common separately.

Learning Unit 20-2

1. Dividends represent cash, stock, or other assets distributed to stockholders. The board of directors has the authority to declare dividends.
2. Three important dates associated with the dividend process are date of declaration, date of record, and date of payment.
3. A cash dividend results in a reduction of Retained Earnings and an eventual reduction in Cash.
4. Retained earnings doesn't mean cash.
5. A stock dividend will not reduce stockholders' equity like a cash dividend. The end result is a transfer of retained earnings to Paid-in Capital.
6. Common Stock Dividend Distributable is a stockholders' equity account that is recorded at par value. It is not a liability account.
7. A stock split has no effect on Retained Earnings or any other ledger account. It increases the number of shares outstanding as well as reducing par or stated value.

Learning Unit 20-3

1. Treasury Stock is a contra-stockholders' equity account that is recorded at cost. It represents stock that was previously issued and is now reacquired or received as a gift by a corporation.
2. Treasury stock is recognized as issued but not outstanding for dividends or voting situations.
3. Paid-in Capital from Treasury Stock can never have a negative balance. Any additional "loss" is reduced in Retained Earnings.

Learning Unit 20-4

1. Appropriations of Retained Earnings can be contractual or voluntary.
2. Appropriations restrict the amount of Retained Earnings available for dividends.
3. Common practice today is to use footnotes on the balance sheet to reveal any appropriations of Retained Earnings.
4. The statement of retained earnings is made up of (1) beginning balance, (2) corrections of prior periods, (3) net income, and (4) dividends.

KEY TERMS

Appropriated (Restricted) Retained Earnings That portion of Retained Earnings that is not available for dividends.

Book value per share Amount of net assets that a stockholder would receive on a per-share basis, assuming no gain or loss on the sale of the assets.

Cash dividend Dividend that is paid in cash.

Common Stock Dividend Distributable Stockholders' equity account that accumulates stock dividend that has been declared but not yet issued and distributed.

Date of declaration The date upon which the board of directors of a corporation formally declares a dividend.

Date of payment The date the dividend is paid.

Date of record The date of ownership that determines which stockholders will receive the dividend.

Dividend Cash or other assets that a corporation distributes as earnings to stockholders.

Dividend Payable Liability showing amount of cash dividend owed.

Market value The price that a buyer pays to purchase shares of capital stock in the open market. Of course for every buyer there is a seller.

Paid-in Capital from Treasury Stock Stockholders' equity account that records amounts more or less than par value of treasury stock sold. The balance of this account can never be negative.

Prior period adjustment Correction made in the current year of a mistake made in previous years. The adjustment is updated on the statement of retained earnings.

Redemption value The price per share a corporation pays to redeem or retire capital stock.

Statement of retained earnings A financial report that reveals the changes in retained earnings for a particular period of time.

Stock dividend Stock that is distributed to stockholders instead of cash or other assets.

Stock split Issuing of additional shares of stock to stockholders; total par or stated value remains the same.

Treasury stock Stock that has been issued but has been bought back by the corporation or received as a gift.

QUESTIONS, MINI EXERCISES, EXERCISES, AND PROBLEMS

Discussion Questions

1. What is the difference between market value and book value?
2. List the three important dates that are associated with the dividend process.
3. Why is no journal entry needed at the date of record?
4. Explain some possible reasons a company may declare a stock dividend instead of a cash dividend.
5. Explain why stock dividends will not reduce total stockholders' equity.
6. Common Stock Dividend Distributable is a liability. Accept or reject. Defend your position.
7. Explain the difference between a stock dividend and a stock split.
8. Treasury stock is really an asset. Defend or reject. Support your argument.
9. All treasury stock is recognized as issued and outstanding for dividends. True or false? Please explain.
10. Explain the purpose of the account Paid-in Capital from Treasury Stock.
11. Appropriation of retained earnings is always done for a contractual reason. Accept or reject. Defend your position.
12. Restrictions on retained earnings have to be updated in the ledger. Agree or disagree. Why?
13. What elements make up the statement of retained earnings?

Mini Exercises

(The forms you need are on page 101 of the *Study Guide and Working Papers*.)

Book Value per Share for Preferred and Common

1. Given the following prepare the book value per share for preferred and common stock:

BLUEPRINT—LEGAL CAPITAL APPROACH

MOOSE COMPANY PARTIAL BALANCE SHEET			
Stockholders' Equity			
Paid-in Capital:			
Preferred Stock 12%, $10 par value,			
authorized 30,000 shares, 9,000 shares			
issued and outstanding		XX	
Common Stock, $10 par value,			
authorized 100,000 shares, 40,000			
shares issued and 29,000 shares			
outstanding, 11,000 shares in treasury	XX		
Common Stock Dividend Distributable	XX	XX	
Additional Paid-in Capital:			
Paid-in Capital in Excess of Par			
Value—Preferred	XX		
Paid-in Capital in Excess of Par			
Value—Common	XX		
Paid-in Capital in Excess of Par			
Value—Stock Dividend	XX		
Paid-in Capital from Treasury Stock	XX		
Total Additional Paid-in Capital		XX	
Total Paid-in Capital		XX	
Retained Earnings		XX	
Deduct: Treasury Stock		XX	
Total Stockholders' Equity			XX

Note that legal capital is listed first. See page 685 for blueprint example of the source-of-capital approach. Both approaches are acceptable, and in the real world both are used.

◆ Preferred Stock $80,000; 1,000 shares issued
◆ Common Stock $150,000; 800 shares issued.
◆ Retained Earnings, $8,500
◆ Dividend in Arrears, $4,000
◆ Paid-in capital in excess of par — preferred, $5,000
◆ Paid-in capital in excess of par — common, $6,000
◆ Redemption value on preferred stock, $16

Cash Dividend

2. On March 15, 19XX, the board of directors of Vision Corporation declared $3 cash dividend per share on the 6,000 shares issued and outstanding. The dividend will be paid on April 18, 19XX, to stockholders of record on March 19, 19XX. Record journal entries for date of declaration and date of payment.

Stock Dividend

3. On December 24, 19XX, Fress Corporation declared a 5 percent stock dividend distributable January 18 to stockholders of record on January 8. Currently Fress has 5,000 shares of common stock issued and outstanding. The stock has a par

value of $20. The current fair market value of the stock is $35. Journalize (a) the declaration of the dividend and (b) the issuance of the stock dividend.

Treasury Stock

4. Journalize the following transactions:

   a. Janson Co. acquired 50 shares of its own $5 par-value common stock at $10 per share.

   b. Twenty-five of the Treasury shares are reissued at $13 per share.

   c. Twenty of the Treasury shares are reissued at $4 per share.

Prior Period Adjustment

5. Seven months after its closing, Brooks Co. discovered that depreciation was understated by $8,000. Provide the journal entry to adjust the prior period error (ignore any tax effects).

Exercises

(The forms you need are on pages 102 and 103 of the *Study Guide and Working Papers.*)

20-1. From the following determine the book value for preferred and common stocks assuming $15,000 of dividends are in arrears on the preferred stock.

Calculating book value of preferred and common.

STOCKHOLDERS' EQUITY

Preferred Stock 12 percent cumulative and non-participating, $20 par value, $19 redemption value, 10,000 shares issued and outstanding	$200,000
Common Stock, $10 par value, 40,000 shares issued and outstanding	400,000
Retained Earnings	80,000
Total Stockholders' Equity	$680,000

Cash dividend.

20-2. Poole Corporation has 300,000 shares of common stock issued and outstanding. On June 9, 19X6, the board of directors declared a $.50 per share dividend, payable on July 16, 19X6, to stockholders of record on June 29, 19X6. Record the appropriate journal entries on June 9 and July 16.

Stock dividend.

20-3. On July 31, 19X1, Harvey Corporation has the following stockholders' equity:

Common Stock, $10 par value, authorized 90,000 shares, 60,000 shares issued and outstanding	$600,000
Retained Earnings	200,000
Total Stockholders' Equity	$800,000

On August 5, 19X1, the board of directors declared a 10 percent stock dividend to be issued on September 6, 19X1, to the stockholders of record on August 19, 19X1. At time of declaration the market price was $17 per share. Prepare the appropriate journal entries for this stock dividend.

20-4. Given the following stockholders' equity:

Common Stock, $7 par value, authorized 100,000 shares, 80,000 shares issued and outstanding	$ 560,000
Retained Earnings	500,000
Total Stockholders' Equity	$1,060,000

Journalize the following entries:

Treasury stock.

19XX
Apr. 3 Issued 5,000 shares at $12 per share.
      9 Reacquired 200 shares at $8 per share.
     15 Reissued 100 shares of treasury stock at $10 per share.
     17 Reissued 50 shares of treasury stock at $7 per share.

Statement of retained earnings.

20-5. From the following, prepare in proper form a statement of retained earnings for Williams Company for the year ended December 31, 19X4.

		Prior period adjustment increase in recording expense for Land in	
Retained Earnings, January 19X4	$40,000	19X2 (disregard taxes)	$14,000
Net Income, 19X4	$60,000	Dividends Paid, 19X4	$20,000

Group A Problems

(The forms you need are on pages 104–114 of the *Study Guide and Working Papers.*)

20A-1. The stockholders' equity of Oscar Company is as follows:

STOCKHOLDERS' EQUITY

Calculating book value with and without dividends in arrears.

Check Figure:
Book value preferred $108

Paid-in Capital:		
Preferred 10 percent Stock, $100 par value, authorized 5,000 shares, cumulative and nonparticipating, 4,000 shares issued and outstanding	$400,000	
Paid-in Capital in Excess of Par Value — Preferred	50,000	
Total Paid-in Capital by Preferred Stockholders		$450,000
Common Stock, $50 par value, authorized 15,000 shares, 6,000 shares issued and outstanding	$300,000	
Paid-in Capital in Excess of Par Value — Common	60,000	
Total Paid-in Capital by Common Stockholders		360,000
Total Paid-in Capital		$810,000
Retained Earnings		160,000
Total Stockholders' Equity		$970,000

Given a redemption value of $108, calculate the book value of preferred and common stock, assuming

a. No dividends in arrears.

b. Two years' dividends in arrears.

Cash and stock dividends.

20A-2. Lance Corporation has 400,000 shares of $7 par-value common stock issued and outstanding. Record the following entries into the general journal for Lance:

Check Figure:
Aug. 4 Paid-in capital in excess of par value—stock dividend $80,000 Cr.

19XX
July 2 Declared a cash dividend of $.60 per share.
Aug. 1 Paid the 60 cents cash dividend to the stockholders.
Aug. 4 Declared a 4 percent stock dividend. The current market price is $12 per share.

Sept. 12 Issued the stock dividend declared on August 4.

Oct. 1 Declared an 8 percent stock dividend. The current market price is $17 per share.

Nov. 2 Issued the stock dividend on October 1.

20A-3. At the beginning of January 19XX, the stockholders' equity of Long View Corporation consisted of the following:

Cash and stock dividend; treasury stock; preparation of stockholders' equity section and statement of retained earnings.

Paid-in Capital:

Common Stock, $25 par value, authorized 50,000 shares, 13,000 shares issued and outstanding	$325,000	
Paid-in Capital in Excess of Par Value — Common	70,000	
Total Paid-in Capital by Common Stockholders	$395,000	
Retained Earnings	160,000	
Total Stockholders' Equity		$555,000

Check Figure:

Total stockholders' equity
$614,300

1. Record the following transactions in general journal form.

2. Prepare the stockholders' equity section at year-end using the blueprint layout on page 711 as a guide.

3. Prepare a statement of retained earnings at December 31, 19XX.

Accounts are provided in the *Study Guide and Working Papers.* Be sure to put in the beginning balances.

19XX

June 4 Long View Corporation purchased 1,000 shares of treasury stock at $28.

20 The board of directors voted a $.20 per share cash dividend payable on July 15 to stockholders of record on July 2.

July 15 Cash dividend declared on June 20 is paid.

Sept. 5 Sold 300 shares of the treasury stock at $36 per share.

29 Sold 700 shares of the treasury stock at $27 per share.

Oct. 10 The board of directors declared a 6 percent stock dividend distributable on January 2 to stockholders of record on November 2. The market value of the stock is currently $38 per share.

Dec. 31 Closed the net income of $60,000 in the Income Summary account to Retained Earnings.

20A-4. The following is the stockholders' equity of Piersal Corporation on October 1, 19XX:

Paid-in Capital:

Journalizing and Posting various stockholders' equity situations and preparing stockholders' equity section by a legal capital approach.

Preferred 14 percent Stock, $10 par value, authorized 6,000 shares, 3,000 shares issued and outstanding		$ 30,000
Common Stock, $10 par value, authorized 20,000 shares, 10,000 shares issued and outstanding		100,000
Additional Paid-in Capital:		
Paid-in Capital in Excess of Par Value—Preferred	$10,000	
Paid-in Capital in Excess of Par Value—Common	5,000	

Check Figure:

Total stockholders' equity
$419,500

Paid-in Capital in Excess of Par Value—Stock Dividend	4,000	
Total Additional Paid-in Capital	19,000	
Total Paid-in Capital	$149,000	
Retained Earnings	200,000	
Total Stockholders' Equity		$349,000

1. Journalize the following transactions in general journal form.
2. Prepare the stockholders' equity section of the balance sheet using the legal capital approach as of December 31, 19XX.

Your *Study Guide and Working Papers* has accounts to update ledger balances. Be sure to put in the beginning balances. Use the blueprint on page 711 as a guide to the setup of stockholders' equity.

19XX

Oct.	3	Declared a $.40 per share dividend on the common stock and a $1.20 per share dividend on the preferred. (The Dividends Payable account will record amounts for both common and preferred, although companies could set up Common Dividend Payable and Preferred Dividend Payable accounts.)
Nov.	15	Dividends were paid that were declared on October 3.
	18	Purchased 300 shares of its own common stock at $13 per share.
	25	Reissued 50 shares at $16 per share.
	26	Declared a 20 percent stock dividend on common. Market value of stock is $40 per share.
Dec.	29	Distributed stock dividend declared on November 26.
	30	Reissued 100 shares of treasury stock at $12 per share.
	31	Closed the Income Summary account, which had net income of $80,000, to Retained Earnings.

Group B Problems

(The forms you need are on pages 104–114 of the *Study Guide and Working Papers*.)

Calculating book value with and without dividends in arrears.

20B-1. Given a redemption value of $105, calculate the book value of preferred and common stock, assuming (1) no dividends in arrears, (2) two years' dividends in arrears, from the following stockholders' equity of Oscar Company:

STOCKHOLDERS' EQUITY

Check Figure:
(a) Book value preferred $105

Paid-in Capital:		
Preferred 12 percent Stock, $100 par value, authorized 3,000 shares cumulative and nonparticipating, 1,000 shares issued and outstanding	$100,000	
Paid-in Capital in Excess of Par Value— Preferred	80,000	
Total Paid-in Capital by Preferred Stockholders		$ 180,000
Common Stock, $75 par value, authorized 12,000 shares, 8,000 shares issued and outstanding	$600,000	
Paid-in Capital in Excess of Par Value— Common	70,000	
Total Paid-in Capital by Common Stockholders		670,000

Total Paid-in Capital	$ 850,000
Retained Earnings	300,000
Total Stockholders' Equity	$1,150,000

20B-2. Lance Corporation has 200,000 shares of $10 par value common stock issued and outstanding. Record the following entries into the general journal for Lance:

19XX

Aug. 3 Declared a cash dividend of $.30 per share.

Sept. 4 Paid the $.30 cash dividend to the stockholders.

6 Declared a 5 percent stock dividend. The current market price is $14 per share.

29 Issued the stock dividend declared on September 6.

Nov. 1 Declared a 10 percent stock dividend. The current market price is $17 per share.

29 Issued the stock dividend declared on November 1.

20B-3. At the beginning of January 19XX, the stockholders' equity of Long View Corporation consisted of the following:

Paid-in Capital:

Common Stock, $30 par value, authorized 70,000 shares, 15,000 shares issued and outstanding	$450,000
Paid-in Capital in Excess of Par Value — Common	60,000
Total Paid-in Capital by Common Stockholders	510,000
Retained Earnings	300,000
Total Stockholders' Equity	$810,000

1. Record the following transactions in general journal form.

2. Prepare a stockholders' equity section, using the blueprint layout on page 711.

3. Prepare a statement of retained earnings at December 31, 19XX.

Accounts are provided in *Study Guide and Working Papers.* Be sure to put in the beginning balances.

19XX

May 3 Long View Corporation purchased 2,000 shares of treasury stock at $40.

15 The board of directors voted a $.70 per share cash dividend payable on July 9 to stockholders of record on June 13.

July 9 Cash dividends declared on May 15 is paid.

Sept. 15 Sold 200 shares of treasury stock at $50 per share.

Oct. 10 Sold 300 shares of treasury stock at $38 per share.

Nov. 1 The board of directors declared a 20 percent stock dividend distributable on January 2 to stockholders of record on November 17. The market value of the stock is $60 per share.

Dec. 31 Closed the net income of $75,000 in the Income Summary account to Retained Earnings.

20B-4. The following is the stockholders' equity of Piersal Corporation on November 1, 19XX:

Paid-in Capital:

| Preferred 12 percent Stock, $10 par value, authorized 8,000 shares, 2,000 shares issued and outstanding | $ 20,000 |

Common Stock, $10 par value, authorized 15,000 shares, 10,000 shares issued and outstanding		100,000
Additional Paid-in Capital:		
Paid-in Capital in Excess of Par Value — Preferred	$30,000	
Paid-in Capital in Excess of Par Value — Common	10,000	
Paid-in Capital in Excess of Par Value — Stock Dividend	7,000	
Total Additional Paid-in Capital		47,000
Total Paid-in Capital		$167,000
Retained Earnings		86,000
Total Stockholders' Equity		$253,000

1. Journalize the following transactions in general journal form.

2. Prepare the stockholders' equity section of the balance sheet using the legal capital approach (see the blueprint on p. 711) as of December 31, 19XX.

Your *Study Guide and Working Papers* has accounts to update ledger balances. Be sure to put in beginning balances.

19XX

Nov. 3 Due to increased sales, the board of directors of Piersal declared a $3 per share dividend on the common stock and a $1.50 per share dividend on the preferred. (The Dividends Payable account records both common and preferred.)

8 Purchased 500 shares of its own common stock at $16 per share.

15 Reissued 200 shares at $18 per share.

16 Declared a 10 percent stock dividend on common. Market value is $25 per share.

Dec. 15 Dividends were paid that were declared on November 3.

28 Distributed stock dividend declared on November 16.

30 Reissued 200 shares at $15 per share.

31 Closed the Income Summary account, which had net income of $55,000, to Retained Earnings.

REAL WORLD APPLICATIONS

20R-1.

Moose Corporation has the following stockholders' equity prepared by Jesse Ross, head bookkeeper:

Paid-in Capital:	
Common Stock, $5 par, 3000 shares authorized, 1,600 shares issued, of which 900 shares are in the treasury	$ 4,500
Paid-in Capital in Excess of Par Value—Common	2,000
Total Paid-in Capital	5,500
Retained Earnings	2,000
Total	7,500
Add: Cost of Treasury Stock	7,000
Total Stockholders' Equity	$14,500

Explain what error(s) Jesse has made in the preparation of stockholders' equity. Also Moose Corporation wants to declare a cash dividend of $3 per share. Is it feasible? Show your calculations along with a written explanation.

20R-2.

Margaret Jones owns 100 shares of Johnson Corporation. She receives in the mail a notice that a 2-for-1 stock split is being declared. Currently the stock is trading on the open market at $120 per share. After the split 600,000 shares will be outstanding. Margaret is very worried that this split will reduce her book value, resulting in a loss of market value. She feels her preemptive right has been ignored. She believes that a stock dividend is the best way for the corporation to go. Respond in writing specifically to Margaret's concerns.

YOU make the call

Critical Thinking/Ethical Case

20R-3.

Alan Homes serves on the Board of Directors of Flynn Company. The president of Flynn told him that in three weeks the corporation would announce a 25 percent increase in dividends. Alan called his neighbor to tell him to buy some stock. The neighbor told his friend about the stock and the friend told him that Alan was acting unethically. The neighbor called Alan back and Alan told him that no one will know the difference, that in business this happens all the time, that he shouldn't be left out. Do you feel that Alan's behavior is appropriate? You make the call. Write down your recommendation to Alan's neighbor.

ACCOUNTING RECALL
A CUMULATIVE APPROACH

THIS EXAM REVIEWS CHAPTERS 1 THROUGH 20

Your *Study Guide and Working Papers* (pp. 118–119) has forms to complete this exam, as well as worked-out solutions. The page references next to each question identify what page to turn back to if you answer the question incorrectly.

PART 1   Vocabulary Review

Match the terms to the appropriate definition or phrase.

Page Ref.

(700)	1. Stock split	A. Can never be a negative balance
(678)	2. Subscriptions receivable	B. Stock held and owned by stockholders
(697)	3. Dividends payable	
(669)	4. Dividends in arrears	C. A stockholders' equity account
(701)	5. Treasury stock	D. Cannot be withdrawn by stockholders
(711)	6. Legal capital	
(674)	7. Organization cost	E. Dividends owed to preferred stockholders
(702)	8. Paid-in capital from Treasury stock	F. Debit balance

(668) 9. Outstanding capital stock   G. An intangible asset
(699) 10. Common stock dividend   H. A liability
          distributable   I. An asset
                                        J. Total par or stated value
                                           remains the same

PART II   True or False (Accounting Theory)

(697) 11. Declaration of dividends increases retained earnings.
(696) 12. The date of record is the date when a dividend is actually paid.
(697) 13. Retained earnings does not mean cash.
(702) 14. Treasury stock is a contra-asset.
(702) 15. Treasury stock increases the number of shares outstanding.

CORPORATIONS AND BONDS PAYABLE

21

THE BIG PICTURE

The Eldorado Computer Center ended its year with a net profit of $168,500. As stockholders, Freedman and West each received 10 percent of that profit as dividends. The remaining 80 percent was retained in the business, with over $90,000 going for additional inventory. Freedman and West set aside $40,000 to expand the business, but they knew they would need much more. They explored many options to help raise additional funds. They considered selling Eldorado Computer Center stock, but at this point neither Freedman nor West wanted anyone else to have a right to vote or have an interest in the profit of the company. They also considered obtaining a long-term loan or selling bonds.

A bond is a form of long-term debt. Selling bonds raises additional funds by incurring long-term debt, which must be repaid. Bondholders are people or businesses that have a claim against the business until the bond is repaid. Their claim against the business takes priority over the stockholders of the business.

In this chapter you will explore the different ways to raise capital and the detail involved in issuing, amortizing, and discounting a bond.

Learning Objectives	◆ **Journalizing the recording of bonds as well as interest payments.** (p. 721) ◆ **Amortizing bond discounts and bond premiums by the straight-line method and by the interest method.** (p. 725, 732) ◆ **Journalizing year-end adjusting entries for bonds.** (pp. 732–733) ◆ **Journalizing entries related to retirement of bonds and to sinking funds.** (p. 735)

A corporation can raise funds by issuing stock or long-term notes payable. Notes or stock are good sources of funds when a company borrows from only one bank or other type of lending institution, but they may not provide the total amount of funds needed. In the last two chapters we've seen how companies issue stock. Now our attention shifts to notes. After all, businesses like IBM and General Motors may need to borrow millions of dollars. This chapter looks at how corporations can raise large amounts of money from groups of lenders by issuing a type of long-term interest-bearing note payable called a **bond.**

LEARNING UNIT 21-1
Structure and Characteristics of a Bond

Each **bond certificate,** usually issued in denominations of $1,000, contains the following:

1. **Face value** (principal) — the amount that the corporation must repay to the lender at maturity date.
2. **Contract rate** (stated interest rate) — the annual interest rate, which is based on face value. Usually this interest is paid *semi*annually. The dates of interest payment are also printed on the certificate.

For example, if Joe Rosse owns a $1,000, 12 percent, 20-year bond that is issued by Von Corporation, it means:

1. At end of 20 years Joe will receive the $1,000.
2. Every six months Joe will receive an interest check for $60 ($1,000 × .12 × $\frac{6}{12}$).

There is also another way to calculate semiannual interest:

$$\frac{12\%}{2} = \text{semiannual rate of 6\%}$$

$$.06 \times \$1,000 = \$60$$

The information on the bond certificate is written by the corporation into a more formal agreement called the **bond indenture.** This agreement is usually monitored by a **trustee** (often a bank), who represents the group of bondholders.

If, before the 20 years have passed, Joe wants to cash in the bond, he can sell it on the securities exchange (like the stock exchange, but dealing in the buying and selling of bonds rather than stock). Bonds are negotiable and generally transferable. Let's assume Joe calls his broker, who indicates that the current market price of the bond is quoted at 94, a percentage (94 percent) of the bond's face value. This price can be higher or lower than the face amount (100, or 100 percent), depending on current rates of interest as well as other market factors. If market interest rates are high compared to the current

Trustee (usually a bank) monitors bondholders' interest as stipulated in the bond indenture.

A bond quote of 70 would mean that a bond with a face value of $1,000 is selling for $700 (.70 × $1,000).

bond's interest rate the percentage would be lower. Why? The bond's interest is not as attractive as current rates. The 94 means that a buyer is willing to pay $940 (.94 × $1,000) for the bond. If the quote were 104, then Joe could receive $1,040 (1.04 × $1,000) for the bond.

The following is a list of different types of bonds. Keep in mind that each bond issue may have special arrangements besides the customary repayment plans. Don't memorize this list—use it as a reference.

TYPES OF BONDS

Corporations can offer many types of bonds. The following are some examples.

Secured Bonds: The corporation issuing the bonds pledges specific assets such as equipment or property as security for meeting the terms of the bond agreement.

Debenture Bonds: The issuing corporation pledges no specific assets as collateral; thus the bonds are unsecured. Risk is higher than with secured bonds; these bonds will generally require a higher rate of interest to make them attractive to the investor.

Serial Bonds: These bonds are made up of a series, each having its own maturity date. For example, a bond issue of $2,000,000 could be made up of a series of twenty $100,000 bonds, one series maturing at the end of each year for a period of 20 years.

Registered Bonds: Owners of bonds are registered with the issuing company, and interest is mailed to the owners of record.

Callable Bonds: These bonds have a provision stating that they can be called in by a corporation after a certain date. When a bond issue is called in, the corporation has to pay a price above the face value of the bond.

Convertible Bonds: The bondholder may be allowed to convert bonds into shares of stock. For this right, the bondholder gives up fixed interest payments for what he or she hopes will be higher stock prices.

STOCKS VERSUS BONDS

Why would a corporation prefer to raise money by selling bonds rather than by issuing and selling stock? Let's look at an example: Should Rojer Corporation obtain long-term funds by selling $500,000 worth of 12 percent bonds, or issue 12 percent preferred stock for $500,000? Rojer Corporation wants to make the most of its tax savings as well as earnings per share of common stock:

$$\text{EPS} = \frac{\text{after-tax earnings} - \text{dividends for preferred}}{\text{number of shares of common stock outstanding}}$$

We are assuming Rojer Corporation has earnings of $700,000 and we assumed a tax rate of 40 percent. The table at the top of page 723 is a worked-out solution to this problem by the corporation's accountant.

Looking just at the numbers, Rojer Corporation would be better off issuing *bonds,* because the $60,000 of bond interest that the corporation would pay to bondholders would serve to reduce earnings that the corporation would have to pay tax on. On the other hand, *dividends* paid to stockholders would not reduce earnings on which the corporation would pay taxes (the dividend for preferred stock is not an expense, as bond interest is, but a distribution of net income *after* tax). With bonds the common stockholders have an earnings per share of $4.80 versus $4.50.

	$500,000 12 Percent Preferred Stock Issued	$500,000 12 Percent Bond (10-Year) Issued
Earnings before Taxes or Finance Costs	$700,000	$700,000
Less: Bond Interest	—0—	60,000 (.12 × $500,000)
Earnings Subject to Income Tax	$700,000	$640,000
Less: Income Tax (40%)	280,000	256,000
Net Income	420,000	384,000
Less: Preferred Dividend	60,000 (.12 × $500,000)	—0—
Earnings Available to Common Stockholders	360,000	384,000
Number of Common Stock Shares Outstanding	80,000	80,000
Earnings per Share	$4.50 $\left(\dfrac{\$360,000}{80,000}\right)$	$4.80 $\left(\dfrac{\$384,000}{80,000}\right)$

However, other factors should be considered when deciding whether to issue stocks or bonds to raise money, such as how interest rates are moving in the economy, or whether the corporation can meet the bond interest payments each period for ten years. If interest rates are high, it may be that the bond issue should be delayed to get more favorable interest rates.

For a comparison of stocks and bonds, see the blueprint on page 740.

Before concluding this unit, let's see how Rojer Corporation would record the sale and pay interest on the 12 percent, $500,000 bonds.

On January 1, Rojer Corporation issued its bonds:

Bonds Payable is a long-term liability on the balance sheet.

Jan.	1	Cash	500 000 00	
		Bonds Payable		500 000 00
		Records issuance of bonds.		

It then made semiannual interest payments to its bondholders:

$500,000 × .12 × $\frac{6}{12}$ = $30,000, or 12%/2 = .06 × $500,000 = $30,000.

June	30	Bond Interest Expense	30 000 00	
		Cash		30 000 00
		Paid semiannual interest expense.		

This entry will be recorded twice a year for ten years. At end of ten years Rojer will record the bond maturity.

On the year of retirement, this is the way the journal entry would look:

Dec.	31	Bonds Payable	500 00 0 00	
		Cash		500 00 0 00
		Retired bonds.		

The face value of the bond, $500,000 has been repaid on maturity date.

BONDS SOLD BETWEEN INTEREST DATES

What would happen if Rojer Corporation issued the bonds on January 1 but did not actually sell them until March 1? Interest would have to be paid for January and February — how is this handled? And what happens if a person buys a bond that was issued in August, but the person buys it in November? As stated earlier, bond issuers only pay interest every six months. So, when a buyer purchases a bond between the six-month interest dates, the buyer pays the purchase price of the bond *plus* the interest that has built up since the last interest payment date. Keep in mind interest is being paid only twice a year. Think of it as an adjustment as the interest accrues. On the next payment, the buyer will receive the full interest payment for the six-month period. Let's show this by seeing how Rojer Corporation records the sale of bonds on March 1 that were issued on January 1:

Accrued Interest

($500,000 × .12 × $\frac{2}{12}$ = $10,000) or $500,000 ×

.06 × $\left(\dfrac{2 \text{ months}}{6 \text{ months}}\right)$

↑ semiannual rate

Accrued interest originally collected is returned to investor.

March	1	Cash		510 0 0 0 00	
		Bonds Payable			500 0 0 0 00
		Bond Interest Payable			10 0 0 0 00
		Bond issue plus 2 months' accrued interest.			

Note the buyer pays $510,000 instead of $500,000, since $10,000 of the accrued interest has been accumulated. On June 30, the $10,000 is repaid along with interest earned for four months.

($500,000 × .12 × $\frac{4}{12}$ = $20,000) or $500,000 ×

.06 × $\left(\dfrac{4 \text{ months}}{6 \text{ months}}\right)$

↑ semiannual rate

June	30	Bond Interest Payable		10 0 0 0 00	
		Bond Interest Expense		20 0 0 0 00	
		Cash			30 0 0 0 00
		Record semiannual interest payment.			

In the next unit we will look at how to record bond issues when the selling price is less or more than the face value.

LEARNING UNIT 21-1 REVIEW

AT THIS POINT you should be able to

- Explain face value and contract interest rate. (p. 721)
- Calculate the cost of a bond from a bond quote. (p. 722)
- Explain the different classifications of bonds. (p. 722)
- Explain the pros and cons of financing with preferred stock versus bonds. (p. 722)
- Record accounting entries to record issuing of bonds at par as well as semiannual interest payment. (p. 723)
- Explain and record an accounting entry for accrued bond interest. (p. 724)

(The forms you need are on page 121 of the *Study Guide and Working Papers.*)

Prepare general journal entries to record the following (treat items 4 and 5 as a separate situation from items 1–3):

1. Issued 20 $10,000 12 percent bonds that mature in ten years at face value on January 1.
2. Paid semiannual interest on June 30.
3. Bonds retired at end of tenth year.
4. Bonds sold on May 1 instead of January 1 due to poor market conditions.
5. Paid semiannual interest on June 30 from bonds issued on May 1.

Solution to Self-Review Quiz 21-1

		Debit	Credit
1	Cash	200 000 00	
	Bonds Payable		200 000 00
2	Bond Interest Expense	12 000 00	
	Cash		12 000 00
	(I = $200,000 \times .12 \times \frac{6}{12}$		
	or $200,000 \times .06$ semiannual rate)		
3	Bonds Payable	200 000 00	
	Cash		200 000 00
4	Cash	208 000 00	
	Bonds Payable		200 000 00
	Bond Interest Payable		8 000 00
	(Accrued interest = $200,000 \times .12 \times \frac{4}{12}$		
	or $200,000 \times .06 \times \frac{4}{6} = \$8,000$.)		
5	Bond Interest Payable	8 000 00	
	Bond Interest Expense	4 000 00	
	Cash		12 000 00
	(Bond Interest Expense = $200,000 \times .12 \times \frac{2}{12}$		
	or $200,000 \times .06 \times \frac{2}{6} = \$4,000$.)		

LEARNING UNIT 21-2
Bonds Issued at a Discount or Premium; Amortization by the Straight-Line Method

When a corporation issues bonds, it must

1. Receive approval from the board of directors of the corporation as well as from a governmental regulatory agency, the Securities and Exchange Commission.
2. Print the bonds.
3. Advertise the bond issue.

The problem is that by the time this has been done, the rate of interest stated on the bond, the *contract* rate, may be lower or higher than the current *market* rate of interest. Investors may require higher rates of interest if the bond issue appears to be different than others offered by companies who may have had fewer financial difficulties.

For example, let's assume that Jossy Corporation is attempting to sell its 12 percent bond issue. The current market rate is 13 percent. To make its bonds more attractive (investors are looking for best return on their investment), Jossy decides to sell the bonds for less than face value (91, or 91 percent of the face value of $1,000). The bondholder will still receive yearly interest of $120 per bond (.12 × $1,000) but will only pay $910 (.91 × $1,000) per bond. Thus investors' annual or **effective rate** of interest is 13.2 percent ($120/$910). The difference between the *issue price* ($910) and the face value ($1,000) is called the *discount*.

Conversely, if Jossy Corporation sells the bond for *more* than the face value (if its contract rate is higher than the market rate), the difference between issue price and face value is called a *premium*.

RECORDING AND AMORTIZING BONDS ISSUED AT A DISCOUNT

To illustrate how to record a bond discount, let's look at the Ronson Corporation, which on January 1, 19XX, issued 200, 12 percent, $1,000, ten-year bonds at 97 (97 percent of face value). The discount is used because the current market rate is 12.4 percent, and Ronson has to be competitive to make its bond attractive to investors. Bondholders will receive a yearly dividend of $120, with an effective rate of 12.4 percent ($120/$970). The accounts that will make up the journal entry include:

.97 × $200,000

Cash	Asset	↑	Dr. $194,000
Discount on Bonds Payable	Contra-Liability	↑	Dr. $6,000
Bonds Payable	Liability	↑	Cr. $200,000

($200,000 − $194,000)
Face value

The journal entry will look like this:

Jan.	1	Cash	194 0 0 0 00		
		Discount on Bonds Payable	6 0 0 0 00		
		Bonds Payable			200 0 0 0 00
		Record Bond Issue.			

Let's look at how the Discount on Bonds Payable would look on the balance sheet.

Long-Term Liabilities:

12 percent Bonds Payable	$200,000	
Less: Discount on Bonds Payable	6,000	$194,000

For bonds sold at a discount, the **carrying value** (also called **book value**) of $194,000 is the face value of $200,000 minus the discount on bonds payable of $6,000. At maturity (after ten years), carrying value will be the same as face value ($200,000).

When each interest payment is made, a portion of the **Discount on Bonds Payable** is transferred to increase Interest Expense. This is called **Amortization of Discount on Bonds Payable.** Bond discount causes the total interest expense to increase, since the bond is sold for less than face value, resulting in higher costs of borrowing.

Before looking at how to amortize the discount, let's prove that the interest expense will be more than the contract amount of interest of $240,000 (.12 × $200,000 × 10 years) for ten years.

Total amount to be paid to bondholder	$440,000 ($200,000 bonds + $240,000 interest)
Total amount to be received from sale of bond	−$194,000
Interest to be paid over life of bond	$246,000
Average interest expense per year	$24,600 ($246,000 ÷ 10 yr)
Semiannual interest expense	$12,300

If no discount has been made, the semiannual payment will be $12,000 ($200,000 × .12 × $\frac{6}{12}$ or $200,000 × .06). Now the discount results in an additional $300 of interest expense *each* semiannual payment $6,000 ÷ 20 periods).

The journal entry for each semiannual payment and amortization of discount will be as follows:

June	30	Bond Interest Expense	1230000	
		Discount on Bonds Payable		30000
		Cash		1200000
		Semiannual interest and amortization of		
		discount.		

After posting, the ledger would look as follows:

Discount on Bonds Payable	Bond Interest Expense
6,000 | 300	12,300 |
5,700 |	

After this amortization the carrying value (book value) of the bond has increased from $194,000 to $194,300. By the end of ten years the carrying value will be back to $200,000, or the amount due at maturity.

In this unit we will calculate amortization of the bond's discount by the **straight-line method;** in the next unit we will use the *interest* method. The straight-line method transfers an equal amount of bond discount to interest expense over equal periods of time.

Table 21-1 shows the straight-line method of amortizing a bond discount over the life of the bond for each semiannual period. At the end of the life of the bond, the Discount on Bonds Payable has a zero balance, and the original $6,000 has been transferred to Interest Expense. At this point, the book value or carrying value of a bond ($200,000) is what is paid at maturity.

Year-End Adjusting Entry: Accrued Interest and Amortization of Discount on Bonds Payable. Let's consider what would happen if the semiannual interest payment were on April 1 and October 1. On December 31, $6,000, three months' interest would be accrued ($12,000 × $\frac{3}{6}$). The amount of dis-

---

Sidebar (left margin):

If there were no discount or premium, the semiannual interest payment would be $12,000.

$200,000	Face value of bond
5,700	Bond discount
$194,300	New carrying value

After ten years, the balance on Discount on Bonds Payable will be zero.

Straight-line allocates equal amount of discount to Interest Expense each period.

Note: Ten years with interest semiannually means 20 periods (10 years × 2).

TABLE 21-1 AMORTIZATION SCHEDULE FOR BOND DISCOUNT USING STRAIGHT-LINE METHOD FOR EACH SEMIANNUAL PERIOD

Period	Carrying Value, Beg. of Period	Total Interest Expense	Interest To Be Paid Bondholders (.06 × Face Value)*	Amortized Discount Transferred to Increase Interest Expense	Carrying Value, End of Period
1	$194,000 (200,000 − 6,000)	$12,300	$12,000 (200,000 × .06)	$300 (6,000 ÷ 20 periods)	$194,300 (194,000 + 300)
2	194,300	12,300	12,000	300	194,600
3	194,600	12,300	12,000	300	194,900
4	194,900	12,300	12,000	300	195,200
19	199,400	12,300	12,000	300	199,700
20	199,700	12,300	12,000	300	200,000

The balance in the Discount on Bonds Payable account should be equal to zero at the end of the 20 periods.

* Half of annual rate of 12% = 6% semiannual rate.

Bond Interest Expense:
$12,300 \times \frac{3}{6} = \$6,150$

Bond Interest Payable:
$12,000 \times \frac{3}{6} = \$6,000$

Bond Discount Adjustment:
$300 \times \frac{3}{6} = \$150$

count to be amortized would be $150 ($300 \times \frac{3}{6}$). The journal entry would be recorded as follows:

Dec.	31	Bond Interest Expense	6 1 5 0 00		
		Discount on Bonds Payable		1 5 0 00	
		Bond Interest Payable		6 0 0 0 00	
		Accrued interest and amortization.			

Note that the Discount on Bonds Payable does indeed increase total bond interest expense from $6,000 to $6,150. This adjusting entry would then be reversed on January 1, as follows:

Jan.	1	Bond Interest Payable	6 0 0 0 00		
		Discount on Bonds Payable	1 5 0 00		
		Bond Interest Expense		6 1 5 0 00	
		Reversing entry			

The regular payment made on April 1 would look like this:

April	1	Bond Interest Expense	12 3 0 0 00		
		Discount on Bonds Payable		3 0 0 00	
		Cash		12 0 0 0 00	
		Semiannual interest and amortizaton of discount.			

RECORDING AND AMORTIZING BONDS ISSUED AT A PREMIUM

Bonds are issued at a premium if the contract rate is greater than the market rate.

The Premium on Bonds Payable is added to the face value of the bond.

To illustrate bonds issued at a premium, let's look at Ronson Corporation again, but assume that on January 1 it issued its 200, 12 percent bonds at 102 (102 percent of face value). This premium occurred because the current market rate was 11.8 percent and Ronson's bonds were thus very attractive to investors. The bondholders would receive per bond the yearly interest payment of $120 (.12 × $1,000 bond) with an effective rate of 11.8 percent ($120/$1,020). The accounts that will make up the journal entry include:

1.02 × $200,000

Cash	Asset	↑	Dr. $204,000	
Premium on Bonds Payable	Liability	↑	Cr. $4,000	($204,000 − $200,000)
Bonds Payable	Liability	↑	Cr. $200,000	Face value

The journal entry will look like this:

Jan.	1	Cash	204 00 0 00	
		Premium on Bonds Payable		4 00 0 00
		Bonds Payable		200 00 0 00
		Issued bond at premium		

Note that the Premium on Bonds Payable is *added* to Bonds Payable to arrive at the carrying value of $204,000.

Let's see how the Premium on Bonds Payable would look on the balance sheet:

Long-Term Liabilities:

12 Percent Bonds Payable	$200,000	
Add: Premium on Bonds Payable	4,000	$204,000

When each interest payment is made, a portion of the Premium on Bonds Payable is transferred to *reduce* Interest Expense. This is called **Amortization of Premium on Bonds Payable.** Let's prove that the interest expense will be less than the contractual amount of $240,000 for ten years.

Total amount to be paid to bondholders	$440,000	($200,000 bonds + $240,000 interest)
Total amount to be received from sale of bonds	−204,000	
Interest to be paid over life of bond	$236,000	
Average interest expense per year	$ 23,600	($236,000 ÷ 10 yr)
Semiannual interest expense	$ 11,800	

If there were no discount or premium, the semiannual interest would be $12,000.

If no premium were made, the semiannual interest expense would be $12,000 ($200,000 × .12 × $\frac{6}{12}$ or $200,000 × .06). Now the premium results in *reducing* the interest expense for each semiannual payment by $200 ($4,000 premium ÷ 20 periods).

The journal entry for semiannual payment will look like this:

June	30	Bond Interest Expense	11 8 00 00	
		Premium on Bonds Payable	2 00 00	
		Cash		12 00 0 00
		Semiannual payment and premium		
		amortization.		

Period	Carrying Value, Beg. of Period	Total Interest Expense	Interest to Be Paid to Bondholder (.06 × Face Value)	Amortized Premium to Decrease Interest Expense	Carrying Value, End of Period
1	$204,000 (200,000 + 4,000)	$11,800	$12,000 (.06 × 200,000)	$200	$203,800 (204,000 − 200)
2	203,800	11,800	12,000	200	203,600
3	203,600	11,800	12,000	200	203,400
4	203,400	11,800	12,000	200	203,200
19	200,400	11,800	12,000	200	200,200
20	200,200	11,800	12,000	200	200,000

The balance in the Premium on Bonds Payable account should be equal to zero at the end of the 20 periods.

After posting, the ledger will look like this:

Premium on Bonds Payable	Bond Interest Expense
200 | 4,000	11,800 |
| 3,800	

We're using the straight-line method of amortizing the bond premium over the life of the bond for each semiannual period. This is shown in Table 21-2. Note that at the end of the schedule, the carrying value is reduced to $200,000 and the balance in the premium account is zero.

LEARNING UNIT 21-2 REVIEW

AT THIS POINT you should be able to

◆ Calculate effective rate. (p. 726)
◆ Explain why a bond will sell at a discount or premium. (p. 726)
◆ Define and explain Discount on Bonds Payable. (p. 726)
◆ Explain why a discount will increase interest expense when semiannual interest is paid. (p. 727)
◆ Journalize the recording of bonds issued at a discount. (p. 727)
◆ Journalize year-end adjusting entries. (p. 728)
◆ Prepare an amortization schedule of bond discount by the straight-line method. (p. 728)
◆ Define and explain Premium on Bonds Payable. (p. 729)
◆ Explain why a premium on bonds payable will decrease interest expense when semiannual interest is paid. (p. 729)
◆ Journalize the recording of bonds issued at a premium. (p. 730)

◆ Prepare an amortization schedule of bond premium by straight-line method. (p. 730)

SELF-REVIEW QUIZ 21-2

(The forms you need are on page 122 in the *Study Guide and Working Papers*.)

Prepare a partial amortization schedule as on page 728 using the straight-line method for the first three semiannual periods based on the following facts: 100 14 percent, ten-year bonds issued at 98. Each bond has a $1,000 face value.

Solution to Self-Review Quiz 21-2

Period	Carrying Value, Beg. of Period	Total Interest Expense	Interest Paid to Bondholders (.07 × Face Value)	Amortized Discount Transferred to Increase Interest Expense	Carrying Value, End of Period
1	$98,000	$7,100	$7,000	$100 (2,000 ÷ 20 periods)	$98,100 (98,000 + 100)
2	98,100	7,100	7,000	100	98,200
3	98,200	7,100	7,000	100	98,300

LEARNING UNIT 21-3
Amortization of Bond Discounts and Premiums by the Interest Method

In the last unit we amortized the discount or premium by the straight-line method. The problem with this method is that it recognizes an equal amount of interest expense each period, even though the bond's carrying value changes. Accountants think that it is inconsistent for interest expense to stay the same while the amount owed changes. They feel that interest should be a *constant percentage of the carrying value*. For this reason, another method, called the interest method, is used in amortizing bond discounts and premiums. The Accounting Principles Board has ruled that the straight-line method be used only if the results do not materially differ from those of the interest method.

AMORTIZING THE BOND DISCOUNT BY THE INTEREST METHOD

The **interest method** makes interest expense a constant percentage of the bond carrying value.

The goal of the interest method is to calculate the interest expense to be recorded each year as a constant percentage of the carrying value of the bonds. The interest amount will thus not be the same each period. There are two formulas to use to reach this goal:

a. Carrying value of bonds at beginning of period × market interest rate = interest expense of carrying value to be recorded.

Period	(1) Carrying Value, Beginning of Period	(2) Interest Paid to Bondholders (.06 × Face Value)*	(3) Interest Expense to Be Recorded (.07 × Carrying Value)	(4) Discount to Be Amortized	(5) Carrying Value, End of Period
1	$178,808 (200,000 − 21,192)	$12,000	$12,517 (.07 × 178,808)	$517	$179,325 (178,808 + 517)
2	179,325	12,000	12,553	553	179,878
3	179,878	12,000	12,591	591	180,469
19	196,373	12,000	13,746	1,746	198,119
20	198,119	12,000	13,881	1,881	200,000

Adjusted for rounding

* Use 6 percent, since 12 percent is for the whole year and the calculations are made semiannually.

Note: Column 4 is the difference between columns 2 and 3.

b. Face value × contract rate = interest expense to bondholders. The discount to be amortized is the difference between a and b.

To illustrate this method, let's assume that Yang Corporation is issuing $200,000 of 12 percent, ten-year bonds on April 1. Interest is to be paid on October 1 and April 1. The selling price of the bonds is $178,808. The market rate is 14 percent.

Look at the amortization schedule shown in Table 21-3. Note that the discount amount to be amortized is not constant, as it is in the straight-line method. As a matter of fact, to prove that the interest expense is a constant percentage of the carrying value, let's look at semiannual periods 2 and 19.

Discount on bond:
$200,000 − $178,808 = $21,192.

$$\text{Period 2: } \frac{\$12,553}{\$179,325} = .07 \qquad \text{Period 19: } \frac{\$13,746}{\$196,373} = .07$$

On October 1, the date of the first semiannual interest payment, the following entry would occur:

Oct.	1	Bond Interest Expense		12 5 1 7 00	
		Discount on Bonds Payable			5 1 7 00
		Cash			12 0 0 0 00
		Semiannual payment and amortization.			

YEAR-END ADJUSTMENT

Bond Interest Expense:
$12,553 × $\frac{3}{6}$ = $6,276.50

Bond Interest Payable:
$12,000 × $\frac{3}{6}$ = $6,000

On December 31, three months' interest of $6,000 ($\frac{3}{6}$ × $12,000) has accrued, as well as $276.50 ($\frac{3}{6}$ of $553), the second-period discount shown on the amortization schedule. The following adjusting year-end entry is prepared:

Dec.	31	Bond Interest Expense	6276 50			
		Discount on Bonds Payable		276 50		
		Bond Interest Payable		6000 00		
		Year-end adjustment.				

The reversing entry on January 1 and the entry to record payment of interest on April 1 would look like this:

Jan.	1	Bond Interest Payable	6000 00			
		Discount on Bonds Payable	276 50			
		Bond Interest Expense		6276 50		
		Reversing entry				
April	1	Bond Interest Expense	12517 00			
		Discount on Bonds Payable		517 00		
		Cash		12000 00		
		Semiannual interest and amortization of discount.				

AMORTIZING THE BOND PREMIUM BY THE INTEREST METHOD

Yang Corporation issues on April 1 $200,000 of 12 percent bonds with interest paid on October 1 and April 1. The selling price of the bonds is $224,926. Marked interest rate is 10 percent. The amortization schedule is shown in Table 21-4.

On April 1 the following entry records the semiannual payment:

Oct.	1	Bond Interest Expense	11246 00			
		Premium on Bonds Payable	754 00			
		Cash		12000 00		
		Semiannual interest and premium amortization.				

YEAR-END ADJUSTMENT

It should be noted that on December 31, three months' interest accrues as well as the need to amortize half the premium (for the second period). The following journal entry records this year-end adjustment:

Dec.	31	Bond Interest Expense	5604 50			
		Premium on Bonds Payable	395 50			
		Bond Interest Payable		6000 00		
		Year-end adjustment.				

Bond Interest Expense:
$\frac{3}{6} \times \$11,209 = \$5,604.50$

Premium on Bonds Payable:
$\frac{3}{6} \times \$791 = \$395.50$

Bond Interest Payable:
$\frac{3}{6} \times \$12,000 = \$6,000$

Period	(1) Carrying Value, Beg. of Period	(2) Interest Paid to Bondholder (.06 × Face Value)	(3) Interest Expense to Be Recorded (.05 × Carrying Value)	(4) Premium to Be Amortized	(5) Carrying Value End of Period
1	$224,926	$12,000	$11,246	$754	$224,172
2	224,172	12,000	11,209	791	($224,926 − $754) 223,381
19	203,726	12,000	10,186	1,814	201,912
20	201,912	12,000	10,088	1,912	200,000

Note: Column 4 is the difference between columns 2 and 3. Column 5 is column 1 minus column 4.

The reversing entry on January 1 and the payment of interest in April would look like this:

Jan.	1	Bond Interest Payable		6 0 0 0 00	
		Premium on Bonds Payable			3 9 5 50
		Bond Interest Expense			5 6 0 4 50
		Reversing entry			
April	1	Bond Interest Expense		11 2 0 9 00	
		Premium on Bonds Payable		7 9 1 00	
		Cash			12 0 0 0 00
		Semiannual interest and amortization of			
		premium.			

LEARNING UNIT 21-3 REVIEW

AT THIS POINT you should be able to

◆ Prepare an amortization schedule for bond discounts using the interest method. (p. 732)
◆ Prepare an amortization schedule for bond premiums using the interest method. (p. 734)
◆ Journalize year-end adjustments. (p. 733)

SELF-REVIEW QUIZ 21-3

(The forms you need are on page 122 of the *Study Guide and Working Papers.*)
    Prepare a partial amortization schedule like the one on p. 732 using the interest method for the first three periods based on the following facts: 100, 12 percent ten-year bonds issued at a selling price of $89,404. Assume a market rate of 14 percent.

Solution to Self-Review Quiz 21-3

Period	(1) Carrying Amount, Beg. of Period	(2) Interest Paid to Bondholders (.06 × Face Value)	(3) Interest Expense to Be Recorded, (.07 × Carrying Value)	(4) Discount to Be Amortized	(5) Carrying Amount, End of Period
1	$89,404	$6,000	$6,258	$258	$89,662
2	89,662	6,000	6,276	276	89,938
3	89,938	6,000	6,296	296	90,234

LEARNING UNIT 21-4
Retirement of Bonds and Bond Sinking Funds

In the first unit of this chapter we mentioned callable bonds, which permit the corporation to reacquire bonds at a price based on a percentage of face value. Some corporations retire them and issue new bonds (called *bond refunding*) to take their place paying a lower rate of interest. If this call provision doesn't exist, a company can repurchase its bonds in the open market and then retire them. By retiring bonds, companies can decrease the amount of debt they owe. If interest rates are high, the retirement of bonds could result in substantial cash savings, even if new bonds are issued at lower rates.

When the bonds are retired before they reach maturity, the following points have to be recognized:

1. Any amortization of discount or premium must be brought up to date at the time of retirement.
2. The premium or discount as well as the bond liability account must be removed.
3. Any gain or loss is recognized on the retirement of the bonds as an extraordinary item that will be shown on the income statement.

Let's use Roberts Corporation as an example. On June 30, the corporation retired a $500,000, 10 percent bond issue that had an unamortized premium of $19,000. The bonds were called in at 105 (105 percent of face value). All journal entries relating to interest payments and premium amortization were completed before the bonds' retirement. The entry to record the retirement of the bonds by Roberts Corporation would look like this:

Bonds Payable	500 0 0 0 00	
Premium on Bonds Payable	19 0 0 0 00	
Loss on Bond Retirement	6 0 0 0 00	
Cash		525 0 0 0 00
Retirement of bond.		

Note that the difference between the bond carrying value of $519,000 ($500,000 + $19,000) and actual cash paid results in the loss of $6,000. Of course, if the carrying value were greater than the cash paid, a gain would be realized.

Often a corporation will agree to establish a fund that will accumulate assets over the life of the bond in order to pay off the bondholders at maturity. In fact, such a fund is often a requirement stated in the bond indentures. This fund is called a **sinking fund.**

For example, Morrel Corporation issued 8 percent, 15-year bonds for $80,000, agreeing to deposit $2946.40 at the end of the year, so that by the end of the fifteenth year the fund would contain $80,000 to pay off bondholders. Sinking fund tables are available that make these periodic deposits easy to calculate. For example, Morrel's accountant would go to a sinking fund table and look up 8 percent for fifteen periods and find a table factor of .0368295. By multiplying the $80,000 × .0368295, one comes up with a yearly deposit of $2946.40, which, at this rate of interest compounded annually, will at the end of fifteen years bring a total of $80,000.

The following would be the journal entries for Morrel Corporation for establishing the sinking fund:

The Analysis:

Long-term investment ──→

Sinking Fund	Asset	↑	Dr.
Cash	Asset	↓	Cr.

The Journal Entry:

Sinking Fund	2946 40	
Cash		2946 40
Establishing sinking fund.		

When interest is earned on the balance in the sinking fund, the following entry results:

The Analysis:

Sinking Fund	Asset	↑	Dr.
Sinking Fund Earned	Other Revenue	↑	Cr.

The Journal Entry:

Sinking Fund	235 00	
Sinking Fund Earned ($2,946 x .08)		235 00
Interest earned.		

When the bonds are paid off, there may be a little more or less cash than is needed in the sinking fund. The entry to record the payment of the bonds by Morrel is as follows (assume $50 extra in the sinking fund):

Cash			5 0 0 0		
Bonds Payable		80 0 0 0 00			
Bond Sinking Fund				80 0 5 0 00	
Payment of bonds.					

Keep in mind the money in the sinking fund cannot be used to meet other current expenses or liabilities. Thus the sinking fund is recorded in the long-term investment section of the balance sheet. Any cash left over is returned to the Cash account.

LEARNING UNIT 21-4 REVIEW

AT THIS POINT you should be able to

◆ Journalize the gain or loss on retirement of bonds. (p. 735)
◆ Explain as well as journalize entries relating to sinking funds. (pp. 736–737)

SELF-REVIEW QUIZ 21-4

(The forms you need are on page 123 of the *Study Guide and Working Papers*.)
     Journalize the following transactions:

(A) Retired $300,000 of bonds that had a $20,000 premium for 106.
(B) Set up a sinking fund account with an initial deposit of $3,000.
(C) Earned $325 interest on sinking fund balance.
(D) Sinking fund of $90,000 was used to retire bond holders amount to $89,900.

Solution to Self-Review Quiz 21-4

(A)	Bonds Payable	300 0 0 0 00		
	Premium on Bonds	20 0 0 0 00		
	Cash		318 0 0 0 00	
	Gain on Retirement		2 0 0 0 00	
(B)	Sinking Fund	3 0 0 0 00		
	Cash		3 0 0 0 00	
(C)	Sinking Fund	3 2 5 00		
	Sinking Fund Earned		3 2 5 00	
(D)	Bonds Payable	90 0 0 0 00		
	Sinking Fund		90 0 0 0 00	

Check Figure:

Discount to be amortized
period 1 $456.96

**Amortization schedule; interest
method of amortization of premium; year-end adjusting entry.**

Check Figure:

Premium to be amortized
period 1 $815.50

2. Prepare journal entries to record:

   a. Bond issuance on January 1.

   b. Semiannual interest payments on July 1 and December 31 as well as amortization of discount.

3. If the bond were issued on March 1 and interest was paid on September 1 and March 1, what would be the year-end adjusting entry on December 31, 19X7, to record accrued interest and amortization of discount?

21A-4. On April 1, 19X6, Potter Corporation issued $200,000 of 10 percent, five-year bonds for $204,100, yielding a market rate of 9 percent. Interest is paid on October 1 and April 1. Potter Corporation uses the interest method to amortize the premium.

1. Prepare an amortization schedule for the first three semiannual periods.

2. Prepare journal entries to record

   a. Bond issuance on April 1.

   b. Semiannual interest payment and amortization of premium on October 1.

   c. The year-end adjusting entry to record expense and premium amortization.

Group B Problems

(The forms you need are on pages 130–134 in the *Study Guide and Working Papers.*)

**Amortization schedule; bond
issue, straight-line amortization
of discount.**

Check Figure:

Amortized discount $1,200

21B-1. On January 1, 19X6, Angel Corporation sold $300,000 of 12 percent, ten-year bonds at 92. Interest is to be paid on June 30 and December 31. The straight-line method of amortizing the discount is used. Prepare (1) an amortization schedule for the first three semiannual periods, and (2) journal entries to record (a) the bond issue on January 1 and (b) semiannual interest payments on June 30 and December 31 for interest and amortization of discount. (c) If the bonds were issued on March 1 and interest was paid on September 1 and March 1, what would be the year-end adjusting entry on December 31 to record interest payment and amortization of discount?

**Amortizaton schedule; bond
issue; accrued interest; straight-
line amortization of premium;
year-end adjusting entry.**

Check Figure:

Amortized premium $1,200

21B-2. On April 1, 19X6, Deever Corporation issued $600,000 of 6 percent, ten-year bonds at 104. The interest is payable on October 1 and April 1. The premium is amortized by the straight-line method. Prepare an amortization schedule for the first three semiannual periods and journalize the following transactions:

19X6		
Apr.	1	Bonds issued.
Oct.	1	Paid semiannual interest and amortization of premium.
Dec.	31	Accrued bond interest and amortization premium.

**Amortization schedule; interest
method of amortization of premium; year-end adjusting entry.**

Check Figure:

Discount to be amortized
$565.59

21B-3. On January 1, 19X8, Vex Corporation issued $400,000 of 12 percent, ten-year bonds for $350,937, yielding a market rate of 14 percent. Interest is paid on July 1 and December 31. Vex uses the interest method to amortize the discount. Prepare an amortization schedule for the first three semiannual periods and prepare journal entries to record:

   a. Bond issuance on January 1.

   b. Semiannual interest payment on July 1 and December 31 as well as amortization of discount.

If the bonds were issued on March 1 and interest was paid on September 1 and March 1, what would be the year-end adjusting entry on December 31, 19X7, to record accrued interest and amortization of discount?

21B-4. On March 1, 19X7, Potter Corporation issued $100,000 of 12 percent, ten-year bonds for $104,408, yielding a market rate of 10 percent. Interest is paid on September 1 and March 1. Potter Corporation uses the interest method to amortize the premium.

1. Prepare an amortization schedule for the first three semiannual periods.
2. Prepare journal entries to record:
   a. Bond issuance on March 1.
   b. Semiannual interest payment and amortization of premium on September 1.
   c. The year-end adjusting entry to record interest expense and premium amortization.

Amortization schedule; interest method of amortization of discount; year-end adjusting entry.

Check Figure:
Premium to be amortized
period 1 $779.60

REAL WORLD APPLICATIONS

21R-1.

Ryan Small, president of Janis Corporation, has hired you as a financial consultant to analyze three proposals made by the Board of Directors to raise additional funds of $3,000,000.

The Plans:

1. Issued 12 percent preferred stock.
2. Issued additional common stock at $10 par.
3. Issue 14 percent, 20-year bonds.

Given:

◆ Tax rate, 48 percent.
◆ Estimated corporation earnings, $1,800,000 annually before bond interest.

Assume:

◆ Before plan 300,000 shares of $10 par outstanding all new stock would be issued at par.

Please submit a written recommendation with supporting data to Mr. Small as soon as possible.

21R-2.

The Board of Directors of French Corporation are planning to announce a new ten-year bond issue of $300,000. The contract rate of the bonds is 12 percent. Owing to several delays, the bonds in the marketplace are now 14 percent.

French feels that this bond issue has to raise at least $280,000 in cash to meet their financial needs. As their financial consultant, could you calculate the actual selling price of the bonds and make appropriate written recommendations to the Board of Directors of French regarding the pros and cons of the bond issue.

Given:

1. Present value of $1.00 at compound interest for 20 periods at 7 percent equals .2584.
2. Present value of $1.00 received periodically for 20 periods at 7 percent equals 10.5940.

YOU make the call
Critical Thinking/Ethical Case

21R-3.
Alice wants to buy bonds, but her husband Pete thinks stocks would be a better deal. Pete was watching a finance show on cable TV that said stocks would be going up and that now is the time to buy stock. He called Alice over and said, "I told you so." Alice told her husband this was no time to take a risk with their money. Do you think Pete is correct in his thinking? You make the call. Write down your recommendations to Alice and her husband.

ACCOUNTING RECALL
A CUMULATIVE APPROACH

THIS EXAM REVIEWS CHAPTERS 1 THROUGH 21

Your *Study Guide and Working Papers* has forms (p. 139) to complete this exam, as well as worked-out solutions. The page references next to each question identify what page to turn back to if you answer the question incorrectly.

PART 1   Vocabulary Review

Match the terms to the appropriate definition or phrase.

Page Ref.

(725)	1. Straight-line method	A. A liability
(736)	2. Sinking fund earned	B. True rate of interest
(698)	3. Common stock dividend distributable	C. Contra-stockholders' equity
		D. Account that accumulates stock dividends that have been
(732)	4. Discount on bonds payable	declared but not yet issued
(736)	5. Interest method	E. Equal amounts of interest
(727)	6. Carrying value	expense
(354)	7. Purchases	F. Part of cost of goods sold
(729)	8. Premium on bonds payable	G. Other revenue account
(701)	9. Treasury stock	H. Constant percentage of the carrying value
(729)	10. Effective rate	I. Face value of bond less bond discount or plus bond premium
		J. Contra-liability account

PART II   True or False (Accounting Theory)

(727)   11. A bond discount means the issue price of bond is more than face value.

(728) 12. The straight-line method is a constant percentage of the carrying value of the bonds.

(728) 13. The carrying value of a bond is face value of bond plus bond discount.

(736) 14. A sinking fund accumulates cash to pay off bonds when they are retired.

(724) 15. If bonds are sold between interest dates the buyer pays the price of the bonds plus accrued interest.

22

STATEMENT OF CASH FLOWS

THE BIG PICTURE

Freedman and West asked each other, "Can you show me the money?" The Eldorado Computer Center had been extremely profitable over the last two years but there never seemed to be enough cash for anything outside of normal expenses. Both stockholders wondered how a business could be so highly profitable and not have enough cash.

Managers must ensure that their business can meet all of its cash demands. A *statement of cash flow* summarizes the increase and decrease in cash in relationship to operating, investing, and financing activities. Using this financial report, Freedman and West can manage their operations better.

In this chapter you will learn how to prepare a cash flow statement. A business's main source of continuing operations is to have a working capital of funds. Working capital will increase and decrease as demands are placed on payment of debt. Owners as well as creditors always want to know a company's cash position. Measuring profit is meaningless if you do not have cash flowing into the business.

Learning Objectives	◆ Converting the net income figure from an accrual basis to a cash basis for the statement of cash flows. (p. 749) ◆ Preparing a statement of cash flows. (p. 753) ◆ Understanding what causes working capital to increase or decrease. (p. 756)

In preceding chapters we have analyzed as well as prepared balance sheets, income statements, and statements of retained earnings. Let's quickly review the purposes of each statement:

◆ *Balance sheet:* Shows the end-of-period financial position of a company at a particular date (close of business on any given date).

◆ *Income statement:* For a given period it shows the results of the company's operation. The net income or loss results in an increase or decrease to retained earnings.

◆ *Statement of retained earnings:* Summarizes the changes in retained earnings of a company during a period of time.

In this chapter, we turn our attention to the fourth type of major statement that is used to better understand the financing and investing activities of a company. It is called a **statement of cash flows,** and it summarizes the changes in the sources and uses of cash by the company during the period covered by the income statement for that company.

LEARNING UNIT 22-1
Statement of Cash Flows

We will use as our example in this chapter Conway Company, which sells stationery products. In order to prepare a statement of cash flows, we need to obtain information from the other financial statements prepared for the company—the income statement, the statement of retained earnings, and the balance sheet. These statements are shown in Figures 22-1, 22-2, and 22-3. Note

FIGURE 22-1

CONWAY CORPORATION
INCOME STATEMENT
FOR YEAR ENDED DECEMBER 31, 19X7

Sales		$190 000 00
Cost of Goods Sold		106 000 00
Gross Profit		$ 84 000 00
Operating Expenses:		
Salaries Expense	$51 040 00	
Insurance Expense	7 200 00	
Depreciation Expense	11 000 00	
Miscellaneous Expense	4 800 00	
Total Operating Expenses		74 040 00
Net Income		$ 9 960 00

FIGURE 22-2

CONWAY CORPORATION
STATEMENT OF RETAINED EARNINGS
FOR YEAR ENDED DECEMBER 31, 19X7

Retained Earnings, January 1, 19X7		$ 38 140 00
Net Income for Year	$ 9 960 00	
Less: Cash Dividends	8 000 00	1 960 00
Retained Earnings, December 31, 19X7		$ 40 100 00

FIGURE 22-3

CONWAY CORPORATION
COMPARATIVE BALANCE SHEET
AS OF DECEMBER 31, 19X7 AND 19X6

Assets	19X7	19X6	Increase Decrease
Current Assets:			
Cash	$ 2 900 00	$ 2 480 00	$ 420 00
Accounts Receivable, Net	19 560 00	14 720 00	4 840 00
Merchandise Inventory	30 000 00	32 000 00	(2 000 00)
Prepaid Insurance	600 00	400 00	200 00
Total Current Assets	$ 53 060 00	$ 49 600 00	$ 3 460 00
Plant and Equipment:			
Office Equipment	$ 96 000 00	$ 66 000 00	$ 30 000 00
Accum. Dep., Office Equipment	(37 200 00)	(26 200 00)	(11 000 00)
Total Plant and Equipment	$ 58 800 00	$ 39 800 00	$ 19 000 00
Total Assets	$111 860 00	$ 89 400 00	$ 22 460 00
Liabilities			
Current Liabilities:			
Notes Payable	$ 17 400 00	$ 14 800 00	$ 2 600 00
Accounts Payable	360 00	460 00	100 00
Total Current Liabilities	$ 17 760 00	$ 15 260 00	$ 2 500 00
Long-Term Liabilities:			
Mortgage Payable	$ 28 000 00	$ 20 000 00	$ 8 000 00
Total Liabilities	$ 45 760 00	$ 35 260 00	$ 10 500 00
Stockholders' Equity			
Common Stock, $10 par	$ 11 000 00	$ 10 000 00	$ 1 000 00
Paid-in Capital in Excess of Par	15 000 00	6 000 00	9 000 00
Retained Earnings†	40 100 00	38 140 00	1 960 00
Total Stockholders' Equity	$ 66 100 00	54 140 00	$ 11 960 00
Total Liabilities and Stockholders' Equity	$111 860 00	$ 89 400 00	$ 22 460 00

† Cash dividends paid out were $8,000

that the balance sheet shown in Figure 22-3 is slightly different from the one we have shown in the past. This is a comparative balance sheet, which shows figures from two separate years side by side, for purposes of comparison. We will discuss this type of statement in more detail in Chapter 23.

The statement of cash flows consists of three main sections: (1) net cash flows from operating activities, (2) cash flows from investing activities, and (3) cash flows from financing activities. Let's take each of these in turn to show where the figures come from and how they are put together to make up the statement of cash flows.

NET CASH FLOWS FROM OPERATING ACTIVITIES

A business needs a positive cash flow to survive. A company's ability to raise money for financing activities is often tied to how the company can generate cash from operations. This section of the statement of cash flows, therefore, is important to potential investors and to creditors.

This section includes all cash flows other than those associated with investment and financing activities. It takes the figure for Net Income from Operations from the income statement (see Figure 22-1) and converts it from an accrual basis to a cash basis. As you will remember, in earlier chapters we discussed the difference between the accrual and the cash basis of accounting. If the accrual basis is used in preparing an income statement, it means that revenue and expenses will be listed (under Accounts Receivable or Accounts Payable, for example) that did *not* involve the receipt or payment of cash. Since we are concerned here only with cash, we must add or subtract the amounts that do not reflect this concern. Let's show this section of the statement and then explain how we arrived at these figures.

CONWAY CORPORATION STATEMENT OF CASH FLOWS		
Net Cash Flows from Operating Activities:		
Net Income from Operations	$ 9 960 00	
Add (Deduct) items to Convert Net Income from		
Accrual Basis to Cash Basis:		
Depreciation	11 000 00	
Accounts Receivable — Increase	(4 840 00)	
Inventory — Decrease	2 000 00	
Prepaid Insurance — Increase	(2 00 00)	
Notes Payable — Increase	2 600 00	
Accounts Payable — Decrease	(1 00 00)	
Net Cash Flows from Operating Activities		$ 20 420 00

In addition to the figure from net income from operations, which is taken from the income statement, we need to look at what happened to the following accounts on the comparative balance sheet: Accumulated Depreciation, Accounts Receivable, Inventory, Prepaid Expenses, Notes Payable (current), and Accounts Payable. The aid sheet shown in Figure 22-4 on page 752 indicates whether to add or subtract from the net income figure, depending on whether these accounts showed an increase or a decrease on the comparative balance sheet.

Our first step, then, is to take the figure of $9,960 for net income from the income statement. To that we add depreciation of $11,000 from the comparative balance sheet. The rationale for adding here is that although depreciation requires no cash payment, it increases the total expenses in accrual accounting, and thus should be added here.

FIGURE 22-4
Aid Sheet for Converting from
Accrual Basis to Cash Basis

	Add to net income if this account has	Deduct from net income if this account has
Current Assets	Decreased	Increased
Current Liabilities	Increased	Decreased

Looking again at the comparative balance sheet, we see that Accounts Receivable increased by $4,840. Using the aid sheet in Figure 22-4, when Accounts Receivable *increases,* we deduct that amount from net income. We do so because the increase in Accounts Receivable means that Credit Sales are increasing more than collections, thus decreasing the amount of cash received. This same procedure applies to Prepaid Insurance ($200) and Accounts Payable ($100). Conversely, decreases in Inventory ($2,000) and increases in Notes Payable ($2,600) are added to net income. If Inventory decreases, the company is selling more goods than it is buying, and thus the $2,000 is added to net income.

In this way we arrive at the Net Cash Flows from Operating Activities figure of $20,420.

CASH FLOWS FROM INVESTING ACTIVITIES

This section of the statement of cash flows includes (1) the purchase and sale of stocks, bonds, etc.; (2) the buying and disposal of plant assets; and (3) the collecting as well as lending of monies for investment activities. We analyze the noncurrent accounts to find these activities. For example, the following transactions could be recorded in this section:

1. Sale or purchase of equipment.
2. Sale or purchase of land.
3. Cash purchases to buy stocks and bonds.
4. Cash received from sale of stock investments.
5. Loaning cash to borrowers.

On the balance sheet for Conway Corporation we see an increase in plant and equipment assets from 19X6 to 19X7 of $30,000. Thus this section of the cash flows statement would look like this:

Cash Flows from Investing Activities		
Purchase of Plant Asset	$(30 0 0 0 00)	
Net Cash Flows Provided by Investing Activities		(30 0 0 0 00)

The figure of $30,000 is put in parentheses because we are going to subtract this amount from the net cash from operating activities—it represents an outflow of cash, not an inflow. Let's now look at how the cash flow is affected by financing activities involving long-term notes, stock, and bond transactions.

CASH FLOWS FROM FINANCING ACTIVITIES

This section of the statement of cash flows records transactions such as the following:

1. Issuance of long-term notes.
2. Issuance of common stock.
3. Payment of dividends.

4. Retirement of bonds payable.

5. Repurchase of Treasury Stock.

From the comparative balance sheet for Conway Corporation we see the Mortgage Payable increased by $8,000. This is shown as an *increase* to cash flows. Why? An increase to Note Payable means that more cash has been borrowed and therefore has come in. Also note that the issuance of $10,000 of common stock has *increased* the cash flows, while the payment of an $8,000 dividend results in a *decrease* to the cash flows. The end result is that net cash provided by financing activities has increased by $10,000, as shown below:

Cash Flows from Financing Activities		
Issuance of Long-Term Note	$ 8 0 0 0 00	
Issuance of Common Stock	10 0 0 0 00	
Payment of Dividends	(8 0 0 0 00)	
Net Cash Flows Provided by Financing Activities		$ 10 0 0 0 00

To arrive at the net increase in cash for the overall statement, we perform the following calculation:

Net Cash Flow Operating Activities	$20,420
− Cash Flow Provided by Investing Activities	(30,000)
+ Net Cash Provided by Financing Activities	10,000
= Net Increase in Cash	$ 420

We now show all three sections together in the statement of cash flows, in Figure 22-5.

FIGURE 22-5
Statement of Cash Flows

CONWAY CORPORATION STATEMENT OF CASH FLOWS* FOR YEAR ENDED DECEMBER 31, 19X7		
Net Cash Flows from Operating Activities		
Net Income from Operations	$ 9 9 6 0 00	
Add (Deduct) Items to Convert Net Income from		
Accrual Basis to Cash Basis:		
Depreciation	11 0 0 0 00	
Accounts Receivable — Increase	(4 8 4 0 00)	
Inventory — Decrease	2 0 0 0 00	
Prepaid Insurance — Increase	(2 0 0 00)	
Notes Payable — Increase	2 6 0 0 00	
Accounts Payable — Decrease	(1 0 0 00)	
Net Cash Flows from Operating Activities		$ 20 4 2 0 00
Cash Flows from Investing Activities		
Purchase of Plant Asset	$(30 0 0 0 00)	
Net Cash Flows Provided by Investing Activities		(30 0 0 0 00)
Cash Flows from Financing Activities		
Issuance of Long-Term Note	$ 8 0 0 0 00	
Issuance of Common Stock	10 0 0 0 00	
Payment of Dividends	(8 0 0 0 00)	
Net Cash Flows Provided by Financing Activities		10 0 0 0 00
Net Increase in Cash		$ 4 2 0 00

* Significant noncash investing and financing activities must be reported on the statement or in a supplementary schedule.

"Wow!" said Fred, impressed.

"Did you call the Brand Intelligence Department with that news?"

"I never thought of it, Fred! I should call right now," said Lou. "Everyone will need to hear this right away. Thanks for reminding me."

Lou had just told Fred that a major competitor was selling some prime locations and scaling back its business. This was the kind of competitive information that Dunkin' Donuts Inc. needed to know—and to get to its franchisees immediately.

Dunkin' Donuts has divided the USA into 13 market areas. Franchisees and corporate personnel work together in each of these market areas to examine the competitive landscape for that region. In addition, there is a Corporate Intelligence Department that oversees trends for the entire country and disseminates this information back to the local market area and the franchisees.

Prime locations are rare; few are available. A prospective buyer needs to move quickly. Dunkin' Donuts Inc. helps with a "site approval process," which is an in-depth analysis that includes traffic counts and projecting break-even points.

Headquarters personnel at Dunkin' Donuts do a lot to help local shops stay competitive. Everyone concerned with the finance function plays a role in evaluating competitive information. The Finance Department works closely with the Retail Operations Department and the Accounting Department to project the effect of different recommended pricing strategies on the individual franchisee, as well as on Dunkin' Donuts Inc. When

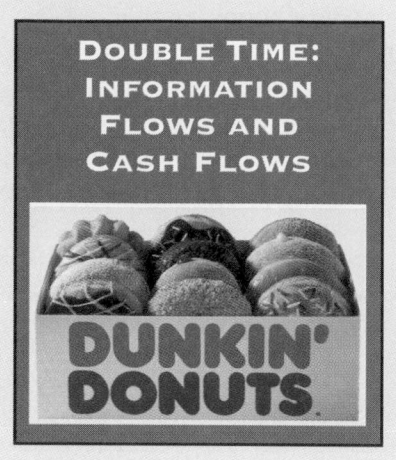

DOUBLE TIME: INFORMATION FLOWS AND CASH FLOWS

a new promotion is planned, this team calculates exactly how much additional product a franchisee would need to sell to break even. Everyone pays special attention to the effect on cash flow—vital for a small business.

The Accounting Department monitors the quarterly and annual financial statements of publicly held competitors for information on what successes or problems they are having. Accumulating large amounts of cash, for example, may signal that they plan an acquisition. Management reports, also contained in Annual Reports, contain clues to what companies are planning, and so are examined as well. The Accounting Department reads the *Journal of Accountancy* for information on new accounting regulations, new strategies, and research results, and *The Wall Street Journal* for economic trends and real estate news.

So when opportunity knocks—Dunkin' Donuts Inc. is ready!

DISCUSSION QUESTIONS

1. Why does Dunkin' Donuts Inc. do traffic counts? How might traffic affect cash flow? How might it affect profit?
2. Why would the Accounting Department monitor the financial statements of publicly held competitors? Why just publicly held?
3. Why does the Accounting Department get involved with pricing strategies? Isn't pricing a marketing function?

Note at the bottom of the statement of cash flows that the cash has increased by $420 (just as shown for cash on the comparative balance sheet), but this report gives us a complete breakdown of just what caused the cash to increase by $420.

When this statement of cash flows is complete, it should be quite helpful for evaluating, comparing, and predicting future cash flows. By breaking this report into three sections, creditors as well as investors can better judge how cash flows from operations compared with those from investing or financing activities. For example, in the case of Conway Corporation, an investor or a creditor can see that there has been a substantial reduction in cash, and that it was the result of investing activities on the part of the corporation and not of operating or financing activities. Keep in mind this statement of cash flows helps a company monitor how cash is increased or decreased from all aspects of a company's operation.

LEARNING UNIT 22-1 REVIEW

AT THIS POINT you should be able to

◆ Explain the components of a statement of cash flows. (p. 751)
◆ Calculate (a) net cash flows from operating activities, (b) net cash flows provided by investing activities, and (c) net cash flows provided by financing activities. (p. 751)
◆ Prepare a statement of cash flows. (p. 753)

SELF-REVIEW QUIZ 22-1

(The forms you need are on page 142 of the *Study Guide and Working Papers.*) From the following, calculate net cash flows from operating activities.

JOHNSON CORPORATION
INCOME STATEMENT
FOR YEAR ENDED DECEMBER 31, 19X2

Sales		$150 000 00
Cost of Goods Sold		90 000 00
Gross Profit		$ 60 000 00
Operating Expenses:		
Salaries Expense	$40 000 00	
Depreciation Expense	3 000 00	
Advertising Expense	8 000 00	51 000 00
Net Income		$ 9 000 00

Additional Data	19X2	19X1
Accounts Receivable	$ 10 600 00	$ 4 000 00
Prepaid Advertising	1 400 00	3 000 00
Accounts Payable	36 000 00	15 000 00
Salaries Payable	1 800 00	1 900 00

Solution to Self-Review Quiz 22-1

Net Cash Flow from Operating Activities:	
Net Income from Operations	$ 9 000 00
Add (Deduct) Items to Convert Net Income to Cash Basis from	
Accrual Basis:	
Depreciation	3 000 00
Accounts Receivable — Increase	(6 600 00)
Prepaid Advertising — Decrease	$ 1 600 00
Accounts Payable — Increase	21 000 00
Salaries Payable — Decrease	(1 000 0)
Net Cash Flows from Operating Activities	$27 900 00

LEARNING UNIT 22-2
Working Capital

Working capital = current assets − current liabilities.

Each corporation closely monitors what is called its working capital. **Working capital** is the total of current assets that exceeds the total of current liabilities. As a business operates, much of the merchandise is obtained by incurring current liabilities (accounts payable and notes payable). When the goods are sold, the accounts receivable are eventually turned into cash. The cash is then used to pay off bills or to buy additional merchandise. Thus much of the current assets and current liabilities of a company are continually circulating, as shown in Figure 22-6.

A sound level of working capital allows a company to:

1. Carry adequate inventory.
2. Meet current debts.
3. Take advantage of cash discounts and offer favorable credit terms to its customers.

Do not think of working capital as only cash. Think of cash as one part of working capital. A corporation's ability to pay the cost of everyday operations and liabilities due is directly related to how other current assets are converted into

FIGURE 22-6 Working Capital Circulation: Operating Cycle for the Purchase and Sale of Goods

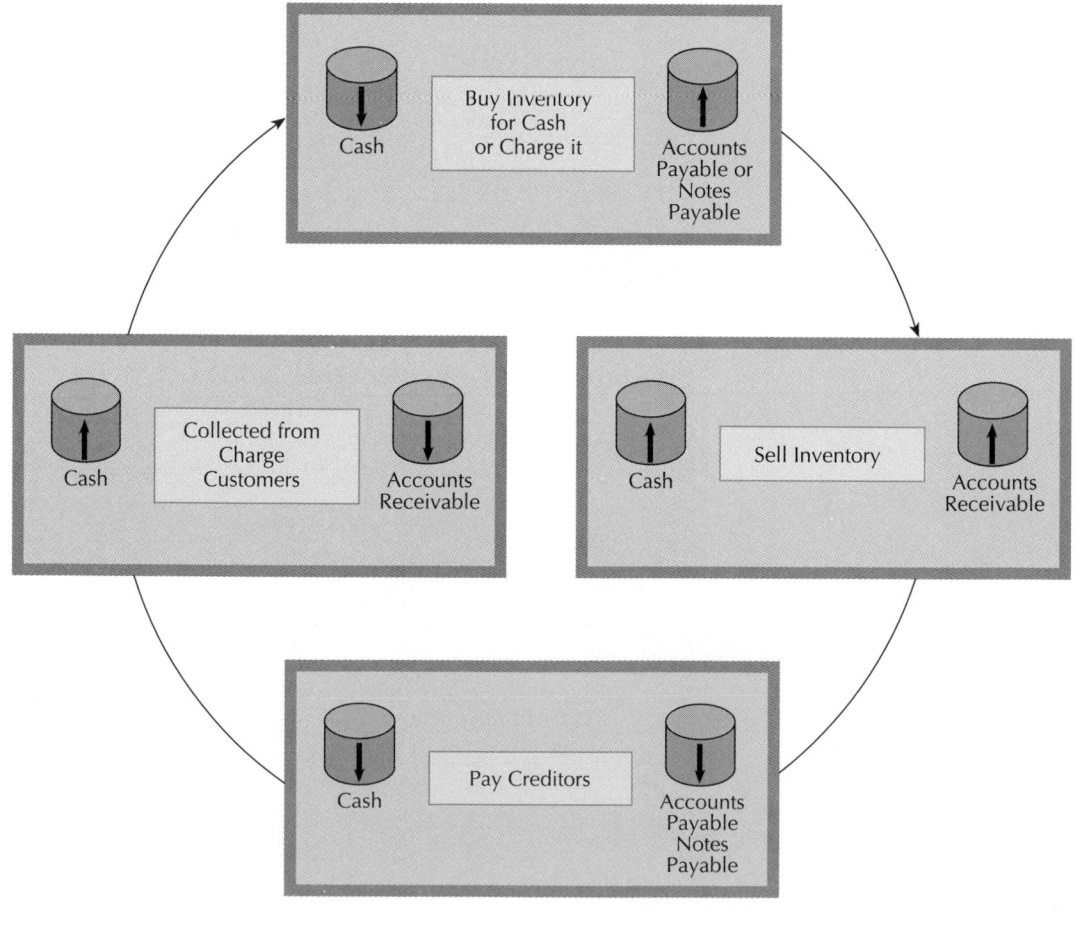

TABLE 22-1   REFERENCE TABLE

Situation	↑	↓	Unchanged	Working Capital Increase	Working Capital Decrease	Working Capital No Change
(A) Current Assets	↑		Current Liab.	X		
(B) Current Assets		↓	Current Liab.		X	
(C) Current Liab.	↑		Current Assets		X	
(D) Current Liab.		↓	Current Assets	X		
(E) If only current assets or liabilities are affected						X
(F) If only noncurrent assets affected						X

cash. Of course, if working capital is not sufficient, long-term financing (stock, bonds, etc.) may be necessary. The key to many successful companies is that in the operating cycle of a business, working capital is successfully generated.

Let's now take a closer look at those activities that increase and decrease working capital.

WHAT CAUSES WORKING CAPITAL TO CHANGE

Working capital will not change unless a transaction affects both current and noncurrent accounts.

Current assets − current liabilities = working capital.

For working capital to change, it will require events and transactions that affect both current and noncurrent accounts. A **noncurrent account** is any balance sheet account that is not a current asset or current liability. When working capital changes, it is a result of one or more noncurrent accounts changing along with a current asset and/or a liability. For example, if cash is received from accounts receivable, the total of current assets is the same. All that has happened is a shift in assets. Keep in mind that if a current asset is changed and there is a corresponding change in current liabilities, the two changes cancel each other out and working capital remains the same. If both changes occur in noncurrent accounts, the current accounts, and thus working capital, are unaffected. Use Table 22-1 for future reference.

Transactions that result in increases to working capital are **sources of funds;** conversely, those transactions causing a decrease in working capital are **uses of funds.** Figure 22-7 shows the sources and uses of funds.

We will now look at how some sample transactions would affect working capital. The key point to remember here is that every change in working capital is a result of a change in one or more of the **noncurrent accounts** accompanied by a change in a current account.

FIGURE 22-7
Sources and Uses of Funds

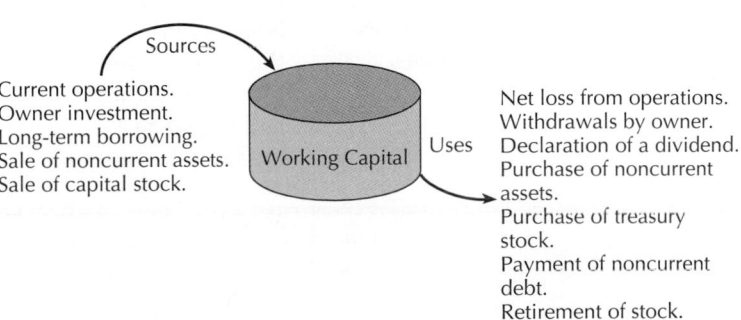

Sources:
Current operations.
Owner investment.
Long-term borrowing.
Sale of noncurrent assets.
Sale of capital stock.

Working Capital

Uses:
Net loss from operations.
Withdrawals by owner.
Declaration of a dividend.
Purchase of noncurrent assets.
Purchase of treasury stock.
Payment of noncurrent debt.
Retirement of stock.

(1) Company Issues Stock for $10,000.

Accounts Affected	Current/Noncurrent	↑	↓	Working Capital		
				Source	Use	No Effect
Cash	Current	↑		╳		
Common Stock	Noncurrent	↑		╳		

Note that working capital increases, because cash is a current asset increasing while the current liabilities *remain the same.* The stock is a *non*current asset, thus confirming that *every change in working capital requires a change in one or more of the* non*current accounts.*

(2) Bought $12,000 of Equipment for Cash.

Accounts Affected	Current/Noncurrent	↑	↓	Working Capital		
				Source	Use	No Effect
Equipment	Noncurrent	↑			╳	
Cash	Current		↓		╳	

(3) Borrowed $2,000 to Buy Merchandise by Issuing a Note Payable Due *Within* a Year:

Accounts Affected	Current/Noncurrent	↑	↓	Working Capital		
				Source	Use	No Effect
Cash	Current	↑				╳
Notes Payable	Current	↑				╳

(4) Billed Customers $50,000 for Grocery Sales:

Accounts Affected	Current/Noncurrent	↑	↓	Working Capital		
				Source	Use	No Effect
Accounts Rec.	Current	↑		╳		
Grocery Sales	Noncurrent (Revenue closed to Income Summary and closed to Retained Earnings— a noncurrent account)	↑		╳		

(5) Paid Operating Expenses:

Situation (B) from Table 22-1.

Accounts Affected	Current/Noncurrent	↑	↓	Working Capital		
				Source	Use	No Effect
Operating Expense	Noncurrent (Expense closed to Income Summary and closed to Retained Earnings—as noncurrent account)	↑				✕
Cash	Current		↓			

(6) Recorded Depreciation of $4,000.

Situation (F) from Table 22-1.

Accounts Affected	Current/Noncurrent	↑	↓	Working Capital		
				Source	Use	No Effect
Dep. Expense	Noncurrent	↑				✕
Acc. Depreciation	Noncurrent	↑				

The Depreciation Expense lowers net income, which is closed to retained earnings, a noncurrent account. As the Accumulated Depreciation increases, the book value of plant assets, a noncurrent asset, decreases. When depreciation is recorded and added back to net income (since it originally reduces net income) only noncurrent assets are affected. Therefore, depreciation has no effect on working capital.

LEARNING UNIT 22-1 REVIEW

AT THIS POINT you should be able to

◆ Explain working capital in relation to the operational cycle of a business. (pp. 756–757)
◆ Identify which situations cause working capital to increase. (p. 757)
◆ List specific uses and sources of working capital. (p. 757)
◆ Explain the effects of transactions on working capital. (pp. 758–759)

SELF-REVIEW QUIZ 22-2

(The forms you need are on page 143 of the *Study Guide and Working Papers.*)
   Explain how each of the transactions will affect working capital (source, use, no effect).

1. Paid $1,000 on accounts payable.
2. Recorded annual depreciation $500.
3. Borrowed $120,000 by issuing a mortgage payable.
4. Declared dividends.
5. Sold additional stock $10,000.

Solution to Self-Review Quiz 22-2

1. No effect.   **2.** No effect.   **3.** Source.   **4.** Use.   **5.** Source.

SUMMARY OF KEY POINTS

Learning Unit 22-1

1. In the statement of cash flows, net increase in cash equals net cash from operating activities plus or minus cash from investing activities plus or minus cash from financing activities.

2. In figuring the net cash from the operating activities section of the statement, it is necessary to convert the net income from the operations figure on the income statement from an accrual basis to a cash basis. This affects the following accounts: Depreciation, Accounts Receivable, Inventory, Prepaid Expenses, Notes Payable, and Accounts Payable. (Note that we are analyzing current assets and current liabilities to see their effect on net income.)

3. Cash flows from investing activities would include the following: purchase and sale of stock and bonds; buying and selling of plant assets; collecting and lending money for investment.

4. Cash flows from financing activities would include the following: issuing long-term notes; issuing common stock; payment of dividends; retiring bonds.

Learning Unit 22-2

1. Working capital is defined as current assets less current liabilities. Cash is one part of working capital.

2. A sound level of working capital allows a company to (a) carry adequate inventory, (b) meet current debts, (c) take advantage of cash discounts and offer favorable credit terms to its customers.

3. Sources of funds increase working capital. Uses of funds decrease working capital.

4. When working capital changes, it is a result of one or more noncurrent accounts changing along with a current asset or liability.

5. Sources of working capital include: current operations, owner investment, long-term borrowing, sale of noncurrent assets, and sale of capital stock.

6. Uses of working capital include: declaration of dividends, purchase of noncurrent assets, purchase of treasury stock, payment of noncurrent debt, and retirement of stock.

7. Working capital can increase without any increase in cash.

8. Depreciation affects only noncurrent accounts and is added back to net income, since it originally reduced net income. Depreciation has no effect on working capital.

KEY TERMS

Noncurrent account Any balance sheet account that is not a current asset or current liability.

Source of funds Transactions that increase working capital.

Statement of cash flows A financial report that pro-vides a detailed breakdown of the net increase or decrease in cash. Cash flows are divided into operating, investing, and financing activities.

Use of funds Transactions that decrease working capital.

Working capital Current assets less current liabilities.

Net Cash Flows from Operating Activities			
Net Income from Operations		XXX	
Add (Deduct) Items to Convert			
Net Income to Cash Basis:			
Depreciation	XXX		
Gain on Sale of Land	(XXX)		
Accounts Receivable — Increase	(XXX)		
Current Assets and Current Liabilities — Inventory — Decrease	XXX		
Prepaid Expenses — Increase	(XXX)		
Notes Payable — Increase	XXX		
Accounts Payable — Increase	XXX		
Wages Payable — Decrease	(XXX)		
Income Tax Payable — Increase	XXX		
Net Cash Flows from Operating Activities		XXXX	
Cash Flows from Investing Activities			
Purchase of Investment Securities	(XXX)		
Proceeds from Sale of Investments	XXX		
Loans Made	(XXX)		
Collections on Loans	XXX		
Sale of Land	XXX		
Purchase of Plant Assets	(XXX)		
Less Equipment acquired by issuing stock	XXX		
Net Cash Flows Provided by Investing Activities		XXXX	
Cash Flows from Financing Activities			
Issuance of Long-Term Note	XXX		
Issuance of Common Stock	XXX		
Less: Common Stock Issued to Acquire Equipment	(XXX)		
Payment of Dividends	(XXX)		
Retirement of Bonds Payable	(XXX)		
Net Cash Flows Provided by Financing Activities		(XXXX)	
Net Increase in Cash		XXXX	

QUESTIONS, MINI EXERCISES, EXERCISES, AND PROBLEMS

Discussion Questions

1. List the three main sections of the statement of cash flows.
2. Explain how net cash flows from operating activities is calculated.
3. The issuance of stock is an investing activity. Agree or disagree. Support your answer.
4. Explain how a creditor might analyze a statement of cash flows.
5. Explain how working capital circulates.
6. For working capital to change, only current assets or current liabilities can be affected. Accept or reject. Why?
7. List five examples of sources of funds.
8. Depreciation affects working capital. True or false? Why? What is a noncurrent account?

Mini Exercises

(The forms you need are on pages 144–146 of the *Study Guide and Working Papers*.)

Effective Net Income in Calculating Net Cash Flows from Operating Activities

1. The following accounts showed an increase or a decrease from the comparative balance sheet. Explain which account will be added to net income and which will be subtracted in calculating net cash flows from operating activities.
    a. Accounts Receivable — Increase.
    b. Inventory — Decrease.
    c. Notes Payable — Increase.
    d. Accounts Payable — Decrease.

Net Cash Flows from Operating Activities

2. From the following calculate the net cash flow from operating activities:

	19X1	19X2
Accounts Receivable	500	700
Prepaid Expenses	400	300
Accounts Payable	1,000	600
Salaries Payable	500	700

For Year Ended 19X2:
Net Income	$1,900
Depreciation Expense	$500

Net Cash Flows Provided by Financing Activities

3. From the following calculate net cash flows provided by financing activities:

Payments of Dividends	$ 6,000
Issuance of Common Stock	2,000
Issuance of a Long-Term Note	14,000

Calculating Change in Cash

4. Given the following, calculate:
- **a.** Net cash flows from operating activities $3,000
- **b.** Net cash flow from investing activities   (1,000)
- **b.** Net cash flows provided by financing activities   600

Working Capital

5. Explain how each transaction will affect working capital (source, use, no effect).
- **a.** Sold additional stock, $5,000.
- **b.** Declared a dividend.
- **c.** Borrowed $10,000 by issuing a mortgage payable.
- **d.** Recorded $400 annual depreciation.
- **e.** Paid $500 to reduce Accounts Payable.

Exercises

(The forms you need are on pages 145 and 146 of the *Study Guide and Working Papers.*)

Converting to cash basis.

22-1. Complete the following chart:

	Add to net income	Deduct from net income
?	Decrease	Increase
?	Increase	Decrease

Net cash flow from operating activities.

22-2. From the following calculate the net cash flow from operating activities:

	19X1	19X2
Accounts Receivable, Net	$ 5,900	$ 7,900
Prepaid Expenses	19,000	16,000
Accounts Payable	19,000	16,000
Salaries Payable	1,200	2,200

For Year Ended 19X2:
    Net Income, $17,000
    Depreciation Expense, $4,000

Statement of cash flows.

22-3. Explain how each of the following transactions would be recorded on the statement of cash flows:
- **a.** Issuance of common stock.
- **b.** Retirement of bonds payable.
- **c.** Purchase of a plant asset.
- **d.** Payment of dividends.

Calculate working capital.

22-4. From the following calculate Lancaster Corporation's working capital:

Mortgage Payable	$115,000
Accumulated Depreciation, Equipment	48,000
Merchandise Inventory	66,000
Notes Payable (due in eight months)	20,000

Buildings		95,000
Accounts Receivable, Net		39,000
Land		60,000
Office Supplies		1,460
Accounts Payable		60,400
Cash		30,000

Transactions affecting working capital.

22-5. Complete the following chart by placing an "X" in the appropriate column.

Transactions	Source of Working Capital	Use of Working Capital	No Effect on Working Capital
A. Paid operating expenses.			
B. Borrowed $6,000 by issuing a note payable due within a year.			
C. Depreciation recorded.			
D. Bought equipment for $20,000 in cash.			

Group A Problems

(The forms you need are on pages 147 – 149 of the *Study Guide and Working Papers*.)

Preparing a statement of cash flows.

22A-1. From the following income statement, balance sheet, and additional data for Joron Corporation, prepare a statement of cash flows.

JORON CORPORATION
INCOME STATEMENT
FOR YEAR ENDED DECEMBER 31, 19X7

Sales		$ 96 500 00
Cost of Goods Sold		69 100 00
Gross Profit		$ 27 400 00
Operating Expenses:		
Rent Expense	$ 7 500 00	
Depreciation Expense	7 000 00	
Salaries Expense	6 600 00	
Miscellaneous Expense	3 200 00	
Total Operating Expenses		24 300 00
Net Income		$ 3 100 00

JORON CORPORATION COMPARATIVE BALANCE SHEET AS OF DECEMBER 31, 19X7 AND 19X6		
Assets	19X7	19X6
Current Assets:		
Cash	$ 3 400 00	$ 2 600 00
Accounts Receivable, Net	5 600 00	4 500 00
Merchandise Inventory	2 200 00	2 000 00
Prepaid Rent	1 000 00	1 200 00
Total Current Assets	$ 12 200 00	$ 10 300 00
Plant and Equipment:		
Store Equipment	$ 58 000 00	$ 50 000 00
Accum. Dep., Store Equipment	(12 000 00)	(5 000 00)
Total Plant and Equipment	$ 46 000 00	$ 45 000 00
Total Assets	$ 58 200 00	$ 55 300 00
Liabilities		
Current Liabilities:		
Notes Payable	$ 6 800 00	$ 5 200 00
Accounts Payable	4 400 00	4 800 00
Total Current Liabilities	$ 11 200 00	$ 10 000 00
Long-Term Liabilities:		
Bonds Payable	$ 12 500 00	$ 15 000 00
Total Liabilities	$ 23 700 00	$ 25 000 00
Stockholders' Equity		
Common Stock, $1 par	$ 22 500 00	$ 20 000 00
Retained Earnings	12 000 00	10 300 00
Total Stockholders' Equity	$ 34 500 00	$ 30 300 00
Total Liabilities and Stockholders' Equity	$ 58 200 00	$ 55 300 00

Additional data:

1. All plant and equipment were paid for in cash.
2. Sold additional 2,500 shares of stock for cash at par value.
3. A $1,400 dividend was declared and paid.

Preparing a statement of cash flows.

22A-2. From the following income statement, balance sheet, and additional data for Dean Corporation, prepare a statement of cash flows.

DEAN CORPORATION
INCOME STATEMENT
FOR YEAR ENDED DECEMBER 31, 19X9

Sales		$24 300 00
Cost of Goods Sold		14 400 00
Gross Profit		$ 9 900 00
Operating Expenses:		
Depreciation Expense, Equip.	$ 6 000 00	
Depreciation Expense, Mach.	3 000 00	
Advertising Expense	6 300 00	
Salaries Expense	2 000 00	
Miscellaneous Expense	4 000 00	
Total Operating Expenses		7 530 00
Net Income		$ 2 370 00

Hint: Note Plant and Equipment recorded at *net* on balance sheet. Be sure to add back depreciation expense to cost of equipment.

DEAN CORPORATION
COMPARATIVE BALANCE SHEET
DECEMBER 31, 19X9 AND 19X8

Assets	19X9	19X8
Current Assets:		
Cash	$ 1 640 00	$ 510 00
Accounts Receivable, Net	2 700 00	2 880 00
Merchandise Inventory	3 000 00	2 400 00
Total Current Assets	$ 7 340 00	$ 5 790 00
Plant and Equipment:		
Office Equipment, Net	$ 6 000 00	$ 4 500 00
Machinery, Net	4 800 00	3 000 00
Land	600 00	450 00
Total Plant and Equipment	$11 400 00	$ 7 950 00
Total Assets	$18 740 00	$13 740 00
Liabilities		
Current Liabilities:		
Accounts Payable	$ 2 250 00	$ 1 950 00
Accrued Liabilities	90 00	120 00
Total Current Liabilities	$ 2 340 00	$ 2 070 00
Long-Term Liabilities:		
Mortgage Payable	$ 2 100 00	$ 1 740 00
Total Liabilities	$ 4 440 00	$ 3 810 00

Stockholder's Equity		
Common Stock, $1 Par	$ 950000	$ 750000
Retained Earnings	480000	243000
Total Stockholder's Equity	$ 1430000	$ 993000
Total Liabilities and Stockholder's Equity	$ 1874000	$ 1374000

Additional data:

1. All increases in Plant and Equipment were paid for in cash.
2. No dividend was declared in 19X9.
3. Sold 2,000 shares of stock for cash at par value.

Transactions affecting working capital.

22A-3. Explain how the following transactions will affect working capital. Do this by drawing transactional analysis charts.

a. Reynolds Company issued stock for $35,000.

b. Reynolds Company borrowed $6,000 by issuing a note payable due within one year.

c. Billed customers for $60,000 for services rendered.

d. Recorded depreciation of $7,000.

e. Bought $20,000 worth of equipment for cash.

Group B Problems

(The forms you need are on pages 147 – 149 of the *Study Guide and Working Papers*.)

Preparing a statement of cash flows.

22B-1. From the following income statement, balance sheet, and additional data for Dean Corporation, prepare a statement of cash flows.

DEAN CORPORATION INCOME STATEMENT FOR YEAR ENDED DECEMBER 31, 19X9		
Sales		$ 3600000
Cost of Goods Sold		2500000
Gross Profit		$ 1100000
Operating Expenses:		
Depreciation Expense, Equip.	$ 80000	
Depreciation Expense, Mach.	50000	
Advertsising Expense	66000	
Salaries Expense	180000	
Miscellaneous Expense	360000	
Total Operating Expenses		736000
Net Income		$ 364000

DEAN CORPORATION
COMPARATIVE BALANCE SHEET
AS OF DECEMBER 31, 19X9 AND 19X8

Assets	19X9	19X8
Current Assets:		
Cash	$ 2 040 00	$ 540 00
Accounts Receivable, Net	2 680 00	2 910 00
Merchandise Inventory	3 200 00	2 430 00
Total Current Assets	$ 7 920 00	$ 5 880 00
Plant and Equipment:		
Office Equipment, Net	$ 6 030 00	$ 4 530 00
Machinery, Net	4 830 00	3 030 00
Land	1 180 00	480 00
Total Plant and Equipment	$12 040 00	$ 8 040 00
Total Assets	$19 960 00	$13 920 00
Liabilities		
Current Liabilities:		
Notes Payable	$ 2 080 00	$ 1 980 00
Accounts Payable	100 00	150 00
Total Current Liabilities	$ 2 180 00	$ 2 130 00
Long-Term Liabilities:		
Mortgage Payable	$ 2 120 00	$ 1 770 00
Total Liabilities	$ 4 300 00	$ 3 900 00
Stockholders' Equity		
Common Stock, $1 par	$ 9 530 00	$ 7 530 00
Retained Earnings	6 130 00	2 490 00
Total Stockholders' Equity	$15 660 00	$10 020 00
Total Liabilities and Stockholders' Equity	$19 960 00	$13 920 00

Additional data:

1. All increases in Plant and Equipment were paid for in cash.
2. No dividend was declared in 19X9.
3. Sold 2,000 shares of stock for cash at par value.

Preparing a statement of cash flows.

22B-2. From the following income statement, balance sheet, and additional data for Joron Corporation, prepare a statement of cash flows.

JORON CORPORATION
INCOME STATEMENT
FOR YEAR ENDED DECEMBER 31, 19X7

Sales		$ 24 50 0 00
Cost of Goods Sold		16 00 0 00
Gross Profit		$ 8 50 0 00
Operating Expenses:		
Rent Expense	$ 1 80 0 00	
Depreciation Expense	1 70 0 00	
Salaries Expense	1 55 0 00	
Miscellaneous Expense	90 0 00	
Total Operating Expenses		5 95 0 00
Net Income		$ 2 55 0 00

JORON CORPORATION
COMPARATIVE BALANCE SHEET
AS OF DECEMBER 31, 19X7 AND 19X6

Assets	19X7	19X6
Current Assets:		
Cash	$ 97 5 00	$ 70 0 00
Accounts Receivable, Net	1 45 0 00	1 17 5 00
Merchandise Inventory	60 0 00	55 0 00
Prepaid Rent	30 0 00	35 0 00
Total Current Assets	$ 3 32 5 00	$ 2 77 5 00
Plant and Equipment:		
Store Equipment	$18 00 0 00	$12 55 0 00
Accum. Dep., Store Equipment	(3 00 0 00)	(1 30 0 00)
Total Plant and Equipment	15 00 0 00	11 25 0 00
Total Assets	$18 32 5 00	$14 02 5 00
Liabilities		
Current Liabilities:		
Notes Payable	$ 1 75 0 00	$ 1 35 0 00
Accounts Payable	1 20 0 00	1 25 0 00
Total Current Liabilities	$ 2 95 0 00	$ 2 60 0 00
Long-Term Liabilities:		
Bond Payable	$ 3 15 0 00	$ 3 80 0 00
Total Liabilities	$ 6 10 0 00	$ 6 40 0 00
Stockholders' Equity		
Common Stock, $1 par	$ 7 50 0 00	$ 5 00 0 00
Retained Earnings	4 72 5 00	2 62 5 00
Total Stockholders' Equity	$12 22 5 00	$ 7 62 5 00
Total Liabilities and Stockholders' Equity	$18 32 5 00	$14 02 5 00

Additional data:

1. All increase in Plant and Equipment were paid for in cash.
2. A $450 dividend was declared and paid.
3. Sold 2,500 shares of stock for cash at par value.

22B-3. Explain how the following transactions will affect working capital. Draw transactional analysis charts to show this.

  a. Recorded depreciation of $6,000.

  b Issued stock for $15,000.

  c. Billed customers for $8,000 for services rendered.

  d. Borrowed $24,000 by issuing a note payable due within one year.

  e. Reynolds Company bought $30,000 worth of equipment for cash.

REAL WORLD APPLICATIONS

22R-1.

Frank Smith is trying to convert income statement items from an accrual basis to a cash basis. Accounts Receivable at the beginning of the year totaled $205,000. At the end of the year receivables were $240,000. On the income statement using accrual accounting, sales were $360,000. Depreciation Expense is $18,000 on the accrual income statement.

    Frank calculates his cash sales received from customers to be $305,000. Do you accept his calculation? What written recommendations could you suggest to Frank? How would Frank calculate advertising expense on a cash basis if Accrued Advertising was reduced by $43,000 and Prepaid Advertising increased from $16,000 at beginning of year to $19,000 at end of year?

22R-2.

Martin Blake is trying to calculate how much cash is being paid to suppliers of his firm's inventory during 19X9. In 19X9 cost of goods sold was reported at $190,500. Martin feels he needs more data than are provided. From the following facts, could you show Martin how to calculate cash paid to suppliers as well as explain this approach versus the accrual approach? If you feel there are insufficient data, explain in writing what data are needed.

	December 31, 19X9	December 31, 19X8
Accounts Receivable	$39,000	$37,000
Merchandise Inventory	50,400	53,000
Accounts Payable	28,500	30,700
Notes Payable	17,000	15,000
(used for all merchandise)		
Salaries Payable	11,000	11,200

YOU make the call

Critical Thinking/Ethical Case

22R-3.

Avone Co. each year prepares an income statement and balance sheet. The controller issued a memo to Stan Smith, VP, that the company should prepare a statement of cash flow. Stan called the controller and told him that there is "no way" he will let a cash flow statement be published, that this type of information is for internal purposes only, and that the public has no right to these data. He said that the competition would kill them if they got this information. Do you agree with Stan's position? You make the call. Write down your recommendation to Stan.

ACCOUNTING RECALL

A CUMULATIVE APPROACH

THIS EXAM REVIEWS CHAPTERS 1 THROUGH 22

Your *Study Guide and Working Papers* has forms (p. 153) to complete this exam, as well as worked-out solutions. The page references next to each question identify what page to turn back to if you answer the question incorrectly.

PART 1 Vocabulary Review

Match the terms to the appropriate definition or phrase.

Page Ref.

(756)	1. Working capital	A. Decrease working capital
(727)	2. Carrying value	B. Contra-revenue account
(757)	3. Noncurrent account	C. A financial report
(701)	4. Treasury stock	D. An asset
(314)	5. Sales returns and allowances	E. Increase working capital
(757)	6. Use of funds	F. Issuance of a long-term note
(678)	7. Subscriptions receivable	G. Face value of bond less bond discount
(753)	8. Statement of cash flows	
(752)	9. Cash flow from financing activities	H. Current assets–current liabilities
		I. Reduction to stockholders' equity
(757)	10. Source of funds	J. Equipment

(505)   11. Allowance for doubtful accounts has a normal balance of a credit.

(752)   12. Purchase of a plant asset is listed under cash flow from financing activities.

(759)   13. Depreciation has an effect on working capital.

(752)   14. If a current asset decreases it is added to net income.

(757)   15. Source of funds will decrease working capital.

23

ANALYZING FINANCIAL STATEMENTS

THE BIG PICTURE

The third year for Eldorado Computer Center has come to an end. Although the company did not reach its budgeted goals of growth and profit, the year was still successful.

In order to judge their position in the marketplace, Freedman and West want to take a detailed look at the company. Since neither owner is an accountant by trade, they choose to take the year-end financial statements to their accountant to provide the interpretation. They write several questions down that they want clear answers to — such questions as:

◆ Will we have enough cash to pay the bills in the near future?

◆ Are we effectively utilizing the resources of the firm?

◆ How does our debt to equity position compare across the years, and to other similar companies?

◆ And if this were a public company would you invest in stock?

The accountant's responsibility, as you will learn in this chapter, is to provide a financial interpretation by analyzing the financial statements. This is done through calculating ratios, by providing a horizontal and vertical analysis of the statements, and by preparing comparative balance sheets. The computer center uses this information as a basis for making decisions. The comparisons to industry standards give them an idea of how they are doing within the industry. Comparisons can also be used to determine patterns or trends.

Financial reports are used by investors, creditors, and management to assist in making business decisions. Typical business decisions might involve such questions as:

◆ *For investors:* How profitable is the company when compared with competing companies? Will dividends be paid? Can the company expand with adequate financing?

◆ *For creditors:* Does the company have enough cash to pay back periodic interest payments as well as balance on maturity?

◆ *For management:* Is the company operating as efficiently as possible? How can we do better?

The four financial statements that we have discussed in earlier chapters — the balance sheet, the income statement, the statement of retained earnings, and the statement of cash flows — help provide the answers to these questions. In this chapter we will discuss how to analyze the numbers that appear on these statements.

Numbers on a financial statement may not have meaning in and of themselves — they must be placed in a context. This context may be a comparison with last year's figures, a comparison with other companies in the same industry, or even a comparison with other figures on the same report.

In the following units we will look at what the numbers mean as well as how to apply that meaning toward making useful business decisions.

LEARNING UNIT 23-1
Horizontal and Vertical Analysis of Balance Sheets

In the **comparative balance sheet,** a statement showing data from two or more periods side by side, shown in Figure 23-1 (p. 776), the accountant has placed the current year's balance sheet figures next to figures from the preceding year's balance sheet. The third column shows the amount of increase or decrease in the 19X8 figures over the 19X7 figures, and the last column shows the percentage of decrease or increase of 19X8 over 19X7. This type of analysis, in which each item on the report is compared with the same item in other periods, is called **horizontal analysis.**

HORIZONTAL ANALYSIS OF THE BALANCE SHEET

Let's perform a sample horizontal analysis on one of the items on Scrupper's comparative balance sheet. Look at the entry for Cash in Figure 23-1. In 19X8 it is $3,040 and in 19X7 it was $4,080. This equals a decrease of $1,040, which is placed in parentheses on the report to show that it is a decrease

SCRUPPER SUPPLY COMPANY
COMPARATIVE BALANCE SHEET
AS OF DECEMBER 31, 19X8 AND DECEMBER 31, 19X7

Note: Most recent year is shown first. ⟶ Assets	December 31 19X8	December 31 19X7	Amount of Increase or Decrease During 19X8	Percent Increase or Decrease During 19X8
Current Assets:				
Cash	$ 3 040 00	$ 4 080 00	$ (1 040 00)	(25.5)
Accounts Receivable, Net	20 000 00	16 000 00	4 000 00	25
Merchandise Inventory	24 160 00	26 120 00	(1 960 00)	(7.5)
Prepaid Expenses	800 00	600 00	200 00	33.3
Total Current Assets	$ 48 000 00	$ 46 800 00	$ 1 200 00	2.6
Plant and Equipment:				
Office Equipment, Net	$125 200 00	$116 800 00	$ 8 400 00	7.2
Total Assets	$173 200 00	$163 600 00	$ 9 600 00	5.9
Liabilities				
Current Liabilities:				
Notes Payable	$ 20 960 00	$ 17 320 00	$ 3 640 00	21
Accounts Payable	240 00	280 00	(40 00)	(14.3)
Total Current Liabilities	$ 21 200 00	$ 17 600 00	$ 3 600 00	20.5
Long-Term Liabilities:				
Mortgage Payable	60 000 00	60 000 00	–0–	–0–
Total Liabilities	$ 81 200 00	$ 77 600 00	$ 3 600 00	4.6
Stockholders' Equity				
Common Stock, $10 par value	$ 60 000 00	$ 60 000 00	–0–	–0–
Retained Earnings	32 000 00	26 000 00	6 000 00	23.1
Total Stockholders' Equity	$ 92 000 00	$ 86 000 00	$ 6 000 00	7.0
Total Liabilities and Stockholders' Equity	$173 200 00	$163 600 00	$ 9 600 00	5.9

FIGURE 23-1
Comparative Balance Sheet

and not an increase. To figure the percentage that this decrease represents, you use this equation:

$$\text{percent} = \frac{\text{amount of change}}{\text{base (old year)}}$$

Thus in this case it would be

$$\frac{\$1,040}{\$4,080} = 25.5 \text{ percent}$$

This type of analysis is called horizontal analysis because in each case you are comparing two figures across columns, from one period to another, rather than comparing figures within a column. Although cash decreased by 25.5 percent,

Scrupper's retained earnings increased by 23.1 percent. You can see that the percentages in the last column in Figure 23-1 cannot be added down the column to total 100 percent—each figure relates only to the figures for the same item across the other columns. These percentages provide us with a quick way of monitoring specific accounts.

VERTICAL ANALYSIS OF THE BALANCE SHEET

In **vertical analysis,** each item on a report is shown as a percent of a total base. The base will be either total assets or total liabilities and stockholders' equity on a balance sheet, and it can be total sales on an income statement. Look at the comparative balance sheet in Figure 23-2. Each item is listed for

FIGURE 23-2
Vertical Analysis of a
Comparative Balance Sheet

SCRUPPER SUPPLY COMPANY COMPARATIVE BALANCE SHEET DECEMBER 31, 19X8 AND DECEMBER 31, 19X7				
Assets	19X8		19X7	
Current Assets:				
Cash	$ 3 0 4 0 00	1.8%	$ 4 0 8 0 00	2.5%
Accounts Receivable, Net	20 0 0 0 00	11.5	16 0 0 0 00	9.8
Merchandise Inventory	24 1 6 0 00	13.9	26 1 2 0 00	16.0
Prepaid Expenses	8 0 0 00	.5	6 0 0 00	.4
Total Current Assets	$ 48 0 0 0 00	27.7%	$ 46 8 0 0 00	28.7%
Plant and Equipment:				
Office Equipment, Net	125 2 0 0 00	72.3%	116 8 0 0 00	71.4%
Total Assets	$173 2 0 0 00	100.0%	$163 6 0 0 00	100.0%
Liabilities				
Current Liabilities:				
Notes Payable	$ 20 9 6 0 00	12.1%	$ 17 3 2 0 00	10.6%
Accounts Payable	2 4 0 00	.1	2 8 0 00	.2
Total Current Liabilities	$ 21 2 0 0 00	12.2%	$ 17 6 0 0 00	10.8%
Long-Term Liabilities:				
Mortgage Payable	60 0 0 0 00	34.6%	60 0 0 0 00	36.7%
Total Liabilities	$ 81 2 0 0 00	46.9%	$ 77 6 0 0 00	47.5%
Stockholders' Equity				
Common Stock, $10 par value	$ 60 0 0 0 00	34.6%	$ 60 0 0 0 00	36.7%
Retained Earnings	32 0 0 0 00	18.5	26 0 0 0 00	15.9
Total Stockholders' Equity	$ 92 0 0 0 00	53.1%	$ 86 0 0 0 00	52.6%
Total Liabilities and Stockholders' Equity	$173 2 0 0 00	100.0%	$163 6 0 0 00	100.0%*

* Total equals 100% due to rounding.

"F RED DID IT!" shouted Dwayne. "Number 1 in sales this month!" He was busy at his desk, pouring over Fred's monthly report. He was smiling broadly as he announced Fred's success to the world.

Fred does a monthly management report to Dwayne, consisting of an Income Statement. A Balance Sheet is done quarterly. Dwayne does a horizontal analysis of Fred's Balance Sheet, comparing each line to its budget and to last year. This tells him if Fred is on target and points up any weak areas in the business. Then he does a vertical analysis of Fred's Balance Sheet to arrive at percents of the totals.

Dwayne compares Fred's results (in percentages) to each of the other shops in his zone, using a common-size statement. This is a useful exercise because, while each shop is different in size, a common-size statement deals only in percentages. This comparison quickly points up exceptions, which may be good or bad. In either case, Dwayne then has the clues he needs to discover a strength other shops can copy, or a weakness Fred can fix.

Everyone in the zone looks forward to seeing how they are doing in comparison to the others in their

COMPARISON TIME

DUNKIN' DONUTS

zone. There is a good deal of friendly rivalry—and a good deal of mutual help. Owners regularly share successful strategies, as well as news about the competition.

Dwayne also does a quarterly report for Dunkin' Donuts Inc. on all the shops he supervises. These are then folded into Dunkin' Donuts Inc.'s internal management reports to Allied Domeq Retailing USA. They, in turn, report to Allied Domeq headquarters in England. As the financial picture grows more inclusive, it is less detailed. So while Fred's shop is unknown outside his zone, his success is reflected all the way up the line.

DISCUSSION QUESTION

1. Why does Dwayne use a common-size statement to compare shops in his zone?
2. Why does he use both horizontal and vertical analysis of the Balance Sheets for the shops in his zone?
3. As the financial statements at the various levels of Dunkin' Donuts and Allied Domeq include more shops, they become less detailed. Why?

19X8, and next to it is a percentage, which is that item's percentage of total assets or total liabilities and stockholders' equity. In the next column each item is listed for the preceding year, 19X7, and then the item is listed as a percentage of total assets or total liabilities and stockholders' equity.

Take the item Cash as an example again. In 19X8, Cash is $3,040 and total assets $173,200; thus Cash represents 1.8 percent of total assets for this year. In 19X7, Cash was $4,080 and total assets $163,600; thus Cash was 2.5 percent of total assets in that year.

Note how in this type of analysis you do add down the columns to total 100 percent, unlike horizontal analysis. Keep in mind that vertical analysis provides us with *another* way of analyzing financial reports that contain data for two or more successive accounting periods.

A shorter version of this report can be seen in Figure 23-3, in which are listed just the percentages of two columns that have been analyzed. Such a report in general is called a **common-size statement;** this particular one is a common-size comparative balance sheet.

The common-size statement makes it easy to see, for example, that from 19X7 to 19X8 there was a drop in inventory (it went from 16 percent to 13.9 percent as a percent of total assets), and an increase in accounts receivable (from 9.8 percent to 11.5 percent). The common-size statement is often used to compare companies of different sizes — that way the dollar amounts do not get in the way, and it is easier to see each item as a percent of the base in each company.

SCRUPPER SUPPLY COMPANY COMMON-SIZE COMPARATIVE BALANCE SHEET DECEMBER 31, 19X8 AND DECEMBER 31, 19X7		
	December 31	
Assets	19X8	19X7
Current Assets:		
Cash	1.8%	2.5%
Accounts Receivable, Net	11.5	9.8
Merchandise Inventory	13.9	16.0
Prepaid Expenses	.5	.4
Total Current Assets	27.7%	28.7%
Plant and Equipment:		
Office Equipment, Net	72.3%	71.4%
Total Assets	100.0%	100.0%
Liabilities		
Current Liabilities:		
Notes Payable	12.1%	10.6%
Accounts Payable	.1	.2
Total Current Liabilities	12.2%	10.8%
Long-Term Liabilities:		
Mortgage Payable	34.6%	36.7%
Total Liabilities	46.9%	47.5%
Stockholders' Equity		
Common Stock, $10 par value	34.6%	36.7%
Retained Earnings	18.5	15.9
Total Stockholders' Equity	53.1%	52.6%
Total Liabilities and Stockholders' Equity	100.0%	100.0%*

FIGURE 23-3
Common-Size Comparative
Balance Sheet

* Total equals 100% due to rounding.

LEARNING UNIT 23-1 REVIEW

AT THIS POINT you should be able to

◆ Explain the items making up a comparative balance sheet. (p. 775)
◆ Compare and contrast vertical and horizontal analysis. (pp. 776 – 777)
◆ Explain the advantage of a common-size statement. (p. 778)

SELF-REVIEW QUIZ 23-1

(The blank forms you need are on page 155 of the *Study Guide and Working Papers.*)

Complete the following Comparative Balance Sheet:

Assets	December 31 19X5	December 31 19X4	Amount of Increase or Decrease During 19X5	Percent Increase or Decrease During 19X5
Current Assets:				
Cash	$ 5 000 00	$ 4 000 00		
Accounts Receivable, Net	4 000 00	2 500 00		
Merchandise Inventory	6 000 00	5 600 00		
Prepaid Expenses	2 000 00	400 00		
Total Current Assets				
Plant and Equipment:				
Store Equipment, Net	146 000 00	125 000 00		
Total Assets				

Solution to Self-Review Quiz 23-1

Assets	December 31 19X5	December 31 19X4	Amount of Increase or Decrease During 19X5	Percent Increase or Decrease During 19X5
Current Assets:				
Cash	$ 5 000 00	$ 4 000 00	$ 1 000 00	25 $\left(\frac{\$1,000}{\$4,000}\right)$
Accounts Receivable, Net	4 000 00	2 500 00	1 500 00	60
Merchandise Inventory	6 000 00	5 600 00	400 00	7.1
Prepaid Expenses	2 000 00	400 00	1 600 00	400
Total Current Assets	$ 17 000 00	$ 12 500 00	$ 4 500 00	36
Plant and Equipment:				
Store Equipment, Net	146 000 00	125 000 00	21 000 00	16.8
Total Assets	$163 000 00	$137 500 00	$ 25 500 00	18.5

LEARNING UNIT 23-2

Horizontal and Vertical Analysis of Income Statements; Trend Analysis

In the last unit we showed how to perform a horizontal and a vertical analysis of the balance sheet for Scrupper Supply Company. We will now show how to perform the same two types of analysis on the income statement for Scrupper Supply Company.

HORIZONTAL ANALYSIS OF THE INCOME STATEMENT

Figure 23-4 shows a comparative income statement for Scrupper Supply using horizontal analysis. As in horizontal analysis for the balance sheet, each item on the income statement is compared with the same item for the preceding year; the amount of increase or decrease is recorded and then shown as a percent. Looking at net sales, it was $302,000 in 19X7 compared with $317,600 in 19X8; that is an increase of $15,600, which comes out to a 5.2 percent increase ($15,600/$302,000). The percent increase or decrease is the amount of increase or decrease divided by the figure for the base year of 19X7.

VERTICAL ANALYSIS OF THE INCOME STATEMENT

Figure 23-5 (p. 782) shows the vertical analysis of a comparative income statement for Scrupper Supply Company. In the case of an income statement, the base used is net sales. (On a balance sheet, it is assets or total liabilities and stockholders' equity.) Thus on the vertical analysis of an income statement, each item is calculated as a percentage of net sales.

From such an analysis of a comparative income statement we can easily see that cost of goods sold decreased (from 64.2 to 62.3 percent) from 19X7 to 19X8, selling expenses increased (from 18.2 to 20.0 percent), and profit before tax was up (7.5 to 10.0 percent). If we had listed just the percentages (each

FIGURE 23-4
Horizontal Analysis of a
Comparative Income
Statement

	December 31		Amount of Increase or Decrease During 19X8	Percent of Increase or Decrease During 19X8	
SCRUPPER SUPPLY COMPANY COMPARATIVE INCOME STATEMENT FOR YEARS ENDED DECEMBER 31, 19X8 AND 19X7					
	19X8	19X7			
Net Sales	$317 600 00	$302 000 00	$ 15 600 00	5.2	
Cost of Goods Sold	198 000 00	194 000 00	4 000 00	2.1	
Gross Profit from Sales	$119 600 00	108 000 00	11 600 00	10.7	
Operating Expenses:					
Selling	$ 63 600 00	$ 55 000 00	8 600 00	15.6	
General and Administrative	20 000 00	26 000 00	(6 000 00)	(23.1)	
Total Operating Expenses	$ 83 600 00	$ 81 000 00	$ 2 600 00	3.2	
Operating Income	$ 36 000 00	$ 27 000 00	9 000 00	33.3	
Less Interest Expense	4 200 00	4 300 00	(1 00 00)	(2.3)	
Income before Taxes	$ 31 800 00	$ 22 700 00	$ 9 100 00	40.1	
Income Taxes	15 900 00	11 350 00	4 550 00	40.1	
Net Income	$ 15 900 00	$ 11 350 00	$ 4 550 00	40.1	

SCRUPPER SUPPLY COMPANY
COMPARATIVE INCOME STATEMENT
FOR YEARS ENDED DECEMBER 31, 19X8 AND 19X7

Assets	19X8		19X7	
Net Sales	$317 6 0 0 00	100 %	$302 0 0 0 00	100 %
Cost of Goods Sold	198 0 0 0 00	62.3	194 0 0 0 00	64.2
Gross Profit from Sales	$119 6 0 0 00	37.7%	108 0 0 0 00	35.8%
Operating Expenses:				
Selling	$ 63 6 0 0 00	20.0%	$ 55 0 0 0 00	18.2 %
General and Administrative	20 0 0 0 00	6.3	26 0 0 0 00	8.6
Total Operating Expenses	$ 83 6 0 0 00	26.3%	$ 81 0 0 0 00	26.8 %
Operating Income	$ 36 0 0 0 00	11.3%	27 0 0 0 00	8.9
Less Interest Expense	4 2 0 0 00	1.3	4 3 0 0 00	1.4
Income before Taxes	$ 31 8 0 0 00	10.0%	$ 22 7 0 0 00	7.5 %
Income Taxes	15 9 0 0 00	5.0%	11 3 5 0 00	3.75
Net Income	$ 15 9 0 0 00	5.0%	$ 11 3 5 0 00	3.75%

FIGURE 23-5
Vertical Analysis of a Comparative Income Statement

item as percentage of net sales) and left out the dollar amounts, we would have produced a common-size comparative income statement.

TREND ANALYSIS

There is a special type of horizontal analysis that is called **trend analysis.** Trend analysis deals with the percentage of changes in a certain item over several years. For example, if we want to understand why sales in 19X8 are 118 percent of 19X5 of Scrupper Supply Company, we have to look at figures for several years. Following are listed figures for sales, cost of goods sold, and gross profit for 19X5 to 19X8:

	19X8	19X7	19X6	19X5
Sales	$317,600	$302,000	$290,000	$270,000
Cost of Goods Sold	198,000	194,000	184,000	142,000
Gross Profit	$119,600	$108,000	$106,000	$128,000

When the trend analysis is developed, a base year is chosen. We will choose 19X5 (the base year is usually the earliest year listed). For each of the following years each item is stated as a percentage of the amount of the base year. For example, sales in 19X8 as a percentage of the base year equal 118 percent. This is calculated as follows:

$$\text{Base} \longrightarrow \frac{\$317,600}{\$270,000} = 118 \text{ percent}$$

This means that sales in 19X8 have increased by 18 percent since 19X5. Over a period of years these percentages are analyzed in relation to a company's history as well as to industry averages that are supplied by companies like Robert Morse Associates and Dun & Bradstreet.

The following is the trend analysis for Scrupper Supply for sales, cost of goods sold, and gross profit.

	19X8	19X7	19X6	19X5
Sales	118%	112%	107%	100%
Cost of Goods Sold	139	137	130	100
Gross Profit	93	84	83	100

Note that in 19X6 sales increased 7 percent from 19X5, but cost of goods sold was up 30 percent, resulting in gross profit being down 17 percent. Such analysis can reveal internal problems in Scrupper Company or industry-wide problems in a certain year. For example, Scrupper might want to investigate why cost of goods sold has risen 39 percent in the last three years.

LEARNING UNIT 23-2 REVIEW

AT THIS POINT you should be able to

◆ Analyze income statement items by vertical and horizontal analysis. (pp. 781–782)
◆ Prepare a trend analysis. (p. 782)

SELF-REVIEW QUIZ 23-2

(The blank forms you need are on page 155 of the *Study Guide and Working Papers.*)

From the following prepare a trend analysis (round to nearest whole percent using 19X3 as the base year).

	19X6	19X5	19X4	19X3
Sales	$189,000	$165,000	$142,000	$130,000
Cost of Goods Sold	85,000	124,000	99,000	88,000
Gross Profit	$104,000	$ 41,000	$ 43,000	$ 42,000

Solution to Self-Review Quiz 23-2

	19X6	19X5	19X4	19X3
Sales	145%	127%	109%*	100%
Cost of Goods Sold	97	141	113	100
Gross Profit	248	98	102	100

$$* \ \frac{\$142,000}{\$130,000}$$

LEARNING UNIT 23-3
Ratio Analysis

Another method for understanding the numbers on the financial statement is the use of ratio analysis.

A **ratio** is the relationship of two quantities or numbers, one divided by the other. **Ratio analysis** looks at the relationship of figures on the financial statement. For example, if Broome Company's net income is $10,000 and sales are $100,000, the ratio of sales to net income may be expressed as follows:

a. Net income is $\frac{1}{10}$ or 10 percent of sales ($10,000/$100,000 = .1 = $\frac{1}{10}$ = 10 percent).

b. Ratio of sales to net income is 10 to 1 or 10 times net income (10:1).

c. For every $10 of sales, Broome Company earns $1.00 of net income.

In this unit we will look at a number of different ratios that are used to analyze different aspects of a business. To be meaningful, ratios are often compared with other standards, such as past company ratios or industry-wide ratios. The ratios we will discuss fall into four general categories:

◆ **Liquidity ratios** measure a company's ability to meet short-term obligations.

◆ **Asset management ratios** measure how effectively a company is using its assets.

◆ **Debt management ratios** measure how well a company is using debt versus its equity position.

◆ **Profitability ratios** measure a company's ability to earn profits.

Let's now do the calculations, as well as provide an explanation of each ratio. All calculations for the ratios come from the financial reports of Scrupper Supply presented in the last two units.

LIQUIDITY RATIOS

Current Ratio

The **current ratio** expresses the relationship of Scrupper's current assets to its current liabilities, as follows:

19X8

◆ Total current assets, $48,000.

◆ Total current liabilities, $21,200.

$$\text{current ratio} = \frac{\text{current assets}}{\text{current liabilities}} = \frac{\$48,000}{\$21,200} = 2.26:1$$

Thus for each $1 of debt, Scrupper has $2.26 of current assets to meet its short-term debt obligations.

It is important to note that this ratio should be evaluated in terms of (1) the type of business Scrupper is in, (2) the composition of current assets, and (3) the type of credit terms Scrupper extends. Ratios can also be compared from year to year, to spot trends in a company or in an industry. For example, in 19X7 the current ratio for Scrupper Corporation (p. 777) was 2.66 ($46,800/$17,600). This year's current ratio is 2.26, which means that Scrupper's ability to pay off short-term debts has decreased from last year to this year. This is something that creditors and investors will be interested in, as well as the management of Scrupper Corporation.

Depending on the inventory or prepaid expenses, the current assets might not be worth what is shown on the balance sheet. For example, if Scrupper Supply has overstocked amounts of inventory, a high current ratio could occur. Or if Scrupper has a large amount of prepaid insurance or rent, it will not be possible to convert these assets into cash, since they have already been paid for. Thus current ratio is not a very rigorous test of Scrupper's ability to pay its short-term debts. The next ratio we will discuss will show this more clearly.

Acid Test Ratio (Quick Ratio)

The **acid test ratio** divides those assets that are most easily converted into cash (called **"quick" assets**) by the current liabilities. In order to determine "quick" assets, we subtract Merchandise Inventory and Prepaid Expenses from current assets (this usually leaves Cash, Notes Receivable, and Accounts Receivable). Thus the acid test ratio would look like this:

$$\text{acid test ratio} = \frac{\text{current assets} - \text{merchandise inventory} - \text{prepaid expenses}}{\text{current liabilities}}$$

$$= \frac{\$23,040}{\$21,200} = 1.09:1$$

Thus for each $1 of short-term debt there is $1.09 of current or quick assets to meet them. This ratio should be at least 1:1 in order to pass the acid test, or be acceptable. If you compare this 1.09:1 ratio with the current ratio figure of 2.26:1, you will see what a difference the inclusion of Merchandise Inventory and Prepaid Expenses makes.

ASSET MANAGEMENT RATIOS

Accounts Receivable Turnover

The **accounts receivable turnover ratio** shows how many times in a year Scrupper is able to convert its accounts receivables into cash. Usually the higher the turnover the better, because a company does not want its money tied up in something that is not yielding any revenue. The turnover rate depends on the length of the credit period that Scrupper gives its customers (for Scrupper, all sales are on credit). Scrupper's income statement is on page 781.

$$\text{accounts receivable turnover} = \frac{\text{net credit sales}}{\text{average accounts receivable}}$$

At the end of 19X7 Accounts Receivable was $16,000; at the end of 19X8 it was $20,000. We will thus take $18,000 as a figure for *average* accounts receivable.

$$\text{accounts receivable turnover} = \frac{\$317,600}{\$18,000} = 17.6$$

This means that Scrupper is able to turn over its accounts receivable 17.6 times a year. Of course, this turnover rate has to be compared with industry standards and must be seen in the context of how aggressive Scrupper is in its attempts to collect the accounts receivable. The next ratio breaks this down into the number of days per collection period for accounts receivable.

Average Collection Period

In 19X8, Scrupper Supply Company turns its accounts receivable into cash every 20.7 days:

$$\text{average collection period} = \frac{365 \text{ days}}{\text{accounts receivable turnover}} = \frac{365}{17.6} = 20.7$$

If Scrupper's **average collection period** increases, although its credit terms have not changed, it may necessitate a greater emphasis on collecting outstanding accounts receivable.

Inventory Turnover

The **inventory turnover ratio** calculates the number of times the *inventory* turns over in one period. Usually a high inventory turnover means that the

KEY TERMS

Accounts receivable turnover ratio This ratio indicates the number of times accounts receivables are converted to cash within a given period and the effectiveness of a company's credit policy.

Acid test ratio A liquidity ratio; those assets that are most easily converted to cash are divided by current liabilities to indicate ability to pay off short-term debt. Also called **quick ratio.**

Asset management ratios Those ratios — accounts receivable turnover, average collection period, inventory turnover, and asset turnover — that measure how effectively a company uses its assets.

Asset turnover ratio This ratio indicates how efficiently a company uses its assets to generate sales and thus helps measure the overall efficiency of the company.

Average collection period This ratio shows how quickly moneys owed are received from customers and thereby measures how effectively a company collects its accounts receivables.

Common-size statements Comparative reports in which each item is expressed as a percentage of a base amount without dollar amounts.

Comparative balance sheets Current and past financial reports covering two or more successive periods that place data in single columns side by side.

Current ratio A liquidity ratio; current assets are divided by current liabilities to indicate a company's ability to pay its short-term debt. This ratio does not provide as much certainty as the acid test ratio.

Debt management ratios Those ratios — debt to total assets, debt to stockholders' equity, and times interest earned — that measure a company's mix of debt and equity financing.

Debt to stockholders' equity Total liabilities are divided by the amount of stock that is owned to measure the risk creditors run in comparison with stockholders.

Debt to total assets ratio This ratio shows how much of a company's assets are financed by creditors.

Gross profit rate A profitability ratio that indicates how well net sales cover administrative and selling expenses.

Horizontal analysis Amounts of items compared on the same line of comparative financial reports. Horizontal analysis can also be in the form of a trend analysis.

Inventory turnover ratio An asset management ratio that indicates how quickly inventory moves off the shelf and therefore how well a company sells its product.

Liquidity ratios The two ratios — current ratio and acid test ratio — that measure a company's ability to pay off short-term debts.

Profitability ratios Those ratios — gross profit rate, return on sales, return on total assets, and return on common stockholders' equity — that measure a company's ability to earn a profit.

Quick assets Those assets — mainly cash, accounts receivable, and notes receivable — that can be easily turned into money.

Ratio A relationship of two quantities or numbers, one divided by the other. See Ratio Blueprint (pp. 794–795).

Ratio analysis An examination of the relationship between two numbers or sets of numbers on financial reports. Analyses of ratios, especially over time, can give a fairly clear picture of how well a company conducts its business.

Return on common stockholders' equity A profitability ratio that indicates how well a company is managing debt financing to earn a profit for holders of common stock.

Return on sales ratio A profitability ratio that shows the relationship of net income before taxes to net sales and thereby the effectiveness of a company's pricing policy.

Return on total assets ratio A profitability ratio that measures how wisely a company has invested in and managed its assets. This can be arrived at in two ways: (1) net income before interest and taxes divided by total assets; and (2) return on sales multiplied by asset turnover.

Times interest earned ratio A debt management ratio indicating the degree of risk to lenders that a company will default on its interest payments. Also called *interest coverage ratio.*

Trend analysis A type of horizontal analysis that deals with percentage changes in items on the financial reports for several years. This analysis uses a base year to calculate the percentage change of each item.

Vertical analysis Comparing items in a financial report by expressing each item as a percentage of a certain base total.

Questions, Mini Exercises, Exercises, and Problems

Discussion Questions

1. Compare and contrast the needs of investors, creditors, and management as they relate to financial statement analysis.
2. Horizontal analysis cannot be presented on comparative financial statements. True or false? Please explain.
3. What is meant by vertical analysis?
4. Common-size statements use horizontal analysis. True or false? Please explain.
5. Why is a base year chosen in trend analysis?
6. How can ratios be expressed?
7. Explain the following types of ratios:
   a. Liquidity.
   b. Asset management.
   c. Debt management.
   d. Profitability.
8. What current asset accounts are deleted in the calculation of the acid test ratio? Why?
9. What could a low accounts receivable turnover rate indicate?
10. Stockouts could easily result if inventory is higher than it should be. True or false? Please explain.
11. What does possible liquidation have to do with the ratio of debt to total assets?
12. Rate of return on assets is affected by return on sales and asset turnover. Agree or disagree.

Mini Exercises

(The blank forms you need are on page 158 of the *Study Guide and Working Papers*.)

Horizontal Analysis Balance Sheet

1. Calculate the amount of increase or decrease as well as the percentage of increase or decrease (round to nearest tenth of a percent).

	19X8	19X7	Amount	%
a. Accounts Receivable	$600	$500		
b. Accounts Payable	400	600		

Vertical Analysis Balance Sheet

2. Complete a vertical analysis of the assets. (Round to nearest tenth of a percent as needed.)

a. Cash	$ 500
b. Accounts Receivable	600
c. Merchandise Inventory	900
d. Office Equipment	1,000
Total Assets	$3,000

(Cont. on page 796)

BLUEPRINT: RATIOS

Ratio	Formula	What Calculation Says	Key Points
1. Current ratio	$$\dfrac{\text{current assets}}{\text{current liabilities}}$$	For each $1 of current liabilities how many dollars of current assets are available to meet the current debt.	The ratio should be evaluated based on the type of business credit terms, along with the composition of the current assets.
2. Acid-test ratio	$$\dfrac{\text{current assets} - \text{merchandise inventory} - \text{prepaid expenses}}{\text{current liabilities}}$$	For each $1 of current liabilities how many dollars of cash and near-cash assets are available to meet the current debt.	Since inventory and prepaid expenses may not be easily converted into cash, they are not used in the calculation.
3. Accounts receivable turnover	$$\dfrac{\text{net credit sales}}{\text{average accounts receivable}}$$	How many times accounts receivable is collected and turned into cash.	Cash sales not included in calculation. High turnover is often the best unless the credit terms cause a reduction in sales.
4. Average collection period	$$\dfrac{365 \text{ Days}}{\text{accounts receivable turnover}}$$	The number of days that it takes a business to collect its accounts receivable.	If average collection period goes up and the credit terms remain the same, increased collection attempts should be emphasized.
5. Inventory turnover	$$\dfrac{\text{cost of goods sold}}{\text{average inventory}}$$	The time period it takes from the purchase of inventory until its sale.	High turnover indicates low amounts of inventory. Care must be taken if frequent stockouts occur.
6. Asset turnover	$$\dfrac{\text{net sales}}{\text{total assets}}$$	How effectively the company is using its assets to generate sales.	A low turnover could mean excessive investment in assets or that the sales volume is too low.
7. Debt to total assets	$$\dfrac{\text{total liabilities}}{\text{total assets}}$$	Amount of assets financed by the creditors.	Low percent, reduces creditors' risk if liquidation occurs. The higher the percentage, the more coverage a company is using.

Ratio	Formula	What Calculation Says	Key Points
8. Debt to stockholders' equity	$$\frac{\text{total liabilities}}{\text{stockholders' equity}}$$	Amount of debt in relation to total stockholders' equity.	The higher the percentage, the more interest cost result for stockholders.
9. Times interest earned	$$\frac{\text{income before taxes and interest expense}}{\text{interest expense}}$$	Degree of risk to creditors if a company defaults on interest payments.	A high times interest earned means a company can have declines in earnings but have ability to meet its annual interest obligations.
10. Gross profit rate	$$\frac{\text{gross profit}}{\text{net sales}}$$	Profit from a sales dollar that will be used to cover expenses (general, selling, etc.)	This rate could drop if stiff competition results in price cuts.
11. Return on sales	$$\frac{\text{net income before taxes}}{\text{net sales}}$$	How much a company earns on each sales dollar.	A company with a low inventory turnover rate usually prices goods with a high return on sales.
12. Rate of return on total assets	$$\frac{\text{net income before interest and taxes}}{\text{total assets}}$$	Without looking at how assets are financed, this ratio measures how productively total assets have been used.	The rate of return can be increased by controlling costs and expenses as well as increasing asset turnover.
13. Rate of return on common stock-holders' equity	$$\frac{\text{net income before taxes} - \text{preferred dividends}}{\text{common stockholders' equity}}$$	Measures company's ability to earn profits for the common stockholder.	If this rate is higher than a a return on total assets, it means the company is using financial leverage to its benefit.

Common-Size Income Statement

3. Prepare a common-size income statement from the following (use net sales as 100 percent).

Net Sales	$500
Cost of Goods Sold	300
Gross Profit from Sales	200
Operating Expenses	60
Net Income	$140

Trend Analysis

4. Complete a trend analysis from the following data of Blue Corporation using 19X5 as the base year (round to nearest percent).

	19X8	19X7	19X6	19X5
Sales	800	700	600	500
Gross Profit	600	200	500	300
Net Income	100	60	25	50

Ratios

5. From the following data calculate (round to nearest hundredth or hundredth of a percent as needed):
   a. Current Ratio
   b. Acid Test Ratio
   c. Asset Turnover Ratio
   d. Gross Profit Rate

Net Sales	$300,000
Current Assets	42,000
Gross Profit	104,000
Current Liabilities	17,000
Total Assets	149,000
Merchandise Inventory	5,000
Prepaid Expenses	3,000

Exercises

(The blank forms you need are on pages 159 and 160 of the *Study Guide and Working Papers.*)

Comparative income statement.

23-1. From the following, complete a comparative income statement for Auster Co. for December 31, 19X8 and 19X9. (Round to nearest hundredth of a percent as needed.)

	19X9	19X8
Net Sales	$70,000	$40,000
Cost of Goods Sold	30,000	20,000
Operating Expenses	17,000	12,000
Interest Expense	5,000	4,000
Net Income (loss)	18,000	4,000

Common-size income statement.

23-2. From the following, prepare a common-size income statement for Ted Co. by converting the dollar amounts into percentages (round to nearest tenth of a percent). Use net sales as 100 percent.

	19X9	19X8
Net Sales	$500,000	$400,000
Cost of Goods Sold	400,000	355,000
Gross Profit from Sales	100,000	45,000
Operating Expenses	60,000	30,000
Net Income	$ 40,000	$ 15,000

Common-size comparative balance sheet.

23-3. From the following comparative balance sheet of Hoster Co., prepare a common-size comparative balance sheet (round all percentages to nearest tenth of a percent).

December

	19X9	19X8
Current Assets	$ 90,000	$ 50,000
Plant and Equipment	450,000	310,000
Total Assets	$540,000	$360,000
Current Liabilities	$ 10,000	$ 30,000
Long-Term Liabilities	30,000	100,000
Common Stock	300,000	200,000
Retained Earnings	200,000	30,000
Total Liabilities and Stockholders' Equity	$540,000	$360,000

Trend analysis.

23-4. Complete a trend analysis from the following data of Band Corporation using 19X5 as the base year (round to nearest percent).

	19X8	19X7	19X6	19X5
Sales	$600,000	$500,000	$400,000	$300,000
Gross Profit	166,000	141,000	112,000	124,000
Net Income	48,000	41,000	22,000	38,000

Asset turnover; inventory turnover; accounts receivable turnover.

23-5. From the following income statement of Canry Co., as well as additional data compute:

a. Asset turnover for 19X7.

b. Inventory turnover for 19X7.

c. Accounts receivable turnover for 19X7.

	19X7	19X6
Net Sales	$800,000	$700,000
Cost of Goods Sold	710,000	490,000
Gross Profit	$ 90,000	$210,000
Operating Expenses (includes taxes)	70,000	160,000
Net Income	$ 20,000	$ 50,000

Additional data:

	19X7	19X6
Year-End Accounts Receivable	$ 60,000	$ 50,000
Year-End Inventory	90,000	70,000
All sales were on credit		
Total Assets	230,000	160,000

Group A Problems

(The blank forms you need are on pages 161–170 of the *Study Guide and Working Papers.*)

Horizontal and vertical analysis of a balance sheet.

23A-1. From the following comparative balance sheet of Hesler Corporation: (a) prepare a horizontal analysis of each item for the amount of increase or decrease as well as the percent increase or decrease (to nearest tenth of a percent), (b) vertically analyze the 19X8 column of the balance sheet (to nearest tenth of a percent).

Check Figure:
Cash increase   5.4%

HESLER CORPORATION
COMPARATIVE BALANCE SHEET
DECEMBER 31, 19X8 AND DECEMBER 31, 19X7

	December 31	
Assets	19X8	19X7
Current Assets:		
Cash	$ 3 9 0 0 00	$ 3 7 0 0 00
Accounts Receivable, Net	28 0 0 0 00	16 1 0 0 00
Merchandise Inventory	47 0 0 0 00	15 0 0 0 00
Prepaid Expenses	1 6 0 0 00	1 3 0 0 00
Total Current Assets	$ 80 5 0 0 00	$ 36 1 0 0 00
Plant and Equipment:		
Office Equipment, Net	$115 0 0 0 00	$110 0 0 0 00
Total Assets	$195 5 0 0 00	$146 1 0 0 00
Liabilities		
Current Liabilities:		
Notes Payable	$ 20 0 0 0 00	$ 26 0 0 0 00
Accounts Payable	21 2 0 0 00	24 0 0 0 00
Total Current Liabilities	$ 41 2 0 0 00	$ 50 0 0 0 00
Long-Term Liabilities:		
Mortgage Payable	$ 50 0 0 0 00	$ 40 0 0 0 00
Total Liabilities	91 2 0 0 00	90 0 0 0 00
Stockholders' Equity		
Common Stock, $10 par value	$ 50 0 0 0 00	$ 30 0 0 0 00
Retained Earnings	54 3 0 0 00	26 1 0 0 00
Total Stockholders' Equity	$104 3 0 0 00	$ 56 1 0 0 00
Total Liabilities and Stockholders' Equity	$195 5 0 0 00	$146 1 0 0 00

Horizontal, vertical, and
common-size preparation
of an income statement.

Check Figure:
Cost of goods sold increase
15.9%

23A-2. From the comparative income statement of Oper Co. prepare:

a. A horizontal analysis with the amount of increase or decrease during 19X8 along with the percent increase or decrease during 19X7 (to nearest tenth of a percent).

b. A vertical analysis of the 19X8 column of the income statement (to nearest tenth of a percent).

c. A common-size comparative income statement (to nearest tenth of a percent).

OPER COMPANY
COMPARATIVE INCOME STATEMENT
FOR YEARS ENDED DECEMBER 31, 19X8 AND 19X7

	Years Ended December 31	
	19X8	19X7
Net Sales	$288 000 00	$275 000 00
Cost of Goods Sold	197 000 00	170 000 00
Gross Profit from Sales	$ 91 000 00	$105 000 00
Operating Expenses:		
Selling	$ 50 000 00	$ 51 000 00
General and Administrative	21 000 00	23 000 00
Total Operating Expenses	$ 71 000 00	$ 74 000 00
Operating Income	$ 20 000 00	$ 31 000 00
Less Interest Expense	6 000 00	8 000 00
Income before Taxes	14 000 00	23 000 00
Income Taxes	5 600 00	9 200 00
Net Income	$ 8 400 00	$ 13 800 00

23A-3. From the accompanying income statement and balance sheet of Austin Company compute for 19X8: (a) current ratio, (b) acid test ratio, (c) accounts receivable turnover, (d) average collection period, (e) inventory turnover, (f) asset turnover, (g) debt to total assets, (h) debt to stockholders' equity, (i) times interest earned, (j) gross profit rate, (k) return on sales, (l) return on total assets, and (m) return on common stockholders' equity.

Check Figure:
Current ratio   2.22

	Years Ended December 31	
	19X8	19X7
Net Sales	$430 000 00	$376 000 00
Cost of Goods Sold	238 000 00	221 000 00
Gross Profit from Sales	$192 000 00	$155 000 00
Operating Expenses:		
Selling	$ 1204 000 00	$110 000 00
General and Administrative	21 600 00	22 400 00
Total Operating Expenses	$142 000 00	$132 400 00
Operating Income	$ 50 000 00	$ 226 000 00
Less Interest Expense	8 200 00	8 600 00
Income before Taxes	$ 418 000 00	$ 14 000 00
Income Taxes	12 540 00	5 600 00
Net Income	$ 29 260 00	$ 84 000 00

AUSTIN COMPANY
COMPARATIVE INCOME STATEMENT
FOR YEARS ENDED DECEMBER 31, 19X8 AND 19X7

AUSTIN COMPANY
COMPARATIVE BALANCE SHEET
DECEMBER 31, 19X8 AND DECEMBER 31, 19X7

Assets	December 31 19X8	December 31 19X7
Current Assets:		
Cash	$ 11 000 00	$ 24 400 00
Accounts Receivable, Net	416 00 00	362 00 00
Merchandise Inventory	612 00 00	624 00 00
Prepaid Expenses	56 00 00	32 00 00
Total Current Assets	$1194 00 00	$1262 00 00
Plant and Equipment:		
Office Equipment, Net	$ 656 00 00	$63 00 00
Total Assets	$185 000 00	$189 200 00
Liabilities		
Current Liabilities:		
Notes Payable	$ 368 00 00	$ 352 00 00
Accounts Payable	170 00 00	158 00 00
Total Current Liabilities	$ 538 00 00	$ 510 00 00
Long-Term Liabilities:		
Mortgage Payable	$ 396 00 00	$ 300 00 00
Total Liabilities	$ 934 00 00	$ 810 00 00
Stockholders' Equity		
Common Stock, $10 par value	$ 560 00 00	$510 00 00
Retained Earnings	356 00 00	572 00 00
Total Stockholders' Equity	$ 916 00 00	$1082 00 00
Total Liabilities and Stockholders' Equity	$185 000 00	$189 200 00

23A-4. From the accompanying information about Vargo Corporation:

   a. Calculate for each year its current ratio and acid test ratio.

   b. Prepare for each year the income statement in common-size percentages (round to nearest tenth of percent).

   c. Prepare a trend analysis of the balance sheet using 19X6 as the base year (round to nearest percent).

VARGO CORPORATION
COMPARATIVE INCOME STATEMENT
FOR YEARS ENDED DECEMBER 31, 19X8, 19X7, 19X6

	19X8	19X7	19X6
Net Sales	$ 320000	$ 280000	$ 244000
Cost of Goods Sold	234500	196000	172000
Gross Profit from Sales	$ 85500	$ 84000	$ 72000
Operating Expenses:			
Selling	$ 46000	$ 48200	$ 34560
General and Administrative	24000	22800	24820
Total Operating Expenses	$ 70000	$ 71000	$ 59380
Operating Income before Taxes	$ 15500	$ 13000	$ 12620
Income Taxes	6200	5200	5040
Net Income	$ 9300	$ 7800	$ 7580

VARGO CORPORATION
COMPARATIVE BALANCE SHEET
FOR YEARS ENDED DECEMBER 31, 19X8, 19X7, 19X6

Assets	19X8	19X7	19X6
Current Assets*	$ 20460	$ 17820	$ 28420
Plant and Equipment	100000	90000	84000
Total Assets	$ 120460	$ 107820	$ 112420
Liabilities and Stockholder's Equity			
Current Liabilities	$ 10000	$ 9600	$ 9200
Common Stock	70000	62000	64000
Retained Earnings	40460	36220	39220
Total Liabilities and Stockholders' Equity	$ 120460	$ 107820	$ 112420

* 19X8 Inventory, $484; 19X7, $310; 19X6, $600.

Group B Problems

(The blank forms you need are on pages 161–170 of the *Study Guide and Working Papers.*)

Horizontal analysis, vertical analysis, and common-size preparation of a balance sheet.

Check Figure:
Cash   3.3%

23B-1. From the following comparative balance sheet of Hesler Corporation:
  a. Prepare a horizontal analysis of each item for the amount of increase or decrease as well as the percent increase or decrease (to nearest tenth of a percent).
  b. Vertically analyze the 19X8 column of the balance sheet (to the nearest tenth of a percent).

			HESLER CORPORATION COMPARATIVE BALANCE SHEET DECEMBER 31, 19X8 AND DECEMBER 31, 19X7		
			December 31		
Assets			19X8	19X7	
Current Assets:					
Cash			$ 16 5 0 0 00	$ 12 3 0 0 00	
Accounts Receivable, Net			5 25 0 0 00	4 4 7 0 0 00	
Merchandise Inventory			6 60 0 0 00	7 8 0 0 0 00	
Prepaid Expenses			9 30 0 0 00	5 7 0 0 00	
Total Current Assets			$14 43 0 0 00	$140 7 0 0 00	
Plant and Equipment:					
Office Equipment, Net			$35 16 0 0 00	$330 0 0 0 00	
Total Assets			$495 9 0 0 00	$470 7 0 0 00	
Liabilities					
Current Liabilities:					
Notes Payable			$ 72 0 0 0 00	$ 54 0 0 0 00	
Accounts Payable			45 0 0 0 00	28 5 0 0 00	
Total Current Liabilities			$117 0 0 0 00	$ 82 5 0 0 00	
Stockholders' Equity					
Common Stock, $10 par value			$300 0 0 0 00	$300 0 0 0 00	
Retained Earnings			78 9 0 0 00	88 2 0 0 00	
Total Stockholders' Equity			$378 9 0 0 00	$388 2 0 0 00	
Total Liabilities and Stockholders' Equity			$495 9 0 0 00	$470 7 0 0 00	

Horizontal analysis, vertical analysis, and common-size preparation of an income statement.

23B-2. From the accompanying comparative income statement of Oper Company (p. 804):
  a. Prepare a horizontal analysis with the amount of increase or decrease during 19X8 along with the percent increase or decrease during 19X7 (to nearest tenth of a percent).

b. Vertically analyze the 19X8 column of the income statement (to nearest tenth of a percent).

c. Prepare a common-size comparative income statement (to nearest tenth of a percent).

Check Figure:

19X8   Net sales increase   38%

OPER COMPANY COMPARATIVE INCOME STATEMENT FOR YEARS ENDED DECEMBER 31, 19X8 AND 19X7	Year Ended December 31	
	19X8	19X7
Net Sales	$ 12 25 0 00	$ 8 88 0 00
Cost of Goods Sold	6 05 0 00	4 24 0 00
Gross Profit from Sales	$ 6 20 0 00	$ 4 64 0 00
Operating Expenses:		
Selling	$ 2 70 0 00	$ 1 92 0 00
General and Administrative	1 05 0 00	9 60 00
Total Operating Expenses	$ 3 75 0 00	$ 2 88 0 00
Operating Income	$ 2 45 0 00	$ 1 76 0 00
Less Interest Expense	2 25 00	2 20 00
Income before Taxes	$ 2 22 5 00	$ 1 54 0 00
Income Taxes	8 90 00	6 16 00
Net Income	$ 1 33 5 00	$ 9 24 00

Calculating ratios from financial reports.

Check Figure:

Current ratio   2.12

23B-3. From the income statement and balance sheet of Austin Company, compute for 19X8: (a) current ratio, (b) acid test ratio, (c) accounts receivable turnover, (d) average collection period, (e) inventory turnover, (f) asset turnover, (g) debt to total assets, (h) debt to stockholders' equity, (i) times interest earned, (j) gross profit rate, (k) return on sales, (l) return on total assets, and (m) return on stockholders' equity.

AUSTIN COMPANY COMPARATIVE INCOME STATEMENT FOR YEARS ENDED DECEMBER 31, 19X8 AND 19X7	Years Ended December 31	
	19X8	19X7
Net Sales	$ 99 00 0 00	$ 89 25 0 00
Cost of Goods Sold	50 50 0 00	55 00 0 00
Gross Profit from Sales	$ 48 50 0 00	$ 34 25 0 00
Operating Expenses:		
Selling	$ 27 05 0 00	$ 25 90 0 00
General and Administrative	3 55 0 00	4 00 0 00
Total Operating Expenses	$ 30 60 0 00	$ 29 90 0 00
Operating Income	$ 17 90 0 00	$ 4 35 0 00
Less Interest Expense	4 55 0 00	2 25 0 00
Income before Taxes	$ 13 35 0 00	$ 2 10 0 00
Income Taxes	5 34 0 00	8 40 00
Net Income	$ 8 01 0 00	$ 1 26 0 00

AUSTIN COMPANY
COMPARATIVE BALANCE SHEET
DECEMBER 31, 19X8 AND DECEMBER 31, 19X7

	December 31	
Assets	19X8	19X7
Current Assets:		
Cash	$ 3 400 00	$ 5 400 00
Accounts Receivable, Net	9 750 00	8 700 00
Merchandise Inventory	14 500 00	14 900 00
Prepaid Expenses	1 200 00	850 00
Total Current Assets	$ 28 850 00	$29 850 00
Plant and Equipment:		
Office Equipment, Net	$ 14 900 00	$ 11 000 00
Total Assets	$ 43 750 00	$40 850 00
Liabilities		
Current Liabilities:		
	$ 9 750 00	$ 9 050 00
Notes Payable	3 850 00	3 400 00
Accounts Payable	$ 13 600 00	$12 450 00
Total Current Liabilities		
Long-Term Liabilities:		
Mortgage Payable	$ 10 000 00	$ 7 500 00
Total Liabilities	$ 23 600 00	$19 950 00
Stockholders' Equity		
Common Stock, $10 par value	$ 14 050 00	$12 000 00
Retained Earnings	6 100 00	8 900 00
Total Stockholders' Equity	$ 20 150 00	$20 900 00
Total Liabilities and Stockholders' Equity	$ 43 750 00	$40 850 00

23B-4. From the following information about Vargo Corporation:

a. For each year, calculate its current and acid test ratios.

b. Prepare the income statement in common-size percentages (round to nearest tenth of a percent).

c. Prepare a trend analysis of the balance sheet using 19X6 as the base year (round to nearest percent).

VARGO CORPORATION COMPARATIVE INCOME STATEMENT FOR YEARS ENDED DECEMBER 31, 19X8, 19X7, 19X6,			
	19X8	19X7	19X6
Net Sales	$ 55 50 0 00	$ 50 40 0 00	$ 38 70 0 00
Cost of Goods Sold	40 20 0 00	37 20 0 00	23 70 0 00
Gross Profit from Sales	$ 15 30 0 00	$ 13 20 0 00	$ 15 00 0 00
Operating Expenses:			
Selling	$ 7 20 0 00	$ 4 80 0 00	$ 5 40 0 00
General and Administrative	5 70 0 00	2 73 0 00	3 75 0 00
Total Operating Expenses	$ 12 90 0 00	$ 7 53 0 00	$ 9 15 0 00
Operating Income before Taxes	2 40 0 00	5 67 0 00	5 85 0 00
Income Taxes	96 0 00	2 26 8 00	2 34 0 00
Net Income	$ 1 44 0 00	$ 3 40 2 00	$ 3 51 0 00

VARGO CORPORATION COMPARATIVE BALANCE SHEET DECEMBER 31, 19X8, 19X7 AND 19X6			
Assets	19X8	19X7	19X6
Current Assets*	$ 6 72 0 00	$ 5 55 0 00	$ 4 95 0 00
Plant and Equipment	18 00 0 00	12 00 0 00	10 50 0 00
Total Assets	$ 24 72 0 00	$ 17 55 0 00	$ 15 45 0 00
Liabilities and Stockholders' Equity			
Current Liabilities	$ 2 40 0 00	$ 1 80 0 00	$ 1 56 0 00
Common Stock	11 70 0 00	10 80 0 00	7 50 0 00
Retained Earnings	10 62 0 00	4 95 0 00	6 39 0 00
Total Liabilities and Stockholder's Equity	$ 24 72 0 00	$ 17 55 0 00	$ 15 45 0 00

* Inventory: 19X8, $1,350; 19X7, $1,800; 19X6, $1,200.

REAL WORLD APPLICATIONS

23R-1.

You have been hired as a consultant to determine which of the two following companies is in overall better shape. From the accompanying information, prepare a schedule of ratio calculations that can be derived from the facts along with your recommendations. Both companies are in the same industry.

	Joyne Co.	Smokey Co.
Cash	$ 17,000	$ 28,000
Accounts Receivable, Net	18,000	55,000
Inventory	80,000	96,000
Plant and Equipment, Net	90,000	170,000
	$205,000	$349,000
Current Liabilities	$ 58,000	$ 89,000
Mortgage Payable	40,000	60,000
Common Stock	79,000	175,000
Retained Earnings	28,000	25,000
	$205,000	$349,000
Sales (all credit)	$230,000	$380,000
Cost of Goods Sold	160,000	275,000
Interest Expense	8,000	12,000
Income Taxes	10,000	16,000
Net Income	24,000	40,000

23R-2.

The bookkeeper of Blue Co. is trying to determine (a) amount of average inventory, (b) accounts receivable average balance, (c) balance of cash from the following information:

Prepaid Rent	$ 16,000
Accounts Receivable Turnover	9 times
Cost of Goods Sold	$270,000
Inventory Turnover	27
Current Liabilities	$ 90,000
Credit Sales	$270,000

Her assistant believes there is not enough information available to complete the calculations. Accept or reject the assistant's remarks. Please provide a written response.

make the call

Critical Thinking/Ethical Case

23R-3.

Jill Land, President of Loon Co., is happy to report to the company's stockholders that the company has increased its cash position by 20 percent from last year. Their average collection period has decreased by 12 days. Jill knows some customers are unhappy about the new credit terms, but believes that you cannot please everyone — that's business. Do you think Loon Co. is on the right track? One shareholder is quite upset to learn that the company is holding so much cash. Do you agree with the company's belief that increasing the cash position by 20 percent is sound? You make the call. Write down your recommendation to Jill.

ACCOUNTING RECALL
A CUMULATIVE APPROACH

THIS EXAM REVIEWS CHAPTERS 1 THROUGH 23

Your *Study Guide and Working Papers* has forms (p. 175) to complete this exam, as well as worked-out solutions. The page references next to each question identify what page to turn back to if you answer the question incorrectly.

PART 1   Vocabulary Review

Match the terms to the appropriate definition or phrase.

Page Ref.

(781)	1. Horizontal analysis	A. No dollar amounts
(784)	2. Quick assets	B. Asset management ratio
(787)	3. Profitability ratio	C. CA − CL
(667)	4. Retained earnings	D. Uses a base year
(782)	5. Trend analysis	E. Return on sales
(702)	6. Treasury stock	F. Items comparison on same line as comparative reports
(785)	7. Inventory turnover	
(784)	8. Current ratio	G. Credit balance
(778)	9. Common-size statement	H. Cash, accounts receivable
(784)	10. Liquidity ratios	I. Contra-stockholder equity
		J. Ability to pay short-term debts

PART II   True or False (Accounting Theory)

(775)   11. Vertical and Horizontal analysis can only be used to analyze Balance Sheets.

(784)   12. Liquidity ratios measure the ability to meet long-term obligations.

(784)   13. Merchandise inventory and prepaid expenses are not included in calculating the acid-test ratio.

(784)   14. The gross profit rate indicates how well net sales cover administrative and selling expenses.

(784)   15. Industry standards are never used in ratio analysis.

24

THE VOUCHER SYSTEM

THE BIG PICTURE

When Tony Freedman began the Eldorado Computer Center, he had done all the work himself, including marketing and accounting. As the business grew, he'd hired two hourly employees and eventually a bookkeeper, acquired a partner, and then hired three additional full-time employees.

Lately the business had been receiving phone calls from several creditors notifying Eldorado that they were past due on their payments. Neither Freedman nor Charles West could understand this, so they met with their bookkeepers at each location. They discovered that the system used to track inventory and payment to the suppliers was not sufficient. Although cash was plentiful, their company rarely took advantage of any cash discounts. They also discovered that invoices were not paid on time because they were misplaced or lost. They decided, as a result, to implement a new measure of internal control by starting a voucher system and hiring Summer Lipe, a new staff accountant.

In this chapter you will learn how to prepare vouchers, record them in a voucher register, and take advantage of your discounts when paying your invoices.

◆ **Preparing vouchers, recording them in a voucher register, and recording payment of vouchers in a check register. (p. 811)**
◆ **Recording revised vouchers to handle nonroutine transactions in a voucher system. (p. 816)**
◆ **Using the net amount method to record invoices and payment. (p. 817)**

In small companies owners may be able to do or look at every step of their business themselves. But as such companies grow larger, and as the sheer number of business transactions multiplies, this becomes impossible. How, then, do owners or managers keep control over the activities of a company? If they don't sign every check themselves or approve every purchase themselves, how do they know if money is being spent in approved ways, or where it's going? Some rules have to be formulated for employees in order to impose order—such rules and procedures are referred to as *internal control,* and one type of system used to implement this internal control is called a *voucher system.*

In Chapter 10 we discussed the steps taken when a company purchases goods. You might take a moment to look back at those pages (pp. 357–359), because we will use these steps in this chapter to explain how a voucher system works. The steps include:

1. Preparing a purchase requisition — and getting it authorized.
2. Preparing a purchase order, which specifies details such as company, number of items, etc. — and getting it authorized.
3. Company receiving the purchase order prepares a sales invoice specifying number and type of goods and price.
4. Company receiving the goods inspects the shipment, checks it against the purchase order and the sales invoice, and completes a receiving report.
5. Someone in the accounting department verifies the numbers — checks the purchase order, the invoice, and the receiving report to make sure the numbers are in agreement and no steps are left out. This person then issues a voucher for payment, which is authorized.
6. Payment is issued in the form of a check.

These steps show internal control, in the form of a voucher system, at work. Other procedures that we have discussed in other chapters of this text also are part of internal control, including banking procedures and petty cash and change funds.

What is a voucher? A **voucher** (see the sample shown in Figure 24-3, p. 813) is a written authorization form that is used for every cash payment the company makes. It contains all the details of the transaction in question along with the signatures of appropriate employees as authorization. A **voucher system,** then, is a system in which no payment is made without an approved voucher.

CHARACTERISTICS OF A VOUCHER SYSTEM

A number of principles of internal control are embedded in the voucher system. Perhaps the most important is the separation of duties. In a voucher system, no one person in a company is in control of all transactions or of everything to do with one transaction. The person who approves purchase and payment is different from the person who makes the accounting entries related to these functions, and that person is different from the person who signs and mails the checks. In this way no one can do anything without other people supplying approval.

A second important principle, perhaps the backbone of a voucher system, is the rule that no purchases are made without an approved voucher backed up by documentation. There are several layers of documentation and authorization here, beginning with a purchase requisition, moving on to a purchase order, and ending up with actual payment by a check. At every layer and step the appropriate documents are presented, checked, and approved before going further.

There is a lot of cross-referencing and cross-checking in a voucher system. Every document is numbered; transactions are recorded in different places by different people and backed up by reference to numbers of other documents. In this way it is always possible to trace one transaction all the way through the system. After a purchase is made and paid for, the documents and forms are kept on file for a certain period of time to allow such checks to be made.

In the next two learning units we will show how a voucher system works in a specific company, and then how certain transactions are handled that don't fit into the voucher system. The specific company we will use is Jones Company.

LEARNING UNIT 24-1
Handling Transactions in a Voucher System

Jones Company is a medium-sized merchandise business that believes in strong internal control practices and procedures. It uses the voucher system to control all cash payments except payments out of the petty cash fund. Company rules state that all invoices must be compared with purchase requisitions, purchase orders, and receiving reports before payment; and all payments must, of course, be supported by appropriate documents and authorizations.

Jones Company's voucher system is made up of the following elements:

1. Vouchers.
2. Voucher register.
3. Unpaid voucher file.
4. Check register.
5. Paid voucher file.

To see this system in action, we will follow one transaction all the way through. To begin with, Jones Company decides to buy $4,500 worth of merchandise from Beam Enterprise. The purchase order is shown in Figure 24-1 (p. 812). When the merchandise is received, along with an invoice (Figure 24-2), a special serially numbered form called a voucher is prepared (Figure 24-3, p. 813).

THE VOUCHER

In preparing the voucher, the invoice from Beam Enterprise is compared with the purchase requisition, purchase order, and receiving report to be sure that it matches the specific requirements and prices of the order. For example, the information in Figure 24-1, the purchase order, does indeed match the information on the invoice shown in Figure 24-2. The original supporting documents (purchase orders, etc.) are attached to the voucher. Note that there is a front

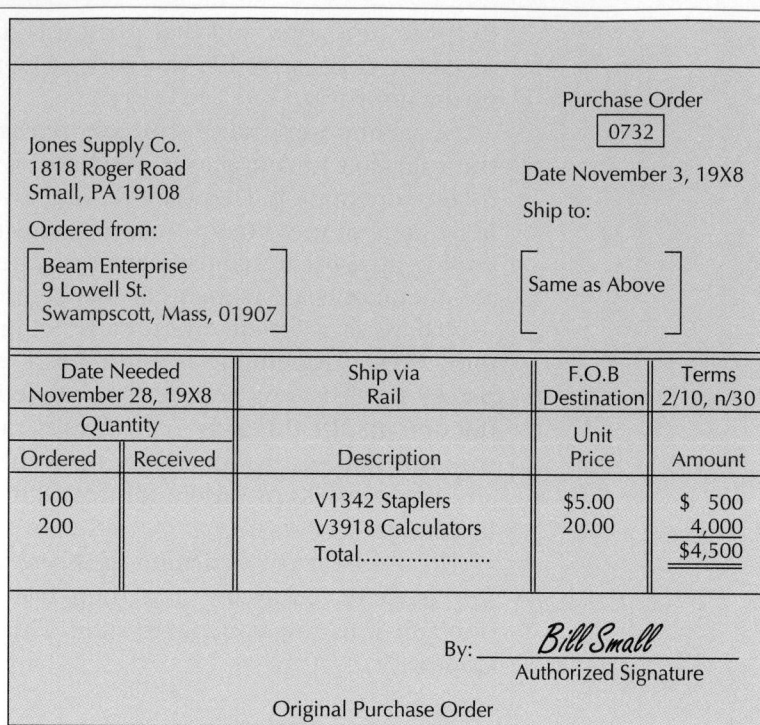

FIGURE 24-1
Purchase Order

and back side to the voucher. The front side indicates the voucher number, invoice number and date, purchase order number, to whom amount will be paid, and verification steps. For Jones Company, all supporting documents are attached to the front of the voucher and folded. The back side shows the account distribution along with space to complete the payment summary and final approvals as needed.

FIGURE 24-2
Invoice

Invoice
Invoice Number: B20
Date: November 28, 19X8

Beam Enterprise
9 Lowell St.
Swampscott, Mass, 01907

Sold to: Jones Supply Co.
1818 Roger Road
Small, PA 19108

Ship to: Same

Your Purchase Order Number 0732	Invoice Number B20	Salesman Munroe	Terms 2/10, n/30	Shipped via: Rail (PPD) F.O.B. Destination
Quantity			Unit Price	Amount
Ordered	Received	Description		
100	100	V1342 Staplers	$5.00	$ 500
200	200	V3918 Calculators	20.00	4,000
		Total......................		$4,500

Original Invoice

FIGURE 24-3
Voucher, front

FIGURE 24-3 (cont.)
Voucher, back

THE VOUCHER REGISTER

Using the approved account distributions, the voucher is recorded in a special journal called the **voucher register** (Figure 24-4, p. 814). This journal replaces the purchases journal. Note that the vouchers are entered in the voucher register in numerical order at the time the liability is *incurred*. For Jones, the **Vouchers Payable** credit column records the amount due on each voucher

FIGURE 24-4 Voucher Register

VOUCHER REGISTER

Date	Voucher Number	Payable to	Date of Payment	Check Number	Voucher Payable Cr.	Purchases Dr.	Supplies Dr.	Repair Expense Dr.	Account	PR	Sundry Accounts Dr.	Cr.
19X8 Dec.												
2	22	Petty Cash	12/4	53	5000				Petty Cash	114	5000	
3	23	Beam Enterprise	12/5	55	450000	450000						
3	24	Ron Co.	12/4	54	42500		42500					
7	25	Rose Co.	12/9	56	2800			2800				
9	26	Blew Co.	12/30	67	100000				Equip.	121	100000	
15	27	Security Bank	12/27	58	515000				Note Payable	211	500000	
									Int. Exp.	531	15000	
28	42	Internal Revenue Service	12/28	65	90000				FICA Tax* Payable	212	25000	
									FIT Tax Payable	216	65000	
9	43	Payroll	12/29	66	400000				Salary and Wages Payable	210	400000	
					2066500	795000	60000	101500			1110000	
					(212)	(513)	(116)	(562)			(X)	

* Includes Medicare and Social Security

(before any discounts) for purchases of merchandise, services, or other assets. Special debit columns have been set up for Jones's accountant based on how often they're used. The sundry column, as in other special journals, records amounts that do not have special columns set up. The posting rules are the same as we covered in the past for special journals. Keep in mind that the columns for date of payment and check number are *not* filled in until *time of payment.*

When a balance sheet is prepared, the term "Accounts Payable" is used instead of Vouchers Payable, because users of financial reports are more used to the term "Accounts Payable."

UNPAID FILE VOUCHER

The voucher remains in the unpaid file until paid.

Each voucher, once it has been recorded in the voucher register, is filed in an **unpaid voucher file** according to due date. This is often referred to as a **tickler file.** Although the amount owed Beam is $4,500, there is a $90 cash discount available if Beam receives payment by December 8, 19X8. Thus the voucher is filed on a *December 5 due date,* anticipating that it will take three days in the mail for Beam to receive it.

In the voucher system, the accounts payable ledger is not used — for Jones, the unpaid file is its subsidiary ledger for the controlling account Vouchers Payable in the general ledger. At the end of the month Jones Company will prepare a schedule of vouchers payable, just as we discussed in Chapter 7 for the schedule of accounts payable, with the total of all unpaid vouchers being equal to the ending balance in Vouchers Payable in the general ledger.

Payment requires notation in three places:

1. Check register.
2. Voucher register payment column.
3. Back of voucher.

CHECK REGISTER

On December 5, Jones Company records the payment to Beam in a special journal called a **check register.** The check register replaces the cash payments journal in recording the payment of vouchers payable. Note in Figure 24-5 that the

FIGURE 24-5 Check Register

		Check Number	Payable to	Voucher Number	Vouchers Payable Dr.	Purchases Discount Cr.	Cash in Bank Cr.	Bank Deposits	Bank Bal.
	Date								
19X8 Dec.	1	52	Broom Co.	21	460 00		460 00		1 200 00
									740 00
	2	53	Moore Co.	22	600 00	12 00	588 00	400 00	552 00
	4	54	Ron Co.	24	425 00		425 00	1000 00	1 127 00
	5	55	Beam Ent.	23	4500 00	90 00	4410 00	400 00	717 00
	28	65	Internal Revenue	42	900 00		900 00		820 00
	29	66	Payroll	43	400 00		400 00		420 00
					(212)	(514)	(111)		

Vouchers Payable account is debited for $4,500, while Purchases Discount is credited for $90 and Cash in Bank for $4,410. The date of payment along with check number is updated in the voucher register. Posting of the check register follows the same rules as other special journals. (*Note:* Once the voucher has been paid, it should be marked "Paid" so as to avoid duplication of payments.)

PAID VOUCHER FILE

After Beam's voucher is paid, it is filed by Jones in a **paid voucher file.** The voucher is filed in sequential order according to the voucher numbers. Some companies will file the voucher alphabetically based on the creditor's name. Jones keeps all paid vouchers for six years. This amount of time will vary from company to company.

LEARNING UNIT 24-1 REVIEW

AT THIS POINT you should be able to

◆ List and define the components of a voucher system. (p. 811)
◆ Explain the steps to record and pay a voucher. (p. 814)
◆ Discuss why the unpaid file voucher is recorded by due dates. (p. 815)

SELF-REVIEW QUIZ 24-1

(The blank forms you need are on page 177 of the *Study Guide and Working Papers*.)

True or false:

1. All companies use the same voucher system.
2. Supporting documents are attached to a voucher.
3. The account distribution is used to record the voucher in the voucher register.
4. Vouchers are recorded in the voucher register in alphabetical order.
5. A schedule of vouchers payable can be prepared from the unpaid voucher file at end of month.

Solution to Self-Review Quiz 24-1

1. F   **2.** T   **3.** T   **4.** F   **5.** T

LEARNING UNIT 24-2
Recording Additional Transactions in Jones's Voucher System

Situation 1: Purchases Returns and Allowances After Voucher Has Been Recorded

On December 26, Jones Company prepared voucher no. 32 for merchandise that was bought from Booth Company for $400. The accountant records the voucher in the voucher register as a debit to Purchases and a credit to Vouchers Payable for $400. On December 28, $100 of the merchandise is found to be defective and is returned to Booth Company. The procedure that Jones Company uses is to cancel the original voucher and prepare a new voucher for $300. Figure 24-6 (p. 818) shows how Jones Company records the cancellation of voucher 32 and the recording of the revised voucher no. 39. The end result is a debit to purchases of $400, a credit of $300 to Vouchers Payable, and a credit to Purchases Returns and Allowances of $100. Another way of handling this is to modify the original voucher and make a *general journal* entry that debits Vouchers Payable $100 and credits Purchases Returns and Allowances $100.

Situation 2: Partial Payments Planned After Voucher Prepared for Full Amount

On January 18, voucher no. 64 was prepared by Jones Company on the assumption that they would pay Ron Co. $15,000 for office equipment in one payment. The top section of Figure 24-7 (p. 818) shows a debit to Office Equipment and a credit to Vouchers Payable for $15,000.

Owing to a cash shortage, on January 29 it was decided by Jones Company to pay Ron Company in three equal installments on February 8, 19, and 21. Thus the original voucher on January 18 is canceled and a *new* voucher is prepared for each installment. Note in Figure 24-7 how the old voucher is canceled and the new vouchers are prepared. In the date of payment column, the January 18 line shows the cancellation along with the new date recording the new voucher (1/29). The check number column indicates which new vouchers are replacing the canceled voucher. Note in the sundry column how Vouchers Payable is debited three times to cancel the original voucher.

RECORDING PURCHASES AT NET AMOUNT

The net approach means that a Purchases Discount account is not needed.

In this chapter Jones Company recorded all invoices at the gross amount, although the check register did show a Purchases Discount column. Many companies, on the other hand, record purchases at net. When a discount is missed using the net approach, a title called Discount Lost is shown in the payment column of the voucher register.

Let's look at journal entries showing the same purchase recorded at gross and at net.

(A) Mill Company Buys merchandise on account from Ryan Company for $8,000. Terms are 2/10, n/30. Mill Company issues voucher no. 299.

	Gross			Net		
(A) Purchases	8,000		(A) Purchases	7,840		
Vouchers Payable		8,000	Vouchers Payable		7,840	

Both would be recorded in
voucher register

If Discount Is Taken on Time

(B) Mill Company issues check no. 531 in payment of voucher no. 299 less the cash discount.

VOUCHER REGISTER

Date	Voucher Number	Payable to	Date of Payment	Check Number	Voucher Payable Cr.	Purchases Dr.	Account	PR	Sundry Accounts Dr.	Cr.
Dec.	32	Booth Co.	Cancelled Voucher	See No. 39	40000	40000				
28	39	Booth Co.			30000		Voucher Payable	212	40000	
							Purchases Returns and Allowances	515		10000

FIGURE 24-6 Voucher Register with Purchases, Returns, and Allowances

VOUCHER REGISTER

Date	Voucher Number	Payable to	Date of Payment	Check Number	Vouchers Payable Cr.	Account	PR	Sundry Accounts Dr.	Cr.
Jan. 18	64	Ron Co.	Cancelled 1/29	V69-71	150000	Office Equip.	121	150000	
29	69	Ron Co.			500000	Vouchers Payable	212	500000	
29	70	Ron Co.			500000	Vouchers Payable	212	500000	
29	71	Ron Co.			500000	Vouchers Payable	212	500000	

FIGURE 24-7 Voucher Register with Partial Payments

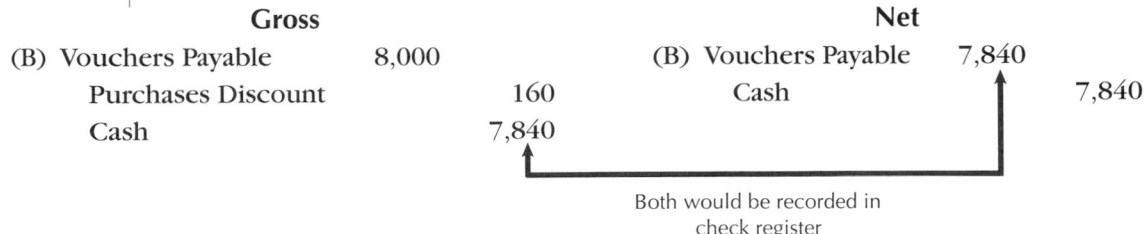

	Gross				Net	
(B) Vouchers Payable	8,000			(B) Vouchers Payable	7,840	
Purchases Discount		160		Cash		7,840
Cash		7,840				

Both would be recorded in
check register

If Discount Is Missed

(C) Mill Company issues check no. 531 in payment of voucher no. 299. Discount date has passed.

	Gross				Net	
(C) Vouchers Payable	8,000			(C) Vouchers Payable	7,840	
Cash		8,000		Discount Lost	160	
				Cash		8,000

Note that when the discount is missed in the net method, the Purchases Discount Loss account is used. (The end-of-chapter problems and exercises record all vouchers at gross unless otherwise stated.)

LEARNING UNIT 24-2 REVIEW

AT THIS POINT you should be able to

◆ Record transactions in a voucher system involving purchases returns and allowances and/or partial payments. (p. 816)
◆ Explain how the Discount Lost account could be used in a voucher system. (p. 819)

SELF-REVIEW QUIZ 24-2

(The blank forms you need are on page 178 of the *Study Guide and Working Papers.*)

Record the following entries in the voucher register for Joe Corporation.

19X8
Oct. 10 Prepared voucher no. 82 for purchase of merchandise for $3,000 from Rose Co.

Oct. 15 Returned $400 of the merchandise purchased from Rose Co. on October 10 due to poor workmanship. Joe Corp. canceled voucher no. 82 and replaced it with voucher no. 95.

DEPARTMENTAL ACCOUNTING

25

THE BIG PICTURE

During Freedman and West's meeting with the Eldorado Computer Center's outside accountant, he suggested that the company departmentalize its financial reports. Although Freedman and West do not operate a retail store with many departments and lines of merchandise, they do have three separate aspects of the business. The one thing they have not measured is how each department in the business is doing and whether each is truly profitable.

Tracking purchases, sales, and operating expenses by department allows managers to see what segments of the business are succeeding. This is the only way the company can control expenses and determine which departments need to be improved or eliminated.

◆ Preparing income statements focusing on gross profit by departments. (p. 831)
◆ Preparing income statements focusing on departmental net income. (p. 834)
◆ Preparing income statements focusing on departmental contribution margin. (p. 838)

Many large companies find it necessary to keep separate accounting records for its various departments so that management can see how efficient each department is and how each contributes to the overall performance of the company. This chapter focuses on various accounting and reporting aids that allow management to do this.

We will use as our example Catlin's Department Store, which sells mainly clothing. The manager of the Adult Clothes Department at the store is quite concerned about the department's performance — there has been talk by upper management of the possibility of reducing the space of the Adult Department in favor of expanding the Children's Department.

LEARNING UNIT 25-1

The Income Statement: Focus on Gross Profit by Department

Each department of Catlin's Department Store is a unit in which the manager has the responsibility for controlling and incurring certain costs as well as generating revenue. Each unit, or department, is known as a **profit center.** If a manager had the responsibility for controlling costs, but not that for directly generating revenue, the unit would be called a **cost center** (an example would be the office maintenance department at Catlin's).

Figure 25-1 (p. 832) shows the income statement for Catlin's Department Store. As you can see from this figure, the total gross profit of the company is $373,800 ($841,300 − $467,500), and the operating expenses are $170,000.

In order to break down the gross profit figure by department, a company must gather information about each department. It does this by setting up separate accounting records for each department — separate accounts for Sales, Sales Returns and Allowances, Sales Discount, Merchandise Inventory, Purchases, Purchases Returns and Allowances, and Purchases Discount. Once this information has been separated by department, we can calculate the gross profit of each department. The use of a computer makes it possible to record and gather information for many departments easily and quickly.

Let's look at an example. Figure 25-2 (p. 832) shows how in the sales journal of Catlin's Department Store there is a Sales account for the Children's Department and one for the Adult Department.

Figure 25-3 (p. 833) is an income statement showing the gross profit for each department and the combined totals. You would not see a balance sheet prepared in this way, broken down by department — only an income statement is done like this. Keep in mind an income statement indicates how well a business or department is performing.

> Income statements can be broken down by departments; balance sheets are not.

FIGURE 25-1
Income Statement for Catlin's Department Store

CATLIN'S DEPARTMENT STORE INCOME STATEMENT FOR YEAR ENDED DECEMBER 31, 19X8			
Revenue from Sales:			
Sales		$870 0 0 00	
Less: Sales Returns and Allowances	$14 7 0 0 00		
Sales Discount	14 0 0 00	28 7 0 0 00	
Net Sales			$841 3 0 0 00
Cost of Goods Sold:			
Merchandise Inventory, January 1, 19X8		$143 0 0 0 00	
Purchases	$499 0 0 0 00		
Less: Purchases Returns and			
Allowances	15 4 0 0 00		
Purchases Discount	16 1 0 0 00	467 5 0 0 00	
Cost of Goods Available for Sale		610 5 0 0 00	
Less: Merchandise Inventory,			
Dec. 31, 19X8		143 0 0 0 00	
Cost of Goods Sold			$467 5 0 0 00
Gross Profit on Sales			373 8 0 0 00
Operating Expenses			170 0 0 0 00
Income Before Taxes			203 8 0 0 00
Income Tax Expense			89 5 2 0 00
Net Income			$114 2 8 0 00

FIGURE 25-2 Sales Journal of Catlin's Department Store

	Date		Account Debited	Invoice Number	Post. Ref.	Accounts Receivable Dr.	Children's Sales Cr.	Adult Sales Cr.
CATLIN'S DEPARTMENT STORE SALES JOURNAL								
	Nov.	3	Marsie Rose	325	✔	1 9 0 00	1 0 0 00	9 0 00
		8	Bill Stone	326	✔	1 8 5 00	1 7 5 00	1 0 00
						(115)	(411)	(412)

CATLIN'S DEPARTMENT STORE
INCOME STATEMENT SHOWING DEPARTMENTAL GROSS PROFIT
FOR YEAR ENDED DECEMBER 31, 19X8

	Children's		Adult		Total	
Revenue from Sales:						
Sales		$580 000 00		$290 000 00		$870 000 00
Less: Sales Returns and Allowances	$ 6 500 00		$ 8 200 00		$ 14 700 00	
Sales Discounts	8 000 00	14 500 00	6 000 00	14 200 00	14 000 00	28 700 00
Net Sales		$565 500 00		$275 800 00		$841 300 00
Cost of Goods Sold:						
Merchandise Inventory, Jan. 1, 19X8		75 000 00		$ 68 000 00		$143 000 00
Purchases	$289 000 00		$210 000 00		$499 000 00	
Less: Purchases Returns and Allowances	6 900 00		8 500 00		15 400 00	
Purchases Discounts	8 200 00	273 900 00	7 900 00	193 600 00	16 100 00	467 500 00
Cost of Goods Available for Sale		348 900 00		$261 600 00		$610 500 00
Less: Merchandise Inventory, Dec. 31, 19X8		79 000 00		64 000 00		143 000 00
Cost of Goods Sold		$269 900 00		$197 600 00		467 500 00
Gross Profit on Sales		$295 600 00		$ 78 200 00		$373 800 00
Operating Expenses						170 000 00
Income Before Taxes						203 800 00
Income Tax Expense						89 520 00
Net Income						$114 280 00

FIGURE 25-3 Income Statement with Gross Profit Broken Down by Department

LEARNING UNIT 25-1 REVIEW

AT THIS POINT you should be able to

♦ Explain the difference between a cost center and a profit center. (p. 831)
♦ Prepare an income statement focusing on gross profit by department. (p. 833)

SELF-REVIEW QUIZ 25-1

(The blank forms you need are on page 195 of the *Study Guide and Working Papers.*)

Indicate whether each statement is true or false.

1. In a cost center, a manager directly generates revenue.
2. Each department can have its own separate accounts for Sales, Sales Returns and Allowances, etc., to record information for the income statement.
3. A balance sheet is always separated by departments.

Solution to Self-Review Quiz 25-1

1. False   **2.** True   **3.** False

LEARNING UNIT 25-2

The Income Statement: Focus on Departmental Net Income

DEPARTMENTAL INCOME FROM OPERATIONS

So far we have shown how gross profit has been accumulated by departments. In this unit we will look at how the $170,000 of operating expenses can be allocated by departments if we want to extend departmental reporting beyond gross profit.

The operating expenses of Catlin's Department Store that can be traced and identified directly to a separate department are called **direct expenses.** An example would be the salaries of the salespeople who work only for the Children's Department at Catlin's. The operating expenses that cannot be identified with a specific department but are incurred on behalf of the company are called **indirect expenses.** An example would be the expense incurred in the upkeep of the building in which Catlin's is located.

We can see in Figure 25-4 a sample of operating expenses that can now be apportioned to the Children's and Adult Departments. Note that the total is still $170,000. Now let's see how these calculations for operating expenses were arrived at. Figure 25-5 is a summary of how the expenses were apportioned. Following this is a detailed explanation. Use Figure 25-5 as a reference sheet as you read the explanation that follows.

1. Sales Salaries

The payroll records of Catlin's show that salespeople in the Children's Department were paid $25,000, and salespeople in the Adult Department were paid

CATLIN'S DEPARTMENT STORE
INCOME STATEMENT SHOWING DEPARTMENTAL INCOME BEFORE TAX
FOR YEAR ENDED DECEMBER 31, 19X8

	Children's	Adult	Totals
Net Sales	$565 500 00	$275 800 00	$841 300 00
Cost of Goods Sold	269 900 00	197 600 00	467 500 00
Gross Profit on Sales	$295 600 00	$ 78 200 00	$373 800 00
Operating Expenses:			
Sales Salaries	$ 25 000 00	$ 15 000 00	$ 40 000 00
Building Expense	12 000 00	4 000 00	16 000 00
Delivery Expense	6 000 00	4 000 00	10 000 00
Advertising Expense	9 000 00	5 000 00	14 000 00
Depreciation Expense	22 500 00	7 500 00	30 000 00
Administrative Expense	40 000 00	20 000 00	60 000 00
Total Operating Expenses	$114 500 00	$ 55 500 00	$170 000 00
Income Before Taxes	$181 100 00	$ 22 700 00	$203 800 00
Income Tax Expense			89 520 00
Net Income			$114 280 00

FIGURE 25-4
Operating Expenses Apportioned by Department

$15,000. These expenses can be identified with specific departments, so they are considered direct expenses.

2. Building Expense

The costs relating to the occupancy of Catlin's building are lumped into an account called Building Expense. Building Expense is an indirect expense, apportioned on the basis of square footage. Catlin's allocates the total cost of Building Expense of $16,000 on the basis of the number of square feet that each department occupies. Catlin's total space is 40,000 sq. ft., with the Children's Department occupying 30,000 sq. ft. and the Adult Department 10,000 sq. ft. Building

FIGURE 25-5 Direct and Indirect Operating Expenses by Department

	Children's		Adult		Total Operating Expense	
	Direct	Indirect	Direct	Indirect	Direct	Indirect
(1) Sales Salaries	$25,000.00		$15,000.00		$40,000.00	
(2) Building Expense		$12,000.00		$4,000.00		$16,000.00
(3) Delivery Expense	6,000.00		4,000.00		10,000.00	
(4) Advertising Expense	7,000.00	2,000.00	4,000.00	1,000.00	11,000.00	3,000.00
(5) Depreciation Expense		22,500.00		7,500.00		30,000.00
(6) Administrative Expense		40,000.00		20,000.00		60,000.00
	$38,000.00	$76,500.00	$23,000.00	$32,500.00	$61,000.00	$109,000.00
					$170,000	

Expense is allocated to each department as follows:

Children's	Adult
$\dfrac{30,000 \text{ sq. ft.}}{40,000 \text{ sq. ft.}} = .75 = 75$ percent	$\dfrac{10,000 \text{ sq. ft.}}{40,000 \text{ sq. ft.}} = .25 = 25$ percent
$.75 \times \$16,000 = \$12,000$	$.25 \times \$16,000 = \$4,000$

Thus of the $16,000 in Building Expense, the Children's Department is allocated $12,000 and the Adult Department $4,000.

3. Delivery Expense

The Children's Department shipped 60 percent of all merchandise, and the Adult Department shipped 40 percent of the merchandise. The total cost of Delivery Expense is $10,000. Since the exact amount of Delivery Expense is traceable to each department, it is considered a direct expense. If the cost of delivery is *not* specifically traceable to each department, it is considered an indirect expense and can be charged to departments based on past delivery records. Delivery Expense is calculated as follows:

Children's	Adult
$.60 \times \$10,000 = \$6,000$	$.40 \times \$10,000 = \$4,000$

4. Advertising Expense

Advertising Expense for Catlin's totaled $14,000. Out of that total, $4,000 was spent on advertising adult clothes and $7,000 on advertising children's clothes. The remaining $3,000 ($14,000 − $11,000) was spent on advertising the store's image in general. Thus, this $3,000 is an indirect expense. How would you divide this expense by department? One common way is to apportion it based on gross sales of each department, as follows:

gross sales:	$580,000	Children's
	290,000	Adult
	$870,000	Total Gross Sales

Children's	Adult
$\dfrac{\$580,000}{\$870,000} \times \$3,000$	$\dfrac{\$290,000}{\$870,000} \times \$3,000$
$= \tfrac{2}{3} \times \$3,000 = \$2,000$	$= \tfrac{1}{3} \times \$3,000 = \$1,000$

Thus out of the $3,000 of indirect expenses, $2,000 is charged to the Children's Department and $1,000 to the Adult Department.

5. Depreciation Expense

Depreciation Expense is an indirect expense.

Catlin's Department Store apportions depreciation on its building based on the square footage each department occupies. (Some companies apportion depreciation based on the average cost of the equipment in each department.) Catlin's has 40,000 square feet, of which the Children's Department takes up 30,000 (3/4) and the Adult Department takes up 10,000 (1/4). The amount of Depreciation Expense charged to each department is calculated as follows:

Children's	Adult
$\tfrac{3}{4} \times \$30,000 = \$22,500$	$\tfrac{1}{4} \times \$30,000 = \$7,500$

6. Administrative Expense

Administrative expenses are incurred for the company as a whole and not broken down by department—they are thus indirect expenses. In the case of Catlin's, it was decided that the Administrative Expense of $60,000 would be divided on the basis of each department's gross sales. We saw this method of alteration used in Advertising Expense. The calculation for indirect expenses charged to each department is as follows:

$580,000	Children's
290,000	Adult
$870,000	Total Gross Sales

Children's	Adult
$\dfrac{\$580,000}{\$870,000} = \dfrac{2}{3}$	$\dfrac{\$290,000}{\$870,000} = \dfrac{1}{3}$
$\dfrac{2}{3} \times \$60,000 = \$40,000$	$\dfrac{1}{3} \times \$60,000 = \$20,000$

Now take a moment to review Figure 25-4 to make sure that you understand how we arrived at the total operating expenses of $170,000.

LEARNING UNIT 25-2 REVIEW

AT THIS POINT you should be able to

- Explain the difference between direct and indirect expenses. (p. 834)
- Explain how operating expenses are allocated to specific departments. (pp. 834–836)
- Prepare, in proper form, an income statement showing departmental income before tax. (p. 835)

SELF-REVIEW QUIZ 25-2

(The blank forms you need are on page 196 of the *Study Guide and Working Papers*.)

Given the following, apportion the Rent Expense on the basis of floor space:

	Dept. A	Dept. B	Total
Floor space	208,000	112,000	320,000
Rent expense			$ 30,800

Solution to Self-Review Quiz 25-2

Apportionment of Rent Expense:

Dept. A	Dept. B
$\dfrac{208,000}{320,000} \times \$30,800 = \$20,020$	$\dfrac{112,000}{320,000} \times \$30,800 = \$10,780$

The Income Statement Showing Departmental Contribution Margin

In this approach, indirect expenses are *separated* from direct expenses.

Referring back to Figure 25-4 (p. 835), income before taxes for the Children's Department equaled $181,100, and the Adult Department showed $22,700. Some accountants feel that these figures are misleading, since the indirect expenses in Figure 25-5 were apportioned to the total operating expenses of each department. An alternative to this approach to indirect expense allocation is shown in Figure 25-6, which lists direct departmental expenses and the contribution each department makes to cover indirect expenses. This is called the **contribution margin,** which can also be defined as the gross profit of a department minus its direct expenses. This approach charges to a department only those expenses that are directly traceable to it. Note in Figure 25-6, the Children's Department contributes $257,600 to cover indirect expenses and net income. This is quite different from the $181,100 listed in Figure 25-4.

Supporters of this approach feel that indirect expenses are not controlled by the department manager and thus should not be used in evaluating departmental performance. Some accountants contend that even if a department is eliminated, the indirect expenses would not be decreased. For example, Catlin spends $3,000 in advertising that is basically aimed at advertising the store's overall image—that expense would still remain if the Adult Department or the Children's Department were eliminated.

Determining whether certain departments at Catlin's should be expanded or reduced would involve investigation of the financial reports presented in the chapter along with topics such as (see next page):

FIGURE 25-6
Income Statement Showing Departmental Contribution Margin

CATLIN'S DEPARTMENT STORE INCOME STATEMENT SHOWING DEPARTMENTAL CONTRIBUTION MARGIN FOR YEAR ENDED DECEMBER 31, 19X8	Children's	Adult	Totals
Net Sales	$565 500 00	$275 800 00	$841 300 00
Cost of Goods Sold:	269 900 00	197 600 00	467 500 00
Gross Profit on Sales	$295 600 00	$ 78 200 00	373 800 00
Direct Departmental Expenses			
Sales Salaries	$ 25 000 00	$ 15 000 00	$ 40 000 00
Advertising Expense	7 000 00	4 000 00	11 000 00
Delivery Expense	6 000 00	4 000 00	10 000 00
Total Direct Departmental Expenses	$ 38 000 00	$ 23 000 00	$ 61 000 00
Contribution Margin	$257 600 00	$ 55 200 00	$312 800 00
Indirect Departmental Expenses			
Building Expense			$ 16 000 00
Advertising Expense			3 000 00
Depreciation Expense			30 000 00
Administrative Expense			60 000 00
Total Indirect Expenses			$109 000 00
Income Before Taxes			$203 800 00
Income Tax Expense			89 520 00
Net Income			$114 280 00

1. The effect that dropping a department would have in terms of loss of its contribution margin. For example, would closing a jewelry department in a clothing store reduce the store's total administrative expenses?
2. The effect one department has in drawing customers to other departments. Do customers who come into the store to look at jewelry go on to look at dresses in another department?
3. Trends in the industry. Even though a certain department is not doing well, all of the competing stores have such a department; the answer may be to cut down on the size of the department rather than eliminating it.
4. Ability of suppliers to meet increasing demand for items. For example, it would not be a good idea to open a pastry shop in Catlin's until one had lined up a number of good, reliable suppliers.

We conclude this unit with an example that shows how eliminating a department that has a net loss may in fact cause an even greater loss in the overall net income for the company. The situation is given below:

	Depts. A, B, C	Dept. D Only	Totals for Depts. A–D	Totals if Dept. D Is Eliminated
Sales	$1,469,000	$130,000	$1,599,000	$1,469,000
Cost of Goods Sold	869,000	182,000	951,000	869,000
Gross Profit	600,000	48,000	648,000	600,000
Direct Expenses	340,000	31,000	371,000	340,000
Contribution Margin	260,000	17,000	277,000	260,000
Indirect Expenses	130,000	26,000	156,000	156,000
Net Income (Loss)	$ 130,000	$ (9,000)	$ 121,000	$ 104,000

Note that if Department D is eliminated, net income of the other departments is reduced by $17,000, from $121,000 to $104,000. This is the result of losing the contribution margin of $17,000 from Department D.

LEARNING UNIT 25-3 REVIEW

AT THIS POINT you should be able to

◆ Explain why an income statement might report departmental contribution margin rather than listing all direct and indirect expenses under total operating expenses. (pp. 838–839)
◆ Prepare an income statement showing the contribution margin. (p. 838)

SELF-REVIEW QUIZ 25-3

(The blank forms you need are on page 196 of the *Study Guide and Working Papers*.)
    Indicate whether each statement is true or false.

1. Allocating indirect expenses will never be subjective.
2. A direct expense is traceable to a respective department.

3. Direct expenses of a department in the contribution margin approach are combined with indirect expenses.
4. Eliminating one department could reduce sales of another department.
5. Contribution margin equals gross profit on sales plus direct department expenses.

Solution to Self-Review Quiz 25-3

1. False   **2.** True   **3.** False   **4.** True   **5.** False

CHAPTER REVIEW

SUMMARY OF KEY POINTS

Learning Unit 25-1

1. A profit center means that a manager is responsible for controlling certain costs as well as generating revenues.
2. Separate accounts for Sales, Purchases, etc., can be set up for each department in order to calculate departmental gross profit.
3. Income statements can be broken down by departments; balance sheets are not.

Learning Unit 25-2

1. Direct expenses can be directly identified with a specific department.
2. The method used to apportion indirect expenses to departments may vary from company to company; there is no one absolute method.
3. One department's direct expense may be another department's indirect expense.
4. One way to apportion indirect expenses such as Advertising Expense or Administrative Expense by department is on the basis of each department's gross sales.

Learning Unit 25-3

1. Indirect expenses are *not* combined with direct expenses when preparing an income statement showing departmental contribution margin.
2. Gross profit on sales minus direct departmental expenses equals contribution margin.

KEY TERMS

Contribution margin A department's net profit used to cover indirect expenses.

Cost center A unit or department that incurs costs but does not generate revenues.

Direct expenses Expenses that can be traced directly to a specific department.

Indirect expenses Expenses that cannot be traced directly to one department.

Profit center A unit or department that incurs costs and generates revenues.

BLUEPRINT OF DEPARTMENTAL ACCOUNTING

Situation 1:
Income statement showing departmental gross profit

	DEPT. A	DEPT. B	TOTAL
Net Sales	1	2	3 (1 + 2)
− Cost of Goods Sold	4	5	6 (4 + 5)
= Gross Profit on Sales	7 (1 − 4)	8 (2 − 5)	9 (3 − 6)
− Operating Expenses			10
= Income before Taxes			11 (9 − 10)
− Income Tax Expense			− 12
= Net Income			13

Situation 2:
Income statement showing departmental income before tax

Direct and indirect expenses allocated →

	DEPT. A	DEPT. B	TOTAL
Net Sales	1	2	3 (1 + 2)
Cost of Goods Sold	4	5	6 (4 + 5)
Gross Profit on Sales	7 (1 − 4)	8 (2 − 5)	9 (3 − 6)
Operating Expenses			
⎰ Salaries Expense	10	11	12 (10 + 11)
⎱ Delivery Expense	13	14	15 (13 + 14)
⎱ Depreciation Expense	16	17	18 (16 + 17)
Administrative Expense	19	20	21 (19 + 20)
Total Operating Expenses	22 (10 + 13 + 16 + 19)	23 (11 + 14 + 17 + 20)	24 (12 + 15 + 18 + 21)
Income before Taxes	25 (7 − 22)	26 (8 − 23)	27 (9 − 24)
Income Tax Expense			28
Net Income			29 (27 − 28)

Situation 3:
Income statement showing departmental contributions to indirect expenses

	DEPT. A	DEPT. B	TOTAL
Net Sales	1	2	3 (1 + 2)
Cost of Goods Sold	4	5	6 (4 + 5)
Gross Profit on Sales	7 (1 − 4)	8 (2 − 5)	9 (3 − 6)
Direct Departmental Expenses			10
Sales Salaries	10	11	12 (10 + 11)
Advertising Expenses	13	14	15 (13 + 14)
Delivery Expenses	16	17	18 (16 + 17)
Total Direct Expenses	19 (10 + 13 + 16)	20 (11 + 14 + 17)	21 (12 + 15 + 18)
Contribution to Indirect Expenses	22 (7 − 19)	23 (8 − 20)	24 (9 − 21)
Indirect Departmental Expenses			
Building Expense			25
Advertising Expenses			26
Depreciation Expenses			27
Total Indirect Expenses			28 (25 + 26 + 27)
Income before Taxes			29 (24 − 28)
Income Tax Expense			30
Net Income			31 (29 − 30)

QUESTIONS, MINI EXERCISES, EXERCISES, AND PROBLEMS

Discussion Questions

1. What is the difference between a cost center and a profit center?

2. Explain how gross profit is calculated.

3. Special journals are not used in departmental accounting. True or false? Please explain.

4. Compare and contrast indirect expenses and direct expenses.

5. Explain how advertising expense could be both a direct and an indirect cost for a company.

6. Square footage is often used to allocate indirect costs to various departments within a company. True or false?

7. An income statement showing departmental income before tax does not list individual operating expenses for each department. True or false? Please explain.

8. Explain why a company might prepare an income statement showing each department's contribution margin.

Mini Exercises

(The blank forms you need are on pages 198 and 199 of the *Study Guide and Working Papers.*)

Appropriating Rent to Departments Based on Sales

1. The cost of rent of $6,000 for Moore Co. is appropriated to each department based on sales. Given the following, assign the cost of rent to each department.

Rent	Toys	Clothing
$6,000	$20,000	$40,000

Appropriating Fire Insurance Based on Square Footage

2. Calculate the assignment of fire insurance of $16,000 to each department:

INDIRECT EXPENSE	BASIS OF ASSIGNMENT	BAKERY	GROCERY
Fire Insurance	4,000 Total Square Feet	1,000 Sq. Ft.	3,000 Sq. Ft.

Calculating Net Income from Total Operating Expenses

3. Given the following, calculate net income:

	Dept. 1	Dept. 2
Net Sales	$4,000	$6,000
Cost of Goods Sold	1,000	2,000

(Cont. on p. 844)

Operating Expenses		$2,500
Income Tax Expense, 40 percent rate		

Calculating Departmental Net Income

4. From the following, calculate departmental income before tax. Assume a tax rate of 40 percent.

	Dept. A	Dept. B
Net Sales	3,000	4,000
Cost of Goods Sold	1,000	1,200
Delivery Expense	500	700
Advertising Expense	400	500
Depreciation Expense	200	300

Calculating Contribution Margin

5. Calculate the contribution margin for each department and income before taxes, based on the following:

	Dept. A 1,000 Sq. Ft.	Dept. B 2,000 Sq. Ft.
Net Sales	$5,000	$10,000
Cost of Goods Sold	2,000	6,000
Sales Salaries	$800 (30 percent directly related to Dept. A and 70 percent related to Dept. B)	
Rent Expense	$400	
Advertising Expense	900 ($400 directly related to Dept. A and $200 related to Dept. B)	

Exercises

(The blank forms you need are on pages 200 and 201 of the *Study Guide and Working Papers*.)

Appropriating rent to departments based on sales.

25-1. The cost of rent of $8,000 for Poller Company is appropriated to each department based on its sales. Given the following, assign the cost of rent to each department.

	Jewelry	Hardware	Automotive
Sales	$30,000	$50,000	$20,000

Appropriating fire insurance based on square footage.

25-2. Complete the assignment of fire insurance to each department.

Indirect Expense	Amount	Basis of Assignment	Candy Sales		Ice Cream Sales		Pizza Sales	
Fire Insurance	$90,000	30,000 total sq. ft.	18,000 sq. ft.	A	7,500 sq. ft.	B	4,500 sq. ft.	C

| | Calculating net income from total operating expenses. | **25-3.** Given the following, calculate net income: |

25-3. Given the following, calculate net income:

	Dept. 1	Dept. 2
Net Sales	$30,000	$40,000
Cost of Goods Sold	14,000	26,000
Operating Expenses		$16,000
Income Tax Expense, 30 percent rate		

Calculating departmental income.

25-4. From the following, calculate departmental income before tax. Assume a tax rate of 30 percent.

	Dept. A	Dept. B
Net Sales	$200,000	$250,000
Cost of Goods Sold	100,000	125,000
Delivery Expense	24,000	28,000
Advertising Expense	23,000	22,000
Depreciation Expense	25,000	24,000

Calculating contribution margin.

25-5. Calculate the contribution margin for each department and income before taxes, based on the following:

	Dept. A 10,000 Sq. Ft.	Dept. B 20,000 Sq. Ft.
Net Sales	$60,000	$90,000
Cost of Goods Sold	25,000	50,000
Sales Salaries	8,000 (40 percent directly related to Dept. A and 60 percent to Dept. B)	
Rent Expense	5,000	
Advertising Expense	18,000 ($3,000 directly related to Dept. A and $9,000 to Dept. B)	

Group A Problems

(The blank forms you need are on pages 202–207 of the *Study Guide and Working Papers.*)

Preparing an income statement showing departmental gross profit.

Check Figure:

Total net income $4,950

25A-1. From the following data, prepare in proper form an income statement showing departmental gross profit (assume a 25 percent tax rate) for Bill's Variety for the year ended December 31, 19X9.

Cash	$12,000
Accounts Receivable	6,000
Allowance for Doubtful Accounts	1,500
Merch. Inventory, Jan. 1, 19X9 — Grocery	7,000
Merch. Inventory, Jan. 1, 19X9 — Pizza	5,000
Merch. Inventory, Dec. 31, 19X9 — Grocery	19,000
Merch. Inventory, Dec. 31, 19X9 — Pizza	7,000
Equipment	15,000

Acc. Depreciation, Equipment	9,100
Accounts Payable	10,200
B. Smith, Capital	10,500
B. Smith, Withdrawals	3,100
Sales, Grocery	20,000
Sales, Pizza	18,000
Sales Returns and Allowances, Grocery	2,000
Sales Returns and Allowances, Pizza	3,000
Purchases, Grocery	22,400
Purchases, Pizza	14,500
Purchases Returns and Allowances, Grocery	800
Purchases Returns and Allowances, Pizza	400
Total Operating Expenses	4,700

Constructing a departmental expense sheet.

25A-2. Given the following information about the clothing and hardware departments of Sally Company, prepare a Departmental Expense Allocation sheet showing expenses by department.

Account	Indirect	Direct	
		Clothing	Hardware
1. Rent Expense	$14,000		
2. Insurance Expense	7,000	$1,400	$2,600
3. Depreciation Expense		300	700
4. Advertising Expense	2,000		
5. Supplies Expense	3,000		
6. Salaries Expense	6,400		

Check Figure:
Total indirect expenses $32,400

Additional facts:

	Clothing	Hardware
Net sales	$70,000	$30,000
Cost of goods sold	50,000	18,000
Floor space	200 sq. ft.	500 sq. ft.

Appropriation basis:

Rent and Insurance:	Floor space
Advertising and Supplies:	Net sales
Salaries:	Gross profit of clothing and hardware departments

Assigning direct expenses and preparing an income statement showing departmental income before tax.

25A-3. From the following partial data, prepare an income statement showing departmental income before tax along with net income for Pete's Corporation for the year ended December 31, 19X9.

Net Sales — TV's	$60,000
Net Sales — Washers	30,000
Cost of Goods Sold — TV's	39,000
Cost of Goods Sold — Washers	18,000
Income tax rate 30 percent	
TV Dept. — 5,000 sq. ft.	
Washers — 3,000 sq. ft.	

Check Figure:
Net income $14,140

		Basis of Appropriation
Sales Salary Expense	$4,500	Net sales
Building Expense	4,800	Square footage
Delivery Expense	2,700	Net sales
Depreciation Expense	800	Square footage

Appropriating indirect expenses and preparing an income statement showing departmental contribution margin.

25A-4. Educator Company has requested that you (1) assign indirect expenses to its jewelry and fur departments as appropriate, and (2) prepare an income statement for November 19X9 showing departmental contribution margins along with net income. Assume a 30 percent tax rate.

	Jewelry: 30,000 Sq. Ft.	Fur: 10,000 Sq. Ft.	Indirect Cost
Net Sales	$280,000	$220,000	
Merchandise Inventory (Nov. 1)	50,000	70,000	
Merchandise Inventory (Nov. 30)	35,000	30,000	
Purchases	200,000	100,000	
Purchases Discount	10,000	20,000	
Salaries	2,900	2,100	$10,000
Depreciation	25,000	21,300	
Advertising	1,000	2,000	20,000
Administrative			32,000
Rent Expense			12,000

Check Figure:

Total indirect expenses $20,400

Appropriations of indirect expenses:

Salaries are based on net sales. All other indirect expenses are based on square footage.

Group B Problems

(The blank forms you need are on pages 202-207 of the *Study Guide and Working Papers.*)

Preparing an income statement showing departmental gross profit.

25B-1. From the following data, prepare in proper form an income statement showing departmental gross profit (assume a 25 percent tax rate) for Randy Company for the year ended December 31, 19X9.

Check Figure:

Net income $2,625

Cash	13,100
Accounts Receivable	6,200
Allowance for Doubtful Accounts	2,400
Merch. Inventory, Jan. 1, 19X9 — Cosmetics	8,000
Merch. Inventory, Jan. 1, 19X9 — Jewelry	6,000
Merch. Inventory, Dec. 31, 19X9 — Cosmetics	19,000
Merch. Inventory, Dec. 31, 19X9 — Jewelry	8,000
Equipment	19,000
Acc. Depreciation, Equipment	9,200

Accounts Payable	13,500
R. Glade, Capital	14,000
R. Glade, Withdrawals	5,000
Sales, Cosmetics	20,000
Sales, Jewelry	18,000
Sales Returns and Allowances, Cosmetics	2,000
Sales Returns and Allowances, Jewelry	1,500
Purchases, Cosmetics	24,800
Purchases, Jewelry	15,100
Purchases Returns and Allowances, Cosmetics	900
Purchases Returns and Allowances, Jewelry	500
Total Operating Expenses	5,500

Constructing a departmental expense sheet.

25B-2. Given the following information about the toys and clothing departments of Avery Company, prepare a Departmental Expense Allocation sheet showing expenses by department.

Check Figure:

Total indirect expenses $79,000

Account	Indirect	Direct	
		Toys	Clothing
1. Rent Expense	$15,000		
2. Insurance Expense	21,000	$1,900	$1,700
3. Depreciation Expense		1,000	700
4. Advertising Expense	3,000		
5. Supplies Expense	10,000		
6. Salaries Expense	30,000		

Additional facts:

	Toys	Clothing
Net sales	$20,000	$30,000
Cost of goods sold	10,000	20,000
Floor space	1,000 sq. ft.	2,000 sq. ft.

Allocation basis:

Rent and Insurance:	Floor space
Advertising and Supplies:	Net sales
Salaries:	Gross profit of toys and clothing departments

Assigning direct expenses and preparing an income statement showing departmental income before tax.

25B-3. From the following partial data, prepare an income statement showing departmental income before tax along with net income for Logan Corporation for year ended December 31, 19X9.

Net Sales — Rugs (10,000 sq. ft.)	$180,000
Net Sales — Furniture (30,000 sq. ft.)	220,000
Cost of Goods Sold — Rugs	55,000
Cot of Goods Sold — Furniture	69,000
Income tax rate, 30 percent	

	Basis of Appropriation	
Sales Salary Expense	$60,000	Net Sales
Building Expense	20,000	Square footage
Delivery Expense	80,000	Net sales
Depreciation Expense	16,000	Square footage

Check Figure:

Net income $70,000

Assigning indirect expenses and preparing an income statement showing departmental contributions to indirect expenses.

25B-4. Lonestar Company has requested that you (1) assign indirect expenses to its candy and grocery departments as appropriate, and (2) prepare an income statement for November 19X9 showing departmental contribution margins along with net income. Assume a 30 percent tax rate.

Check Figure:

Total indirect expenses $7,075

	Candy: 20,000 Sq. Ft.	Grocery: 30,000 Sq. Ft.	Indirect Cost
Net Sales	$18,000	$22,000	
Merchandise Inventory (Nov. 1)	1,000	1,500	
Merchandise Inventory (Nov. 30)	2,000	2,500	
Purchases	9,250	8,450	
Purchases Discount	250	450	
Salaries	750	1,500	$2,500
Depreciation	1,250	250	
Advertising	250	1,500	
Administrative			7,500
Rent Expense			2,000

Appropriations of Indirect Expenses:

Salaries are based on net sales. All other indirect expenses are based on square footage.

REAL WORLD APPLICATIONS

25R-1.

Dot Jenson received the following memorandum:

MEMO

To: Dot Jensen—Manager of Children's Clothing

From: Bill Barnes

Re: Annual evaluation

Based on the following data (attached), I am sorry to inform you that you will not be rehired at the end of your current contract. Your department's performance was far below the budgeted level we had projected for this period.

Dot is quite upset and feels her evaluation is not justified. Analyze the data to see whether Dot's evaluation is indeed not justifiable. What additional factors might be considered? Please respond in writing.

ATTACHMENT—ANNUAL EVALUATION DATA

Clothing Sales		$320,000
Cost of Goods Sold		170,000
Gross Profit		$150,000
Operating Expenses:		
Hourly Wages	$75,000	
Manager's Salary	40,000	
Depreciation of Building	15,000	
Interest on Long-Term Bonds	12,000	
Payroll Taxes	16,000	
Total Operating Expenses		158,000
Departmental Loss		(8,000)

25R-2.

Moore Markets is considering the elimination of the Bakery Shop. Based on the following data, make your written recommendations to Jim Moore, president of Moore Markets.

	Produce	Dairy	Bakery
Sales	$60,000	$90,000	$82,000
Cost of Goods Sold	19,000	58,000	67,000
Gross Profit	$41,000	$32,000	$15,000
Direct Expenses	12,000	6,000	8,000
Indirect Expenses	6,000	12,000	4,000
Total Operating Expenses	18,000	18,000	12,000
Net Income Before Tax	$23,000	$14,000	$ 3,000

YOU make the call

Critical Thinking/Ethical Case

25R-3.
Hernando Favor had been working in the bakery department of Long Company for four years when he was promoted to the accounting department. Since his promotion, sales in the bakery department have slipped and management is considering cutting the department in half. Hal Moore, who works in the bakery, will be laid off. Hernando has thought about shifting some of his sales figures in his accounting records to the bakery department from other departments, so as to save his friend, Hal, from losing his job. Hernando feels no one will find out in the long run, since he knows the bakery can increase sales. Do you feel Hernando has clear justification for his actions? You make the call. Write down your recommendation to Hernando.

ACCOUNTING RECALL

A CUMULATIVE APPROACH

THIS EXAM REVIEWS CHAPTERS 1 THROUGH 25

Your *Study Guide and Working Papers* has forms (pp. 213–214) to complete this exam, as well as worked-out solutions. The page references next to each question identify what page to turn back to if you answer the question incorrectly.

PART 1 Vocabulary Review

Match the terms to the appropriate definition or phrase.

Page Ref.

(831)	1. Cost center	A. Unit or department that incurs costs and generates revenue
(819)	2. Discount lost	B. Contra-cost of goods sold account
(813)	3. Vouchers payable	C. Cannot be identified with one department
(315)	4. Net sales	D. Traced directly to a specific department
(834)	5. Direct expenses	E. Gross sales less returns, discounts, and so on
(355)	6. Purchases discount	F. Net profit used to cover indirect expenses
(838)	7. Contribution margin	G. Contra-asset
(505)	8. Allowance for doubtful accounts	H. Used in net approach
(831)	9. Profit center	I. A liability
(834)	10. Indirect expenses	J. Unit or department that incurs costs but does not generate revenues

(838)   11. Contribution margin equals gross profit plus departmental expense.

(834)   12. A department's net profit is used to cover direct expenses.

(838)   13. Gross profit on sales minus direct departmental expenses equals margin contribution.

(834)   14. Depreciation expense is a direct expense.

(838)   15. A balance sheet is not broken down by department as an income statement is.

26

MANUFACTURING ACCOUNTING

THE BIG PICTURE

Many companies manufacture what they sell and therefore need more complicated accounting systems than those we have discussed to track their business. The Eldorado Computer Center does not plan to manufacture its own goods now or in the near future, but there are some important concepts to understand about manufacturing accounting.

This chapter will provide an overview of the field of cost accounting. Cost accounting provides methods for tracking and compiling cost flows associated with goods sold and goods on hand. A cost must be determined for each product manufactured. Because there are so many details involved in tracking this type of accounting, most companies now use computer accounting software systems to do the tracking.

Learning Objectives	◆ Preparing a cost of goods manufacturing schedule. (p. 854)
	◆ Journalizing transactions recording the manufacturing process. (p. 859)
	◆ Preparing a worksheet for a manufacturing company. (p. 865)

Manufacturing accounting refers to the specialized accounting concepts and techniques that are required to properly record, report, and control the operations of a manufacturing company. The financial accounting procedures discussed in the previous merchandising chapters are all still valid in a manufacturing firm, but they are supplemented by the manufacturing accounting to be presented in this chapter, including some new terms and techniques that were not considered or required in the accounting for merchandising operations.

LEARNING UNIT 26-1
Cost of Goods Manufactured and the Income Statement

In a manufacturing company, it is necessary to separate the manufacturing costs from all other selling and administrative expenses, because product costs, inventory costs, and even gross profit come from the manufacturing process. One way of thinking about this is to imagine manufacturing costs being incurred in one building, and the other costs in another building, as shown below:

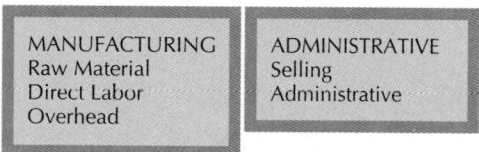

All the costs incurred in the manufacturing building are manufacturing costs, including the managers' salaries, maintenance, all the labor, all materials, supplies, electricity, rent, and the depreciation of manufacturing property and machinery. In addition, it is necessary to allocate a portion of the accounting, personnel, purchasing, and data processing departments each month based on their contribution to manufacturing.

The administrative building would house top management, sales personnel, and other administrative personnel and their supplies and expenses.

ELEMENTS OF MANUFACTURING COST

Once we have determined which are administrative and which are manufacturing costs, we can break the manufacturing costs down into three elements: raw material, direct labor, and manufacturing overhead.

Raw material (or direct material) consists of all the items of material that will become a part of the product, or will change the quality or characteristics of the product. For example, for a furniture manufacturer, the raw material includes lumber, metal parts, fabric, epoxy, finishing material, and even nuts and bolts. In a company that manufactures aluminum products, raw material includes the pure aluminum and the additives that are inserted to make the aluminum shiny or dull, or rigid or flexible.

Direct labor includes the wages of those *personnel* whose efforts directly change the quality or characteristics of the products. In a furniture manufacturing company, the direct labor would include the person who saws the table top, the person who paints the furniture, the person who attaches the handles to the drawers, and so on. However, in that same company, the foreman, the maintenance person, and the forklift driver are *not* direct labor.

Manufacturing overhead consists of all other manufacturing costs not included in raw material or direct labor. Manufacturing overhead includes many diverse items such as indirect labor, maintenance, engineering, manufacturing supervision, and supplies. Some of the most common items of manufacturing overhead are as follows:

◆ Maintenance wages and supplies
◆ Production supervision and expenses
◆ Depreciation expense of manufacturing assets
◆ Rent expense for buildings or machinery
◆ Electricity for manufacturing
◆ Insurance expense for manufacturing
◆ Indirect labor — material handlers
◆ Manufacturing clerical wages

MANUFACTURING INVENTORIES

In a merchandise firm there is basically an inventory made up of goods for sale. In a manufacturing firm there are *three* major inventories: raw material, work-in-process, and finished goods. (In addition, there are other minor inventories for such things as maintenance supplies and operating supplies.)

The *raw material inventory* consists only of the cost of the items of raw material being held for production, plus the freight cost to bring the material in. The acquisition of raw material is recorded as Purchases, the account reserved for the purchase of raw material.

The *work-in-process inventory* represents the cost of the products being processed (this is the step before becoming finished goods) and includes the raw material, direct labor, and the manufacturing overhead costs incurred at the time of the inventory.

The *finished goods inventory* consists of the manufacturing cost of the products that have been completed and are awaiting shipment to customers.

COST OF GOODS SOLD

In order to prepare an income statement for a manufacturing company we first must figure the cost of goods sold. This section of the income statement for a manufacturing company is somewhat different from that of a merchandise company. The following diagram shows how cost of goods sold is calculated for a merchandise firm and for a manufacturing company.

LAYOUT TO CALCULATE COST OF GOODS SOLD

Merchandising Company	Manufacturing Company
Beginning Merchandise Inventory	Beginning Finished Goods Inventory
+ Net Purchases	+ Cost of Goods Manufactured
= Cost of Merchandise Available for Sale	= Cost of Goods Available for Sale
− Ending Merchandise Inventory	− Ending Finished Goods Inventory
= Cost of Goods Sold	= Cost of Goods Sold

As you can see in the diagram, the cost of goods manufactured replaces the purchases of the merchandise company statement. The purpose of the cost of goods sold section is to properly match the manufacturing costs with the sales, and for this reason it is necessary to include the beginning and ending finished goods inventories in order to calculate the cost. For example, the sales may have been for 500 units of product, whereas the company manufactured only 400 units this month. In this case there would be a 100-unit reduction in inventory. Thus, by adding the cost of goods manufactured to the beginning inventory, and subtracting the ending inventory, the result will be the cost of 500 units of product. Similar reasoning is applied if the units manufactured for the month exceed the units sold.

The cost of goods manufactured is figured on a separate form or schedule. This statement is shown in Figure 26-1. There are a few key points to be remembered when preparing this figure:

1. Cost of raw materials equals beginning raw materials inventory plus purchases less ending inventory of raw materials.
2. Total manufacturing costs incurred equals:
   cost of raw material used
   + direct labor
   + factory overhead
3. Cost of goods manufactured equals:
   total manufacturing costs
   + beginning work-in-process
   − ending work-in-process

The first step in preparing the cost of goods manufactured is the calculation of the raw material cost for the month. If the accounting department has its records on a computer, the raw material cost may be readily available. If it is not, the cost must be calculated as shown by adding purchases to the beginning raw material inventory and then subtracting the ending inventory. The

FIGURE 26-1
Statement of Cost of Goods Manufactured

DUKE MANUFACTURING COMPANY STATEMENT OF COST OF GOODS MANUFACTURED FOR THE MONTH ENDED 6/30/X8			
Direct Materials:			
Raw Material Inventory, 6/1/X8		$ 5 0 0 0 00	
Plus: Net Purchases	55 0 0 0 00		
Less: Raw Material Inventory, 6/30/X8	8 0 0 0 00	47 0 0 0 00	
Raw Material Cost			$ 52 0 0 0 00
Direct Labor			90 0 0 0 00
Overhead:			
Factory Supervision			
Maintenance Labor	$ 37 0 0 0 00		
Electricity	15 0 0 0 00		
Maintenance Supplies	6 0 0 0 00		
Operating Supplies	5 0 0 0 00		
Depreciation of Machinery	3 0 0 0 00		
Total Overhead	4 0 0 0 00		70 0 0 0 00
Total Manufacturing Costs			212 0 0 0 00
+ Work-in-Process Inventory, 6/1/X8			7 0 0 0 00
− Work-in-Process Inventory, 6/30/X8			9 0 0 0 00
Total Cost of Goods Manufactured			$210 0 0 0 00

DUKE MANUFACTURING COMPANY INCOME STATEMENT FOR THE MONTH ENDED 6/30/X8			
Sales			$400 0 0 0 00
Cost of Goods Sold:			
Finished Goods Inventory 6/1/X8	$ 25 0 0 0 00		
Plus: Cost of Goods Manufactured	210 0 0 0 00		
Cost of Goods Available for Sale	235 0 0 0 00		
Less: Finished Goods Inventory 6/30/X8	15 0 0 0 00		
Cost of Goods Sold		220 0 0 0 00	
Gross Profit		180 0 0 0 00	
Operating Expenses:			
Selling Expenses	$ 55 0 0 0 00		
Administrative Expense	65 0 0 0 00	120 0 0 0 00	
Net Income (before taxes)		$ 60 0 0 0 00	

FIGURE 26-2
Income Statement for a Manufacturing Firm

direct labor cost is normally a single figure found on the payroll or the labor distribution report. The overhead costs are then totaled and added to the raw material and direct labor to arrive at the total costs for the month. *The final step is to add the beginning work-in-process inventory and subtract the ending inventory.* Keep in mind we subtract ending inventory since it is not part of the cost of goods manufactured (yet).

Let's see how this figure is then used in preparing the income statement (Figure 26-2).

LEARNING UNIT 26-1 REVIEW

AT THIS POINT you should be able to

♦ Define and explain the three elements of manufacturing costs: raw material, direct labor, and manufacturing overhead. (p. 859)
♦ Define and explain the three major inventories in a manufacturing company — raw material, work-in-process, and finished goods. (p. 855)
♦ Compare the cost of goods sold section on an income statement for a merchandising company with the cost of goods manufactured section for a manufacturing company. (p. 856)
♦ Prepare a cost of goods manufactured schedule. (p. 856)

SELF-REVIEW QUIZ 26-1

(The blank forms you need are on page 216 of the *Study Guide and Working Papers*.)

Using the accounts and amounts below, prepare a separate statement of cost of goods manufactured and a cost of goods sold section of the income statement:

Finished Goods Inventory, June 1	$ 45,000
Depreciation of Machinery	15,000
Purchases (Net)	250,000
Maintenance Labor	15,000
Raw Material Inventory, June 1	15,000
Direct Labor	320,000
Work-in-Process Inventory, June 1	30,000
Factory Foremen Salaries	45,000
Finished Goods Inventory, June 30	60,000
Raw Material Inventory, June 30	20,000
Indirect Factory Labor	120,000
Work-in-Process Inventory, June 30	40,000
Factory Electricity Expense	15,000

Solution to Self-Review Quiz 26-1

Statement of Cost of Goods Manufactured

Raw Material Inventory, June 1	$ 15,000	
Plus: Net Purchases	250,000	
Less: Raw Material Inventory, June 30	20,000	
Raw Material Cost		$245,000
Direct Labor		320,000
Overhead:		
Depreciation	$ 15,000	
Maintenance Labor	15,000	
Factory Foremen	45,000	
Indirect Labor	120,000	
Electricity Expense	15,000	210,000
Total Manufacturing Costs		$775,000
Plus: Work-in-Process Inventory, June 1		30,000
Less: Work-in-Process Inventory, June 30		40,000
Total Cost of Goods Manufactured		$765,000

Cost of Goods Sold

Finished Goods Inventory, June 1	$ 45,000
Plus: Cost of Goods Manufactured	765,000
Cost of Goods Available for Sale	810,000
Less: Finished Goods Inventory, June 30	60,000
Cost of Goods Sold	$750,000

LEARNING UNIT 26-2
The Flow of Manufacturing Costs

THE ACCUMULATION OF MANUFACTURING COSTS

As the raw material, direct labor, and overhead are charged into the manufacturing process, they must be recorded. The issuance of material from the warehouse, the assignment of labor to departments, and the movement of the products through the process must be provided to the cost accountants as the basis for journal entries.

Source Documents: The required data is submitted to the cost accountants through various source documents. The timely receipt of legible documents is often a problem in some companies, and employees must be made aware of their importance.

Receiving reports are prepared by the receiving department to acknowledge receipt of all material and supplies from vendors. A typical receiving report is shown in Figure 26-3. The accounting copy becomes a part of the vendor payment voucher, along with the purchase order and the vendor invoice.

Material requisitions are the documents initiated by the manufacturing personnel, or other users, to request material from the inventory warehouse. The requisition (Figure 26-4) is presented to the storekeeper as the materials are issued. Copies of the requisitions are kept in accounting as a basis for charging material into production.

A **clock card** is a card used by each hourly based employee to clock in and out of the factory each day. A typical clock card is shown in Figure 26-5. The

FIGURE 26-3
Receiving Report

RECEIVING REPORT			
Received From Adams Company		Receiving Report No. 1031 Date: 6/20/X8	
Quantity	Description	Unit Price	Total Price
50 Gals.	Paint	$6.50/Ga.	$325.00
	Revilo Manufacturing Co. Inspected By MS Received By BJ		

FIGURE 26-4
Material Requisition

MATERIAL REQUISITION			
Department Finishing		Requisition No. 3648 Date: 6/20/X8	
Quantity	Description	Unit Price	Total Price
8 Gals.	White Paint	$6.50	$52.00
	Revilo Manufacturing Co. Inspected By CY Received By FU		

FIGURE 26-5
Clock Card

cards are collected each week by the payroll department and become a basis for the payroll check, and for charging labor into production.

Lot tickets, or move tickets, are documents that are written by departmental managers to reflect the movement of products, or parts of products, from one department to another. The department receiving the products must verify the quantity and quality of the products. These tickets become the basis for transferring costs between departments and to finished goods inventory. An example of a lot ticket is shown in Figure 26-6.

A **labor distribution report** is a byproduct of the payroll that has been reassembled into the categories of direct labor, maintenance labor, etc. Based on this report the cost accountants charge labor into departments. An example of a typical labor distribution report is shown in Figure 26-7.

FIGURE 26-6
Lot Ticket

FIGURE 26-7
Labor Distribution Report

FIGURE 26-8
Bill of Lading

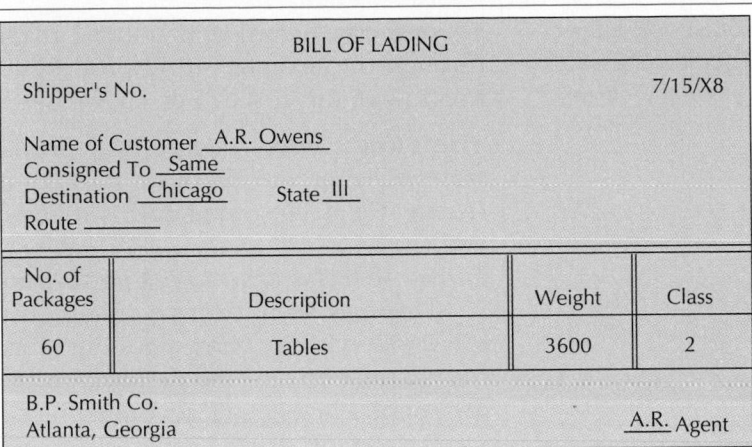

BILL OF LADING			
Shipper's No.			7/15/X8
Name of Customer A.R. Owens			
Consigned To Same			
Destination Chicago State Ill			
Route			

No. of Packages	Description	Weight	Class
60	Tables	3600	2

B.P. Smith Co.
Atlanta, Georgia   A.R. Agent

Bills of lading are documents that are used to show the shipment of products to customers. The cost accounting copies of the bills become the basis for recording the transfer of the cost of the products from the finished goods inventory to the cost of goods sold. A typical bill of lading is shown in Figure 26-8.

THE FLOW OF MANUFACTURING COSTS

FIGURE 26-9
Flow of Costs

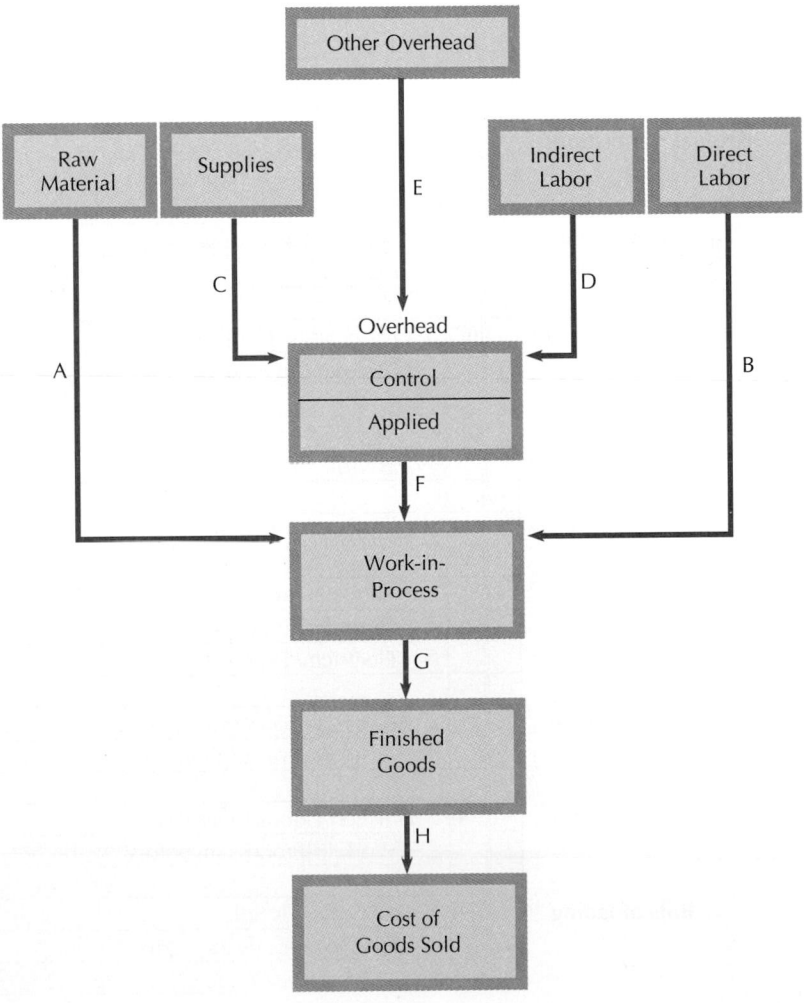

To properly record and control manufacturing costs as the products move through the manufacturing process, it is necessary to establish the pattern of the flow of the costs. To do so, we use a flow chart.

The Flow Chart: Figure 26-9 on page 861 illustrates the movement of the material, labor, and overhead through the operation. Each step of the flow, from (A) to (H), is illustrated and is followed by an example of the journal entries and the source documents for each step. *It should be noted that the journal entries reflect a debit to the destination and a credit to the source.*

This may seem overwhelming, so take the time to match each step in Figure 26-10 with its corresponding journal entry. Remember that the debit is to the destination and the credit is to the source. See the blueprint on page 872 for samples involving T accounts.

Overhead Application: As shown in the flow of cost journal entries (C), (D), and (E), the debit is to an account called Overhead — Control and in (F) the credit is to the account Overhead — Applied. It is desirable to maintain both of these overhead accounts in order to avoid errors and confusion. Overhead — Control is used for the accumulation of all actual overhead costs as debits, and the Overhead — Applied is credited for the application of overhead to production.

FIGURE 26-10 Journal Entries

SOURCE DOCUMENTS

			Debit	Credit
Material requisitions	(A)	Work-in-Process Inventory	2 0 0 0 00	
		Raw Material Inventory		2 0 0 0 00
Labor distribution report	(B)	Work-in-Process Inventory	1 8 0 0 00	
		Payroll		1 8 0 0 00
Material requisitions	(C)	Overhead — Control	4 0 0 00	
		Supplies Inventory		4 0 0 00
Labor distribution report	(D)	Overhead — Control	1 0 0 0 00	
		Payroll		1 0 0 0 00
Various	(E)	Overhead — Control	1 0 0 0 00	
		Supervision Salaries		6 0 0 00
		Rent Expense		1 0 0 00
		Depreciation Expense		2 0 0 00
		Electricity Expense		1 0 0 00
None	(F)	Work-in-Process Inventory	25 0 0 00	
		Overhead — Applied		25 0 0 00
Lot tickets	(G)	Finished Goods Inventory	22 0 0 00	
		Work-in-Process Inventory		22 0 0 00
Bills of lading	(H)	Cost of Goods Sold	24 0 0 00	
		Finished Goods Inventory		24 0 0 00

It is necessary to apply overhead each week in order to determine the total costs for that week. However, some overhead accounts, such as electricity, supervision, and depreciation, are not known until the end of the month. For this reason, an overhead rate must be established as a basis for applying the overhead. There are several methods of determining a rate, depending on the type of operation of the company.

The most common and practical methods are based on direct labor or machine hours. A rate can be developed from the annual budget of the overhead costs and the *direct labor dollars* (wages of those persons whose efforts *directly* affect the characteristics of the products manufactured) as follows:

annual overhead ÷ annual direct labor dollars

$500,000 ÷ $1,000,000 = 50 percent

Based on this calculation, overhead can be applied to production each week or month at a rate of 50 percent of the direct labor cost charged to production. For example, if the direct labor this month is $20,000, overhead would be applied at $10,000, as follows:

Work-in-Process Inventory	10 0 0 0 00	
Overhead — Applied		10 0 0 0 00

Another much-used rate is based on *direct labor hours:*

annual overhead ÷ annual direct labor hours

$500,000 ÷ 200,000 hours = $2.50/hour

In this case, the rate of $2.50 per direct labor hour would be applied as overhead. If direct labor hours this month were 2,000 hours, the applied overhead would be $5,000, as follows:

Work-in-Process Inventory	5 0 0 0 00	
Overhead — Applied		5 0 0 0 00

Still another method that is convenient in some companies is based on *machine hours,* as follows:

annual overhead ÷ annual machine hours

$500,000 ÷ 100,000 machine hours = $5.00/hour

Using the $5.00 per machine hour rate, if the machine ran 3,000 hours, the overhead applied would be $15,000.

DEMONSTRATION PROBLEM

To further illustrate the journal entries and overhead application, consider the following transactions and the resulting journal entries for the month of August:

(A) Issued raw material from the storeroom costing $69,000.

(B) Charged direct labor into production, $60,000.

(C) Issued supplies from the storeroom costing $6,000.

(D) Incurred indirect labor costs of $15,000.

(E) Charged the following expenses to overhead: rent — $3,000; supervision — $12,000; depreciation — $4,000; electricity — $6,000.

(F) Applied overhead at 85 percent of direct labor dollars.

(G) Transferred completed products costing $200,000 to finished goods.

(H) Sold products costing $208,000.

Journal Entries

			Debit	Credit
(A)	Work-in-Process Inventory		69 00 00	
	Raw Material Inventory			69 00 00
(B)	Work-in-Process Inventory		60 00 00	
	Payroll			60 00 00
(C)	Overhead — Control		6 00 00	
	Supplies Inventory			6 00 00
(D)	Overhead — Control		15 00 00	
	Payroll			15 00 00
(E)	Overhead — Control		25 00 00	
	Rent Expense			3 00 00
	Supervision Expense			12 00 00
	Depreciation Expense			4 00 00
	Electricity Expense			6 00 00
(F)	Work-in-Process Inventory		51 00 00	
	Overhead — Applied			51 00 00
(G)	Finished Goods Inventory		200 00 00	
	Work-in-Process Inventory			200 00 00
(H)	Cost of Goods Sold		208 00 00	
	Finished Goods Inventory			208 00 00

LEARNING UNIT 26-2 REVIEW

AT THIS POINT you should be able to

◆ List the six source documents covered in this unit and explain the function of each in the accounting process. (p. 859)
◆ List the steps of the flow chart showing the movement of raw materials through the manufacturing process. (p. 861)
◆ Explain the difference between Overhead — Control and Overhead — Applied. (p. 862)

SELF-REVIEW QUIZ 26-2

(The blank forms you need are on page 217 of the *Study Guide and Working Papers*.)

Prepare the general journal entries required to record the following transactions (omit explanations):

(A) Charged raw material into production, $6,000.

(B) Charged direct labor into production, $8,000.

(C) Issued operating supplies, $2,000.

(D) Charged indirect labor into production, $5,000.

(E) Incurred the following overhead: supervision, $4,500; rent, $1,000; depreciation, $500; electricity, $1,500; maintenance, $2,500.

(F) Applied overhead to production at 180 percent of direct labor dollars.

(G) Transferred products to finished goods, $9,000.

(H) Sold products costing $10,000.

Solution to Self-Review Quiz 26-2

(A)	Work-in-Process	6 000 00	
	Raw Material		6 000 00
(B)	Work-in-Process	8 000 00	
	Payroll		8 000 00
(C)	Overhead — Control	2 000 00	
	Supplies Inventory		2 000 00
(D)	Overhead — Control	5 000 00	
	Payroll		5 000 00
(E)	Overhead — Control	10 000 00	
	Supervision		4 500 00
	Rent		1 000 00
	Depreciation		5 00 00
	Electricity		1 500 00
	Maintenance		2 500 00
(F)	Work-in-Process	14 400 00	
	Overhead — Applied		14 400 00
(G)	Finished Goods Inventory	9 000 00	
	Work-in-Process		9 000 00
(H)	Cost of Goods Sold	10 000 00	
	Finished Goods		10 000 00

LEARNING UNIT 26-3
Worksheet for a Manufacturing Company

In past chapters we have seen worksheets for a service company as well as a merchandise company. We now examine and explain the preparation of a worksheet for a manufacturing company. Figure 26-11 on the next page shows a worksheet for Roe Corporation. We have changed companies to provide you with more insight into other account titles used by different companies. The

FIGURE 26-11 (cont.)

FIGURE 26-11 Worksheet for a Manufacturing Company

Account Titles	Trial Balance Dr.	Trial Balance Cr.	Adjustments Dr.	Adjustments Cr.	① Statement of Cost of Goods Manufactured Dr.	Statement of Cost of Goods Manufactured Cr.	Income Statement Dr.	Income Statement Cr.	Balance Sheet Dr.	Balance Sheet Cr.
Cash	135000								135000	
Accounts Receivable	153000								153000	
Allowance for Doubtful Accounts		48000		(B) 66000						114000
Raw Materials Inventory	57000				② 57000	② 96000			② 96000	
Work-in-process Inventory	123000				② 123000	② 159000			② 159000	
Finished Goods Inventory	75000						③ 75000	54000	54000	
Factory Supplies	99000			(A) 78000					21000	
Prepaid Factory Insurance	105000			(D) 75000					30000	
Factory Machinery	648000								648000	
Acc. Dep., Factory Mach.		120000		(C) 84000						204000
Note Payable (due within 30 days)		225000								225000
Common Stock $10		225000								225000
Retained Earnings		180000								180000
Sales (Net)		2430000						2430000		
Raw Material Purchases (Net)	540000				540000					
Direct Labor	330000		(E) 132000		462000					
Indirect Labor	102000		(E) 48000		150000					
Heat, Light and Power	174000				174000					
Machinery Repairs	45000				45000					
Rent Expense — Factory	180000				180000					
Selling Expense — Control	261000					④	261000			
Administrative Expenses (Control)	201000		(E) 33000				234000			
	3228000	3228000								
Factory Supplies Expense			(A) 78000		78000					
Bad Debts Expense			(B) 66000				66000			
Dep. Expense — Factory Mach.			(C) 84000		84000					
Factory Insurance Expense			(D) 75000		75000					
Accrued Payroll Payable				(E) 213000						213000
			516000	516000	1968000	255000				
Cost of Goods Manufactured						1713000	1713000			
					1968000	1968000	2349000	2484000	1296000	1161000
Net Income							135000			135000
							2484000	2484000	1296000	1296000

theory is the same. We will then see how reports are prepared from the worksheet. Let's first look at some key points to remember when a worksheet is prepared. Keep in mind that the steps of the accounting cycle for a manufacturing company are the same as those used for a merchandise company.

KEY POINTS TO LOOK AT ON THE WORKSHEET

See number of key points circled on the worksheet (Fig. 26-11).

1. New set of columns for statement of cost of goods manufactured.
2. Beginning balances of raw materials inventory, $570, and work-in-process, $1,230, are listed in debit column of statement of cost of goods manufactured. Ending balances of $960 and $1,590 are entered in the credit column.
3. Finished goods inventory is not listed on statement of cost of goods manufactured. The beginning figure of finished goods, $750 is listed in the debit column of the income statement, while the ending balance of finished goods, $540 is listed on the credit column of the income statement and debit column of the balance sheet.
4. These are expenses that are not part of the cost of manufacturing and thus are not listed on the statement of cost of goods manufactured.

REPORTS PREPARED FROM THE WORKSHEET

ROE CORPORATION STATEMENT OF COST OF GOODS MANUFACTURED FOR YEAR ENDED DECEMBER 31, 19XX		
Direct Materials:		
Raw Materials Inventory (Beg.)	$ 570 00	
Raw Materials Purchased (Net)	5 400 00	
Cost of Available Raw Materials	5 970 00	
Less: Raw Materials Inventory (End.)	960 00	
Cost of Raw Materials Used		$ 5 010 00
Direct Labor		4 620 00
Factory Overhead:		
Indirect Labor	$ 1 500 00	
Heat, Light and Power	1 740 00	
Rent Expense	1 800 00	
Machinery Repairs	450 00	
Factory Supplies Expense	780 00	
Dep. Exp., Factory Machinery	840 00	
Factory Insurance Expense	750 00	
Total Factory Overhead		$ 7 860 00
Total Manufacturing Cost Incurred		17 490 00
Plus: Work-in-Process (Beg.)		1 230 00
Less: Work-in-Process (End.)		1 590 00
Cost of Goods Manufactured*		$ 17 130 00

* This will go on the cost of goods sold section of the income statement, as shown on page 857.

THE INCOME STATEMENT

Figure 26-12 is the income statement for Roe Corporation. Note how the $17,130 from the statement of cost of goods manufactured is listed below the beginning finished goods inventory. Note that the operating expenses, which were not part of the cost of the goods sold, are listed below gross profit. For example: Bad Debts Expense, a selling expense, had no part in the production of bean bag chairs for Roe. Remember that the cost of goods manufactured is not the same as cost of goods sold.

FIGURE 26-12
Income Statement

ROE CORPORATION INCOME STATEMENT FOR YEAR ENDED DECEMBER 31, 19XX		
Net Sales		$ 24 3 0 0 00
Cost of Goods Sold:		
Finished Goods Inventory (Beg.)	$ 7 5 0 00	
Cost of Goods Manufactured	17 1 3 0 00	
Cost of Goods Available for Sale	$17 8 8 0 00	
Less: Finished Goods Inventory (End.)	5 4 0 00	
Cost of Goods Sold:		$ 17 3 4 0 00
Gross Profit on Sales		$ 6 9 6 0 00
Operating Expenses:		
Selling Expense*	$ 3 2 7 0 00	
Administrative Expense	2 3 4 0 00	
Total Operating Expenses		$ 5 6 1 0 00
Net Income (before taxes)		$ 1 3 5 0 00

* Includes the $660 of bad debt expense.

THE BALANCE SHEET

Figure 26-13 is the completed Balance Sheet of Roe Corporation. The net income of $1,350 in Figure 26-12 helps update retained earnings in Figure 26-13. Note how under current assets the manufacturing company lists out its raw materials and work-in-process, as well as finished goods.

ROE CORPORATION
BALANCE SHEET
DECEMBER 31, 19XX

Assets			
Current Assets:			
Cash			$ 1 3 5 0 00
Accounts Receivable	$ 1 5 3 0 00		
Less: Allowance for Doubtful Accounts	1 1 4 0 00		$ 3 9 0 00
Inventories			
Raw Materials	$ 9 6 0 00		
Work-in-Process	1 5 9 0 00		
Finished Goods	5 4 0 00		$ 3 0 9 0 00
Prepaid Expenses:			
Factory Supplies	$ 2 1 0 00		
Prepaid Factory Insurance	3 0 0 00		$ 5 1 0 00
Total Current Assets			$ 5 3 4 0 00
Plant and Equipment			
Factory Machinery	$ 6 4 8 0 00		
Less: Accum. Depreciation, Factory Machinery	2 0 4 0 00		$ 4 4 4 0 00
Total Assets			$ 9 7 8 0 00
Liabilities and Stockholders' Equity			
Current Liabilities:			
Notes Payable	$ 2 2 5 0 00		
Accrued Payroll Payable	2 1 3 0 00		$ 4 3 8 0 00
Stockholders' Equity			
Common Stock, $10 par 225 shares	$ 2 2 5 0 00		
Retained Earnings*	3 1 5 0 00		$ 5 4 0 0 00
Total Liabilities and Stockholders' Equity			$ 9 7 8 0 00

FIGURE 26-13
Balance Sheet

* Beginning Retained Earnings + Net Income.

LEARNING UNIT 26-3 REVIEW

AT THIS POINT you should be able to

◆ Explain the key points to consider of a worksheet for a manufacturing company. (pp. 865 – 867)
◆ From the worksheet, prepare a statement of cost of goods manufactured, along with the income statement and balance sheet. (pp. 867 – 869)

SELF-REVIEW QUIZ 26-3

(The blank forms you need are on page 217 of the *Study Guide and Working Papers.*)

Answer the following true or false.

1. The figure for cost of goods manufactured is always placed on the credit column of the income statement on the worksheet.
2. Finished goods are not listed on the statement of cost of goods manufactured.
3. All expenses are listed on the cost of goods manufactured.
4. The ending balances of raw materials inventory and work-in-process are entered in the debit columns of cost of goods manufactured.

Solution to Self-Review Quiz 26-3

1. False   **2.** True   **3.** False   **4.** False

CHAPTER REVIEW

SUMMARY OF KEY POINTS

Learning Unit 26-1

1. Manufacturing costs are broken down into raw materials, direct labor, and manufacturing overhead.
2. A manufacturing firm has three major inventories: raw materials, work-in-process, and finished goods.
3. Cost of goods manufactured is prepared first, before the income statement is completed.

Learning Unit 26-2

1. When journal entries are prepared to record the movement of material, labor, and overhead through the operation of a company, each debit is the destination and each credit is the source.
2. Overhead may be applied based on direct labor hours, direct labor dollars, or machine hours.

Learning Unit 26-3

1. The steps of the accounting cycle for a manufacturing company are the same as those used for a merchandise company.
2. The worksheet for a manufacturing company has columns for items used to calculate the statement of cost of goods manufactured. This figure is then updated on the income statement debit column of the worksheet.

KEY TERMS

Bill of lading A formal document issued to the carrier of the finished product. It is the basis for charging cost of goods sold.

Clock card The card used by employees when clocking in and out for the factory; it becomes the basis for the payroll.

Direct labor The wages of those persons whose efforts directly affect the quality or other characteristics of the products manufactured.

Labor distribution report A report issued by the payroll department to categorize all the types of labor incurred during the week.

Lot ticket A document prepared to show the movement of materials or products between departments.

Manufacturing overhead All the manufacturing costs except raw material and direct labor.

Material requisition A document used to order material or supplies from the storeroom and the basis for charging material into production.

Raw material Material that is to be processed into a finished product or that changes the quality or characteristics of the product.

Receiving report A document prepared by the receiving department to evidence the receipt of material or supplies that were ordered.

Blueprint: MANUFACTURING ELEMENTS

QUESTIONS, MINI EXERCISES, EXERCISES, AND PROBLEMS

Discussion Questions

1. Into what three elements can manufacturing costs be broken down?
2. Direct labor includes the wages of those personnel whose efforts indirectly change the quality or characteristics of the product. True or false? Please explain.
3. What are the three major inventories of a manufacturing firm?
4. Explain how to calculate total cost of goods manufactured.
5. Explain the purpose of receiving reports, as well as materials requisitions.
6. What tickets become the basis for transferring costs between departments to finished goods inventory?
7. What is the purpose of a bill of lading?
8. Draw a diagram to show the flow of manufacturing costs.
9. Explain how overhead may be applied.
10. Compare and contrast the structure of a worksheet for a merchandise company and a manufacturing company.

Mini Exercises

(The blank forms you need are on page 219 of the *Study Guide and Working Papers.*)

Classifications of Raw Material, Direct Labor, and Overhead

1. Classify each of the following as raw material, direct labor, or overhead:
   a. Finishing material for a furniture manufacturer.
   b. Depreciation expense of manufacturing assets.
   c. Person who paints furniture for a furniture manufacturer.
   d. Pure aluminum in a company that manufactures aluminum products.

Calculating Cost of Raw Materials

2. From the following calculate the cost of raw materials used:

Raw materials Inventory, Jan. 1	$ 5,000
Raw materials Inventory, Dec. 31	12,000
Purchases of raw materials	70,000

Calculating Total Manufacturing Costs

3. From the following calculate total manufacturing costs:

Direct Labor	$ 7,000
Raw materials inventory, June 30	4,500
Raw materials purchases	15,000
Raw materials inventory, June 1	3,000
Overhead	4,000
Finished goods	8,000

Journal Entries to Record Manufacturing Costs

4. Journalize the following transactions:

   (A) Storeroom issued raw materials costing $5,000.

   (B) Direct Labor of $3,000 was charged into production.

   (C) Supplies costing $2,000 were issued by the storeroom.

   (D) Indirect labor cost of $4,000 was incurred.

   (E) Rent of $1,000 and Depreciation of $400 was charged to overhead.

5. Identify where each title is placed on the worksheet.

   1. Cost of goods manufactured column

   2. Income Statement column

   3. Balance Sheet

      _____ **a.** Raw materials purchases

      _____ **b.** Ending finished goods inventory

      _____ **c.** Ending raw materials inventory

      _____ **d.** Sales

Exercises

(The blank forms you need are on page 220 of the *Study Guide and Working Papers*.)

Classifications of raw material, direct labor, and overhead.

26-1. Classify each of the following as raw material, direct labor, or overhead:

   a. The lumber in making furniture.

   b. The insurance for a factory.

   c. The wages of a forklift driver.

   d. A manufacturing foreman's salary.

Calculating raw materials costs.

26-2. From the following balances, calculate the cost of raw material used:

Raw materials inventory, Jan. 1	$ 60,000
Raw materials inventory, Dec. 31	90,000
Purchases of raw materials	800,000

Calculating total manufacturing costs.

26-3. From the following, calculate total manufacturing costs:

Direct labor	$ 80,000
Raw materials inventory, May 30	9,600
Raw materials purchases	70,000
Raw materials inventory, May 1	9,000
Overhead	75,000
Finished goods	120,000

Journal entries to record flow of manufacturing costs and the application of overhead.

26-4. From the following transactions, prepare the appropriate general journal entries for the month of May:

   (A) Raw materials costing $75,000 were issued from the storeroom.

   (B) Direct labor of $65,000 was charged into production.

   (C) Supplies costing $7,000 were issued from the storeroom.

   (D) Indirect labor costs of $18,000 were incurred.

   (E) Rent of $3,000 and depreciation of $500 were charged to overhead.

   (F) Eighty percent of the direct labor dollars used were applied to overhead.

(G) Completed products costing $70,000 were transferred to finished goods.

(H) Products costing $39,000 were sold.

26-5. (a) In which columns on the worksheet would the following additional data be placed?

	Year-End Figures	Column
Raw materials	$34,000	
Goods-in-process	19,500	
Finished goods	30,000	

(b) In which columns would the beginning-of-year figures be placed?

Group A Problems

(The blank forms you need are on pages 221–222 of the *Study Guide and Working Papers.*)

26A-1. An analysis of the accounts of Harwood Manufacturing reveals the following data for the month ended July 31, 19XX:

Inventories	Beginning	Ending
Raw materials	$18,000	$19,000
Work-in-process	13,000	17,000
Finished goods	15,000	14,000

Costs incurred: Raw materials purchased, $130,000; direct labor, $130,000; manufacturing overhead, $52,000. These specific overheads included: indirect labor, $20,000; factory insurance, $9,000; depreciation on machinery, $10,000; machinery repairs, $4,000; factory utilities, $6,000; miscellaneous factory costs, $3,000.

Instructions: Prepare a cost of goods manufactured statement.

26A-2. As the bookkeeper of Ace Manufacturing, you are to record the following transactions in the general journal for the month of November:

(A) Raw materials of $80,000 were issued from the storeroom.

(B) Charged $60,000 of direct labor to production.

(C) Supplies costing $7,000 were issued from the storeroom.

(D) Incurred indirect labor costs of $15,000.

(E) The following expenses were charged to overhead: rent, $3,000; supervision, $8,000; depreciation, $4,000; electricity, $6,500.

(F) Overhead was applied at 90 percent of direct labor dollars.

(G) Transferred completed products costing $160,000 to finished goods.

(H) Sold products costing $198,000.

26A-3. From the figure at the top of the following page, prepare a worksheet for Keep Corporation (assume no adjustments):

Additional data:

Year-End Figures:

Raw materials	$11,400
Goods-in-process	8,280
Finished goods	10,200

TRIAL BALANCE	Cr.	Dr.
Cash	6240.00	
Raw Materials Inventory	8880.00	
Goods-in-Process Inventory	7440.00	
Finished Goods Inventory	10320.00	
Factory Supplies	3240.00	
Prepaid Factory Supplies	360.00	
Desks	960.00	
Machinery	57240.00	
Acc. Depreciation, Machinery		8280.00
Accounts Payable		3120.00
Common Stock $10 Par		60000.00
Retained Earnings		8040.00
Sales		115680.00
Raw Materials Purchases	38400.00	
Direct Labor	22320.00	
Indirect Labor	9960.00	
Machinery Repairs	720.00	
Selling Expenses	14760.00	
Administrative Expense	10080.00	
Factory Supplies Expense	1320.00	
Depreciation of Machinery	2880.00	
	195120.00	195120.00

Group B Problems

(The blank forms you need are on pages 221 and 222 of the *Study Guide and Working Papers*.)

Preparing a cost of goods manufactured schedule.

26B-1. An analysis of the accounts of Harwood Manufacturing reveals the following data for the month ended July 31, 19XX:

Check Figure:

Total cost of goods manufactured
$249,000

Inventories	Beginning	Ending
Raw materials	$16,000	$22,000
Work-in-process	12,000	16,000
Finished goods	16,000	14,000

Costs incurred: Raw materials purchased, $130,000; direct labor, $90,000; manufacturing overhead, $39,000. These specific overheads included: indirect labor, $9,600; factory insurance, $8,000; depreciation on machinery, $7,600; machinery repairs, $6,000; factory utilities, $6,300; miscellaneous factory costs, $1,500. *Instructions:* Prepare a cost of goods manufactured statement.

Journalizing entries to record manufacturing costs and application of overhead.

26B-2. From the following transactions for May for Ace Manufacturing, please record the appropriate general journal entries:

(A) Raw materials of $70,000 were issued from Ace's storeroom.

(B) Charged $75,000 of direct labor to production.

(C) Supplies of $4,000 were issued from the storeroom.

(D) Indirect labor costs were incurred for $20,000.

(E) The following expenses were charged to overhead: rent, $5,000; supervision, $9,000; depreciation, $6,200; electricity, $9,000.

Check Figure:

(D) Dr. Overhead control
$20,000
Cr. Payroll $20,000

(F) Overhead was applied at 80 percent of direct labor dollars.

(G) Completed products costing $180,000 were transferred to finished goods.

(H) Sold products costing $208,000.

Preparing a worksheet for a manufacturing company.

26B-3. From the following, prepare a worksheet for Keep Corporation (assume no adjustments).

Check Figure:

Net income $2,055

	TRIAL BALANCE	
	Cr.	Dr.
Cash	1310 00	
Raw Materials Inventory	2220 00	
Goods-in-Process Inventory	1860 00	
Finished Goods Inventory	2580 00	
Factory Supplies	560 00	
Prepaid Factory Insurance	590 00	
Desks	240 00	
Machinery	14310 00	
Acc. Depreciation, Machinery		2070 00
Accounts Payable		780 00
Common Stock $10 Par		15000 00
Retained Earnings		2010 00
Sales		28920 00
Raw Materials Purchases	9600 00	
Direct Labor	5580 00	
Indirect Labor	2490 00	
Machinery Repairs	180 00	
Selling Expenses	3690 00	
Administrative Expense	2520 00	
Factory Supplies Expense	330 00	
Depreciation of Machinery	720 00	
	48780 00	48780 00

Additional data:

Year-End Figures:

Raw materials	$ 285
Goods-in-process	2,070
Finished goods	2,550

REAL WORLD APPLICATIONS

26R-1.

Peter Roel had to leave the office on urgent business and asked you to close the costs into the manufacturing summary account. Please do so. Why do you think Peter forgot to close the accounts? Provide a written response.

MEMO

TO: Peter Roel, Bookkeeper

FROM: M. V. Rooy, Vice-President

RE: Closing Entries

I notice that you forgot to close the costs that appeared in the statement of cost of goods manufactured into the manufacturing summary account. Here is a blueprint of the form. Please provide them to me as soon as possible.

Manufacturing Summary	XXX	
Raw Materials Inventory		XXX
Raw Materials Inventory	XXX	
Manufacturing Summary		XXX
Manufacturing Summary	XXX	
Work-in-Process Inventory		XXX
Work-in-Process Inventory	XXX	
Manufacturing Summary		XXX

YOU make the call

Critical Thinking/Ethical Case

26R-2.

Dot Lovet works in the receiving department of a leading publishing company. She has become good friends with many of the suppliers. At 4 P.M., Joe Andrews delivered a truckload of art supplies. Joe was in a hurry and asked Dot to accept the order. He promised that everything was there. Dot signed the receiving report without verifying the specifics of the order. Two weeks later the art department called complaining that their department was being charged for items they never received. The accounting department has already processed the payment to this vendor. If you were Dot's supervisor, what would you do in this situation? You make the call. Write down your recommendation to Dot.

ACCOUNTING RECALL

A CUMULATIVE APPROACH

THIS EXAM REVIEWS CHAPTERS 1 THROUGH 26

Your *Study Guide and Working Papers* has forms (pp. 225–226) to complete this exam, as well as worked-out solutions. The page references next to each question identify what page in the text to turn back to if you answer the question incorrectly.

PART 1   Vocabulary Review

Match the terms to the appropriate definition or phrase.

Page Ref.

(861)	1. Bill of lading	A. Material that is to be processed into a finished product
(505)	2. Allowance for doubtful accounts	B. Face value of bond less bond discount
(854)	3. Direct labor	C. Wages of people who directly affect the products manufactured
(831)	4. Gross profit	D. Contra-stockholders' equity account
(855)	5. Manufacturing overhead	E. Applied based on direct labor, dollars, hours, and so on
(726)	6. Carrying value	F. A formal document
(860)	7. Lot ticket	G. Contra-asset
(862)	8. Overhead	H. Shows movement between departments
(701)	9. Treasury stock	I. Net sales less cost of goods sold
(854)	10. Raw material	J. All the manufacturing costs except raw materials and direct labor

(867)   11. Cost of goods manufactured is prepared after the Income Statement.

(855)   12. Raw materials, work-in-process and finished goods are three major inventories.

(855)   13. Manufacturing overhead are all the manufacturing costs except raw material and direct labor.

(868)   14. Beginning finished goods inventory plus cost of goods manufactured equals cost of goods available for sale.

(855)   15. Finished goods inventory is added to cost of goods sold.

How Companies Record Credit Card Sales in Their Special Journals

A

Recording Bank Credit Cards

Example—Credit Card Sale of \$100, Master Card: It is interesting to note that for bank credit cards (Master Card, Visa) the sales are recorded in the seller's Cash Receipts Journal, since the slips are converted into cash immediately. Bank credit cards are not treated as accounts receivable. The fee the bank charges, $2\frac{1}{2}$ to 6 percent, is usually deducted, and the bank credits the depositor's account immediately for the net. The end result for the seller is:

Accounts Affected	Category	↑ ↓	Rule
Cash	Asset	↑	Dr. \$94
Credit Card Expense	Expense	↑	Dr. 6
Sales	Revenue	↑	Cr. 100

				CASH RECEIPTS JOURNAL					
Date	Cash Dr.	Credit Card Expense Dr.	Accounts Receivable Cr.	Sales Credited	Sales Tax Payable Cr.	Sundry Account Name	Sundry Amount Cr.
	94 00	6 00		100 00			

It is the responsibility of the credit card company to sustain any losses (bad debts) from customers' nonpayment. If the bank waits to take the discount until the end of the month, the seller makes a nonpayment entry in the cash payment journal to record the credit card expense; the end result would be credit card expense up and cash balance down. Usually, the bank would send the charge on the monthly statement. *Remember: bank credit cards are not treated as accounts receivable.*

RECORDING PRIVATE COMPANY CREDIT CARDS

Private companies such as American Express and Diners Club are considered by sellers as accounts receivable. The seller periodically summarizes the sales slips and submits them to the private credit card company for payment (which the company will pay quickly). Let's look at two situations to show how a company would handle its accounting procedures for these credit sales transactions.

Situation 1: On May 4, Morris Company sold merchandise on account of $53 to Bill Blank. Bill used American Express. Assume Morris Company has a low dollar volume and few transactions.

Note in Figure A-1 how the sale of $53 is recorded in the sales journal. Keep in mind that Morris is treating American Express, not Bill Blank, as the accounts receivable. In Figure A-2 we see on June 8 payment is received from American Express and results in

1. Cash increasing by $50.35.
2. Credit card expense rising by $2.65.
3. Accounts receivable being reduced by the $53 originally owed by American Express.

Situation 2: On March 31, Blue Company summarized its credit card sales for American Express. Payment was received on April 13 from American Express. Assume Blue Company has a high dollar volume and many transactions.

Note in Figure A-3 how each credit company has its own column set up. In the ledger there is an account set up for each as well; the posting to the ledger would be done at the end of the month. With high volume and the need to record many transactions, the use of these additional columns (versus Figure A-1) will result in increased efficiency. Figure A-4 shows the receipt of money from American Express less the credit card expense charge.

FIGURE A-1

		Date	Invoice	Description of Accounts Receivable	PR	Accounts Receivable Dr.	Sales Tax* Payable Cr.	Sales Cr.	
				SALES JOURNAL					
		May 4	692	American Express		53 00	3 00	50 00	
				(Bill Blank)					

* Assume a 6% sales tax.

FIGURE A-2

		Date		Cash Dr.		Sales Discount Dr.		Credit Card Expense Dr.		Accounts Receivable Cr.		Sales Tax Payable Cr.		Account Name		PR		Amount Cr.	
								CASH RECEIPTS JOURNAL							Sundry				
		June 8		50 35				2 65*		53 00				American Express					
														(Bill Blank)					

* Assume credit card expense of 5%. Note the $2.56 is 5% × $53.

BLUE COMPANY SALES JOURNAL

Date	Invoice Number	Description of Accounts Receivable	PR	Accounts Receivable Dr.	Credit Cards American Express Dr.	Credit Cards Diners Club Dr.	Sales Tax Payable Cr.	Credit Card Sales Cr.	Sales Cr.
March 31		Summary of American Express			1197000	5300	57000	1140000	
					(112)	(113)		(401)	

BLUE COMPANY CASH RECEIPTS JOURNAL

Date	Cash Dr.	Sales Discount Dr.	Credit Card Expense Dr.	Accounts Receivable Cr.	Credit Card Accounts Rec. American Express Cr.	Credit Card Accounts Rec. Diners Club Cr.	Sales Cr.	Sales Tax Payable Cr.	Sundry Account Name	Sundry PR	Sundry Amount Cr.
April 13	1125 1800		718 200		1197000				Summary of American Express payments		

COMPUTERIZED ACCOUNTING

B

PART *A*
An Introduction

Accounting procedures are essentially the same whether they are performed manually or on a computer. The following is a list of the accounting cycle steps in a manual accounting system as compared to the steps in a computerized accounting system.

STEPS OF THE ACCOUNTING CYCLE

Manual Accounting System	Computerized Accounting System
1. Business transactions occur and generate source documents.	1. Business transactions occur and generate source documents.
2. Analyze and record business transactions in a journal.	2. Analyze and record business transactions in a computerized journal.
3. Post or transfer information from journal to ledger.	3. Computer automatically posts information from journal to ledger.
4. Prepare a trial balance.	4. Trial balance is prepared automatically.
5. Prepare a worksheet.	5. No worksheet is necessary.
6. Prepare financial statements.	6. Financial statements are prepared automatically.
7. Journalize and post adjusting entries.	7. Record adjusting entries in a computerized journal; posting is automatic.
8. Journalize and post closing entries.	8. Closing procedures are completed automatically.
9. Prepare a post-closing trial balance.	9. Trial balance is prepared automatically.

The accounting cycle comparison shows that the accountant's task of initially analyzing business transactions in terms of debits and credits (both routine business transactions and adjusting entries) is required in both manual and computerized accounting systems. However, in a computerized accounting system, the "drudge" work of posting transactions, creating and completing worksheets and financial statements, and performing the closing procedures is all handled automatically by the computerized accounting system.

In addition, computerized accounting systems can perform accounting procedures at greater speeds and with greater accuracy than can be achieved in a manual accounting system. It is important to recognize, however, that the computer is only a tool that can accept and process information supplied by the accountant. Each business transaction and adjusting entry must first be analyzed and recorded in a computerized journal correctly; otherwise, the financial statements generated by the computerized accounting system will contain errors and will not be useful to the business.

Before a business can begin to use a computerized accounting system, and specifically the Simply Accounting system, it must have the following items in place:

1. A computer system
2. Computer software
   a. Operating system software
   b. Applications software
      (1) Accounting applications software
      (2) Simply Accounting

COMPUTER SYSTEM

A computer system consists of several electronic components that together have the ability to accept user-supplied data; input, store, and execute programmed instructions; and output results according to user specifications. The physical computer and its related devices are the hardware, while the stored program that supplies the instructions is called the software.

To understand how a computer system works, we must first look at a conceptual computer that demonstrates the major components and functions of a computer system. The conceptual computer shown in Figure B-1 has four major elements—input devices, processing/internal memory unit, secondary storage devices, and output devices. The illustration also shows the flow of data into the computer and of processed information out of the computer.

Input devices are used to feed data and instructions into the computer. Once the data and instructions are entered, the computer must be able to store them internally and then process the data based on the instructions. Storage and processing occur in the processing/internal memory unit.

There are two types of internal computer memory: random-access memory (RAM) and read-only memory (ROM). RAM is the largest portion of the memory but still has limited capacity; consequently, secondary storage devices are needed. In addition, RAM is temporary—anything stored in RAM is erased when power to the computer is interrupted. Therefore, data stored in RAM must be saved to a secondary storage medium through the use of a secondary storage device before the power is turned off. ROM is permanent memory and consists of those instruction

FIGURE B-1
Conceptual Computer

FIGURE B-2
Typical Configuration of a
Microcomputer System

sets necessary to start the computer and receive initial messages from input devices. ROM takes up only a small portion of the total internal memory capacity of a computer system.

Finally, the results of processing must be made available to computer users through output devices. These components form a collection of devices referred to as computer hardware because they have physical substance.

In a typical microcomputer system (see Fig. B-2) a keyboard and mouse are used for input and a printer and monitor are used for output. The processing/internal memory unit is housed inside a box along with secondary storage devices consisting of a hard drive unit, one or more floppy disk drives, and a CD-ROM drive.

Computer hardware can do nothing without a computer program. Computer programs are supplied on floppy disks or CD-ROMs, which are secondary storage media used in floppy disk or CD-ROM drives. Figure B-3 shows an example of a floppy disk and of a CD-ROM.

To operate a particular computer program you must first load the program into the system's internal memory (RAM) through the use of a floppy disk or CD-ROM drive or by accessing the program that has been installed and stored on the system's hard drive. Once a program is accessed by RAM, the computer can execute the program instructions and process data as directed by the user through the keyboard or mouse. At the end of a processing session, the results may be viewed on the monitor, printed on the printer, and/or stored permanently on a floppy disk or hard drive.

COMPUTER SOFTWARE

The computer can do nothing without a computer program. Computer programs control the input, processing, storage, and output operations of a computer. Computer programmers write the instructions that tell the computer to execute certain

FIGURE B-3
Storage Media

procedures and process data. There are two broad categories of computer software: operating system software and applications software.

Operating System Software

Operating system software provides the link between the computer hardware, applications software, and the computer user. It consists of programs that start up the computer, retrieve applications programs, and allow the computer operator to store and retrieve data. Operating system software controls access to input and output devices and access to applications programs. There are several popular operating systems for microcomputers. They include Windows 95, DOS, DOS combined with Windows 3.XX, OS/2, the Macintosh operating system, and UNIX.

Applications Software

Applications software refers to programs designed for a specific use. The five most common types of business applications software are database management, spreadsheets, word processing communications, and graphics. Spreadsheet software allows the manipulation of data and has the ability to project answers to "what if" questions. For example, a spreadsheet program could project a company's profit next year if sales increased by 10 percent and expenses increased by 6 percent. Word processing software enables the user to write and print letters, memos, and other documents. Graphics software displays data visually in the form of graphic images, and communications software allows your computer to "talk" to other computers. But to accomplish communications you need additional hardware: a modem to transmit and receive data over telephone lines. Database management software stores, retrieves, sorts, and updates an organized body of information. Most computerized accounting systems are designed as database management software. Accounting information is data that must be organized and stored in a common base of data. This allows the entry of data and the retrieval of information in an organized and systematic way.

Applications software is frequently linked with a particular operating system. Database management, spreadsheet, word processing graphics, communication, accounting, and other software applications are available in versions that work with most of the popular operating systems. For example, if your computer system is using Windows 95 you would purchase the Windows 95 version of a word processing program. If you were using a Macintosh computer and operating system you would purchase the Macintosh version of a spreadsheet program.

Accounting Applications Software Most computerized accounting software is organized into modules. Each module is designed to process a particular type of accounting data such as accounts receivable, accounts payable, or payroll. Each module is also designed to work in conjunction with the other modules. When modules are designed to work together in this manner, they are referred to as integrated software. In an integrated accounting system each module handles a different function but also communicates with the other modules. For example, to record a sale on account, you would make an entry into the accounts receivable module. The integration feature automatically records this entry in the sales journal, updates the customer's account in the accounts receivable subsidiary ledger, and posts all accounts affected in the general ledger. Thus in an integrated accounting system, transaction data are only entered once. All of the other accounting procedures required to bring the accounting records up-to-date are performed automatically through the integration function.

Simply Accounting The educational version of Simply Accounting has been selected for use in this text to demonstrate and help you learn how to use a computerized accounting system. It is easy to use, fully integrated, and is also available in versions that work with several different operating systems. Simply Accounting includes six modules: General, Receivables, Payables, Inventory, Payroll, and Project.

Two modes of operation are available in Simply Accounting: Ready and Not Ready. The Not Ready mode is used when you are converting a manual accounting system to a computerized accounting system. The Ready mode is used for regular accounting purposes. The educational version is the complete commercial program package with one restriction: The program will not accept dates after January 1, 1998. The payroll functions of the educational version are based on the federal and state tax laws in effect as of April 15, 1997.

WORKING WITH SIMPLY ACCOUNTING

Before you begin to work with Simply Accounting you need to be familiar with your computer hardware and the Windows 95 operating system. When you are running Windows 95, your work takes place on the desktop. Think of this area as resembling the surface of a desk. There are physical objects on your real desk and there are windows and icons on the Windows 95 desktop.

A mouse is an essential input device for all Windows 95 applications. A mouse is a pointing device which assumes different shapes on your monitor as you move the mouse on your desk. According to the nature of the current action, the mouse pointer may appear as a small arrow head, an hourglass, or a hand. There are five basic mouse techniques:

- ◆ Click — To quickly press and release the left mouse button.
- ◆ Double-click — To click the left mouse button twice in rapid succession.
- ◆ Drag — To hold down the left mouse button while you move the mouse.
- ◆ Point — To position the mouse pointer over an object without clicking a button.
- ◆ Right-click — To quickly press and release the right mouse button.

The Windows 95 Desktop

Figure B-4 shows a typical opening Windows 95 screen. Your desktop may be different, just as your real desk is arranged differently from those of your colleagues.

- ◆ **Desktop icons:** Graphic representations of drives, files, and other resources. The desktop icons that display will vary depending on your computer setup.
- ◆ **Start button:** Clicking on the Start button displays the start menu and lets you start applications.
- ◆ **Taskbar:** Contains the Start button and other buttons representing open applications.

FIGURE B-4
Windows 95 Desktop

Applications Window (the Company Window)

As you work with Simply Accounting two kinds of windows will appear on your desktop: the application window (called the Company Window — see Fig. B-5), and windows contained within the Company Window (called dialog boxes). An application window contains a running application. The name of the application and the application's menu bar will appear at the top of the application window. Regardless of the windows that are open on your desktop, most windows have certain elements in common.

FIGURE B-5
Simply Accounting Application (Company) Window

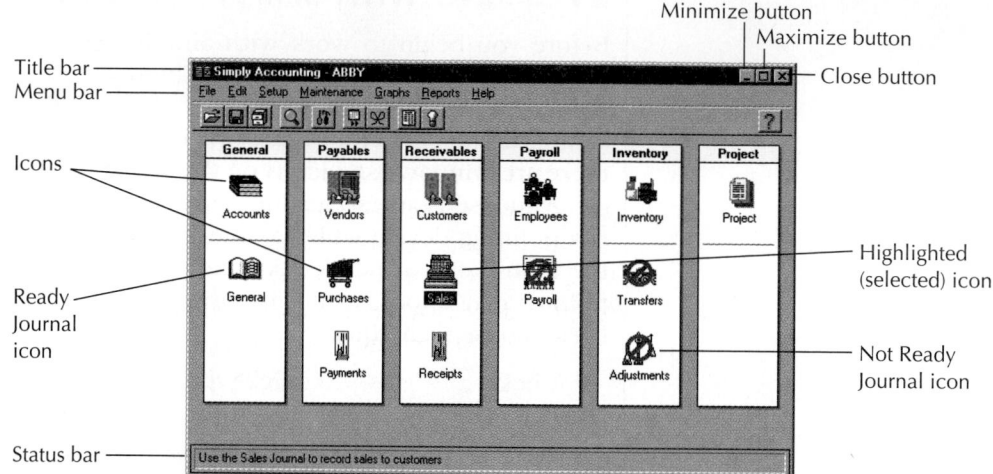

- ◆ **Minimize button:** Clicking on this button minimizes a window and displays it as a task button on the taskbar.
- ◆ **Maximize button:** Clicking on this button enlarges the window so that it fills the entire desktop. After you enlarge a window, the maximize button is replaced by a **Restore button** (a double box, not shown) that returns the window to the size it was before it was maximized.
- ◆ **Close button:** Clicking on this button will close the window.
- ◆ **Title bar:** Displays the name of the application.
- ◆ **Menu bar:** This window element lists the available menus for the window.
- ◆ **Icons:** The Company Window displays the icons that represent a company's accounting books — the full set of Ledgers and Journals that you use to record accounting transactions. The top row contains the Ledgers; the bottom two rows contain the Journals aligned vertically with their related Ledgers.
- ◆ **Highlighted (selected) icon:** The active icon in the Company Window.
- ◆ **Not Ready Journal icon:** A Journal icon is shown with a no-entry symbol if its status is Not Ready.
- ◆ **Ready Journal icon:** A Journal icon is shown without a no-entry symbol if its status is Ready.
- ◆ **Status bar:** A line of text at the bottom of many windows that gives more information about a field, button, or menu item. If you are unsure of what to enter in a field or what a button is for, point to it with your mouse and read the status bar.

Dialog Boxes

A dialog box appears when additional information is needed to execute a command. There are different ways to supply that information; consequently, there are different types of dialog boxes. Most dialog boxes (see Fig. B-6) contain options you can select. After you specify options, you can choose a command button to carry out a command. Other dialog boxes (see Fig. B-7) may display additional information, warnings, or messages indicating why a requested task cannot be accomplished.

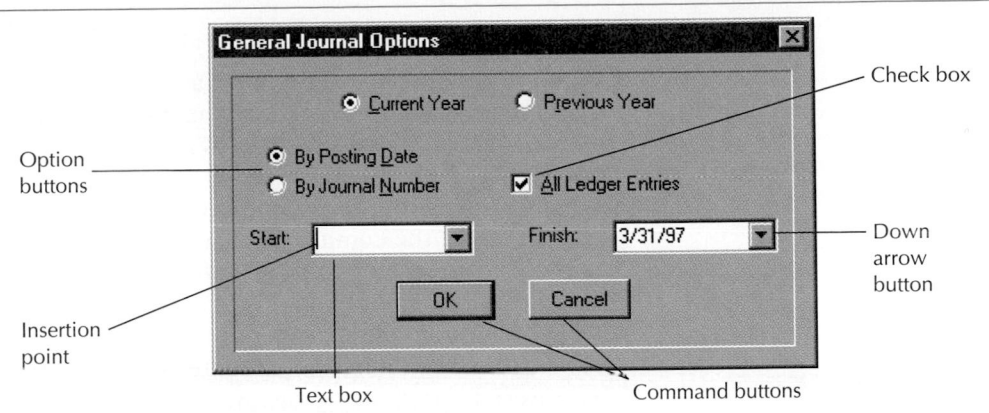

◆ **Insertion point:** This element shows where you are in the dialog box. It marks the place where text will appear when you begin typing.

◆ **Check box:** A small square that represents an option. When you select an option (click on the empty check box), the check box contains an X; when you turn off the option (click on the check box to remove the X), it is blank.

◆ **Option buttons:** A small circle that represents an option. When you select (click on the button) an option from a group, that button contains a large black dot; the remaining buttons in the group are blank. Option buttons represent mutually exclusive options. You can select only one option button at a time.

◆ **Text box:** When you move to an empty text box, an insertion point appears at the far left-hand side of the box. The text you type starts at the insertion point. If the box you move to already contains text, this text is selected (highlighted), and any text you type replaces it. You can also delete the selected text by pressing the DELETE or BACKSPACE key.

◆ **Command buttons:** Choose (click) on a command button to initiate an immediate action such as carrying out or canceling a command. The **OK, Cancel, Yes, No,** and **Post** buttons are common command buttons.

◆ **Down arrow button:** Click on this button to display a list of choices.

◆ **Highlighted (selected) item:** To highlight or select an item in a displayed list, click on the item.

◆ **Scroll bar:** A bar that may appear at the bottom and/or right side of a window or dialog box if there is more text than can be displayed at one time within the window.

◆ **Scroll arrow:** A small arrow at the end of a scroll bar that you click on to move to the next item in the list. The top and left arrows scroll to the previous item; the bottom and right arrows scroll to the next item.

◆ **Scroll box:** A small box in a scroll bar. You can use the mouse to drag the scroll box left or right, or up or down. The scroll box indicates the relative position in the list.

◆ **Mouse pointer:** The mouse pointer is shown as a small arrow head in this example.

Using Menus

Commands are listed on menus, as shown in Figure B-8. Each application has its own menus which are listed on the **Application menu bar.** To display a complete menu, click on the **Menu title.** When a menu is displayed, choose a command by clicking on it or by typing the **Underlined letter** to execute the command. You can also bypass the menu entirely if you know the **Keyboard equivalent** shown to the right of the command when the menu is displayed.

A **Dimmed command** indicates that a command is not currently executable; some additional action has to be taken for the command to become available. Some commands are followed by **Ellipses** (. . .) to indicate that more information is required to execute the command. The additional information can be entered into a dialog box, which will appear immediately after the command has been selected.

FIGURE B-8
Sample Menu

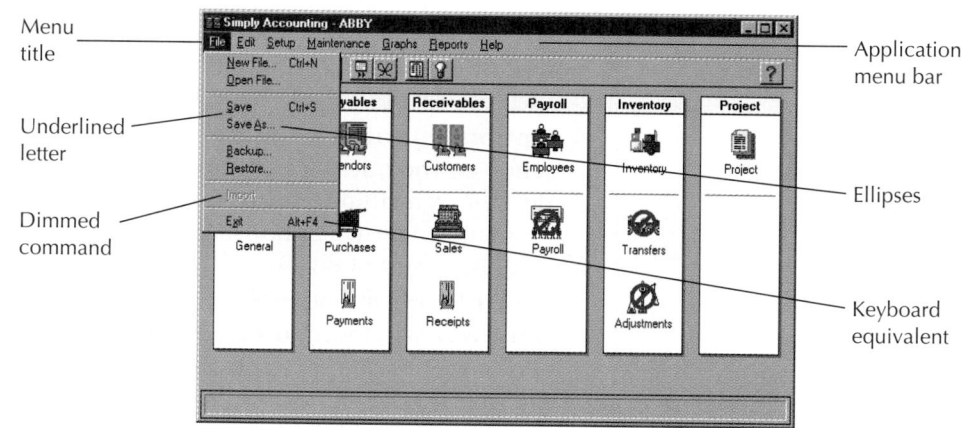

Working in the Windows 95 Environment

You can use a combination of mouse and keyboard techniques to navigate within the Windows 95 environment. For example, you can click on an item to select it, and then press the ENTER key to choose it, or you can just double-click on the item. Simply Accounting is designed for a mouse, but it also provides keyboard equivalents for almost every command. It may seem confusing at first that there are several different ways to do the same thing. You will find this flexibility useful. For example, if your hands are already on the keyboard, it may be faster to use the keyboard equivalent of a mouse command. Alternatively, if your hand is already on the mouse, it may be faster to use a mouse technique to carry out a command. When a procedure in an assignment says to select or choose an item, generally use whichever method you prefer. Alternative procedures are often provided as well. It is not necessary to memorize any particular technique, just be flexible and willing to experiment. As you gain experience with the program, you will develop personal preferences, and the various techniques will become second nature.

Windows 95 Tour

Windows 95 includes a tour to acquaint new users with mouse techniques and the Windows 95 operating environment. Use the following instructions to access the Windows Tour on your computer system.

1. Click on the Start button; then click on Run.
2. Type tour.exe into the **Open** text box; then click on the **OK** button.
3. Follow the instructions on your screen to complete the tour.

PART *B*
Installing Simply Accounting/Creating a Student Data Files Disk

This section of the appendix discusses several basic operations that you need to complete to install the Simply Accounting program and create a Student Data Files disk for use in completing the Computer Workshop assignments in this text.

SYSTEM REQUIREMENTS

The recommended minimum software and hardware your computer system needs to run both Windows and Simply Accounting successfully are:

◆ Microsoft Windows 3.1 or 3.11, or Windows 95.
◆ A personal computer with an 80486/33 processor.
◆ A hard disk with 12 MB of free disk space.
◆ One 3.5 inch high density floppy disk drive.
◆ A CD-ROM drive (optional, the Simply Accounting program and the Student Data Files are also available on 3.5 inch high density floppy disks).
◆ 8 MB of RAM.
◆ A VGA, or similar high-resolution monitor that is supported by Windows.
◆ A printer that is supported by Windows.
◆ A mouse that is supported by Windows.

CD-ROM CONTENTS

The Simply Accounting installation and program files (in condensed form) and the Student Data Files (not in condensed form) for use in completing the Computer Workshops are on the CD-ROM that accompanies this text.

Installation Procedures

To install Simply Accounting on your hard disk, follow these instructions:

1. Start Windows.
2. Make sure that no other programs are running on your system.
3. Insert the CD-ROM in your CD-ROM drive.
4. Click on the Start button; then click on Run.
5. Type d:setup and press the ENTER key. For d, substitute the letter of your CD-ROM drive.
6. Follow the step-by-step instructions as they appear on the screen. Enter your Name and your school's name as the Company when requested. Enter the following serial number when requested: 252160230500. Install all of the Simply Accounting components. Read the ReadMe text file; then click on the Close button.
7. Put your CD-ROM away for safekeeping.

Installing Simply Accounting on a Network

Simply Accounting can be used in a network environment as long as each student uses a separate Student Data Files disk to store his or her data files. Refer to the *Instructor's Resource and Solutions Manual for College Accounting*, seventh edition, for specific network installation instructions.

Students should consult with their instructor and/or network administrator for specific procedures regarding program installation and any special printing procedures required for proper network operation.

Creating a Student Data Files Disk

The Student Data Files for use in completing the Computer Workshops are on the CD-ROM that accompanies this text in a special folder called Student. You need to copy these files from the CD-ROM to a 3.5 inch high density floppy disk. You will need a blank, formatted 3.5 inch high density floppy disk labeled "Student Data Files Disk."

1. Insert the CD-ROM in your CD-ROM drive.
2. Insert your blank, formatted 3.5 inch high density floppy disk into your 3.5 inch disk drive.
3. Double-click on the My Computer icon on your Windows 95 desktop. The My Computer window will appear.
4. In the My Computer window double-click on the icon for your CD-ROM drive. The contents of the CD-ROM will be displayed.
5. Right-click on the Student folder; point to Send To; then click on the icon for $3\frac{1}{2}$ Floppy. The copying window will appear. When your system has finished copying the files, close the CD-ROM window, then close the My Computer window.
6. Put your CD-ROM away for safekeeping. Use your Student Data Files disk to complete the Computer Workshop assignments.

PART C
Correcting a Posted Transaction

Once a transaction is posted in Simply Accounting, the journal entry will be permanently reflected in the accounting records. This feature of Simply Accounting is designed to ensure that a good audit trail of all transactions is constantly maintained within the program. Consequently, the only way to correct a posted transaction is to reverse the original entry. After this is accomplished, the accounting records will be in the same position as if the transaction had not been posted in the first place, but a complete record of the original entry and the reversing entry will be maintained by the program. After the reversing entry is posted, enter the correct journal entry.

The term reversing entry as it is used here should not be confused with the optional way of handling certain adjusting entries. The optional reversing entry procedure for adjusting entries is designed to help prevent errors. Reversing an incorrect entry in a computerized accounting system is a required procedure designed to correct an error that has already occurred.

The following procedures for reversing an incorrect journal entry and re-entering the correct journal entry are not intended to be exhaustive, but to give you the general idea of how to correct transactions posted in error. It is impossible to predict the particular error or combination of errors you might make in an assignment.

You will need to have a printed copy of a General Journal report listing the entry you intend to reverse on hand as you work through the following reversing and correcting procedures.

Reversing an Entry Made in the General Journal Dialog Box: Use the General Journal

1. Open the General Journal; enter the word "Reverse" into the **Source** text box; press the TAB key; enter the **Using** date into the **Date** text box; press the TAB key; enter an explanation for the transaction into the **Comment** text box; then press the TAB key.

2. Refer to your printed copy of the General Journal report. With the flashing insertion point positioned in the **Account** text box press the ENTER key to bring up the Select Account dialog box. Double-click on the account that you credited in the incorrect journal entry; enter the amount used in the credit portion of the incorrect journal entry into the **Debits** text box; then press the TAB key.

3. If you are reversing a compound journal entry, skip this step and go to the next step. With the flashing insertion point positioned in the **Account** text box, press the ENTER key to bring up the Select Account dialog box. Double-click on the account that you debited in the incorrect journal entry; then press the TAB key to accept the default **Credits** amount.

4. If you are reversing a compound journal entry, press the ENTER key with the flashing insertion point positioned in the **Account** text box to bring up the Select Account dialog box. Double-click on the first account that you debited in the incorrect compound journal entry. The program will offer a default **Credits** amount and the **Credits** amount will remain highlighted. Override the default **Credits** amount by entering the amount used in the debit portion of the incorrect compound journal entry. Press the TAB key; then press the ENTER key to bring up the Select Account dialog box. Double-click on the second account that you debited in the incorrect compound journal entry. The program will offer a default **Credits** amount; press the TAB key to accept the default **Credits** amount.

5. Click on the General Journal Report menu; then click on Display General Journal Entry. Verify that the reversing entry is correct. The reversing entry should be the exact opposite of your incorrect journal entry. Accounts and amounts originally debited should be credited, and accounts and amounts originally credited should be debited.

6. Close the General Journal Entry Display window. Make editing corrections if necessary.

7. Click on the **Post** icon to post the entry.

8. Re-enter the journal entry correctly. Enter the word "Correct" in the **Source** text box to indicate that it is a correcting entry; enter the **Using** date into the **Date** text box.

NOTE: Simply Accounting will not accept duplicate invoice or check numbers in the Sales, Receipts, Purchases, Payments, or Payroll Journals. This feature of the program is designed to prevent the error of entering invoices and checks twice. Consequently, invoice and check numbers must be modified when reversing and correcting entries are entered. Insert the letter R after the invoice or check number to indicate a reversing entry. Insert the letter C after the invoice or check number to indicate a correcting entry.

Reversing an Entry Made in the Payroll Journal Dialog Box: Use the Payroll Journal

1. Click on the Company Window Setup Menu; then click on Settings. The Settings dialog box will appear. Click on the **Payroll** tab; click on the **Automatic Payroll Deductions** check box to de-select this option (the X will disappear from the check box); then click on the **OK** button.

2. Open the Payroll Journal; click on the arrow key to the right of the **To the order of** text box; select the employee from the list displayed; then press the TAB key.

3. Enter the check number into the **No.** text box inserting the letter R after the check number to indicate that this is a reversing entry; then press the TAB key.

4. Enter the Using date into the **Date** text box; then press the TAB key.

5. Accept the **Period Start** and **Period End** dates offered by pressing the TAB key.

6. Refer to your General Journal report listing the incorrect payroll journal entry. Enter amounts into the following text boxes overriding any default amounts offered:

Wages Enter the amount debited to the Wages account as a negative number.

FIT Enter the amount credited to the FIT Payable account as a negative number.

SIT Enter the amount credited to the SIT Payable account as a negative number.

Medicare Tax Enter the amount debited to the Medicare Tax Expense account as a negative number.

Soc Sec Tax Enter the amount debited to the Social Security Tax Expense account as a negative number.

7. Press the TAB key; click on the Payroll Journal Report menu; then click on Display Payroll Journal Entry. Verify that the entry is correct. It should be the exact opposite of your incorrect payroll entry. Accounts and amounts originally debited should be credited, and accounts and amounts originally credited should be debited.

8. Close the Payroll Journal Entry window. Make editing corrections if necessary.

9. Click on the **Post** icon to post the entry.

10. Click on the Company Window Setup menu; then click on Settings. The Settings dialog box will appear. Click on the **Payroll** tab; click on the **Automatic Payroll Deductions** check box to re-select this option (the X will re-appear in the check box); then click on the **OK** button.

11. Re-enter the payroll journal entry correctly. Insert the letter C after the check number in the **No.** text box to indicate that this is a correcting entry; enter the **Using** date into the **Date** text box.

REVERSING AND CORRECTING ENTRIES MADE IN SPECIAL JOURNALS

You must know for certain which dialog box you originally used (Sales Journal, Receipts Journal, Purchases Journal, or Payments Journal) to record a transaction prior to attempting to use the reversing procedures described in the following sections for special journals. If you are uncertain about which dialog box you used to record the journal entry you wish to reverse and correct, print a Sales Journal, Receipts Journal, Purchases Journal, and Payments Journal report.

1. **To print a Sales Journal,** click on the Sales Journal icon to highlight the icon; click on the Company Window Reports menu; then click on Display Sales Journal. Enter 3/1/97 into the **Start** date text box; leave the **Finish** date text box set at 3/31/97; then click on the **OK** button. The Sales Journal Display window will appear. Click on the Sales Journal Display File menu; then click on Print to print the report. After you have printed the report, close the Sales Journal Display window.

2. **To print a Receipts Journal,** click on the Receipts Journal icon to highlight the icon; click on the Company Window Reports menu; then click on Display Receipts Journal. Enter 3/1/97 into the **Start** date text box; leave the **Finish** date text box set at 3/31/97; then click on the **OK** button. The Receipts Journal Display window will appear. Click on the Receipts Journal Display File menu; then click on Print to print the report. After you have printed the report, close the Receipts Journal Display window.

3. **To print a Purchases Journal,** click on the Purchases Journal icon to highlight the icon; click on the Company Window Reports menu; then click on Display Purchases Journal. Enter 3/1/97 into the **Start** date text box; leave the

Finish date text box set at 3/31/97; then click on the **OK** button. The Purchases Journal Display window will appear. Click on the Purchases Journal Display File menu; then click on Print to print the report. After you have printed the report, close the Purchases Journal Display window.

4. **To print a Payments Journal,** click on the Payments Journal icon to highlight the icon; click on the Company Window Reports menu; then click on Display Payments Journal. Enter 3/1/97 into the **Start** date text box; leave the **Finish** date text box set at 3/31/97; then click on the **OK** button. The Payments Journal Display window will appear. Click on the Payments Journal Display File menu; then click on Print to print the report. After you have printed the report, close the Payments Journal Display window.

Review each report to determine which report contains the journal entry you wish to reverse; then use the following chart to determine which set of instructions to use to reverse the journal entry and enter the correct entry.

If the journal entry you wish to reverse appears on the:	Use these instructions to reverse the entry and enter the correct entry:
Sales Journal	Reversing an Entry Made in the Sales Journal Dialog Box: Use the Sales Journal
Receipts Journal	Reversing an Entry Made in the Receipts Journal: Use the Sales Journal
Purchases Journal	Reversing an Entry Made in the Purchases Journal: Use the Purchases Journal
Payments Journal	Reversing an Entry Made in the Payments Journal: Use the Purchases Journal

Reversing an Entry Made in the Sales Journal Dialog Box: Use the Sales Journal

1. Open the Sales Journal; click on the arrow button to the right of the **Sold to** text box; select the customer from the list displayed; then press the TAB key until the Invoice text box is highlighted.

2. Enter the invoice number used in the incorrect entry into the **Invoice** text box followed by the letter R to show that you are reversing this entry; then press the TAB key.

3. Enter the Using date into the **Date** text box; then press the TAB key until the insertion point is positioned in the **Amount** text box.

4. Enter the same **Amount** as used in the incorrect entry, preceded by a minus sign if the incorrect amount was originally entered as a positive amount. Enter the amount as a positive amount if the original amount entered was negative. Press the TAB key.

5. Enter the same **Acct** number as used in the incorrect entry (do not use the Accounts Receivable account number); then press the TAB key.

6. Click on the Sales Journal Report menu; then click on Display Sales Journal Entry. Verify that the entry is correct. The entry should be the exact opposite of your incorrect entry. Accounts and amounts originally debited should be credited, and accounts and amounts originally credited should be debited.

7. Close the Sales Journal Entry window. Make editing corrections if necessary.

8. Click on the **Post** icon to post the entry.

9. Re-enter the journal entry correctly. Insert the letter C after the invoice number to show that this is a correcting entry; enter the **Using** date into the **Date** text box.

Reversing an Entry Made in the Receipts
Journal Dialog Box: Use the Sales Journal

1. Open the Sales Journal; click on the arrow button to the right of the **Sold to** text box; select the customer from the list displayed; then press the TAB key until the **Invoice** text box is highlighted.

2. Enter the customer's check number used in the incorrect entry into the **Invoice** text box followed by the letter R to show that you are reversing this entry; then press the TAB key.

3. Enter the Using date into the **Date** text box; then press the TAB key until the flashing insertion point is positioned in the **Amount** text box.

4. Enter the amount debited to the Cash account in the incorrect journal entry into the **Amount** text box; then press the TAB key.

5. Enter the Cash account number into the **Acct** text box; then press the TAB key.

6. If necessary, enter the amount debited to the Sales Discounts account in the incorrect journal entry into the **Amount** text box; then press the TAB key.

7. Enter the Sales Discounts account number into the **Acct** text box; then press the TAB key.

8. Click on the Sales Journal Report menu; then click on Display Sales Journal Entry. The entry should debit the Accounts Receivable account and credit the Cash account (and the Sales Discounts account, if necessary) for the amount of the entry you are reversing. Verify that the entry is correct.

9. Close the Sales Journal Entry window. Make editing corrections if necessary.

10. Click on the **Post** icon to post the entry.

11. Re-enter the customer's payment correctly using the Receipts Journal dialog box. Insert the letter C after the customer's check number to show that this is a correcting entry; enter the **Using** date into the **Date** text box. Enter amounts as necessary into the **Disc Taken** and **Payment Amt** text boxes to record the correct amount received from the customer.

Reversing an Entry Made in the Purchases
Journal Dialog Box: Use the Purchases Journal

1. Open the Purchases Journal; click on the arrow button to the right of the **Purchased From** text box; select the vendor from the list displayed; then press the TAB key until the flashing insertion point is positioned in the Invoice text box.

2. Enter the invoice number used in the incorrect entry into the **Invoice** text box followed by the letter R to show that you are reversing this entry; then press the TAB key.

3. Enter the Using date into the **Date** text box; then press the TAB key until the insertion point is positioned in the **Amount** text box.

4. Enter the same **Amount** as used in the incorrect entry, preceded by a minus sign if the incorrect amount was originally entered as a positive amount. Enter the amount as a positive amount if the original amount entered was negative. Press the TAB key.

5. Enter the same **Acct** number as used in the incorrect entry (do not use the Accounts Payable account number); then press the TAB key.

6. Click on the Purchases Journal Report menu; then click on Display Purchases Journal Entry. Verify that the entry is correct. The entry should be the exact opposite of your incorrect entry. Accounts and amounts originally debited should be credited, and accounts and amounts originally credited should be debited.

7. Close the Purchases Journal Entry window. Make editing corrections if necessary.

8. Click on the **Post** icon to post the entry.

9. Re-enter the journal entry correctly. Insert the letter C after the invoice number to show that this is a correcting entry; enter the **Using** date into the **Date** text box.

Reversing an Entry Made in the Payments Journal Dialog Box: Use the Purchases Journal

1. Open the Purchases Journal; click on the arrow button to the right of the **Purchased From** text box; select the vendor from the list displayed; then press the TAB key until the flashing insertion point is positioned in the **Invoice** text box.
2. Enter the check number used in the incorrect entry into the **Invoice** text box followed by the letter R to show that you are reversing this entry; then press the TAB key.
3. Enter the Using date into the **Date** text box; then press the TAB key until the insertion point is positioned in the **Amount** text box.
4. Enter the amount credited to the Cash account in the incorrect journal entry into the **Amount** text box; then press the TAB key.
5. Enter the Cash account number into the **Acct** text box; then press the TAB key.
6. If necessary, enter the amount credited to the Purchases Discount account in the incorrect journal entry into the **Amount** text box; then press the TAB key.
7. Enter the Purchases Discount account number into the **Acct** text box; then press the TAB key.
8. Click on the Purchases Journal Report menu; then click on Display Purchases Journal Entry. The entry should debit the Cash account (and the Purchases Discount account, if necessary) and credit the Accounts Payable account for the amount of the entry you are reversing. Verify that the entry is correct.
9. Close the Purchases Journal Entry window. Make editing corrections if necessary.
10. Click on the **Post** icon to post the entry.
11. Re-enter the payment issued to the vendor correctly using the Payments Journal dialog box. Insert the letter C after the check number to show that this is a correcting entry; enter the **Using** date into the **Date** text box. Enter amounts as necessary into the **Disc Taken** and **Payment Amt** text boxes to record the correct amount of the payment issued to the vendor.

PART *D*
How to Repeat or Start Over on an Assignment

You always have the option to repeat an assignment for additional practice or start over on an assignment. To repeat or start over on an assignment, make a new Student Data Files disk using the procedures listed in the Creating a Student Data Files Disk section of this appendix. Relabel your first Student Data Files disk "Student Data Files #1" and label your new copy "Student Data Files #2." Store your disk labeled "Student Data Files #1" in a safe place; then use the disk labeled "Student Data Files #2" to repeat the assignment or start over on the assignment.

After you have repeated or started over on an assignment, you can continue to use the disk labeled "Student Data Files #2" to complete the remaining assignments in this text.

PART *E*

How and When to Use the Backup Copy of a Company's Data Files

At certain times in the assignments you are asked to make a backup copy of a company's data files. There are several reasons why you might wish to access the backup copy of a company's data files. For example, you may not have printed a required report in an assignment before advancing the **Using** date to a new month, or you may want to start an assignment over at the point where the backup copy was made rather than at the beginning of an assignment.

To use the backup copy of a company's data files complete the following procedures. The backup data files for Valdez Realty for June are used to explain the process in the following procedures.

1. Click on the **Start** button. Point to Programs; point to Simply Accounting; then click on Simply Accounting in the final menu presented. The Simply Accounting-Open File dialog box will appear.

2. Insert your Student Data Files disk into disk drive A. Enter the following path into the **File name** text box: A:\student\valdjune.asc.

3. Click on the **Open** button; leave the **Using Date for this Session** set at 6/30/97; then click on the **OK** button. The Company Window for Valdjune will appear on your screen. If you only need to print reports for Valdez Realty for June, print those reports now; click on the Company Window File menu; then click on Exit to end the current work session and return to your Windows desktop. If you want to start the Valdez Realty assignment over at the point where you made the June backup copy (i.e., you completed the June transactions and adjusting entries correctly, but made an error in the June closing process and/or made errors in the July transactions) continue with the following instructions.

4. Click on the Company Window File menu; click on Save As; then enter the following new file name into the **File name** text box: A:\student\valdez.asc.

5. Click on the **Save** button. Click on the **OK** button in response to the question "Replace existing file?" Note that the company name in the Company Window has changed from Valdjune to Valdez.

6. Continue with the Valdez Realty Mini Practice Set starting with instruction #17 under Part A: The June Accounting Cycle.

If you want to use the backup copy of a company's data files in a situation other than that described in the preceding section, substitute the desired backup file name for valdjune. asc and the desired current data file name for valdez. asc into the procedures described in the preceding section. A summary of the substitutions appears at the top of page B17.

PART *F*

Print and Display Settings in Simply Accounting for Windows

When you install Simply Accounting, the program automatically installs the default printer established in Windows as the default printer for Simply Accounting. If you have not yet installed a default printer in Windows, you will need to do so prior to attempting to print any reports from the Simply Accounting program. Refer to your Windows manual for information on installing a printer. You do not need to re-install Simply Accounting for Windows. The next time you access Simply Accounting, the Windows default printer will automatically be established as the default printer for Simply Accounting.

Backup You Want to Use	Substitute in Prior Procedures	Using Date	Continue Assignment Starting With
1. valdjuly.asc	valdjuly.asc for valdjune.asc	7/31/97	Valdez Realty Mini Practice Set Part B, instruction #15
2. petejan.asc	petejan.asc for valdjune.asc pete.asc for valdez.asc	1/31/97	Pete's Market Mini Practice Set, instruction #20
3. petefeb.asc	petefeb.asc for valdjune.asc pete.asc for valdez.asc	2/29/97	Pete's Market Mini Practice Set, instruction #30
4. petemar.asc	petemar.asc for valdjune.asc pete.asc for valdez.asc	3/31/97	Pete's Market Mini Practice Set instruction #42
5. dressmar.asc	dressmar.asc for valdjune.asc dress.asc for valdez.asc	3/31/97	The Corner Dress Shop Mini Practice Set instruction #15

The installation process for the Windows default printer does not ensure that the default printer and display settings within Simply Accounting will work to your satisfaction; consequently, you must test and if necessary adjust your printer and display settings before you complete any of the assignments in the text. Once the print and display settings are adjusted, they will become the default printer and display settings for each set of company data files. You need only make these adjustments once.

HOW TO TEST AND ADJUST THE DEFAULT PRINTER AND DISPLAY SETTINGS FOR SIMPLY ACCOUNTING

1. Click on the **Start** button. Point to Programs; point to Simply Accounting; then click on Simply Accounting in the final menu presented. The Simply Accounting-Open File dialog box will appear.

2. Insert your Student Data Files disk into disk drive A. Enter the following path into the **File name** text box: A:\student\printest.asc

3. Click on the **Open** button. The program will respond with a request for the **Using Date for this Session.** Leave the **Using Date for this Session** text box set at 12/1/97; then click on the **OK** button. The Company Window will appear.

4. Click on the Company Window Setup menu; then click on Settings. The Settings dialog box will appear.

5. Click on the Display tab; then adjust the display features based on the following definitions and suggestions:

   ◆ **Display Font:** Click on the arrow button to the right of the **Display Font** text box to display a list of available fonts. Select the font you want to see on the screen when you display reports.

   ◆ **Size:** Click on the arrow button to the right of the **Size** text box to display a list of available type sizes. Select the type size you want to see on the screen when you display reports.

   NOTE: It is suggested that you adjust the display settings to agree with **Display Font** and **Size** used for the screen illustrations in the text. These settings are:

   ◆ **Display Font:** MS Sans Serif
   ◆ **Size:** 8

6. Click on the **OK** button to return to the Company Window. These display settings will become the new display settings for all sets of company data files.

7. Click on the Company Window Reports menu; point to Financials; then click on Trial Balance. The Trial Balance Options dialog box will appear. Leave the **As at** date set at 12/1/97; then click on the **OK** button. The Trial Balance report window will appear.

8. The scroll bar can be used to advance the display to view other portions of the report.

9. Click on the Trial Balance File menu; then click on Print to print the Trial Balance.

10. Click on the Close button to close the Trial Balance window and return to the Company Window.

11. Review your printed Trial Balance report. If the font, type size, and/or margins are not satisfactory continue with the following instructions. If the font, type size, and margins are satisfactory, click on the Company Window File menu; then click on Exit to end your current work session and return to your Windows desktop.

12. To adjust the printer settings, click on the Company Window Setup menu; then click on Printers. The Printers dialog box will appear.

13. Click on the Reports & Graphics tab; then adjust the printer settings as necessary based on the following definitions:

   ◆ **Printer:** Click on the arrow button to the right of the **Printer** text box to display a list of available printers. These are the printers you set up in Windows. If you want to use a printer that is not on the list, you must install the new printer in Windows. Select the printer you want to use.

   ◆ **Font:** Click on the arrow button to the right of the **Font** text box to display a list of available fonts. Select the font you want to use.

   ◆ **Size:** Click on the arrow button to the right of the **Size** text box to display a list of available type sizes. Select the type size you want to use. The larger the type size selected, the larger the type will appear on your printed reports. If no type size options appear, make sure that you have selected a font in the **Font** text box; then select the type size for the **Font** you have selected.

   ◆ **Top Margin:** Enter the amount you want the top margin of the text to be lowered or raised if your reports are being printed too high or too low on the page. The amount should be expressed in inches and decimal fractions of an inch (up to two decimal places). Positive amounts lower the top margin; negative amounts raise it.

   ◆ **Left Margin:** Enter the amount you want the left margin of the text to be moved to the right or left if your reports are being printed too far to the left or right. The amount should be expressed in inches and decimal fractions of an inch (up to two decimal places). Positive amounts move the left margin to the right, negative amounts move it to the left.

14. After you have established the desired printer settings, click on the **OK** button to return to the Company Window. These printer settings will become the new printer settings for all sets of company data files.

15. To test your adjusted printer settings, click on the Company Window Reports menu; point to Financials; then click on Trial Balance. The Trial Balance Options dialog box will appear. Leave the **As at** date set at 12/1/97; then click on the **OK** button.

16. Click on the Trial Balance File menu; then click on Print to print the Trial Balance.

17. Click on the Close button to close the Trial Balance window and return to the Company Window.

18. Review your printed Trial Balance report. If the font, type size, and/or margins are still not satisfactory go back to instruction #12 and make new adjustments. If the font, type size, and margins are satisfactory, click on the Company Window File menu; then click on Exit to end your current work session and return to your Windows desktop.

Procedure	Page no.	Procedure	Page no.
Add your name to the company name	110	Install Simply Accounting	B9
Advance the Using date	201	Invoice lookup	600
Automatically reverse an entry in the		Make a backup copy	155
Purchases Journal	601	Modify the fiscal end date	202
Sales Journal	601	Open company data files	110
Change display settings	B17	Post an entry in the	
Change printer settings	B17	General Journal	112
Close the accounting records	200	Payments Journal	398
Correct a posted transaction		Payroll Journal	308
Original entry made in the:		Purchases Journal	396
General Journal	B10	Receipts Journal	395
Payments Journal	B15	Sales Journal	394
Payroll Journal	B11	Record	
Purchases Journal	B14	Adjusting entries	153
Receipts Journal	B14	Cash receipts from all sources other	
Sales Journal	B13	than credit customers (use	
Create a Student Data Files disk	B10	General Journal)	111
Display and Print		Cash payments for all purposes other	
Balance Sheet	154	than payments to credit vendors	
Chart of Accounts	114	(use General Journal)	111
Customer Aged Detail	398	Cash payments to credit vendors	396
Employee Detail	308	Cash receipts from credit customers	394
General Journal	113	Closing entry for withdrawals account	200
General Ledger	113	Compound general journal entries	152
Income Statement	154	Credit memos	394
Inventory Activity Detail	599	Debit memos	396
Inventory Synopsis	601	General journal entries	111
Payments Journal	B13	Inventory adjusting entries	501
Purchases Journal	B12	Payment of payroll liabilities and taxes	307
Receipts Journal	B12	Payroll journal entries	307
Sales Journal	B12	Purchases discount	396
Trial Balance	114	Purchases on account	395
Vendor Aged Detail	398	Sales discounts	394
941 FIT Summary	310	Sales on account	392
941 Social Security/Medicare Summary	310	Repeat or start over on an assignment	B15
Drill-down	115	Review an entry prior to posting	
Edit an entry prior to posting		General Journal	112
General Journal	112	Payments Journal	397
Payments Journal	395	Payroll Journal	307
Payroll Journal	308	Purchases Journal	396
Purchases Journal	393	Receipts Journal	394
Receipts Journal	395	Sales Journal	393
Sales Journal	393	Save your work	115
Exit from the program	115	Use a backup copy	B16

INDEX